OXFORD HISTORY OF
MODERN EUROPE

General Editors
LORD BULLOCK *and* SIR WILLIAM DEAKIN

Oxford History of Modern Europe

THE STRUGGLE FOR MASTERY
IN EUROPE 1848–1918
By A. J. P. TAYLOR

THE RUSSIAN EMPIRE 1801–1917
By HUGH SETSON-WATSON

FRANCE 1818–1945
By THEODORE ZELDIN *Available in paperback in five volumes:*
AMBITION AND LOVE
POLITICS AND ANGER
INTELLECT AND PRIDE
TASTE AND CORRUPTION
ANXIETY AND HYPOCRISY

GERMANY 1866–1945
By GORDON A. CRAIG *Available in paperback*

THE LOW COUNTRIES 1780–1940
By E. H. KOSSMAN

SPAIN 1808–1975 *Available in paperback*
By RAYMOND CARR

GERMAN
HISTORY
1770–1866

BY

JAMES J. SHEEHAN

CLARENDON PRESS · OXFORD
1989

Oxford University Press, Walton Street, Oxford OX2 6DP
Oxford   New York   Toronto
Delhi   Bombay   Calcutta   Madras   Karachi
Petaling Jaya   Singapore   Hong Kong   Tokyo
Nairobi   Dar es Salaam   Cape Town
Melbourne   Auckland
and associated companies in
Berlin   Ibadan

Oxford is a trade mark of Oxford University Press

Published in the United States
by Oxford University Press, New York

British Library Cataloguing in Publication Data
Sheehan, James J. (James John), 1937
German history 1770–1866.—(Oxford history of modern
Europe).
I. Germany, history
I. Title   943
ISBN 0 19–822120–7

Library of Congress Cataloging in Publication Data
Sheehan, James J.
German history, 1770–1866/by James J. Sheehan.
p.—cm.—(Oxford history of modern Europe)
Includes bibliographical references and index.
1. Germany—History—1740–1806. 2. Germany—History—1806–1815.
3. Germany—History—1815–1866. I. Title. II. Series.
DD203.S48 1989
943—dc20
89–23023
CIP
ISBN 0–19–822120–7

Typeset by Pentacor Ltd, High Wycombe, Bucks
Printed and bound in
Great Britain by Biddles Ltd,
Guildford and King's Lynn

This book is for Michael

PREFACE

THIS book is part of the Oxford History of Modern Europe and is meant to cover the period preceding Gordon A. Craig's *Germany, 1866–1945*, which was first published in 1978. While Craig's starting-point established the year in which my book would end, I have purposely avoided selecting a significant event with which to begin: 1770 is no more than a notational convenience. It seems to me that to have begun with a particular date, such as the start of Frederick the Great's reign or the outbreak of the French revolution, would have given my story a predetermined shape and structure. I do not think modern German history began with Frederick or the revolution or any other single phenomenon. As I shall argue at length in this book, German history between the mid-eighteenth century and the formation of the Bismarckian Reich was shaped by three separable, but closely linked developments: the rise of sovereign territorial states, the expansion of economic activity and social mobility, and the emergence of what I shall call a literary culture.

My first three chapters treat each of these developments in their eighteenth-century setting. Thereafter, I have used political events as a chronological frame. The reader will find, therefore, a series of familiar dividing points: the revolution of 1789, the defeat of Prussia and the dissolution of the old Reich in 1806, the Congress of Vienna in 1815, the revolutions of 1830 and 1848, the so-called 'new era' created in 1859 by dynastic change in Prussia and military defeat in Austria, and, finally, the Austro-Prussian war of 1866. Although my treatment of society and culture is set within this chronological frame, I want to insist that social and cultural developments should not be subordinated to politics, and especially that they should not be seen as part of an emerging German nation-state. No doubt both society and culture were affected by, and in turn affected, the course of political change, but they also had an autonomy that German historiography has sometimes overlooked or underestimated. This autonomy was an important source of

German history's richness and variety, which has made writing this book both fascinating and frustrating.

It is a pleasure to be able to thank those who have helped me while I was writing this book.

The American Council of Learned Societies and the National Endowment for the Humanities financed two years of leave. By making me a Visiting Fellow during the autumn of 1981, Wolfson College, Oxford, provided a splendid setting in which to work. Grants from the Pew Foundation and the School of Humanities and Sciences at Stanford paid for research and editorial assistance. For these funds and many other acts of generosity, I am grateful to Deans Norman Wessells and Ewart Thomas, and to James F. Dickason.

Inez Drixelius, Iris Massion, and Jim Saliba worked on the bibliography. Richard Wetzell and Douglas Klusmeyer read the entire manuscript with great care and attention. Priscilla Hayden Roy offered some valuable advice about the section on romanticism. Robert Kunath and Dirk Rotenberg helped with the proofreading and index. Paul W. Schroeder gave me the benefit of his extraordinary knowledge of international relations in the nineteenth century. At the Oxford University Press, Dan Davin and then Ivon Asquith managed to be both attentive and patient. Alan Bullock, whose biography of Adolf Hitler was one of the first books I ever read about German history, was a model editor—supportive, permissive, and demanding. Ron Davies performed Herculean editorial labours with unfailing good humour and without telling me more about the mysteries of the computer than I wanted to know.

On three occasions members of the European History Discussion Group at Stanford dissected sections of the book and did their best to prevent me from becoming over-confident. While I owe a great deal to many of my colleagues, both at Northwestern and Stanford, I want to acknowledge a special debt to Gordon Craig and Gordon Wright, who have been important to me for three decades. Margaret Lavinia Anderson, Felix Gilbert, Van Harvey, Hans-Ulrich Wehler, and Robert Wiebe read the manuscript, gently pointed out its numerous errors, and made many wise and useful suggestions for improvement; but much more important than this scholarly assistance has been their affection and encouragement.

Finally, I would like to record my sorrow that two people are not alive to read what I have written: Hans Rosenberg, who died at the end of a long, productive career, and James Allen Vann, who did not live to realise his full promise as a scholar. Both men enriched my life with their friendship and left it much diminished by their deaths.

J.J.S.

Stanford, California
September 1988

CONTENTS

LIST OF MAPS

LIST OF TABLES

ABBREVIATIONS

AfK	*Archiv für Kulturgeschichte*
AfS	*Archiv für Sozialgeschichte*
AHR	*American Historical Review*
AJS	*American Journal of Sociology*
CEH	*Central European History*
CEHE	*Cambridge Economic History of Europe*
CSSH	*Comparative Studies in Society and History*
DVLG	*Deutsche Vierteljahrsschrift für Literaturwissenschaft und Geistesgeschichte*
DSB	*Dictionary of Scientific Biography*
DV	*Deutsche Vierteljahrs-Schrift*
EGK	*Europäischer Geschichtskalender*
EHQ	*European History Quarterly*
GGB	*Geschichtliche Grundbegriffe*
GuG	*Geschichte und Gesellschaft*
HJ	*Historical Journal*
HJb	*Historisches Jahrbuch*
Huber	E. R. Huber, *Deutsche Verfassungsgeschichte* (4 vols.; Stuttgart, 1957–69).
Huber, *Dokumente*	E. R. Huber, *Dokumente zur deutschen Verfassungsgeschichte* (3 vols.; Stuttgart, 1961–6).
HWSG	*Handbuch der deutschen Wirtschafts- und Sozialgeschichte*
HZ	*Historische Zeitschrift*
IASL	*Internationales Archiv für Sozialgeschichte der deutschen Literatur*
IRSH	*International Review of Social History*
JbbNs	*Jahrbücher für Nationalökonomie und Statistik*
JbG	*Jahrbuch für Geschichte*
JbGMO	*Jahrbuch für die Geschichte Mittel- und Ostdeutschlands*
JbW	*Jarhbuch für Wirtschaftsgeschichte*
JCEA	*Journal of Central European Affairs*
JEH	*Journal of Economic History*
JHI	*Journal of the History of Ideas*
JMH	*Journal of Modern History*

JSH	*Journal of Social History*
PJbb	*Preussische Jahrbücher*
PP	*Past and Present*
PV	*Politische Vierteljahrsschrift*
RV	*Rheinische Vierteljahrsblätter*
SH	*Social History*
SJb	*Schmollers Jahrbuch*
StL	*Staatslexikon*
SR	*Studies in Romanticism*
VSWG	*Vierteljahrsschrift für Sozial- und Wirtschaftsgeschichte*
ZBL	*Zeitschrift für bayerische Landesgeschichte*
ZfG	*Zeitschrift für Geschichteswissenschaft*
ZGO	*Zeitschrift für Geschichte des Oberrheins*
ZGS	*Zeitschrift für die gesamte Staatswissenschaft*

Introduction

JULES MICHELET began his lectures on British history by reminding his audience that 'l'Angleterre est une île'. We can begin this book on German history from 1770 to 1866 by stating the equally obvious and no less significant fact that 'Germany' did not exist. In the second half of the eighteenth century, as in the second half of the twentieth, there is no clear and readily acceptable answer to the question of Germany's political, social, and cultural identity. To suppose otherwise is to miss the essential character of the German past and the German present: its diversity and discontinuity, richness and fragmentation, fecundity and fluidity. Our history, therefore, cannot be the single story of a fixed entity, a state or a clearly designated landscape. We must instead try to follow the many different histories that coexisted within German-speaking central Europe, histories that led Germans towards and away from one another, at once encouraging them to act together and making such common action virtually impossible.[1]

The problem of German identity begins with the land itself. Nowhere on the Continent is there greater variety than in German-speaking central Europe, which stretches from the sandy soil and pine forests of the northern coast to the hidden valleys and snow-capped peaks of the southern mountains, from the sheer gorges cut by the river through the Rhine massif to the seemingly endless flatlands of the east. Fishermen and shepherds, foresters and vintners, dairy farmers and grain growers have all sought to sustain themselves from this diverse terrain. Before modern times, when technology enabled people to break through the limits imposed by the natural world, most Germans lived in islands defined by their geographical limits, distinctive in speech and custom, disconnected from any common life. It used to be possible, Werner Sombart wrote, to identify 'cultural zones, tribal areas and settlement patterns by the type of farmhouses' built there. This geographical

---

[1] The reference to Michelet is from Kolakowski, *Main Currents of Marxism* i. 1. For a fuller version of the argument presented here, see Sheehan, 'What is German History?'

diversity forms our starting-point, not only because it is the setting for the Germans' histories, but also because it symbolizes the multiplicity of their condition.[2]

Central Europe, as is often pointed out, lacks natural frontiers. The northern littoral, itself divided by Jutland, did not serve as an effective barrier to foreign intruders during the Middle Ages; in modern times, Germans living along the coast have frequently been drawn outwards, linked more closely to the commerce and culture of the Baltic and the North Sea than to the life of the interior. In the south, the Alps are a formidable natural barrier, but they cannot serve as a national frontier since they are themselves divided by impediments to movement and by no less impenetrable 'hidden frontiers' of ethnicity that can cut one village off from its neighbours. In the west, the Rhine serves as a clear line of cartographical demarcation but does not separate Germans from other nationalities; if anything, the Rhine drew Germans away from one another, north towards the Low Countries and the sea, south towards Switzerland and the Alps. In the east, the distinctive openness of the German lands can be most clearly felt: part of those vast continental lowlands that begin at the mouth of the Rhine, the German east extends, in an ever-widening arc, towards the Urals; here the only barriers are those built and sustained by human hands.[3]

If, in one sense, Germans had too few frontiers, in another they had too many. Some of the great natural barriers in central Europe are internal ones, dividing and isolating Germans from each other. The major rivers rarely define ethnic or linguistic groups, but they often break up the interior landscape. For instance, the Danube, the region's most impressive waterway, frames the northern edge of the Bavarian plateau and helps to set this region apart from the German north. Similarly, the central mountains that reach from the Ardenne to the Bohemian massif disrupt the core of German

---

[2] Sombart, *Volkswirtschaft*, p. 13. On the geography of central Europe, see E. Ambrosius, *Andrees Allgemeiner Handatlas* (7th edn., Bielefeld and Leipzig, 1921); Robert Dickinson, *The Regions of Germany* (London, 1945), and *Germany*; Jean Gottmann, *A Geography of Europe* (4th edn. New York, 1969); E. de Martonne, *Europe Central* (2 vols.; Paris, 1930–1); Mutton, *Central Europe;* Pounds, *Geography. . . 1500–1840*; Smith, *Geography*.

[3] Hermann Aubin, *Staat und Nation an der deutschen Westgrenze* (Berlin, 1931); Andrew F. Burghardt, *Borderland: A Historical and Geographical Study of Burgenland, Austria* (Madison, Wis., 1962), John Cole and Eric Wolf, *The Hidden Frontier: Ecology and Ethnicity in an Alpine Valley* (New York and London, 1974); A. Demangeon and L. Febvre, *Le Rhin: Problèmes d'histoire et d'économie* (Paris, 1935).

Europe and divide the Alpine forelands from the northern plain. Germans have often complained, as Goethe did to Eckermann in 1830, that they had no centre, no Paris or London, 'no city . . . nay, no country of which we could decidedly say: '*Here is Germany.*''[4] This is a geographical as well as a cultural and political condition.

'History', Fernand Braudel once remarked, 'is not made by geographical features but by the men who control or discover them.' For more than four centuries German geographers sought to discover a terrain that would be distinctively their own. As early as 1599 the humanist scholar Matthias Quad reluctantly concluded that 'there is no country in all of Christendom which embraces so many lands under one name'. In the late seventeenth and eighteenth centuries, geography became an intellectually vigorous field of enquiry as Germans tried to map their homeland, describe its character, define its shape. But this search for boundaries remained a vexed and contentious enterprise. In 1809, for example, Heusinger's *Handatlas* was greeted by a storm of criticism when it maintained that, because all true borders are 'wet', Germany must be defined by the Rhine and Oder Rivers and by the Baltic and Adriatic seas. Even after the political question of boundaries was apparently settled in 1871, the geographical debate about the nation's spatial dimensions, what geographers tended to call its *Raum* or *Boden*, continued. This debate is, of course, still with us.[5]

Perhaps because the central European landscape proved so difficult to define in national terms, many scholars tried to find the essence of German nationality in culture rather than geography, in the lives of people rather than the shape of the terrain. The humanist Johann Stumpf looked for Germany in 'customs, character and language', while Ulrich Mutius believed that the nation occupied the territory 'in which the German language or any of its dialects was spoken'.[6] The study of linguistics, like the study of geography, flourished in the German lands, because it was so easily allied to the national search for identity. In the eighteenth century, as we shall see, Herder and his contemporaries blended

---

[4] J. W. Goethe, *Conversations with Eckermann (1823–1832)* (San Francisco, 1984), 291.

[5] Fernand Braudel, *The Mediterranean and the Mediterranean World in the Age of Philip II* (New York, 1966), i. 225; Gerald Strauss, *Sixteenth-Century Germany: Its Topography and Topographers* (Madison, Wis. 1959), 40–1; Emil Meynen, *Deutschland und Deutsches Reich: Sprachgebrauch und Begriffenswesenheit des Wortes Deutschland* (Leipzig, 1935), 45 ff.   [6] Pounds, *Geography . . . 1500–1840*, p. 14.

linguistics and cultural history to produce the concept of the *Volk*, which they believed to be the basic unit of national existence, at once the expression and the guardian of the nation's distinctive individuality.

As an answer to the question of German identity, the concept of the *Volk* leaves a great deal to be desired. In the first place, the German *Volk*'s historical existence is very doubtful. From the Renaissance until today, some Germans have persisted in regarding as their ancestors those 'German tribes' supposedly described by Tacitus; but this genealogy is the product of faith, imagination, or habit rather than of scholarly research. There are no clear and direct connections between the tribes who arrived on Rome's northern borders and modern Germans.[7] Even as a purely linguistic concept, the *Volk* poses some serious empirical difficulties. In language, as in the landscape, the problem of boundary-making is acute. The lines between the speakers of Dutch and *Plattdeutsch* are hard to draw; the distance between the dialects of Hamburg and Swabia is surely no less significant. Like the drawing of national borders, the defining of a national language is essentially a political process which creates more than it reflects 'natural' entities.[8] Even after German has been defined as a linguistic unit, its utility as a source of national identity remains open to question. In the east, centuries of population movements and intermingling produced extraordinarily complex linguistic patterns: Count Czoernig, who prepared an ethnography of Austria in the middle of the nineteenth century, found no less than eleven different frontiers separating German-speaking Austrians from other language groups. Moreover, on both sides of these frontiers were 'linguistic islands' (*Sprachinseln*), where various minorities lived in relative isolation. In the 1860s there were 2,500 Polish communities with some half million inhabitants on the German side of the German–Polish linguistic frontier and at least as many Germans on the Polish side. Unless some political force— either the state or a popular movement—intervened, these various linguistic borders and islands tended to be relatively porous and malleable, subject to a variety of cultural, economic, and demographic pressures. Can one talk of a German *Volk* in such a setting? I very much doubt it.[9]

[7] Frank Borchardt, *German Antiquity in Renaissance Myth* (Baltimore and London, 1971); Lewis Spitz, *Conrad Celtis: The German Arch-Humanist* (Cambridge, Mass., 1957).

[8] Dickinson, *Germany*, pp. 312–13; Karl Bernhardi, *Sprachkarte von Deutschland* (2nd edn., Kassel, 1849).

[9] Karl Czoernig von Czernhausen, *Ethnographie der Oesterreichischen Monarchie*

   Names, Harold Isaacs reminds us, often lead 'to where the heart
[of the matter of group identity] can be found, leading us deep into
the history, the relationships, and emotions which lie at the centre
of any such affair'. In the German case, names lead us in many
different directions. Consider, for instance, the identities suggested
by the names given to the city that Germans call Pressburg, the
Slovaks Bratislava, the Hungarians Pozsony, and the Croats
Pozun—a terminological variety appropriate for a town once
inhabited by Germans, Magyars, and Jews but set in the middle of a
Slovak hinterland.[10] The national nomenclature is no less varied:
German has Latin roots and once referred to all those tribes who
eventually inundated Roman Europe from Spain to the Danube. In
the Renaissance, 'German' scholars often included among their
ancestors a bewildering variety of groups, including the occasional
Phrygian, Scythian, and Celt. *Deutsch* is more recent in origin, but
no more precise in denotation. It comes from the Latin adjective
theotisca, which seems to have been used in the eighth century to
describe the civic and legal language of the Frankish empire. The
gradual transformation of this linguistic term into a geographical
and political one was long, complex, and never free from
confusion. In the eighteenth century the most common meaning of
Deutschland was the Holy Roman Empire, whose full title—
Heiliges Römisches Reich der deutschen Nation—underscores the
ambiguity of its national character and aspirations. Nor did matters
much improve in modern times: throughout the nineteenth century
the proper name of the Habsburgs' realm was a matter of persistent
uncertainty, while the title to be given the new German emperor in
1871 provoked a bitter quarrel between William of Prussia and
Bismarck at the very moment of the Kaiserreich's creation. Much
weightier and more intractable disputes about names continue
within and between the German states of our own time. 'Titles',
Lord Bryce wrote, 'sum up the political history of nations.'[11]

(3 vols.; Vienna, 1857). On the Polish frontier, see Böckh, *Volkszahl*; William
Hagen's important monograph, *Germans, Poles and Jews: The Nationality Conflict in
the Prussian East, 1772–1914* (Chicago and London, 1980). Another interesting
example of ethnic variety can be seen in Gary Cohen's *The Politics of Ethnic Survival:
Germans in Prague, 1861–1914* (Princeton, 1981).

   [10] Harold Isaacs, *Idols of the Tribe: Group Identity and Political Change* (New York,
1975), 73. The Pressburg example is from Deak, *Revolution*, p. xviii.
   [11] Bryce, *Empire*, p. 420. On the vocabulary of German national identity, see
Eugen Rosenstock-Huessy, *Frankreich-Deutschland: Mythus oder Anrede* (Berlin,
1957), especially pp. 17, 54, 61; Poliakov, *The Aryan Myth*, ch. 5; Zollner,
'Formen'; Karl Zeumer, *Heiliges Römisches Reich Deutscher Nation: Eine Studie über
den Reichstitel* (Weimar, 1910).

The problem of national identity is not peculiar to Germany. There is something 'unnatural' about the physical and cultural geography of almost every nation. However neat and permanent boundaries may look when they appear as lines on a map, most of them exist as standing violations of the landscape's logic, the historical products of war and politics. Furthermore, as the histories of Britain and the Iberian peninsula amply demonstrate, even the possession of geographical integrity does not make nation-building easy. For most of European history, people's language, culture, and politics were not defined in national terms; indeed these basic patterns of human life usually resisted being forced into or subsumed under a national unit. Only gradually did the nation's advocates acquire the political and cultural power to convince a majority of their contemporaries that the nation was the proper, natural, inevitable way of organizing public life. Often enough the resistance to this process of persuasion and compulsion has not been given its proper place in the nation's histories, which were most often written, as histories usually are, by the winners.

While national identity is everywhere an inherently problematic concept and nation-building is always a conflict-ridden process, the German case may have a special claim to our attention. In part this is because of the German nation-state's obvious importance during the second half of the nineteenth century and the first half of the twentieth. Furthermore, we can find in the German experience an especially intense conflict between variety and communality, between the obdurate facts of multiplicity and a stubborn struggle to attain or impose unity. German history has long been seen as an example of the nation's power and irresistibility. It is also an example of the nation's incompleteness and fragility. As W. H. Riehl observed in the middle of the nineteenth century, 'The sharp conflict between a natural, deeply-rooted spirit of dissension and an equally intense impulse towards unity has made our social life extremely interesting and instructive, but also extremely troubled.'[12]

In this book I shall try to do justice to the diversity of German historical experience, as well as to their struggles for unity and to what Ranke once described as the 'thousand kinds of co-operation' which lie between what he called *Einheit und Zerfallenheit* ('unity and fragmentation').[13] German history from the middle of the eighteenth century until 1866 must be, first of all, the history of the

---

[12] Riehl, *Gesellschaft*, p. 27.   [13] Ranke, 'Trennung', p. 136.

Germans' various efforts to master their political, social, and cultural worlds, the history of their separate achievements and defeats, institutions and innovations. It must also be the history of the emerging questions about Germany's collective identity and its future as a national community. Finally, it must be the history of the multitude of answers to this question which Germans formulated and sought to act upon. The book's fundamental problem—and it is at once a conceptual, analytical, and organizational problem—is how to do justice to all three of these themes. I have tried, on the pages that follow, to describe diversity without creating chaos, to acknowledge the importance of the 'national question' without assuming its primacy or overestimating its significance, and to assess the competing answers to this question without accepting the inevitability of any one of them. I have, in other words, tried to build into my story a sense of national diversity, of open alternatives, and of uncertain outcomes, which I take to be compatible with the historical realities of the past and with the political possibilities of the present.

PART ONE

Eighteenth-century Background

1
Eighteenth-century politics

IN the introduction to his *History of Osnabrück*, first published in 1768, Justus Möser noted that the vocabulary of contemporary politics did not fit the traditional institutions he was trying to describe. As a result, he lamented, 'my words often have to struggle with my feelings'. Especially troublesome were terms like *Freiheit* and *Eigentum*, 'freedom' and 'property', because they no longer conveyed the cluster of meanings Möser needed to recreate his fatherland's past. Möser recognized that this disjunction between language and institutions was a product of the political transformations which he watched from his vantage point in Osnabrück, the small north German city-state where he spent most of his life. With an area of forty-five square miles and a population of about 125,000, Osnabrück retained a set of institutions that represented what Friedrich Meinecke called 'the very epitome of all that was old fashioned in the old German empire'. Outside its jealously guarded frontiers, however, powerful forces were at work, creating the basis of a new kind of politics and a new political language. Möser, a lawyer in the service of his city, was intensely aware of these changes and of the threat they posed to everything he loved and admired. His history was a struggle to preserve, at least in words, a way of life he felt was swiftly slipping away.[1]

Like Möser, we are forced to use contemporary terminology to describe a distant past and, like him, we are struck by the apparent 'poverty of our language with regard to certain political and constitutional expressions'. Our modern conceptions of sovereignty and statehood make it difficult for us to talk about and understand the politics of the Holy Roman Empire and the territorial units of which it was composed. Similarly, our assumptions about the clarity and primacy of political authority obscure a world in which political, social, and economic power had an undifferentiated and deeply personal existence. Also, and perhaps most importantly, we

---

[1] Justus Möser, *Osnabrückische Geschichte* (1768–80), xii. 33–4. On Möser, see Meinecke, *Historicism*, pp. 251 ff.; Epstein, *Genesis*, pp. 297–338; Walker, *Home Towns*, especially pp. 2–3; Jonathan Knudsen, *Justus Möser and the German Enlightenment* (Cambridge, 1986). On Osnabrück, see Renger, *Landesherr und Landstände*.

MAP 1. The Holy Roman Empire

Accepted boundary of the Empire

Principal ecclesiastical states

Prussian gains by partition of Poland in 1772

Prussia from the 1740's

The Monarchy from the 1740's

Gains by the Monarchy in the 1770's

Military frontier regions

Königsberg

EAST PRUSSIA

Vistula

POLAND

0   100   200 miles
0   100   200   300 km

SILESIA

SILESIA

GALICIA

MORAVIA   ZIPS

BUKOVINA

na   Danube

H U N G A R Y   TRANSYLVANIA

BANAT

SLAVONIA

CROATIA   Save   Danube

OTTOMAN

EMPIRE

can easily be taken in by words that seem familiar but which refer to conditions radically different from our own: the eighteenth-century state, for example, has a family resemblance to modern political forms, but was far less integrated and much weaker. If we are to understand traditional politics, therefore, we must struggle to grasp concepts that were firmly embedded in a vanquished ensemble of assumptions and institutions. 'To imagine a language', Wittgenstein wrote, 'means to imagine a form of life.' The reverse is no less true: to imagine a form of life means to imagine its language.[2]

i. REICH AND STAAT

Among traditional Europe's political structures none is more difficult for us to imagine than the Holy Roman Empire. It does not fit any of our political categories; it was not a nation or a state, nor was it an international organization. In dealing with the old Reich, our assumptions about sovereignty do not work; the distinction we customarily make between foreign and domestic affairs does not apply. To impose these categories, assumptions, and distinctions on the empire, as did generations of nineteenth-century historians, is to make it appear grotesque, pathetic, and unintelligible. But, if we view it from the other direction, as the last expression of a long, universalist tradition in European public life, we can begin to grasp the Reich's distinctive character and to appreciate the reasons it held the loyalties of so many for so long. The Reich came from a historical world in which nationality had no political meaning and states did not command total sovereignty. Unlike nations and states, the Reich did not insist upon pre-eminent authority and unquestioning allegiance. Its goal was not to clarify and dominate but rather to order and balance fragmented institutions and multiple loyalties.[3]

[2] Möser in a letter to Friedrich Nicolai (5 Apr. 1767), quoted in Justus Möser, *Gesellschaft und Staat. Eine Auswahl aus seinen Schriften*, ed. K. Brandi (Munich, 1921), 73; Ludwig Wittgenstein, *Philosophical Investigations* (Oxford, 1972), 8. On changing patterns of usage and their social meaning, see Wulf Damkowski, *Die Entstehung des Verwaltungsbegriffes: Eine Wortstudie* (Cologne, 1969); Reinhart Koselleck, 'Sprachwandel und sozialer Wandel im ausgehenden Ancien Regime', in B. Fabian *et al.* (eds.), *Deutschlands kulturelle Entfaltung* (Munich, 1980), 15–30; and the articles in *GGB*.

[3] There is a good discussion of recent work on the Reich in Gerald Strauss, 'The Holy Roman Empire Revisited', *CEH* 11:3 (Sept. 1978), 290–301. The standard account of the Reich's last years is Aretin, *Reich*. See also Benecke, *Society*; Gagliardo, *Reich*; Hanns Gross, *Empire and Sovereignty: A History of the Public Law*

Many eighteenth-century Germans regarded the Reich as their second fatherland—it was the most widely used synonym for *Deutschland*. But while it was located in the heart of German Europe, the Reich was not really a German polity. As the geographer Anton Büsching recognized in 1762, 'the empire has not one and the same extent with Germany'. In the first place, it included a significant number of non-Germans—Flemings and Walloons in the Austrian Netherlands, Italians in the south, Czechs in Bohemia, and Slovenes along the southern frontier. Foreign monarchs, including the kings of England, Denmark, and Sweden, had a part in imperial affairs by virtue of their possessions within the Reich. Moreover, a great many Germans lived outside the Reich's borders, especially in the east. Antwerp and Prague, therefore, were imperial cities, but Danzig and Königsberg were not. No wonder that those who came to view the nation as the 'normal' unit of political organization found these anomalies outrageous.[4]

Even those who knew it best and loved it well were concerned that the Reich did not seem to fit Aristotelean political categories: thus Samuel Pufendorf, a seventeenth-century admirer, called the Reich a 'monstrosity' and thereby gave its enemies a label they could use against it. Imperial institutions were a labyrinth of overlapping jurisdictions and special privileges; they had no well-defined centre, just as the Reich itself had neither a capital nor a single source of sovereignty. This was why the author of a guidebook for English visitors wrote in 1787 that the empire, 'when considered as one single power or state . . . is of no great political consequence in Europe'. The 'inequality and weak connection of its parts' make it impossible for its power to be 'united, compact, and uniform'. The more people expected political authority to be 'united, compact, and uniform', the more difficulty they had understanding and accepting the Reich.[5]

Since the fifteenth century imperial traditions and institutions

Literature in the Holy Roman Empire, 1599–1804 (Chicago, 1973), and 'Empire'; and the essays collected in the special issue of *JMH* 58 (1986). Mack Walker uses the career of J. J. Moser to illustrate certain aspects of the empire; see his *Moser*, especially sects. 13, 14, 15.

[4] A. F Büsching, *A New System of Geography* (London, 1762), iv. 4; in volumes iv, v, and vi, Büsching gives a useful survey of the empire's territories.

[5] Eberhardt August Wilhelm von Zimmermann, *A Political Survey of the Present State of Europe* (London, 1787), 126. On the Reich's lack of an institutional centre, see Wilhelm Berges, 'Das Reich ohne Haupstadt', *Jahrbuch für die Geschichte des deutschen Ostens*, 1 (1952), 1–30.

had been engaged in a series of complex struggles with the values and aspirations of its member states. These struggles intensified during the sixteenth and seventeenth centuries when they fused with religious conflicts and European-wide dynastic rivalries. Confessional hatreds and dynastic ambitions split the Reich internally at the same time they pulled its members into external alliances with powers all along the imperial frontier—France, the papacy, the Ottoman Empire, and Sweden. These antagonisms culminated in the Thirty Years War that devastated central Europe during the first half of the seventeenth century. The Peace of Westphalia, which finally ended this disastrous sequence of events in 1648, reaffirmed the empire's existence, but also significantly strengthened its members by recognizing their separate sovereignty and their right to act independently in military and foreign affairs. The settlement of 1648, therefore, acknowledged without seeking to resolve the historical conflicts between universality and parti-cularism, between the imperial ideal and the reality of state power.[6]

These conflicts were not only fought between the Reich and its opponents; they raged within imperial institutions themselves. Consider, for example, the office of emperor. He was the Reich's chief executive, ceremonial head, and feudal overlord. But he was also the sovereign of a particular part of the Reich—except for one brief interval between 1742 and 1745, the emperor came from (or in one instance had married into) the ruling branch of the Habsburg dynasty. Throughout the seventeenth and eighteenth centuries the two roles united in the emperor's person often came into conflict. Increasingly, the Habsburgs were inclined to use their imperial authority to enhance their own power and to further their dynastic ambitions. In the 1780s the Emperor Joseph II seriously considered abandoning his imperial crown in return for more tangible political ends. Needless to say, as the emperor's particularist ambitions grew, his imperial position was challenged by the rulers of rival states and was criticized by the defenders of the old imperial ideal.

The traditional foil to the emperor within the imperial system was the *Reichstag*, a cluster of representative bodies consisting of a Council of Electors (the seven or eight rulers who elected the emperor), a Council of Princes (divided according to complex rules and including all the rulers of imperial territories except the knights), and a Council of Cities. At the time of the Westphalian settlement, some of the Reich's partisans had hoped that the

[6] Aretin, *Reich*, has a good summary of these developments.

Reichstag would provide a source of reform and renovation. The emperor, afraid of potential competition, called the body together only twice during the decade and a half after 1648. At the second of these meetings, in 1663, the *Reichstag* refused to disband and went into permanent session. This made it possible for the various elements in the Reich to keep their eyes on the emperor and, no less important, on one another. But the *Reichstag's* power over imperial affairs did not substantially increase. As the most important states consolidated their authority, the *Reichstag* began to reflect their particular interests and antagonisms. Its business was conducted by ambassadors, whose energies were absorbed by social and symbolic rather than legislative functions. At times as few as twenty-five heavy-lidded delegates sat in the council chambers discussing some fine point of imperial jurisprudence. Except for the Law on Military Organization of 1681 and the Guild Ordinance of 1731, the 143 years life of the 'eternal *Reichstag*' were not marked by great legislative achievements.[7]

For administrative purposes, the Reich was divided into ten circles (*Kreise*). As in all imperial affairs, this was a complex and inconsistent arrangement. A few areas, such as Bohemia and Silesia, did not belong to a circle, while some territorial states were scattered across several. The criteria for membership in the circles' representative institutions were similar to, but not exactly the same as, those for the *Reichstag*. Moreover, the institutional vitality and effectiveness of the circles varied greatly. Some, especially in the south and west, provided mutual support for their members and created the basis for an active corporate life. These circles tried to comply with the Military Organization of 1681, which made them the primary source of recruitment and supply. They raised armies, both for their own protection and as a contribution to imperial defence. Other circles, however, were empty forms. Those dominated by states with their own armed forces—Brandenburg Prussia, for example—simply ignored the law of 1681. In the course of the eighteenth century, as the army became increasingly significant for both the substance and the symbols of statehood, the political implications of the Reich's military deficiencies steadily increased.[8]

[7] Benecke gives a convenient list of the territories, institutions, and families represented in the *Reichstag*: *Society*, app. III, pp. 394–9.

[8] James Vann's book on Swabia describes an area where imperial institutions functioned relatively well: *The Swabian Kreis: Institutional Growth in the Holy Roman Empire* (Brussels, 1975).

The empire's special character and distinctive strength were not to be found in its legislative, administrative, or military capacities, but rather in its symbolic and judicial functions. The Reich was, first of all, a symbolic community, which provided its members with a set of symbols and ceremonies through which they could escape or extend the bounds of particularism. As the British representative to the *Reichstag* was warned in the 1760s, 'Ratisbon is so full of ceremony, you cannot spit out of the window without offending the head or paraphernalia of an excellence. . . . Ceremonial there is looked upon as essential and subject to contests.'[9] The election and coronation of the emperor, the meeting of the *Reichstag*, and the sessions of the imperial judiciary were all marked by complex rituals through which the empire's purpose and identity could be reaffirmed. Furthermore, the emperor's position in the Reich derived in no small measure from his ability to create new nobles and to fill a range of honorific offices for which members of the aristocracy yearned. To be made a *Hofpfalzgraf* lifted a minor nobleman above his fellows, just as being the site of an imperial celebration linked a particular town with the wider world. Goethe's famous description of Joseph II's coronation as King of the Romans in 1764 nicely captures the way the empire's ceremonies enabled Frankfurt to transcend without surrendering its autonomous existence '[Frankfurt's] equerry opened the procession; chargers with armorial trappings . . . followed him; then came attendants and officials, drummers and trumpeters, and deputies of the council, accompanied by the clerks of the council, in the city livery, on foot.' For a moment at least, the citizens of Frankfurt could feel at the very heart of European affairs, basking in the reflected glory of the universal Reich while simultaneously celebrating their own independent sovereignty.[10]

In addition to being a symbolic community, the Reich was a 'community of justice'. All of its institutions, including the emperor and the *Reichstag*, had judicial functions, but two were of particular importance. The Aulic Council *Reichshofrat* met in Vienna and was sometimes regarded as the 'Emperor's court'. It carried out both legal and administrative tasks, with particular responsibility for the imperial cities, whose affairs it was empowered to investigate. The Cameral Tribunal, which met at Speyer before moving to Wetzlar, had a different if sometimes overlapping

---

[9] W. Doyle, *The Old European Order, 1660–1800* (Oxford, 1978), 268.
[10] Benecke, 'Ennoblement'; Goethe, *Autobiography*, i. 200. By being crowned King of the Romans, Joseph automatically became emperor when his father died.

jurisdiction. It was supported by a tax from the various states but its members, unlike those of the Aulic Council, did not end their term in office when the emperor died.[11]

Our picture of the imperial courts is often drawn from the account left by Goethe, who spent a few months at Wetzlar in the early 1770s. 'One often cannot understand,' he wrote in *Dichtung und Wahrheit*, 'how men could be found for such thankless and melancholy employment. But what a man does everyday he puts up with . . . even if he does not see exactly that anything will come of it. The German especially is of this persevering turn of mind.' Surely there was something thankless and melancholy about the courts, which were chronically understaffed and frequently challenged by those they sought to regulate. Even after reforms were introduced in the 1780s, proceedings could sometimes move so slowly that they seemed to be standing still. One famous case, involving the property of an imperial count, lasted almost two centuries, leaving a record of judicial sluggishness which might have consoled even the litigants in Dickens's *Bleak House*. Nevertheless, despite these manifest deficiencies, imperial justice could help to protect smaller states from their larger neighbours, and even subjects from their lords. Often enough, as is so frequently the case in judicial affairs, imperial institutions worked best by keeping something from happening, by preventing rather than creating. Slow, stately, perhaps lethargic, the mechanisms of the Reich were designed to balance and contain political forces within a web of formal rules and informal understandings, laws and customs, court proceedings and unofficial consultations H. A. L. Fisher grasped the meaning of this arrangement when he wrote that a successful public servant in the empire did not need the talents of a modern politician but rather those 'of the skilled solicitor who knows the intricacies of a large family estate'.[12]

The empire's judicial role was most highly valued by the rulers of small principalities, patriciates of cities, and holders of imperial estates. To those with the most to lose from a consolidation of power, universalism appeared as the best guarantee of particularism and autonomy, the best defence against greed and aggression. In small states and independent towns, the empire made sense,

[11] See the works by Gross cited in n. 3, and F. Hertz, 'Die Rechtsprechung der höchsten Reichsgerichte', *Mitteilungen des Instituts für österreichische Geschichtsforschung*, 69 (1961), 331–58.
[12] Goethe, *Autobiography*, ii. 152; Carol M. Rose, 'Empire and Territories at the End of the Old Reich', in Vann and Rowan (eds.), *Reich*, p. 72.

participation in the *Reichstag* was an honour and a mark of sovereignty, the imperial circle a responsible form of mutual defence, and the imperial courts a refuge from predatory neighbours. The ecclesiastical princes, for example, looked to the empire for protection from larger states, from Protestant influences of various sorts, and also from papal interference. The imperial counts and knights, the smallest and therefore the most vulnerable holders of sovereign power, knew that the only thing separating them from territorial nobles was their *Reichsunmittelbarkeit*, the fact that no intermediate authority stood between them and the emperor. Finally, the fifty officially-defined imperial cities buttressed their independence with their separate council of the *Reichstag* and with their ties to the Aulic Council. In addition, over a hundred other towns fiercely defended the special privileges and immunities they had gained from the Reich. As Mack Walker has so beautifully demonstrated, the Reich was the 'incubator' necessary to keep these often fragile political organisms alive in an increasingly hostile environment.[13]

John Gagliardo has argued that 'the intensity of devotion' to the Reich among its members 'tended to be in inverse proportion to the size and power of the territories themselves'. The larger the polity, the more likely it was to be in a position to do without imperial rituals and legal protection. In the courts of the new absolutist states, princes turned to Versailles rather than Vienna or Ratisbon for their symbols and ceremonies; after mid-century, secular rulers of imperial states no longer sought investiture by the emperor. At the same time, the more important sovereigns sought to create their own nobility and thus create a social hierarchy dependent only on themselves. The states also began to draft sets of uniform laws designed to override both local custom and imperial jurisdiction. The existence of these codification projects, undertaken by both Austria and Prussia in the late eighteenth century, struck at the heart of the Reich's claim to be a 'community of justice'.[14]

To those German states eager to expand their territories or influence, imperial institutions often seemed troublesome or irrelevant. In the decades after the Peace of Westphalia several states pursued foreign policies at odds with their responsibilities to the Reich: between 1658 and 1668, for example, a number of western principalities, joined for a time by Brandenburg Prussia, belonged

---

[13] Walker, *Home Towns*, pp. 18 ff. See also Benecke, *Society*, pp. 374 ff.

[14] Gagliardo, *Reich*, p. 9. On state law and the imperial 'community of justice', see Gross's cogent analysis in 'Empire'.

to a Rhenish alliance closely tied to France. Bavaria, always eager to move into the ranks of the major powers, also defied the Reich with a French alliance. In the late seventeenth and early eighteenth centuries these various centrifugal pressures decreased as the Reich united against the Turks in the east and the expansionary policies of Louis XIV in the west. But in 1740 a new set of conflicts and divisions erupted when the king of Prussia, Frederick II, success-fully invaded and occupied Austrian Silesia. During the twenty-three years of intermittent dynastic warfare which followed, the Reich's failure to keep the peace became painfully apparent. Instead, both sides displayed contempt for imperial institutions and ideals, which they either ignored or sought to manipulate for their own advantage. Perhaps the nadir was reached in 1757, when the imperial armies, joined in an unpopular alliance with France, were badly beaten by Prussian troops at Rossbach. Even after 1763, when the so-called Seven Years War came to an end, the distrust and antagonism between Prussia and Austria went on; any move by the one was sure to provoke a countermeasure by the other. In the 1770s, therefore, when the Habsburgs tried to establish the basis for a claim to the Wittelsbachs' Bavarian lands, the Hohen-zollern opposed them with a series of countermoves. After fighting a desultory war in 1778–9, Prussia sponsored the so-called League of Princes, which at first included the electors of Brandenburg, Saxony, and Hanover and was eventually joined by a number of other German states. The League dominated German diplomacy for a few years, then began to lose significance as Prussia became involved in an alliance with England, and Austria once again went to war against the Turks. The situation drastically changed in 1790 when, as we shall see in Chapter 4, new monarchs in Vienna and Berlin faced new challenges, first in Poland and then in revolution-ary France.[15]

The dynastic rivalries of Habsburg and Hohenzollern were not the first round in that long 'struggle for supremacy in Germany' which preoccupied generations of German historians. In the first place, the Austro-Prussian conflict was fought on a European rather than a German stage: neither power saw itself as a German state. In so far as the conflict did centre on the Reich, it was less a rehearsal for the future than the culmination of deeply rooted historical antagonisms between the emperor and the Reich, between Catholics and Protestants, and between the ambitions of

[15] Aretin, *Reich*, has the details of this struggle.

individual dynasties and the restraints imposed by imperial institutions. One thing about this conflict was unprecedented: for the first time, a struggle within the Reich involved two states which, while by no means equal in size and significance, were both willing and able to play an independent role on the European scene. After the emergence of Prussia as a second major German power, the Reich contained two potential centres of hegemony. In this situation, the other states had every reason to fear being trampled during a conflict between the superpowers, especially when this conflict engaged, as it did after 1770, imperial institutions. At the very time when the Austro-Prussian rivalry displayed the empire's weakness, therefore, it underscored the need for some means through which the interests of the weak might be protected from the ambitions of the strong. The result was a series of reform proposals brought forward by the small states throughout the 1780s.

That the struggle between Vienna and Berlin created a crisis within the empire is clear enough, but it is no less important to remember that imperial institutions survived this struggle as they had survived so many others. The League of Princes, which was surely antithetical to the Reich's theory and practice, none the less explicitly committed its members to the Reich's preservation. Frederick II, however cynical and selfish his motives may have been, acknowledged the empire's indispensability. Others contrived to see the League as a potentially rejuvenating source for the imperial ideal. And almost everyone, admirers and critics of the Reich alike, assumed that it would, in some form, continue to provide the framework for Germans' public life. As Ernst Moritz Arndt recalled from his youth in the 1780s, even when people wondered what had happened to it, they still had 'das alte Reich' imprinted on their hearts.[16]

Throughout the eighteenth century, the Reich never lacked defenders. For example, in *Project de Paix perpetuelle de Monsieur l'Abbé de Saint-Pierre*, Jean-Jacques Rousseau presented the empire as an essential source of support for the equilibrium upon which the European international system rested. The Reich 'holds every other power in check and perhaps can serve the security of others more than its own. . . . [A]s long as [the Reich] remains, the European balance cannot be destroyed and no ruler need fear being dethroned by another.' The Swiss jurist Johannes von Müller also believed

---

[16] Arndt, *Erinnerungen*, p. 79.

that the Reich preserved an equilibrium in Europe because, as he put it, Germany was 'free through its fragmentation' (*frei durch seine Zerteilung*). The most elaborate defence of the imperial ideal was provided by a string of legal theorists who, from Hermann Conring in the seventeenth century to Johann Pütter at the end of the eighteenth, tried to show how the empire's public law held aggressive power in check. In works such as Johann Jacob Moser's monumental *Teutsches Staatsrecht*, whose twenty volumes appeared between 1766 and 1775, these scholars traced the intricate web of law and custom which connected local and imperial institutions. Even in 1795, when the Reich's last agony had already begun, C. M. Wieland could declare that anyone who knew the Reich realized how, 'from its elected monarch to the mayor, masters, council, and community of the imperial city of Zell am Hammersbach', the authority of every German ruler was limited by imperial customs, laws, and procedures.[17]

After the Reich collapsed in 1806, these signs of loyalty were soon forgotten. Nineteenth-century writers looked upon the Reich as something pathetic or absurd: conservatives decried its weakness, liberals its irrationality, Protestants its ecclesiastical connections, and nationalists its disunity. Treitschke spoke for the entire German nationalist school of historians when he called the empire 'a hateful lie', imposed upon a reluctant *Volk* by the Habsburgs. Only recently have scholars realized that the Reich's critics were blaming it for not being a nation or a state and thus for failing at a game it never intended to play. Now that we have had a century or more of experience with nation-states, it is hardly surprising that we can view the Reich with greater sympathy and understanding.[18]

But, however much we may appreciate the Reich's universal ideals and decentralized institutions, and however much we might regret their ultimate failure to contain the forces at work in Europe, we cannot doubt that in the course of the eighteenth century the Reich's relative position declined. Power shifted to the states, and especially to what one contemporary called the 'predator states', like Frederick's Prussia. More important than this shift in the location of power was the change in its nature and purpose.

[17] Vierhaus, *Deutschland*, p. 152; Paul Stauffer, *Die Idee des europäischen Gleichgewichts im politischen Denken Johannes von Müllers* (Basel and Stuttgart, 1960), 40–4; Johann Pütter, *An Historical Development of the Present Political Constitution of the Germanic Empire* (English trans. London, 1790); Aretin, *Reich*, i. 103.

[18] Treitschke, *History*, i. 8.

Ultimately, the Reich declined because what it could do best—restrain, limit, and conciliate—seemed less desirable than what states could do—consolidate, expand, and initiate. While the Reich could slow and deflect conflict, settle certain kinds of disputes, and help smaller polities defend themselves, the states could regulate, conquer and control. The Reich depended on custom and complexity, the states promised codification and rationality. Imperial institutions were diverse and elusive, the state administration tried to be integrated and apparent. In the end, the Reich was overcome because it could not do what people began to demand from their political institutions: it failed because the definition of political success had been radically rewritten. For this reason, the story of the Reich is inseparable from the subject to which we now must turn, the long, complex struggle between the representatives of the old corporate order and the advocates of new political forms and values. It is within the context of this struggle that we can best understand how the Reich, sometimes as participant, sometimes as pawn, and finally as victim, played a central part in the decline and fall of traditional Europe.

ii. *HERRSCHAFT* AND *VERWALTUNG*

'The three central concepts in modern political theory', Otto Brunner wrote, 'are the state's power, territory, and citizens [*Staatsgewalt, Staatsgebiet, und Staatsvolk*].' The state takes precedence over competing agencies beyond and within its own territories; it yields to neither supranational nor internal organizations. We grant it a monopoly over the legitimate use of violence to protect itself from foreign enemies and to impose its will on domestic dissidents. We assume, moreover, that the whole world is divided into separate sovereign states, whose boundaries take precedence over other kinds of frontiers. We tend to find exceptions to this rule—post-war Berlin, for instance—deeply disturbing; everything, we think, should clearly belong to some state. On our maps and in our minds, the state is firmly entrenched as the primary unit of political thought and action.[19]

[19] Brunner, *Land,* p. 139. Although Brunner's analysis of traditional society has helped to shape my own views, his work should not be read uncritically: see David M. Nicholas, 'New Paths of Social History and Old Paths of Historical Romanticism: An Essay Review on the Work and Thought of Otto Brunner', *JSH* 3/3 (spring 1970), 277–94. Edmund Leach has some interesting comments on what

In order to understand politics in traditional central Europe we must imagine a world in which these assumptions about state sovereignty do not obtain. In this world, the basic unit is not the state, but the *Land*. The term is from that political vocabulary whose passing Möser mourned; it has no modern equivalent. A *Land* was, first of all, a territorial entity, a particular kind of landscape, to be distinguished from cities, which were thought to belong to a different socio-political realm, and from uncultivated terrain, which belonged to no realm at all. A *Land* was also a collection of institutions, laws, and customs peculiar to itself. Unlike a modern state, however, a *Land* asserted its identity but not its primacy; it was enmeshed with, rather than self-consciously superior to, a variety of institutions beyond and within itself. As Henry Strakosch has written, the *Land* did not possess sovereignty in our sense because it was 'composed of social bodies living by their special laws' and because it was 'open . . . towards integration into a system of more universal scope'. Authority in a *Land* was diffuse, shared by a number of semi-autonomous bodies, such as guilds or aristocratic landholders, or by specially defined communities, such as the Jews. At the same time, the boundaries of a *Land* were porous, easily penetrated by outside elements, such as the Catholic Church or the Holy Roman Empire.[20]

In the *Länder* of traditional central Europe, the distinction between public and private institutions was much less distinct than it would become in the world of sovereign states. Families, guilds, urban communities, and landholders all combined functions which we tend to divide between governmental and private agencies. Similarly, what we think of as political and economic powers tended to be fused: a father had power over his children, a master over his apprentices, and a landlord over his peasants not just because they controlled economic resources but also because they possessed a special kind of authority, which often included the right to enforce their will with violence. Following Otto Brunner, we can call this kind of authority *Herrschaft*, a concept which combines political, economic, and social powers and which locates them in

he calls 'the dogma of sovereignty' in 'The Frontiers of "Burma"', *CSSH* 3/1 (1960), 49–68. For more on the German situation, see Benecke, *Society*, especially p. 7. On the concept of sovereignty, see F. H. Hinsley, *Sovereignty* (2nd edn., Cambridge, 1986), especially pp. 137 ff.

[20] Strakosch, *Absolutism*, pp. 30 ff; Dietrich Gerhard, 'Regionalismus und ständisches Wesen als ein Grundthema europäischer Geschichte', *HZ* 174/2 (1952), 307–38.

the person of the *Herr*, the individual lord and master. *Herrschaft* adhered to a person rather than an office; it was something to be possessed rather than borrowed from a higher power. While everyone knew that authority came in different quantities and could be used for different purposes, it was thought to be diffused throughout the social order. For example, in his work on the *Theatrum iurisdictionis Austriae* of 1752, F. J. Greneck set out to describe the rights of 'every *Stand* from the mightiest prince [*Landesfürsten*] to the most modest head of a household [*Hausvater*]'. To Greneck, prince and father were part of a single complex of institutions, each joined together and limited by the same web of customs, traditions, and laws.[21]

Contrary to the image of pre-modern stability created by conservative social theorists in the nineteenth century, the world of *Herrschaft* was inherently contentious. Because boundaries were porous and uncertain, ownership was constantly in dispute. The bishops of Mainz and Würzburg, for instance, carried on a prolonged struggle over a forest; Meiningen and Coburg once came to the brink of war over the tiny city of Wasungen. Similarly, because authority was diffuse and ill-defined, rights and obligations were often in conflict. Princes and prelates, city governments and guilds, administrators and estate owners fought over who had the power to do what to whom. During the eighteenth century, when authority was being redefined and power redistributed, these various conflicts became increasingly intense, overloading corporate bodies within the *Länder* and flooding the imperial courts with litigation.[22]

In this atmosphere of persistent jurisdictional conflict, the possession of *Reichsunmittelbarkeit*—a position directly under the authority of the Reich—carried enormous advantages. *Unmittelbarkeit* enabled a *Herr* to assert his superiority over competing sources of *Herrschaft*. Moreover, by being directly subject to the emperor and legally entitled to a voice in some imperial institution, a ruler could use the authority of the Reich to support his claims against a fellow sovereign or his own subjects. The more contentious eighteenth-century politics became, the more some rulers would cleave to the trappings of independence. The Bishop of Olmütz, for example, insisted on his right to mint coins,

---

[21] Brunner, *Land*, p. 279.
[22] Examples can be found in Biedermann, *Deutschland*, i, pt. 1, p. 37; and H. H. Hofmann, *Herrschaft*.

dispense justice, and maintain an armed guard—much to the annoyance of the Habsburg monarchs whose territories surrounded his small realm. While diminutive in scale, the bishop's mint and army proclaimed his legal equality with the mightiest princes in the land. Without such symbols of independent sovereignty, he would become just another link in the chain of authority leading from the individual household to the emperor's court.

Nowhere were the privileges of *Unmittelbarkeit* more strongly defended than on the estates of the imperial nobility. During the eighteenth century there were well over a thousand imperial counts and knights, who ruled about 5 per cent of the Reich's territory and population, mostly in Swabia, Franconia, and parts of the Rhineland. Their estates were usually quite small. The Stein family, for example, had about 1600 acres on the left bank of the Rhine; since the family had acquired this land over time and had had to sell parts of it, their 'estate' was divided into two dozen separate parcels. The Steins occupied a modest palace in Nassau, which was also the seat of their 'government', the *Freiherrlich Steinsche Amt*. Recognizing no authority between themselves and the emperor, they demanded sovereign power over their lands and the people living on them. They or their agents acted as judge and policeman, tax collector and ecclesiastical authority. In the course of the eighteenth century, families like the Steins were frequently under siege, their authority challenged by their more powerful neighbours, their legal status questioned by those who denied them true sovereignty.[23]

Most theorists continued to acknowledge the nobility's political independence. In 1786, for example, Johann Georg Kerner defined the *Reichsritterschaft* as a 'state [*Staatskörper*] made up of many small, particular states'. But, while Kerner may have intended his definition as a defence of the nobility, there is something absurd about thinking of their properties as minuscule states. Neither in theory nor in practice did their authority easily translate into the language of states and state sovereignty; the imperial counts and knights belonged to the world of *Herrschaft*, the world of the Reich. Within these institutions they could flourish, defending themselves in the *Reichstag*—to which counts had direct access—and in the corporate organs of their *Kreis*, accepting honorific and profitable positions in the imperial service and sending their sons to serve as

[23] Max Lehmann, *Freiherr vom Stein* (Leipzig, 1921), 2–3.

members of cathedral chapters or even to become the ordained ruler of an ecclesiastical state.[24]

Like the imperial nobility, upon whom they depended for personnel and support, the ecclesiastical territories were deeply entrenched in the life of the Reich. These entities varied enormously in size and significance. The Abbey of St George, which was located in the small (population 1,300) Swabian imperial city of Isny, claimed independent sovereignty and was duly represented as an imperial estate in the *Reichstag* despite its minuscule size. Mainz, on the other hand, was an important small state, with 6,000 square kilometres scattered in five separate parcels. As Chancellor of the Reich, the Archbishop Elector of Mainz was an important figure in central European affairs as well as the ruler of a large and luxurious court. But even small ecclesiastical states could be of considerable significance: in 1780, for instance, the Habsburgs paid almost a million gulden in gifts and bribes to have Maria Theresa's twenty-four-year-old son, Max Franz, elected bishop of Cologne-Münster, where he was supposed to block the westward movement of Prussian influence.[25]

Together with the nobility and the ecclesiastical territories, the imperial free cities represented the political and moral heart of the old Reich. There were fifty-one *Reichstädte* in the eighteenth century, ranging in size from internationally recognized urban centres like Frankfurt and Hamburg to small towns with narrow horizons like Bopfingen, Pfullendorf, and Überlingen. In addition to these cities, which had a clear legal status and immediate representation in the *Reichstag*, many more had managed to acquire some measure of self-government that they jealously guarded from their larger neighbours. Large and small, formally or informally autonomous, these cities all struggled to assert their independence and to determine who had the right to live within their walls. When the town fathers of Nördlingen embellished their public buildings with the motto 'Senatus populusque Nordlingensis', they intended to tell the world that their power was no less legitimate than that of the greatest state.[26]

---

[24] Vierhaus, 'Eigentumsrecht', p. 234. On the imperial nobility, see Thomas J. Glas-Hochstettler, 'The Imperial Knights in Post-Westphalian Mainz: A Case Study of Corporatism in the Old Reich', *CEH*, 11/2 (June 1978), 131–49; Reif, *Adel*.

[25] Braubach, *Sohn*, ch. 2. The transaction was arranged by Count Metternich, the future Chancellor's father.

[26] On the variety of urban life in the eighteenth century, see below, Ch. 2, sect. iii. Aretin, *Reich*, i. 90 ff., has a good account of the cities' role in imperial institutions.

The political and social structure of the free cities varied as widely as their size and economic significance. Some, like Nuremberg, were ruled by a closed caste of patricians, others, like Hamburg, by a somewhat more open commercial oligarchy, and a few, like Frankfurt, by what one observer called 'a moderate aristocracy, a combination of democracy and aristocracy', Many of the small and medium-sized cities were governed by a relatively large group of citizens, whose influence in municipal affairs reflected and affirmed their position in the guilds and their prestige in urban society. As was characteristic in the world of *Herrschaft*, the political, social, and economic élites and institutions in these 'home towns' were braided together to create a distinctive form of self-government, which was at once extremely cohesive and virtually unintelligible to outsiders.[27]

Throughout the eighteenth century, urban affairs in central Europe were marked by endemic constitutional and jurisdictional disputes. In Frankfurt, for example, an intramural struggle began in 1725 when a delegation of citizens complained to the emperor—through his representative—that their rights were being violated by the aristocratic town council. Despite the council's unyielding opposition and the emperor's initial hostility, the citizens managed to engage the empire on their behalf. After more than a quarter century of litigation, investigation, and manipulation, imperial institutions helped to effect what one historian has called 'a kind of equilibrium between the urban aristocracy and the leading elements of the citizenry', which lasted throughout the century. On a much smaller scale, Nördlingen carried on a series of disputes with a multitude of small states, free cities, and ecclesiastical entities that shared its corner of northern Swabia. Within its walls, Nördlingen's authority was reasonably secure but, like most cities, it claimed scattered territories in the surrounding area. One of these was the village of Pflaumloch, whose thirty-six farms were owned by seven different sovereignties. Who controlled the people living on these farms? In whose courts were they to be tried? According to whose laws were they to be married and buried? Needless to say, the opportunities for disagreement on these matters were virtually without limit.[28]

The majority of the Reich's inhabitants, roughly 80 per cent,

[27] The classic account is Walker, *Home Towns*, ch. 2. Two examples: Adolf Laufs, *Die Verfassung und Verwaltung der Stadt Rottweil, 1650–1806* (Stuttgart, 1963); Renger, *Landesherr und Landstände*.

[28] Soliday, *Community*; Friedrichs, *Society*, pp. 20–1.

lived in one of fifty dynastic states. Many of these states are difficult
to distinguish from an important city or large estate; some were so
small that, as Justus Möser once remarked, they seemed to be made
up entirely of boundaries. Nassau Weilung, for example, was really
no more than a *Reichsgrafschaft*, whose ruler had bought a princely
title in 1737; its population of 35,000 was comparable to that of a
medium-sized city-state. Lippe had a better legal claim to sovereignty but not a much larger population; a hard day's ride was
sufficient to cross its lands. Ansbach-Bayreuth, with a population
of 400,000 on a territory of 116 *Quadratmeilen*, was clearly in a
different category, although still far too small to play the
independent role on the European stage to which Bavaria, Saxony,
Hanover, or the Palatinate aspired. All these states possessed, or
had possessed, enough resources to lift them well above their
smaller neighbours, but none of them made it into the ranks of the
major powers. For reasons that should become clear as we proceed,
these ranks were closed by mid-century. Only two German states
would qualify, the Habsburg monarchy and Brandenburg
Prussia.[29]

Disaster awaited the eighteenth-century state at every turn.
States in the German west, which was a major theatre of combat
throughout the early modern period, were frequently devastated
by war. The Palatinate, for instance, was battered beyond repair,
first by the Thirty Years War, then by the struggles between the
Reich and France. An important polity throughout the seventeenth
century, the Palatinate's influence dwindled to insignificance by the
middle of the eighteenth. States were also subject to the sudden
rekindling of religious passion. In both Saxony and Württemberg
the ruler's conversion to Catholicism set off a series of debilitating
confessional struggles. Moreover, every dynasty, great and small,
had to contend with the grim realities of pre-modern demography.
If a ruler did not produce an heir or live long enough to ensure an
uncontested succession, then the integrity of his state was immediately open to attack from aggressive outsiders and competing
members of his own family. Few states escaped the trauma of a
succession crisis in the seventeenth and eighteenth centuries; some
did not survive. In sum, when we review the vicissitudes
confronting rulers in this period we are inclined to say about
traditional statecraft what Moltke once said about war: even to be
mediocre was quite an accomplishment.

[29] Aretin, *Reich*, i. 24, n. 77. Some examples: on Lippe, Benecke, *Society*,
pp. 162–3; on Nassau-Weilburg, Rössler, *Revolution*, pp. 43 ff.; on Weingarten,
Scherer, *Reichsstift*.

Many German rulers were satisfied with mediocrity. They lived in comfortable if not splendid circumstances, enjoying as best they could the varied pleasures traditional society provided for its most privileged members. A few princes wanted more—more prestige, glory, land, power. They wanted these things, above all, for themselves and for their families. They thought of state power as inseparable from their own authority—a special kind of *Herrschaft*—and saw the state itself as an extension of their own dynastic lands. However, this drive for personal glory and dynastic aggrandizement helped to set into motion political forces that would eventually bring to an end the identification of ruler and state, creating in its place a new theory and practice of politics, a new kind of state.

At the end of the seventeenth century the cost of living as a prince significantly increased when German rulers, like their counterparts throughout Europe, took Louis XIV of France as their model of what a monarch should look like and how he should live. The Sun King's standards were very high; many lesser dynasties went bankrupt trying to keep up with the Bourbons. Following Louis's example required, first of all, the proper setting for a princely life, a palace suitable for court ceremonies and dynastic display, located away from the dirt and noise of the capital city. As a result, copies of Versailles were built throughout the Continent, at Schönbrunn, Potsdam, Mannheim, Schleissheim, Rastatt. Once constructed, these new buildings were filled with loyal retainers, who had to be entertained brilliantly and fed lavishly. Hundreds, sometimes thousands of servants were needed to provide for the court's sustenance. However thin its substance might be, power had to be given symbolic expression and ceremonial affirmation. Thus Casanova could regard Dresden as 'the most brilliant court in Europe' at precisely the time when Saxony's real significance was swiftly sinking. Mistresses, a necessary status symbol, were to be found at every court, where they frequently put great demands on the princely purse as well as on other royal resources. To be sure, some rulers accepted their amatory obligations with reluctance— Casanova, for one, complained bitterly about the Dresden court's high moral tone but others devoted themselves to their mistresses with great enthusiasm. Karl Eugen of Württemberg, it was said, had so many illegitimate children that he considered forming a regimental officer corps solely from his bastards.[30]

---

[30] Casanova, *Life*, iii. 218. Compare Boswell's impressions, in Pottle (ed.), *Boswell*, p. 167. Fauchier-Magnan, *Courts*, is filled with gossip about court life.

In many states, the army was another serious drain on a ruler's finances. Of course princes had always maintained soldiers, just as they had always lived in palaces. In the course of the seventeenth century, however, armies tended to become larger, while changes in military tactics required them to be better trained and more highly disciplined. To supply and co-ordinate the activities of this fighting force required complex organizations and, if possible, uniform clothing, weapons, and procedures. As we shall see presently, the impact of these military institutions on a state like Prussia was profound. But even smaller states maintained standing armies, sometimes in order to increase their international position, sometimes just to amuse their rulers. Karl August of Weimar, for instance, kept an army well beyond his means and needs; he finally had to be content with command over a Prussian regiment. The prince of Zerbst took great pleasure in drilling his 150 foot soldiers and thirty cavalrymen, whom he mobilized to defend his realm when he thought it threatened by Prussia. Lippe-Detmold, as the famous drinking song assures us, had but a single soldier, whose valiant and untimely death brought some tiny conflict to a sudden end.[31]

The princes' new standing armies, like their newly built copies of Versailles, had both practical and symbolic importance. The palace's characteristic architectural arrangement, with its buildings extending outwards along an axis centred in the court, represented the centralization of royal authority, just as the palace's ceremonial arrangement reproduced the prince's domination of the social hierarchy. In addition to being an instrument of royal power, the ideal army was also an image of how the state should be. After all, the qualities most admired in an army—discipline, loyalty, rational organization—were exactly those most sought in a well-run polity.

Mannlich, *Rokoko*, provides an insider's view of princely conduct at Zweibrücken. For a recent case study, see Aloys Winterling, *Der Hof der Kurfürsten von Köln 1688–1794. Eine Fallstudie zur Bedeutung 'absolutistischer' Hofhaltung* (Bonn, 1986). Jürgen von Kruedener, *Die Rolle des Hofes im Absolutismus* (Stuttgart, 1973), emphasizes the court's function in controlling the nobility. On court architecture, see Eberhard Hempel, *Baroque Art and Architecture in Central Europe* (Baltimore, 1965); Renate Wagner-Rieger, 'Gedanken zum fürstlichen Schlossbau des Absolutismus', in Engel-Jánosi *et al.* (eds.), *Fürst*, 42–70.

[31] There is a splendid account of these developments in Howard, *War*. Biedermann, *Deutschland*, i, pt.1, pp.198 ff., has data on the size of various states' armies. On Weimar, see Bruford, *Germany*, pp. 33–4; on Zerbst, Pottle (ed.), *Boswell*, p. 104. I am grateful to Gordon Craig for calling my attention to the fate of Lippe-Detmold's solitary trooper.

The fact that more and more monarchs began to dress in military uniforms suggests the degree to which the new armies were becoming enmeshed with the theory and practice of statecraft. 'Military discipline', Max Weber once wrote, 'gave birth to all discipline.'[32]

Palaces and armies, together with all the other expensive paraphernalia of princely rule, cost a great deal of money. Johann Justi, who served Frederick II of Prussia, declared in 1767 that 'Money is the blood of the state, just as the government is its heart. Taxation brings blood to the heart and in a healthy system the government would pump it back into the veins.' The metaphor is striking but inexact: the heart, after all, pumps but does not expend the body's vital resources. Governments, by contrast, characteristically consumed more than they circulated, drawing wealth and talents from society which they used for their own rather than society's well-being.[33]

Money—for whatever purpose—was the dominant force behind the construction of the modern state. Whether it was to defend themselves against aggression, invest in cultural splendour, or feed their own carnal appetites, princes needed more funds than they ever had before. To obtain these funds, they had a limited set of choices. They could try to increase the productivity of their own personal domains. Various sorts of manufacturing enterprises, such as the great royal porcelain works in Saxony and Prussia, might bring in additional cash. More often, princes had to borrow, especially from the international bankers whose rise to prominence coincided with state-making. But, even if such measures were possible, they were rarely sufficient. To support their courts and pay their soldiers, rulers needed a steady, inexhaustible supply of income and that, more and more of them came to recognize, could only be found by increasing the revenues they drew from society itself. Of course states had always collected some kinds of taxes, but these were usually constrained by a tangle of special privileges and customary exemptions. Filtered through the intervening network of *Herrschaft*, only a limited amount of society's resources found their way into the ever-empty coffers of the state. Taxation required that rulers penetrate their territories more deeply than ever before, and thereby cut through or circumvent the web of institutions separating them from their subjects. The result was a

---

[32] Weber, *Economy*, ii. 1155.

[33] Ursula A. J. Becher, *Politische Gesellschaft: Studien zur Genese bürgerlicher Öffentlichkeit in Deutschland* (Göttingen, 1978), 84–5.

century-long struggle between the centralizing power of the prince
and the defenders of *Herrschaft*.[34]

German princes in the seventeenth and eighteenth centuries did
not set out to build a new kind of state—certainly not the kind of
state their policies eventually produced. With neither the altruism
nor the foresight sometimes attributed to them by patriotic
historians, most princes were caught up in the day-to-day business
of making ends meet. They had no grand design; usually they were
too busy finding troops for their armies and cash to pay their debts.
In time, however, the princes' advisers formulated a political
theory to justify their claim that the state's power was separate
from, and inherently superior to, the other sources of authority in
society. In contrast to the diffuse and porous boundaries that
characterized the world of *Herrschaft*, the theoretical defenders of
the state insisted on clear distinctions between the power of princes
and their subjects, between public and private institutions, and
eventually between the state and society. Each of these institutional
spheres had its own special character and rights, but theorists and
practitioners insisted on the primacy of state as the single
instrument of legitimate authority and the source of social
regulation and reform.[35]

When they wrote about the new state, theorists reached for
metaphors to capture its special qualities and virtues. In contrast to
the organic, corporeal images employed to describe traditional
polities, these metaphors often evoked mechanical devices. 'A well-
organized state must be like a machine,' Johann Justi wrote, 'all the
wheels and gears must mesh exactly. The ruler should be a master
mechanic—the primary spring or soul, one might say—which sets
everything in movement.' Justi's language reflects his assumption
that states can be created, they need not grow slowly over time.
They stand, as a machine does, apart from the human world
around them. Since states are the products of human ingenuity,
their workings are complex but intelligible, intricate but rational.

---

[34] The importance of finances for state-building is a central theme in the
important collections of essays edited by Charles Tilly, *Formation*, and Peter
Christian Witt, *Wealth and Taxation in Central Europe: The History and Sociology of
Public Finance* (New York, 1987). Biedermann, *Deutschland*, i, pt. 1, pp. 205 ff., has
data on state finances.

[35] For an example of princely motivation, see Roland-Götz Foerster, *Herrschafts-
verständnis und Regierungsstruktur Brandenburg-Ansbach, 1643–1703* (Ansbach, 1975).
On the language of state-building, see Wulf Damkowski, *Die Entstehung des
Verwaltungsbegriffes: Eine Wortstudie* (Cologne, 1969).

To grasp the essence of a state does not require deep and subtle knowledge about its past, but rather a scientific understanding of its internal logic.[36]

If the intended product of the state's machinery was usually money, its essential lubricant was information. To control society, rulers had to know more about their territories than they ever had before. They had to know how many men were available to serve in their armies, how much grain could be levied, how much money passed through a merchant's hands. This information had to be gathered, remembered, communicated; files, forms, statistics became more extensive and more important for decision making. As this happened, custody over the state's information became a full-time task, carried out by those who devoted themselves to its acquisition and accumulation. Just as this information was meant to enhance the state's power over society, so its guardians used it to enhance their own position within the ruling councils of the state. Knowledge, as Max Weber pointed out in his classic formulation, is at the heart of bureaucratic power.[37]

The development of a professional corps of information-keepers was slow and uneven. At first, most princes used whatever reliable agents were at hand: courtiers, soldiers, local officials, and the like. The degree to which central authorities overlapped with, and depended upon, traditional institutions has often been under-estimated by historians anxious to sanctify the state. Gradually, however, states acquired a staff of professional administrators, whose growing number helps us track the states' growing aspirations. This process was by no means confined to great states like Prussia: by the end of the eighteenth century even the small principality of Leiningen, with a population of 70,000, employed fifty councillors, eighteen secretaries, and fifty-four subaltern officials. Max Franz of Electoral Cologne, no less than Frederick II of Brandenburg Prussia, was convinced that the duty of a prince required the formation of the best possible administration. By the end of the eighteenth century, bureaucrats had become the chief instruments of the state's authority and the personification of its distinctive character. 'The power interests of the bureaucracy', Weber wrote, 'give a concretely exploitable content' to the

[36] Justi quoted in Parry, 'Government', p. 182. On Justi, see Mack Walker, 'Rights and Functions: The Social Categories of Eighteenth-Century German Jurists and Cameralists', *JMH* 50/2 (June 1978), 234–51.
[37] Weber, *Economy*, especially ch. 11.

ambiguous ideal of *raison d'état* and, he added, 'in dubious cases, it is always these interests which tip the balance'.[38]

In almost every German state the development of centralized authority led to a conflict between the ruler and the privileged corporations within his realm. Characteristically, the immediate issue was fiscal: did the ruler have the right to tax a particular social group, region, or economic activity? Both sides knew, however, that more than money was at stake. To the prince and his officials, the right to tax was the purpose of state power, the chief goal and product of state-building. To their opponents, financial obligations were an inseparable part of a complex set of rights and customary privileges which defined them as a special status group. By trying to alter these obligations, the state was attacking not only a group's economic interests but also the basis of its social identity and political position. Every element within the world of *Herrschaft* was affected by the states' insatiable search for funds, but the landed nobility were the group most likely to resist: their traditional power and privileges made them formidable opponents at the same time that their wealth made them tempting targets.

The arenas in which the conflict between the central authority and the world of *Herrschaft* took place were the *Stände*, the corporately organized representative institutions that had been created in almost every central European *Land* during the fourteenth and fifteenth centuries. The *Stände* traditionally advised the prince, exercised certain administrative and judicial functions, and provided financial assistance by approving new kinds of taxation. As we should expect, the character and composition of the *Stände* varied greatly from *Land* to *Land*. Some retained the classic tripartite division of clergy, aristocracy, and towns; elsewhere the clerical estate had disappeared; occasionally, the nobility withdrew, leaving the towns dominant, but more often the second estate was able to play a leading role. Some *Stände* convened regularly, others had to be called by the prince; some met as separate estates, others had evolved forms of common action. A few *Stände* were vigorous institutions, many more were not. This diversity, it should be remembered, often existed within the territories of a prince, since *Stände* were connected to a particular *Land* and dynastic states were often composed of several Länder.[39]

---

[38] Ibid. ii. 979. On Max Franz, see Braubach, *Sohn*, p. 109. Data on state administrations can be found in Biedermann, *Deutschland*, i, pt. 1, p. 101; Wehler, *Gesellschaftsgeschichte*, i. 261–2.

[39] Carsten, *Princes*, is a good introduction. See also H. G. Koenigsberger,

The fate of the *Stände* varied almost as much as their character and composition. In several states, including some of the Reich's most important polities, the ruler's victory over his estates was virtually complete. After a few bitter skirmishes, the central authority was able to introduce and collect new taxes—usually some form of excise tax—without reference to corporate rights and privileges. With these sources of funds, princes could expand their armies and increase the ranks of officials under their immediate control. Occasionally, when the *Stände* lost their fiscal power and administrative functions, they simply ceased to exist; more often, they settled into a clearly subordinate role. For example, by the early seventeenth century, the Bavarian Estates had stopped meeting as a formal institution, even though their members continued to exercise some influence on governmental affairs. The Saxon *Stände* managed to hold out somewhat longer—their key defeat came in the 1690s when the elector was able to impose an excise tax—but they also were reduced to a subsidiary role by the early eighteenth century.[40]

In ecclesiastical territories, corporate institutions survived if only for the obvious reason that they were necessary to elect a new ruler. Such elections were usually the right of the Cathedral Chapter, a body of aristocratic clergymen who enjoyed considerable formal influence and controlled a good deal of church property. During the interregnum following the death of one ruler and the election of his successor, the chapter effectively ruled the state. But even with these formidable statutory and practical advantages, many chapters gradually lost influence to the ruler and his administration. In Mainz, for instance, the electors and their chief ministers dominated political affairs throughout the second half of the eighteenth century. The Chancellery and council, both directly under electoral control, usurped the chapter's functions and undermined its authority. So when a progressive elector like Emmerich Joseph

'Monarchies and Parliaments in Early Modern Europe: Dominum Regale and Dominum politicum regale', *Theory and Society*, 5/2 (Mar. 1978), 191–218; the essays edited by Gerhard, *Vertretungen*; Rudolf Vierhaus, 'Ständewesen und Staatsverwaltung in Deutschland im späten 18. Jahrhundert', in Vierhaus and M. Botzenhart (eds.), *Dauer und Wandel der Geschichte* (Münster, 1966), 337–60.

[40] On Bavaria, see Carsten, *Princes*, ch. 5; the somewhat more positive view in Aretin, *Bayerns*; Wolfgang Quint, *Souveränitätsbegriff und Souveränitätspolitik in Bayern: Von der Mitte des 17. bis zur ersten Hälfte des 19. Jahrhunderts* (Berlin, 1971). On Saxony, see Fritz Hartung, *Das Grossherzogtum Sachsen unter der Regierung Carl Augusts, 1775–1828* (Weimar, 1923).

introduced policies which the chapter vigorously opposed, his will eventually prevailed.[41]

Stände were usually better able to defend themselves in the north-western sector of the Reich, where we find territories belonging to dynasties whose core lands were elsewhere: the western possessions of the Hohenzollern, some smaller entities owned by the Arch-bishop of Cologne, a state belonging to Denmark, and, most important of all, Hanover, whose elector became king of England in 1714. In most of these territories, which Rudolf Vierhaus has called *Nebenländer*, rulers had neither the inclination nor the need to achieve total victories over the estates. Even as resolute a state-builder as the Great Elector of Brandenburg Prussia was willing to work out local accommodations which would have been unthink-able closer to home. Similarly, Hanover's absentee ruler allowed a peculiar mix of bureaucratic and corporate rule, in which a few aristocratic families dominated both the *Stände* and the upper ranks of the administration.[42]

Mecklenburg was not a *Nebenland*, but it also retained a corporate regime in the eighteenth century. The *Stände* in this state were dominated by a cohesive aristocratic élite which, with the aid of the imperial Aulic Council, was able to halt the duke's effort to curtail their power. In 1755, the estates forced him to grant them 'complete security and maintenance of their rights, freedoms, privileges, customs and traditions'. In effect, this limited the authority of the duke to his own domains and left the rest of the state in the hands of the landed nobility.[43]

The constitutional situation in Württemberg was especially complex. Although involved with state government in many ways, Württemberg's nobility claimed *Reichsunmittelbarkeit* and therefore did not participate as an estate within the state. Instead, the Württemberg *Stände* were dominated by local notables, clergymen, urban élites, and rural magistrates. In the seventeenth century these groups were involved in a series of conflicts with the prince, who was eager to extend his power and increase his revenues, and with the Privy Council, which had originally been an

[41] On Mainz, see Blanning, *Reform*; Dreyfus, *Sociétés*. Rudolfine Freiin von Oer's essay in Gerhard (ed.), *Vertretungen* (1969) has further examples.

[42] See Vierhaus's essay in Gerhard, (ed.) *Vertretungen*; Joachim Lampe, *Aristo-kratie, Hofadel und Staatspatriziat in Kurhannover* (2 vols.; Göttingen, 1963).

[43] Quoted in Rudolf Vierhaus, 'Land, Staat und Reich in der politischen Vorstellungswelt deutscher Landstände im 18. Jahrhundert', *HZ*, 223/1 (1976), 49. See also Peter Wick, *Versuche zur Erreichung des Absolutismus in Mecklenburg in der ersten Hälfte des 18. Jahrhunderts* (Berlin, 1964).

administrative instrument of the crown but was now a semi-independent agent in what James Vann has called a 'triangle of antagonists'. Relations between prince, estates, and council deteriorated in the late 1750s and 1760s, when Duke Karl Eugen embarked on a vigorous campaign of cultural aggrandizement and foreign political adventure. In 1770, after Karl Eugen's excesses had provoked strenuous domestic protest and imperial intervention, he was forced to accept the so-called *Erbvergleich*, which restored the constitutional rights of the estates and the administrative power of the Privy Council. From then until the end of the old regime a quarter of a century later, Württemberg was ruled by an often restless coalition of princely, corporate, and bureaucratic authority.[44]

The situation in Württemberg reminds us that we should not view state-building as uniform or unilinear. Nevertheless, in the course of the seventeenth and eighteenth centuries, most German princes were able to achieve some measure of financial independence from their *Stände*. Almost everywhere, the organs of central government increased their role in the political life of many states. Officials began to produce written rules, sometimes complete legal codes, which replaced the complex of customary law and tradition upon which the world of *Herrschaft* had depended. Taxation, administration, and legal codification combined to form the basis of a new kind of state power, a new kind of sovereignty. With these instruments of rule, states could assert their independence against the intrusive pressures of the Reich and the subversive influence of competing authorities within their lands. Boundaries were clarified, loopholes closed, institutional ambiguities clarified. The outlines of the sovereign state in its modern form began to take shape on the landscape of the old Reich.

We should not become so fascinated by the emerging outlines of the future that we overlook persisting contours of the past system. In the south-west, consolidation had hardly begun. Swabia remained a cartographer's nightmare: its nine hundred square miles contained the overlapping and fragmentary lands of four ecclesiastical and thirteen lay principalities, nineteen prelacies and abbeys, twenty-six earldoms and lordships, and thirty-one free cities. Mainz, the largest and most cohesive of the ecclesiastical states, was

[44] This paragraph is based on James Vann's masterful *Making*. For another example of the interaction of prince, officialdom, and *Stände*, see Charles Ingrao's recent study of *The Hessian Mercenary State: Ideas, Institutions, and Reform under Friedrich II, 1760–1785* (Cambridge, 1987).

composed of five distinct territorial units, most of which contained smaller sovereignties. And even Prussia, that paradigmatic eighteenth-century state, was actually a collection of non-contiguous territories scattered across central Europe. In fact, the term 'Prussia' was no more than diplomatic shorthand for 'his royal majesty's estates and provinces', which were separated by boundaries not clearly distinguishable from those of foreign governments. As late as 1794, the *Allgemeines Landrecht* spoke in terms of the 'Prussian states'. Efforts made three years later to introduce free trade within the monarchy proved impossible to enforce. The Hohenzollern, like most of their fellow princes, ruled over a collection of Länder, still internally broken by sovereign enclaves and imperfectly knitted into a single political unit.[45]

State sovereignty remained attenuated as well as fragmented. The *Landstände* were in retreat, but many other traditional institutions were still active. Sometimes this was because the prince had no desire to remove them: as long as they could collect the revenues they needed, many rulers were willing to compromise with guilds, urban communities, church authorities, and noble landlords. Even when they had the desire to challenge these groups, most states did not possess the means. Because trained officials were difficult to find and expensive to maintain, bureaucracies were much too small to control fragmented lands with notoriously poor systems of communication. The closer one got to the local realities of life, therefore, the more important traditional institutional arrangements were likely to be. State theorists may have wanted to have centralized systems of education, justice, and social control, but most schools, judicial disputes, and police matters were settled by local élites in a customary fashion. Justi's machine was a theoretical fantasy, not a reflection of institutional reality. The government remained, as Treitschke once put it, 'high above the people'.[46]

While we should not overestimate either the cohesion or the power of the pre-revolutionary state, we cannot doubt that the expansion of bureaucratic authority was the most important development in German politics. Throughout the eighteenth century, local institutions were infiltrated and undermined by the central administration; almost everywhere, the world of *Herrschaft* was slowly giving way to the forces of *Verwaltung*. In their long,

[45] Riesbeck, *Travels*, i. 58 ff., provides a contemporary account of Swabia. On Mainz, see Dreyfus, *Sociétés*, p. 13.

[46] Treitschke, *History*, i. 183. See also Gerhard Oestreich, 'Strukturprobleme des europäischen Absolutismus', in Oestreich, *Geist*, 179–97.

uneven, and discontinuous struggle to penetrate the social and political order, the leaders of the bureaucratic states had a number of important advantages. The institutions they commanded, while small and inefficient by our standards, were formidable instruments indeed when they could be brought to bear on the diffuse and disparate organs of the old regime. The world of *Herrschaft* was, by definition, locally rooted, regionally specific, socially divided. Few of its institutions were able to develop the organizations or self-image necessary to create a common basis for action. The advocates of the states, therefore, could claim to speak for unity, order, and initiative, and could condemn their opponents for representing particularity, irrationality, and inaction. Like the institutions of the Reich, traditional institutions declined because more and more Germans came to believe that what they did was not enough. In order to fulfil the new purposes of politics—to maintain the monarch in the manner to which he had become accustomed, to raise and sustain an adequate military establishment, and to preserve social order and encourage economic prosperity—a new kind of political institution appeared to be necessary. When the nature and purpose of political power changed, so did its distribution and location: away from the Reich and towards the territorial states, away from local institutions and towards the central administration, and, as we shall see in the next two sections, away from the fragmented lands of the west and towards the major states of the north and east.[47]

iii. AUSTRIA

In 1684, when Philip Wilhelm von Hörnigk published his treatise, *Österreich über alles, wenn es nur will,* he used the term *Österreich* to refer to all of the German Habsburgs' territories: the *Erbländer,* which Ferdinand I had received from his brother Charles V in 1519, the Bohemian and Hungarian crown lands acquired in 1526, and territories conquered from the Turks in the sixteenth and seventeenth centuries. During the early eighteenth century the Habsburgs added a substantial part of the Low Countries and northern Italy to these extensive areas. At the apex of its power, therefore, the Habsburg realm included the hereditary lands (the Archduchy of Austria, the duchies of Styria, Carinthia, and Carniola, the counties of Tirol, Istria, Vorarlberg, and Gorizia-Gradisca, and the

---

[47] Marc Raeff, *The Well-Ordered Police State: Social and Institutional Change through Law in the Germanies and Russia, 1600–1800* (New Haven and London, 1983), examines this process in a European context.

city of Trieste), the Bohemian and Hungarian crown lands (Bohemia, Moravia, Silesia, Hungary, Croatia, Transylvania, the military frontier, and Fiume), a handful of small *Länder* in the western part of the empire, the Austrian Netherlands, Lombardy and Mantua, Galicia and some other fragments of Poland, and Bukovina.[48]

The Habsburgs commanded the allegiance of a dozen nationalities, their authority stretched across a bewildering variety of social and cultural landscapes, their servants came from throughout Europe. No single set of institutions, no one ideal could possibly contain these various elements; each one owed its allegiance to the dynasty, but each interpreted this allegiance in a different way and expressed it through a distinctive set of institutions. No wonder that the baroque, which sought the 'concordia discordantium, the triumph of unity over diversity, and the reconciliation of opposites', became the dynasty's most effective mode of symbolic self-presentation.[49] German conversation, Italian music, Spanish ceremony filled every Habsburg's day, forming a multifaceted legacy to be enjoyed, manipulated, and preserved. Even after the principle of nationality took hold throughout the Continent, the Habsburgs had no choice but to preserve multinational—perhaps it would be more accurate to say, supranational—politics and culture.

Since we will mainly be concerned with the German inhabitants of the Habsburgs' domain, we will use the term Austria in its narrower, more modern sense, as a shorthand for the Alpine and Danubian heartland of the dynasty's central European possessions. Nevertheless, we must keep in mind the full extent of the Habsburgs' domain because only then can we recognize their problematic relationship to German history. Always an important part of our story, they constantly transcend its limits; always a force in German affairs, they were never a German dynasty. Too often, Austrian history has been distorted by seeing it within the restrictive confines of a struggle for mastery over 'Germany'. This misses the essential character of the Habsburgs' historical condition, the range of interests and commitments which provided the foundation for their glory and the source of their ultimate destruction.[50]

[48] There is a selection from Hörnigk in Macartney (ed), *Habsburg*, pp. 70 ff.

[49] Heer, *Kampf*, p. 91. On the formation of baroque culture, see Evans, *Making*, pp. 442 ff.; Hantsch, *Geschichte*, i, ch. 8.

[50] There is a convenient summary of the Habsburgs' territories in Macartney, *Habsburg Empire*, p. 2; Dickson, *Finance*, i. 21. On the dynasty's European scope, see Wandruszka, *House*, pp. 10–11.

During the sixteenth and seventeenth centuries the Habsburgs tried to master their realm with family ties and religious loyalties; they hoped that the dynasty and the church would provide institutional connections flexible enough to contain diversity but cohesive enough to prevent chaos. Unfortunately, both dynastic interests and Catholic religiosity lured the Habsburgs beyond their own borders, embroiling them in conflicts which sapped their resources and inhibited their efforts to create a stable political order. From the division of the family lands in 1519 until the War of Spanish Succession two centuries later, the dynasty expended its subjects' blood and treasure to further the Habsburg cause throughout the Continent. Similarly, the post-reformation church encouraged the Habsburgs' universalistic ambitions by using them to defend the faith against Christian heretics and Turkish infidels. Perhaps the highpoint of Austrian history came when the Habsburgs broke the Turkish siege of Vienna in 1683 and led Christian Europe on a new crusade against its ancient foes. But these were costly victories, which drew the dynasty into an endless series of conflicts along its extensive eastern frontier.[51]

By the end of the seventeenth century, some of the Habsburgs' advisers had begun to recognize that their realm could not be sustained with courtly ceremony, dynastic ties, and religious faith. The monarch, these men were convinced, needed stronger institutions to exercise his authority and a stronger army to enforce his will. They wanted to turn the organizations that served the court—the Chancellery, the *Hofkammer*, and the *Hofkriegsrat*—into instruments for consolidating central power over administrative, fiscal, and military policy. The strongest advocate of these policies was Prince Eugene of Savoy, one of the greatest soldiers of his age and a quintessential Habsburg hero. Eugene, unlike many of those who fought for the dynasty, was not committed to some universal ideal nor did he merely pursue his own narrow self-interest; his primary loyalty was to the state and to the dynasty as its true embodiment. He wanted the monarchy to be regarded as a *totum*, a unity to be sustained by an integrated administration and a powerful standing army. Eugene and his fellow centralizers had some successes in the late seventeenth and early eighteenth centuries, but a great deal remained to be accomplished when the Habsburgs were confronted with that most perilous of dynastic conditions, a succession crisis.[52]

[51] Karl Roider's *Austria's Eastern Question, 1700–1790* (Princeton, 1982) analyses the monarchy's persistent engagement with south-eastern Europe.

[52] The basic work on Prince Eugene is Max Braubach's monumental *Prinz Eugen*

In 1711 the Emperor Joseph I died without a male heir and was succeeded by his brother, Charles VI, who immediately set out to ensure that the realm would pass to his children rather than Joseph's surviving daughters. The so-called Pragmatic Sanction, first announced at a secret council meeting in 1713 and published five years later, proclaimed the indivisibility of the Habsburgs' territories and guaranteed their passage to Charles's heirs. When it became clear that he would leave only female descendants, Charles set about getting the various *Stände* to accept the Pragmatic Sanction; they eventually did so, but usually with the condition that their own special rights and privileges be preserved. While the emperor worked tirelessly to ensure that his daughter's claim be honoured, he did little to leave her the means with which to enforce this claim. Instead he became involved in a series of wars that cost a great deal and gained little. In October 1740, with the weakness of his realm revealed to a watchful Europe, Charles died, the victim of an autumn chill or the inexpertly chosen contents of some mushroom soup.

The emperor's eldest daughter, Maria Theresa, was just twenty-three when she became the first female heir in five hundred years of Habsburg history. Educated by Jesuits, who had stuffed her mind with useless bits of information dredged out of antiquated texts, persistently excluded by her father from affairs of state, and married to the charming but feckless Francis Stephan of Lorraine, Maria Theresa was ill-prepared for her responsibilities. When she ascended the throne, the new monarch was pregnant, as she would be no fewer than sixteen times during the first twenty years of her marriage. Because of her prodigious fertility, her affectionate loyalty to her husband, and her sweet temper, Maria Theresa has often been contrasted to Elizabeth Tudor and Catherine the Great, neither of whom, for opposite reasons, conformed to what were once the accepted standards of domestic virtue. Hugo von Hofmannsthal, writing on the bicentenary of her birth, maintained that her qualities as a sovereign were inseparable from her femininity: 'She was a great ruler in that she was an incomparable, good, and naively generous woman.' In fact, Maria Theresa's strengths had little to do with gender. She was a great ruler because

von Savoyen: Eine Biographie (5 vols.; Munich, 1963–5). Evans, *Making*, pp. 146–51, has a survey of the monarchy's institutions at the beginning of the eighteenth century.

she had a profound and unyielding faith in her own authority, considerable courage and determination, a shrewd sense of people's abilities, and a well-developed instinct for effective gestures.[53]

She needed all of these qualities to survive the first decade of her reign. A few weeks after her succession, the Prussians marched into Silesia, easily defeated the Habsburg armies, and occupied the major towns. At the same time, the elector of Bavaria, invoking rights of inheritance from a distant dynastic tie, invaded Austria from the west. His claims were supported by France, the Habsburgs' long-time rival, as well as by dissident groups within the monarchy itself. Together these challenges represented the most serious threat to the Habsburg's power between the Thirty Years War and the European revolutions of 1848. In the end, Maria Theresa prevailed, largely because of her opponents' divisions and incompetence; the Bavarian challenge collapsed, the alliance woven by France unravelled, and the domestic dissidents were won over or suppressed. When the fighting finally stopped in 1748, the Prussians still held Silesia, Parma had been lost to Spain, but the rest of the monarchy was intact and Francis Stephan had been safely installed as Holy Roman Emperor.

The struggles of the 1740s made clear to the empress and her advisers that basic changes were necessary if the monarchy was to survive. Gradually, traditional bonds of dynasty and religion were supplemented and sometimes absorbed by other sources of power and authority. From this point on, the basis of Habsburg politics began to shift towards what R. J. W. Evans has called 'the middle ground between provincialism and cosmopolitanism', the ground occupied by a consolidating bureaucracy, a uniform legal code, a standing army—in short, the ground upon which states were being built everywhere in central Europe. Maria Theresa accepted the institutional imperatives of the new situation without difficulty; only on religious issues did she show some reluctance. A devout, indeed narrowly pious Catholic throughout her life, Maria Theresa never abandoned her ultimate dependence on God and His church.

[53] Walter Koschatzky (ed.), *Maria Theresia und ihre Zeit* (Salzburg and Vienna, 1979), 11. Alfred Ritter von Arneth's biography of Maria Theresa is filled with information and colourful detail: *Geschichte Maria Theresias* (10 vols.; Vienna, 1863–79). A good insight into the empress's character and opinions can be found in her 'Political Testament' of 1749, which is reprinted in Macartney (ed.), *Habsburg*, pp. 94–131. On the period as a whole, see Richard Plaschka *et al.*, (eds.), *Österreich im Europa der Aufklärung: Kontinuität und Zäsur in Europa zur Zeit Maria Theresias und Josephs II.* (2 vols.; Vienna, 1985).

Eventually, however, her political vision came down to earth. 'Duty' and 'the best welfare of my lands' were, she told her children, 'my two chief maxims'. These came from God, but required for their defence the construction of a powerful, integrated state.[54]

The foundation of this state was the army. Although Austrian military institutions never penetrated politics and society as deeply as their Prussian counterparts, they were a fundamental aspect of Theresian reform. Maria Theresa recognized that military force was 'indispensable for the preservation of the monarchy'; her son and heir, Joseph II, the first Habsburg to appear regularly in uniform, declared on his deathbed that 'the development of the strength, courage, and prestige of the army [was] the principal object of my life'. From the 1740s on, the government struggled to improve the quality of its armed forces: a training academy was established, new uniforms issued, the order of command rationalized. The monarch bolstered the morale of the officer corps by increasing its prestige in the state and ennobling those who served for thirty years. But above all, the army needed men—Maria Theresa's advisers reckoned that she should command 108,000 by the late 1740s—armed, trained, and ready to move. To recruit and equip these men required a great deal of money, which in turn demanded major changes in the fiscal system, constitutional readjustment, and administrative innovation.[55]

In the mid-eighteenth century the Habsburgs' fiscal institutions, like just about everything else in their realm, were a jumble of uncertain jurisdictions, regional diversity, and imperfect administration. Two things were true everywhere: the richest group in society, the landed nobility, was the least likely to be taxed, and the *Stände*, which usually reflected the nobility's views, were prepared to resist any threats to their wealth and power. In 1748 Count Haugwitz, a Saxon officer's son who had emerged as the leading architect of the first phase of Theresian reform, proposed a plan to increase the nobility's tax burdens and to reduce the estates' control over new revenues. He met bitter and determined opposition, first within government circles in Vienna, then in *Stände* throughout the monarchy. This was not, of course, the first time the Habsburgs had clashed with the estates of their realm. But now the crown

[54] Evans, *Making*, pp. 448–50. On Maria Theresa's reform programme, see the documents and analysis in Walter, *Zentralverwaltung*.

[55] Joseph quoted in W. Doyle, *The Old European Order, 1660–1800* (Oxford, 1978), 266. On military institutions, see Duffy, *Army of Maria Theresa*.

confronted the *Stände* on a new set of issues and with a new set of goals: as Otto Hintze put it, the dynasty acted on behalf of an administrative rather than a confessional state. When the struggle intensified, Maria Theresa would not give in. She was sometimes prepared to recognize a region's special status, but she did not compromise her basic demands. One by one, the *Stände* were either persuaded or compelled to go along; all eventually agreed, except for the Carinthians, whose obduracy made them subject to changes by decree.[56]

In order to enforce the agreements so reluctantly accepted by the *Stände*, the government needed direct access to its subjects' social and political lives. The men in Vienna could not count on the estates or their representatives to tell them what there was to be taxed, how much tax had actually been paid, and whether these payments had found their way into the imperial treasury. In a realm as large and diverse as the Habsburgs', such knowledge was hard to come by, but it was vital if the state were to gather the resources it required. The best source of knowledge and control was obviously an administration loyal to the crown. Maria Theresa, therefore, presided over the division of her western possessions (that is, the hereditary lands and the Bohemian crown lands) into districts, which were governed by a royal official whose responsibilities included many duties once performed by local notables and corporate bodies. At the same time, the government's legal and administrative functions were separated. State courts took over most important judicial matters. A Directory supervised the affairs of each *Land*, while central institutions co-ordinated bureaucratic and legal activities in the realm as a whole. Needless to say, this brief summary oversimplifies a complicated and prolonged process; as always in dealing with bureaucratization, we must be careful not to confuse intention with results or formal pronouncements with real accomplishments. Throughout the eighteenth century the centralization of authority and control was incomplete; the administration of Habsburg lands remained untidy and irregular. State agencies were usually understaffed and overworked; officials were not always loyal to the crown, in fact they were

---

[56] Otto Hintze, 'Der österreichische und der preussische Beamtenstaat im 17. und 18. Jahrhundert', in his *Abhandlungen*, i. 349. On the composition and character of the *Stände*, see Beidtel, *Geschichte*, i. There is a good deal of material on the conflict between *Stände* and state in Walter, *Zentralverwaltung*, which is summarized in his *Verfassungs-und Verwaltungsgeschichte*, pp. 89 ff. The most recent account of administration and finances is in Dickson, *Finance*.

known to express their hostility to royal decrees by ostentatiously ripping them to shreds; on the local level, the old élites often retained a great deal of formal and informal influence. Nevertheless, in his efforts to overcome what Maria Theresa gently called 'the unbusinesslike methods' of the *Stände*, Haugwitz established an expanding pattern of control over the traditional social and political order.[57]

Haugwitz's enemies hoped that this pattern would shift when Count Kaunitz, the empress's chief foreign policy adviser, turned his attention to domestic affairs in the late 1750s. But, despite his bitter attacks on Haugwitz, Kaunitz made only minor revisions in his predecessor's policies; the direction of reform remained the same. 'I cannot agree to return the nobility and the *Stände* to their former power,' Kaunitz wrote to his sovereign, 'I am myself a Bohemian aristocrat and landowner, but my duty to Your Majesty stands above that.'[58] For four decades, from the 1750s to the 1790s, Kaunitz served the empress and her heirs. He was joined by a characteristically international set of advisers: Ignaz Koch, an Austrian of humble birth who functioned as Maria Theresa's secretary, Count Tarouca, a Portuguese who ran her household, and Gerhard von Swieten, a Dutch physician with considerable influence on educational institutions.

In the 1760s the monarchy's affairs were directed by the following agencies: the *Staatskanzlei*, which handled foreign policy and dynastic concerns; the *Oberste Justizstelle*, which functioned as a central judicial organ and highest court of appeals; a variously named central administrative agency, best known as the *Vereinigte österreichisch-böhmische Hofkanzlei*; the *Hofkammer* and *Hofrechnungskammer*, both of which dealt with fiscal matters; and the *Hofkriegsrat*, which continued to control the military. Kaunitz put at the top of all these institutions the so-called *Staatsrat*, a council of leading officials and great nobles, which served as a deliberative body called to discuss matters of state and advise the crown. The practical significance of the *Staatsrat* varied over time, but its very existence points out the differences between Austrian and Prussian governmental development: Maria Theresa and her sons were much more dependent on their advisers than were Frederick William I or Frederick II, who would never have allowed a deliberative body to threaten their own, highly personal power.

---

[57] In addition to Hintze's brilliant summary (cited in n. 56) and Walter's documents (n. 54), see Beidtel, *Geschichte*, i.

[58] Walter, *Verfassungs-und Verwaltungsgeschichte*, p. 105.

For the last fifteen years of her reign, from Francis Stephan's death in 1765 until her own in 1780, Maria Theresa's most important collaborator was her son, Joseph, who succeeded his father as Holy Roman Emperor. The empress, deeply grieved by her husband's sudden death and exhausted by four decades of turmoil and travail, eagerly shared her authority with Joseph, whom she viewed with both admiration and concern. From childhood, Joseph seems to have been a difficult and wilful person; the early death of his first wife and a wretched second marriage did nothing to sweeten his personality. There was always something hard and cold about Joseph; everything he did had an edge to it. 'I flattered myself', his mother wrote to him in 1776, 'that your numerous family [and] your states would lose nothing by my death, but would, on the contrary, gain by it. Can I nurse this hope if you indulge yourself in tones which repel all tenderness and friendship?' But friendship and tenderness were foreign to Joseph; reason and knowledge mattered. A great king did not need to be loved, he only needed to be right.[59]

Unlike his mother, who had been reared in the twilight of baroque piety and courtly culture, Joseph was trained by men committed to the new state. Christian August Beck, for instance, lectured his royal pupil on the fundamental importance of natural and civil law for an understanding of human institutions. Beck believed that faith and revelation belonged to a purely religious realm, necessary to lead a Christian life but separate from civil society. Joseph did not see himself, therefore, as the anointed head of a divinely sanctioned order but rather as the first servant of a secular state, the guardian of its laws and the chief of its administration. He remained a Catholic, but made few connections between his private faith and public duties. Nor was he much interested in ceremonial expressions of royal power, those rituals and displays that had been so central to Habsburg rule in the age of the baroque. He dressed simply, usually in uniform, kept a rather small and modest court, and opened his palace grounds to the public. For a time he even thought about burning the court archives in order to save money. Religion, ritual, even dynastic traditions meant less to him than organizational efficiency, clarity, and

[59] Quoted in Macartney (ed.), *Habsburg*, pp. 185–6. The first volume of Derek Beales's definitive biography of Joseph II appeared after this chapter had been written: *Joseph II, i. In the Shadow of Maria Theresa, 1741–1780* (Cambridge, 1987). In his introduction, Beales provides a useful discussion of the literature on Joseph and Josephism.

coherence. These were the virtues he hoped to impose upon his realm.

Some contemporaries and many historians have praised Joseph for the simplicity of his tastes. In comparison to the corrupt overindulgence so common among eighteenth-century monarchs, his austerity and sense of duty seems appealingly democratic. We should not forget, however, that Joseph kicked away the religious and ceremonial props of his position in order to strengthen his real power. He wanted to create a political machine to unify and co-ordinate his lands and thus to enable him to touch the lives of all his subjects. When he talked about 'Wir Beamten', he was not simply associating the crown with the rest of the state's servants, he was placing it at the head of an institution that aspired to a monopoly of legitimate authority over state and society, a kind of power his most ceremonially fastidious forebears could not have imagined.

Although they differed greatly in personal style and temperament, Joseph and Maria Theresa shared the same political goal, the same desire to ground Habsburg rule on a firm bureaucratic foundation. Much of what the son did merely continued or extended his mother's policies. Consider, for example, the vexed matter of church–state relations. Maria Theresa's deep religious feelings did not prevent her from pushing the state into areas traditionally claimed by the church. She knew that the church, like the other privileged corporations in her realm, undermined the state's ability to mobilize and extract the resources it required. Thus she supported Kaunitz's efforts to limit clerical influence to spiritual issues by extending political control over education, charitable institutions, and other cultural matters. When a cardinal protested at her educational policies in 1770, the empress tersely replied: 'The school is and remains a *politicum*.' During the 1770s the government revoked the clergy's fiscal privileges, closed some monasteries, and expelled the Jesuits, the élite corps of counter-reformation Catholicism. After his mother's death, Joseph expanded the process of secularization, first by dissolving the monastic orders, then by effecting large-scale parish and diocesan reorganization, and finally by taking over the education of the clergy. Together, these measures weakened the alliance between dynasty and church which had been central to the Habsburg system of rule throughout the sixteenth and seventeenth centuries.[60]

[60] Fritz Valjavec, *Der Josephinismus. Zur geistigen Entwicklung Österreichs im achtzehnten und neunzehnten Jahrhundert* (2nd edn., Munich, 1945), analyses Joseph's religious policies and their significance for the evolution of Austrian liberalism. See

In one important respect, Joseph went beyond his mother: not only did he remove the church's privileges, he also tried to take away its power to impose its teaching on unwilling subjects. In 1781 the emperor issued the famous Toleration Patent, which declared that, while Catholicism remained the public religion of the realm, members of the two Protestant denominations and the Greek Orthodox Church could worship as they wished. Moreover, in another Toleration Patent of 1782, Joseph set out to improve the position of Austria's Jews, so that 'all of our subjects, without regard for their nationality or religion . . . might share in the public welfare that we wish to improve through our care'. To this end, the edict destroyed the tangle of special laws governing Jewish life, removed many social restrictions, and opened a number of educational opportunities. By narrowing the differences between them and Christians, Joseph hoped to make Jews 'more useful to the state'.[61]

Joseph believed that religion should be a private matter, but he did not believe in the value of freedom *per se*. He was quite prepared to repress opinions that did not fall within the accepted limits of his toleration. In 1783, for instance, he ordered that a number of Bohemian Deists be whipped until they abandoned their heretical views. He also created institutions to oversee and control his subjects. The political police, established under Count Pergen in the 1780s, spread a net of surveillance over public life, gathering information and arresting suspected dissidents. These policemen are as important for an understanding of Josephism as the Edicts of Toleration; each is an authentic element in his regime. Their coexistence helps to explain why both liberals and absolutists looked to Joseph's reign for their roots, and why some historians hail him as an emancipator while others condemn him as a despot. In fact, he was the ancestor of both liberalism and absolutism; his policies were at once tolerant and repressive, sources of emancipation and domination. In Josephism, as in other systems of enlightened despotism, new kinds of freedom were inseparable from new kinds of restraint.[62]

also Ferdinand Maass's monumental *Josephinismus*; Winter, *Der Josephinismus;* Klaus Gottschall (ed.), *Dokumente zum Wandel im religiösen Leben Wiens während des Josephinismus* (Vienna, 1979).

[61] Katz, *Ghetto*, pp. 161 ff; and the documents in Macartney (ed.), *Habsburg*, pp. 148 ff.

[62] Paul Bernard, *The Limits of Enlightenment: Joseph II and the Law* (Urbana, 1979), ch. 2, discusses police and censorship. For a contemporary view, see Riesbeck, *Travels*, i. 244–5.

This interplay of freedom and restraint can be clearly seen in the social and economic policies pursued by Maria Theresa and continued by Joseph. In 1749 the government established the *Universalkammerdirektorium*, a central office in charge of commercial policy, manufacturing, and transportation. To encourage economic productivity, improve her subjects' standard of living, and expand the resources available to the state, the empress tried to cut back on the power of the guilds and to reward new, dynamic enterprises. Joseph continued these policies which in effect substituted state regulation for corporate authority, central supervision for local control. At the same time, he lengthened the tariff wall that his mother had begun to construct around her lands so that domestic industries might profit at the expense of foreign goods.[63]

Because agriculture was the most important sector of the economy, the key to Austria's prosperity was to be found in the tangled relationships between landowners and their peasants. Here, both Maria Theresa and Joseph realized, was the problem which their state must ultimately resolve. In her testament of 1749, the empress noted that administrative reforms gave the monarch

the opportunity of acquiring personal knowledge of the nature of her domains . . . and withal of promoting a just relationship, such as is pleasing to God, between lords and their subjects, but especially of watching closely that the poor, and particularly the unfree population, be not oppressed by the rich and by their masters.

Neither mother nor son wanted to destroy the nobility's special privileges by dismantling completely the peasantry's bondage. But in order to create a prosperous, contented rural labour force, they had to invade the realm of *Herrschaft*. Throughout the second half of the century, the authorities in Vienna struggled to find an acceptable balance between their own aspirations and the interests of the aristocracy. At first, the process was halting and uneven, filtered through the complex skein of local needs and relationships. After a series of piecemeal changes in the 1760s and 1770s, Joseph tried to enforce a consistent, rational policy; his Edicts of 1781 and 1782 restricted patrimonial justice and removed some of the restrictions on peasants' rights to move, marry, and change occupations. In return, peasants were expected to obey the state, pay taxes, and serve in the army. As the burdens of *Herrschaft* were lifted, the demands of the bureaucratic order increased.[64]

---

[63] Hantsch, *Geschichte*, i. 208 ff.
[64] Macartney (ed.), *Habsburg*, p. 130. See below, Ch. 2, sec. ii.

State-building involved legal as well as fiscal, administrative, and constitutional reform. In order to absorb or destroy the rules and customs defended by church, guilds, and landowners, the government had to establish the primacy of public law, which it alone could codify, interpret, and enforce. An important step in this direction occurred during the first phase of Theresian reform when judicial and administrative functions were separated and a new court structure was established. In 1753 the empress set up a commission to codify civil law throughout much of her realm (the dynasty's possessions in the Netherlands, Italy, and Hungary were excluded). The commission struggled with this formidable task until 1766, when it issued eight huge volumes covering well over eight thousand points of law—an extraordinary compendium that tried to balance a respect for existing statutes with the need for clarity and conciseness. Both conservatives and progressives attacked this compromise during Maria Theresa's last years; it was finally abandoned by Joseph, who committed himself to making the laws of his lands conform to reason. The first instalment, known as the *Josephinisches Gesetzbuch*, appeared in 1786; some significant changes in the judicial system and several legal innovations, such as civil marriage, were also introduced in the 1780s.[65]

Joseph's ultimate object was machine-like uniformity. He wanted to turn his varied dominions into 'une province égale dans toutes les dispositions et charges'. Stubbornly he pushed ahead, centralizing and regularizing whenever he could. Regional peculiarities that his mother had tolerated now came under attack, as Joseph imposed a standard form on the departments governing the Netherlands and Lombardy. His new system of administration in the lands of the Hungarian crown undermined the Magyar nobility's pre-eminence in state and society.[66]

Inevitably, this drive for administrative uniformity raised problems of language that had been easily avoided in the local world of personal relationships. No longer could people choose the language that suited them, shifting from one to another as the situation required. Bureaucratic regulations and reports demanded that there be one official language, a single medium for privileged messages and official records; the ambiguities and flexibility of oral communications were now intolerable. In 1784, therefore, German was officially designated as the internal language of the bureaucracy, the

---

[65] Strakosch, *Absolutism*, chs. 4, 6, 7.

[66] Quoted in Fritz Hartung, 'Der aufgeklärte Absolutismus', in Hofmann (ed.), *Entstehung*, p. 168.

Amtssprache for the Habsburg realm. Few realized it at the time, but a fateful link between Germanization and centralization had been forged. Austrian politics would never be the same.[67]

We should not become so enthralled with Joseph's domestic innovations that we lose sight of his ambitions for glory. 'L'empereur', wrote an observer in 1784, 'croit que le plus grand prince pour l'histoire, comme pour ses contemporains, sera toujours celui qui aura le plus accru son territoire.' He tried, therefore, to strengthen the Habsburgs' position in German affairs by engineering an exchange of the Netherlands for the electorate of Bavaria. At the same time, he allowed himself to become involved in a Russian alliance against the Turks. Both these ventures ended badly: forced to abandon the Bavarian exchange, he soon confronted a rebellion in the Netherlands, encouraged by his European rivals; the Turkish war proved to be both expensive and unproductive. Foreign setbacks were then joined by domestic defeats. Joseph's most ambitious reform programme the decrees of 1789 abolishing the distinction between noble and non-noble land tenure, had to be abandoned in the face of angry protests from the aristocracy and scattered violence from disappointed peasants. In January 1790 the emperor was forced to abandon his reorganization of the Hungarian lands and to acknowledge the Magyar nobility's special status. The great drive for uniformity and cohesion had stalled; the forces of regional autonomy were once again on the move.[68]

By this time Joseph was gravely ill, suffering from a fever caught during his luckless Turkish campaign. His last weeks have a kind of tragic grandeur: beset by a battalion of troubles and ravaged by disease, he remained chained to his duties, sustained only by years of habit and his own unbending will. Joseph died in February 1790, at the end of his forty-ninth year, lamenting that his years of struggle had brought so little happiness to his subjects and evoked gratitude from so few. Even as he lay dying, no longer in control of events, rebellion spread throughout his lands. When his death was announced, there were some who offered prayers of thanksgiving for their deliverance from his rule.[69]

[67] Hantsch, *Geschichte*, i. 232.

[68] Quotation from Aretin, *Reich*, i. 24. On the Bavarian exchange, see Paul Bernard, *Joseph II and Bavaria: Two Eighteenth-Century Attempts at German Unification* (The Hague, 1965); on the Turkish war, Karl Roider, *Austria's Eastern Question* (Princeton, 1982).

[69] S. K. Padover, *The Revolutionary Emperor: Joseph II of Austria* (New York, 1967), has a moving account of Joseph's last days.

In his history of the Habsburg monarchy C. A. Macartney names 28 January 1790 as the date when the tide turned against the dynasty. From that day, when Joseph retreated in the face of Hungarian resistance, Macartney traces the start of the political decline which would end with the monarchy's dissolution 128 years later.[70] One cannot help but wonder if 'decline' is quite the right word for a process that lasted so long. The Habsburgs did, after all, rule another twelve decades; of course they perished in the end, but only after fighting and losing the most destructive war in human history. However, in politics, as in nature, motion is a relative condition, and relatively speaking the Habsburgs did decline after 1790, in comparison with both their own glorious past and the future fortunes of their arch-rivals in central Europe, the Hohenzollern rulers of Brandenburg Prussia.

iv. PRUSSIA

When Joseph Riesbeck listed the great powers in 1780, he did not mention Prussia.[71] Many of Riesbeck's contemporaries would not have quarrelled with this omission, however impressed they might have been with the character and achievements of Prussia's great king, Frederick II. Thoughtful observers of eighteenth-century politics knew that one great monarch did not make a great power: Sweden, after all, had played a major role on the European scene under Gustavus Adolphus and had then swiftly shrunk into the status of a secondary, peripheral state. A military defeat, an unfortunate alliance, an inept heir, or a contested succession might reverse the fortunes of any but the greatest state. Even at the end of Frederick's reign, therefore, many Europeans viewed Prussia as no more than a potential great power.

One had only to compare Vienna and Berlin in order to sense the differences in scale and significance between Habsburg and Hohenzollern. Vienna's history stretched to Roman times; by the seventeenth century it was a city of world renown, the only central European rival to Paris or London. Its streets were crowded with the relics of a rich and complex past; outside its walls, new suburbs developed, gradually enveloping the palaces built by nobles drawn to the Habsburg court from throughout the Continent. Berlin, on the other hand, was newer and smaller. While Vienna had commanded the Danube for Rome, Berlin was a small fishing

---

[70] Macartney, *Habsburg Empire*, p. 1.
[71] Riesbeck, *Travels*, ii. 77.

village on the Spree. Little of historical importance or architectural distinction could be found in Berlin when the Hohenzollern began to turn the city into the small, tidy capital of a minor dynasty. Writing in 1804, Madame de Staël complained that 'one sees [in Berlin] no traces of earlier times . . . an entirely modern city, beautiful as it is, makes no impression; it reveals no marks of the history of the country, or the character of its inhabitants. . . '. While Vienna seemed to burst with the richness of its heritage, Berlin reflected the glory of its most recent king and the skills of a few great builders.[72]

The contrast between Vienna and Berlin points to an important difference between the two dynasties' historical positions. With an extended and unruly legacy to defend, the Habsburgs had to find a way to consolidate and contain their territorial possessions and to restrain their historical pretensions. Habsburg history in the eighteenth and nineteenth centuries is the history of reluctant but unavoidable choices between the dynasty's universal mission and its narrow self-interests, between influence in central or southern Europe, between enemies in the east or west. The Hohenzollern started from a much more modest base: they had no universal mission to look back on, no dynastic glories to maintain. Unburdened with the legacy of greatness, they had to create their own history and thus to find a set of ideals and a sense of purpose with which they could embellish their struggle for survival. Perhaps the best artistic expression of this process can be seen in Andreas Schlüter's splendid equestrian statue of the Great Elector, which once stood on Berlin's Lange Brücke and is now in the courtyard of the Charlottenburg Palace. The sculptor has caught his subject's remarkable personal power and energy, but the iconography, roughly based on the Capitoline statue of Marcus Aurelius, is derivative and empty.

The Hohenzollern's link to Brandenburg was forged at the beginning of the fifteenth century when Frederick, count of Nuremberg and ruler of Ansbach-Bayreuth, agreed to administer the electorate for his old friend and comrade in arms, the Emperor Sigismund. Frederick's sons inherited the land and established it as a separate part of the family domains. In 1539 the Hohenzollern

[72] Bab and Handl, *Wien*, is a stimulating comparison of the two capitals. Staël is quoted by Hermann Pundt, *Schinkel's Berlin: A Study in Environmental Planning* (Cambridge, 1972), 16. Compare Nathaniel Wraxall, *Memoirs of the Courts of Berlin, Dresden, Warsaw and Vienna in the Years 1777, 1778, and 1779* (2 vols.; London, 1799), 97 ff.

joined the Lutheran cause, which they supported with the caution and restraint dictated by their meagre resources. What territorial gains they made over the next century came from marriage or purchase, not conquest. Eventually they ruled the counties of Cleves, Mark, and Ravensberg in the west and, as vassals of the Polish king, the duchy of Prussia in the east. In all of these scattered *Länder*, the dynasty's power was strictly limited by the estates, whose members jealously protected their political rights and fiscal privileges. For the Hohenzollern, as for so many other German rulers, the Thirty Years War was a disaster. By 1640 their lands had lost half their inhabitants and much of the countryside was wasteland; Berlin contained no more than 6,000 unhappy souls. Foreign soldiers were everywhere—the Dutch in the west, the Swedes in the north, the Poles in Prussia. The dynasty's survival was in doubt.[73]

It is difficult not to be impressed by Prussia's growth from these most unpromising beginnings. Franz Schnabel, not someone to be counted among the Hohenzollern's uncritical admirers, called the creation of their state 'the greatest political deed in German history'. Before turning to the specifics of this story, we should note three advantages which set the Hohenzollern apart from many of their less fortunate competitors. First, their lands, while neither immense nor laden with wealth, were large and rich enough to sustain powerful political and military institutions. They were large enough—but not too large to be controlled with the means available to early modern statesmen. One of the Great Elector's more important accomplishments was his refusal to accept the crowns of Sweden and Poland; this saved his state from the pains of overextension so apparent, for example, in the history of Saxony. Second, because the dynastic core of the Hohenzollern's territories was not in the centre of late-seventeenth- and early eighteenth-century geopolitics, they escaped the devastation suffered by the Palatinate and allowed the electors to pursue a flexible foreign policy. While Austria was engaged in enormously expensive wars against France and the Ottoman Empire, Brandenburg Prussia was consolidating its position against a much less formidable set of opponents in the north. Finally, from 1640 to 1786, the Hohenzollern beat the demographic odds of their age by producing an unbroken series of male heirs, each of whom lived long enough to ensure an orderly succession. No other major dynasty had this

---

[73] Carsten, *Origins*, provides a useful account of early Prussian history.

good fortune. Moreover, throughout this long period no Hohen-zollern ruler was either hopelessly stupid or totally mad, and three of them were men of quite extraordinary ability.[74]

The first of these extraordinary rulers was Frederick William, known even during his lifetime as the 'Great Elector'. Only twenty years old when his father died in 1640, Frederick William had experienced the disruptions and humiliations which war brought to a state unable to defend itself. Like the energetic new proprietor of some faltering family business, he resolved to succeed where his predecessors had so obviously failed. His reign, it should be noted, was not without disasters: at times the elector's diplomacy was unproductively devious; some of his greatest military victories brought little or no return. Nevertheless, he left his lands significantly stronger than he found them. In 1648 he came away from the negotiations that ended the Thirty Years War with Lower Pomerania and two western bishoprics, Minden and Halberstadt. Eventually he managed to acquire full sovereignty over the duchy of Prussia and to annex from Poland a strip of land along the Oder. But more important than these territorial gains was the army the elector created to defend them. This, he told the counsellors who gathered around his bed on the day before he died, was the simple lesson upon which all of his achievements rested: to live in an armed world, one must have arms. In 1640 he had inherited 5,000 unruly and unreliable troops; he bequeathed to his heir an effective force of 35,000.[75]

To build such an army with the resources available to him, the Great Elector had to become involved in a process familiar from our earlier accounts of state-building: soldiers required money, money had to come from taxes, taxes had to be collected by a central agency, often in defiance of local interests and privileges. This process, we should emphasize once again, was neither inevitable nor irreversible. The elector did not have a preconceived masterplan; he did not function like a master architect laying

---

[74] Schnabel, *Geschichte*, i. 96. The single best account of Prussia's rise is still the work of Otto Hintze. In addition to the essays collected in his *Abhandlungen*, see *Die Hohenzollern und ihr Werk*. Felix Gilbert has edited an English translation of some of Hintze's most important studies: *The Historical Essays*. Hans Rosenberg's extra-ordinarily influential *Bureaucracy* builds on Hintze but reverses many of his ideological positions. A good introduction to recent scholarship can be found in Puhle and Wehler (eds.), *Rückblick auf Preussen.* There is an interesting comparative analysis of Prussian institutions in C. B. A. Behrens, *Society, Government and the Enlightenment: The Experiences of Eighteenth-century France and Prussia* (New York, 1985).

[75] Ferdinand Schevill, *The Great Elector* (Chicago, 1947).

foundations upon which his descendants might build; he was a beleaguered leader trying to resolve the day-to-day problems of political and military survival. While recognizing that the contingent and improvisational character of his reign may undermine patriotic conceits about Prussia's predetermined path towards greatness, it does nothing to diminish the elector's accomplishment.

During the bleak period just preceding Frederick William's reign, many of the *Stände* in his territories had been badly battered, first by invasion then by belated efforts at self-defence. In the early 1640s the estates began to recover their former power and once again were in a position to inhibit the elector's efforts to raise taxes and mobilize resources. After mid-century, however, the initiative clearly shifted to Berlin. By taking advantage of the estates' social and regional divisions, Frederick William was able to acquire the revenues necessary to form an army against which no domestic forces could prevail. Roughly speaking, the same pattern was repeated throughout the Hohenzollern lands: in Brandenburg in 1651–3, then in Prussia and the western *Länder* ten years later, the elector presented a general meeting of the estates with a higher tax bill; after a good deal of haggling, a compromise was achieved through which the state got some funds but the *Stände*'s rights were confirmed; thereafter, the state collected the money but tended to ignore the rights. This process was most complete in Brandenburg, where the *Stände* virtually disappeared; in Prussia, the elector's hegemony was slowed by local resistance; in the west, the *Stände* paid their dues but retained considerable autonomy, thus following the pattern of the other *Nebenländer* in their region.

The cities in the Hohenzollern's eastern lands suffered most from the elector's triumph over the estates. Revenues from urban areas came from excise taxes, which the state levied and collected on most economic transactions. This system provided the central government with a wedge that it eventually drove into the entire structure of municipal life. By the end of the century most cities had lost almost all control over their own affairs. Governed by tax officials, these cities existed on the political periphery, regarded by the ruler and his advisers only as sources of support for the true embodiments of the state, its soldiers and bureaucrats.

The countryside turned out to be much harder to dominate than the cities. Here, despite the decline of the *Stände*, the aristocracy's local power persisted. There were, to be sure, bitter clashes between nobles and the elector—harsh words, lasting antagonisms, frequent threats, and occasional violence. But gradually the two sides learned to live with one another: in Otto Hintze's summary phrase, 'the nobles abandoned their resistance to the standing army and to the cost that this entailed, and in return the elector was willing to strengthen and affirm their social and economic interests as well as their local authority..' Eventually the institutional terrain on which central and local authority met displayed a distinctive mixture of corporate and bureaucratic offices and interests. The *Landrat*, for example, was appointed by the state but had close ties to local élites, thus institutionalizing a complex and often unstable balance of forces in state and society. Often enough tensions between the government and the nobility were resolved at the expense of the peasantry. In contrast to the cities, the excise tax was not used in rural areas; instead a land tax enabled estate owners to shift much of the new fiscal burden on to the already heavily laden shoulders of their dependents.[76]

Throughout the Great Elector's reign the army played a central role, not simply as the end but also as the means of state-building. The first officials to enforce central authority in the country were *Kriegskommissare*, Military Commissars, who began by supervising local support for the army forces, but gradually became involved in a wide range of social and economic activities. In Berlin, the main co-ordinating agency was the *Generalkommissariat*, which had originally been devoted to purely military matters but soon began to direct district officials, oversee urban tax collection, and instruct those in charge of the elector's personal estates. The lands of the seventeenth-century Hohenzollern were still fragmented and diverse, but in the *Generalkommissariat* one can see the faint beginnings of a unified, central state apparatus.[77]

In what would become a Hohenzollern family habit, the Great Elector's relationship to Frederick, his eldest son and heir, was filled with distrust and animosity. When Frederick finally came into his inheritance in 1688, he immediately set about writing his own chapter in the dynasty's history. If the Great Elector resembled a vigorous new owner out to save the old firm from bankruptcy, his son was like another familiar type in literature and life, the heir who wants to spend what the preceding generation had earned. And spend he did—on wars, large and small, on the

---

[76] Hintze, 'Geist und Epochen der preussischen Geschichte', in his *Abhandlungen*, iii. 39. There is an account of the struggle between ruler and *Stände* in Carsten, *Origins*, Chs. 13, 14, 15.

[77] Hintze, 'Der Commissarius und seine Bedeutung in der allgemeinen Verwaltungsgeschichte', in his *Abhandlungen*, i. 242–74, also available in *Essays*.

construction of palaces and churches, on the creation of important centres of learning, and on the pomp and ceremony of his court. He managed to add a few parcels of land to the family domain, but his most lasting impact was, appropriately enough, a symbolic one. In 1700 he took advantage of the Habsburgs' need for help during the War of Spanish Succession by sending eight thousand soldiers to the emperor, who repaid him the following year with royal status for himself and his descendants. Henceforth, the Hohenzollern would be known as 'Kings in Prussia', a title which set them apart from the herd of dukes and counts which roamed central Europe. Frederick died in 1713, leaving this title and some fine buildings as his principal achievements.[78]

The new king, Frederick William I, was as different from his father as Frederick had been from the Great Elector. While Frederick had been personally refined and cultivated but politically aggressive and bellicose, his son was the opposite. Frederick William firmly opposed war for prestige or conquest. In his famous testament of 1722, he warned future rulers that 'God has forbidden unjust wars and one day you will have to account for every man who has fallen in [one].' A peaceful monarch, Frederick William was a violent man—crude, loud, and given to terrible rages. He was not simply without cultural interests, he actively opposed them. For one thing, culture cost money that might be better spent elsewhere. Furthermore, the king believed that, since what passed for culture in his times was manifestly satanic, its pursuit was a sure sign of predestined damnation. Work was the true purpose of life; from dawn to late evening, Frederick William devoted himself to affairs of state. For relaxation, he hunted, drank prodigious quantities of beer, and enjoyed the antics of his court buffoon, whom he eventually appointed to be Leibniz's successor as president of the Berlin Academy.[79]

The psychological differences between Prussia's first two kings left a lasting mark on their state's public style and political culture. Frederick had tried to import into his lands the baroque forms and courtly ceremonies that flourished throughout the Continent. His son, however, wanted nothing to do with 'mistresses, comedies, operas, ballets, masquerades, balls, gorging and guzzling'. Instead,

[78] There is a good account of Frederick in Carl Hinrichs's biography of his son, *Friedrich Wilhelm I., König in Preussen: Jugend und Aufstieg* (Hamburg, 1941).

[79] Robert Ergang's biography of Frederick William is a much better book than its title would lead one to expect: *Potsdam Führer* (New York, 1941). There is a more up-to-date account in Gerhard Oestreich, *Friedrich Wilhelm I.* (Göttingen, 1977).

Frederick William sought to revitalize the traditions of reformed piety that he believed had been part of the Hohenzollern family since its conversion to Calvinism in the early seventeenth century. Hard work in one's calling, duty, puritanical restraint—these were the virtues he preached and tried to live by, these were the political values that his appointed spokesmen were supposed to spread throughout his state. We should not overestimate the spread of these virtues among Prussian bureaucrats; there was plenty of room for corruption and incompetence behind official protestations of austerity and industriousness. But Frederick William's peculiar brand of *raison d'état* remained among his most important legacies.[80]

For Frederick William, this *raison d'état* was inseparable from his own personal desire for mastery. He did not care if this mastery was ceremonially embellished, as his father's had been, nor did it have to be rationally defined, as it was for an enlightened despot like Joseph II. Frederick William's impulse to control events was personal, direct, immediate. He wanted to know everything, watch everyone, reward loyal service, and punish malefactors—if possible with a few swift blows from the royal cane. He approached his realm as he had approached the estate his father gave him when he was crown prince. Like a vigorous and profit-seeking rural businessman, he drained swamps, built canals, improved housing, encouraged enterprise, and tried to find the best possible people to do the job. Many of his subjects doubtlessly benefited from his efforts, as did the skilled refugees who came to Prussia from everywhere in Europe. But for the king himself, these benefits were means to other ends: his own authority, the steady increase of his treasury, and the impressive expansion of his military might.

Mastery, the king realized, required institutional extensions of his individual energy and will. In December 1722 he created what came to be called the General Directory, an agency designed to supervise and co-ordinate military, fiscal, and judicial activities throughout his lands. The Directory was divided into four departments, each responsible for certain territories and functions (for example, the affairs of Minden, Ravensberg, and the budget, or of Prussia, Pomerania, and agriculture), a combination which reminds us that the Hohenzollern still did not rule a state cohesive

[80] See the literature on pietism cited below, Ch. 3, sect. iii, n. 61. The classic account of Calvinism and Prussia is by Hintze, *Essays*; see also Rudolf von Thadden, *Die brandenburgisch-preussischen Hofprediger im 17. und 18. Jahrhundert* (Berlin, 1959).

enough to be run without regard for its territorial diversity. The king did not usually attend the Directory's daily meetings, but he left careful instructions about how each hour was to be spent, even going so far as to plan what was for lunch ('four good courses, with wine and beer') and how it was to be eaten ('half the heads and members of the departments is to eat while the other half works'). Frederick William also tried to consolidate institutions within his territorial units by centralizing taxes and extending the excise system. But he was careful not to enhance bureaucratic power at his own expense: 'We remain King and Lord,' he wrote at the end of his decrees on the General Directory, 'and do as We please.' To be sure that he could do as he pleased, Frederick William gathered around him a 'cabinet' composed almost entirely of commoners, who recorded his commands and delivered them as he instructed.[81]

Frederick William was interested in everything in his realm, but he was fascinated, even obsessed by the army. From the first moment when he was given the command of a small band of troops, he lavished on every detail of military life his passionate attention. No doubt these military interests had a practical source, as anyone who looked at his lands' vulnerable geographical position could easily see. But pragmatic considerations do not explain the depth and intensity of Frederick William's commitment to the army. Perhaps he loved his soldiers because his mastery over them seemed so clear and unambiguous. Unlike his officials, who always seemed ready to deviate from his rigorous plans, or his nobility, who remained stubbornly tied to their own interests, the king's troops obeyed, their columns turned upon command, their muskets fired in single salvos. The complex drills to which eighteenth-century armies devoted so much time (and none more so than his) certainly had tactical value, but they were also metaphors for organizational co-ordination and political mastery. No wonder that Frederick William combined his love for soldiers with a hatred for war, that most unpredictable and potentially chaotic of human activities. He much preferred the fine points of soldiering in peacetime, when he could devote himself whole-heartedly to rules and regulations about the length of an infantry-man's pigtail and the proper position of his buttonholes.

Under Frederick William, the army consolidated its position as a pre-eminent force in state and society. The king increased the

[81] Macartney (ed.), *Habsburg*, pp. 299 ff. On administrative developments, see the works by Hintze and Rosenberg cited in n. 74, and the concise summary in Johnson, *Frederick*, ch. 1.

prestige of the officer corps at every opportunity: officers dominated the court, served in local government, staffed royal commissions, and held important ministerial positions. Lower levels of administration also took on a military cast because veterans received preference in the assignment of minor bureaucratic posts, such as school teaching. But more important than this interweaving of military and political institutions were two steps which Frederick William took to engage the army in the day-to-day life of rural society. First, he forbade his nobility from serving in foreign armies and did everything he could to encourage them to serve for a time in his own. By meshing officer corps and aristocracy, he hoped to increase the former's prestige and the latter's loyalty. Second, in 1733 Frederick William changed the way ordinary soldiers were recruited by introducing the so-called canton system. Each of his eastern lands was divided into districts, cantons, which were responsible for providing a certain number of troops. The army was to be filled with able-bodied peasants instead of misfits, mercenaries, and the unfortunate victims of press gangs or unscrupulous recruiting agents. But, since he did not want to disrupt agricultural production, the king allowed his recruits to remain in their cantons and to work the land when they were needed most, at planting and harvesting times. This meant that the army became an integral part of the social structure. When church bells rang to announce that a soldier had deserted, for example, the entire village was supposed to help return him to his unit. Moreover, the canton system gave Prussia's characteristic blend of state power and aristocratic privilege a military dimension: just as the aristocratic officer affirmed his loyalty by his service to the king, so the peasant trooper reaffirmed his obedience to his master, who was both his military and social superior.[82]

Given what we know of Frederick William's taste and temperament, we should not be surprised by the fact that he was an extraordinarily difficult father. As soon as it was clear his eagerly awaited son and heir, Frederick, would survive infancy, he set about making the child into a copy of himself. But in this, his most important effort at mastery, the king's will was thwarted. The young prince disliked his father's habits, remained indifferent to religion, affected courtly manners and elegant dress, was physically

---

[82] Craig, *Politics*, remains a fine introduction to the development of Prussian military institutions. On the army and society, Otto Büsch, *Militärsystem und Sozialleben im alten Preussen, 1713–1807: Die Anfänge der sozialen Militarisierung der preussisch-deutschen Gesellschaft* (Berlin, 1962), is still unsurpassed.

delicate and intellectually ambitious. Every one of his interests and mannerisms seemed to be a calculated affront to his father, a challenge to Frederick William's notion of how a young Hohenzollern should behave. 'I cannot abide an effeminate chap,' he wrote to his sixteen-year-old son, 'who has no manly leanings, who, to his shame, can neither ride nor shoot, and at the same time is personally unclean, wears his hair long and curled like a fool.'[83] In 1730 the conflict between the two reached a crisis. When Frederick tried to flee the country, he was arrested, imprisoned, and finally forced to watch the decapitation of his friend and companion, Lieutenant Katte. The prince survived only because he was willing to submit to his father's commands and devote himself to learning his duties in a bureaucratic office. Ten years later, when Frederick William, sick and exhausted by his labours, died at the age of fifty-two, he and his son had been reconciled. But Frederick's unhappy childhood and the traumatic events of 1730 left their mark on his character. They helped to harden his will, to fortify his courage in the face of adversity, and to sustain his profound confidence in himself, but they also contributed to the dark side of his personality, his deviousness, deep cynicism, and abiding loneliness.

Whatever its source in the complex chemistry of personality and circumstance, individual talent and historical opportunity, Frederick's character fascinated his contemporaries and ensured him a formative role in the history of his state. By the second half of his long reign he had become a kind of tourist attraction, drawing travellers to Berlin with the hope that they might see or even speak to him. Boswell, for example, watched him walk around Potsdam in the summer of 1764 and was deeply impressed by his simplicity of manner and 'air of iron confidence'. Goethe disliked his politics but was enthralled by his personality and praised him as a truly heroic figure. Soon after his death, Frederick's greatness took on legendary stature. Georg Friedrich Rebmann, who later devoted himself to the service of revolutionary France, was deeply moved by the memories of Frederick which were evoked during his visit to the Prussian capital in 1793, an experience he compared to seeing the sites of classical heroism in Rome. Frederick's practical importance for the growth of the dynasty was certainly less than the Great Elector's, nor did he have King Frederick William's

[83] Macartney (ed.), *Habsburg*, p. 323. The literature on Frederick is gigantic: the best account in English is Peter Paret's translation of Gerhard Ritter's *Frederick the Great*; the most recent biography is Schieder, *Friedrich der Grosse*.

impact on the growth of Prussian institutions. But as symbol and personification of his state, he was the most significant of all. His deeds and, still more important, the historical narrative of these deeds eventually gave Prussians a sense of themselves; in him, they came to see both evidence and promise of their own greatness. But, while Frederick's historical legacy was persistent and powerful, it was also diverse and ambiguous. As often happens with national heroes, his admirers disagreed about the historical nature and contemporary meaning of his heroism. When it was time to build a monument to his achievements, Frederick's heirs bitterly disagreed over whether he should be portrayed as an enlightened thinker, political reformer, or military conqueror.[84]

When his reign began, thoughtful people hoped that he would serve as the instrument for enlightenment values. Since childhood he had been interested in literature and philosophy and, after his marriage in 1735, he had spent four years at his estate, Rheinsberg, where he had read widely, writtten on various subjects, and corresponded with some of the best minds of the age. In his first letter to the new king, Voltaire reflected enlightened thinkers' hopes and expectations when he addressed Frederick as 'Votre majesté ou votre Humanité', and added, 'The French have all become Prussians.' Even after he became king, Frederick wrote a great deal, and while we may doubt Dilthey's overly enthusiastic estimate that he was one of the four greatest authors of his generation, he did write extraordinarily well considering everything else he had to do. As king, Frederick also encouraged the life of the mind throughout his realm, revitalized the Prussian Academy, improved education, and sponsored various cultural institutions. He was famous throughout Europe for his tolerance, perhaps because he was especially tolerant of foreigners. Rousseau, for instance, kept the king's picture in his room and once fled to the Prussian enclave of Neuchatel because he was sure he could find refuge there. Neuchatel was also the place where that quintessential enlightenment product, the *Encyclopédie*, was published.

Our age is the age of enlightenment, the century of Frederick [Immanuel Kant proclaimed], He deserves to be praised by a grateful present and posterity as the man who first liberated mankind from immaturity (as far

[84] Pottle (ed)., *Boswell*, p. 24; Georg Friedrich Rebmann, *Wanderungen*, pp. 69–70. Compare Riesbeck, *Travels*, iii. 1; Joseph Marshall, *Travels through Holland . . . in the Years 1768, 1769, and 1770* (London, 1772), 242 ff. On the debate over Frederick's monument, see Nipperdey, 'Nationalidee'.

as government is concerned), and who left all men free to use their own reason in all matters of conscience.[85]

Frederick's conception of the state was shaped by enlightened ideas. He had even less taste for the ceremonial dimensions of kingship than did his father. Religiously indifferent, he also rejected that sense of God-given duty and responsibility so important to Frederick William's conception of the state. Nor was he much interested in the dynasty, and evidently made no particular effort to produce an heir of his own. Frederick, like his admirer and rival Joseph II, believed that his authority came from the state itself, not from rituals or God or even the royal blood in his veins. Monarch and people were bound by the laws of the state, had to serve it as best they could, and remained subordinate to its purpose.[86]

Frederick sometimes acted as if the purpose of the state was to increase the welfare of its inhabitants. After all, he once said, how can people love their country if it does nothing for them? He devoted time and energy to improving the material conditions of his lands, especially after the appalling destruction caused by the Seven Years War. He encouraged enterprises, financed economic innovations, and embarked on a massive campaign of colonization that brought 300,000 new inhabitants to the Prussian provinces. On his own private estates, he gave many of his peasants land and freed them from their seigneurial obligations. But, despite all of these accomplishments, one could not argue that Frederick regarded the state as merely an instrument of public welfare. He made it clear often enough that people existed to further the state's ends, not to be served by the state. 'I view my subjects like a herd of stags on some noble's estate,' he once wrote to Voltaire, 'their only function is to reproduce and fill the space.' And, he might have added, to fight and die when called upon to do so.[87]

Stripped of its ceremonial, religious, and dynastic functions, the Frederician state emerges as the instrument of its own power. 'The first hallmark of a prince should be to survive,' Frederick wrote in his testament of 1768, 'the second, to expand.'[88] Enlightenment

[85] Wilhelm Dilthey, 'Friedrich der Grosse und die deutsche Aufklärung', in his *Schriften*, iii. 83–205. Jean-Jacques Rousseau, *Confessions* (Baltimore, 1954), 547–8; Kant, *Writings*, p. 58. On Kant's political views, see below, Ch. 3, sects. iii and iv.

[86] The best sources for Frederick's own views are his political testaments: see Hintze's essays on the testaments of 1752 and 1768 in his *Abhandlungen*, iii.

[87] Marcel Reinhard *et al.*, *Histoire générale de la population mondiale* (Paris, 1968), 225.

[88] Aretin, *Reich*, i. 24.

and public welfare were surely parts of his agenda, but at the core of his regime were motives as old as human society, the desire for power, glory, and conquest. Within a few months of becoming king, Frederick began his first war, sending his armies into Silesia and thereby adding to his lands a rich province that increased the number of his subjects from two and a half to four million. Easy to take, Silesia was painfully hard to hold. Twice in the 1740s and again during the Seven Years War (1756–63), the Habsburgs fought to regain what they had lost; each time they were defeated, but only at great cost.

In the course of these wars Frederick showed himself to be a gifted strategist and brilliant field commander. Because he was willing to abandon the conventional emphasis on position and manœuver in favour of swift, energetic offensive action, he was able to win some impressive victories. At Rossbach, for instance, he inflicted heavy losses on a French and Austrian force while suffering minimal casualties; a month later, at Leuthen, he produced what Napoleon would call 'a masterpiece of movement, manœuvers, and resolution' in which he defeated a badly led imperial army. In Frederick's best battles we can sometimes catch a glimpse of the strategic revolution that would occur in the decades after his death. But he himself remained very much within the framework of old-regime warfare and accepted its assumed limitations on the size and mobility of forces. These limitations often prevented Frederick from converting victory in battle to victory in war: after Rossbach and Leuthen, for example, the fighting went on for five more years. Of course these same limitations also prevented Frederick's enemies from taking full advantage of his frequent defeats.[89]

The centrality of war for the Frederician state shaped the king's vision of the social order. Ordinary men, he believed, would only fight if compelled to do so; soldiers required iron discipline and constant intimidation. Their officers, however, had to be inspired by personal honour and the love of glory, qualities that were only to be found in the aristocracy. A strong, loyal nobility was, therefore, a military necessity. To strengthen his noblemen, Frederick lent them money, affirmed their exclusive right to own an estate, and preserved their power over the peasantry. At the same time, he tried to widen the gap between nobles and the rest of

---

[89] Fuller, *Battles*, pp. 194 ff., describes Frederick's qualities as a commander. See also Duffy, *Army of Frederick the Great*, and the concise analysis in Howard, *War*.

society by prohibiting them from 'inappropriate' commercial and industrial activities. In the officer corps, aristocratic rank was a prerequisite for advancement. By the end of Frederick's reign 90 per cent of the corps was titled; the commoners who had been commissioned during the Seven Years War had been forced to resign or were relegated to unfashionable artillery, engineering, and supply units. From the benefits and privileges heaped upon them, from the opportunities they received in the government and army, and perhaps most of all, from the shared glories and dangers of combat, the Prussian nobility developed a loyalty to the king and to the state he embodied. Antagonisms between state and nobility remained, as did the landed élite's well-honed sense of their own self-interest; but during Frederick's reign the Prussian aristocracy acquired an ethos of state service that remained part of their collective identity as long as they existed as a social group.[90]

Frederick's aristocratic preferences were also felt in the administrative hierarchy, where titles and family connections improved an official's opportunities for promotion. But in the bureaucracy, unlike the military or local government, aristocratic influence meet powerful counterpressures. By the second half of the eighteenth century there were several hundred men in what has been called Prussia's 'core bureaucracy'. Under Frederick, the core bureaucracy grew in size and significance. The acquisition of new territories, the growth of the state's role in education and economic affairs, and the extraordinary demands of continued military campaigns all required more officials and new forms of administrative organizations. Although these officials were divided by personal, social, and departmental rivalries, they did share a sense of collective identity created by their training, recruitment, and experience. This identity could, for some men and on some occasions, override other values and interests. In short, the bureaucracy had begun to develop social and political interests of its own.[91]

Frederick recognized that a self-conscious bureaucracy was a challenge to his own authority. The transformation of 'royal servants' into 'state servants' threatened the desire for mastery

[90] Hintze, 'Die Hohenzollern und der Adel', in his *Abhandlungen*, iii. 30–55; Rosenberg, *Bureaucracy*, pp. 155 ff.; Demeter, *Officer Corps*. The most recent survey of the Junkers' long history is F. L. Carsten, *Geschichte der preussischen Junker* (Frankfurt, 1988).

[91] In addition to Hintze and Rosenberg, see Johnson, *Frederick*. Johnson estimates that in the middle of the eighteenth century there were no more than three thousand Prussian civil servants, including subalterns (pp. 15 ff.).

which he inherited from his father. Unlike Frederick William, however, Frederick did not try to dominate the administrative apparatus by concentrating its authority. Instead he added new departments, jumped over chains of command, and even allowed some power to devolve upon local institutions. As a result, the administration became increasingly fragmentary and disorderly. A man of Frederick's intelligence and drive could sometimes make it work, but he had much less control than conventional treatments of his regime would lead us to believe. To get results, he had to work with or around his chief officials and, even with their support, the practical effect of his commands depended on a thinly spread, overworked, and undertrained band of subordinates, many of whom were tightly bound to communities far from Berlin. The closer we get to what policies meant in these localities, the more often we find the king's commands were evaded, reinterpreted, or simply ignored. As one official noted in 1749, Frederick's directions were always in danger of remaining confined to a 'platonic republic, so good on paper, but impossible to put into practice'.[92]

The tension between command and execution, theory and practice, can be seen in Frederick's greatest and most lasting political reform, the reorganization of the Prussian legal system. Like Joseph II, he wanted to create a new community of justice, flowing from and administered by the state. He began with the court system, which was reorganized and greatly improved under the leadership of Samuel von Cocceji, a veteran jurist who became head of the legal department in 1746 and served until his death, at seventy-eight, nine years later. Frederick also wanted a new code, a 'masterpiece of the human spirit' resembling a clock 'in which all the gears have but one purpose'. Yet in Prussia, as in Austria, codification was immensely complex, not simply because of the variety of statutes it had to contain and the diversity of interests it had to please but also because Frederick and his legal advisers came to their task with ambivalent intentions and incompatible motives. They wanted to create clock-like order and coherence, but also to preserve special rights and social privileges. The final code, the *Allgemeines Landrecht*, published in 1794, eight years after Frederick's death, asserted the principles of uniformity in its general passages only to undermine and negate them with innumerable exceptions, redefinitions, and qualifications. As Günter Birtsch has

[92] Walter Mertineit, *Die fridericianische Verwaltung in Ostpreussen* (Heidelberg, 1956), 181; Mertineit's study is an important attempt to examine the impact rather than merely the intentions of state policy.

written, the Prussian Code was 'not a radical, enlightened–absolutist will to reform, but rather the coexistence of an absolutist conception of the state with a preservation of corporate rights'.[93]

In his fascinating essay on the *Allgemeines Landrecht*, Wilhelm Dilthey noted that, just as the early church sought to objectify its religious spirit in dogma, so the eighteenth century sought to put its spirit into practice through law.[94] Dilthey is characteristically insightful, even though he underestimates the internal tensions and limitations within the century's political spirit and its legal accomplishments. In its aspirations, the drive for legal reform expressed the state's desire to overcome universalist communities of justice like the old Reich and local islands of custom, privilege, and special status, like guilds, cities, corporate institutions, and religious communities. Moreover, the new laws sought to create a new kind of man, a citizen—what, significantly enough, Germans called a *Staatsbürger*—who would exist outside the particularist confines of family, caste, or community. The state promised these citizens freedom from the restraints imposed by intermediate institutions, but in return demanded that they obey its laws, pay its taxes, and serve in its armed forces.

As we have seen, no pre-revolutionary state was able to fulfil these promises of emancipation or to realize these desires for control. Both the old Reich and the intermediate spheres of *Herrschaft* remained, limiting state sovereignty from the outside or weakening it from within. Most states were still knit together from *Länder* that retained some measure of local power. And every state, large or small, contained corporate institutions which its central authorities would not or could not dominate. The unfulfilled aspirations and implicit compromises so vividly expressed in the Prussian legal code have their counterparts throughout central Europe. Why that should have been the case will become clearer after we have examined the social context of eighteenth-century politics.

---

[93] Frederick quoted in Aretin, 'Einleitung', in Aretin, *Absolutismus*, p. 17; Günter Birtsch, 'Eigentum und ständische Gesellschaft im 18. Jahrhundert', in Berding *et al.* (eds)., *Staat*, p. 67. On the *Landrecht*, see Birtsch, 'Gesetzgebung und Repräsentation im späten Absolutismus: Die Mitwirkung der preussischen Provinzialstände bei der Entstehung des Allgemeinen Landrechts', *HZ*, 208/2 (Apr. 1969), 265–94; and especially Koselleck's now classic account in *Preussen*.

[94] Wilhelm Dilthey, 'Das Allgemeine Landrecht', in his *Schriften*, xii. 132.

II
Eighteenth-century Society

IN 1765, when Goethe went from Frankfurt to Leipzig to begin studying law, his clothes, speech, and manners marked him as a foreigner; some female companions told him, none too gently, that he looked as if he had 'dropped down out of another world'. Karl Heinrich Lang had a similar experience when he and his family moved from one Swabian village to another in the 1770s; although their journey lasted no more than four hours, the Langs found themselves in an 'island of different customs, dialects, and manners'. The same sort of thing struck Georg Forster when he travelled through the Rhineland in 1791. Even in neighbouring towns such as Boppard and Andernach, Forster discovered that people spoke and behaved quite differently. Nowhere else, wrote Freiherr von Knigge, is it harder to know how to act than in Germany, since 'nowhere else can one find such a great multiplicity of conversational tones, educational methods, opinions on religion and other matters, and such a great diversity of conditions which claim the attention of various social groups in the different provinces'.[1]

This fragmentation of social experience reflected and was reinforced by the backwardness of the communications system throughout central Europe. Goethe's trip from Frankfurt to Leipzig, for instance, was filled with delays and discomforts; even so, he was more fortunate than Casanova, who once had to spend three long days trying to traverse eighteen short leagues. Under the best of circumstances, it took nine days to go from Berlin to Frankfurt, two from Augsburg to Munich. And of course circumstances were often not of the best, particularly at those legendarily difficult spots that experienced travellers learned to dread. One of these was the steep and perilous track between Bohemia and Saxony, which terrified Lady Montagu in 1716 and had not been noticeably improved when Nathaniel Wraxall made the same journey sixty years later. Water transport was usually preferable to overland routes, although river traffic was also slowed

---

[1] Goethe, *Autobiography*, i. 268; Lang, *Zeit*, i. 25; Forster, *Ansichten*, pp. 11–12; Adolf Knigge, *Über den Umgang mit Menschen* (5th edn., Hanover, 1796), 23–4.

by navigational hazards and political harassment. To go down the Rhine from Mainz to Cologne took thirty hours (and at least three days going the other way), while a trip on the Danube from Regensburg to Vienna lasted almost six days. For those who had to do without the comforts that only great wealth could buy, even the swiftest journey could seem interminable because of the vehicles and accommodations that were available. The German postal coach is a 'barbarity', wrote Boswell. 'It is just a large cart, mounted on very high wheels, which jolts prodigiously. It has no covering and three or four deal boards laid across it serve as seats.' After a day in one of these conveyances, the traveller found refuge in some dingy, unhygienic inn with cuisine to test the hardiest digestions. No wonder that the authors of adventure stories did not feel obliged to send their characters to far-off lands; a damsel like Johann Hermes's Sophie could find more than enough distress on the road from Memel to Saxony.[2]

Traditional society's deplorable communications system did not prevent people from moving. The rich travelled in search of amusement and adventure, the poor in search of nourishment and work. But the difficulties of travel did inhibit the development of sustained relationships extending beyond village, city, or region, and without such relationships there could not be an easy exchange of capital, labour, or commodities; there could not be, in other words, a cohesive society or economy. As we shall see, supra-local relationships grew slowly in the course of the eighteenth century, promoted in part by commerce and manufacturing, in part by the political forces just described and by the cultural movements to be considered in Chapter 3. Nevertheless, at the end of the century we can find no more than the faint beginnings of an institutional network uniting different parts of German Europe. Most Germans remained locked in their insular social worlds—or were forced to wander in desperate search of a world in which they might find a place.

i. CHARACTERISTICS OF THE TRADITIONAL SOCIAL ORDER

Let us begin our consideration of the traditional social order with the most fundamental facts about human existence: fertility and

[2] Casanova, *Life*, x. 55; Montagu, *Letters*, i. 281–2 and n. 2; Pottle (ed.), *Boswell*, p. 50. For additional examples, see Biedermann, *Deutschland*, i, pt 1, pp. 300 ff; Sombart, *Volkswirtschaft*, ch.1.

mortality, birth and death, the beginning and the end of life. We tend to think of these as intimate, individual events, isolating and isolated experiences that set us apart from one another. 'The memory of birth and the expectation of death', E. M. Forster once wrote, 'always lurk within the human being, making him separate from his fellows and consequently capable of intercourse with them.' In traditional society, birth and death were social events that affirmed people's interdependence rather than their individuality. Fertility and mortality, and especially the balance between them, reflected and determined the community's fate. A decline in the number of births and an unnatural increase in the number of deaths were signs of trouble—famine, plague, or war. But in time, such declines in population might bring new opportunities—vacant lands to till, widows in need of husbands, masters without apprentices. The reverse was also true: an increase in the birth-rate and a decline in mortality were signs of current prosperity, but also harbingers of future scarcity. Eventually, there would be too many people and not enough land, food, or work. Throughout the second half of the eighteenth century, communities tried to respond to these alternating patterns of privation and opportunity. When some disaster cut down the competition for resources, the number of births increased since more people could get married and others could marry at an earlier age. However, when competition became too intense, the number of marriages declined, some people moved away, and the population contracted. Behind these figures about marriage and migration, behind the lines of fertility and mortality on our charts, is the largely unwritten story of ordinary people's hopes and disappointments, struggles and misfortunes, happiness and pain.[3]

At the beginning of the seventeenth century there were between fifteen and twenty million people in the German states; fifty years later, their numbers may have been reduced by as much as 30 or 40 per cent. The fighting, famine, and disease surrounding the Thirty Years War left scars on the social landscape that took decades to heal. In Pomerania, Brandenburg, and the Palatinate, cities shrank, villages were abandoned, fields left untilled. The city of Augsburg, which had about 50,000 inhabitants in 1600, had fewer than 20,000

[3] DeVries, *Economy*, provides a good introduction to early modern demography. In addition to the material cited below, n. 5, see Tilly (ed.), *Studies*, and the various works by Arthur Imhof, especially *Jahre*, *Historische Demographie*, *Einführung*, and *Die verlorenen Welten: Alltagsbewältigung durch unsere Vorfahren—und weshalb wir uns heute so schwer damit tun* (Munich, 1984).

fifty years later; it did not reach its former size until the nineteenth
century. The state of Württemberg suffered even more dramatically. Its population was 400,000 when war engulfed it in the 1630s;
by the end of the decade, hardly one-quarter of that number
remained. Of course, the sufferings caused by the war were
unevenly distributed. Some areas, such as the Alpine regions, parts
of Saxony, and the Rhineland, were virtually untouched. Others
actually benefited from the war; Hamburg, for instance, grew from
40,000 to 50,000 during the first half of the century.[4]

In the German lands, as in the rest of Europe, a new
demographic era began around the middle of the eighteenth
century. Almost everywhere, the pace of population growth
significantly accelerated. Moreover, for the first time in human
history, growth was sustained, unbroken by major crises and
catastrophes. As the data in table 2.1 show, the process that would
culminate in the unparalleled demographic movements of the
nineteenth century was clearly under way.

TABLE 2.1. *Population growth in the eighteenth century*
(millions)

	1700	1750	1800
Europe	115	140	187
Germany[a]	16	16–18	23–24
Württemberg	0.340	0.472[b]	0.660
Prussia[c]	5.1	6.4	8.8

Notes:
  [a] Boundaries of 1914.
  [b] 1740.
  [c] Boundaries of 1846.
Source: Wehler, *Gesellschaftsgeschichte*, i. 69–70.

While demographic historians agree about the importance of this
'vital revolution', they are divided and uncertain about its origins.
Most now acknowledge that the revolution was not primarily the
result of changes in either fertility or nuptiality; the available

[4] The demographic impact of the Thirty Years War is a much debated subject.
Günther Franz, *Der dreissigjährige Krieg und das deutsche Volk* (Jena, 1940), is the
classic account, which has been much criticized. Pounds, *Geography . . . 1500–1840*
p. 77, has a regional map summarizing Franz's data. Wehler (in *Gesellschaftsgeschichte*, i. p. 54) is sceptical about the extent of the damage inflicted by the war on
German Europe as a whole.

evidence does not suggest that after 1750 women had more children, married earlier, or were more likely to be married—at least not in numbers sufficient to explain demographic growth. If fertility and nuptuality are excluded as explanations, then the main answer must lie in changes in the mortality rate. Although, by modern standards, mortality rates remained terrifyingly high until well into the nineteenth century, what Michael Flinn calls a 'stabilization of mortality' seems to have occurred after 1750. On charts measuring demographic change, the jagged lines that plot the incidence of death gradually straighten. We are not sure why. For some reason, the bubonic plague no longer threatened western and central Europe. Moreover, a series of marginal improvements in public health and nutrition somewhat increased people's chances for survival. Still, the essential forces behind the vital revolution remained shrouded in mystery. Louis Henry, one of the greatest demographers of modern times, modestly admitted that 'we still do not know whether this reduction in disasters was produced by man, the result for instance of economic progress, or whether it was just a piece of good luck.'[5]

As we should expect, the effect of the vital revolution on central Europe was uneven. Both Austria and Prussia grew rather rapidly (at annual rates of 0.84 and 0.86 per cent); Bavaria stagnated or even declined. Within Prussia, significant regional variations can be found: in the course of the eighteenth century the population of Pomerania expanded by 138 per cent, of Silesia by 100 per cent, and of East Prussia by 132 per cent, while the more densely settled western territories grew much more slowly. Such large regional differences were almost always the result of population movements. There were also, however, important variations in fertility and mortality. In Bavaria, for instance, local aversion to breast-feeding produced endemic intestinal disorders and a murderously high incidence of mortality among infants. In Prussia, the number of children per family tended to be somewhat higher than in the south. Both the age and incidence of marriage—which, in the absence of contraception are very powerful demographic forces—could also vary widely. For instance, Jacques Houdaille found that the number of unmarried adults ranged from between 19 and 29 per cent in Bavaria to between 3 and 11 per cent in Hesse.[6]

[5] Flinn, *System*, p. 95; Post, *Crisis*, p. 122. On the 'vital revolution' in the German lands, see the works of W. R. Lee, especially *Growth* and the essays in *Demography*.

[6] Lee, *Growth*, pp. xx, 8, 63 ff.; Marcel Reinhard *et al.*, *Histoire générale de la*

Behind these regional variations and chronological fluctuations loomed the fact that all eighteenth-century Europeans had to face: death was to be expected at every age. Infancy was the most dangerous time of life. In some areas, one-third of all babies died before their first birthday; as many as one-half of all children died during their first ten years. This meant that one's life expectancy was considerably higher at age ten than at birth: according to Halley's famous computations of data from late-seventeenth-century Breslau, 39.9 as compared to 33.5 years. Famine, disease, accidents at work, or misfortunes in childbirth thinned the ranks of every age cohort. Somewhere between 5 and 10 per cent of the population lived past sixty; only a handful reached what we have come to think of as old age, the natural end of life.[7]

Often enough death struck communities and regions in epidemic form. Warfare, while surely less destructive than it had been in the seventeenth century, continued to create turmoil and disruption. Prussia, for example, suffered greatly during the Seven Years War, which briefly reversed demographic growth in places such as Pomerania, whose population declined from 368,996 in 1734 to 339,947 in 1766. Although better disciplined than Wallenstein's mercenaries eighteenth-century armies still brought hunger and sickness in their wake, causing townsmen to seek refuge behind their walls and peasants to build their houses away from potential lines of march. Famine, that other familiar apocalyptic beast, remained a danger for most Europeans. Because so many lived so close to the level of subsistence, crop failures, such as those that occurred during the terrible winters of 1708–9 and 1740–1, could easily lead to starvation, and because transportation remained poor, local problems could have fatal consequences. In 1771–2, for example, poor harvests sent prices skyrocketing in the Erzgebirge; the cost of rye rose tenfold, of bread, sixfold. Those with barely enough to get by in good times had to sell everything just to stay alive. Those with nothing to sell had to beg, steal, or starve. No wonder that lines measuring the changing price of food and the incidence of death usually move in tandem. But even without the stimulus of war or hunger, epidemic disease could strike with

population mondiale (Paris, 1968), 224; Pounds, *Geography . . . 1500–1840*, pp. 99 ff.; Jacques Houdaille, 'Quelques résultats sur la démographie de trois villages d'Allemagne de 1750 à 1789', *Population*, 25/3 (1970), 649–54.

[7] On child mortality, see Imhof, *Jahre*, pp. 41 ff.; Halley's data are reproduced in Louis Dublin and Alfred Lotka, *Length of Life: A Study of the Life Table* (New York, 1936), 42–3.

sudden and devastating effect. In Berlin, for instance, five hundred children died from a brief but virulent outbreak of measles in 1751. Smallpox killed one of every thirteen children in Württemberg during the 1770s. In such a world, death was an ever-present companion, not some gradually approaching destination.[8]

To many of life's dangers, the poor were much more vulnerable than the rich. The poor had no reserves of food, no hoarded gold to use when prices rose, no walls to hide behind or well-placed kinsmen to call upon for aid. Their sons could fall into the hands of a recruiting officer, who might send them off to fight in some far-distant war. Their daughters could fall prey to the amorous attentions of a lecherous master and then be left to pay the price for their dishonour. The poor were subject to the whims of the powerful, taxed to support the luxurious life of their betters, forced to watch silently as noblemen rode across their fields in pursuit of game.

To some vicissitudes, however, the rich were as vulnerable as the poor. Fire, for example, was a constant threat, which could swiftly destroy an entire village or neighbourhood or even, as in the case of Neuruppin in 1797, an entire city. There was little anyone could do to stop a fire; only a few had insurance—that characteristically modern form of security—to compensate them for their losses. Nor was wealth much help in the case of sickness. The children of the rich died almost as often as those of the poor. Among eighteenth-century Europe's ruling families, where the survival of children was a matter of the greatest possible concern, twenty-nine out of every thousand infants were stillborn, another forty-seven died during their first week, and 106 during the remainder of their first year of life. Kaunitz, the great Austrian statesman, had ten brothers, not one of whom lived to adulthood.[9] To those seriously sick, money could buy comfort but not health. Even the best physicians were as apt to make their patients worse as better; their treatments, whether successful or not, were often extraordinarily painful. A bad set of teeth, an improperly healed fracture, failing eyesight, poor digestion—these and countless other sources of pain or discomfort were a permanent part of many, perhaps most people's lives.

[8] The standard work on famine is Abel's *Massenarmut*. François's study of Koblenz traces the parallel course of food prices and mortality rates: 'Population', especially p. 306 and the graph on p. 338. Biedermann, *Deutschland*, i, pt. 1, has a great deal of data on disease.

[9] See Preller's essay in Glass and Eversley (eds.), *Population*; and Klingenstein, *Aufstieg*, pp. 112 ff., 127 ff.

In their own bodies, as well as in the worlds of nature and society, people confronted forces they could neither understand nor control. About many essential things, Europeans seemed to know little more at the beginning of the eighteenth century than they had in the ancient world: medical students still read Galen, strategists studied Caesar, architects followed Vitruvius. People still travelled as the Romans had, sometimes on roads less well constructed; the techniques of farming had not improved much since the Middle Ages; other technological advances, while often impressive individually, were scattered and uneven. As Fernand Braudel has written, the ordinary citizen of traditional Europe remained 'an unconscious prisoner of the frontier marking the inflexible boundaries between the possible and the impossible. Before the eighteenth century, his sphere of action was tightly circumscribed, largely limited to what he could achieve by physical effort.'[10]

The principal purpose of traditional institutions was to help people to live within these limitations and thus to survive in a hostile, unpredictable, largely unmanageable universe. People did not expect the social order to make them healthy, happy, and successful; such expectations are distinctly modern, the products of eighteenth-century ideas and nineteenth-century institutions. In traditional Europe, people were content if the social order could shield them from disaster, or at least soften its inevitable blow and provide consolation after it had struck. Institutions, therefore, were supposed to protect their members, by erecting real or symbolic walls between them and those outside. In this context, *liberties* were not general rights to engage the outside world as one might wish; they were restricted rights to enjoy the privileges and protection within a particular community. These liberties—to gather wood in a certain part of the forest, to farm a particular piece of land, to make shoes for a town or music for a prince—were necessarily limited to a specific group; they had no meaning if they belonged to everyone.[11]

At the heart of the traditional social order was that most restrictive and supportive of human institutions, the family. Here, if one were fortunate, life began and ended. To be born or to die outside one's home, and especially in some public place or institution, was almost always an indication of displacement and disgrace. The family was supposed to provide the first and most reliable line of defence against the world outside. Like any refuge,

---

[10] Braudel, *Capitalism*, p. xiv.
[11] See Schlumbohm, *Freiheit*, especially ch. 1.

the family was a source of both protection and restraint; it kept outsiders at bay, but in return demanded obedience and confirmity.[12] conformity.[12]

In the nineteenth and twentieth centuries, social theorists often contrasted what they took to be the stability of the traditional family with the unhappy instability of modern marriage. Like so many other images of the pre-modern world, this image reflects contemporary discontents rather than historical realities. The demographic data just considered make clear why the traditional family was anything but stable; families were continually disrupted by death, usually of children, but also of one or both parents. Moreover, in most families childhood was brief; boys and girls of twelve or thirteen had to leave home to go to work. Even when the parents survived, older children would depart from the household while their younger siblings were still being born. This instability had an obvious impact on the emotional climate of family life; although there was surely a good deal of love and affection in many households, one does not find the highly charged emotional bonds and affective expectations we associate with modern families. Similarly, the sentimental cult of the child, so powerful in both romantic and *Biedermeier* culture, is foreign to traditional ways of thinking.[13]

Most households in western and central Europe were based on the so-called nuclear family, that is, one set of parents and their offspring. Extended families, including several generations and married siblings, were rare. Except among the very rich, households tended to be fairly small, one or two parents, some young children, and a few lodgers, workers, or servants. Lutz Berkner has called our attention to what he calls the 'stem family', a pattern most often found in rural areas where the family lands passed undivided to a single heir. In this situation, it sometimes made sense for the heir to take over the land while the original owner was still alive and to provide him (or her) with a place to live and some kind of income. As Berkner makes clear, this arrangement was usually quite unlike the idyll of extended kinship one sometimes comes upon in nostalgic accounts of pre-modern family life; often

---

[12] After decades of neglect, the family has become a subject of great interest to German historians. Hausen, 'Familie', is an introduction to the problems and literature of family history. Sieder, *Sozialgeschichte*, is a good brief account, with an up-to-date bibliography. Conze (ed.), *Sozialgeschichte*, and Evans and Lee (eds.), *Family*, are valuable collections of recent scholarship. See also Hubbard, *Familiengeschichte*; Rosenbaum, *Formen*; and Mitterauer and Sieder, *Family*.

[13] Mitterauer, *Sozialgeschichte der Jugend*.

enough family life was fraught with strains and tensions between the heir and his parents and between the heir and his siblings.[14]

The family's size, structure, and atmosphere were determined by economics and demography, the need to produce and to reproduce. In contrast to its modern counterpart, therefore, the traditional family was more apt to be shaped by trade regulations, land tenure patterns, and inheritance laws than by sexual attraction and personal satisfaction. It was an economic rather than an emotional unit. This was reflected in the original meaning of *economics*, whose roots are in the Greek term *oikos*, household. 'The Oeconomia', wrote Wolf Helmhard von Hohberg in his *Georgica curiosa* of 1682, 'is nothing other than the prudent wisdom necessary to run a successful household.' In this book, which Hohberg referred to as an *Oeconomica*, *Hausbuch*, and *Wirtsehaftsbuch*, he dealt with problems of estate management, agricultural practice, and various domestic affairs. To him, these things were all closely related matters having to do with running a household economically. Only gradually does the term *family* take on its modern connotations, paralleling the changing meaning of *economics*, which comes to be used to refer to a set of activities centred in markets rather than households. As we shall see, this terminological division between economics and family reflects the emergence of a separation between the family's productive and reproductive functions, between home and work, affection and interest, private and public life.[15]

The traditional household was dominated by the *Hausvater*: 'Herr bist du als Mann', as one treatise of family life put it early in the nineteenth century. As a *Herr im Haus*, the father's authority, his *Herrschaft*, was linked with a hierarchy of other authorities, ranging from the noble lord to the prince to the divine source of all legitimate rule. Like the other earthly *Herren*, the father could enforce his will by violence over his children and over other members of his household. In all matters of importance, his word was law: 'Bravely, the man and father presents himself as what he is by nature, the head of his family, the lord of his home. . . . He apportions the household jobs and makes sure that everyone gets his due. . . . As far as his position allows, he likes to be at home, so

[14] Berkner, 'Stem Family'. See also Mitterauer, 'Familiengrösse'.

[15] Brunner, *Landleben* pp. 237 ff.; Brunner's influential essay on 'Das "ganze Haus" ' in *Wege*. There is an excellent discussion of these terminological shifts in M. I. Finley, *The Ancient Economy* (Berkeley and Los Angeles, 1973), 17 ff. See also the relevant articles in *GGB*.

that he can fully supervise and lead the domestic unit.'[16] To count for something in the outside world, to have a say in the life of the community or corporation, required that one be a *Hausvater* or, in some cases, his widow. Full membership in most guilds, political office, and many kinds of work were reserved for males, either by law or tradition.

The *Hausfrau*, whose identity and authority derived from her husband's, played an equally important role in the household. She had primary responsibility for the family's reproductive functions. In contrast to her modern counterpart, a woman in traditional society would spend most of her adult life caring for her own (or other people's) children. She would also prepare the food, care for the house, make and mend the family's clothing, and help to manufacture many necessities of life, such as soaps, candles, and utensils. Only affluent families in urban settings had the means and opportunity to buy prepared foods and manufactured goods. In addition to her domestic tasks, the *Hausfrau* participated in the household's productive activities, not simply by helping to feed and supervise the apprentices or hired hands, but also by directly performing certain kinds of work. The character of her economic role varied from trade to trade and place to place, since both necessity and custom helped to determine what was 'women's work'. In some regions, for instance, women spun but did not weave; when the chief farming implement was the hoe, women worked together with men, whereas only men operated the plough. Everywhere, women were expected to pitch in when the rhythm of work intensified; at harvest time, they joined the rest of the family in the fields, where they helped to save the crops while they continued to perform their other duties. As Arthur Imhof has recently shown, this seasonal pattern affected every aspect of family life: in the village he studied, the number of conceptions declined sharply during the busiest time of the agricultural cycle.[17]

[16] Möller, *Familie*. p. 10.

[17] The history of German women is just beginning to be written. Ute Frevert discusses the state of the subject in 'Bewegung und Disziplin in der Frauen-geschichte: Ein Forschungsbericht', *GuG* 14/2 (1988), 240–62. Frevert's *Frauen-Geschichte* is a good place to start. Barbara Becker-Contatino, *Die Frau von der Reformation zur Romantik* (Bonn, 1980), and Priscilla Robertson, *The Experience of Women: Pattern and Change in Nineteenth-Century Europe* (Philadelphia, 1982), are useful general surveys. Joeres and Maynes (eds.), *Women* and John Fout (ed.), *German Women in the Nineteenth Century: A Social History* (New York, 1984), contain selections from recent research. For an interesting discussion of some traditional views, see Peter Petschauer, 'Eighteenth-Century Opinions about Education for Women', *CEH* 19/3 (1986), 262–92.

Except among the wealthy, children began to work at a very early age. In Johann Baptist Schad's family, for instance, children were assigned carefully defined tasks of increasing difficulty; by the time he was eight Schad was helping to bring in the harvest. In Schad's affectionate portrait of his early years we can see the way in which the household could give work a familial quality; we should not forget, however, that the productive household also infused familial relations with the demands and discipline of work.[18] Child labour was an essential part of traditional economic life, not an invention of the factory system. What made child labour so disagreeable to nineteenth century reformers were changes in the work children had to do and in what people believed was the proper nature of childhood.

Because the traditional family was an economic unit, to start a household required access to some means of production, usually land or the right to practice a trade. The acceptance of this necessity produced what J. Hajnal has called the 'European marriage pattern', a situation in which most people married fairly late in life and a substantial number of people did not marry at all. In the Bavarian town of Durlach, for instance, the mean age of men and women at the time of their first marriage remained twenty-seven and twenty-five throughout the eighteenth century. In late-seventeenth and early-eighteenth Nördlingen, first marriages occurred at twenty-nine and thirty. The same situation obtained in rural areas: in the Austrian parish of Abtenau, only one-third of the men and two-fifths of the women married before they were thirty. Almost half the women and more than half of the men were still unmarried at thirty-five; of these, a significant number would remain celibate for life.[19]

Most households needed two active adults to function properly. Few men or women were strong enough to carry on alone, especially if they had children dependent on them. Considering the incidence of mortality, this meant that second and sometimes third marriages were required so that the surviving partner might keep the household intact. The stepmother, that familiar figure in traditional folk literature, was an economic and demographic

[18] Irene Hardach-Pinke and G. Hardach (eds.), *Deutsche Kindheiten: Autobiographische Zeugnisse, 1700–1900* (Kronberg, 1978), 72 ff. Other examples can be found in Möller, *Familie*, ch. 1.

[19] Hajnal, 'Patterns' (the data on Durlach are on p. 110); Friedrichs, *Society*, p. 69; Mitterauer and Sieder, *Patriarchat*, pp. 52–3. See also Lutz Berkner and Franklin Mendels, 'Inheritance Systems, Family Structure, and Demographic Patterns in Western Europe, 1700–1900', in Tilly (ed.), *Studies*, pp. 219–20.

necessity. In the Austrian market town of Stockerau, for example, more than half the marriages recorded between 1670 and 1709 involved at least one partner who had been married before. Because they were more likely to be economically independent, men found it easier to find second spouses than did women; widowers were able, therefore, to marry younger, single females.[20]

Many households contained people who were not blood relatives. Sometimes these people were boarders, labourers who worked elsewhere but slept and ate with the family. Such arrangements remained common throughout the nineteenth century for unmarried wage-earners of both sexes. In traditional society, however, unrelated household members were more likely to be functioning members of the domestic economic unit: helpers, apprentices, journeymen, field hands, servants, and the like. In the more strictly organized trades, apprenticeship was carefully regulated by contracts governing the range of economic and domestic rights and obligations to be assumed by both master and apprentice. But in many trades and most rural areas, the relationship between master and dependant was ill-defined and fluid. A handbook published in 1781 refers to these dependents as 'Gesinde oder Domestiques und Arbeitsleute', a categorical jumble that suggests the combination of domestic and economic functions these people must have performed: taking care of children, doing the housework, and participating in the household's productive enterprise. Even in households that did not operate a farm or trade, dependants did a variety of jobs, acting as servants as well as live-in seamstresses, bakers, and handymen. Probably most young people who entered a household as a dependant hoped that this would be a temporary condition, to be endured while they acquired the means to establish their own families. Many did manage to marry and escape the authority of *Hausvater* and *Hausfrau*. But others remained dependent, forced to live their entire lives tending other people's fields, cleaning other people's houses, and nurturing other people's children.[21]

Getting married was not a matter to be left to the individuals

[20] Jean Paul Lehners, 'Die Pfarrei Stockerau im 17. und 18. Jahrhundert', in H. Helczmanorski, *Beiträge zur Bevölkerungs- und Sozialgeschichte* (Munich, 1973), 394; Friedrichs, *Society*, p. 67. For some images of the stepmother, see Weber-Kellermann, *Die deutsche Familie*, pp. 32 ff.

[21] In the Austrian area that Lutz Berkner studied, 31% of the households had servants, 19% had lodgers, and 5% both: 'Stem Family', p. 410. On the legal and social status of servants, see Engelsing, 'Personal'; on agricultural servants, Walter Hartinger, 'Bayrisches Dienstbotenleben auf dem Land vom 16. bis 18. Jahrhundert', *ZBL* 38/2 (1975), 598–638.

directly involved. Since families were potential burdens on their kin, their neighbours, and perhaps even on their states, all of these institutions might be expected to take a hand in regulating when and if a new household could be formed. In rural areas the most powerful way of doing this was by controlling the land. Sometimes, according to what he took his interest to be, the lord would try to encourage or discourage marriage among his dependants; in other regions, peasants did this themselves through complicated laws of inheritance. Guilds also tried to control marriage, not simply to limit the number of potential masters, but also to protect their members from improper or immoral alliances. In parts of central Europe where governments were concerned about over-population, the states restricted marriage, usually by demanding some sort of a means test for those seeking to wed.[22]

In the traditional social order, communal power was affirmed at every stage in the life of an individual and his family. Birth, marriage, and death were all marked by public rituals that brought people together to express their dependence upon one another. The rules governing courtship were enforced by sharp-eyed adults, as well as by the couple's peers who subjected transgressors to elaborate rites of humiliation. At the same time, courtship and marriage were usually regulated by some higher authority, the local lord, the church, the city government, sometimes the state. Whatever form they took, these efforts to control people's sexual desires were successful as long as people felt they had no alternative but to obey. After all, considering the facts of life in this society, it took a peculiar kind of strength or foolhardiness to break the rules and run the risk of losing the help only a community could provide. Where else could people turn for help in times of trouble, to put out a fire, raise a barn, help deliver a baby, wash a corpse, and pray for a departed soul? At its source, therefore, the characteristic solidarity of traditional society came from the stark and simple necessities of life.

Unfortunately, we know very little about the human costs this solidarity imposed. The data about families, households, and communities tell us something about their size and structure but very little about their emotional texture and psychological climate. What was it like to live in a traditional household? Did villages provide companionship as well as mutual assistance? Did guilds

---

[22] For a vivid example of community-imposed marriage restrictions, see the case of Flegel the tinsmith, which is described in Walker, *Home Towns*, pp. 73 ff. On changing state regulations, see Mitterauer and Sieder, *Patriarchat*, pp. 148–9.

soften competition and help to close the gap between family and work? How close to reality were those idealized pictures of pre-modern existence we find in the works of conservative social theorists like Justus Möser? The answers to such questions must in large part have depended on the character of the individuals involved, the psychological condition of those men and women forced to live and work together in spaces far smaller and more confined than most of us could tolerate, often without proper nourishment, usually without adequate medical care. If times were good and the people decent, the traditional household was probably a bearable place, but when things went wrong, when the crops failed or the soldiers came, when people broke under the burdens of overwork or undernourishment, when disease or disappointments became unbearable, then the close spaces of the household could become the scene of endless torment. We find vivid accounts of such situations in the novels and memoirs of the period. In Moritz's autobiographical novel, *Anton Reiser*, for instance, the hero had to live with a slightly mad hatmaker, who could be genial one moment and dangerously angry the next. Johann Probst suffered under a brutal, ignorant master who beat his wife when she could not nurse their child; after weeks of these violent quarrels, the child eventually died—all in the midst of a household that shared the agonies of this domestic tragedy.[23]

To those caught in such situations, the alternatives were few and unappealing. To whom could the exploited apprentice turn? Where might a battered wife find aid? The authorities could rarely be counted on to help; most often, they would send the victim back to suffer more. Running away meant crossing the deepest and clearest division in the traditional social order, the division between those who had a place and those who did not. Greater than the difference between aristocrat and commoner, townsman and peasant, free-man and serf, perhaps even greater than the difference between men and women, this gap divided the population into two distinct groups. To be outside the confines of a household, a trade, or a community was to be in the ranks of those without somewhere to go, a last resort, a final source of sustenance.

Some people accepted homelessness as a necessary but temporary condition. Each spring, for example, boys and girls anywhere between ten and fourteen years old left their crowded villages in

[23] Moritz, *Anton Reiser*, pp. 52 ff.; Lahnstein (ed.), *Report*, pp. 62–4, 258 ff. See also Johann Dietz's autobiography, *Master Johann Dietz: Surgeon in the Army of the Great Elector and Barber to the Royal Court* (New York, 1923).

Switzerland, walked along the Rhine until they came to a town, and then stood in the market place waiting to be chosen by some peasant in need of a maid or cowherd. From these same villages came the strong young men who served in many European armies during the old regime. Other people left their home to find some real or alleged opportunity elsewhere. Because of their high mortality rate, European cities depended on migration in order to survive. Hungarian nobles tried to entice skilled farmers, especially from the German south west, to come and work lands left depopulated by the long war against the Turks. Other Germans went east to the mining areas of Bohemia, the growing commercial centres along the Baltic, and new farm lands of southern Russia. Both the Habsburgs and Hohenzollern were eager to promote colonization: Frederick the Great brought into Prussia 300,000 new inhabitants, almost 60,000 families grouped in some 900 new settlements. More hesitantly, some Germans moved farther, across the sea: by the end of eighteenth century about 200,000 had settled in the New World. Virtually all of those who moved, whether by necessity or choice, whether it was to the next valley or to the American wilderness, did so in the hope of finding a more secure and comfortable place for themselves and their families.[24]

For some people, however, homelessness was a permanent condition. A servant who found herself pregnant and without a husband might lose her place and slip to the fringes of society, perhaps into prostitution or petty criminality. When faced with this possibility, many women resorted to infanticide, a crime that contemporaries found both horrible and fascinating. Some people lost their place simply because they were old. Johann Hechen-berber, whose fate Lutz Berkner has rescued from historical oblivion, spent sixty years as a hired hand in a village in northern Austria; when he could no longer work, he was forced to leave and had no choice but to become a beggar. There must have been hundreds of thousands of people like him in traditional Europe: elderly men and women without children to care for them, children without parents, discharged servants, disabled soldiers, disgraced women—the list of those who might be without a home is as long and as varied as the list of catastrophes with which life was so

[24] On the mobility of early modern populations, see DeVries, *Urbanization*; Hans Fenske, 'International Migration: Germany in the Eighteenth Century', *CEH* 13/4 (1980), 332–47; Steve Hochstadt, 'Migration in Preindustrial Germany', *CEH*, 16/3 (1983), 195–224. There is a contemporary account of the Swiss experience in Lahnstein (ed.), *Report*, p. 234. Frederick's efforts are discussed in Ritter, *Frederick the Great*, p. 179.

amply supplied. These people lived in city slums or wandered the countryside in search of temporary employment, they became prostitutes or thieves, beggars or casual labourers. When they grew too feeble to move, they died in the streets or highways or in the cold discomfort of some public asylum. Their lives help us to understand why the etymological root of the word for misery, *Elend*, is the word for being away from home.[25]

The eighteenth century was fascinated by people who lived outside society. *Robinson Crusoe*, that archetypical tale of social isolation, was widely read and imitated in German-speaking Europe. On another level, highwaymen, adventurers, and others who managed to exist on their own were frequently heroes of folk tales and popular literature. But with this fascination went fear of the poor and homeless themselves, who might fall upon the unwary in a dark alley or deserted road, and fear of the condition of poverty and homelessness, which remained for all but the richest and most powerful a possibility never entirely to be ignored.[26]

In the second half of the eighteenth century, the fear of homelessness increased, largely because the most immediate and manifest impact of the vital revolution was to swell the ranks of those on the fringes of the social order. From the middle of the eighteenth century until the middle of the nineteenth—an era of unparalleled social turmoil almost everywhere in Europe—the population grew faster than the economy. In densely populated rural areas, farms became more crowded and places harder to find. Despite large-scale emigration, the population of Württemberg increased from 51.8 per square kilometre in 1712 to 54.8 sixty years later—three times greater than the density of an eastern area such as Pomerania.[27] The population of Berlin grew by about 60 per cent during the second half of the century, while the number of the city's indigents grew ninefold. As populations expanded, local communities found it more difficult to control their members. This weakening of social controls is apparently behind the dramatic increase in illegitimacy, another mysterious demographic phenomenon that occured throughout Europe. Rare in traditional society, illegitimacy became more and more common after 1750: in

[25] Berkner, 'Stem Family', p. 413. There is a good discussion of infanticide in Möller, *Familie*, pp. 291 ff.

[26] On these groups, see Carsten Küther, *Räuber und Gauner in Deutschland: Das organisierte Bandenwesen im 18. und frühen 19. Jahrhundert* (Göttingen, 1976), and *Menschen auf der Strasse: Vagierende Unterschichten in Bayern, Franken und Schwaben in der zweiten Hälfte des 18. Jahrhunderts* (Göttingen, 1983).

[27] Kellenbenz, 'Germany', p. 195.

some areas, the number of illegitimate births per 100 live births grew from 2.5 before 1750 to 11.9 between 1780 and 1820; at the same time, pre-marital conceptions went from 13.4 to 23.8.[28]

As demographic growth strained and eventually disrupted the institutional structure of traditional society, contemporaries began to realize that the old forms of protection and domination would not be sufficient. Families, villages, and guilds would no longer be able to contain those who wished to belong. As a result, those without a place would increase; vagrancy, crime, prostitution, and infanticide would reach epidemic proportions. Some Germans recognized that the new scale of poverty and homelessness required new countermeasures. Christian charity and occasional repression would no longer be enough to ease the plight of the unfortunate and to protect the social order. In a number of German states, therefore, administrators established commissions to assist and control the poor. Workhouses, designed to contain and to improve the indigent, were opened throughout central Europe. In Berlin, for example, both begging and giving alms were prohibited by a royal order of December 1774. Instead, the poor were to be confined in a new workhouse where 'the genuinely needy and the poor deserving sympathy shall be cared for better than hitherto', while the 'deliberate beggars' will be forced to work.[29] In this royal decree, as in many other theoretical and practical statements about poverty from the second half of the eighteenth century, we find a characteristic combination of amelioration and repression, charity and coercion. Equally important, the very existence of public institutions to deal with social discontents points to the growing failure of traditional social order to regulate, improve, or even to live with its least fortunate members. Slowly and often with great reluctance, social theorists and practical reformers were groping towards a formulation of what a later generation would call 'the social question'.[30]

---

[28] Flinn, *System*, p. 82. See also Otto Ulbricht, 'The Debate about Foundling Hospitals in Enlightenment Germany: Infanticide, Illegitimacy, and Infant Mortality Rates', *CEH* 18/3/4 (1985), 211–56.

[29] Pollard and Holmes (eds.), *Documents*, pp. 166–7. The original is reprinted and discussed in Horst Krüger, *Zur Geschichte der Manufakturen und der Manufakturarbeiter in Preussen: Die mittleren Provinzen in der zweiten Hälfte des 18. Jahrhunderts* (Berlin, 1958), 369 ff., 615–17. See also Christoph Sachsse and F. Tennstedt, *Geschichte der Armenfürsorge in Deutschland: Vom Spätmittelalter bis zum 1. Weltkrieg* (Stuttgart, 1980).

[30] For examples of these changing attitudes, see François, *Koblenz*, pp. 183 ff.; Dreyfus, *Sociétés*, pp. 347 ff.

ii. AGRICULTURAL AND RURAL SOCIAL RELATIONS

Frederick the Great regarded agriculture as 'the first of all the arts' and was convinced that the 'only true wealth comes from the earth'. Germans, like everyone else in eighteenth-century Europe, depended on the earth for sustenance and raw materials; the agricultural cycle was the basis of their religious rituals and the source of their literary symbols. Eighty per cent of central Europe's population lived in a rural community, at least half earned their living directly from agriculture. Even in cities, the agrarian world was never far away. Many towns included surprisingly large quantities of open space that people cultivated. Townsmen also raised animals; the citizens of Hanover, a city of about 20,000 in the 1770s, shared their streets with nearly four hundred cows and oxen. Since manufacturing usually required agricultural materials—wood for furniture, wool for clothing, leather for harness-making, barley and hops for brewing beer—craftsmen were closely tied to their suppliers in the countryside. Wealthy townsmen owned land as an investment or a source of status; bankers provided credit to farmers; and merchants were more likely to trade in a farm commodity than any other product. Nothing affected the quality and character of traditional social life with as much power and immediacy as agriculture.[31]

Since the land had to yield fuel, fodder, and food, it was usually divided into forest, pasture, and fields. Roughly 25 per cent of eighteenth-century German Europe was wooded, enough to yield the forest products people needed and to shelter the game noblemen spent their leisure-time pursuing. In some densely-settled regions, where wood had begun to be in short supply, the traditional right to gather fallen branches had become a cherished liberty; elsewhere, great tracks of timber supplied lumber that could be shipped to the expanding markets of the west. Almost every farm had a copse or a small stand of trees in a gully where the land was hard to plough or along a line of demarcation between the fields.

[31] Frederick quoted by Wilhelm Abel in *HWSG*, i. 512; data on the distribution of population are from Benecke, *Society*, p. 13. In addition to Abel's chapter in *HWSG* and his *Geschichte*, there are introductory accounts of German agriculture in Slicher van Bath, *History*, and his contribution to *CEHE* v; and in F. W. Henning, *Landwirtschaft und ländliche Gesellschaft in Deutschland* (2 vols.; Paderborn, 1978–9). A good collection of recent scholarship can be found in Evans and Lee (eds.), *Peasantry*, which has a useful historiographical essay by Ian Farr. See also Rosenberg, *Probleme*, for a trenchant critique of the traditional literature.

Then, overall, about 20 per cent of the land was devoted to pasture or meadow. Most farms had some grazing land; in a few regions, animal husbandry was the principal occupation. Along the fringes of German-speaking Europe, in Schleswig and on the Hungarian plain, animals were raised extensively, that is, they were grazed on large tracks of lands and then driven to market, where they were sold for their meat and hides. Elsewhere, animals were raised intensively in pastures that had been planted and maintained for the purpose. Intensively raised animals usually provided products to be sold, such as milk, cheese, or wool.

While every prosperous farmer needed a few animals, most devoted themselves to growing crops. About 40 per cent of the land, therefore, was cultivated to produce specialized crops, like the grapes so carefully tended in the valleys of the Rhine and Mosel, legumes and other vegetables in garden plots, and most of all cereals, which made up nearly two-thirds of eighteenth-century produce. Where the weather was mild and the soil rich, farmers grew wheat, but in most of the north and east they had to be content with rye, and, where the winters were harsh and the land poor, people planted oats, barley, or buckwheat, which were not suitable for bread but glutinous enough to make cakes or porridge, those rough and heavy staples of the peasant diet.[32]

Most German farmers employed some form of the three-field system, which left at least one-third of their land fallow each year. In especially difficult areas a two-field system had to be used, while, along the Baltic coast and in Saxony, cultivators had figured a way of rotating crops so that a four- or even five-field arrangement was possible. Only where demand was high and manure supplies sufficient could farmers use their lands without a break. At any given moment, therefore, about a third of the arable soil (just over five out of almost thirteen million hectares) was fallow. Cultivated land was usually open and divided into strips of varying length; these strips were farmed in furlongs (*Gewanne*), which were gathered into fields, the primary unit for planting and rotation. If the furlongs were long enough, they were cultivated with a heavy Saxon plough; the so-called *Blockflur* system of shorter strips required the lighter *Hakenpflug*. Like the shape and pattern of field cultivation, types of settlement varied from one part of central Europe to another. In the Black Forest and the pasture lands of the

[32] Kellenbenz, 'Germany', pp. 196–8; Pounds, *Geography* . . . *1500–1840*, pp. 32 ff., 172 ff.

north, people lived in isolated farms or small hamlets made of three or four houses. In the west, there tended to be large, enclosed villages from which farmers went out each day to work their land. In the east, which had been settled by colonists, villages often had a regular arrangement and were gathered around an estate, whose owner dominated them politically as well as economically. How peasants' houses were built, the shape of their roofs, and the character of their decoration depended on the availability of materials and the weight of custom. As one moved across the German-speaking lands, the houses, like the dialects and costumes of their inhabitants, were as varied as the natural landscape itself.[33]

Behind this variety, however, was one depressing uniformity: almost everywhere the earth yielded no more than enough to enable people to walk a slender path between subsistence and want. Except in a few fertile and prosperous areas, the total yield from the land did not much increase between the end of the Middle Ages and the beginning of the eighteenth century. Most cultivators lacked the capital and the expertise to improve their fields. Nor could they increase their yields by cultivating pastures or meadows, not simply because these areas were often commonly held but also because they supported the animals necessary for farm work and manure. The best way of increasing the harvest was by bringing new land into cultivation, by working abandoned fields, draining marshes, or pushing back the sea. But such land reclamation was extremely expensive and was usually limited to wealthy land-owners or reformist governments.

Stable over the long run, crop yields could fluctuate dramatically from one year to the next. Weather accounted for many of these fluctuations—during the eighteenth century, approximately one growing season in four was especially unfavourable for agriculture. But weather was only one among many sources of trouble: plant blights and animal epidemics, military action or social unrest, accidents or sickness in the household could also disrupt the delicate arrangements upon which a peasant's survival might depend. To confront these difficulties people had to rely on their own and their livestock's energy, water from rain and rivers, fertilizers from human and animal waste. To these natural forces they could add a few rude tools and a storehouse of custom and folklore handed

[33] Abel in *HWSG*, i. 502–3; Smith, *Geography*, chs. 4, 5; Pounds, *Geography* . . . *1500–1840*, p. 178; Mutton, *Central Europe*, pp. 262–5; Pfeifer, 'Quality', p. 258.

down from their ancestors: neither their tool supply nor their technical knowledge was substantially better in 1700 than it had been four hundred years earlier.

A farmer's fixed costs remained high. Since the yield ratio of crop to seed was rarely more than 4 : 1, a grower had to set aside one-quarter of his harvest if he wanted to maintain a steady yield.[34] Out of the remaining three-quarters, he had to provide food for his household and animals, and enough surplus to pay a variety of debts, dues, and rents. Because most growers were locked into local markets, they were vulnerable to bad times and poorly positioned to take advantage of good fortune. When a poor harvest prevented them from covering their needs, they had to buy at high prices, whereas the value of their surplus was usually depressed by local abundance.

How well—or, in some cases, *whether*—people survived the rigours of traditional agriculture depended on the quality and location of their fields, their own skill and luck, and, perhaps most of all, how much land they held and how much of its produce they were able to keep for themselves. This last consideration brings us to the most important question to be asked about any agrarian social order: who controls the land? In traditional Europe this turns out to be an extremely difficult question to answer. Land, apparently so solid and visible a commodity, was never simply a 'piece' of property; owning land meant having access to one or more of what Henry Sumner Maine called a 'bundle' of property rights, privileges, and obligations.[35] For instance, even if a family owned land in the sense that it had the right to sell or bequeath it, these owners might have to recognize someone else's right to cultivate the land and share in its products. More often, people might have cultivation rights without ownership in the modern sense. Because land was the basis of wealth, the primary source of employment, and the means of subsistence, its possession and use had been the subject of economic, social, and political developments for centuries. Both ownership and usufruct, therefore, were burdened by a number of different taxes, rents, and other obligations, some imposed from above, others sanctioned by local custom. No wonder that when eighteenth-century reformers set

---

[34] Slicher van Bath, *CEHE* v. 81. By the middle of the seventeenth century the yield ratio in England and the Low Countries was 9 : 3; by the middle of the eighteenth it was 10 : 1.

[35] On the character of rural property, see Jack Goody's introduction and E. P. Thompson's essay in Goody (ed.), *Family*.

about codifying rural laws, they were always frustrated and often defeated by the thicket of special obligations and liberties which confronted them. In one Prussian province, for instance, Johann von Justi discovered no less than eight different types of tenancy, each of which might be held by one of five different kinds of farmer—and neither the type of his tenancy nor his status was an infallible indicator of a peasant's economic position.[36]

We can best begin our consideration of rural law and custom by dividing eighteenth-century German farmers into two categories: those who had enough land to support themselves and those who did not. At the top of the first group, we find *Grossbauern*—in Schleswig and southern Bavaria, the Black Forest and some parts of Thuringia—who had farms large enough to sustain a secure and independent existence. Some of these peasants were rich: Ewer Iwerson had seventy-seven fertile hectares on the Hadersleber Damm in Schleswig, from which he earned a gross annual income of 1,200 taler (he paid his hired hands between twelve and seventeen taler a year). People like the Iwersons lived well; they had warm houses with glass windows, meat on their tables, and a good suit of clothes to wear to church. They could provide dowries for their daughters and some capital for their sons; when they grew too old to work, they retired and left the running of the farm to their heirs. Even in the most prosperous regions, such successful farmers were rare; in German Europe as a whole, they represented a tiny minority.[37] A larger group of peasants were able to coax an adequate if not abundant return from their lands, but even if we define this group broadly, it certainly represented fewer than half the total number of rural households. F. W. Henning has estimated that families with enough land to qualify as *Bauern* made up about 37 per cent of the Prussian population. In the north-western principality of Paderborn, 21 per cent of the farmers had a full or half parcel of land, which ranged between five and twenty hectares; in Saxony, 51 per cent had this much land, while in Bavaria only 28 per cent worked more than ten hectares. Obviously we cannot make too much of these figures: because the quality of the land and the nature of the crop varied so greatly, there is no clear minimum figure below which subsistence was impossible. None the less, we must bear in mind that the smaller the holding, the greater the chances that a family would have too much labour and not enough food. Once this happened, peasants had no choice but to move or

---

[36] Abel, *Geschichte*, p. 219.
[37] Ibid. 220–1.

to supplement their income by working someone else's land or engaging in some other kind of employment.[38]

How could those with just enough land ensure the survival of their children as independent cultivators? Peasants faced with this question had only two alternatives: they could try to keep their land intact, bequeath it to a single heir and thereby leave the rest of their children landless, or they could divide the property and run the risk of leaving everyone with too little. Roughly speaking, the first strategy, which is called impartible inheritance, was common in the north and east, while the second, partible inheritance, predominated in the west. Lutz Berkner's examination of two Hanoverian regions illustrates the impact of these strategies on landholding patterns: in the villages around Calenberg, where impartible inheritance was common, the number of holdings increased by 18 per cent between 1664 and 1766; in the Göttingen region, on the other hand, partible inheritance produced an increase of over 400 per cent during this same period. Clearly both strategies had unpleasant consequences: under the first, those who were not heirs had to leave the farm or work as permanent dependants, whereas under the second, the land eventually became fragmented and inefficient. Needless to say, the choice of strategies was rarely a free one. Often enough it was imposed on families by the landlord, who usually tried to keep plots intact. After mid-century, governments sometimes tried to regulate inheritance practices, although they seem to have had only limited success enforcing laws which went against the authority of local notables or the customs of established communities.[39]

Under both inheritance systems, the proportion of those who could support themselves from their land remained fairly constant; when the population expanded, those beneath the subsistence level necessarily increased. In Saxony, the number of farms actually declined from the mid-sixteenth to the mid-eighteenth centuries, whereas the number of smallholders and tenants rose from 4,000 to 36,000. Contemporaries used a variety of terms for these marginal people—*Brinksitzer, Gärtner, Kotter, Häusler, Warfsleute*. Their situation differed greatly from one region to another: sometimes, as the name suggests, *Brinksitzer* held land along the edge of the

[38] Henning's important research is summarized in his article, 'Betriebsgrössen-struktur'. See also his specialized studies, *Ostpreussen* and *Paderborn*. The best account in English is Blum, *End*, especially pp. 104–6.

[39] Berkner in Goody (ed.), *Family*, especially the table on p. 81; Pfeifer, 'Quality', especially the map on p. 257.

commons, rough and rocky soil no one else wanted to cultivate; sometimes they had a few strips in an open field. Occasionally, they were regular members of the village community; more often they remained marginal, both socially and economically. In practice, *Brinksitzer* were hard to distinguish from hired hands, who worked full-time as agricultural labourers, just as hired hands were hard to distinguish from *Gesinde*, servants who lived and worked within the household. Together, *Brinksitzer*, labourer, and servant shared the common experience of being dependent. They all had to look to their more established neighbours for land, work, and perhaps a place at the dinner table. To some degree, they all occupied a precarious position within the community; during hard times, they were the ones who suffered first and longest. By the 1780s, 45 per cent of the peasantry in the Hochberg district of Baden were either landless or held only a small plot, another 40 per cent worked fewer than seven acres; in Paderborn, just over 40 per cent had a smallholding, 18 per cent were labourers, 5 per cent shepherds; in East Prussia, less than half the rural population was self-sufficient.[40]

Even among the most prosperous eighteenth-century peasants, only a minority were free to buy, sell, or lease their property. Freeholders could be found along the French frontier, in a few eastern regions where some of the descendants of German colonists had managed to retain their rights, and in those parts of the Alps where a seigneurial system had never taken hold. Hereditary lessors usually had most of the same rights as a freeholder, even if the land did not formally belong to them. Their tenure was regulated by a complex set of rights and obligations defined in the so-called *Meierrecht*, a contractual arrangement between them and the seigneur. From freehold and hereditary lease, the quality of tenure declined through a scale of gradations, each one shading off into the next: lifetime leaseholds, leaseholds for a given period of time, sharecropping, annual renting at the whim of the lord or his agent. These gradations in tenure overlapped, but by no means coincided with the quantity and quality of the land held and the personal status of the tenant.[41]

[40] Slicher van Bath, *CEHE* v. 128; Blum, *End*, p. 106; Henning, *Paderborn*, p. 33. See also the interesting analysis of the rural labour force in Saalfield, *Bauernwirtschaft*, p. 128. There is a useful glossary of German terms in Mayhew, *Settlement*, pp. 218–20.

[41] Lütge, *Geschichte*, especially the survey of the situation at the end of the eighteenth century on pp. 182 ff. See also Blum, *End*, pp. 29–31, 96 ff.; Mayhew, *Settlement*; Achilles, *Vermögensverhältnisse*, p. 61.

Freeholders and some lessors were legally free, even if the latter were often caught in a web of servile obligations because of the way they held their land. But many, and probably most, German peasants were personally subject to one or more lords; they lived in *Erbuntertänigkeit*, hereditary subjection, which limited their rights to move, marry, and do certain kinds of work. To the west of an imaginary line running south from Flensburg and then along the Elbe River, hereditary serfdom had declined in the early modern period, but to the east, landlords in the fifteenth and sixteenth centuries had tended to impose servile status and precarious tenancy on what had once been a relatively free and prosperous peasantry. Pockets of serfdom remained scattered across eighteenth-century central Europe, but as a general rule peasants in the west were legally freer and often economically better off than their eastern counterparts.[42]

In return for their land, most peasants had to make payments, in money or kind, annually or on certain occasions; they also had to provide labour, in their lord's fields or in some special capacity, to assist him during the hunting season, as beater or dog handler, to transport his crops and repair his roads and bridges, to send their children to work in the manor house, to use the lord's mill and acknowledge his rights to sell certain products, and so on through a list which in one locality ran to 138 separate obligations, each with its own name and carefully described character. The severity and enforcement of these obligations varied from region to region, often from one estate to another. But in this matter, as in the case of personal status, we are struck by the contrast between east and west. Peasants living west of the Elbe line characteristically fulfilled their seigneurial duties with payments of some sort; their labour services were usually limited and easily converted into cash. Sometimes these total payments were light, elsewhere they might take up to half a farmer's gross income: for example, in the four Brunswick villages studied by Diedrich Saalfeld, tenants paid between 32 and 52 per cent of their crops in various kinds of rents, dues, taxes, and converted services. Not surprisingly, the larger a farmer's holding, the smaller his cost per acre and the greater his chances of avoiding labour services. In the east, the overall picture was quite different. Peasants, especially those who were personally unfree, often worked almost full-time for their lords, perhaps as

[42] In addition to Lütge, *Geschichte*, see Blum, *End*; Mayhew, *Settlement*, pp. 135 ff.; and the works on the landed nobility cited below, sect. iv.

many as six days per week. But even east of the Elbe there was considerable variety: on a selected number of East Prussian estates, F. W. Henning found that 7 per cent of the peasantry had virtually no labour obligations, about half gave less than 15 per cent of their time, and a third worked more than 40 per cent for their lords.[43]

The hereditary obligation to work without pay infuriated critics of traditional rural society. Karl Biedermann, who viewed the situation from the perspective of a nineteenth-century liberal, quoted with approval the following contemporary condemnation of seigneurial duties:

What is to be said when the peasant must transport last year's harvest belonging to someone else while his own current crop needs attention, when he must help build some ceremonial structure while his own hut falls in, when he must act as a messenger with some polite note while his dying mother needs him . . . when he must remain in service while his own house burns down.

This last example actually occurred, Biedermann assures us, on 18 March 1790, when peasants working in their master's fields were not given permission to fight a fire in their village. Often enough such things must have happened, foolish and infuriating expressions of selfish and irrational domination. But labour services were not simply the silly remnants of a dying system; to landlords who could extract them fully and use them profitably, they had great value. When, for instance, the Brandenburg estate of Wustrau was appraised for tax purposes in 1696, its fields, livestock, game, and vineyards were valued at 2,434 taler, while the services and dues its commanded 'from its own and foreign subjects' were valued at 3,001 taler. Significantly, when landlords became more concerned with commercial agriculture in the second half of the eighteenth century, many of them tried to increase the amount of labour owed them by their dependants.[44]

Whether in the form of direct payments or of services rendered, the rural population supported an immense array of institutions. Goethe once compared the peasantry with plant lice, who feed themselves only to be sucked dry by other insects: 'Things have gone so far now', he wrote in 1782, 'that more is consumed in a day at the top than can be produced in a day at the bottom.' Of course, the individual's share of this burden varied: a freeholder only had to

[43] Saalfield, *Bauernwirtschaft*, p. 46; Henning, *Dienste*, p. 42. There is a good summary of the recent literature on dues and services in Blum, *End*, chs. 3, 4.

[44] Biedermann, *Deutschland*, i, pt. 1, p. 245; Abel in *HWSG*, i. 497. See also Brinkmann, *Wustrau*.

pay taxes to the state, whereas some serfs worked full-time for their lords. Most cultivators were somewhere in between these two extremes. Neither free landholder nor totally dominated serf, they had to confront a wide array of superiors: their landlords, whom they had to compensate for the fields they worked and usually for the house in which they lived; their *Leibherr*, their direct master, if they were personally unfree; the appropriate religious authorities, who would extract support for the parish and sometimes special payments; and, finally, the village community, which would expect its members to help finance education, poor relief, care of the common lands, and so on. As the central government became more powerful and more expensive, its representatives joined the ranks of those demanding direct payments and various services. A great many of the conflicts that divided rural society turned on who had the right to absorb the largest share of the hard-earned fruits of the peasantry's labour.[45]

Some scholars have recently begun to insist that we should not regard the peasantry as merely the passive subject of these conflicts. Winfried Schulze has drawn our attention to the social protests, ranging from individual acts of insubordination to communal rebellions, which were endemic in traditional society. Where institutional channels for social action existed, it is clear that peasants used them to assert their interests against state and local authorities. As Peter Blickle has shown in convincing detail, ordinary people in the south-western sectors of the Reich participated in corporate representative institutions in order to resist unfair taxes, encroachments on their customary rights, and limitations on their personal liberties. Even in Brandenburg Prussia, peasants were far from impotent. So great was their willingness to seek legal redress from their landlords' excessive demands that in 1787 King Frederick William II was moved to issue a public decree in which he expressed his 'highest displeasure that in recent times lawsuits and quarrels between landlords and their subjects have greatly multiplied in Our provinces'. What the king called 'unbridled passion for litigation' challenged, and in some cases may have halted, estate owners' efforts to increase the labour services owned by their tenants.[46]

[45] Bruford, *Germany*, p. 41. Henning, *Dienste*, p. 103, has a chart showing the various obligations that peasants had to fulfil. For a good example, see Hofmann, *Herrschaft*, pp. 81 ff.

[46] See Winfried Schulze (ed.), *Aufstände, Revolten, Prozesse: Beiträge zu bäuerlichen Widerstandsbewegungen im frühneuzeitlichen Europa* (Stuttgart, 1983); Peter Blickle,

We tend to think of the seigneur as an individual nobleman, but that was by no means always the case. The landlord might be a lessor acting as a nobleman's agent, a monastic order or other religious body, a town, or a charitable corporation. The largest individual landholders in central Europe were the rulers of various states. The Hohenzollern, for example, had vast estates throughout their realm: in Brandenburg about a third, and in East Prussia over a half of all peasants worked royal land. The traditional social order had made no distinction between the monarch's private demesne and public lands; in the world of *Herrschaft* clear lines were rarely drawn between the private and public sphere. During the second half of the eighteenth century, however, some sovereigns began to think of their land as state property, the source of public revenue and places where state policies could be directly enforced. The prince's estates were run by agents, who leased them for a set period of time. These men were usually not nobles and often brought to their positions new agrarian techniques, a vigorous managerial style, and strong profit motives. They were sometimes important forces for innovation on the local scene.[47]

The church also held large quantities of land. The south German Reichsstift of Weingarten, for example, covered 160 square kilometres and had a population of 50,000. Around the silent cloisters forming Weingarten's religious core extended a large and productive estate, which provided for the monastery's material needs and yielded valuable cash crops. The monks worked two hundred hectares themselves and let out the rest on long leases to their tenants, who were also their subjects, since Weingarten, even though it was pressed on all sides by Habsburg land, was a sovereign territory directly under the emperor. In Bavaria, the church controlled 50 per cent of the total number of farms, as compared to the nobility's 24 per cent and the sovereign's 13 per

Landschaften im alten Reich: Die staatliche Funktion des gemeinen Mannes in Oberdeutschland (Munich, 1973), and *Aufruhr und Empörung? Studien zum bäuerlichen Widerstand im alten Reich* (Munich, 1980); and on Prussia, the recent work by William Hagen, 'How Mighty the Junkers? Peasant Rents and Seigneurial Profits in Sixteenth Century Brandenburg', *PP* 108 (1985), 80–116, 'The Junkers' Faithless Servants: Peasant Insubordination and the Breakdown of Serfdom in Brandenburg-Prussia, 1763–1811', in Evans and Lee (eds.), *Peasantry*, pp. 71–101, and 'Working for the Junker: The Standard of Living of Manorial Laborers in Brandenburg, 1584–1810', *JMH* 58/1 (1986), 143–58. On peasant protests in Austria, see Georg Grüll, *Bauer, Herr und Landesfürst: Sozialrevolutionäre Bestrebungen der oberösterreichischen Bauern von 1650–1848* (Graz and Cologne, 1963).

[47] Blum, *End*, p. 209.

cent. Much of this church land was in the hands of a few important prelates, such as the Bishop of Freising, whose estate at Massenhausen gave him seigneurial rights over one thousand peasants.[48]

In most of German Europe the aristocracy controlled the largest portion of the land. Of the almost five thousand villages in Silesia at the end of the eighteenth century, individuals—most of them nobles—held just over 3,500, the state or sovereign 340, the cities 250, and religious corporations around 840. As will be seen later in this chapter, the quantity and character of aristocratic landholding varied enormously. A few large magnates ruled over huge estates, while many squires just barely managed to sustain themselves. Some estates, especially in the colonized lands of the east, were coherent units that could be worked as a single agricultural enterprise. Often, however, an 'estate' was no more than a notational convenience for someone's collected .properties and rights. A family's parcels of lands might be scattered across a fairly large area, overlapping and interweaving with those of other lords: just 10 per cent of the villages in Austrian Styria had a single owner, the rest were shared by several individuals and corporations. Moreover, seigneurial rights did not necessarily cohere. Since it was possible for a lord to sell or bequeath some of his rights, several seigneurs might possess a portion of one village's obligations.[49]

The sheer complexity and impenetrable interdependence of traditional rural society retarded innovation. Aristocratic landowners, although often desperately eager to increase their incomes, usually lacked an adequate system of accounting that could tell them how much wealth they had and how much they needed. Since they were in no position to make economically rational decisions about investment and consumption, many found it easier just to keep borrowing as long as someone was willing to lend them what they needed. Peasants, on the other hand, had neither the knowledge nor the capital with which to innovate, and, even if they did, they had to face powerful counterpressures from their social superiors and neighbours. Open fields and common pastures required co-operative farming techniques and made individual experimentation with new tools or techniques virtually impossible. Together, the web of values and institutions upon which most rural communities depended created customs which, as one agricultural reformer put it, 'long ruled with irresistible power over arts and sciences'. After reviewing five centuries of agrarian history, Jerome

[48] Scherer, *Reichsstift*; Blum, *End*, p. 21; Lee, *Growth*, p. xxix and app. 6.
[49] Ziekursch, *Agrargeschichte*, p. 65; Blum, *End*, p. 26.

Blum concluded that in the middle of the eighteenth century, 'The face of rural Europe looked much as it had in the Middle Ages. . . . The great mass of people . . . lived at the narrow margin of subsistence, as much at the mercy of a shortage of food as their forebears had been in the thirteenth century.'[50]

After 1750 things began to change. Whereas the pioneer agronomist Johann Georg Leopoldt had found it impossible to acquire a basic knowledge of farming from the literature available at mid-century, within a few decades books, periodicals, and local agricultural societies spread useful information throughout the German-speaking world. Albrecht Thaer's justly famous *Einleitung zur Kenntnis der englischen Landwirtschaft in Rücksicht auf Vervollkommung deutscher Landwirtschaft*, first published in 1798, was part of a burgeoning literature which sought to import western ideas about agricultural processes and farming techniques. Seeds and cereals, ploughs and manure became fashionable topics of conversation in elegant drawing rooms and the subjects of learned papers to scholarly academies. Johann Christian Schubart's essay on the usefulness of clover won him a prize from the Berlin Academy and eventually a title from the Emperor Joseph II, who made him Edler von dem Kleefeld. Of course knowledge *per se* is necessary but rarely sufficient to effect innovation. Knowledge makes change possible, but is powerless unless people have the desire and ability to apply it. To understand agricultural developments, therefore, we must examine, not simply the work of men like Thaer and Schubart, but also the conditions that made their ideas relevant and applicable.[51]

Many German historians have stressed the state's role in creating the conditions for innovation in the second half of the eighteenth century. As we have seen, many states did seek to improve their subjects' lives and increase their own revenues by engaging in various social reforms. Officials sometimes helped to spread useful knowledge about agronomy. Governments drained swamps, reclaimed land from the sea, encouraged the cultivation of abandoned fields, and made loans to those willing to adopt new techniques. With these direct and immediate measures, states were

[50] Blum, *End*, pp. 128, 154. DeVries, *Economy*, pp. 41 ff., summarizes the inhibitions to innovation in traditional rural society. Ilien and Jeggle, *Leben*, trace the historical development of a Swabian village community.

[51] Abel, *Geschichte*, pp. 281 ff. Joachim Nettelbeck recalled that, when Frederick the Great sent a load of potatoes to his village as a gift, people immediately began to eat them raw and, not surprisingly, found them quite unpleasant; even the dogs ignored them: *Mein Leben* (Zeulenroda, 1938), 44.

often the instruments of progress. Many governments wanted to do more: enlightened rulers and their advisers believed that agricultural innovation required changes in the rural social order. Some of them viewed common land as inefficient and hoped to enclose or divide it. Others believed that peasants would never be productive farmers until they were freed from the unreasonable burdens of serfdom. In short, some German statesmen became convinced that economic growth required some measure of social emancipation.[52]

The states' emancipatory efforts are extremely difficult to evaluate; as is always the case with government policies, we must be careful not to confound what was intended with what actually took place. Frederick the Great, for example, was able to improve the peasantry's social status and to encourage higher productivity on his own estates: in 1763 he revoked his agents' seigneurial rights to labour services; fourteen years later, he converted peasant holdings into hereditary tenure. However, Frederick's efforts to effect changes outside the royal demesne were limited in scope and significance. Legislation to curtail the expropriation of peasant holdings by their lords was ignored or circumvented in most of the Prussian east. Joseph II, who did not have Frederick's high regard for the landed nobility and was therefore less inhibited in his reforms, was also frustrated in his plans to transform rural society. His decrees of September 1781 provided peasants with protection from some seigneurial power and gave them the right to move and engage in other occupations; in 1789 he issued a patent equalizing the taxation on noble and peasant land, allowing peasants to convert labour services into cash, and limiting the total obligation any dependant might owe his lord. But these measures, certainly the most progressive to be suggested anywhere in pre-revolutionary central Europe, were never put into effect. In the Habsburgs' lands, as in most German states, the landed nobility remained powerful enough to defy or at least to deflect decrees that seemed to go against their own interests.[53]

The most effective stimuli for agricultural innovation came, not from above, but from below, not from monarchs and states, but from a large number of noblemen, estate agents, and peasants who saw new opportunities for personal advantage. The clearest

[52] Mayhew, *Settlement*, pp. 143 ff.

[53] Blum, *End*, has a good summary of these various measures. On Austria, see W. E. Wright, *Serf, Seigneur, and Sovereign: Agrarian Reform in Eighteenth-Century Bohemia* (Minneapolis, 1966); on Prussia, Johnson, *Frederick*, pp. 72 ff.

measure of these opportunities was the ascending curve of agricultural prices in the last half of the eighteenth century. After comparing the price of rye in selected German cities for the periods 1721–45 and 1750–99, Slicher van Bath found increases of between 20 and 57 per cent. The price of land also rose sharply: in Silesia, estates doubled in value between the 1750s and the turn of the century; in Brunswick, the average price per morgen of land went from 48.5 talers in the 1750s to 120 talers in the 1790s. Equally impressive is the velocity of sales, which led to complaints that noblemen were now trading their land the way they had once traded horses. People coined words—*Ackersucht, Ackergier*—to describe the hunger for fertile fields that seemed to grip many of their contemporaries. As Hartmut Harnisch has recently shown, even the dependent peasantry living east of the Elbe was drawn into the expanding agricultural market during the last decades of the eighteenth century, thereby setting into motion profound changes in the social and economic order. When commercial consider-ations, market calculations, and the drive for profit penetrated the German countryside, more and more landholders came to agree with Albrecht Thaer's underlying assumption that 'the object of agriculture is to produce a profit. . . . The greater the retained profit the better is this accomplished. . . . Accordingly, the teachings of rational agriculture must demonstrate how the highest pure profit can be obtained from the enterprise under all conditions.'[54]

The effects of this commercialization on agricultural produc-tivity are most impressive. Some farmers began to experiment with new crops: in Brandenburg, for example, the potato harvest increased from 5,200 tons in 1765 to 103,000 tons in 1801. Improvements in the growing of fodder made larger herds of livestock possible—in parts of Prussia the number of cattle grew by over 150 per cent between 1750 and 1800. More animals produced more manure, which, together with new techniques of crop rotation, enabled farmers to decrease the land left fallow and raise the total productivity of their fields. In some regions, growers began to specialize, focusing their efforts on the most appropriate

[54] Blum, *End*, pp. 284–5. On prices, see Slicher van Bath, *History*, pp. 222 ff.; on estate sales, Ziekursch, *Agrargeschichte*, pp. 23 ff., and Abel, *Fluctuations*, ch. 7; on the role of peasant farmers, Hartmut Harnisch, 'Peasants and Markets: The Background to the Agrarian Reforms in Feudal Prussia East of the Elbe, 1760–1807', in Evans and Lee (eds.), *Peasantry*, 37–76, and the works of William Hagen, cited above, n. 46.

or marketable crops rather than trying to be as self-sufficient as possible. By the end of the century, 300,000 tons of grain each year were shipped from Danzig, Elbing, and Königsberg.[55]

We should not overestimate the rate or extent of change in the German countryside. Even where the traditional social order was no longer intact, the influence of traditional values and élites persisted. The restrictive web of institutions that kept the vast majority of central Europeans on the edge of subsistence was just beginning to unravel. Nevertheless, many thoughtful observers recognized that population growth, state efforts at social reform, and increases in the value and productivity of the land had begun to transform rural society and to reorder the relationship between agriculture and manufacturing, between city and countryside.

iii. CITIES, MARKETS, AND MANUFACTURING

There were over two thousand German 'cities' in the eighteenth century. Some could trace their lineage back to Roman times, but most were the battered survivors of medieval urbanization. As the data from early nineteenth-century Prussia suggest, a majority of cities were quite small, characteristically with less than 3,500 inhabitants (see table 2.2). Many of these towns were separated

TABLE 2.2. *Prussian cities in the early nineteenth century*

Size of town	Number	Population (000s)
over 10,000	26	836
3,500–10,000	136	765.9
2,000–3,500	194	508.9
1,000–2,000	407	597.9
less than 1,000	258	186.9

Source: Pounds, *Geography . . . 1500–1840*, p. 145.

from the countryside by walls; even in peacetime, visitors were watched carefully as they passed through gates that would be closed from dusk to dawn. Cities, like other traditional institutions, faced inwards, husbanding their resources, limiting their membership,

[55] Pounds, *Geography . . . 1500–1840, p. 185*; Abel, *Fluctuations*, p. 209; Abel, in Lütge (ed.), *Situation*, p. 241.

and protecting their special privileges. Wealthy and influential citizens preferred to live in the centre of town, concentrating their economic and political resources at the urban core, as far away as possible from the dangers that lurked beyond the walls. It would take time for cities to dismantle their walls—and abandon the habits of mind they expressed—and for urban élites to move their houses out to the expanding periphery. Before 1800 only a few German cities had begun to display the appetite and capacity for growth that we associate with modern urbanism.[56]

Despite this self-conscious insularity, eighteenth-century cities were tied to their hinterlands. None of them was self-sufficient, all had to form some kind of partnership with the countryside, upon which they depended for food, fuel, raw materials, customers, and new inhabitants. As we have seen, the rural world intruded on the towns in many ways; even in a large city, rustic sights, sounds, smells, and habits were never far away. The 'essential problem' in understanding town life, Fernand Braudel has written, is 'the division of labour between the countryside and urban centres, a division which has never been perfectly defined and which calls for constant reassessment, because the position of the partners changes incessantly'.[57] To understand both the city and its surroundings, therefore, we must abandon a sharp dichotomy between the urban and rural worlds.

All cities interacted with their surroundings, but few had the resources to reach very far beyond their immediate hinterlands. Cities were held captive by those obdurate natural and man-made barriers that divided Germans from one another: poor roads and treacherous rivers, political fragmentation and social unrest, omnipresent tolls and tariffs, and a monetary system so complex that, as one bewildered traveller complained, 'it would require profound skill in calculation to pass without detriment from Düsseldorf to Mayence'. The circle of a city's influence was

---

[56] Abrams and Wrigley (eds.), *Towns*, Jürgen Reulecke and Gerhard Huck, 'Urban History Research in Germany: Its Development and Present Condition', *Urban History Yearbook* (1981), 39–54, and DeVries, *Urbanization*, provide good introductions to new trends in urban history. On German cities, see the essays in Rausch (ed.), *Städte, . . . im 19. Jahrhundert*, and Press, (ed.), *Städtewesen*. The two best case studies of early modern cities are both by French scholars: Dreyfus, *Sociétés*, and François, *Koblenz*. Also of interest are Mauersberg, *Wirtschafts- und Sozialgeschichte*, *Wirtschaft und Gesellschaft Fuldas*, and *Wirtschaft und Gesellschaft Fürths*; Soliday, *Community*; Bátori, *Reichstadt*; Friedrichs, *Society*.

[57] Braudel, *Capitalism*, p. 376. 'A city', Max Weber wrote, 'is always a market centre': *Economy*, ii. 1213.

characteristically bounded by radial routes along which people could walk in a day. Within this region, rarely more than about fifty square miles in size, townsmen bought most of what they needed and sold most of what they made. For goods not available locally—necessities of life like salt, luxury items like coffee or precious metals—towns frequently depended on regional fairs, whose continued importance was a sign of central Europe's economic fragmentation and commercial insularity. Long after they had begun to die out in the west, fairs flourished in the German states: along the Rhine, for example, six hundred of them were held annually in the early nineteenth century.[58]

Since the urban economy was shaped by local markets, most manufacturing was directed towards supplying the everyday needs of the town and its hinterland. Consider, for example, the situation in Fürth, a town of almost 9,000 inhabitants in the mid-eighteenth century. Fürth's records list seventy different occupations, by far the most popular of which were bakers, butchers, tailors, brewers, innkeepers, and shoemakers, most of whom catered to a local clientele. Only the unusually large number of people engaged in a few speciality trades, such as goldworking, glassblowing, and textiles, point to production for a larger market. In Nördlingen, which was known throughout the early modern period as a textile centre, weavers of one sort or another made up the largest occupational group, but butchers, bakers, innkeepers, and shoe-makers were as numerous and commercially as important.[59] In both cities, as in the rest of central Europe, enterprises were small, composed of a master, often working alone, sometimes with a journeyman and one or two apprentices. Most craftsmen required little capital: their equipment was simple, and they did not have to accumulate either raw materials or an inventory of finished goods. Since manufacturers dealt directly with both suppliers and customers, they remained in a world of face-to-face relationships, without the need for complex accounting and marketing procedures. The local orientation of urban economics, therefore, influenced not only what was produced but also the scale and character of productive relations.

In most of the German lands, urban commerce and manufacturing

[58] Owen, *Travels*, i. *153*. Compare Riesbeck, *Travels*, iii. 284, who describes the nine tolls he had to pay between Mainz and Koblenz. On fairs, see Pounds, *Geography . . . 1500–1840*, pp. 290–1.

[59] Mauersberg, *Wirtschaft und Gesellschaft Fürths*, pp. 49–55; Friedrichs, *Society*, p. 80.

were organized in guilds. Guilds were, first of all, economic associations that regulated the recruitment and qualifications of their members, licensed the practitioners of a trade, and upheld the standards of its production. To be a shoemaker in Fulda required, among other things, demonstrating one's skills to the shoemakers' guild. These organizations also protected their members' 'liberties', that is, their corporate rights and privileges. They made certain, for example, that only carpenters used iron nails (cabinetmakers could not), and that no more than the stipulated number of loaves were baked or swords manufactured. Their collective goal was not to maximize their members' individual profits but to ensure that there was sufficient work and enough demand for the group to prosper and reproduce. Given the realities of the traditional social order, this required setting and defending limits on who could belong and on what members were allowed to do.[60]

But guilds were much more than just occupational interest groups; as part of the world of *Herrschaft*, they did not distinguish between occupation and family, economics and politics, the public and private realms. Guild ceremonies, carefully planned and elaborately performed, asserted the primacy of the corporation at every stage in a member's life, from the first day of his apprenticeship until his death. Guilds were centres of sociability, where people could celebrate feast days and other joyous occasions, and they were sources of consolation, to which people might turn in times of grief. They offered charitable assistance and moral support, fellowship and protection. They also exercised authority and imposed conformity. An apprentice, as we saw earlier in this chapter, lived under the familial guidance of his master, subject to him both as employer and as *Hausvater*. Every member was expected to uphold the moral standards of the guild, to live respectably and marry properly. To defy one's guild by breaking its rules or ignoring its customs was to invite a host of countermeasures, ranging in severity from subtle social pressures to banishment from the guild's protective community.

To their admirers, guilds appeared to be the quintessential expression of traditional society's stability and harmony. C. W. Dohm, for one, believed that the master craftsman was uniquely blessed with security and contentment: 'His soul is troubled by

---

[60] The best introduction to the guilds can be found in the work of Wolfram Fischer, especially *Handwerksrecht*, and the essays in *Wirtschaft*. The case studies cited above in n. 56 all have material on corporate life. Here, as on many issues, Dreyfus is particularly informative: *Sociétés*. Stadelmann's and Fischer's *Bildungswelt* remains the essential starting-place for a study of artisans' culture and values.

neither nagging fears nor delusive hopes concerning the future,'
Dohm wrote in 1781; 'he enjoys the present with a pure and perfect
joy, and expects tomorrow to be exactly like today.' The
craftsman, declared another contemporary, 'is the true burgher, the
law which binds him, protects him too; his place is in the middle
[of society], here he is secure, as he is needed everywhere, so he is
free; honor and worth are in perfect correspondence'.[61] Privilege
and protection, freedom and security, honour and value—the
guilds brought together many of the most distinctive features of
traditional social life. No wonder that a guild term like *Gesellen*
provided the roots for the word *Gesellschaft*, society, or that guild
ceremonies were adopted by organizations as different as the Free
masons and the early labour movement.

When they functioned properly, the guilds could provide a
reasonably healthy blend of stability and mobility. But we would
do well not to overestimate the contentment or cohesion which
they provided. We have already noted that the familial bonds of
master and apprentice could produce anguish and exploitation as
easily as affection and co-operation. Moreover, like other traditional institutions, guilds were highly contentious and involved
themselves in endless jurisdictional disputes with municipal authorities, states, and others guilds. Far from the harmonious social
universe pictured by its admirers, the real world of the guild was
persistently disrupted by conflicts and competing interests. Guild
rituals, designed to promote harmony and cohesion, could just as
easily be occasions for confrontations with those who threatened
the organization's sacred privileges or violated its cherished
liberties. If slighted, a guild member's honour, upon which his
standing ultimately depended, could require elaborate acts of
retribution or revenge. In 1786, for example, when a journeyman
mason put a dead cat in another man's bucket of lime, the insulted
party stopped work and convinced his colleagues to do the same;
before long, masons had left construction sites all over Berlin,
setting off a week of violence and agitation that required military
action to repress. Similar outbreaks frequently took place all along
the complex internal and external boundaries of corporate life,
between masters and apprentices, between trades and the political
authorities, between guildsmen and students, and between members of different guilds.[62]

The most vulnerable, and therefore often the most volatile

---

[61] Epstein, *Genesis*, p. 219.
[62] Stadelmann and Fischer, *Bildungswelt*, pp. 82–3.

members of the guild structure were the journeymen. In most trades, an apprentice had to complete his training by leaving his home town and working under a series of masters elsewhere; after this tour, he could return home and apply for full admittance to the guild. Journeymen were enmeshed in guild values and institutions: from their arrival in a strange city until their departure, how they should speak and behave was carefully defined by custom and regulation. As future masters, they had a powerful stake in the system. However, their intermediate position between apprentice and master and the supra-local connections they made during their *Wanderschaft* created a sense of solidarity among journeymen that cut across the guild's vertical structure. This solidarity was institutionalized in associations that catered to journeymen's practical needs and represented their special interests. As the position of the guilds deteriorated and the opportunities for journeymen to become masters decreased, journeymen became increasingly militant and their organizations increasingly prone to violent protests. Not surprisingly, a number of historians have traced the roots of the nineteenth-century labour movement to these institutions, which overlapped but did not coincide with traditional corporate order.[63]

Of all the institutions that composed the world of *Herrschaft*, the guilds were most susceptible to the expanding power of the new bureaucratic states. Unlike the landed nobility, they could not use court connections, family ties, and shared values to absorb or deflect hostile officials. Nor did they have the doctrinal and institutional leverage the church could use to influence government religious policy. Because many bureaucrats viewed the guilds as purely fiscal instruments, when alternative sources of tax money presented themselves governments were quite willing to circumvent or undermine the guild's authority. When the guilds provoked, or failed to contain, social unrest, administrators were ready to limit their jurisdiction and take over their functions. Like the other institutions of municipal self-government, the autonomous power of guilds usually declined whenever states consolidated and centralized their authority.

An important legislative milestone in the extension of state

[63] On the social position of *Gesellen*, see Stadelmann and Fischer, *Bildungswelt*, pp. 68 ff. Andreas Griessinger, *Das symbolische Kapital der Ehre: Streikbewegungen und kollektives Bewusstsein deutscher Handwerksgesellen im 18. Jahrhundert* (Frankfurt, 1981), describes strikes and protests; Klaus Schwarz, *Die Lage der Handwerksgesellen in Bremen während des 18. Jahrhunderts* (Bremen, 1975), is a good case study.

control over guilds was one of the Reich's last important laws, the decree 'To Remedy Abuses among the Guilds' issued in 1731. The purpose of this decree was to assert the primacy of political authority over the guilds' corporate life: 'In no place', stated Article One, 'shall any guild articles, practices, or customs be sustained unless they have been confirmed and ratified after prior and sufficient consideration and adjustment, according to the existing state of things, by the appropriate authorities of the land.' But the framers of the law recognized that the guild's role in economic and social life could not be abolished—there were, after all, no institutions on hand to take their place. The masters, therefore, were given 'wise and healthy power' over journeymen, whose rebellious activities the decree explicitly condemned. Nevertheless, the decree severely limited the ability of masters to impose, and of journeymen to resist, corporate authority. In case of disputes, the parties involved should 'bring the matter to the attention of the authorities, and patiently and peaceably await their investigation, knowledge, and judgment . . . '. Public insults, work stoppage, banishment, and ostracism were forbidden; the guilds were supposed to turn to political authorities to resolve their legal disagreements. Whether this actually happened depended on the strength and character of the local authorities. Where governments were eager to interpose their own jurisdiction between guild and subject, the imperial decree strengthened tendencies to turn corporations into agents of state power. But if the government was unwilling or unable to assume the guilds' role, the decree remained without real significance—as renewed imperial efforts in 1764 and 1772 tacitly acknowledged.[64]

Brandenburg Prussia is the best example of a state that asserted its hegemony over the guilds. In 1731 the Prussian government published the imperial decree at once and followed it with a series of special laws covering the behaviour of guilds within the Hohenzollern's realm. These statutes preserved corporate mono-polies and allowed masters to supervise and control their employees, but the ultimate authority rested in the hands of the state. In the *Allgemeines Landrecht* of 1794, the guilds continued to be recognized as 'privileged corporations', but were firmly placed under the direct and complete power of the state. The diffusion of authority, so characteristic of *Herrschaft*, was thereby contained; the

[64] Walker reprints the law in *Home Towns*, pp. 435 ff. and discusses it on pp. 93–7. See also Karl H. Wegert, 'Patrimonial Rule, Popular Self-Interest, and Jacobinism in Germany, 1763–1800', *JMH* 53/3 (1981), 440–67, especially p. 451.

line between economics and politics was more clearly drawn. At the same time, when guildsmen turned to the government for protection against economic enterprises developed outside the guild structure, they were often rebuffed. For example, when Berlin's calico printers complained to the king in 1783 that manufacturers were hiring journeymen without regard to guild customs and the current oversupply of labour, they were told that 'no calico printer can order his employer which journeymen he is to keep, what work he is to give to any of them and how many apprentices he shall train . . . all this depends entirely on the arbitrary decision of the entrepreneur'. Entrepreneurial autonomy, backed in this case by the full power of the Prussian state, violated the basic social and economic assumptions upon which the corporate world of the guilds had rested.[65]

The institutional climate was much more favourable for the guilds in the 'home towns' of the south and west, where there was no external authority to which the guild's jurisdictions might be transferred. In these autonomous or semi-autonomous municipalities, the guilds themselves were part of the government, inseparable from the political and social as well as the economic order. Master craftsmen, by virtue of their positions as home-owners and citizens, were also the leaders of city government. Family ties, longstanding personal relationships, and a relatively homogeneous set of values sustained functionally differentiated but not rigidly hierarchical social structures. Of course there were differences of wealth, status, and opinion in the home towns, but the style and substance of public life tended to blur these differences and to keep them from hardening into lasting cleavages. In these cities, therefore, political independence, economic localization, and social cohesion combined to reinforce one another, acting together to seal urban institutions from external interference.[66]

In contrast to the home towns, central Europe's few large cities were internally diverse and externally extended. To borrow a distinction suggested by Edward Fox, the home towns, like most small cities, had a 'territorial, areal extent', more or less limited to their immediate surroundings. Big cities had a 'linear dimension' that connected them to distant markets, cultures, and polities.

---

[65] Pollard and Holmes (eds.), *Documents* pp. 171–4. On Prussian guilds, see Gustav Schmoller, 'Das brandenburg-preussische Innungswesen von 1640–1800', *Umrisse und Untersuchungen zur Verfassungs-, Verwaltungs- und Wirtschaftsgeschichte* (Leipzig, 1898); Schieder, *Friedrich der Grosse* p. 93.

[66] The classic account of this situation is Walker, *Home Towns*.

Needless to say, the distinction is not absolutely clear-cut: a small city did engage in some supra-local commerce, just as a metropolis had to function in local markets. Nevertheless, a great city like Hamburg and a home town like Goslar, while both recognizably urban in character, had little in common.[67]

German cities' linear extensions did not have a single center. Instead, central European cities reached in a number of different directions, often responding to stimuli from more advanced regions or acting as intermediaries between west and east. A map of central European commerce, therefore, would show regional and international connections; there would be nothing 'German' about it. For instance, towns along the Baltic from Lübeck to Memel traded grain, salt, fish, lumber, flax, and hemp on sea lines through the Danish Sound into the North Sea and beyond. Hamburg exported grain that had been moved north on the Elbe, and served as an entry port for goods shipped to central Europe from throughout the Atlantic economy. Just outside Hamburg, the great cattle market at Wedel supplied beef and hides to Hanover, Saxony, and points south. Leipzig and Frankfurt, two important inland cities, each had a famous fair and was connected to a network of roads, the one leading south to Italy and west towards France, the other south and east, towards Silesia, Poland, and Bohemia. Sometimes a city's goods moved along a natural corridor, like the river traffic between Cologne and the Low Countries, and sometimes along paths determined by local needs and material resources, such as the copper trade between the Thuringian mines and the brass makers of Aachen.[68]

Cities that operated within an international market were not simply larger than their insular counterparts, they had qualitatively distinctive economic and social structures. Since long-distance trade required people who had the skills and resources to buy, store, and transport large quantities of valuable goods, big cities had bankers, merchants, and shippers, who were willing and able to provide capital and connections. In short, these cities had to have a complex commercial élite with interests and experiences markedly different from the owners of locally based, small-scale manufacturing enterprises. Moreover, social distinctions in big cities were apt to be broader and more clearly expressed than they

[67] Edward Whiting Fox, *History in Geographic Perspective: The Other France* (New York, 1971).
[68] Zorn, 'Schwerpunkte'; Glamann in *CEHE* v; Kellenbenz in Lütge (ed.), *Situation*.

were in most towns. David Hume was shocked by the gulf between rich and poor he found in mid-century Vienna, a city 'compos'd entirely of nobility, and of lackeys, soldiers, and priests'. Forty years later, Georg Friedrich Rebmann called Berlin 'a spectacle of human elegance and misery, a place where great wealth and great poverty meet, interact, and coexist'. Then Rebmann anticipated a sentiment that has come to be identified with modern urbanism by recording his 'feeling of being alone amid this crowd'. Isolation was, of course, a feeling which the institutions and atmosphere of a small city made virtually impossible.[69]

Big cities lacked a common life in which a large sector of their population might participate. The scale and heterogeneity of their social institutions precluded the informal interaction and personal ties upon which the home town's cohesion depended. The public world of these urban centres tended to be fragmented, composed of overlapping but clearly separate organizations and groups. Metropolitan élites, for example, were usually set apart from the rest of the population, sometimes by formal regulations, more often by their style of life and occupations. In many cities there were several élites, each one tied to a particular sphere: commercial activities, the court, and the government. Guilds of different sizes and substance provided fellowship for their members but did not, as in the home towns, collectively contribute to municipal self-rule. Finally, big cities contained separate groups, such as the Jews, who often lived in isolated communities, and whose relationships with the rest of urban society were carefully regulated by special laws.[70]

In most big cities, a substantial portion of the population did not belong to a corporate group and thus remained outside, or at least on the margins of urban social, economic, and political life. Half of Mainz's inhabitants, for instance, lacked the skills and connections to become part of the guild hierarchy. These people were usually forced to seek casual labour, which was subject to the vagaries of the weather or the market. They were boatmen, stevedores, porters, stable boys, kitchen workers, serving-maids—wage labourers without a secure position, sometimes unable to work, often underemployed, always dependent on someone else. In Mainz the urban poor were scattered in cellars and attics through-

[69] Mossner, *Life*, p. 211; Rebmann, *Wanderungen*, p. 75.
[70] The best source for Jewish life in German Europe is the collection of documents edited and with informative introductions by Monika Richarz, *Leben*. Katz, *Ghetto*, is a good introduction.

out the city; in Koblenz they were segregated in crowded tenements facing the town walls and in ramshackle houses along the river. Everywhere their dwellings were damp and cold, their nutrition insufficient, their death-rate unusually high.[71]

Closely related to the casual labourer were those listed in the city census as 'servants'. This was usually the largest single occupational category, and often included over 10 per cent of the adult work-force. Servants had a hierarchy that replicated the social structure as a whole: at the top were the major-domos of large establishments, the élite servants of the rich and powerful; next came the staff of stable, moderately well-off households; finally, and by far the largest group, were those who fulfilled a variety of tasks for people just slightly better off than themselves. Like the rural *Gesinde*, urban servants did more than domestic tasks; they would often be expected to work part-time in the family's enterprise as well as to perform household chores. The overwhelming majority of servants were females—only quite grand establishments could afford a butler, coachman, or footman. As we have seen, the most fortunate servants managed to found an independent household, but the majority were destined for a lifetime of dependence.[72]

Of course there were worse fates than secure dependence: if things went badly, for themselves or for their masters, servants could easily be pushed to the fringes of respectability or into that shadowy underworld of beggars, prostitutes, and thieves that could be found in every European city. When the population grew in the second half of the eighteenth century, those on the margin of urban society became more numerous and began to occupy an increasingly important place in respectable people's social consciousness. As we shall see in a later chapter, the shadowy, 'mysterious' side of city life frightened and fascinated contemporaries all over Europe, for whom it became one of the most emotionally charged aspects of the 'social question'.[73]

In the eighteenth century most German cities did not grow as swiftly as their western European counterparts, nor did the percentage of Germans living in cities increase as quickly as the population at large. Nevertheless, in absolute terms the expansion of the urban population was impressive. By 1800, sixty-one German cities had more than 10,000 inhabitants; their total population was over 1.6 million. Berlin (150,000) and Vienna

[71] Dreyfus, *Sociétés*, p. 300; François, *Koblenz*, pp. 161 ff.
[72] Engelsing, 'Personal'.
[73] See below, Ch. 10, sect. iv, n. 90.

(231,000) were German Europe's two largest cities at the end of the century. Other capitals and smaller *Residenzstädte*, which also benefited from the process of state-building and monarchical self-aggrandizement, increased in size between 1700 and 1800: Munich's population went from 21,000 to 34,000, Stuttgart's from 13,000 to 20,000, Mannheim's from 13,000 to 22,000, Dresden's from 40,000 to 55,000, Hanover's from 11,000 to 17,000. Most of central Europe's old commercial centres did not participate in this accelerated urbanization; a few actually declined—Nuremberg's population, for example, fell from 40,000 in 1700 to 30,000 in 1750, and then to 27,000 in 1800. Most of the fastest-growing economic centres were newly prominent towns like Barmen and Elberfeld, whose combined population increased almost five fold, from 5,000 to 23,000.[74]

Since these numbers do not tell us anything about the character and variety of urban life in eighteenth-century central Europe, let us consider in somewhat greater detail four German cities: two political capitals, Berlin and Mainz, and two commercial centres, Hamburg and Nuremberg.

Alone among central European cities, Berlin matched the extraordinary pace of urban growth to be found in the west. Vienna was still the largest German city, but the Prussian capital was uniquely dynamic: a town of 12,000 in the bleak aftermath of the Thirty Years War, its population doubled between 1650 and 1700 and doubled again between 1700 and 1750; even in the second half of the eighteenth century, when its growth slowed, it increased from 90,000 to 150,000. The city's character and appearance reflected this frantic pace. John Owen, an English traveller who was there in 1792, complained about Berlin's oppressive drabness and squalor. A native, writing a few years later, lamented the dark and dangerous streets, the absence of decent bridges, and the conditions of the pavements, 'which alternate between mountains and valleys, so that in the dark of night a pedestrian is perpetually in danger of falling and breaking a leg'. Berlin's social structure, like the pace and scale of its growth, was shaped by Prussia's rise as a European power. Over 30,000 of its inhabitants—20 per cent of the total population—were either soldiers or their dependants. Twenty thousand craftsmen and merchants, together with their employees, apprentices, and servants, made up the core of Berlin's economic life. But they had only an indirect role to play in city government.

[74] This is based on DeVries, *Urbanization*.

Since the 1720s the *Magistrat* had been composed of civil servants led by a royally appointed president; the *Magistrat* chose the members of a council that played a largely advisory role. Thus, while guilds and privileged corporations continued to exist, Berlin's administration rested on what Friedrich Nicolai called the 'repression of traditional corporate municipal self-government'. Moreover, many of the city's richest and most influential inhabitants were *eximierte*—aristocrats, courtiers, and civil servants who were subject not to local institutions or the city courts, but rather to state authority and legal jurisdiction.[75]

Mainz was obviously not in the same league as Berlin, any more than the territories of the Archbishop Elector could be compared with the Hohenzollern's state. The elector's capital, defended by a less than formidable force of 3,000 troops, had neither a military nor a bureaucratic caste. But it was the symbolic centre of central Europe's largest and richest ecclesiastical polity, the setting for costly ceremonies of church and court, and thus a magnet for aristocratic families in search of lavish entertainment and lucrative employment. The city, like the electorate, was run by the twenty-four canons of the Cathedral Chapter, who acted with and through a growing cadre of administrative officials. Mainz's social structure was dominated by the electoral court and local aristocracy, together with the craftsmen and merchants who supplied their needs. Economic life continued to be run by the guilds, whose representatives on the City Council helped to shape local affairs. In the second half of the eighteenth century, however, a new group of entrepreneurs began to exploit Mainz's strategic location at the confluence of Main and Rhine. Many of these men were outsiders without ties or commitments to the city's corporate structure; their success in building new enterprises and broadening Mainz's commercial role was necessarily won at the expense of the old guilds, whose economic role and political position steadily declined.[76]

To move from electoral Mainz to Hamburg is to be reminded once again of how many different social worlds coexisted in the eighteenth century. Hamburg was one of the century's most impressive success stories. The principal German participant in an expanding Atlantic economy that stretched along an arc from Denmark to Cadiz, Hamburg's population grew from 70,000 to

[75] Owen, *Travels*, ii. 523 ff.; Sombart, *Volkswirtschaft*, p. 17; Möller, *Aufklärung*, pp. 265 ff. Helga Schultz's *Berlin, 1650–1800: Sozialgeschichte einer Residenz* (Berlin, 1987) is the best social history of the city.

[76] In addition to Dreyfus, *Sociétés*, see Blanning, *Reform*.

100,000 between 1700 and 1800. Foreigners like Charles Burney were impressed by the 'air of cheerfulness, industry, plenty, and liberty' they found there, while progressive Germans marvelled at the openness of the city's social and political structures. Hamburg's élite was self-consciously anti-aristocratic: nobles were barred from public life, no special privileges protected the city's leaders. As one inhabitant put it just after the turn of the century: 'All real Hamburgers know and have only one status, that of Bürger.' We should not, however, take this often-quoted phrase too literally. Limited to those who met certain qualifications, citizenship was difficult for newcomers to acquire; in the 1750s less than four hundred new citizens were created annually. This meant that the city contained a large number of people totally excluded from public life: Jews, recent arrivals, as well as thousands of day labourers, servants, and indigents. Moreover, active political participation was further restricted. After 1710, only those citizens with 1,000 Reichstaler of urban property, or 2,000 Reichstaler worth of rural property could take part in the citizens' conventions where office holders were chosen. In fact, the city was run by some 350 honorary officials, who were supported by twenty legally trained officials and perhaps fifty clerks. While not legally closed, the ranks of this élite were practically limited to a relatively small number of merchant families, whose names appear over and over again on the rolls of the most important government institutions. 'The Hamburg constitution', wrote Johann Jakob Rambach in 1801, 'is neither totally aristocratic, nor totally democratic, nor totally representative, but is all three at once.'[77]

The same people who sang Hamburg's praises often pointed to Nuremberg as an example of what was wrong with too many German cities; Karl Biedermann, for instance, called it 'the eldorado of the patriciate'. In comparison with Hamburg's dynamic growth, Nuremberg had steadily declined from its Renaissance glory; by the end of the eighteenth century its population was substantially less than it had been three hundred years earlier. Contemporary critics associated this decline with the sorry state of Nuremberg's political institutions, which had enabled a few patrician families to monopolize power and use the city's wealth for

[77] Burney, *Tour*, p. 208; Möller, *Aufklärung*, p. 268; Kopitzsch, 'Hamburg', p. 197. For a positive account of Hamburg society, see Schramm's classic *Hamburg*, and *Generationen*. Joachim Whaley's *Religious Toleration and Social Change in Hamburg (1529–1819)* (Cambridge, 1986) gives a balanced picture of the city's strengths and weaknesses.

their own aggrandizement. Extending downwards from this corrupt and exclusive élite was a rigid status hierarchy, resistant to innovation and intolerant of dissent. But Nuremberg's problems were not solely institutional in origin. After suffering dreadfully from the effects of war and disease during the seventeenth century, Nuremberg's recovery had been hindered by the mercantile policies of its neighbours, Austria, Prussia, and Bavaria, who had closed their borders to the city's goods in the 1720s and 1740s. Even the most progressive of systems would have had trouble responding to this combination of external disasters. For Nuremberg's stagnant oligarchy, these troubles eventually led to a state of economic and political bankruptcy best illustrated by the city's efforts to have itself annexed by Prussia in 1796.[78]

Considering the range of historical examples from which they had to choose, it is not surprising that scholars have come to quite different conclusions about the role of cities in German economic development. One school, following the traditional association of urbanism and progressive ideals, has argued that cities were both instruments and products of economic growth; indeed, some writers conflate urbanization, industrialization, and 'modernization' into a single process. Another group of scholars, reacting to the often disastrous role of cities in many parts of the non-western world during the twentieth century, has emphasized the parasitic character of urban concentrations, which seem to drain resources from the countryside in order to support swollen bureaucracies and privileged élites. As is often the case in such controversies, there is no need to commit ourselves to either position; both contain an element of truth. 'Cities', as Jan DeVries has recently shown, 'did not, by themselves, constitute a superior economy whose relative growth would transform society.'[79] Sometimes they were barriers to development, sometimes sources of innovation. How cities functioned economically depended on their own social and political structures and, more importantly, on the nature of the regional system within which they operated. To understand the relationship between urbanization and development, therefore, we must broaden our concern beyond the city's walls and enquire how the urban economy interacted with the various elements—agriculture,

---

[78] Biedermann, *Deutschland*, i, pt.1, pp.182–3. See also Ingomar Bog, 'Wirtschaft und Gesellschaft Nürnbergs im Zeitalter der Merkantilismus (1648–1806)', *VSWG* 57/3 (1970), 289–322; Ekkehard Wiest, *Die Entwicklung des Nürnberger Gewerks zwischen 1648 und 1806* (Stuttgart, 1968).

[79] DeVries, *Urbanization*, p. 246.

rural manufacturing, and commerce—in its economic environment.

An important first step in this enquiry is to recognize that cities never had a monopoly on manufacturing; even at the highpoint of their power, urban crafts accounted for only a small portion of the total goods produced. Since most families had to be as self-sufficient as possible, a great deal of simple manufacturing went on in the household. If they possessed the time, skills, and equipment necessary to make things for their neighbours, some peasant families could extend household production into a modest form of village industry. Thatchers, smiths, shoemakers, weavers, and the like were to be found in most communities, where they worked full- or part-time to meet local needs for their goods and services. Under the right conditions, these rural craftsmen could direct their skills and resources towards larger markets. Another, very different sort of non-urban manufacturing involved enterprises that depended on the location of natural resources. Quarrymen, charcoal burners, miners, and some metal-workers had to live and practise their crafts where their stones, timber, ore, and minerals were to be found. While they were linked to cities in many ways, these producers, like the practitioners of village industry, operated in a regionally based market.[80]

The expansion of the eighteenth-century economy was not exclusively urban or rural; it depended upon and affected both cities and countryside. Urban élites and institutions provided the resources to support new enterprises and the marketing mechanisms to distribute their goods, but agriculture was no less indispensable for any successful economic upswing. Agricultural products were essential for manufacturing and commerce, farm surpluses were necessary to feed growing populations and to sustain the increasing portion of rural society that was devoting its time and energies to non-agrarian pursuits. Regional economic units worked best when these various elements were mobilized and co-ordinated. Often this was the work of an entrepreneur, who provided the capital and the connections rural enterprises needed in order to expand their production and market their goods. The larger the market—and the greater the distance between producer and consumer—the more important it became to have someone to purchase raw materials and distribute finished products. Sometimes entrepreneurs became directly involved in production by

[80] There is a summary of regional manufacturing in Smith, *Geography*. On mining, see Zorn in *HWSG* i. 542–3.

gathering craftsmen together in a single unit; more often, they preferred to use some form of the putting-out system, through which craftsmen sold to the entrepreneur what they produced separately. This system was especially appropriate in the textile trade, which required several, quite distinct steps. Characteristically, a merchant would provide materials to weavers, buy the cloth they produced, and then have it finished before marketing it himself.[81]

If they sensed a rising demand, entrepreneurs wanted as many goods as they could get and would buy them wherever they could, at the lowest possible price. They had no interest in maintaining the guilds; when these corporate institutions got in the way, they simply turned to places where customary restrictions could not interfere with the pressures of the market. For example, one contemporary found that Aachen was 'dominated by the most disadvantageous guild restrictions that paralyse the wings of industry', whereas in the surrounding countryside a businessman has 'free reign in his endeavours and selects his workers and their numbers as he sees fit'. Over the course of the century, therefore, guild production stagnated while rural manufacturing flourished. By 1800 roughly one-half of all Prussian craftsmen lived 'free' in villages or the countryside. As production shifted away from cities, complicated networks evolved through which rural manufacturers were tied to one another and to regional, sometimes international markets.[82]

The growth of rural manufacturing, a process that scholars sometimes call 'protoindustrialization', had obvious importance for the organization of society. By introducing a degree of occupational diversity into village life, protoindustrialization freed some people from their dependence on agriculture. Longstanding limits on marriage and fertility began to ease as the traditional cycles of scarcity and death became somewhat less apparent; often the demographic results were dramatic. Some historians have portrayed these rural craftsmen as the first authentic proletariat since they were virtually landless, no longer controlled the means of production, and were subject to the forces of the market and the interests of an entrepreneur. It is equally important, however, to note how the protoindustrial craftsman remained tied to the traditional order, both as a member of the village community and as the head of a familial productive unit. Protoindustrialization,

[81] DeVries, *Economy*, pp. 94 ff., has a good analysis of this process.
[82] Kisch, 'Deterrents', p. 536; Pollard, *Conquest*, pp. 62–3.

therefore, is a characteristically transitional phenomenon, combining residues of artisanal practices with adumbrations of a new industrial order.[83]

Most of the large manufacturing enterprises that developed in the eighteenth century also combined traditional and innovative elements. These *Manufakturen*—manufactures—were usually staffed by craftsmen gathered together in a single place but working separately. In scale, the manufacture resembled a modern factory, but the organization of production was usually set by artisanal techniques and procedures. These enterprises, whose number increased markedly in the second half of the century, were widely used in the final stages of textile manufacture, as well as in those large-scale ventures, like shipbuilding and some metal working, where a number of different stages were required. Many state-run enterprises were also of this type, such as the Lagerhaus that supplied uniforms for the Prussian military and the Royal Porcelain works in Vienna and Berlin.[84]

The most important economic innovations in eighteenth-century central Europe were in the organization rather than the technology of production. However, as the economy expanded, businessmen began to look for better machines with which to increase their output. Some firms used water wheels to provide power for wire-pulling devices and metal-splitting mills. Textile producers employed new treadle-operated spinning wheels, dutch looms, and knitting frames. In 1753 a lead mine at Lintorf near Duisberg put into operation a steam engine of English design. The first coke blast furnace was established at the Royal Ironworks in Gleiwitz in 1796. Generally speaking, however, technological change was not

[83] Scholarly interest in this process was stimulated by Mendels's important article, 'Proto-Industrialization'. Recent work can be found in Kriedte *et al.* (eds.), *Industrialization*. For a sceptical view, see E. Schremmer, 'Industrialisierung vor der Industrialisierung', *GuG* 6 (1980), 420–8, and Rab Houston and K. D. M. Snell, 'Proto-Industrialization? Cottage Industry, Social Change, and Industrial Revolution', *HJ* 27/2 (1984), 473–92. The best summaries are Pollard, *Conquest*, pp. 62 ff., and William Hagen, 'Capitalism and the Countryside in Early Modern Europe: Interpretations, Models, Debates', *Agricultural History*, 62/1 (1988), 13–47.

[84] These enterprises are analysed in Hassinger, 'Stand'; Horst Krüger, *Zur Geschichte der Manufakturen und der Manufakturarbeiter in Preussen. Die mittleren Provinzen in der zweiten Hälfte des 18. Jahrhunderts* (Berlin, 1958); Ortulf Reuter, *Die Manufaktur im fränkischen Raum. Eine Untersuchung grossbetrieblicher Anfänge in den Fürstentümern Ansbach und Bayreuth als Beitrag zur Gewerbegeschichte des 18. und beginnenden 19. Jahrhunderts* (Stuttgart, 1961); Gerhard Slawinger, *Die Manufaktur in Kurbayern: Die Anfänge der grossgewerblichen Entwicklung in der Übergangs-Epoche vom Merkantilismus zum Liberalismus, 1740–1833* (Stuttgart, 1966). There is a good summary in Wehler, *Gesellschaftsgeschichte*, i. 106–7.

impressive until after the turn of the century. Scarcities of both skilled labour and venture capital, together with the guilds' vigorous opposition to threatening innovation, inhibited that combination of technology and entrepreneurship which would be so prominent in the future emergence of German economic power.[85]

Not many eighteenth-century enterprises had either the machinery or the organization of labour we normally associate with a 'factory'. Occasionally contemporaries used this term to refer to large manufacturing plants but, like so much of the period's vocabulary, *Fabrik* had a range and fluidity of meanings that reflected the unsettled character of social reality.[86] Contemporaries also spoke of 'workers', but here too we must be careful about using nineteenth-century categories to describe traditional society: few eighteenth-century workers would fit the now classical, Marxian definition of the proletariat. However, we do find a large and heterogeneous group of people who were no longer part of the old corporate order. This group included the lower strata in large cities, wage labourers in both rural and urban settings, and the majority of those engaged in some kind of protoindustry. Some of these people were destitute, others managed to scrape by with casual labour, a few were reasonably well off. Since the rising price of agricultural products depressed real wages throughout the second half of the century, the condition of these groups probably deteriorated, especially after 1770. But, whatever their material condition, they all lived outside the protective restrictions around which the traditional social order had been built. These men and women were free and vulnerable in new ways: they were able to move, to marry, to set up a trade; they were also fully exposed, both to the harsh forces of economic circumstance and to the regulative authority of the bureaucratic state.[87]

In their efforts to explain the decline of traditional institutions and the rise of new economic and social forces, several generations of German historians emphasized the government's role as a source of demand, technological innovation, and entrepreneurial energy. Gustav Schmoller, who was one of the founding fathers of this tradition, argued that, when the old order stagnated, only the state—and of course he had Prussia in mind—was strong enough to effect change:

[85] DeVries, *Economy*, pp. 91 ff.; Landes, *Prometheus*, p. 142.
[86] Hassinger, 'Stand', p. 115; Hilger, *GGB*, 229 ff.
[87] Slicher van Bath, *History*, pp. 222 ff., has some data on real wages.

As the medieval city-states and great lordships became more and more incapable of serving as the adequate organs of social life [Schmoller wrote], it became necessary that all conceivable means should be employed, if need be, through blood and iron—to erect territorial and national states. Enlightened princely despotism was the representative of this great progressive movement.

A *kleindeutsch* patriot, historical economist, and editor of publications from the Prussian archives, Schmoller was committed to a view of the state as an instrument of social progress and national greatness.[88]

It is clear enough that enlightened state policy did help to weaken the guilds and sometimes promoted innovative new enterprises. Firms like Splitgerber and Daum in Berlin prospered by supplying the needs of Prussia's ever-growing military machine. Elsewhere royal patronage facilitated the development of porcelain works and silk producers, iron foundries and coal mines, shipyards and textile mills. The Prussian state trading company, the so-called Seehandlung, encouraged a wide variety of business through investment and direct intervention. The collieries of the Ruhr, in whose service Freiherr vom Stein first won his bureaucratic spurs, were largely the product of state support. It would be a mistake, however, to overestimate the beneficial effects of the state on economic development. While we are in no position to draw up a balance sheet on the state's role, it would be surprising if, in sum, its interventions did more good than harm. In the first place, officials sometimes encouraged productive enterprises, but sometimes protected the unproductive—out of ignorance, inattention, or self-interest. In Silesia, for instance, Frederick the Great sacrificed the interests of the linen weavers to the privileges of a few powerful merchants, thus initiating a policy with disastrous long-run implications for the region's textile industry. Similarly, Frederician efforts to promote the Berlin silk industry had only intermediate success, especially when these enterprises are compared to silk manufacturing in Krefeld, which triumphed in spite of government harassment. Overall, economic growth in eighteenth-century central Europe was most vigorous and sustained when it was fed by autonomous social forces and engaged in expanding international markets. The pull of these growing economies, usually in combination with marginal improvements in domestic prosperity and some local advances in agricultural productivity, were more important stimuli for economic activity than the mixed blessings of

[88] Kisch, *Mercantilism*, pp. 42–3.

state action. Eighty per cent of Krefeld's silk, for example, went to customers in the Low Countries, Scandinavia, Britain, and even America.[89]

For our purposes, however, there is no need to choose between explanations which stress state and those which stress private initiative. Since we are concerned with broadly defined processes of social change, rather than technical questions of economic development, it is sufficient for us to recognize that state action and autonomous market forces were both at work and that, in the long run at least, both worked in the same direction. The state and the market, in different ways and at different times, undermined traditional social values, weakened existing institutions, and challenged established élites.

iv. OLD AND NEW ÉLITES

At the beginning of the eighteenth century the nobility occupied positions of unquestioned pre-eminence in German social, political, and economic life. Anchored by their status as a privileged caste, they virtually monopolized political power and, through their control of the land, economic resources as well. Their influence was felt throughout the social order, from village common to imperial court, from parish church to prelate's palace, from craftsman's shop to officers' mess. In the course of the century, however, the growing importance of bureaucratic states and expanding markets created new challenges to aristocratic pre-eminence. Strains developed within the nobility itself, especially between traditional landed families and those drawn into state service or commercial activities. Moreover, along the complex frontier that separated the nobility from the rest of society, there was friction between old and new élites, each representing different values, tastes, and claims to status and power. By the last decades of the century some Germans were talking about a crisis of the aristocracy. Few, to be sure, could imagine a world without nobles—except perhaps in some far-off land like America. But more and more contemporary thinkers were beginning to wonder if hereditary privileges were compatible with the modern age. 'In an enlightened era,' wrote a contributor

---

[89] Kisch offers a refreshingly sceptical view of the benefits of state initiative: *Mercantilism* and 'Industries'. See also Max Barkhausen, 'Government Control and Free Enterprise in Western Germany and the Low Countries in the Eighteenth Century', in Earle (ed.), *Essays*, 212–73. For more on this issue, see below, Ch.7, sect.iii, n. 66.

to the *Teutscher Merkur* in 1774, 'and in a refined nation, a citizen's rank and standing should be personal, not inherited, earned, not accidental.'[90]

The essence of traditional status was its hereditary, unearned character. Precisely because they were unearned, the nobility's privileges were inalienable. This was why Goethe's Wilhelm Meister believed that 'universal and personal cultivation is beyond the reach of anyone except a nobleman'. Noble status was defined and guaranteed by a core of medieval laws which had been added to and explicated over the centuries. In theory, only the emperor and the rulers of independently sovereign states could create new nobles, although other princes struggled to share this right and aristocratic corporations sought to protect themselves from interlopers.[91] As with everything else in the old Reich, the character and gradations of noble rank were extraordinarily complex and subject to endless political wrangling and litigation. The nobility was an extremely diverse social group that included Count Kaunitz, whose authority stretched across central Europe, and Friedrich Gabriel von Clausewitz, a poorly paid tax collector with a questionable title, Prince Wallenstein, who ruled 36,000 people in a territory of 320 square miles, and Ottilie von Pogwisch, a well-born but impoverished lady-in-waiting, whose only domain was her small attic room near the court of Weimar. Theoretically, these people all had rights and privileges that set them apart from the rest of society. In most states they could claim immunity from the local courts and had the right to be tried in special tribunals, with a different set of penalties; if the worst came to worst, they could choose to be beheaded rather than hanged. They sat apart from commoners in churches, theatres, and university lecture halls. They were allowed to wear swords and hats of a certain style. They demanded to be addressed with titles—*Hochgeborene*, *Edelgestrenge*, *Gestrenger Herr*—complicated enough to bewilder their fellow countrymen as much as they amused foreign visitors.

The nobility's claim to political power was rooted in their

[90] Quoted by Conze in *GGB* i. 26. On the eighteenth-century German aristocracy, see Bruford, *Germany*, pt. II, chs. 1, 2; and two recent local studies: Reif's *Adel*, and Pedlow, *Survival*.

[91] Benecke, 'Ennoblement', is a lucid introduction to this issue. T. H. Marshall defines *status* as a 'position to which is attached a bundle of rights and duties, privileges and obligations, legal capacities and incapacities, which are publicly recognized and which can be defined and enforced by public authority and in many cases by courts of law': quoted in G. Poggi, *The Development of the Modern State* (Stanford, 1978), 43.

Herrschaft, a concept which, as we know, fused various forms of authority with the person of the individual, the *Herr*, who possessed them. *Herrschaft* in its purest form was exercised by aristocrats immediately under the emperor: princes, ecclesiastical rulers, and imperial counts. Below these wielders of semi-sovereign power were the territorial nobility who owed their primary allegiance to an intermediary sovereign. Nevertheless, the territorial nobility's position as landlords gave them direct authority over their dependants and an array of other rights and privileges. They served in representative bodies, as patrons of church and school, inspectors of dikes and roads, directors of charitable trusts, and officers in the local militia. Even if sometimes attenuated by intervening agencies, *Herrschaft* and nobility remained inseparable.[92]

In addition to these sources of local authority, which they exercised directly or indirectly over their subjects, aristocrats were guaranteed positions of importance in religious, administrative, and military institutions throughout the German lands. The younger sons of Catholic families were especially fortunate in being able to find lucrative and influential posts in the church. For instance, at the end of the seventeenth century, five members of the Fürstenberg family held high offices, as Bishop of Münster, Dean of Salzburg, and Prebendaries of Mainz, Paderborn, and the Teutonic Order in Mühlheim; in addition, four of their sisters became canonesses. To the well-born Catholic, ecclesiastical honours came quickly and without great effort: Franz Ludwig, son of the Elector of the Palatinate, was a bishop at nineteen, and soon rose to be Grand Master of the Teutonic Order and then Archbishop of Mainz. The Canons of the Cathedral Chapter in Mainz, who were recruited exclusively from aristocratic families, owned as much as one-fifth of the electorate's total wealth and could hope for substantial bribes when the time came to elect a new archbishop.[93]

Most rulers chose their ministers and army officers from the aristocracy, and often from families with international ties and loyalties. Until well into the nineteenth century, many German nobles served several different princes: the Bennigsens, for instance, were based in Hanover but had members active throughout central Europe; the Gagerns fought for both the king of Sweden and the emperor before establishing themselves in the

---

[92] See above, Ch.1 secs. i, ii, on the concept of *Herrschaft*.
[93] Sagarra, *History*, pp. 39–40.

Rhineland. Moreover, all the major states attracted an international élite of nobles from Ireland, Scotland, Italy, and Spain, who came in search of glory, wealth, and power. Despite their efforts to bring the native nobility into the government, even the kings of Prussia took some of their most illustrious servants from outside their lands—Stein, Hardenberg, and Moltke are just the most obvious examples. Of course, once in the Hohenzollern's service, many nobles became Prussians; this happened, for instance, to the Boyen family, a migrant clan of warriors, who eventually settled down, acquired estates and intermarried with the local landed élite.[94]

To propertyless families like the Boyens, some form of state service was a necessity, but to great landowners like the Kaunitzes, high office was a duty, an opportunity to play the great game of politics, and an excuse to enjoy the pleasures of capital and court. The various members of the Kaunitz family who served the Habsburgs continued to hold their estates in Moravia and, when they could, used their political position to further their economic interests. But Wenzel Anton Kaunitz did not think of himself primarily as a *Grundherr*; his power and self-esteem came from his position within the state and near the throne. Some aristocrats even began to argue that state service would turn out to be the best defence of their privileges. 'I cannot repeat too often', wrote Max Franz von Habsburg to a noble friend, 'that the prestige which once surrounded and enhanced our rank is diminishing and that clergy and nobles must therefore make the effort to place themselves above other strata through real and essential services.' Indeed, to the author of the article on 'Adel' in the *Deutsche Encyclopädie* of 1778, nobility was 'an honour and dignity that comes not only from birth but also from an office'. In practice, however, birth and office, influence and ability, ascriptive status and personal achievement were often difficult to distinguish.[95]

Aristocrats frequently enhanced their political power through their positions at court, where they tried to influence the decisions of the ruler and his entourage. The court was both the real and the symbolic centre of political power, and thus, in the words of one contemporary, functioned as the 'theatre where everyone wants to make his fortune'. In the courts, nobles gathered around the person of the prince, whose position as the centre of the state they acknowledged in repeated rituals. Within the nobility itself, the court established a strict hierarchy which descended from the ruling

[94] Oncken, *Bennigsen*, i. 48 ff.; Rössler, *Revolution*; Meinecke, *Leben*, i. 4 ff.
[95] Braubach, *Sohn*, p. 112; Conze, in *GGB* i. 21. On Kaunitz, see Klingenstein, *Aufstieg*.

family through the ranks of officials and holders of honorary office to mere hangers-on. In addition to celebrating the primacy of the prince, court ceremonies also affirmed people's position in the social hierarchy of these little worlds. Men paid handsomely to acquire some functionless post that might elevate them one rung closer to the throne; their wives battled fiercely to defend their position, refusing to yield an inch to someone they judged an inferior. Most travellers agreed that the Viennese had the most obsessive notion of ceremonial nuance. Writing from the Austrian capital in 1716, Lady Montagu reported the story of two ladies whose carriages met on a narrow street; because they could not agree on who had precedence, they sat immobile until the next morning when they were removed by the imperial guard. Even at less formal courts, the rules of precedence and procedure were extremely complex. Goethe, who would never fully master the courtly game being played at Weimar, provided a classic description of the commoner's inability to grasp these aristocratic rules in his *Sorrows of Young Werther*.[96]

At court, nobles could bask in the reflected glory of the prince; on their own estates they could play the part of minor monarchs. Throughout the eighteenth century, land remained the most acceptable source of an aristocrat's wealth and the most secure foundation for his family's honour. After all, that magical particle, the noble *von*, which identified the caste, had originally been the expression of a link between person and place, between the *Herr* and his *Herrschaft*. When he sat in the family pew at his village church, returned the greetings of his deferential peasants, and acted as local judge or policeman, an aristocrat's authority took on a specificity and immediacy unavailable to the courtier and civil servant. For many noblemen, the hunt best captured that sense of power and self-esteem so important to their caste. Hunting embellished real privileges with the symbolic trappings of former glory: mounted and armed, the hunter evoked memories of feudal warriors, just as the peasants, pressed into service for the occasion, represented the docile serfs of days gone by. Noblemen, therefore, defended with the harshest penalties their exclusive right to certain sorts of game and pursued with no regard of cost this most aristocratic of sports.[97]

---

[96] Elias, *Process.* i. 9; Montagu, *Letters*, i. 273, Goethe, *Sorrows*, pp. 77–9. (Goethe of course wrote his novel before he went to Weimar. (See also Jürgen von Kruedener, *Die Rolle des Hofes im Absolutismus* (Stuttgart, 1973) and, on Weimar, Bruford, *Culture*.

[97] Blum, *End*, summarizes landowners' privileges in chs. 1 and 4. On hunting,

There were, of course, many aristocrats without estates. Others had only a modest manor house and garden, hardly more land than a well-off peasant farmer. In the north-east, medium-sized holdings seem to have been the rule: in Brandenburg, for instance, estates yielded between one and five thousand taler annually, that is, roughly the equivalent of a senior official's salary. Some magnates, however, drew princely sums from their holdings. The Reventlows' estate in eastern Schleswig-Holstein, founded in the fifteenth century, consisted of 5,000 fertile hectares which produced enough to maintain a splendid palace built according to French models and decorated by painters imported from Italy. The Schloss Hardenberg, near Göttingen in Hanover, dominated fourteen villages, 3,000 morgen of forest, vast fields of corn, and extensive pasture land. Finally, consider the success story of the Reichenbach family. In 1727 the twenty-two-year-old Leopold Freiherr von Reichenbach acquired a Silesian estate consisting of five villages, a market town, and five large farms. Over the next several years, the Freiherr (later Count) picked up eight more estates and a free city, expanded his arable land by cutting down forests, built a papermill, enlarged his fisheries, and sought every other means to increase his income. The Reichenbachs lived in a magnificent rococo mansion, entertained lavishly, and claimed all the traditional rights and privileges of the landed élite.[98]

Roughly speaking, the noble's relationship to his land and its inhabitants corresponded to the east–west bisection that we observed in our discussion of rural society. To the west of the Elbe line, landowners were principally concerned with the rents and other cash payments they could extract from their tenants. When they could afford it, western aristocrats lived in townhouses, usually near a court, returning to their estates only when the hunting was good or urban life dull. A very different situation obtained in most of the north-east. Here the nobility exercised their authority not only over the land—*Grundherrschaft*—but also over the estate as a social and economic unit—*Gutsherrschaft*. In part because of their colonial origins, in part because of their owners'

see Hans Wilhelm Eckardt, *Herrschaftliche Jagd. Bäuerliche Not und bürgerliche Kritik: Zur Geschichte der fürstlichen und adligen Jagdprivilegien vornehmlich im südwestdeutschen Raum* (Göttingen, 1976).

[98] Fritz Martiny, *Die Adelsfrage in Preussen vor 1806 als politisches und soziales Problem* (Stuttgart and Berlin, 1938), 9 ff.; Mayhew, *Settlement*, p. 142; Lang, *Zeit*, i. 218 ff.; Ziekursch, *Jahre*, pp. 12 ff. On the wealth of the Austrian nobility, see Dickson, *Finance*, i, ch. 5.

aggressive expansion of their demesnes in the seventeenth and eighteenth centuries, eastern estates tended to be consolidated agricultural enterprises rather than scattered farms and open fields. Using the labour of his dependent peasants, the *Gutsherr* worked his land and lived off what he could make by marketing the produce. In contrast to the absentee landlords of the west, therefore, eastern estate owners had a sustained relationship with their property, exercised personal authority over their dependants, and were directly involved in an agricultural market.[99]

Among the nobles of the north-east, the Prussian Junkers were distinctive because they combined *Gutsherrschaft* with an active role in state politics. As we have seen, after 1650 the Prussian landed élite gradually lost their corporate influence over the monarch but retained most of their authority over local affairs. In fact, the Junkers' compliance with the state often affirmed their power in the countryside: for instance, the militarization of rural society through the so-called canton system simultaneously tied aristocratic officers to the dynasty and enforced these officers' domination over their peasant soldiers. Similarly, the *Landrat* simultaneously served the state and defended the interests of the aristocratic stratum to which he almost always belonged. Unlike their counterparts in most German states, therefore, the Junkers established a tradition of state service without abandoning their position in the rural world of *Herrschaft*. Even if they themselves did not run an estate and hold an office at the same time, many Junkers were tied to both local and state hierarchies through military service or family connections. Their character as a social group was shaped by these experiences in a variety of institutions, all of which they were willing to use in pursuit of their individual interests and collective survival.[100]

Despite the efforts of Frederick the Great to preserve the Junkers as a separate landowning caste, more and more of their estates fell into the hands of commoners after 1750. Even generous subsidies and legal protection could not help incompetent or unfortunate aristocrats from having to sell their lands to wealthy businessmen, efficient agricultural capitalists, or aggressive speculators. At the end of the century, Silesian estates were held by about 1,350 noble

[99] Lütge, *Geschichte*, summarizes these differences, see especially pp. 145 ff., 188 ff. For some examples, see Hofmann, *Herrschaft*; Reif, *Adel*; and Brinkmann, *Wustrau*. There were, of course, pockets of *Grundherrschaft* in the east and *Gutsherrschaft* in the west.

[100] On the Junkers, see Hans Rosenberg's classic essays, reprinted in *Probleme*, and the literature cited above, Ch. 1, sect. iv.

and 250 non-noble families; in 1800 commoners owned 13 per cent of the estates in Brandenburg and between 4 and 10 per cent in Pomerania. Outside Prussia, the alienation of the aristocracy from its agrarian base was even more apparent: in the Saxon Diet, for instance, the number of commoners steadily increased as they bought up noble properties; by the 1720s thirty-two out of fifty-eight estates in the area around Leipzig had been acquired by non-nobles.[101]

The movement of commoners into the rural world of *Herrschaft* was just one of several ways in which the old aristocracy's position was threatened by new groups. In the countryside and at court, in administrative offices and urban drawing rooms, in universities and on the pages of periodical publications, the old élites were confronted by people unwilling to accept without question traditional rank and privilege. These people based their own claims to power and prestige on different grounds: wealth, political competence, educational accomplishment, moral superiority. They came from various places in society: commerce and manufacturing, the civil service and free professions, education and publishing. While it is awkward to refer to them as 'non-noble élites', there is no more positive term that adequately describes them. *Bürgertum*, which best fits their nineteenth-century successors, is inappropriate because in the eighteenth century it still retained its connections with the corporate realm of traditional urban élites. *Middle class* is certainly misleading, since these groups had neither a common relationship to the market nor a consciousness of themselves as a collective entity. *Bourgeoisie*, with its participatory, even revolutionary connotations, is completely out of place on the German scene. It may even be a mistake to think of these élites as belonging to a social stratum, if by that one imagines a clearly defined category of people 'in between' the aristocracy and lower orders. Perhaps their position can best be imagined with another geological metaphor: neither class nor stratum, non-noble élites were comparable to a vein of ore running through the social structure, discontinuous, uneven in quality and strength, often cutting across and sometimes disappearing into more readily apparent strata.[102]

[101] Blum, *End*, p. 18; Carsten, *Princes* p. 254.; Biedermann, *Deutschland*, i, pt. 1, p. 266.

[102] On the problem of definition, see the essays in Kocka, (ed.), *Bürger*, and Riedel's article in *GGB* i. Significantly, the Prussian legal code of 1794 defined the *Bürgerstand* negatively as 'all the inhabitants of the state not born into the aristocracy or the peasantry . . .'.

The diversity of these élites can be clearly seen even if we confine our attention to the citizens of German cities, those whom a conservative social theorist like Justus Möser would have called *Bürger*. Some cities were dominated by patricians who seem virtually indistinguishable from the traditional aristocracy: in Nuremberg, for instance, the leading families held office by hereditary right, demanded to be addressed as 'your grace', and claimed the exclusivè right to bear arms and wear special clothes. The leadership of the small 'home towns', on the other hand, was a relatively open stratum of craftsmen and merchants who lived modestly and without pretension. Neither the Nuremberg patriciate nor the home town notables had much in common with Hamburg's ostentatiously *bürgerliche* leaders who prided themselves on their aversion to aristocratic values and barred nobles from participating in urban affairs. But these differences represent only a preliminary summary of urban diversity. No less important was the contrast between independent cities and those in territorial states: unlike the leading citizens of Hamburg or Nuremberg, the *Bürger* of Hanover, Munich, or Berlin did not have independent political power. Nevertheless, in all of these cities a well-established and prosperous collection of businessmen, lawyers, physicians, and clergymen played important roles in social and economic affairs, belonged to the best clubs, held office in religious and charitable institutions, and participated in whatever municipal self-government was left to them by the states.[103]

Entrepreneurial élites overlapped but did not coincide with the urban *Bürgertum*. Financiers, bankers, and government contractors had direct ties to court or bureaucracy; they frequently had little interest in municipal affairs. David Hirsch, for instance, was a Jew from Potsdam who made a fortune after King Frederick William I gave him the exclusive right to produce velvet in the Prussian territories; ignoring the guilds, Hirsch imported skilled craftsmen and drew the rest of his work-force from local charitable institutions. Johann Heinrich Schüle, although a Christian, was no less an outsider than Hirsch. His textile enterprise was opposed by the town fathers of Augsburg because he imported unfinished cloth from the East Indies; eventually he won a suit against the city in the

---

[103] Material on individual cities was cited in the preceding section. For some additional examples, see Margareta Edlin-Thieme, *Studien zur Geschichte des Münchner Handelsstandes im 18. Jahrhundert* (Stuttgart, 1969); Rainer Koch, *Grundlagen bürgerlicher Herrschaft. Verfassungs- und sozialgeschichtliche Studien zur bürgerlichen Gesellschaft in Frankfurt am Main (1612–1866)* (Wiesbaden, 1983).

imperial courts and proceeded to create a giant concern which employed 3,500 people by the 1770s. Energetic, aggressive families like the Schüles and the von der Leyens from Krefeld broke with or simply ignored the traditional world in which the German *Bürger* had felt most at home. Not surprisingly, these new commercial élites frequently came from groups outside the established urban élite: Jews, Protestants in the Catholic west, Mennonites, and Huguenots.[104]

The economic expansion described earlier created new opportunities for these entrepreneurs and further attenuated their ties to corporate traditions. But we should not be too quick to identify these people as the vanguard of a 'rising' bourgeoisie. Both the von der Leyens and the Schüles, for example, were eventually ennobled and set themselves up with the trappings of the landed élite. Like many of their counterparts elsewhere in central Europe, their social ambitions were directed towards the aristocracy, whose lands and offices they acquired in order to diversify their investments and feed their vanities. Nor was this a peculiarly German phenomenon: 'In most European economies', Jan Devries has argued, if bourgeois families rose, they 'rose out of the bourgeoisie and into the aristocracy'.[105]

Eighteenth-century businessmen were pulled in several different directions—towards the nobility, towards the restrictive confines of the corporate order, and towards risky opportunities for industrial expansion or international trade. Some stayed in one or another of these worlds; others lived in several, moving from court to landed estate to commercial enterprise as required by the demands of the situation or the scope of their own ambitions. Paradoxically, the most clearly and consistently *bürgerlich* of German businessmen were those who combined strong local roots with broad international connections: the merchants of Hamburg or Danzig, for example, furnished their homes in the English style, dressed their womenfolk in Paris gowns, and peppered their talk with French phrases—all the while remaining deeply aware of their local traditions and regional loyalties. Thomas Mann captured the

---

[104] Kisch, *Mercantilism*, p. 5; Helen Liebel, 'The Bourgeoisie in Southwestern Germany, 1500–1789: A Rising Class?', *IRSH* 10/2 (1965), 293. For other examples, see Stefi Jersch-Wenzel, *Juden und Franzosen in der Wirtschaft des Raumes Berlin-Brandenburg zur Zeit des Merkantilismus* (Berlin, 1978), and the material on Jews in Vienna in Dickson, *Finance*, i. 142 ff.

[105] DeVries, *Economy*, p. 214. On literary treatment of the merchant as parvenu, see Ernst Baasch, 'Der Kaufmann in der deutschen Romanliteratur des 18. Jahrhunderts', *Aus Sozial- und Wirtschaftsgeschichte: Gedächtnisschrift für Georg von Below* (Stuttgart, 1928), 279–98.

nuances of this cosmopolitan provincialism in the marvellous opening scene of *Buddenbrooks*, in which the family's long association with Lübeck is celebrated with a poem by the town laureate, Jean-Jacques Hoffstede.[106] A similar combination—although with different components—might have been found in Frankfurt and Leipzig, as well as in Milan, Barcelona, and Amsterdam. Everywhere in Europe, businessmen, like the economies in which they operated, were regionally situated but internationally connected. A *German* economic élite did not exist.

The other principal category of non-noble élites in the eighteenth century was defined by office and educational attainment rather than by wealth or entrepreneurial energy. Like businessmen, the élites of office and education originated within the corporate order; clerks, clergymen, physicians, and lawyers were familiar figures in traditional society. By the beginning of the eighteenth century, however, the expanding bureaucratic states gave these groups new duties and opportunities. As a result, they grew beyond or tested the limits of their traditional place in the social and political structure. Just as economic growth eroded the bonds of corporate Europe by creating new paths to wealth, the states disrupted the existing order by opening up new chances for prestige and power.[107] But before we consider the growth of these élites, we must take a quick look at the educational system upon which they all depended.

Most eighteenth-century German schools were ill-equipped, poorly run, and badly attended. The village schoolmaster might be a pensioned non-commissioned officer, an underemployed craftsman, or the church sexton. Since they could almost never live on the fees paid by a reluctant community, teachers had to work in a variety of other jobs. The 'school' itself was rarely a separate structure; pupils met in the teacher's house, the local church, or some other temporary shelter. In Burg, the Prussian town where Carl von Clausewitz spent his childhood, seventy students between six and sixteen were exposed to the rudiments of grammar,

---

[106] Another good example is Joseph Marshall's description of Danzig in the late 1760s: *Travels through Holland . . . in the years 1768, 1769, and 1770* (London, 1772), 254.

[107] For the most recent research on these groups, see the collections edited by Conze and Kocka, *Bildungsbürgertum*; Ulrich Herrmann, 'Die Bildung des Bürgers'. *Die Formierung der bürgerlichen Gesellschaft und die Gebildeten im 18. Jahrhundert* (Weinheim and Basel, 1982); Ulrich Engelhardt, *Bildungsbürgertum: Begriffs- und Dogmengeschichte eines Etiketts* (Stuttgart, 1986). See also R. Steven Turner, 'The Bildungsbürgertum and the Learned Professions in Prussia, 1770–1830: The Origins of a Class', *Histoire sociale–Social History*, 13 (1980), 105–35.

arithmetic, and religion, with a little Latin thrown in. Even in a relatively prosperous and enlightened town like Mainz only about half the school-aged population got any instruction at all. In most parts of German Europe, schools did improve during the second half of the century, when governments tried to regulate teachers' training, strengthen the curriculum, and increase attendance. But progress was slow, in part because both material resources and qualified personnel were scarce, in part because many people had no great interest in schools. The poor could not afford to do without their children's labour; the rich could provide for their children with private tutors and personal instruction.[108]

Throughout the century the best-supported schools served a particular function or catered to a specific social group. Young aristocrats, for example, frequently attended one of the so-called *Ritterakademien,* founded in the late seventeenth and early eighteenth centuries to teach courtly manners, martial arts, and a smattering of scholastic subjects. Seminaries prepared young men to be priests or pastors. Cadet schools provided officers. Most towns had some sort of a Latin school, where artisans and merchants sent their sons for a few years before sending them out to learn a trade. The condition of these Latin schools was often execrable. In 1766, for instance, when Anton Büsching became head of the Graues Kloster in Berlin, he found its classrooms 'all looked like cellars, dark, unpleasant and unhealthy. . . . the writing class did not even possess a few tables . . . [and] though a minimum of candles were available there were no candlesticks, so the pupils had to hold the candles in their hands.' Eventually, educational reformers like Büsching were able to make some modest improvements. A few cities had schools that tried to teach young people to do more than read, write, count, and recite biblical passages from memory. But such schools were rare, merely a few scattered oases in an arid pedagogical landscape.[109]

[108] Paret, *Clausewitz,* p. 18; Dreyfus, *Sociétés* pp. 390 ff. For some other examples, see Lahnstein (ed.), *Report,* pp. 144 ff; Jung-Stilling, *Lebensgeschichte,* bk. 2. Peter Lundgreen's *Sozialgeschichte der deutschen Schule im Überblick, i. 1770–1918* (Göttingen, 1980), and Georg Jaeger, *Schule und literarische Kultur i. Sozialgeschichte des deutschen Unterrichts an höheren Schulen von der Spätaufklärung bis zum Vormärz* (Stuttgart, 1981), are good introductions to German education. For a local study of Baden, see Maynes, *Schooling* ch. 2; On Prussia, see ch. 2; LaVopa, *Schoolteachers;* Wolfgang Neugebauer, *Absolutistischer Staat und Schulwirklichkeit in Brandenburg-Preussen* (New York, 1985).

[109] Büsching quoted in Mark Boulby, *Karl Philipp Moritz: At the Fringe of Genius* (Toronto, 1978), 61. On school reform, see Jeismann, *Gymnasium.*

Since German schools differed enormously in what and how well they taught, there was no well-defined and generally accepted sequence of instruction, and no clear path from one educational level to the next. Very few people stayed in school for long; Clausewitz, for instance, left at twelve to join the army. Not many found their way to university; in fact, university enrolments seem to have declined over the course of the century: from 4,180 in 1700 to 3,700 in 1780. Most of German Europe's thirty universities (six in Austria, twenty-four in the other German states) were quite small: in the 1780s Leipzig had about 359 enrolments each year, Halle around 400. Göttingen, one of the most dynamic institutions, enrolled 810 students in 1787; Rostock, an academic backwater, had only about 40.[110]

After reading a few descriptions of student life in the eighteenth century, one has no difficulty understanding why many families were reluctant to send their sons to a university. Drinking, duelling, and rowdiness were the rule in many places; students were legendary for their eccentric dress, loose morals, and irresponsible behaviour.[111] Any effort to impose discipline was hampered by the fact that universities tried to function as separate corporations, each with its own governance and mores. Like other traditional institutions, universities were eager to defend their boundaries against intrusions from the outside, and were often willing to sacrifice new opportunities rather than endanger old privileges. The endemic conflicts between town and gown—as well as the pitched battles occasionally fought between students and apprentices—were the natural result of the tensions created by autonomous institutions coexisting within the same enclosed space. By mid-century most states had imposed some degree of control over the universities in their own territories. Since it was clearly in the state's interest to monitor and if possible to monopolize the production of educated élites, officials tried to regulate appointments, oversee examinations, and enforce certain rules of behavior. But, as in the case of the state's influence over city government, rural society, the church, or guilds, its control of university affairs was more limited than reading the relevant statutes might lead one to believe. Residues of academic autonomy remained.

There were about eight hundred university professors at the end

---

[110] McClelland, *State*, is a convenient summary of the eighteenth-century university. Enrolment data are from Turner, 'Reformers', p. 498.

[111] For an example, see Fr. Ch. Lankhard, *Leben und Schicksale* (Stuttgart, 1908), i. 95 ff., which describes student life at Giessen in the 1770s.

of the century. Most of them were poorly paid; a majority probably had some other job or source of income. When making new appointments, one contemporary complained, the faculty was concerned 'more with its relatives and personal friends, more with religious, fraternal, or collegiate relationships . . . than with true learned capability. . . . [I]t was only a fortunate coincidence when a really skilful man ever found his way to a teaching post.'[112] This emphasis on personal qualities and connections is not surprising when we recall that there were neither professional organizations nor well-defined disciplines through which scholarly credentials might be established and evaluated, just as there was no clearly marked path leading towards an academic career. Pressures to raise the professoriate's intellectual level came not from scholarly disciplines but from bureaucratic reformers. First at Halle, then at Göttingen, government officials set out to hire gifted academics, often by paying them enough to change jobs. Teachers were encouraged to do research and to publish, so that their reputations might attract other eminent intellectuals as well as more and better students. In these two institutions, therefore, we see foreshadowed the pre-eminence which German scholarship was to enjoy throughout the nineteenth century.

But if reformers' accomplishments at Halle and Göttingen point towards future academic developments, their motives were a product of the contemporary scene. E. A. von Münchhausen, for example, poured resources into the University of Göttingen because he wanted to attract the sons of wealthy and powerful families. In fact, both Halle and Göttingen did manage to increase the number of aristocrats among their student population. Throughout central Europe more and more young nobles studied law as a preparation for a governmental career; a young man as rich and well connected as Kaunitz spent time at Leipzig in the 1730s. Nevertheless, even at Göttingen, aristocrats remained a minority— never more than about 15 per cent. The largest single source of students was the university-trained élite itself: at Halle in the 1780s, 17 per cent came from the families of officials and lawyers, 31 per cent from professors, clergymen, and other professionals. The universities could also serve as a path towards social ascent: some 40 per cent of the Halle students were the sons of minor officials, schoolmasters, tradesmen, and artisans. This path, however, was steep and narrow, open only to those with unusual talents and energy.[113] Characteristically, it took several generations to move into range of a university education: for example, Freiherr von Lang's great-grandfather was a gamekeeper, his grandfather a minor official, his father and uncles pastors and professors; Ernst Moritz Arndt's grandfather was a shepherd, his father a prosperous estate agent. Without family resources or a reliable patron, attending a university was an extraordinarily difficult endeavour. 'The status of the lowest craftsman's helper', exclaimed Karl Philipp Moritz's Anton Reiser, 'is better than someone who must live from charity in order to study.' Moritz, whose own painful journey through the social order provided the basis for his widely read book, knew whereof he spoke.[114]

Because most men attended the university to prepare themselves for a career in medicine, theology, or government, the philosophical faculties were of minor importance, their teachers poorly paid, their students usually in transit to some other course of study. In both the humanities and sciences, most of what we would now recognize as scholarly research was carried out by someone in either a professional faculty or a royal academy. One of the most significant reforms introduced at Göttingen was the attempt to improve the teaching of history, languages, and mathematics and thereby change the philosophical faculty into something more than a preparatory course for ill-equipped applicants. But even when things began to improve towards the end of the century, a scholarly career was a risky business; most intellectuals had to support themselves as private tutors, seminary teachers, or librarians before they finally found a university appointment.[115]

Medicine was the smallest of the professional faculties—at Halle there were only about thirty medical students a year in the 1750s— and usually the least distinguished. According to one Hanoverian official, medical education existed to provide 'ten or fifteen young angels of death so that people can be buried methodically'. A few physicians did occupy positions of great importance; one suspects they were judged by the social position of their patients rather than by the quality of their treatment. Most medical men, however, worked for the state and had to compete for patients and prestige

---

[113] On Göttingen, see McClelland, *State*, p. 47; on Halle, Mueller, *Bureaucracy*, p. 89.

[114] Moritz, *Anton Reiser*, p. 156.

[115] See the material on this in Gerth, *Lage*, and Ludwig Fertig's collection of evidence on private tutors, *Die Hofmeister: Ein Beitrag zur Geschichte des Lehrerstandes und der bürgerlichen Intelligenz* (Stuttgart, 1979).

with a complicated array of other practitioners, including barber-surgeons, midwives, itinerant healers, herbalists, and the like.[116]

Theology was larger (at Halle it enrolled an average of 250 students a year between 1750 and 1774) and more intellectually vigorous than medicine. In Protestant territories, the clergy's social background, training, and status as government employees made them part of the professional élite. In contrast to the Catholic priesthood, which was largely staffed with men from rather modest backgrounds, Protestant ministers came from educated families. For example, of the forty-four pastors serving in the county of Sondershausen at the turn of the century, twenty two were the sons of pastors, eight of officials, seven of teachers, six of craftsmen, and one of a worker.[117] To those with talent and connections, the clerical life offered many opportunities: pastors in rural areas were often powerful and prestigious men, while the dean of an important city church could expect to move in the highest social circles. But the number of posts was small—only about 584 pastoral appointments were made in Prussia between 1786 and 1806—and the dangers of being passed over were considerable. For example, it took Friedrich Schleiermacher, a gifted but poor young man, several years, including a term as private tutor for a noble family, before he found a position as a parson in Landsberg.[118]

Law was the most attractive course of study for men with secure backgrounds, ample resources, and high ambitions. In his efforts to improve the social and academic scene at Göttingen, Münchhausen knew that jurisprudence was of primary importance: 'That the legal faculty be filled with famous and excellent men is necessary, above all, because the faculty must induce many rich and distinguished people to study in Göttingen.' In fact, almost four-fifths of the aristocrats at the university in 1777 were enrolled in the law faculty. A similar situation obtained at Halle where the sons of landowners and high officials were disproportionately well represented in law.

---

[116] J. Conrad, 'Die Entwicklung der Universität Halle', *JbbNS* 11/1 (1885), 110; McClelland, *State*, p. 30. See also Frevert, *Krankheit*, pp. 36 ff.

[117] Hans Eberhardt, *Goethes Umwelt: Forschungen zur gesellschaftlichen Struktur Thüringens* (Weimar, 1951), 100; Günther Bormann, 'Studien zu Berufsbild und Berufswirklichkeit evangelischer Pfarrer in Württemburg: Die Herkunft der Pfarrer: Ein geschichtlich-statistischer Überblick von 1700–1965', *Social Compass*, 13/2 (1966), 117, 129–30. Compare the material on Catholic priests in Rainer Müller, 'Sozialstatus und Studienchance in Bayern im Zeitalter des Absolutismus', *HJb* 95 (1975), 120–41.

[118] Brunschwig, *Enlightenment*, p. 133; Dilthey, *Leben*, pp. 49–50, 68 ff.

The popularity of legal studies among the 'rich and distinguished' was largely due to the association of jurisprudence and state service. Over the course of the eighteenth century, more and more German governments came to insist that their officials be university-trained before they could be appointed to important positions. By doing so, the states had taken an important step towards making education—and this meant, essentially legal education—the prerequisite for, and a clear indication of, a place in the political élite.[119]

This emphasis on formal training was only one of the ways in which states tried to ensure that their servants had the knowledge, skills, and personal characteristics necessary to run the increasingly complicated machinery of government. Some states also tried to establish formal procedures to measure these qualifications. The Prussian administration, wrote Ludwig von Hagen in 1770, must 'recruit young, able, and lively people as in-service trainees, and examine them thoroughly before they are recommended for appointment to determine whether they have acquired a basis of scientific knowledge'. Hagen introduced examinations at both the entry level and at the point of promotion to full-time service. 'No one who has not passed the examination in the prescribed manner will be admitted . . . and no one, regardless of status or background, shall be dispensed from taking the examination.'[120]

Examinations did not, of course, take the place of status and background as sources of political authority. Increasingly, however, an official's ascriptive status had to be supplemented, reaffirmed, and validated by educational attainments and measurable achievements. The result was what one scholar has called a system of 'limited competition', in which family ties and personal connections combined with talent and knowledge to determine who made it up the bureaucratic ladder. The effects of this limited competition on the social character of the bureaucracy varied over time and from state to state. In the early stages of Prussian state-building, the Hohenzollern had tended to recruit their bureaucrats from legally trained commoners, who were sometimes more able and invariably more reliable than the native nobility. Frederick the Great, as we have seen, reversed this tendency and gave preference to aristocrats in the civil service. But just as nobles were important in some sectors before 1740, so commoners continued to find a place thereafter. Frederick drew his immediate advisers from 'new

[119] McClelland, *State*, p. 43. See above, Ch. 1, and below, Ch. 7, sect. iii.
[120] Mueller, *Bureaucracy*, pp. 77–8.

men', who were completely dependent upon, and therefore totally loyal to himself. Furthermore, the judicial branch of the state continued to be staffed by commoners: only about 10 per cent of those appointed to junior judicial posts between 1786 and 1800 had a title, even though the proportion of titled individuals did increase in the upper ranks of the judiciary.[121]

Almost every German state was governed by a combination of men from the élites of birth and education. The relative weight and particular character of these élites varied: sometimes legally trained commoners acquired titles and moved easily into the old aristocracy, sometimes the lines between new and old nobles were sharply drawn. In Württemberg top civil servants, most of them with imperial titles, seem to have ignored court life, whereas at Gotha high-ranking officials were welcomed members of the prince's entourage. A newly ennobled Prussian official caused an unpleasant scene by trying to sit in one of the aristocracy's special church pews, but the daughter of a civil servant might marry into a family as old and distinguished as the Bismarcks.

More important than these particulars, however, is the fact that a new bureaucratic élite was taking shape throughout central Europe. In some places, this élite was joined by complex familial bonds: Johann Jakob Moser, for example, was married to the daughter of a Württemberg official; while he served this state, his sons held high positions in Hesse-Darmstadt and Baden Durlach, one daughter married a professor, and three others married clergymen and officials. Even when they lacked these dynastic ties, officials were joined by common educational experiences and career expectations. Above all, they came to be united by their commitment to and identification with the state. They were still servants of their prince, and dependent upon his whims and favour—as Johann Jakob Moser discovered when disobedience earned him five years of confinement. But they began to think of themselves as *Staatsdiener*, servants of the state, from which their authority derived and through which they advanced the common good. As the state's theoretical and practical power increased, its servants became more aware of their own importance and of their cohesion as a social group.[122]

Like businessmen and urban *Bürger*, the élites of office and

[121] For a sceptical view of this process, see Rosenberg, *Bureaucracy*. Mueller, *Bureaucracy*, takes the reform more seriously.

[122] Biedermann, *Deutschland*, i, pt. 1, p. 101, has data on the number of officials in the various states. For some examples, on Prussia, see Johnson, *Frederick*; on Hanover, Joachim Lampe, *Aristokratie, Hofadel und Staatspatriziat in Kurhannover* (Göttingen, 1963); on Württemberg, Vann, *Making*.

education still straddled corporate institutions. Civil servants in a small state, lawyers for aristocratic *Stände*, physicians at court, professors in the unreformed universities, all lived in deeply traditional social worlds. Furthermore, successful civil servants and professional men, like successful entrepreneurs, often aspired to membership in the old aristocracy. In government service, as in commerce, social ascent might mean ascent into another social stratum. At the other end of the scale, minor officials, school-teachers, and some physicians were difficult to distinguish from the craftsmen and small merchants whom they served and among whom they lived. And, of course, as great a social space separated minor official and royal minister as lay between the urban élite of a home town and the merchant princes of Augsburg or Krefeld.

Despite their diversity and discontinuity, non-noble élites had begun to develop a set of attitudes and values that would eventually become the moral core of a new social order. In the first place, the élites of commerce and of office began to develop an ethos based on individual achievement—on acquisition of knowledge, the performance of tasks, the fulfilment of duties. These achievements, they believed, could be measured by profits accumulated, promotions earned, or examinations passed. But these achievements also represented a vocation, a calling, a sign of devotion and commitment: in this sense, as Otto Hintze once wrote, *raison d'état* and *raison d'économie* have the same historical roots and produce similar social formations.[123] Second, the professional life of these élites was often combined with a new set of private relationships. The traditional tie between household and economy began to weaken, especially among the educated élites for whom work and family life usually took place in separate spheres. One result of this was a growing appreciation for the affective side of family relations, an increased sense of the emotional bonds between men and women, as well as between parents and children. Finally, these élites tended to operate in networks that extended beyond the local social worlds to which most traditional institutions had been confined. Their education, position in a bureaucratic hierarchy, and economic connections gave them wider social horizons and an enlarged awareness of their political identity. As we shall see in the chapter to follow, among these new élites of property and education are to be found the chief creators and consumers of a new, national culture, which at once drew upon and helped to clarify their social experience and private sensibilities.

[123] Hintze, *Essays*. p. 92.

III
Eighteenth-century Culture

JOHANN GOTTFRIED HERDER, a teacher's son in the Prussian town of Möhringen, swiftly exhausted the meagre intellectual resources available to him at home and in the local school. By the time he was ten or eleven he had begun to wander the streets looking for new books; when he saw one through a window, he would ask to borrow it at once. Towards the end of his life, when he was a venerable figure on the cultural scene, Herder told an audience of schoolboys how joyfully he recalled his earliest encounters with authors old and new: 'Scarcely anything in later years matched this pleasure, this sweet astonishment.' Since we live in a culture awash with printed matter, we may find it difficult to share that sense of awe and wonder that books produced in intellectuals of Herder's generation. For them the written word was sacred. While Herder may have praised folk culture in his theories, the culture to which he belonged was the culture of print. For every hour he spent watching peasants dance and recording their songs, he spent thousands pouring over the latest publications, writing responses to what he liked or disliked, discussing what he had just read or written.[1]

Born in 1744, Herder belonged to one of the first generations for which the printed word could be the primary means of cultural exchange. Of course printing had existed for three hundred years, but only in the mid-eighteenth century were there enough readers, writers, and books to support a sustained, secular reading public in the German lands. By this time, the centre of cultural gravity had clearly shifted from oral communications to written links between author and audience. The written word had acquired practical power and distinctive symbolic force. To write down rules, define ideas, and describe emotions was to give them a potent legitimacy and authenticity. We have already observed this phenomenon in the political realm, where the emergence of bureaucratic institutions involved the production of an unprecedented volume of secret records and public pronouncements, administrative regulations and judicial compilations. An apparently similar process was at work in

---

[1] Herder, *Werke*, xxx. 222. For another example, see Möller, *Aufklärung*, p. 18.

the private sphere, where people explored their emotional worlds in journals, diaries, and autobiographies. To put intimate thoughts and feelings down on paper, to capture them in ink or print, seemed to make them at once more vivid and more controllable. This era was also what one scholar has called the 'century of the letter', when people spent enormous amounts of time and energy creating written ties across time and space and, as Heine mockingly noted, put their 'Herzblut ins Briefcouvert', The novel, often constructed in the form of a journal or correspondence, gradually emerged as the characteristic literary genre for this new culture of print. No wonder that eighteenth-century intellectuals were fascinated by the nature of language, which, as Fichte was to argue, 'accompanies the individual into the most secret depths of his mind' and 'unites within its domain the whole mass of men who speak'. The eighteenth century is the great age of dictionaries as well as law codes, grammars as well as autobiographies, linguistic theories as well as novels.[2]

Like Herder, we live in a culture based on the printed word. When we think of eighteenth-century cultural life, therefore, we usually have in mind those great monuments that stand in intimidating bulk upon our shelves, the multi-volume works of Herder and Kant, Lessing and Klopstock, Goethe and Schiller. Much of what follows in this chapter will concern these writers and their achievements. But if we are to understand their historical position, we must trace the origins of their culture and examine how it coexisted and competed with other cultural forms.

i. CULTURES: POPULAR, ÉLITE, AND LITERARY

When Gustav Freytag called eighteenth-century German culture 'the miraculous creation of a soul without a body', he was expressing a nineteenth-century nationalist's amazement that cultural distinction was possible without political unity. In fact, for most of human history cultural and political boundaries have not coincided; cultures do not need nations or states in order to flourish. But every culture does need some kind of an institutional foundation. Since culture is a set of shared values and symbols, it requires a network of relationships within which the sharing can take place. Culture, therefore, is always both spiritual and

---

[2] Steinhausen, *Geschichte*; Leo Balet and E. Gerhard, *Die Verbürgerlichung der deutschen Kunst, Literatur und Musik im 18. Jahrhundert* (Berlin, 1972), 190; Fichte, *Addresses*, p. 68.

institutional, content and context, message and medium. The medium is not the message, but messages presuppose a means of delivering them. Message and mode of delivery are inseparable; together they make up what L. K. Frank called the 'activity of culture'. In this life, souls cannot live without bodies.[3]

In the eighteenth century there were many cultures in the German lands, many different networks through which people shared ideas and assumptions about the world. The same geographical, political, and technological barriers that divided Germans into separate social and economic units kept them apart culturally. Since most cultural activity was oral, it was necessarily limited to a small group of people who could communicate directly with one another. These cultural networks were not hermetically sealed; people moved across them, and sometimes lived in more than one. Certain kinds of activities, especially religious ones, linked islands of cultural contact. Nevertheless, just as it is misleading to talk about *a* German society or economy in the eighteenth century, so we should be aware that no single German culture can be found.[4]

We know very little about the cultural activities of most eighteenth-century Germans. We have a few scattered remnants of their lives, some artefacts, musical instruments, buildings, and utensils, but most of our evidence is indirect, the testimony of travellers, pastors, or officials who, for reasons of their own, decided to describe some festivity or custom. These outsiders, sometimes sympathetic, sometimes disdainful, always inexpert, provide us with what little we can learn about the vast majority of the population. An example of such a guide is Charles Burney, an Englishman who toured Europe in the early 1770s to gather material for his classic work on contemporary music. Burney was mainly interested in operas and sacred liturgies, but occasionally he gives us a glimpse of a world quite different from the courts and cathedrals to which most of his account is devoted. Here is his description of what happened when he stopped to change horses at Jülich:

In my way through this town . . . I was entertained at the post house . . . by two vagabonds, who in opposite corners of the room, imitated, in dialogue, all kinds of wind instruments, with a card and the corner of their

---

[3] Freytag, *Bilder*, xxi. 7; Frank quoted in Karl Deutsch, *Nationalism and Social Communication* (Cambridge, Mass., 1966), 283–4, n. 6. See also the valuable discussion of these issues in Walter J. Ong, *Rhetoric, Romance, and Technology. Studies in the Interaction of Expression and Culture* (Ithaca and London, 1971), 290.

[4] On the concept of 'popular culture', see Peter Burke, *Popular Culture in Early Modern Europe* (New York, 1978), chs. 1, 2; Kaschuba, *Volkskultur*.

hats, so exactly that if I had been out of their sight, I should not have been able to distinguish the copy from the original, particularly in the clarinet, French horn, and bassoon, which were excellent.

Men and women like this pair must have existed everywhere in Europe: singers and storytellers, acrobats and musicians, actors and clowns, who devoted their talents to distracting tired travellers like Mr Burney or providing some entertainment for ordinary people. Of course not all popular culture was beautiful or benign. We may regret the disappearance of Burney's musical vagabonds, but we are well rid of the show to which he was invited in Vienna, where thousands turned out to see a wild Hungarian ox tormented with fire and then set upon by dogs. Such debased spectacles, accompanied by drunkenness, violence, and cruelty, were as much a part of everyday cultural activity as folk-songs, storytellers, and travelling minstrels.[5]

Because most people lived close to the edge of subsistence, they had little to spend on entertainment or superfluous ornamentation. A devotional picture or two, perhaps a Bible and a few precious objects would be the extent of most people's non-essential possessions. Those few resources that could be spared from the arduous task of staying alive were usually lavished on important milestones in private or public life, the celebrations of births, weddings, and deaths, planting and harvesting, saints' days and religious feasts, military victories and royal visits. F. Friese, a schoolteacher in Altenburg, was one of the first Germans to devote himself to gathering information about these festivities. From his work we can assemble a picture of the complicated rituals and symbols that people constructed to explain and embellish their existence. Marriage ceremonies, for example, acted out the movement of the bride from one family to another, and thus reaffirmed the mutual dependence between individual families and their community. A couple's neighbours joined in the celebration as observers and guests, but also as the necessary source of social approval and support. Similar ceremonies marked the events in a craftsman's life: the beginning of his apprenticeship, his entry into the world as a journeyman, and, if he were fortunate enough, his achievement of master's status. Here also rituals were simultaneously public and private, turning-points in an individual's life and assertions of a community's power and legitimacy.[6]

---

[5] Burney, *Tour*, pp. 24, 112–13.

[6] Friedrich Friese, *Historische Nachricht von den merkwürdigen Ceremonien der Altenburgischen Bauern* (1703, repr. Schmöller, 1887). See also the material in Möller, *Familie*, especially pp. 254–6.

Religion played a central role in these festivities and in most other aspects of popular culture. 'The common man's entire life', Helmut Möller has written, was 'still embedded in the church'. The parish was the primary unit for celebrating weddings and burying the dead; farmers gathered to pray for bountiful crops; guildsmen had their patron saints and special churches; no business contract was signed or battle fought without calling upon divine assistance. Saints and shrines, parish organizations and travelling preachers, the consolations of prayer and the expectation of eternal life were all of the greatest importance to the overwhelming majority of the population. Since German Catholics put more emphasis on public ritual than private prayer, Catholic communities could exert enormous pressures on their members to attend mass and receive the sacraments; only a few individuals were stubborn enough to resist. In some Catholic regions, church ceremonies became massive and carefully arranged popular movements, such as the processions, sometimes two or three miles long, which moved through the streets of Vienna singing hymns in praise of the Virgin. The great pilgrimage churches in the south, such as the rococo masterpieces at Die Wies and Steinhausen, were built to mark places where the devout venerated sacred relics and prayed for miraculous cures.[7]

Religious and state authorities often viewed this popular piety with considerable uneasiness, since, in both Protestant and Catholic areas, the intense religiosity of ordinary life could easily lead to heterodoxy and disorder. Many cherished popular beliefs and rituals were theologically suspect expressions of some pre-Christian past or local custom rather than manifestations of orthodox faith and conventional piety. Bavarian villagers, for example, knew that the best protection from violent storms was to ring the church bells; they scorned lightning rods until well into the nineteenth century. In the province of Prussia, farmers protected their animals from evil spells by putting a cross made from certain flowers in their barns. Snake bites and sour milk, headaches and nosebleeds, infertility and madness, these and hundreds of other complaints had specific magical remedies known to every sensible person. While the authorities might have been contemptuous of some popular delusions, they could themselves have trouble drawing a line between prayer and magic, faith and superstition. In

[7] Möller, Familie, p. 214; Phayer, Religion, p. 30; Burney, Tour, p. 105; Karstein Harries, The Bavarian Rococo Church: Between Faith and Aestheticism (New Haven, 1983).

1749 Daniel Schleiermacher, the great theologian's grandfather, was forced to flee from his parish because he was suspected of sorcery. That same year, the superior of a nunnery in Würzburg was beheaded and her body burned after she was convicted of having commerce with the devil. The last German witch was executed in 1775.[8]

Christianity was the great unifying force in traditional Europe. In both its Protestant and Catholic forms, it provided the strongest links among ordinary people's oral cultures. But popular religion, like entertainment, festivity, and dialect, had local configurations. Every Catholic may have prayed to the Virgin, but most villages had their particular saint or form of supplication. Most people believed that they were surrounded by supernatural dangers and magical possibilities, but the nature of their charms and incantations varied from region to region. Weddings were celebrated everywhere, but the ceremonies were different, the songs and stories locally based. In popular cultures, as in the unwritten rules of social life, communities had their own language, carefully passed from generation to generation, difficult to learn, and impossible to forget.

In contrast to the locally rooted cultures of ordinary people, the culture of the aristocratic élite was internationally extended. Whereas a practised eye can easily detect the regional identity of peasant houses, nobles' residences usually reflected fashions common throughout Europe. Young villagers learned the traditions of their community; young aristocrats were tutored in the international code of their caste, and then taken on a grand tour to meet their counterparts throughout the Continent. In the course of the seventeenth century the international flavour of élite culture increased as foreign influences became dominant at most German courts; Italian music and theatre, French literature, architecture, and fashions were imported and emulated by every prince. In 1721 over four hundred foreign noblemen spent some time at the court

[8] Chadwick, *Popes*, ch. 1, has a concise account of popular religion. See also Möller, *Familie*, pp. 230 ff., Wolfgang Brückner, 'Popular Piety in Central Europe', *Journal of the Folklore Institute*, 5/2/3 (1968), 158–74; Ludwig Andreas Veit and Ludwig Lenhart, *Kirche und Volksfrömmigkeit im Zeitalter des Barocks* (Freiburg, 1956). We badly need a study of eighteenth-century German religiosity comparable to J. B. Neveux's *Vie spirituelle et vie sociale entre Rhin et Baltique au XVIIe siècle* (Paris, 1967). Daniel Schleiermacher's case is discussed in Dilthey, *Leben*, pp. 3 ff. Hermann Frischbier, *Hexenspruch und Zauberbann: Ein Beitrag zur Geschichte des Aberglaubens in der Provinz Preussen* (Berlin, 1970), provides material on local customs and magical beliefs.

of Saxony, while in Brunswick the ruling duke brought so many Frenchmen to his palace that one of them was moved to remark, 'Your grace is the only foreigner here.'[9]

The culture of the baroque court was shaped by the assumption that political power and social hierarchy could not be taken for granted but had to be expressed over and over again, with ceremonies and symbols, architectural monuments and festive display. Theatricality, therefore, was the essential characteristic of the courtier's world. The court itself was a setting for pageants of power and prestige, just as the baroque church was designed as a theatre wherein the sacred drama of the mass could be enacted. At court, as in church, there were no lines between participant and observer; everyone was meant to join the rituals that reaffirmed the social, political, and divine order. Life at court was filled with receptions and parades, banquets and balls, an endless variety of fêtes and galas that amused the courtly entourage and displayed the ruler's wealth and power. Foremost among these courtly cere-monies were those surrounding the person of the ruler, rituals that involved elaborate and often strenuous expressions of homage and respect. When David Hume was presented to Maria Theresa at Vienna, he found the rites more than his portly body could perform and had to be excused from the practice of backing away from the royal presence—much to the relief of his companions who feared that he might fall over on them.[10]

The theatre was the genre most characteristic of the baroque court. Indeed, theatre was a specialized and intense expression of court life. Dramatic performances offered unlimited opportunities for the conspicuous consumption of the ruler's money and the direct exercise of his authority. The content of the plays and operas, often devoted to the narration of Greek myths and the celebration of classical virtues, did nothing to call into question the social or cultural status quo. In the course of the eighteenth century, as many princes' cultural ambitions steadily increased, their theatricals became more extravagant and more burdensome for the public purse. The duke of Württemberg, for example, built a theatre at Ludwigsburg in 1750 with a stage large enough to contain a squadron of cavalry; a lake nearby could be used for complex

[9] Bendix, 'Province', p. 132; Fauchier-Magnan, *Courts*, p. 28, n. 2. Klingenstein, *Aufstieg*, pp. 220 ff., discusses the grand tour.
[10] Mossner, *Life*, p. 211. There is an earlier view of Viennese court life in Montagu, *Letters*, especially i. 273. See also Hubert Ehalt, *Ausdrucksformen absolutistischer Herrschaft: Der Wiener Hof im 17. und 18. Jahrhundert* (Munich, 1980).

nautical displays. Charles Burney, when he visited Württemberg a few years later, was overwhelmed by the amount of money lavished on plays, operas, and music. Perhaps, Burney suggested, these things can become a vice when half the state is composed of 'stage players, fiddlers, and soldiers'.[11]

Most rulers did not view the writers, composers, set designers, architects, and actors who provided them with drama and music as being fundamentally different from the other craftsmen who supplied luxury goods for the court's consumption. Johann Christian von Mannlich's move from goldsmith to court painter for the duke of Zweibrücken was, therefore, easy and natural. Nevertheless, with enough fortitude and good luck, a talented person could significantly better his social and economic position. Karl Ditters von Dittersdorf, for instance, used his musical ability to rise from a family of court tailors into the aristocracy; Josef Haydn, who spent most of his career as the valued employee of the Esterhazy family, started life as one of an impoverished cartwright's twenty children. Highly successful court artists like Mannlich, Ditters von Dittersdorf, and Haydn occupied an intermediate place in the social hierarchy, well above the rank of servant but clearly below the charmed circle of the aristocratic courtiers. In the last decades of the century, as the demand for talent grew and its rewards increased, this intermediate position frustrated many ambitious young artists, who were no longer content to view what they did as a craft and did not think of themselves as mere servants of the court. The exemplary figure here is Mozart, whose father, a court musician in the traditional mode, had dined with his master's valets, but who himself struggled to become more than just another purveyor of luxury goods. Even though his art transcended the limits set by court and church, Mozart himself was never able to achieve personal independence or financial security.[12]

A vast social distance separated the court musicians from the unknown mimics who hoped that Charles Burney would buy them a mug of wine in the coach house at Jülich. They lived in different worlds, as far apart as the crude entertainments of travelling players

---

[11] Burney, *Tour*, p. 38. See Bruford, *Theatre*, and *Germany*, pp. 83 ff. on court theatricals, and Raynor, *History*, pp. 164 ff., 296 ff., on opera.

[12] Mannlich, *Rokoko*; Karl Ditters von Dittersdorf, *Autobiography* (London, 1896); Vernon Gotwals (ed.), *Haydn: Two Contemporary Portraits* (Madison, 1968). For a positive view of the court's cultural role, see Martin Warnke, *Hofkünstler: Zur Vorgeschichte des modernen Künstlers* (Cologne, 1985).

and the lavish spectacles put on to amuse Duke Karl Eugen at Ludwigsburg. But, while the cultures of élite and populace were obviously distinct, they were never totally separate. For one thing, élites needed the common folk to admire their splendour, celebrate their victories, and pray for the salvation of their souls. The cheering throngs in Frankfurt's streets were almost as necessary for the imperial coronation as the notables who gathered close to the emperor's throne. When members of the court celebrated the coronation by tossing specially minted coins into the crowd, it was not just an amusing diversion (amusing, that is, for the observers, not for the unfortunate participants who were hurt and sometimes killed in their struggle for one of these prizes), it was also a symbol of power and social superiority. At times the élites entered the world of popular festivity. For instance, during carnival, the celebrations preceding the beginning of Lent, the theatrical mode so common to court life absorbed everyone and drew social groups together in a special realm. What one observer called 'the comedy of carnival' in Cologne took its actors from all of society, from every age and both sexes: 'the stage is the entire city, inside houses and on the street, in public squares and private balls'.[13]

People sometimes moved between cultures, but never as equals. The masked aristocrats who mingled with the crowds at carnival knew they were trespassing—that was part of the fun and excitement. The boisterous spectators at royal pageants derived their own pleasure from the show but recognized that they were there at the behest of their betters. In baroque churches, as in the theatres they resembled, élite and populace viewed the same performance, but sat in different places and had a different relationship to those on stage or at the altar. Traditional cultures, like the social institutions on which they depended, were restrictive. The particular characteristic they demanded for entry—noble birth, command of a local dialect, knowledge of unwritten rules and customs—set them apart from the rest of the world. Traditional communities—villages, guilds, cities, universities, or courts—were held together by what their members shared and by what divided them from those outside. Cohesion and exclusiveness were inseparable elements of the same social process.

In the course of the eighteenth century a new kind of culture emerged in central Europe. For want of a better term, we shall call

[13] Anton Fahne, *Der Carnival mit Rücksicht auf verwandte Erscheinungen* (Cologne and Bonn, 1854), 158. The coin-throwing scene is described in Mannlich, *Rokoko*, p. 42.

this a 'literary culture', a culture of readers and writers for whom print had become the essential means of communication and printed matter the primary source and subject of cultural activity. Such a culture had, to be sure, begun to take shape in the sixteenth century; as Elisabeth Eisenstein and others have demonstrated, printing was important for both Renaissance and Reformation. But books and printing were a necessary, not a sufficient cause for the triumph of literary culture as it is here defined. Equally important were innovations that did not occur in German Europe until after 1700. These innovations included a dramatic increase in the sheer number of books available, as well as in the velocity and extent of their circulation. People had once read intensively; those who had owned books, had usually owned only a few, which they had tended to read again and again. Now, in a literary culture, people read extensively, expending a great deal of time and effort to keep up with new publications and to gain access to as many books as possible. At the same time, the social role of reading was transformed. During the first two centuries after the invention of printing, most people had continued to employ books as supplements to oral communication; they had read them aloud, perhaps as the basis for religious devotion or court spectacle. Now, reading became an increasingly private activity—as David Riesman once wrote, the book is a door that one closes against the world. Riesman's phrase reminds us that the growth of a reading public coincided with an architectural emphasis on private domestic spaces where one might read alone. The primacy of print and its distinctive social function are essential elements in a literary culture, setting it apart from the oral communications that characterized the cultures of both élite and populace in traditional Europe.[14]

The emergence of a German literary culture is most clearly reflected in the data on publishing. In 1700 the Leipzig Book Fair catalogue listed 978 titles, almost half of which were on theological subjects; by 1780, the number of titles had increased to over 2,600 and the relative importance of religious works had declined

[14] On the initial impact of print, see Elizabeth Eisenstein's pioneering work, *The Printing Press as an Agent of Change: Communications and Cultural Transformation in Early Modern Europe* (Cambridge, 1979). Möller, *Familie*, pp. 258 ff., describes the role of reading in traditional society; the distinction between intensive and extensive reading is from Rolf Engelsing, 'Die Perioden der Lesergeschichte in der Neuzeit', *Archiv für Geschichte des Buchwesens*, 10 (1969), 945–1002. An introduction to the historiography of 'literary culture' can be found in Gerhard Sauder, 'Sozialgeschichtliche Aspekte der Literatur im 18. Jahrhundert', *IASL* 4 (1979), 197–241, and Kiesel and Münch, *Gesellschaft*.

significantly. Over this same period the proportion of books in German to those in Latin changed from about 2 : 1 to 10 : 1. By the 1750s there were large bookshops in many cities; at the same time, cash sales replaced the barter system that had traditionally limited a bookseller's ability to expand and reinvest his capital.[15] When businessmen realized that money could be made by serving the new literary public, some energetic and ambitious entrepreneurs entered the publishing trades. Of course, like all eighteenth-century commerce, dealing in books was risky: not only was the public's taste hard to predict, but ineffective copyright laws made it difficult to benefit from successful ventures. Respectable publishers complained endlessly about literary piracy, that insidious practice of *Nachdruck* which deprived them of hard-earned profits. Nevertheless, some literary entrepreneurs flourished. Johann Thomas Edler von Trattner became a major figure in Austrian public life by supplying enlightened literature to interested readers in Vienna; Friedrich Nicolai, the author of some widely read novels and travel books, dominated the publishing scene in Berlin; Johann Jakob Kanter founded a famous bookstore in Königsberg; and Georg Joachim Göschen, who started a printing firm with borrowed funds in 1785, eventually controlled a thriving enterprise based on the Weimar classics. Firms like Schott of Mainz (founded in 1770), André of Offenbach (the purchasers of Mozart's unpublished works), and Simrock of Bonn (Beethoven's publisher after 1796) did well by printing musical scores, which were much in demand from concert societies and other amateur musical groups.[16]

Publishers also began to market a variety of newspapers, magazines, and guides to the literary scene. One of the first signs of the newly expanded audience for literature was the extraordinary success of the so-called 'moral weeklies', which were based on English models and combined instruction, entertainment, and edification. About ten new moral weeklies appeared every five years between 1700 and 1740, twenty-eight between 1741 and 1745, twenty-seven from 1746 to 1750, and forty-four from 1751 to 1755, after which their popularity began to wane. In 1721 the

---

[15] Ward, *Production*, pp. 29 ff.; Hans Widmann, *Geschichte des Buchhandels vom Altertum bis zur Gegenwart* (new edn. Wiesbaden, 1975); R. Wittmann, *Die frühen Buchhändlerzeitschriften als Spiegel des literarischen Lebens* (Frankfurt, 1973).

[16] Klingenstein, *Staatsverwaltung*, pp. 93–4; Möller, *Aufklärung*, pp. 198 ff.; Vorländer, *Kant*, i. 181 ff.; Raynor, *History*, p. 331. A good introduction to the development of publishing and bookselling is Paul Raabe, *Bücherlust und Lesefreuden: Beiträge zur Geschichte des Buchwesens im 18. und frühen 19. Jahrhundert* (Stuttgart, 1984).

Berlinische Privilegierte Zeitung (later famous as the *Vossische Zeitung*) began its long career; enterprising editors in other cities swiftly followed its example. By the 1770s there were over seven hundred periodicals being published in German, as compared to just fifty-eight at the beginning of the century. Some of the most important and influential of these publications were designed to keep readers informed about the world of books and authors. From 1770 to 1800 H. A. O. Reichard put out a *Theater-Kalender* in which he discussed the new dramatic literature. Friedrich Nicolai, always quick to spot a market, published the *Allgemeine deutsche Bibliothek*, which reviewed some 80,000 titles between 1765 and 1805. In 1767, Georg Christoph Hamberger prepared an 800–page list of German writers which had to be emended by Johann Meusel seven years later. By the second half of the century, therefore, we can find the emergence of German literary criticism, which was perhaps the surest indication that a literary culture had been formed. After all, books about life require a common language, but books about books demand common literary tastes, interests, and knowledge.[17]

Reading freed people from the inevitable interdependence of oral communication, but it also helped to foster new kinds of relationships. An extraordinary amount of correspondence seems to have taken place in the eighteenth century, among writers and between writers and readers. Letters were a model for other kinds of writing, such as the epistolary novel or the published report on a particular subject addressed directly to the reader. Books also helped to create certain kinds of institutions and face-to-face encounters. Some of these were informal, such as the gathering that took place each day at Kanter's bookshop, where regular customers looked over the new books and magazines in the morning mail. Kanter created a small shrine to the new literature; his shop provided newspapers, refreshments, and desks at which to write; on the walls were pictures of famous authors, including Kanter's best-known patron and neighbour, Immanuel Kant. Literary culture was also sustained by formal organizations, such as lending libraries and reading societies, which combined the attributes of private clubs, libraries, and discussion circles: 'reading together with congenial conversation', according to the by-laws of the Stuttgart Reading Society founded in 1784. At the end of the century there were over three hundred of these organizations in

---

[17] Ward, *Production*, p. 23; Martens, *Botschaft*; Schenda, *Volk*, pp. 288–9; Joachim Kirschner, *Das deutsche Zeitschriftenwesen. Seine Geschichte und seine Probleme* (2 vols., Wiesbaden, 1958–62).

central Europe, many of them thriving centres of literary activity
where people came to borrow books, read newspapers, have a glass
of wine, and listen to a lecture on some recent publication. In
traditional society, books had been ancillaries of oral communication; in literary culture, people met to discuss books or to acquire
materials that they could read in private.[18]

Unlike the cultures of élites and populace, literary culture was
not inherently restrictive. Since it was not limited by either the
practical restraints of oral communication or the social barriers of
status, the culture of reading and writing was theoretically
accessible and potentially universal. It was not tied to a particular
regional dialect, shrouded by the secrets of a guild, or locked
behind the walls of a ruler's palace. It was open, public—as the
term *Öffentlichkeit*, so critical to the culture's self-definition,
suggests. The ruler of this public sphere was the *Publikum*, the
public, a self-selected audience whose tastes and opinions were
supposed to determine success or failure. To join the public
required neither noble birth nor arcane knowledge: as the by-laws
of the Stuttgart Reading Society proudly proclaimed, 'status and
external qualities', did not count; what mattered were 'qualities of
the heart and spirit'.[19]

In reality, of course, 'qualities of the heart and spirit' were not
enough, either for the Stuttgart Reading Society, whose fees were
high and membership limited, or for the literary culture as a whole.
Books were expensive and often hard to get, libraries and reading
societies were private organizations that most people could not
afford to join. Much more important, participation in the literary
culture demanded skills that only a minority of Germans possessed.
We do not have data on literacy rates for the eighteenth century, so
we cannot say with any precision how many Germans could read
and write. We do know that the quality of schooling was low,
teachers were poorly trained and badly paid, pupils unruly and
reluctant. Even among those willing and able to attend school, only
a minority could have learned enough to move with ease into the
new culture. To do this required more than an ability to write one's

[18] Dann, *Lesegesellschaften*; Erning, *Lesen*, p. 116; Gerteis, 'Bildung'; Gustav
Klemm, *Zur Geschichte der Sammlungen für Wissenschaft und Kunst in Deutschland*
(Zerbst, 1837); Milstein, 'Societies'; Richard van Dülmen, *Die Gesellschaft der
Aufklärer. Zur bürgerlichen Emanzipation und aufklärischen Kultur in Deutschland*
(Frankfurt, 1986). For an exhaustive local study, see Franklin Kopitzsch, *Grundzüge
einer Sozialgeschichte der Aufklärung in Hamburg und Altona* (2 vols.; Hamburg, 1982).
[19] Erning, *Lesen*, p. 116. The classic work on the significance of *Öffentlichkeit* is
Habermas, *Strukturwandel*.

name in the parish register or laboriously read some well-known passages from the family Bible. Access to the literary culture demanded the mastery of a complex language with its own references and specialized vocabulary. In fact, despite some marginal improvements in elementary education over the course of the century, the increasing complexity of literary communications may have put printed culture further away from ordinary men and women than it had been before 1700. The meaning of *Publikum* captures the ambiguities surrounding the public quality of literary culture: on the one hand, the *Publikum* meant every potential reader or spectator, on the other, it was confined to those able to pay the price of a book or a ticket of admission.[20]

Only a small minority of German speakers were part of the eighteenth-century literary culture. Contemporary estimates of its size range from 20,000 (Friedrich Nicolai in 1773) to 300,000 (Jean Paul two decades later). The best, although still very imprecise measure is the size of editions and subscription lists. Contemporaries regarded anything over one thousand as impressive. Nicolai's *Deutsche Bibliothek* reached its peak in 1777 with 2,500 subscribers; its chief competitor, the *Allgemeine Literarische Zeitung*, never got over 2,000. Schlözer's *Staatsanzeiger*, probably the most successful periodical of the era, managed to acquire some 4,000 subscribers in the 1780s. Individual titles rarely did so well. Nicolai's *Sebaldus Nothanker*, considered a runaway best-seller, sold about 12,000 copies in four editions; Goethe's and Schiller's *Xenien*, written when both poets were famous, sold about 3,000; the first edition of Goethe's collected works (1787–90) did not come close to that figure.[21] There were, to be sure, more readers than these figures suggest: since books were still rare and costly, almost every volume was read by several people. If we accept Rolf Engelsing's estimate of about twenty readers for each copy, we arrive at a literary public of somewhere between 100,000 and 200,000, less than 5 per cent of the total population. The overwhelming majority of Germans,

---

[20] On measuring literacy, see Pierre Chaunu, *La Civilisation de l'Europe des lumières* (Paris, 1971), 17 ff. The best introduction to these issues is the work of Rolf Engelsing, especially *Bürger*, and the essays in *Sozialgeschichte*. German education is discussed above in Ch. 2, sect. iv.

[21] Some examples can be found in Ward, *Production*, and Möller, *Aufklärung*, pp. 203–4. The most successful books of the period, such as R. Z. Becker's *Noth und Huelfsbüchlein*, which Göschen brought out in an extraordinary first edition of 30,000 copies in 1788, were up-dated versions of the old chapbooks. Becker's 'best seller' seems to have been written to be read aloud and was thus intended for those still accustomed to oral communication.

therefore, remained outside this 'national culture', either because they were functionally illiterate or because they confined their reading to a few religious tracts, the Bible, and perhaps, some of those crudely printed pamphlets offered by travelling peddlers or displayed in local markets such as the one on Berlin's Mühlendamm.[22]

The core of the literary culture was composed of teachers, pastors, officials, and other members of the educated élite. Consider, for example, the occupations of the three hundred contributors to the *Berlinische Monatsschrift* during the last third of the eighteenth century: about eighty of them, by far the largest group, were educators, about sixty high-ranking civil servants, fifty clergymen or church officials, ten army officers, five businessmen, two booksellers, one master craftsman, and about fifteen 'writers' whose other sources of income are unknown. Forty-five of these authors had a noble title; five were female. A rather similar occupational distribution is to be found among contributors to the moral weeklies earlier in the century and among the authors of articles on social issues studied by Johanna Schultze. For obvious reasons, it is easier to examine the social composition of writers than of readers. But what little we can discover suggests that here too educated élites predominated. Officials, theologians, professors, writers, and private tutors made up a majority of those who ordered advance copies of Nicolai's *Reisebeschreibung*. The same social mix seems to have provided the social basis for most literary organizations. Even in Mainz, where the presence of an active court meant that noblemen and church dignitaries played an unusually large role in urban life, officials and academicians were over-represented in the Reading Society. Almost everywhere, the available data suggest, businessmen were not much involved in literary life; even the court nobility seems to have played a proportionately larger part.[23]

In assessing these figures, it is necessary to bear in mind that the data on authors, subscribers, and society memberships are likely to

[22] Erning, *Lesen*, p. 38; Möller, *Aufklärung*, pp. 260 ff. For a description of the Mühlendamm's booksellers, see Anton Friedrich Büsching, *Beschreibung seiner Reise von Berlin über Potsdam nach Rekahn unweit Brandenburg welche er vom dritten bis achten Junnis 1775 gethan hat* (2nd edn., Frankfurt and Leipzig, 1780), 12–13.

[23] Möller, *Aufklärung*, pp. 188 ff., 251–4; Johanna Schultze, *Die Auseinandersetzung zwischen Adel und Bürgertum in den deutschen Zeitschriften der letzten drei Jahrzehnte des 18. Jahrhunderts (1773–1806)* (Berlin, 1925); Martens, *Botschaft*, pp. 128–9 and 145 ff.; Ernst Manheim, *Die Träger der öffentlichen Meinung. Studien zur Soziologie der Öffentlichkeit* (Brünn, 1933); Dreyfus, *Sociétés*, pp. 497 ff.

be biased in favour of the more prosperous and prominent elements within literary culture. We do not, therefore, discover quantitative evidence about those people from relatively modest backgrounds whose contributions to German intellectual development will concern us later on in this chapter. For men like Herder, Kant, Winckelmann, and many others, reading and writing were a means of escape from the spiritual as well as the material limitations of their social situation. 'The world is too narrow for me,' wrote Ulrich Bräker, an impoverished textile merchant from Toggenburg, 'so I'll create a new one in my head.' But such creations were difficult; upward mobility was rare. As the biographies of those who made it clearly show, to master literary culture without sufficient funds and family support required a heroic and sometimes psychologically debilitating struggle.[24]

To belong to the literary culture usually meant being estranged from the cultures of village and guild. By virtue of their training, tastes, and social position, the educated élites were cut off from popular culture. They recoiled in horror from the crude jokes of travelling players, were outraged by barbarous spectacles, and viewed popular piety with undisguised contempt. In order to appreciate popular art or oral literature, they would need translators and guides such as Herder and, in the nineteenth century, the brothers Grimm. The educated élites were also alienated from the culture of the courts, which seemed to them corrupt, trivial, and shallow. We do not want to be read by some 'half dressed beauty at her dressing table', wrote Nicolai in the preface to *Sebaldus Nothanker*, 'nor by some prancing little master . . . nor by a courtier . . . nor gambler, nor kept woman'. But if there is, somewhere, a 'haggard teacher, a brave superintendent, a wise scholar, a student, or well-read country parson', they are welcome to enjoy his book. A similar blend of social and moral categories— given a characteristically national configuration—can be found in Herder's evocation of those who live in every German province 'without French vanity or English elegance, obedient, often suffering, accomplishing things which anyone would admire if they were known'. For these courageous souls, Herder continued, he wished neither court nor capital, but 'only an altar of honest loyalty, at which heart and spirit might gather. It can only exist in the realm of the spirit, that is, in writing.' These writings would strengthen men's hearts and inflame their souls so that 'the German

[24] Ulrich Bräker, *The Life Story and Real Adventures of the Poor Man of Toggenburg* (Edinburgh, 1970), 37.

name, now so little valued among nations, would perhaps appear as the first among Europeans, without pomp or pretension, but strong, firm, and great in itself.'[25]

Educated élites set the tone for literary culture because they were the masters of the written word—poetic keepers of the sacred texts, recorders of public life, compilers of law, guardians of grammar. As people most at home in the realm of print, these élites formed a clerisy upon whose skills many of the new developments in politics, society, and culture had to depend. As we shall see in the rest of this chapter, the great eighteenth-century German poets and philosophers looked to these elites for their audience and drew from them their most important themes and values. The new German literature, the flowering of enlightenment philosophy, and the emergence of political ideologies are all unimaginable without this clerisy and the cultural institutions it created.

ii. LANGUAGE AND LITERATURE

In *The Sorrows of Young Werther*, Goethe's hero first experiences the full force of his tragic infatuation when he and his beloved watch the movement of a storm across the horizon:

We walked over to the window. It was still thundering in the distance, the blessed rain was falling on the land, and the most refreshing scent rose up to us with a rush of warm air. She stood there, leaning on her elbows, her gaze penetrating the countryside; she looked up at the sky, at me, and I could see tears in her eyes. She laid her hand on mine and said, 'Klopstock'.

Werther, like most of the book's contemporary readers, knew at once that Lotte was referring to Klopstock's ode, 'Die Frühlingsfeier', written in 1759 and reissued in a collection of the poet's work shortly before Goethe began to write his novel. Drawn together by a common language of allusion and symbols, Werther and Lotte expressed their feelings for nature with this shared vocabulary, and thus affirmed their common membership in literary culture.[26] Of course this incident's illustrative power is enhanced by the fact that Goethe's characters themselves swiftly become part of the century's

[25] Friedrich Nicolai, *Das Leben und die Meinung des Herrn Magisters Sebaldus Nothanker* (1773–6, rep. Berlin, 1960), 15–16; Herder, *Humanitätsbriefe* (1793), quoted in Kemiläinen, *Auffassungen*, p. 85.
[26] Goethe, *Sorrows*, p. 41. For an interesting account of the role of reading in Goethe's novel, see Ralph-Rainer Wuthenow, *Im Buch der Bücher, oder der Held als Leser* (Frankfurt, 1980).

growing reservoir of literary references. Not many Germans fully emulated Werther's fatal love, but many did copy his mode of dress and manners. Werther became for them the emblem of a certain sort of sensibility, the personification of feelings and desires somehow connected to their own. As vividly as the statistical data on book publishing and periodical circulation, this mingling of literary reference and quotidian emotion illustrates the arrival of a national literature.[27]

With the creation of Goethe's youthful works, what Friedrich Schlegel once called 'die Zeit der deutschen Nichtliteratur' had clearly come to an end. By the 1770s, Germans had begun to achieve a vernacular literary tradition comparable to that of the French and English. We saw in the preceding section the social groups and cultural institutions that the development of this literature required. No less important a prerequisite was the formation of a literary language capable of describing and evoking the social situations and emotional states which contemporaries could recognize as relevant to their own experience. Such a language had to be precise and uniform in the narrowly grammatical sense, but also rich and supple enough to transcend the confines of convention and to sustain new genres, modes of expression, and reservoirs of reference.[28]

Most histories of German as a literary language begin, quite properly, with Luther, who provided the foundation upon which modern German could be built. But Luther's achievement was not followed by a sustained literary development. In contrast to the situation in England and France, sixteenth- and seventeenth-century German writers did not establish a powerful, autonomous national literature, no doubt because of the political fragmentation, civil unrest, and social turmoil that we observed earlier.[29] Not until the late seventeenth and early eighteenth centuries do we find signs that Luther's linguistic accomplishments were being further developed. New philosophical achievements created a powerful

[27] A good introduction to eighteenth-century German literature, with an emphasis on the relationship between literature and society, can be found in the essays edited by Horst Albert Glaser, *Deutsche Literatur. Eine Sozialgeschichte* (Reinbek bei Hamburg, 1980), iv, v.

[28] Schlegel quoted in Reed, *Centre*, p. 11. On the evolution of 'literary language', see Blackall, *Emergence*.

[29] Of course one should not underestimate the quality or diversity of German literature in the seventeenth century: see Leonard Forster, *The Temper of Seventeenth Century German Literature* (London, 1951), for an analytical introduction; Gerhard Dünnhaupt, *Bibliographisches Handbuch der Barockliteratur* (Stuttgart, 1980–1), for a bibliographical guide.

vernacular language of speculation, while religious innovations, especially the emergence of pietism, generated an emotionally charged language of devotion and introspection. During the 1720s and 1730s Johann Christoph Gottsched, a professor of morals and metaphysics at Leipzig, devoted himself to popularizing and codifying language reform. He tried to encourage his contemporaries to write clear, straightforward but elegant prose, purged of affectation and heaviness, and designed to reach as large an audience as possible.[30]

Educated Germans came into contact with these modes of discourse in university classrooms—where instruction began to be given in German rather than Latin—and in a variety of new periodicals, such as the increasingly popular moral weeklies. Translations of foreign works, particularly from England, helped to elevate Germans' tastes. *Robinson Crusoe*, for example, was an immediate success when it was translated soon after its first appearance in 1719. Among Defoe's many imitators was J. G. Schnabel, whose *Insel Felsenberg* (1731–43), perhaps the first German best seller, remained popular throughout the century. Schnabel's laborious celebration of domestic virtue, defended under the most strenuous of circumstances, marked an important shift in public tastes and sensibility away from the courtly romances and scandalous fiction characteristic of baroque literature.[31]

Many of the same readers who applauded the virtuous restraint of Schnabel's protagonists were also drawn to the early religious poems of Friedrich Gottlieb Klopstock. Born into a family of lawyers and pastors, Klopstock attended the Schulpforta, the famous Saxon academy that would later have Ranke and Nietzsche among its pupils. At the university, Klopstock soon abandoned his theological studies for the literary life, supporting himself with a poorly paid position as private tutor. *Der Messias*, his poetic cycle on the life of Christ, was a great success when it began to appear in the 1740s. Christian Friedrich Daniel Schubart, who read the poems as a boy of twelve, compared the profundity of their impact with the religious awakening so central to pietist thought. While much of Klopstock's later work was neither artistically successful

---

[30] Pietism is discussed in the next section. On Gottsched and his contemporaries, see Blackall, *Emergence*, chs. 5, 6.

[31] Ward, *Production*, pp. 18 ff., discusses *Robinson Crusoe* and its imitators. The hero and heroine of Schnabel's novel lived together on a deserted island for four years without even mentioning their love for one another.

nor popularly accepted, his reputation persisted. Coleridge, for example, considered him 'the venerable father of German poetry', and made a pilgrimage to see him soon after arriving on the Continent in 1798. Klopstock, Eric Blackall has written, 'laid the foundations of a new grand style, giving to the German language a whole new register of voice', Without abandoning a concern for harmony and restraint, his best poetry extended the emotional range of literary expression as he sought to evoke in his readers authentic feelings about God, nature, or love. In the process, Klopstock helped to create a new image of the poet as a social and psychological type. He wrote, as his first wife once described him, 'with the most nobly dignified expression of devotion, pale with emotion and with tears in his eyes'. Here was no court entertainer, no contriver of clever embellishments or elegant artefacts, here was the artist as keeper of a sacred flame, the embodiment and expression of emotional depth and authenticity. No wonder that Goethe, who had read him as a youth, chose Klopstock's ode to seal poor Werther's obsessive passion for the lovely Lotte.[32]

In 1748, when Klopstock's *Messias* was gaining popularity and Gottsched's *Grundlegung einer deutschen Sprachkunst* first appeared, Gotthold Lessing abandoned his medical studies and some bad debts in Leipzig to pursue a literary career in Berlin.[33] Lessing was not quite twenty when he arrived in the Prussian capital. The son of a poor pastor from the small Saxon town of Kamenz, Lessing had great talent, energy, and ambition, but few resources. Eventually, his writing brought him fame but not security: he worked as a journalist, private tutor, and theatre director before finally becoming royal librarian at Wolfenbüttel. Like so many of his contemporaries, Lessing was eventually obliged to accept the mixed blessings of patronage in order to survive. Undoubtedly the practical difficulties of his own life imparted a particular sense of urgency to his cultural mission, which was to create the basis for a flourishing national literature. From his earliest days as a literary journalist for the *Berlinische Privilegierte Zeitung*, Lessing tried to sort out the healthy and unhealthy elements in German literature. With his friends Friedrich Nicolai and Moses Mendelssohn, he

[32] Erning, *Lesen*, p. 33; Samuel Taylor Coleridge, *Collected Letters* (Oxford, 1956–71) i. 442; Blackall, *Emergence*, p. 350; Menhennet, *Order*, p. 108.

[33] Among the other important literary works to appear in the 1740s were C. F. Gellert's novel, *Leben der schwedischen Gräfin von G.* (1747–8) and a collection of C. M. Wieland's poems. On the achievements of this decade, see Martini, 'Aufklärung', pp. 429 ff.

raised the level of Germans' literary taste and awareness just when the public was most in need of such direction. At the same time, he gathered material for a dictionary and studied etymology and grammar because he believed that literature required a refined language, free from foreign intrusions and structural impurities. Improvements in taste and linguistic reform would, he hoped, create the foundation for a national culture like the ones that had sustained Sophocles and Shakespeare. Lessing's vigorous objections to French influences, therefore, had both an aesthetic and a patriotic purpose; he found French literature sterile and rigid, and also an unfortunate impediment to the German search for cultural identity.[34]

Lessing, together with many of his contemporaries, viewed the theatre as the most effective instrument for building a national literary culture. The drama's impact on its audience was direct and immediate; it could stir the public's emotions, encourage their moral sensibilities, and shape the language of their everyday lives. His own plays all sought to enlighten and elevate as well as to entertain their viewers. *Miss Sara Sampson* (1755) is a domestic tragedy about the destruction of innocence; *Minna von Barnhelm* (1767), his masterpiece, examined the relationship of love and honour; *Emilia Galotti* (1772), another tragedy of destroyed innocence, provided an oblique criticism of courtly morals; and *Nathan the Wise*, written during the last, unhappy years of his life, is Lessing's famous plea for tolerance and understanding. These plays, and particularly the first two, had a powerful impact on Lessing's contemporaries. *Sara Sampson*, subtitled 'ein bürgerliches Trauerspiel', may seem mawkish and contrived to us, but its original audience found it realistic and familiar. Set in a simple inn of a kind familiar to everyone in the audience, the play concerned people not unlike themselves. It was *bürgerlich* in its domesticity, in the social location of its subject, and in the moral and emotional tone it intended to evoke. When the audience wept for Sara Sampson, their tears came from empathy and recognition.[35]

---

[34] Wilfried Barner *et al.*, *Lessing. Epoche—Werk—Wirkung* (Munich, 1975), is an introduction to works by and about Lessing. See also H. B. Garland, *Lessing, the Founder of German Literature* (2nd edn., London, 1962); Paul Rilla, *Lessing und sein Zeitalter* (Munich, 1977). For his impact on language, see Blackall, *Emergence*, pp. 315 ff. Cassirer, *Philosophy*, pp. 357 ff., puts him in the context of Enlightenment thought.

[35] On Lessing's dramatic achievements, see R. R. Heitner, *German Tragedy in the Age of Enlightenment* (Berkeley and Los Angeles, 1963), especially ch. 6 on *Sara Sampson*.

By the time Lessing died in 1781, a new generation had taken up his struggle to create a national literature. Among these younger critics and writers, Johann Gottfried Herder most deserves to be considered Lessing's successor. Born to a poor and pious family of teachers and craftsmen, Herder escaped the restraints imposed by his background because he found a patron, a Russian surgeon who paid his tuition at the same fine school in Königsberg from which Immanuel Kant had graduated a few years earlier. Herder went on to the University of Königsberg, studied medicine and then theology, attended Kant's lectures, and perused the latest books and magazines in Kanter's bookshop. In 1769 he took a post preaching to the German-speaking population of the Russian town of Riga. He left soon thereafter, toured France, served briefly as a tutor, was court preacher at Schaumburg-Lippe, and finally moved to Weimar, where he remained from 1776 until his death in 1803. Herder was one of the Enlightenment's greatest polymaths, at home in seven languages and literatures, actively interested in art and natural science, and the author of major works on history, literary criticism, theology, philology, and philosophy.[36]

Not long after arriving in Riga, Herder delivered a speech entitled 'Do we now have a Public and Fatherland like the Ancients?' He concluded that, while nothing like the ancients' public existed, the fatherland remained—but by *fatherland* he meant the same sort of small community to which Justus Möser was committed, in Herder's case, Riga. Over the next few years, however, his concept of fatherland broadened to include all Germans and his notion of the public was superseded by the idea of the *Volk*, a national community through which history, culture, and individual life acquired meaning. 'Unless we have a *Volk*, we lack also a public, a nation, a language, and a literature.' Herder, like Lessing, devoted himself to building the foundation for a new national culture, which he also saw as a social as well as a spiritual enterprise. But Herder's *Volk* is socially wider and spiritually deeper than the enlightened public for which Lessing yearned. The *Volk* is 'the invisible, hidden medium that links minds through ideas, hearts through inclinations and impulses, the senses through impressions and forms, civil society through laws and institutions, generations through examples, modes of living and education'. The *Volk* is the most important of the circles of collectivity—family,

[36] Although obviously out of date, Rudolf Haym's *Herder* remains a fine introduction to his career. See also Isaiah Berlin's splendid essay in *Vico and Herder* (New York, 1977); Clark, *Herder*; Barnard, *Herder*.

tribe, community, *Volk*, species—from which humans acquire their identity and purpose.[37]

Because the *Volk* is a living organism, it is best understood developmentally; its essence is expressed and can be found in its history. The historian's task is to trace the evolution of a *Volk's* particular character over time, and thus to establish its distinctive morphology and purpose. The primary focus for such history is not politics and statecraft—as we shall see, Herder viewed states with considerable misgiving—but rather art, religion, and literature. The culture of a *Volk*, he believed, 'was the flower of its being', most vividly and powerfully expressed by the nation's artists.[38]

Herder regarded language as the key to a group's identity and development. Language made both personality and community possible. It linked individuals to one another, established boundaries between peoples, and separated humanity from the rest of creation. In his famous prize essay on the origins of language, written in 1770 and published two years later, Herder argued that, 'since the definition of humans is the creation of the group, the development of language was natural, essential, necessary'.[39] Like Klopstock, who regarded each language as 'a shrine containing the *Volk's* essence', Herder viewed language as the clearest expression of national identity. Like Johann Georg Hamann, who saw language as a mirror of a nation's history, Herder searched in literature, folk-tales, and linguistic development for the key to the nation's past and the promise of the nation's future.[40]

This belief in the centrality of language came naturally enough to the members of an élite whose cultural identity and social significance depended on their mastery of the correct language of the new grammars and the symbolic language of the new literature. Language established the ties that joined this clerisy together and the boundaries that separated it from the illiterate mass and the Frenchified nobility. The great literary achievements of the 1770s and 1780s seemed to confirm the power of language to stir people's emotions, elevate their sentiments, and consolidate their inter-

[37] Wellek, *History*, i. 192; Barnard, *Herder*, p. 117. On the context of Herder's Riga speech and trip to Paris, see Haym, *Herder*, i. 109 ff., 313 ff.

[38] On Herder's historical views, see Berlin's essay cited in n. 36; Rudolf Stadelmann, *Der historische Sinn bei Herder* (Halle/Saale, 1928); Meinecke, *Historicism*, ch. 9. The quotation is from Stadelmann, p. 68.

[39] *Werke*, v. 112.

[40] Klopstock quoted in Poliakov, *Aryan Myth*, p. 96. On Hamann, see Blackall, *Emergence*, pp. 426 ff.

connections. 'It was truly a poetic epoch', Ernst Moritz Arndt recalled, 'when, after long, dull dreams, our dear Germany awoke to a new literary and political existence.'[41]

This epoch was, above all, the epoch of the young Goethe. Like Dante, Shakespeare, and Cervantes, Goethe is a national poet, whose work has had a deep and lasting impact on his nation's language and literature. Without him, Friedrich Meinecke once wrote, 'we [Germans] should not be what we are', But, as E. M. Butler astutely noted, Goethe is the most modern and therefore the least cohesive of the great national authors. Despite his own titanic efforts to unify his life and thought, individual impulses and historical situation, his work does not represent a dense, coherent world like Shakespeare's but rather a fragmented, often incoherent world like our own.[42]

Goethe was born in 1749 into what he liked to describe as the Frankfurt patriciate. On his father's side, however, patrician status was newly won, the result of his marriage into a well-established Frankfurt family. Goethe early on displayed the wit and playfulness, love of make-believe and illusion, selfishness and inconstancy which remained central to his character. His father, who counted on him to consolidate the family's place in the urban élite, viewed the boy's preoccupations with some uneasiness. When his sixteen-year-old son left for Leipzig to study law, the elder Goethe must have felt with unusual acuity that blend of relief, hope, and anxiety so characteristic of such occasions. From his father's point of view, Goethe's time at Leipzig was not a success; he enjoyed an active social life, went to the theatre, wrote lyrics, and explored the contemporary literary scene, but he did not study much law. When he returned to Frankfurt in 1768, his health was uncertain and his academic record bleak. After two years at home, convalescing, writing, and experimenting with alchemy, he set off again to pursue his studies, this time at the University of Strassburg.[43]

Strassburg did not do much for Goethe's legal career, but his stay there turned out to be absolutely crucial for his artistic development. In the company of a talented group of like-minded young men, Goethe first became aware of the power and possibilities of

[41] Arndt, *Erinnerungen*, p. 43.

[42] Meinecke, *Historicism*, p. 373; Butler, *Tyranny*, pp. 85 ff. See also the stimulating remarks about Goethe in Beenken, *Jahrhundert*, pp. 133 ff.

[43] The basic source, at once indispensable and unreliable, for Goethe's life up to 1775 is his autobiography, *Dichtung und Wahrheit*. Friedenthal's *Goethe* is a good modern biography.

literary culture. By far the most important among these compan-ions was Herder who, after abandoning plans to travel with a young nobleman, was in Strassburg recovering from a painful eye operation. Their long conversations in Herder's darkened room and a careful reading of Herder's essays enabled Goethe to put his growing artistic ambitions into a broader cultural context. Poetry, he learned, 'was a gift to the world and to nations, and not the private inheritance of a few refined, cultivated men'. This new conception of art's roots and functions inspired Goethe's essay on the Strassburg cathedral, which he celebrated as a prime example of Gothic architecture, a distinctly German style. Erwin von Stein-bach, the shadowy figure whom Goethe credits with building the cathedral, was praised as a national genius, able to capture in stone the profound feelings and aspirations of the *Volk*.[44]

When Goethe returned home from Strassburg he began writing *Götz von Berlichingen mit der eisernen Hand*, a play based on the life of a sixteenth-century knight. Goethe's Götz represented what would become a familiar type of German hero, a man of great strength and courage caught in a hopeless struggle against wicked intrigue and his own fate. The play has an emotional intensity almost without precedent in earlier German drama: unlike Sara Sampson, Götz does not meekly meet his doom, but rages against it until the end. The world, one feels, is diminished by his death. *Götz* was published in 1773. A year later, Goethe's epistolary novel about obsessive love, *The Sorrows of Young Werther*, appeared. Werther, like Götz, is engulfed by forces he cannot control, but the forces are inner impulses rather than external enemies. In contrast to most contemporary German novels—Hermes's *Sophiens Reise von Memel nach Sachsen* (1769–73), for instance—the locus of action in *Werther* is the hero's mind, the world he finds within himself. This inner world, reached by a process of secularized pietist introspection, is the novel's true setting and main subject.

Some established critics were not pleased by these works. Lessing dismissed *Götz* as 'Wischiwaschi', while Frederick the Great, who saw it performed in Berlin in 1774, thought it was a pitiful imitation of some inferior English drama. Friedrich Nicolai

---

[44] J. G. Herder *et al.*, *Von deutscher Art und Kunst* (1773), ed. E. Purdie (Oxford, 1924). In addition to Goethe's essay on the cathedral, the volume contains Herder's comparison of Ossian and Shakespeare, Möser's introduction to his history of Osnabrück, and an obscure essay on the Gothic by an equally obscure Italian. For the context, see Franklin L. Ford, *Strasbourg in Transition, 1648–1789* (Cambridge, Mass., 1958). Goethe's account of his relationship with Herder is in Book 10 of his autobiography. See also Haym, *Herder*, i. 380 ff.

ridiculed Werther's emotional excesses in a biting parody entitled 'The Joys of Young Werther', and Lessing lamented the main character's lack of classical restraint. But to many younger readers, Goethe's works represented a release from formal restrictions and emotional blandness. They welcomed *Götz*'s ramshackle structure and passionate language and applauded Werther's intense preoccupation with his own psyche. With uncanny accuracy, Goethe had absorbed the mood of the time. The young dramatists of the *Sturm und Drang*—Lenz, Merck, and Klinger—duplicated his concern with passion and shared his restlessness with convention, and the writers of spiritual autobiography—Moritz, Jung Stilling, and Bräker—followed his path into the inner realm of feelings.[45] Still in his twenties, Goethe must have caught a glimpse of the cultural figure he would eventually become: 'One only knows that one exists', he wrote, 'when one finds oneself again in others.' But, unlike most of his admirers and imitators, Goethe was neither chained to, nor destroyed by the themes and styles of the 1770s. As he would do so often in the course of his long life, he moved on, prepared to abandon the basis of past accomplishments in search of new challenges and experiences.[46]

In December 1774 Goethe met the young duke of Weimar, who was passing through Frankfurt on a grand tour of the Continent. After two brief but cordial encounters, he accepted the duke's invitation to join his court. When Goethe arrived in November 1775, he had no clear sense of purpose, other than to serve as a 'favourite' and amuse the duke. The young citizen of Frankfurt found himself in a difficult position: the principality's most distinguished intellectual, Christoph Wieland, had been understandably annoyed by a nasty little satire that Goethe had once published about his work; the chief figures at court, busy jockeying for influence over the new ruler, viewed him with dislike and distrust. Often frustrated and sometimes repelled by courtly life, Goethe was also fascinated by his new environment: 'Was weiss ich, was mir hier gefällt| In dieser engen kleinen Welt| Mit leisem Zauberband mich hält!' Much to everyone's surprise, Goethe became more than a jovial companion for the duke; after taking an

---

[45] For some examples of the contemporary response to Goethe: on Lenz, see Allen Blunden, 'Language and Politics: The Patriotic Endeavors of J. M. R. Lenz', *DVLG* 49 (Sonderheft, 1975), 168–89; on Möser, Menhennet, *Order*, p. 5. Leppmann, *Image*, provides a convenient summary of the poet's impact over time. Compare Goethe's own account in Books 14 and 15 of his autobiography.

[46] Friedenthal, *Goethe*, p. 174.

active interest in the administration of the state, he was named a Privy Councillor in June 1776. For ten years he published little and finished no major works, devoting himself to caring for Weimar's tiny army, muddy roads, inactive mines, and chaotic finances.[47] He remained 'in love with the real' until September 1786, when he fled to Italy, leaving behind the unbearable burden of his public duties and private entanglements. He spent two years in the south, refreshing his spirit and gathering his strength for a new and more prolonged period of artistic creativity.[48] By the 1790s he had begun to finish fragmentary projects and to begin new, yet more ambitious works. In all of these enterprises he was immeasurably assisted by Friedrich Schiller, who became—in T. J. Reed's words—'a practical ally, a sympathetic audience, and a perceptive analyst of [Goethe's] work alike in its finest detail and its broadest cultural significance'.[49]

Schiller was born in 1759 in the town of Marbach, where his father was a low-ranking officer in the service of Karl Eugen of Württemberg. Eventually the family moved to Ludwigsburg, the site of the duke's court and the setting for his spectacular self-aggrandizements. Nothing within his orbit escaped Karl Eugen's attention, not even the career objectives of a minor official's talented son; contrary to his own desire to study theology, therefore, Schiller was sent off, at fourteen, to begin a seven-year course at the Karlsschule, an institution sponsored by and closely watched over by the duke. Bored by his studies and hemmed in by the semi-military discipline imposed at the Karlsschule, Schiller found release in a few passionate friendships, intense pietist Christianity, and the new German literature. During his last year at school he wrote his first play, *The Robbers*, which was performed at Mannheim in 1782, just after he had taken up his duties as a regimental surgeon. When, contrary to orders, Schiller left his post to see a production, Karl Eugen had him arrested and forbade him to write on anything other than medical subjects. The choice was clear and unavoidable: on the one hand, military discipline, obedience, security, on the other, artistic freedom, rebellion, and risk. Late in the evening of 22 September 1782 Schiller fled Stuttgart and, without personal resources or an alternative position, began the difficult life of a writer. 'The public', he wrote a

---

[47] On Goethe in Weimar, see Bruford, *Culture*; Friedenthal, *Goethe*, pp. 204 ff.

[48] Once again, Goethe himself provides the basic account, reprinted, with a useful commentary, in his *Werke*, xi.

[49] Reed, *Centre*, p. 68.

few years later, 'is now everything to me, my source of study, sovereign, and friend. . . . Before no other tribunal will I stand.' In fact, the public was unable to support Schiller. Like most of his contemporaries, he wandered from one post to another until 1789, when, through the influence of well-placed friends, he was made professor of history at the University of Jena.[50]

Between the ages of twenty and twenty-eight, Schiller wrote four extraordinary dramas, all of which explore the conflicts he had experienced as a child, conflicts between the brittle glamour of the court and the supportive domesticity of home, between the powerless authority of his real father and the formidable paternalism of the duke, between the moral imperative of individual desire and the crushing force of external circumstance. Although their subject matter and tone vary, *The Robbers*, *Fiesko*, *Love and Intrigue*, and *Don Carlos* are all concerned with some kind of intrigue, betrayal, and rebellion. In three of them, the troubled relationships of fathers and sons have a central role. By the end of all of them, human failing and blind fate have joined to litter the stage with death and destruction. Schiller leaves no doubt that he knows the pains of rebellion and freedom's terrible costs.[51]

Things did not come easily to Schiller, in life or in art. He had not enjoyed Goethe's comfortable childhood, he lacked his friend's good health and his instincts for self-protection. Nowhere in Schiller's work do we find those apparently effortless, breathtakingly beautiful passages that Goethe could make seem so easy. But suffering and discipline combined to give Schiller his own special genius, a depth and authenticity of feeling, a sureness of moral purpose, and a vigorous intellectual engagement. Both a poet and a philosopher, Schiller was as committed to truth as he was to beauty, and he recognized that such commitments were difficult to sustain and reconcile. As he wrote to Goethe in August 1794, 'characteristically I am overcome by poetry when I should philosophize and by philosophy when I want to be a poet', But, even if Schiller was never quite able to fuse his quests for truth and beauty, his aspirations were, as we shall see, of great importance to the generation of artists and philosophers who came of age in the 1790s.[52]

Schiller looked to the ancient world as a model. Here, he

---

[50] Wiese, *Schiller*, is a good biography. The quotation is from p. 220.

[51] For an intelligent and stimulating reading of Schiller's plays, see Ilse Graham, *Schiller's Drama: Talent and Integrity* (London, 1974).

[52] Wiese, *Schiller*, p. 97. See also Goethe's and Schiller's *Briefwechsel*.

believed, art and thought, aesthetics and philosophy flowed from a common source and nourished an integrated culture. It was a 'happier generation', he wrote in his great poem of 1788, when the Gods of Greece 'still ruled the beautiful world'.

> Da der Dichtkunst malerische Hülle
> Sich noch lieblich um die Wahrheit wand!
> Durch die Schöpfung floss da Lebensfülle,
> Und, was nie empfinden wird, empfand.

Similar feelings of reverence and nostalgia for classical civilization can be found in many eighteenth-century German writers. Johann Joachim Winckelmann, the extraordinary self-taught classical scholar and enthusiast, believed that 'the only way for us to be great, and if at all possible, immortal, is by imitating the ancients'. Lessing, who was critical of Winckelmann's theories, had no doubt about the importance of the ancients for modern times. Similarly Herder, while opposed to all cultural imitations, acknowledged Greece as 'the type and exemplar of all beauty, grace, and simplicity'. As a result of his experience in Italy, Goethe also entered a classical phase, most clearly to be seen in his play, *Iphigenie auf Tauris*, which he completed in 1787.[53]

So pronounced were these classical enthusiasms that some scholars have called the late eighteenth century the age of 'neo-classicism'. As a stylistic category, however, neo-classicism is of limited usefulness. Even in the visual arts, where the influence of ancient models is undeniable, the classical style conveyed a complex range of feelings and intentions. Thus Robert Rosenblum, after considering the variety of classical influences on late-eighteenth-century painting and architecture, wondered if 'neo-classicism may properly be termed a style at all, or whether it should not be termed, to use Giedion's phrase, a "coloration"'.[54]

In literature even 'coloration' may be too strong a term to cover the extent of the ancient world's influence or to account for the different ways in which classical subjects and motifs were used. Among eighteenth-century German intellectuals, it is not easy to

---

[53] W. D. Robson-Scott, *The Literary Background of the Gothic Revival in Germany* (Oxford, 1965), 70. There is a brilliant but eccentric account of German classicism in Butler, *Tyranny*. Hugh Honour's *Neo-Classicism* (Harmondsworth, 1968), provides a useful introduction to the style. On Winckelmann, see Rudolf Pfeiffer, *History of Classical Scholarship: From 1300 to 1850* (Oxford, 1972), 167 ff.

[54] Robert Rosenblum, *Transformations in Late Eighteenth Century Art* (Princeton, 1967), 4.

find anyone who did not admire the ancients and borrow from them some theme, character, or stylistic device.

German admiration for classical culture had less to do with style and artistic form than with moral tone and artistic function. In contrast to the conventions and sensibilities of the baroque and rococo, classical art seemed harmonious, serious, and authentic. Greek tragedies were not written to amuse a privileged élite, they sought to edify and inspire the entire nation; Greek statues were not simply decorations, they served religious and political purposes. Germans were drawn to the organic quality of the ancient world, to what they saw as its unification of art and life, poetry and public purpose. Winckelmann's account of the Greeks seemed to convey the same message as Herder's analysis of the Volk: art should be the expression and celebration of a nation's aspirations, the product and protector of its collective identity. It was perfectly possible, therefore, to esteem Sophocles and Shakespeare, Homeric epics and Norse sagas, because all seemed to draw their greatness from their connections with a living folk and all held the promise that someday the German nation might find poets worthy of itself. 'If we are able to have a national theatre,' Schiller wrote in 1784, 'then we will be a nation. What held Greece together? What drew the Greeks so irresistibly to their theatres? Nothing but the plays, which were infused with the Greek spirit, the great interests of the state and of a better humanity.'[55]

In the decades between the 1740s and the 1770s, between the publication of Klopstock's 'Messias' and Goethe's *Werther*, some Germans sensed that they were witnessing the birth of a national literature. Readers and writers shared the belief that they belonged to a cultural community beyond the reaches of their states or cities. In addition to our home towns, Justus Möser wrote, we now have a 'literary fatherland'. But with these hopes and aspirations went disappointments and anxieties. The public was an essential but often unreliable source of material support and spiritual nourishment. Rarely could a writer live from his books. 'We direct our writings into thin air,' lamented Wieland in 1776, 'towards all mankind and our dear neighbours—and thus towards no one at all.'[56] This separation of author and audience occurred wherever print replaced oral communication as the primary literary medium. But perhaps the public's elusiveness was especially troublesome to

[55] 'Schaubühne', p. 98.
[56] Haferkorn, 'Entstehung', p. 164.

German writers. Unlike their French and English counterparts, they had no geographical centre for their efforts; nor had German literary culture a political base. 'We are working in Germany as if in that confusion of Babel,' Herder wrote in 1767, 'There is no capital, no interest of general concern. There is no great general, furthering agency and no legislative genius.' Scattered across central Europe, isolated between a francophile aristocracy and an illiterate mass, German readers and writers were forced to live from their own resources, to create their own connective tissues, to defend their own cultural mission.[57]

From this historical situation arose two impulses within German literary culture: first, a widespread belief among German writers that they were public figures whose work had a profound moral purpose and national significance; and, second, an equally pervasive sense of authorial isolation and cultural fragmentation. These aspirations and anxieties were among the eighteenth century's most potent legacies to modern German literature. Sometimes in conflict, but often moving in tandem, aspiration and anxiety remained inseparable from the way German writers viewed themselves, their work, and their audience.

iii. PHILOSOPHY AND RELIGION

The same social groups and cultural institutions that supported the new German literature provided the basis for innovations in philosophy and religion. While German poets and critics were creating a literary language to express their feelings and experience, contemporary philosophers and theologians were establishing a vernacular discourse to express their ideas about faith and reason. Eighteenth-century literature and philosophy had a great deal in common. Both, for instance, were deeply influenced by pietism. Some of the same individuals, such as Lessing and Herder, played a significant part in the history of both developments. Perhaps most important, the makers of modern German literature and philosophy shared a sense of their own historical position: Kant, like Goethe, believed that he was helping to lay the foundations for an intellectual enterprise particularly appropriate for his own time and place. Contrary to what is sometimes argued, most eighteenth-century writers and thinkers were interested in, and respectful of the past. Nevertheless, they were convinced that they lived in a

[57] Clark, *Herder*, p. 62.

new and different age, which was, as J. C. Adelung wrote at the end of the century, 'without doubt the most important and brilliant time in the whole history of culture'. Eighteenth-century thinkers recognized that their historical burden and opportunity was to provide this age with the spiritual nourishment it required.[58]

To a greater degree than German literature, eighteenth-century German philosophy was linked to international developments, and remained essentially inseparable from intellectual developments throughout Europe. The evolution of Kant's thought was, as we shall see, fundamentally shaped by the ideas of Hume and Rousseau. The German *Aufklärung*, like the rest of the European Enlightenment, involved what Diderot called 'a revolution in men's minds to free them from prejudice'. Most enlightened Germans, like enlightened Britons and Frenchmen, would usually have considered religion to be the most widespread and dangerous source of prejudice. Kant, for example, regarded 'religious immaturity' as the 'most pernicious and dishonourable' of the childhood diseases from which enlightened people had to free themselves.[59]

But while German thinkers shared enlightened Europe's hostility to dogmatism and intolerance few of them were opposed to religion *per se*. It is difficult to find anti-clerical pagans like the Baron D'Holbach east of the Rhine; even discreet non-believers like David Hume were rather rare. Instead, the *Aufklärer* usually accepted the significance of religion for culture and society. Many of them had close ties to the Protestant clergy, who occupied an important place in the new educated élite; pastors' sons, former students of theology, and ordained ministers were prominent among the leaders of the German Enlightenment as well as of the new literary movements. Far from wanting to eradicate Christianity, they wanted to see it improved, purged of its imperfections, brought up to date. Their goal was a spiritual realm in which faith and reason might coexist, each strengthening and strengthened by the other. They sought, as Ernst Cassirer wrote, 'not the dissolution of religion, but its transcendental justification and foundation'.[60] The origins of this close relationship between

---

[58] Quoted in Schober, *Spätaufklärung*, p. 49.

[59] Isser Woloch, *Eighteenth-Century Europe: Tradition and Progress, 1715–1789* (New York, 1982), 233; Kant, *Writings*, p. 59.

[60] Cassirer, *Philosophy*, p. 136. Cassirer's book remains the richest and most challenging analysis of eighteenth-century philosophy, with a particular emphasis on epistemology. For a somewhat different approach and emphasis, see Gay, *Enlightenment*.

enlightened aspirations and religious faith can be seen in both of the main sources of the *Aufklärung*, pietism and early rationalist thought.

Pietism was the German version of that deeply personal, often anti-establishment brand of religiosity that emerged all over Protestant Europe in the late seventeenth and eighteenth centuries. Pietists had little interest in the official church's ceremonies, hierarchical institutions, and complex doctrinal disputes. Such things were irrelevant, perhaps harmful to authentic religious experience, which was based on direct, immediate, and emotionally charged bonds between individual believers and God. Philip Spener (1635–1705) formulated the main spiritual elements in pietism, but it was August Hermann Francke (1663–1727) who provided the organizational talents to spread these ideas everywhere in central Europe. Francke founded schools and orphanages, sponsored travelling preachers, and established the University of Halle as an important centre for pietist studies and devotion. As often happens when religious enthusiasms find institutional expression, Francke's success drained some of pietism's original spiritual energy and fervour. In some places it began to resemble the orthodoxies against which it had originally been launched. Nevertheless, the influence of pietist ideas and attitudes was felt throughout German Protestantism, from separate communities like Count Zinzendorf's Moravians at Herrnhut to thousands of ordinary parishes where it affected the emotional tone and theological content of everyday religious practices.[61]

Although many devout pietists would have been scandalized by the thought, Karl Biedermann was surely correct when he maintained that the movement was 'at once the prelude and the signal' for the German Enlightenment. The pietists' emphasis on the immediacy of an individual's religious experience prepared the way for a secularized belief in personal autonomy and independence, as well as for that powerful introspective impulse which we have already seen at work in German literature. Thomas Mann once wrote that *Werther* 'is inconceivable without a long tradition of pietistic introspection'. The same thing could be said about

---

[61] There is an admirably clear and concise account of pietism in Sagarra, *History*, pp. 111 ff. Hartmut Lehmann's 'Der Pietismus im alten Reich', *HZ*, 214/1 (1972), 58–94, summarizes the historical literature and provides a good analysis of Spener and Francke. Mary Fulbrook, *Piety and Poetics: Religion and the Rise of Absolutism in England, Württemberg, and Prussia* (Cambridge, 1983) underscores the way in which pietism could be used for quite different political goals. The classic account of Prussian pietism is C. Hinrichs, *Preussentum und Pietismus* (Berlin, 1971).

Kant's critical philosophy. Moreover, by encouraging its adherents to express their feelings in written form, pietism helped to link them to the emerging literary culture. This is not to suggest that pietist education advanced free thought—far from it. But its schools did teach people to explore their spiritual sensibility and to describe it in journals and autobiographies, letters and spiritual statements. These modes of self-expression taught some Germans a new language of poetic sensibility and led others to a personal search for truth.[62]

Rationalist philosophers, like pietist theologians, set out to free Christianity from institutional abuse and thus return it to what they regarded as its proper basis in the autonomous consciousness of the individual. Christian Thomasius (1655–1728), for example, was deeply involved in religious issues during his long career as a philosophy professor at Leipzig and then Halle, where he preached a brand of enlightened religion that left no room for witch hunts and superstitious ritual, legal torture and doctrinal intolerance. He was committed to rational discourse, but always qualified this commitment with an awareness that faith and revelation brought higher forms of truth. Christian Wolff (1679–1754), for a time Thomasius's colleague at Halle, also advocated a reconciliation of logic and theology. Wolff had been influenced by both Leibniz and medieval scholasticism, which he combined with a Thomistic confidence that faith and reason could be joined. In his aptly titled *Vernünftige Gedanken von Gott, der Welt, und der Seele der Menschen*, published in 1720, he argued that reason was man's most divine faculty and could lead him to God, the highest form of reason. Wolff expressed his ideas with a vigorous and lucid style that found many admirers: Friedrich Nicolai, for example, was drawn to what he called 'the uncommon orderliness, clarity, and directness which reigns in these works'. Like Thomasius, who was the first academic philosopher to announce his intention of lecturing in German, Wolff helped to popularize rationalist thought and to create a vernacular language of philosophy. In the process, Wolff managed to earn the enmity of the pietist faculty at Halle, who forced him to leave Prussian territory and take a position in Marburg. He finally returned, in triumph, when Frederick the Great became king and inaugurated a policy of religious toleration.[63]

By the time Wolff was restored to his post at Halle, the social

[62] Biedermann, *Deutschland*, ii, pt. 1, p. 346; Blackall, *Emergence*, p. 54.

[63] On German rationalism, see Beck, *Philosophy*. The Nicolai quote is from Menhennet, *Order*, p. 71.

support and intellectual contours of the *Aufklärung* had begun to take shape. In philosophy, as in literature, during the 1740s and 1750s an older generation consolidated its accomplishments while another began to produce its first important works. The young people who came of age around the mid-century were exposed to both pietism and rationalism, each of which undermined the smooth certainties of the established church. Consider, for example, the case of Lessing, a clergyman's son with deep theological interests, who broke with his family's orthodoxy because it seemed intellectually and emotionally unsatisfying. Echoing pietist and rationalist attitudes, he argued that an individual could not simply inherit religion as though it were family property; everyone had to find his own way to God. Lessing never stopped searching for a rationally consistent and ethically compelling set of beliefs that would fill his need for faith and moral sustenance. During the last years of his life, when he was plagued by family problems, ill-health, and theological controversy, he wrote his touching declaration of principles, *Die Erziehung des Menschengeschlechts* (1779), which presents Christianity as an important, but not final, stage in the inevitably progressive education of the race. In language that reflects a characteristic blend of rationalism and piety, Lessing evoked the promise of a new, enlightened order he realized that he would never see: 'It will come, it will surely come . . . this time of a new eternal gospel.'[64]

A similar combination of rationality and religiosity can be seen in the work of Lessing's friend and admirer, Moses Mendelssohn. Born in 1729, the son of a teacher, scribe, and employee of the Dessau synagogue, Mendelssohn moved to Berlin as a young boy and remained there until his death in 1786. By the end of the 1750s Mendelssohn was a well-known writer, prolific reviewer, and valued participant in Berlin's cultural affairs. In many ways, Mendelssohn's background and experience seem totally different from the educated circles in which he eventually moved: after a largely religious training, he served as the private tutor for a wealthy Jewish family, and eventually supported himself by managing a silk factory. Nevertheless, Mendelssohn's writings on theology, literature, and politics, like those of his friends among the *Gebildeten*, were based on the belief that education and

[64] Gay, *Enlightenment*, i. 333. Lessing's early religious beliefs can be seen in a letter to his father from May 1749, quoted in Henry Allison, *Lessing and the Enlightenment* (Ann Arbor, 1966), 51.

enlightenment provided the keys to social, economic, and eventually political progress.[65]

Mendelssohn became more important for what he represented than for his specific contributions to eighteenth-century thought. To educated German Jews, he personified the blend of cultural identity and assimilation that characterized what David Sorkin has called the 'German-Jewish subculture'. This group 'read its own history and actions in his work and, perhaps even more, through his life'. Mendelssohn's life and work also had representative significance for his non-Jewish contemporaries. Mendelssohn's role in Berlin's cultural élite seemed to offer the promise of healthier relations between Jews and non-Jews throughout German society; he was an important source of C. W. Dohm's famous pamphlet of 1781 'On the Civil Improvement of the Jews', which urged the destruction of those barriers separating the Jews from mainstream German life. But Mendelssohn's career is no less important as an illustration of assimilation's limits. Despite his reputation and accomplishments, he received no official recognition from the Frederician state; his nomination to the Prussian Academy was firmly rejected by the king. Furthermore, even some of his closest friends had difficulty accepting Mendelssohn's Jewishness: either they continued to hope that he might convert to Christianity (as his children in fact would) or they simply ignored his true beliefs and treated him as a kind of honorary Christian.[66]

If Immanuel Kant had died at the end of the 1770s, he would have been remembered as one of several enlightened writers in late eighteenth-century Prussia, less influential than Lessing or Mendelssohn, less popular than Nicolai, less poetic than Thomas Abbt. Between 1781 and 1790, however, Kant published a series of works that guaranteed him a place among the greatest philosophers who have ever lived: *The Critique of Pure Reason* (1781, with a revised edition six years later), *Prolegomena to any Future Metaphysics* (1783, a summary and partial revision of the first critique), *Foundations of the Metaphysics of Morals* (1785), *Critique of Practical*

---

[65] Alexander Altmann, *Moses Mendelssohn. A Biographical Study* (University of Alabama, 1973).

[66] Sorkin, *Transformation*, p. 8. On Dohm: see Ilsegret Dambacher, *Christian Wilhelm von Dohm. Ein Beitrag zur Geschichte des preussischen aufgeklärten Beamtentums und seiner Reformbestrebungen am Ausgang des 18. Jahrhunderts* (Frankfurt, 1974). Katz, *Ghetto*, analyses these developments in ch. 4. See also H. I. Bach's stimulating essay, *The German Jew: A Synthesis of Judaism and Western Civilization, 1730–1930* (Oxford, 1984).

Reason (1788), and *Critique of Judgement* (1790). 'No decade in the life of any philosopher', Lewis White Beck has written, 'even approaches this one in quantity, variety and importance of what Kant did in these nine years.'[67]

Kant was born in 1724, the son of a pious harness-maker. His parents' pastor, a former student of pietism and rational philosophy at Halle, recognized the boy's talents and enabled him to attend the Fridericianum, an excellent Königsberg preparatory school that was at once intellectually rigorous and religiously intense. From there, Kant went to the university and then put in some time as a private tutor before securing an academic appointment, first as Privat Dozent and then, in 1770, as a professor. During his early years Kant produced a series of books and articles on the sort of issues that interested his enlightened contemporaries: Newtonianism, logic, natural theology, and aesthetics. His professorial salary of 236 talers enabled him to live as a bachelor in a pleasant if by no means opulent style; always well dressed and at home among the city's best families, he cut a rather elegant figure in Königsberg society. He liked stimulating conversation and good food, but kept to a rigorous schedule of reading and writing. As he grew older, his routine grew rigid, and the punctuality of his daily walk became a legend. 'Change makes me uneasy,' he wrote to a friend in 1778, 'all I want is a tranquil life suited to my needs, with alternating spells of work, speculation, and sociability.' But with this compulsion for external harmonies went a willingness to tackle the most intellectually challenging and spiritually perilous questions of the age. '*Sapere aude!*'—dare to know—was the motto Kant took for his famous essay on the question, 'What is Enlightenment?'[68]

Reading David Hume, as Kant wrote in his *Prolegomena*, 'interrupted my dogmatic slumbers and gave a completely different direction to my enquiries'. Hume's corrosive scepticism undermined the metaphysical assumptions on which the Enlightenment seemed to rest; after reading him, Kant could no longer admire the logical order and placid confidence so apparent in a rationalist philosopher like Wolff. But Kant also recognized—and this was the key to his greatest achievements—that Hume's attack on metaphysics could easily be turned back against itself, destroying in its

---

[67] Beck, *Philosophy*, p. 434.

[68] Kant, *Briefwechsel*, pp. 170–1. Karl Vorländer's biography (2 vols. 1924) remains the basic source for the philosopher's career. Cassirer, *Philosophy*, and *Kant's Life and Thought* (New Haven and London, 1981), set his work within the context of Enlightenment thought.

wake the possibility of all knowledge and moral action. Because he could not imagine a world without knowledge and morality, Kant sought to find 'for human reason safe conduct between these rocks' of rationalist metaphysics and scepticism, the one promising too much, the other offering too little, the first encouraging excessive confidence, the second evoking dark despair. The image of a passage between the rocks is just one of many similar metaphors Kant used to describe his task, which he called an effort to find a 'secure path', to point out 'the highway of science', or 'to clear and level what has hitherto been wasteground'. As this geographical imagery suggests, Kant helped to turn philosophy into what Richard Rorty calls a 'foundational discipline', which takes as its major purpose showing people the basis and boundaries of knowledge.[69]

Each of Kant's three critiques—of pure reason, practical reason, and judgement—begins by asking how knowledge of the world, ethical choices, and aesthetic appreciation are possible. How can we discover what is true, right, and beautiful? Reading Hume had persuaded Kant that experience alone cannot lead us to a world beyond ourselves, even the 'regularity in the appearances which we entitle nature, we ourselves introduce'. No actions are intrinsically good, no objects inherently beautiful. It follows from this that philosophy must begin, not with the external order of things, but with individual consciousness—with an introspective turn that clearly links Kant to his own pietist origins and to the later development of romanticism and idealism. Yet for Kant introspection was always a means, never an end. He sought to escape from both skepticism and subjectivity by establishing universal principles of epistemology, ethics, and aesthetics. These principles provide a firm foundation of knowledge, moral action, and judgements. Without indulging in flights of metaphysical fancy or seeking recourse in a divine order beyond human experience, Kant endeavoured to transcend the Enlightenment but not to deny it, to remain true to both faith and reason but be uncritical of neither.[70]

'Two things', Kant wrote in his *Critique of Practical Reason*, 'fill

[69] Kant, *Prolegomena*, p. 9; *Critique of Pure Reason*, pp. 128 and 147; Rorty, *Philosophy*, p. 132.

[70] On Kant's thought, see P. F. Strawson, *The Bounds of Sense: An Essay on Kant's Critique of Pure Reason* (London, 1966); Paul Guyer, *Kant and the Claims of Taste* (Cambridge and London, 1979). There is a stimulating discussion of Kant's language in Marshall Brown, 'The Pre-Romantic Discovery of Consciousness', *SR*, 17 (1978), 387–412.

the mind with ever new and increasing admiration and awe . . . the starry heavens above me, and the moral law within me.' Even more than he desired to find a belief in the order of the physical universe, Kant wanted to establish a philosophical basis for human morality. For him, the great moral teacher of the age was Rousseau—whom he called 'another Newton' and whose picture adorned his study wall. Rousseau's work gave Kant the hope that by exploring our hidden selves, we could discover the transcendent principles on which a scientific ethics might be based. Here also Kant found the strongest foundation for religious belief: 'Morality', he argued in the preface to *Religion within the Limits of Reason Alone*, 'leads ineluctably to religion, through which it extends itself to the idea of a powerful moral lawgiver, outside mankind, for whose will that is the final end [of creation] which at the same time can and ought to be man's final end.' Thus, from man's ethical nature, Kant proceeded to a faith in God and the immortality of the soul. But beyond these austere convictions, he did not venture. For instance, while he admired the ethical teachings of the Bible, he saw no way of establishing its historical validity. Much of what the churches preached, and especially what he called the intellectual 'cobwebs' surrounding official doctrines, were unfortunate impediments to enlightened faith. For Kant himself at least, it was enough to believe in a divine lawgiver who gave moral direction for this world and hope for a world to come.[71]

The initial response to Kant's critical philosophy was disappointing, especially in the light of his own conviction that he had revolutionized philosophical enquiry. But gradually the significance of the Kantian enterprise became clear—although, from the start, readers took very different things from his work. Friedrich Schiller, for instance, spent several years studying Kant in the 1780s so that he might acquire intellectual order and discipline. Jung Stilling, on the other hand, was exhilarated by a sense of freedom in Kant, who liberated him from the narrow determinism of Leibniz and Wolff. Goethe, who had initially found little of interest in critical philosophy, was eventually drawn to what he took to be the strong parallels between Kant's writings and his own. By the end of the 1780s, therefore, Kant was a major cultural force. Academic philosophers considered his ideas in university classrooms throughout central Europe, while in reading societies, drawing rooms, and even around the dinner tables in aristocratic country houses, people

[71] Beck, *Philosophy*, p. 501; Vleeschauwer, *Development*, pp. 39–40; Kant, *Religion*, pp. 5–6.

argued about the meaning and validity of Kantianism. Visitors from Königsberg were pressed for news of his habits and opinions, travellers to that city tried to catch a glimpse of the philosopher or, if they were bold enough, to spend a few hours in his company. By 1802 almost three thousand separate pieces had been published about Kant's life and thought.[72]

Kant, supported by a growing number of would-be disciples, spent the last decade of his life defending his ideas from two groups of critics. Followers of Wolff and other rationalists charged him with betraying the cause of reason by setting such sharp limits on what reason could accomplish. From Halle, Johann August Eberhard, an admirer of both Leibniz and Wolff, tried to demonstrate that there was nothing new in Kant's thought: the best things had already been said by the rationalists, the rest was sophistry. In 1789 Eberhard founded the *Philosophisches Magazin*, which was devoted to printing refutations of Kant's ideas. But Kant was also attacked from the opposite direction, by those who believed that his ideas were too rational, his rhetoric too cold, his faith too narrow and arid. If Eberhard saw Kant as a traitor to the *Aufklärung*, these critics viewed him as its personification. If Eberhard wanted a broader field for reason than Kant allowed, these critics doubted that reason could lead to truth. They looked instead for a deeper, more authentic kind of knowledge, uncorrupted by the arrogant pretensions and false promises of Enlightenment thought.[73]

One of the earliest representatives of these anti-rationalist opponents of Kantianism was J. G. Hamann. Born in 1730 in Königsberg, Hamann travelled the familiar path from youthful pietism to adult enlightenment. For a time he worked as a publicist, producing essays similar to those written by his friends Lessing and Mendelssohn. Then Hamann experienced a religious conversion to the emotive piety of his early years. 'Feeling alone', he now believed, 'gives to abstractions and hypotheses hands, feet, and wings.' His God was not the Wolffians' abstract reason or the Kantians' distant lawgiver. He was the great universal poet who spoke to people 'in poetical words, addressed to the senses, not in abstractions for the learned.' Hamann, no less than Kant, acknowledged the power of Hume's scepticism, which confirmed his intuitive conviction that rationality was an illusion, logic a blind

[72] Jung Stilling, *Lebensgeschichte*, p. 351. On the reception of Kant, see Vleeschauwer, *Development*, pp. 89 ff. and the bibliography in Beck, *Philosophy*.

[73] Vleeschauwer, *Development*, ch. 4, summarizes these controversies.

alley. Kant tried to show Hamann the error of his ways, but found it virtually impossible to communicate with him. Please write to me 'in the language of mankind', Kant pleaded in 1774. 'I am a poor son of the earth and am simply not equipped to use the divine speech of illuminating reason.' In a sense, the two men did speak different languages, the one that of reason and enlightenment, the other that of intuition and poetic mysticism. Eventually Kant recognized that Hamann was a lost cause and let him go his own, eccentric way.[74]

Kant was more deeply distressed by the defection of another former friend and student, J. G. Herder. As we know, Herder came from circumstances similar to Kant's, followed his footsteps to the Fridericianum, and attended his lectures at the university. By the time Herder left to take up his post in Riga, he had a secure place among Kant's growing circle of admirers. Gradually, however, the two men drifted apart. Kant first sensed Herder's deviation when he read the *Fragmente über die neue deutsche Literatur* in the late 1760s. By 1774 Herder was prepared to challenge the Enlightenment directly—in his words, to pour 'hot coals on the century's forehead'. Relations between teacher and former student were finally broken when Kant reviewed critically Herder's *Ideen zur Philosophie der Geschichte der Menschheit* in 1784. By then, Herder had obviously moved closer to Hamann's camp: intuition and poetry, not reason and philosophy, were the royal roads to truth. For Herder, the confines of subjectivity could not be transcended with critical analysis, but only through the language of poetry and metaphor. 'Our whole life', he maintained, 'is a poetics. We do not see, we create images ourselves.'[75] We should not, of course, underestimate Herder's debt to Kant and the *Aufklärung*: as Cassirer has argued, his conquest of the Enlightenment was 'a genuine self-conquest'. Nevertheless, Herder's celebration of art and intuition, like his attacks on Kant and the claims of rationality, helped to prepare the ground for the next generation's more rigorous and consistent revolt against the Enlightenment.[76]

With the arrival of what Isaiah Berlin has called the 'counter Enlightenment', most histories of pre-revolutionary German thought come to an end. Tracing a line of development from

[74] Isaiah Berlin, 'The Counter-Enlightenment', *Current*, p. 8; Kant, *Briefwechsel*, p. 120. See also Vorländer, *Kant*, i. 90 ff.
[75] Haym, *Herder*, i. 538 ff.; Wellek, *History*, i. 188. See also Vorländer, *Kant*, i. 145 ff., 172 ff., 317 ff.
[76] Cassirer, *Philosophy*, p. 233.

pietism and rationalism through Kant and his critics, the history of eighteenth-century 'German philosophy' is usually presented as Protestant in origin and evolution, the German Enlightenment as an exclusively Protestant phenomenon. This version of the *Aufklärung* has deep roots: 'There was a light', wrote F. C. von Moser in 1787, 'that shone on us all during the Reformation. Protestants let themselves be led further by this light, but Catholics were afraid and fled from it.' In the nineteenth century it became the conventional account, part and product of the Protestants' increasing cultural hegemony over German Europe. Like the rest of *kleindeutsch* historiography, this view of the eighteenth century leaves out a great deal. There was a Catholic Enlightenment. German Catholics read and were influenced by Wolff and Kant, Klopstock and Lessing, Goethe and Schiller. Many of the same books that were admired in Berlin found an eager audience in Munich or Vienna. Like its Protestant counterpart, the Catholic Enlightenment was part of a European phenomenon, linked to developments in Italy, France, and other Catholic lands. Moreover, Catholic *Aufklärer* also struggled to find a balance between religion and reason, the traditions of their faith and the demands of the new age.[77]

The Catholic Enlightenment started slowly, without the powerful support Protestants could draw from academic institutions and élites. There were no Catholic equivalents to Halle and Göttingen, no centres of learning equal in prestige to Kant's Königsberg. While these universities were experimenting with new curricula and promoting new ideas, most Catholic schools were stuck with outdated texts and a rigid, enervating course of study, the so-called *ratio studiorum*. Moser blamed the Jesuits for this situation—'They think Paraguay is everywhere.' Others pointed to the unhealthy influence of the ecclesiastical states or the corrupting power of the papacy. But, whatever the reason, even some German Catholics acknowledged that Protestant education was far ahead. Why else would Catholic aristocrats like the Kaunitz family choose a young graduate from Halle as the tutor for their talented young son, Wenzel? Cardinal Garampi, who travelled through the German states on papal business during the 1760s, had to conclude that Catholic universities were in a 'state of scholarly stagnation'.[78]

[77] Moser quoted in Hammerstein, *Aufklärung*, p. 16. On the Catholic Enlightenment, see Chadwick, *Popes*; Epstein, *Genesis*, pp. 153 ff.; and the historiographical discussion in Klingenstein, *Staatsverwaltung*, pp. 88 ff.

[78] Hammerstein, *Aufklärung*, p. 13; Haass, *Haltung*, p. 14.

By the time Garampi delivered this bleak appraisal, educational institutions had begun to improve in some Catholic states. Speyer's 30,000 inhabitants for example, had one of the best systems of instruction in Europe, with forty schools staffed by well-qualified teachers. In Mainz, Friedrich Karl von Erthal, elector from 1774 to 1802, introduced a series of enlightened reforms and devoted considerable resources to improving the university. Beginning with the reign of Maria Theresa and accelerated by Joseph II, educational progress was also under way in the Habsburg realm. In 1773 the empress reluctantly approved legislation expelling the Jesuits, thus introducing the possibility of curricular reform in the universities formerly dominated by that order. During the 1770s and 1780s journals, reading societies, and other organizations expanded throughout Catholic regions, where they encouraged the spread of new literary works and enlightened ideas. Periodicals such as the *Journal von und für Deutschland* from Fulda or *Der Freymüthige* from Freiburg published articles advocating religious tolerance and theological renewal.[79]

During the first half of the century scattered writers like the Czech Jansenist, Count Sporck, and the enlightened Italian, Ludovico Antonio Muratori, had urged German Catholics to abandon what they viewed as the ecclesiastical establishment's sterile orthodoxies. By the end of the 1740s these calls for innovation were reinforced by the work of Christian Wolff, whose brand of enlightened Christianity was not difficult to absorb into the eclectic Thomism popular among many Catholic philosophers. In Benedictine monasteries from Innsbruck to Melk, at episcopal courts like Salzburg, and in the most progressive universities of the west, young men debated Wolff's significance for their faith.[80] Even the Jesuits were not immune to rationalism. Benedikt Sattler, who taught at several Catholic universities, used Wolff to combat the ossified propositions of what one scholar has called 'baroque

[79] G. Benecke, 'The German *Reichskirche*', in W. J. Callaghan and D. Higgs (eds.), *Church and State in Catholic Europe in the Eighteenth Century* (Cambridge, 1979), 84; Dreyfus, *Sociétés*. On university reform see, Haass, *Haltung*; Hammer-stein, *Aufklärung*. Max Braubach, 'Die kirchliche Aufklärung im katholischen Deutschland im Spiegel des 'Journal von und für Deutschland' (1784–1792)', *HJb*, 54 (1934), 1–63, 178–220, discusses contemporary Catholic periodicals. See also T. C. W. Blanning, 'The Enlightenment in Catholic Germany', in R. Porter and M. Teich (eds.), *The Enlightenment in National Context* (Cambridge, 1981), 118–26; James Melton, 'From Image to Word: Cultural Reform and the Rise of Literate Culture in Eighteenth-Century Austria', *JMH*, 58 (1986), 95–124.
[80] Chadwick, *Popes*; and Winter, *Josephinismus*, pp. 20 ff.

scholasticism'. Sattler's *Philosophia methodo scientiis propria explanata* (1769–1772) was an eloquent defence of free thought and the possibilities of its reconciliation with the true faith. By the 1770s baroque scholasticism was in retreat, challenged almost every-where by enlightened ideas drawn from both Catholic and Protestant sources. There was reason to hope, as Marcus Anton Wittola wrote in the Vienna *Kirchenzeitung* on 2 January 1789, that these ideas would lead the church back to 'long forgotten truths' and her 'original beauty and dignity'.[81]

Perhaps the most impressive manifestation of a Catholic *Auf-klärung* was the reception of Kantian ideas by Catholic thinkers. Two Benedictines, Maternus Reuss and Conrad Stang, lectured on Kant to appreciative audiences in Würzburg. Reuss's *Soll man auf katholischen Universitäten Kants Philosophie erklären?*, published in 1789, was a stirring defence of the critical philosophy from a Catholic perspective. 'Even the ladies are taken with you,' wrote Father Reuss to the master in Königsberg: 'I myself am receiving many a friendly glance from the ladies now.' In some places, however, Kant's advocates found much greater resistance. When a priest in Heidelberg used Kant to show that God's existence could not be proved rationally, he was ordered to be silent and then dismissed. In Bavaria and Austria, Kant's books were hard to find and his positions vigorously attacked by academic philosophers. Clearly Kantianism was much more difficult to reconcile with traditional Catholic thought than Wolffian rationalism had been.[82]

In the Catholic *Aufklärung*, philosophical questions about faith and reason often became entangled with institutional questions about religious authority. In contrast to the Protestant lands, where state control over ecclesiastical affairs was an accepted fact of life, the Catholic Church's constitutional position was unsettled and complex. Although the Pope claimed ultimate authority in matters of faith and morals, his supremacy was challenged, not only by the states, who wanted to extend their power over local religious institutions, but also by German bishops, who wanted a greater say in church affairs. Because enlightened Catholics viewed the Pope and his Jesuit agents as the chief opponents of religious reform, they were inclined to look to the states or the bishops as potential allies.

The close connections between spiritual enlightenment and

[81] Klingenstein, *Staatsverwaltung*, pp. 97 ff. See also Fries and Schwaiger (eds.), *Theologen*, i. for a chapter on Sattler.
[82] Kant, *Correspondence*, pp. 222–3. See also Vorländer, *Kant*, i. 406 ff., ii. 239 ff.

ecclesiastical governance can be seen in Febronism, perhaps the most influential movement for change within eighteenth-century German Catholicism. 'Febronius' was the pseudonym used by Johann Nikolaus von Hontheim, whose *De statu ecclesiae* created a sensation throughout Catholic Europe soon after its appearance in 1763. Like many young German noblemen destined for high church office, Hontheim had received an international education: he studied at Louvain, where he came into contact with Jansenism, as well as at Leyden, Vienna, and Rome. He rose steadily in the service of the Archbishop of Trier, taught at the university there, was made a Privy Councillor, then suffragan bishop and vicar general. *De statu ecclesiae*—or to translate the book's complete title, 'Febronius's book on the condition of the church and the legitimate authority of the Roman Pope, for the purpose of uniting in religion contrary-minded Christians'—was the result of more than two decades of scholarly research and practical experience in church affairs. The papal monarchy, Hontheim contended, was the chief source of corruption in the church and the major barrier to a reconciliation with Protestantism. In its place, he recommended establishing a council of bishops representing the church as a whole. Hontheim did not raise doctrinal questions, but he did condemn Jesuitical scholasticism and drew on both rational and historical criticism in an effort to restore Catholicism to its true mission. Moreover, he advocated co-operation with civil authorities in the campaign for religious reform. Not surprisingly, the papacy put *De statu ecclesiae* on the index of forbidden books as soon as a copy reached the Vatican. State censors were more lenient; translations quickly appeared and were readily available. Hontheim, unable to conceal his identity in the face of his work's great fame, was put under enormous pressure to recant. He finally yielded in 1778—in terms that left his true belief open to question—but the debate over his ideas continued to divide the German church until it was resolved by the declaration of papal infallibility almost a century later.[83]

Despite the breadth and vitality of the Catholic Enlightenment, it remained qualitatively and quantitatively inferior to the developments in Protestant lands. There were no Catholic Kants or Herders; moreover, the ranks of Catholic *Aufklärer* were thinner. 'I can always count on ten Protestant correspondents for every one

[83] There is a good brief treatment of Febronius in Chadwick, *Popes*. See also Ludwig von Pastor, *The History of the Popes* (London, 1950), xxxvi. 250 ff.

Catholic,' complained the editor of a journal directed at both denominations.[84] One reason for this inferiority was certainly the difference between the leading Catholic and Protestant states. While we should be sceptical about identifying Prussia with the Enlightenment, Frederick the Great did introduce a policy of tolerance—perhaps indifference would be a better term—at precisely the time when German literature and philosophy were entering a decisive phase of their development. The contrast with Austria is impossible to overlook. Here a cumbersome, often ineffective, but nevertheless annoying system of censorship persisted. Joseph II reduced the list of forbidden titles from 4,500 to 900, but many classics, among them several works by Goethe and Lessing, remained officially banned from the Habsburg lands. Throughout central Europe, Protestant authorities were usually more receptive to literary culture than Catholics—even when they were no more enlightened or progressive on other issues.[85]

Another reason for Protestants' greater receptivity to the Enlightenment was their clergy's social position. As we have seen, pastors were more often part of the educated élite than were priests, who were more at home with the nobility on one extreme and the common folk on the other. By background, training, and experience, most Catholic clergymen belonged to the traditional oral cultures of court or village, not the literary culture of civil servants, professors, and publicists. Catholic intellectuals had less impact on the public: the Benedictines debated rationalism in their cloisters at Innsbruck and Melk rather than the lecture halls of Halle and Göttingen; Sattler and Hontheim, both of whose major works first appeared in Latin, did not have direct access to the audience addressed by Lessing, Mendelssohn, or Kant. Even when the culture of print became increasingly important in German life, Catholicism remained a religion of ritual, firmly committed to the universal language and sacred gestures of the Latin mass. To Protestants, Luther's Bible was a foundational text, Gutenberg a major hero. The Catholic hierarchy viewed the written word with some suspicion: indeed a papal bull of 1713 explicitly condemned the proposition that 'the reading of the Bible is for everyone'. There was no Catholic equivalent to pietism, with its emphasis on individual experience and autobiographical reflection; the great,

---

[84] P. A. von Bibra, editor of the *Journal von und für Deutschland*, quoted in Braubach, 'Aufklärung', p. 10.
[85] Klingenstein, *Staatsverwaltung*.

autonomous spiritual movements within Catholicism produced pilgrimages and group devotions, architecturally captured in the final flowering of south German rococo.[86]

If it had continued for a few more decades, the Catholic Enlightenment might have closed the distance between the two denominations. By the 1780s powerful political, social, and intellectual forces within German Catholicism were undermining old restrictions. The decline of censorship and increase of toleration in the Habsburg empire, the growth of a reading public throughout Catholic areas, significant improvements in education, and a flurry of creative activity in philosophy and theology all suggested that Catholics were becoming more open to new ideas. But these innovative developments did not survive the impact of the French revolution on central Europe. The Catholic *Aufklärung*, like so many other features of eighteenth-century German life, was a casualty of war and revolution.

iv. THE ORIGINS OF A POLITICAL PUBLIC

In December 1784 two ministers of the Prussian crown, displeased by some critical articles in the *Journal von und für Deutschland*, wrote that 'a private individual does not possess the right to issue public judgements (let alone unfavourable judgements) upon the actions, procedures, laws, proclamations or decrees of sovereigns, their ministers, administrative boards or courts of justice'. When they argued that private individuals do not know enough about public policies and public figures to have worthwhile opinions, the ministers were using the concept of 'public' to designate political affairs that were too complex, arcane, and sensitive for private consumption. Such 'public' matters had to be secret. By the 1780s, however, this usage had already begun to give way to a very different one: as we have seen, within the literary culture the realm of the 'public' was held to be necessarily open and universally accessible. Most enlightened Germans believed that ideas— including ideas about political affairs—belonged in this public

---

[86] On counter-reformation Catholicism, see Evans, *Making*. Klingenstein, *Staatsverwaltung*, pp. 33 ff., has some interesting remarks on Catholics' distrust of the printed work. R. Wittmann, *Die frühen Buchhändlerzeitschriften als Spiegel des literarischen Lebens* (Frankfurt, 1973), gives some tentative data on the regional distribution of booksellers.

realm, where they could be freely evaluated by 'public opinion'.[87] Our age, Kant wrote in the preface to his *Critique of Pure Reason*, is 'the age of criticism, and to criticism everything must submit'. Religion and law may seek to exempt themselves, but then they 'cannot claim the sincere respect which reason accords only to that which has been able to sustain the test of free and open examination'. A few years earlier, Friedrich Gabriel Resewitz had defined the purpose of civil education as convincing citizens that they should evaluate and become involved in public matters, which belong to them. A new meaning of *public*, and with it a new kind of politics, was slowly taking shape.[88]

In the second half of the century, and especially after 1770, participants in German literary culture were deeply concerned with 'public matters'.[89] Authors such as Friedrich Carl von Moser, Thomas Abbt, and Friedrich Nicolai produced widely-read works on politics. Periodicals such as Wieland's *Teutscher Merkur* (founded in 1773), Schubart's *Deutsche Chronik* (founded in 1774), Schlözer's *Briefwechsel meist historischen und politischen Inhalts* (founded in 1776) and his *Staatsanzeigen* (founded in 1783) provided material on policy-making and public personalities in the German states and abroad. Moreover, many books and periodicals devoted to subjects like agriculture and theology treated political issues, if only because governments were so directly and deeply involved in the operation of both the economy and the churches. Like the literature and philosophy described in the preceding two sections, these political writings fed an expanding public discourse, held informally in coffee houses and bookstores and institutionalized in lending libraries and reading societies. The line between literary and political concerns was often difficult to draw: both literature and politics sought, as the founders of the 'Deutsches Museum' society declared in 1777, 'to make Germans better acquainted with themselves and direct their attention to their own national affairs'. In its earliest manifestations, therefore, a participant political

---

[87] Epstein, *Genesis*, p. 77. On the changing meaning of *public*, see Habermas's seminal study, *Strukturwandel*; Lucian Hölscher, *Öffentlichkeit und Geheimnis: Eine begriffsgeschichtliche Untersuchung zur Entstehung der Öffentlichkeit in der frühen Neuzeit* (Stuttgart, 1979).

[88] Kant, *Critique of Pure Reason*, p. 9; Haltern, 'Bildung', p. 63.

[89] Dreitzel, 'Ideen', provides a good introduction to the recent literature on German political thought in the eighteenth century. See also Epstein, *Genesis*; Valjavec, *Entstehung*; Vierhaus, 'Bewusstsein'; Schlumbohm, *Freiheit*; and the essays in Franklin Kopitzch (ed.), *Aufklärung, Absolutismus und Bürgertum in Deutschland* (Munich, 1976).

culture was formed within the context of literary culture; public opinion was inseparable from the literary public.[90]

In addition to explicitly literary institutions, a number of other organizations also served as the basis for political discourse. In the 1780s, for instance, Prussian officials used the 'Mittwochgesellschaft,' a small, informal gathering of notables, to sample and influence public opinion on the matter of legal reform. In Hamburg, the Gesellschaft zur Beförderung der Manufakturen, Künste und nützlichen Gewerbe (the so-called Patriotische Gesellschaft) was founded in 1765 by a group of academics, lawyers, and administrators to gather information on public issues and to sponsor good works. Among aggressive textile entrepreneurs in the Rhineland we can find the first, faint signs of interest organizations, formed to affect government economic policy.[91] Perhaps most significant of all, there were a large number of secret societies, many of which had definite political orientations. Soon after it was imported from England to Hamburg in the late 1730s, Freemasonry spread across central Europe, some Lodges were socially élitist and politically conservative, but others identified with the *Aufklärung*. 'To think freely . . . is the spirit of our royal arts,' declared some Berlin Freemasons in 1786. We 'abhor the intrigues which seek to rob men of their noble rights and bar from our sanctuary the enemies of healthy reason and true enlightenment'. As Mozart so gloriously demonstrated in *The Magic Flute*, masonic ritual and ideals could be used to celebrate human liberation. The Illuminati, members of a secret society formed by Adam Weishaupt at Ingolstadt in 1776 to encourage enlightened values, were extremely popular in Bavaria and then spread northward under the leadership of Adolf von Knigge.[92]

By the last decade of the century, every German city and many

---

[90] Schneider, *Pressefreiheit, p.* 82. For more on the literary public and politics, see Dann, *Lesegesellschaften.*

[91] Günther Birtsch, 'Zum konstitutionellen Charakter des preussischen Allgemeinen Landrechts von 1794', in Kluxen and Mommsen (eds.), *Ideologien*, pp. 97–116, describes the *Mittwochgesellschaft*; Elly Mohrmann, 'Studie zu den ersten organisatorischen Bestrebungen der Bourgeoisie in einigen Städten des Rheinlandes', *Beiträge zur deutschen Wirtschaft- und Sozialgeschichte* (Berlin, 1962), 189–249, discusses early interest groups. For more on organizational life, see Dann, 'Anfänge'; Imhof, *Jahrhundert.*

[92] The quotation is from Vierhaus, 'Aufklärung', p. 26. In addition to this splendid article, see Ludz (ed.), *Gesellschaften*; Manfred Agethen, *Geheimbund und Utopie. Illuminaten, Freimauer und deutsche Spätaufklärung* (Munich, 1984). The political meaning of Mozart's opera is examined in Jean Starobinski, *1789: The Emblems of Reason* (Charlottesville, 1982).

towns had a variety of public institutions, reading societies, discussion groups, and masonic lodges. These institutions were not all critical of the status quo; some had the express purpose of countering criticism and combating the *Aufklärung*. But their very existence represented a radical break from the past. There were no historical precedents for the associations that grew up in the eighteenth century: unlike parishes or villages, they were voluntary; unlike guilds or *Gesellenvereine*, they were open to a variety of social groups; and unlike monasteries or convents, they were not cut off from the world. As public associations of private individuals, these organizations straddled state and society. As social associations of equals, they offered a mode of sociability that was not rooted in the corporate order. As cultural associations of readers and writers, they supported a new kind of political discourse.[93]

In this discourse, as in the related realms of literature and philosophy, educated élites played a predominant role. To be sure, a variety of social groups were drawn to the various organizations within the public sphere: landowners, businessmen, a few upwardly mobile craftsmen and small merchants. But the most important element, both quantitatively and qualitatively, was the clerisy, those academicians, civil servants, and clergymen who provided the basis for the literary culture at large. These people had the training, experience, and opportunity to formulate ideas about contemporary politics and society. Their education made them aware of intellectual developments at home and abroad; their social position separated them from the traditional worlds of village, guild, or court; and their role within the state linked them to the most powerful instrument for change in both political practice and political theory.[94]

As we have seen, bureaucratic practice encouraged people to believe that politics could be codified, standardized, and subsumed under certain general propositions. The theoretical implications of this were clear: politics was based on a set of principles that could be studied, formalized, and taught to future practitioners. By the eighteenth century, cameralism, the science of bureaucratic practice, had become an academic subject. Professorial chairs for cameralists were established at Halle and Frankfurt/Oder in 1727. At Göttingen, Königsberg, and eventually throughout German

[93] There is a stimulating analysis of this process in Koselleck, *Kritik*.
[94] On the social basis of eighteenth-century politics, see the works cited above, nn. 91, 92 and the discussion in Ch. 2, sect. iv, and in sect. i of this chapter.

Europe, scholars in traditional subjects like law and in newer ones like *Polizeiwissenschaft* and political Economy devoted their attention to problems of statecraft. 'The study of politics', A. L. Schlözer wrote in 1793, 'emerged in the seventeenth century as an autonomous, wide-ranging discipline comparable in importance to the study of law in the twelfth century and of medicine in the sixteenth.'[95]

Cameralism, as Keith Tribe has recently argued, was the science of political management, an effort to define the principles according to which officials could regulate social life and encourage its improvement. From the start, the theoretical formulations of cameralism were inseparable from the practical problems of state-building. In late seventeenth-century Vienna, for example, Philip Wilhelm von Hörnigk, the author of *Österreich über alles, wenn es nur will*, and his brother-in-law, Johann Joachim Becher, wrote treatises on politics at the same time that they were making their careers in the Habsburgs' service.[96] J. H. G. von Justi, whose *Grundriss einer guten Regierung* of 1759 was another important milestone in the evolution of bureaucratic theory, was also a state servant. Justi believed that the purpose of the state was to promote the 'common good', which he defined in purely secular terms as prosperity and happiness. But for him, the common good was inseparable from the state's own well-being. 'Every law must have as its goal increasing the state's strength, power, and prosperity to the highest possible extent.' Similarly, freedom was inseparable from obedience. 'As long as the citizens have to obey only laws which promote the common welfare, they are truly free.' Like Hörnigk and Becher, Justi was an outsider, a young man on the make, who identified his own quest for status and power with the state's expanding role in social and political life. Ambitious, energetic, and ruthless, Justi resembles a hero out of the pages of Balzac. He died in prison, unjustly accused of financial malfeasance by that difficult master and prototypical state-builder, Frederick the Great.[97]

[95] Dreitzel, 'Ideen', p. 21.

[96] Tribe, 'Cameralism'. See also Jutta Brückner, *Staatswissenschaften, Kameralismus und Naturrecht. Ein Beitrag zur Geschichte der politischen Wissenschaften im Deutschland des späten 17. und frühen 18. Jahrhunderts* (Munich, 1977). Small, *Cameralists*, and Sommer, *Kameralisten*, are still worth reading. For the relationship between cameralism and the theory and practice of 'mercantilism', see the essays in D. C. Coleman (ed.), *Revisions in Mercantilism* (London, 1969).

[97] On Justi, see Krieger, *Essay*, pp. 40 ff. The quotations are from Valjavec, *Entstehung*, p. 54; J. Garber, in Steinbach (ed.), *Probleme*, p. 30.

The Austrian writer Josef von Sonnenfels gave eighteenth-century cameralism its fullest expression. Sonnenfels's grandfather was chief rabbi in Brandenburg; his father, eager for an academic career, converted to Catholicism and in 1745 was appointed Professor of Oriental Languages at the University of Vienna. He was ennobled the following year. After an unsettled youth, Josef studied law, was an active figure on the Austrian literary scene, and became Professor of *Polizeiwissenschaft* at Vienna in 1763. For the next fifteen years he was one of the most influential men in the Habsburg realm; he taught scores of civil servants, advised the empress and her closest associates, and shaped public opinion with scholarly treatises and a widely read periodical entitled *Der Mann ohne Vorteil*. Like Justi, Sonnenfels viewed politics in purely secular and pragmatic terms. He was convinced that the power of the state existed to promote its citizens' welfare and happiness. But citizens also existed for the state: 'In the monarchy, the citizens perceive the centre of power, concentrated in one, as the centre of welfare.' To a greater degree than most cameralists, Sonnenfels was also concerned with moral reform; on the pages of *Der Mann ohne Vorteil*, he condemned the excesses of aristocratic immorality and the crudities of popular culture. 'Libertinism', he wrote in 1767, 'must be punished as a political crime.' But in the struggle for moral progress, as in the pursuit of material well-being, Sonnenfels looked to the state to provide effective leadership.[98]

Among the cameralists' major achievements was their recognition that the size and prosperity of the population were as essential for political success as the character of the ruler and the condition of his armies. J. J. Becher, for instance, defined national wealth in productive rather than monetary terms and thus took an important step towards uncovering the state's dependence on, and responsibility for, its population's material well-being. Justi also believed in the economy's significance as both an instrument and a goal of statecraft. Like many contemporary theorists, he favoured loosening the restraints inherent in the traditional social order; he was willing to retain the guild system, but he wanted guild authority limited and economic opportunity increased. 'The way should be open for every poor but talented man to acquire a Master's status.' Moreover, the government should do everything possible to encourage manufacturing, expand arable land, and

[98] Robert Kann, *A Study in Austrian Intellectual History* (New York, 1960), 170, 173. See also K. Osterloh, *Joseph von Sonnenfels und die österreichische Reformbewegung im Zeitalter des aufgeklärten Absolutismus* (Lübeck and Hamburg, 1970).

promote demographic growth. Sonnenfels agreed: he condemned serfdom as socially degrading and economically regressive, distrusted guilds, and opposed restrictions on entrepreneurial energy. Economic prosperity and civil liberty went together.[99]

The impact of the French physiocrats and British classical economists in the German states can best be understood as the extension rather than the antithesis of these cameralist assumptions. The economists' analysis of the systematic relationships of production, consumption, and commerce was applauded by many German political theorists and practitioners. For example, soon after Adam Smith's *Wealth of Nations* was published in 1776, it was translated into German by J. F. Schiller, a cousin of the poet. In 1777, J. G. Feder wrote an extensive review of Smith's work for the *Göttinger Gelhrter Anzeiger*. At Göttingen, where Feder was a professor, and at Königsberg under the leadership of Christian Jakob Kraus, British economics was taught to a sympathetic and influential audience of future civil servants. With its emphasis on the advantages of economic freedom, western thought served as a powerful theoretical weapon against the old order: enlightened thinkers and reform-minded bureaucrats could use these ideas to discredit the guilds, the corporate authority of the home towns, and the entrenched privileges of the landed nobility. The staunchest practical advocates of economic liberty, therefore, were not German businessmen, eager to be free from state control, but rather civil servants, intent on using state power to effect social and economic emancipation. As a result, French and British economics took on a subtly different form within the German context, where theorists did not defend the complete autonomy of the market because they continued to accept the importance of the state as a force in economic affairs.[100]

Just as German thinkers often viewed economic emancipation as a contribution to, and sometimes as the result of, state power, so they tended to fuse discussions of individual freedom with considerations of political authority. Christian Thomasius, for example, was greatly influenced by Locke's notion of inviolable human rights existing beyond government control. But this principle—like the ideas of classical economics—was extremely difficult to translate into German theory or practice. Increasingly,

[99] Klein, 'Justi', p. 161.
[100] Wilhelm Treue, 'Adam Smith in Deutschland:. Zum Problem des "politischen Professors" zwischen 1776 und 1810', in Werner Conze (ed.), *Deutschland und Europa (Rothfels Festschrift)* (Düsseldorf, 1951), 101–34; Vopelius, *Ökonomen*.

Thomasius associated rights and power, freedom and subordination. He ended up by arguing that obedience was the citizen's
freest act and thus, as Leonard Krieger shrewdly noted, managed to
use the concept of rights 'to intensify rather than challenge the
power of the absolutely-ruled state'. Christian Wolff, with
Thomasius the other great transplanter of western rationalism to
German soil, was also firmly committed to individual liberty at the
outset of his career as a political theorist. His work remained an
eloquent defence of freedom, the virtues of democracy, and even
the right of resistance to unjust authority. But Wolff's account of
governmental power is both more comprehensive and more
convincing than his discussion of individual rights. In his
Vernünftige Gedanken vom gesellschaftlichen Leben der Menschen,
published in 1721, Wolff articulated the essential elements of
enlightened absolutism: since the state exists to 'promote the
common welfare and security', it can and must bend its citizen to
the pursuit of these goals. The state's authority, and the obligations
of its citizens to obey, are limited only by the rationality of its
purposes.[101]

While Thomasius and Wolff looked for a defence of individual
freedom in rationalism and the doctrine of natural rights, Johann
Jakob Moser turned to pietism and the traditional corporate order.
Moser came from a family of jurists and bureaucrats in Württemberg; during his long life he served a number of German princes,
including Prussia's Frederick William, occupied several academic
posts, and produced an extraordinarily large and difficult body of
work on law and statecraft. After becoming involved in the
controversy between the ruler of Württemberg and his *Stände*,
Moser spent five years in prison—a testimony to his flinty courage
and epic intransigence. As a devout Christian, Moser abhorred the
moral corruption he found at many courts and the spiritual poverty
of the bureaucratic states. 'We live in a century',,' he wrote in 1772,
'when many great men get the urge—not from necessity, but
because it pleases them—to introduce a strict military code and to
rule their lands in a military manner.' Against this military model,
Moser offered the ideal of the German territorial institutions, in
which the prince enjoyed 'his proper privileges' and the subject had
'his proper freedom'. Representative institutions, such as those that
still survived in Württemberg, provided the best defence against
despotism. Natural rights and rational principles, Moser believed,

---

[101] Krieger, *Idea*, pp. 59 ff.

were theoretically without foundation and practically without effect.[102]

Friedrich Carl von Moser, Johann Jakob's son, also served a number of states and produced an important body of work on contemporary politics. Like his father, Friedrich Carl hated 'the blind and unlimited obedience' demanded by the military state, condemned the perversions of power, and celebrated the checks and balances of the traditional order. But the younger Moser was much closer to the ideals of enlightened absolutism than his father. 'A truly free person', he wrote in 1763, 'is someone who is no more subordinate than the order and maintenance of his government requires.' His best hope for progressive change was spiritual transformation: in his *Der Herr und sein Diener*, published in 1761 while his father languished in a prison cell, he called for a ruler with the religious sensibility and enlightened opinions necessary to promote his subjects' material and ethical improvement. Similarly, Moser believed that the problems of political order in central Europe could best be resolved by moral renewal. His widely discussed pamphlet of 1765, *Von dem deutschen Nationalgeist*, lamented the decline of imperial institutions, then being badly battered by the Habsburg–Hohenzollern conflict, but found solutions in pedagogical and personal changes rather than institutional reform. To invigorate the national spirit, Moser argued, required better instruction in German law and goodwill among the princes of the German states.[103]

In his critical review of *Von dem deutschen Nationalgeist*, Justus Möser rejected the idea that princely power or professorial eloquence could renew the nation's spirit. Like the Mosers, Justus Möser was a lawyer, and like them a vigorous participant in the public sphere. But he was no itinerant administrator, servant to many states, adviser to kings and emperors. Justus Möser's fatherland, as we know, was Osnabrück; the city's boundaries measured his political universe. The German spirit, he admonished Moser, lived not in university lecture halls and royal courts, but in organic peasant communities, the cohesive society of the home towns, the free associations of men gathered to defend their lands. Political wisdom was to be found in the rich plenitude of these institutions, not among scholars who wanted to govern states with 'academic theories'. To reduce politics to such theories was, Möser

<hr/>

[102] Valjavec, *Entstehung*, p. 47.

[103] Hammerstein, 'Denken', p. 322; Schlumbohm, *Freiheit*, p. 86. In addition to Walker's *Moser*, see Gagliardo, *Reich*, pp. 43 ff.

insisted, a violation of nature, 'which reveals its wealth through its manifold character' and a move towards despotism, 'which always seeks to straitjacket life by confining it to a few rules.'[104] Möser's defence of regional diversity, traditional liberties, ancient wisdom, and human scale was extraordinarily influential among his contemporaries and successive generations. Goethe and Herder admired his ideas about art and culture, Niebuhr and Savigny learned from his historical writings, Marwitz and Stein drew ideological lessons from his criticism of enlightened absolutism. But Möser's strategies for overcoming what he disliked are not clear; indeed the emotional power of his work comes in part from his recognition that the world he most admired was ebbing, that the future belonged to Vienna and Berlin, not Osnabrück.

Among Möser's admirers was a group of writers whose political views had been shaped by Hanover's English connections and corporate continuities. The best known of these men was A. L. von Schlözer, Professor of History at Göttingen and editor of two important political journals. Like Möser, Schlözer was a sworn enemy of despotism, the self-appointed scourge of petty tyrants throughout central Europe. He was, however, rather more restrained in his treatment of matters closer to home; after having been reprimanded for printing an article critical of the Hanoverian postal service, he wrote no more about his own state. It is also extremely difficult to tease Schlözer's personal preferences out of his voluminous, complex, and often contradictory writings. Many of his journal articles seem to favour a rational, enlightened government, which would be free from the nasty buffoonery so common in the smaller states. Some of his lectures and theoretical works, on the other hand, appear to favour a mixed constitution in which prince and *Stände* work together. 'This ideal of a supremely fortunate form of government is of course more than ideal,' he wrote, 'England really has it, and Rome had it in its first epoch.' But Schlözer did not advocate the introduction of such a constitution into the German lands; like so many critics of the established order, he advanced alternatives that were hazy and uncertain.[105]

The critical assault on despotism and corruption, so central to the thought of the Mosers, Möser, and Schlözer, was reinforced and

---

[104] Möser, *Phantasien*, pp. 240–3; Epstein, *Genesis*, p. 313.
[105] McClelland, *Historians*, p. 17. On Schlözer, see Krieger, *Idea*, pp. 76 ff.; James Melton, 'From Enlightenment to Revolution: Hertzberg, Schlözer, and the Problem of Despotism in the Late *Aufklärung*', *CEH*, 12/2 (June 1979), 103–23.

extended by a number of important German writers during the second half of the century. Lessing, for instance, based his *Emilia Galotti* on a Spanish play set in ancient Rome, but he moved the story to contemporary Italy so that he might turn his audience's attention to the abuses of courtly society in their own states. The *Sturm und Drang* writers of the 1770s were direct and outspoken in their attacks on tyranny, while in Vienna dramatists like Paul Weidmann criticized judicial torture and the misuses of privilege. Even Goethe, in many ways the least political of the great German writers, set his *Egmont* in the politically charged atmosphere of the Dutch conflict with Spain and had his hero struggle for personal fulfilment within the context of his nation's struggle for liberty. Although these plays all express the frustrations and aspirations of their age, their political meaning is characteristically uncertain. *Emilia Galotti* focused on the malevolence of evil advisers, but leaves the prince, and with him the political system as a whole, relatively unscathed. In *Egmont*, Goethe's political intentions swiftly give way to his concern for his hero's personal fate. The action may have political consequences, but these lie outside the dramatic frame; what we see are the roots and expression of Egmont's own destiny, against which he is powerless to struggle.[106]

A deep uncertainty also pervades the work of Friedrich Schiller, who is frequently regarded as the most profoundly political of the major eighteenth-century poets. We have already observed how the theme of rebellion in his early plays mirrored his own unhappy experiences as a cadet in the service of a petty tyrant. Like their creator, Schiller's protagonists revolt against the forces of injustice and the confines of social restraint. Many of his contemporaries must have identified with Schiller's own cosmic restlessness as it found expression in his characters' tragic struggles against the evils of intrigue. Nevertheless, the political significance of these struggles remains obscure: *The Robbers* is set in some primeval wilderness without a polity; in *Fiesko*, the meaning of the hero's conspiracy is unclear—in fact his doom is sealed when he chooses public action over personal commitment; and, while the political system provides the setting for *Love and Intrigue*, the action of the play leaves the system itself unchanged. The duke, an unseen presence at the heart of the intrigue, remains apparently untouched

---

[106] H. B. Garland, *Lessing, the Founder of German Literature* (2nd edn., London, 1962), 29 and 130 ff.; Paul Bernard, *Jesuits and Jacobins: Enlightenment and Enlightened Despotism in Austria* (Urbana, Ill., 1971), 54 ff.; Friedenthal, *Goethe*, pp. 342 ff.

by the destruction he has caused. In contrast to the conclusions of classical or Shakespearian tragedies, the death of Schiller's hero does not purge the polity of its discontents and thus lay the basis for a new order. The only positive impact of the action is on the character of the villain, Ferdinand's father, who finds moral redemption—but at the expense of his political power.

In Schiller's work, as in that of his contemporaries, the central conflicts are spiritual and moral rather than social and institutional. As its title suggests, *Kabale und Liebe* presents the clash of two opposing sensibilities; the one manipulative, disingenuous, and evil, the other authentic, sincere, benevolent, 'My thoughts of greatness and happiness are not akin to yours,' Ferdinand tells his father in the second scene of act one. 'The ideal of my happiness I seek more modestly within myself. My wishes all lie buried in my heart.'[107] Schiller did not, however, intend his plays to advocate a flight from the public world. As he made clear in his lecture of 1784 on 'The Stage as a Moral Institution', art had a profoundly important public purpose. By portraying the human condition in all its splendour and misery, theatre teaches people to love virtue and hate vice, to appreciate courage and overcome weakness, to embrace wisdom and eschew folly. The theatre is 'a school of practical wisdom, a guide through civil life, an infallible key to the innermost secrets of the human soul'. Viewed from our perspective, this statement might seem like a substitute for 'real politics', but to Schiller political change and moral reform were inseparable because he believed that states were essentially moral associations, rooted in religion, law, and culture.[108]

Schiller's image of the poet as moral preceptor was just one of the ways eighteenth-century intellectuals portrayed the public purpose and social function of culture. Herder, for example, saw his scholarly activities as an extension of his calling as a preacher, a profession he had chosen because, he wrote to Kant in 1768, 'under our existing civil constitution, this is the best way to spread culture and human understanding among those honourable people whom we call the Volk'. Herder's later advocacy of German language and literature was a contribution to the *Volk*'s political awareness and

---

[107] The limits of Schiller's political vision can be seen by setting *Kabale und Liebe* next to Beaumarchais's *Figaro*, a play with which it has sometimes been compared. Whereas Beaumarchais's hero personifies an alternative social order, based on wit and accomplishment, Schiller's Ferdinand stands for an alternative moral order, based on the authenticity of feeling.

[108] Schiller, 'Schaubühne' p. 94.

ethical improvement. His 'Idee zum ersten patriotischen Institut für den Allgemeingeist Deutschlands', written in 1788, begins with the problem of German fragmentation and how it might best be overcome. After praising the political and cultural achievements of the age—'the rays of light that have penetrated every German province'—he turned to language which, 'seen as either an intellectual or political instrument, serves as the unifying force for all our provinces'. An institute to foster linguistic education and reform, therefore, would bring Germans together, encourage political co-operation, and spread ethical values. The implications of such a project for the nation's future were enormous: 'History shows that every dominant *Volk* has ruled not only with weapons, but with intelligence, art, and a fully developed language . . . ' For Herder, cultural reform was neither surrogate nor pre-condition for political strength: the two went together, each sustaining and sustained by the other.[109]

In his famous response of 1784 to the question, 'What is Enlightenment?', Kant gave the interdependence of culture and politics a somewhat different, but clearly analogous formulation. Enlightenment, Kant argued, was not a quality or condition, but a way of thinking: to be enlightened was to be willing and able to think critically and independently—something only a few can do, even in this age of enlightenment. If this number is to increase, people must be free to express their views and debate the issues before them. The public sphere, the sphere of *Öffentlichkeit*, must be open to everyone and be free from restrictions by the state. Kant obviously hoped that the development of enlightened minds within this public sphere would have important consequences for politics and society, which were, he knew, filled with injustice and irrationality. Nevertheless, Kant did not specify the institutional implications of public enlightenment. Indeed, he maintained that, while the process of enlightenment was going on, institutional authority should remain intact. Only in the privileged sphere of literary discourse was freedom unabridged; a pastor, for example, could challenge dogma as an author but in his Sunday sermons he must toe the line of accepted orthodoxy. This combination of intellectual freedom and political restraint was, Kant believed, Frederician Prussia's distinctive strength: 'Only a ruler who is himself enlightened and has no fear of phantoms, yet who likewise has on hand a well-disciplined and numerous army to guarantee

---

[109] Kant, *Briefwechsel*, p. 60; Herder, *Werke*, xvi. 600 ff.

public security, may say what no republic would dare to say: Argue as much as you like and about what you like, but obey!'[110]

A number of eighteenth-century intellectuals shared Kant's willingness to combine 'public' criticism and practical accommodation. Herder, for instance, condemned 'all inquisition' as harmful to the 'republic of learning', but none the less admitted that 'licentiousness or moral indifference' must be banned and further was convinced that, if freedom of expression 'stops the wheel of state', it must be repressed. Carl Friedrich Bahrdt, frequently cited as a radical, put the matter even more baldly: 'Everything that does not injure the state can be freely spoken and written; but whatever directly and really injures the state . . . must be forbidden.'[111] These views reflect the widespread recognition of the state's power and authority; to many eighteenth-century Germans, the state was the best hope for reform, the ultimate defence against reaction on the one hand and mob violence on the other. Furthermore, a reluctance to challenge the state came from the dependent relationship writers often had with established authority. Unable to live from their work, a majority of intellectuals held office, occupied an academic post, or were supported by a well-placed patron. The sort of critical acquiescence one finds in Kant's life and thought perfectly expressed the difficult position of someone deeply embedded in, but not especially comfortable with, his political order.

Closely connected to these mixed attitudes about political authority were intellectuals' views of society. Although many writers cited the *Volk* as the ultimate source of culture and regarded the universality of the new German literature as one of its great strengths, they viewed with distaste what Herder called 'the rabble of the streets which never sings or creates, but roars and mutilates'. In contemporary literature it is as a rabble that the common people are most often portrayed: in Goethe's *Götz*, for instance, the citizens who appear in the fourth act are cowardly and treacherous, while in Schiller's *Fiesko* the populace seem without direction or restraint, fully deserving the contempt with which the hero treats them. Kant did not think that the critical philosophy had implications for popular religion, 'in view of the unfitness of the common human understanding for such subtle speculation'. Words like *Aufklärung* and *Kultur*, Moses Mendelssohn wrote, belong to

---

[110] Kant, *Writings*, pp. 54–60. For an example of the philosopher's willingness to accept authority, see his letter of 27 Mar. 1789: *Briefwechsel*, p. 370.
[111] Barnard, *Herder*, p. 245; Krieger, *Idea*, p. 74.

literary speech [*Büchersprache*], 'the mob scarcely understands them'.[112] Like their view of political authority, these social attitudes mirror the historical position of eighteenth-century intellectuals, who prided themselves on being the representatives of the *Volk*, but at the same time wanted to be a new élite, set apart from the unenlightened masses.

In his answer to the question, 'What is Enlightenment?', Mendelssohn linked the terms *Aufklärung* and *Kultur* with *Bildung*: all three, he wrote, were 'modifications of social life, the results of people's attempts to improve their social condition'. *Bildung*, with its roots in pietism and its connections with such central eighteenth-century concerns as art, education, and culture, best expressed eighteenth-century intellectuals' various efforts at moral reform. People used the concept in many ways and gave it different philosophical and emotional colorations; to Kant and Mendelssohn, *Bildung* was enlightened thought, to Herder and Schiller it had a more cultural, artistic character. *Bildung* was politically and socially multivalent: it could be associated with protest and obedience, criticism and accommodation; it represented universal values and the particular claims of a new élite. Whatever its specific formulation, *Bildung* represented eighteenth-century intellectuals' hopes and aspirations, for themselves and for their society.[113]

Seen as a whole, German political discourse corresponded to the political experience of German educated élites. Cameralism, for example, provided the servants of the bureaucratic states not only with a theory of administrative management but also with the means to legitimate their claims to political authority. *Bildung* in all its variations buttressed intellectuals' aspirations to assume the moral leadership of their communities. Of course, theory tended to be weakest where experience was thinnest: few German thinkers tried to define the character and limitations of political authority or to establish institutional alternatives to the existing order. As a result, those constitutional questions that dominated nineteenth-century political thought and action were rarely posed before 1789. Germans were usually not much interested in the location of sovereignty, the scope of governmental power, or the degree of popular participation. But this does not mean that they were as 'non-political' as some scholars have claimed. Many eighteenth-

---

[112] Robert Ergang, *Herder and the Foundations of German Nationalism* (New York, 1931), 195; Kant, *Critique of Pure Reason*, pp. 30–1; Vierhaus, 'Bildung', p. 508.

[113] Mendelssohn quoted in Vierhaus, 'Bildung', p. 508. This is an excellent introduction to the concept. See also the essays in Herrmann (ed.), *Bildung*.

century thinkers were very much engaged with politics, but their engagement was necessarily shaped by the political world in which they lived. Given the opportunities for action available in this world, they had to think and act like bureaucrats and publicists rather than like party leaders and parliamentarians.[114]

Both the extent and limitations of late eighteenth-century political thought can be seen in the Germans' response to the events surrounding the rebellion of the American colonies against England. Despite the difficulties created by their distance and complexity, these events on the far shore of the Atlantic captured the imaginations of many members of the German reading public. Political newspapers, Johann Heinrich Voss wrote in 1782, were 'full of America'. Moreover, most German observers seemed quite sympathetic to the colonists' struggle, in which they saw their own attempt to combat despotism and privilege. Even the most sympathetic, however, had trouble grasping the constitutional issues at stake. Few understood the American notion of federalism; no one recognized the theoretical or practical significance of popular sovereignty.[115]

The American revolution, together with the unmistakable evidence of political, social, and cultural transformations closer to home, helped foster some Germans' conviction that the world would never be the same again. In government offices and business enterprises, in Masonic Lodges and reading societies, on noble estates and in university classrooms, people discussed the nature and direction of change. Writers on many different subjects provided guides to what they often called *Verbesserung*, the improvement promised by C. W. Dohm to the Jews and, much more radically, by Theodor von Hippel to women.[116] Improvement would come from both understanding and action, from seeing the world as it is and from taking steps towards how it should

[114] In his essay on 'The Vocabulary of a Modern European State', *Political Studies*, 22 (1975), Michael Oakeshott distinguishes three kinds of political questions– questions about the location of authority, about the instruments of power, and about the mode of association. It seems to me that eighteenth-century German political theorists were only slightly concerned with the first, but were considerably engaged with the second and third, although they characteristically viewed them from what might be called a pedagogical perspective.

[115] Horst Dippel, *Germany and the American Revolution, 1770–1800* (Chapel Hill, 1977), 8; this is the best account. Wehler, *Gesellschaftsgeschichte*, i. 347 ff., presents a convincing case for the American revolution's importance in German Europe.

[116] Theodor Gottlieb von Hippel, *Über die bürgerliche Verbesserung der Weiber* (Königsberg, 1792). On Hippel and the debate his work provoked, see Epstein, *Genesis*, pp. 229 ff. Ruth Dawson's essay, 'Emerging Feminist Consciousness in the

be. As Rudolf Becker wrote in his widely read *Noth- und Huelfs-büchlein*, 'if one wishes, one can use understanding, skill, and industry to improve everything in the world, to make one's self better and thereby happier'. Becker was in no way politically radical, but the message of his book rested on deeply radical assumptions. Because the social and political order were not mere products of providence or chance, they could be observed, analysed, and improved. And because changes in the social and political order might hold out the promise for progress, happiness, those who resisted these changes could be held responsible for stagnation and the persistence of misery. These assumptions, so central to political consciousness and to political action, had come to German Europe well before events in France transformed the contours of political discourse and the conditions of public life.[117]

Late Eighteenth Century', in Joeres and Maynes (eds.), *Women*, discusses two female writers on emancipation, Marianne Ehrmann and Emilie Berlepsch. On Dohm, see above, sec iii, n. 66.

[117] Rudolf Z. Becker, *Noth- und Hülfsbüchlein, oder Lehrreiche Freuden- und Trauer-Geschichte der Einwohner zu Wildheim* (2 pts., new edn., Gotha, 1798–9), pt. 1, p. 414.

PART TWO

Germans and the French Revolution, 1789–1815

IV
Confrontation and defeat

IN the summer of 1789 Heinrich Steffens was a sixteen-year-old schoolboy living in Copenhagen. He heard that the Bastille had fallen from his father, an army surgeon down on his luck, who tearfully told him, 'You are to be envied—what beautiful, happy times lie ahead.' And so, Heinrich later recalled, 'I was pulled from the quiet solitude of childhood.' Long after he had become disillusioned with the revolution, Steffens remembered his initial enthusiasm as 'something pure, even sacred'. Johanna Schopenhauer, the young wife of a wealthy businessman, learned about the Bastille when her husband rushed home to their suburban villa near Danzig with the news. Like Steffens, Schopenhauer was drawn into the world of politics by the events of 1789. From then on, she wrote in her memoirs,

a new life, filled with unprecedented hopes for total change throughout the world, surged inside me. . . . Perhaps only a few of my contemporaries will immediately recall this event, but after a moment they too will bring to mind the burning enthusiasm and that sublime, reckless sense of Freedom which inflamed the sensibility of the noblest youth. . . .

For Steffens, Schopenhauer, and thousands of other Germans, the outbreak of the revolution in France was an unforgettable confrontation with history, the dawn of a new age.[1]

The initial influence of the revolution on Europeans' political imagination came from the fact that it was located in France, which most people regarded as the greatest nation in the world, the centre of fashion, arbiter of taste, and source of new ideas. What happened there was bound to seem more significant than the interesting but distant events in America or the recurrent upheavals that disrupted the periphery of Europe. But the drama that began in 1789 did not

---

[1]Steffens, *Was ich erlebte*, pp. 41–3; Johanna Schopenhauer, *Ihr glücklichen Augen: Jugenderinnerungen, Tagebücher, Briefe*, ed. R. Weber (Berlin, 1978), 264. Another example: Arndt, *Erinnerungen*, p. 68. For the revolution's impact on German life, see Aris, *History*; Jacques Droz, *L'Allemagne et la Révolution française* (Paris, 1949), Epstein, *Genesis*, ch. 9; Gooch, *Germany*, Alfred Stern, *Der Einfluss der Französischen Revolution auf das deutsche Geistesleben* (Stuttgart and Berlin, 1928). Träger (ed.), *Revolution*, is a useful collection of sources.

remain in France; during its quarter-century run, it left no corner of the Continent untouched. The revolution's duration and extent, apparently limitless energy, and inexhaustible ambition had a global resonance. No less important, however, was the specificity and immediacy of the revolution's impact on local communities, those thousands of villages and towns that were the settings for most people's experience. Here, in these small worlds, the forces of change shattered familiar institutions and disrupted old loyalties; and here too the price of change was paid, in taxes levied by ever more demanding states, in supplies requisitioned to feed armies' boundless hunger, and in the lives of young men sent off to fight in distant wars.

The next three chapters all deal with the revolutionary era's meaning for German history. In this chapter we shall view the revolution as an external force, a phenomenon to be understood, a military enemy to be fought, a political power to be courted or contained. Chapter 5 examines the domestic effects of the revolution on German politics and society, and Chapter 6 traces the changes it produced in art, philosophy, and political thought.

i. INITIAL RESPONSES

The French revolution reverberated through German intellectual life, Heine wrote, just as the tides seem to echo in a shell far from the sea. 'The most isolated author, living in some out-of-the-way corner of Germany, took part in the movement; sympathetically, without being exactly informed about its political developments, he felt the revolution's social significance and expressed it in his writing.'[2] Klopstock, the one-time pioneer of poetic sensibility, who was now living on a pension from the Danish crown, called the revolution 'the century's most noble deed' and lamented his own country's relative passivity: 'Ach, du warst es nicht, mein Vaterland, das der Freiheit| Gipfel erstieg, Beispiel strahlte den Völkern umher;| Frankreich war's.' Wieland, whose position as editor of the *Teutscher Merkur* made him one of the most influential publicists in central Europe, was equally enthusiastic. It is a blessing, he wrote to a friend in 1790, to be able to witness 'this greatest and most interesting of dramas'. That year he published an essay in the *Merkur* urging his readers to avoid hasty judgements;

---

[2] Heinrich Heine, 'Über Ludwig Börne', (1840), in *Werke*, ii. 779.

some excesses, he pointed out, are inevitable in the pursuit of great goals. Kant was unfailingly positive about the revolution in private conversations, but since his run-in with the royal censors in 1787 he was even more discreet than usual in his public pronouncements.[3]

Of course, not all German intellectuals were so enthralled by the news from France. Justus Möser, as we might expect, doubted that any good could come from rapid change. In his analysis of the first French constitution, he argued that since inequalities were endemic in social order, all this talk about abstract rights belonging to every person merely encouraged dangerous illusions. At first, Goethe was mildly hostile but not extremely interested in the revolution. In an epigram of 1790 he admitted that 'alle Freiheitsapostel, sie waren mir immer zuwider; | Willkür suchte doch nur jeder am Ende für sich. | Willst du viele befrein, so wag es, vielen zu dienen. | Wie gefährlich das sei, willst du es wissen? Versuch's!' Preoccupied with his study of colour and optics and busy with his new duties as director of the court theatre, Goethe did not have much time or energy for distant political dramas; at the end of 1791 he noted that he had enjoyed 'a calm year, at home and in the city'. Somewhat more surprisingly, Schiller, who eventually was named an honorary citizen of the French nation, seems to have been sceptical about the revolution from the start. Like Goethe, during 1789 and 1790 he was absorbed with his own affairs: a new position at Jena, marriage, and a serious illness. As we shall see later, when Schiller turned again to public concerns in his great essays of 1795, he reiterated his pre-revolutionary emphasis on the political significance of art.[4]

As far as we call tell, Möser, Goethe, and Schiller were in the minority; most German artists and intellectuals seem to have responded to the first stages of the revolution with considerable sympathy and often unrestrained enthusiasm. Sympathy and enthusiasm were especially prevalent among the young, who identified the dawn of a new order in Paris with the opening of new opportunities in their own lives. Friedrich Gentz, a former student of Kant's and now a junior Prussian official, called the revolution 'the first practical triumph of philosophy . . . the hope and consolation for so many of those ancient ills under which mankind has suffered. If the revolution is defeated, these ills will become ten

---

[3] Klopstock and Wieland quoted in Träger (ed.), *Revolution*, pp. 27–8, 39–40.

[4] See the essays on the revolution in Möser, *Phantasien*, especially pp. 145 ff. The Goethe quotes are from Träger (ed.) *Revolution*, p. 241, and Friedenthal, *Goethe*, p. 370. On Schiller, see below, Ch. 6, part iii.

CONFRONTATION AND DEFEAT

times harder to cure.' Georg Forster, soon to be caught up in the
political upheavals of the revolution in Mainz, responded to the fall
of the Bastille in terms significantly similar to Gentz: 'It is beautiful
to see', he wrote to his father-in-law in July 1789, 'what philosophy
nurtures in the mind and then realizes in the state.' To Hermann
von Boyen, a Prussian subaltern attending a regimental school in
Königsberg, the revolution appeared to be a sort of practical
Christianity: 'What we have pompously started to call "human
rights"', he believed, 'are no more nor less than our duties to our
neighbour defined politically.' Like most of his fellow students,
Boyen followed events in France with care and judged them
positively.[5]

A similar spirit prevailed at the Tübingen Seminary, which
numbered among its pupils a remarkable cluster of geniuses: the
future philosophers Hegel and Schelling and the poet Friedrich
Hölderlin. The Tübingen seminarians had long been sympathetic
to enlightened ideas; beneath their long, monkish robes, they had
concealed forbidden works by Rousseau and Voltaire. When the
Bastille fell, it seemed to them that these ideas had taken historic
shape. Hegel later remembered the revolution's outbreak as a
'glorious sunrise', which all thoughtful people celebrated. 'A
sublime emotion reigned over the epoch, the world was thrilled
with spiritual enthusiasm, as if the divine had now really
conciliated itself with the world.' In the spring of 1793 Hegel and
his colleagues were still avidly reading revolutionary pamphlets
and meeting secretly to sing a German version of the *Marseillaise*.
These experiences find powerful expression in Hölderlin's early
poems, such as his hymn 'An die Freiheit', written sometime in late
1791:

> Wonne sang' ich an des Orkus Thoren,
> Und die Schatten lehrt' ich Trunkenheit,
> Denn ich sah', vor tausenden erkohren,
> Meiner Göttin ganze Göttlichkeit,
> Wie nach dumpfer Nacht im Purpurscheine
> Der Pilote seinen Ozean,
> Wie die Seeligen Elysens Haine,
> Staun' ich dich geliebtes Wunder! an.
>
> Ehrerbietig senkten ihre Flügel,
> Ihres Raubs vergessen, Falk und Aar,
> Und getreu dem diamantnen Zügel

[5] Träger (ed.), *Revolution*, pp. 861–2; Vierhaus, 'Bewusstsein' p. 193; Meinecke,
Leben, i. 32–4.

Schritt vor ihr ein trozig Löwenpaar;
Jugendliche wilde Ströme standen,
Wie mein Herz, vor banger Wonne stumm;
Selbst die kühnen Boreasse schwanden,
Und die Erde ward zum Heiligtum.[6]

Hölderlin's rich blend of classical allusion and revolutionary fervour, like Gentz's and Forster's philosophical formulations, illustrates the way in which German intellectuals translated their feelings about the revolution into familiar idioms of moral reform and spiritual renewal. As they watched the complex, inchoate process of change unfold west of the Rhine, these people had to make sense of it within their own frame of reference, which was the emotionally charged but institutionally limited realm of the German political public. A good example of this kind of analysis is Wieland's essay, 'Betrachtungen über die gegenwärtige Lage des Vaterlandes', which he wrote in January 1793, when his own revolutionary ardour was starting to cool. Wieland began by trying to set recent events into their proper historical context— 'humanity's culture and education [*Ausbildung*], which over three centuries had climbed from one stage to another in most of Europe'. The men of 1789, he argued, were trying to bring culture and education to a new stage. In the process, they have done some unfortunate things, but counter-revolution cannot stop freedom's progress: 'every violent attempt to halt the advance of the human spirit' will turn out to be morally wrong and practically impossible. 'Only reason can heal the evils which the misuse of reason has created.' No wonder Carl Leonhard Rheinhold believed that 'Germany, among all the nations of Europe, is most likely to have a spiritual revolution and least likely to have a political one'.[7]

By viewing 1789 as a new chapter in the history of cultural progress, German intellectuals could celebrate freedom's triumph abroad without taking a position on its practical implications for their own political institutions. Joachim Campe, for instance, who was in Paris during the summer of 1789, watched at first hand the mortal blow 'struck at the heart of the dragon', and announced that the death of this beast marked 'the happiest day of my life'. But when Campe published his report on the revolution, he prefaced it

---

[6] Hegel in Frederick Hertz, *The Development of the German Public Mind* (London, 1957–62), ii. 420; Friedrich Hölderlin, *Sämtliche Gedichte* (Bad Homburg, 1970), i. 118.

[7] Wieland, *Werke*, xv. 558, 561. See the analysis by Horst Stuke in *GGB* i. 254. Reinhard quoted in Vierhaus, 'Bewusstsein', p. 195.

with laudatory words about his own prince, the duke of Brunswick, and with a warning that rebellion is a terrible act that only the
most severe oppression could justify. Georg Friedrich Rebmann,
who would eventually serve the French occupation, insisted in 1793
that, despite his commitment to the ideals of liberty, equality, and
fraternity, he did not 'belong to the party that wants to have a
popular revolt in Germany'.[8] Finally, consider the case of Immanuel Kant: long after most Germans had turned against France, Kant
remained loyal to the revolution, but he maintained, with equal
consistency, that citizens do not have the right to rebel.

Is rebellion a rightful means for a people to use in order to overthrow the
oppressive power of a so-called tyrant?' The rights of the people have been
violated, and there can be no doubt that the tyrant would not be receiving
unjust treatment if he were dethroned. Nevertheless, it is in the highest
degree wrong if the subjects pursue their own rights in this way, and they
cannot in the least complain of an injustice if they are defeated in the
ensuing conflict and subsequently have to endure the most severe penalties.

Pro-revolutionary from a French perspective, but anti-revolutionary
at home, Kant's statement provides a remarkably concise
formulation of the paralysis to which his politics of critical
accommodation could easily lead. In Albert Sorel's memorable
phrase, Kant 'led his disciples up to the giddy heights where his
critique held sway, so that they could better admire the scaffolding
of balustrades, parapets and guard rails he had so carefully erected
to keep them from the abyss'.[9]

The revolution's enemies, like its admirers, tended to view it in
spiritual terms. A minister in Trier, for example, blamed the
'terrible events in France' on the Enlightenment, which made
people 'too clever' and too sensitive to the governments' 'minor
crimes and the authorities' errors'. In 1791 a former member of the
Illuminati wrote an essay warning 'of the dangers which threaten
thrones, states, and Christianity from the system of enlightenment,
its so-called philosophers, secret societies, and sects'. A Jacobin,
declared a contributor to the *Wiener Zeitschrift* in 1792, 'is nothing
more nor less than a practical Illuminist'. Ever since there have been
reading societies, another writer argued, 'there has been one

[8] Gooch, *Germany*, pp. 41 ff.; Rebmann, *Wanderungen*, p. 42.
[9] Albert Sorel, *Europe and the French Revolution: The Political Traditions of the Old
Regime* (London, 1969), 457. Kant's remark is from *Perpetual Peace* (1795), repr. in
Writings, p. 126. Lewis White Beck, 'Kant and the Right of Revolution', *JHI* 32/3
(1971), 411–22, is an ingenious but ultimately unsuccessful attempt to find a
consistent line of argument in Kant's view of the revolution.

revolution after another in our minds'.[10] Some intellectuals began to worry about what they called *Lesesucht*, an epidemic of compulsive reading leading to physiological, psychological, and social disabilities, to which disrespectful servants, overtrained teachers, nervous youths, and loose women were especially susceptible. As a result of these anxieties, the repressive pressures that had already begun to be felt in parts of central Europe before 1789 were greatly intensified; various governments banned secret societies, closed periodicals, and censored newspapers.[11]

Conservatives' fears about the Enlightenment's corrosive effect on the social order were doubtless increased by the tremors of unrest which shook various central European states after 1789. One centre of trouble was the Rhineland, the region closest to France and therefore most likely to be infected by revolutionary ideals. A few weeks after the fall of the Bastille, for example, peasants and burghers gathered in Saarbrücken, where they protested against high taxes and unfair labour services, and then presented the duke with a list of forty specific demands for reform. That summer the elector of Trier was confronted by the angry citizens of Boppard, one of his Rhenish possessions, with whom he had a longstanding feud over the ownership of a forest. In October there was rioting in Trier itself when the town's tailors learned that washerwomen were mending clothes and thereby threatening their guild's cherished liberties. In Aachen, the spread of unrest after 1789 further exacerbated the turmoil that had existed ever since the bitterly contested mayoral election of 1786. In contrast to these trouble spots, Mainz, the largest of the Rhenish polities, was quiet in 1789. When rumours of trouble led the elector to dispatch troops to Aschaffenburg in early 1790, their arrival came as an unpleasant surprise to the town's tranquil citizens. During the summer of 1790, however, serious riots broke out in the city of Mainz, where students and journeymen battled one another and the authorities. Peace finally had to be restored by armed force. Overall, these various disturbances in 1789 and 1790 were occasionally troublesome and perhaps temporarily frightening to the governments, but they did not amount to much. Even the rioting in Mainz was,

---

[10] Hammerstein, *Aufklärung*, p. 258; Vierhaus, 'Aufklärung', p. 23, Engelsing, *Bürger*, p. 222.

[11] Helmut Kreuzer, 'Gefährliche Lesesucht? Bemerkungen zu politischer Lektürekritik im ausgehenden 18. Jahrhundert', in *Arbeitsstelle Achtzehntes Jahrhundert: Leser und Lesen im 18. Jahrhundert* (Heidelberg, 1977), 62–75. On the government response, see Epstein, *Genesis*, chs. 9, 10.

according to a sympathetic observer like Georg Forster, 'merely a farce'.[12]

A more serious situation existed in Saxony, where news of the events in France threatened to ignite an already volatile situation. For decades, Saxon peasants had objected to the seigneurial obligations imposed upon them by the nobility. Their grievances grew in the late 1780s when poor weather and an unusually large population of deer harmed their crops. Sporadic protests that began in the spring of 1790 had spread throughout the electorate by early August. A broadside, claiming to represent the views of 'twenty thousand conspirators of the land of Saxony', suggests the depths of the peasants' discontents but also the limits of their political consciousness. The document begins with a prayer for 'our dear Elector Frederick August, his friends and relations', but then swiftly turns to the nobility, 'those fiends calling themselves Lordships in our country and attempting to be Gods on earth'. If the nobles do not free their subjects from all dues, rents, and services, their estates will be destroyed, they will be hunted down, and 'the tongues of these hounds of hell shall be torn from their mouths'. The peasants' mood was clearly revolutionary, their tone defiant, their anger genuine, but the blend of specific demands and eschatological rhetoric seems more like the rural rebellions of the sixteenth century than the revolutionary debates going on in contemporary Paris. Using a judicious combination of armed force and vague promises, the Saxon government was able to repress the rebellion within a few weeks.[13]

Events in France certainly did raise the level of political awareness among many Germans and thus helped to create a climate conducive to the expression of discontents. While many reports of secret revolutionary agents were probably the work of some official's overactive imagination, there undoubtedly were many people like Christian Benjamin Geissler, a ropemaker from the Saxon village of Liebstadt, who wanted to import revolutionary ideas and tactics into the German lands. In general, however, the disturbances of 1789, 1790, and 1791 were extensions of pre-revolutionary developments rather than echoes of the forces at

---

[12] Quoted in Blanning, *Reform*, p. 266, which provides the best single account. Hansen (ed.), *Quellen*, is a fine collection of documents. See also Kyösti Julku, *Die revolutionäre Bewegung im Rheinland am Ende des achtzehnten Jahrhunderts* (2 vols.; Helsinki, 1965–9).

[13] There is a summary of the Saxon unrest in Epstein, *Genesis*, pp. 441 ff. The document is reprinted in Pollard and Holmes (eds.), *Documents*, pp. 175–7.

work in France. This was manifestly the case in western cities like Boppard and Aachen, where the revolution merely underscored persistent conflicts. Similarly, the antagonisms in Mainz that led to violence during the summer and fall of 1790 were deeply rooted in traditional urban life: journeymen against students, townsmen against university, popular piety against alleged secularization. The social strife in Rhenish cities and in rural Saxony came from efforts to defend guild privileges or to be free from seigneurial obligations—both well-established sources of contention in the eighteenth century. At stake in these struggles were the liberties on which the old order had rested rather than the Liberty for which people were killing and dying on the other side of the Rhine. Well into 1792, therefore, alert and thoughtful observers could believe that however powerful the revolution's impact might be in the realm of the German spirit, its political consequences were limited and could be controlled.[14]

In July 1793 the *Schleswig'sches Journal* published an article by Adolf Freiherr von Knigge on 'why Germany probably did not expect a dangerous, major political revolution'. Knigge, a well-known author, prominent member of the Illuminati, and admirer of the French revolution, was obviously not a disinterested party. He wrote in order to calm the fears that were beginning to spread among some German governments and thereby ease the growing pressures for censorship and repression. But Knigge was also an astute social commentator, whose analysis pointed to some important differences between the situations in France and central Europe. In the first place, Knigge tentatively suggested, the governments of most German states were not harsh enough to provoke rebellion by a populace 'grown accustomed to a certain degree of poverty and domination'. Secondly, even if rebellions did occur, the fragmentation of German life would inhibit the outbreak of full-scale revolution and thus enable the authorities to isolate and defeat the rebels. Thirdly, Knigge pointed out that there was no German equivalent to the French 'Third Estate', which had 'effected the revolution and energized the masses'. The Third Estate in Germany, Knigge wrote, was composed of bureaucrats, court officials, contractors, lawyers and physicians, 'who all more or less live from the crumbs that fall from the tables of their betters'. These people were much too deeply embedded in the existing order to lead a revolution. Finally, the German *Volk* was

[14] Some examples: on the Rhineland, Forster, *Ansichten*, p. 108; on Leipzig in November 1792, Owen, *Travels*, ii. 512.

218 CONFRONTATION AND DEFEAT

more 'sensible' than the French, less spoiled by what Knigge called 'the corruptions of enlightenment', less moved by 'adventurous spirits', and more infused with a 'reasonable religiosity—especially in Protestant areas'. A revolution, Knigge concluded, was not inevitable east of the Rhine, especially if German rulers learned from the events in France and introduced reform while there was still time. In what would become an ever more insistent refrain during the following decades, Knigge urged reform from above to pre-empt revolution from below.[15]

Knigge's diagnosis of German politics and society was quite accurate: indigenous rebellions from 1789 to 1792 were scattered, easy to isolate, badly led, and unevenly supported. But his prognosis could not have been more in error. He failed to see that many of the same characteristics that inhibited domestic revolutions would make the German states vulnerable to external attack. What he had called the 'phlegmatic disposition' of the *Volk*—what we have described in early chapters as the traditional, locally based character of German public life—may have limited the appeal of revolutionary ideals but it also limited the governments' ability to mobilize their population for national defence. The political fragmentation that isolated popular discontent also rendered effective military co-operation extremely difficult. The same small armies that had worked so well against Rhenish journeymen and Saxon peasants proved to be no match for the revolutionary soldiers sent into the field by the French. Soon after Knigge's attempt to reassure his contemporaries was printed, much of what he had to say became irrelevant: when the revolution finally arrived in German Europe, it came not as a spiritual awakening or a social transformation, but in the baggage train of a conquering army.

ii. A NEW KIND OF WAR: FROM VALMY TO JENA

Since it is difficult to imagine how the Reich's brittle western frontiers could have contained the extraordinary forces unleashed in 1789, the eastward expansion of revolutionary France may have been inevitable. In the years immediately following the fall of the Bastille, however, few contemporaries expected a Franco-German conflict, and no one imagined a war that would last more than two decades. As late as April 1792—after France had already declared

[15] Alfred Freiherr von Knigge, 'über die Ursachen, warum wir in Deutschland vorerst wohl keine gefährliche politische Haupt-Revolution zu erwarten haben', *Schleswig'sches Journal*, 2 (1793), 273–90.

war—Archduke Charles wrote from Brussels that 'no one here considers war likely'. German statesmen, like German intellectuals, viewed the events of 1789 within the context of their own, immediate concerns. And they had plenty to worry about besides someone else's constitutional embarrassments. The smaller German states, still shaken by the crisis within the empire produced by the Habsburg–Hohenzollern rivalry, were trying to reckon the significance of Frederick the Great's death for German politics and to understand the course his heir, Frederick William II, would set for the Prussian monarchy. In 1789 the Habsburg monarchy faced political upheavals in the Austrian Netherlands and Hungary, where Joseph II's ambitious reforms had provoked passionate protests. Equally disturbing were the signs of instability in eastern Europe, where Austria and Russia were fighting the Ottoman Empire and where Poland, a persistent source of tension among the great powers, was edging towards another constitutional crisis. If German statesmen expected trouble in 1789, they expected it to come from the east, not the west.[16]

Even after the death of Frederick the Great, the Austro-Prussian antipathy remained the pivot of central European power politics. Kaunitz, who was still directing Austrian foreign affairs, hoped to exploit the manifest weakness of the new Prussian monarch and thus push his kingdom back into the ranks of secondary states. Frederick William II, however, retained his uncle's advisers, who urged him to continue an activist, anti-Austrian policy. In 1787 Prussia sent troops into the United Provinces after the Dutch rebels had arrested the king's sister, the wife of Prince William of Orange. At the same time, Prussian diplomats, eager to take advantage of the Habsburgs' domestic and military troubles, signed an alliance with England and laid plans for a broad coalition directed against Vienna. The Prussians were also active in Poland, where they encouraged the political ferment that had begun after the removal of Russian forces in 1788. But the drift towards what many feared would be a new German war was halted by Joseph II's death in February 1790. Since Joseph's heir, Leopold, was eager to consolidate his position both at home and abroad, he adopted a series of conciliatory policies that included a *rapprochement* with Berlin. In July 1790 the two states signed the Treaty of Reichenbach, in which Vienna promised to end the Turkish war without

[16] For a good introduction to the issues covered in this section, see Howard, *War*, ch. 5; Geoffrey Best, *War and Society in Revolutionary Europe, 1770–1870* (New York and Oxford, 1986).

annexations and to respect the territorial integrity of Poland, while Berlin acquiesced in the restoration of Habsburg rule in Belgium. This Austro-Prussian *détente* was extended in 1791 with several other agreements, including the Declaration of Pillnitz, issued in August, which pledged the two states to defend monarchical principles against revolutionary upheavals.[17]

Although the Pillnitz statement hinted at intervention against France, neither Vienna nor Berlin wanted to put their eloquent expressions of monarchical solidarity into practice. Both governments were more immediately interested in what was happening in the Low Countries, the Reich, and in the increasingly volatile Polish situation. When the French king accepted the new constitution in September 1791, Austrian and Prussian statesmen were relieved; a potentially dangerous situation seemed to have passed. Nor did the other German states want war. Even in the Rhineland, where French *émigré* nobles were busy agitating for the creation of a counter-revolutionary coalition, most governments were reluctant to be drawn into a conflict against France. In January 1792 Prince Klemens Wenzeslaus of Trier, whose territories were subject to intense political pressures from France and from the *émigrés*, wrote to Emperor Leopold that the worst seemed to be over. A month later Vienna informed German princes in the west that they could expect Austrian aid only in the event of an unprovoked French attack.[18]

In Paris, however, an increasingly powerful group in the National Assembly viewed the German situation with alarm. These men, led by Jacques Pierre Brissot, were outraged by the aggressive rhetoric of the Pillnitz Declaration, frightened by the *rapprochement* between Austria and Prussia, and obsessed with visions of a counter-revolutionary conspiracy between the king and his *émigré* supporters. In late 1791 and early 1792 the French and Austrian governments exchanged charges of aggressive intent and threats of retaliatory action. On 24 January 1792 the Assembly issued an ultimatum demanding that Austria renounce any treaty directed against France's security. The Austrians could not but respond in kind; the tone and substance of their note of 17 February strengthened the hand of the war party in Paris. Meanwhile, Prussia, Austria's new ally, was more than willing to join in a move towards war, largely because Frederick William's advisers were

---

[17] This section concentrates on Prussia and Austria; the Reich and the smaller states are discussed in sect. iii, and Ch. 5, sect. i.
[18] Aretin, *Reich*, i. 260.

eager for territorial gains at France's expense. Thus in 1792 traditional great power rivalries, newly minted ideological antagonisms, and—perhaps most important of all—fundamental miscalculations on both sides drew the two major German powers into war with revolutionary France. As so often happens in the history of armed conflicts, when France declared war on 20 April no one could have imagined how long it would last and what consequences it would have.[19]

In the midst of the final crisis that led to war, Leopold.II died suddenly and was succeeded by his son, Francis II, who was crowned with traditional pomp in July 1792, while the Prussian and Austrian forces were gathering for the invasion of France. A few days later Francis met Frederick William II in Mainz to discuss military and political affairs and to enjoy those concerts, theatricals, and banquets that ornamented public life under the old regime. There seemed to be reason to celebrate: the Habsburgs' troops, who had easily routed a disorganized and dispirited French army in the Austrian Netherlands earlier in the year, were now joined by a formidable Prussian force under the command of the duke of Brunswick, widely regarded as the finest soldier of his day. Brunswick's manifesto, inspired by the *émigrés* and issued to the people of France on 25 July, set the tone for the counter-revolutionary crusade about to begin. Should any harm come to the royal family, Brunswick warned, he would take 'unprecedented, never to be forgotten revenge' on France and particularly on the city of Paris.[20]

The Austro-Prussian alliance was not quite as potent as July's splendid festivities and stirring rhetoric might have suggested. Old antagonisms and new ambitions divided Vienna and Berlin. At Mainz, Austrian and Prussian statesmen had debated the problems raised by the Habsburgs' ambitions in Bavaria and the Hohenzollern's appetites for more Polish land. The duke of Brunswick, despite his uncompromising 'Manifesto', was not pleased to be starting a campaign so late in the year, and with troops so hastily assembled and so poorly prepared. Always a cautious strategist, the duke would have been content with a few brief engagements and then a long lull in winter quarters. Francis and Frederick William, however, demanded that he press on; they dreamed of a triumphant promenade westward to the French capital. Had Brunswick

[19] See Blanning, *Origins*.
[20] Hansen (ed.), *Quellen*, ii. 297. For a contemporary description of the coronation, see H. A. O. Reichard, *Seine Selbstbiographie* (Stuttgart, 1877), 271 ff.

moved swiftly and decisively enough, he might have been able to destroy the French army and thus open the road to Paris. But his advance was slow and deliberate, hampered by bad weather, senseless squabbles among his subordinates, shortages of vital supplies, and an epidemic of dysentery.[21]

On 20 September Brunswick finally made contact with the enemy under General Dumouriez, near the town of Valmy, in hilly country between the Bionne and Auve Rivers about a hundred miles from Paris. When the morning fog lifted, the armies exchanged artillery fire. Neither risked an all-out attack on the other's position, although Brunswick was pressed to do so by the king. When darkness fell, the shooting stopped and the battle was virtually over. That evening, Goethe, who had accompanied Karl August of Weimar on the campaign, joined some discouraged Prussian officers around a campfire. His report of their conversation, published almost thirty years later, has become the battle of Valmy's most famous epitaph: 'Someone asked me what I thought of the situation,' Goethe wrote in his *Campagne in Frankreich*, 'and I replied, "Here and now a new epoch in world history has begun and you can say that you were there."' Was Goethe right? The battle was surely not much in military terms: of the seventy thousand troops involved, there were five hundred casualties on both sides, fewer than the number who had died of dysentery during the preceding week. But the results of this minor engagement were significant enough to earn it a chapter of its own in Fuller's *Decisive Battles*. Valmy broke the momentum of the allied advance and thereby gave the French a chance to regroup, mobilize their resources, and survive. It was, to borrow General Fuller's somewhat inflated classical comparison, the revolution's Marathon. The counter-revolutionary promenade to Paris, which seemed so effortless in the late summer of 1792, would be delayed for twenty-two years.[22]

The immediate aftermath of Valmy provided a preview of the years ahead. After a brief truce Brunswick conducted a peaceful and orderly retreat along his line of march, surrendering the forts he had captured a few weeks earlier. By mid-October the last German soldier had left French soil. The revolutionary armies, however,

---

[21] On the campaign, see Fuller, *Battles*, ch. 11. Fr. Ch. Lankhard, *Leben und Schicksale* (Stuttgart, 1908), ii. 49 ff. has a vivid eyewitness account.

[22] *Campagne in Frankreich*, in *Werke*, x. 234–5. For some shrewd remarks on Goethe's historical perceptions, see Stern, *Re-Interpretations*, pp. 350–1. There is more on Goethe's views of contemporary events below, Ch. 6, sect. iii.

went on the offensive. In the south, troops under the command of General Custine invaded imperial territory, captured Speyer on 30 September, Worms on 4 October, and Mainz on 20 October. Meanwhile, Dumouriez turned his army north into the Low Countries, defeated the Austrians at Jemappes, occupied much of Belgium, and pushed into the neighbouring German states. The revolution's expansion abroad was entwined with its radicalization at home. The day after Valmy, the newly elected National Convention abolished the monarchy; two days later, Year 1 of the new republican age began. Over the next few weeks, decrees flowed from Paris promising aid to the cause of liberation everywhere. In the first months of 1793, following the trial and execution of Louis XVI, France went to war with most of Europe.

France's enemies, shocked into action by the revolution's military victories and domestic violence, gathered into what is usually called the First Coalition, a potentially formidable but ultimately fragile alliance. In the first months of 1793 France's situation deteriorated. The Austrians defeated Dumouriez in the Low Countries and moved their troops into French territory. The duke of Coburg, with a force of 100,000 men, threatened Paris from the north. At the same time, the Prussians drove Custine from his bases in the Rhineland; Mainz was recaptured on 23 July. Had they pressed their advantage, the allied commanders could probably have destroyed the revolutionary regime. But they were men trained in the orthodoxies of traditional warfare, which emphasized careful manœuvres and marginal advantage rather than decisive battles and total victory. As a result, the revolution survived, and managed not only to stop the slow advance of its foreign enemies but also to defeat a full-scale rebellion among its own citizens in the Vendée. With an extraordinary combination of physical coercion and patriotic enthusiasm, the beleaguered government in Paris mobilized enormous resources, and thus revealed for the first time the potential power that could be generated by the new regime. There seemed to be no limits to what the state could demand of the nation; the new French army, unprecedented in size and dedication, was sustained by civil institutions completely devoted to pressing the war against the revolution's ubiquitous enemies. In the face of this concentration of national energy and political will, the armies of the old regime fell back. The French reconquered the Low Countries, penetrated the German lands of the north-west, and once again raised the tricolore over key strongholds along the Rhine.

From the start, the counter-revolutionary alliance was weakened by the way in which Polish affairs divided and distracted its two most important continental members, Austria and Prussia. These two states, together with Russia, had been involved in Poland throughout the century; in 1772 they had carved off about a third of the kingdom for themselves. In May 1792, just as hostilities were getting under way in the west, a new round of conflicts began among those who wished to establish themselves as the chief beneficiaries of Poland's anticipated demise. Between the second partition of Poland in 1793 and her political extinction two years later, Polish affairs poisoned Austro-Prussian relations, engaged an important part of both states' armies, and finally, in the summer of 1794, caused Frederick William to lead fifty thousand troops into Poland to support his territorial ambitions. That fall, with the military situation still uncertain and rumours of a secret agreement between Austria and Russia circulating in Berlin, Frederick William decided, with considerable reluctance, that he had to abandon his allies and seek peace in the west. Thus, as Georges Lefebvre wrote, 'Poland contributed to the salvation of the revolution . . . at the price of her independence.'[23]

Negotiations between France and Prussia began in November 1794 and dragged on until the Treaty of Basel was signed in April 1795. As with every important policy in post-Frederician Prussia, the government was deeply divided about both the ends and the means of these negotiations. The king's older advisers, most of them former servants of his uncle, still believed that Prussia's principal interests were in the east and thus wanted to deal with France as quickly as possible. However, some younger men, such as Karl von Hardenberg, the chief administrator of the Hohenzollern's Franconian lands, were reluctant to abandon the French war because they did not want to jeopardize Prussia's influence over the smaller states of the west. In the end, Frederick William's own desire for peace carried the day. At Basel, Prussia not only acknowledged the legitimacy of the revolutionary government but also accepted the French occupation of the Rhineland, thereby deferring the ultimate fate of these territories until some future agreement between France and the Reich. In a secret codicil to the treaty, Prussia promised to support French annexations in the west, for which it was promised compensation on the right bank of the

[23] Georges Lefebvre, *The French Revolution* (New York, 1962–4), ii. 11. On the Polish situation, see Norman Davies, *God's Playground: A Short History of Poland* (New York, 1984), ii.

Rhine. Another secret agreement established a neutral zone in the north-east, which was to remain undisturbed by French forces as long as Prussia could guarantee it would not engage in acts hostile to France. In 1795, therefore, Prussia set off on a neutralist course, taking with it, in direct violation of the imperial constitution, a cluster of states given over to its care by the French conquerors.[24]

With the withdrawal of Prussia from the war, Austria had to shoulder the full weight of the anti-revolutionary struggle on the Continent. For the next decade, war raged along the vulnerable arc of the Habsburgs' possessions extending from the Low Countries, down the Rhine, and into Italy. Initially, the main theatre of operations was the German west, but in the second half of 1796 Napoleon Bonaparte, a newly minted general of twenty-seven, shifted the focus of strategy to Italy, where he won a series of striking victories against the Austrians. In March 1797, after having secured his base in the south, Napoleon crossed the Alps and within weeks was eighty miles from Vienna. At that point, because neither the French nor the Austrians were willing to risk a full-scale engagement, they suspended hostilities and, after considerable delay and complex negotiations, signed the Treaty of Campo Formio in October 1797. But within a year the Habsburgs were again at war, this time as members of the Second Coalition, which included England, Russia, and the Imperial *Kreise* of Swabia, Bavaria, and Franconia. At first things went well for the allies, but, as so often happened, political disagreements and military incompetence prevented them from taking full advantage of their successes. The Russians turned out to be difficult partners, the British, without substantial ground forces, had only limited influence on events, and the Austrians suffered from their characteristic problems of logistical insufficiency and strategic uncertainty. As the coalition started to dissolve, Napoleon returned from Egypt, brushed aside the Directory, declared himself First

[24] Agatha Ramm gives the following concise description of the boundary demarking the neutral zone:
> The line began at the frontier of East Friesland and then followed the course of the River Ems to Münster, then turned west to the frontier of Cleves, followed the Rhine, so as to include Cleves, to Duisburg, then turned southwards and eastwards away from the Rhine so as to exclude Hesse Cassel and Hesse Darmstadt. It followed the valley of the Lahn and crossed the Main, reached the Necker at Eberbach, followed it to Wimpffen, then ran eastwards so as to exclude Baden and Württemberg, but bent southwards towards Nördlingen so that some of the Franconian Circle as well as both the Saxon Circles were included, but Bavaria and the Upper Palatinate and Bohemia excluded. (*Germany, 1789–1919* [London, 1967], 40).

Consul of the Republic, and then brought new energy to the French war effort. In 1800 the French won a series of victories, culminating on 3 December, when a badly led Austrian force was mauled in the Hohenlinden forest a few miles east of Munich. The Treaty of Lunéville, signed by Austria and France in February 1801, completed the Habsburgs' extrusion from their spheres of influence in the western Reich.[25]

Like a broad-beamed, cumbersome galleon, the Habsburg monarchy was both hard to steer and hard to sink. Despite a series of costly defeats, which narrowed its influence and diminished its prestige, the monarchy remained a major power with enormous resources. After 1801 the Habsburgs made a concerted effort to improve their military establishment with reforms introduced under the direction of the Archduke Charles, the only military commander to survive the débâcles of 1800 with his reputation intact. Unfortunately, these reforms did not have time to take effect. In 1805 Francis agreed to join the Third Coalition, which had been formed by Britain and Russia in a new effort to liberate the Continent from the newly created Napoleonic empire. He then sent his brother Charles, who had warned against a premature resumption of hostilities, off to lead Austrian forces in Italy, and made General Mack commander of the northern armies. Mack was a terrible choice: despite his high reputation, he was neither a sound strategist nor a gifted leader. At the end of the summer, without a clear plan to direct their operations and further confused by some last minute efforts at reorganization, the Habsburgs' armies moved into the field against Napoleon, whose troops were close to the peak of combat readiness. Austria's German allies deserted even before the campaign had begun; when they caught the scent of a disaster in the making, they moved their forces as far away as possible. Their expectations were fulfilled: after three weeks of pointless manœuvering around Ulm, Mack surrendered to Napoleon without a fight. The French occupied Vienna in November and then defeated a combined Austrian and Russian force at Austerlitz. With its army in shambles and its allies in disarray, the monarchy had no alternative but to accept the peace imposed by Napoleon at Pressburg.[26]

How were the French able to win such an impressive string of

[25] For the territorial effects of Lunéville, see below, sec. iii.
[26] On the Austrian army, see Rothenberg, *Napoleon's Great Adversaries*; Craig, 'Command'. There is a vivid account of Austerlitz in Christopher Duffy, *Austerlitz, 1805* (London, 1977).

victories during the decade following the Treaty of Basel? Like most of history's winners, they were blessed with incompetent opponents. The various alliances formed against France were, as we have seen, deeply divided within themselves. Militarily, the allies were not well led. Brunswick and Coburg were no better than average soldiers and both were past their prime by the time they assumed command against the revolution. Mack was an unqualified disaster. Archduke Charles, the best of this lot, was never able to acquire the resources and authority he needed to prepare and lead a successful campaign. But, even if they had been better led and more co-operative, the allies could not have defeated the French, who had learned to wage a new kind of war.

Unlike later changes in the art of war, the military revolution that occurred between 1792 and 1815 was not caused by technological change. During this period, there was no dramatic progress in communications or transportation, no new weapons or means of defence. Napoleon's troops marched to battle just as men had for centuries; they fought with smooth-bore muskets, sabres, and lances; the most important innovations in artillery had taken place under the old regime. What changed was not the machinery of war, but rather the spirit and organization of the men who did the fighting. Like most of the developments that transformed European politics and society in this period, the emergence of a new kind of war involved changes in scale and tempo as well as style and substance. Most obviously, wars were now bigger—and, as the fighting in 1805 demonstrated, could be settled with extraordinary speed. The highly-trained, very expensive professional armies of the old regime had tended to be small; battles involving more than 50,000 men were rare. In contrast, Napoleon had used over 180,000 troops to humiliate the unfortunate General Mack at Ulm; he would march to his own humiliation in Russia with three times that many. Half a million men fought at Waterloo.

The French had raised these mass armies through conscription; according to the famous law of 23 August 1793, 'From this day until that when our enemies have been chased off the territories of the Republic, all Frenchmen are on permanent requisition for military service.' As soon as it became clear that this conscript army would not be cut to shreds by its professional opponents, some German soldiers and statesmen began to call for a mobilization of their own populations. In 1794, for example, Friedrich von Bock, an officer in the army of the Westphalian circle, argued that the French threat required the formation of a new imperial German army, drawn from the Reich as a whole. As we shall see in the next chapter, the trail of French victories evoked an increasing number of pleas to break what Bock called 'the fetters of tradition and custom'. Most German governments, however, were extremely reluctant to follow the French model. Few princes felt able to impose on their societies the sort of demands that had led to a mobilization of 500,000 French troops during the second half of 1793. Moreover, to hand out muskets indiscriminately seemed politically dangerous and militarily useless. 'I would rather pay my last *ecu* to the Elector of Saxony to have a couple of his good regiments march', wrote Karl August of Weimar in 1794, 'than to arm five hundred of my peasants.' Most generals schooled in the warfare of the old regime did not see how mass armies could be supplied and commanded since they were convinced that unrestricted foraging would encourage mass desertion. Moreover, traditional tactics required soldiers to stand in a line firing volley after volley while being shelled by the enemy's guns and assaulted by his cavalry. Most military experts believed that only long-serving professionals, subjected to endless drill and threatened with draconian punishment, would be able to serve as what Frederick the Great once called 'moving batteries' amid the terrible chaos of combat. A general like the duke of Brunswick did not want an army of untrained civilians. His ideal was a manageable body of professionals, whose slow movement, careful manœuvring, well-chosen positions, and secured lines of march could minimize the cost and reduce the unpredictability of battle. The goal of strategy, for Brunswick and his colleagues, was to keep war as much like the drill-field as possible.[27]

The French had abandoned the assumptions of conventional warfare because they had no choice. The revolutionary armies, composed of masses of conscripts plus a core of high-quality professionals from the old regime, did not have the skills and self-discipline necessary to maintain a firing line in the face of experienced troops. But they were able to develop flexible, open order tactics, in which the firing line was combined with attack columns, skirmishers, and light cavalry. Revolutionary officers were willing to use small combat units that had great mobility and independence. As can be seen in this description of the Prussian infantry at Jena, regular troops were sometimes pathetically vulnerable to an enemy unwilling to play by the rules:

[27] Howard, *War*, p. 80. Gagliardo, *Reich*, pp. 154–56.

This magnificent infantry, some 20,000 strong, stood out in the open for two whole hours whilst exposed to the merciless case and skirmishing fire of the French, who behind garden walls offered no mark at all for their return fire. In places the fronts of the companies were marked by individual files still loading and firing, while all their comrades lay dead and dying around them.

We should not overstate the suddenness of this tactical revolution: armies had used skirmishers before 1789 and, as Wellington would demonstrate at Waterloo, the firing line could still be a formidable tactical device. Nevertheless, the apparent political enthusiasm and unmistakable military effectiveness of the new French armies transformed the nature of battle.[28]

Napoleon's greatness came from his ability to understand the opportunities and resolve the problems presented by the changing scale and tempo of war. Like Frederick the Great, Napoleon regarded battles as the true purpose and culmination of a campaign, not—as so many eighteenth-century professional soldiers believed—necessary evils to be avoided if at all possible. But while Frederick had defined the purpose of battles as compelling 'your opponent to yield you his position', Napoleon knew that victory meant nothing less that the destruction of the enemy's ability and will to resist further. Frederick pushed old orthodoxies to their limits; Napoleon grasped and manipulated the possibilities of a new age. But to will new goals is useless without developing new means to achieve them. In order to lead his massive forces to decisive victories, Napoleon had to resolve profound problems of logistics and command. To supply an army as large as his required carefully organized supply depots, dispersed lines of march—his troops moved eastward in 1805 along a hundred-mile front—and ruthless requisitioning policies. To coordinate his armies and concentrate them at the decisive moment required flexibly organized units, independent but not irresponsible subordinates, and—most important of all—Napoleon's own energy, powers of concentration, and force of personality.[29]

Even before Napoleon demonstrated its full significance, some

[28] Fuller, *Battles*, p. 433. An excellent discussion of tactical innovations can be found in Paret, *Yorck*, ch. 2.

[29] Ritter compares Frederick and Napoleon in *Frederick the Great*, ch. 8. See also Robert Palmer, 'Frederick the Great, Guibert, Bülow: From Dynastic to National War', in Earle (ed.), *Makers*, 49–76. On the Napoleonic revolution in war, see Chandler, *Napoleon*, and two recent works by Van Creveld, *Supplying War*, and *Command in War*.

Europeans tried to come to terms with the new style of war. Archduke Charles, temporarily retired after the bruising campaigns of 1794, wrote a treatise entitled 'On War against the New Franks', which sought to explain how 'a well-equipped, balanced, and disciplined army had been defeated by an enemy with raw troops, lacking cavalry, and with inexperienced generals'. A few years later, Heinrich Dietrich von Bülow devoted his *Geist des neueren Kriegssystems* to the same problem. Bülow, a minor noble with limited military experience but considerable literary flair, was a characteristically transitional figure, whose work combined brilliant analysis with hopeless eccentricity. To his credit, he understood that the revolution in war's scale involved a new strategy; he also had some astute comments on tactical innovations and helped to clarify what would become the conventional distinctions between strategy and tactics. But to these insights he added a doctrine in which victory depended upon the application of a set of geometrical formulae.[30]

A more solid and convincing diagnosis of the French triumphs was provided by Gerhard von Scharnhorst, whose essay of 1797 on the 'Entwicklung der allgemeinen Ursachen des Glücks der Franzosen in dem Revolutionskriege und insbesondere in dem Feldzuge von 1794' emphasized the political and psychological advantages of the revolutionary armies. Scharnhorst had begun his career in the Hanoverian army but accepted a Prussian commission in 1801. Soon after his arrival in Berlin, he joined with a few other soldiers and civilians to form the *Militärische Gesellschaft*, an organization devoted to the discussion and publication of new ideas about military affairs. The society's proceedings published the work of young officers like Hermann von Boyen, who had been carefully studying the course of events while serving as a company commander in a provincial Prussian garrison. Scharnhorst was also responsible for setting into motion the career of Carl von Clausewitz, who became a student at the academy for the training of young officers not long after Scharnhorst took over as its director and principal instructor.[31]

Clausewitz was born in 1780, the son of a former Prussian officer

[30] Rothenberg, *Napoleon's Great Adversaries*, p. 43. On Bülow, see Palmer's article cited in n. 29; Paret, *Yorck*, pp. 80 ff., and 'Napoleon as Enemy', *Proceedings of the Consortium on Revolutionary Europe, 1983* (Athens, Ga., 1985), 49–61.

[31] Scharnhorst's essay is reprinted in his *Ausgewählte militärische Schriften*, ed. Freiherr v.d. Goltz (Berlin, 1881), 192 ff. The best brief treatment of his ideas and influence is in Paret, *Clausewitz*, ch. 4.

who held a minor post in the revenue administration. Clausewitz joined the army at the age of twelve and from then on had no other career and knew no greater passion. But he was never a typical officer: the uncertainty of his background—his title was probably illegitimate—and the complexity of his character set him apart from most of his fellows. After his first taste of combat as a thirteen-year-old ensign in the French campaign, Clausewitz spent five years in a garrison at Neuruppin, where he read widely and was active in various educational programmes, before being transferred to Scharnhorst's academy in 1801. Four years later he published his first theoretical essay, a sharp critique of Bülow's strategic writings, which appeared in the *Neue Bellona*, a journal edited by the Badenese officer and military publicist Heinrich Philip von Porbeck. Over the next quarter century, except when he was actively involved in combat, Clausewitz read, thought, and wrote about the nature of war. He did not live to finish the summation of his life's work, but even in their uncompleted form, Clausewitz's writings (published posthumously as *On War*) remain the finest formulation of revolutionary warfare's character and significance.[32]

Like many of his most gifted contemporaries, Clausewitz tried to use reason to study what he recognized as a deeply irrational world. His style is restrained and straightforward, his tone cool and diffident. When war is stripped of idealistic bombast and rhetorical fancy, Clausewitz tells us, it has a terrible simplicity: it is 'an act of force to compel our enemy to do our will'. In this most violent and dangerous of human activities, there is no room for humanitarian distractions. 'The mistakes which come from kindness are the very worst.' Honour is of psychological interest but has no intrinsic value as an ideal. Courage matters, foolhardiness does not. Clausewitz had no use for those 'whose idea of war is summed up by a galloping hussar waving his sword'. To view war rationally requires that we understand rationality's limitations. 'No other human activity is so continuously and universally bound up with chance.' Moreover, in the course of a battle, innumerable opportunities arise for error and miscalculation, physical weakness and psychological collapse. 'Everything in war is very simple, but the simplest thing is difficult.' Any theory of war must, therefore,

---

[32] Paret's introduction to the new edition of *On War* (1976) describes the work's evolution, while his *Clausewitz* is a brilliant analysis of the thinker in his historical setting. Raymond Aron's *Penser la guerre. Clausewitz* (2 vols.; Paris, 1976) views Clausewitz in the context of modern military theory.

allow for what Clausewitz calls 'friction', the resistance of events to human understanding and control. To study war is like having a swimming lesson on dry land: one can see the strokes clearly but one must also recognize that things will be different in the water.[33]

On War touched on almost every aspect of military operations, from details of supply to the broadest strategic considerations, but the book's most famous passages are those dealing with the relationship between war and politics. Characteristically, Clausewitz sought to give this relationship the clearest and most general formulation possible: 'war is not a mere act of policy but a true political instrument, a continuation of political activity by other means. . . . The political object is the goal, war is the means of reaching it, and means can never be considered in isolation from their purpose.' War is an intrinsically political activity since politics determines war's goals and character—as Clausewitz writes in another famous passage, 'Its grammar, indeed, may be its own, but not its logic.' Clausewitz saw that this fact had special significance in the current era because the quality of revolutionary warfare can best be understood in political rather than military terms: 'the tremendous effects of the French revolution abroad were caused not so much by new military methods and concepts as by radical changes in policies and administration' . . . Of these changes, the most important were those that enabled the state to mobilize its resources behind the war effort. Because of the contribution that 'the heat and temper of a nation can make to the sum total of its politics, war potential and fighting strength', states can wage war on the basis of their total strength, not just the strength of their standing armies. Once the revolutionary state tapped this source of strength, its enemies had to do the same, or they would continue to endure the defeats such as were suffered by the old regime at the hands of the French armies. In a particularly sombre passage, Clausewitz acknowledges the implications of this for the future: 'If war is part of policy, policy will determine its character. As policy becomes more ambitious and vigorous, so will war, and this may reach the point where war attains its absolute form.'[34]

Clausewitz, together with the other gifted young officers whom Scharnhorst gathered around him in the early 1800s, grasped the meaning of the revolution for warfare and recognized the tasks this imposed upon the revolution's enemies. These men, working with

[33] *On War*, pp. 75, 438, 85, 119.
[34] Ibid. 87, 605, 609–10, 220, 606.

like-minded individuals in the civil administration, pressed the Prussian government to introduce reforms while there was still time. Only a transformed social and political order, they believed, could support an army sufficient for the inevitable conflict with France which lay ahead. Cassandra-like, the Prussian reformers saw what was coming but were powerless to do much about it. For reasons that will be considered at length in the next chapter, the Prussia of Frederick William II and, after 1797, of Frederick William III, was not receptive to calls for basic reform. Indecisiveness at court, opposition to change from the landed nobility, and a false sense of confidence in the military establishment combined to limit the reformers' influence.

As we have seen, after 1795 Prussia stood on the sidelines while the various European coalitions fought unsuccessfully against the French. Unless one believes that by remaining neutral Prussia was shirking some pre-ordained historic mission, there is no reason to repeat the harshly critical attacks on this policy made by generations of patriotic historians. Neutrality *per se* was not a poor policy. Considering Prussia's position, it had not done badly in the Treaty of Basel, and considering the quality and fate of the anti-French coalitions, it had not been altogether unwise to remain aloof from their undertakings. The difficulty with Prussian foreign policy after 1795 was not its neutrality, but rather the weakness of will and obscurity of vision this neutrality attempted to mask. Perhaps more than most diplomatic postures, neutrality in time of war demands firm resolve and clear goals; it cannot be the result of indecision and an excuse for inaction. By the turn of the century this was precisely what neutrality had come to be in Berlin, where the government was bitterly divided, uncertain of its true interests, incapable of mobilizing forces for its self-defence. Confusion, vacillation, and dissension were at their worst in the months preceding the final struggle between Napoleon and the Third Coalition in 1805. King Frederick William was wooed and threatened by both sides, but joined neither. His delay gained little, his ultimate indecision helped defeat the coalition without improving his relations with the French. After Austerlitz, Napoleon's demands for Prussian support increased. He did not want to fight, but he did want Berlin to become a compliant partner in the continental order that he was in the process of creating. After being forced to agree to a humiliating treaty with France in February 1806, Frederick William's willingness to compromise began to ebb. A slow drift towards war began during the summer when the king allowed a partial mobilization of his army and thus evoked a comparable response from France. Finally, on 13 September, Prussian troops crossed into Saxony and hostilities began.[35]

The autumn of 1806 was not a good time for Prussia to confront France militarily. The Austrians, badly beaten in their last campaign, were in no position to fight again; the Russians had withdrawn their troops; Britain, the most persistent of Napoleon's enemies, had declared war on Berlin following the Prussian invasion of Hanover. Eventually, both the Russians and the British would have been willing to support another anti-French coalition, but, once war had become inevitable, Napoleon was not in the habit of giving his enemies the gift of time. His army, re-equipped and its ranks replenished with new conscripts, moved immediately into central Europe. Against this formidable military machine, Prussia had to fight alone, with an army which had as the chief legacies from its great past a false sense of confidence and an outmoded set of tactics. Scharnhorst and the others who saw what was coming could not make themselves heard among the cacophony of voices around the king.

After crossing the Elbe to offer battle to the enemy, the Prussians were soon engaged by the three French forces that had moved northward through the Frankenwald with remarkable speed. Early in the morning of 14 October Napoleon's troops clashed with what he took to be the main Prussian army on a plateau near Jena. The issue was never in doubt. By late afternoon the outnumbered and outmanœuvred Prussians had been soundly defeated. Meanwhile, twelve miles north an even greater disaster was in the making. While Napoleon was winning his battle at Jena, Marshall Davout fought and defeated the rest of the Prussian army near Auerstädt. As darkness fell the disorganized survivors from this battle mingled with defeated remnants from Jena and thus added to the chaos of defeat. Hermann von Boyen, badly wounded and cut off from his own unit, watched the army disintegrate as men dropped their weapons, deserted wounded comrades, and fled the pursuing French. 'The carefully assembled and apparently unshakable military structure', Boyen wrote, 'was suddenly shattered to its very foundations.' Clausewitz, who was also there, devoted a few emotion-charged pages of *On War* to the defeat, in which 'the most extreme poverty of the imagination to which routine had ever led'

---

[35] On the Prussian situation, see Paret, *Clausewitz*, pp. 110 ff.

ruined the Prussian army 'more completely than any army has ever been ruined on the battlefield'.[36]

The ruin of its army left Prussia without the ability to play an autonomous role in the continuing war between France and Russia. From mid-October 1806 until the following June, Frederick William was reduced to being the tsar's junior partner, and, after Napoleon defeated the Russians at Friedland on 14 June 1807, the Prussian being was forced to wait impatiently on the shore while Napoleon and Alexander met on a raft anchored in the Niemen River to decide Prussia's future. The Treaty of Tilsit, signed on 9 July, stripped Prussia of all her territory west of the Elbe, as well as most of her Polish lands. Reduced to just four provinces, occupied by French troops, saddled with a large war indemnity, and compelled to join an alliance against the British, Prussia seemed about to slip back into the ranks of minor German states from which several generations of Hohenzollern had tried to raise it. Napoleon, on the other hand, was triumphant: with Russia now his ally, Austria defeated and temporarily compliant, and Prussia in shambles, he was free to complete his plans for a new European order.[37]

iii. THE END OF THE OLD REICH AND THE REORGANIZATION OF CENTRAL EUROPE

On the morning of 6 August 1806 the herald of the Reich, resplendent in the ceremonial robes of his office, rode through the streets of Vienna to perform his last imperial duty. At the Church of the Nine Choirs of Angels, he sounded the traditional trumpet fanfare and then read a proclamation announcing that Francis II, 'by God's grace elected Roman emperor, for all times guardian of the Reich, hereditary emperor of Austria, king in the Germanies', had laid down his imperial crown and released the members of the Reich from their constitutional obligations. This abrupt and illegal act ended the existence of institutions that had provided some measure of order to the German lands for centuries and had preserved a filament of historical continuity reaching back through

[36] Van Creveld, *Command in War*, pp. 78 ff., describes the campaign from the French perspective. Fuller, *Battles*, has an account of Jena. Quotations are from Hermann von Boyen, *Denkwürdigkeiten und Erinnerungen* (rev. edn. Leipzig, 1899), i. 171–2; *On War*, pp. 154–5.
[37] The conditions of the Tilsit peace can be found in Georges Lefebvre, *Napoleon* (New York, 1969), i. 273.

the settlements of 1648 to the medieval Imperium and the lingering memories of ancient Rome. Considering its venerable age and the allegiance it had once evoked, the Reich's end was remarkably quick and curiously uncontested. Goethe, who was on a journey that August, noted in his journal, 'Conflict between the servant and coachman on the coachbox, which excited us more than the dissolution of the Roman Empire.'[38]

Historians who shared Lord Bryce's opinion that the Reich was like 'a corpse, brought forth from some Egyptian sepulchre, ready to crumble at the touch', felt no need to explain its sudden collapse in 1806, nor were they surprised that this collapse was greeted by such apathy. More recently, however, the Reich's scholarly defenders have insisted that its passing was the result of the revolution's formidable power rather than its own endemic weakness. 'Far from being the gale which blew away the desiccated feudal leaves,' T. C. W. Blanning has argued, 'the French revolution is better likened to a chainsaw, which felled an ancient, gnarled, but still flourishing oak.' Blanning is surely closer to the mark than those who have traditionally underestimated the Reich's vitality. Nevertheless, we should not overlook how the growth of state power in the eighteenth century had weakened imperial institutions and diluted imperial loyalties. By sapping the strength and exposing the roots of the imperial oak, this long-term process of erosion made the Reich's destruction after 1789 that much easier.[39]

On the eve of the revolution, even the Reich's most devoted admirers were concerned about its future. 'The empire is an ill-cohering, clumsy mass,' lamented Johannes von Müller in 1788, 'where the strong do what they will, and the others not what they should.' A year later, a citizen of Augsburg provided this gloomy but prescient picture of the future: 'If one imperial city falls, several will follow, and if several fall, all will. If the cities go under, the small states will too. Then there will be only two governments in Germany and since they are everlasting rivals, eventually there will be but one.' In 1792, when there were already signs that the Reich would have trouble withstanding external threats and internal dissension, Friedrich Carl von Moser, who had been one of the imperial ideal's most eloquent spokesmen for decades, republished

[38] Aretin, *Reich* i. 506; J. W. Goethe, *Gesamtausgabe*, xi, pt. 1. *Tagebücher, 1770–1810* (Stuttgart, 1956), 686. The proclamation is reprinted in Huber, *Dokumente*, i. 35–6. See the literature on the Reich cited above, Ch. 1, sect. i.
[39] Bryce, *Empire*, p. 407; Blanning, *Revolution*, p. 20.

his famous pamphlet of 1765 on the German National Spirit. In a deeply pessimistic preface to this new edition, Moser wrote that the time for reform had passed. Let us wait a century or so, he argued, 'until the ark in which so many small and large, clean and unclean creatures are shut up together springs a leak and everyone saves himself or is gobbled up . . .'. Moser's leisurely fatalism had no place in the historical era that began in 1789. Never again would institutions like the Reich have a century in which to seek self-renewal.[40]

The first confrontation between the Reich and the revolution took place in Alsace, one of those areas where the overlapping sovereignties of the old regime still survived. When the French estates abolished 'feudalism' during their famous session on the night of 4 August 1789, they took away the seigneurial rights of those German aristocrats whose Alsatian properties had once been an imperial territory but were now part of the French monarchy. Since the proprietors of these estates were still imperial nobles, they appealed to the emperor for protection and compensation. However, they did not find much interest in their plight; the emperor was unresponsive, the other imperial institutions too slow-moving to be of help. Before long, the more powerful of these landowners, such as the duke of Württemberg, entered into direct negotiations with Paris. In effect, the conflict between France and the so-called imperial enclaves brought to a new level the long-term struggle between state and local power. It marked, therefore, the opening of a new—and final—chapter in the story of the Reich's declining ability to protect the realm of *Herrschaft* from the central state's drive for total sovereignty.[41]

No one had more reason to be concerned about the problem of imperial self-defence than the rulers of the small states scattered along the Reich's western frontier. Although they were able to maintain order within their own territories, these states were in no position to defend themselves against foreign aggression. Cumbersome and inefficient under the best of circumstances, imperial military institutions were appropriate weapons against brigands, but were ill-suited to large and sustained campaigns. The sombre assessment of the empire's war making potential made by Johann Jakob Moser in the 1760s was no less true thirty years later: 'The

---

[40] Gagliardo, *Reich*, pp. 96, 140; Aretin, *Reich*, i. 108.

[41] There is a clear account of these developments in S. Biro's informative if rather eccentric *The German Policy of Revolutionary France: A Study in French Diplomacy during the War of the First Coalition, 1792–1797* (Cambridge, Mass., 1957), i. 39–42.

deficiencies which are exposed in an imperial war and in an imperial army are so great', Moser concluded, 'that as long as the German Empire remains in its present constitution, it should forever be forbidden to wage an Imperial War . . .' In 1790 some western governments considered calling upon the French *émigré* nobles who had streamed into their territories for assistance—a sure sign of desperation when one considers the level of political talent and military skill common among these gentlemen. 'We German princes have only laws, treaties, and solemn, sworn promises to set against this expanding power,' wrote Elector Max Franz of Cologne, 'only morality can save us.'[42]

The obvious places for the small states to look for military protection were Prussia and Austria, the only two central European states large enough to fight a great power like France. However, most German rulers had good reason to distrust the governments in Vienna and Berlin. Present Prussian policy, wrote a Hanoverian diplomat in May 1791, holds that 'the imperial tie is important and worth maintaining only in so far as it improves the House of Brandenburg's position against Austria'. A few months later an observer in Dresden reported that the Saxon government viewed any Austrian initiative on the Reich's behalf as a cover for its own self-interest. The alliance between the two major states did little to assuage the anxiety their policies aroused among their smaller neighbours. For decades German statesmen had worried they would be trampled in the conflict between Habsburg and Hohen-zollern; now they worried that a great power condominium might seek its own advantage at their expense. 'All of Germany is an uproar,' wrote Max Franz in June 1792, 'one fears the French less than these two powers, and one generally finds the cure worse than the malady.'[43]

Threatened by an unpredictable new set of forces in the west, afraid of the major powers in the east, too weak to act alone, and too divided to act together, the German states had only one real option: do nothing and hope the crisis would pass. Most governments were not displeased, therefore, when France carefully excluded the Reich from its declaration of war on Austria and Prussia in April 1792. They had no desire to finance an invasion from which they had nothing to gain. Nor, it should be said, were Austria and Prussia anxious for the Reich's military involvement—

---

[42] Gagliardo, *Reich*, p. 148; Braubach, *Sohn*, pp. 207–8.
[43] Aretin, *Reich*, ii. 206, 212; Gagliardo, *Reich*, p. 144.

they did not want to share the spoils of war with unnecessary allies. Desultory efforts to mobilize the Reich during the fall of 1792 remained inconclusive, and, even after the military situation had changed, many western states clung to the hope that they might remain on the sidelines. In February 1793 the *Reichstag* agreed to provide limited financial support for the war effort, but restricted the use of imperial troops to defensive operations. At the same time, within the states themselves people were often reluctant to recognize the crisis into which they had stumbled. The *Stände* of Electoral Cologne, for instance, refused to vote the taxes necessary to support the war. In Zweibrücken, Duke Karl August II was too distracted by the strenuous pleasures of courtly life to be interested in the movement of invading armies, and so ignored the signs of impending catastrophe until French soldiers arrived at his palace gates.[44]

The *Reichstag* finally declared war in March 1793, well after the empire's western territories had been overrun by the enemy. Almost from the start, most governments found the uncertainty and cost of war oppressive. Even those who had learned to hate the French conquerors continued to distrust their Austrian and Prussian allies. Neither the victories of 1793 nor the defeats of 1794 made war seem attractive. Max Franz of Cologne, as loyal an imperial patriot as one could find in the Rhineland, complained that he had barely been able to afford the allies' victorious march into the Low Countries and would surely be bankrupted by their defeat and withdrawal. As the revolutionary armies' momentum increased, defeatism spread. 'It is indescribable how successfully the French advance on all fronts,' wrote a Rhenish statesman in October 1794; 'if things keep up like this, they will be in Vienna by spring time.' The Reich's response to this situation was to seek to end the war as swiftly as possible. In October the elector of Mainz, acting in his capacity as Imperial Chancellor, attained a *Reichstag* majority in favour of his peace proposals. Two months later a similar majority formally requested the emperor to co-operate with the king of Prussia in negotiating an end to the hostilities. Unfortunately, the Reich was as powerless to compel peace as it had been to wage war. The shape of the fighting in the west was not determined by *Reichstag* resolutions but rather by the self-interest of the two major states.[45]

[44] See the eyewitness account in Mannlich, *Rokoko*, pp. 241 ff.
[45] Braubach, *Sohn*, pp. 302 ff., 311.

As we have seen, in the fall of 1794 Frederick William II withdrew from the war and in April 1795 signed the Treaty of Basel with France. The provisions of this treaty showed the degree to which Berlin was willing to undermine the imperial system by sacrificing the smaller states for its own aggrandizement and advantage. With the formation of a neutral zone under its own protection, Prussia directly challenged both the sovereignty of the northern states and the authority of imperial institutions. 'Since Prussia has gone ahead with the truce line,' wrote one observer in August 1795, 'there is no more Reich *in corpore* which can participate in the war against France.' Even more subversive for the Reich were the treaty's other secret provisions. By acknowledging French annexations west of the Rhine and seeking compensation at the expense of German states, Prussia participated in the first stage of a process that would eventually transform the entire structure of central European politics. Once it had begun, this interlocking process of annexation and compensation became a standing invitation to aggression by encouraging states to expand, sweep aside established boundaries, and absorb smaller polities. In this situation, which left the weak at the mercy of the strong, the Reich's ability to restrain its members simply collapsed. 'At the very moment when co-operation is more necessary than ever before,' lamented Max Franz in September 1796, 'each [state] lets itself be driven along its own path by the fear that has conquered all of them, thinking only of the present, not the future. God knows what will come of this.'[46]

As early as the summer of 1795, when the rulers of Hesse-Kassel and Brunswick signed separate peace treaties with the French, fear and greed had led some smaller German states to abandon the imperial war. In August 1796 Baden, Bavaria, and Württemberg all made agreements with France in which the link between French annexations in the Rhineland and German compensation among the ecclesiastical territories was once again established. Meanwhile Austria continued to fight in the Reich's name, but did little to promote co-operation among the German states. The Habsburgs' generals treated their allies with contempt, disregarded their material interests, and exploited their territories. Even before the military disasters of 1797, many imperial patriots regarded Vienna as the Scylla to Berlin's Charybdis. To be sure, Austria, unlike Prussia, did not simply abandon the French war to pursue other

---

[46] Aretin, *Reich*, i. 334; Braubach, *Sohn*, pp. 339–40.

interests; it had been forced to make peace by a victorious enemy just a few days' march from its capital. But the Treaty of Campo Formio, like the Treaty of Basel, clearly displayed its signatories' willingness to sacrifice imperial interests for their own particular advantage. While publicly promising to respect the Reich's integrity, the parties at Campo Formio secretly accepted French annexations along the Rhine—including the occupation of the key fortresses at Mainz, Ehrenbreitstein, and Mannheim—for which Austria was to be compensated with Salzburg and some Bavarian territories.[47]

The Treaty of Campo Formio stipulated that the ultimate fate of the Reich would be decided by direct negotiations between France and imperial representatives. These negotiations began at Rastatt in November 1797 and continued until April 1799. The Rastatt Congress is one of those historical occasions when the paths of many important people cross: Napoleon was there, briefly, as was the poet Hölderlin; Goethe accompanied his duke; Clemens von Metternich came with his father, the chief of the Austrian delegation. The elder Metternich, whom Ritter von Lang described as 'a stately, plump, and polished old German gentleman', tried his best to run the congress according to pre-revolutionary standards. He organized the seventy representatives of the empire according to rank, insisted on proper protocol, gave fancy parties, and presided over the preparation of elaborate memoranda. The small French delegation clearly came from another world: plainly dressed, with unpolished shoes and unpowdered hair, their appearance and manners shocked the fashionable sensibilities of the young Metternich. 'Good God,' he wrote, 'how this nation has changed!' The chief French delegate reminded Lang of a notary in a play, who arrives to write one of the character's last will and testament. Indeed, that was exactly what he was there to do. Calmly, without ceremony or extensive consultation, the French insisted on their territorial claims, which they combined with an offer of compensations from the territories of the ecclesiastical states. With this, Lang noted, 'the signal for plundering had been given'. No wonder the French representatives could barely conceal the contempt they felt for their German counterparts.[48]

As they watched developments at Rastatt, many Germans

[47] There is an excellent analysis of these developments in Aretin, *Vom Deutschen Reich*.

[48] Lang, *Memoiren*, pp. 155 ff. describes the Congress; the quotations are from pp. 164 and 174. Metternich quoted in Srbik, *Metternich*, i. 83 ff.

recognized for the first time just how powerless imperial institutions had become. The Reich's admirers responded with sorrow and anger, thus beginning a prolonged period of mourning that had virtually run its course by the time the empire was formally dissolved seven years later. Joseph Görres, for instance, provided the following bitter obituary:

On 30 December 1797, the day of the transfer of Mainz [to France], at three p.m., the Holy Roman Empire, at the ripe old age of nine hundred and fifty-five years, five months, and twenty-eight days, fully conscious and consoled with all the sacraments, died peacefully and piously as the result of a total paralysis and attendant apoplexy.

To Hegel, who eagerly followed the proceedings from his post in Frankfurt, Rastatt demonstrated that the old world was over. In his first political essay, written sometime during late 1798 and early 1799, Hegel maintained that the Congress deprived German patriots of the hope that reform was possible. 'Germany', as he put the matter in a later version of this essay, 'is no longer a state' because it lacks the power to defend itself. As a result, its members are reduced to insanity, 'which is nothing other than the perfected isolation of the individual from his kind'. Elector Max Franz of Mainz, who had lost his lands and seemed about to lose his sovereign status, was forced to acknowledge that the empire could no longer protect its subjects. Perhaps, he had come to believe, the era of small states was finished and it would be better if Prussia and Austria were to impose on central Europe a solution 'à la polonaise'.[49]

The Rastatt Congress was still in session when France once again declared war on the empire and Austria. Aware of the extent of French ambitions and encouraged by the Austrian armies' early successes, the smaller states participated in the campaign of 1799 with uncharacteristic enthusiasm. The *Reichstag* voted full war credits and, in the summer of 1799, imperial troops even managed to drive a French force under Marshall Augereau back across the Rhine. But, as we know, the German states could not sustain these initial victories. Following the defeats of Marengo and Hohenlinden, Francis II had no choice but to agree to the terms incorporated in the Treaty of Lunéville, which he signed on his own and the Reich's behalf. But, because Francis refused to serve as the Reich's plenipotentiary in the final settlement, the *Reichstag*

[49] Aretin, *Vom Deutschen Reich*, p. 84; Hegel, *Werke*, i. 61; Braubach, *Sohn*, p. 342.

appointed a delegation which deliberated from the summer of 1802 until the following February.

The Imperial Deputation was composed of the elector of Mainz, the Master of the Teutonic Order, and representatives of Bohemia (ruled, of course, by the Habsburgs), Brandenburg (i.e. the king of Prussia), Württemberg, Saxony, Bavaria, Hesse, and Würzburg. The deputation's final report, the *Reichsdeputationshauptschluss*, which was passed by the Reichstag with unprecedented alacrity and proclaimed as law by the emperor on 27 April 1803, runs to some twenty-six closely printed pages in E. R. Huber's collection of constitutional documents. One of the greatest territorial rearrangements in all of European history, the *Hauptschluss* decided the destiny of major polities and tried to settle a bewildering set of claims by scores of lesser rulers. The middle-sized states, which would be of crucial importance for nineteenth-century German history, were given their basic shape; at the same time, the Princes Hohenlohe were awarded six hundred gulden (half to Schillings-fürst, half to Bartenstein) in return for their share in the Rhenish custom duties collected at Boppard. In a single destructive sweep, the number of imperial cities was reduced to six: only Hamburg, Bremen, Lübeck, Frankfurt, Nuremberg, and Augsburg retained their independence, while the rest, together with all their lands, were absorbed by various states. No less dramatic was the damage done to the ecclesiastical territories, of which only three remained: a reconstituted electorate of Mainz, with its headquarters at Regensburg, and the Estates of the Teutonic Order, and of the Order of Malta. The others, from the electorate of Cologne to the tiny Abbey of Guttenzell, were gone forever. On the right bank of the Rhine, three electorates, nineteen bishoprics, and forty-four abbeys, totalling some ten thousand square kilometres with about three million subjects disappeared.[50]

The *Hauptschluss* was written in Regensburg and proclaimed in Vienna, but its source was in Paris, where the future of German Europe was actually determined. Most of those who gained from the reorganization of 1803 were states large enough to negotiate separately with France and thus qualify for the compensation offered by the conquerors in return for their annexations.[51] Prussia, for example, lost some scattered lands west of the Rhine, but

---

[50] Huber, *Dokumente*, i. 1–26. See also the analysis in Huber, i. 42 ff.
[51] For an example, see Rössler's account of Hans Christoph von Gagern's mission to Paris on behalf of Nassau: *Revolution*, pp. 76–7.

gained substantially at the expense of the ecclesiastical states and free cities; in return for 48 *Quadratmeilen* with 127,000 inhabitants, Prussia acquired 234 *Quadratmeilen* with over half a million inhabitants. This land was lost following the Prussian defeat in 1806 but regained in 1815: the *Hauptschluss* anticipated, therefore, the future extension of Berlin's power across the northern arc of central Europe. In the south, the settlement of 1803 confirmed Bavaria's position as the third German power; in return for 255 *Quadratmeilen* and 730,000 subjects, the Wittelsbachs received 290 *Quadratmeilen* and 880,000 people, including the rich lands of the bishops of Würzburg, Bamberg, Freising, Augsburg, and Passau. Württemberg gave up only 7 *Quadratmeilen* and 14,000 people but got 29 *Quadratmeilen* and over one hundred thousand new subjects. Relatively speaking, Baden did even better, for 8 *Quadratmeilen* and 25,000 people, she took over the former bishoprics of Constance, Basel, Strassburg, and Speyer, as well as parts of the Palatinate with Mannheim and Heidelberg, altogether 59 *Quadratmeilen* and 237,000 people. Hesse-Kassel, Hesse–Darmstadt, the dynastic lands of Nassau, Oldenburg, and Hanover also expanded.[52]

That the ecclesiastical territories would be the main victims of the reorganization of 1803 was clear well before the imperial deputation began its work. For decades, these religious polities had been under attack from enlightened Germans, who regarded them as sinks of moral corruption, intellectual backwardness, and political inefficiency. Their vulnerability to the French seemed to confirm that they were hopelessly cut off from the forces of statecraft and philosophy at work in the modern world. States now evidently found it easier to seize church lands if they could claim to be executing the verdict of history and advancing the cause of progress: the monasteries of Bavaria, Count Montgelas wrote in 1802, 'have encouraged the perpetuation of superstition and of the most baneful errors; they have built up obstacles against the spread of enlightened principles, and they have sown suspicion against every institution working for true moral education . . . '.[53] More important, although statesmen like Montgelas were not likely to dwell on the matter, the church was rich, its lands fertile, its

[52] There is a convenient summary of the territorial changes in Huber, i. 46 ff., 67, 77–8.

[53] Epstein, *Genesis*, p. 607. On Montgelas, see below, Ch. 5, sect. i. Peter Wende, *Die geistlichen Staaten und ihre Auflösung im Urteil der zeitgenössischen Publizistik* (Lübeck and Hamburg, 1966), summarizes opinion for and against the ecclesiastical states. Rudolfine von Oer discusses the legal aspects of secularization in Vierhaus (ed.), *Eigentum*.

treasuries filled with precious metals; in short, it was a source of the wealth badly needed by governments to pay for their own bills and to meet the never-ending needs of the French. Against the onslaught of their enemies, the ecclesiastical authorities could construct only the flimsiest of rhetorical barriers. Their defenders insisted that to secularize and absorb these lands would undermine the whole structure of the Reich, compromise the principle of legitimacy, and deprive imperial institutions of their most committed supporters. All these arguments were true, but they did not count for much in the face of the states' political ambition, moral righteousness, and greed.

Secularization significantly weakened Catholicism's political position in German Europe. Among the major states, only Austria and Bavaria had a Catholic majority ruled by a Catholic dynasty. Because the ecclesiastical polities had been so closely connected to the social, cultural, and religious life of German Catholics, their demise had ramifications well beyond the narrowly political realm. By abolishing many of those offices to which young Catholic nobles had so naturally aspired, secularization severed the close ties that bound the church hierarchy to the landed aristocracy. In the place of the courtier–cleric, whose position fused religious and secular authority, the governance of the church passed into the hands of the clergy and the state, each persistently seeking to clarify and control its own sphere of activity. Moreover, secularization undermined many of the church's most active intellectual centres, including those seminaries, universities, and monasteries where the Catholic *Aufklärung* had taken root. This meant that at the same time that Catholicism's political position was weakened, its intellectual resources were diminished, thereby widening the cultural gap between Protestants and Catholics that had seemed to be narrowing in the 1770s and 1780s.[54]

The church's loss was the states' gain, not simply in land and subjects, but also in control over property, organizations, and social relationships. The states had little difficulty occupying church buildings, removing the gold from sacristies, and selling monastic fields. To replace or supervise the church's role in social and cultural life, however, turned out to be much harder. For almost a century, church and state would be engaged in a persistent, costly battle all along the complex institutional frontier that separated the religious from the political world. This battle

---

[54] Morsey, 'Auswirkungen'.

was intensified because the reorganization of 1803 had broken the rough coincidence between denominational and political divisions that had been imposed in the sixteenth century. Most states now had both Catholic and Protestant subjects. Over the course of the century, this confessional mixture would take on a profound political significance as Catholics organized to defend their cultural values and religious institutions from what they regarded as the illegitimate intrusion of outside forces.[55]

According to Article 28 of the *Hauptschluss*, the imperial nobility would continue to exist, although the question of how they were to be compensated for lost territories was postponed indefinitely. For a time the *Reichsadel* seemed to be the last residue of the old imperial order, but everyone knew that its position was extremely precarious. Like the ecclesiastical authorities, the imperial knights had been consistently attacked by enlightened publicists, while their lands were coveted by greedy princes. In the early 1790s the new Prussian administration in Ansbach and Bayreuth had severely limited nobles' rights and privileges. In the west, their estates were battered by the destructive powers of war and revolution. After 1803 the states began to move against the nobles, sometimes by sending troops on to their lands in order to destroy their pretensions of sovereignty. The knights sought protection from the Reich and, in what would turn out to be the last imperial campaign to protect the weak from the strong, the Reich tried to respond. In 1805 the emperor was able to restore the imperial nobility's privileges in Bavaria, where attacks upon them had been particularly brutal and blatant. However, the Austrian defeats at Ulm and Austerlitz removed the last impediments to the nobility's destruction. In January 1806 Napoleon told three of their representatives that he would guarantee their lands as private property but would not protect their special rights and privileges as semi-sovereign seigneurs. Thus, another outpost of *Herrschaft* fell to the expanding sovereignty of the states.[56]

Even during the Reich's last days, when its institutions were under attack on every front, some Germans continued to formulate plans for imperial renewal and reform. Johann Gottfried Pahl, for

---

[55] Huber, i. 51 ff., and the documents in Huber and Huber (eds.), *Staat*, i. Hubert Jedin *et al.*, *Atlas zur Kirchengeschichte. Die christlichen Kirchen in Geschichte und Gegenwart* (Freiburg, 1970), has maps showing the changing religious composition of the states. The best account of this process in English is Chadwick, *Popes*, pp. 494 ff.

[56] Heinrich Müller, *Der letzte Kampf der Reichsritterschaft um ihre Selbstständigkeit (1790–1815)* (Berlin, 1910). See also Vierhaus's essay in Vierhaus (ed.), *Eigentum*.

instance, sent to the negotiators drafting the Treaty of Lunéville a memorandum in which he proposed a reorganization of the Reich into a streamlined, more efficient set of national institutions. A little later Karl von Soden suggested that the old imperial circles be used to consolidate political and military power and thus to protect German diversity. Even a young radical as critical of the Reich as Hegel still used it as the frame within which to think about the future. After Rastatt had convinced him that 'Germany is no longer a state', Hegel could only hope for a conqueror strong enough to prevail against the forces of disunity within the empire, but wise enough to share his power with the people he had united.[57]

While these schemes suggest that the Reich still had a hold over some Germans' political imagination, by the turn of the century the odds against imperial reform were overwhelming. Imperial institutions continued to exist, but they proved incapable of absorbing the massive changes imposed upon them. The Reichstag spent most of its last three years debating how a new system of voting could restore the religious parity so badly disturbed by the disappearance of the ecclesiastical territories. The various *Kreise* were no more effective; only in Swabia did the *Kreistag* hold a brief, turbulent session. North of the truce line, Prussia was busy pursuing its own interests, while the middle-sized states of the south and west were fully occupied trying to digest their new acquisitions. In Vienna, the longstanding tensions between Austrian interests and imperial loyalties had entered the final stage. When Francis II declared himself to be the Hereditary Emperor of Austria in 1804, he hoped to establish a claim to imperial dignity independent of the Reich. And after the defeats of 1805, Austrian statesmen became increasingly convinced that the costs of the old imperial connection outweighed the benefits. In May 1806 Count von Stadion prepared a 'report on the question whether it is advisable to retain the Roman–German crown under current conditions', in which he argued that the crown had no value in itself, but rather was only a means of defending the Habsburgs' own interests. The Reich, therefore, could be abandoned whenever it seemed advantageous to do so.[58] With the emperor quickly backing away from his imperial responsibilities, the Reichstag in disarray, and the other German states absorbed with their own interests, the Reich's only possible ally was France.

[57] In addition to the works by Aretin and Gagliardo (cited above in n.40), see Berney, 'Reichstradition'.
[58] The memorandum is reprinted in Aretin, *Reich*, ii.

In the spring of 1806 Karl von Dalberg, Archbishop–Elector of Regensburg-Aschaffenburg, tried to persuade Napoleon that he should accept the imperial crown. By the time he made this last, desperate effort to save some remnant of the old Reich, Dalberg had established himself as Napoleon's most enthusiastic German supporter. Born in 1744 to a distinguished family of imperial aristocrats, Dalberg's life touched many of the main currents of late-eighteenth-century politics and culture. He had studied law and been a member of the Illuminati, knew Herder, Goethe, and Schiller, was an admirer of Febronius and a highly successful clerical statesman. After taking Holy Orders, he had entered the service of Electoral Mainz in 1772 and then rose steadily to become governor of Erfurt, rector of the University of Würzburg, and finally coadjutor bishop under the Elector Friedrich Karl von Erthal, whose long reign coincided with the last flowering of old-regime culture as well as the crises of the revolution. When Friedrich Karl died in mid-1802, on the eve of his territory's dissolution, Dalberg took his place and was able to save his electoral dignity and his office as imperial Chancellor by arranging the move from Mainz to Regensburg-Aschaffenburg, a territorial unit created for him by the *Hauptschluss*. Fascinated by Napoleon's personality, awed by his power, and persuaded of his good intentions, Dalberg hoped that the French conqueror might recreate a realm 'such as it was under Charlemagne, composed of Italy, France, and Germany'. The southern and western states, he believed, would be better off tied to France than they had been in an empire dominated by Prussia and Austria.[59]

Napoleon evidently considered but finally rejected Dalberg's invitation to assume the Roman crown. Instead, on 12 July 1806, he established the Rhenish Confederation, a league of sixteen states locked into close alliance with France. Napoleon wanted the Confederation to be a buffer between himself and his potential enemies in the east, a set of allies large enough to defend their independence but too small to be a threat to France. In return for their unrestricted loyalty and military assistance to the French imperium, the Rhenish states were given full sovereignty over their own territories, including the property of the formerly independent imperial nobility. To his more important allies, Napoleon also guaranteed new titles (the electors of Bavaria and Württemberg

---

[59] Gagliardo, *Reich*, p. 275. The most recent work on Dalberg is Arnulf Jürgens, *Emmerich von Dalberg zwischen Deutschland und Frankreich* (Stuttgart, 1976).

became kings, the ruler of Baden a grand duke), arranged dynastic ties to his own extended family, and provided a few additional pieces of land. Dalberg, now installed in a principality centred at Frankfurt, was named Prince Primate, Bonaparte's chief spokesman in the Confederation and chairman of the diet that was to decide the details of its future. Article Two of the Confederation charter separated the member states from the Reich and thus forced the imperial abdication announced in Vienna on 6 August.[60]

Eventually twenty-three other states joined the original sixteen members of the Rhenish Confederation. All of the old Reich, with the exception of Prussia, Austria, Danish Holstein, and Swedish Pomerania, now belonged. Some Germans tried to see the Confederation as the Reich's legitimate heir, a source of order and independence for central Europe's small states. Nicholas von Gönner, for instance, a legal scholar and devoted imperial patriot, believed that the Confederation had given Germany 'a better form, without which it would perhaps have become only a province of foreign states'. A significant number of other theorists, with varying degrees of enthusiasm, accepted Napoleon's creation as the new basis for German politics. Anything, these people realized, would be better than the violent great-power rivalries that had disrupted and finally destroyed the imperial system. The Confederation did not, however, fulfil the hopes of its admirers; its diet never met, its collective institutions were never formed. Between the rapacious demands of the French war machine and the relentless struggle of the new states for independent sovereignty, there was not much room for a German common life.[61]

Napoleon's reorganization of central Europe permanently transformed German politics. Of the hundreds of sovereign and semi-sovereign polities in the old Reich, only about forty had survived the maelstrom of defeat, secularization, and annexation. Historians have often viewed this consolidation of power as part of the process of nation building. But, while the map of 1806 may look like a transitional stage between the old regime and the national unification, it is by no means clear that this was the case. The creation of several medium-sized, relatively well-integrated states, ready and willing to preserve their identity, did not make the formation of a nation-state any easier. The settlement of 1806 deserves a place among the few historic turning points in German history not because it represented a tentative step towards a new nation but rather because it was a decisive step away from the traditional political order. In 1806 the heirs of the Reich and *Herrschaft* were the various German states, not some future German nation.

V
Mastering the Revolution

Almost 60 per cent of the German population changed rulers during the revolutionary period. Among them were the inhabitants of Hausen, a village that had once been part of the Habsburgs' western lands and then was given by Napoleon to Frederick of Württemberg in return for his support during the campaign of 1805. To mark the beginning of his rule, Frederick ordered special religious ceremonies to be held throughout his new domain. On 19 January 1806, therefore, the villagers of Hausen gathered to hear Pastor Knoblauch pray for their new monarch:

Francis, He the most excellent emperor, was our father and with childlike love we were loyal to him. . . . Frederick, He the most glorious and merciful father of our Land, will be your father, with care and mercy he will regard you as his children. . . . We have lost one father, God has given us in him, our Frederick, another.

Perhaps the people of Hausen were soothed by the familiar patriarchal imagery of the pastor's speech; perhaps they believed the political world of 1806 was just another version of the old. Like Germans everywhere, however, they would discover that they were now part of a larger world, subject to forces at work far beyond the horizon of their village. Twenty-nine Hausener marched with the Grande Armée into Russia, sixteen—almost two complete age cohorts of the village's young men—did not return. 'Grimmige Kälte und Mangel an Brot übergab uns in Russland dem Todt', reads the sentence above their names in the cemetery chapel.[1]

By 1806 German statesmen had no doubt that they lived in a political era filled with new dangers and opportunities. The military success of the revolution and its Napoleonic heir had left no German state, from Justus Möser's Osnabrück to Frederician Prussia, untouched. Every German government had to discover ways to deal with the expansion of French power, to fulfil its demands, and to withstand its destructive impact. But as the most creative and resourceful Germans recognized, political survival would require more than an ability to endure. To exist in a

[1] Ilien and Jeggle, *Leben*, pp. 40–3.

revolutionary age demanded mastering the revolution itself, acquiring the revolution's power by turning to one's own uses the forces it had unleashed. 'The power of these [revolutionary] principles is so great, so universally recognized and widespread,' wrote Karl von Hardenberg in 1807, 'that a state that does not embrace them must face either their forcible imposition or its own extinction.'[2]

The German states responded to the French threat in many different ways, but their responses all displayed certain common characteristics. First, while the intensity of outside influence varied widely—from the annexed lands in the west to the still autonomous great powers in the east—everywhere pressures from the victorious French armies were decisive in establishing the direction of domestic political development. The costs of war and the burdens of defeat created a set of problems to which all governments had to respond. Second, everywhere these problems played into the hands of a relatively small group of reformers, who operated within the narrow confines of the ruling elite and without strong ties to broader social movements. Most of these reformers were experienced bureaucrats, even if they came from outside the states they served. Imperial nobles like Stein and Stadion, émigrés from other states like Hardenberg and Scharnhorst, aristocrats with European connections like Montgelas were all willing and able to take over in a time of crisis, to exact compliance from reluctant sovereigns, and temporarily to triumph over the longstanding opposition of established élites. The narrowness of the reformers' social base helps to explain the third characteristic they shared: the persistent need to compromise and limit their ambitions. Almost everywhere, established élites, and especially the landed nobility, turned out to be tougher, more resilient, and better able to defend their privileges than many of their enemies had expected. Moreover, every reformist administration also had trouble creating the representative institutions most of them wanted, in large part because these institutions were not supported by the social groups they were designed to serve. In the end, therefore, the reformers' aspirations were never wholly realized, their work remained incomplete, their legacy ambiguous. The reforms that worked best and lasted longest were those most in line with the historical currents at work in German Europe before 1789: the affirmation of

---

[2] Erwin Hölzle, 'Das napoleonische Staatssystem in Deutschland', in Hofmann (ed.), *Entstehung*, p. 270.

state power, the reduction of intervening sovereignties, and the consolidation of bureaucratic rule. Tocqueville's remark that the French revolutionaries 'used the debris of the old order for building up the new' is an even more appropriate description of the German reformers' accomplishments and limitations.[3]

i. NAPOLEONIC GERMANY: 'ALLIES AND VICTIMS'

By the middle of 1807, Albert Sorel once wrote, Napoleon had 'only allies and victims' on the Continent. Sorel might have added that the distinction between them was sometimes very subtle indeed. One indication of Napoleon's hegemony is the fact that when they write about this period, historians usually classify the former lands of the Holy Roman Empire according to their relationship with France: first, the two territorial units directly annexed to the French state, the west bank of the Rhine, occupied since the mid-1790s and subject to French law since 1802, and the land along the north coast taken by Napoleon in 1810; second, the three satellite states established after the victories of 1806, the King-dom of Westphalia, ruled by Napoleon's brother Jerome, the Grand Duchy of Berg, ruled first by the emperor's brother-in-law, Joachim Murat, then by Napoleon himself as regent for his nephew, Prince Louis Napoleon, and the Grand Duchy of Frankfurt, created for the Prince Primate of the Confederation of the Rhine, Karl von Dalberg; third, the medium-sized states in the south and west, of which the most important were Bavaria, Württemberg, Baden, and Hesse-Darmstadt, all greatly enlarged polities grouped around a pre-existing dynastic core and ruled by one of Napoleon's German allies; fourth, a heterogeneous collec-tion of states, mostly small northern territories, which had not been much changed by the process of reorganization but were closely tied to France through their membership in the Rhenish Confedera-tion; and finally, the two major eastern powers, Prussia and Austria, both reduced in size and sometimes allied to France.[4]

---

[3] For further examples of continuity, see the essays in Weis ed., *Reformen*, especially the contribution by Rudolf Vierhaus.

[4] Aretin's *Vam Deutschen Reich* is a fine introduction to the period as a whole. Fehrenbach, *Gesellschaft*, is especially good on legal reform and social change. Surveys of recent scholarship can be found in Weis ed., *Reformen*; Berding and Ullmann eds., *Deutschland*; and Hans Schmitt, 'Germany without Prussia: A Closer Look at the Confederation of the Rhine', *German Studies Review*, 6/1 (1983), 9–39. H. A. L. Fisher's *Studies in Napoleonic Statesmanship* (Oxford, 1903) is a classic, but now quite out of date.

MAP 2. Central Europe in 1806

That France should demand economic and military support from its allies and victims was only to be expected. Victorious powers had rarely done otherwise: why else should victory be preferable to defeat? What differed in the present case was not the fact of exploitation but its magnitude and duration. The changes in the scale of war discussed in the preceding chapter meant that the demands imposed by the victor on the vanquished had grown significantly. During the 1790s for instance, the Rhineland had been expected to support an occupying force that, together with its dependents, totalled about a quarter of a million people. The charter establishing the Rhenish Confederation contained a detailed list of military services that France's allies were required to provide in the case of war. Following their defeats in 1805 and 1807, Austria and Prussia were saddled with enormous indemnities; Prussia was also expected to pay over two hundred million francs to support the occupation of its lands by French troops. Finally, in November 1806 Napoleon issued a decree from occupied Berlin that established the so-called 'Continental System'. Essentially this intensified the economic policies France had pursued for more than a decade: an anti-British commercial blockade and an attempt to subordinate the entire European economy to the needs of the French military machine.

Almost as important as these material demands were the pressures for political conformity imposed first by the revolutionary governments and then by Napoleon. Unlike most conquerors in European history, the French were not content to consolidate their conquests with fortresses and treaties. In addition to these traditional military and diplomatic measures, they wanted to impose or encourage institutional changes that would render their allies and victims more like themselves. In a famous declaration of 15 December 1792, the National Convention instructed its newly victorious troops to proclaim 'in the name of the French nation, the sovereignty of the people, the suppression of all established authorities . . . and generally of all privileges', thereby fusing military conquest and political revolution. Napoleon abandoned the democratic ideals of 1792, but retained the belief that military alliances should be based on political compatibility: he insisted, therefore, that the Code Napoleon be introduced into the satellite states and encouraged its adoption by his other allies in the Rhenish Confederation. This blurring of the distinction between foreign and domestic politics, surely one of the revolutionary era's most enduring and dangerous legacies, is a key to understanding the issues considered in this chapter.[5]

From the start, France brought to its conquered German territory promises of reform and emancipation as well as demands for material and military support. In the early days of the National Convention, the French government and a few of its German admirers may have thought that emancipation and support were inextricably linked, the one encouraging and reinforced by the other. But before long it was clear that the two dimensions of French occupation policy were not easily reconciled: neither the attitude of the German population nor the expanding requirements of the French military machine made it possible for the revolutionary armies to play the role of liberators, who could freely join with the peoples of Europe against their reactionary enemies. The emancipatory element was never completely lost; almost everywhere, the French did sponsor reforms. But the threat and often the reality of coercive violence were also ever-present, deflecting the impact of liberation, mitigating the effect of reform, and poisoning the relationship between ruler and ruled. Nowhere were the tensions between emancipation and exploitation more apparent than in the Rhineland, the area conquered first and held longest by the revolutionary forces.

Following its victories in late 1792, the French army occupied part of the Rhine, was forced to withdraw in 1793, returned the next year, and finally consolidated its hold on the area with the provisions forced upon Austria and the Reich at Campo Formio and Lunéville.[6] From then until 1814, France ruled about one million former subjects of the old imperial states, including the archbishoprics of Cologne, Trier, and Mainz, the bishoprics of Worms and Speyer, the electorate of the Palatinate, the duchies of Cleves, Geldern, Jülich, Simmern, and Zweibrücken, the counties of Sponheim and Saarbrücken, the free cities of Aachen, Cologne, Worms, and Speyer, and various other small entities—in short, everything to the west of a line running along the river from Cleves in the north to the Swiss frontier. Even before the consolidation of

---

[5] The declaration is quoted in Jacques Godechot, *La Grande Nation. L'Expansion révolutionnaire de la France dans le monde, 1789–1799* (Paris, 1956), ii. 702, and analysed in Blanning, *Revolution*, pp. 64–5.

[6] Blanning, *Revolution*, is the standard account, but is perhaps too harshly critical of France. Hansen (ed.), *Quellen* is an invaluable collection of source materials. See also Roger Dufraisse, 'Das Napoleonische Deutschland. Stand und Probleme der Forschung unter besonderer Berücksichtigung der linksrheinischen Gebiete', *GuG* 6/4 (1980), 468–96, J. Hashagen, *Das Rheinland unter der französischen Herrschaft* (Bonn, 1908).

its military position in 1797, the revolutionary government sought to do more than merely occupy these rich lands. Both ideological fervour and practical necessity required changes in the political and social structure. Eventually seigneurial obligations were ended, tithes and special privileges abolished, guilds dismantled and freedom of occupation introduced, the clergy reorganized according to French civil law, church lands secularized and sold, tolls and fees along the river discontinued, and tariff boundaries redrawn. In 1804 the Code Napoleon was applied to the Rhenish lands, which were now reorganized into four departments: Donnersberg, Saar, Rhine-Mosel, and Roer. Despite these transformations, lines of continuity did remain. The nobility were stripped of their legal privileges but not of their social existence; many nobles held on to their property, some even improved their economic position by buying up church lands. A surprisingly large proportion of the administration also survived. In 1800 more than half of the nine hundred judicial and civil officials in the four French departments had held some kind of a post before the invasion; no more than 15 per cent of the administration and only a handful of judges and notaries came from outside the region.[7]

Some Rhinelanders prospered under French rule. People with capital could buy the church lands at bargain prices. Certain industries, such as metal-working in the Eifel and textile manufacturing around Aachen and Krefeld, improved their market position by becoming part of France and thus protected from traditional competition. A few peasants in the short run and almost all in the long run benefited from the destruction of seigneurialism. In the cities, a new élite of manufacturers, lawyers, publicists, and civil servants began to fill the social, political, and cultural vacuum left by the forced removal of the old regime courts and their aristocratic appendages. These gains, however, came at a very high price. The guilds bitterly regretted their lost privileges, the purveyors of luxury goods mourned their missing customers, some firms languished without the protection of the Reich's customs barriers, others lost essential markets or sources of raw material. More important, the cost of the military occupation—and frequently the behaviour of the occupying troops—fuelled anti-French feelings.

[7] Karl-Georg Faber, 'Verwaltungs-und Justizbeamte auf dem linken Rheinufer während der französischen Herrschaft. Eine personengeschichtliche Studie', in Max Braubach *et al.* (eds)., *Aus Geschichte und Landeskunde (Franz Steinbach Festschrift)* (Bonn, 1960), 350–88. On economic developments in the Rhineland, see François Crouzet, 'Wars, Blockade, and Economic Change in Europe, 1792–1815', *JEH* 24 (1964), 567–88.

Townsmen were forced to find room for unruly soldiers in their houses. Peasants discovered that what they had once paid to their lords now went to support the French army. Revolutionary religious policy was also an important source of animosity. In 1793, for instance, some citizens of Aachen rejected the oath required by the French republic, swearing instead 'to maintain the Roman apostolic religion in all its purity and to support with all our power, the sovereignty, freedom and welfare of the people of Aachen'. Devout Protestants and Catholics resisted or evaded efforts to regulate their worship; monks refused to vacate their cloisters, the faithful marched in illegal processions, and priests led congregations in defiance of anti-clerical legislation.[8]

In 1792 and 1793 some Rhinelanders had welcomed the French as liberators. The men in the Jacobin Club of Mainz, so carefully studied by Heinrich Scheel, eagerly joined what they hoped would be a European democratic revolution. But as one of the best of them, Georg Forster, recognized, they represented 'a tiny little group', surrounded by an indifferent or hostile population. In time, many of the revolution's most passionate supporters had their doubts about French rule. Other Rhinelanders were consistently hostile, sometimes violently opposed—even though the area was never the scene of the guerrilla fighting against the occupation which broke out in the Tirol and Spain. The majority of the population, however, was neither enthusiastic in its support nor violent in its opposition. Especially when it seemed that the French were there to stay, most people tried to survive under the new regime just as they had under the old; and, given the persistent problems of subsistence and the new demands of the occupation, survival was difficult enough. As one careful student of the popular mood has concluded, 'the relative domestic tranquillity [along the Rhine] was not the product not of broad, active acceptance but rather of passivity and conformity—much as it had been in the last decades of the old regime'.[9]

[8] Hansen (ed.), *Quellen*, ii. 702, n. 2.

[9] Hansgeorg Molitor, *Vom Untertan zum Administré: Studien zur französischen Herrschaft und zum Verhalten der Bevölkerung im Rhein-Mosel-Raum von den Revolutionskriegen bis zum Ende der napoleonischen Zeit* (Mainz, 1980), 212. Historical debates over German Jacobinism, once poisoned by nationalist animosities, are now enmeshed in ideological anatagonisms. Some scholars have been so eager to establish a democratic tradition in Germany that they have greatly overestimated the extent and quality of German Jacobinism. The most industrious spokesman for this position is Walter Grab, whose views can be found in *Ein Volk muss seine Freiheit selbst erobern:Zur Geschichte der deutschen Jakobiner* (Frankfurt, 1984). For a Skeptical review of Grab and the other 'Jacobins', see T. C. W. Blanning, 'German Jacobins

The other major set of annexations by the French state in the German lands was undertaken during the final stages of imperial glory and thus had a very different tone and character from the ideologically-charged and promise-laden conquests along the Rhine. In 1810, as he gathered his resources for a decisive battle against Russia on land and England at sea, Napoleon took over a series of states that extended along the northern littoral from the mouth of the Rhine, connecting a corridor to Lübeck in the east and reaching south to contain Münster, Osnabrück, and Lüneburg. This move was an attempt to consolidate French control over these important commercial centres, buttress sagging finances within the empire, and police the exclusion of English goods from European ports. Hardest hit by annexation were Hamburg, Bremen, and Lübeck, which had already suffered from the combined effects of an English blockade and French harassment. Throughout 1811 a commission of three leading French officials, including Davout, Napoleon's most austere and uncompromising marshal, supervised the destruction of local institutions and the imposition of Napoleonic law and administration. By this time, the exploitative face of French policy was unmistakable. Under Davout, the Hansa towns were deprived of their old institutions, without being allowed to become full members of the French economy.[10]

Although they were nominally autonomous, the Grand Duchy of Berg, the Grand Duchy of Frankfurt, and the Kingdom of Westphalia were also products of Napoleon's hegemony and instruments of his direct control over German territory. Of the three satellites, Westphalia deserves our particular attention, because of its size (in 1807 it was roughly as large as post-Tilsit Prussia) and its special role as a model state.

Napoleon created the Kingdom of Westphalia, from territories formerly held by Prussia, Hanover, and a dozen smaller states, in order to anchor the Rhenish Confederation's northern flank.[11] Always eager to find gainful employment for his large family, the emperor made his younger brother Jerome king of the new state. Jerome was twenty-three years old in 1807; he had spent the past

---

and the French Revolution', in R. Porter and M. Teich (eds.), *The Enlightenment in National Context* (Cambridge, 1980). In addition to Hansen's sources cited in n.8, see Heinrich Scheel (ed.), *Die Mainzer Republik* (2 vols.; Berlin, 1975–81), which reprints the protocols of the Jacobin Club and the Rhenish National Convention of 1792 and 1793.

[10] See the literature on Hamburg, cited above, Ch. 2, sect. iii, n. 57.
[11] Berding, *Herrschafts-und Gesellschaftspolitik*, is the best account.

decade in the relentless and reckless pursuit of adventure, military glory, and beautiful women—not necessarily in that order. By the time he ascended the Westphalian throne, he had shed his first wife, a young lady from Baltimore, Maryland, and had done his part to consolidate the Napoleonic alliance system by marrying Princess Katharina of Württemberg. Considering his character and experience, Jerome turned out to be a better king than might have been expected. Always loose-living and unpredictable, he could also be generous, brave, and shrewd. Many of his subjects seem to have regarded him with amused affection. His reign, however, was brief, turbulent, and unhappy. After the Austrians were defeated in 1809, Westphalia expanded to the north, then contracted again after the annexations of 1810. By 1812 there were rumours that the emperor would force Jerome to abdicate, perhaps in order to become king of a new Polish state recreated from lands taken from Russia. But within a year the entire French imperium had begun to unravel; Cossacks had penetrated Westphalian lands from the east, Swedish troops from the north. When Napoleon retreated across the Rhine following the battle of Leipzig in October 1813, the kingdom, like the other French satellites, sank without a trace. Unlike his realm, Jerome himself was a survivor. He lived until 1860, long enough to enjoy the reign of another Bonaparte.

Characteristically, Napoleon brought to Westphalia not only his tawdry dynastic ambitions but also a profound belief in the political superiority of the French system. He wanted the kingdom to be a model state, a bridgehead for the moral conquest of central Europe. Westphalia was, as an official of the new regime declared, a state without a past, 'a creation, like the universe itself, in which the creator, turns primary materials into a finished object'. The kingdom's institutions were based on the first constitution in German history, issued by decree in November 1807, which embodied the emancipatory promises of the revolutionary age: civil equality and religious liberty, the abolition of guilds, serfdom, and aristocratic privilege, and the introduction of the French legal code, open courts, and trial by jury. With an efficient administration, a free society, and a rational polity, Westphalia was supposed to be a stable and prosperous state, loyal to the Bonapartes and willing to support the further extension of their power. 'What nation would want to return to arbitrary Prussian rule', the emperor wrote to his royal brother, 'after it has enjoyed the benefits of a wise and liberal administration. The peoples of Germany, France, Italy, and Spain demand civil equality and liberal ideas.'[12] Unfortunately, when equality and liberalism were incompatible with the demands of French foreign policy, they had to be qualified or abandoned. Thus the representative institutions promised by the constitution met only twice and had little significance. Military power and bureaucratic control, not political participation and civil liberties, were the true hallmarks of the regime. Instead of the promised prosperity, the people of Westphalia confronted tax collectors who had to raise money to pay for military adventures, recruiters who extracted from them more soldiers per capita than anywhere else in Europe, and greedy politicians and soldiers who took over confiscated land as rewards for their services to France. The absence of a past, presented as an opportunity for liberation in 1807, swiftly became an excuse for manipulation and exploitation.

The way in which reformist impulses were deflected by other considerations can be seen with particular clarity in the kingdom's agrarian policy. A royal decree of January 1808 lifted some of the peasants' heaviest seigneurial obligations and gave them the right to own land, move freely, and educate their children as they wished. These reforms, however, altered the system of *Grundherrschaft* without destroying it: specific services were not abolished but could be replaced by cash payments; the settlement of debts, as well as questions about land use, fees, and interest payments, was left to the lord to decide. In short, while peasants were free to move—or to be removed—from the land, their masters were equally free to manipulate their residual privileges to full advantage. Moreover, when Napoleon handed out large parcels of land to his supporters, he granted them tax exemptions and other special privileges, which further increased the burdens and restricted the rights of many peasants. As a result, the agrarian structure in Westphalia, in contrast to that on the west bank of the Rhine, survived the revolution relatively unscathed. In rural policy, and in many other aspects of Westphalian reform, we are struck by a distance between aspiration and accomplishment that can, to some degree, be found throughout Napoleonic Germany. If Jerome's short-lived kingdom was a model for the other German states, it was more because of its contradictions and limitations than its achievements.[13]

The largest and most important of the Confederation's newly enlarged states was Bavaria. As we saw in Chapter 1, during the

[12] Ibid. 20; Fehrenbach, *Gesellschaft*, p. 16.
[13] In addition to the works by Berding and Fehrenbach just cited, see Fehrenbach's summary article, 'Reformen', especially pp. 290 ff.

last third of the eighteenth century uncertainties surrounding the Wittelsbachs' succession had encouraged the Habsburgs to consider trading their own possessions in the Low Countries for Bavaria. The French conquest of the Netherlands finally put an end to this project, but since the Elector Karl Theodor remained without an heir, the fate of the Wittelsbachs' lands was still in doubt. After Karl Theodor's death in 1799, his cousin, Max Joseph of Zweibrücken managed to make good his claim to the family territory. The new elector clearly saw that the future belonged to France: 'I ask you', he told the French representative at the outset of his reign, 'to communicate to the Directory that they have no more loyal friend than I. On the occasion of every French victory, I feel like a Frenchman.' Over the next few years Max Joseph profited handsomely from his friendship with Paris. Between 1803 and 1810 he acquired the ecclesiastical states of Augsburg, Bamberg, Eichstädt, Freising, Passau, and Regensburg, the cities of Augsburg, Lindau, Nördlingen, Nürnberg, Regensburg, and Rothenburg, the counties of Ansbach and Bayreuth, and a variety of smaller principalities. These acquisitions enabled the Wittelsbachs to consolidate and extend the core of Electoral Bavaria from the Alps to the Main River. In 1806 Bavaria became a kingdom, Max Joseph its first king.[14]

Whereas Bavaria had long been a significant, if never quite first-rate power, Baden's rise from the ranks of minor polities was rapid and without precedent. In 1771 Margrave Karl Frederick of Baden-Durlach inherited the lands of his family's Catholic branch and thus added Baden-Baden to his domain. Ruling from Karlsruhe, whose carefully planned streets symbolized his taste for order and control, Karl Frederick had established a reputation for administrative efficiency and enlightenment. But his lands, which stretched on a north-south axis along the Reich's western frontiers, were especially vulnerable to the expansion of French power after 1793. Fortunately, Baden had an extraordinarily effective representative in Paris, Freiherr Sigismund von Reitzenstein, a young career civil servant who managed to link his state to France's rising fortunes. Under Reitzenstein's leadership, Baden made the largest gains of any German state, adding the Austrian Breisgau, the principalities of Fürstenberg, Leiningen, and Löwenstein-Werthelm, the parts of

---

[14] The origins and character of the Wittelsbachs are discussed in Gollwitzer's fine biography of *Ludwig I.* On state-building, see Aretin, *Bayerns*; Waeser Demel, *Der Bayerische Staatsabsolutismus, 1806/08–1817: Staats-und gesellschaftspolitische Motivationen und Hintergründe der Reformära in der ersten Phase des Königreichs Bayern* (Munich, 1983).

the Palatinate and the bishopric of Strasburg that were east of the Rhine, the bishopric of Constance, the abbey of St Blasien, and the cities of Offenburg, Gengenbach, and Zell. Now a grand duke, Karl Frederick ruled a string of territories stretching from Lake Constance to the Main. The slender shape of his realm reflected less the character of its dynastic core than Napoleon's desire to have no more than a thin territorial membrane between France and the strategically significant routes to the east.[15]

Eighteenth-century Württemberg, the reader will recall, had not followed the German states' characteristic path towards bureaucratic absolutism but rather had adhered to a complex compromise in which the *Stände* preserved an important share of power. During his long and stormy reign, Duke Karl Eugen had challenged, thwarted, raged against, but finally accepted the necessity of co-operating with the *Stände*. His brothers, whose two brief reigns followed his own, did nothing to disrupt the constitutional settlement. But when Frederick II became duke in 1797, the old order was threatened by both the French army and a group of radicals whose Reform Party wanted to extend the power of the *Stände*. Had France aided the reformers, politics in Württemberg might have been transformed; instead, Frederick was able to use France's support to purge the government, put down the divided and uncertain opposition, and move his state towards administrative centralization. Like the rulers of Bavaria and Baden, the duke expanded his lands, annexing the former Austrian enclaves in Swabia, together with those free cities, counties, and other small entities that had once given the fragmented political landscape of the south-west its distinctive character. Neither in these new lands nor in the old dynastic core did Duke—and, after 1806, King—Frederick allow the *Stände* to play their traditional role. Together with so much else from traditional central Europe, Württemberg's 'gutes altes Recht' did not survive the revolutionary upheaval.[16]

With the exception of Frederick's Württemberg, in most of the Rhenish Confederation political initiative was retained by civil servants who sometimes had to act without their monarch's full support or approval. Among these bureaucratic reformers, Count Maximilian Montgelas deserves our particular attention, not simply because of his importance for the evolution of modern

[15] Becker *et al.* (eds.), *Geschichte*; Lee, *Politics*. On the historical background, see Helen Liebel, *Enlightened Bureaucracy versus Enlightened Despotism in Baden, 1750–1792* (Philadelphia, 1965).

[16] E. Hölzle, *Württemberg im Zeitalter Napoleons und der deutschen Erhebung* (Stuttgart and Berlin, 1937).

Bavaria but also because his career so clearly illustrates the forces at work in the lives of many contemporary statesmen. Montgelas was born in 1759 and thus belonged to that key generation of leaders who were old enough to have some political experience before 1789 but young enough to grasp the extraordinary opportunities offered by the revolutionary era. Like Reitzenstein, Metternich, Stein, Gagern, and many others, Montgelas came from an aristocratic family with connections beyond the borders of any single state. His ancestors were French-speaking landowners from Savoy, his father was a soldier who fought for both the Habsburgs and Wittelsbachs. Reared in the Frenchified atmosphere of the courts, Montgelas did not learn to write correct German until the 1780s. After attending schools in Nancy and Strasburg, he entered the Bavarian bureaucracy and rose rapidly through the ranks until his membership in the Illuminati aroused the suspicion and anger of his prince, Elector Karl Theodor. As a result, Montgelas transferred to the service of the duke of Zweibrücken, Karl Theodor's presumptive heir. At Zweibrücken, he enjoyed the life of the court so vividly described in Mannlich's memoirs and became an effective administrator and accomplished courtier. A favourite of the duke, Montgelas returned to Munich in his entourage when Max Joseph inherited the Wittelsbach lands in 1799.[17]

Montgelas had the tastes and manners of a courtier, but the values and political instincts of an enlightened bureaucrat. His loyalty to what he called 'ma patrie' was distinct from his affection for the prince and his devotion to the dynasty. 'Ma patrie' was more than a collection of dynastic lands, gradually acquired by a ruling family through the fortunes of war or the accidents of birth and death. Montgelas had no difficulty, therefore, writing off the Wittelsbachs' Rhenish possessions that had to be ceded to France. Nor was his fatherland the product of historical traditions, such as those which Bavaria's official historians tried to create after the formation of the kingdom in 1806. A man like Montgelas was not much impressed by arguments that legitimized the Wittelsbachs through alleged links to Charlemagne. A true state, he believed, was a stable set of institutions, a cohesive polity to which citizens— Staatsbürger—were joined by bonds of loyalty and self-interest, what one official called Nationalgeist and Nationalinteresse. In the extraordinary situation created by the Napoleonic conquests, the need for such institutions acquired a new urgency; if a state like Bavaria was to survive at all, it had to be strong enough to integrate

[17] Weis, Montgelas, is the standard biography.

its new acquisitions, to absorb their resources, and to create the basis for a common future. Enlightened, centralized administration might have been an available option under the old regime, but, to Montgelas and his counterparts in the other newly enlarged states of the south and west, it was an unavoidable necessity.[18]

Without dynastic loyalties, common religious institutions, or historical traditions these states had to base their legitimacy on new foundations. Following the example of both eighteenth-century absolutists and the French conquerors, the *Rheinbund* states sought such foundations in constitutions and legal codes. In May 1808, for example, King Max Joseph issued a constitution for Bavaria, which the French ambassador praised as 'the first of its kind' in Europe, because it was based on France's example but formulated without its direct influence. King Frederick of Württemberg formally—and illegally—abrogated the old corporate constitution in December 1805 and issued a manifesto declaring the old and new parts of his territory to be a single state. Baden, the least integrated of the states and the one most susceptible to French influence, adopted the Code Napoleon, which, in a translated and slightly amended form, remained the basis for Badenese law from 1809 until 1900. The aim of all these various constitutions, decrees, and codes was to clear away the intervening loyalties and jurisdictions separating citizen and state, and thus, in the words of a constitutional draft from Baden, 'tighten the knot in the bonds between the ruler and his citizens'. In the long run, most reformers hoped that the constitutional order could be enhanced with representative institutions, such as those called for in the Bavarian constitution of 1808. But in Bavaria, as in the 'model kingdom' of Westphalia, the parliament was of no real importance. Throughout the Rhenish Confederation, innovation was not the product of public participation; it was carried out by, and often for, civil servants. As Ernst Rudolf Huber has rightly noted, 'State-building in the south German lands was an explicitly bureaucratic achievement, a process of administrative integration.' Everywhere, therefore, the first step towards a reform of the state was reform of the administrative apparatus.[19]

[18] For efforts to build an alternative source of legitimacy, see Ferdinand Seibt, 'Die bayerische 'Reichshistoriographie' und die Ideologie des deutschen National-staats, 1806–1918', in Karl Bosl (ed.), *Gesellschaft, Staat, Kultur in Bayerns Geschichte: Max Spindler zum 70. Geburtstag* (Munich, 1965).

[19] The quotations are from Möckl, 'Konstitution', p. 152; Fehrenbach, 'Reformen', p. 296; Huber, i. 316–17. For more on the Bavarian constitution, see Möckl's *Staat*. Franz-Ludwig Knemeyer surveys the administrative reforms in *Regierungs-und Verwaltungsreformen in Deutschland zum Beginn des 19. Jahrhunderts* (Cologne and Berlin, 1970).

Montgelas had recognized the importance of administrative reorganization even before he returned to Munich as Max Joseph's chief adviser. 'One of the most serious weaknesses of the Bavarian administration', he wrote in a memorandum to the duke in September 1796, 'is the defective organization of the ministries.' Soon after taking power in 1799, Montgelas began to replace the regionally rooted administrative bodies with four (later five) ministries that had functionally divided responsibilities for the entire state. Over the next several years, he and his colleagues extended the principle of centralized administration into local government and at the same time encouraged the development of a professionally trained, honest, and hard-working cadre of officials. In place of poorly-paid, ill-trained favourites who struggled for influence, accepted bribes, and wallowed in incompetence, the reformers wanted an orderly and efficient administration directed towards clearly defined tasks and staffed by the most talented men available.[20]

Similar efforts were made in the other *Mittelstaaten*. Johann Friedrich Brauer, a leading Badenese official since the 1790s, was responsible for a series of reform edicts issued by the grand duke in 1803 and 1807–09. But since Brauer lacked Montgelas's vision, energy, and drive—qualities all the more necessary in a state as fragile and overburdened as Baden—it was only after Reitzenstein began to play a central role in Karlsruhe in May 1809 that the situation significantly improved. Reitzenstein surrounded himself with tough, ambitious men who shared his commitment to creating a single, integrated state with a functionally organized government. In the place of the four provinces with which Brauer had tried to keep regional traditions alive, Reitzenstein divided the state into ten circles, comparable to French departments, each of which was placed under a director with almost complete control over his subordinates.[21]

In Württemberg, the struggle for administrative centralization was shaped by the fact that the prince, rather than a group of civil servants, played the leading role. In Stuttgart, therefore, the central ministries did not have the same weight that they acquired in Munich and Karlsruhe; the king and his immediate advisors always retained the final say. But, away from the center, administrative reform in Württemberg followed a familiar pattern; the state was divided into twelve units, which were defined without regard to

[20] Weis, *Montgelas*, p. 224. See also Wunder, *Privilegierung*.
[21] The best account of this is Lee, *Politics*.

regional traditions or social character and ruled by *Landvögte*, whose power was comparable to the Bavarian *Generalkommissare* and Badenese *Kreisdirectoren*.[22]

Throughout the Confederation, as in the centralizing polities of the old regime, administrative reform was inseparable from the state's fiscal needs, which were now greatly increased by the demands of the French and the costs of political consolidation. The Bavarian public debt was nearly 120 million gulden in 1811; the Badenese, eight million in 1806, eighteen million twelve years later. To meet their expenses, states needed reliable tax records and honest tax collectors, an orderly budgetary process, and legally defined, commercially effective sources of credit. Frequently, the changes introduced in central and local administration were the means to these ends: to inventory and extract social resources required effective local institutions, to regulate spending and expand income demanded efficient policy-making, to write and market bonds presupposed a loyal and confident group of buyers. Furthermore, reformers recognized that their financial needs were ultimately tied to the economic prosperity of their lands, another assumption of cameralist theory carried over and intensified during the critical years of Napoleonic hegemony. The Rhenish states, therefore, tried to further both economic growth and political integration by dismantling internal customs barriers, limiting the restrictive power of traditional corporations, and encouraging productive and innovative enterprises.[23]

Financial security, like political integration, involved the states in a series of struggles with a variety of corporate institutions that wanted to protect their autonomy. Like advocates of pre-revolutionary bureaucratic reform, Montgelas and the other reformers believed that a state had to be sovereign, which one contemporary defined as 'tolerating no competing state within itself'. Even the concept of *state*, this writer continued, 'excludes every independent association, every alien purpose, every inter-mediate authority'.[24]

Throughout the south, the most formidable of these competing institutions was the Catholic Church. Tensions between church and state were nothing new: as we know, the expansion of bureaucratic power in the eighteenth century had triggered bitter

[22] Wunder, *Privilegierung*.

[23] For a general introduction to these issues, see Obenaus, 'Finanzkrise'; Ullmann, 'Schulden'. Additional material can be found in the articles in Berding and Ullmann (eds.), *Deutschland*.

[24] Weinacht, *Staat*, p. 193.

struggles over ecclesiastical property and jurisdictions. Writing in 1796, Montgelas extended the ambitions of the enlightened states by calling for a ministry of religious affairs that could affirm 'the rights of the prince over the Catholic and Protestant clergy'. This must include, Montgelas argued, 'the direction over hospitals, almshouses, boarding schools, and other pious institutions, a re-examination of the accounts of churches and abbeys, and the supervision over the administration and use of the clergy's wealth'. Montgelas had already begun to put these measures into effect when Napoleon's territorial reorganization transformed Catholicism's political position. After 1804 the new states had to absorb the territories once ruled by ecclesiastical authorities; at the same time, they had to establish the legal and institutional means to deal with various confessions. Bavaria, for instance, added to its traditionally Catholic core some important Protestant lands in Franconia, while in Baden a Protestant dynasty and administration found themselves governing a majority of Catholic citizens. Secularization thus became a necessity.[25]

A special dimension of the state's religious policy was the issue of Jewish emancipation. This also was not a new problem: since the 1770s enlightenment ideas, as well as changes in Jews' social and economic position, had led some Germans to argue that this minority's legal position should be revised. Before 1789, however, not much had happened. Even Joseph II's famous edict of 1782 had had quite limited practical consequences. After 1806, however, the German states could not easily avoid the problem. Confronted by a tangle of existing laws on Jews within their newly acquired lands, aware of the possible economic advantages of emancipation, and committed to the creation of a secular state based on civil equality, the reformers had every reason to add Jewish emancipation to their agenda of necessary changes. But hostility towards Jews was much too deeply rooted in German culture and society for equality to be so easily achieved. Only in the Rhenish lands annexed to France and in the satellite states of Berg and Westphalia was full emancipation introduced, and even here it was then qualified by Napoleon's restrictive decree of March 1808. Among the German states, the most progressive measures were passed in Baden, but

---

[25] Weis, 'Montgelas', pp. 249–50. Huber, i. 51 ff., has a clear and concise analysis of secularization. See also Chadwick, *Popes*, pp. 505 ff.; for a detailed case study, see Harm Klueting, *Die Säkularisation im Herzogtum Westfalen 1802–1834* (Vienna, 1980).

they still stopped short of guaranteeing full civil equality. In 1813 Bavaria, which had excluded Jews entirely before its expansion, passed a law that granted Jews state citizenship but retained some important restrictions on their activity. With a few minor exceptions, the other states took even longer to come to terms with the 'Jewish question'.[26]

No such delay and equivocation was possible in the state's relationship to the Catholic Church. Article Sixty-three of the *Reichsdeputationshauptschluss*, which supposedly guaranteed church property, had expressly excluded from its protection the property of formerly independent ecclesiastical territories, religious orders, and those charitable foundations that had passed from religious to civil jurisdiction. After 1803 all of the southern and western states passed edicts affirming their right not simply to the church's authority but also to its property. Officials moved in and assumed control over bishoprics, abbeys, and cloisters. Monastic lands were either confiscated or sold. Monks and nuns were expelled from their communities and, if possible, directed to some other form of spiritual or charitable activity. On occasion, art objects and precious metals were auctioned off; vestments, which seemed to have little practical value, were sold at absurdly low prices. Tons of books and manuscripts were carted away to become the core of new, state-run libraries. Often this happened without difficulty, since many religious institutions were insignificant communities, composed of a few nuns or monks living in pious squalor. But at times the arrival of the state's representatives provoked protests, even violence; when Württemberg officials took over the lands of the Grand Master of the Teutonic Order, for instance, people living nearby resisted and eventually had to be subdued by government troops. Generally speaking, Catholic regimes were harsher than Protestants and none was harsher than Montgelas's in Bavaria, where the church had owned vast tracts of agricultural land, as well as mills, breweries, and other enterprises. Unfortunately, neither Bavaria nor the other states profited greatly from secularization; they put too much land on the market at once, exhausted the available capital, and drove down prices. In the long run, perhaps the most valuable acquisition turned out to be the forest land which the states usually did not try to sell; even today, one-third of

---

[26] The standard works on emancipation during this period are by Rürup: 'Judenemanzipation', *Emanzipation*, and 'Kontinuität' See also Berding, 'Emanzipation'.

Bavaria's state forests were origanally ecclesiastical lands acquired during the Napoleonic era.[27]

In addition to exerting their control over the church, the states also moved against the organs of municipal self-government. Here too political and fiscal considerations worked together: to tax the cities, they had to be governed, to pay the cost of government, they had to be taxed. In the case of the former free imperial cities, the imposition of state power meant destroying institutions that had been independent for centuries. Consider, for example, the case of Augsburg, a sovereign city-state with a glorious past, but a conflict-ridden present and uncertain future. Although vigorous diplomacy and generous bribes enabled Augsburg to keep its independence in 1803, the city found itself locked in an expensive and apparently endless conflict with Bavaria, which had taken over the urban properties of the bishop of Augsburg along with the rest of his secularized territories. By the time Bavarian troops occupied Augsburg in December 1805, therefore, many of its citizens had come to recognize that their independence was a costly anachronism. Swiftly, Montgelas' officials took over the city's public business and destroyed the ancient constitution with all its attendant restraints, privileges, and liberties. No longer an island of separate sovereignty. Augsburg, together with *Reichsstädte* all over central Europe, became a city like any other.[28]

States had an easier time establishing control in a city like Augsburg, with its clearly articulated institutions and well-defined political alignments, than they did in the smaller, more cohesive home towns. Soon after scores of these towns lost their sovereignty in 1803, various governments issued edicts designed to limit the autonomy of all urban communities. The home towns' cherished and idiosyncratic politics, hallowed by custom and sustained by collective memory, thus came under assault from centrally appointed officials, who sought to apply, uniform laws and procedures. To these outsiders, the personal relationships and delicate distinctions upon which town life was based meant nothing. Nor were officials sympathetic to the townsmen's insistence that they must be able to limit and control their own community. Under the sovereign state, all citizens should be equally free to settle where they wished, enter a trade, or hold an office; similarly, all citizens

[27] In addition to the works cited in n. 25, see the documents in Huber and Huber (eds.), *Staat*, i.
[28] There is a good account of this in Epstein, *Genesis*, pp. 639 ff. For a case study, see Bátori, *Reichsstadt*.

should be equally responsible to support the state, pay taxes, and provide military service. During the highpoint of reform following Napoleon's victories in 1805 and 1806, representatives of the new states pushed hard to impose their will on these reluctant communities, but, by the time French power began to ebb seven years later, there were signs that the states were having considerable trouble triumphing over the obdurate complexities of town life. The Bavarians, for instance, simply could not find a way of regulating the ten thousand guilds within their territory; attempts at bureaucratic supervision and state-run licensing failed. In Bavaria, as in the other states, the 'terrible variety' of the towns defeated reform. Mack Walker, the home towns' eloquent historian, has written:

Not everything could be foreseen by a code, the result was impossible floods of litigation and administrative inquiry, and the machinery stalled and broke down. Bureaucratic resources were not enough to master the details of local life: state officials succeeded neither in reconciling local issues with general policies nor in forcing local affairs into a uniform pattern.[29]

For somewhat different reasons, the states had difficulty penetrating the domains of the landed aristocracy, whose *Herrschaft* had long attracted the ire of civil servants eager to promote unqualified sovereignty. The reorganizations of 1803 and 1806 seemed to deal as great a blow to the nobility as they had to the *Reichskirche*: like the ecclesiastical territories, the estates of sovereign and semi-sovereign imperial counts and knights passed into the hands of Napoleon's German allies. But while the imperial nobles lost their political independence, they remained a special status group, whose residual rights and privileges were guaranteed by the articles of the Rhenish Confederation. More important, the nobility, unlike the church, kept their property, and thus retained a foundation upon which their wealth, prestige, and position in local society could ultimately be rebuilt. The old imperial nobles, who came to be called *Standesherren*, managed to insulate their estates from bureaucratic control and full taxation; in Baden they held almost 25 per cent of the land. Even without the special privileges of the *Standesherren*, the territorial nobility managed to use their position at court and their influence in the countryside to undermine efforts at centralization and reform. An aristocratic fronde in Bavaria helped to prevent the introduction of the Code Napoleon in 1808

[29] Walker, *Home Towns*, p. 210.

and, three years later, was able to force a revision of the constitution to its advantage. One hundred estate owners in Baden's new territories also retained a special status that released them from the jurisdiction of local judges, guaranteed their own police and judicial rights, and gave them the power to appoint pastors and teachers. King Frederick of Württemberg smashed the *Stände*, but he did not demolish the seigneurial rights and local power of his nobles. Overall, the landed nobility emerged from the era of revolution and reform without political autonomy, but with most of their wealth and some of their privileges. In the Rhenish Confederation, as in most of the German lands, the decline of *Herrschaft* brought the redefinition rather than the destruction of the aristocracy's elite status.[30]

It should come as no surprise that the cost of the aristocracy's persistence was borne by the peasantry, which was still by far the largest group in German society. In Bavaria, the Montgelas regime had set out to create a free and mobile agrarian society by abolishing serfdom, but since few peasants could afford to buy their freedom from seigneurial obligations, most remained in some kind of dependent relationship to their landlords until 1848. The peasants in the old dynastic lands of Baden had been among the freest in central Europe, but their material condition was less enviable; backward techniques, demographic pressures, and fragmented holdings kept many Badenese farmers at a low level of subsistence. When the Code Napoleon was introduced into the new Grand Duchy of Baden, this situation was not essentially changed; peasants consolidated their legal position as independent landholders without substantially improving their productivity or prosperity. Unlike Baden, Württemberg did not have a tradition of agrarian reform; as late as the 1790s the dukes had rejected calls to revise the existing system of *Grundherrschaft*. Under King Frederick, however, the state's need for money and the monarch's commitment to change produced some reforms, but no significant improvement in the peasantry's material condition. Emancipation did not get under way in Württemberg until after Frederick's death in 1816; it was still incomplete in 1848.[31]

When we follow the history of Bavaria, Baden, and Württemberg during the Napoleonic era, we are continually struck by the

[30] Fehrenbach, *Gesellschaft*, describes this process.

[31] Conze's classic article, 'Wirkungen', is still the best introduction. For a more critical analysis, see Christof Dipper, *Die Bauernbefreiung in Deutschland, 1790–1850* (Stuttgart, 1980). The impact of emancipation on rural society is treated below, Ch. 8, sect. ii.

distance between aspiration and accomplishment. To be sure, even under the best of circumstances, reform is difficult, old privileges die hard, and institutions resist change. While the situation created by the collapse of the Reich seemed to favour, perhaps even to mandate, reform, the pervasive atmosphere of crisis and upheaval did not make it easy to formulate clear and sustained policies. Considering the historical context in which they had to work, the reformers managed to accomplish a great deal. They laid the administrative foundations for states that had been swiftly created from heterogeneous territorial components. They articulated the ideals of civil equality and social liberty and made some progress in implementing these ideals. If we judge them by what they promised, Montgelas, Reitzenstein, and the rest appear to be no more than qualified successes, but when we bear in mind their slender resources, the pressures imposed upon them from abroad, and the opposition they faced at home, the scope and significance of their achievements seem impressive.

We can now move to summarize quickly the condition of the other states in the Rhenish Confederation. In addition to the three satellites and the three *Mittelstaaten* just discussed, the confederation had thirty-three (after the annexations of 1810, twenty-nine) members. Hesse-Darmstadt and Nassau were smaller versions of the newly enlarged states of the south west. Like their neighbours, these two states had formed alliances with France, grown by absorbing territories from the old Reich, and then introduced a number of domestic reforms.[32] Under the gifted leadership of Hans von Gagern, Nassau managed to establish itself as the most effective of the other small states which, for one reason or another, had not been swallowed up during the reorganizations of 1803 and 1806: these included the Saxon duchies (Weimar, Eisenach, Coburg, and so on), as well as Anhalt, Schwarzenburg, the various Reuss principalities, Waldeck, Lippe-Detmold, and Schaumburg-Lippe. In the north, the two Mecklenburgs retained their sovereignty, thus displaying an ability to resist political reform that would persist for over a century. Finally, mention should be made of the electorate of Saxony. Although Saxony had fought on the losing side in 1806, its common border with Prussia, Russia, and Bohemia made it a strategically valuable ally for France. Napoleon, therefore, turned the electorate into a kingdom, gave it some territory taken from Prussia, and made its monarch the titular ruler

---

[32] On Hesse-Darmstadt, see Ulmann (ed), *Denkwürdigkeiten*; on Nassau, Rössler, *Revolution*.

of his Polish satelite, the duchy of Warsaw. In return, Saxony became one of France's most reliable German allies, but, like the Mecklenburgs, its geographical and institutional character was not much altered.

The Saxon case suggests a pattern with which to order the Confederation's political multiformity. In the centre and north of the old Reich, where existing political boundaries were not significantly redrawn, states like Saxony and the Mecklenburgs could keep their old constitutions intact. In the south and west, however, territorial transformations produced a new political landscape and an inescapable set of institutional reforms. In both cases, diplomatic and military considerations were inseparable from constitutional and administrative developments. Thus Eberhard Weis's remark that Montgelas was 'primarily concerned with foreign policy' could also be applied to Reitzenstein, King Frederick, Gagern, and many of their contemporaries.[33] To master the revolution required the ability to move along the seam between domestic and foreign affairs, shifting from one to the other without losing sight of their intense and dangerous connections.

ii. AUSTRIA: THE ORDEAL OF SURVIVAL

In Vienna, as in Munich, Karlsruhe, and Stuttgart, the government had to master the forces unleashed by the revolution. The domestic political condition of the vast Habsburg empire was no less influenced by international relations than that of Bavaria, Baden, or Württemberg. After 1792 Austrian statesmen and soldiers found themselves locked in a series of unexpected and unequal battles with new enemies, whose victories enabled them to strip away valuable territories and impose painful burdens. Austria was large enough, and far enough away from the centre of the fighting, to avoid the drastic changes imposed upon the newly enlarged states in the Rhenish Confederation. Nevertheless, to survive in this unhappy time required institutional reform, as well as the expenditure of vast quantities of human and material resources. But, while the cost of survival was high, the rewards were elusive: at the end of the revolutionary era, neither the monarchy's international position nor its domestic condition was much improved by its costly victories.

During the first stage of the revolution, most Austrians were

---

[33] Weis, *Montgelas*, p. x.

distracted from the events in France by more immediate concerns: the eastern war, the protest evoked by Josephian reforms, and then, in early 1790, by Joseph's terminal illness. So great was the animosity towards the emperor that his brother and heir, Archduke Leopold, refused to come to Vienna while Joseph was still alive. 'I am determined', Leopold told his sister, 'not to get mixed up in public affairs. . . . It would give the people and foreign govern- ments the idea that I shared the emperor's principles and systems.' When Leopold did finally begin his journey north to accept the crown, he was met along the way by the notables of his realm, who pressed upon him grievances collected during Joseph's long and difficult reign. After arriving in the capital, the new emperor went into seclusion, surrounded by the administrative documents his varied lands produced in such abundance. He emerged a few weeks later determined to correct the errors which seemed to have brought the Habsburgs to the brink of disaster.[34]

Although Leopold was not afflicted by his brother's pathological insensitivity, he also was a rather unlovable character. Suspicious to the edge of paranoia, subject to fits of black depression and other maladies, he was a demanding master and a difficult man. Nevertheless, in Tuscany he had earned a reputation as an energetic and enlightened ruler. Moreover, unlike most of the rulers who have earned the label 'enlightened', he was not an absolutist, interested in augmenting his own power as the state's first servant. He was prepared to acknowledge that all authority had to be limited by the dictates of reason and by the influence of legitimate interests within the state.

I believe [he wrote a few weeks before his coronation] that every country ought to possess a constitution . . . a contract which defines the authority and sets the limits to the competences of the [prince] . . . and that while the executive power belongs to the ruler, the legislative power belongs to the people and their representatives. [35]

Considering these convictions, it is not surprising that Leopold had long been critical of Joseph's enlightened absolutism and that he began at once to defuse the anger building throughout his realm.

After achieving a *rapprochement* with Prussia and thus depriving his restless subjects of their most powerful foreign ally, Leopold set out to win them over with a skilful blend of promises and threats. He affirmed the concessions Joseph had reluctantly made to the

[34] Hantsch, *Geschichte*, ii. 258.
[35] Epstein, *Genesis*, p. 415. The standard biography is Adam Wandruszka, *Leopold II*. (2 vols.; Munich and Vienna, 1965).

rebellious Hungarian nobility, acknowledged the special place of Hungary among his possessions, but refused to compromise his ultimate authority. He then began to encourage the representation of other national groups within Hungary and thus put pressure on the Magyar nobility in Budapest to abandon their most radical demands and come to an accommodation with Vienna. The Bohemian estates, which had been as outraged by the direction of Joseph's policy as the Hungarians, used the occasion of his death to demand a restoration of their corporate privileges and seigneurial rights. Here, too, Leopold granted some concessions: he revoked the hated tax reforms of 1789, but held on to the Peasants' Patent of 1781; he agreed to be crowned king of Bohemia in Prague, but would grant no greater local rights than those existing in 1764. A similar pattern of compromise and resolution governed Leopold's dealings with his Austrian lands. While he eased some of the controls his brother had imposed on teachers and clergymen, he left no doubt that schools and churches were ultimately under the state's authority. And while he allowed a few monastic orders to return and promised some changes in the marriage laws, he retained Joseph's Edict of Toleration. Towards the Austrian nobility the new imperial policy was less ambiguously accommodating: after allowing the provincial estates to meet in 1790 and to express their complaints, Leopold cancelled the tax legislation of 1789 and returned the financial burden of the state to its traditional resting place on the backs of the peasantry.

If Leopold had reigned longer and in quieter times, he might have transformed the monarchy into a constitutional state. There are some tantalizing indications that he was on the verge of extensive reforms when he died suddenly in March 1792, at the age of forty-five. By this time, however, the revolution in France had begun to have an impact on the Habsburgs' western lands; soon any constitutional experiments within the monarchy would have been extraordinarily difficult. Prince Kaunitz, nearing the end of his long career in the Habsburgs' service, seems to have sensed what lay ahead. When asked by a visiting delegation how Leopold's son and heir should be shown in his official portrait, Kaunitz replied, 'Have the new lord painted in marshal's uniform and armour; let there be a reddish-blue sky and an army in the background. . . . Emperor Francis will, against his wishes and judgement, become involved in wars . . .'[36]

Francis was twenty-four in 1792. A year older than Napoleon

---

[36] Langsam, *Francis*, p. 107.

and Wellington, he was one of the first members of his generation to play a leading role on the political scene. But, unlike his great contemporaries, this role came to him through the accident of birth, not because of his qualities and achievements. Francis was ill-suited by nature and training to assume the burdens of his office; unimaginative, narrow-minded, and painfully shy, he had been overwhelmed by his father's educational efforts and intimidated by the attentions shown him by his uncle, the Emperor Joseph. Contemporaries found him peculiarly colourless, 'without virtues or vices, without any kind of passion, nothing seems able to stir him from his natural apathy'.[37] In fact, Francis could be drawn from apathy only by the formidable sense of duty that compelled him to sit for hours with his stacks of official papers or to see endless numbers of petitioners. Stories about his industriousness are legion. On a trip to his Italian lands, he supposedly received 20,000 subjects; at home in Vienna, he averaged eighty a week. It was as though Francis hoped to transform statecraft into bureaucratic detail and individual audiences, and thereby acquire a sense of mastery over a task too great for him to imagine. Devoted to the specifics of government, he had no sense of the large historical forces at work around him, no vision of the extended network of institutions and loyalties of which he was the centre. The passage of the Habsburgs' legacy from Leopold to Francis, like the shift from Frederick II to Frederick William II of Prussia, was a sign that the great age of monarchy had come to an end. The era of Frederick William I and Frederick II, Maria Theresa and Joseph II, Karl Eugen of Württemberg and Karl August of Weimar was giving way to a period of almost uninterrupted monarchical mediocrity.

Because, as he wrote rather plaintively on his first day as emperor, he was 'so young' and had 'so little experience', Francis clung to those he had known in his youth, the wise old men in whose charge his father had put him. Chief among these advisers was Franz von Colloredo, who had served as Francis's tutor and now became head of the Privy Council. A genteel man with a flawless pedigree, Colloredo remained close to the throne for more than a decade, giving advice, encouraging the emperor's hopes and fears, controlling access to his presence. Historical opinions about Colloredo vary; his admirers portray him as honest and hard-working, his critics hint at corruption and moral turpitude. No one accuses him of being intelligent or politically astute. The one important new figure in Francis's circle was Johann Amadeus von

[37] Aretin, *Reich*, i. 276.

Thugut, who became director of foreign affairs in March 1793. In contrast to Colloredo, Thugut was vigorous and talented; without background or connections, he had worked his way to the centre of power with energy, skill, and a finely honed sense of his own interests. He had made enemies along the way, not simply because he was a parvenu but also because his apparent lack of principles shocked even the most cynical Viennese courtiers. A small state in peaceful times might have gotten along with a monarch like Francis and statesmen like Colloredo and Thugut, but, for the Habsburg realm at this historical juncture, they were a disastrous trio. Aretin is probably correct when he writes that Francis's 'fatal apathy', Colloredo's 'practical incompetence', and Thugut's 'immorality' made up 'one of the most unfortunate political constellations in history'.[38]

Observant contemporaries quickly recognized that Franciscan Austria lacked direction and resolve. 'So powerfully supplied with territory, population, and resources,' the Bavarian ambassador wrote from Vienna in May 1795, 'Austria cannot make up its mind; the only thing it can do is select what other powers want to give it.' At about the same time, Thugut compared his government to the tower of Babel, where any semblance of order was drowned out by the confusion of competing voices. 'We would be lost,' he noted, 'if our enemies realized the full extent of the evil and lamentable condition into which the monarchy has fallen.'[39] From our discussion of international relations between 1793 and 1805, we know some of the results of this political weakness: the promotion of gross incompetents like General Mack at the expense of talented soldiers like Archduke Charles, the weakness of Austrian diplomacy at critical moments, and the general decline in the Habsburgs' influence throughout central Europe. These foreign political disasters had profound domestic results: ambitious, self-serving men tried to get what they could for themselves, while dedicated, well-intentioned officials became discouraged. 'Who rules Austria?' asked the author of a critical contemporary pamphlet. By the turn of the century, no one was quite sure. Unfortunately, the worse the situation became, the more closely Francis stuck to his old advisers,

[38] On Colloredo, see Langsam, *Francis*, p. 143; Springer, *Geschichte*, i. 111 ff. Aretin's remark about Thugut is from *Reich*, i. 277. Karl A. Roider, in *Baron Thugut and Austria's Response to the French Revolution* (Princeton, 1987), has recently attempted to revise the overwhelmingly negative view of Thugut in the historical literature, but even he must admit that one reason why Thugut failed to defeat revolutionary France was 'others' perceptions of his character and goals' (p. xx).

[39] Aretin, *Reich*, p. 79; Hantsch, *Geschichte*, ii. 272.

resisted change, and allowed the routine of government to carry him along. To the emperor, difficulties at home and abroad were reasons to keep things as they were, to avoid the agonies of choice, and to preserve what could be preserved. These conservative instincts, already deeply rooted in his character, were greatly strengthened in mid–1794 by the discovery of allegedly revolutionary forces within his own capital.

In July 1794 an agent of the Austrian police reported that Franz von Hebenstreit, a young army officer with an interest in literature and a low tolerance for alcohol, had revealed to him a plot to overthrow the monarchy. Arrests swiftly followed, first in Vienna, then in Budapest. Those involved included a cross-section of the political public—writers, teachers, officers, a few civil servants, and businessmen. Some had been involved in Leopold's constitutional ventures; all had become disillusioned with the new emperor, whose personal qualities and political values seemed certain to end decades of reform from above. Significantly, one of the best-known conspirators was Andreas Freiherr von Riedel, who had once been called upon to teach the future emperor the principles of mathematics, surely not a task easily reconcilable with an unwavering faith in monarchical institutions. Riedel and his collaborators—there were about eighty of them in Vienna—belonged to a loose network of reading clubs and discussion groups in which they had circulated forbidden literature, exchanged subversive views, and may even have made some tentative plans to act. They did not represent a real threat to the established order; even within the thin stratum of society to which they belonged, they were a minority. Nevertheless, their discovery, trial, and punishment had a profound effect on the young emperor, who was further alienated from the progressive programmes and personnel favoured by his uncle and father.[40]

Francis's growing conviction that his realm was awash with dangerous ideas led him to tighten governmental controls over his subjects. In every corner of Austrian society, the power of the policeman and censor became more intrusive. The net of spies that had snared the unfortunate Lieutenant von Hebenstreit was expanded Clubs, secret societies, and even some religious organizations were banned. Above all, the war against subversive opinion was intensified. To say anything even remotely positive about the

[40] Helmut Reinalter, *Aufgeklärter Absolutismus und Revolution: Zur Geschichte des Jakobinertums und der frühdemokratischen Bestrebungen in der Habsburger Monarchie* (Vienna, Cologne, and Graz, 1980).

French revolution was expressly forbidden; no comments could be made about pending legislation; eventually permission was needed just to own a book printed outside Austria. After 1801 censorship was placed under the jurisdiction of the police, who broadened its scope to cover even the decorations on toys and snuff-boxes. In 1803 a commission reviewed all the books that had somehow managed to be published during the two preceding years and as a result an additional 2,500 titles were banned. To be sure, these repressive policies lacked both the means and the will to match the standards set by tyranny in the twentieth century; most of those accused of subversion were given fair trials and, except for the 'Jacobins' of 1794, prison terms were usually short. Traffic in forbidden books and periodicals continued; if one knew where to look, anything was available. Nevertheless, the impact of these policies was considerable. First, Franciscan repression provided the basis for the stereotype of a reactionary Austria that alienated many progressive Germans, both inside and outside the monarchy. Second, censor and spy interfered with the development of political discourse, narrowed the ranks of an informed public, and isolated Austrians from their counterparts throughout Europe. In the only slightly hyperbolic words of an English visitor in 1805, the Austrian 'public mind is dull and torpid, or rather no public mind exists'.[41]

The reactionary climate of the 1790s created confusion and dismay among those who sought to perpetuate the traditions of Josephism. The members of the commission charged with drafting a new legal code, for example, found themselves locked in a bitter struggle with Francis's advisers over the proper role of law in society. In 1794, when Karl Anton von Martini presented his revisions of the code to the emperor, Francis created another commission to review Martini's work. In the end, the new code was only introduced into Galicia, the monarchy's recently acquired Polish lands, where the pressing need for a legal system allowed no time for delay or revision. Discussions about applying the code to the rest of the monarchy dragged on, while conservative jurists scrutinized every statute to be sure that it did not compromise monarchical authority. *Das allgemeine bürgerliche Gesetzbuch* was not published until June 1811; it went into effect the following January and remained in force 'for the German hereditary lands of the Austrian monarchy' until the end of the monarchy. In this final

---

[41] Quoted in Langsam, *Francis*, p. 56. For two detailed and passionately critical accounts of Austrian censorship, see Springer, *Geschichte*, i. 64 ff.; Beidtel, *Geschichte*, ii. 95 ff.

version, written under the supervision of Franz Edler von Zeiller, the rule of law was narrowly defined to exclude questions of natural rights and limitations on state power. The principle of civil equality was retained, but only in relationships among private individuals; in public affairs, Zeiller insisted, inequalities of rank and function had to remain.[42]

Francis's absorption with a new set of enemies at home and abroad led him to reassess the problems facing the Austrian state. His grandmother and, much more decisively, his uncle had hoped to extend the state's power over intermediate, competing authorities, especially the nobility and the church. Francis, however, seemed prepared to co-operate with these groups in his struggle against Jacobin subversion and French aggression. He halted the Habsburgs' longstanding campaign to make peasants the direct subjects of the state by undermining the practice of *Grundherrschaft*. The Legal Code of 1811, therefore, declared rural social relations to be in the public realm and not subject to the principle of civil equality.[43] The aristocracy, of course, would have liked much more. But, while they were disappointed that Francis would not undo his predecessors' reforms, they accepted the partnership he offered them, backed away from their most extreme demands, and cherished their remaining privileges and power. In the Franciscan era, the nobility seem to have become increasingly aware of their social status, more exclusive in its values and self-image, and content to live in a world of their own. At the same time, the ideological image of the aristocracy began to change: in place of the bitter critiques of luxury and decadence we find in the work of enlightened writers like Sonnenfels, there are stirring defences of aristocratic virtues by conservatives like Adam von Müller, for whom the nobility were a necessary source of stability and order.[44]

The church also benefited from Francis's search for allies. The secular spirit and tolerant atmosphere of Josephism was replaced by a greater emphasis on piety and orthodoxy. The educational reforms sponsored by Francis gave religious instruction a central role in the curriculum; the clergy were used to oversee what was taught and to ensure that Austrian youngsters were not seduced by dangerous ideas from the west. Nevertheless, the partnership offered by the monarchy to the church remained an unequal one. Although the clergy were given authority over the minds of the

---

[42] Strakosch, *Absolutism*, chs. 10, 11.
[43] Brunner, *Land*, pp. 288–9.
[44] See Beidtel, *Geschichte*, ii. 46. On Müller, see below, Ch. 6, sect.iii.

faithful, they did not get greater autonomy within the state. Francis, no less than his forebears, viewed priests as civil servants, forbade them to have direct contact with their superiors in Rome, and did not give them control over their property. In some ways, secular authority over the church increased after 1792, since a sharp decline in the quality and quantity of candidates for the priesthood prompted the government to supervise reforms in the teaching of theology and the administration of seminaries.[45]

Under Francis, as under his three predecessors, the foundation of Habsburg government was the bureaucracy. The new emperor and his advisers tried to turn the state's machinery in a different direction, but they could not change the machinery itself. Nor did Francis want to do so: he may have surrounded himself with grandees and devout churchmen, but he was, above all else, an imperial bureaucrat, deeply committed to the institution that could feed his appetite for detail and assuage his passion for immobility. Although its critics regarded the administration as a 'machine that turns over with enormous noise but never moves', the Austrian bureaucracy actually worked fairly well at the lower and middle ranks, where it continued to be staffed by men trained in the traditions of enlightened government.[46] The weakness of Austrian politics was at the top, where those in charge, unable to set a clear direction for policy, issued a cascade of decrees and a bewildering multiplicity of rules which even the most dedicated officials could not grasp well enough to administer properly.

Finances remained the Habsburgs' most critical domestic problem, simultaneously the cause and the symptom of their inability to master the rich resources at their disposal. By 1790 the state had an annual budget deficit of about twenty-seven million gulden and a debt of almost four hundred million. To cover its expenses, the government had resorted to the irresistible but irresponsible expedient of printing more currency, the first step towards increasingly serious inflationary disruptions. Leopold had managed to decrease the annual deficit, but his gains were soon eroded by the cost of the French wars. Because he was reluctant to impose new taxes, Francis met his fiscal needs by issuing more paper money and selling government bonds; in 1795 and 1796 the banknotes in circulation increased from thirty-five and a half million to almost

---

[45] Ernst Tomek, *Kirchengeschichte Österreichs,* iii. *Das Zeitalter der Aufklärung und des Absolutismus* (Innsbruck, Vienna, and Munich, 1959), pt. 5; Maass, *Josephinismus,* v.

[46] Springer, *Geschichte,* i. 120.

forty-seven million. If war was costly, defeat was disastrous. Following Austria's military setbacks, public confidence in the government eroded and the market for government paper shrank. In the spring of 1797, when a French invasion of Vienna seemed likely, redemption of notes in silver had to be suspended. At the same time, Austria's extrusion from her western markets disrupted the economy by cutting off important sources of tax revenues and blocking access to the loans supplied by the private banking houses in Frankfurt. The Habsburgs were now hopelessly trapped in a vicious circle: as military defeat sapped their financial strength, fiscal weakness made a successful war effort more and more difficult.[47]

Eventually even Francis was prepared to acknowledge the need for reform. In response to impassioned pleas from his brother Charles, in 1801 the emperor established a *Staats-und Conferenz-ministerium*, which was to co-ordinate affairs of state under three large ministries—Foreign Affairs, Defence, and Internal Affairs— and thus allow 'the entire administration of the state to run by itself, like a well-made clock set on its proper course'. Alas, the machinery of state did not tick on like clockwork. Once Francis realized that the new arrangement improved the co-ordination of policy and strategy at the expense of his own freedom of movement, he began to deal with each department head individually, following the advice of the one who suited him best. Charles, the most consistent and effective champion of reform, was eased to one side and left without either the time or the resources necessary to renovate the army.[48]

Francis's belated and half-hearted efforts at reform pale in comparison to the massive changes imposed upon the monarchy from outside. We have seen how Napoleon took away the dynasty's western lands and weakened its authority in the Reich. Increasingly, the Austrian government was turned in upon itself, forced to recognize that its power required the consolidation of a cohesive state rather than the control of diffuse and scattered territories. An important symbolic expression of this recognition came in August 1804, when Francis declared himself to be emperor of the Habsburgs' German lands, Hungary, and Galicia. The

[47] The classic account is Adolf Beer, *Die Finanzen Österreichs im XIX. Jahrhundert* (1877, repr. Vienna, 1973); for a more modern view, see Volker Press, 'Das "Droit d'Épaves" des Kaisers von Österreich: Finanzkrise und Stabilisierungspolitik zwischen Lunéviller und Pressburger Frieden', *GuG*. 6/4 (1980), 559–73.

[48] Quoted in Springer, *Geschichte*, i. 62. For a summary of administrative reforms, see Walter, *Verfassungs-und Verwaltungsgeschichte*.

immediate occasion for this proclamation was Napoleon's self-coronation in May—the Habsburgs were surely not going to risk being outranked by a ragtag family of Corsican adventurers. Equally important, however, was the government's desire to achieve 'a consolidation of the united Austrian polity [*des vereinigten österreichischen Staatskörpers*]'. As most contemporaries were aware, this consolidation came at the expense of the Holy Roman Empire. The establishment of the new imperial title, Friedrich Gentz wrote to Metternich, is an act of 'unspeakable meanness . . . a true political solecism, for Austria is a province subordinated to the empire by feudal ties; one could just as well speak of an emperor of Salzburg, Frankfurt, or Passau'. Long accustomed to such humiliations, the representatives of the Reich did not protest; when the Swedish representative raised the issue of the compatibility of Francis's new title with his old responsibilities, the *Reichstag* went into immediate recess. Two years later, as we have seen, Francis abandoned the imperial crown and affirmed his primary dynastic identity as 'Francis I, by the grace of God emperor of Austria'.[49]

By this time, sensible Austrian statesmen must have known that it would take more than a new dynastic label to keep their state intact. The military disaster of Austerlitz, the Treaty of Pressburg's harsh provisions, the creation of the Rhenish Confederation, the defeat of Prussia, and the formation of a Franco-Russian *entente* each marked a severe decline in the Habsburgs' international position. But, while the emperor's advisers agreed that reform was inevitable, they were divided about the direction it should take. The Minister of the Interior, Count Sinzendorff, wanted an absolutist solution—greater administrative efficiency, increased centralization, closer supervision of social and cultural affairs. Until such measures could take hold, Sinzendorff recommended co-operation with Napoleon, whose hegemonic position seemed unassailable, at least for the immediate future. The chief opponents of this viewpoint were the Archduke Charles and the new Foreign Minister, Count Philip Stadion. An imperial noble, whose background and career brings to mind his Prussian counterpart, Freiherr vom Stein, Stadion had combined a career in state service with a commitment to representative institutions. Like Stein, he wanted a renewal of state and society through a revitalization of the *Stände*, which he hoped would reconcile government and social order. In contrast to Sinzendorff, Stadion wanted decentralization and

---

[49] Gentz quoted in Epstein, *Genesis*, p. 659. On the end of the Reich, see above, Ch. 4, sect. iii.

greater regional autonomy. Moreover, he believed that peace with Napoleon was out of the question: 'Napoleon wants to destroy us, because our principles and size are incompatible with a single, universal hegemony.'[50]

Stadion and Charles, like the Prussian reformers after Jena, hoped to turn the weapons of the revolution against France. Their success was limited. The Austrian police remained autonomous, the censor pervasive, the bureaucracy all powerful. The local government act of 1808 may even have weakened the role of representative institutions at the expense of the administration. Only in military affairs, where reform seemed most pressing and unavoidable, was Charles able to use his new title as Commander-in-Chief to make some important organizational improvements, dismiss incompetent officers, and strengthen the command structure.[51] In 1808 Stadion persuaded Francis to establish a militia based on universal military service, thus bringing to the monarchy the possibility of a citizen–soldier so close to the hearts of military reformers everywhere in Europe. Moreover, since the militia was locally supported, its creation led to the revitalization of corporate bodies in many of the Habsburgs' territories. Predictably, Francis was not enthusiastic about these changes; he acted with great reluctance and only because he sensed there was no alternative. Many men still close to the throne shared their master's distrust of change: 'One defends feudal society against the revolution,' wrote an official in 1807, 'but what is to be gained from this struggle if it requires that revolution to be introduced into society?'[52]

Throughout 1808 the reformers tried to create a climate of patriotic fervour to support the war they hoped to fight against France. Periodicals such as the *Vaterländische Blätter für den österreichischen Kaiserstaat* and *Österreichischer Plutarch*, as well as scores of pamphlets, poems, and hymns, urged the Habsburgs' subjects to express their love for the fatherland by joining the struggle against French despotism. On the occasion of Francis's wedding to his cousin, the beautiful Maria Ludovica, the Austrian élite, who reminded Madame de Staël of 'the old teutonic nobility', expressed their commitment to national values by ostentatiously abandoning French fashions in favour of what they took to be German costumes. Throughout the empire, men rushed to join the

---

[50] Quoted in Hantsch, *Geschichte*, ii. 282. The standard biography is Hellmuth Rössler, *Graf Johann Philipp Stadion: Napoleons deutscher Gegenspieler* (2 vols.; Vienna and Munich, 1966).

[51] Rothenberg, *Napoleon's Great Adversaries*, ch. 6.

[52] Kübeck, *Tagebücher*, i. pt. 1, p. 211.

militia; in Vienna alone, six volunteer battalions were recruited. But as impressive and sincere as these patriotic sentiments may have been, we should not accept the conventional view that they represented an opportunity for Austria to assume the leadership of a nationalist crusade. First, while it is by no means clear just what Stadion and his colleagues meant by the German nation, their ideas were certainly closer to the old Reich than to the nineteenth-century nation-state. Second, patriotic feelings did not penetrate very deeply into the social order. What popular support for the war did exist, came from remote areas such as the Tirol, where people fought for local autonomy and religious convictions, not for a 'Germany' about which they knew little and cared less.[53]

'We are fighting for the autonomy of the Austrian monarchy, in order to recreate Germany's independence and national honour. . . . Our cause is Germany's cause.' These words, issued by Archduke Charles as he led his armies across the Inn in the spring of 1809, expressed his hopes that Napoleon's victims and allies in the Rhenish Confederation would rally in support of the Habsburgs. Unfortunately for the Austrians, their intense diplomatic manœuvrings had failed to persuade the princes of the German states to switch sides. Although there was a war party in Berlin, Prussia was still too weak to fight; Russia was not yet ready to abandon her erstwhile French ally. Nevertheless, Stadion still hoped that he could speak over the heads of the governments and evoke popular movements comparable to those supporting the guerrilla war in Spain. Friedrich Schlegel, a leading Habsburg propagandist, composed a 'Proclamation to the Bavarians' in which he declared that 'we [Austrians] are Germans every bit as much as you are. . . . All those who are imbued with a true German patriotism will be powerfully supported, and, if they so deserve, richly rewarded by their former emperor, who did not resign his German heart along with his German crown.'[54] Except in the Tirol, no one responded to these entreaties. When Charles's army faced Napoleon's near Ratisbon in April, the Austrians fought alone. After suffering heavy casualties in this engagement, Charles withdrew towards the east, leaving the French a clear path to Vienna, which they occupied in May. Later that month, however, Charles defeated Napoleon at Aspern, on the banks of the Danube, and forced him to withdraw

[53] Hellmuth Rössler, Österreichs Kampf um Deutschlands Befreiung. Die deutsche Politik der nationalen Führer Österreichs. 1805–1815 (Hamburg, 1945), greatly overestimates the effectiveness of these efforts. For a sober and more convincing account, see Kraehe, Metternich's German Policy, i. 78–80.

[54] Hantsch, Geschichte, ii. 286 and Langsam, Francis, p. 67.

his forces to the island of Lobau. But Charles did not follow through and seek to destroy the enemy; instead, by delaying, he gave Napoleon time to regroup and gather reinforcements. This same hesitancy characterized the archduke's conduct of the battle fought on the plains of Wagram in July, when he disengaged his forces and called for negotiations well before the outcome of the action was clear. Throughout the campaign, Charles was unwilling to risk his army to gain total victory, perhaps because he realized that, despite all the patriotic rhetoric, the Austrian state ultimately rested upon its soldiers. 'The first lost battle', he had written in June, 'is the death sentence of the monarchy and the present dynasty.'[55] Charles's calculations may well have been correct: the Treaty of Vienna was harsh, more territory was lost, a huge indemnity was imposed, and the size of the army was limited, but monarchy and dynasty survived.

Wagram brought to an end the era of national idealism personified by Stadion and Charles, both of whom left their posts in 1809. The new architect of Austrian policy was Clemens von Metternich, who had been recalled to imperial headquarters from his ambassadorial post in Paris while the fighting was still going on. At thirty-six, Metternich now moved into the position of power and influence that he would retain for the next four decades.[56] Like the Stadions and the Steins, the Metternichs were imperial aristocrats; their estates had once nestled in the Mosel valley between Koblenz and Trier. Clemens's father, Franz Georg, was a quintessentially rococo figure: indolent, sensual, delighted to play a major role in the minor ecclesiastical courts of the old regime. He reared his son in an atmosphere where the pleasures of aristocratic society easily coexisted with the intellectual products of the French Enlightenment. In many ways, Metternich never abandoned the tastes and values of his early years. A patron of conservative ideology and religious orthodoxy, his own view of the world remained dispassionate, calculating, and resolutely secular. A skilled practictioner of power politics, he retained a courtier's mastery of social rituals and a proclivity for the joys of ballroom and boudoir. Throughout his life, he was, as one shocked

[55] Kraehe, *Metternich's German Policy*, i. 86. On the war, see Rothenberg, *Napoleon's Great Adversaries*, chs. 7,8.

[56] The classic account of Metternich remains Srbik's monumental biography (3 vols; 1925–54); the most recent is G. de Bertier de Sauvigny, *Metternich* (Paris, 1986). Paul Schroeder's 'Metternich Studies since 1925', *JMH* 33/3 (Sept. 1961), 237–60 analyses the literature published between 1925 and 1960. On Metternich's foreign policy, I am especially indebted to Kraehe's fine study, *Metternich's German Policy*.

Englishman reported, 'most intolerably loose and giddy with women'.[57] But, like Bismarck, the only other nineteenth-century German statesmen of comparable stature, Metternich knew how to draw on the strengths of his background without being trapped by its weaknesses. Just as Bismarck was always more than the gruff Junker he sometimes pretended to be, Metternich was always more than the elegant dandy, whose impeccably dressed appearance he presented to the world. Metternich recognized that politics was a perilous and violent game, not a matter of polite gestures and elegant ceremonies. He hated the revolution, but he had, at some considerable cost, learned its lessons.

His first contact with the new age had come a week after the Bastille's fall, when, as a university student, he watched an angry crowd storm the Strasburg city hall, plunder its wine cellar, and carry on a rampage of looting until put down by troops. The following year, when he attended the coronation of Leopold II, the memories of this event returned, underscoring the contrast between the values of the old regime and the destructive fury of the new, between order and chaos, decorum and violence.[58] Two years later, at Francis's coronation, Metternich shared the common belief that Brunswick's troops would put an end to the political pestilence in Paris. Instead, French victory brought personal disasters to the Metternich family. With their estates occupied, their properties confiscated, and their place in the Rhenish courts destroyed, Franz Georg and his son had no choice but to seek their fortune in Vienna. Young Clemens did his part by marrying Prince Kaunitz's granddaughter and thereby establishing a connection with one of the most powerful families in the Habsburgs' service. Meanwhile, however, the revolution's destructive force continued to destroy Metternich's world. 'Everything is going to the devil,' he wrote to his wife from the Rastatt Congress, 'and the time has come when everyone must save from the wreckage what he can.'[59] These words would make a fitting motto for Metternich's career, and for the future course of the monarchy he would soon begin to serve.

The governmental reorganization that followed the Treaty of Lunéville gave Metternich's patrons the chance to find him a suitable appointment. In 1801 he was named ambassador to

---

[57] Edward Cooke, quoted in Nicolson, *Congress*, p. 35.
[58] Metternich, *Memoirs*, i. 7–8.
[59] Srbik, *Metternich*, i. 84–5; Kraehe, *Metternich's German Policy*, i. 22. On Rastatt, see above, Ch. 4, sect. iii.

Saxony, three years later was given the Berlin Embassy, and three years after that was sent to Paris as the Habsburgs' representative at the most important and difficult diplomatic post in Europe. His French assignment did not begin auspiciously. As he was about to cross the frontier on 14 July 1806, he was detained and compelled to stay in Strasburg until the final negotiations over the Rhenish Confederation were completed. When he got to Paris, the French refused to accept his credentials as the representative of the Holy Roman Empire, and would only accredit him as ambassador of Austria. Over the next months, Metternich watched helplessly as Bonaparte's fortunes soared—military victories over Prussia and Russia, the alliance with the Tsar, the Treaty of Tilsit, and the steady extension of French influence over the German states. Metternich was repelled by the behaviour of France's German allies—'that rabble of crowned prefects . . . [who] pay for their doubtful and precarious privileges with the blood and money of their subjects'—and appalled by Napoleon's own brutality and ambition. 'Peace', he came to believe, 'does not exist with a revolutionary system,' whether it be under the leadership of a Robespierre or a Bonaparte.[60] He was, therefore, easily drawn into the war party around Stadion. In December 1808 his memoranda emphasizing France's military weakness and the German situation's volatility helped convince Francis that the time for a new war was at hand.

Six months later Metternich returned to Austria to pick up the pieces left after Napoleon's shattering victory. The events of 1809—Austria's diplomatic isolation, the total absence of a national uprising, and the invincible military power of France—convinced Metternich that the monarchy was no longer able to act independently. 'Whatever the stipulations of the peace may be,' he wrote in August, 'the result will be the same, namely that we seek our security only in adapting ourselves to the triumphant French system.' To do this, Francis must be prepared to participate in the Continental System, accept Napoleon's territorial demands, and embark on a policy of 'tacking, evading, and flattering'.[61] When he became Foreign Minister in October, Metternich set out to put this distasteful strategy into practice. Did he view this as a temporary measure, necessary only as long as France was strong and Austria weak? Or did he believe that the balance of power had permanently

---

[60] Kraehe, *Metternich's German Policy*, i. 63.
[61] Ibid. 104.

shifted in favour of the French? There is no way to answer these long-debated questions about the Foreign Minister's motives— most likely he himself was uncertain about the future. There is no doubt, however, that in 1809 Metternich set out to displace Russia as France's chief ally, a process that included, among other accommodations, the marriage of the emperor's daughter Maria Louise to Napoleon. In 1811, as Franco-Russian relations began to deteriorate, Metternich backed the French, and in early 1812, when war seemed unavoidable between the two powers, he signed an alliance with Napoleon. A relatively small contingent of Austrian troops marched with the *Grande Armée* into Russia.

While Metternich struggled to define a new role for Austria on the international scene, Francis's domestic advisers tried to come to terms with the monarchy's chronic political weaknesses. As usual, state finances were the most obvious and immediate source of trouble. Count O'Donnell, who had taken charge of fiscal affairs in 1808, described in sombre terms the problem and its roots: 'Those happy days, when the state had credit because it was the state, when firm confidence in the state's power and resources encouraged people to lend the state money, those days are gone.' O'Donnell saw what had to be done, but he could not do it. The value of the currency continued to decline, prices rose rapidly, and economic activity languished. Governmental indecision, declining public confidence, and the growing cost of rearmament in 1809 aggravated the inflation that had been gathering steam since the turn of the century. The cost of war and defeat brought the state to the edge of economic chaos. In December 1809 the government was forced to call in all the silver held by its subjects (except in Hungary) in order to pay off the French. This did nothing to bolster the *Bankozettel*, which continued to deteriorate in value. Finally, Count Joseph Wallis, the energetic if inexperienced official who took over after O'Donnell's death in 1810, introduced drastic deflationary measures. The *Finanzpatent* of February 1811 replaced the *Bankozettel* with a new currency and established revised schedules for the payment of public and private debts. This stopped the worst of the inflation and may have benefited some social groups, but many Austrians were ruined by the deflation, which they saw, not unreasonably, as a concealed form of state bankruptcy. Within a few weeks, the new currency was being sold at a discount on European financial markets.[62]

The period between 1790 and 1812, from Joseph's death until

[62] Springer, *Geschichte*, i. 51. On the reforms, see Adolf Beer, *Die Finanzen Österreichs im XIX. Jahrhundert* (1877, repr. Vienna, 1973), ch. 2.

Napoleon's Russian campaign, forms a bleak chapter in Austrian history. Led by an uninspiring monarch and ineffective statesmen, defeated in battle and frustrated at home, the Habsburg realm reeled from one crisis to the next. But all the unhappy features of this unhappy time should not conceal the monarchy's single, extraordinary accomplishment: it survived, ready to emerge again at the end of the revolutionary era as a major force in European affairs. We tend to undervalue persistence as a historical achievement; it impresses us less than dramatic victories or revolutionary transformations. Yet to survive in times as dangerous as these was not easy, especially for those who paid survival's heavy costs. .

iii. PRUSSIA: HUMILIATION AND RENEWAL

Patriotic historians have so often stressed the unique character of Prussia's response to the revolution that it is worthwhile underscoring the ways in which the Hohenzollern monarchy shared the fate of its neighbours. Prussia, like the other German states, was alternately a victim and an ally of France. Defeated in 1793–4, neutral from 1795 to 1806, defeated again in 1806–7, junior partner of the French imperium from 1807 until 1813, the Hohenzollern were no more successful in their efforts to withstand the revolution than the Habsburgs or the Wittelsbachs; and for them, military failure was also attended by political disruption, territorial rearrangement, and fiscal catastrophe. There is no reason to suppose that Prussia's efforts to master this situation were any more authentic or progressive than those of the states in the Rhenish Confederation. In some important respects, Montgelas and Reitzenstein went further and accomplished more than Stein and Hardenberg. Nor should we overestimate the contrast between Prussian achievements and Austrian failures. To be sure, the reformers in Berlin effected a more sustained and cohesive programmes than their counterparts in Vienna, but this was in part because of the extraordinarily desperate situation in which Prussia found itself after the Treaty of Tilsit. The Prussian reformers had the chance to push their state in a new direction because sixteen months of war had done to Prussia what sixteen years had not done to Austria: brought the state to the edge of extinction as a major power.[63]

Frederick the Great's death, like the death of his admirer Joseph II four years later, ended an era of monarchical accomplishment. But,

---

[63] The works by Hintze, Rosenberg, and Koselleck, cited in Ch. 1, sect. iv, provide accounts of the reform era within its historical context. For an astute

while he was much mourned by his foreign admirers, Frederick's passing was greeted with a sense of relief, almost of jubilation, by many of his own subjects, who had been burdened by the cost of his military glory, repelled by the coldness of his public personality, and upset by the blatantly irreligious atmosphere of his court. Since Frederick, again like Joseph, was childless, his crown passed to his nephew, Frederick William II. As so often in the history of the dynasty, we are struck by the differences that separated one Hohenzollern from his successor. Whereas Frederick had been withdrawn, calculating, and rational, the new monarch was gracious and amiable, with an inclination towards mysticism. The uncle had had no interest in women, the nephew surrounded himself with mistresses, two of whom he married, both bigamously. Weak-willed, pliable, without political talent, and anything but industrious, Frederick William quickly dissipated the goodwill with which Prussians had initially greeted his reign. Increasingly, he fell under the influence of his advisers, especially Johann Rudolf von Bischoffwerder and Johann Christoph Wöllner, who were, like him, members of the Rosicrucian order. Bischoffwerder, a Saxon nobleman and Prussian officer, had been an important part of Frederick William's entourage since the two men first met in 1778. He had no official government post, but exercised considerable influence on the king, particularly in the realm of foreign policy. Wöllner was a more complicated and talented figure: born in modest circumstances, he had followed a not unfamiliar path of social mobility, as scholarship student, private tutor, and pastor. Eventually he had managed to marry his patron's daughter and set himself on a landed estate. His influence over Frederick William came from the coincidence of their views of society and religion: like the king, he cherished a vision of an obedient and pious folk, who had to be protected from heterodox ideas and moral contamination. Under Wöllner's direction, Frederick the Great's tolerant and permissive religious policies were dismantled; governmental pressure for orthodoxy and conformity increased. Among those who felt the sting of censorship and the threat of repression was the greatest living German philosopher, Immanuel Kant of Königsberg.[64]

An uncertain king, a well-born confidant, and a talented but

analysis of the era's lasting political significance, see Bernd Faulenbach, *Ideologie des deutschen Weges. Die deutsche Geschichte in der Historiographie zwischen Kaiserreich und Nationalsozialismus* (Munich, 1980), especially pp. 200 ff. on the 1920s.

[64] On Frederick William, see Häusser, *Geschichte*, i. 195 ff. and the cogent summary of his reign in Hintze, *Hohenzollern und ihr Werk*, pp. 405 ff.

unstable parvenu—the combination of Frederick William, Bischoffwerder, and Wöllner, like that of Francis, Colloredo, and Thugut, was not up to the task of leading a state through the perils of war and revolution. After first ignoring the troubles in the west, Frederick William and his advisers heedlessly supported the ill-fated military campaigns of 1792. At the same time, they responded to protests within their own state with contemptuous repression. Conventional piety, traditional deference, and brute force were the weapons of choice against any signs of discontent. The more restless Prussians became, the more necessary it was to keep them isolated from dangerous ideas. The governor of Silesia, for example, reacted to journeymen's demonstrations in Breslau by ordering the immediate arrest of anyone who went so far as to mention that a revolution was going on in France. But, while repression and censorship might keep a fragile peace at home, the Prussian army could not defeat the revolution abroad. As the military and diplomatic pressures from France increased, the more manifest became the weaknesses of the government in Berlin. 'From the wretched and dirty intrigues that pervade this court,' wrote the British ambassador in 1793, 'the transaction of all business becomes everyday more difficult.'[65]

Historians, like some contemporary observers, have been tempted to explain Prussia's political problems in biographical terms. 'Everything has collapsed into smallness,' wrote Count Mirabeau about the death of Frederick the Great, 'as everything had once expanded into greatness.'[66] But, while it is no doubt true that Frederick William lacked his uncle's extraordinary intellect and will, the roots of Prussian weakness in the 1790s were deeply embedded in the political structures that Frederick himself had helped to create. The notorious disorder at the centre of policy-making, for example, was not simply due to the incompetence of the king and his Rosicrucian cronies; it was also the product of a persistent tendency towards administrative fragmentation that Frederick had accentuated by using his own circle of advisers as a foil to the ambitions of the regular bureaucratic organization. Similarly, the Hohenzollern's inability to mobilize their resources for a successful military campaign came in part from their longstanding compromises with the landed élite, whose privileged position had been enhanced during Frederick's reign.[67]

When Frederick William II died in November 1797, he was

---

[65] Gooch, *Germany*, p. 400.
[66] Dilthey, *Leben*, p. 213.
[67] See above, Ch. 1, sect. iv.

succeeded by his son, Frederick William III, who would rule Prussia for the next forty-three years. In some ways, the new king was as different from his father as Frederick William II had been from Frederick II. Modest and restrained in his personal habits, Frederick William's private life was Victorian in its sensible domesticity. No mistresses adorned his court; no outlandish Rosicrucian rituals disturbed the tranquil beauty of Charlottenburg's gardens. Bischoffwerder retired from the army and withdrew from public life; Wöllner was forced to resign. Unfortunately, however, the most important differences between father and son were matters of taste, style, and moral standards. The new Frederick William was a no better king than the old, no more skilled politically, no quicker and more resolute in making decisions. He was, at best, an ordinary man who found himself living in extraordinary times. His reign, which began the same year as Bonaparte's first great victories, very nearly saw the end of the Hohenzollern as a major German dynasty.[68]

Among Frederick William's advisers were men who recognized the dangers facing Prussia and realized that reform was necessary.

The creative revolution was made in France from below [Minister Johann Struensee told the French chargé d'affaires in 1799]; in Prussia it will be made slowly and from above. The king is a democrat in his own way—he is working untiringly to restrict the privileges of the nobility, and will follow Joseph II's plans, only with slower means. In a few years there will be no privileged class in Prussia.

Part hyperbole to impress the French, part wishful thinking to encourage himself, Struensee's remark none the less points to the reformist energies present in Berlin around the turn of the century. The energies were not completely without effect. The king did agree to improve the situation of the peasants working on his own, extensive domain; between 1799 and 1805 he emancipated his serfs in order to encourage emulation among the landed nobility. Frederick William's advisers also began to reform the administration and the tax structure. We have already mentioned how Scharnhorst and others tried to bring the army up to date and prepare it for a new kind of war. Before 1806, however, these various changes remained fragmentary and incomplete. In part this was because of what Otto Hintze, in his authoritative summary of the subject, called 'the irresolution of the monarch, the subordinate position of the royal assistants, the atrophy in ministerial energy

[68] Häusser, Geschichte, ii. 117 ff. Hintze, Hohenzollern und ihr Werk, pp. 423 ff.

and in responsibility'. No less important were the powerful social forces arrayed against reform, at court, in the aristocracy, and in the bureaucracy itself.[69]

While the authorities in Berlin were struggling with the problem of domestic reform, they endeavoured to remain aloof from the military and political convulsions taking place in the rest of central Europe. Even when Napoleon raised the price of neutrality, the king's nearly pathological reluctance to act, combined with the disorderly and divided policy-making apparatus at his disposal, made any effective diplomatic response virtually impossible. As a result, Prussia went to war in 1806, at the least favourable moment. As quickly became clear, the army suffered from the same weaknesses as the government: half-hearted and insufficient reforms, poor leadership, an incoherent command structure, and a surfeit of special privileges.[70]

Perhaps the most striking characteristic of the Prussian officer corps in 1806 was the age distribution of its members; half of the 142 generals were over sixty, 13 over seventy, 4 over eighty. Almost the entire corps came from an aristocratic background; non-noble officers usually were given low-prestige assignments in garrisons, the engineers, or the supply corps. With few exceptions, the ageing, well-born veterans of Frederick's wars found memories of past glory more vivid and instructive than the recent record of French triumphs. And some of those who did understand the reasons for France's victories refused to consider following her example: 'it would be perilous', wrote an official in 1794, 'to take an ordinary man from his daily tasks, give him a weapon, and set him against an enemy who could easily become his most dangerous seducer.' Most Prussian officers wanted to lead an army of mercenaries and long-term conscripts, who fought, not for glory or patriotism, but because, in Frederick the Great's well-known phrase, they feared their officers more than the enemy. Once the instrument and symbol of Prussia's strength, the army by 1806 had become the most dangerous manifestation of her political vulnerability.[71]

---

[69] Hintze, 'Preussische Reformbestrebungen vor 1806', in his *Abhandlungen*, iii. 504–29; the quotations are from the translation in *Essays*, pp. 69, 86. On Prussian domestic politics in this period, see also Otto Tschirch, *Geschichte der öffentlichen Meinung in Preussen vom Baseler Frieden bis zum Zusammenbruch des Staates* (Weimar, 1934).

[70] See above, Ch. 4, sect. ii.

[71] Quotation in Aretin, *Reich*, ii. 275. On the decline of Frederick's army, see Craig, *Politics*, pp. 22 ff.

'The king has lost a battle—calm is the citizen's first duty.' These words, part of a proclamation he issued after the disastrous defeats of 1806, reflected the governor of Berlin's hope that the future of the state would not depend on the fortunes of war. A possibility during the limited engagements of the old regime, such a hope was anachronistic in the revolutionary era, when the scale of fighting had long since transformed both the instruments and the stakes of combat. In predictable fashion, Prussia's military catastrophe was followed by territorial dismemberment, economic disruption, and financial ruin. The king, whose vacillation had helped to paralyse foreign and domestic policy before 1806, now had to acknowledge that reform was necessary if his state was to survive. The enemies of reform in the aristocracy, army, and civil service were in disarray.

In this desperate situation, the men who had been pressing for change from the fringes of the administration and officer corps were able to move into the centre of decision-making. During the months following Jena, therefore, Frederick William came to depend on the advice of Karl von Hardenberg, a vigorous and skilful official who urged continued resistance to the French. When Napoleon insisted on Hardenberg's removal, he was replaced by Karl Freiherr vom Stein, who served as leading minister for just over a year, before he too was dismissed as the result of French pressures. After an interim ministry under Count Dohna and Karl Altenstein, Hardenberg returned to power in 1810 and remained in office through the highpoint and gradual devolution of reform. The Prussian reforms were conceived by men trained in the old regime and were based on policies long advocated by progressive administrators; but the primary impulse for reform, and the main reason for its success, came from the irresistible pressure of the events following Jena. In the short run, reform—and especially military reform—enabled Prussia to survive as a great power. In the long run, the reformers' achievements, and perhaps even more the historiographical celebration of these achievements, helped to provide the basis for Prussia's claim to primacy in German Europe.

'Where is Stein?' asked Queen Luise in 1807 'He is my last hope. A great heart, an encompassing mind, perhaps he knows remedies that are hidden to us.'[72] There is no better evidence for the truly

[72] Quoted in Meinecke, *Age*, p. 49. On the changing historical image of Stein, see Klaus Epstein's 'Stein in German Historiography', *History and Theory*, 5/3 241–74. The best biography is still Ritter, *Stein*. For a sympathetic treatment of Stein's ministry, see Marion Gray, *Prussia in Transition: Society and Politics under the Stein Reform Ministry of 1808* (Philadelphia, 1986).

desperate situation in which Prussia found itself than the fact that the king heeded his wife's advice and, in October 1807, made a man as difficult and self-willed as Karl vom Stein his chief minister. Born in 1757 to an old family of imperial knights with estates scattered along the Lahn River, Stein had been in the Prussian bureaucracy since 1780. After serving in the Hohenzollern's western territories, Stein had acted as the Minister for Economic Affairs from 1804 until he was dismissed for insubordination in January 1807. In October he brought to his new appointment the profound conviction that Prussia's ability to avenge the humiliations of defeat would require a transformation of the political and social order. Neither a systematic nor an original thinker, Stein's vision of reform was the product of deep personal convictions, an eclectic reading of contemporary theorists, and decades of practical experience. At the root of his personality were two centuries of family history, the traditions of proud and independent aristocrats who had served many princes but felt inferior to none. From these traditions came Stein's strengths and weaknesses as a political leader: his self-confidence, courage, and high moral character, but also his wilfulness, inflexibility, and tactlessness.

While a student at Göttingen, Stein had been influenced by the distinctive *mélange* of ideas then current at this continental outpost of British thought: classical economics, a Whiggish sort of aristocratic liberalism, and a belief in the value of corporate institutions. Stein's career in Westphalia helped to reconfirm his faith in the *Stände* since these bodies continued to function there long after they had been broken in the Hohenzollern's eastern provinces. But no less important than these various ideas and experiences was the fact that, for more than a quarter century, he had served as a Prussian civil servant, mastering the details of mining operations, tax structures, local administration, and fiscal policies. Despite Stein's frequently caustic remarks about his own profession, we should not forget that, by choice and by conviction, he was a bureaucrat who had worked his way up the administrative hierarchy and who accepted the state's role as a key instrument for social change and moral progress.

The centrality of the bureaucracy for Stein's view of politics can be clearly seen in the two memoranda he prepared on the eve of the reform era, the first written in April 1806 while he was still Minister for Economic Affairs, the second in June 1807 as he watched the final stages of Prussia's collapse from his estate in Nassau. The thrust of the April memorandum is suggested by its characteristically direct and unadorned title: 'Presentation of the mistaken organization of the cabinet and of the necessity of forming a ministerial conference.' The cabinet, Stein argued, allows the incompetent favourites of the king to wield enormous power, without 'legal constitution, responsibility, orderly ties to the administration, and participation in the execution of policy'. Behind this criticism of the cabinet as an institution was a much more serious attack on the very foundation of monarchical authority. The king's advisers, he charged, 'have all the power, the final decisions in every decision and appointment, but no responsibility, since the person of the king legitimizes their actions'. The key word here is *responsibility*: for Stein, a responsible minister was someone with a clearly defined place in a legally sanctioned administrative apparatus. Loyalty to, and the confidence of, the king was not enough. In his memorandum of June 1807, the famous *Nassauer Denkschrift*, Stein extended this line of analysis to other administrative problems, especially on the provincial and local level. Within the context of bureaucratic reforms for province and community, he addressed questions of popular participation, which he viewed as a source of valuable knowledge and expertise for the state and of patriotism and self-confidence for the citizenry. Although the Nassau memorandum is sometimes cited as a demonstration of Stein's commitment to representative government, it has little or nothing to say about national participatory institutions or popular sovereignty. Stein justifies participation on functional and pedagogical grounds: it will promote inexpensive, effective local government at the same time as it teaches people to be loyal and committed citizens.[73]

Stein's desire to replace the arbitrary and irresponsible rule of royal cronies with orderly and responsible ministerial government was shared by many other talented and ambitious Prussian officials who had been frustrated by the political ineptitude so characteristic of both Frederick Williams. By making Hardenberg his chief adviser in 1807, the king had tacitly acknowledged the need for clearer lines of authority. When Stein took over that October, he tried to clarify jurisdictional divisions, advance the careers of effective civil servants, and construct a new policy-making apparatus. After months of intense debate, Stein finally persuaded the king to dissolve his cabinet of personal advisers and, in

[73] Karl Freiherr vom Stein, *Briefe und amtliche Schriften*, ed. Erich Botzenhart and Walther Hubatsch (Stuttgart, 1957–74), ii. pt. 1, pp. 206 ff., 380 ff.

November 1808, to issue an edict establishing a central administration run by five ministers, each heading a functionally defined
department. The ministers had direct access to the king, but drew
their authority from their positions within the bureaucracy itself. In
theory, the king remained absolute; in practice, his authority was
circumscribed by his ministers' monopoly over the formulation
and execution of policy. The situation that the great eighteenth-
century rulers had warned against was now at hand—in Hintze's
famous phrase, 'the absolute monarchy was transformed into a
bureaucratic monarchy'.[74]

To Stein and his collaborators, the reorganization of governmental authority was a pre-condition for turning the state into an
effective instrument for social change. The ideal of a free,
progressive, and productive society had long attracted civil
servants, while the immediate disruptions of war and the inevitable
burdens of defeat made some social rearrangements unavoidable.
Even before Stein became first minister, therefore, a group of
officials was at work on various plans for social emancipation and
economic development. These plans became the basis for the edict,
'On the Facilitation of Property Ownership, the Free Use of Land,
and the Personal Condition of Peasants', issued by the king on 9
October 1807. According to its preamble, the October Edict rested
on the belief that every individual should be free 'to achieve as
much prosperity as his abilities allow'. Over the next three years,
this same principle was applied in legislative measures designed to
weaken the guilds and ease restrictions on various types of
commercial activity. Taken together, these various reforms
furthered the project outlined in the *Allgemeines Landrecht*: civil
equality, social mobility, and economic freedom, all directly
guaranteed by the state. But, like the legal code, the reforms were
not without internal inconsistencies and qualifications. The dense
network of *Herrschaft* inherited from the old order was substantially
weakened but not totally destroyed; even when the reforms
significantly reduced or drastically redefined old privileges and
traditional restraints, residues of the traditional social order
remained part of Prussian life.

'After 11 November 1810', the edict of 9 October boldly

---

[74] On Stein's administrative reforms, see Hintze, 'Das preussische Staats-
ministerium im 19. Jahrhundert', in id., *Abhandlungen*, iii. 530 ff., Rosenberg,
Bureaucracy ch. 9, Eckart Kehr, 'Zur Genesis der preussischen Bürokratie und des
Rechtsstaats', in his *Primat*, pp. 31–52.

declared, 'there will be only free people' throughout the kingdom. This was an extraordinary promise, but also an ambiguous one. What did freedom mean in the rural world of early nineteenth-century Prussia? What were its advantages? Who paid its costs? In short, how could freedom be reconciled with the complex blend of rights and obligations upon which rural social and economic relationships had traditionally been based? Even the reformers were not in agreement about how to answer these questions. Leopold von Schroetter, the chief of the East Prussian ministerial office, favoured a consistent policy of economic freedom that would turn all questions about services and land tenure into matters of contractual agreement between landlord and tenant. Theodor von Schön, a member of the transition committee charged with preparing for Stein's ministry, recognized that Schroetter's plan would allow landlords simply to turn their former serfs into landless labourers. He advocated, therefore, protecting peasants' rights to remain on and work their lands. In its final version, the October Edict said little about protection. Peasants were freed from their hereditary servitude, from labour services and payments in kind, and from seigneurial restrictions on their rights to own land, but they were also left exposed to the forces of the market and required to compensate their lords for the loss of their seigneurial dues. As a result, only a few former serfs were able to consolidate their holdings and become independent farmers; many more were legally free, but still economically and socially dependent.[75]

The October Edict promised equality as well as freedom. It abolished all restrictions on the buying and selling of noble estates, and opened all occupations to noble and commoner alike. 'Every noble, without injury to his status, is free to enter any occupation; every burgher and peasant has the right to move out of and into the status of burgher or peasant.' In effect, this legalized the already significant incursion of market forces into the Prussian countryside. Land speculation, together with the movement of wealthy commoners into the Junkers' domain, could now be carried on without restriction or subterfuge. Deprived of the last shreds of legal protection and forced to do without the services of their serfs, some aristocratic landowners lost their family estates. But as a social

---

[75] The edict is reprinted in Huber, *Dokumente*, i. 38–40. Marion W. Gray's 'Schroetter, Schön, and Society: Aristocratic Liberalism versus Middle-Class Liberalism in Prussia, 1808', *CEH* 6/1 (Mar., 1973), 60–82, provides a good summary of the intragovernmental debate.

group, the Junkers survived, in part because they were eventually able to reclaim some of their lost privileges, in part because they were able to profit from the introduction of economic freedom. According to one estimate, about four million morgen of land were absorbed by Prussian estate owners after 1807, as compensation, through direct purchase, or by annexation. Equality, like freedom, turned out to be difficult to realize; even without their legally defined status, the Prussian nobility remained prosperous, privileged, and powerful.[76]

In order to create a nation of citizens, the reformers knew that it would be necessary to have not only freedom and equality, but also opportunities for people to participate in government. Unlike the cameralists, who had usually seen reform in economic and social terms, Stein and his colleagues recognized the need to give people sufficient stake in their nation so that they would be willing to fight and die for it. Here too there was a great deal of disagreement among the reformers about how much participation was necessary and how it might best be institutionalized. Stein himself was extremely eloquent about participation's advantages, but elusive about its specific character and function. His ideas were drawn from two quite separate realms, the corporate *Stände* which provided representation based on occupation or status, and 'self-administration', which he described in his Nassau memorandum as a way for propertied citizens to become involved in the management of their local affairs. After returning to office in October 1807, Stein worked on plans for an elaborate national representative assembly that was to be indirectly elected by corporate bodies throughout the kingdom; this assembly was to have the right to debate, even to initiate laws, but its power over the government was limited. It was never instituted. Instead, Stein had to be content with two different kinds of participatory institutions: in December 1807 the government convened the provincial estates in order to raise more taxes, and in November 1808, just before he left office, Stein had the king issue a *Städteordnung*, an edict on municipal government, which included provisions for electing officials and popular representation. Neither of these modes of representation turned out as the reformers might have hoped: the

[76] The classic account of the reforms' impact is Georg Friedrich Knapp, *Die Bauernbefreiung und der Ursprung der Landarbeiter in den älteren Theilen Preussens* (2 vols.; Leipzig, 1887); the most up-to-date are Schissler, *Agrargesellschaft*, and Harnisch, 'Oktoberedikt'. See below, Ch. 8, sec. ii for more on rural Prussia.

provincial *Stände* provided a forum for the reformers' reactionary enemies, whereas the new organs established by the *Städteordnung* evoked no enthusiasm from the population.[77]

The reformers' intellectual uncertainty about political participation and their failure to create effective representative institutions were both symptoms of the shallow support for reform in Prussian society. The reformers spoke to, and for, a nation that did not exist. While they had some support among the enlightened public, the overwhelming majority of Prussians had little understanding for what was being done in their name. For the peasants on a Pomeranian estate or the citizens in occupied Berlin, edicts promising freedom and decrees extolling equality had only limited application to the problems of everyday life. In a sense, the very sluggishness with which Prussian society responded to the reformers' efforts added a sense of urgency to their work. But at the same time, the reformers' social isolation left them vulnerable to growing opposition at court, in the landed aristocracy, and among other civil servants.

In Prussia, as in the other German states, the conflict between the reformers and their enemies continued a longstanding struggle between the advocates of state sovereignty and the defenders of *Herrschaft*. Both sides knew that the stakes had increased and that the price of failure was high. To its enemies, reform endangered religion, property, and authority. Friedrich August Ludwig von der Marwitz, for example, who had condemned the *Allgemeines Landrecht* as 'the legal expression of the revolution', believed that Stein's rural reforms involved 'the revolutionary transformation of the fatherland . . . the war of the impoverished against the propertied, industry against agriculture, mobility against stability, crass materialism against divinely-instituted order'.[78] Men like Marwitz had been temporarily displaced by the disasters of 1806–7, but they gradually constructed positions from which they could carry out a war of attrition against reform. They exploited their influence in the provincial *Stände*, supported periodicals sympathetic to their views, and lost no opportunity to warn the king and his entourage about the dangers ahead. On one level, their arguments were simple and straightforward: monarchy and aristocracy were bound together; to threaten one was inevitably to endanger the

---

[77] The relevant documents are in Engeli and Haus (eds.), *Quellen*. Heffter's *Selbstverwaltung* is the basic work for the issue of local government.

[78] Berdahl, 'Aristocracy' has a good account of Marwitz. The quotations are from Koselleck, *Preussen*, p. 44; Schissler, *Agrargesellschaft*, p. 116.

other. 'If your royal highness robs me and my children of our rights,' Yorck von Wartenburg asked Prince William, 'on what, pray, do your own rights rely?'[79] But beyond this assertion of common interests, the enemies of reform tried to weave a defence of their own economic interests and social privileges into a complex ideological defence of *Herrschaft*. The result, as we shall see in the next chapter, was a significant clarification of German political discourse.

Many of Stein's Junker antagonists rejoiced when he was forced from office in 1808. After Bonaparte's agents intercepted documents linking Stein with advocates of a new war against the French, the emperor used them as an excuse for increasing the already sizable indemnity imposed at Tilsit. Stein wanted to respond by joining with Vienna in a national crusade to liberate central Europe from foreign rule. Not unreasonably, Frederick William III took a dim view of such an enterprise, which was almost certainly doomed without Russian help. In November 1808, therefore, he dismissed Stein and replaced him with Dohna and Altenstein, two able but not especially energetic civil servants.[80] Napoleon, in an extraordinary proclamation, declared Stein an international criminal, confiscated his estates, and ordered his immediate arrest. Stein fled, first to Austria and then to Russia, where he became part of a multinational group in opposition to the French imperium. But, contrary to his enemies' hopes, Stein's fall did not bring the era of reform to an end. Dohna and Altenstein continued some of his policies, passed an important decree separating the administrative and judicial bureaucracies, and presided over some changes in educational and military institutions. They were not, however, able to provide the kind of leadership and inspiration a coherent policy of reform required. Frederick William, still unsure of himself and of the future, needed a clear and decisive person to keep him moving along a reformist path.

The advocates of change, therefore, were generally encouraged when, in June 1810, the king named Karl von Hardenberg to head the ministries of finance and the interior and gave him the new title of *Staatskanzler*, thus formally designating him as Prussia's first prime minister. Born in 1750 to a family with extensive estates in Hanover, Hardenberg had studied at Göttingen, done a brief tour

[79] Demeter, *Officer Corps*, p. 14.
[80] R. C. Raack, *The Fall of Stein* (Cambridge, Mass., 1965) is a detailed account of Stein's dismissal with particular emphasis on the personalities of those involved.

of duty at the imperial court in Wetzlar, and then served as an official in Hanover, Brunswick, and finally Prussia, where he had run the administration of the Hohenzollern's newly acquired lands of Ansbach-Bayreuth. By the mid-1790s Hardenberg had become an important figure in Berlin, where he was one of the mixed chorus of voices around Frederick William II. His power and prestige increased under the new king, who appointed him to the General Directory in 1798. Eventually he was given charge of foreign affairs and thus had to co-ordinate the diplomatic salvage operation that followed the defeats of 1806. After his forced retirement in 1807, he waited restlessly on the sidelines until his reappointment three years later.[81]

Hardenberg was carefully groomed, gracious in manner, and fond of brief flirtations; his style of life was closer to that of courtiers like Montgelas and Metternich than to the austere and blunt figure of Stein. Hardenberg also lacked Stein's moral fervour and passionate idealism. His admirers claimed he was flexible and realistic, his detractors that he was devious and unprincipled—there is probably some truth in both propositions. He was certainly a man much closer to the king's tastes than the mercurial Stein, whose vigour and frankness always made Frederick William nervous. But more important than the differences in personality between the two leading Prussian reformers were the personal differences in their political visions. Hardenberg was much closer to the traditions of eighteenth-century enlightened absolutism; his approach to politics tended to be cooler, more rational, less burdened by eloquent exhortations and idealized imagery. In contrast to Stein, Hardenberg did not have much use for corporate representative bodies—he had made his reputation breaking the power of the local nobility in Ansbach, a struggle that turned out to be a kind of dress rehearsal for the final destruction of the imperial nobility after 1803. Since he worried less about the fragmentation of communal bonds and the isolation of the individual, Hardenberg was also a more consistent advocate of social and economic freedom than Stein had been.

Hardenberg's political views were best expressed in the lengthy memorandum he wrote in the summer of 1807, shortly after his own resignation and before Stein's appointment. This document, the so-called *Rigaer Denkschrift*, ranks with Montgelas' memorandum of 1796 and Stein's of 1806 and 1807 as one of the most

---

[81] Thielen, *Hardenberg*, is a good, concise biography. For a comparison of Stein and Hardenberg, see Krieger, *Idea*, pp. 147 ff.

important formulations of the German reformers' aspirations. After acknowledging the centrality of the French experience and the necessity of learning its lessons, Hardenberg defined the purpose of reform as:

a revolution in a positive sense, one leading to the ennoblement of mankind, to be made not through violent impulses from below or outside, but through the wisdom of the government. . . . Democratic principles in a monarchical government—this seems to me to be the appropriate form for the spirit of our age.

By 'democratic', Hardenberg meant economic freedom and social emancipation, the opening of careers to all men of talent, religious toleration and civil liberty for Jews, freedom of opinion and education. About the participatory elements in democracy, he had much less to say. Beyond acknowledging that public opinion was important and that people should be involved in state administration, he seems to have been uncertain or unconcerned about representative institutions. Within the context of the Riga memorandum, 'Democratic principles in a monarchical government' meant freedom for individuals in the economic and social realm—and virtually unlimited power for the state in the conduct of public affairs.[82]

The immediate cause of Hardenberg's appointment was the fiscal crisis produced by mounting state debts and persistent French demands for indemnity payments. Ever since 1807 financial problems had shadowed the Prussian government, forcing it to increase taxes, issue paper money and debase the coinage, and borrow at high rates from Berlin bankers. None of these measures proved sufficient. When Dohna and Altenstein suggested abandoning territory in Silesia to clear the debt, Frederick William replaced them with Hardenberg, who pledged himself to full payment of the French indemnity and total reorganization of the state's finances. The chancellor introduced new taxes and increased income from tariffs, but he was not able to break Prussia's dependence on private loans or to halt inflationary pressures. Nor did Prussia's overall financial picture significantly improve: the state debt, which had been 53 million gulden before the war of 1806 and was about 100 million in 1810, increased to 112 million in 1811 and 206 million four years later. Hardenberg's efforts to master the fiscal crisis did,

---

[82] Thielen, *Hardenberg,* p. 207. See also Hans Hausherr, 'Hardenbergs Reformdenkschrift Rigas 1807', *HZ* 157/2 (1938), 267–307.

however, include some legislative achievements with lasting importance for Prussian political and social development.[83]

In a cluster of edicts issued in October 1810, Hardenberg tried to improve the state's financial situation by removing exemptions from taxation and restrictions on economic activity. The *Finanz-edikt* of 27 October promised an equalization of the tax burdens, the introduction of freedom of enterprise, a reform of the tariff and toll system, secularization of church properties, and further sale of the royal domains. The next day, 'an edict on the introduction of a universal tax on enterprises [*Gewerbesteuer*]' required anyone carrying on a business to purchase a licence from the state, thereby shifting from the guilds and towns the authority to regulate economic activity. Two days later, the government nationalized the land belonging to both Catholic and Protestant churches and assumed control over all ecclesiastical institutions. In March 1812, after much of his reformist energy had been spent, Hardenberg added to these regulations an edict 'concerning the civil condition of Jews in Prussia', which removed the special restrictions and privileges governing Jews' social and economic activities and declared them 'natives and citizens' (*Einländer* und *Staatsbürger*). The political meaning of citizenship, however, was left open, since Article Nine declared that the question of Jews' access to public duties and state offices would be decided at some future time.[84]

The political meaning of citizenship, explicitly set to one side for Jews, was also a matter of uncertainty for the rest of the Prussian population. In an effort to soften the blow of the financial obligations outlined in the *Finanzedikt*, the king had called for the creation of 'appropriately organized representations, both for the provinces and the state as a whole', which could provide advice and participate in further financial discussions. In 1811 Hardenberg attempted to deflect the growing opposition to his policies by calling an assembly of notables, which he hoped would outflank the hostile, Junker-dominated *Stände*. When the sixty representatives

---

[83] Ernst Klein, *Von der Reform zur Restauration. Finanzpolitik und Reformgesetz-gebung des preussischen Staatskanzlers K. A. von Hardenberg* (Berlin, 1965). On the financial problems Hardenberg inherited, see Schissler's introduction and the documents in Eckart Kehr, *Preussische Finanzpolitik, 1806–1810: Quellen zur Verwaltung der Ministerien Stein und Altenstein*, ed. Hanna Schissler and Hans-Ulrich Wehler (Göttingen, 1984).

[84] The relevant edicts are reprinted in Huber, *Dokumente*, i. 41 ff. See the analysis in Barbara Vogel, *Allgemeine Gewerbefreiheit. Die Reformpolitik des preussischen Staatskanzlers Hardenberg, 1810–20* (Göttingen, 1983).

nominated from various leading social groups gathered in Hardenberg's palace in February, he told them to view themselves 'as
representatives of the entire nation', and called upon them to assist
in the creation of a free and equal society. But, since the assembly
was not sympathetic to his cause, the chancellor dissolved it as soon
as he could. It was replaced by an 'interim national representation',
elected by local governmental assemblies, which met in Berlin in
1812 and again in 1814 to advise the government. Like the assembly
of notables, however, this body had little practical significance.
Under Hardenberg, as under Stein, the participatory dimensions of
reform proved impossible to realize—and for essentially the same
reason: neither Hardenberg nor Stein could establish ways to
represent a nation that was either apathetic or hostile towards his
political goals.[85]

In comparison to Stein, Hardenberg was more willing to bow to
the pressure exerted against him by powerful social groups. As
early as September 1811, the chancellor compromised with the
Junkers by reinstating many of the tax exemptions for nobles
abolished the preceding October. Moveover, in time, an edict
regulating the questions of land tenure which had been left
unresolved in Stein's emancipation decrees, Hardenberg attempted
to accommodate the interests of landowners at the expense of the
peasantry. Finally and most important, the chancellor had to limit
efforts to clarify and centralize the lines of state authority in local
affairs. His *Gendarmerie-Edikt* of July 1812 had tried to break the ties
of the *Landrat* to local interests and to create a bureaucratized
system of rural government on the French model. So great was the
outcry among the Junkers that the edict proved impossible to
enforce; in 1814 it was abandoned altogether.[86]

Hardenberg and his collaborators were sustained in their
struggles against the enemies of reform by the hope and expectation that their policies would enable Prussia to become, once again,
a major power. Like Montgelas and the reformers in the south and
west, Hardenberg was primarily a diplomat, committed to
liberating his nation from French domination and restoring it to its
former position of independence. Military defeat had made reform
possible by making it essential; the need for recovery drove
Hardenberg's social, economic, and fiscal policies just as it had
driven Stein's. Military reform, therefore, was a critical element in

[85] Koselleck, *Preussen*, p. 194.
[86] Schissler, *Agrargesellschaft*.

the minds of every reformer, who regarded a revitalized army as both the product and the instrument of national regeneration.

Like their civilian counterparts, the military reformers were a group of kindred spirits who had struggled against the institutional inefficiencies and weaknesses which had threatened the state and frustrated their own ambitions. This group included many men from the traditional Prussian élites, but the leading personalities were, like Stein and Hardenberg, outsiders. We have already had occasion to mention Gerhard von Scharnhorst, the Hanoverian peasant's son who joined the Prussian army after the turn of the century and quickly became the driving force behind reform. Neithardt von Gneisenau came from a family of jurists and minor civil servants; his father, a junior officer in the service of the bishop of Würzburg, had appropriated his title on the basis of some questionable ties to a noble house. After serving various German princes, Gneisenau had joined the Prussian army. In 1806 he was a middle-aged captain with unusual intellectual interests but not much hope for advancement. After being catapulted into prominence in 1806 by his heroic defence of Kolberg against overwhelming odds, he became an effective supporter of military renewal and later one of Prussia's finest combat commanders.[87]

The military reformers' initial base of operations was the Military Reform Commission, which had been established by the king in the summer of 1807. Acting through this commission, they purged those who had led the army to disaster; within a year, 208 officers, including seventeen generals, lost their jobs. Their next step was to overcome the institutional incoherence that had inhibited the military command structure no less than it had hindered the political decision-making apparatus. Like the civilians, the army reformers wanted clear, efficient lines of 'responsible' authority, which would help take power away from the king's cronies and keep it in the hands of expert professionals operating within an official hierarchy. In December 1808 they convinced the king to establish a war ministry with control over all aspects of military affairs. Even though a minister was not appointed until 1814, this new structure gave Scharnhorst and his associates the authority they needed to improve the overall organization of the army and to introduce various changes in the details of military life.

To have an effective officer corps, the reformers believed,

---

[87] Craig, *Politics*, pp. 37 ff., has a good summary. On the social background of the reformers, see Paret, *Yorck*, pp. 125–6.

required removing outdated privileges and harmful restrictions. Their ideal, incorporated in an order of August 1808, was a military career open to talent: 'aspirations to officer's rank should be based, in peacetime, on knowledge and training, and in war, on bravery and vision.' To further this goal, the reformers dissolved the old cadet schools and founded new training institutes to provide nine-month courses for prospective subalterns. An élite academy was established in Berlin, where the most promising young officers could receive a three-year preparation for staff responsibilities. But more important than these efforts to improve the quality of the army leadership was the reformers' campaign to bring the army into what Scharnhorst called 'a more intimate union' with the nation. Here social, economic, political, and military reforms combined in an effort to create free, independent, prosperous, and patriotic men, ready and able to fight and die for their state. 'We must interject a feeling of independence,' Scharnhorst wrote in September 1807, 'to destroy the old forms, to dissolve the bonds of privilege, to lead and nurture and unfetter the free development of regeneration—there can be no higher purpose.'[88] The culmination of this process was to be the nation in arms, a citizen army led by the most talented professionals society could produce. To Frederick William, however, such a mass army seemed dangerous and expensive, a provocation to the French and a peril to domestic order. Neither he nor Hardenberg had the kind of faith in the *Volk* that inspired Scharnhorst and his idealistic fellow officers. The government, therefore, was willing to allow some adjustments in the old modes of recruiting but refused to follow the soldiers' call for a national mobilization.

By 1812 the military reformers were frustrated by the king's resistance to a *Volksarmee* and appalled by the direction of Prussian foreign policy. Convinced that the nation would rise in their support and impatient with what they saw as overly subtle diplomatic manoeuvering, the soldiers were eager to renew the battle against Napoleon. But the king remained cautious. The Austrian defeat in 1809 had convinced him that he had been right to ignore those who had wanted to join Stadion's ill-fated national crusade. Furthermore, following the sudden death of his wife in 1810, Frederick William withdrew from public life and became preoccupied with grief and consoled only by prayer. Hardenberg was also reluctant to follow an aggressive course. He wanted to

[88] Huber, i. 235, 240.

restore Prussian independence, but he was not convinced that a national war of liberation was either desirable or possible. In any case, the time did not seem right. With Austria defeated and apparently prepared to compromise with France, the Rhenish Confederation firmly under French control, and England still alienated from Prussia by a series of commercial and political disputes, Berlin was isolated and Napoleon's power apparently unassailable. To the war party, the deterioration of Franco-Russian relations in 1811 seemed a perfect opportunity; they wanted an immediate alliance with the tsar. Hardenberg, however, had no desire to trade Russian for French hegemony, nor did he want his state to become the arena for a final struggle between the two great powers. After negotiating with both emperors and finding neither willing to offer him anything substantial, Hardenberg took what seemed like the safest of two unattractive paths. At the end of February 1812 Prussia signed a new agreement with Napoleon, to whom it promised limited aid in the event of a Russian war.

The reformers now faced the prospect of having the army they had so painfully rebuilt commandeered to help Napoleon destroy the last major barrier to French hegemony. Stein, who had joined the court at St Petersburg, argued that the Franco-Prussian alliance raised central questions about the loyalty any citizen owed his state. 'At this moment', he wrote in March 1812, 'it is very difficult to reconcile the duties of the citizen with those of a moral man.' Scharnhorst must have had the same sort of thing in mind when he told an officer who had joined the Russian army, 'I cannot condemn your decision, because everyone must first see that he remains true to himself.'[89] Several reformers resigned during the first half of 1812. Scharnhorst, who had been forced from his military post by Napoleon in 1810, withdrew completely from public life; Clausewitz, Scharnhorst's most talented protégé, joined Hermann von Boyen, Stein, and several other patriots in St Petersburg. The era of reform was apparently over, its sacred mission abandoned and unfulfilled.

iv. THE END OF NAPOLEONIC HEGEMONY

During the spring of 1812, when some Prussian patriots, in despair

---

[89] Paret, *Clausewitz*, p. 219. Bernd von Münchow-Pohl provides a careful analysis of the depressed public mood in Prussia on the eve of the war: *Zwischen Reform und Krieg. Untersuchungen zur Bewusstseinslage in Preussen, 1809–1812* (Göttingen, 1987).

over the declining fortunes of reform, left to serve foreign governments, their arch-enemy Napoleon was at the peak of his power. His relatives occupied thrones throughout the Continent; his dependants ruled states of his own creation along France's much advanced eastern frontiers; he had intimidated Prussia and Austria into becoming his allies. When the emperor travelled through his domain, whole villages emptied to catch sight of him. 'Rich and poor, nobleman and commoner, friend and foe all rush out,' wrote Philippe de Segur, a member of the imperial staff, 'with alert curiosity these masses fill the streets, roads, and public squares, waiting through the day and even through the night to get a glimpse [of Napoleon].' The object of the crowd's fascination was not the imperial dignity, not the office or the crown, but the man himself. People waited to see a hero, a great personality, a historical figure 'whose features were impressed in their souls, so that they could tell their less fortunate children and fellow citizens that they had gazed upon Napoleon'.[90] This deeply personal character of Napoleon's fame and power made the trapping of traditional kingship with which he surrounded himself largely irrelevant. His own personal qualities of character and intelligence were the primary sources of his success, just as they would be the ultimate cause of his downfall. 'Your sovereigns born on the throne can let themselves be beaten twenty times and return to their capitals,' he once told Metternich. 'My domination will not survive the day when I cease to be strong and therefore feared.'[91]

In May 1812, as the *Grande Armée* began to deploy for the invasion of Russia, Napoleon summoned his German clients and allies to Dresden for what would turn out to be the last great celebration of his European imperium. All of them came. Francis of Austria was given pride of place, less because of his imperial rank and dynastic dignity than because of his position as Napoleon's father-in-law, grandfather of the infant king of Rome. Francis and Metternich, Frederick William and Hardenberg, together with the rulers of the other states watched the massive display of French power that their host had carefully prepared. As usual, Napoleon managed to evoke a mixture of avarice and awe from the more gullible of his German dependants. Christian von Voigt, a minister of Weimar, had looked forward to the Dresden meetings 'with astonishment and wonder. . . . What heroes will be there assembled! What diplomatists! Certainly everything will end with

---

[90] Klessmann (ed.), *Napoleons Russlandfeldzug*, p. 35.
[91] Chandler, *Napoleon*, p. 140.

globally blessed treaties: Egypt, Greece, the archipelago will be ours. If the great emperor offers to each prince an island, which one should I take?' In fact, Napoleon did not have any territory with which to feed his allies' Gargantuan appetites. He could offer his guests no more than flattering attention, newly minted decorations, and lavish banquets. Never one to be taken in by the shows he so hugely enjoyed, Metternich recognized that the Dresden meeting would be without political content. He knew that no important changes could take place on the continent until the final conflict between France and Russia had been resolved.[92]

The Dresden conference ended on 28 May. The German sovereigns journeyed back to their capitals; Napoleon joined his troops. If he had hoped to intimidate the tsar into accepting his terms for living on a continent dominated by France, he was disappointed. There remained no alternative but war on a scale without precedent; on 24 and 25 June Napoleon's army crossed the Niemen. Among its 600,000 men were 180,000 Germans, including 20,000 Prussians under Yorck and 30,000 Austrians under Schwarzenberg. Characteristically, Napoleon hoped to win the war with a swift and total victory over the Russian army, preferably in Poland. But the Russians would not stand and fight; instead they retreated deeper and deeper into their own territory, stretching the invader's supply lines, draining his troops' morale, slowly chipping away at his awesome numerical superiority. As the months went by without a decisive battle, sickness, desertions, and constant harassment by Russian irregulars took a terrible toll, especially among some of the badly trained and poorly motivated soldiers provided by Napoleon's allies—after three months, for example, less than 1,500 of the original 16,000 troops from Württemberg remained. As Clausewitz, always sensitive to the ironies of war, later remarked: 'The highest wisdom could never have devised a better strategy than the one the Russians followed unintentionally.' The Russian strategy's results are well known: after an inconclusive victory at Borodino in September, the French advanced to Moscow, which was then destroyed by its own inhabitants; without supplies or shelter, the invaders had to make a long, painful retreat through the terrible Russian winter. By the time the last French infantryman had dragged himself across the Niemen in December, the *Grande Armée* was reduced to 40,000

---

[92] Klessmann (ed.), *Napoleons Russlandfeldzug*, p. 35. See also Kraehe, *Metternich's German Policy*, i. 143 ff.

dispirited survivors, the tragically small remnant of what had once been the most formidable fighting force in modern military history.[93]

The Russian disaster left Napoleon's regime critically, but not fatally wounded. By rushing back to Paris in December, the emperor had managed to consolidate his political position before the full extent of the Russian débâcle became clear. Moreover, the Russians' victory had been purchased at a high price: with their battered army, chaotic finances, and devastated homeland, they could not hope to defeat Napoleon on their own; their forces were too weak to move too far westward, where they would suffer from the same logistical problems that had undone the *Grande Armée*. In effect, Napoleon's fate depended on the German states. If they remained loyal, he could rally enough support in France and mobilize sufficient resources in the rest of Europe to withstand any military threat from the Russians. But if the Germans turned against him, he would have to face a formidable coalition of enemies with only the manpower and material wealth of France at his disposal.

In the various German capitals, the news from Russia had provoked great interest but no clear convictions about the future. In the Rhenish Confederation, most rulers were much too closely tied to Napoleon to set off on an independent course. Prussia's Frederick William was predictably irresolute; perhaps he remembered how Napoleon's defeat at Aspern in May 1809 had been followed by his victory at Wagram two months later. Metternich was intent on keeping his options open, not merely because he was uncertain about the military balance, but also because he feared a Russian victory no less than the persistence of French domination.

In contrast to these cautious assessments by the various German governments, the German contingent at the Russian court pressed for a full-scale war of European liberation. Shortly after his arrival in Russia, Stein had formed a committee for German affairs and then a German legion to fight against the French. In the wake of Napoleon's defeat, he argued that if the tsar would lead a crusade to rid Europe of its Corsican oppressor, the German *Volk* would rise to aid him in this noble work. As he looked for ways to reach the *Volk* over the heads of their timid and short-sighted rulers, Stein was once again trying to turn the weapons of the revolution against their French inventors: like the decrees from Paris in 1792, Stein's

[93] Clausewitz, *On War*, p. 615. See Chandler, *Campaigns*, chs. 13, 14.

proclamations two decades later suggest the degree to which some contemporaries were prepared to ignore the traditional divisions between foreign and domestic politics.[94]

The first great success of the German patriots in Russia's service was the defection of General von Yorck at the end of December 1812. Yorck had managed to preserve 14,000 Prussian troops from the Russian catastrophe. Long an avowed enemy of Napoleon, he had been in contact with the Russians since September. In December, during the final retreat of the main French force under MacDonald, Yorck found himself in a key position: with his assistance, MacDonald could try to stop the Russian advance at the Niemen, without him there would be no alternative but full-scale retreat. On Christmas Day, Yorck met with the commander of the advance Russian force. The intermediary in these negotiations was Clausewitz, now a Russian staff officer, who has left us a dramatic account of the events. Initially, Yorck hoped that his superiors in Berlin would agree to let him change sides, but when no such orders arrived, he decided to violate his oath of obedience and act on his own. 'You've got me,' he told the delighted Clausewitz late in the evening of 29 December. The following day, at a mill in Poscherun, near Tauroggen, Yorck signed a document severing his connections with the French. Within a few days, the Russians were across the Niemen and in Prussian territory. For Stein and his collaborators, winning over Yorck was a major psychological boost that helped to steel their resolve during the difficult weeks ahead.[95]

When word of Yorck's defection reached Berlin, Frederick William relieved him of his command and ordered his immediate arrest. The general ignored the king and quickly became an active partner of the Russians. 'Now or never is the time to regain liberty and honour,' he declared on 13 January, 'with a bleeding heart, I tear the bonds of obedience and wage war on my own.'[96] Stein, who had arrived in Königsberg with the Russian forces, also began to wage his own war. In order to mobilize support for the campaign, he summoned the East Prussian Stände and persuaded them to raise a militia to reinforce Yorck's troops. Meanwhile, Frederick William continued to hesitate, while Hardenberg, who had by now realized that it was time to change sides, worried that a

---

[94] For more on this issue, see below, Ch. 6, sect. iv.

[95] Paret, Yorck. Clausewitz's account is reprinted in Klessmann (ed.), Napoleons Russlandfeldzug, pp. 361 ff.

[96] Paret, Clausewitz, p. 331.

premature move might provoke effective French countermeasures. On 22 January the king moved away from the French garrison occupying Berlin and established his court in Breslau, where his attention was monopolized by the war party. After establishing an armaments commission under Scharnhorst, Frederick William issued an order on 9 February removing all exemptions from military service 'for the duration of the war'. This was followed some weeks later by decrees setting up a militia (*Landwehr*) and reserve (*Landsturm*). Meanwhile Hardenberg began negotiating with the Russians on the conditions for an alliance. After some hard bargaining, Frederick William and Alexander agreed to join in a campaign for the liberation of Europe. On 17 March the Prussian king issued a proclamation announcing that his soldiers 'will fight for our independence and the honor of the *Volk*. Both will only be secured if every son of the fatherland participates in this battle for honour and freedom. . . . My cause is the cause of my *Volk*, and of all well-intentioned Europeans.'[97] These words show how the pressure of events had led Frederick William to adopt the reformers' rhetoric, but they should not obscure the traditional goals of statecraft that continued to motivate the king and his chief adviser. The alliance with Russia was based on a common struggle against France, but also included a series of territorial arrangements through which Frederick William ceded his Polish lands in return for the promise of acquisitions in the north and east. From the start, the war of liberation combined secret diplomacy and public proclamations, devotion to the familiar interests of the states and unprecedented appeals for patriotic involvement.

While Frederick William and Hardenberg were becoming the somewhat reluctant patrons of national liberation, Francis and Metternich remained on the sidelines. In October 1812, at a time when Napoleon's forces seemed almost certain to defeat the Russians, Metternich had written to Hardenberg that 'we must seek the instrument of our salvation in our own resources, we cannot gamble our existence on a single card'. This strategy involved a willingness to negotiate with everyone and a reluctance to be committed to anyone. Those who regarded unwavering hostility to Napoleon as the only legitimate German policy were understandably outraged by Metternich's position. From his perspective, however, it made a great deal of sense, even after the defeat of the *Grande Armée*. France, after all, was still a great power

[97] Huber, *Dokumente*, i. 49.

with an apparently unshakeable grip on much of Europe, whereas Russia was an unpredictable and potentially dangerous ally, no less worrisome in victory than it had been in defeat. Moreover, Metternich viewed the German *Volk*, whose support loomed so large in the reformers' rhetoric, with the gravest suspicion. 'The first, the most unalterable of all Austrian interests is independence,' he wrote in January 1813. Shortly thereafter he rejected both Prussian and Russian alliances. He did, however, slowly and cautiously begin to disengage himself from France; in April he renounced his formal agreement with Napoleon and declared Austria a free agent, ready to assist either side to advance the cause of peace. Throughout this period he hoped to convince the French emperor to offer concessions and thus bring the war to an end without a final victory for either side. This would have created what Metternich viewed as the best possible situation: a strong, but not predominant France that could balance Russian power and thus leave Austria able to manoeuvre in between.[98]

Although they were in no position to defy him, Bonaparte's German allies now feared that he would not be strong enough to protect them. Needless to say, they regarded the advance of the Russian and Prussian troops with horror, especially after the release on 25 March of a 'Proclamation to the German People and Princes', signed at the military headquarters at Kalisch by the Russian commander, and issued in the names of Tsar Alexander and King Frederick William. In this remarkable document, directed to both the governments and people of the German states, General Kutusow promised 'honour and freedom' in the hope that 'every German worthy of the name would quickly and forcefully accept his offer'. Although the language was evasive, the dangers of non-compliance were unmistakably defined: king and tsar hoped, the proclamation stated, that no prince would reject a chance to support the German cause and thus risk 'destruction through the strength of public opinion and the power of righteous arms'.[99] With the exception of Mecklenburg, whose duke was a relative of the tsar, no German state responded positively to the mixture of promises and threats contained in the Kalisch proclamation. King Frederick of Saxony, whose lands were especially vulnerable to Russian and Prussian ambition, found refuge from their invading armies on Austrian soil. In a treaty signed at Prague on 20 April, he obtained full Austrian support against any attempted annexations.

[98] Kraehe, *Metternich's German Policy*, i. 148, 153.
[99] Huber, *Dokumente*, i. 72.

Although not yet directly threatened by enemy troops, Bavaria followed a similar course. On 25 April the government in Munich announced its neutrality and prepared to enter a treaty with Austria. As the eager recipient of territory taken from Prussia in 1807, the Wittelsbachs had good reason to worry about a Prussian victory over France. Metternich meanwhile continued to try to mediate between the belligerents and to lure Prussia away from Russia and towards Austria.

Without the help of either Austria or the smaller German states, the allied struggle against Napoleon would have to be decided by the Prussian and Russian armies, backed, as usual, by British naval and economic power. When the spring offensive began in April 1813, the Prussians could field 80,000 men who were much better trained, motivated, and commanded than the troops over whom Napoleon had triumphed so easily seven years before. The Russians had an army of 110,000, including the 30,000 cossack cavalrymen who had been harassing the French lines since the beginning of the year. In the north, a Swedish force under Bernadotte and a small Anglo–German contingent were ready to close the circle of Napoleon's antagonists. But, despite his defeat in Russia, the continued deterioration of the situation in Spain, and the painful effects of the British blockade, Napoleon had not lost hope in total victory. During the first months of 1813 he reached deeply into France's reserves of manpower and material to rebuild his army. By April he had moved his troops into the heart of German Europe, between the Saale and Elbe, where he searched for an opportunity to isolate and destroy his enemies before they had a change to consolidate their forces. At Lutzen on 2 May and at Bautzen three weeks later, he managed to defeat the allied armies. These victories were enough to send the German princes hurrying back to their French patron. Frederick of Saxony left his new Austrian allies, while Max Joseph of Bavaria abandoned his negotiations with Vienna. Nevertheless, neither Lutzen nor Bautzen were decisive enough to end the campaign. Both sides, therefore, were willing to accept an armistice in early June.[100]

During this lull in the fighting, Metternich acted as a mediator recognized by both sides. Convinced that a decisive victory of either Napoleon or his enemies would be against Austrian interests, he urged compromise, conciliation, and peace. However, while he feared the consequences of a French defeat, Metternich knew that he could not remain on the sidelines much longer. The growing

[100] Fuller, *Battles*, pp. 450 ff.; Chandler, *Campaigns*, pp. 865 ff.

strength of the allies, together with Wellington's triumph over Joseph Bonaparte in Spain, suggested that the balance had begun to tip against France. Although Metternich did not abandon his campaign to convince Napoleon that compromise was essential if he were to survive, the chancellor did sign a treaty with the allied powers on 27 June. Finally, after the failure of his best efforts to force concessions from Napoleon, Metternich declared war on 12 August. A few days later the belligerents began to move their troops into position for what they knew would be the decisive struggle for Europe's future.[101]

Austria's entry into the war brought the allies an additional 127,000 men. By August Prussia's new conscription laws and the military reformers' tireless activity had produced an army of 228,000 infantry, 31,000 cavalry, and thirteen thousand artillery-men with 376 guns. Scharnhorst's death in May deprived the army of its finest soldier, but his work was carried on by Gneisenau, whose own abilities as a military leader were just being recognized. Blücher, Prussia's best known combat commander, was a tough, seventy-year-old veteran, whose hatred of Napoleon and eagerness to fight provided the allies with some badly needed energy and *élan*. In August Blücher commanded the army of Silesia, a force of 90,000 men operating south of Breslau. To the north, Bernadotte's army of 110,000 Swedes and Prussians had retaken Berlin. Schwarzenberg led a multinational force of allied troops on the upper Elbe. Against these enemies, Napoleon had 442,000 combat troops, many of them poorly trained conscripts, just recently called to the colours. Contrary to his inclinations, he was forced by political considerations to keep a sizeable number of his men in garrisons, such as Dresden, where King Frederick, who had ill-advisedly returned to the French side, was in need of protection. But Napoleon did have the advantage of moving from interior lines against a coalition of enemies whose record of strategic and military co-operation was less than inspiring. After he had won a bitter engagement near Dresden at the end of August, the emperor attempted to concentrate his armies and attack the enemy before they had a chance to bring their forces together—a classic Napoleonic strategy. This time the strategy did not work. Finally, on 16 October he had to accept battle at Leipzig, where the fighting raged for three days across a broad sweep of ground circling the city. Outnumbered and outgunned, Napoleon eventually had no choice but to withdraw, leaving the allies victorious in what would

---

[101] The best defence of Metternich's position is in Srbik, *Metternich*, i. 157 ff.

enter the mythology of national liberation as 'the battle of nations'.[102]

The price of victory was high. The allies lost 54,000 killed or wounded, another 5,000 defected to the French in the course of the battle. The French lost over 38,000 troops in combat and another 30,000 who were taken prisoner when a frightened sapper corporal stranded the entire rearguard by blowing up the last escape route. Napoleon also had to abandon more than three hundred cannon and much of his transport and supplies. For days the fields around the city were covered with dead bodies, a macabre scene that Wilhelm von Humboldt tried to describe in a letter to his wife of 20 October:

Crowds of corpses lay around, most of them partially clothed or completely naked, often piled one on top of another. Most lie with outstretched arms over the face, so that one grasps for the first time the meaning of Homer's lines, bite the earth with the teeth. A poor dog searches here and there and won't be dragged away. . . . he has probably found his master's scent. [103]

Within the city, little could be done to comfort the wounded who filled hospitals, churches and schools, and, as usual, disease was war's handmaiden. Typhus soon spread through Leipzig's overcrowded streets, killing off the wounded and infecting those who were charged with their care. Among the dead was Friedrich Wagner, a conscientious policeman, who left a wife and a six-month-old son named Richard.

The battle had clearly ended Napoleon's European hegemony. Although he was able to conduct a brilliant retreat along his main supply lines and by early November was safely across the Rhine, his imperium collapsed. As the French garrisons surrendered, their satellite regimes disintegrated. At this point, questions about the future organization of the German lands could no longer be avoided. What would happen to Napoleon's allies? What mode of organization would replace the Rhenish Confederation? Could the Reich or something like it be restored? What, if anything, might be salvaged from the political reorganizations of 1803 and 1806? How would the ambitions of the victorious allies be fulfilled and at whose expense? What would happen to the Austro-Prussian alliance once the Napoleonic danger had passed? From the autumn of 1813 until the final settlement at Vienna almost two years later,

[102] Chandler, *Campaigns*, pp. 903 ff. See also Craig, *Problems*.
[103] Klessmann (ed.), *Befreiungskriege*, p. 188. For an eloquent statement of the battle's significance, see Meinecke, *Age*, p. 119.

these questions would plague the victors, threatening their coalition, undermining their co-operation, and sometimes bringing
them to the brink of war. Like the war of liberation itself, answers
to questions about the German future combined passionate
patriotic rhetoric and hard-edged statecraft, the dreams of reformers like Stein and the calculations of diplomats like Metternich.

In 1813 and 1814 Stein enjoyed the tentative and perhaps
disingenuous support of Tsar Alexander, who apparently had
embraced the cause of national liberation. No longer tied to
Prussia, or to any other state, Stein was free to envision a new
Germany unified, reformed, and powerful. To build this nation he
was prepared to sacrifice those 'thirty-six petty despots' who had
forfeited their right to rule by gorging themselves at the tyrant's
table. For a time, he even supposed that Prussia might be dissolved.
'I have but one fatherland, and that is Germany,' he wrote in
December 1812. 'I am completely indifferent, in this historic
moment, to the fate of the dynasties. . . . you may do with Prussia
what you like. . . .' But once Prussia and then Austria had entered
the war, Stein had to adjust his views: now he was dealing with
Tsar Alexander's allies, not Napoleon's. By the fall of 1813 he had
come to imagine three 'Germanies'—the old western territories
reclaimed from the Rhenish Confederation, Austria, and Prussia—
which would be joined in a military alliance. Stein's Central
Administrative Committee, set up in March 1813, was supposed to
lay the foundation for this new 'Germany' by taking over areas as
they were liberated from France. This committee, Stein hoped,
would destroy the existing political order and mobilize the
population for the continued struggle against Napoleon.[104]

To future generations of German nationalists, Stein's vision of a
unified nation seemed an attractive adumbration of their own
political goals. But within the context of 1813 and 1814, Stein
found few supporters; indeed the breadth of his vision was in part
the result of this isolation. Without connections with any state,
Stein was in a position to imagine a total reorganization of central
Europe, but he was not in a position to do anything to bring it
about. As a result, the great patriot was frustrated at every turn by
the apathy of the *Volk* he wished to mobilize and by the
antagonism of the statesmen who were not about to sacrifice their

[104] Walter M. Simon, 'Variations in Nationalism during the Great Reform Period
in Prussia', *AHR* 59/2 (1954), 307. For a stirring expression of Stein's views, see his
proclamation to the duke of Nassau, who had annexed his ancestral lands in 1803,
quoted in Epstein, *Genesis*, p. 631. On the work of the *Zentralverwaltungsrat*, see
Huber, i. 487 ff.

concrete interests for the sake of his vague ideals. As different as they were in so many ways, both Hardenberg and Metternich agreed that Stein's plans were unacceptable. After all, both men were servants of their states, conscious of past rivalries, alert to present opportunities, fearful of future disadvantage. Once Austria entered the war, they shared a common objective, but they never lost sight of the potential for discord any post-war settlement must involve.

On 9 September 1813, as their soldiers prepared for the decisive battle against France, the rulers of Austria, Prussia, and Russia met at Teplitz and signed a series of treaties in which they committed themselves to fighting until Napoleon's final defeat and promised to return Austria and Prussia to their size and status of 1805. The three rulers also agreed to dissolve the Rhenish Confederation, but they guaranteed 'the entire and absolute independence of the intermediate states between the frontiers of the Austrian and Prussian monarchies . . . and the Rhine and the Alps'.[105] The vague phrasing of this final clause was meant to obscure the differences between Hardenberg and Metternich. The former viewed the smaller German states as a potential source of territorial aggrand-izement; he was prepared to trade Austrian gains in the south for a massive extension of Prussian power in the north and east. Metternich, on the other hand, took a more cautious, defensive tact. He had not yet given up the hope of negotiating a settlement that would keep France as a balance against Russia and foresaw the smaller states as useful buffers between east and west. He did all he could, therefore, to undercut efforts to mobilize the population of the western states against their own rulers.

On 8 October Metternich achieved an extremely consequential diplomatic victory when Prince Henry of Reuss, the commander of the Austrian army of the Danube, and Count Wrede, the commander of the Bavarian army, signed an agreement at Ried. In return for renouncing membership in the Confederation, contribu-ting at least 36,000 troops to the allied cause, and promising not to sign a separate peace with France, Bavaria was granted 'full and entire sovereignty' by the Austrian emperor, 'in his own name as well as in the name of his allies'. The Ried agreement was denounced by Prussian patriots, who were furious at what seemed to be a significant limitation on their own freedom of manœuvre, by Stein, who condemned it as betrayal of the German cause, and even by some Austrian statesmen, who complained that it seemed

[105] Kraehe, *Metternich's German Policy*, i. 203–4.

to preclude a recovery of the Habsburgs' western lands. But Metternich was able to prevail. Indeed, in November and December he signed comparable treaties acquiring the assistance and guaranteeing the sovereignty of Württemberg, Hesse-Darmstadt, Baden, Nassau, Saxe-Coburg, and Hesse-Kassel. These treaties drove the final nails into the coffin of the old Reich; if the new states remained intact, the imperial territories of the abbots, bishops, counts, and knights could not reappear. Napoleonic Germany would survive the defeat of its creator.

Although Metternich succeeded in keeping the western states from being swept away, he could not prevent Napoleon's downfall. Following the victory at Leipzig, the chancellor had renewed his efforts at mediation, which were made all the more urgent by Tsar Alexander's growing ambitions for Russian influence in Europe. But Napoleon would not grant the concessions necessary to satisfy the allies, even when their armies moved into France. Determined to fight on, Napoleon managed to win a few small victories, all the more remarkable considering the exhausted condition of the veterans and raw recruits whom he led into battle. But he could do no more than delay the inevitable. On 30 March 1814 Blücher and Schwarzenberg joined forces on the heights of Montmartre and after a brief engagement accepted the surrender of the city from the emperor's two brothers, the former kings Joseph and Jerome. The next day, the allied monarchs rode in triumph through the streets of Paris, thus bringing to its destination the long journey that had begun, under very different auspices, twenty-two years earlier. Napoleon made a desperate attempt to disrupt Schwarzenberg's lines of communication and thus force him to turn back, but without effect. On 6 April, therefore, the emperor abdicated and surrendered to the British. The peace signed with the restored Bourbon regime on 30 May called for a congress of belligerents to meet in Vienna to determine a comprehensive settlement.

There remained one final act of the Napoleonic drama to be played, one last spasm of reckless ambition and all-consuming will. At the end of February 1815 Bonaparte escaped from Elba, landed in France, and began to move north towards Paris. The allies, still meeting in Vienna, branded him an outlaw and vowed to fight until he was unconditionally defeated. But in France Napoleon was welcomed as a hero, the troops sent to arrest him joined his cause, the representatives of the newly restored monarchy fled in terror. Once safely installed in the Tuilleries, Napoleon demanded from his nation yet another army, and the nation once again responded. In eight weeks, veterans, young volunteers, and a hodge-podge of customs officers and policemen combined to give him a force of 280,000 men. Napoleon knew he had to strike before the massive weight of the allied armies could be brought to bear against him. Early in June he moved his troops north into the Low Countries, where he hoped to engage Wellington and Blücher. He met and badly battered Blücher's Prussians at Ligny on 16 June and then turned to isolate and destroy Wellington the following day. But the two armies did not meet until the 18th, when they fought all day along a quarter mile front between the village of La Belle Alliance and the ridge of Mont Saint Jean, just south of Waterloo. This was, of course, one of the most famous battles in the history of war, ultimately decided by the extraordinary discipline of Wellington's regulars and the timely arrival of the Prussians, whom Blücher had rallied and redeployed after Ligny. By evening the French army was in full retreat, pursued by Blücher's cavalry. The Napoleonic era was finally over.[106]

For almost a quarter of a century, the greatest armies in European history had fought on German soil. Here the revolutionary troops had won their first victories in 1793–4, and here Napoleon suffered the decisive defeat at Leipzig that sent him reeling backwards across the Rhine. No aspect of German public life was left untouched by these years of violence and upheaval. The Holy Roman Empire, which had defined the basis for national politics at the beginning of the era, was gone. Scores of minor sovereignties had also disappeared, usually without a trace. A number of new states, created by the co-operation of established dynasties and the French conqueror, replaced the patchwork of imperial lands in the south and west. The two great German powers, Austria and Prussia, survived the revolutionary era, but with different boundaries and altered institutions. Less obvious, but perhaps no less significant, than these profound changes in political geography and institutional structure were the changes effected by the revolutionary era on the cultural landscape, where we find new directions in literature, philosophy, and art, as well as transformations in private sensibilities and public expectations.

[106] There is a brilliantly rendered account of Waterloo in John Keegan, *The Face of Battle* (New York, 1976), ch. 3.

VI
Culture in the Revolutionary Era

On New Year's Day 1792, as the impact of the political revolution was just beginning to be felt east of the Rhine, Franz Dautzenberg, the editor of the *Aachener Zuschauer*, published an essay on 'the spirit of our age', which he defined as 'the almost universal drive for a new existence'. There is hardly anywhere on earth, he went on, 'where the disagreeable urge to change civil conditions has not expressed itself, either forcefully or hesitantly.' Eight years later, a Protestant pastor greeted the new century with the same sentiments: 'The unmistakable character of our era', he told his congregation, 'is the vital, free struggle for something new and better.' In 1804 Hermann von Boyen, then a junior officer in the Prussian infantry, began his prize-winning essay on tactics by expressing the conviction that 'the first, holiest law of the human spirit' is 'tireless progress'.[1]

In the last two chapters we have observed how, during the quarter century after 1789, a sense of political possibility quickened the blood of ambitious men throughout Europe, men eager to take advantage of apparently unprecedented opportunities for power, wealth, and glory. Innovation also was at work in some people's private lives, which seemed to be charged with new, intensified feelings about love and betrayal, sorrow and joy, achievement and loss. At the same time, some people were moved by enlarged dreams of artistic accomplishment and cultural renewal. A young man like Hegel, who set out to grasp the meaning of the spirit's journey from its creation to the present, was fired by aspirations no less extraordinary than those that drove an obscure Corsican subaltern to his own triumphs and defeats. From its most talented and energetic children, the age seemed to demand nothing less than greatness.

Greatness always has a price and a boundless desire for something new and better can often lead to failure and disappointment. The biographies of our protagonists in this chapter are filled with personal tragedy—unbearable sorrow, incurable madness, sickness, and early death. Dilthey's remark that Friedrich Schlegel

---

[1] Hansen (ed.), *Quellen*, ii. 3; Sheehan, *Liberalism*, p. 8; Meinecke, *Leben*, i. 123.

'tore himself apart with his unrestrained demands on life' might also have been made about many of Schlegel's contemporaries whose existences were shattered by the demands they placed upon themselves, their associates, and the world in which they lived.[2] It should not surprise us, therefore, to find that, coexisting with the drive for innovation were longings for synthesis, reconciliation, and security. As passionately as men and women desired a new and better world, they hoped for new sources of certainty and repose. Such hopes were reflected in the concept of organic unity so important to Friedrich Schlegel, the 'unifying power' that Hegel sought to restore to human existence, and the harmony that Adam Müller believed could be found in the political order of the medieval world.

Revolutionary culture is characterized by a quest for innovation and a search for peace, restlessness and homesickness, rebellion and reconciliation. Goethe, best remembered as the creator of *Faust*, that epic testimony to human ambition, was also the author of *Hermann und Dorothea*, an idyllic celebration of domestic tranquillity. Schiller, who so often depicted men's violent struggles for glory and freedom, understood that such struggles usually ended in disaster. His pilgrim, who leaves the comforts of his father's house to find some distant reward, comes to realize that his search will have no end:

> Ach, kein Steg will dahin führen,
> Ach, der Himmel über mir
> Will die Erde nie berühren,
> Und das dort ist niemals hier.

Hölderlin knew the sad answer to the question posed in his incredibly beautiful poem, 'Die Heimath':

> Ihr holden Ufer, die ihr mich auferzogt,
>   Stillt ihr der Liebe Laiden? ach! gebt ihr mir,
>   Ihr Wälder meiner Kindheit, wann ich
>   Komme, die Ruhe noch Einmal wieder?

To those caught up in Europe's unprecedented revolutionary journey, going home meant finding a stable place to stand, something authentic to believe in, a nourishing community to belong to. Philosophy, wrote Novalis, 'is actually homesickness— the desire to be at home everywhere'. Considering how different the two men were, Hegel's definition is strikingly similar: 'The aim

---

[2] Dilthey, *Leben*, p. 252.

of knowledge is to divest the objective world that stands opposed to us of its strangeness, and, as the phrase is, to find ourselves at home in it.'[3]

i. ROMANTICISM

The conflicting impulses within revolutionary culture are nowhere better expressed than in the lives and works of those publicists, poets, and painters whom we call 'romantics'.[4] Romanticism is so notoriously hard to define because it lacks the centre of authority, transcendent goals, and internal cohesion that would enable us to establish its core beliefs and determine who 'belonged' and who did not. Romanticism is a movement, not a school; by nature, it was dynamic, inchoate, and multivalent. It was directed towards stylistic innovation rather than reaffirmation, it sought the dramatic extension rather than the careful cultivation of conventional forms. The romantics' identity came from their historical situation. They were, in Hugh Honour's phrase, 'united only at their point of departure'. They shared questions and aspirations, not answers and accomplishments.[5]

The first generation of romantics was born around 1770, and therefore was composed of people old enough to have some memory of the pre-revolutionary world but too young to have found a settled place in it. This group included A. W. Schlegel (born in 1767), Hölderlin (1770), Friedrich Schlegel (1772), Novalis (1772), Tieck (1773), and Wackenroder (1773), all of whom began to publish their first important works at the end of the 1790s when the significance of revolutionary change was becoming increasingly apparent. These young people were bound together in a series of overlapping relationships. Tieck and Wackenroder were fellow-

[3] 'The Pilgrim' is analysed in Abrams, *Supernaturalism*, pp. 194–5. Novalis quoted by Mason in Prawer (ed.), *Period*; Hegel, in Hegel, *The Essential Writings*, ed. by Frederick G. Weiss (New York, 1974), 89.

[4] Alan Menhennet, *The Romantic Movement, 1795–1830* (Totowa, New Jersey, 1981), and Glyn T. Hughes, *Romantic German Literature* (London, 1979), are convenient guides to German romanticism. The essays in Prawer (ed.), *Period*, treat various aspects of the literary movement; Brinkmann (ed.), *Romantik*, covers its political and social, as well as cultural, dimensions; Honour, *Romanticism*, is especially good for the visual arts.

[5] Honour, *Romanticism*, p. 19. Arthur O. Lovejoy, 'The Meaning of Romanticism for the Historian of Ideas', *JHI* 2/3 (1941), 257–78 is the classic statement of the problem of definition. See also the survey of usage in Hans Eichner (ed.), *'Romantic' and its Cognates: The European History of a Word* (Manchester, 1972). The distinction between a 'school' and a 'movement' is from Renato Poggioli, *The Theory of the Avant Garde* (Cambridge, 1968), 17 ff.

students at Erlangen and were collaborating on a novel when the latter died. Tieck later knew Schlegel in Berlin, where they frequented the same salons. In 1799 August Wilhelm Schlegel's house in Jena was a gathering place for his brother Friedrich, Tieck, Novalis, the philosopher Schelling, and several other leading intellectuals. A second generation, sometimes called the 'late romantics', was born roughly a decade after the first: Clemens Brentano (1778), Arnim (1781), Chamisso (1781), Peter Cornelius (1783), Eichendorff (1788), Franz Pforr (1788), and Friedrich Overbeck (1789). This group also was linked through a network of connections; Brentano, Arnim, and Joseph Görres (born in 1776) worked together in Heidelberg gathering material on folk culture, while Overbeck, Pforr, and later Cornelius lived in a Roman monastery where they established a group of painters known as the Nazarenes.

Since few of the romantics had a steady job, they had to live from small inheritances, what they could earn from their work, or the charity of friends. Patronage, still central to the lives of men like Goethe, Schiller, Herder, and Lessing, had begun to be less important by the turn of the century; in any case, the young romantics would have found subordination to a patron's will hard to bear. 'I do not belong to the Berlin Academy', wrote the painter Asmus Jakob Carstens, 'but to humanity.' When Heinrich von Kleist was about to resign his commission so that he could devote his life to literature and philosophy, he told his former tutor that, while he might someday seek a state position, 'I doubt such a possible step; for once I have been fortunate enough to win back my golden independence . . . I would be forever reluctant to offer it up for sale again.' Often poor, almost always insecure and unsettled, the romantics paid dearly for the artistic autonomy they celebrated in their work.[6]

Members of the romantic generation also sought new freedom in their personal lives. Just as they refused to fit into established career patterns, so they would not conform to conventional morality or be content with formal social relations. They wanted more: more satisfying work, more intense friendships, more passionate love affairs, more fulfilling marriages. Some formed clandestine circles like the *Tugendbund*, which brought together a number of bright young people from Berlin's élite. Others joined artistic communities like the Nazarenes. In art and life, romantics turned friendship into a cult, a set of bonds to be displayed, deepened, and reaffirmed

[6] Beenken, *Jahrhundert*, pp. 81 ff.; Kleist, *Abyss*, p. 24.

with song and ceremony. Some men and women were able to create a new kind of marriage in which friendship and erotic love might be fused. Many more searched in vain for sexual fulfilment; Hölderlin, Kleist, and Schleiermacher all suffered from the frustrations of unrequited passion.[7]

Among the romantics were a few courageous women who tried to shape their own destinies. Caroline Michaelis, for example, dreamed of independence: 'I would much rather not marry', she wrote at eighteen, 'if I could be my own master, have a decent, pleasant life, and be useful to the world in some other way.' After her first husband died, she had a liaison with a French officer, was imprisoned by Prussian troops in Mainz, eventually married August Wilhelm Schlegel, whom she divorced in order to marry Friedrich Wilhelm Schelling. Moses Mendelssohn's daughter Dorothea left her banker husband of twenty years for Friedrich Schlegel, whom she helped to support with her writings, many of which were published under his name. Dorothea Mendelssohn Veit, together with Rahel Levin, Henriette Herz, and other well-to-do and cultured young Berlin Jews, established salons during the 1790s, which attracted a number of the most lively people in the Prussian capital. These open houses represented a quintessential form of romantic sociability. For Friedrich Scheiermacher, the salons were precious because they were unconstrained by 'domestic and civil relations' and thus left everyone to be the 'legislator' of his own condition. August Varnhagen von Ense, who married Rahel Levin, remembered the turn of the century in Berlin as a time when 'the rules to which life in society conformed' were defined by 'intelligence, talent, and the actions of individuals'.[8]

The personal relationships between the romantics and the older generation of German writers were often clouded by jealousy and misunderstanding. Schiller, for instance, was appalled by Caroline Schlegel's vigorous intelligence, which seemed so far from the conventions of feminine domesticity he celebrated in poems like 'Das Lied von der Glocke'. Nor was Goethe especially open to the young and talented; he ignored Hölderlin and treated Kleist in a particularly cruel and patronizing manner. The romantics, however, realized that their ideas were built upon the achievements of

[7] On romantic friendship, see Brunschwig, *Enlightenment*, pp. 200 ff.

[8] Frevert, *Frauen-Geschichte*, p. 56. Otto Dann, 'Gruppenbildung und Gesellschaftliche Organisierung in der Epoche der deutschen Romantik' in Brinkmann (ed.), *Romantik*, p. 118; Brunschwig, *Enlightenment*, p. 232. On the salons, see Arendt, *Varnhagen*, especially pp. 56 ff., Deborah Hertz, *Jewish High Society in Old Regime Berlin* (New Haven, 1988).

their predecessors. Friedrich Schlegel admired Goethe and, for a time, collaborated with Schiller. Hölderlin and Kleist were both deeply influenced by Kant, whose importance they acknowledged even after they had rejected his philosophical principles. Novalis and many others reflected the influence of pietism in their work, and continued the long process through which pietist sensibility was absorbed into secular thought. The romantics' view of folk culture, like their admiration for wild nature and primitive societies, had roots in the ideas of Hamann and Herder, just as their image of the rebellious hero was based on works by the *Sturm-und-Drang* writers. Romantic ideas about the autonomy and centrality of art were clearly foreshadowed in Goethe's essay on the Gothic, Herder's views of poetry, and Kant's discussion of the aesthetic realm in his third critique. Finally, the romantics took from earlier writers a commitment to moral and spiritual reform, which they then sought to redefine in order to meet the crisis of their own age.

The most important link between the romantics and the eighteenth-century tradition of moral reform was provided by Friedrich Schiller, whose essays on 'The Aesthetic Education of Mankind' and 'Naïve and Sentimental Poetry' had an immediate and powerful effect when they appeared in the mid-1790s. The first essay, written in the form of letters to the duke of Schleswig-Holstein and published in a revised version in *Die Horen* during 1795, was a reaffirmation of the political primacy of culture, and especially of art, in the face of revolutionary change. 'If man is ever to solve the problem of politics in practice,' Schiller wrote at the end of the second letter, 'he will have to approach it through the problem of the aesthetic, because it is only through Beauty that man makes his way to freedom.' To this conviction about beauty's civic task, Schiller adds his influential diagnosis of contemporary society's peculiar maladies. Everywhere we look, he argued, we find division and fragmentation—in scholarship, art, society, and the state. Since the roots of this malady are cultural, so must be the cure. Only beauty, Schiller was convinced, could restore humanity to the energies of its natural state without sacrificing the refinements of civilization.[9] In the essay on 'Naïve and Sentimental Poetry', also published in *Die Horen* in 1795, Schiller picked up a similar theme. After contrasting the energy and spontaneity of natural, primitive beauty with the sophisticated modes of modern

---

[9] F. M. Wilkinson's and L. A. Willoughby's edition of *On the Aesthetic Education of Man* (Oxford, 1967) is a good translation with a useful introduction; the quote is from p. 9.

aesthetics, he argued that true art must have both primitive energy and classically imposed harmony, natural authenticity and skilful artifice. To escape the sterility and fragmentation of the present, we must recapture what we have lost from our earlier selves: 'our culture should lead us back to nature along the path of reason and freedom.' Again and again, the romantics searched for this path, which they hoped would allow them to link culture and nature, community and personality, art and life.[10]

Schiller's essays appeared just when the members of the first romantic generation were formulating their views of the world. Friedrich Schlegel, for example, was twenty-three years old in 1795 and hard at work on his book about Greek literature. Schlegel came from a distinguished north German family; his father was a pastor and scholar, his uncle a critic, a dramatist, and one of the earliest German exponents of Shakespeare. Since it was assumed that his elder brother, August Wilhelm, would carry on the family's intellectual traditions, Friedrich was meant to be a merchant. But the commercial life did not suit him, so he turned to law, then to literature. He soon made contact with young people with similar tastes and sensibilities and by 1797 was an established figure in the fashionable salons of Berlin. Friedrich read widely, wrote a great deal, edited the famous journal, *Athenäum*, and knew everyone worth knowing, but he never found a project worthy of his talents. He spent the last fifteen years of his life as a hired publicist for various reactionary interests. The chief source of his historical influence was the work of his brother, August Wilhelm, a less original but more orderly mind, whose lectures *Über dramatische Kunst und Literatur* (given in Vienna during 1808 and published in 1809–11) became, together with his friend Mme de Staël's *De l'Allemagne*, the basis for Europe's notion of German romanticism.[11]

Like Schiller in 1795, Friedrich Schlegel devoted himself to overcoming the painful fragmentation he perceived in the world around him. In his early essays he seems to suggest that harmony could be restored through a reintegration of past and present, 'the unification of the essentially modern with the essentially classical'. He ends his book *Über das Studium der griechischen Poesie*, for instance, by invoking Winckelmann and the other classicists who

[10] Schiller, *Werke*, xx. 414.

[11] There is a good brief sketch of Schlegel's life in Dilthey's *Leben*, pp. 229 ff. A definitive edition of his work is now being prepared by Ernst Behler (Paderborn, Darmstadt, and Zurich, 1958 ff.). Schlegel, *Schriften*, is a convenient collection of his most important writings.

had sought a new, creative understanding of Greek literature. Increasingly, however, Schlegel's classical preoccupations give way to a concern for the dynamism of the future, a dynamism inherent in what he sometimes called 'romanticism'. Romantic literature, he wrote in his famous fragment of 1798, is always becoming, 'that is its true essence, it eternally becomes, and can never be completed'. But the function of romanticism, like the function of classical ideals, is to synthesize the scattered elements of modern existence and thus restore harmony to human life:

Romantic poetry is a progressive universal poetry. Its mission is not merely to reunite all separate genres of poetry and to put poetry in touch with philosophy and rhetoric. It will and should, now mingle and now amalgamate poetry and prose, genius and criticism, the poetry of art and the poetry of nature, render poetry living and social, and life and society poetic. [12]

At the centre of this titanic struggle to build a new synthesis of life and art, Schlegel put the figure of the artist himself, clothed in the moral legislator's heroic garb which he will wear for the next century. 'Artists', he wrote in 1799, 'make humanity into individuals by bringing together past and future in the present. They are the higher organs of the soul, where the spirit of life among public persons meets, and in which the private spirit then works.' The artist must be free, so the first law of romantic literature is that 'the poet's arbitrary will tolerates no higher law'. [13] Schlegel hoped, however, that freedom would be tempered by what he called the artist's sense of irony, that quality of mind which distanced him from his material and helped him to restrain his imaginative energies. In fact, neither Schlegel nor his contemporaries were able to resolve the tension between their belief in artistic freedom and their concern for art's social mission. From this time on, artists who defined their calling in the romantic mode found themselves carrying a double burden—the special, unqualified commitment to their own, personal vision and the universal responsibilities imposed by an obligation to serve humanity.

The romantics' fascination with the artist led them to assign him a central role in literary theory and practice. Schlegel, for example, helped to make the relationship of art and artist into a prime critical concern. He was also one of the first to use literary works like Shakespeare's sonnets as a source of biographical information. At

[12] *Schriften*, pp. 37–8. See Behler, 'Origins'.
[13] Beenken, *Jahrhundert*, p. 87.

the same time, romantic writers used the artist as a subject for their work. Wackenroder's *Herzensergiessungen eines kunstliebenden Klosterbruders*, Tieck's *Franz Sternbalds Wanderungen*, Novalis's *Heinrich von Ofterdingen*, and Hölderlin's *Hyperion* are all portraits of an artist's quest for beauty. When Goethe, in his *Wilhelm Meisters Lehrjahre*, dared to portray a young man who abandoned art, some denounced him as a heretic. Novalis regarded Goethe's novel as 'an odious book', which should have had the subtitle 'pilgrimage to a patent of nobility'—a low blow from the scion of an aristocratic family (Novalis was the pen-name of Friedrich von Hardenberg) to the newly ennobled son of Frankfurt burghers.[14]

Novalis believed that the true source and most interesting subject of art was the artist himself. 'The more personal, local, peculiar, of its own time, a poem is, the nearer it stands to the centre of poetry.' And what could be more personal and peculiar than the poet's own experience, the inner world to which he alone had access and of which he alone was king? When Goethe's Werther turned within himself to find a world, his creator set him on a journey to isolation, madness, and death. But for the romantic hero the turn inward was a turn towards true feelings and authentic life. 'We are not acquainted with the depths of our spirits,' Novalis wrote, 'The most mysterious path leads inward [*nach innen*].' The direction to which Novalis points is the one towards which almost all the romantic heroes must move on the path of self-discovery. Like the protagonist in Hoffmann's tale, they had to descend deep into the mine shafts of their consciousness, where they would find what the painter Caspar David Friedrich called 'the only true source of art . . . our own heart'.[15]

In comparison to the realm of feeling, many romantics found the so-called real world grey and uninteresting. Friedrich Schlegel, for example, argued that 'the best part of the best novels is nothing other than the more or less concealed self-awareness of the author'. The English novel of manners, he believed, was of interest only if one wanted to know something about fashions, boredom, and the swear words popular among the squirearchy. The true novel was concerned with emotions, not events, states of consciousness, not states of society. In Novalis's *Heinrich von Ofterdingen* the hero seeks

[14] Quoted by Eichner in Prawer (ed.), *Period*, p. 80. On romantic literary theory, see Abrams, *Mirror*.

[15] Honour, *Romanticism*, p. 18; John Neubauer, 'The Mines of Falun: Temporal Fortunes of a Romantic Myth of Time', *SR* 19 (winter 1980), 475; Beenken, *Jahrhundert*, p. 96.

the blue flower that will become one of romanticism's most enduring symbols. Moving in a kind of double dream, he loses the flower when he is recalled to the world of work and family and must then pursue it again on a journey filled with myth and fable. The portrayal of external reality is not one of Novalis's concerns. 'By giving what is common a deeper meaning, what is everyday a mysterious aspect, what is known the dignity of the unknown, what is finite the appearance of infinity, I romanticize it.' Much the same thing is true of Eichendorff's *Ahnung und Gegenwart*, which is supposed to be a 'picture of this storm-tossed time', but which persistently slips away from the *Gegenwart* to *Ahnung*, from the condition of the present to those forebodings, presentiments, and intuitions which crowd the hero's mind. The novel tells us relatively little about the years between 1810 and 1812, but quite a lot about the impact of these years on the sensibilities of a young man who stood on the edge of an uncertain future.[16]

Many romantics regarded depictions of nature and society as ways to express their own poetic feelings. In Eichendorff's poem 'Zwielicht', for example, the details of the forest are blurred by gathering darkness until they become a fantasy landscape filled with vague menace. The same lack of specific detail characterizes Brentano's 'O kühler Wald', where our attention is focused on the emotions that the forest evokes.[17] In landscape painting, of course, the complete obliteration of detail was impossible, but in the canvases of Philip Otto Runge and Caspar David Friedrich sentiment is none the less of primary importance. Our generation, wrote Runge in 1802, 'is driven to landscape, seeks something definite in this indeterminacy, but does not know how to begin'. Throughout his short life Runge searched, without success, for a way of fusing landscape and feeling, the worlds of nature and emotion. Friedrich also subordinated observation to introspection. That is why, in the portrait of Friedrich by his friend, G. F. Kersting, the artist is pictured gazing at his canvas in a room without a view. His subject is himself. 'It is not the faithful representation of air, water, rocks, and trees, which is the task of the artist,' Friedrich explained, 'but the reflection of his soul and emotion in these objects.' In contrast to traditional landscapes, the human figures in Friedrich's paintings are not there to provide scale or to give a sense of man's mastery of nature; they are observers,

---

[16] Schlegel, *Schriften*, pp. 319–20; Trainer in Prawer (ed.), *Period*, p. 100.
[17] See the fine analysis in Prawer, *Poetry*, pp. 131 ff.

whose forlorn posture anticipates the feelings that the painting is likely to arouse in the viewer himself.[18]

The supremacy of feeling could best be achieved in music, the mode of expression least encumbered by the distracting details of the everyday world. Whereas, to a man of the *Aufklärung* like Kant, music was less valuable than the other arts precisely because its impact was purely emotional, to the romantics music was the purest art, to be imitated as far as possible in poetry and prose. 'Music, plastic art, and poetry are synonyms,' Novalis believed, 'Painting, plastic art—objective music, music—subjective music or painting,' E. T. A. Hoffman regarded music as 'the most romantic of all the arts—one might even say it is the only genuinely romantic art' because it has 'nothing in common with the world of sensuous reality around us'. For Hoffmann, the greatest of the romantics was Beethoven, whose music 'opens the floodgates of fear, of terror, of horror, of pain, and aroused that longing for the eternal which is the essence of romanticism'.[19] Hoffmann was right about Beethoven's greatness and about music's distinctive affinity for romanticism. Long after most romantic poets had fallen silent or turned against their earlier work, romantic composers continued to produce art of the highest order. As Paul Robinson has recently shown, Schubert's great song cycles, *Die schöne Müllerin* and *Winterreise*, written in the 1820s, perfectly capture that sensibility 'in which consciousness has displaced both God and society as the principal object of artistic and intellectual contemplation'.[20]

Writers could not achieve this same distillation of emotional essences, but they were able to lead their readers into new, unexplored realms of feeling. They could, for instance, address subjects artists had long ignored, as Friedrich Schlegel did in his novel *Lucinde*, which shocked contemporaries both because of the author's candour about the importance of sexuality and because his plot was so clearly based on his own relationship with Dorothea Veit. Neither the baroque novel of courtly romance nor eighteenth-century explorations of domestic virtue prepared people for Schlegel's portrayal of the erotic love, sentimental attachment, and true friendship possible between a man and a woman. By inventing new ways of talking about physical desire and psychological

[18] Beenken, *Jahrhundert*, pp. 143 ff.; Robson-Scott in Prawer (ed.), *Period*, p. 269. See also William Vaughan, *German Romantic Painting* (New Haven and London, 1980); Otto von Simson, *Der Blick nach Innen. Vier Beiträge zur deutschen Malerei des 19. Jahrhunderts* (Berlin, 1986).

[19] M. H. Abrams, *Mirror*, p. 94; Taylor in Prawer (ed.), *Period*, p. 285.

[20] Paul Robinson, *Opera and Ideas: From Mozart to Strauss* (New York, 1985), 64.

torment, companionship and hatred, the promise of love and the presence of death, Schlegel and his contemporaries enriched the language of poetic sensibility crafted by men like Klopstock and Goethe. They created an extensive private mythology of symbols, metaphors, and allegory which we still associate with the romantic vision—the blue flower, the dark forest, the mysterious double, the cave and mine shaft, and many others. These combined to produce what S. S. Prawer calls 'a nearly coherent system of tales, partly invented and partly adapted, which tell of man's relationship to the demonic and the divine'.[21]

The romantics' achievements often came at a great personal cost. The realm of subjectivity, whose primacy they ceaselessly asserted, was both fascinating and terrifying, familiar and treacherous. Novalis may sometimes have longed to live in an inner world that was 'so intimate, private . . . so much one's own nation [vater-ländisch]', but he also knew that this world was 'dreamlike' and 'uncertain' because it lacked clear lines between reason and irrationality, sickness and health. For Novalis, the journey 'nach innen' passed through a landscape of lust and cruelty, sickness and death. 'Life', he once wrote in a line foreshadowing so many later thinkers, 'is a disease of the spirit.' The same dark forces that dwell in Novalis's works are also just behind the surface of those deceptively tranquil settings we find in E. T. A. Hoffmann's tales. 'Der Sandmann', for example, is a story about that familiar romantic figure, the 'uncanny guest', who intrudes into a family circle, bringing disorder and destruction in his wake. And yet, as the story's heroine tells us, the real source of danger is 'a dark, psychic power. . . . It is the phantom of our own selves, whose close connection with and deep impact on our feelings casts us into hell or transports us up to heaven.' Hoffmann knew about these forces at first hand. Trained as a civil servant, his career was disrupted by the revolutionary wars and he was forced to support himself with his writing; he remained conventional and respectable in appearance, but inwardly was tormented by ill health, mental breakdowns, and disastrous love affairs.[22]

Romantics sought isolation, which they knew was essential for their art, but often endured loneliness, a terrible sense of estrangement from the rest of humanity. To explore the depths of

[21] Prawer (ed.), Period, p. 9.
[22] Mason in Prawer (ed.), Period, pp. 219, 224; S. S. Prawer, 'Hoffmann's Uncanny Guest: A Reading of Der Sandmann', German Life and Letters, 18/4 (1965), 297–308.

consciousness or to experience the full grandeur of the external world, it was necessary to be free from quotidian distractions. One had to be on one's own, standing like the single figure in Friedrich's great painting, *The Wanderer above the Mists*, who confronts the scenery below him, moved by, yet clearly separate from, its majesty. But in this painting, as in so much of romantic art and literature, there is a certain ambiguity about the wanderer's position, something in the way he stands that makes us aware of his vulnerability and loneliness. The pain of this condition is a recurrent subject for the romantics, who portray lonely heroes on a quest, travellers frightened in the night, lovers abandoned or estranged. Behind a great deal of romantic art seems to be an urge to ease the pains of isolation and break the bonds of subjectivity. 'From childhood on,' Philip Otto Runge wrote in 1801, 'I have always yearned to find words or drawings or something, through which I could make clear to others my inner feelings.'[23] Runge longed for a community in which misunderstanding would be impossible, a family joined by love and a sense of common purpose. His painting, *We Three*, captures this longing by showing the artist with his brother and sister-in-law in an atmosphere of tenderness and love. But even here, the artist's ability to belong is attenuated—husband and wife merge into a single figure, while Runge stands apart, joined to the couple, but clearly separate from their more compelling intimacy.

For some romantics, especially after the turn of the century, religion began to replace art as the best relief from the pains of subjectivity, the surest source of value and community. Once again, the careers of the brothers Schlegel are exemplary. Friedrich's *Gespräch über die Poesie*, first published in 1800, contained a section on mythology, in which he argued that, while the modern world lacked an ordering myth, 'we are near to receiving one, or more accurately, it is time that we began to work together in order to evoke one'. At this point, Schlegel seems to have believed that the new myths were to be found in 'the most artful of all art', which could serve as 'course and container for poetry's eternal spring'. Soon thereafter he set out to search for a modern myth in the rich religious soil of the east, but in 1808, the same year he published his pioneering work on Indian philosophy, Friedrich and his wife were received into the Roman Catholic Church. Meanwhile, August Wilhelm was also moving closer to religion. He began his famous lectures on dramatic art and literature with the

---

[23] Runge, *Schriften*, i. 3.

premise that 'religion is the root of the human being'. If religion is corrupted, all of humanity's emotional and cultural life will be adversely affected, as happened to the ancient world before the introduction of Christianity. This 'sublime and philanthropic religion' renewed European culture and then prepared the way for the great achievements of the Middle Ages, which Schlegel presented as equal in quality to the best of the classical heritage.[24] The Schlegels' turn backwards to Christian medievalism signalled their new political conservatism and their desire to find a source of cultural stability and order beyond the eternally unfulfilled promise of romantic art. 'The present appalled him and the future terrified him,' Heine wrote about Friedrich Schlegel, 'so he could only turn his prophet's gaze towards the past, which he loved.'[25]

Other romantics took, or thought about taking, the Schlegels' road to Rome. Clemens Brentano had been reared a Catholic but lapsed during his youth. His keenly felt agonies of disbelief pervade his poem, 'Frühlingsschrei eines Knechtes aus der Tiefe':

> Meister, ohne dein Erbarmen
> Muss im Abgrund ich verzagen,
> Willst du nicht mit starken Armen
> Wieder mich zum Lichte tragen.

Eventually Brentano returned to the church. His friend Joseph Görres, whose intellectual development will be discussed later in this chapter, also rediscovered his family's faith, which he used as a reservoir of literary symbols and political values. Religion was equally important to Eichendorff, for whom romanticism and Catholicism were inseparable: he once defined the romantic movement as the expression of Protestants' longing for reconciliation with the true church. Even writers who did not convert were often moved by religion's power as an integrating force. Writing from Leipzig in 1801, Heinrich von Kleist told his betrothed how moved he was by a Catholic ceremony, which, unlike the Protestant, 'speaks to the senses'. Kleist loved the way music and the other arts embellished the mass, but above all he was impressed by the phenomenon of faith itself.

At the centre of the altar, at its lowest step, a wretched man, apart from all the others, remained kneeling . . . praying with conviction. No doubts tortured him, he believes. I felt an indescribable longing to throw myself

---

[24] F. Schlegel, *Schriften*, p. 301; A. W. Schlegel, *Vorlesungen*, pp. 22–4.
[25] Heine, 'Schule', p. 157. On Heine's view of romanticism, see below, Ch. 9, sect.iv.

down beside him and weep. Ah, a single drop of forgetfulness, and I would embrace Catholicism with a passion.[26]

Because Kleist was never vouchsafed that drop of forgetfulness, he had to live without the certainties of faith. Born in 1777 into a family with a distinguished military tradition, Kleist joined the army at fifteen and served seven years until, unable to bear the numbing discipline of a soldier's life, he resigned his commission. When he began studying at the small university of Frankfurt-on-the-Oder in 1799, his aim was to seize control of his destiny and to avoid being what he called a 'puppet on the wire of fate'. Kleist found freedom, but not peace. Against the turbulent backdrop of revolutionary Europe, he could not establish a secure position, a place where he was totally at home, a task to which he could devote himself without qualification, a person whom he could love and trust wholeheartedly. His hopes and ambitions fluctuated wildly. At one point he wished only to 'cultivate a field, plant a tree, engender a child', but he quickly jettisoned these pastoral inclinations to seek artistic fame and political influence. Sometimes contemptuous of religion, he was drawn to Catholicism; he once considered enlisting in the French army, then toyed with the idea of assassinating Napoleon; he longed for love and companionship, but abandoned his fiancée and quarrelled with all who came too near him; intensely private, he became engaged in a series of impressive, but short-lived, collaborative ventures.[27]

Like many of his contemporaries, Kleist found the philosophy of the *Aufklärung* both liberating and terrifying. As soon as he realized that, by locating all knowledge within the consciousness of the knower, Kant had apparently undermined the possibility of absolute truth, Kleist lost his own commitment to science as a vocation. 'We can never really be certain that what we call Truth is really Truth, or whether it does not merely appear so to us,' he wrote in 1801 'If the latter, then the Truth we acquire here is not Truth after death, and it is all a vain striving for possession that may never follow us into the grave.' If there is no Truth, then there can be no way of avoiding misunderstandings, no way 'to reach into my breast, seize my thought, and with my hands place it with no further addition in your breast', Kleist's obsession with the essential uncertainty of our perceptions echoes through his work,

[26] Clemens Brentano, *Werke* (4 vols.; Darmstadt, 1963–8), i. 329; Kleist, *Abyss*, p. 106.
[27] Hamburger, *Reason*, p. 113. For a brief account of Kleist's career, see Richard March, *Kleist* (Cambridge, 1954).

which is filled with masquerades, unreliable reports, false witnesses, and masked identities. These are not the errors and intrigues of which comedy had been made since ancient times, but rather the results of people's tragic isolation from one another, their inability to communicate, their failure to understand. When Kleist saw Friedrich's landscape entitled *Der Mönch am Meer*, he recognized at once what the painter had in mind: 'Nothing can be sadder and more uncomfortable than this position in the world; the only spark of life in the vast realm of death, the lonely central figure in the lonely circle.'[28]

The plots in Kleist's plays and stories are often driven by his protagonists' struggles to break out of their isolation by finding solace in love's embrace, by showing compassion for a stranger's need, or by seeking justice for a wrong endured. These efforts invariably end in disaster: in 'Die Verlobung in St Domingo' the heroine's passion eventually kills the object of her love; in 'Der Findling' a charitable deed ends in devastation; and Michael Kohlhaas's quest for justice leads him on a rampage of destruction. But, while his characters' struggles end badly, Kleist never denies the authenticity or value of their feelings. He admired love, compassion, and a thirst for justice, but recognized that in a world like ours these emotions can easily be transformed into destructive forces. For love, compassion, and justice to flourish, a new social order was necessary; change could not be limited to the realm of feeling. This conviction is best expressed in Kleist's last play, *Prinz Friedrich von Homburg*, which follows a trajectory from dream to reality, from the hero's absorption with self to his acceptance of public responsibility, from the confines of isolated subjectivity to the freedom of active choice. Read this way, the play stands as a critique of the primacy given to private feelings by so many of his contemporaries.[29]

Like Kleist, Friedrich Hölderlin combined an appreciation of true feeling with the realization that it had to be nourished by a new social order. We have already cited Hölderlin's 'Hymne an die Freiheit', written in praise of the revolution while he was a student at the seminary in Tübingen. Hölderlin was a most unlikely seminarian: without religious faith, restless under any discipline, he

---

[28] Kleist, *Abyss*, p. 95; Marshall Brown, *The Shape of German Romanticism* (Ithaca, 1979), 81; Glaser, *Mind*, p. 192.

[29] There is a useful introduction to Kleist's major works in John Gearey, *Heinrich von Kleist: A Study in Tragedy and Anxiety* (Philadelphia, 1968). On *Prinz Friedrich*, see Herbert Lindenberger, *Historical Drama: The Relation of Literature and Reality* (Chicago and London, 1975), 144 ff.

attended the Tübinger *Stift* only because he had no other means of getting an education. Since he would not become a minister, he left school without a secure position. Forced to follow that rocky path which so many contemporary intellectuals had to walk, he struggled to support himself as a tutor, part-time student, sometime publicist. While teaching the children of a Frankfurt banker, he fell in love with his employer's young wife, the woman who, as Diotima, inspired his great love poems. But the affair, if we can call it that, ended as it had to, with Hölderlin's dismissal. He then taught in a few more private houses, lived with friends, tried a desperate publishing scheme, and finally, through the influence of some well-placed admirers, was given a sinecure as the court librarian in Homburg, which he had to abandon because of his deteriorating mental health.[30]

In Hölderlin's unhappy career we can see the characteristic disjunctions of his age—between ambition and opportunity, hope and achievement, talent and recognition, the promise of romantic love and the unyielding restraints of conventional morality. Much of the energy in Hölderlin's poetry is generated by the frustration he felt with his inability to find fulfilment as a citizen, an artist, and a man.

> Doch uns ist gegeben,
> Auf keiner Stätte zu ruhn,
> Es schwinden, es fallen
> Die leidenden Menschen
> Blindlings von einer
> Stunde zur andern,
> Wie Wasser von Klippe
> Zu Klippe geworfen,
> Jahr lang ins Ungewisse hinab.

From his own disappointments and frustrations, Hölderlin constructed a statement about modern culture as a whole. Like Schiller, he perceived the fragmentation at work in the contemporary world, the divisions among people, the estrangement of humans from their own true nature. The poet's task is to restore a sense of wholeness to humanity, to find 'the holy path' to cultural health and social renewal. From all the greatest elements in western thought—classical Greece, the Old Testament, Christianity—he built a vision of outstanding poetic power. But this, he knew, would not be enough. In his novel, *Hyperion*, written while the

[30] L. S. Salzberger, *Hölderlin* (Cambridge, 1952), is a good place to start reading about the poet. Hamburger, *Reason*, analyses the poetry.

Rastatt Congress was debating Europe's future and Hölderlin was waiting in vain for a revolutionary movement to break out in the German south-west, the heroine asks the hero, 'Do you know what you are striving for, the one thing you lack?' And then she answers her own first question: 'It is a better world that you are seeking, a more beautiful world.' But to create a better world would not be easy. Hyperion's efforts to lead his people to freedom deteriorate into terror and chaos; at the end of the novel he is isolated, with only the world of nature to console him. Yet, as difficult as it might be to achieve in the contemporary world, the reconciliation of individual and society remained Hölderlin's ideal.[31]

On stylistic grounds, literary critics may object to the inclusion of Kleist and Hölderlin among the romantics. For our purposes, however, here is where they belong. Their personal experience, intellectual orientation, and artistic preoccupations all join them to the other thinkers and artists conventionally called 'romantic'. More clearly than all but the very greatest of the romantics, Kleist and Hölderlin speak to us across the moat of time: their work remains fresh and moving. Both of them led unhappy lives, with tragic ends. In 1806, after his removal from his librarian's post, Hölderlin had to be confined in an asylum and then was set up as a lodger in a carpenter's house in Tübingen, where he remained until his death in 1843. Hopelessly insane, his solitude was occasionally interrupted by curious visitors. Kleist's end was swifter, but no less tragic. On the morning of 21 November 1811, after having suffered a series of setbacks and disappointments, he travelled to Wannsee, near Berlin, in the company of a woman who was terminally ill. After a few hours writing letters of farewell, he shot his companion and then himself. He was thirty-four.

Several other romantics also died young: Wackenroder at twenty-five, Novalis at twenty-nine, Runge at thirty-three. Many of those who lived longer lost the creative energies of their youth. The personal ties that had drawn them together in Jena or Berlin tended to be broken. The Schlegels, Tieck, Eichendorff, Brentano, and the others went their separate ways in search of their own style and unique source of meaning. The romantic synthesis for which Friedrich Schlegel yearned never materialized. Instead, as hopes and dreams of the revolutionary age gave way to the sober realities of restoration Europe, romanticism became increasingly fragmented, idiosyncratic, and internally inconsistent.

---

[31] Friedrich Hölderlin, 'Hyperions Schiksaalslied', in *Poems*, p. 79. Abrams, *Supernaturalism*, p. 345.

The romantics left behind no 'universal poetry', no single style, no core beliefs. But their themes and motifs—the healing power of art, the primacy of feeling, the pain of loneliness, the search for community—influenced writers as different as Heinrich Heine, Richard Wagner, and Thomas Mann. And, while the romantics were deeply enmeshed in their own distinctive historical experience, they also have a distinctly 'modern' quality: it comes as no surprise, therefore, to learn that Nietzsche was drawn to Hölderlin, that Freud analysed Hoffmann's 'Der Sandmann', or that Kafka greatly admired Kleist. Finally, as we shall see in the rest of this chapter, elements in the romantic response to the revolutionary age overlapped with, and were absorbed by, German philosophers, theologians, and political theorists, who brought to their own particular concerns many of the same hopes, demands, and anxieties.

ii. PHILOSOPHY AND RELIGION

'Kant is our Moses', Hölderlin wrote in January 1799; 'he has led us from our Egyptian slumbers into the free, lonely desert of his speculations and brings us vigorous laws from the holy mountain.' But a few weeks later Hölderlin complained about the feelings of dissatisfaction and depression which his philosophical studies had brought him; he longed for poetry, he told his mother, as a Swiss mercenary might long for the cool meadows of his homeland.[32] This combination of attitudes was common among intellectuals of Hölderlin's generation, many of whom shared his admiration for Kant's intelligence, yet found the philosopher's austere style and relentless logic emotionally hollow and unsatisfying. Even those who recognized that Kant had helped to free Germans from the bondage of unexamined orthodoxy were not at home in the arid landscape of Kantian speculation. By the turn of the century, younger philosophers had begun to reopen the questions Kant hoped that he had definitively resolved, questions about the relationship between faith and reason, emotion and .intellect, objective and subjective knowledge, German traditions and Enlightenment ideals. The new generation felt the need to formulate their own answers, which they believed would be more appropriate for an era of revolutionary change.

The fate of the Kantian project can be seen with particular clarity in the life and thought of Johann Gottfried Fichte. Like Kant, Fichte

[32] Hamburger, *Reason*, p. 16.

was born in modest circumstances, received help from a generous patron, studied theology, and was then forced to support himself with a series of positions as a private tutor. In 1790, when Fichte read Kant for the first time, he wrote to a friend, 'I am living in a new world.' By lifting the belief in determinism that had long burdened Fichte's mind and heart, Kant's philosophy opened the way to a rational, free ethical system, which Fichte welcomed as 'a blessing for an age in which morality has been destroyed down to its very foundations'. So great was the pull of Kant's writings that Fichte decided to go to Königsberg to seek the great man's assistance. At first Kant showed little interest in the impoverished ex-tutor who arrived on his doorstep. With just enough money to last a few frugal weeks, Fichte set out to win Kant's favour by writing a philosophical critique of revelation. Eventually, Kant was somewhat more receptive, and gave Fichte a meal and some encouraging words, even though he did not find time to read more than a few pages of what would eventually be published as *Versuch einer Kritik aller Offenbarung*. Finally, when his funds were almost totally exhausted, Fichte's luck changed; with Kant's help, the *Versuch* was published and was an immediate success, establishing its author's reputation as a leading Kantian. In 1794 he was named to the chair of philosophy at Jena, which recently had been vacated by K. L. Reinhold, one of Kant's foremost academic admirers.[33]

Soon after Fichte was settled in Jena he began to drift away from Kant. But, even though the evolution of his ideas philosophy after 1794 can be read as a persistent and increasingly harsh struggle against the critical philosophy, Fichte remained on what Kant had defined as the proper terrain for philosophical debate. Like Kant, Fichte viewed philosophy as a foundational study, the science of science, whose task was to determine what could and could not be known. Moreover, Fichte accepted Kant's emphasis on the role of the knower in the formation of knowledge. But he did not accept the complex compromises Kant offered between subjectivity and objectivity, between our knowledge of the world and the existence of things-in-themselves. For Fichte, the source of all reality was the ego, the self, which at once perceived and created the only world there is. The operation of this ego would remind Heine of 'an ape sitting on a hearth with his tail in a copper kettle, who says, "true cookery is not cooking something objectively, it is subjectively cooking oneself." ' Needless to say, Fichte would not have been

---

[33] Johann Gottlieb Fichte, *Attempt at a Critique of all Revelation*, ed. Garret Green (Cambridge, 1978), 2. See also Vorländer, *Kant*, ii. 261 ff.

amused by this summary of his position. He denied that his ideas led to hopeless subjectivity by insisting that every ego was part of a larger spiritual realm: 'It is not the individual but the one immediate spiritual Life which is the creator of all phenomena, including phenomenal individuals.' Nevertheless, Fichte's early epistemology, like the literary theory and poetry being written by his friends and contemporaries among the romantics, could easily be viewed as a celebration of pure subjectivity. This is what it seems to have meant to Novalis, for example, who attended Fichte's lectures in 1795 and 1796 and left notebooks demonstrating how intensely he tried to come to terms with the meaning of Fichte's thought.[34]

For both Fichte and Kant, epistemology was inseparable from ethics. Thus Fichte saw the absolute ego as a moral agent, the source of those ethical intuitions that enable people to recognize their social obligations and live an ethical life. In his ethics, as in his epistemology, Fichte tried to avoid Kantianism's inherent compromises. Whereas Kant had posited a tension between our moral nature and our instincts, Fichte declared that our instincts are themselves moral. The ethical principle is the 'drive to the complete self', the 'drive to freedom for freedom's sake'. In order to act morally, we must become aware of these impulses and of the law based on our 'intuition of self-activity and freedom.'[35] Fichte, like Novalis, directed our attention *nach innen*, where morality and freedom, as well as true knowledge were to be found. Unlike the romantics, however, Fichte never abandoned the *Aufklärung's* commitment to philosophical analysis as the way to knowledge and morality. Despite his occasional flights of mystical fancy and the subjectivity implied by his emphasis on the ego, at the centre of Fichte's thought was a hard core of rationality.

During the period from 1794 to 1799, while he was trying to formulate the fundamental principles of his philosophical system, Fichte was also searching for ways to influence a broader public. Kant had believed that he could effect a revolution in philosophy through the sheer power of his thought, but the younger man realized that it would be necessary to create a basis for support in the *Öffentlichkeit*. The range and vigour of his activities during these years are evidence of Fichte's own extraordinary energy and also of his generation's ambition to seize the apparently limitless oppor-

---

[34] Heine, 'Geschichte', p. 85; Copleston, *History*, vii. 64. Copleston provides a good introduction to Fichte's thought. See also Hartmann, *Philosophie*; Kroner, *Kant*.

[35] Copleston, *History*, vii. 77; Hartmann, *Philosophie*, p. 81.

tunities offered by a revolutionary era. In 1794–5, at the same time that Schiller was writing his essays on aesthetics and Schlegel was finishing his work on Greek literature, Fichte delivered a series of lectures on the scholar's social duties. More than any other social group, Fichte maintained, the scholar exists 'through and for society'. Scholarship is a 'branch of human education [*Bildung*]' that seeks to make people aware of their purpose in life, to cultivate their character as well as their mind. The academy, therefore, imparts knowledge, but 'at the same time should be a school of action'. To the young people who thronged into Jena's largest lecture hall to hear him, Fichte seemed like a modern prophet. Heinrich Steffens called him 'the most powerful concentration of the era's self-awareness', while to another admirer, 'Fichte's words in his lectures sweep along like a storm cloud that sheds fire in separate strokes. He does not move, but he uplifts the soul. Reinhold wanted to make good men; Fichte wants to make great men.'[36]

Calls to greatness make many people nervous, so it is not surprising that Fichte's spiritual message evoked animosity from the authorities. Even before his arrival, officials in Jena had been worried about his articles defending the French revolution. They were further upset by the success of his lectures, as well as by his habit of scheduling them on Sunday mornings. In 1798 Fichte's enemies decided that they could proceed against him on the basis of his essay, 'Über den Grund unseres Glaubens an eine göttliche Weltregierung', a rather tame exposition of his doubts about the philosophical foundations for a belief in divine providence. When the Saxon minister in charge of religious and educational affairs accused Fichte of atheism and demanded a retraction, the philosopher's reply was harsh, uncompromising, and tactically unwise: 'I could not be silent without sacrificing all my influence. . . . I am a professor at the university. . . . I am a philosophical writer, who believes in his ability to bring some new ideas before the public.' To compare Fichte's statement with Kant's unctuous defence of his own, not dissimilar, views a decade earlier, is to get a sense of how the tone of German intellectual life had changed by the late 1790s. The outcome of the controversy was also different: whereas Kant had survived, Fichte was removed from his post and forced to leave

---

[36] Fichte, *Von den Pflichten der Gelehrten: Jenaer Vorlesungen, 1794/95*, ed. R. Lauth *et al.* (Hamburg, 1971), 38, 112–13; Heinrich Steffens, *Was ich erlebte* (Munich, 1956), 65; Bruford, *Tradition*, p. 266. Bruford's book examines Fichte's ideas about *Bildung* in their historical context.

Jena. During the final stages of this controversy, when all the forces of repression were arrayed against the young professor, the great men in neighbouring Weimar did nothing. He wants to be burned at the stake, Herder joked, but wood is now too expensive. Goethe, whose religious beliefs were even less orthodox than Fichte's, was indignant about his lack of discretion: I would vote against my own son, the *Geheimrat* wrote, 'if he allowed himself to address the government in such a fashion'. The students were more courageous than their elders; twice they protested about Fichte's dismissal with petitions to the duke, but to no avail.[37]

Among the other intellectual luminaries at Jena in the 1790s was Friedrich Wilhelm Joseph von Schelling, who for a time thought of himself as one of Fichte's disciples. Even in an age as rich in prodigies as this one, Schelling seems remarkably precocious: born to a pastor's family in 1775, at fifteen he was a fellow student of Hegel and Hölderlin in Tübingen; he wrote his dissertation at seventeen and began to publish scholarly articles a year later. By the time he was twenty-three he had a chair of philosophy at Jena, where he knew Fichte, the Schlegels, and Novalis, as well as Goethe and Schiller; in 1803 he married August Wilhelm Schlegel's former wife, Caroline. Unlike many of his contemporaries, Schelling had a long, successful academic career, first at Würzburg, then Erlangen, Stuttgart, and finally Berlin. During his more than six decades as a philosopher, Schelling produced a large and complex body of work in which each stage of intellectual development is laid upon the last like a geological stratum.[38]

In the late 1790s Schelling sketched a world view that would, despite innumerable changes in language and emphasis, remain intact throughout his long career. At the centre of this world was the Absolute—in his later, more orthodox work, he identified it with God—which provided the beginning and end of all reality. History, he once wrote, is 'an epic composed in the mind of God', an epic that tells of mankind's journey to the farthest point of alienation and of our return to the divine centre. 'The first part is the *Iliad*, the second the *Odyssey* of history. In the first the movement was centrifugal, in the second it was centripetal.' Like Schiller and many other contemporaries, Schelling defined the

[37] Frank Böckelmann, *Die Schriften zu J. G. Fichtes Atheismus-Streit* (Munich, 1969), 94, 248, 251.

[38] The works by Copleston, Hartmann, and Kroner cited in n. 34 also contain useful analyses of Schelling.

human condition as the painful but unavoidable alienation of man from God, nature, and society. Reflective self-consciousness helped to cause, but can also help to cure this alienation. Philosophy's task is to restore unity to life, to reconcile humankind with its place in the theological, natural, and social order. 'Then there will no longer be any difference between the world of thought and the world of reality. There will be one world, and the peace of the golden age will make itself known for the first time in the harmonious union of all sciences.'[39]

From early in his career Schelling assigned art a privileged part in the philosopher's struggle to understand and unify the human condition. Because the world was generated by what he called 'the power of divine imagination', humans' artistic imagination gives them access to the secrets of the universe. Like the romantics, Schelling regarded art as a sacred activity, not as entertainment, adornment, or an imitation of the real world. 'The highest stage of reason, in which all ideas are embraced, is the aesthetic. . . . The philosopher is as much in need of aesthetic power as the poet.' At times he seemed to suggest that there was no important difference between art and philosophy, which in turn merged with myth and religion to provide the source of knowledge and meaning.[40]

Religion is art's most compelling subject, the richest source of symbols for individual and community. Like many of his contemporaries, Schelling first regarded classical Greek culture as the greatest historical example of art's fusion with religious values. After the turn of the century, however, he joined the movement back to Christianity and began to insist that humans needed a personal God. The ego 'demands God himself. Him, him will it have, the God who acts, who exercises providence, who can meet the reality of the Fall.' The *Aufklärung*, especially in its Kantian formulation, was 'negative philosophy', useful as a way of dissolving error but insufficient to bring us the truth we need. 'Without an active God . . . there can be no religion, for religion presupposes an actual, real relationship of man to God.'[41] Kant's chilly, impersonal creator, like the abstract God of absolute reason, the distant myths of ancient Greece, or the rich but foreign

---

[39] Copleston, *History*, vii. 161; Abrams, *Supernaturalism*, p. 31.

[40] Wellek, *History*, i. 367. Compare Schlegel's assertion that 'all art should become science and all science art': *Schriften*, p. 22. On Schelling's view of art, see James Engell, *The Creative Imagination. Enlightenment to Romanticism* (Cambridge, Mass., 1981), ch. 20.

[41] Copleston, *History*, vii. 169–70.

religions of the east, could not fulfil Schelling's need for an emotionally satisfying, culturally nourishing deity.

A former schoolmate and longtime friend of Schelling, Georg Wilhelm Friedrich Hegel arrived in Jena at the end of January 1801 to begin his own career as a professional philosopher. Born the son of a Württemberg civil servant in 1770, Hegel enjoyed none of Schelling's early success. At the Tübingen seminary, in his posts as tutor in Bern and Frankfurt, and in his first few publications, he appeared to be a moderately intelligent, but in no way outstanding young man. Yet to read through his unpublished writings from this period is to confront an extraordinarily active, tirelessly curious mind, remarkably sensitive to cultural trends and political developments, and deeply committed to understanding the hopes and fears of his age. We have already mentioned Hegel's early enthusiasm for the revolution in France, acquired while at Tübingen and sustained throughout his life. To this he added the admiration of classical Greece so characteristic of his time, Christian values, especially in their pietist formulation, the vision of a true folk religion like that in the Old Testament, and the *Aufklärung's* commitment to rational enquiry. Many of these various themes flow together in a remarkable letter he wrote to Schelling in January 1795. After describing his disappointment with Kant, whose ideas seemed of interest 'only for theoretical reasons', Hegel reported that he heard great things from Hölderlin about Fichte, a Titan 'who struggles for humanity and whose influence will certainly not be contained by the wall of a lecture room'. He then gives us one of those poignant expressions of hope and expectation so widespread among the German intellectuals of his age. 'The kingdom of God is coming', he assured his friend, 'and we must not sit by with our hands in our laps. . . . Reason and freedom remain our motto, and our meeting place is the invisible church.' Here, in this blend of Enlightenment principles and pietist imagery, we find the goals to which Hegel remained faithful, in his fashion, throughout his life. 'Reason' and 'Freedom' were the lodestars of his thought, the ideals with which he tried to plot a course through a world he came to see as manifestly irrational and unfree.[42]

Hegel accepted the diagnosis of the human condition offered in Schiller's great essays of 1795. 'The need for philosophy', Hegel

---

[42] G. W. F. Hegel, *Briefe von und an Hegel*, ed. Karl Hegel (Leipzig, 1887), 13 ff. There is a challenging exposition of Hegel's early years in Harris, *Hegel's Development: Toward the Sunlight*. The most recent account is Laurence Dickey's

once wrote, arises 'when the unifying power has disappeared from human life'. But Hegel saw, more clearly than Schiller and most of his contemporaries, that to restore harmony to life was both a spiritual and a social task. From the start, Hegel rejected subjectivity in all its forms; empiricist, rationalist, idealist, and romantic. Human beings cannot live in isolation; without others, we cannot think or act or even imagine our own existence. Throughout his career, therefore, Hegel was concerned with the necessary but problematic relationship between the self and other, lover and beloved, master and servant, brother and sister, guildsman and apprentice, citizen and ruler. He never stopped looking for ways in which people could live together without abandoning their individuality, enjoy freedom without enduring chaos, participate in the common life without being stifled by its demands.

During the first stage of his intellectual development, Hegel searched for a faith appropriate to his times, a source of meaning and direction for individual and community. Although he was by no means an orthodox Christian, he conducted this search along religious lines. As he wrote at the beginning of a fragmentary essay in 1793, 'Religion is the most important thing in our lives'; it consoles us in our private sorrows and links us to others through ritual and shared belief. He wanted a *Volksreligion* as cohesive as the ancient Hebrews', but also a religion compatible with his ideals of reason and freedom. Built upon the rational foundations laid by Kant, Hegel's new religion was also to contain the qualities of 'heart and imagination' necessary to win over ordinary people; and it would have to be freely chosen by the folk, who were to be won over by a prophet, not compelled by a tyrant. In the late 1790s Hegel's search for a rational and free faith merged with his growing interest in the political situation. Like his most alert contemporaries, Hegel recognized that German public life was being transformed by war and revolution. For a time he seems to have hoped that Austria might take the lead in restoring German freedom and independence, but more and more he came to see that there was no source of German power strong enough to withstand the French. As a result, his religious and political interests began to give way to philosophical concerns. He still hoped to create a new faith and he continued to recognize the need for political reform, but he began to think of these tasks philosophically. As he wrote to

Hegel. Religion, Economics, and the Politics of Spirit,. 1770–1807 (Cambridge, 1987), which appeared after this section had been written. Rosenzweig, *Hegel*, is still worth reading for the historical background.

J. H. Voss, the great German translator of Homer, 'I should like to say of my aspirations, that I shall try to teach philosophy to speak German. Once that is accomplished, it will be infinitely more difficult to give shallowness the appearance of profound truth.' Never one to be excessively modest in his choice of tasks, Hegel hoped to do for philosophy what Luther had done for the Bible and Voss had recently accomplished for Greek poetry.[43]

By the spring of 1805, what one of Hegel's biographers called his 'apocalyptic consciousness of the present' was heightened by the Reich's continued decline, Austria's military defeat, and the growing danger of war between France and Prussia. Over the next few months the political situation further deteriorated. Hegel told those who attended his last lecture in Jena in the summer of 1806: 'The entire mass of existing assumptions and concepts, the connecting bonds of the world are dissolved and have collapsed like images in a dream.' Within a short time the decisive battle between France and Prussia occurred outside Jena, and Hegel's town was filled with casualties and conquerors. During the tension-filled months of late 1805 and early 1806 Hegel had worked feverishly on his first great philosophical statement, the book that would launch his career and that remains one of the monuments of western thought, *The Phenomenology of the Spirit*. Hegel finished the *Phenomenology* before the battle of Jena began—for a while he worried that the manuscript might be lost or damaged by the fighting. The book survived unharmed, but in the chaos following the battle his university appointment collapsed and he was forced to move on in search of another post.[44]

Among the major classics of philosophy, the *Phenomenology* has a richly deserved reputation for being unusually enigmatic and elusive. Written at great speed by a man not blessed with much stylistic grace, the book places enormous demands on its readers. Although deeply historical in character, Hegel's analysis has little narrative structure, few names, and no dates. Instead, Hegel gives us what might be called a historical geography of the spirit's evolution from the beginning of human history to the present, a geography that describes the multiple layers of experience beneath the contemporary cultural terrain. To do this, Hegel must treat the mind in all its manifestations: as the source of knowledge and reasoning, private emotion and public commitment, religious faith

---

[43] Hegel, *Werke*, i. 37; Harris, *Hegel's Development: Night Thoughts*, p. 409.
[44] Rosenzweig, *Hegel*, i. 204, 220.

and artistic achievement. He must also make clear how the Absolute—the world spirit, the divine—intersects with the history of human thought and the spiritual development of individuals. The story is complex because the spirit's journey does not follow a straight path; there are setbacks and defeats, each victory is temporary, every resting place must crumble. Again and again, the spirit must 'return out of its confusion to itself as spirit, and win for itself a still higher consciousness'. History, Hegel realized, can be read as the story of recurrent failure, and the pages of the *Phenomenology* are littered with the wreckage of uprooted faiths and broken hopes. He sets himself the task of showing us the rational pattern that gives meaning to this tragic history and thus transforms it into the story of the spirit's progress towards higher forms of self-knowledge.[45]

Hegel shared his contemporaries' conviction that the spirit's journey had now entered a new, unprecedented stage. Before the eighteenth century mankind had had 'a heaven adorned with a vast wealth of thought and imagery'; then the *Aufklärung* had expelled religion and fixed mankind's attention on earthly things. Much good came of this, but the Enlightenment's denial of heaven proved to be as unsatisfactory as the medieval world's denial of earth had been. Without religiously grounded values, human relationships became utilitarian, politics was turned into negation, even terror. For all its great accomplishments, therefore, the Enlightenment left us without the power to understand ourselves and to order our lives. 'The spirit shows itself so impoverished that, like a wanderer in the desert craving for a mere mouthful of water, it seems to crave for its refreshment only the bare feeling of the divine in general. By the little which now satisfies the Spirit, we can measure the extent of its loss.'[46] Among these pale satisfactions, Hegel lists the ideas of most contemporary philosophers, whose vague and mystical ramblings provide 'edification' but not true knowledge. No wonder that Schelling, who grasped the meaning of the book more readily than most, was deeply offended when he read the *Phenomenology*.

Hegel regarded Enlightenment self-consciousness as mankind's greatest burden and only hope. It has left us vulnerable and uncertain, but also conscious of what has been lost and thus able to pass to a new stage of consciousness. This is why Hegel, despite his

[45] Hegel, *Phenomenology*, p. 319.
[46] Ibid. 5, see also pp. 328 ff.

profound admiration for the world of classical antiquity, believed that modern culture was potentially superior. The ancient world had been integrated, its values were beautifully expressed in artistic form, but contemporary fragmentation and disorder have revealed with a terrible clarity the essentially problematic character of all culture. In his well-known passages based on Diderot's *Rameau's Nephew*, Hegel clearly sympathized with the nephew's rejection of values and his ridicule of convention. Men such as this 'will find in their subversive depths the all-powerful note which restores the spirit to itself'.[47] The *Phenomenology* does not tell us how this restoration will occur. For all its length and complexity, it remains a preliminary reconnoitring of the terrain, a prelude to more systematic attempts to find a faith beyond irrational superstition and empty doubt, beyond anachronistic medievalism and sterile rationality.

That Hegel, Schelling, Fichte, and the romantics all belonged to the same intellectual generation is perhaps most readily apparent in their various attitudes towards religion. While few of them were orthodox and most were highly critical of current religious practice, all acknowledged the social power and cultural significance of religious belief. There was, therefore, an intensity to their religious feelings that one rarely finds even among the more theologically inclined *Aufklärer*. Unlike Kant, for example, who had believed as much and no more than was necessary to sustain an ethical life, these younger men wanted to have a faith that could inspire, console, and satisfy. This is why so many of them were fascinated by mythology, comparative religion, and the aesthetic function of the idea of divinity. Moreover, they recognized that an ebbing of belief would have incalculable consequences for both the inner life of individuals and the public life of the community. Since the members of the romantic generation refused to accept the prospects of a life without faith, many of them either embraced some form of Christianity or continued to search for a surrogate. This is why Friedrich Schleiermacher praised his most secular contemporaries for underscoring just how essential religion was. 'Whether you wish to or not,' he wrote in 1799, 'the goal of your present efforts is also the resurrection of religion . . . I celebrate you as, however unintentionally, the rescuers and guardians of religion.'[48]

---

[47] Ibid. pp. 317 ff. There is a striking analysis of this passage in Lionel Trilling, *Sincerity and Authenticity* (Cambridge, 1971), 26 ff.
[48] Gerrish, *Prince*, p. 44.

Schleiermacher, the most important theologian of his age, was also a member of the romantic generation. Born in Breslau in 1768, the son of an army chaplain, he attended schools which were deeply imbued with pietist religiosity. 'Religion', he once recalled, 'was the maternal womb in whose sacred darkness my young life was nourished.' But the influence of the secular world was present at Schleiermacher's seminary just as it had been at Hegel's; in addition to the Bible and the classics of ancient literature, Schleiermacher and his fellow students read the modern works of Wieland, Goethe, and Kant. The result for the young seminarian was a shattering religious crisis, which he reported to his father in an anguished letter of January 1787: 'Alas, dearest father, if you believe that without this faith [in the Godhead] no one can attain to salvation in the next world, nor to tranquillity in this . . . then pray to God to grant it to me, for to me it is now lost.' Eventually, however, his faith returned, he was ordained a minister, and served as a pastor, first in a small town and then, from 1796 to 1802, at the Charité hospital in Berlin.[49]

While in the Prussian capital, Schleiermacher came to know many of the leading romantic writers of the day, and for a time shared a flat with Friedrich Schlegel. How extraordinary it must have been for this sensitive young clergymen to be plunged into the highly charged world of romantic sensibility, now at its most brilliant and seductive stage. How far away from the seminary and rural parish must have seemed Berlin's salon life, which sparkled with wit and basked in the warmth of shared celebrity. That Schleiermacher was not unmoved by the values of this world can be seen in his *Confidential Letters on Lucinde*, a defence of Schlegel's scandalous book which has often been something of an embarrassment to the theologian's pious admirers. But as is so often the case, Schleiermacher found it easier to write about romantic love than to enjoy it in his life. He received little pleasure from his tempestuous attachment to Eleonore Grunow, who could not bring herself to dissolve her unhappy marriage in order to marry him. In 1802, when he left his post at the Charité for a small parish in Pomerania, his personal affairs were in disarray and his relationship to his ecclesiastical superiors severely strained.

With his faith tested and reshaped by his philosophical doubts,

---

[49] The quotations are from Gerrish, *Prince*, pp. 24–5. In addition to this essay, see Gerrish's chapter on Schleiermacher in Smart *et al.* (eds.), *Thought*, i. Dilthey's *Leben* is not only the best single book on Schleiermacher; it is also one of the best intellectual biographies ever written.

Schleiermacher considered himself a 'Moravian of a higher order', who was both a man of his time and a committed Christian. Even in his Berlin days, when he was most receptive to the secular currents swirling around him, he retained his belief in the primacy of theology and continued to perform his clerical duties. He was well read in philosophy, but unlike Fichte or Hegel, he did not see philosophical reason as the main road to truth. He was deeply moved by literature, but unlike the romantics, he did not identify art and true knowledge. Both reason and beauty were subordinate to theology, whose message he sought to convey to his contemporaries—and especially, as the subtitle of his first major work expressed it, 'to the cultivated despisers of religion'. These are the people, Schleiermacher lamented, for whom 'suavity and sociability, art and science' have left no room 'for the eternal and holy being that lies beyond the world'. To address this audience, Schleiermacher used the idiom of Fichte and the romantics, not the crisp complexities of Wolffian rationalism or the ethical arguments of Kant's second critique. 'Religion neither seeks like metaphysics to determine and explain the nature of the universe, nor like morals to advance and perfect the universe by the power of freedom and the divine will of man. It is neither thinking nor acting, but intuition and feeling.' The nature of religion and, therefore, the proper subject of theology are to be found in the pious sensibility of the believer. But Schleiermacher did not intend this appeal to emotion, with its characteristic introspective impulse, as a defence of mysticism or pure subjectivity. By getting to know one's self, one learns about God's universe: 'The examination of self and the examination of the universe are interchangeable concepts.'[50] Moreover, Schleiermacher was deeply committed to social life in all its forms, including, as we will see presently, the relationship of nation and state.

There was no Catholic theologian of Schleiermacher's stature during the revolutionary era; the Protestant pre-eminence in German literary culture, already apparent in the eighteenth century, increased during the 1790s and early 1800s. In a sense, this decline in the creativity of Catholic thought is curious, since most scholars agree that romanticism revitalized Catholicism's influence over literature and the visual arts. But cultural revival did not produce philosophical renewal. In part this was because the romantics' emphasis on art, myth, and feeling was much easier to

[50] Schleiermacher, *Religion*, pp. 1, 277; Dilthey, *Leben*, p. 330.

express aesthetically than philosophically. Moreover, the harsh anti-clericalism of the revolution deepened the antagonism many church leaders felt for enlightened ideas and strengthened the ties between hierarchy and reactionary political regimes. Those Catholic institutions that had survived the process of secularization were often intolerant of rational enquiry and philosophical speculation. Owen Chadwick called this movement of the church to the right 'the curse the revolution bequeathed to the popes', because it alienated many Catholics from the enlightened ideas and further divided them from their Protestant contemporaries.[51] A brief look at the two most interesting Catholic thinkers around the turn of the century, Franz von Baader and Bernard Bolzano, will suggest how these intellectual and institutional restraints inhibited the growth of Catholic philosophical discourse.

Franz von Baader was born in 1765, the son of a well-connected Munich physician. He intended to follow his father's profession, but when he found the pain of his patients too much to bear, he became a mining engineer, thus putting into practice a pervasive romantic metaphor for penetrating the surface of both earth and psyche. During a four-year stay in England, Baader became aware of social problems and was one of the first to write about the dangers of what he called the 'proletariat'. After his return to Bavaria, he worked in the department of mines, operated a glass factory, was engaged in a number of political projects, and wrote on a variety of theological and philosophical topics. When he retired from the civil service in 1820, he devoted himself full-time to intellectual pursuits and, in 1826, was appointed to the chair of speculative theology at the University of Munich.[52]

In the opening pages of the diary he began to keep in 1786, Baader posed the question that troubled so many of his contemporaries: if our own self-knowledge is the primary source of certainty, how do we gain knowledge of the external world? 'Here is the knot, here is the greatest, deepest secret of all our knowledge, as I saw it expressed in Kant.' Baader's solution was a curious blend of natural science and religious mysticism, already apparent in his

[51] Chadwick, *Popes*, p. 610. As evidence of how far Catholic thought is outside the canon, consider the marginal role it plays in the authoritative three-volume collection, Smart, *et al.* (eds.), *Thought*. There is a more positive account of the revolution's impact on the church in Epstein, *Genesis*, p. 674.

[52] See Hans Grassl, 'Franz von Baader (1765–1841)', in Fries and Schwaiger (eds.), *Theologen*, i, for a good introduction; Grassl, *Aufbruch zur Romantik: Bayerns Beitrag zur deutschen Geistesgeschichte, 1765–1785* (Munich, 1968), for the historical context.

dissertation on *Wärmestoff*, a problem in physical chemistry which he transformed into a question of metaphysical reality. Thus began Baader's search for 'the world soul', that 'general connection that binds and weaves together all being in the universe'. For half a century he looked for this source of unity, the common principles that would return mankind to harmony and order. Like Hegel, whom he visited in Berlin, and Schelling, with whom he worked in Munich, Baader was a vigorously eclectic thinker, as interested in medieval mysticism as he was in modern science. The result was a peculiar mixture of science and alchemy, sharp social analysis and eccentric obscurantism, theosophy and logic. When reading his works, one senses a receptivity and ambition equal to Hegel's, but not the creative, ordering intelligence that enabled Hegel to construct his majestic philosophical system.[53]

As was the case for Catholic philosophers in the eighteenth century, Baader's speculations led him to think about questions of religious organization. Because he believed in the religious primacy of the individual, he had a low regard for the trappings of ecclesiastical hierarchy and the realities of papal power. The true church was the invisible community of the faithful, who had been divided into different denominations by a series of unfortunate historical accidents. Baader hoped that, as a layman and a theologian, a scientist and a believer, he would be in a position to lay the foundations of a new, unified Christianity. Unfortunately, Baader's ecumenical enthusiasms were more than a century ahead of their time. His efforts to bring the denominations together were without success, with the ironic exception of his idea for a so-called 'Holy Alliance' of Protestant Prussia, Catholic Austria, and Orthodox Russia, which Metternich manipulated on behalf of reactionary goals contrary to Baader's own sympathies. The Catholic authorities largely ignored Baader. His writings were not put on the index of forbidden books, nor were they taken seriously as blueprints for reform. The religious establishment seems to have been convinced, quite accurately as it turned out, that Baader was eccentric and isolated enough to be harmless. However, as a look at the career of Bernard Bolzano demonstrates, when it was necessary to do so, the church could move decisively against dangerous ideas and influences.

The Bolzano family illustrates the rich and varied strands from which Austrian culture was woven: Bernard's father was born in

[53] Franz von Baader, *Sätze aus der erotischen Philosophie und andere Schriften*, ed. G. K. Kaltenbrunner (Frankfurt, 1966), 31; Grassl, 'Baader' (cited in n. 52), p. 275.

Lombardy and settled in Prague, where he married the daughter of a local merchant, achieved some success as an art dealer, and reared his children as members of the enlightened, German-speaking *Bürgertum*. Born in 1781, Bernard was a gifted but troubled young man, who excelled at mathematics as well as philosophy and theology. Despite his own misgivings and his father's strenuous objections, he became a priest, and was soon appointed to a chair in theology at the University of Prague, where he exerted a powerful influence as both a lecturer and a preacher. Unlike Baader and many of the romantics, Bolzano's scientific interests were in mathematics rather than biology, chemistry, or geology; he holds a small, but secure place in the history of calculus. However, he was never exclusively interested in abstract thought and always tried to use his philosophical analysis to probe the moral and practical questions of the age. Furthermore, Bolzano shared the romantics' concern for the emotional side of religious life. His best known work, the *Athanasia*, is a defence of the idea of immortality, written to console his housekeeper for the death of her young daughter. Although he remained a Catholic, he had as little sympathy for the institutional structure of the church as did Baader. He opposed 'the secular authority of the pontiff in the Papal states, and above all, the priesthood's earthly power and glory'.[54]

Bolzano's ideas won him few friends among the ecclesiastical and political authorities in Prague. When one of his students was arrested in 1819, Bolzano was removed from his post and, after a series of investigations and trials, forced into permanent retirement. He lived for almost thirty years in relative isolation, supported by a small pension and the kindness of his friends. Due in large part to the heroic scholarly efforts of Eduard Winter, we can now see that, despite his isolation, Bolzano's ideas were of considerable importance for the development of nineteenth-century thought, especially in the Habsburg lands. Winter is able to assemble an impressive list of people who were touched by Bolzano's work. Much of his influence, however, was surreptitious or indirect, often forced underground by the pressures of political and religious repression. Bolzano's accomplishments, therefore, illustrate both the lingering vitality of Catholic thought and the profound difficulties Catholic thinkers had to face.

---

[54] Edward Winter, 'Bernard Bolzano', in Fries and Schwaiger (eds.), *Theologen*, i. 334. In addition to this essay, see Winter's monograph, *Bernard Bolzano und sein Kreis* (Leipzig, 1933).

iii. INTELLECTUALS AND POLITICS

At the end of the conversation they had in October 1808, Napoleon told Goethe that the time for writing tragedies of fate had passed. 'What do we want with fate now?' said the emperor to the poet, 'Politics is our fate.'[55] Few German intellectuals would have wished to dispute the great politician's lapidary pronouncement; for almost two decades they had been pursued by political fates as remorseless as those Aeschylus unleashed upon his tragic heroes. As a distant spectacle or, more often, as a forceful intrusion into their lives, revolutionary politics demanded contemporaries' attention, affected their careers, reshaped their sense of the possible. The romantics' awareness of emotional power, like the philosophers' search for an alternative system of belief, was a response to the political passions and commitments that swept across central Europe from the French side of the Rhine. Burden or opportunity, disaster or triumph, occasion for celebration or lament, politics in the revolutionary era was everybody's *Schicksal*.[56]

No German intellectual regretted the fateful primacy of revolutionary politics more deeply than Goethe. After he had freed himself from his own political responsibilities by fleeing to Italy, he returned to Weimar in June 1788 with the intention of devoting himself to writing, scientific research, and other cultural enterprises. Although he had exposed himself to the strenuous dangers of war in 1792, Goethe's engagement with these events was more limited and half-hearted than his oft-quoted assessment of Valmy's global significance might lead one to conclude. Throughout the campaign he had spent more time in his tent working on a translation of 'Reynard the Fox' into hexameters than he did observing the world-shaking events going on around him. From 1795 until 1805, while Weimar was shielded from war by the armistice line established in the Treaty of Basel, Goethe was completely absorbed by his own affairs; neither his voluminous correspondence nor his *Annalen* give many indications that he was interested in day-to-day political developments. But Goethe's response to politics was one of antipathy rather than of apathy. He saw as much of what was going on as he wanted to see, and what he saw, he disapproved of. Radical change, he believed, was risky, ideals illusory, the populace a fickle mob. He much preferred the sort of political neutrality possible in a well-run, benevolent

---

[55] Goethe, *Werke*, x. 546.

[56] The political history of these years is treated above in Chs. 4 and 5.

authoritarian regime—a neutrality that was tantamount to accepting the status quo. He hated the revolution for threatening this neutrality with its seductive promises and terrifying threats. The revolution pulled people from their private lives and distracted them from what really mattered. 'Franztum drängt in diesen verworrenen Tagen, wie ehemals| Luthertum es getan, ruhige Bildung zurück.'[57]

Goethe was never able to create an artistic idiom to express his feelings about the revolution. Scattered throughout his work are various political references, epigrams, and verses, but his major attempt to treat the subject directly, a play entitled 'Natürliche Tochter', was never finished. The best representation of his political views, therefore, remains his long pastoral poem of 1797, *Hermann und Dorothea*, in which intruding political forces are finally expelled so that hero and heroine can enjoy the sweet fruits of private bliss. As Wilhelm Mommsen once wrote, 'The basic political tone of this poem is protective and conservative.' The plot, like the direction of Goethe's thought, is anti-political, the wilful assertion of personal needs in the face of powerful external pressures. Politics, even history, was less interesting to Goethe than the specific but everlasting realm of human values and emotions. This was why, as he wrote to Schiller in March 1799, the last play of Schiller's Wallenstein trilogy pleased him most of all: 'everything stops being political and becomes only human, indeed, history itself becomes a veil through which we see the purely human [*Reinmenschliche*].'[58]

While he shared Goethe's instinctive dislike and increasing antagonism to the events in France, Schiller remained much closer to politics and history. While Goethe had fled the responsibilities of power, Schiller had once fled its oppressive imposition. Because he had felt the tyrant's lash and suffered the pains of stateless isolation, his fascination with power and his fear of its misuse were rooted in deep personal memories. Schiller's work after 1789, therefore, never displays Goethe's self-consciously Olympian disdain for the political realm. Schiller's historical works, several of his major poems, and many of his plays, especially *Wilhelm Tell* and the great Wallenstein trilogy, all have to do with power and freedom. Yet Schiller also refused to grant politics the primacy its immediacy seemed to claim; he remained convinced that moral worth and

[57] There is a sympathetic treatment of Goethe's politics in Mommsen, *Anschauungen*. Butler, *Tyranny*, and Stern, *Idylls*, are both critical.
[58] Mommsen, *Anschauungen*, p. 102; Goethe and Schiller, *Briefwechsel*, p. 397.

inner freedom must always take precedence. This was why, as we have seen, his essays on aesthetics in 1795 pointed to art as the proper foundation of human liberty. In order to have a good state, men had to be morally good; the purpose of the state was to encourage, but not compel morality.[59]

Schiller shared Goethe's sense that politics was an unwelcome intrusion into the realms of art and culture. In a letter written in the summer of 1799, he compared contemporary events to the Puritan revolution and remarked that 'such times are apt to ruin literature and art, because they excite and inflame the spirit, without giving it a subject'. But for Schiller the revolution was not just a distraction. Its false ideals had unleashed deeply rooted destructive urges, dark instincts that always threatened mankind's long, perilous journey from barbarism to civilization. In his remarkable poem of 1795, 'Der Spaziergang', he used a dazzling series of natural images to evoke the dangers that attend us on this journey. In 'Das Lied von der Glocke' written five years later, the evils of revolution are displayed without metaphorical costume. When the bell tolls 'Freedom and Equality', the streets are filled with an armed and angry mob,

> Da werden Weiber zu Hyänen
> Und treiben mit Entsetzen Scherz,
> Noch zuckend, mit des Panthers Zähnen,
> Zerreissen sie des Feindes Hertz.

These angry lines display the bitterness with which Schiller, his health gone and his hopes for cultural renewal fading, railed against the political developments of his day. In *Demetrius*, his last, unfinished play, the hero seems virtually powerless, condemned to suffer from forces against which he lacks the strength to struggle. All we have left, Schiller tells us in a sad poem on the dawn of a new century, is flight 'into the heart's holy stillness' since 'Freedom is only in the realm of dreams, | And beauty blooms only in song.'[60]

Goethe's and Schiller's dislike of the revolution became widespread among German intellectuals after the first blush of their enthusiasm faded. In April 1793, for example, Karoline Herder, who had once celebrated 'the healthy winds blowing from across the Rhine', condemned 'these lawless, impassioned, vain, and

---

[59] The literature on Schiller is cited in Ch. 3, sects. ii and iv. For a brief introduction to his political views, see Gordon A. Craig, 'Friedrich Schiller and the Problems of Power', in Krieger and Stern, eds., *Responsibility*, pp. 125–44.

[60] Goethe and Schiller, *Briefwechsel*, p. 424; Wiese, *Schiller*, p. 410.

intolerant men' who have done us all 'irretrievable harm' and have dishonoured 'the noblest nation on earth'. About the same time, Klopstock wrote a poem entitled 'Mein Irrthum', in which he regretted that Freedom, once praised as the 'mother of salvation', had now become the rallying cry for a war of aggression:

> Ach des goldenen Traums Wonn' ist dahin'
> Mich umschwebet nicht mehr sein Morgenglanz,
> Und ein Kummer, wie verschmähter
> Liebe, kümmert mein Herz.

What had seemed like the culmination of the Enlightenment, now appeared as a dark and dangerous drama, dominated by what one contemporary called 'the lower classes, that is, the craftsmen and peasants', who were, 'taken as a group, only half human'. Conquest, regicide, sacrilege, and terror—these were the images which many German thinkers identified with the French struggle for liberty, equality, and fraternity.[61]

Some German intellectuals responded to the failure of the French experiment by reformulating their traditional commitment to moral reform. This was, as we know, the inclination of men like the Schlegels, Novalis, Fichte, and Schelling, all of whom, in different ways, tried to find a spiritual antidote to the political poison at work in Europe. The result, some liked to claim, was 'a revolution no less glorious, no less rich in consequences than the one from which has come the government of the French republic. This revolution is in the country of the mind.' In 1798, the same year that the Rhenish journalist J. B. Geich made this assessment, Friedrich Schlegel named the French revolution, Fichte's epistemology, and Goethe's *Wilhelm Meister* as 'the three greatest forces of the age'. Whoever doubts this, Schlegel went on, and believes that 'no revolution can be important unless it is noisy and materialistic, has not yet reached a broad enough perspective on human history'. By 1807 even Hegel, who never lost his admiration for the revolution, wrote to a student that 'fatherland, princes, constitutions, and the like do not seem to be the means to raise up the German folk; it is a question what would happen if religion were used'. In these remarks, and in many others that might be quoted, we can see how the tradition of moral reform survived into the revolutionary era. Even when confronted by the inescapable realities of political change, some Germans continued to insist that

---

[61] Valjavec, *Entstehung*, pp. 166–7; Klopstock, 'Mein Irrthum', in *Ausgewählte Werke* (Munich, 1962), 148–50.

the place to begin—and for a few of them, the place to end—was the human spirit, which could be led on a journey to true freedom under the banners of beauty, philosophy, or religion.[62]

But it was not always easy to live in the realm of the spirit during the revolutionary age, when the magnetic force of political realities pulled men towards the world of action and compelled them to accept the responsibilities of power or to seek the possibilities of influence. Consider, for example, the case of Wilhelm von Humboldt, in whose life and thought the poles of spirit and power, contemplation and action appear with exemplary clarity. Born in 1767, Humboldt was reared in and around Berlin, where he enjoyed all the material comforts and intellectual opportunities his wealthy and well-established family could provide. He had access to the best society in the Prussian capital and for a time was part of the first flowering of the salon culture to which the romantics would later be drawn. With Henriette Herz, Dorothea Veit, and Carl Laroche, he founded a secret society devoted to 'the pursuit of happiness through love'—which meant, it should be said, sentimental intimacy but physical chastity; the members of this so-called *Tugendbund* were as observant of conventional morality as the professedly democratic Freemasons were of existing social hierarchies. At the University of Göttingen, Humboldt was fortunate in his circle of friends, which included the classicist Heyne, his daughter Therese and son-in-law Georg Forster, as well as two interesting young women, Caroline von Beulwitz, who was soon to become Schiller's sister-in-law, and Caroline von Dacheröden, who would eventually become Humboldt's wife.[63]

Humboldt was a committed intellectual, fascinated by Greek culture, widely read, interested in a variety of subjects, and much given to passionate discussions deep into the night. Nevertheless, in April 1790 he set foot on the lowest rung of the Prussian bureaucratic ladder by joining the judicial service in Berlin's municipal court. He found the work confining and distasteful, a personal burden and a violation of his belief in the complexity and sanctity of the individual. How, he asked himself, could he ever judge someone like the woman who stood before him accused of infanticide—how could he get to know her feelings and values

[62] Epstein, *Genesis*, p. 448; Schlegel, *Schriften*, pp. 45–6; Rosenzweig, *Hegel*, ii. 22.

[63] Sweet, *Wilhelm von Humboldt,* is the most recent biography. Kaehler's *Humboldt* remains a challenging and powerful analysis. For a good brief treatment, see Sorkin's article, 'Humboldt'.

from the incomplete dossier on which he had to base his verdict? After little more than a year he resigned his post and set out to live a life of private study and cultivation, first on his wife's estates, then in Jena and finally in Paris.

During the months following his resignation from government service, Humboldt confronted theoretically the tension between politics and culture he had just tried to resolve in his own life. An essay, 'Ideen über Staatsverfassung, durch die neue französische Constitution veranlasst', a fragment 'Über die Gesetze der Entwicklung der menschlichen Krafte', and a short book, *Ideen zu einem Versuch, die Grenzen der Wirksamkeit des Staates zu bestimmen*, all turn on the problem of how a deeply individualized culture can best contribute to, and coexist with, the demands of the state. Humboldt's point of departure is the conviction that 'what should thrive in human beings must flow from their inner selves, not be given them from the outside—and what else is a state but the sum of creating and suffering human forces?'[64] Political authority, he argued in his *Ideen zu einem Versuch . . .* , should be restrained as much as possible so that individuals can realize their full spiritual potential.

Although finished at the end of 1792, *Ideen zu einem Versuch . . .* , was not published until after Humboldt's death, when it was immediately taken up as a defence of human freedom from the state—John Stuart Mill, the reader may recall, took a quotation from Humboldt as the epigraph for *On Liberty*. This is not an illegitimate interpretation, since Humboldt did intend to criticize eighteenth-century bureaucratic absolutism, which had just entered a new phase of intolerance and repression under Frederick William II. But Humboldt's political ideal was not the kind of state Mill would have much admired. 'Properly speaking,' he wrote, 'free constitutions do not seem to me so important or salutary. A moderate monarchy on the whole puts far less straitening effects on the education of the individual.'[65] For Humboldt, it was as important to assert the interests of the private over the public as to defend the rights of the individual *vis-à-vis* the state. He remained, therefore, much closer to the eighteenth-century ideal of moral reform than to the nineteenth-century politics of liberalism. *Bildung*—the moral, spiritual, and aesthetic cultivation of the personality—was the highest value towards which individuals

[64] Humboldt, *Werke*, i. 36.
[65] Aris, *History*, p. 157.

should strive and by which the actions of the state should be judged.

Humboldt's commitment to *Bildung* was deepened by the close relationship to Schiller that he established after moving to Jena in 1794. During this crucial period in the poet's own intellectual development, Humboldt saw him almost every day, read drafts of his essays, discussed his new ideas, and shared with him the invigorating cultural climate of classical Weimar. Humboldt discharged his debt to the Weimar notables in a long analysis of Goethe's 'Hermann und Dorothea', written after he and his family had gone to Paris in 1797. The very fact that, so soon after arriving in the political centre of the European world, Humboldt would devote his time and energy to studying this pastoral denunciation of political action underscores his own values and priorities. 'Hermann und Dorothea', Humboldt wrote, is an epic for our time, Homeric in its grace and simplicity, but contemporary in its preference for what he called *bürgerlich* life. By *bürgerlich* he appears to have meant the private and personal rather than the public and political sphere—this was the aspect of life to which poets must turn in these unpoetic times. In a passage that recalls Schiller's essays of 1795, Humboldt concluded his account with a plea for a new aesthetics: 'it has never been more necessary to shape [*bilden*] and consolidate the inner form of character than now, when external circumstances and habits are threatened by the terrible power of universal upheaval.' But this does not mean that art should have a political purpose: art is and should be an autonomous act, in which only aesthetic judgments can be brought to bear. Art, like *Bildung*, must have an existence beyond politics.[66]

Humboldt himself, however, could not live outside the political world. After a decade of private indulgence, he was ready once again to serve his state. This time he found a place more congenial than the municipal court: in 1802 he was appointed Prussian minister to Rome, a position he occupied with great skill and considerable pleasure, in part because he could combine his diplomatic duties with scholarly and artistic pursuits. From the relative peace and isolation of the Prussian embassy he watched the destructive sweep of the French conquests, whose scale seemed to threaten not only the state he served but also the culture he so admired. 'It is sad to see', he told Madame de Staël in August

---

[66] Humboldt, *Werke*, ii. 342, 356. See the analysis in Hans-Wolf Jäger, *Politische Kategorien in Poetik und Rhetorik der zweiten Hälfte des 18. Jahrhunderts* (Stuttgart, 1970), 28–9.

1808, 'that the present crisis menaces our literary glory, the only national glory we possess.'[67] Just weeks after writing this, Humboldt found himself caught up in the crisis. In October 1808 he left Rome to take care of some long-neglected family business concerning his own and his wife's properties. As he had feared, once in Berlin he was quickly drawn into the work of the reformers. Personal honour and reputation, an awareness of the unique possibilities at hand, and a desire to test himself in the field of action combined to make it impossible for him to refuse the king's appointment as chief of educational and ecclesiastical affairs in the newly-reorganized Ministry of the Interior. Over the next two years he helped to achieve a series of basic reforms at all levels of Prussian education, tried to reshape elementary schools in the light of Pestalozzi's humane and ethical concerns for individual growth, introduced a classical curriculum into a reconstituted type of secondary school called the Gymnasium, and established at Berlin a new university which would become a model for higher education throughout much of the world. We will consider in a later chapter these various attempts to 'inoculate the Germans with the Greek spirit', as Humboldt once called his efforts to bring Prussian educational institutions into line with the ideals of *Bildung*. For the present, it is sufficient to point out how quickly and completely Humboldt's struggle for spiritual reform became enmeshed with the state's struggle for political survival. Within the historical world of revolutionary central Europe and as the servant of a state with Prussia's problems and traditions, Humboldt found it impossible to resist using bureaucratic power to realize his cultural ideal. As a result, he presided over a marriage of *Staat* and *Bildung* that would have lasting consequences for German politics, culture, and society.[68]

A different sort of engagement with the world of political reality can be seen in the life of Humboldt's friend from his Göttingen days, Georg Forster. Although he was only thirty-four when he met Humboldt at his father-in-law's house, Forster had already lived a life filled with adventure and accomplishment. His father had been a famous traveller, who took him first on a long trip up the Volga and then on Captain Cook's second great voyage of discovery. Forster's account of Cook's voyage, written when he

---

[67] Humboldt, *Werke*, ii. 240; Kaehler, *Humboldt*, p. 512.

[68] See Kaehler, *Humboldt*, bk. 2, ch. 1; Sorkin, 'Humboldt'. A concise statement of Humboldt's own views is his 'Antrag auf Errichtung der Universität Berlin' (July 1809), in *Werke*, iv.

was barely twenty, made him famous. But literary fame was not enough to live on, so Forster had to search for a satisfactory position. Finally, in 1788, he found employment as librarian for the Archbishop Elector of Mainz, whose enlightened old-regime court was soon to be directly in the path of the revolution's eastward march. As an opponent of organized religion, Forster was politically radical in the institutionally vague style of the day, and, like so many of his contemporaries, he greeted the revolution, abstractly but enthusiastically. But, as Custine's troops drew closer to Mainz, he recognized that 'the hour of decision is approaching and I shall have to take sides'. In the end he joined the minority who welcomed the French troops and agreed to serve in their administration. The choice was a difficult one, easy to regret, hard to undo. Forster knew that he would be condemned by those who 'find me detestable because I have gone to work to apply principles which they applauded'. He also had difficulties with his French allies, who resented his efforts to deflect their self-serving and exploitative policies. Nevertheless, he held to his commitments and did not fear to take responsibility for his choice. While he was in Paris, representing his district at the Convention, German troops reconquered Mainz, and thus left him stranded in a city quickly slipping into the grip of terror. He died there in January 1794, discouraged by the course of events but not without hope for the final triumph of his ideas.[69]

By the time Forster died, most German intellectuals had abandoned their support for the revolution; even some German Jacobins were beginning to rethink their alliance with the conquerors. As T. C. W. Blanning has shown in such convincing detail, one reason for this shift away from the revolution was the behaviour of the French, whose identification of their own interests with the ideals of revolution opened the way for exploitation and repression. But the movement of German political opinion to the right was not merely a reaction to French excesses. Equally important, especially in territories not under foreign occupation, were the anti-revolutionary measures taken by many German states, which tightened censorship, arrested suspected radicals, and

[69] The Berlin Academy of Sciences is publishing what will be the definitive edition of Forster's writings (1958 ff.). R. R. Wuthenow has edited a convenient collection of his work from 1791 to 1794 under the title *Anblick*. For a concise, sympathetic treatment of Forster's politics, see Gordon A. Craig, 'Engagement and Neutrality in Germany: The Case of Georg Forster, 1754–94', *JMH* 41/1 (1969), 1–16. The quotations are from Gooch, *Germany*, p. 308; Craig, p. 12.

dissolved allegedly subversive organizations. These policies, some of which were under way even before 1789, had an understandably chilling effect on a political public as ideologically uncertain and institutionally fragile as eighteenth-century central Europe's.[70] Moreover, the governments' reaction to the French menace was not merely repressive: 'Against an enemy like the one the revolution has brought to this age,' Friedrich Gentz wrote to Metternich in January 1806, 'our military and political skills cannot prevail. . . . we will soon be destroyed unless we bring entirely new weapons into the field.' Gentz had in mind the ideological weapons he himself had forged and was eager to set against the false ideals of liberty, equality, and fraternity.[71]

Born in 1764 into a family of successful, upwardly mobile Prussian civil servants, the young Friedrich Gentz seemed to be an exemplary Enlightenment figure. Well-educated, a student and friend of Kant, popular member of Berlin society, and promising administrator, Gentz became Humboldt's close friend and companion soon after the two men met in 1790. At that point, it will be recalled, Gentz admired the French revoution, whose proclamations of freedom for humanity seemed to fit his own restless search for a great cause. In 1791, Gentz read Edmund Burke's *Reflections on the Revolution in France*, at first with distaste, then with growing enthusiasm, as the radicalization of French politics and the drift towards war with the German states seemed to validate Burke's critique of revolutionary radicalism. In 1793 Gentz's translation of the *Reflections* helped to establish his reputation as an anti-revolutionary publicist; over the next decade he became a prolific polemicist and editor of various conservative journals. Like so many other Berlin intellectuals around the turn of the century, he moved with ease in the social world of the salons, sought influence on the fringes of political power, and indulged his taste for close friendships and brief flirtations. His life was marked by an undercurrent of instability—divorce, bankruptcy, scandal, and disappointment. He left Berlin in 1802 for Vienna, where he found a government job and eventually, under the protection of Metternich, an important if subordinate position in the councils of the great. But, despite his gifts and influence as an ideologue, he remained dependent on the help of his well-placed friends. At once

[70] Blanning, *Revolution*, especially ch.7, 'The Alienation of the Left'. On the development of conservatism, see Valjavec, *Entstehung*, pp. 258 ff.
[71] Quoted in Srbik, *Metternich*, i. 112.

propagandist and courtier, Gentz represents a transitional figure.[72]

Burke's *Reflections* was neither the first nor the most popular attack on the French revolution, but in the long run this book did more than any other to bring the traditions of German conservatism to bear on the immediate problemms of the revolution. In some important ways, Burke resembled Justus Möser: both men had a rich, emotionally charged vision of politics, were deeply suspicious of abstract analysis and impractical theorists, and used historical analysis to defend tradition and celebrate organic communities. But Burke's vision had greater intensity, persuasive power, and political specificity. To him, and to his translator, the values of the old order were not simply anachronisms, whose passing should evoke nostalgic affection and regret; they were a programme around which men could rally and for which battles must be won. Burke's ideas, therefore, helped to create an ideological justification of the old order, which could be turned against the revolutionaries in France and the reformers closer to home.[73]

The most sustained, consistent, and intellectually powerful German formulation of conservative principles was the work of Adam Müller, a friend of Gentz and, like him, a denizen of the Berlin salons. Müller was born in 1779, the son of a subaltern official in the Prussian bureaucracy. He owed his opportunity to rise above his father's station to a patron, his stepmother's father, who helped him to attend Berlin's famous Gymnasium-am-Grauen-Kloster, where he mixed with the local élite and learned to use his wits to overcome the limits of his background. After studying at Göttingen, he accepted a bureaucratic appointment in Berlin. An aesthete, something of a dandy, ready to talk about the latest fashions or the newest book, Müller frequented the salons at the same time as devoting himself to his career. After four years, he resigned his post and went to live on a friend's estate in order to finish his first major work, *Die Lehre von Gegensätzen*. In 1805, for reasons that puzzled even those who knew him well, he converted to Catholicism, but kept this decision hidden from the various Protestant princes whose favour he courted. Probably the most productive years of Müller's life were those he spent in the service of Saxe-Weimar from 1806 to 1809: here he delivered a series of

---

[72] Paul R. Sweet's *Friedrich von Gentz: Defender of the Old Order* (Madison, 1941) is balanced and informative, while Golo Mann's *Secretary of Europe: The Life of Friedrich Gentz: Enemy of Napoleon* (New Haven, 1946) is lively and psychologically acute. For Gentz and the salons, see Arendt, *Varnhagen*, pp. 80–3.

[73] Gooch, *Germany*, pp. 91 ff.; Aris, *History*, ch. 8.

lectures on philosophy, literature, and politics, edited (with Heinrich von Kleist) a periodical, and served as tutor to the ruler's heir. A measure of his importance was the fact that he was on Madame de Staël's itinerary in the summer of 1808 when August Wilhelm Schlegel took her around the German states to meet the leading minds of the day. In 1809 French pressure drove Müller from Dresden, first to Berlin, where he participated in the famous Christlich-Deutsche Gesellschaft, and then to Vienna, where he became part of Metternich's stable of conservative ideologues. Throughout his long career, few people who knew Müller doubted his great gifts, but even some of his admirers distrusted him; Varnhagen von Ense once remarked that Müller was insincere even when he was telling the truth. Despite his talent and accomplishments, he never quite lost the reputation of being a young man on the make, unreliable, too clever for his own good, always ready to trim his sails to catch a favourable wind.[74]

Unlike Gentz and many of the other thinkers who have concerned us in this chapter, Müller was too young to have experienced the initial euphoria evoked by the revolution. By the time he became politically aware, the tide of pro-revolutionary opinion had receded; he suffered no disappointments, no loss of faith. However, he never lost sight of what he called in his first book 'the intellectual and social revolutions that characterize our age'. Against the destructive forces of these revolutions he set the image of an organic community, in which all men must live and from which true harmony and order must arise. As he told the distinguished audience of statesmen, diplomats and courtiers who gathered to hear his lectures on *Elemente der Staatskunst* in 1808: 'Do not all the unfortunate errors of the French revolution come together in the illusion that the individual can truly step out of his social bonds?' There is, Müller insisted, no Archimedean point from which one might move the world, no place to stand outside society itself. Nor should we seek one; our humanity depends upon our membership in families, communities, and polities. And at the heart of these collective entities, embracing and sustaining all of them, is the state, 'the totality of human affairs, their connection to a single living whole'. Outside of the state, 'mankind is unthinkable'.[75]

---

[74] The most recent analysis of Müller is Koehler, *Ästhetik*, which contains an extended critique of the scholarly literature. There is a good treatment of his ideas in Meinecke, *Cosmopolitanism*, ch. 7.

[75] Koehler, *Ästhetik*, p. 42; Müller, *Elemente*, i. 26, 48, 29.

Müller was the most romantic of the major political theorists. His religious beliefs, emphasis on organic communities, and admiration for medieval institutions linked him to a number of the romantic poets and thinkers who turned towards Catholicism after the turn of the century. Like them, he used the vocabulary of art, family, and love to talk about the purposes and character of politics. Müller represented not just a reaction against the French revolution but also a rejection of German bureaucratic absolutism, with its emphasis on the state as a machine designed to produce, as efficiently as possible, the conditions for material prosperity and spiritual enlightenment. Müller and his romantic contemporaries did not want a political machine, they wanted a loving family, a community of the faithful, a work of art. Members of this generation turned away from the coolly rational state of a Justi or a Sonnenfels for the same reasons that they had rejected Kant's theology or Lessing's classical aesthetics; all these products of the *Aufklärung* lacked the emotional power and heightened sense of possibility that the romantics demanded from life.

These people wanted political poetry and poetic politics, and looked to the state with the same emotional intensity they brought to religion, friendship, and sexual passion. Novalis expressed these feelings in an essay entitled 'Glaube und Liebe', which he dedicated to the new king of Prussia, Frederick William III, and his bride, Queen Luise, in 1797. For too long, Novalis proclaimed, the Prussian government has been run like a factory; now it must be turned into a work of art with the ruler acting as 'the artist of artists'. In his 'Die Christenheit oder Europa', written two years later, Novalis turned from art to religion; his ideal is the Middle Ages, 'that beautiful, brilliant time, when Europe was a Christian land', united in its faith and institutions. Although Friedrich Schleiermacher's political imagination was rooted in pietist sensibility rather than medieval Catholicism, he shared Novalis's belief that the state should not be like a factory or a machine. In his *Monologen* of 1800, Schleiermacher lamented that many believed that the *best* state was 'a necessary evil, an unavoidable piece of machinery'. Where, Schleiermacher asked, is the state we read about in the ancient sages, 'where is the power to be drawn from this most sublime source of humanity, the consciousness that each of us should have of being part of its strength and reason and imagination?'[76]

Müller gave political shape and direction to these diffuse

[76] Novalis, *Werke*, ii. 303, 734; Kluckhohn, *Idee*, p. 63.

longings for a transcendent political community and also helped to relate them to the aggressive patriotism that engaged German intellectuals after 1806. War, Müller argued, was an inevitable part of international affairs, the necessary product of political growth, development, and decline. Moreover, war had profound domestic benefits because, in a genuine conflict, 'the most essential and beautiful aspect of the nation's existence, that is, the idea of the nation, becomes exceptionally clear to all who share its fate'. By *nation*, Müller meant a state, like Prussia or Austria, not a politicized cultural community like Germany; he regarded 'national feelings' as the patriotic attachment of people to their states, an escape from isolation and selfishness, a path to the joys of true community. But while Müller continued to think of Germany in cultural terms and doubted that 'the German could ever be disentangled from the European', his concept of patriotism and the connection he drew between patriotism and war were important intermediate steps between romantic ideas of community and the civic nationalism of the nineteenth century.[77]

iv. NATIONALISM: IDEAS AND MOVEMENTS

So great is the conceptual confusion in the scholarly literature on nationalism that we must begin this section with a few general remarks about this peculiarly misunderstood subject. Much of the confusion arises from the pervasive belief that nations and nationalism are natural phenomena, the one based on objective realities, the other on people's growing awareness of these realities' existence and importance. That this belief has no historical basis should be particularly apparent in the German case, where geography, language, culture, and politics combine to confound attempts to find a natural, objectively defined nation. Nations are inventions, the products of particular historical circumstances and movements; they are not the causes and objects of national self-consciousness, but rather its products and projections. Typically, nations get defined in the course of social, cultural, or political struggles in which one side uses its identification with 'national values' or the 'national cause' as a weapon against its enemies at home and abroad. For example, an important stage in the growth of German national awareness occurred when Renaissance humanists used Tacitus's description of supposedly 'Teutonic' virtues to affirm their own superiority over the corruptions of the Roman

---

[77] Müller, *Elemente*, i. 81; *Schriften*, pp. 85, 113–14.

church and its German allies. Similarly, in the eighteenth century German writers contrasted the authenticity and depth of their language and values with the shallow artificiality of French culture and its admirers among the court aristocracy. During the revolutionary era, the Franco-German *Kulturkampf* was intensified and partially transformed. For the first time, some German writers began to associate the defence of their national interests with the creation of a nation-state. Moreover, the proclamation of national values went beyond the sphere of literary culture and, in a tentative and limited fashion, became a political movement. Although the change is less dramatic and irreversible than some scholars have argued, both the theory and practice of German nationalism were transformed in the course of the long struggle against revolutionary France.[78]

German theoreticians of national identity, like nationalists everywhere, constructed their image of the nation from the materials at hand. In the eighteenth century these materials were most often linguistic and literary—as was to be expected among men whose sense of themselves as Germans came from their participation in the culture of print that had drawn them into a network of relationships above social and political particularities. 'What binds me to Germany', Humboldt once told Goethe, 'is nothing else but what I have drawn from life with you and with our circle. . . .' We have, Justus Möser had written some years earlier, a home town and a literary fatherland.[79]

People in the eighteenth century often gave the language of nationality an essentially moral or cultural meaning. For instance, when Friedrich Nicolai spoke of the 'patriots' he met on his tour of central Europe in 1781, he had in mind enlightened, reasonable men, who were concerned with the common good. But this cultural orientation should not distract us from the potential political significance of national self-consciousness even before 1789. To some Germans, membership in the 'fatherland' was part of a struggle against the Frenchified nobility for cultural authority

---

[78] A good introduction to German views of the nation can be found in Kemiläinen, *Auffassungen*. Kluckhohn's *Idee* is a valuable anthology despite its unwholesome political complexion. In the vast theoretical literature on the subject, I find the work of Ernest Gellner of particular value: *Thought and Change* (Chicago and London, 1964) and especially *Nations and Nationalism* (Ithaca and London, 1983). John Breuilly's *Nationalism and the State* (Manchester, 1982) correctly insists on the centrality of politics. The most up-to-date bibliography is in Peter Alter, *Nationalismus* (Frankfurt, 1985).

[79] Meinecke, *Cosmopolitanism*, p. 44.

and social status. Others might use their literary skills to sing the praises of a particular German state, as Thomas Abbt did in his famous work of 1761, 'Vom Tod für das Vaterland', which was about dying for Prussia.[80]

Until the turn of the century, however, virtually no one argued that the German nation's existence required the creation of a German nation-state. As C. M. Wieland pointed out in May 1793, German patriotism was difficult to find, even after French troops had begun to move east of the Rhine. 'I see Saxon, Bavarian, Württemberg, and Hamburg patriots,' Wieland wrote, 'but German patriots, who love the entire Reich as their fatherland . . . where are they?' Wieland suspected that to create national patriotism in a state with such 'heterogeneous and loosely connected parts' would take 'a moral and political miracle'. Only through common culture, language, and religion—the same forces that helped the ancient Greeks transcend their differences—can Germans think and act as one. They must, Wieland concluded, listen to their poets, not their princes.[81]

Throughout the following two decades, as the conditions for national existence became ever more problematic, some Germans followed Wieland's advice and sought to root their nationality in the familiar soil of cultural community. In his unfinished poem, 'Deutsche Grösse', Schiller declared that '*Deutsches Reich* and *deutsche Nation* are different things'; German greatness is 'moral, it lives in the culture and in the character of the nation, independent of its political fate'. Everything now depends, wrote Johannes von Müller in 1807, 'on keeping our language and a national literature filled with a healthy spirit'. A year later Friedrich Niethammer called for 'a national book to serve as the basis for a universal national education'. By making available German classics, Niethammer hoped to instil national feelings in German youth.[82]

The conflict with France strengthened some Germans' commitment to the cultural concept of nationality, just as the political pressures of the revolution led some intellectuals to reaffirm the eighteenth-century tradition of moral reform. Indeed, there were those who maintained that the absence of common political institutions enabled German nationhood to be particularly pure and potentially creative. While the rest of Europe has been caught up with 'war, speculation, and partisan conflicts', Novalis wrote in

[80] Vierhaus, 'Deutschland', p. 432; Prignitz, *Vaterlandsliebe,* pp. 18ff.
[81] Wieland, 'Patriotismus', p. 591.
[82] Valjavec, *Entstehung*, p. 339; Erning, *Lesen*, pp. 95 ff.

1799, Germans have devoted themselves to the creation of a culture that was 'incomparably diverse, wonderfully deep, with a brilliant polish, all-encompassing knowledge, and a rich, powerful imagination'. For Hölderlin, the fact that Germans were 'poor in deeds but rich in thought' would help them assume the cultural leadership once held by Greece:

> Aber kommt, wie der Strahl aus dem Gewolke kommt,
> Aus Gedanken vielleicht, gestig und reif die That?
> Folgt die Frucht, wie des Haines
> Dunkelm Blatte, der stillen Schrift?

In another poetic appeal 'To the Germans', this one written by Friedrich Schlegel in 1800, the idea of a cultural mission is even more clearly set forth: 'Was Hellas schlau ersann, was Indien blühte,| German'scher Männer Lied wird's neu entfalten,| Wie zornig blinder Pöbel gegenwüte.' For Schlegel, this mission takes its immediacy both from the Germans' strength and their neighbours' unhappy decline: 'Europas Geist erlosch; in Deutschland fliesst| Der Quell der neuen Zeit. Die aus ihm tranken,| Sind wahrhaft deutsch. . . .'[83]

After the turn of the century Joseph Görres formulated a more aggressive and politically engaged version of Germany's cultural mission. Görres was born in 1776 and reared in Koblenz, close to the epicentre of the upheavals that destroyed the old Reich. An admirer of Kant and Rousseau, the young Görres greeted the invading French as instruments of enlightenment, the harbingers of liberation from Rhenish provincialism and ecclesiastical misrule. He laid his pamphlet of 1798 on 'Universal Peace' at 'the altar of the fatherland', by which he meant the French republic. Eventually, however, Görres began to recognize that France was not really his fatherland. A visit to Paris in 1799 left him with a deep feeling of uneasiness about the revolution: 'I saw the actors undressed behind the curtains,' he wrote; 'passions loosed from the chains imposed by social decency rushed about the empty stage, paying scant attention to the audience that gazed in amazement at the Bacchanale.' To this political uneasiness Görres added a characteristic set of national stereotypes. The French, he discovered, were warm-blooded, quick, witty, but also unreliable, fickle, and shallow. The Germans, on the other hand, were slow, persistent, and deep.[84]

[83] Novalis, *Werke*, ii. 745; Hölderlin, *Poems*, pp. 122–3; Schlegel, *Ausgabe*, v. 298–301.

[84] Joseph Görres, *Gesammelte Schriften*, i. *Politische Schriften der Frühzeit (1795–1800)* (Cologne, 1928), 18, 555, 591 ff. See also Aris, *History*, ch. 11; Blanning, *Revolution*, pp. 283 ff.

The Franco-German frontier, which he had once seen as an artificial barrier to be erased by common political ideals, now appeared to be based on profound and immutable cultural differences. At first, however, Görres's disaffection with the French did not have any political consequences. In 1800 he abandoned his career as a journalist to teach in a secondary school in Koblenz, where he devoted his spare time to reading romantic literature and idealist philosophy. Six years later he joined Brentano and Arnim in their efforts to recover German folk art; his *Volksbücher* of 1807 were an important contribution to this enterprise. After he returned to the Rhineland in 1808, he became increasingly depressed and pessimistic: the Germans, he wrote in 1811, do not have the character for acts of valour, 'they are a herd of sheep that the wolf can scatter as he wishes.'[85]

When Napoleon's fortunes began to decline in 1812 and 1813, Görres was inspired by the possibility of a national revival, an uprising of the people, which 'surprisingly, admirably, astoundingly, will be the basis of the form of the world and the destiny of the species for many generations'. In 1814 he became an influential figure in the propaganda campaign being waged against the French and their German allies. His journal, *Der Rheinische Merkur*, preached a remarkable blend of cultural romanticism and national hatred, on the one hand extolling the beauties of the medieval order, while on the other demanding a war to the knife against Bonaparte. 'We have been since time immemorial a German *Volk*,' cried Görres in 1814, and this entitles us to the lands we have always held. The *Volk* has kept its identity, he went on, even when princes served foreign invaders, the nobility chased alien honours, the clergy traded their principles, and the scholars bowed down before imported idols. Now was the time to enshrine and protect this genuine national identity with common institutions and a constitution that could hold together other German ancestral lands.[86] To those statesmen eager to mobilize opinion against Napoleon, Görres' views had a certain usefulness, but, when the conqueror was defeated, he became a nuisance, and eventually a threat. With Bonaparte safely in exile, Görres was expendable; the authorities closed his periodical, confiscated his writings, and forced him to flee across the frontier to Strasburg, where he sought refuge among those whose characters he had so often maligned.

[85] Droz, *Romantisme*, p. 196; Kluckhohn, *Idee*, pp. 103–4.
[86] Krieger, *Idea*, p. 212; Kluckhohn, *Idee*, pp. 103–104.

Like Görres, J. G. Fichte created a blend of cultural self-consciousness and political commitment from his experiences with war and revolution. During the first phase of his intellectual development, roughly coinciding with the period at Jena that was discussed above, Fichte's politics were as individualistic as his ethics and epistemology. The primary philosophical question, he argued in 1796, must be 'what is necessary in order that anyone be free and an individual?' The state, as far as he was concerned, had to 'remain within its limits'; political life was not 'among the absolute purposes of mankind.'[87] Gradually, however, the state began to take on greater importance for Fichte; by the time he wrote *Der geschlossene Handelsstaat* in 1800 he was willing to declare that the polity had full responsibility for its citizens' welfare. 'The duty of the state does not consist only in protecting the mass of goods accumulated by somebody . . . its true aim is to procure for its subjects that which is their due as members of mankind.' *Der geschlossene Handelsstaat* is by no means an appeal or an apology for despotism; the state Fichte had in mind was a republic, not a bureaucratic machine like Frederician Prussia. He remained convinced that the collectivity's claim to control the lives of individuals must rest on the individuals' collective control over political institutions.[88]

Fichte's discovery of the political community was not initially accompanied by national commitments. Far from it. His bitter experiences with the authorities at Jena soured him on German politics and prolonged his enthusiasm for the French revolution. 'If the French do not acquire a dominance and make changes in Germany', he wrote in 1799, 'in a few years no one in Germany who is known to have practised freedom of thought will find a haven'. But eventually two things led him to change his mind about France. The first was the rise to power of Napoleon, whom Fichte viewed as the revolution's liquidator. The second was the philosopher's increasing intellectual and personal identification with Prussia, the state in which he eventually found a home after having been forced out of Jena in 1799. By the summer of 1806, as France and Prussia edged towards war, he acknowledged for the first time that patriotic sympathies were as valuable as cosmopolitanism: the former led towards humanity through a particular

---

[87] Reiss, *Thought*, p. 46; Schnabel, *Geschichte*, i. 293–4. On Fichte's politics, see Krieger, *Idea*, ch. 5; Meinecke, *Cosmopolitanism*, ch. 6.

[88] Aris, *History*, p. 130.

community, the latter through the love of mankind as a whole.[89] When the war began, Fichte fled from Erlangen to Berlin, watched with dismay as the French army occupied the city, accompanied the court to Königsberg, and then returned to the capital, where, during the winter of 1807–08, he delivered his *Reden an die deutsche Nation* in the amphitheatre of the Berlin Academy. To some of the patriotic men and women who were trying to reform and rearm Prussia, Fichte personified patriotism in its purest and most intellectually potent form. Clausewitz, for instance, called him 'the great philosopher, the priest of this holy flame of truth, to whom a beautiful privilege had granted access to the innermost—to the spirit of every art and science'.[90] In 1810 he was appointed to the chair of philosophy and served as first rector of the new University of Berlin. But he did not live to see the final triumph of his adopted state over Napoleon: in 1814 his wife contracted typhus while nursing wounded soldiers from the front; Fichte was infected at her bedside and swiftly succumbed to the disease.

Contrary to the patriotic legend about them, Fichte's *Reden* did not have much immediate impact, but they deserve our attention because they so vividly express the various elements from which German national consciousness was formed. Like Herder and so many other eighteenth-century theorists, Fichte believed in the primacy of language: 'men are formed by language far more than language is formed by men.' Since language is the key to human identity, its purest expression is the most sublime form of collective existence. 'For a people with a living language,' Fichte told his audience, 'poetry is the highest and best means of flooding the life of all with the spiritual culture that has been attained.' On this linguistic and cultural foundation, Fichte then erected structures more reminiscent of romanticism than of eighteenth-century thought. In the first place, he described the experience of nationhood in intensely emotional terms. His new national élite is an élite of sensibility: 'love has been ignited in them; it burns down into the roots of their living impulse, and from now on will grip everything which touches this living emotion.' Second, Fichte had picked up the idea of Germany's special mission to redeem human culture. While this mission may affect all mankind, it engages Germans in a particularly powerful way because they have their ancestral lands, their traditional moral code, and above all else, their original language. At a time when the very existence of

[89] Anderson, *Nationalism*, p. 30; Kluckhohn, *Idee*, p. 110.
[90] Paret, *Clausewitz*, p. 169.

German politics and culture seemed in question, Fichte had the courage to celebrate his nation's continuity and cohesion. We owe our character and our strength, he wrote, to the Germans described in Tacitus; 'it is they whom we must thank—we, the immediate heirs of their soil, their language, and their ways of thinking—for being Germans still, for still being borne along on the stream of original and independent life.'[91]

About the specifics of Germany's political future, Fichte was uncertain. In the *Reden* he opposed a centralizing autocracy and praised the existing multiplicity of states for their potential encouragement of educational reform. The concept of German unity, he wrote in 1813, is 'a general concept for the future'. All that can now be said is that this unity would 'realize the citizens' freedom'. But the immediate pressures of occupation and war compelled Fichte to acknowledge the importance of the state as a defender of culture and freedom. Like Humboldt, he feared that the scope of France's power might threaten Germans' cultural existence. Without political independence, he warned in 1808, we could lose our language and, with that, the foundation of our identity. At the same time, Fichte assigned to the state the task of building schools and teaching people about their national character and responsibilities. In his *Staatslehre* of 1813, he suggested that a despot should use his power to impose enlightenment. This would, he insisted, be temporary; 'the state with all its means of compulsion must be considered as an educational institution to make compulsion eventually unnecessary'. Nevertheless, the fact that even a man as committed to freedom as Fichte would accept such a conception of change underscores the state's increasing influence over political theory and practice.[92]

Many of Fichte's contemporaries were also propelled along a path from Enlightenment cosmopolitanism to intense national enthusiasm by the experiences of war and upheaval. Heinrich von Kleist, for instance, had had little interest in political matters during the 1790s—as we know, he resigned his commission in order to pursue his private intellectual goals. But politics would not leave Kleist alone. In 1806 he had to flee from Berlin; the next year he was arrested and imprisoned in France, apparently by mistake; even his greatest literary triumph, the performance of his play *Der zerbrochene Krug* in Vienna, was shadowed by the fact that it was

[91] There is a useful edition of the *Reden*, edited by G.A. Kelly (1968). The quotations are from pp. 48, 68, 123–4, and from Anderson, *Nationalism*, pp. 52–3.
[92] Kluckhohn, *Idee*, p. 126; Reiss, *Thought*, pp. 118–19 (from Fichte's *Staatslehre* of 1813).

presented in honour of Napoleon's marriage to a Habsburg princess. By 1808 Kleist had conceived an obsessive hatred for Napoleon, which he expressed in his 'Hermannsschlacht', a most disagreeable piece of propaganda ostensibly about the ancient 'Germans' ' struggle against Rome, but obviously paralleling contemporary struggles against France. With a rhetorical violence that now strikes us as sinister and sickening, Kleist demands a war without quarter, in which enemies were to be exterminated like beasts and rivers dammed with corpses. But Kleist could also evoke the progressive side of patriotism; in his essay, 'Über die Rettung Österreichs', written in 1809, he argued that 'every great, general danger, if it is fairly faced, gives the state for a moment a democratic appearance'. Kleist's distress over the Austrians' defeat in 1809, his disappointment with the excessive caution of Prussian foreign policy under Hardenberg, and his own failures as a political publicist helped cause the depression that led to his suicide in 1811.[93]

Schleiermacher, like Kleist, was uprooted and blown about by the winds of war. In 1806 he was forced to leave Halle, where he had taken refuge after leaving the Pomeranian parish to which he had been exiled from Berlin. Eventually he found his way back to the Prussian capital and soon established contacts with the patriotic intellectuals and reformist bureaucrats who were rebuilding the state. After securing an appointment at the University of Berlin, he devoted himself to arousing popular support for the next round of war against France. Schleiermacher's religious feelings and national loyalties issued from the same source and flowed in the same direction; to abandon the nation to a foreigner, he proclaimed in a sermon given in January 1808, was a violation of the divine order of the universe. By June 1813, as the war of liberation was entering its decisive stage, he had come to believe that Germans should strive for some kind of new Reich, a unified political community that would combine both cultural identity and state patriotism.

My greatest wish after liberation [he wrote Friedrich Schlegel], is for one true German Empire, powerfully representing the entire German folk and territory to the outside world, while internally allowing the various *Länder* and their princes a great deal of freedom to develop and rule according to their own particular needs.[94]

[93] Anderson, *Nationalism*, p. 134. See also Gordon A. Craig, 'German Intellectuals and Politics, 1789–1815: The Case of Heinrich von Kleist', *CEH* 2/1 (Mar. 1969), 3–21.

[94] Kluckhohn, *Idee*, p. 74. On the religious element in German nationalism, see Kaiser, *Pietismus;* Pinson, *Pietism*.

The most influential attempt to create a national concept that fused culture and politics was made by Ernst Moritz Arndt, whose efforts on Germany's behalf stretched from the Napoleonic wars to the revolutions of 1848. Born and reared on his family's farm on the island of Rügen, which was then part of Sweden, Arndt was torn between his youthful ambitions to be a writer and his reluctance to leave the security of home. After studying theology at Greifswald and Jena, he returned to Rügen, where he helped to work the land and tutored his younger brothers. Two years later he left to accept a teaching job, but personal tragedy—his wife died in childbirth just a year after their marriage—and his own restlessness turned him into a wanderer. Arndt longed for security and commitment, but rarely stayed very long in one place and persistently failed to find a permanent position. For many years his spiritual condition was as unsettled as his career. At first attracted by the *Aufklärung*, he soon turned against rationalism and what he took to be its twin political expressions, bureaucratic absolutism and the French revolution. Like Hegel and so many others, Arndt brought to his early work an acute sense of cultural crisis and personal estrangement, which he articulated in terms of the modern spirit's separation from the world: 'The two worlds are divided, it seems forever, the spiritual one which the spirit has forsaken, and the heavenly one above which lights and blesses the one below'. But, unlike Hegel, Arndt did not seek to overcome this alienation through some new synthesis of faith and reason. For him, salvation was to be found in the emotions: 'It is an eternal rule that when one speaks of the highest [things], of love and friendship, one should not think, but let the heart reign.'[95]

Arndt did not at first realize that Germany was the realm over which his heart should reign. In 1799 he regarded himself as Swedish; three years later, in his *Germanien und Europa*, he included Scandinavia among the Germanic peoples. In 1806, when Napoleon's armies swept into Pomerania, Arndt fled north and spent the next three years in Sweden, where, as so often happens to exiles, Arndt began to develop a feeling for his own, distinctively German nationality. 'We live in a beautiful, large, rich land, a land of glorious memories, undying deeds, unforgettable service to the world in remote and recent times. We are the navel of Europe, the centre of north and south. . . . Germans! What a name and what a

---

[95] Anderson has a good treatment of Arndt in *Nationalism*; the quotations are from pp. 83 and 87. Arndt's *Erinnerungen* is an essential source for his life and thought.

people!'[96] Amid the personal hardships of exile and the disruptions he observed following the Prussian defeat, Arndt discovered an object for his affections and a new sense of purpose for his life. At last he had found a home to replace the family farm from which his restlessness had lured him, a faith to which he would be willing to devote the rest of his long career.

Arndt's concept of nationality contains a number of familiar elements. Like Herder, he believed that the true basis of a nation was language: 'The only legitimate frontiers are linguistic.' His claims for German superiority were based on the same assertion of cultural purity and continuity so important to Fichte: 'Germans have not been bastardized by foreign nations . . . they remain in their original purity and have been able to develop from this purity their own character and nature, slowly and in accord with eternal laws.' The fortunate Germans are an original *Volk*. Arndt shared Schleiermacher's conviction that national commitments had the same sacred authenticity as religion: 'To be a nation, to have one feeling for one cause, to come together with the bloody sword of revenge, is the religion of our times.'[97]

Far more clearly than most of his contemporaries, however, Arndt recognized the political implications of these national emotions. As early as *Germanien und Europa*, he made some tentative references to the association of *Volk* and state. By the final stage of the Napoleonic wars he had worked out a programme for national unification. His *Über die künftigen ständischen Verfassungen in Teutschland*, published in 1814, called for a single monarchical state, with its own army, laws, and representative institutions. Because he believed that Berlin rather than Vienna was the new centre of national energies, he assigned Prussia a leading role in this new Germany, which would also contain the various other German princes and their states. Nevertheless, Arndt retained an essentially populist view of the nation: 'People have older and more irreversible duties towards fatherland and folk than towards their princes,' he wrote in 1813, 'Princes are only the servants and administrators of fatherland and folk . . . the land and people do not exist in order that there be princes.' The basis of the nation had to be democratic, but such a democracy has nothing to do with the rule of the mob: 'The folk is as holy as the mob is profane.' The nation, according to Arndt, offers the perfect reconciliation of ruler

[96] Anderson, *Nationalism*, p. 91.
[97] Kluckhohn, *Idee*, pp. 151, 136; Krieger, *Idea*, p. 193. See also the analysis in Kaiser's *Pietismus*, p. 44.

and ruled: national loyalties purges the one of despotism, the other of unreason. Thus Arndt formulated what would become a persistent ideal of German liberals: a nation-state in which just authority and rational democracy coexist, their potential conflict cleansed by a common commitment to the *Volk*.[98]

Arndt's influence came from his remarkable sensitivity to the intellectual and emotional atmosphere of contemporary intellectual life and from his ability to express pervasive ideas and longings in a direct, dramatic, and accessible way. Far less gifted than Fichte or Schleiermacher, he nevertheless had a genius for capturing the national cause, especially at the moment when it had begun to shift from poetry to propaganda, from peace to war, from the call for a cultural mission to the demand for a crusade of national revenge. Consider, for instance, his famous 'Vaterlandslied' of 1812, whose strident lines contrast so sharply with the hymns that Hölderlin and Schlegel had written 'to the Germans' a dozen years earlier:

> O Deutschland, heil'ges Vaterland!
> O deutsche Lieb' und Treue!
> Du hohes Land! Du schönes Land!
> Dir schwören wir aufs neue:
> Dem Buben und dem Knecht die Acht,
> Der füttre Krähn und Raben!
> So zieh wir aus zur Hermannsschlacht
> Und wollen Rache haben.

Arndt also understood the psychology of national commitment well enough to know that people needed more than poetic appeals and propaganda; he was one of the first to develop the rituals and symbols with which national feeling might be expressed and encouraged. Ceremonies, monuments, festivals, even a so-called 'Germanic' style of dress could be used to make people aware of their membership in the *Volk*.[99]

In his efforts to organize national movements, Arndt was joined by Friedrich Ludwig Jahn, a pastor's son who had become involved in patriotic politics soon after arriving in Berlin to teach in 1809. Like many early nationalists, Jahn came from a family steeped in pietist religiosity. He had studied theology, but found his true

---

[98] Kluckhohn, *Idee*, pp. 142, 146.

[99] Arndt, *Erinnerungen*, i. 101. Arndt wanted to use the anniversary of the battle of Leipzig as the occasion for patriotic ceremonies: see *Ein Wort über die Feier der Leipziger Schlacht* (Frankfurt, 1813). George L. Mosse, *The Nationalization of the Masses. Political Symbolism and Mass Movements in Germany from the Napoleonic Wars through the Third Reich* (New York, 1975), is a pioneering effort to understand the ritualization of national identity.

vocation in the *Volk*, to whose liberation he wholeheartedly devoted himself, and whose praises he sang in manifestly religious terms. 'With the state, through it, for it, and in it, the citizen will feel, think, and act; he will be one with state and *Volk* in life, passion, and love.' In his pamphlet, *Deutsches Volkstum*, published in 1810, Jahn purged the nation of the humanitarian and cosmopolitan residues still present in the writings of Fichte and Schleiermacher. Driven by a hidden core of identity, 'an unnamable something', the *Volk* suffered but did not die; its holiest hour would come when it expelled the foreign elements in its midst, proclaimed its purity, and established the conditions for its independence. Mystical, even racial in its essence, Jahn's *Volkstum* is unambiguously political: 'The state is the essential *Volk*, the continuing external confirmation of the *Volk's* true being [*Volkstum*]. Like Arndt, Jahn tried to organize popular movements to spread national awareness and mobilize resistance to France. In 1811, on Berlin's Hasenheide, he formed a gymnastic society that blended paramilitary drills and spurious teutonic symbols with classical ideals of bodily strength.[100]

More and more writers were drawn towards the national cause in 1813; patriotic poems and articles filled contemporary periodicals; reading societies and other cultural associations considered how best to aid the struggle against France. In Jena, Heinrich Luden's course on the history of the German *Volk*, which had once languished for want of listeners, became so popular that students overflowed the lecture hall into the corridors. In Breslau, Heinrich Steffens spoke to an excited crowd of students about the defence of their fatherland and then left his post to volunteer for the front. Even a man as sensitive to his own interests as Varnhagen von Ense realized that now was the time 'to be personally and particularly involved'. I am, he wrote in 1813, 'intoxicated by the jubilation I have experienced, by the strength I see before me, by the happy outcome of our undertaking, which cannot fail'. It should be noted that Varnhagen's intoxication did not prevent him from using the wars of liberation to full personal advantage; after securing an appointment as an aide to a Russian colonel, he contributed to the war effort with a series of published letters praising the patriotic efforts of well-placed members in all the allied governments.[101]

---

[100] Kaiser, *Pietismus*, p. 113; Kluckhohn, *Idee*, p. 160. In addition to Mosse's book just cited, see the treatment of Jahn's organizational efforts in Düding, *Nationalismus*.

[101] Brinkmann, *Nationalismus*, see p. 36 on Luden; Steffens, *Was ich erlebte*, pp. 314 ff.; Arendt, *Varnhagen*, pp. 190–3.

By 1813 young men in search of adventure, romantics eager for experience, sincere patriots willing to sacrifice for the nation, careerists anxious to prove their devotion to the state, all looked for ways to become involved in the final round of national liberation. Some found their place in the corps of volunteers under the command of Adolf Freiherr von Lützow, a Prussian officer whose troops were the source of one of the most important legends born in 1813. The laureate of this legend was Theodor Körner, who left a promising literary career to fight with the Free Corps. Before he was killed in a minor action in Mecklenburg, Körner wrote a series of patriotic verses celebrating the fellowship of combat:

> Doch Brüder sind wir allzusamm'
> Und das schwellt unsern Mut,
> Uns knüpft der Sprache heilig Band,
> Uns knüpft ein Gott, ein Vaterland,
> Ein treues, deutsches Blut.

To these familiar sentiments the poet added a disquieting fascination with death which recalls the most morbid aspects of romanticism and anticipates some of the least wholesome aspects of German political rhetoric. We are marching out at once, he wrote to his beloved and 'in two days we expect our deadly nuptials [*Todeshochzeit*]'. Death, Körner seems to have thought, should not be accepted bravely as a necessary sacrifice but rather should be embraced eagerly, like an impatient bride.[102]

Some German intellectuals found the intense patriotism of 1813 most unattractive. Goethe, for instance, could not understand why a talented young man like Körner would want to waste his time galloping around the countryside playing soldier. At the highpoint of nationalist sentiment following the battle of Leipzig, Goethe responded without enthusiasm to an invitation to contribute to a new national magazine. The Germans, he believed, were 'admirable as individuals but miserable as a group'. He continued to be convinced, as he had written in 1799, that 'for an impartial thinker, who can raise himself above his time, the fatherland is nowhere—and everywhere'. Hegel remained equally unaffected by national passions. Like Goethe, he was in awe of Napoleon, 'the world-soul on horseback', whose victory he had witnessed in 1806. For as long as possible, Hegel argued that the emperor could not be

---

[102] Hasko Zimmer, *Auf dem Altar des Vaterlandes: Religion und Patriotismus in der deutschen Kriegslyrik des 19. Jahrhunderts* (Frankfurt, 1971), 35; Heer, *Kampf*, pp. 177–8. See also the treatment in Prignitz, *Vaterlandsliebe*.

defeated. When the news of Bonaparte's abdication did reach him, he wrote to a friend that

[I]t is a tremendous spectacle to see an enormous genius destroy himself. That is the most tragic thing there is. The whole mass of mediocrity with its absolute leaden gravity keeps pressing its leaden way, without rest and reconciliation, until it finally brings down what is higher—to its own level or lower.'[103]

There is, of course, no way of knowing how many German writers shared Goethe's and Hegel's viewpoint. We do know that the image of armed students and intellectuals riding off to battle with Lützow is pure legend: as the data gathered by Rudolf Ibbeken show, the overwhelming majority of the men who fought with the Free Corps were craftsmen and labourers; no more than 12 per cent were university or high school students and other academicians. If these groups seem more numerous, it is because more of them wrote books about their experience.[104]

Throughout central Europe, most people remained impervious to the national agitation carried out by Arndt, Jahn, and the others. For example, the wife of one Prussian landowner reported that the militia had not been warmly received by the rural population: 'What has that got to do with our quiet peasantry, who for eight years have taken care of the French with conscientious hospitality?' In most cities, the local officials, merchants, and guildmasters viewed mobilization of a citizen army as economically burdensome and socially disruptive. To be sure, some people rushed out to contribute their family silverware to the war effort, but many more stayed as far away from it as they possibly could. The same was true of the farmers in Hesse, along the Weser, and in the Harz mountains, where Blücher and Wittgenstein's cavalry found few supporters among local residents.[105]

Most of the popular antagonism towards the French does not seem to have been the result of national loyalties. In Oldenburg, for example, inhabitants of the coastal villages resisted the occupation because they suffered directly from Napoleon's tariff policies and disliked the impressment of their young men to serve on French ships. In other regions, both Catholics and Protestants were

[103] Friedenthal, *Goethe*, p. 501, and the analysis in Mommsen, *Anschauungen*, pp. 143 ff. On Hegel, see Rosenzweig, *Hegel*, ii. 2 ff. The quotation is from a letter of 29 Apr. 1814, printed in Walter Kaufmann (ed.), *Hegel: A Reinterpretation* (Garden City, 1966), 341.

[104] Ibbeken, *Preussen*, pp. 405 ff., and the tables on pp. 442 ff.

[105] Meinecke, *Leben*, i. 282 ff. On the popular mood, Ibbeken, *Preussen*.

sometimes ready to defend their churches from French anti-clericalism.[106] Elsewhere, populations might try to protect their goods from the excessive demands of Napoleon's quartermasters or the petty larceny of common soldiers. Overall, however, the number of spontaneous uprisings in the German lands was small; with the exception of the Tyrol, guerrilla warfare on the Spanish model did not occur. Instead, the decisive battles were won by troops who fought for the same reasons soldiers had always fought—a combination of diffuse loyalty to state and sovereign, the habits of discipline, and the fear of punishment. If Prussian troops were more effective in 1813 than they had been in 1806, it was because they were better trained, better equipped, and better led, not because they had been suddenly infused with national passions. There is more than a little truth in Heine's sardonic comment that, during the wars of liberation, 'we were told to be patriots, and we became patriotic because we always do what our princes tell us'.[107]

Prussia in 1813, like Austria in 1808, did try to harness patriotic passions behind its military efforts. As we know, reformers in both states insisted that patriotism was an essential element in the kind of wars being fought in the revolutionary age. But, while Frederick William's proclamations of February and March 1813 had evoked the folk and fatherland as values around which Prussians should now rally, the king made clear that he was speaking to and about 'my folk', the patriotic subjects of the Prussian crown, not the cultural community of Germans so important to Arndt, Jahn, and others. If Frederick William seemed to sponsor Stein's more broadly based national appeals, he did so because he reluctantly recognized the advantage of putting pressure on the German princes still allied to Bonaparte, not because he wished to assume leadership over a national political movement. As would happen so often in the history of modern nationalism, in 1813 the relationship between state and nation was clouded by misunderstandings and false hopes.

The *Volk's* role in its own 'liberation' was, at best, a minor one. Napoleon was defeated by regular armies, not patriotic poets and quaintly attired gymnasts. Eventually, however, the apostles of nationalism were able to create a historical memory of 'liberation'

[106] Wolfgang von Groote, *Die Entstehung des Nationalbewusstseins in Nordwest-Deutschland, 1790–1830* (Göttingen, 1954), 53–4. Blanning, *Revolution*, emphasizes the role of religion in stimulating popular opposition to the French.
[107] Heine, 'Schule', p. 134.

which projected their own enthusiasms on to the nation. 'Those were days, yes glorious days', remembered Ernst Moritz Arndt, 'young hopes for life and honour sang, echoing through every heart, ringing from every street, sounding from pulpit and podium.'[108] In memoirs and stories, paintings and pageants, festivals and scholarly histories, the war against France assumed a central role in the emergence of national consciousness. It was, people came to believe, a time when nation and state had joined in a single struggle, inspired by the same goals, acting together until victory was theirs. Liberals gave this image its most influential form, in which they celebrated both the progressive reform of the states and the popular enthusiasm this reform evoked. The heroes of their account were Lützow's poetic volunteers or men like Joachim Nettelbeck, an ordinary citizen of Kolberg, who had helped to defend his home-town against the French. But, as is always the case with patriotic myths, the historical memory of liberation took many forms and had many different heroes. Some celebrated it as a victory of traditional Prussian values, best personified by Blücher, the grizzled veteran of Frederick's armies, who had helped defeat Napoleon at Waterloo. Others emphasized the triumph of German culture over the Enlightenment, and saw in the ideas of Arndt and Jahn weapons to be turned against the superficial rationalism of western thought. As an image of liberal reform and emancipation, of traditional military virtues and state power, or of xenophobic antagonism to the west, the era of liberation became part of Germans historical consciousness and contemporary discourse.[109]

In most of its various formulations, the historical myth of liberation tended to obscure the essential significance of the revolutionary era for German history. In the first place, France's role in the transformation of the German states was much more complicated than the rhetoric of 'liberation' might lead one to believe. In the Rhenish Confederation, France had been the ally and at times the instrument of important political reforms. Even in Austria and Prussia, where the drive for independence and revenge gave impetus to reform, reformers had tried to emulate the French politically so that they might defeat them militarily. Second, the revolutionary era's most important product was not the mobilization of the *Volk* but rather the reform and reorganization of the

[108] Ibbeken, *Preussen*, pp. 395–6.
[109] Düding, *Nationalismus*, has some interesting material on the myth of liberation. See also the highly critical analysis in Heer, *Kampf*, pp. 163 ff.

states. By 1815, Prussia, Austria, and the various middle-sized states had emerged as the dominant forces in German public life. They had clearly—if not completely—triumphed over the competing sovereignties of Reich and *Herrschaft*.

PART THREE

The Limits of Restoration, 1815–1848

VII
Restoration Politics,
1815–1830

In 1815 Heinrich Olivier, just returned from military service with the Free Corps, painted a picture celebrating the Holy Alliance formed by Austria, Russia, and Prussia. In the foreground of the painting stand the Emperors Francis and Alexander and King Frederick William, their hands joined in an expression of solidarity, which was meant to recall their common victory over Napoleon and to affirm their common stand against further upheavals. The sovereigns are dressed in the cumbersome ceremonial armour of the late Middle Ages, crusaders' crosses adorn their cloaks, a heavy Gothic altar-piece stands behind them. Here Catholic, Orthodox, and Protestant came together in an enterprise whose symbols evoked the Christian heritage they shared.[1] Olivier's *Holy Alliance* is not a very good painting, but it does exemplify the medieval idiom through which some people in restoration Europe tried to express their distaste for revolutionary change. Architecture and design, the settings of novels and the background of paintings, the subject-matter of historical monuments and the focus of scholarly research all reflected this fascination for the Middle Ages. To be sure, medievalism was sometimes merely a temporary refuge, an escape from contemporary cares into the apparently more cohesive and peaceful world of chivalry and cathedrals. The fake castle built by William IX of Hesse-Kassel was supposed to provide an ambience in which such escapism might flourish, as was Franzenburg, constructed by the Emperor Francis outside Vienna. We probably should not make too much of these masquerades. But for some Europeans, the medieval world was more than a refuge; it provided a standard against which current shortcomings might be judged, a set of symbols with which deep-seated longings might be captured, and a model of how society and culture should be organized. The Middle Ages, seen through this historical lens, appeared to be a time when faith was secure and social hierarchies unchallenged, when people believed in God and obeyed their betters. Especially to those who

[1] Ludwig Grote, *Die Brüder Olivier und die deutsche Romantik* (Berlin, 1938).

yearned for the world before 1789, the medieval setting of Olivier's painting stood for the hope that once again men and women might live without an infectious desire for change.

Of course, even during the early stages of 'restoration', perceptive Europeans recognized that there was no returning to the supposedly simpler, more cohesive world of the Middle Ages. The revolution, these people knew, was not a temporary break in the orderly flow of history but a permanent part of the modern experience. G. W. F. Hegel, once an enthusiastic admirer of the French revolution, soon to become a not uncritical exponent of the Prussian *Beamtenstaat*, told a friend in 1819: 'I am just fifty years old, and have lived most of my life in these eternally restless times of fear and hope, and I have hoped that sometime these fears and hopes might cease. But now I must see that they will go on forever, indeed in moments of depression I think they will grow worse.' In 1820, Metternich, the man who presided over and seemed to personify the age of restoration, lamented that he had been born 'too early or too late'. Earlier he might simply have enjoyed life, later he could have helped build a new society, but 'today I must devote myself to propping up rotten buildings'. A few months later he wrote, 'My most secret thought is that old Europe is at the beginning of the end. Determined to go down with it, I will know how to do my duty. Elsewhere the new Europe is still taking shape. Between end and beginning there will be chaos.'[2] Hopes and fears, a deeply felt sense of lasting change, and the terror of chaos— these sentiments are close to the heart of the age of restoration.

In each of the next four chapters we will examine a different facet of the age, and in each we will see how powerful political, social, and cultural changes frustrated efforts at restoration. In this chapter our focus will be on the international, constitutional, and bureaucratic institutions through which Germans tried to bring order to central European politics. Chapter 8 follows the development of German social and economic life from the end of the revolutionary wars to the structural crises of the 1840s. Chapter 9 treats the further evolution of cultural institutions and the emergence of new modes of expression and self-understanding. Finally, in Chapter 10 we shall trace the emergence of the conflicts that disrupted German politics and society between the revolutions of 1830 and 1848.

---

[2] Joachim Ritter, *Hegel und die Französische Revolution* (Cologne, 1957), 15–16; Schnabel, *Geschichte*, ii. 64. For a stimulating introduction to the period as a whole, see Rudolf Vierhaus, '"Vormärz": Ökonomische und soziale Krisen, ideologische und politische Gegensätze', *Francia*, 13 (1985), 355–68.

i. THE CONGRESS OF VIENNA AND THE GERMAN QUESTION

'History teaches us, and invariably we disregard her lesson, that coalitions begin to disintegrate from the moment that the common danger is removed.' Harold Nicolson wrote these lines in the summer of 1945, as he thought about the post-Napoleonic settlements in the light of his own experience with peacemaking in 1919 and his growing uneasiness about the post-war world taking shape around him. Nicolson knew that every great power brought different interests to a coalition and that 'the jealousies, rivalries, and suspicions which in any protracted war arise between the partners in an alliance generate poisons which war-wearied arteries are too inelastic to eliminate'. His classic study of the Vienna Congress, subtitled 'a study in allied unity', was meant to show that a victorious coalition could hold together, even when its members were acutely conscious of the separate interests that divided them.[3]

That the leaders of Britain, Russia, Austria, and Prussia had quite different interests no informed statesman could doubt. Castlereagh, who represented Napoleon's most persistent foe, wanted a continent free from any single state's hegemony, security for Britain's dominions overseas, and the economic freedom required by her commercial and manufacturing enterprises. Tsar Alexander's aims were more grandiose and magnanimous but also less precise and stable: he saw himself as Europe's liberator, whose conquest of Napoleon would be followed by a massive expansion of Russian influence in the west. This Metternich feared above all else. Indeed, as we have seen, the Austrian chancellor had hoped to keep Napoleon on the throne so that France might balance Russia, thus leaving Austria free to defend her central position by playing one against the other. Metternich did not want the sort of instability in central Europe that might encourage the tsar's continental ambitions. Hardenberg, on the other hand, viewed the weakness of the smaller German states as possible sources of Prussian strength. While he recognized the need to work with Austria, Hardenberg also realized that, in order to consolidate Prussia's great power status, he would have to employ the leverage won by its military contributions in order to acquire additional territory and influence. About how they should expand their territory and influence, the

---

[3] Nicolson, *Congress*, pp. 262, 49.

Boundary of German
Confederation

1 Holstein
2 Oldenburg
3 Palatinate
4 Grand Duchy of Baden
5 Kingdom of Württemberg

0   100   200 miles
0   100   200   300 km

MAP 3. Central Europe in 1815

Prussians were sharply divided, not only from their allies but also among themselves.[4]

Peacemaking in 1814 was complicated by the fact that it was by no means clear who should be involved. The initial agreements ending the war were signed by the four major powers, together with France and Spain. Representatives of the big four had then met in London during the summer, but were unable to formulate a set of principles with which to resolve their own differences and settle the claims of the other parties. Thus, the leaders of the major powers were still divided among themselves when they gathered in Vienna to confront the motley collection of princes and plenipotentiaries who had converged on the Austrian capital. From the states of the defunct Rhenish Confederation came princes and would-be princes who had once been Napoleon's allies but were now eager to elbow their way to a place among the victors. The imperial nobility, whose lands had been swallowed up by these states, lobbied for special status if not a restoration of their independence. Among their spokesmen was old Franz Georg Metternich, the chancellor's father, displaced *Reichsgraf*, and erstwhile diplomatist. Altogether some fifty plenipotentiaries represented various interests, which ranged in size and significance from the German Catholic Church to the city of Mainz's Chamber of Commerce, and included the German book trade, the Jewish communities of several cities, and the Teutonic Order. Friedrich Gentz, an important member of Metternich's staff, was correctly cynical about these suppliants' chances for success: 'All eyes are turned on the Congress', he wrote on 5 September, 'and everybody expects of it the redress of his grievances, the fulfilment of his desires, and the triumph of his projects. For the most part all these expectations are unfounded and illusory.'[5]

For generations of progressive Europeans, the true character of the Vienna proceedings was best summarized by Prince de Ligne's oft-quoted line that 'Le Congres danse et ne marché pas.' An extraordinary amount of money and effort was expended to feed and entertain the participants and their entourages. Throughout the autumn and winter, banquets and balls, private dinners and public concerts, fireworks displays and parades took up a great deal of time. These affairs ranged from the sublime to the outrageous— from a gala performance of Beethoven's Seventh Symphony, with

[4] Kraehe, *Metternich's German Policy*, ii, is the best account of the German question at Vienna.
[5] Ibid. ii. 119.

the composer in attendance, to a hunt in which six hundred wild boars were driven into the Linzer Tiergarten so that the dignitaries, lined up according to rank, could shoot as many animals as they pleased. In addition to these official functions, many of the participants pursued clandestine joys on the frontiers of respectable society. The Countess Aurora de Marasse, who was as poor as she was beautiful, filled her attic apartment with ambassadors, officials, and courtiers, while at a somewhat different social level, one lovely lady of the night captured the heart of Denmark's king during one of his strolls through the city. Much to the displeasure of the Viennese police, she became known to her friends and neighbours as 'the queen of Denmark'. Together with coachmen, wine merchants, and purveyors of luxury goods, these ladies may have been the true beneficiaries of Congress diplomacy.

But we should not make too much of the Congress's collective festivities or its participants' individual foibles. Among the major figures only the tsar was an indefatigable party-goer, always ready to dance and ever eager for a new amorous conquest. Francis and Frederick William were serious men, not given to excessive play. Hardenberg was too deaf to dance, King Frederick of Württemberg too fat. Humboldt, who had a taste for brief encounters with women from the lower social orders, tried to avoid high society, which he found 'more negative, empty, and monotonous than ever'. Metternich usually liked the convivial dimensions of diplomacy, but was much distracted by his central role in the negotiations and his troubled relationship with the fickle Wilhelmina von Sagan. Whether they enjoyed it or not, however, all of these men saw the Congress's social life as an essential part of the proceedings. Elaborate, carefully planned entertainments provided settings where they might meet informally, helped to occupy the scores of participants who were kept away from the actual decision-making, and gave everyone a chance to display the wealth and status naturally associated with political power. In any case, the difficulties faced by the peacemakers in 1814 and 1815 did not come from their indolence or moral lassitude, but were, as Varnhagen von Ense put it, 'deeply rooted in the matter at hand'—in the political and personal conflicts among the participants, the scope of their various ambitions, and the awesome complexity of their task.[6]

Among the issues confronting the Congress the fate of German

[6] There is a convenient collection of contemporary descriptions in Spiel (ed.), *Kongress.* Sydow (ed.), *Humboldt,* is a splendid source; the quotation is from p. 375.

Europe had particular weight, because in 1814–15, as in 1919 and 1945, it pulled into a knot the various strands of the great powers' interests. At one point, disagreements over German affairs brought the Congress to the point of dissolution; once a compromise solution to the German problem had been reached, the diplomats were able to conclude their deliberations with a show of allied unity.

The most obvious question about the German future concerned the legitimacy of Napoleon's reorganization. Now that the French imperium was broken, how much of its structure would remain? If new political boundaries were to be drawn, according to what principles should this be done? In a political setting as battered and disrupted as central Europe, what did legitimacy entail? How was sovereignty to be defined? When the Congress opened, only a few tentative answers to these questions were apparent. It was clear, for example, that the Rhenish lands annexed by France would be returned to German rule and that the satellite states of the north and west were finished. It was not apparent, however, who would get this territory. Nor was it certain what would happen to the kingdom of Saxony, whose ruler had returned to Napoleon's side after the French victories in the spring of 1813 and had been taken captive after the French defeat at Leipzig. The other middle-sized states had, as we know, managed to attain some measure of protection by rushing into the anti-Napoleonic coalition during the autumn of 1813. But would this protection be enough to withstand the territorial ambitions of the major powers and the demands from the various *Herrschaften* which the states had absorbed. The interactive process of compensation and annexation, from which the *Mittelstaaten* had benefited under Napoleon, could easily be turned against them by an Austro-Prussian condominium.[7]

Inseparable from the question of how German territories were to be distributed was the issue of German Europe's overall political organization. Here too the debris left by two decades of war made the situation perilously unstable. The old Reich, almost everybody knew, was gone forever. The Rhenish Confederation, whose collective existence had always been thin to the point of transparency, had evaporated as soon as its patron met defeat. On the eve of the Congress, therefore, the old questions about the German situation returned. How was the delicate balance of co-operation and diversity in German affairs to find institutional expression? How could the smaller states be protected and the larger ones be

[7] On the background to this, see above, Ch. 4, sect. iii, and Ch. 5, sect. iv.

given room to realize their ambitions? Who merited protection, and from whom—for instance, were the interests of the imperial nobility and the church to be protected from the states? Or should Napoleon's former partners be made the basis of a new German order? How would the rivalry between Berlin and Vienna, so disruptive in the last stages of the Reich, affect the political character of the Reich's nineteenth-century successor?

From the moment of Napoleon's first defeats in the autumn of 1813 until the Congress met a year later, various German statesmen tried to draft proposals to answer these questions. Stein, who viewed the German situation from the vantage point of the tsar's entourage, had originally hoped for a total reordering of central Europe. After Prussia and Austria entered the war, he proposed amalgamating the states of the Rhenish Confederation into a 'third Germany', separate from, but closely tied to, the two major German powers. In December 1813 Wilhelm von Humboldt, since 1810 the Prussian ambassador in Vienna, prepared a long memorandum on Stein's ideas. Germany, Humboldt wrote, must be 'free and strong' in order to nourish and protect its existence as a nation. But such freedom and strength had to come gradually; unity could not be forced; longstanding habits and differences should not be ignored. For the present, Humboldt proposed a voluntary association in which states would pool their resources for common defence and arrange treaties to co-ordinate their domestic policies. Humboldt did not overestimate Prussia's ability to shape this new German association, but rather acknowledged that 'the firm, consistent, and unwavering agreement and friendship of Austria and Prussia is the only cornerstone for this entire structure'.[8] About this Humboldt was surely right, both for the long-term development of German political affairs and for the immediate resolution of the German question in 1814. Until Austro-Prussian agreement was attained, German Europe's future would remain as uncertain and ill-defined as the phrasing of the Paris treaty, which had stated only that 'Les états de l'Allemagne seront indépendants et unis par un lien fédératif.'

Hardenberg tried to provide the basis for a discussion about what independence and federation might mean in a memorandum that he prepared, in consultation with Stein and others, during the summer of 1814. In its final form, this document, conventionally called the 'Forty-one Articles', represented the Prussian chancellor's efforts to

---

[8] Humboldt, *Werke*, iv. 302ff., and the analysis in Sweet, *Wilhelm von Humboldt*, ii. 142 ff. For some other plans, see Huber, i. 510 ff.; Gruner, *Frage*, pp. 60 ff.

reach a compromise between the interests of the various states and Stein's desire for a cohesive, unified replacement for the old Reich. Hardenberg proposed the creation of an 'Eternal Confederation' of German states, divided into seven circles (*Kreise*), each of which would be under the chairmanship of one, or in some cases two, of its leading princes. The Confederation was to have two institutions, a council of the *Kreise* heads, under the joint direction of Prussia and Austria, and a larger diet, which would include all the states and the mediatized imperial nobility. But, while Hardenberg's plan gave Prussia and Austria considerable influence over the Confederation's affairs, important parts of both states were to remain outside its boundaries, so it was by no means clear how much influence the Confederation could exert over its two most powerful members. 'The whole system can only be constructed on the foundation that Austria and Prussia are and remain united, and that they decide to place the other [states] in an essentially consultative position'. In effect, Hardenberg was offering Metternich joint hegemony over the smaller states in return for his acceptance of Prussia as Austria's equal partner in German affairs.[9]

Such a position was not acceptable to the other states, who feared the combined power of Vienna and Berlin even more than they feared domination by one or the other. Deprived of their Napoleonic protector, several of the middle-sized states had begun to look around for other allies; Württemberg had the advantage of dynastic ties with Russia, Hanover with Britain. Such foreign connections became all the more necessary when Metternich proposed that the final disposition of German affairs be left in the hands of the big six—Britain, Russia, Austria, Prussia, France, and Spain—who were to be guided by a German committee, composed of Austria and Prussia, plus Bavaria, Württemberg, and Hanover, which would in turn consult all of the assembled German princes and their representatives. If they had retained a united front, such a procedure would have enabled the major states to formulate the peace behind closed doors and impose it as they wished. But, as soon became apparent, divisions among the big six gave the smaller states considerable room to manoeuvre among them.

Metternich received Hardenberg's 'Forty-one Articles' in September, soon after the Prussian delegation arrived in Vienna. Without consulting the other German states, the Austrian chancellor, together with Humboldt, Count Münster, the Hanoverian representative, and a few aides, tried to work out an acceptable

[9] Thielen, *Hardenberg*, p. 305.

revision of Hardenberg's proposals which would blunt the inevitable opposition from the *Mittelstaaten* and protect the interests of
the Habsburg monarchy. The result was the 'Twelve Articles',
finally finished on 12 October and presented to the various German
representatives two days later. While retaining the main contours
of Hardenberg's Confederation, Metternich's plan involved several
important revisions: all of Austria's and Prussia's German territories were made part of the federal system, the presidency was to
be in Austrian hands alone, and the power of the *Kreise* chiefs was
increased. Most of the German statesmen at Vienna were not
pleased when they learned the details of Metternich's plan. On the
German committee itself, both the Bavarian and Württemberg
delegates objected to the limitations placed on the sovereignty of
their states. King Frederick of Württemberg instructed his representative to make clear that 'there could be no thought of decreasing
or limiting the existing sovereign power now held by his supreme
majesty'. Until Metternich suspended them in mid-November,
acrimonious and unproductive discussions in the German committee dragged on.[10] But by the time these deliberations ground to
a halt, they were completely overshadowed by the much more
serious conflict that had erupted among the great powers over the
future of Saxony and Poland.

As the reader will recall, in 1806 Napoleon consolidated his
influence over Saxony by making it a kingdom and naming its king
the absentee ruler of his Polish satellite, the duchy of Warsaw.
Following the French defeat at Leipzig in October 1813, the Saxon
and Polish territories immediately became the objects of Russian
and Prussian ambitions. The latter were eager to annex the
kingdom itself, which they saw as the best compensation for the
lands they had abandoned to the new *Mittelstaaten* and for the Polish
territories they were prepared to cede to Russia. Hardenberg raised
the issue several times with Metternich, who was encouraging but
noncommittal. In October 1814, as the bargaining over the future
organization of Germany intensified, the Austrian chancellor
seemed prepared to give Hardenberg most of what he wanted, in
return for his co-operation in dealing with Russia. At this point
Castlereagh was also prepared to back Prussia, if it would in turn
support a British move to frustrate Russian ambitions in Poland.
But this front could not hold against the fury of the tsar; Metternich .

[10] The protocols of the Committee are printed in Johann Ludwig Klüber, *Akten
des Wiener Kongresses in den Jahren 1814 und 1815* (1815-35; repr. Osnabrück, 1966),
ii. 64 ff. The quotation is from pp. 97-8.

eventually had to withdraw his promise of Saxony, and thus precipitated a crisis that threatened the entire process of peacemaking. 'I witness every day', wrote Castlereagh in mid-December, 'the astonishing tenacity with which all the powers cling to the smallest points of separate interest.' As the political climate deteriorated, there was talk of war in Vienna, while in Berlin patriots began to suggest that now was the time for Prussia to assert its rights with force. Early in the new year, when Austria, England, and France stood firm against both Prussia and Russia, a compromise settlement was reached. Hardenberg had to be content with the northern part of Saxony rather than the kingdom as a whole; as compensation, Prussia was to receive extensive territories in the west. The tsar did not get the reunited Polish kingdom for which he yearned, but he did receive virtually all of the duchy of Warsaw, which became 'Congress Poland', a nominally independent state under Russian control.[11]

In the meantime, Metternich had resumed negotiations with the *Mittlestaaten* in an effort to achieve a consensus on his Confederation Napoleon's return from Elba put the entire enterprise at risk when Napoleon's return from Elba put the entire enterprise at risk and thus provided a substantial impetus for a final compromise, which was hammered out in a series of meetings in May. The agreements on the territorial organization and federal structure of the German states were accepted by most of the participants on 8 June, and were included in the treaty signed by the major European powers on 9 June, just ten days before the battle of Waterloo. Despite efforts by the Prussian military to impose a punitive peace on France following Napoleon's defeat, the June settlement was reaffirmed when the allies gathered in Paris to sign a second peace treaty on 20 November. At the same time, allied solidarity was underscored by two additional agreements, the 'Holy Alliance' of Christian powers inspired by the tsar's recently enkindled religiosity and the Quadruple Alliance of the four victorious states designed by Castlereagh as a buttress for the status quo.

The map of German Europe drawn in 1815—together with some minor revisions and emendations made during the next four years—lasted until 1866 and, in many important respects, until 1919. Among the German states, Prussia was doubtlessly the big winner: the Hohenzollern received two-fifths of Saxony, with a

[11] Nicolson, *Congress*, p. 175. A good description of the climate in Prussia and in the Prussian delegation can be found in Sydow (ed.), *Humboldt*, see especially the letters of 5 Jan. on pp. 448 ff.

population of about 850,000, some Polish land around Danzig, Swedish Pomerania (including Arndt's birthplace, the island of Rügen), most of the area lost in the Treaty of Tilsit, and extensive territories in the Rhineland and Westphalia. These Rhenish and Westphalian lands, taken with some reluctance as compensation for Prussia's thwarted ambitions in Saxony, were of particular long-term significance since they enabled Berlin to build an arc of influence across central Europe, stretching from the Hohenzollern's traditional bastions in the east to the rich and progressive provinces in the German west. Bavaria received Berchtesgaden, Ansbach and Bayreuth, Würzburg and Aschaffenburg, but not, as its leaders had hoped, the important fortress of Mainz (which had also been coveted by Prussia and eventually went to Hesse-Darmstadt) or all of the Electoral Palatinate. Hanover, now recognized as a kingdom but still dynastically tied to Britain, expanded into some former Prussian territory and annexed several small northern states. Saxony, although territorially truncated, remained a kingdom and kept its most important lands around Leipzig. Baden and Württemberg neither gained nor lost much territory—their achievement was to survive the Congress with most of their Napoleonic legacy intact. Austria, which had initially asserted its claims to some western territories, eventually used these lands to compensate some of the other states during the process of adjustment that culminated in the *Territorialrezess* of June 1819. The Habsburgs' main aims in 1815 were a consolidation of their dynastic lands and a strengthening of their influence in northern Italy. Metternich had decided that Austria's influence over German affairs could best be achieved through a series of diplomatic arrangements rather than a broken bridge of territories connecting Vienna to the Rhine.[12]

In the closing days of the Congress, as the opposing armies were taking their position in the Low Countries, Metternich hurriedly drafted a proposal for a German organization which, with Prussia's backing, he presented to the states for their approval on 23 May. Slightly revised, this became the basis for the *Bundesakte*, originally signed by thirty-seven states on 8 June and then, some weeks later, by Baden and Württemberg. In comparison to the proposals circulated earlier by Stein, Humboldt, Hardenberg, and Metternich himself, the final plan was simple and straightforward. Gone were the efforts to limit how much Austrian or Prussian territory might come under federal jurisdiction; gone were the *Kreise* that had been the occasion for so many complicated negotiations; gone were the

[12] There is a summary of the territorial changes in Huber, i. 576–82.

executive, the bicameral representative institutions, the court, and many of the other measures designed to unify German public life. Instead, the 'sovereign princes and free cities of Germany' established a confederation of independent states, a *Staatenbund* rather than a *Bundesstaat*.

Among the original thirty-nine members of the Confederation were Prussia and Austria (or, more accurately, those possessions of the Habsburgs and Hohenzollern that had previously belonged to the Holy Roman Empire), the kingdoms of Saxony, Bavaria, Hanover, and Württemberg, the electoral principality of Hesse, the grand duchies of Baden and Hesse, assorted other duchies and principalities, and the four free cities of Lübeck, Frankfurt, Bremen, and Hamburg. Most of these entities were quite small: in 1818 only seven members of the Confederation had populations of more than one million, whereas twenty-one had populations of less than 100,000, and thirteen less than 50,000; Liechtenstein, the smallest member, had just over 5,000 inhabitants. Since many of the smaller entities were enclaves in a larger state, their autonomy, especially in foreign affairs and commercial relations, was highly qualified. In the course of the Confederation's existence, several minor principalities fused; in 1866 there were only thirty-four members left.

The Confederation had only one statutory institution, the *Bundesversammlung*, a diet of delegates appointed and instructed by their governments. The diet could meet in a small council, composed of the eleven largest members (Austria, Prussia, Bavaria, Saxony, Hanover, Württemberg, Baden, Electoral Hesse, the Grand Duchy of Hesse, Denmark, and the Netherlands) and representatives of the rest grouped in six composite voting blocs, or in full assembly. In the latter, which was supposed to deal with all matters having to do with the character of the Confederation itself, either a two-thirds majority, or, on the most important issues, unanimity was necessary for a decision. This meant that, while Austria, Prussia, Hanover, Württemberg, Saxony, and Bavaria—each with four votes—could never be overwhelmed by a united front of the small states, neither could they overwhelm their neighbours. Austria provided the *Bundesversammlung*'s president, but he functioned as the chairman of its proceedings, not as a chief executive. In effect, the German states had not got much further than the formulaic promise of a 'lien fédératif' contained in the Paris peace of May 1814. Almost everything substantive about the future, including common provisions for defence, economic policies, legal institutions, the legal status of the Jews, the position of the mediatized nobility, and a variety of other issues was left open, subject to subsequent discussion and decision by the diet.[13]

Most of those who signed the *Bundesakte* in June 1815 did so without much enthusiasm. While representatives from the smaller states felt left out of the decision-making and objected to the lack of adequate debate, the advocates of a more cohesive national polity were disappointed that the Confederation was so loose and ill-defined. Humboldt, for instance, wrote to his wife that it was only 'a shadow' of what he had wanted. Nevertheless, Humboldt recognized that the new organization had potential. In September 1816, after he had finished a year's tour of duty as Prussian representative to the diet, Humboldt reported to Hardenberg that, despite its deficiencies, the Confederation could develop from a federation of states into a federal state. Prussia should work towards this end, remaining ever mindful of hostile coalitions, but also alert to the possibilities of influencing other states 'through dignity, justice, and firmness'. In the long run, Humboldt was convinced, greater unity among Germans would certainly come: 'It will never be possible to stop Germany from wanting to be One state and One nation; the inclination, if not towards unity at least towards some kind of association remains . . . in every heart and mind.'[14]

There were, however, powerful counterpressures to the process of unification. In the first place, the Confederation, like the old Reich, contained foreign sovereigns (the king of England, in his capacity as ruler of Hanover; the king of Denmark, as ruler of Holstein; the king of the Netherlands, as ruler of Luxemburg), whose closer amalgamation into a federal state would have strained their dual sovereignties. Second, and much more important, the smaller states, although pleased to have their sovereignty recognized and protected by the Confederation, feared that any expansion of federal power would have to come at their expense.[15] As we shall see in the next two sections, after 1815 these states directed their energies and resources towards internal integration, not international co-operation. Finally, Metternich was not in favour of a more cohesive structure. From the beginning of the last war against Napoleon, Metternich had favoured retaining the

[13] Huber, i. 583–4; Huber, *Dokumente*, i. 75 ff. On the distribution of populations, see Lutz, *Habsburg*, pp. 20–1.

[14] Sydow (ed.), *Humboldt*, pp. 553 ff. Humboldt's September memorandum is printed in *Werke*, iv. 547 ff.

[15] Gruner, 'Einzelstaaten'.

sovereignty of the most important *Mittelstaaten* in order to stabilize central European affairs; nothing had happened since 1813 to change his mind. For him, the Confederation was a regional security system, designed to control Prussia by tying it to the other German states in an association that was then itself to be enmeshed in a series of other agreements with the status-quo powers.

To Humboldt, the Confederation was a foundation upon which future institutions might be built, to the rulers of the smaller states, it was a way of protecting their fragile sovereignty; to Metternich, it was one piece in a larger plan for the European order Austrian interests demanded. But, to the patriots inspired by the rhetoric of Arndt and Jahn, the Confederation stood for the reactionary particularism they wanted to destroy. After the heady excitement of war, these enthusiasts found the peace dispiriting. In 1814 Arndt had tried to keep alive the sacred flame of nationalism with ceremonies marking the anniversary of the battle of Leipzig, but the climate had changed, governments were no longer sympathetic, the need for patriotic energy had passed. When asked for ideas about a monument for the heroic Scharnhorst, Caspar David Friedrich replied, 'So long as we remain the menials of princes, nothing great of this kind will be seen. Where the people have no voice, the people will not be allowed to be conscious of, and honour themselves.' Soon Friedrich's paintings began to reflect this political mood: in *Die Gescheiterte Hoffnung*, for instance, the remnants of a lost ship litter a landscape as glacially barren as the artist's view of public life. 'Where is the Germany', asked the young men back from the war, 'that was worthy of our common struggle?'[16]

A small minority of Germans, most of them students or intellectuals, responded to this diminution of political hopes by establishing themselves as the personification of nationhood. The institutional expression of their identification with the nation was the *Burschenschaft* movement, formed at Jena in June 1815, when some students, dressed in what they took to be old German costumes and carrying the black–red–gold colours of the Lützow volunteers, pledged themselves to work for the ideals defined by Arndt and the other poets of patriotic commitment. The Jena *Burschenschaft* soon had between 500 and 650 members; within a few months affiliated groups had been formed at other major universities. Everywhere, the *Burschenschaftler* shunned the ribald pleasures of traditional student life and sought to overcome the

---

[16] Honour, *Romanticism*, p. 222; Steffens, *Was ich erlebte*, pp. 372 ff.

regional divisions embodied in the old organizations. They wanted
to be German, in dress and custom, virtue and deportment, heart
and soul. They believed themselves to be the best representatives of
the present, the true hope of the future. The movement, Heinrich
von Gagern told his father, who had helped to organized a defence
of the small states at the Congress of Vienna, speaks 'to the best
youth' and gives them 'substance and nourishment'. We are moved
above all, Gagern went on, by our love of the fatherland. .'We want
more communal spirit among the individual German states, greater
unity in their policies and values, the closest federal co-operation
rather than independent policies of each state. Above all, we desire
that Germany as a land, and the German people as a folk, can be
esteemed.'[17]

The great public expression of the *Burschenschaft* spirit was the
festival held at the Wartburg in October 1817 to celebrate the allies'
victory at Leipzig and the tricentenary of the Reformation—the
freedom of the nation from foreign domination and the freedom of
thought from doctrinaire restraints. Four hundred and sixty-eight
German students gathered at the castle where Luther had translated
the Bible into the vernacular. At this shrine to the emergence of the
German language, the participants heard speeches extolling them to
represent the nation, transcend particularism, and defy reaction.
'You should be clear that the moment you decide to attend a
university', they were told, 'all of Germany is open to you.' As
heirs of the German literary culture of the eighteenth century, these
young academicians searched for the symbols and institutions with
which to express their commitment to a political nation. They did
not find them. Despite the emotional fervour and rhetorical elan
displayed at the Wartburg, the German national movement was
obviously uncertain and divided. How would it be possible to
create symbols of national unity at a place which stood for the
division of Germans into different confessions? How would the
majority of Germans who still owed their religious allegiance to
Rome respond to Friedrich Forster's festive song, 'Dreht uns der
Papst die Nase nicht| So giebt's noch manchen Lumpengewicht|
Den wir darnieder schlagen'? Nor were the *Burschenschaftler* in
agreement about the practical direction their institutions should
take. Some, like Heinrich von Gagern, believed they had an
educational function to provide their membership with ideals they

[17] Letter of 17 June 1818, printed in Gagern, *Liberalismus*, pp. 57–61. There is an
extensive collection of documents on the *Burschenschaften* in Wentzcke *et al.* (eds),
Darstellung. The best analysis is Hardtwig, 'Mentalität'.

could bring with them 'into civil society . . . which they could try to make conform to these ideals'. Others, however, took a much more activist line and hoped for 'swift and violent' acts by individuals against the nation's enemies.[18]

The most radical sector of the national movement was led by Karl Follen at Giessen. The more frustrated Follen became with the narrowness of public life in the duchies of Hesse and Nassau, the more radically he envisioned a free, united, Christian nation. In 1818 he moved from Giessen to Jena because he hoped to broaden his influence over the *Burschenschaften*.[19] But he was never able to attract more than two dozen eccentric followers, and would very likely have been forgotten had it not been for Karl Sand, a fringe member of his group, who in March 1819 stabbed to death August von Kotzebue, a playwright, reactionary publicist, and sometime political agent then employed by the Russian legation at Mannheim.

Karl Sand was twenty-three years old in 1819, a veteran of the Napoleonic war, member of a *Burschenschaft*, and student of theology. He had no doubt that murdering Kotzebue would bring him immortality: 'Thank you, God, for the victory', he cried as he drove a second dagger into his own body. In a sense, of course, he was right. Sand did earn himself a place in history, even though his posthumously published writings reveal him to be politically confused, mentally unbalanced, and artistically untalented. His attempt at suicide failed and he recovered enough to stand trial and be executed. Everyone whose life had touched his was hurt by Sand's deed; for example, even though Follen's connection with the murder was never proven, he was hounded by the police, stripped of his position at the university, and forced into exile. Eventually, he moved to the United States where he died in 1840. Despite some efforts to turn Sand into a hero of political romanticism, most of those aware of what he had done viewed it with undisguised horror. Stein, for example, believed that the murder underscored the need for vigorous action against radicalism: as he wrote to Görres in July 1819, 'it is the duty of every moral and religious man to insist that this accursed sect be punished and that it become the object of public repugnance'.[20]

---

[18] Robert Keil and Richard Keil, *Die burschenschaftlichen Wartburgfeste von 1817 und 1867* (Jena, 1868) prints the most important documents; my quotations are from pp. 14–15 and 18. Gagern, *Liberalismus*, pp. 59–60, Krieger, *Idea*, p. 263.

[19] Krieger, *Idea*, pp. 266 ff. Karl Wegert, 'The Genesis of Youthful Radicalism: Hesse-Nassau, 1806–19', *CEH* 10/3 (Sept. 1977), 185–205, emphasizes the connections between Follen's movement and the local situation.

[20] Huber, i. 730, 731, n. 2.

Metternich recognized immediately that the fear and anger provoked by Kotzebue's murder could be used to mobilize the Confederation against radicalism, contain south German constitutionalism, and derail Prussian reform. On 1 August Metternich met with King Frederick William at Teplitz and secured his co-operation before proceeding to a larger conclave, attended by the representatives of ten German states, held from 6 to 31 August at the fashionable resort town of Karlsbad. The decrees formulated at Karlsbad were then presented to, and unanimously passed by, the German diet when it met at Frankfurt in late September. The first decree called for closer supervision of universities throughout the Confederation: governments should ensure that no teacher misused his authority 'by spreading harmful ideas which would subvert public peace and order and undermine the foundations of the existing states'. Should a subversive teacher be dismissed by one university, he could not be hired by another. A second decree demanded tighter regulation of the press through the creation of a central commission, charged with the co-ordination and enforcement of censorship throughout the Confederation. Finally, the so-called *Untersuchungsgesetz* established a federal bureau of investigation to handle 'revolutionary agitation discovered in several states'.[21]

In November 1819 Metternich moved to consolidate the reactionary functions of the Confederation by calling a meeting of German ministers who, after six months of deliberations, agreed to the *Wiener Schlussakte*, a revised version of the federal constitution defined at Vienna four years earlier. The *Schlussakte*, which was accepted by the diet in July 1820, stripped the Confederation of the potentially progressive impulses that had been part of its original charter: there was no more talk about Jewish emancipation, religious toleration, or economic reforms. The institutional impediments to change within federal institutions were reinforced—the plenum was to be used only for voting, not discussion, and unanimity was required for the most important matters. While it was protective of its members' independence and sovereignty in most respects, the *Schlussakte* set limits on the possibility of change within the German states. Article Twenty-six made clear that the Confederation would intervene in a state's domestic affairs to preserve public order, especially if 'the state's government was rendered unable to seek help by the situation'. And Article Fifty-eight prohibited German princes from agreeing

---

[21] Ibid. i. 732 ff. Huber, *Dokumente*, i. 90 ff.

to a constitution 'that would limit or hinder them in the fulfilment of their duties to the Confederation'. In its final form, the Confederation, which Humboldt had once hoped would develop into the vehicle for political reform and national cohesion, became a kind of counter-revolutionary holding company through which Metternich could co-ordinate governmental action against his political enemies. Instead of protecting citizens from the abuse of state power, the Confederation made sure that even relatively progressive governments would have to accept responsibility for stamping out dissent.[22]

Only in one respect did the Confederation retain some shred of the national cohesion for which patriots had hoped: Article Two defined it as 'a community of independent states in domestic matters . . . but in its external relations a politically unified, federated power [*eine in politischer Einheit verbundene Gesammt-Macht*]'. That this would mean little in practical terms became clear when the federal states set out to define a common military policy. The *Kriegsverfassung*, adopted by the federal states in April 1821 and amended in July 1822, called for the creation of a single wartime army, under one commander to be chosen by the Confederation. This army was to be composed of contingents to be supplied by the member states according to a set formula. But since the state's armies would remain separate until a federal war had been declared, there were no incentives to common military planning or co-ordination. In fact, no one was especially interested in creating federal military institutions. The smaller states, burdened with debt and fearful of becoming the instruments of their larger neighbours, kept their military expenses low and their forces separate. Few Austrian or Prussian officers were ready to abandon their distinct traditions and special social role for some ill-defined German army. Only in the five federal fortresses did soldiers from several states serve together.[23]

Once the final version of the territorial settlement of 1815 and the newly defined federal constitution had been accepted by the German states in 1819 and 1820, the German Confederation moved to the fringes of national life. The diet continued to rent crowded quarters in the Taxis family palace on Frankfurt's Eschenheimer Gasse. It conducted its official business slowly, with a small staff of twenty-seven secretaries, clerks, and other office personnel. The various state representatives often led active social lives, but their

[22] Huber, *Dokumente*, vol. i. 81 ff.
[23] Ibid i. 108 ff.

public duties were usually limited since the diet rarely met in full session and, especially after the appointment of Count Munch-Bellinghausen as presiding ambassador in 1822, the smaller council's proceedings became increasingly dull, predictable, and inconsequential. Except for a few issues—such as conventions regulating river traffic—most governments bypassed the diet and used bilateral arrangements, dynastic marriages, and shifting alliances to regulate their relations with other German states. Even the repressive measures with which the Confederation became so closely identified had been worked out through a series of special meetings before they were presented to the diet. The Confederation, therefore, had little impact on most Germans, who could safely ignore what Treitschke contemptuously referred to as that 'busy idleness' on the Eschenheimer Gasse.[24]

That the Confederation did not provide a lasting basis for Germans' national existence is clear enough; that it could not have done so is much more debatable. The Confederation had the three elements that are essential for any effective solution to the 'German question.' First, it was part of an international settlement, guaranteed by the major states of east and west. It could function, therefore, as what Paul Schroeder called an 'intermediary body', which ordered central European affairs at the same time as it discouraged great power interference. Second, its institutions balanced the major German powers' need for independence with the smaller states' need for security and protection. At least potentially, the diet might have provided Metternich's goal of concord without unity, 'Einigkeit ohne Einheit'. Finally, in its original form the settlement of 1815 acknowledged that a satisfactory national existence would have to include some common social, economic, and cultural institutions. Here of course the Confederation's failure was most manifest and consequential: by setting to one side the reforms promised in 1815 and turning federal institutions into instruments of reaction, Metternich and his collaborators alienated the Confederation from the most progressive forces in German politics and society. As we shall see, this identification of the Confederation with political reaction encouraged many Germans both to identify progress and nationhood, domestic freedom and national unification.[25]

[24] See, for example, the account in George S. Werner, *Bavaria in the German Confederation, 1820–1848* (Cranbury, NJ, 1977); Katzenstein, *Partners*, pp. 38–9.

[25] Paul W. Schroeder, 'The 19th-Century International System: Changes in Structure', *World Politics*, 39 (1986), 22. For a defence of the Confederation's potential, see Gruner, *Frage*.

ii. CONSTITUTIONAL CONFLICTS

'Among all worldly things,' Friedrich Christoph Dahlmann wrote in 1815, 'nothing is more important than the fatherland's constitution.'[26] Dahlmann was not referring to the political organization of the German nation; his 'fatherland' was Holstein, where a bitter constitutional conflict was going on between the estates and the king of Denmark. But this struggle for power in the far northern tip of German Europe was also a part of the German question. Like the diplomats at the Vienna Congress, people in Holstein, and in most other German states, were trying to come to terms with the redefinition and redistribution of political power that was produced by years of war and revolution. Princes who had been forced to compromise with Napoleon in order to survive were now reconsidering their options, looking for new advisers, weighing different policies; élites who had been frightened into silence by the pressure of events were hoping to reassert their privileges and power; reformist bureaucrats who had benefited most from the years of upheaval were desperately trying to stay in office and keep their hard-won gains. At Vienna, the constitutional issues raised by these various groups often touched the diplomats' debates over the German future. Defenders of state sovereignty, mediatized nobles in search of special status, monarchs jealous of their prerogatives had all sought to have their views expressed in the final treaties. But in these matters, as in so much else, the *Bundesakte* of 1815 ended with a compromise vague enough to inspire hope in many camps: Article Thirteen tersely stipulated that 'in every federal state there will be a *landständische Verfassung*'.[27]

In order to understand contemporary constitutional discussions, we must avoid reading them anachronistically, in the light of later debates between liberal constitutionalists and their enemies. In 1815 exponents of constitutional government came from two distinct, if sometimes overlapping groups. First there were the defenders of the traditional estate system—the *altständische Verfassung*—who saw constitutional government and representative institutions as a way of protecting their position from the encroachment of the

[26] F. C. Dahlmann, 'Ein Wort über Verfassung', in his *Schriften*, p. 13. For a general introduction to German constitutional history, see Dieter Grimm, *Deutsche Verfassungs geschichte, 1776–1866: Vom Beginn des modernen Verfassungsstaats bis zur Auflösung des Deutschen Bundes* (Frankfurt, 1988).

[27] On the constitutional question at Vienna, see W. Mager, 'Das Problem der landständischen Verfassungen auf dem Wiener Kongress, 1814/15', *HZ* 217/2 (1973), 296–346.

bureaucratic states. Among this group the former imperial nobility, the *Standesherren*, were especially important; they were, for
example, in the forefront of those who wanted the Vienna
Congress to take a position in favour of *Stände*. Second there were
advocates of state sovereignty, who saw constitutions as a way of
integrating and consolidating the polities which had been stitched
together from various *Länder*. Among this group, the officials from
the states of the Rhenish Confederation were prominent, as were
many of those associated with the Prussian reform movement.
Representative institutions appealed to these people as an antidote
to, rather than a defence of, social privilege and local particularism.
Wilhelm von Humboldt, for instance, believed that properly-
constructed representation would increase people's 'independence'
but also 'tie them more firmly to the state'.[28] Liberal constitutionalism, as we shall see, did not involve a choice between one or the
other of these positions; it drew on and wove together aspects of
both.

Roughly speaking, the advocates of the old *ständische* constitutions were strongest in the northern and central German states,
many of which had been able to maintain corporate institutions
throughout the eighteenth century and had not been as disrupted
by Napoleonic intervention as had most states in the south-west.
Although diminished by Prussia's acquisitions in 1815, these states
remained the bastions of the old *Stände*. Nowhere was this more
obviously true than in the two Mecklenburgs, where the compromise effected between prince and *Stände* (the so-called *Erbvergleich* of 1755) was reintroduced after 1815 without a significant
effect on the landed nobility's predominant position. A similar
situation obtained in Brunswick, where a renewed *Landschaftsord-
nung* in 1820 provided a slightly reformed version of the estates
which had exercised political power there since the 1770s. When
Hanover was resurrected in 1815, its traditional élites once again
flourished under their absentee ruler, the king of England. In
1819 the Prince Regent issued a royal patent that created a bicameral legislature, the *Allgemeine Stände-Versammlung*, whose upper
chamber was completely dominated by aristocrats. The Saxon
Landtag also retained its corporate form; the first chamber was
limited to the upper clergy and higher nobility, the second to
landholders and a few urban delegates; the peasantry had no
representatives at all. Traditional constitutional patterns remained
in the four free cities that had survived the destruction of the Reich:

[28] *Werke*, iv. 316.

in 1814–15 the patriciates of Hamburg, Bremen, Lübeck, and Frankfurt reasserted their authority and established highly restricted representative bodies in these urban republics.[29]

An *altständische Verfassung* could not be so easily restored in states which had dramatically expanded as clients of the French; indeed any serious attempt to recreate the estates in Bavaria or Baden would have put the entire political order at risk. The governments of these states, therefore, wanted constitutions that would affirm their own sovereign authority, integrate recently acquired territories, and centralize political and legal institutions. In this respect, constitutional developments in the south and west were extensions of the reform administrations established during the Napoleonic era. After 1815, however, the balance of power within these states shifted, their political atmosphere changed, and governments became more willing to compromise with traditional élites. As a result, the bureaucratic integration of the reform era acquired a corporate component, usually in the form of representative institutions that acknowledged aristocratic privilege, but at the same time anchored it in the state.[30]

The political history of Bavaria after 1815 offers the clearest example of this process at work. In 1808 King Maximilian, acting on Napoleon's advice, issued a constitution providing his subjects with basic rights and freedoms, religious toleration, and a

[29] Huber, i. 656–7, gives the following summary of German constitutional development:

i. Corporate municipal constitutions were restored in Lübeck (1813), Hamburg (1814), Bremen (1816–18), and Frankfurt (1816).

ii. Corporate constitutions remained in Mecklenburg-Schwerin and Mecklenburg-Strelitz (*Erbvergleich* of 1755), Hohenzollern-Hechingen (*Landesvergleich* of 1796), the three Anhalt states (*Landtagsabschied* of 1625), and the four Reuss states (*Erbvereinigung* of 1668).

iii. New constitutions, often combining corporate and representative elements were established in Nassau (1814), Schwarzburg-Rudolstadt (1816), Schaumburg-Lippe (1816), Waldeck (1816), Sachsen-Weimar (1816), Sachsen-Hildburghausen (1818), Bavaria (1818), Baden (1818), Liechtenstein (1818), Württemberg (1819), Hanover (1819), Brunswick (1820), Hesse-Darmstadt (1820), Sachsen-Meiningen (1824, united with Hildburghausen in 1829).

iv. After 1830, Brunswick (1832) and Hanover (1833–6, 1840) amended their constitutions, while new constitutions were established in Electoral Hesse (1831), Sachsen-Altenburg (1831), Holstein (1831), Saxony (1831), Hohenzollern-Sigmaringen (1833), Lippe (1836), Schwarzburg-Sondershausen (1830, 1841), Luxemburg (1841).

v. The following states were without constitutions: Austria, Prussia, Oldenburg, and Hesse-Homburg. Limburg belonged to the Confederation but was governed according to the Netherlands' constitution.

[30] Huber, i. 314 ff.; Huber, *Dokumente*, i. 141 ff.

centralized governmental structure. This constitution mentioned but did not create representative institutions, since, to a bureaucratic reformer like Montgelas, political participation had little appeal. Everyone, he once wrote, needs civil liberty, 'but how many men are there in the state who can enjoy the rights of political freedom, who indeed can even understand what it is?' The common people, whom Montgelas viewed as the beneficiaries of his policies, were too ignorant for politics; traditional élites would have used their political rights to combat the forces of reform. After 1814, however, a number of Bavarian officials realized that bureaucratic integration was not sufficient. Montgelas, with some reluctance, participated in the drafting of a new constitution, but it was not completed until after his dismissal in 1817. The final document, decreéd by the king in May 1818, had been prepared hastily and secretly by a special ministerial committee, in which Crown Prince Ludwig and Georg Friedrich von Zentner, a veteran bureaucrat, played the leading roles.[31]

The Bavarian constitution of 1818 established a representative body, whose character and composition clearly reflected the impulses at work in most of the German south-west. The legislature's name, *Stände-Versammlung*, evoked the corporate estates of traditional Europe, but it was charged with representing the state as a whole, not particular regions or a collection of social groups—thus it was universal, an *Allgemeine Versammlung der Stände*. The legislature consisted of two chambers. Membership in the upper chamber, the *Reichs-Räthe*, was hereditary (adult members of the royal family and the heads of imperial noble houses), ex officio (the two Catholic archbishops and certain royal officials), or granted by royal appointment. In all three categories, the aristocracy was predominant. The chamber of deputies was chosen by electors, who were themselves elected by five separate categories of voters: estate owners, academicians, clergy, representatives of 'markets and cities', and landowners not included in the first category. But while this separate and indirect mode of selection had a corporate cast, the chamber of deputies functioned like a modern parliament; its members met and deliberated together and voted as individuals.

The Bavarian constitution also contained a statement of *Grundrechte*, basic rights that had been part of administrative reformers' vocabulary since the late eighteenth century. These rights, reformers had long been convinced, would increase the state's sovereignty

[31] Montgelas quoted by Weis in Spindler (ed.), *Handbuch*, iv. 77. See also Aretin, *Bayernsweg*, chs. 3 and 4, and the fine treatment in Möckl, *Staat*.

by clearing away competing privileges, encourage èconomic prosperity by removing restraints on trade and manufacturing, and win popular approval by guaranteeing equal rights and civil liberties. But behind formulaic promises of freedom and equality lay considerable uncertainty about how they could be defined and administered. All citizens, for example, were promised 'freedom of conscience', but, according to Article Nine of Part IV, the question of civil rights for Jews was postponed until it could be worked out by further legislation. Similarly, the constitution called for 'legal equality and equality before the law', but this was qualified in a section on 'Special Rights and Privileges' which guaranteed patrimonial justice and granted the nobility certain special prerogatives. Finally, on the critical question of local government, and especially the right of communities to decide who could acquire local citizenship rights, the constitution evasively promised to grant communities the administration of matters of interest to them, but said nothing about who would decide what these matters were.[32]

Three months after Max Joseph decreed his new constitution, the grand duke of Baden issued a similar document. Baden, it will be remembered, was the most fragile and vulnerable of the new medium-sized states. The dukes of Baden-Durlach had held their core lands for just three decades when Napoleon gave them a chance to quadruple their holdings with a narrow band of acquisitions along France's eastern frontier. The reformist regime in Baden during the era of the *Rheinbund* had had considerable success integrating these territories, but in 1814 the task was by no means completed. At that point the government in Karlsruhe not only had to contend with the immediate post-war problems of fiscal collapse and administrative confusion, it also was involved in a bitter dispute with Bavaria over the Palatinate and, tied to that conflict, the possibility of a contested succession. This dangerous situation enabled a small group of officials, led by Reitzenstein and his protégé Karl Nebenius, to create a settlement without significant interference from other social groups. The constitution of August 1818, therefore, was by far the most 'modern' existing in any German state. Like its Bavarian counterpart, the Badenese constitution established a bicameral legislature, with an upper house heavily weighted towards the old nobility. But, unlike any other contemporary German parliament, the sixty-three members of the Chamber of Deputies were elected by all of those who met

[32] See the essays in G. Birtsch (ed.), *Grund- und Freiheitsrecht im Wandel von Gesellschaft und Geschichte* (Göttingen, 1981).

the economic and legal qualifications of citizenship within geographically defined districts. In Baden, therefore, the traditional association of political participation and social status was replaced by a concern for property and legal position.[33]

In contrast to Baden, whose rulers had to build a state virtually without traditions, Württemberg's government had to find a way of reconciling its own ambitions with the historical memories of the 'gutes altes Recht'. King Frederick, as we have seen, exploited the historical situation in 1805 and 1806 in order to increase his own power at the expense of the estates. In 1814, however, Frederick needed a constitution in order to blunt the mediatized nobility's counteroffensive against his authority. In January 1815 the king announced elections for a *Landtag* in whose single chamber the *Standesherren* would be overwhelmed by deputies elected from the rest of Württemberg society. Much to Frederick's displeasure, however, the newly elected parliament refused to endorse his constitution and demanded a say in the definition of its own future composition and function. In this controversy, members of the traditional nobility, eager to reclaim lost privileges, joined with young liberals like Friedrich List, who wanted to use the estates as a stepping-stone to a more progressive constitution. As had so often happened in Württemberg's past, the government exploited the divisions among its opponents, allying itself first with the left, then with the right. Finally, Frederick's successor, William I, effected a compromise with the conservative wing of the opposition. The constitution of 1819, promulgated by the crown and endorsed by the *Landtag*, balanced the interests of bureaucratic authority and aristocratic privilege: a bicameral legislature carefully protected the landed élite's position, while the declaration of universal *Grundrechte* was qualified by specific exceptions and left open to further limitation.[34]

Despite the prolonged debate and complex negotiations that preceded its proclamation, the Württemberg constitution, like those of Bavaria and Baden, was issued by royal decree. At least in theory, all three constitutions drew their authority from the monarch alone, who held power 'by the Grace of God'. The *Volk* was not involved, except as the grateful recipient of a royal gift. Moreover, the constitutions expressly stated that the prince's power remained undivided and undiminished. 'The king', proclaimed the Bavarian document, 'is the head of the state, unites in

[33] Lee, 'Constitutionalism', and *Politics*.
[34] Brandt, *Parlamentarismus*, surveys these developments in ch. 1.

himself all the rights of state power, and exercises them according to the definition in the present constitutional decree given by him.' Although, as the last phrase suggests, certain restrictions on monarchical authority were inevitable under a constitutional system. However qualified and vague, these documents established an autonomous, impersonal basis for political life which could only be altered within the context of the constitution itself. In this way, the constitutions extended the struggle of eighteenth-century reformers to escape what they called the arbitrariness, the *Willkür*, of the monarch's personal rule.

Equally important, the parliaments established by the south German constitutions introduced into the political system a new, potentially significant element. To be sure, the power of these representative institutions was carefully circumscribed; the composition of the ministry, foreign and military affairs, and effective control over the administration all remained exclusive prerogatives of the crown. Nevertheless, these representative bodies had some impressive sources of influence. First of all, their control over fiscal matters was substantial—indeed one of their essential functions was to legitimize the new forms of revenue required to ease the states' parlous financial conditions. Not only was the parliament's approval of new taxes constitutionally necessary; its supervisory authority over the budget was guaranteed. Second, the parliaments had the right to approve legislation, although in the Bavarian and Württemberg documents this right was restricted to laws concerning individual citizen's freedom or property. Finally, the parliaments could hold individual ministers responsible for unconstitutional behaviour and thus seek to ensure that the government kept within the legal limits of its power. While it was not easy for the new legislatures to use the instruments of power and influence open to them, they—and the constitutions of which they were a part— did represent a new definition of political legitimacy. In the constitutional states, the king still possessed a monopoly of power, but, in order to use this power legitimately, he had to act within the rules laid down by the constitution and in accord with the state's parliamentary representatives.

No one perceived the potential significance of these constitutions more clearly than Metternich, who watched political developments in the south-west with growing apprehension. For him, political opposition in all its forms was part of a seamless web; moderate parliamentarians and radical agitators, respectable journalists and Jacobin fanatics seemed interchangeable. He was afraid, therefore, that parliamentary institutions would provide a forum from which dangerous ideas could be broadcast throughout Europe. Moreover, Metternich feared that constitutional movements in the medium-sized states might gather momentum and create pressures for reform throughout the Confederation. This could only lead to trouble for Austria, which Gentz once called 'the last noble remnant of the old political system'. In the vast and diverse lands ruled by the Habsburgs, Metternich was convinced, any declaration of *Grunrechte* would be an invitation to chaos. Moreover, in a polity held together by dynastic loyalty, any constitutional restraint on monarchical authority would put the entire political system in jeopardy. As Karl von Kübeck had written in 1808, 'The Austrian state is a federal system of states. Every part of it is properly a state, united with the others not by contract or a common constitution, but solely through their common subjection to the reigning house.'[35]

The central question of Austrian domestic politics in the immediate post-war period was how to reorganize the administration, consolidate new territories, and resolve the monarchy's chronic financial difficulties *without* resorting to a constitutional solution. In the territories acquired or regained by the Habsburgs in 1815, Metternich encouraged the formation of estates, regional bodies in line with what he referred to as the 'multiplicity' of a realm composed of 'Länder different in climate, language, culture, and mores'. Each *Land* had 'its own *ständische Verfassung* received from the monarch'. Beyond the level of the individual *Land*, however, Metternich adopted administrative rather than constitutional measures. In 1814 Francis had finally accepted the chancellor's proposed *Staatsrat*, a council of high officials modelled after the Napoleonic *Conseil d'état*, which was supposed to broaden the basis of decision-making and co-ordinate governmental actions. Three years later Metternich suggested a more elaborate scheme for the bureaucratic reorganization in which four separate, territorially based ministries were to report to an *Oberster Kanzler* of domestic affairs. This was never adopted. Metternich also tried to deal with fiscal matters administratively. In 1814 Count Stadion was put in charge of a commission to handle the Herculean task of currency reform and then made head of a ministerial department responsible for finances. After several false starts, Stadion was able to establish a national bank based on private capital but under governmental supervision. Some degree of monetary stability—bought at a very high price for many Austrians—was achieved and the state's revenues gradually increased. Nevertheless, as we shall see, the Habsburgs continued to be plagued by financial problems.[36]

As was always the case, Metternich's domestic and foreign policies were inseparable. He believed that the spread of constitutionalism in the German states would not only endanger Austria's internal order but also weaken its international position. Thus, even if it were possible to halt the constitutional movement at the frontier, Metternich did not want Austria to be isolated in a confederation of constitutional states. In 1817 and early 1818, therefore, he sought to distract other German governments from their constitutional deliberations. He was encouraged when Bavaria, Württemberg, and Prussia instituted some kind of *Staatsrat*, which he had recommended as a surrogate parliament. But in the spring and summer of 1818, when first the Bavarians and then the Badenese proclaimed constitutions, Metternich's fear of Austrian isolation increased. At this point, the key player was Prussia; if the constitutional movement failed in Berlin, then the south-western states could be contained and their constitutions undermined, but if Prussia joined the constitutional ranks, Metternich's influence would be seriously diminished, both at home and abroad.

In mid–1818 there seemed to be reason to fear that Prussia would follow the Bavarian and Badenese example. Officials in Berlin, as in Munich and Karlsruhe, recognized that a constitution would help them to consolidate recent reforms and integrate newly acquired territories. Furthermore, Prussian finances required new fiscal policies that could best be legitimized through representative institutions. As we have seen, in 1811 and again in 1812 and 1815, Hardenberg had tried to use representative assemblies to provide a basis of support for his policies. He believed, as one of his associates told the Interim National Representation in 1815, that 'with representation, provincialism disappears, the different estates fuse into a powerful whole, thus will a nationality be formed'. Patriotic Prussians also hoped that constitutionalism would increase their state's influence over German Europe. Gneisenau, no less than Metternich, saw that constitutional questions had both a domestic and foreign political dimension:

If a new constitution is drafted soon for the revived and expanded Prussian

---

[36] See Metternich's memorandum of 27 Oct. 1817 in Metternich-Winneburg (ed.), *Papieren*, iii. 67–8. On his ideas for a *Staatsrat*, see *Memoirs*, ii. 519 ff.

monarchy, and granted to the people by the king, that will be the strongest bond binding the new acquisitions to the old provinces; the other German states will compare our condition with theirs, and thus the desire will be awakened to be united with us and the way will be clear for new acquisitions, made not by force of arms but by liberality of principles.

The disappointing outcome of the Vienna Congress seemed to make reform in Prussia all the more necessary. For example, Stein, who was disheartened by what he called 'the Confederation's mistaken constitutions', took consolation from the 'example . . . which several princes, and especially Prussia's, seem to want to set by granting their subjects wise and benevolent constitutions'.[37]

King Frederick William had first promised a constitution with representative institutions in his financial edict of 1810. On 22 May 1815, as the allied armies were preparing for their last battle against Napoleon, he issued a 'Verordnung über die zu bilende Repräsentation des Volks', which called for a constitutional commission to draft such a document 'without delay'. This decree stipulated that the parliament would be composed of deputies elected by the estates already existing in Prussia's core provinces and by those to be created in newly annexed territories. Some reformers were disturbed by this link between state and provincial representation; others, like Humboldt, believed that it might be advantageous to have representatives come 'from the provinces to the centre'.[38] No one, however, fully realized that the apparently straightforward language of the May decree actually blurred the distinction between two quite different forms of representation: on the one hand, a corporate arrangement in which a member was elected by, and operated within, a pre-defined status group, and on the other, a parliamentary system in which delegates functioned as representatives of the state as a whole. As we shall see, advocates of Prussian constitutionalism were never able to reconcile the king's commitment to corporately based, local *Stände* with their own hopes for an authentic national parliament.

After 1815 Frederick William's always tentative constitutional inclinations declined markedly. By defeating their foreign enemies, the reformers had lost their best argument for reform. The completion of the post-war settlement in 1815 further eased pressures for political change. At the same time, Hardenberg's enemies in the royal entourage—men like Friedrich Ancillon, the

---

[37] Koselleck, *Preussen*, p. 210; Walter Simon, 'Variations in Nationalism during the Great Reform Period in Prussia', *AHR* 59/2 (Jan. 1954), 309; Huber, i. 562.

[38] Huber, *Dokumente*, i. 56.

crown prince's tutor, and Count Wittgenstein, the court chamberlain—redoubled their efforts to influence the king. In the summer of 1815, for example, Frederick William's reactionary companions pressed into his hands a thin pamphlet by Professor Theodor Schmalz, a member of the University of Berlin's faculty of law. Harmlessly entitled 'Correction of an Item in the Bredow-Venturi Chronicle for 1808', Schmalz's work was a diatribe against the *Tugendbund*, a secret society that he claimed was at work throughout the kingdom. In another pamphlet, written during the constitutional debate itself, Schmalz tried to turn the reformers' patriotism back against their own enterprise. 'Are we', he asked, 'Germans or Frenchmen? This accursed hatching of constitutions has been a characteristically French vice for twenty-six years. Bonaparte created them by the dozen, like decrees; our political scribblers create them by the dozen, like newspaper articles.' This statement marks a moment in the history of German rhetoric that is worth noting: like so many of his heirs, Schmalz tried to discredit political reform by associating it with foreigners, revolutionaries, and intellectuals. In October 1815 he was awarded a medal by his grateful sovereign.[39]

More formidable than intriguers like Ancillon or propagandists like Schmalz were the opponents of constitutionalism in the landed nobility. The Junkers, it will be recalled, had been bitterly opposed to Stein's and Hardenberg's policies. The emancipation of the serfs, revision of local governmental institutions, and imposition of new taxes threatened their political, social, and economic authority. After 1815 they intensified their campaign to bring the process of reform to a stop. In their efforts to affect state policy, the Prussian nobility had a substantial advantage over the landed élites of the south or west; unlike the *Standesherren*, who confronted their states as outsiders, proud of their former sovereignty and disdainful of the polities in which they now found themselves, the Prussian nobility had served the Hohenzollern for more than a century. They could say to their king what most aristocrats in Bavaria, Baden, or Württemberg could not: this is our state, we have purchased our place in it with blood, we stand for its most cherished traditions. With some justification, the Junkers could even claim the victory over Napoleon for their own, since, from Yorck's patriotic treason to Blücher's decisive role at Waterloo,

---

[39] Simon, *Failure*, p. 119. See also Dann, 'Organisierung'; Vogel, 'Beamtenkonservatismus'.

they had played a prominent part in the rebirth of Prussian military power.[40]

When faced with these contrary winds of aristocratic opposition, Hardenberg tried to set a characteristically moderate course. In 1816 he altered his agrarian policies to meet some of the Junkers' objections. At the same time he channelled his constitutional efforts into a series of bureaucratic reforms, culminating in the creation of a Prussian *Staatsrat* in March 1817. Nevertheless, he continued to hope that the king would keep his constitutional promises. After the long-awaited constitutional commission had its first and only meeting in July 1817, government agents spent the rest of the year touring the provinces, gathering data on existing institutions, and testing opinion on proposed changes. In February 1818 Hardenberg assured the other members of the Confederation that, since the preliminary work had been done, the way to a national representation was open. He was wrong. The king, who had not been consulted about Hardenberg's declaration, sharply reprimanded his chancellor and informed him that a constitutional timetable was no longer possible. The balance of power had clearly shifted away from reform.[41]

A critical phase in the conflict over the future of Prussian—and thus of German—constitutionalism was the months between the proclamation of the Bavarian and Baden constitutions in the spring and summer of 1818 and the reactionary decrees issued after Kotzebue's murder the following summer. During this period Hardenberg pressed on with his plans, apparently still in the hope that he could win over his always indecisive sovereign. Humboldt was appointed 'Minister for Estate Affairs [*ständische Angelegenheiten*]' in January 1819 and a few weeks later presented an eloquent memorandum to Frederick William in defence of representative institutions.[42] Unfortunately, Hardenberg and Humboldt were bitter enemies, whose personal animosity hindered their co-operation on behalf of the political goals they shared. But more important than the reformers' uncertainties and divisions was the effectiveness of the campaign Metternich mounted as soon as the south German constitutions were decreed. At the European Congress held at Aachen in September 1818, the Austrian

---

[40] See above, Ch. 5, sect. iii. For more on the Junkers as a social group, see below, Ch. 8, sect. ii.

[41] There is a good clear account of these developments in Simon, *Failure*, chs. 8, 11. Huber, i. 290–311 provides a concise summary, while Koselleck, *Preussen*, gives the richest and most subtle analysis.

[42] *Werke*, iv. 433–500.

chancellor warned of a new wave of revolutionary violence against which the forces of order must stand united. For the next several months he frequently pointed out the connection between radical unrest and constitutional representation. For example, in two memoranda that he sent to the Prussian government and, under separate cover, to King Frederick William in November 1818, he declared: 'A central representation through representatives of the *Volk* will be the dissolution of Prussia . . . because such an innovation cannot be introduced into a great state without a revolution or without leading to a revolution'. Prussia's geographical position and composition, he went on, is incompatible with a central parliament, above all because Prussia needs a 'free and solid military force and this can and will never coexist with a purely representative system'. Here again we see an effort to attack the reformers with their own weapons; military strength, Metternich tried to convince the king, was fundamentally incompatible with, not the necessary by-product of, progressive political change.[43]

Metternich saw Sand's murder of Kotzebue as a godsend. In July 1819 he rushed to Teplitz where Frederick William was on holiday and repeated his insistence that a representative constitution was merely the first step on the road to revolution. This time the king was in full agreement. He summoned Hardenberg and commanded him to join with Metternich in issuing a communiqué that formally renounced efforts to introduce a 'universal representation of the *Volk*', which would be, he claimed, 'incompatible with the territorial and political structure of his realm'. The king's commitment to reaction was now complete. He instructed the Prussian government to enforce fully the Karlsbad decrees; in the autumn he blocked Hardenberg's efforts to get the constitutional process going again. By December, Humboldt and several other veteran reformers, including General von Boyen, resigned. Metternich had won.[44]

Metternich consolidated his victory over the constitutional movement with the Vienna *Schlussakte* of 1820, which, in contrast to the *Bundesakte* of 1815, emphasized monarchical power. Reluctantly, Metternich accepted a phrase acknowledging that a ruler might be 'constitutionally obliged to co-operate with his estates in the exercise of particular rights', but he insisted that this be preceded by a statement of the sovereign's monopoly over

---

[43] Metternich-Winneburg (ed.), *Papieren*, iii. 171.

[44] Metternich's own account of this meeting is in his *Memoirs*, iii. 295. On the decrees, see above, sect. i.

political power: 'Since the German Confederation is composed, with the exception of the free cities, of sovereign princes, it follows that according to this document the entire power of the state must remain united in the sovereign.' (Article Fifty-seven). The next article stipulated that no prince could be constitutionally prevented from fulfilling his duties to the Confederation. Finally, the *Schlussakte* underscored the need to avoid turning parliaments into centres of agitation. According to Article Fifty-nine, neither the proceedings nor the publications of a German parliament could be allowed to threaten the domestic order of any individual German state or of Germany as a whole. Read in the light of the threat of counter-revolutionary intervention made in other articles, these statements in defence of princely authority were supposed to put the south German states on notice that they would have to limit the political possibilities offered by their constitutions. According to Gentz, the acceptance of these articles represented 'the greatest and most significant results of negotiations in our time, a victory more important than the battle of Leipzig'.[45]

With the constitutional option closed, the Prussian government had to follow the Austrian example in seeking solutions to their fiscal and administrative problems. By 1820 financial matters were the most pressing concern in Berlin, since Prussia, like most other states, was deeply in debt. Due to rearmament, war, and indemnities, the national debt had risen from forty-eight million taler in 1979, to one hundred million in 1810, and then to over two hundred million in 1815. The search for a way to deal with this matter had always been an important part of Hardenberg's constitutional endeavours. In 1820 the king issued a series of financial edicts that consolidated the debt, established a schedule of amortization, and reformed the tax structure. Hardenberg did manage to get Frederick William to promise to consult with the estates before incurring any new debts, but the impetus of Prussian fiscal policy had clearly shifted from a constitutional to an administrative solution. In Prussia, as in Austria, the major efforts to master the state's financial difficulties were made by ministers and bankers, not by the representatives of *Stände* or *Volk*.[46]

By the time of Hardenberg's death in 1822 the Prussian constitutional movement had come to a halt. The following year the king formally brought to an end the process begun thirteen years earlier when he issued a series of decrees establishing

[45] Huber, *Dokumente*, i. 88–9; Srbik, *Metternich*, i. 597.
[46] Obenaus, 'Finanzkrise'.

provincial *Stände*, organized 'in the spirit of the old German constitutions'. These bodies, which were corporately elected and organized, had highly restricted memberships and narrowly defined areas of competence. Lest they be thought of as the foundation for the kind of representation suggested in his decree of January 1815, the king expressly disassociated the provincial assemblies from any discussion of a national parliament.[47]

The constitutional conflicts which so occupied German statesmen between 1815 and 1820 helped to clarify the distinctions between corporate and representative constitutions, which had remained obscure in earlier formulations such as Dahlmann's 'Ein Wort über Verfassung', Frederick William's declaration of January 1815, and Article Thirteen of the *Bundesakte*. After 1815 the enemies of reform, led by Metternich, tried to disassociate legitimate, conservative constitutions from the illegitimate and subversive ones. For example, in his essay 'On the Difference between *landständische* and Representative Constitutions', written to guide the discussion at the Karlsbad conference of 1819, Gentz advocated Estates which rested on what he called 'the natural foundation of a well-ordered civil society', take into account corporate rights and relationships, can be legally modified in the course of time, and 'do not transgress the essential rights of the sovereign'.[48] For Gentz and his masters, this final clause was essential; they cared much more about the competence than about the composition of representative institutions. They favoured regional, corporately organized *Stände* because they did not expect these bodies to pose a threat to monarchical authority.

iii. THE CONSOLIDATION OF THE BEAMTENSTAAT

'Freedom', wrote B. G. Niebuhr in 1815, 'depends much more on the administration [*Verwaltung*] than the constitution [*Verfassung*].' Although by *Verwaltung* Niebuhr seems to have had in mind 'self-administration' as envisioned in Stein's municipal government decree, his remark was quickly taken up by contemporaries and has often been cited by historians as an example of Germans' belief in the superiority of bureaucratic over constitutional government.

---

[47] The best account of the provincial *Stände* is Obenaus, *Anfänge*.

[48] Udo Bermbach, 'Über Landstände: Zur Theorie der Repräsentation im deutschen Vormärz', in C. J. Friedrich and B. Reifenberg (eds.), *Sprache und Politik* (Heidelberg, 1968), 246. See also Brandt, *Repräsentation*.

That the bureaucracy played a central role in German political thought and action is beyond dispute. But during the first three decades of the nineteenth century bureaucratic and constitutional developments were not antithetical; both were means to consolidate the sovereign power and political cohesion of states, to limit the arbitrary will of the ruler, and to contain the residual privileges of traditional élites and institutions. To Montgelas, for instance, one purpose of the Bavarian constitution was to provide Bavaria's subjects with 'the advantages of nearer association with administrative authority'.[49] Historically, therefore, the two developments moved in tandem: between 1815 and 1820 several states, mostly in the south-west, achieved both constitutions and laws guaranteeing bureaucrats' rights and privileges; after a relatively unproductive decade on both fronts, another group of states followed in the early 1830s; finally, most of those remaining, including Prussia, acquired constitutions and administrative codes in the wake of the revolution of 1848. The emergence of constitutional government and the consolidation of bureaucratic authority were part of the same historical process, frequently advocated by the same people, opposed by the same enemies, and seeking to advance the same goals.[50]

Nowhere can the interaction of *Verwaltung* and *Verfassung* be better observed than in Baden, which was at once the most highly bureaucratized and the most genuinely constitutional German state. Article Seven of Baden's constitution gave 'ministers of state and the entire civil service' responsibility for 'the precise administration of the constitution'. Article Twenty-four guaranteed the bureaucracy's special legal status, which was then clarified and emended in the *Beamtenedikt* of 1819. This document established a privileged category of civil servants, set apart from state employees such as clergymen, courtiers, and army officers, and from those in the lower ranks of the administration itself, such as clerks, messengers, guards, and other subalterns. To the 'secular, civil state servants' at the top of the administration, the edict of 1819 promised job

[49] Koselleck, *Preussen*, p. 217; Walker, *Home Towns*, p. 201.

[50] The origins of state bureaucracies is discussed above in Ch. 1, their reform and consolidation during the revolutionary era in Ch. 5. On the evolution of bureaucratic institutions after 1815, see the essays in Conze (ed.), *Staat*; Henning, *Beamtenschaft*; Wunder, *Geschichte*. Hubatsch (ed.), *Grundriss*, has a great deal of information on administrative organization and personnel. Lenore O'Boyle, 'Some Recent Studies of Nineteenth Century European Bureaucracy: Problems of Analysis', *CEH* 19/4 (1986), 386–408, examines the problem of bureaucracy in a European context.

security, independence, and an extraordinary amount of autonomy. Article One made their positions 'irrevocable after five years
of service'. Only judicial action—that is, a trial by his peers—could
deprive a bureaucrat of his salary and his status; the ruler could only
remove him from a particular post, not from the service itself. At
the same time, the edict stipulated a complex system of rules
governing appointment and promotion. Training programmes,
regular examinations, and other carefully defined procedures
combined to provide modes of recruitment and advancement that
remained firmly in the hands of the bureaucrats themselves.[51]

In the other constitutional states of the south-west, officials used
the power they had attained during the era of reform to secure their
own special status. As early as 1805 Montgelas issued a decree 'on
state servants' conditions of employment, with special reference to
their status and pay', which contained provisions on bureaucratic
tenure, salary, and self-government. As in Baden, the Bavarian
constitution of 1818 guaranteed officials' social position with an
article on 'Conditions of Service and Pension Rights'. A new
version of the 1805 edict, issued as an amendment to the
constitution, regulated the conduct of Bavarian officials until the
early twentieth century. In Württemberg, the definition of officials'
legal status got caught up in the constitutional conflict between the
king and the *Stände*, and thus became an integral part of the final
settlement. Section Four of the constitution of 1819 gave Württemberg's bureaucrats the same kind of job security and institutional
autonomy that obtained in Baden and Bavaria. In all three states,
therefore, the formulation of a representative constitution was
linked to the bureaucracy's final transformation from an instrument
of the ruler's will into an independent agent of the state.[52]

Although Prussia did not pass a comprehensive set of laws on the
bureaucracy until the early 1850s, Prussian officials managed to
acquire piecemeal most of what their south-western colleagues
achieved in 1818 and 1819. As we know, by the middle of the
eighteenth century the Hohenzollern's servants had begun to think
of themselves as an independent political élite—much to the
consternation of a wilful sovereign like Frederick the Great. An
examination system had been in use for judicial officials since the
1750s and for administrators since the 1770s. The *Allgemeines
Landrecht* of 1794 gave civil servants a social status just below the

---

[51] Huber, *Dokumente*, i. 158–9. In addition to Lee, *Politics*, see Wolfram Fischer's
essay in Conze (ed.), *Staat*.

[52] Wunder, *Privilegierung*; Bleek, *Kameralausbildung*.

traditional nobility, and, in language quite similar to that used in later legislation, established their paramount political importance: 'Military and civil officials are expressly commissioned to maintain and further the state's security, good order, and welfare.' After the turn of the century, Prussian officials were able to use these legal provisions, combined with regulations passed during the era of reform, to secure control over their own institutions. Elaborate internal reviews were necessary before a member of the bureaucracy could be dismissed. Examinations and interviews were required for appointment and promotion. Pension rights and a special tax status assured officials' material well-being. Moreover, Stein's governmental reorganization of 1808 reinforced the bureaucracy's central place in the political system by tightening its line of command, clarifying its internal organization, and strengthening its position *vis-à-vis* the king and his advisers.[53]

Prussian political discourse after 1800 persistently associated the problems of *Verwaltung* and *Verfassung*. Karl Friedrich von Beyme, for instance, wrote in 1818 that the state's bureaucratic structure had enabled Prussia to function 'in the spirit of a representative constitution' and thus 'not to miss its absence in fact'. Hardenberg's *Staatsrat*, established the year before, had been designed as the prelude to, or perhaps the substitute for, a formal constitution. The *Staatsrat* was composed of princes of the royal house, high-ranking officers, officials, and judges, who met together and discussed issues on an equal basis. In the words of one contemporary, this body served as 'an intra-administrative parliament'. Similarly, the office of *Oberpräsident*, the highest official in Prussia's provinces, had representative as well as bureaucratic functions: the president chaired the province's assemblies, co-ordinated its administrative agencies, and provided a channel between province and central government. After the notion of a national parliament had been abandoned, the *Oberpräsident* became the most important spokesman for the province's special interests, which he sometimes defended against the interests of his ministerial superiors in Berlin.

'The strength of the state lies in the constitutional order of the administration', said Eduard Gans in 1832, and 'civil freedom lies in its legal order'. In Prussia, he went on, administrator and subject do not confront each other as one form of power against another, but rather, 'since the administrators are and can only act as organs of the law, they stand for those they administer and are to be seen as their representatives'. Officials could perform this representative

---

[53] The best treatment of these matters is Koselleck, *Preussen*.

function because, as one of them put it, 'in their free activity on behalf of the state's interests, they represent the highest insight which social life could achieve through the progressive movement of the spirit'. As the expression of society's best interests, the Prussian bureaucracy saw itself as providing the kind of reconciliation between society and government granted to the south-western states in their constitutions of 1818 and 1819.[54]

Like its Prussian counterpart, the Austrian bureaucracy was the product of monarchical state-building in the eighteenth century. Under Maria Theresa and even more emphati-cally under Joseph II, the Habsburgs' servants had sought to extend their power over society, limit local authorities, and provide the basis for an efficient, modern polity. But, while the Austrian civil service became an important political force, it did not acquire the autonomy enjoyed by its counterparts elsewhere. Austrian officials continued to be subject to supervision and interference from the monarch and his advisers, who took advantage of the complex and uneven structure of the administration to play one section or group against another. Lines of bureaucratic authority remained unclear, criteria for promotion inconsistent, modes of training unsettled. An Austrian official's career, therefore, was less secure than in many other states, his sense of mastery and institutional independence more fragile. As a result, in the words of one not unsympathetic student of the Austrian scene, 'Deep pessimism crippled the most able officials' pleasure in their work, formalistic routine and a reluctance to take responsibility triumphed.'[55]

Closely connected to the Austrian administration's inability to acquire professional security and institutional self-governance was the failure of the government to effect a rational organization of tasks and jurisdictions. While reformers in other German states were introducing ministerial systems, the Habsburgs kept their eighteenth-century mode of organization, which combined territorial and functional jurisdictions. The same forces that precluded constitutional reform also inhibited bureaucratic reorganization; both were seen as threats to the dynastic hegemony upon which the Habsburg realm ultimately seemed to rest. In no other German

---

[54] Quotations from Koselleck, *Preussen*, pp. 282–3; Hans Branig, 'Wesen und Geist des höheren Verwaltungsbeamten in Preussen in der Zeit des Vormärz', in F. Benninghoven and C. Lowenthal-Hensel (eds.), *Neue Forschungen zur brandenburg-preussischen Geschichte* (Vienna, 1979), 167.

[55] Walter, *Verfassungs- und Verwaltungsgeschichte*, p. 126. On the Austrian administration, see Brunner's essay in Conze (ed.), *Staat*; Srbik, *Metternich*, i. 452 ff.; Brandt, *Neoabsolutismus*, i. ch. 1.

state could someone say with more certainty, 'the state is the court'. Nowhere else could a monarch express the nature of his state more clearly than Francis did in 1813 when, in a manifesto to his people, he crossed out the word 'fatherland' and wrote instead 'emperor'. Metternich, who realized that governmental reform was necessary, was none the less convinced that the emperor was 'the only true centre of the state's power'. An independent bureaucracy, like a constitution, was unacceptable because it might compete with the monarch for that central space.[56]

In most of German Europe, except for the Habsburg lands and some of the smaller, *altständische* polities, the balance of political power after 1815 had clearly shifted from the ruler to the professional civil service. Even though monarchical authority was everywhere important in both theory and practice, the development of well-defined lines of ministerial jurisdiction made it difficult for a ruler to outflank the bureaucracy with his own informal advisers. Similarly, the requirement of ministerial counter-signatures made it harder for him to act on his own and the network of examinations and regulations limited his ability to push forward unqualified favourites. More and more, a monarch acted with and through his ministers, depended upon them for advice and information, and defied them only on the most trivial or the most serious matters. We see here, therefore, the beginning of the process so eloquently described by Max Weber a century later:

The absolute monarch . . . is powerless in the face of the superior knowledge of the bureaucratic expert. . . . Under the rule of expert knowledge, the influence of the monarch can attain steadiness only through continuous communication with bureaucratic chiefs which is methodically planned and directed by the central head of the bureaucracy.

Early nineteenth-century political thinkers were quick to pick up the theoretical significance of this practical dependence of the ruler on his servants. As one observer put it in 1842, the administration has become the real sovereign, the monarch is now only 'sovereignty's representation'. Friedrich Murhard, an influential member of the liberal opposition, was convinced that the bureaucracy had become 'the only active power in the life and institutions of the state'.[57]

The most powerful and influential defence of the bureaucracy's political pre-eminence was provided by G. W. F. Hegel, who

[56] Walter, *Verfassungs- und Verwaltungsgeschichte*, p. 121; Srbik, *Metternich*, i. 433.

[57] Weber, *Economy*, ii. 993; Koselleck in Conze (ed.), *Staat*, p. 87; Wilhelm, *Idee*, p. 11.

became professor of philosophy at the University of Berlin in 1818 and was soon regarded as the intellectual paladin of the Prussian state. In the light of his previous ideas and experience, Hegel was an unlikely spokesman for either Prussia or the bureaucracy—that he became one testifies to the magnetic attraction exerted by Prussia and its institutions over German political thought and action. Between his flight from battle-torn Jena in 1806 and his arrival in the Prussian capital twelve years later, Hegel had held a variety of jobs—as a journalist in Bamberg, a high school teacher in Nuremberg, and finally, at the age of forty-six, as a professor in Heidelberg. Throughout this turbulent time he displayed little sympathy for the Hohenzollern state or for the men running it; he had shed no tears for the losers at Jena, evidently ignored the reform movement under Stein and Hardenberg, and was contemptuous of the 'Cossacks, Bashkirs, Prussian patriots, and all sorts of liberators' who combined to defeat Napoleon. But Hegel was even more hostile to those who hoped to restore the old order. 'We must', he told his students and colleagues in 1815, 'oppose this need which always uselessly misses the past and yearns for it.' On this ground, in 1817 he took the side of King Frederick against the Württemberg *Stände*; the monarch, he believed, represented the common good and the future, while the *Stände* stood for private interests and outmoded tradition. At his inaugural lecture in Berlin, he transferred these preferences to Prussia, which he praised for having saved itself 'through intellectual superiority' and for being a state where 'culture and the flourishing of scholarship are among the essential elements in political life'. The instrument and beneficiary of this fusion of intellect and politics was the bureaucracy.[58]

In 1821, three years after taking up his duties in Berlin, Hegel published the *Grundlinien der Philosophie des Rechts*, an extraordinarily rich and subtle statement of his political convictions. His subject, as the title tells us, is not law in the narrow sense, but *Recht*, a broad and inclusive category embracing the operation of law and the principles of justice in private, social, and political life. In the course of his analysis of European institutions from this perspective, Hegel offered an interconnected set of social, political,

---

[58] Quotations from Avineri, *Hegel's Theory*, pp. 70–1; Hegel 'Anrede an seine Zuhörer bei der Eröffnung seiner Vorlesungen in Berlin am 22. Oktober 1818', in *Sämtliche Werke* (Leipzig, 1911), v. p. lxxvii. Rosenzweig, *Hegel*, ii, has the relevant biographical information. On the development of his philosophy, see above, Ch. 6, sect. ii.

and philosophical arguments for bureaucratic pre-eminence. 'Civil servants and members of the executive', he maintained, 'constitute the greater part of the middle class, the class in which the consciousness of right and the developed intelligence of the mass of the people is found.' Because they do not depend on the market for their income, civil servants are not driven by self-interest; they are conscious of society's needs, but not corrupted by its divisions. The fact that *Beamten* form a 'universal stratum', at once superior to and representative of social interests, enables them to define and defend the general welfare. In the modern world, this political role is especially necessary to balance the dynamism of what Hegel called 'civil society', the realm of economic interests and market relationships. Civil society always presents the danger of chaos: 'Particularity by itself, given free reign in every direction to satisfy its needs, accidental caprices, and subjective desires, destroys itself. . . .'[59] Against these self-destructive forces, the state provides the most effective barrier, not only because its servants stand above society, but also because they represent true reason. Philosophically, the state's system of *Recht*, the law of which the bureaucracy is the agent and expression, takes precedence over the sentimentally based rules of family life or the self-interested calculations of civil society. Unlike the family, which compels obedience through love, or the market, which achieves co-operation through conflict and competition, the state appeals to its citizens on the basis of what is right for all. That is why its laws are rational and why obeying them involves the greatest possible freedom.[60]

One may well wonder how many people worked their way through the complex skein of arguments and analysis out of which Hegel's *Philosophie des Rechts* is woven. Nevertheless, the book is a central text for the evolution of German politics because it captures the assumptions upon which the bureaucracy's claim to power rested. Their alleged neutrality was the heart of the bureaucrats' claim to regulate the social process. Their defence of political stability, guaranteed by their constitutional position, was the basis of their claim to protect society from its own inherent inclination to conflict and chaos. The rationality of their procedures, enshrined in their training and regulations, represented the ultimate justification

[59] *Hegel's Philosophy of Right*, pp. 193, 123. For his formulation of the modern state's 'prodigious strength and depth', see p. 161.

[60] Like Hegel, Max Weber believed that the bureaucracy was 'formally the most rational means of exercising authority over human beings' (*Economy*, i. 223), but of course for him 'rationality' had a very different meaning.

for their claim to legitimacy at a time when religious values and dynastic rights no longer seemed valid.

Whether they liked it or not, after 1815 most contemporaries agreed that the bureaucracy was the dominant political force in German life. Officials, Friedrich Bülau wrote, were 'the most important class of citizens for the conduct of public affairs'. The young Otto von Bismarck, disillusioned by his recent—and brief—experience as a civil servant, lamented in 1838 that 'in order to take part in public life, one must be a salaried and dependent servant of the state, one must belong completely to the bureaucratic caste. . . .' To an English visitor, this bureaucratic monopoly seemed especially striking: 'The political power of the state over private free agency is the basis of all social institutions in Germany.' In order to get a clearer picture of what this power involved, we must now turn from such general statements to a more precise consideration of the bureaucracy's role in Germans' political and social lives.[61]

The obvious place to start is with what we can call the bureaucracy's extractive function. From its very beginning, the administration's chief purpose had been to find resources to support the ruler's military, political, and cultural endeavours. The characteristic servants of the early state were tax collectors, excisemen, and other fiscal agents to whom princes had turned in order to expand their revenues. But, while many states' revenues did increase under the old regime, most of their fiscal efforts were uneven, discontinuous, and inefficient. Rulers continued to rely mainly on their own domains, government monopolies, special levies, and high interest loans from private bankers. By the turn of the century, however, the demands of war and revolution had made these fiscal policies as outmoded as old-regime strategy and statecraft. To meet the expenses involved in being Napoleon's enemy or ally, German states created financial systems that often had to be legitimized through new constitutions and administered through reformed bureaucracies. The relative importance of revenue from royal domains, monopolies, and loans declined significantly. In the Prussian budget of 1821, for example, over 70 per cent of the state's income was derived from taxes, tolls, and tariffs. The formulation of an annual budget, the control over state expenses, and the collection and management of revenues were the bureaucracy's most important tasks, a primary sources of influence

---

[61] Wilhelm, *Idee*, p. 11; Rothfels (ed.), *Bismarck*, p. 4; Laing, *Notes*, p. 61.

over state policy, and significant instruments for controlling social processes.[62]

The state's need for money continued to drive many of its activities. For instance, the *Zollverein*, perhaps the period's most famous bureaucratic accomplishment, was essentially a fiscal measure which began in 1818 when Prussia decreed a tariff law that was designed to increase her revenues and integrate her newly acquired territories. Fiscally, this measure seems to have worked: in 1821 customs dues amounted to over fifteen million taler, by far the largest source of income in the budget. However, by imposing duties and, equally important, by seeking to enforce them, Berlin exerted considerable economic pressure on its neighbours, some of whom were surrounded by Prussian territory. Moreover, since the Hohenzollern's western lands were not contiguous with the rest of the monarchy, complete economic unity naturally involved negoti-ations with other states. The Prussian tariff of 1818, therefore, set off a chain of responses, countermeasures, and negotiations, which resulted in a series of agreements between Prussia and other states, and then in a tariff union that by the mid–1830s embraced Prussia, the medium-sized states, and most of their smaller enclaves and neighbours. Although often absorbed into the story of national unification, the *Zollverein* is better seen in the context of the individual state's struggle for financial solvency and economic consolidation.[63]

After 1815 more and more state revenues went to paying administrative costs and supplying social services. To be sure, in the nineteenth century, as in the eighteenth, the army was the single largest item in the budgets of most major states: military expenses comprised almost half of the Prussian budget of 1821. However, while the absolute cost of the army remained about the same—in Prussia it was 22.8 million taler in 1821 and 25.8 million in 1847—its relative share in the total budget declined and other sorts of expenditures correspondingly increased—in the Prussian case, from 13.2 million taler in 1821 to 23.9 million in 1847. These figures reflect a slow, silent revolution in the relationship of state and society, a revolution intimately tied up with, and no less important than, the constitutional developments and party conflicts to which most political history is devoted. Under the old regime,

[62] See above, Chs. 1 and 5. Ullmann summarizes the financial problems of two *Mittelstaaten* in 'Schulden', pp. 32–67. The Prussian budget is from Zorn, in *HWSG* ii. 174 ff. See also Gerloff, 'Staatshaushalt', iii. 5.

[63] On the *Zollverein*, see below, Ch. 8, sect. iii.

the state apparatus had taken from society what was needed to pay for the monarch's courtly pleasures, military ambitions, and cultural accomplishments. In the nineteenth century, the state became more insistent and inventive about what it could take but also more effective and ambitious about what it should offer in return.

To the officials who laid the groundwork for the *Beamtenstaat*, there was no more important mission for the state than education. Like military service and taxation, education was one of those new rights and obligations that states conveyed and imposed upon their citizens. Teachers should, in the words of a Bavarian document from 1806, further 'the formation [*Bildung*] of the nation and the enlightenment of the Volk over their most sacred and important affairs'. These goals required the creation of a complex apparatus to build schools, train teachers, and define curricula. Progress was slower than official statements of intent might lead one to expect. Prussia, for instance, budgeted just two million taler for all religious and educational expenses in 1821, and less than four million in 1847. Nevertheless, by mid-century there were 29,000 teachers at work in Prussia, where over 80 per cent of the school-age population received some kind of formal training. Most other states did less well, but almost everywhere the state acknowledged its responsibility to educate its subjects and had begun to lay the institutional foundations for fulfilling this responsibility.[64]

Governments also began to expand their role in improving health care. That public health was an administrative task had been one of cameralism's central tenets. As early as 1779, for example, J. P. Frank had begun to publish his classic multi-volume treatise, *System einer vollständigen medizinischen Policey*, which was supposed to cover 'everything having to do with the administration of public health from procreation to death and burial'. But it took states until well into the nineteenth century before they had the institutional or intellectual resources necessary even to begin fulfilling the aspirations of theorists like Frank. Slowly, governments made some limited headway in the struggle against disease: they established districts under a public health officer, passed laws regulating patent

[64] Blessing, *Staat*, p. 30. On Suevern, see Karl Schleunes, 'Enlightenment, Reform, Reaction: The Schooling Revolution in Prussia', *CEH* 12/4 (1979), 315–42. Kenneth Barkin provides an interesting analysis of the state's intentions and accomplishments in his essay on 'Social Control and the Volksschule in Vormärz Prussia', *CEH* 16/1 (1983), 31–52. Additional literature on the history of German education can be found above, Ch. 2, sect. iv, n. 108 and below, Ch. 8, sect. iv, n. 100.

medicines, established standards and issued licenses for various sorts of medical practitioners, gathered statistics on disease and mortality, sponsored epidemiological research, and made a few rudimentary improvements in sanitation systems and water supply. Perhaps the only clear triumph in the field of preventive medicine came from the discovery of inoculation against smallpox, which was being used in some German regions by the 1750s. After inoculation was made compulsory by many states during the first decades of the nineteenth century, the number of deaths from smallpox decreased dramatically—in Prussia, for example, from around 40,000 to 3,000 a year.[65]

As the reader will recall, cameralist theory and practice also defined an important economic role for the state. In the nineteenth century, states continued to own land, operate enterprises, and monopolize the production and distribution of certain products, such as salt. In some places, officials encouraged the dissemination of technical knowledge and assisted what they took to be worthy business enterprises. How much these various activities did in fact promote economic development is now a matter of intense scholarly controversy, but it does seem evident that the importance of the state's role has usually been overestimated by German economic historians.[66] Government support for the economy was probably most effective when it was indirect—and usually unintentional. The creation of unified legal systems, for instance, helped promote larger markets for goods, labour, and capital. Similarly, government participation in the construction of hard surface roads and railroads also served to establish an infrastructure for economic growth. Of course, roads and railroads also enhanced the political and military power of the state: for the expansion of bureaucratic authority, Max Weber wrote, these new means of communication 'frequently play a role similar to that of the canals

[65] Jan Brügelmann, *Der Blick des Arztes auf die Krankheit im Alltag, 1779–1850* (Cologne, 1962), 12–13. On the development of public health, see Frevert, *Krankheit*, especially pp. 69 ff; on smallpox; Evans, *Death*, pp. 218 ff.

[66] For a characteristic statement of the state's positive role in economic development, see W. O. Henderson, *The State and the Industrial Revolution in Prussia, 1740–1870* (Liverpool, 1958). More sceptical assessments can be found in Pollard, *Conquest*, pp. 161 ff.; Hubert Kieswetter, 'Erklärungshypothesen zur regionalen Industrialisierung in Deutschland im 19. Jahrhundert', *VSWG* 57/3 (1980), 305–33; and, on Austria, Komlos, *Monarchy*. For a general introduction to nineteenth-century political economy, see Hans Jaeger, *Geschichte der Wirtschaftsordnung in Deutschland* (Frankfurt, 1988). Wehler, *Gesellschaftsgeschichte*, ibid ii, has a full discussion of these issues and an extensive bibliography.

of Mesopotamia and the regulation of the Nile in the ancient orient'.[67]

Everywhere that governments performed services they also imposed controls. To monitor the quality of education, governments had to provide pedagogical training, administer examinations to both teachers and pupils, and supervise instruction. In order to bring educational advantages to as many of its citizens as possible, the state had to be prepared to compel parents to send their children to school. The same situation existed in the area of public health, where regulation and compulsion were always of central importance. In social and economic matters, too, the new freedoms promised by bureaucratic reform often meant new rules. If, for instance, reformers granted citizens the right to start an enterprise (*Gewerbefreiheit*), they not only had to enforce this right against the resistance of the guilds, they also had to take over the task of licensing and regulation. In a more direct and obvious fashion, the state's rather desultory efforts to protect workers and impose minimal safety standards in the workplace produced new rules and a new group of supervisory personnel. To some degree, therefore, what an English visitor noted about Prussian economic policy was true of the entire range of the bureaucracy's activities: 'The monarch', wrote Thomas Hodgskin in 1820, 'set trade free from the fetters of ancient custom, and he pinioned it with his own. . . . By the abolition of all the ancient regulations, the sovereign increased his own power and influence very much.'[68]

In religious affairs, new responsibilities came to the states as a result of the political transformations effected by Napoleon. The destruction of the old ecclesiastical polities, secularization of church lands, and collapse of imperial institutions produced a constitutional crisis within German Catholicism. Many of the sources of religious influence available in the old Reich were now gone. the number of Catholic princes was significantly reduced; millions of Catholics lived as minorities within Protestant states; even the old diocesan boundaries had lost their meaning. At the Congress of Vienna, some Catholic leaders tried to find a solution to these problems for the entire German church, but their efforts were defeated by an alliance of the smaller states and the papacy. The

[67] Weber, *Economy*, ii. 973.

[68] Hodgskin, *Travels*, i. 98–9. For some examples, see Maynes, *Schooling*, pp. 84–5, Frevert, *Krankheit*, pp. 82–3. Wolfgang Köllmann discusses the state's efforts to regulate labour conditions in his article, 'Die Anfänge der staatlichen Sozialpolitik in Preussen bis 1869', *VSWG* 53/1 (1966), 28–52.

Bundesakte of 1815 said nothing about church matters beyond a brief statement promising political equality to the members of all the Christian denominations. As in so many other aspects of German political life, the Confederation left the settlement of religious affairs up to the individual states, which set out to regulate them through bilateral agreements with the papacy.[69]

The first formal concordat between a German state and Rome was signed by Bavaria in 1817 and issued, together with other decrees regulating the church, as part of the constitutional settlements of 1818. According to this agreement, the Bavarian government recognized the church's authority on religious matters, reopened some institutions closed during the secularization drive, and allowed bishops to communicate directly with the pope. In return, the papacy acknowledged the loss of church properties, brought diocesan boundaries into conformity with the state's, moved an episcopal see from Freising to Munich, and agreed to give the government control over the selection of bishops. During the next decade, the papacy and other German governments reached similar accords, often after intense and complex negotiations. While the details of these agreements varied, everywhere they gave governments a say in the internal workings of the church and made the sovereign states the primary organizational unit for German Catholics. The result was to increase greatly the state's leverage over ecclesiastical affairs, but also, as we shall see in a later chapter, to encourage the transformation of religious conflicts into political ones.[70]

The political reorganization of German Europe also presented the states with the need to formulate policies towards their Jewish minorities. Under the old regime, the social and political status of Jews had been defined by a diverse set of local customs and traditional restraints. Jews were tolerated in some areas, banned from others; they could engage in some occupations, but were excluded from others. When it served their interests, traditional states granted certain Jews special privileges; more frequently, they were kept on the fringes of politics and society. In the last decades of the eighteenth century a few governments tried to develop uniform, coherent rules governing Jews. As we saw in Chapter 5, these efforts increased during the revolutionary era, when states

[69] The best brief introduction to these issues is Chadwick, *Popes*, pp. 539 ff. See also Aubert *et al.* (eds.), *Church*.

[70] Blessing, *Staat*, has a great deal of information on the Bavarian situation. The relevant documents are in Huber and Huber (eds.), *Staat*.

found themselves confronting a bewildering variety of regulations in their newly acquired territories. As a result, several reform administrations abolished some of the most onerous restraints on Jews' freedom. After 1815, however, the movement towards legal emancipation slowed, partly because of conservative pressures within the governments, partly because of resistance from communities where hostility towards Jews continued to be strong. For the next several decades, progress was slow and uneven. Nevertheless, both the advocates and opponents of emancipation looked to the states for support. Like so much else in German Europe, the Jewish question had become a matter of state policy and therefore a political issue.[71]

In their efforts to extract resources, provide services, and regulate social life, early nineteenth-century states were inhibited by a severe shortage of qualified personnel. In Prussia, for instance, there were only about six hundred senior political officials in 1820; over the next decade, their number was further reduced in order to cut costs. According to one rough estimate, in 1846 there were just 7.1 government employees per one thousand inhabitants (by 1913 the figure was 12.5). A more precise picture of the scale of administrative institutions emerges if we consider the situation in Marienwerder, a Prussian administrative district with an area of 318 square miles and a population, in 1816, of 330,000. The district office in Marienwerder, the administrative centre for the region, had fifty-nine employees in 1826; most of them were messengers, clerks, and other subaltern officials. Only a handful of university-trained administrators were available to handle the district's affairs. In addition, there was a *Landrat* in each of Marienwerder's twenty-one subdistricts [*Kreise*], some of which had as many as 36,000 inhabitants. To keep order, the *Landrat* could call on the *gendarmarie*, but since there were only about 1,300 of these rural policeman in the entire kingdom of Prussia, any one subdistrict would have no more than three or four.[72]

[71] See Richarz (ed.), *Leben*; the essays in Mosse *et al.* (eds.), *Revolution*; Hans Liebeschütz and Arnold Paucker (eds.), *Das Judentum in der deutschen Umwelt, 1800–1850* (Tübingen, 1977). Selma Stern's *Das preussische Staat und die Juden* (4 vols.; Tübingen, 1962–75) is the classic work on the political condition of Jews in the old regime. The best study of emancipation is Rürup on Baden, 'Judenemanzipation', pp. 241–300.

[72] Koselleck, *Preussen*, p. 245. Bleek, *Kameralausbildung*, pp. 139–40, estimates that there were about 1,600 salaried employees at the upper levels of the Prussian administration. The figures on Marienwerder are from Horst Mies, *Die preussische Verwaltung des Regierungsbezirks Marienwerder (1830–1870)* (Cologne and Berlin, 1972), 14, 46. Another local study is Peter Letkemann, *Die preussische Verwaltung des*

Considering the thinness of its bureaucratic apparatus, the state had no choice but to co-operate with traditional élites and institutions in order to maintain order, keep records, and regulate trade and commerce. Throughout German Europe, therefore, noble landowners and their representatives still exercised important governmental functions. In some states, such as Bavaria, the clergy functioned as school inspectors, thus recapturing some of the influence they had lost due to the growth of state schools. Throughout much of the south-west, a measure of community control returned to the old home towns because their new rulers could not master local complexities and overcome local resistance. Despite the reformers' commitment to regulating economic and social life, guilds retained regulatory power in many areas. Nor were states able to integrate fully the regions they had acquired after 1800. For example, Prussia, Bavaria, and Hesse-Darmstadt all contained territories which kept their French laws and institutions. Local privileges and exceptions also existed in regions like Swedish Pomerania and cities like Stralsund. Even close to the core of the old states, regional loyalties and particularism resisted administrative domination and central control. 'We are not merely a province,' a mid-century visitor to East Prussia was told, 'we are a *Land*'. Thus the administrative structures of most states, like their constitutional arrangements, continued to be shaped by a series of tactical compromises between bureaucratic power and traditional sources of authority.[73]

Compared to the massive administrative machine that developed later, the German bureaucracies of the early nineteenth century were small and ill-equipped. Nevertheless, the *Beamtenstaat* was clearly in the ascendancy, its century-long struggle with the forces of *Herrschaft* was drawing to a close. Almost everywhere in central Europe, the state's influence over education and religion steadily increased. In the south-west, officials continued their efforts to undermine the autonomy of local communities and corporate economic organizations. Even the Prussian Junkers, whose power and privileges were so deeply rooted in the history of their state, faced the slow erosion of their local authority. But as its power

Regierungsbezirks Danzig, 1815–1870 (Marburg, 1967). On the state's repressive powers, see Alf Lüdtke, *'Gemeinwohl', Polizei, und 'Festungspraxis': Staatliche Gewaltsamkeit und innere Verwaltung in Preussen, 1815–1850* (Göttingen, 1982).

[73] Schieder in Conze (ed.), *Staat*, p. 20. For examples from Bavaria, see Zorn's essay, ibid. 122–3. The best-known instance of localism and integration is probably the Rhineland: see Schütz, *Preussen und die Rheinlande*.

over these traditional sources of authority grew, the bureaucracy found itself confronting a new set of opponents—and sometimes, as in the case of the church and nobility, old opponents with new weapons. This was because the growth of bureaucratic institutions was everywhere attended by the development of political participation. The connection between subject and state, for which reformers like Montgelas yearned, turned out to be reciprocal: the more directly the state affected people's lives, the more people sought to influence state policy. Before the 1830s, however, these participatory forces were still weak, their institutions fragile, their ideological expressions uncertain. Some bureaucrats believed they could repress them completely, while other, more progressive officials hoped that the administration could coexist with, perhaps even absorb, these participatory energies. The first three decades of the century deserve to be thought of as the apogee of the *Beamtenstaat*, therefore, not simply because bureaucrats had won decisive victories over their old enemies but also because their new antagonists had not yet begun to take shape.

iv. PATTERNS OF POLITICAL PARTICIPATION

Most modern theorists view political participation as an instrument of popular sovereignty, a way for people to share in, and have some measure of control over, their governments. Participatory institutions—parties, various organs of opinion-making, pressure groups, and, most important of all, parliamentary assemblies—are supposed to provide a set of channels linking government and citizen, politics and society. In order for these channels to work properly, they must be clear of illegitimate interventions, such as censorship or corruption, and they must be available to all citizens. Moreover, the messages sent through these channels must have an effect on the government, which is required to respond to the will of its citizens. By the middle of the nineteenth century, in the German lands as in the rest of Europe, most constitutional conflicts were about how this model of participation ought to work. What kinds of participatory institutions were proper? Who should participate in them? What were their formal powers over the other organs of government?[74]

In 1815, however, these issues were just beginning to take shape within German theory and practice. At this point, most Germans

[74] For an introduction to these issues see the essays in Kurt Kluxen (ed.), *Parlamentarismus* (Cologne and Berlin, 1967).

viewed the problem of participation in terms of the longstanding conflict between the defenders of local privileges and the advocates of state sovereignty, between what we have called *Herrschaft* and *Verwaltung*. Each side had its own image of participation's character and purpose. Those who admired corporate institutions believed that participation should take place within, and affirm the distinctive existence of, a particular social group or community. To these people, participation was not a universal political right but part of a cluster of specific, restricted liberties. If they used the term *Bürger*, it was to refer to those with a special role within an urban community. To the state-builders, on the other hand, citizenship—*Staatsbürgertum*—always had precedence over an individual's intermediate loyalties to his town, village, or guild. Participation, like taxation, military service, and universal education, was supposed to create a new sort of political consciousness by forging direct ties between citizens and their states. Representative institutions, Carl von Rotteck wrote in 1818, can help a group of people who just happen to live together become 'a vital whole', a *Volk* whose collective loyalties and commitments would take precedence over their local identities and particular preoccupations. As a citizen of Baden, the most contrived and diverse of the new states, Rotteck knew how difficult it would be to create citizens with a single will and common interest.[75]

The representative institutions that existed in the German lands reflected both of these contrasting images of what participation should be. In some states, *Landstände* perpetuated traditional modes of representation in highly restricted, corporately organized assemblies. The provincial estates granted to Prussia in lieu of a constitution followed this same model. In the constitutional states of the south-west, however, representation was clearly linked to the struggle for state sovereignty. In Baden, for example, every member of the *Landtag* had to take the following oath:

I swear allegiance to the grand duke, to obey the law, protect and follow the constitution, and in the Assembly to represent only the general welfare and best interests of the entire land according to my own inner convictions, and without consideration of particular estates or classes. . . .[76]

In the reactionary climate following the Karlsbad decrees, no state, including Baden, was prepared to allow its parliamentarians to follow their 'inner convictions' without careful scrutiny and

---

[75] 'Ein Wort über Landstände', *Schriften*, ii. 407.
[76] Huber, *Dokumente*, i. 167. See above, Ch. 5, sect. i, and Ch. 7, sect. ii.

control. Throughout the 1820s governments everywhere did their best to inhibit the operations of representative institutions and to limit their impact on the public. In most states, for example, the rules of order in the lower chamber forced delegates to take preassigned seats so that they could not form factions; debates were strictly controlled and parliamentary proceedings rarely made public. Ministers sought to deflect the parliament's attention away from politically sensitive matters and to turn them into cheering sections for official policy. The Prussian *Landtage* established in 1823 were also designed so that they could not be centres for political agitation. Summoned by a state official, frequently meeting in the halls of a royal residence, and directed by a member of the upper nobility, the provincial *Stände* were meant to serve the government by providing advice and assistance.[77]

Before 1848, elections, which would become the most important ritualized expression of political participation, were carefully controlled by the states. Except in Baden, voting was done by social group; and even in Baden, voting was indirect, which meant that a layer of notables insulated the electors from their representatives; everywhere, suffrage was restricted to adult males who met certain legal and economic qualifications. Often enough, therefore, voting turned into an affirmation of the traditional order rather than a means through which the public expressed its will. Observed and directed by civil servants, governed by rules favouring the wealthy and well established, and smothered by a blanket of censorship, electoral politics was often greeted by understandable apathy and incomprehension. In Königsberg, for instance, only 203 out of almost 4,000 eligible voters appeared at the polls for a local election in 1816, while in Württemberg a by-election had to be called off because a minimum number of electors failed to show up.[78]

Caught between repression from above and apathy below, few Germans after 1819 were prepared to risk a direct confrontation with their governments. The *Burschenschaften*, which had always been confined to a small if passionate minority of young people, crumbled when faced with the reactionary decrees mandated at

[77] Kramer, *Fraktionsbindungen*; Obenaus, *Anfänge*; and the convenient summary in Botzenhart, *Parlamentarismus*. On the situation in Württemberg, see Brandt, *Parlamentarismus*.

[78] Albert Adam, *Ein Jahrhundert württembergischer Verfassung* (Stuttgart, 1919), 23; Gause, *Stadt Königsberg*, ii. 400. Monika Wölk, 'Wahlbewusstsein und Wahlerfahrungen zwischen Tradition und Moderne', *HZ* 238/2 (1984), 311–52 emphasizes the continuities between electoral behaviour in the old regime and *Vormärz*.

Karlsbad. In a few universities, student societies carried on a shadowy existence, but without the inflated expectations that had inspired some advocates of national liberation after 1814. Other expressions of the national movement also collapsed: Jahn's gymnasts had been disbanded by Prussian authorities even before Kotzebue's murder; Görres and other publicists had either fled abroad or lapsed into prudent silence.[79] In the south-western parliaments, a few brave men stood up and called for an end to censorship, aristocratic privilege, and irresponsible authority. But since their efforts were usually without impact on their fellow parliamentarians or the public at large, they were no more than minor irritations to the government. When a narrow majority of the Baden *Landtag* voted down the military budget in 1823, the grand duke simply brought the session to an end. Two years later, governmental pressure on the electorate prevented the return of all but a handful of the opposition. Throughout the 1820s, therefore, most German representative institutions could have been described with the self-satisfied assessment of the Württemberg official who told his king that the *Landtag* had turned out to be 'the safest way to bring calm and happiness to his subjects'.[80]

With the avenues to political action blocked, most Germans had little choice but to turn once again to the realm of literary interchange, that sphere of *Öffentlichkeit* in which German political discourse had first taken shape. During the years of upheaval between 1789 and 1815 the scope of this discourse had broadened and its quality had substantially improved, but its institutional base had not been strengthened. Indeed, the experience of war and revolution had, if anything, further disrupted the fragile bonds that had united the eighteenth-century public. After 1815, and especially after 1819, political discourse was under attack from reactionary regimes throughout the German Confederation. Once Metternich and his associates had mobilized governments against subversive opinion, policemen and censors interfered with all forms of public activity, watched over associations and clubs, and inspected publications for any trace of radicalism.

Of course the states' tyrannical aspirations were limited by their lack of resources. Censorship was often inconsistent, police control usually uneven. In some places, quite minor infractions might evoke official action: one Austrian civil servant, for example, was

---

[79] Lutz, 'German'; Hardtwig, 'Mentalität'.
[80] Quoted in Brandt, 'Gesellschaft', p. 102. On the situation in Baden, see Kramer, *Fraktionsbindungen*, pp. 42–3.

called to the police station because his daughter had played some unfamiliar music and danced without permission. Sometimes, however, the authorities were surprisingly lenient and permissive. Generally speaking, censors did not molest expensive books and scholarly periodicals, which were likely to be written by and for people like themselves. But they were apt to be strict with cheap pamphlets and newspapers, which might have wider circulation and a direct connection to practical politics. Throughout the 1820s and 1830s, therefore, the free and easy flow of news, the clash of opinions about everyday events, and circulation of ideas about politics—all essential elements in the formation of a politically informed public—were severely restricted by most German states. Those interested in current affairs often had to be content with studying theoretical treatises, reading accounts of politics in other countries, or enjoying the empty gossip satirized in Fallersleben's bitter ode to contemporary journalism.

> Was haben wir heute nicht alles vernommen!
> Die Fürstin ist gestern niedergekommen,
> Und morgen wird der Herzog kommen,
> Hier ist der König heimgekommen,
> Dort ist der Kaiser durchgekommen—
> Bald werden sie alle zusammenkommen—
> Wie interessant! Wie interessant!
> Gott segne das liebe Vaterland![81]

Many observers agreed that the unwholesome impact of censorship was most apparent in Metternich's Austria, where it produced what one contemporary called 'a crippling of national energies'. For a creative playwright and poet like Franz Grillparzer, the authorities were a never-ending source of frustration and despair. In 1819 he was personally summoned to the presence of Count Sedlnitzky, who relayed to him the emperor's displeasure about his poem, 'Campo Vaccino', in which Grillparzer lamented the passing of Rome's greatness. Four years later, his play *König Ottokars Glück und Ende* was rejected by the censors. When Grillparzer finally confronted the official responsible for the ban, he was told that, while nothing seemed wrong with the piece, 'One can never tell.' In fact, Grillparzer was anything but a radical. Above all, he

---

[81] Fallersleben quoted in Hermann, *Biedermeier*, p. 267. On political repression, see Schneider, *Pressefreiheit*; Wolfram Siemann, *Deutschlands Ruhe, Sicherheit und Ordnung.' Die Anfänge der politischen Polizei, 1806–1866* (Tübingen, 1985), and his 'Ideenschmuggel: Probleme der Meinungskontrolle und das Los deutscher Zensuren im 19. Jahrhundert', *HZ* 245/1 (1987), 71–106.

wanted to be a loyal subject of what one of his characters calls 'that wise arrangement instituted by God which men call the state'. But his state did not make such loyalty easy. 'An Austrian writer should be held in higher esteem than any other', Grillparzer wrote in his diary in 1829, 'Anyone who does not completely lose heart under such conditions is truly a kind of hero.' He never lost heart, but the cost of persistence was great. 'Serfdom', he once complained, 'destroyed my youth.'[82]

Starved for information about their own affairs by censorship, inhibited from meaningful participation by formal restrictions and informal intimidation, Germans were understandably slow to develop a clear sense of political objectives and alternatives. William Jacob, who visited Berlin in 1819, was struck by the uncertainty and obscurity of goals he found among 'those men of letters who have assumed the appellation of liberals'. When he pressed them for their solution to political problems, Jacob found that 'the answers I received were such as convinced me that those who were most vehement for a change had the least contemplated the nature of the one they required'.[83]

When Germans gathered to talk about public affairs in the early decades of the nineteenth century, they most often did so in coffee houses and wineshops, clubs and recreational societies, reading groups and lending libraries. Often enough, this kind of political discourse was disconnected from the realm of power and lent itself easily to the satirical contempt so beautifully expressed in Fallersleben's poem 'Cafe National':

> Und sie plaudern, blättern, suchen
> Endlich kommt ein Resultat:
> Noch ein Stückchen Apfelkuchen!
> Zwar der Kurs steht desolat.

Nevertheless, these clubs and cafés served an important political purpose. Within their convivial atmosphere, men read what news they could find, discussed political issues, and began to establish those relationships upon which political action could be based.[84]

[82] Brunner, in Conze (ed.), *Staat*, p. 60; W. E. Yates, *Grillparzer: A Critical Introduction* (Cambridge, 1972), 221. For a bitter attack on Austrian censorship, see 'A. Sealsfield' [Karl Postl], *Austria as it is, or Sketches of Continental Courts* (London, 1828).

[83] William Jacob, *A View of the Agriculture, Manufactures, Statistics, and State of Society of Germany and Parts of Holland and France* (London, 1820), 222.

[84] Fallersleben quoted in Hermann, *Biedermeier*, p. 64. For another satirical portrait, see Glassbrenner's marvellous description of 'Herr Buffey in der Zaruck-Gesellschaft', in *Unterrichtung*, i. 192 ff. The best introduction to organizational life is Nipperdey, 'Verein'. See also Müller, *Korporation*.

In order to mobilize and direct opinion beyond this social sphere, Germans usually had to conceal their organization's political purpose behind some apparently harmless façade. Often enough the authorities were not taken in. For example, when Friedrich List established the *Allgemeiner deutscher Handels- und Gewerbeverein* in 1819 to gather support for progressive political and economic programmes, Metternich condemned such 'practical revolutionaries' who spread subversion under the guise of tariff reform. Governments were also suspicious of the various cultural associations founded in the 1820s and 1830s to celebrate some important figure who was seen as the personification of national virtues and aspirations. These *Vereine*, dedicated to Schiller, Luther, Gutenberg, or Dürer, had to be explicitly unpolitical, but their purpose was clearly to keep alive the ideals of the *Burschenschaften* and to work for a new national community. Together with a few professional societies and economic interest groups, these associations provided the first, thinly spread and informally organized networks within which Germans interested in public affairs could meet, exchange views, and acquire some standing beyond their own communities. But for most Germans politics during the 1820s remained locally based, locked in particular communities by the forces of governmental repression and social fragmentation. The absence of a national centre, the lack of visible representative institutions, the deficiencies of the Press, and the still primitive condition of the communications network combined to inhibit national movements. As the handful of prominent political figures from the era of reform retired or lapsed into silence, only a few men had reputations that extended beyond the walls of their own towns.[85]

The social basis of the political public in the 1820s remained roughly what it had been in the last third of the eighteenth century: a mixture of educated and economic élites in which businessmen, officials, professionals, and publicists were especially prominent. The precise social composition of the public varied widely from one place to another. In economic centres like Leipzig and the more commercially active regions along the Rhine, entrepreneurs were important. In the small market cities of the north-east, the political tone would probably be set by pastors, physicians, and local merchants. Significantly, men in government service played an

---

[85] Gabriele Stadler, *Dichterverehrung und nationale Repräsentanz im literarischen Leben des 19. Jahrhunderts: Studien zur Geschichte der Schillervereine im 19. Jahrhundert* (Munich, 1977). For a sensitive account of social life in an early nineteenth century German city, see Bähr's memoirs of Kassel: *Stadt*, pp. 174 ff.

important role in many participatory institutions. Just as the institutions of *Verwaltung* and *Verfassung* intertwined in the minds of bureaucratic reformers, many sought to combine the roles of civil servant and opinion leader. As we shall see in more detail later, there is perhaps no clearer sign of the *Beamtenstaat's* centrality on the German political scene than the prominent part played by officials in the emergence of an opposition movement.[86]

Judges and administrators, teachers and professional men, industrialists and merchants were drawn into the political sphere because they were convinced that their interests and opinions represented the direction of the future. They wished to sweep away the petty limitations on social life, the senseless restraints on publications, the foolish privileges of outmoded castes, and the irresponsible power of incompetent rulers. In a free society, they would prosper; if opinions were unfettered, their views would triumph; if the polity were reasonably run, their position would be secure. In this sense, they represented not just an opinion but the only opinion rationally possible: public opinion, as one contemporary put it, was 'nothing but reason developed and put into practice'.[87]

By the early twenties, many members of the German political public had begun to think of themselves as 'liberals', a term appropriated from contemporary Spain and applied to progressive forces everywhere in Europe. From the start, liberalism meant different things to different people, but all agreed that to be a liberal was to belong to the party of movement, to oppose tyranny and love liberty, to hate irrationality and celebrate reason, to fight reaction and advance progress. Thus in one of the first histories of liberalism, published by W. T. Krug in 1823, we read that 'what is called liberalism' emerged from the struggle between the defenders of the status quo and 'the evolutionary drive in humanity, which is only the struggle for liberation from limitations of time and place . . .'. Liberalism was movement, progress, emancipation; its advocates stood for the forces of history.[88]

The overwhelming majority of Germans had nothing to do with the liberal movement. They could not hear the muffled voices debating distant issues in parliamentary bodies, they did not read the abstract formulations to be found in most books and periodicals, and they were not welcome in the social clubs and cultural

[86] On the social composition of the political public, see below, Ch. 10.
[87] Quoted in Gall, *Constant*, p. 62.
[88] Quoted in Rosenberg, *Denkströmungen*, p. 36. On liberalism, see below, Ch. 10, sect. i.

associations where progressive notables gathered to discuss politics. But it would be a mistake to regard this 'silent majority' as passive or unpolitical. Their politics was surely different from that taking shape in the liberal public, but it was no less significant for the history of political participation.

Throughout the first half of the nineteenth century, political participation for most Germans was based on traditional communities and attitudes. Whereas liberals directed their energies towards the pursuit of a better future, ordinary men and women were more likely to defend past rights and established standards. For these people, political action took place in, and for, the immediate world, the face-to-face realm of village, neighbourhood, guild, or parish. For them, political action was justified by custom and conventional morality, rather than by abstract rights and ideological principles. By our standards, there is something ephemeral about this kind of politics; it produced no great theoretical statements, passed no laws, adopted no constitutions. We catch sight of it only at times of crisis, when the community, mobilized by some extraordinary event, engages in collective action serious enough to provoke state intervention and thus leave documentary record. Almost always, the targets of such protests were outsiders, people bent upon disrupting the social balance and cultural cohesion upon which the community depended.

A series of such protests accompanied the subsistence crisis which followed the Napoleonic wars. Throughout 1816 a variety of regions in western Europe were disturbed by rioting, brigandage, and other forms of social violence. By the end of the year the trouble had spread to the German states: angry crowds gathered in Ratisbon, Augsburg, and Munich; the following spring, troops had to be called out to restore order in Mainz; in many rural areas, farmers were threatened by vagabonds and armed bands. In form, this violence resembled the grain riots that had erupted during the old regime when food shortages produced high prices and scarcity; hungry, angry people attacked the merchants, bakers, and producers whom they believed were taking unfair advantage of their discontents and profiting from their misery.[89]

In 1819 communal protests were directed against Jews throughout the German west. This movement began at the University of Würzburg, when students—always a volatile group in the old regime—attacked a professor who had written in defence of Jewish rights. Personal assaults on Jews quickly followed and spread to

[89] Post, *Crisis*, ch. 3.

several other cities, most notably Frankfurt, where there was enough disorder to warrant the possible use of federal troops. During these so-called 'Hep! Hep!' riots—named from the insulting slogans shouted at Jews—students, craftsmen, and farmers were caught up in a wave of irrational ethnic violence created by a combination of longstanding social and religious antagonisms and the immediate problems of the post-war years. To Metternich, these 'outbreaks of the vulgar masses' were deeply disturbing: once they had begun to appear, he wrote in 1819, 'no security exists, for the same thing could arise again at any moment over any other matter.'[90]

Despite the repressive efforts of the states, popular protests continued throughout the 1820s. Richard Tilly, using a sample based on reports in the *Augsburger Allgemeine Zeitung*, has counted twenty-nine disorders between 1820 and 1829, of which thirteen involved students; nine, religious conflicts; three, social and economic issues; and four, what Tilly regards as 'political' affairs. In fact, such labels are necessarily arbitrary, since most of these disorders engaged communities that did not clearly distinguish between social cohesion, religious identity, and political interests; together, these attributes often provided the source for collective action.[91]

As was the case with so much else during the first half of the century, political participation in the German lands was a mix of traditional and modern elements. Thus we find some of the last expressions of community solidarity as well as the first indications of ideological awareness. Until the end of the 1820s, however, no form of participatory politics represented a serious threat to the established order: popular protests remained episodic and regionally isolated; ideological opposition was socially shallow and institutionally diffuse. As we shall see in Chapter 10, this system began to change after 1830, when a new wave of unrest demonstrated the limits of restoration. In the decade following the revolutions of 1830, participatory energies significantly increased; popular protests intensified; the political public became more confident and decisive. But before considering these developments, we must turn to equally important changes in German society and culture.

[90] Quoted in ibid. 173 On anti-Jewish protests, see Wirtz, *'Widersetzlichkeiten'*, pp. 60 ff.; Rürup, *Emanzipation*, p. 77.
[91] Tilly, 'Disorders'.

VIII
Growth and Stagnation in German Society

FRIEDRICH ENGELS (1820–95) was born and reared in Barmen, a fast-growing industrial city on the Wupper River, a few miles east of Düsseldorf. The Engels family had lived in the region since the sixteenth century, first as farmers, then as successful textile manufacturers. Like many of their neighbours, they were pious Calvinists, who combined commercial acuity with intense religiosity. But the Engels were also part of an economic network that extended far beyond the Wuppertal; their search for raw materials, markets, and capital led them to the Low Countries, Britain, and overseas. In 1837 Engels's father opened a spinning mill in Manchester, the epicentre of the new industrial order. Here young Friedrich, after several false starts on a career closer to home, took a position in 1842. His observations of Manchester and its labour force were the basis for an influential book, *The Condition of the Working Class in England*, first published in 1845, and for his own life-long commitment to improving the conditions of working people.[1]

Viewed from the perspective of industrial Britain, Engels found German social and economic life depressingly backward. In an essay on the 'German status quo', which he wrote in the spring of 1847, he lamented the fact that in all the German states 'the countryside dominates the towns, agriculture dominates trade and industry'. Every indicator that we have confirms Engels's perception of German backwardness. Consider, for example, these data on per capita production and consumption: if the values for the United Kingdom are indexed at 100, then German pig iron consumption was 10 in 1830, 6 in 1850; cotton yarn 5 in 1840, 7 in 1850; woollen yarn 15 in 1830, 29 in 1850; and coal 6 in 1820, and only 7 in 1850.[2]

As aggregate measures, these figures give an accurate enough

---

[1] Gustav Mayer's *Friedrich Engels: Eine Biographie* (The Hague, 1934) is old-fashioned but still worth reading. On Engels's social thought, see below, Ch. 9, sect. iii, and Ch. 10, sect. iv.

[2] Hoffmann, 'Take-Off', p. 118, the data are for the territories in the *Zollverein*.

indication of how the two economies compared during the first half of the nineteenth century. But men and women do not live in the aggregate; their lives take shape in individual communities, each with its own blend of innovation and backwardness. When we move closer to these particular circumstances, the character of German social and economic institutions appears substantially more complex. Seen from a local perspective, we are struck less by backwardness than by the coexistence of dynamic and stagnate regions, groups, and enterprises. The Engels family, with their Manchester factory and international connections, lived near nailmakers and ironmongers who sold their wares in a single community. Agricultural capitalists, eager to increase their yields and export their grain, lived with subsistence farmers who still struggled to coax a meagre living from the soil. In the villages high above the Rhine, people worked in the vineyards as they had for decades, while on the river the arrival of steamboats signalled the advent of a transportation revolution. Berlin was among the fastest growing cities in Europe, but other German towns still locked their gates and closed their societies against the outside world. This diversity, Engels was alert enough to realize, contributed to what he called 'the poverty of the German status quo':

no single class has hitherto been strong enough to establish its branch of production as the national branch of production par excellence and thus to set itself up as the representative of the interests of the whole nation. All the estates and classes that have emerged in history since the tenth century—nobles, serfs, peasants subject to corvée labour, free peasants, petty bourgeoisie, journeymen, manufactory workers, bourgeoisie and proletarians—all exist alongside one another.[3]

To be sure, such social diversity is not unique. Every age contains old and new groups and institutions; impulses for change always mix with sources of stagnation. But there are historical periods in which the juxtaposition of old and new appears to be especially intense, when values, ideas, habits, and institutions seem to be torn between two orders. In such periods, some people lament an old world in decline, while others yearn for a new one waiting to be born, defenders of tradition feel particularly threatened, and the advocates of innovation are intensely frustrated. This was the situation throughout the German lands between the Napoleonic era and the mid-century revolutions.

[3] Marx and Engels, *Works*. vi. 84.

i. THE CHANGING DIMENSIONS OF LIFE

Nineteenth-century writers often contrasted the stability of traditional society with the turbulence they saw in the world around
them. In fact, the traditional social order was anything but stable:
marauding armies, epidemics, failed harvests, and a host of private
catastrophes were dangers against which people had virtually no
defence. For most of European history, men and women lived with
uncertainties beyond the comprehension of citizens in a modern
western society. The essential difference between the traditional
and modern worlds was not stability, but scale: modern institutions
are bigger, the pace of development swifter, the dimensions of
change broader and more encompassing. Armies, cities, factories,
universities, and governmental agencies all grew so much in the
course of the nineteenth century that they became qualitatively
different from their pre-modern predecessors. At the same time,
these institutions, and the ideas and habits that sustained them,
changed more quickly than at any time in history. The implications
of these changes left no corner of life untouched. Traditional
Europeans lived in a world of immediate uncertainty but long-term
continuity; if they survived, they could assume that tomorrow
would be much like today. For moderns the opposite seemed to be
true: slowly and painfully, they acquired some measure of control
over their personal lives, but they had to live in a world where basic
change was permanent and inescapable. It is not an accident that the
nineteenth century was the great age of historical analysis, in the
study of both human affairs and the natural world.

Central to the expanding scale of modern life was the demographic revolution that began around the middle of the eighteenth
century. When we deal with an event of this magnitude, questions
about cause and effect become hopelessly entangled: the unparalleled expansion of the European population was at once the product
of fundamental changes in social and economic life and an impetus
for further transformations. Battered by the rising demographic
tides, the introspective institutions of traditional society began to
crumble. On the battlefield, within the walls of urban communities, and in corporate organizations like the guilds, Europeans had
to deal with more people than could be directed or protected under
the old rules. The result was a basic realignment of institutions
throughout the social and political order.[4]

[4] The literature on German demography is cited above, Ch. 2, sect. i, n. 1. There

German Europe (the Confederation of 1815 plus the three Prussian provinces outside its borders), which had about 32.7 million inhabitants in 1816, grew to 52.2 million in 1865, an increase of some 60 per cent. Over the same period, the density of the population, measured in inhabitants per square kilometre increased from 38 to 71 in Prussia, from 49 to 78 in the Confederation not including Austria, and from 47 to 71 in Austria. On the basis of calculations for the territories that would become part of the German empire in 1871, it can be determined that there was a surplus of births over deaths every year between 1817 and 1865, although the size of this surplus varied from a high of 17.9 per mille 1821 to a low of 4.1 per mille in 1855. The average annual growth rate for the Confederation (including all of Prussia) was 0.94 per cent. Such levels of growth had been reached before in European history, but their long-term impact had always been blunted by equally dramatic reverses. As Michael Flinn has written, 'What was new about the nineteenth century was not so much the high level of the rate of growth as its being sustained virtually unchecked.'[5]

That this demographic revolution had no single cause should not surprise us. Demographic data, after all, measure the decisions and destinies of millions of people. We should be suspicious, therefore, of explanations that put too much weight on a set of political events, such as the Prussian reforms, or a particular socio-economic process, such as industrialization. Demographic trends in the modern era are the result of multiple, cumulative developments in nutrition and public health, transportation and production, politics and culture. In isolation, each of these developments represented no more than a marginal advantage in people's ability to survive and reproduce, but together they produced a sustained transformation in the quality of life and the nature of society.

By twentieth-century standards, mortality rates after 1800 were still high. Bad harvests, such as occurred in 1816, or agricultural and trade crises, like those of 1846–7, could produce peaks in the line tracing the incidence of mortality. Epidemics continued to strike without warning. The outbreak of cholera that killed Hegel and Clausewitz in 1831 may have infected 1 per cent of the total

is a convenient summary of nineteenth-century developments in Marschalck, *Bevölkerungsgeschichte*. See also Köllmann and Kraus (eds.), *Quellen*, for a useful compilation of data. Some of Köllmann's demographic work can be found in his collection of essays, *Bevölkerung*.

[5] Flinn, *System*, p. 76. The data are from Fischer *et al.*, *Arbeitsbuch*, pp. 17, 26.

population of central Europe. Between the summer of 1831 and the following spring, about 4,300 Viennese contracted the disease; almost 2,200 died. Throughout the nineteenth century, we find heartrending stories of families overshadowed by death. The parents of the composer Michael Dierner, for instance, had seven children after their marriage in 1861; two died as infants, two others succumbed to diptheria, one at three, another at nine. August Bebel, who was born in 1840, lost first his father, than his mother and stepfather to consumption; his sister died in infancy, one brother at age three, another at eighteen. Ludwig Windthorst and his wife had eight children, four of whom died in infancy, another at eleven, two more in their twenties; only one lived to middle age. Overall, the rate of infant mortality was tragically high, indeed it seems to have increased during the first two thirds of the century (see table 8.1).[6]

TABLE 8.1. *Infant mortality in the nineteenth century (deaths in the first year/1,000 live births)*

	Prussia	Saxony	Bavaria
1821–30	174	—	284
1831–40	183	266	296
1841–50	186	261	297
1851–60	197	255	310
1861–70	211	267	326

Source: Fischer *et al.*, *Arbeitsbuch*, p. 33.

But, while progress in combating epidemics and early death was slow, some marginal improvements did occur. As we saw in the last chapter, governments began to make some tentative steps to improve the quality of medical care and sanitation facilities; advances in basic science and clinical procedures enabled physicians to diagnose and treat some diseases; hospital care became available to more people. We should not overestimate the impact of any of these developments, but they may have had some small part in helping to stabilize mortality rates.[7] After 1800, even the most

[6] Flinn, *System*, p. 92. For other examples, see Ilien and Jeggle, *Leben*, pp. 90 ff. On cholera, see Evans, *Death*.

[7] For some data on the impact of medical care, see Robert Lee, 'Medicalization and Mortality Trends in South Germany in the Early 19th Century', in Imhof (ed.), *Mensch*, 79–113. Spree, *Ungleichheit*, takes a generally pessimistic view, while

serious crises did not reverse the process of demographic growth; the mortality peaks of 1816, 1831, and 1847 were lower than those produced by the traumas of plague and starvation before 1750. Moreover, in some regions, death rates began to decline: in Hanover, for example, from 29.4 per mille at the end of the eighteenth century to 26.3 per mille in the 1830s. Furthermore, Germans' average life span slowly increased: in 1816, the life expectancy (at birth) of a Prussian male was 26.5 years, of a female, 28.7; by 1865–7 these figures were 32.4 and 34.9.[8]

Most scholars are convinced that this decline in mortality is a more salient explanation for demographic growth than any changes in fertility. According to the local studies surveyed by W. R. Lee, the birth rate did not increase between the middle of the eighteenth and the middle of the nineteenth centuries. Moreover, as the data in the table 8.2 show, the number of children per marriage did not change in fertility was the unprecedented growth in the number of the population actually declined between 1816 and 1861 (from 36.2 to 32.8). People also continued to marry late in life: in Prussia during the late 1860s, for instance, the average age of those marrying for the first time was 27.9. There were, as always, some important regional variations in these patterns, but overall marital fertility seems to have remained fairly constant.[9]

TABLE 8.2. *Marital fertility in the 1840s and 1850s (children/marriage)*

	1841–50	1851–60
Württemberg	5.1	5.4
Bavarian Palatinate	4.9	4.8
Baden	4.6	4.8
Pomerania	4.2	4.4
East Prussia	3.8	4.2

Source: Harnisch, 'Probleme', p. 307.

In the German lands, as in the rest of Europe, the most dramatic change in fertility was the unprecedented growth in the number of

Frevert, *Krankheit*, is highly critical of the whole process of 'medicalization'. For more on the medical professions, see the essays in Artelt and Rüegg (eds.), *Arzt*.

[8] Marschalck, *Bevölkerungsgeschichte*, p. 20; Lee, *Growth*, pp. 53 ff.; Fischer *et al.*, *Arbeitsbuch*, p. 32.

[9] Lee, 'Germany', pp. 146 ff.; Harnisch, 'Probleme', pp. 281, 299; Flinn, *System*, p. 84.

illegitimate births. According to eight local studies of the period before 1750, 2.5 per cent of live births were illegitimate, between 1740 and 1790 this number increased to 3.9, and from 1780 to 1820 to 11.9. Aggregate figures on the Confederation suggest that this high proportion remained constant until the end of the century: in 1841, 128,713 (11.2 per cent) of 1,151,794 live births were illegitimate; in 1866, 184,075 (12.6 per cent) of 1,456,707.[10] Needless to say, many observers viewed this situation with considerable alarm. In 1833, for example, an official in Oberfranken lamented that 'in the countryside a girl who has preserved her virgin purity to the age of twenty counts as exceptional, and is not at all esteemed for it by her contemporaries'. Depending on their social values and political sympathies, Germans blamed this alleged decline in sexual morality on urbanization, industrialism, secularization, or democracy. In fact, a great deal of illegitimacy was caused by the legal and material barriers to marriage which confronted many young people; there is a clear correlation between the incidence of illegitimate births and the presence of marriage restrictions passed by several states in a vain attempt to control population growth. A significant number of illegitimate children, therefore, were reared in fairly stable family units, formed by men and women who could not legally marry but who did try to maintain a household. Others, however, were born to parents unwilling or unable to support them. The fate of these infants, as the evidence on their mortality makes abundantly clear, was very grim indeed: during the 1870s, the mortality rate for illegitimate infants was 345 per mille as compared with 192 per mille for those born to married couples. In big cities, to which abandoned and destitute women often gravitated to have their babies, the numbers are even more shocking—almost half of those born illegitimately in Berlin did not reach their first birthday.[11]

Throughout our period, every demographic indicator varied widely from one region to another. As can be seen in table 8.3, this variety is visible, first of all, in the population history of the individual states. These data reflect a redistribution of the German population away from the north-west, south, and south-east, towards the north-east and the Rhineland. They provide the first glimpse of what will be an important theme throughout the rest of

[10] Flinn, *System*, p. 81; Fischer *et al.*, *Arbeitsbuch*, p. 29.
[11] The quotation is from Shorter, *Making*, pp. 95 ff. See also Tilly, *Studies*, p. 45; Kraus, ' "Ehesegen" '; Marschalck, *Bevölkerungsgeschichte*, pp. 38–9; John Knodel, 'Law, Marriage and Illegitimacy in the Nineteenth Century', *Population Studies*, 20/3 (Mar. 1967), 279–94.

TABLE 8.3. *Population growth in German states, 1816–1865* (000s)

	1816	1865	Population growth (%)
Baden	1,005.8	1,429.2	42
Bavaria	3,560.0[a]	4,814.7	35
Württemberg	1,410.3	1,752.0	24
Electoral Hesse	567.8	754.1	33
Hesse-Darmstadt	587.9	854.3	45
Hanover	1,328.3	1,927.8	45
Saxony	1,192.7	2,354.0	97
Prussia	10,349	19,445.0	88

Note: [a] Includes Bavarian Palatinate.
Source: Köllmann and Kraus (eds.), *Quellen*.

this book: the relative growth of Prussia's economic power and population within German Europe, especially *vis-à-vis* the medium sized states of the south-west and the Habsburg monarchy (see table 8.4).[12]

While these regional shifts certainly had political implications, it is not clear that they had political causes. For one thing, variations within states were frequently as striking as those between states. In Prussia, for example, where the population as a whole grew by some 87 per cent between 1816 and 1865, the province of West Prussia registered a growth of 121 per cent as compared to 57 per cent in Westphalia. Even greater regional variations existed in the kingdom of Saxony: by the middle of the eighteenth century the development of rural manufacturing in the south-western parts of the state around Glauchau, Chemnitz, and Zwickau and in southern sectors of Oberlausitz enabled these areas to grow significantly faster than the purely agrarian regions elsewhere in the state. This pattern continued into the nineteenth century, so that by 1834, Glauchau had a population density of 177 per square kilometre, more than three times that of districts like Grossenhain and Kamenz and well above the state average of 106.[13]

Some regional differences were the result of variations in fertility and mortality. For example, between 1816 and 1840 the average surplus of births over deaths was 11.9 per mille for Prussia as a whole, 13.6 per mille for West Prussia, 9.5 per mille, Westphalia,

[12] Nipperdey, *Geschichte*, pp. 110 ff.
[13] Blaschke, 'Bevölkerungsgeschichte'.

TABLE 8.4. *Regional distribution of population growth, 1816–1865* (000s)

	1816	1865	Population growth (%)
Confederation	30,446.0	47,689.0	56
Prussian territories	8,093.0	14,785.0	83
Austrian territories	9,290.0	13,865.0	49
southern states[a]	5,976.1	7,995.9	34
western states[b]	1,557.9	2,225.3	43
central states[c]	2,013.1	3,585.2	78
northern states[d]	2,166.8	3,297.1	52
Kingdom of Prussia	10,349.0	19,445.0	88
Habsburg monarchy[e]	25,500.0	34,790.0	36

Notes:
[a] Bavaria, Baden, Württemberg.
[b] Hesse-Darmstadt, Electoral Hesse, Nassau, Waldeck, Frankfurt.
[c] Thuringian States, Saxony, Anhalt.
[d] Hanover, Brunswick, Mecklenburgs, Hamburg, Bremen, Lübeck.
[e] Figures are for 1810 and 1860.

Sources: Köllmann and Kraus (eds.), *Quellen*; Elster *et al.* (eds.), *Handwörterbuch*, pp. 687–8; Nipperdey, *Geschichte*, pp. 103–4.

and 3 per mille for Berlin. Measured for shorter periods, the differences become yet more striking: between 1821 and 1825, the surplus of births was 16.32 per mille for the state, 22.98 per mille for West Prussia, 12.92 per mille for Westphalia, and 6.42 per mille for Berlin. The closer we come to people's immediate environment, the more clearly we can see how particular social, economic, and political conditions shaped their willingness and ability to marry and procreate.[14] Consider, for instance, the data on the range of nuptiality, fertility, and mortality among five Prussian administrative districts in table 8.5.

Migration was another important reason for regional demographic variations. The urban environment, while less lethal than in the eighteenth century, continued to require an influx of new residents in order to grow as quickly as rural areas. For example, of the 26,000 new residents of Cologne between 1835 and 1849, 14,000 were born outside the city. The figures on Berlin (see table 8.6) indicate how the relative importance of migration for urbanization continued even after the 'natural' movement of the population became more favourable. Overall, Prussian cities grew

[14] Marschalck, *Bevölkerungsgeschichte*, pp. 27 ff.; Nipperdey, *Geschichte*, pp. 106 ff.

TABLE 8.5. *Demographic trends in selected Prussian regions, 1801–1871* (per mille)

	Births[a]	Deaths
Münster		
1803–4	28.1	22.6
1816–28	31.1	23.5
1829–40	30.0	25.4
1841–55	29.5	24.0
1856–71	29.9	24.3
Aurich		
1801–5	36.0	23.3
1826–28	31.7	24.7
1829–40	31.5	20.9
1841–55	31.6	19.1
1856–71	31.2	20.6
Lüneburg		
1826–28	32.3	21.7
1829–40	30.2	22.5
1841–55	30.6	22.2
1856–71	30.5	22.8
Osnabrück		
1826–28	33.3	22.5
1829–40	32.8	23.0
1841–55	29.8	22.1
1856–71	33.0	23.0
Köslin		
1816–28	44.2	25.0
1829–40	40.4	25.5
1841–55	40.0	24.7
1856–71	40.8	25.1

Note: [a] Age-specific fertility of women between 15 and 45.

Source: Harnisch, 'Probleme', p. 304.

at an average annual rate of 1.55 per cent during the 1850s; 0.74 per cent was due to a surplus of births, 0.63 per cent to migration, and 0.24 per cent to the incorporation of surrounding territory.[15]

[15] Ayçoberry, *Cologne*, p. 155; Fischer *et al.*, *Arbeitsbuch*, p. 39.

TABLE 8.6. *Source of population growth in Berlin,*
1815–1856/8 (000s)

	Population	Natural increase	Net immigration	Net change
1815	190	−32	+165	+133
1837	283	+25	+ 68	+ 93
1856/8	434/459	+58	+118	+176

Source: DeVries, *Urbanization*, p. 236.

At least until mid-century, migration between rural areas was no less important than migration from the countryside to the city. In Prussia, for example, some of the largest gains from migration before 1850 were made by the agrarian provinces of East Prussia, West Prussia, and Silesia, whose attractiveness to newcomers was comparable to Berlin's (see table 8.7). Blaschke's research on Saxony shows how these migration patterns interacted with other developments: people moved into the economically advanced areas, usually from purely agricultural regions in Saxony, Prussia, or Austria; during periods of economic depression, many of these migrants returned to their place of origin. In German Europe as a whole, the most important losses of population due to migration were suffered by the overcrowded farmlands in the south-west, where demographic pressures were not relieved by the development of rural manufacturing or urban commerce. Between 1826 and 1865 both Baden and Württemberg had substantial migration deficits, which reached their peak in the early 1850s when the average annual rate was 14.85 per cent for Baden and 20.38 per cent for Württemberg.[16]

The south-west was also the most important source of the overseas migration. Although the data on emigration for the period before 1830 are sketchy, it is clear that, when the poor harvests of 1816 drove food prices up, thousands of Germans, especially from Baden and Württemberg, sought to emigrate, mostly by travelling down the Rhine to Amsterdam in hopes of securing passage to the United States. According to one estimate, of the 50,000 Badenese who tried to leave in 1816–17, about 15,000—1.66 per cent of the state's population—made it. The lot of these early immigrants was a sorry one. Often misled and ill-treated, the majority returned

[16] Köllmann, 'Bevölkerung', pp. 218–19; Marschalck, *Bevölkerungsgeschichte*, p. 22.

TABLE 8.7. *Immigration in three Prussian provinces and Berlin,
1816–1861* (000s)

	1816–25	1826–34	1835–43	1844–52	1853–61
East Prussia	+73	+ 1	+ 62	− 9	+14
West Prussia	+38	+31	+ 55	+13	+ 7
Silesia	+75	+37	+162	− 7	−25
Berlin	+12	+36	+ 74	+61	+73

Source: Fischer *et al.*, *Arbeitsbuch*, p. 36.

home in worse shape than they left; many of those who got to
North America found themselves indentured servants or impoverished workers. Not surprisingly, the misfortunes of these people,
together with an improvement in the economic situation, depressed the number of overseas migrants during the early 1820s. By
the end of that decade, however, migration began to rise once again
and continued to grow—albeit unevenly—until the mid-1850s (see
table 8.8). As with every important demographic movement,
emigration did not have a single cause. Bad harvests and rising food

TABLE 8.8. *German emigration overseas, 1816–1864*

	Population of affected Areas[a] (000s)	Emigrants (000s)	Emigrants/ 1,000
1816–19	1,857	25.0	1.35
1820–4	1,936.2	9.8	0.51
1825–9	2,050.2	12.7	0.62
1830–4	4,597.4	51.1	1.11
1835–9	7,151.2	94.0	1.31
1840–4	9,138.8	110.6	1.21
1845–9	13,807.6	308.2	2.23
1850–4	16,192.4	728.3	4.50
1855–9	17,214.4	372.0	2.16
1860–4	17,762	225.9	1.27

Note: [a] 1816–29: Württemberg and the Palatinate, plus Baden after
1830; 1831–35: Bavaria; 1841–6: Rhineland, Westphalia, Hesse, Hesse-
Nassau; 1849–53: Brunswick, Hanover, Mecklenburg. The total .
population is the yearly average for the period.

Source: Marschalck, *Überseewanderung*, pp. 35–7.

prices certainly provided an important impetus, but their effect was often cumulative rather than immediate; when transportation improved and popular knowledge about the new world grew, economic and social pressures led more and more people to consider pulling up their roots and leaving Europe. During this period, the typical emigrant was someone from the middle strata, a man with a little property and some skills, who usually travelled with his family. High prices, limited opportunities for employment, and the dwindling supply of land combined to push these people towards North America, where, in Mack Walker's telling phrase, they sought 'less to build something new than to regain and conserve something old . . .'.[17]

As will be remembered from our discussion in Chapter 2, there was nothing new about migration. Traditional society was filled with people in flight from disaster or in search of security; a significant minority of the European population had always been permanently homeless, forced to wander the roads as vagrants, beggars, or thieves. What changed in the nineteenth century was not the relative size of the migrant population, but rather the dimensions of the world within which they moved. There is no real evidence, Charles Tilly has written, 'that large-scale industrialization increased the frequency with which people changed residence. But the distances they moved increased tremendously.'[18] We can take 'distance' here in both a literal and a symbolic sense: people moved across physical space and from one social world to another. There was no traditional equivalent to the massive overseas migrations of the nineteenth century, or to the movement from village to metropolis and from workshop to factory.

Another difference between the population movements in traditional and modern societies was personified by the tourist, that familiar modern figure who made his appearance in the German lands during the first half of the century. Before 1800 only the very rich and the exceptionally bold travelled without a serious purpose—indeed an important appeal of the aristocratic grand tour or the journey of adventure was the fact that so few were able to travel. In the modern era, however, this changed so dramatically that Karl Immermann could complain, 'it has become exceptional

---

[17] Walker, *Germany*, p. 69. In addition to Walker, see Marschalck, *Überseewanderung*; Wolf-Heino Struck, *Die Auswanderung aus dem Herzogtum Nassau (1806–1866): Ein Kapitel der modernen politischen und sozialen Entwicklung* (Wiesbaden, 1966); Klaus J. Bade (ed.), *Auswanderer. Wanderarbeiter. Gastarbeiter. Bevölkerung, Arbeitsmarkt und Wanderung in Deutschland seit der Mitte des 19. Jahrhunderts* (Ostfildern, 1984).

[18] Tilly, *Studies*, p. 29.

for someone to stay home'. Most people, he went on, seem 'to travel for the sake of travelling. They want to flee the torture of monotony, to see something new, no matter what . . .'[19] Of course Immermann exaggerated. Leisure travel remained difficult and expensive enough to be out of most people's reach. But a growing minority could travel, if not to some elegant spa or scenic landscape, at least to a nearby village or seaside town. At Baden-Baden, Ems, Karlsbad, and other fashionable watering places, enterprising businessmen built hotels to accommodate the throngs who wished to enjoy the mineral waters and gambling casinos that had once been the preserve of kings and noblemen. More modest establishments grew up in places like Helgoland, to which several thousand people journeyed each year to bathe in the sea. Among the first to grasp the commercial possibilities offered by tourism was a young publisher in Koblenz named Karl Baedeker. In 1828 he bought the rights to a book entitled *Rheinreise von Mainz bis Köln: Handbuch für Schnellreisende*, which he re-edited and issued in 1835. So successful was this guide to the sights along the Rhine that Baedeker commissioned a series of similar books; by the time of his death in 1859 there were 'Baedekers' for Belgium, Holland, Paris, the German states, and Austria. A few years later, the Stangen brothers began to offer package tours to Italy and the Middle East, where their guests enjoyed carefully arranged trips down the Grand Canal or camel rides to the pyramids.[20]

Tourists on their way to a spa, emigrants going to the New World, commercial travellers in search of sales, and labourers looking for work, were all part of a growing stream of Germans who moved from one place to another. In the course of the nineteenth century, improvements in the communications network made their journeys cheaper, easier, and swifter. The result was a redefinition of the social world's spatial dimensions which constituted as essential a change in the scale of life as the demographic revolution. When the inhibitions that time and space had traditionally imposed on institutional growth gradually weakened, economic behaviour, political authority, military strategy, and personal relationships were all affected. while the effect of the communications revolution was felt throughout nineteenth-century Europe, its impact may have been especially important in the German lands,

[19] Böhmer, *Welt*, p. 224.
[20] Boehn, *Biedermeier*; A. Sternberger, *Panorama of the 19th Century* (New York, 1977), 47.

where geography and politics had for so long combined to produce social and economic fragmentation.

As contemporary accounts make clear, travel in the first decades of the nineteenth century continued to be expensive, arduous, and slow. Ludwig Börne's *Monographie der deutschen Postschnecke*, for instance, was based on his forty-six hour journey by post wagon from Frankfurt to Stuttgart. Foreign travellers recorded their own unpleasant experiences: 'Scarcely out of the gates of Hanover', wrote Russell in 1828, 'and the wheels already drowned in sand up to the axletree; tedium to the eye, and death to the patience of the traveller, with the added vexation of paying tolls for permission to follow the most convenient track which his postilion can find among the fir trees. . . .' In 1836 Murray's authoritative handbook for travellers described as 'very bad' the roads in Bavaria, where the usual speed of a journey could be no more than one German mile an hour.[21] By mid-century, however, the situation had improved, most significantly in Prussia, where the length of hard-surface roads grew from 3,800 kilometres in 1816 to 7,300 in 1830, 12,800 in 1845, and 16,600 in 1852. As important as the expansion of the road system were changes in people's attitudes towards movement. In 1816 one observer had written from Westphalia that many of the inhabitants opposed building better roads, which they feared would encourage troop movements and deprive innkeepers of their livelihoods. By 1835, however, Heinrich von Gagern could proclaim: 'No one now speaks of military roads [*Heerstrassen*] as instruments of war, repression, and plunder; roads are now frequently called the veins and arteries of the body politic . . .' Roads, Gagerern believed, would promote freedom and independence, peace and prosperity.[22]

Water transportation also improved significantly after 1800. As we have seen, river traffic had always been slowed by navigational hazards, tolls, and the right of certain cities to unload and reship all merchandise that passed their docks. First under Napoleon and then under Prussian rule, these barriers were gradually removed from the Rhine, making it possible to move goods and passengers much more easily. At the same time, the arrival of the steam engine freed riverboats from their dependence on the cumbersome system

---

[21] Russell, *Tour*, ii. 1; J. Murray, *Handbook of Travellers in South Germany* (1st edn.), (London, 1837), 20.

[22] Fremdling, *Eisenbahnen*, p. 106; Pollard, *Integration*, pp. 37–8; Gagern, *Liberalismus*, p. 152.

of men and animals necessary to tow them upstream, usually at a rate of two or three kilometres per hour. By 1846 there were 180 steamers on German rivers. Furthermore, a network of canals connected major waterways, extending from the Danube, Weser, and Elbe.[23]

Despite these achievements, however, water transport could usually not compete with the railroad, which swiftly established itself as the transportation revolution's leading symbol and most significant instrument. The first German rail line, connecting Nuremberg and Fürth, was opened, to the sound of ceremonial cannons and the music of a brass band, in 1835. A single track, six kilometres long, the Nuremberg–Fürth line operated only in daylight. But it was both popular and profitable; many of its passengers were Jews, who worked but could not live in Nuremberg. Within three years, 141 kilometres of track had been laid; by 1840, 462; by 1850, 5,875; and, by 1860, 11,157. At first, rail lines were scattered throughout German Europe, linking, for example, Berlin and Potsdam, Augsburg and Munich, Vienna and Brunn. By mid-century, the lines began to be connected and networks slowly took shape. As with so many other aspects of German social and economic development, the railroad lacked a single centre. Instead, there were separate webs, each tying together different regional systems. Berlin was linked to the north by lines to Stettin and Hamburg, to the east by a line to Breslau, and to the west by a line running through Brunswick and Hanover and then turning south into Westphalia and on to Cologne. At the same time, a south-western line ran from Freiburg north through Baden and on to Frankfurt, with connections to Stuttgart. A Bavarian line ran north from Munich to Bamberg and then on to Hof and Plauen. Vienna was linked to Prague, Budapest, and Oderberg, but not until the 1850s was there direct service from the Habsburgs' capital to most German cities.[24]

As the rail network expanded, the railroad's comparative advantage over other forms of transport increased. In 1850 inland shipping still carried three times more freight traffic than railroads, but by 1870 the railroad had a lead of almost four to one. At the

[23] Pollard, *Integration*, pp. 42 ff.; Böhmer, *Welt*, p. 233.
[24] The best introduction to the development and impact of railroads is Fremdling, *Eisenbahnen*. There is a useful set of maps and schedules in Klaus Kobschätzky, *Streckenatlas der deutschen Eisenbahnen 1834–1892* (Düsseldorf, 1971), and a more detailed collection in Arthur von Mayer's classic *Geschichte und Geographie der deutschen Eisenbahnen von ihrer Entstehung bis auf die Gegenwart* (2 vols.; Berlin, 1891).

same time, the cost of transporting goods by rail declined sharply, from an estimated eighteen Pfennig per ton per kilometre in 1840 to less than ten in 1850, seven in 1860, and five in 1870. As a result, the volume of both passenger and freight traffic grew rapidly (see table 8.9).

TABLE 8.9. *Railroad traffic, 1840–1865[a]*

	Passenger km (millions)	Freight km (millions)
1840	62.3	3.2
1845	308.5	50.8
1850	782.7	302.7
1855	1,090.4	1,094.9
1860	1,732.9	1,675.2
1865	2,676.0	3,671.8

Note: [a] German boundaries of 1867.
Source: Fremdling, *Eisenbahnen*, p. 17.

'The younger generation will soon have forgotten', wrote Carl Gustav Carus in his memoirs, 'how extraordinarily strange, indeed daemonic these great new means of transportation appeared to be.' Germans viewed the railroad with fascination; they recorded the first time they saw a locomotive, smoke billowing from its engine, moving through the landscape; they noted the sensations of excitement and anxiety which their first train trip aroused. Karl Beck's poem, 'Die Eisenbahn', written to commemorate the opening of the Leipzig-Dresden line in 1837, seeks to capture the sights, sounds, and particular rhythms of the railroad:

> Rasend rauschen rings die Räder,
> Rollend, grollend, stürmisch sausend,
> Tief im innersten Geäder
> Kämpft der Zeitgeist freiheitsbrausend.
> Stämmen Steine sich entgegen,
> Reibt er sie zu Sand zusammen,
> Seinen Fluch und seinen Segen
> Speit er aus in Rauch und Flammen.

People of every political persuasion recognized that these machines would leave no facet of life unchanged. Metternich, for instance, was convinced that the effects of the railroad would 'penetrate into the depths of society', and would produce 'a transformation in political and also in social conditions'. Not everyone, to be sure, agreed. Frederick William III remarked that he saw no great advantage in getting from Berlin to Potsdam a few hours sooner. Nor did everyone view the arrival of the railroad as a good thing. To Nikolaus Lenau, it was 'an evil visitor', despoiling the landscape's beauty:

> Mitten durch den grünen Hain,
> Ungestümer Hast,
> Frisst die Eisenbahn herein,
> Dir ein schlimmer Gast.
> Bäume fallen links und rechts
> Wo sie vorwärts bricht;
> Deines blühenden Geschlechts
> Schont die rauhe nicht.

Lenau called this poem 'An den Frühling 1838' in order to locate the exact historical moment when the triumph of machine over nature began.[25]

Most Germans, however, welcomed the railroad as an example of human ingenuity and as the harbinger of progressive change. 'Our joy', wrote Heinrich Brüggemann about the opening of a new line, 'is a liberal joy, a pleasure over new triumphs which will increase the power of liberal and humane principles.' Friedrich List, the apostle of economic growth, called the railroad a Hercules, 'who will deliver nations from the plague of war, inflation, famine, national hatreds, unemployment, and ignorance . . .'. In an essay entitled 'On the Uses of Railroads', List spelled out in detail their material and spiritual benefits. He began by calling the railway and the new Customs Union 'Siamese twins', born together and inseparable, both providing the basis for material co-operation and economic progress. But the railroad was also a contribution to national defence, a way of promoting culture, 'a tonic for the national spirit', and 'a tight belt around the loins of the German nation'. All of this, List concluded, was especially necessary for Germany, which has been 'robbed of almost all attributes of nationality by earlier divisiveness' and therefore 'so desperately needs internal unification of its limbs'.[26]

After the formation of the Bismarckian Reich, patriotic historians stressed the connection between railroads and national unification. 'The German empire was founded' wrote Wilhelm Raabe, with the construction of the first railway . . .'[27] In so far as the

---

[25] Böhmer, *Welt*, pp. 230 and 224–25. On the cultural impact of the railroad, see Riedel, 'Biedermeier'; Schivelbusch, *Journey*.

[26] Sheehan, *Liberalism*, p. 28; Böhmer, *Welt*, p. 228; Glaser, *Mind*, pp. 186–7.

[27] Quoted with approval in Henderson, *Zollverein*, p. 147.

railroad helped is contribute to the growth of Prussian social, economic, and military power, it did contribute to the Hohenzollern's victory in 1866. But it is by no means clear that the railroad made the Bismarckian Reich a natural or necessary political formulation. If one studies a map of the central European rail system in 1860, any number of political, social, economic, and cultural connections seem possible. Furthermore, we should bear in mind that, despite List's confident predictions, a communication system can divide as well as unite. The laying of tracks connects some areas but isolates others; the railroad can produce regional diversity in addition to regional cohesion.

In any event, the railroad is too important to be confined within the narrow context of German nation-building. As perceptive contemporaries sometimes realized, the railroad was comparable to the epoch-making discoveries of the past: in 1837, for example, Eduard Beurmann wrote that the railroad would have the same kind of historical importance as the invention of printing, 'The one transmitted ideas, the other life, the one taught people about one another, the other led them to one another . . .'[28] The railroad was also a quintessentially modern invention. In the first place, it qualitatively differed from the various marginal improvements in transportation made in the preceding centuries. Until the coming of the train, Europeans had moved no more swiftly, and in little more comfort, than they had in Roman times; by mid-century, the speed and character of travel was fundamentally different. Moreover, the effects of the railroad spread throughout the social and political order. As we shall see, railroads encouraged economic activity—directly, by creating demand for commodities like coal, and indirectly, by facilitating commerce. They also changed the scale, economic role and even physical appearance of cities, extended the reach of political institutions, and produced a revolution in the conduct of war. Trains spurred other forms of communication, such as the telegraph, which flourished only when rail travel created the need for the rapid transmission of signals. More clearly than any of the other technological marvels created during the industrial age, trains symbolized the nineteenth century's ability to break the bonds of nature by harnessing power without precedent in human history. They seemed to show that science and reason had done what necromancy had vainly promised: men and women could now transcend the limits imposed by flesh and blood. No wonder that those who celebrated

[28] For this and other examples, see Riedel, 'Biedermeier', pp. 103 ff.

these achievements saw the railroad as a metaphor for progress; like a locomotive speeding towards its destination, European society seemed to be moving along the tracks of change, away from the constraints of the past, towards the blessings of the future.

ii. AGRICULTURE AND RURAL SOCIAL RELATIONS

When the nineteenth century began, most Germans were still entrapped by the bonds of nature. Men and women continued to travel along ill-kept roads, on foot, or with horses. They heated their houses with wood and lit them with candles, fertilized the soil with animal wastes, and powered what few machines they had with animal energy. People lived in structures built in time-honoured ways, grouped in villages or behind the walls of small, inward-looking cities. The rhythm of their lives was set by the sun and the seasons, time was marked by church bells, space by the distance someone could walk in a day. A time-traveller, suddenly transported from the sixteenth century to 1800, would have been amazed at German politics and culture, but would have found the social and economic order quite familiar. While states had risen and fallen, and extraordinary new ideas were under discussion every-where, men and women continued to earn their livings much as they had in Luther's day.

Throughout the first half of the nineteenth century, German Europe remained predominately rural. In 1800, about 75 per cent of the population lived from and on the land. Over the course of the next decades, the number of those engaged in agricultural pursuits declined, but the relative size of rural society remained fairly constant: 73 per cent of the Prussian population was in the countryside in 1816, 72 per cent in 1840, and 71 per cent in 1852. Data compiled by Hartmut Harnisch (see table 8.10) show how this trend operated in some selected administrative districts. In Austria, rural society was even more predominant: over 84 per cent of the Habsburgs' Austrian subjects lived in communities with less than two thousand inhabitants in 1830, 81 per cent in 1851. Everywhere the countryside continued to intrude on urban life: whenever they could, craftsmen worked a small plot of land and city-dwellers raised poultry or livestock. Even in the 1830s, almost 60 per cent of Prussian investment capital went to the land. Overall, German agriculture continued to make up the largest portion of the gross national product until after 1871.[29]

[29] For an introduction to the literature on German agriculture, see above, Ch. 2,

TABLE 8.10. *Relative population growth in selected districts, 1816–1859*

		1816	1831	1849	1859
Prussia	urban	1000	1249	1590	1817
	rural	1000	1269	1461	1672
Königsberg	urban	1000	1221	1374	1582
	rural	1000	1396	1681	1835
Gumbinnen	urban	1000	1154	1329	1505
	rural	1000	1549	1867	1965
Danzig	urban	1000	1228	1588	1749
	rural	1000	1468	1925	2107
Marienwerder	urban	1000	1366	1810	2098
	rural	1000	1407	1952	2142
Köslin	urban	1000	1366	1810	2098
	rural	1000	1393	1911	2116
Oppeln	urban	1000	1396	1808	2022
	rural	1000	1390	1847	2060

Source: Harnisch, 'Probleme', p. 321.

During the first half of the century, Germans' dependence on agriculture was underscored again and again. In the early 1800s agricultural prices fell, which made things hard for farmers, but gave consumers what amounted to an increase in real wages. In 1816, however, this situation swiftly changed. Almost everywhere the crop cycle was a disaster: April was wet, May so cold that the ground froze, between June and September it rained incessantly, sometimes hard enough to ruin orchards and flood what few crops had begun to sprout. By October, when it was time for the harvest, there was bitter cold and heavy snow. In the spring of 1817, after farmers had sold their small surplus at high prices, many people were reduced to the pitiful condition that Clausewitz found in the Rhineland, where 'ruined figures, scarcely resembling men, [prowled] around the fields searching for food among the unharvested and already half rotten potatoes that never grew to maturity'. In parts of the south-west, overpopulation made scarcity especially painful: between 1815 and 1817 the index of wholesale grain prices more than doubled in both Baden and Württemberg.[30]

sect. ii, n. 31. Data on population distribution can be found in Sandgruber, *Agrarstatistik*; on investment and employment, in Fischer *et al.*, *Arbeitsbuch*, especially pp. 52–3 and 100 ff.

[30] Post, *Crisis*, p. 44. See also Walker, *Germany*, especially p. 5.

John D. Post, in a careful study of what he calls 'the last great subsistence crisis in the western world', has argued that 'the violent fluctuation of agricultural productivity and consequently the price of foodstuffs . . . exercised the primary influence on the entire western economy'.[31] Because so much depended on agriculture, particularly on the grain supply, bad harvests led to high prices, declining real wages, and shortages in both food and key raw materials. However, bountiful crops could also produce problems. The excellent harvests that followed the disasters of 1816–17, for example, depressed prices, ruined some farmers, and severely dislocated trade and commerce. As long as the economy rested on an agrarian base, it would be hostage to forces difficult to control and impossible to predict.

The economic and social pre-eminence of the German country-side persisted, but the character of country life significantly changed. Like the demographic revolution, the transformation of agriculture was the product of gradually gathering forces, whose cumulative impact can best be seen over a fairly long period of time. Again like demography, developments in agriculture were locally rooted and regionally diverse. Everything important about agrarian society varied from place to place: the nature of the soil, the climate, the manner of landholding, and the organization of the community. The strength and effectiveness of innovative impulses primarily depended on the character of the local market and the local social structure. Until the development of a powerful communications network pulled these localities together, they evolved separately, each responding in its own way to challenges shaped by the immediate environment.

By the end of the eighteenth century, two powerful forces had begun to sweep across this mosaic of agricultural microcosms: the state, which attempted to regulate rural life so that it might better exploit rural resources, and the market, which offered landowners and tenants an opportunity to maximize their profits and improve their material condition. How state and market affected the countryside depended on an interlocking and interdependent set of conditions which we can call the agricultural system: the character of land tenure and the size of each holding, the way the land was worked and the crops it produced, the regional market for agricultural products, and the availability of capital and labour. Under the traditional social order, the system's interlocking pieces usually resisted both internal and external pressures for change. But

---

[31] Post, *Crisis*, p. 141.

once change began and one element in the system was altered, then the system as a whole had to respond: new legal definitions of land tenure, different crops, or a reorganization of the field system set in motion a transformation of social, economic, and political relationships on the land. The specific timing and character of this transformation varied, but in the long run the direction of change was everywhere the same; power relationships shifted from personal *Herrschaft* to state authority, labour relationships from seigneurial dependence to economic domination. German historians characteristically fuse the political and economic aspects of this process under the rubric of 'land reform' or 'peasant emancipation', terms which must be understood as shorthand for a complex and prolonged series of alterations in the way land was held and worked, and in the social condition of those who held and worked it.[32]

Land reform, the reader will recall, began earliest and went fastest in the Habsburg realm. In order to encourage the evolution of a free, prosperous, and productive peasantry, Maria Theresa and Joseph II had tried to raise the peasant's legal status, regulate the obligations he owed his seigneur, improve the condition of his land tenure, and protect him from eviction or exploitation. By the time of Joseph's death, Austrian peasants were still caught up in a net of servile relationships, but they were no longer serfs and enjoyed some measure of protection from the state. Joseph's successors halted the process of reform, abandoned his ambitious overhaul of the tax system, and moved the state away from its protective role. An edict of 1798, for example, left the regulation of labour services up to free—but extraordinarily unequal—negotiations between landlord and tenant. Nevertheless, enough of the Josephist legacy remained to convince Freiherr vom Stein that 'in the Austrian monarchy infinitely more has been done for the peasant than in Prussia, even by the Edict of 9 October 1807'.[33]

From Joseph's reign until 1848, there were no more dramatic legal reforms in the Austrian countryside. When the elaborate survey of taxable property commissioned by the government was finally finished in 1843, it was never used. The imperial decrees of April and December 1846, issued in response to serious unrest in

[32] The concept of an 'agricultural system' is from Pounds, *Geography...1800–1914*, p. 197. On the process of political emancipation, see Conze's classic article, 'Wirkungen'; Blum, *End*.

[33] E. M. Link, *The Emancipation of the Austrian Peasant, 1740–1798* (New York, 1949), 168.

Galicia and other parts of the monarchy, did little more than catalogue pre-existing rights and obligations. Throughout the first half of the nineteenth century, therefore, most Austrian peasants continued to owe their landlords substantial services as well as rents and other obligations. In Austrian Silesia, for instance, a family had to provide between 108 and 144 days of labour with a team of animals, several additional days at other tasks, and a number of payments in kind and money. On average, a peasant could expect to pay about one-third of his income to his lord and the state.[34]

But beneath the surface of legal continuity and persisting servility, powerful forces for change were at work. The bureaucracy continued to interefer in local affairs, extending its reach further and further into everyday life. Hans Kudlich, the son of a Silesian peasant, recalled in his memoirs how people in his father's village protested about the distance they had to travel in order to haul wood for the landlord. After several setbacks, they won their case in court and forced a redefinition of this aspect of their labour services. At the same time, more and more estate owners responded to new economic opportunities by trying to increase production and sell their produce on an international market. Since many of these progressive agriculturists believed that forced labour was inefficient and uneconomical, they were often eager to convert labour services into cash, with which they could then hire workers by the day.[35]

Because the eighteenth-century Hohenzollern had comparatively limited success in their efforts to regulate rural society, when the Prussian state collapsed in 1806 much of what the Austrians had accomplished under Maria Theresa and Joseph remained to be done. Throughout the era of reform, the issue of rural social, economic, and political organization was a source of bitter animosity between progressive administrators and a landed nobility intent upon defending their privileges, wealth, and authority. The result, as we know, was a complex of compromises reached after the government retreated from its most ambitious plans and sacrificed the peasantry's interests in order to win the aristocracy's reluctant acquiescence. As one scholar has put it, the authorities combined welfare measures for the estate owners with a policy of strict *laissez-faire* towards the peasantry.[36]

---

[34] Blum, *End*, pp. 74 ff.

[35] Kudlich, *Rückblicke*, i. 22 ff.; Brunner, *Landleben*, pp. 313 ff.; Sandgruber, *Anfänge* pp. 36 ff.

[36] Erich Jordan, *Die Entstehung der Konservativen Partei und die preussischen Agrarverhältnisse von 1848* (Munich and Leipzig, 1914), 96.

The political battle over Prussian agrarian policy was intensified by the economic climate in which it took place. By the time the era of reform began, the extraordinary growth and prosperity enjoyed by Prussian agriculture in the late eighteenth century had given way to a prolonged crisis, rendered all the more painful by the greed and speculative fever that had gripped many landowners around the turn of the century. As land values and agricultural prices fell, debtors could not meet their obligations, mortgages came due, and the danger of financial ruin became a reality. When the shortages of 1816 and 1817 inflated prices, things improved somewhat, but then deteriorated again during the 1820s; by 1825 grain prices had fallen to roughly a quarter of what they had been eight years earlier. In some places, land prices did not reach the level of the 1790s until the 1880s. It was a grave misfortune for the reformers, therefore, that their attempt to open the agricultural sector to the free play of economic forces coincided with a period of chronic instability in the international market.[37]

Land reform in Prussia entailed the elimination of personal servitude, the conversion of services into cash payments, and the removal of the traditional restrictions on the sale and purchase of rural property. In some areas, these measures had the effect the reformers wished: peasants established themselves as legally free, independent proprietors with enough land to work efficiently. But only a small minority of Prussian peasants had a chance of realizing this ideal. According to the edict of 1816, those eligible to acquire ownership of their land had to be *spannfähig*, that is, they had to have the resources to support a team of animals. Those who could not—and this was almost always the majority—found themselves without either the slender protection of the seigneurial system or the natural resources necessary to enjoy the newly granted right of property. These marginal peasants were usually forced to make some kind of contractual arrangement with their landlords, to whom they promised to provide labour in return for a house, garden, and the right to gather wood. Emancipation thus changed the form but not the substance of social dependence. Moreover, as the population of the eastern provinces increased, it was in the landlord's interest to rely on hired workers rather than long-term contracts. The result was a growing population of landless agricultural labourers, totally at the mercy of the market.

While the marginal peasant was the major casualty of the

---

[37] Abel, *Geschichte*, pp. 220 ff. has data on prices. For the political context, see above, Ch. 5, sect. iii.

Prussian reforms, even people with a chance to become free and independent farmers faced serious obstacles. In order to gain title to their land, peasants had to make payments to the landlord, usually at a fixed rate over a long period. When prices plummeted during the 1820s, these payments, together with the peasants' other obligations, were often ruinous. The government, usually quite generous with loans to large landowners, was rarely willing to extend credit to small farmers. A number of emancipated peasants, therefore, lost the land they had acquired. In Magdeburg the number of peasant farmers declined by about 8 per cent, from 15,272 to 14, 244, between 1816 and 1851. According to the official statistics, almost one of four Prussian farms was sold during this period, most of them to other peasants, but over 8 per cent either to smallholders or to estate owners.[38]

Scholars now agree that the landed élite turned out to be the principal beneficiary of reform—although how much they benefited is still a matter of dispute. Estate owners were compensated for the services lost by emancipation, received land or long-term payments in return for granting title to peasant farmers, and were in a position to take full advantage of any redistribution of land formerly held in common. Furthermore, since the reforms removed restrictions on the sale of peasant holdings, estate owners could sometimes expand their property at bargain prices. Overall, the landed élite acquired some four million Morgen of peasant land and a disproportionately large share of the divided commons. Even these gains were not enough to save some aristocrats from their own improvidence or the destructive impact of the market. The landed élite as a whole may have improved its relative position, but many individuals and regions did poorly. Thus, of the 594 estates in debt to the mortgage bank in East Prussia, between 1815 and 1826, 98 were subject to a forced sale. According to one authority, the Prussian nobility's total indebtedness doubled during the first half of the century.[39]

Like Prussia, the west German states passed a series of land reforms during the first half of the century. The motives of the reformers were the same in Stuttgart or Munich as they had been in Berlin: as King William of Württemberg put the matter in his decree of 1817, because the state's wealth 'lies in landed property and in its appropriate use, the prosperity of the people must be

---

[38] Berthold, 'Bevölkerungsentwicklung', p. 149.
[39] Blum, *End*, p. 246; Abel, *Fluctuations*, p. 283; Schissler, *Agrargesellschaft*, p. 111.

based upon a freedom of the landowner and of the peasant that is in harmony with the laws and spirit of the time'.[40] But nowhere in the west did reformers face opponents as powerful and stubborn as the Prussian Junker. Moreover, the western system of *Grundherrschaft* was a good deal less resistant to reform than the *Gutsherrschaft* prevalent east of the Elbe. Under *Gutsherrschaft*, emancipation required a partial redistribution of the land and a transformation in the way labourers were hired and compensated, whereas, under *Grundherrschaft*, it was only necessary to redefine what the tenant owed his lord in return for working the land. Nevertheless, reform in the west was not achieved without animosity and conflict. Despite a system of compensation, the nobility lost between 10 and 20 per cent of their income due to emancipation. The peasantry, on the other hand, was still burdened by dues and debts and resentful of the servile residues that remained in many states.

In most of German Europe, demography seems to have had a more powerful impact on rural life than political reform. In the south-west, for example, demographic pressures led to greater fragmentation of the land and therefore produced an increasing number of marginal farmers, who could barely survive in the best of times and were doomed to destitution as soon as prices fell or a harvest failed. In order to prevent what Friedrich List called a *Zwergwirtschaft*, a dwarf economy of minuscule plots insufficient to support the families living on them, some states, including Baden, Nassau, Saxony, and Bavaria, tried to pass laws limiting a peasant's right to divide his land. But even where law or tradition prevented fragmentation, there was an increase in the number of marginal or landless people who had to work as hired labourers or find some other means of livelihood. In the long run, the government could do little to alleviate this situation; only improved productivity might make life better for German farmers. Political reform could not create sustained growth; at best it might help to create the conditions under which growth would be possible.[41]

Beginning in the last decades of the eighteenth century, agricultural productivity slowly improved. Cereal production in Prussia, for example, grew from 4.6 million tons in 1816, to 5.9 million in 1831, and 6.8 million in 1840, before falling back to 4.8 million in 1846. The average weight of Prussian oxen increased from 250 kilograms in 1802 to 274 in 1842, of cattle from 164 to

[40] Rürup, *Deutschland*, p. 369.
[41] Walker, *Germany*, especially pp. 47 ff.; Pounds, *Geography . . . 1800–1914*, p. 225; Mayhew, *Settlement*, has some data on fragmentation.

185. According to the estimates calculated by Gertrud Helling, grain and potato crops in Prussia, Saxony, Bavaria, and Württemberg declined between 1800 and 1818, improved by about 16 per cent in the 1820s, and then by another 10 per cent in the 1830s. The figures available on meat, poultry, milk, eggs, and wool suggest similar gains.[42] Output per worker also displayed moderate improvements (see table 8.11).

TABLE 8.11. *Labour productivity in German agriculture, 1800–1850*

	Total production (1,000 tons)[a]	Labour force (000s)	Average	Index
1800–10	22,055	9,525	2.32	100
1811–20	22,992	9,530	2.41	104
1821–5	27,240	10,100	2.70	116
1826–30	28,797	10,300	2.80	120
1831–5	34,115	10,600	3.22	139
1836–40	37,057	11,057	3.35	144
1841–5	40,544	11,662	3.48	150
1846–50	43,874	11,425	3.84	165

Note: [a] Calculated in equivalent of grain production.
Source: Helling, 'Entwicklung', p. 134.

This growth of agricultural productivity was in part due to spread of the scientific knowledge. Benedikt Weber's *Handbuch der ökonomischen Literatur*, published in 1809, listed some six thousand titles on agriculture, of which 230 were practical guides. In 1810, Johann Heinrich von Thünen bought 460 hectares in Mecklenburg, which he turned into a well-known model of innovative agronomy. Throughout the first half of the century, farmers, academicians, and civil servants founded societies devoted to agricultural progress and enlightenment—by 1852 there were 360 in Prussia alone. In 1837 members of these various societies in German-speaking Europe began to meet annually. The application of scientific theory to agricultural practice was greatly enhanced by the publication of Justus von Liebig's *Die organische Chemie in ihrer Anwendung auf Agrikultur und Physiologie*, which tried to show how an understanding of chemical processes could help farmers improve their productivity. By mid-century the first improvements in equipment began to be adopted by German farmers: the sickle was

[42] Fischer *et al.*, *Arbeitsbuch*, p. 58. See also Helling, 'Entwicklung'.

gradually replaced by the scythe, which allowed a harvester to work four times faster, and heavy wooden ploughs slowly gave way to lighter, stronger, and more mobile metal ones.[43]

Agricultural production also increased because the amount of arable land expanded. This expansion occurred in three ways: first, through land reclamation projects, such as those carried on along the upper Rhine, in the Ditmarschen region, and on the Lüneburg heath; second, through piecemeal extension into uncultivated wasteland, forests, or meadows; and finally, through the cultivation of fallow land through the use of fodder crops, which supported additional livestock, or of legumes, which served to fix the atmospheric nitrogen in the soil. In some areas, gains in productivity were made by a process of enclosure which brought together the open field system's separate strips into a small number of more efficient units. Such rearrangements were passionately advocated by reformers like Albrecht Thaer, but they took place slowly and often painfully, first in Mecklenburg and Schleswig-Holstein, in Prussia after 1821, and eventually in parts of the south and west, where they continued well into the second half of the nineteenth century. Field systems were also affected by improvements in transportation that made it possible for farmers to specialize. Since they no longer had to be self-sufficient, they could replace hemp, flax, herbs, and dyestuffs with the crops best suited to local soil and climate conditions. Regions now began to concentrate on cereals, tobacco, fruits, or other specialities, which were then shipped by railroad to wider markets. In addition to these commodities, root crops became especially popular almost everywhere in central Europe. Highly nutritious and well-suited to sandy soil, the potato, which farmers had begun to plant towards the end of the eighteenth century, was heavily used in fallow fields: in Prussia, for example, the potato crop increased fivefold between 1816 and 1840. So dependent did the population become on this source of food that the first signs of potato blight in 1842 triggered panic in many regions. By the late 1840s, as we shall see, the failure of the potato crop produced widespread misery and unrest.[44]

Since rural society was a set of interlocking pieces, a change in any one aspect of life was bound to alter the system as a whole. The introduction of the scythe, for instance, increased productivity, but

---

[43] Pounds, Geography...1800–1914, pp. 227 ff. and 252 ff.

[44] There is a good summary of these developments in Pounds, Geography...1500–1840. See also the data in Fischer et al., Arbeitsbuch, pp. 58–59 and the discussion below, Ch. 12, sect. ii.

also decreased the demand for agricultural labour and left less residue in the fields for those with the right to glean after the harvest. The consolidation of fields into separate units made innovation easier, but also removed an important source of community solidarity. The distribution of common lands increased output, but deprived a number of marginal families of their last rights and privileges. Even changes in the kind of crops grown had a profound impact on the organization of household and community. Cereals, for instance, demand heavy, intense physical labour when they are planted and harvested, but do not require a great deal of attention in between. Vegetables, on the other hand, need more sustained and intense cultivation. As these crops became more popular, women worked in the fields all year round and not just at harvest time, while men remained committed to the seasonal work patterns imposed by cereal cultivation. Sometimes the result was a new set of strains within peasant households, where wives felt overwhelmed by the amount they were expected to do and husbands were perpetually dissatisfied by what they regarded as a decline in women's domestic obligations.[45]

About the German peasantry's material condition in the first half of the nineteenth century no generalizations are possible. At one extreme were the farmers living on the rich soil in the plain between Karlsruhe and Baden–Baden, where T. C. Banfield was impressed by how 'the marks of ease and even of wealth are easily distinguished in the houses of the greater landed proprietors, although their peasant-like appearance and manner rather belong to a poorer class'. Far less well off were the men and women who approached William Jacob at the Frankfurt market in 1820, 'offering their commodities for sale in very small quantities, some had a few apples, plums, pears, or grapes, the whole value of which could not be more than three pence or four pence'.[46] Worst of all was the condition of the landless labourers in the east, who were legally free but remained caught in a web of poverty and ignorance hardly less constraining than their former servitude. Forced to live in primitive dwellings and work for subsistence wages, these peasants, like their counterparts throughout the German lands, were at the bottom of the rural social order. As the population expanded, their numbers grew and their situation deteriorated.

[45] David Sabean, 'Small Peasant Agriculture in Germany at the Beginning of the Nineteenth Century: Changing Work Patterns', *Peasant Studies*, 7/4 (1978), 218–24.

[46] Pollard and Holmes (eds.), *Documents*, p. 261; Blum, *End*, p. 171. Two other examples: Schurz, *Lebenserinnerungen*, i, chs. 1, 2 on his boyhood in a Rhenish village, and Jeggle, *Kiebingen*.

The condition of the nobility, like that of the peasantry, was extremely diverse. The advance of commercial agriculture, the accelerated turnover of estates due to speculation, and the legal effects of land reform combined to subject landed property to the forces and values of the market place. 'Thirty or forty years ago', wrote G. Hanssen in 1832, 'our whole nation got into a frenzy of buying and selling real estate in a way now reserved only for government stocks.' Among the Junker landlords studied by Fritz Martiny, one in six sold his property between 1800 and 1805. While this speculative fever abated in the years thereafter, the real estate market remained active: according to a government study, the average Prussian *Rittergut* changed hands more than twice between 1835 and 1864; 60 per cent of these transfers were due to sales, 34 per cent to inheritance, and 5 per cent to foreclosure. Among the sellers were doubtlessly many who could not survive in the tough economic environment faced by German agriculture before mid-century. Once they had lost their land, these families could retain their status only by entering an appropriate profession, most often the service of a state. But the commercialization of rural society brought opportunities as well as peril. For example, a Silesian estate owner named von Keltsch prospered through careful and well-informed agricultural practices that enabled him to raise cattle as well as rye, barley, and clover. Similarly, in Carl Brinkmann's study of Wustrau, a Brandenburg estate, we see how landlords and their agents could employ advanced techniques and hired labour to create a flourishing agricultural enterprise.[47]

While they could not take their wealth, authority, and prestige for granted, the landed nobility remained privileged and powerful. Not all seigneurial rights had been lost during the age of reform; the Austrian nobility kept some of their monopolies until well after mid-century, while in Prussia the attempt made in 1810 to tax estates was never enforced and eventually abandoned until 1872. Landlords' political and judicial power over their dependents also remained, not only in Prussia but also in Bavaria, Württemberg, Hanover, and other smaller states. In Mecklenburg proprietors kept these local powers until the 1870s. Even when their authority over rural institutions was formally transferred to the state, the élites' local influence often continued. Symbolically, the persistence of the aristocracy's pre-eminence in the countryside was best expressed in their exclusive right to hunt. As in the waning days of

---

[47] Abel, *Fluctuations*, p. 217; Fritz Martiny, *Die Adelsfrage in Preussen vor 1806 als politisches und soziales Problem* (Stuttgart and Berlin, 1938); Brinkmann, *Wustrau*.

the old regime, hunting recalled the nobleman's function as his dependants' armed protector and thereby affirmed his continued position in the social order. 'I will not deliver a speech in praise of hunting rights,' said Freiherr von Hornstein in 1838, 'but I believe that the nobility must be viewed as a *Stand*, and that if it is a *Stand* it should have its marks of status.' If, the Freiherr continued, aristocrats did not hunt, then 'probably in many places where now the most beautiful villages and cities flourish, we would see the dwellings of bears'.[48]

Nobles might pretend that their status still flowed from their pedigree and adhered to their person, but few could doubt that their power and privilege was dependent on the states. Gone was the imperial nobility, whose existence had stood for the stratum's claim to personal sovereignty; gone too were the independent institutions of the church, those ecclesiastical principalities through which aristocratic families had traditionally found wealth and political power. Even when legal codes and constitutions recognized the nobility's special role, this role was defined by, and set within, the state. Moreover, many states were inclined to see the landed élite in terms of property ownership rather than ancestry: the edicts establishing the provincial *Landtage* in Prussia, for instance, conferred membership—in law if not always in practice—in the *Ritterschaft* to proprietors of a *Rittergut*, regardless of their social origins.

The German aristocracy responded to their absorption by the state in quite different ways. In Westphalia, the revolution stripped the upper nobility of their independence and destroyed the institutions through which they had once exercised ecclesiastical and political power. When their lands were annexed by Prussia, the Westphalian nobles found themselves confronting a alien polity without much sympathy for their social position or religious loyalties. Eventually, they were transformed from an autonomous *Stand* into a regional élite, with localized power and a mandate to defend their province and church against the state. The situation was quite different in Prussia's eastern provinces, where, as we know, the Junkers had been working in tandem with the Hohenzollern state since the late seventeenth century. To the Junkers, land reform was yet another, albeit particularly painful, step in a long historical journey. Not surprisingly, they continued

[48] Hans Wilhelm Eckardt, *Herrschaftliche Jagd. Bäuerliche Not und bürgerliche Kritik. Zur Geschichte der fürstlichen und adligen Jagdprivilegien vornehmlich im südwestdeutschen Raum* (Göttingen, 1976), 279.

to exploit their positions in the bureaucracy and army, while pressing for new versions of the bargain they had so often made with the Prussian state at the expense of their dependants. In contrast to most western nobilities, therefore, the old Prussia élite continued to combine authority in their region with influence over the central institutions of the state.[49]

A distinctive place within the German landed aristocracy was occupied by the *Standesherren*, those eighty-odd families of imperial counts and princes whose sovereignty had been lost in 1806. After having failed to regain their independence at the Congress of Vienna, these aristocrats had to be satisfied with the ambiguous promises offered in Article Fourteen of the *Bundesakte*, which granted them *Ebenbürtigkeit* with the ruling dynasties and a variety of other rights and privileges, but made these dependent on state law and limited by governmental authority. For the next several decades, the *Standesherren* struggled to define a position between sovereignty and citizenship. They retained, as best they could, the trappings and rituals of their own courts, continued to exercise authority over their dependants, and insisted upon their special prerogatives as the state's most privileged group. 'The consciousness', Heinz Gollwitzer wrote, 'of being Herr im Haus, and ruler in country or principality remained powerful for many *Standesherren*.' This consciousness was most difficult to express in the smaller states of the southwest, where most of their lands were located and where they represented possible competitors to state authority. Not surprisingly *Standesherren* and state were often locked in protracted jurisdictional battles.[50]

To many progressive Germans, all of the nobility's privileges seemed unhappy, transitory holdovers from the past. In the eighteenth century, the critics of the aristocracy had stressed its immorality, superficiality, and cosmopolitanism; against these defects, they set the moral power of *Bildung* and national awareness. After the turn of the century, anti-aristocratic sentiments remained important, but the substance of the criticism gradually changed from moral to social. Now the nobility was seen as a temporary inhibition to economic progress and social emancipation, the doomed residue of a declining order. 'The locomotive', the industrialist Friedrich Harkort wrote in the 1840s, 'is the hearse which will carry absolutism and feudalism to the

---

[49] Reif, *Adel*; Pedlow, *Survival*; Rosenberg, 'Pseudodemokratisierung der Rittergutsbesitzerklasse', in *Probleme*.
[50] Gollwitzer, *Standesherren*, p. 77.

graveyard.' A few years later, in his short story 'The Nihilists', Karl Gutzkow described how a group of east Elbian nobles were so outraged by the arrival of a railroad in their region that they decided to race the train and run it into the ground. Needless to say, against the awesome power of steam and steel, their best horses could not prevail.[51]

Some advocates of economic growth extended their criticism of the aristocracy to rural society as a whole. Friedrich List, for example, argued that in an agricultural nation, 'the whole range of intellectual and moral powers is virtually non-existent'. Industry, List believed, 'is the mother and father of science, literature, the arts, enlightenment, freedom, useful institutions, and national power and independence'. In order to foster growth, therefore, trade and manufacturing had to spread through the countryside so that industry and agriculture would be physically as well as economically joined. List wanted to get rid of the traditional peasantry; he would have liked to banish from the language the word *Bauernstand*, with its overtones of subjection and misery. Owners of viable farms, rural businessmen closely tied to markets and allied with the industrial sector, free and independent *Landwirte*— these were to be the rural participants in List's 'natural system of economy'.[52]

Many of List's contemporaries did not share his belief that industry held the key to the countryside's future. Ernst Moritz Arndt, for instance, believed that the peasantry had to be protected from 'the overflow of factories, the riches of trade, and the exaggerated partition of the land'. Because the peasant was close to the earth and at one with the rhythms of nature, he was essential for society's moral and political well-being. Even a liberal like Rotteck considered the peasants to be 'the constantly fresh source of life from which the other classes of society, which all have the inclination to gradual languor or to corruption, draw their continual refreshment or renovation'. By the 1840s writers like Jeremias Gotthelf and Karl Immermann were pursuing what would become a familiar literary theme, the story of hard-working, decent peasants locked in a hopeless struggle against the encroachment of modernity. The more Germans worried about the growth of cities and the spread of industrialization, the more some of them yearned for the virtues and stability traditional rural society seemed to embody.[53]

[51] Sheehan, 'Conflict', p. 4; Riedel, 'Biedermeier', p. 117.
[52] List, *System*, p. 66.
[53] Gagliardo, *Pariah*, pp. 232, 243.

iii. CITIES, MARKETS, AND MANUFACTURING

Many foreign visitors found German cities charming, old-fashioned, and quaint. In 1842, for instance, William Howitt described their 'gabled and picturesque white buildings, old squares and markets [and] people, many of them in the garb of centuries ago'. Viewing urban life across the span of time, Otto Bähr gave a similar impression of the town in which he grew up. During the 1820s, Bähr recalled sixty years later, Kassel was a small, simple place with wooden houses and limited horizons: 'Today one can hardly imagine the isolation in which such communities existed.' In his memoirs, Otto Elben, who was reared in Stuttgart about the same time, wrote that his town's society was 'more modest and more comfortable' than that of a big, modern city. Not surprisingly, when Germans went to the capitals and industrial centres of Britain or France, they were often appalled by the scale and pace of city life, as well as by its monotony and ugliness. 'A large portion of Birmingham', Johann Georg Kohl reported, 'might be described as a wilderness of houses, all equally ugly, an ungainly mass, unbroken by a single building of a pleasing exterior.'[54]

During the first half of the nineteenth century the overwhelming majority of Germans had little or no direct experience with big cities. In 1816 less than 2 per cent of Prussia's population lived in Berlin, that state's only city with more than 100,000 inhabitants; just over 4 per cent lived in the eleven Prussian cities with populations of between 20,000 and 100,000. By 1849, these figures had not changed dramatically: Breslau had now joined Berlin in the largest category, which included 3.3 per cent of the population, while 4.8 per cent lived in the eighteen cities with over 20,000 but less than 100,000 inhabitants. Even if we use a quantitatively more modest definition of 'city', urban growth barely kept up with that of the population as a whole: in 1816, 25.4 per cent of the Prussian population lived in communities larger than 2,000, in 1849, 26.7 per cent. Among the other German states, only Saxony was more urbanized than Prussia; Bavaria, on the other hand, had just 6 per cent of its population in cities with more than over 20,000 inhabitants in 1852, and 13.4 per cent in all communities larger than 2,000.[55]

As always, these aggregate figures blur significant regional differences. In contrast to the sluggish rate of urbanization in

---

[54] Bruford, *Germany*, p. 211; Bähr, *Stadt*, p. 71; Otto Elben, *Lebenserinnerungen, 1823–1899* (Stuttgart, 1931), 5; Lees, *Cities*, p. 64. For another example, see Kussmaul's description of Mannheim in the 1830s: *Jugenderinnerungen*, pp. 48–9.

[55] For an introduction to the literature on German cities and urbanization, see

central Europe as a whole, Berlin continued to grow quickly, from 201,138 inhabitants in 1819 to 378,204 thirty years later. Vienna, still larger than its Prussian counterpart, grew more slowly, from 260,224 in 1821 to 431,147 in 1850. Among the other capitals, Munich, Dresden, and Stuttgart all expanded at rates well beyond the national average, while Karlsruhe, Brunswick, and Saarbrücken did not. As it had in the eighteenth century, Hamburg remained the most dynamic German commercial centre; its population was 132,007 in 1811, 220,968 in 1851. Leipzig, Cologne, and Frankfurt also increased rapidly; Königsberg, Danzig, and Augsburg did not. Finally, we find among early nineteenth-century cities some unfamiliar names, none of them major urban centres, but all with extraordinary rates of demographic expansion. Friedrich Engels's home town of Barmen, for instance, went from a population of 16,289 in 1810 to one of 41,463 forty years later. Essen, which was hardly more than a village at the beginning of the century, had almost 10,000 inhabitants in 1850 and would add another 40,000 before 1871.

As important as the quantitative differences among German cities was the diversity of their style, tone, and social organization. Weimar, according to Russell, who stopped there on his German tour in the 1820s, 'scarcely deserves the name of a town'. Over a quarter of its inhabitants were employed by the government, another third were servants, the rest artisans, merchants, and innkeepers, many of whom were heavily dependent on the court.[56] Berlin, on the other hand, had become an important commercial and manufacturing centre, which impressed visitors with its sober and industrious atmosphere, as well as its size and vitality. But travellers were rarely charmed by the Prussian capital as they were by Vienna, whose grace seemed to one contemporary 'as distant from Berlin's smalltown academic atmosphere as the sun is from the earth'. Still surrounded by walls built to repel the Turks, Vienna's *Altstadt*, with its parks, palaces, and cafés, was easy to enjoy.[57] No less striking than the differences between Berlin and Vienna were those between Hamburg and Frankfurt, or Breslau

above, Ch. 2, sect. iii, n. 56. On nineteenth-century cities, see the essays in Reulecke (ed.), *Stadt*; Jäger (ed.), *Probleme*, Rausch, (ed.), *Städte*; Ada Weber, *The Growth of Cities in the Nineteenth Century* (1899; repr. Ithaca, New York, 1967), is a valuable collection of statistics; Reulecke, *Geschichte*, is a convenient guide to recent themes and interpretations.

[56] Russell, *Tour*, i. 42.
[57] Bab and Handl, *Wien*, p. 201.

and Cologne. In these commercial towns, as in the state capitals, historical traditions, geography, and economics combined to ensure the persistence of particularity.

But across the map of urban particularity moved the same forces we have seen at work in the German countryside: the state, which was eager to subject city-dwellers to its laws and tap urban resources for its own ends, and the market, which wove bonds between cities and their environs, as well as between regions and increasingly extended economic systems. Of course neither state nor market was powerful enough to obliterate urban traditions and personality, but together they altered cities' internal organization as well as their relationship to the outside world. Increased bureaucratic regulations and intensified commercial activity combined to undermine that complex set of customs, rights, and liberties upon which traditional urban society depended. At the same time, these political and economic forces destroyed urban autonomy and opened the city to the movement of goods, people, and ideas from throughout society. Under the old regime, most German cities had been distinctive communities with a restricted corporate structure; by the end of the century, all but a few of them had become administrative units with an open and mobile economic system.[58]

The single most important effort to define a new relationship between cities and the state during the nineteenth century was the Prussian *Städteordnung*, issued towards the end of Stein's ministry in November 1808. Like many of the Prussian reforms, this ordinance had both a participatory and a bureaucratic dimension. It was, as we have seen, part of Stein's efforts to engage citizens in public affairs; he hoped that 'active involvement in public administration' would 'encourage and sustain a sense of community'. To this end, the *Städteordnung* established representative institutions with some important responsibilities. But the ordinance also tightened the state's control over urban life by abolishing the residual privileges of formerly independent cities, curtailing municipal judicial authorities, and transferring police power to the central government. 'The state', declared Article One, 'retains the final right of control over the cities, their constitutions and property, in so far as these jurisdictions are not expressly renounced in the following ordinance.' When the ordinance was revised in 1831, the participatory elements were slightly weakened, the state's power increased. This revised law was then applied to the Prussian territories acquired in 1815, except for Swedish Pomerania and the Rhineland. The latter

[58] Matzerath, 'Stadt'.

province retained the system of local government imposed during
the French occupation until a new *Gemeindeordnung* was finally
introduced in 1845. This law did not distinguish between urban and
rural communities—a distinction retained in the ordinances of 1808
and 1831—and provided for a chief executive appointed by the
government rather than elected by the municipal parliament. In
essence, however, the Rhenish *Gemeindeordnung*, like the ordinance
of 1831, was an explicit statement of the state's ultimate authority
over local affairs.[59]

A number of other German states introduced local government
laws during the first half of the century—Bavaria in 1818,
Württemberg in 1822, Baden in 1831, Electoral Hesse in 1834,
Saxony in 1838. All these laws contained a characteristic blend of
representation and bureaucratization. But in many states, especially
those in the south-west, the relationship between state and city was
more vexed than in the Prussian east. The citizens of most Prussian
cities had lost their autonomy during the early stages of state-
building; they responded slowly and without enthusiasm to the
opportunities for political participation offered them by the
reformers. The citizens of formerly independent imperial cities and
home towns, on the other hand, cherished the memory of self-
government and struggled to preserve as much autonomy as they
could. To them, any centrally imposed definition of the community's institutions seemed like a frontal assault on traditional
rights and privileges. As Mack Walker has written, the 'political
direction of local self-government in Prussia was opposite to the
political direction of self-government in the individualized country
because the starting points were different. Prussian town corporations had been too weak to link their populations into politics;
home town regimes were too strong.'[60] Yet while they may have
been coming from opposite directions, Prussian and south-western
city governments eventually moved closer together as they
struggled to find some balance between state power and formally
defined representation.

By the 1840s there were two main deviants from this pattern:
Austria, where the bureaucracy dominated city government, and
those scattered regions in which traditional urban autonomy

[59] The standard work on local government remains Heffter, *Selbstverwaltung*.
There is a useful document collection edited by Engeli and Haus (eds.), *Quellen*. On
the Rhineland, see Karl Georg Faber, 'Die kommunale Selbstverwaltung in der
Rheinprovinz im 19. Jahrhundert', *RV* 30/1 (1965), 132–51.

[60] Walker, *Home Towns*, p. 265.

survived. In the Habsburg lands all pretence of urban self government had been abandoned under Franciscan absolutism, which directly subjected Austrian cities to the central administration. Vienna, for instance, was governed by a mayor and 'Magistrate of the Royal and Imperial Capital and Residence', all appointed by the state.[61] In the four remaining free cities and a few parts of the north-west, on the other hand, urban self-government was more or less intact. Frankfurt, Hamburg, Bremen, and Lübeck remained independent republics, ruled by a patriciate composed of merchants and lawyers. Hanoverian cities, while under state control, were not subject to a uniform municipal ordinance and managed to retain some of their traditional institutions and privileges. The same was true of cities in Schleswig-Holstein, Mecklenburg, and the parts of Swedish Pomerania taken over by Prussia after 1815. Altogether, however, these outposts of urban autonomy were merely reminders of a vanished era, the vestiges of an age when central Europe was filled with city-states, each conscious of its corporate identity and jealous of its sovereign rights.

At the same time that cities were being subjected to state laws and bureaucratic control, some of them were being pulled into a wider and more vigorous set of market relationships. The spatial dimensions of this economic process are more difficult to establish than those of its political counterpart; markets did not respect state boundaries and did not radiate from a single administrative centre. Moreover, the impact of markets on urban affairs was much less uniform than the impact of bureaucratization: every German city may have been affected by economic change, but these effects were shaped by each city's location and social structure. Some cities flourished, others wilted, some became *Weltstädte*, world cities with ties to global markets, others turned into or remained *Kleinstädte*, small towns of no more than regional importance.

The fate of the cities along the northern coast provides a good example of how expanding markets could affect urban development. In the eighteenth century, trade on the North Sea and Baltic coasts had been served by a score of ports, most of them small harbour towns that shipped raw materials from, and provided imported goods to, their immediate hinterlands. In the nineteenth century, most of these ports declined, sometimes because their harbours could not accommodate the bigger vessels now used for

[61] See the essay by Orgis in Rausch (ed.), *Städte . . . im 19. Jahrhundert.*

international trade, sometimes because their hinterland was not large or prosperous enough to sustain vigorous growth. Eventually, a few major cities began to dominate overseas commerce. Hamburg and Bremen prospered, while Papenburg, at the mouth of the Ems, and Brake, near the mouth of the Weser, both lost ground, as did Lübeck, once the proud and equal partner of the other Hansa cities. Königsberg, which was thirty-seven kilometres from the sea on the Pregel, could not compete with better-placed outlets for eastern grain and timber. Furthermore, Königsberg, like Danzig, was disadvantaged by its distance from growing population centres in Saxony and Prussia. Stettin, on the other hand, benefited from its proximity to Berlin, especially after a rail line linking the two cities was finished in 1843.[62]

Of all the economic forces at work in German urban affairs, the railroad was certainly the most important. Those slender lines of track could help a city transcend the limits of geography by linking its factories with sources of coal and iron, its merchants with markets for their goods, its publishers with readers and writers throughout Europe. An inland city could have access to the sea, a port the means to send its commerce far inland. Moreover, the railroad had a direct economic importance, especially to the state capitals that became centres for construction, maintenance, and repair. Firms like Borsig and Pflug in Berlin, Maffei in Munich, and Kessler in Karlsruhe were significant sources of jobs and money. Finally, railroads affected the character and contours of urban space. In 1838, for instance, when the Leipzig–Berlin line opened, a newspaper reported that the environs of the Leipzig station had been suddenly transformed: 'The solid, massive buildings reverberate from the continuous shocks, and inhabitants who formerly thought to find here a quiet, beautiful street . . . are now moving back into the city to find their lost serenity.'[63] By the middle of the nineteenth century, train stations had replaced city walls as the best expression of what urbanism meant; instead of the protection and separation once guaranteed by fortifications, the railroad promised extension and connection.

The same developments that altered cities' relationship to their political and economic worlds also transformed their inner life. Once again, Stein's municipal reform offers us a particularly clear example of this process. Article Fifteen of the *Städteordnung*

---

[62] Pounds, *Geography . . . 1800–1914*, pp. 462 ff.; Lee, 'Aspects', p. 281.
[63] Shivelbusch, *Journey*, p. 180. See also Reulecke, *Geschichte*, pp. 30–1; Pounds, *Geography . . . 1800–1914*, p. 131.

conferred citizenship on every inhabitant who ran an enterprise or owned property within the city. Everyone else—from ministers of state to the humblest scullery maid—was considered a *Schutz-verwandter*, without the right to participate in urban affairs. By making property the sole criterion for active citizenship, the Prussian law cut away the special rights, privileges, and liberties with which cities had once determined who could belong and who could not. This commercialization of the urban community was intensified by the revised ordinance of 1831, which gave *Schutz-verwandte* the right to own property. The Rhenish *Gemeindeordnung* of 1845 provided this association of property and citizenship a new—and eventually influential—formulation by dividing urban voters into three classes according to the amount of their tax payments.

As we should expect, corporate conceptions of community membership lasted longer in most south-western states, where cities fought vigorously to keep control over citizenship, which was, after all, the heart of local self-government. For more than two decades, the advocates of central authority and local autonomy struggled over this issue, in the state parliaments and in the day-to-day life of the towns. Along the way, each side won some battles and lost others, deals were struck, regulations enforced or evaded. In the long run, however, the direction of change was on the side of the states.

The conflict between state and community over citizenship was inseparable from a cluster of controversies over trade regulations. Here too we are struck by the difference between Prussia and most *Mittelstaaten*. Guild restrictions had been under assault by the Prussian government throughout the eighteenth century; they were, as we have seen, abolished in the Rhineland and Westphalia by the French. In the early nineteenth century, when Prussian cities became purely administrative units, Prussian guilds were turned into economic associations rather than expressions of corporate identity and instruments of social control. However, in those parts of German Europe where guilds and communities had traditionally been more vigorous, they remained able to determine who could practise a craft or open a shop or start a family.[64]

The development of *Gewerbefreiheit*, like the spread of land reform, began in the eighteenth century and continued, with many fits and starts, throughout the first two-thirds of the nineteenth. In

[64] Heffter, *Selbstverwaltung*, p. 218; Stadelmann and Fischer, *Bildungswelt*, pp. 107 ff.

both agriculture and manufacturing, the erosion of traditional restraints was driven by a combination of political, social, and economic forces. Generally speaking, guilds were most likely to survive in states where community autonomy remained, in areas where demographic and market pressures were weak, and in trades whose pace of technological change was slow. They were most endangered when the opposite conditions prevailed: bureaucratic centralization, population growth and intense commercial activity, and rapid alterations in the means of production were all antithetical to the customs, rights, and duties upon which guilds traditionally had depended. Because many states, regions, and trades remained—or moved back and forth—somewhere between these two extremes, the pattern of guild erosion and survival was complex, the movement toward *Gewerbefreiheit* gradual and uneven.[65] In Württemberg, for instance, only about 17 per cent of manufacturing enterprises were organized along guild lines in 1835, but these firms employed some 80 per cent of the masters and apprentices. A list of Fulda's citizens compiled that same year shows almost half (497 of 1,176) to have been *zünftige* craftsmen or innkeepers. Even in Berlin, where guild membership seems to have declined substantially, 80 per cent of the master bakers and 65 per cent of the tailors—as opposed to only 19 per cent of the shoemakers and 14 per cent of the plumbers—belonged to a guild.[66]

Despite the continued vitality of guilds in some areas and certain trades, it seems clear enough that the guilds, like the autonomous urban communities of which they were once so important a part, steadily lost ground to the regulatory power of the state, the relentless pressure of demographic expansion, and the competitive force of industrial production. One clear sign of this decline, apparent almost everywhere, was the growing difficulty apprentices faced in becoming masters. Between 1816 and 1849 the number of masters in Prussia grew by 65 per cent, while the number of journeymen and apprentices increased by 124 percent.

[65] The literature on guilds is given above, Ch. 2, sect. iii, n. 60. On the nineteenth century, see Wilhelm Abel *et al.*, *Handwerksgeschichte in neuer Sicht* (Göttingen, 1970); Abraham, *Strukturwandel*; Kaufhold, 'Umfang'. Schmoller's *Geschichte*, although more than a century old, is still worth reading. Two excellent local studies: Lenger, *Kleinbürgertum*; Jürgen Bergmann, *Das Berliner Handwerk in den Frühphasen der Industrialisierung* (Berlin, 1973). Lenger's *Sozialgeschichte der deutschen Handwerker seit 1800* (Frankfurt, 1988) is a good synthesis.

[66] Langewiesche, *Liberalismus*, pp. 40 ff.; Mauersberg, *Wirtschaft und Gesellschaft Fuldas*, p. 146; Pollard, *Conquest*, p. 62.

This meant that, while there were some 56 apprentices for every 100 masters in 1816, there were over 76 in 1843. By the 1840s many apprentices in the building trades and in some forms of textile production had virtually no chance to become a master. The opposite situation obtained in other trades, especially those producing products for everyday consumption, such as bread, shoes, and clothing, where masters often could not afford an apprentice and therefore had to work alone or with family members. 'A master who works without helpers', observed one contemporary, 'is actually no more than a special kind of wage earner.'[67] Of course the situation was not uniformly bleak: many individuals and some trades flourished, despite—and sometimes because of—demographic pressures and competition. There were masters who grew rich, owned several houses, and employed a score of apprentices, just as there were trades—construction, certain kinds of metalworking and some services—which expanded to meet new demands. Of course, the loosening of corporate bonds could be a blessing for some apprentices, who were now free to live on their own, marry, and demand better wages. But, despite these bright spots, contemporaries painted pictures of the crafts' condition in sombre hues: by the 1840s an increasing number of Germans were worried by what they began to call the dangers of a proletariat, whose ranks were being swollen with the surplus labour that could no longer find a stable place in the corporate order.[68]

The social groups included by contemporaries among the 'proletariat' were familiar features on the social scene. These groups included a large number of hard-working men and women without the skill or resources necessary to create a secure and stable existence: casual labourers of all sorts, such as stevedores, waiters, messengers, and stablehands, many servants and household helpers, and a variety of wage-earners, underemployed apprentices, and the like. Below this large and heterogeneous social stratum was the urban underworld, in which lived victims of temporary misfortune, as well as those unwilling or unable to work: the insane, disabled, or deviant. A considerable social distance separated the top and bottom of this category, between, for instance, an unskilled labourer struggling to support his family and a recipient of public charity. But when seen from the outside,

---

[67] Bruno Hildebrand, quoted in Köllmann, *Bevölkerung*, p. 230. The data are from Kaufhold, 'Umfang', p. 323.

[68] See below, Ch. 10, sect. iv.

these groups tended to blend into one another, their members united by a shared condition of social marginality and material privation. In fact, economic dislocation or personal mishap—a downturn in the trade cycle or a broken bone—could easily defeat people's struggle to be self-sufficient and push them and their family into total indigence.

In many German cities during the first half of the nineteenth century we can find a new social formation, the forerunners of what will become the 'working class'. Members of this group were wage earners, characteristically employed in large enterprises, where they were assigned routine tasks to be performed according to fixed rules. It is important to keep in mind that this was a highly diverse group, with extensive internal divisions: gangs of men moving about the countryside laying track, miners still living on small plots of land, machinists in a railroad repair shop, and children tending mechanical looms might all be considered 'workers', but they had very different social positions. Glassblowers, blacksmiths, and weavers might work in a 'factory' without losing their status as skilled craftsmen. Moreover, the categories with which contemporaries tried to understand the emergence of industrial labour remained fluid and uncertain: the term *factory* continued to be applied to a number of different sorts of enterprises; *worker* was used to refer to skilled and unskilled labourers, hired hands and domestic helpers. It is no wonder, then, that working people's awareness that they shared a common condition and mutual interests should have developed slowly and unevenly. The development of 'class consciousness' grew, as we shall see in a later chapter, from political and social conflicts that were often based on but did not necessarily flow from, people's work experience and economic situation. Family relationships, the social ties arising from neighbourhood associations, and a shared sense of political oppression and social injustice were equally important for the creation of common values among workers from different parts of the economic system.[69]

Workers' communities were more likely to develop outside the

[69] For an introduction to these issues, see Kocka, *Lohnarbeit*; Werner Conze's article on 'Arbeiter', *GGB* i. 216 ff., Hans-Ulrich Wehler, 'Bürger, Arbeiter und das Problem der Klassenbildung 1800–1870. Deutschland im internationalen Vergleich', in Jürgen Kocka (ed.), *Arbeiter und Bürger im 19. Jahrhundert* (Munich, 1986), 1–27. Three important local studies: Marquardt, 'Class'; Zwahr, *Konstituierung*; Klaus Tenfelde, *Sozialgeschichte der Bergarbeiterschaft an der Ruhr im 19. Jahrhundert* (Bonn-Bad Godesberg, 1977).

old urban centres, which continued to be dominated by traditional trades and established élites. Sometimes workers were concentrated on the periphery of large cities, in industrial suburbs that grew up next to, and were eventually absorbed by, the urban core. At the beginning of the century, for instance, Moabit was still a rural settlement, in which the inhabitants of nearby Berlin might keep a weekend retreat; by 1850 Moabit had been transformed by the presence of two large machine works and other related enterprises. In Leipzig's inner city there were thirty-eight manufacturing enterprises as opposed to twenty-three in the suburbs. But among the latter were the largest and fastest growing factories, including two textile mills, with over three hundred workers, a steam-driven rolling mill and a gas works, as well as the railroad yard and a boxcar plant. In addition to these industrial suburbs, communities of workers could be found away from cities, in large villages devoted to textile production or near deposits of coal and other natural resources. Gradually, these communities became urbanized, without ever having been cities in the traditional sense. Indeed, the spread of cities beyond their walls and the growth of new kinds of urban settlements make defining cities more and more difficult.[70]

As the nature of urban life changed, so did the relationship between cities and their hinterlands. Most cities continued to depend on the surrounding countryside for some of their food supply, especially vegetables and dairy products; similarly, most cities supplied their environs with various manufactured goods, now usually sold in shops rather than markets or fairs. Increasingly, however, the urban economy's relationship to its region was shaped by production rather than consumption. In industrial areas, the city drew on its region for supplies of raw material and labour, while importing most of its food from elsewhere. Alternatively, in agrarian areas, cities shipped local agricultural products to distant markets and bought what manufactured goods they needed from areas that could produce them most cheaply.[71]

The expanding connections between cities, regions, and larger markets did not make the economy more uniform. Quite the contrary: as regions became more specialized, they grew less alike. Industrialized areas became more intensely industrial because cities and suburbs spread into what had once been farmland. Agricultural

---

[70] See Hofmann's essay on Moabit in Jäger, *Probleme*; Czok's on Leipzig in Rausch, *Städte . . . im 19. Jahrhundert*.

[71] Hohenberg and Lees, *Making*, p. 176.

regions became more agricultural because marginal manufacturing enterprises failed and inefficient mines closed down. But while the nature of the various regional units changed, their fundamental economic importance did not. In traditional Europe, regions had been significant because they tended to be separate and self-sufficient; in the nineteenth century, their significance derived from their special character and function. Each region was now, in Sidney Pollard's phrase, linked to the rest of the economy 'like an organ within the body'.[72]

German Europe's regional diversity had been increased rather than diminished by Napoleon's efforts to forge a continental economy in support of his warfare state. Napoleonic policies hurt areas that produced linen, commercial regions that depended on English or overseas trade, and marginal enterprises that could not compete with French firms. However, the main centres of the cotton industry, especially in the north-west and Saxony, benefited from the removal of English competition, as did scattered metalworking and machine-building plants throughout the German west. One result of these shifting fortunes was to move the centre of European industry inland, away from the coast and towards a zone stretching across north-western Europe between the Seine and the Elbe. Overall, the economic impact of the French imperium was probably more positive than negative, but it left most German industries well behind their counterparts in England, which emerged from the revolutionary era with a position of global economic hegemony. Throughout most of the nineteenth century the power of the English example and the pressure of English competition were the most important exogenous forces at work on the German economic scene.[73]

As soon as German businessmen and bureaucrats realized that technology was an important source of England's economic strength, they tried to acquire technical experts for their own firms or states. After 1815 Germans eagerly employed Englishmen with mechanical skills, imported English machines, or crossed the

---

[72] Pollard, *Conquest*, p. 115. See also the essays in Hans Pohl (ed.), *Gewerbe- und Industrielandschaften vom Spätmittelalter bis ins 20. Jahrhundert* (Stuttgart, 1986), Sidney Pollard (ed.), *Region und Industrialisierung. Studien zur Rolle der Region in der Wirtschaftsgeschichte der letzten zwei Jahrhunderte* (Göttingen, 1980); R. Fremdling and R. Tilly (eds.), *Industrialisierung und Raum: Studien zur regionalen Differenzierung im Deutschland des 19. Jahrhunderts* (Stuttgart, 1979), Pounds, *Geography . . . 1500–1840*, pp. 119 ff. and, for a local example, Ayçoberry, *Cologne*, especially pp. 110 ff.

[73] François Crouzet, 'Wars, Blockade, and Economic Change in Europe, 1792–1815', *JEH* 24 (1964), 567–88; Berding and Ullmann (eds.), *Deutschland*, pp. 32 ff.

Channel to study and learn in one of the new industrial cities in the Midlands. Many German states subsidized technical training, established schools for machinists and engineers, and encouraged investment in the latest technology. Despite English efforts to limit their diffusion, technological knowledge and often the machines themselves spread swiftly to the Continent. But, while technology was easy enough to transport, it turned out to be difficult to apply successfully. Not surprisingly, English technology worked best in areas that most resembled England's own industrial heartland. Thus, industrialization did not 'spread' from England to the continent, but rather, as Pollard has written, 'jumped from one industrial region to another, though in a general direction outward from the North-West, while the country in between remained to be industrialized, or at least modernized, much later, if at all'.[74]

During the first half of the nineteenth century · the most important beneficiary of the new technology was the textile industry. The reader will remember that textile manufacturing had expanded during the eighteenth century, especially in those 'protoindustrial' enterprises which grew up outside the corporate jurisdictions of city and guild. Throughout the middle decades of the nineteenth century the various branches of the textile industry remained by far the largest source of non-agricultural employment: between 1841 and 1865 textiles and clothing made up over 40 per cent of Austria's industrial production.

The gradual yet cumulative advance of West European capitalism [Herbert Kisch wrote], was in large part epitomized by the developments of its textile trades. They were the first to carry the seeds of economic change into the stagnant preserves of guild conservatism, and subsequently they again proved to be the pioneers of the new factory system.

After 1800, however, the character of textile production changed as the domestic system that had characterized protoindustry gradually lost ground to larger, more centralized modes of production. At the same time, linen and wool declined while cotton manufacturing dramatically increased—between 1834 and 1850, for instance, the consumption of raw cotton in the German Customs Union grew from 7,500 to over 17,000 metric tons.[75]

Although some spinning and weaving went on everywhere in

[74] Pollard, *Conquest*, p. 45. In addition to Pollard, my account of German economic development owes a great deal to Richard Tilly's work, which is conveniently collected in *Kapital*, and to Frank Tipton's brilliant article, 'Consensus'.

[75] Kisch, in Kriedte *et al.* (eds.), *Industrialization*, p. 178; Landes, *Prometheus*, p. 165.

central Europe, the most dynamic and technically advanced forms of production were confined to a few regions. Unlike metal-working and machine-building, the textile industry tended to develop where protoindustry had been strong enough to create a supply of skilled labour and entrepreneurial talent. Moreover, since textile makers—and especially those who produced cotton cloth—needed ready access to imported raw material and to large markets for their goods, they did best in regions near to port cities and heavily populated areas. Finally, mechanized textile producers needed lots of water, not only to process the cloth, but also, at least until the arrival of the steam engine, to power their machines.

All of these conditions existed in the Rhineland, which had an established textile industry and close proximity to Dutch ports and western markets. Like most German textile regions—and unlike their English counterparts—the Rhenish area included several kinds of textile production: the woollen trade flourished around Aachen, silk in Krefeld, and linen in the Wuppertal. But in the Rhineland, as elsewhere in Europe, the relative importance of cotton manufacturing increased, displacing linen from cities such as Barmen and spreading into new industrial areas such as Gladbach. At the same time, textile mills became more common throughout the region, as enterprising businessmen like Friedrich Engels senior looked for ways to match English productivity. Often factories remained linked to domestic industry in the multi-stage production of cloth: the Weerth firm in Bonn, for instance, set up a spinning factory in a secularized monastery in 1804, but continued to send out its yarn to weavers in nearby Cologne and in villages throughout the Eifel until the 1840s.[76] For certain kinds of work, especially high quality weaving and embroidery, protoindustrial systems of production lasted even longer.

Traditionally, metalworking and mining had been done by small-scale, relatively simple enterprises. For example, iron production, which required both ore and charcoal for the refining process, was carried out near mines and forests; when these sources of raw materials were depleted, the industry characteristically moved on. In the 1830s and 1840s metalworking was transformed by a series of interrelated developments. First, the demand for metal, and especially iron and steel, rocketed, in largely because of railroad construction: in the 1830s, one kilometre of railroad track required thirty-five tons of iron, by mid-century eighty-five tons.

[76] Pounds, *Geography . . . 1500–1840*, p. 369.

Second, the technology of production changed, with coal replacing charcoal for puddling and smelting. Finally, the intense, mechanized exploitation of a few, rich fields of high-quality coal replaced the extensive mining operations in small, scattered deposits. The economic geography of the metal industry, therefore, was determined by the location of natural resources and the changing technology of production rather than by the presence of a skilled work force or even the proximity to markets. Metal production eventually was centred in the coalfields of the Ruhr, upper Silesia, and the Saar. By mid-century, Saxony's charcoal burning ironworks were in serious trouble. In Austria, coal production and consumption lagged behind the more advanced areas in the German west, although the per capita production of pig iron (8.8 kilograms) remained higher than that of the *Zollverein* (7.3).[77]

Until well into the nineteenth century, most tools and utensils were made locally by blacksmiths or other craftsmen. A few areas specialized in high quality products, such as the cutlery and arms manufactured in Solingen and Remscheid. Wire, nail, and pin-making enterprises were scattered along the river valleys of the west. Most large and complicated machines were imported; for instance, eleven of the twelve locomotives used on German railroads in 1840 were produced in England. Gradually, however, German firms began to take over; by 1850 only eleven of fifty-three locomotives had been imported. Between 1837 and 1852 the number of machine works in Berlin increased from three to thirty, the work-force from seventy-two to almost nine hundred. A similar pattern could be found in other major German cities where railroads stimulated the development of factories and repair shops. In comparison to England and Belgium, German machine production was still backward, but the foundations for later growth were clearly in place.[78]

Industrial development was painful and disruptive for many firms, trades, and regions. Small manufacturers of wire or nails simply went under when faced with factory competition. The use of steamships threatened the livelihood of boatmen on the Rhine, and then steamships operators were themselves threatened by the pre-eminence of the railroad. Printers who would not or could not

[77] Ibid. 338

[78] Fremdling, *Eisenbahnen*, p. 76; Lothar Baar, *Die Berliner Industrie in der industriellen Revolution* (Berlin, 1966), 89. See also Karl Lärmer, 'Maschinenbau in Preussen. Ein Beitrag zur Problematik Staat und industrielle Revolution', *JbW* (1975) 2 13–32; A. Schröter and W. Becker, *Die deutsche Maschinenbauindustrie in der industriellen Revolution* (Berlin, 1962).

acquire the new mechanical presses sometimes went out of business. Most protoindustrial enterprises, however, were likely to decline slowly rather than collapse. Instead of sudden bankruptcy, these domestic industries underwent a long, slow process of marginalization or were pushed into a few highly skilled, labour-intensive enterprises like lace-making or woodcarving. Of course, decline and dislocation were most painful when they hit entire regions, such as happened in Silesia, where protoindustrial textile production had once flourished. After 1800 the demand for Silesian linen flattened, wool production stagnated, and local cotton manufacturing remained competitive only because of its low labour costs. Competition from more efficient enterprises in the Rhineland and elsewhere pushed the Silesian textile industry into a state of permanent crisis which, as we shall see, produced the famous weavers' uprising of 1844. In the south-west, the problem was not decline but stagnation: because neither agriculture nor manufacturing grew quickly enough to support an expanding population, farms and trades became crowded, underemployment common, and privation a constant danger.

The south-west's stagnant economy provided the setting within which Friedrich List first formulated his influential views on growth and development. Born in 1789, the son of a master tanner and civic leader in the imperial city of Reutlingen, List spent his youth surrounded by the corporate traditions of a prototypical home town. After working as a local official, attending lectures at the University of Tübingen, and participating in the Württemberg constitutional conflict, List received an academic post at Tübingen and a seat in the *Landtag*. A victim of the political repression that gripped the Confederation after 1819, List was charged with subversive activities, lost his position, and had to emigrate; from 1825 until 1831 he lived in the United States, where he engaged in various businesses and participated in the public debate over American tariff policy. After returning to Europe, he served as American Consul in several German cities, helped promote railroad construction, and wrote prolifically on a variety of economic, social, and political issues—his publications, letters, and speeches fill twelve large volumes. In 1841 he published *Das nationale System der politischen Ökonomie*, which was an immediate success. However, none of List's projects brought him the fame and security he sought; disappointed, exhausted, and troubled by ill health, he took his own life in 1846.[79]

[79] On List, see Carl Brinkmann, *Friedrich List* (Berlin and Munich, 1949); and

While List is best known as a critic of the classical economists, he shared a great many of their assumptions. Like them, he viewed the economy as a system of productive forces driven by supply and demand. The goal of economic policies, he believed, should be to help this system grow, become more productive, and therefore bring prosperity to ever greater numbers of people. However, unlike the advocates of what he called 'cosmopolitan economics', List believed that, since nations stand at different levels of economic development, their economic policies must vary. What had seemed like a universal law to British theorists was merely the reflection of Britain's unique historical position as a dominant economic power. In order for Germany to grow, these principles had to be revised—although by no means abandoned. Protective tariffs, for instance, were necessary to preserve and encourage German manufacturers, but such protection was 'only necessary and useful if it is regarded as a first step on the road that eventually leads to the establishment of universal international free trade'.[80] Moreover, while he saw the need for a tariff wall around German industries, List was a tireless opponent of trade barriers within central Europe. In a memorandum to the Confederation's diet, drafted in 1819 on behalf of a group of merchants and manufacturers gathered at the Frankfurt fair, List called for the abolition of all intra-German customs and tariffs and the creation of a customs union to protect German enterprises from unfair foreign competition.

At the time List composed this memorandum, German commercial policies were in a state of flux. During the revolutionary era, some trade barriers had been removed; the French had opened the Rhine to unimpeded traffic and had erased a great many of the 1,800 customs boundaries within, as well as between, German states. From 1807 to 1812 several members of the Rhenish Confederation, including Bavaria, Württemberg, and Baden, created unified customs zones out of their own territories. Nevertheless, impediments to the free movement of goods remained formidable.

'There are no less than twenty-two tolls on the Weser betwixt Münden and Bremen,' [wrote Thomas Hodgskin in 1820], seven of which belong to the

Paul Gehring's *Friedrich List und Deutschlands politisch-ökonomische Einheit* (Leipzig, 1956) and *Friedrich List. Jugend und Reifejahre, 1789–1825* (Tübingen, 1964). The most recent study is Roman Szporluk, *Communism and Nationalism: Karl Marx versus Friedrich List* (New York, 1988). List's writings are available in a twelve-volume edition (1927–35).

[80] List, *System*, p. 113.

sovereign of Hannover. . . . At every toll every vessel is stopped and her whole cargo is examined. . . . The cargo of the raft on which I passed from Munich to Vienna was nothing but trees, deals and three bales of goods; yet we were frequently detained both in Bavaria and Austria for hours to have it examined.[81]

The Vienna *Bundesakte* had included tariff reform among the matters for future action, but in this, as in so much else, the Confederation eventually left the initiative to the states. In 1818, Prussia turned its old and new provinces into a free trade zone, towards which its smaller neighbours—some of them enclaves surrounded by Prussian territory—were irresistibly drawn. Bavaria and Württemberg signed a bilateral customs agreement in 1828; a few months later, Prussia, Hesse-Darmstadt, and several smaller states formed a Central German *Handelsverein*. Once these two blocks had been formed, the other German states were under considerable pressure to join. Finally, in 1833 the Prussian-led *Handelsverein* and the south German states agreed to merge into a *Zollverein* (tariff union), which began on New Year's Day 1834, with a territory of 162,000 square miles and a population of 23.5 million. Baden and Nassau joined the following year, Frankfurt in 1836, Brunswick in 1841, Hanover in 1851, and Oldenburg in 1852. Among the members of the Confederation, therefore, only the two Mecklenburgs, the three Hansa cities, and the Habsburg monarchy remained outside the *Zollverein*.[82]

Because they were convinced that the *Zollverein* had brought both prosperity and national awareness to the peoples of German Europe, its admirers viewed its formation as a turning-point in Germany's emergence as an industrial power and a unified nation-state. In 1842, for example, Hoffmann von Fallersleben began his poem on the *Zollverein* with a litany of commodities—'Schwefelhölzer, Fenchel, Bricken,| Kühe, Käse, Krapp, Papier,| Schinken, Scheren, Stiefel, Wicken,| Wolle, Seife, Garn und Bier'—which, he believed, had done more for German unity than ideas or diplomacy:

---

[81] Pollard and Holmes (eds.), *Documents*, p. 99. On trade, see the essays in Lütge (ed.), *Situation*.

[82] Henderson's *Zollverein* is the standard English account. The most recent treatment is Hahn, *Geschichte*. For a critical analysis of conventional interpretations, see Rolf Horst Dumke, 'Intra-German Trade in 1837 and Regional Economic Development', *VSWG* 64/4 (1977), 468–96; Helmut Berding, 'Die Entstehung des Deutschen Zollvereins als Problem historischer Forschung', in Berding *et al.*(eds.), *Staat*, 225–37.

Und ihr andern deutschen Sachen,
tausend Dank sei euch gebracht!
Was kein Geist je konnte machen,
ei, das habet ihr gemacht:
Denn ihr habt ein Band gewunden
um das deutsche Vaterland,
und die Herzen hat verbunden
mehr als unser Bund dies Band.

Wilhelm Roscher, in a phrase which nicely illustrates German historians' inclination to conflate economics and national politics, called the *Zollverein* 'not only the most beneficial, but also the greatest event in German history between Waterloo and König-grätz'. W. O. Henderson carried on this historiographical tradition when he wrote in the introduction to a new edition of his classic study of the *Zollverein* that he had 'endeavoured to show that the establishment of the customs union—and other economic develop-ments—helped to prepare the way for the subsequent political unification of Germany . . .'.[83]

There are good reasons to be sceptical about this picture of the *Zollverein's* place in German economic and political history. While the creation of a large market certainly encouraged some forms of commerce and significantly benefited certain enterprises, its direct impact on the German economy is hard to measure. Frank Tipton, for example, has argued that the 'available statistical series fail to reveal any decisive shift which might be connected with the establishment of the *Zollverein*'. The best that can be said is that the *Zollverein*, especially in combination with other phenomena, such as railroad construction, helped to promote growth. Moreover, it is important to keep in mind that there were some important limitations on the *Zollverein's* economic cohesion. Since its mem-bers could not agree on how to tax government monopolies in tobacco, wine, and brandy, these items did not move freely across state lines. Weights, measures, and coinage remained diverse. In the south, for example, Austria currency was widely used until the late 1850s. Similarly, the *Zollverein* did not sever economic connections between German regions and overseas markets. Most of Berlin's coal, for example, continued to come from abroad. Even though the German market grew in significance for Barmen's textile industry, international developments continued to have a

---

[83] Böhmer, *Welt*, p. 326; Berding, 'Entstehung', p. 226; Henderson, *Zollverein*, pp. v–vi.

direct and powerful impact on the city's economic condition. Further west, the textile manufacturers on the Rhine remained closely tied to Dutch enterprises, while almost everywhere in German Europe the influence of English goods, raw material, and equipment was prevalent. In short, the *Zollverein* created the basis for a common German market, not a German national economy.[84]

Even more doubtful than the extravagant claims for the *Zollverein's* economic significance are allegations about its contribution to German national unification. As we saw in Chapter 7, the *Zollverein* was created by bureaucrats, who were interested in fiscal reform and administrative consolidation rather than nation-building. These fiscal and administrative goals the union undoubtedly fulfilled. The dissolution of internal tolls and barriers helped to knit together the various states' territorial units; and between 1834 and 1850 the union's gross income from tariffs increased from 14.8 million to 22.9 million talers. Prussia's leading role in the creation of the union was part of its long-term efforts to integrate its own territories and extend its influence over neighbouring north German states. In retrospect, of course, the *Zollverein* seemed to fit perfectly into the story of Prussia's 'national mission' to unify Germany. Actually, the tariff union had little to do with the nation and a great deal to do with the various German states, whose steady rise and consolidation has provided our most compelling political theme.[85]

iv. ARISTOCRATS, BUSINESSMEN, AND BUREAUCRATS

Despite frequent obituary notices, some composed with sorrow, some with satisfaction, the German aristocracy did not succumb to the forces of modernity. Until well into the twentieth century, aristocratic élites continued to impress, fascinate, and outrage their contemporaries. With reserved admiration like Goethe's, open hostility like Gutzkow's, or nostalgic irony like Fontane's, fiction writers tried to capture the nobility's changing position in society. Theorists as distant from one another in time and temperament as Christian Garve and Max Weber analysed the aristocratic character and tried to define its proper social role. Statesmen from Freiherr

[84] Tipton, 'Consensus', p. 202; Pounds, *Geography . . . 1500–1840*, p. 45; Pollard, *Integration*, p. 14; Tilly, 'England'; Milward and Saul, *Development*, p. 385. See also the selection from Alexander Lips's description of German monetary 'chaos' in 1837, repr. in Pollard and Holmes (eds.), *Documents*, pp. 450–1.
[85] Hahn, *Geschichte*, pp. 93 ff.

vom Stein to Leo von Caprivi learned how costly it was to challenge aristocratic interests. Although the nature and relative importance of their status, wealth, and influence changed over time, noblemen retained a disproportionate share of social, economic, and political power. Long after the world of *Herrschaft* had disappeared, the noble *Herren* survived. 'The Germans can be roughly divided into two classes,' John Lothrop Motley wrote from Berlin in 1833, 'the von's and the non-von's.'[86]

Most impressive to their admirers and irksome to their critics was the prestige aristocrats continued to enjoy. A title, particularly an old and distinguished one, gave its bearer a special kind of glamour—no less attractive for being unearned, often undeserved. As a dinner guest or business partner or prospective son-in-law, the nobleman exerted an irresistible charm over many commoners. Part of this charm might come from a distinctive style and manner the nobility affected, but even the dullest and most awkward aristocrat carried with him the promise of connections to the courts, which remained the centres of high society in every German state. Much more diverse than their old-regime predecessors, nineteenth-century courts ranged from the elaborate rigidity still evident in Vienna to the relatively austere, militarized atmosphere prevalent in Berlin, or the artistic and intellectual milieu created by the Wittelsbachs in Munich. But at every court, the nobility kept their place nearest the monarch, provided him counsel and companionship, and carried the main burden of those exhausting rituals of birth, marriage, and death around which courtly life revolved. As long as the monarch continued to be the state's symbolic centre and ultimate source of authority, the aristocracy's special place was assured.[87]

Although nineteenth-century aristocrats remained at the apex of the status hierarchy, the nature of their status had changed. In the traditional social order, nobility was defined by custom, protected by law, and expressed by a number of external signs. Noble status adhered to the person of the noble, who passed it on to his progeny like a physical attribute. After 1800, however, status lost its customary and juridical moorings; its external signs—swords and special dress and separate theatre seats—became less important. In sum, status became what Weber would call 'an effective claim to

[86] Engelberg, *Bismarck*, p. 126.
[87] See the essays in Karl Werner (ed.), *Hof, Kultur und Politik im 19. Jahrhundert* (Bonn, 1985). There is a vivid picture of life at a small court in Kügelgen's *Lebenserinnerungen*, which consists of letters written between 1840 and 1867.

social esteem'.[88] The key word here is *claim*: a claim is not a condition or a possession or a fact of life; a claim must be made, it requires action, and can be granted or ignored. In order for aristocratic status to be effective, therefore, heredity had to be joined with wealth or power.

As was always the case, the nobility included an economically heterogeneous group of people. At one extreme, we find great princely families like the Liechtensteins and Schwarzenbergs, whose vast estates supported establishments as large as the courts of some ruling families. A more characteristic member of the landed élite was Leopold von Hoverbeck, who would eventually achieve fame as a liberal parliamentarian. After Leopold's grandfather brought the family to the edge of ruin, his father married the daughter of a commoner who had become rich managing royal estates. With the financial backing of his in-laws, Ernst von Hoverbeck became a successful agricultural entrepreneur who was able to establish his son on an estate of his own. The Moltke family was not so fortunate: after various failures as a farmer, Friedrich von Moltke joined the Danish army, in which several of his relatives already held commissions. Barely able to support his large family, Friedrich enrolled his son, Helmuth, in cadet school at the age of eleven. As a member of the Prussian officer corps, Helmuth von Moltke was so strapped for funds that he had to take a variety of jobs—including translating Gibbon—in order to supplement his pay. Landless and impoverished families like the Moltkes were so common that many contemporaries feared they would become a serious burden to the state. Stein, for instance, believed that the landed élite had an important role to play in public life, but wanted to restrict noble status to those with property and thus allow the rest to slip back into the ranks of ordinary citizens. 'Wealth', Stein wrote in 1808, 'unites the landowner's special interests with those of the community, while the memory of his ancestors' deeds binds the nation's glory with his family honour.' Fewer and fewer aristocrats, however, possessed enough land to live from or sufficient wealth to be independent. Office rather than property was the base from which most nobles pressed their claim to social esteem.[89]

For many aristocrats, an officer's commission was the most

[88] Weber, *Economy*, i. 305. For some well-informed reflections on the changing character of élites, see Hans Hubert Hofmann, 'Eliten und Elitentransformation in Deutschland zwischen der französischen und der deutschen Revolution', *ZBL* 41/2 (1978), 607–32.

[89] Hannes Stekl, *Österreichs Aristokratie im Vormärz. Herrschaftsstil und Lebens-*

appropriate source of income and security. Noblemen from throughout Europe continued to be drawn to the Habsburgs' service; in the 1840s, one-third of those holding the rank of general were born in a German state other than Austria. At every rank in the Austrian officer corps, aristocrats predominated: only twenty out of 125 major generals and thirty-nine of 216 colonels were without a title. The army's critics charged that noble birth and family connections were more important for a military career than ability and courage. According to one story, a young man, at dinner with his father and some well-placed family friends, ate soup as a cadet, the main course as a lieutenant, and dessert as a captain.[90] In Prussia, as we have seen, the military reformers had tried to banish excessive aristocratic influence by opening the officer corps to talented men from throughout society. By 1818 aristocrats were a bare majority among regular officers. But after these progressive impulses weakened and the most important reformers were forced from office, traditional Prussian élites reasserted their influence. Even though they could not regain the predominant position granted them by Frederick the Great, noblemen were able to control the most prestigious regiments and to occupy an increasingly large percentage of positions as they moved up the ranks. In 1860, for instance, only 14 per cent of Prussian officers with the rank of colonel or above did not have a title.[91]

Aristocrats also continued to find employment in the civil service. Here, as in the army, the possession of a title and family backing facilitated a candidate's rise to positions of power and influence. Friedrich von Blittersdorff, for instance, a member of an impecunious but well-connected family, was greatly aided in his diplomatic career by the efforts of his uncle, Freiherr von Marschall. The higher one rose, the more connections to the court and high society were likely to be useful. Seventy per cent of top administrators in Austria had a title in 1829, 80 per cent in 1847. The Bavarian cabinet of 1817 was composed entirely of nobles; between 1806 and 1848 eighteen out of thirty ministers had titles.

formen der Fürstenhäuser Liechtenstein und Schwarzenberg (Munich, 1973); Parisius, Hoverbeck i. 8 ff.; Eberhard Kessel, Moltke (Stuttgart, 1957), 10 ff.; Werner Conze, 'Adel', in GGB i. 33.

[90] Deak, Revolution, p. 188; Josef Polisensky, Aristocrats and the Crowd in the Revolutionary Year 1848. A Contribution to the History of the Revolution and Counter-Revolution in Austria (Albany, 1980), pp. 46–7; Sked, Survival, ch. 1.
[91] Demeter, Officer Corps, chs. 2, 3; the data are on p. 28. It is important to keep in mind that a number of these titles were acquired as a result of military service.

The Prussian situation was not much different, although here the relative strength of the aristocracy varied from one sector of the government to another. Thus between 1820 and 1847 the proportion of commoners among *Oberlandesgerichtspräsidenten*, high-ranking judicial officials, increased from 32 to 58 per cent, while the commoners' share of the *Regierungspräsidenten*, that is, top administrative officers, declined from 32 to 16 per cent. In the eastern part of the monarchy, the position of *Landrat* continued to be an aristocratic preserve; in the Marienwerder district, for instance, over three-quarters of the *Landräte* between 1818 and 1848 were titled.[92]

We should not make too much of these data on titles. The fact that someone had a 'von' before his name does not, in itself, always tell us very much about either his family background or his social position. Throughout the German lands some of those holding high rank in the army or the bureaucracy had been ennobled for their accomplishments; their status was the result rather than the cause of their climb up the service ladder. Similarly, members of established families could put their institutional loyalties above their other social commitments. Officers and bureaucrats were subjected to an intense process of socialization designed to give them corporate values that would transcend all others. A young man who entered a cadet school as a teenager and thereafter lived in a hermetically sealed military universe was likely to be an officer first, and an aristocrat second; a civil servant who had undergone the long, carefully designed training his calling required would characteristically feel closer to his colleagues than to the members of his caste. While it is no doubt important to note the persistence of aristocratic influence in military and bureaucratic institutions, we should not lose track of how both the army and the bureaucracy developed their own ethos and corporate identities.

The persistence of aristocratic prestige and influence led some contemporaries and many historians to complain about the incomplete or uneven character of German modernization. There is some truth to this argument: in the German states, as in many other parts of Europe, noble élites did help to preserve traditional values and institutions. But their success in preserving these values and institutions required using the forces of modernity to their own

---

[92] Hippel, *Blittersdorff*, pp. 5 ff.; Wandruszka and Urbanitsch, *Habsburgermonarchie*, ii, p. xiii; Wolfgang Zorn in Conze (ed.), *Staat*, p. 117; Reinhart Koselleck in ibid. 89; Bleeck, *Kameralausbildung*, p. 160, n. 156; Horst Mies, *Die preussische Verwaltung des Regierungsbezirks Marienwerder (1830–1870)* (Cologne and Berlin, 1972), 50.

advantage. The German nobility, in contrast to some of their counterparts in southern and eastern Europe, did not withdraw from their own era. However much they may have hated the forces at work around them, aristocrats throughout the German lands were closely tied to both the market and the state. Like the other élites to which this section will be devoted, these nobles had to live in a world where status, wealth, and power no longer coincided. In this dynamic, unstable social situation, the special claim to social esteem conveyed by noble status could do no more than enhance an individual's chances to acquire wealth and power. The nineteenth-century nobility were a product of their age, not the residue of pre-modern times.

For the *Bürgertum*, as for the nobility, the decline of the old regime involved a fragmentation of status, wealth, and political power. As the reader will recall from the discussion in Chapter 2, during the second half of the eighteenth century the traditional German *Bürgertum* had come under attack from two directions: politically, states were destroying or narrowing the urban élites' control over city government, while, at the same time, economic growth was producing a group of entrepreneurs outside, and often actively opposed to, the corporate structure of guild production. In the nineteenth century an acceleration of these developments created a new entrepreneurial élite. No one can accuse this élite of being a relic of an earlier age. To admirers and critics alike, these bankers, manufacturers, and merchants came to personify the world of big cities, unfettered capitalism, and industrial expansion. Their achievements, as Marx wrote in a famous passage of the *Communist Manifesto*, far surpassed Egyptian pyramids, Roman aqueducts, or Gothic cathedrals.[93]

There were fortunes to be made during the first half of the nineteenth century. With extraordinary energy, commercial acumen, and technological ability, Karl Mez turned his family's silk business into a giant enterprise that sold its products throughout Europe and reached for its raw materials into south-east Asia. August von der Heydt and David Hansemann made money in banking, commerce, and insurance at the same time as they took a leading role in the development of railroads. Ludolf Camphausen also invested in railroads, but directed most of his time to establishing a steam tugboat company, which eventually domin-ated the movement of freight on the Rhine. After having been

[93] A good place to begin reading about German businessmen is Zorn's 'Typen'.

trained as a carpenter and attending a government technical school, August Borsig quickly established his reputation as a master mechanic and eventually opened his own machine shop. At first he supplied steam engines for sugar beet refineries, then began to compete with English manufacturers of locomotives; by the time of his death in 1854, Borsig's Berlin factories had produced five hundred locomotives. Werner Siemens laid the foundation of his industrial empire in 1847 when, with borrowed capital and an amateur enthusiasm for technological innovation, he started a firm to manufacture telegraph apparatus.[94]

With the exception of Borsig, whose father was an artisan, none of these men came from the lower orders. Some were from quite prosperous circumstances: Mez, for instance, inherited a well-established textile firm from his father, who had begun as a weaver. Heydt had access to a considerable fortune accumulated by several generations of bankers in the textile town of Elberfeld. Friedrich Harkort, an entrepreneur with widespread interests in metal-working and machines, was a member of a prominent landed family in Westphalia. These men, and many others like them, merely increased already sizeable fortunes, either by expanding family businesses or by shifting capital into new enterprises; it does not make much sense to talk about them as a 'rising' social group. Other entrepreneurs, however, did rise, from the fringes if not the depths of the social order. Without financial assistance from his father, a not very prosperous pastor, David Hansemann began his spectacularly successful career as a fourteen-year-old merchant's apprentice. Camphausen's father was a shopkeeper who died when the boy was ten, leaving him to make his own way.

The scattered quantitative data on the social background of entrepreneurs confirm the impression left by these examples. From his study of 124 Berlin entrepreneurs active during the middle decades of the century, Hartmut Kaelble found that ninety-six (78 per cent) were the sons of bankers, merchants, and manufacturers, twelve (10 per cent) of artisans, innkeepers, and farmers, and fifteen (12 per cent) of officials, teachers, and pastors. As we should expect, businessmen's social origins varied both by industry and region. In relatively new, technically oriented branches like

---

[94] See Fischer's essay on Mez in *Wirtschaft*; Anna Caspari, *Ludolf Camphausens Leben* (Stuttgart and Berlin, 1902); Alexander Bergengrün's *David Hansemann* (Berlin, 1901) and *Staatsminister August von der Heydt* (Leipzig, 1908); Kocka, *Unternehmungsverwaltung*. Kocka's study of Siemens is the best available analysis of a single German firm.

machine building, a skilful craftsman such as Borsig had a better chance of success than in banking or railroads. In commercial cities, merchants usually controlled investment capital, while in Silesia, the landed nobility played an entrepreneurial role. Overall, upward mobility into the economic élite took place within a fairly narrow social range: virtually closed to the poorest and least educated sectors of society, this élite was open to a few highly gifted—and extremely lucky—men from artisanal backgrounds, but was most accessible to those from a well-established, prosperous families. Parents with some wealth and property provided their sons with training and motivation, as well as the capital and connections they needed for success.[95]

Such family ties were especially important in the first half of the nineteenth century, when the institutional structure of economic relationships was not well articulated. A businessman's parents, brothers, or in-laws were the most reliable source of credit to start a firm or keep it afloat. Familial bonds helped establish relationships of trust between trading partners or between branches of the same enterprise. Both Mez and Siemens, for instance, used their kin to expand into new regions, while many others married into families which extended their network of economic influence. This interconnection between economics and kinship had characterized social life in commercial cities like Hamburg for centuries. Now it spread to new economic centres: the mothers of five out of seven leading Leipzig entrepreneurs during the 1840s came from an entrepreneurial family, and five of these businessmen themselves married businessmen's daughters.[96]

Family connections blended with, and were extended by, the various local offices held by members of the economic élite. In the old Hansa cities, urban affairs were still run by a few prominent families whose members monopolized city government and held the key posts in religious, charitable, and cultural institutions. In the Rhineland and Westphalia, businessmen participated in public life by means of the institutions established during the French occupation: chambers of commerce, arbitration boards, and other

[95] Kaelble, *Unternehmer*, ch. 1, especially p. 31. Horst Beau, *Das Leistungswissen des frühindustriellen Unternehmertums in Rheinland-Westfalen* (Cologne, 1959) has a great deal of evidence on the social origins of entrepreneurs, but much of it is difficult to use and evaluate. Some local examples: A. Schröter and W. Becker, *Die deutsche Maschinenbauindustrie in der industriellen Revolution* (Berlin, 1962), 64 ff.; Zunkel, *Unternehmer*, ch. 1; Wutzmer, 'Herkunft'.

[96] Zwahr, 'Klassenkonstituierung'; Kocka, 'Entrepreneur'.

organs of economic self-administration. After the western provinces were taken over by Prussia, these institutions remained and continued to attract members of the economic élite. Similar sorts of institutions gradually took shape elsewhere in German Europe, as businessmen gathered to form useful alliances, defend their special interests, and influence government policy. Economic élites were also increasingly drawn into local representative institutions, which became forums within which they could express their political views and extend their influence over community affairs.[97] Generally speaking, businessmen were most comfortable in local or regional institutions, which served their immediate needs and did not require a large amount of time away from home. When an entrepreneur needed to establish contact with the central administration, he usually did so without an intervening institution. David Hansemann, for example, dealt with the Prussian government about Rhenish railroads by negotiating directly and personally with the ministry in Berlin.

Until mid-century the German economic élite continued to be regionally separate and diverse. In Hamburg, Bremen, and Lübeck, the old commercial elements remained pre-eminent, their ranks joined by new men who were absorbed into traditional values and institutions. Frankfurt was run by an uneasy coalition of wealthy master craftsmen, merchants, and jurists. Leipzig's economic élite, on the other hand, reflected that city's rapidly expanding industrial base. Economically, socially, and politically, Barmen was dominated by energetic textile manufacturers such as the Engels family. Capital cities like Vienna and Berlin contained a large and important banking community, ironworks and similar enterprises connected to railroad building, and a variety of other industries. As these cities expanded, their economic élites converted their houses into stores or office buildings and built new residences outside the centre of town, thus converting villages like Charlottenburg into fashionable suburbs.

Superimposed on this regional diversity was a complex of social and economic differences among German businessmen. The Leipzig publisher Friedrich Brockhaus could afford to buy himself a manor and marry his daughters to titled army officers, but many other manufacturers had incomes and ways of life that were virtually indistinguishable from those of a master craftsman. Of course businessmen also had different economic interests. Frank-

---

[97] Diefendorf, *Businessmen*, ch. 8.

furt's manufacturers and merchants shared a common regard for their city but battled over its economic policy. Cologne's traditional commercial élite, with its orientation towards the Rhine, clashed with the supporters of railroads that would draw the city into new economic orbits. Businessmen dependent on raw materials from abroad or eager to exploit foreign markets characteristically favoured free trade, while those in direct competition with more advanced firms wanted some degree of tariff protection. Mine owners and iron manufacturers pressed for greater investment in railroads; innkeepers and ship builders did not.[98]

There is nothing uniquely German about this diversity within the economic élite. Everywhere in Europe, regional, social, and economic differences divided businessmen into separate, sometimes competing groups. Everywhere the emergence of a cohesive bourgeoisie was slow, uneven, and incomplete. In the German case, however, social and economic diversity was reinforced by deeply rooted geographical and institutional divisions among regions and states. Moreover, the pressure of political repression, never absent from German public life before mid-century, inhibited the development of economic co-operation and consensus. After all, those social groups which we conventionally call *classes* usually become conscious of their identity when their members begin to act together in defence of their common interests and values. Opportunities for such action were not easy to find in Metternichian Germany.

The development of a cohesive German 'bourgeoisie' was further inhibited by the continued division between the élites of property and education. For the *Bildungsbürgertum*, office rather than property was the most important source of prestige, political influence and economic security. Among his fellow students in the 1820s, Heinrich Laube wrote, 'everyone looked to the state for his advancement. The world was enclosed in a fence called office, minor office.' Because the state was the most important employer of educated men, it played a dominant role in determining the course and content of education. In contrast to England, where the administration was small and semi-autonomous corporations

[98] On the problem of definition, see Henning, *Bürgertum*, pt. 1; Lothar Gall, '. . . Ich wünschte ein Bürger zu sein! Zum Selbstverständnis des deutschen Bürgertums im 19. Jahrhundert', *HZ* 245/3 (1987), 601–23. Two local examples are Ayçoberry, *Cologne*, p. 12 and Sharlin, 'Structure', pp. 82 ff. There are excellent analyses of various aspects of the *Bürgertum's* development in Jürgen Kocka (ed.), *Bürgertum im 19. Jahrhundert. Deutschland im europäischen Vergleich* (3 Vol.; Munich, 1988).

regulated the professions, most German governments assumed increasing power over the training for, admission to, and regulation of careers in law, medicine, education, and the church. Thus when the Prussian *Allgemeines Landrecht* stipulated that 'no one should hold an office for which he has not qualified and demonstrated his expertise', it laid the basis for administrative control over how quality should be defined and expertise demonstrated.[99]

During the reform era, many educational innovators had cherished the ideal of universal education as a source of social progress and equality. But the main result of their efforts was to strengthen élite schools and isolate them from the overwhelming majority of the population. First in Prussia, and then in many other states, a uniform education system was established during the first decades of the nineteenth century. Most young people attended school from the ages of six to thirteen, after which they would enter the work-force, acquire some technical training or attend one of the various secondary schools available in most cities. After three or four years of elementary school, a young man destined for the university entered a *Gymnasium*, in which he spent nine years studying a curriculum heavily weighted towards the classical languages. Once he passed the *Abitur*, the final examination given after nine years of *Gymnasium* training, a student could go on to study at a university. Entrance into a university without the *Abitur* became increasingly difficult; in 1834 Prussian universities were virtually closed to those who had not passed this examination. Unlike the primary schools, to which very limited resources were made available, most states devoted considerable money and talent to the training of their élites: one scholar has estimated that each *Gymnasium* student cost 260 times more than his counterpart in the elementary schools. With resources came regulations. Governments decided which schools could grant the *Abitur*, supervised their curriculum, and verified their examination results. According to Fritz Ringer, 'the whole institutional history of the German secondary and higher education during the early nineteenth century must be conceived as a process of bureaucratic rationalization'.[100]

[99] Sagarra, *History*, p. 275; Konrad Jarausch, *Deutsche Studenten, 1800–1970* (Frankfurt, 1984), 15.

[100] Ringer, *Education*, p. 33. More data on education can be found in Fischer *et al.*, *Arbeitsbuch*, pp. 224 ff. The fullest treatment of the subject is now Karl-Ernst Jeismann and Peter Lundgreen (eds.), *Handbuch der deutschen Bildungsgeschichte iii. 1800–1870* (Munich, 1987). Additional literature on education is cited above, Ch. 2, sect. iv, n. 108, and Ch. 7, sect. iii, n. 64.

As the path to higher education became more clearly defined and closely regulated, it also became narrower and steeper. The *Volksschule* and the secondary schools into which their students passed were quite separate from the *Gymnasium* and university. Each track produced its own teachers: the Volksschule faculty was trained in special pedagogical institutes, while Gymnasium teachers came from the universities. Moreover, students found it almost impossible to switch from one track to another.[101] By the age of nine or ten, therefore, the most important decisions about a young person's educational future had been made. Not surprisingly, this arrangement greatly benefited families able to steer their children towards the right goal, assist them with their schoolwork, and support them during the long years when they would be unable to work. Throughout the nineteenth century the number of *Gymnasium* and university students from the lowest social and economic strata was extremely small, while the number of those from within the *Bildungsbürgertum* itself was relatively high.

Nevertheless, the educated élite was not closed; self-recruitment was significant, but not overwhelming. In the Berlin *Gymnasien* studied by Detlef Müller, for instance, almost 30 per cent of the students enrolled between 1832 and 1836 were the sons of merchants and master craftsmen, 18 per cent of entrepreneurs. Margret Kraul's examination of six *Gymnasien* in Prussia's western provinces yields the following results: 19 per cent of the students came from what she calls the 'upper' and 'upper-middle', 36 per cent from the 'middle middle', 42 from the 'lower-middle', and 3 per cent from the 'lower strata'.[102] Attendance at a university, which was more academically demanding and financially burdensome than studying at a *Gymnasium*, drew from a somewhat narrower band on the social spectrum. Overall, the data in table 8.12 remind us of the situation we observed in economic élites:both the *Besitz-* and *Bildungsbürgertum* were virtually closed to the least fortunate members of society, relatively open to intermediate groups, but most accessible to those from families already inside.

The reforms that were first introduced by Humboldt and his collaborators in Berlin and were then taken up by statesmen throughout central Europe revitalized German universities and

---

[101] Fischer, 'Volksschullehrer'; LaVopa, *Schoolteachers*; Kraul, *Das deutsche Gymnasium*; Rainer Bölling, *Sozialgeschichte der deutschen Lehrer. Ein Überblick von 1800 bis zur Gegenwart* (Göttingen, 1983).

[102] Müller, *Sozialstruktur*, p. 524; Kraul, *Gymnasium und Gesellschaft*, especially p. 143.

TABLE 8.12. *Social origins of students at Halle, 1770–1874*

Father's occupation	1770	1821	1834	1852	1874
Academically trained élites	55	46	38	49	. 37
Officers	1	2	1	2	1
Subaltern officials, teachers	14	17	21	19	22
Landowners	4	4	4	5	7
Small farmers	4	7	8	6	6
Industrialists	—	2	2	2	3
Merchants, innkeepers	8	8	11	7	10
Artisans	12	14	12	. 8	8
Workers, servants	1	1	2	1	1
Rentiers	1	1	1 .	1	4

Source: Ringer, *Education*, p. 82.

helped turn them into models for educational innovation through-out the world.[103] But, despite this apparent success, Humboldt's reforms did not accomplish what he had hoped: instead of being centres of learning for its own sake, German universities remained closely tied to professional training for the clergy, medicine, academia, law, and government service. Changes in university enrolments, therefore, were in large measure a product of the changing pattern of demand for personnel in these professions. After dropping sharply during the Napoleonic wars, the number of German university students increased immediately after 1815, peaked at about 0.52 per mille in 1830, and then dropped back to 0.35 per mille when the market for educated men declined during the entire middle third of the century. Between 1830 and 1860, 30 per cent of the student body majored in theology, 30 per cent in law, 15 per cent in medicine, 15 per cent in humanistic subjects, 5 per cent in the natural sciences, and 5 per cent in a variety of smaller, more specialized fields. When clerical posts became increasingly difficult to obtain, the number of theology students declined from a high of six thousand in 1831 to just over three thousand in 1845. The number of students in the arts and sciences, on the other hand, increased after 1850 because the demand for teachers increased.[104]

[103] On the paradigmatic character of the German university, see Lenore O'Boyle, 'Learning', and 'Klassische Bildung und soziale Struktur in Deutschland zwischen 1800 und 1848', *HZ* 207/3 (1968), 584–608.
[104] Ringer, *Education*, pp. 46, 60, 291. See also McClelland, *State*.

Despite its decline in the 1830s and 1840s, theology remained the largest faculty at many German universities until after mid-century. In Halle, for instance, more than half the students were enrolled in the theological faculty between 1817 and 1860. Theology continued to be a path of social mobility: although many future ministers came from clergymen's families (41 per cent as opposed to 28 per cent for the student body as a whole), a disproportionately large number were the sons of families with modest means—minor officials, teachers, small farmers, and craftsmen. Every clergyman was a state employee. At the end of their study, Protestant theologians took an examination administered by the government in order to qualify for a clerical position; their appointment and future promotion remained under state control, although in some regions landowners retained their right to nominate the pastor of 'their' church. Sometimes compromises had to be worked out between bureaucratic authority and the community control so important for some Calvinist congregations.[105]

At the beginning of the nineteenth century the practice of medicine was divided between a small number of university-trained physicians, many of them employed by the state as army doctors or public health officers, and a variety of practitioners such as barbers, midwives, apothecaries, and folk-healers. Among this motley collection of medical craftsmen, the physician was not clearly pre-eminent, either scientifically or socially. Indeed, there was little relationship between formal training and competence. Some of the best medical care available was provided by men like Adolf Kussmaul's father, a respected rural surgeon around the turn of the century, who had learned his craft through practical experience. In the 1820s, however, both the intellectual basis and the institutional structure of medical care began to change. As we shall see in Chapter 13, the quality of scientific research and education in German universities improved dramatically, often due to the work of scholars trained in the medical faculty. The invention of the microscope encouraged physicians to examine the physical basis of disease; the application of percussion and auscultation as clinical techniques enabled them to consider a broader range of symptoms. The possession of new knowledge and

[105] J. Conrad, 'Die Entwicklung der Universität Halle', *JbbNS* 11/1 (1885), 105–24; Günther Bormann, 'Studien zu Berufsbild und Berufswirklichkeit evangelischer Pfarrer in Württemberg. Die Herkunft der Pfarrer. Ein geschichtlich-statistischer Überblick von 1700–1965', *Social Compass*, 13/2 (1966), 95–137; Ringer, *Education*, p. 88.

tools gave formally trained physicians the basis—albeit still rather shaky—on which to claim superiority over their competition; but this claim prevailed only when it was taken up and enforced by the states, which instituted a series of laws establishing the physician's place at the top of the healing hierarchy and limiting the functions of other medical practitioners. By mid-century the relative number of doctors employed directly by the state had declined (in Prussia from 49 per cent in 1827 to 36 per cent in 1842), but the role of the state in the regulation of medical care had substantially increased.[106]

For professors, as for physicians, the achievement of a new professional identity and pre-eminence was the result of state action. The nineteenth-century university was a state-run institution, staffed by civil servants, and ultimately controlled by a government ministry. Faculty participation in professorial appointments was guaranteed, but bureaucratic influence was substantial: in Prussia, for instance, the faculty was either not consulted about, or was actively opposed to, one-third of the full professors of law appointed between 1817 and 1840. In return for these limits on their autonomy, nineteenth-century professors got financial security and social prestige. They now earned enough so that they could devote themselves full-time to teaching and scholarship; their intellectual preeminence—as the guardians of tradition, creators of new knowledge, and educators of the future élite—was universally acknowledged. The path to an academic career led directly through the university itself: regular study, a doctorate, then the *Habilitation* that conveyed the *venia legendi*, the licence to teach. The new emphasis on research provided the faculty with criteria according to which they could select the most promising and co-operative young scholars for positions as *Privatdozenten* and extraordinary (that is, non-tenured and subordinate) professors. Like most professions, the professoriate tried to protect its position by resisting expansion: during the first two-thirds of the century the number of full professors grew slowly while the ranks of the junior faculty expanded to meet the needs of increasing enrolments.[107]

Although clergymen, physicians, and professors were tied to the government, the most direct link between the *Bildungsbürgertum*

---

[106] Claudia Huerkamp, 'Ärzte und Professionalisierung in Deutschland: Überlegungen zum Wandel des Arztberufs im 19. Jahrhundert', *GuG* 6 (1980), 349–82; W. Robert Lee, 'Medicalization and Mortality Trends in South Germany in the Early 19th Century', in Imhof (ed.), *Mensch*, pp. 81 ff.; Kussmaul, *Jugenderinnerungen*, especially pp. 11 ff.

[107] McClelland, *State*, ch. 5; the data on appointments to the Law Faculties are given on p. 185.

and the state ran through the faculty of law. Some lawyers, of course, carried on private practice, while others served as legal advisers to a corporate body. Ludwig Windthorst, for instance, was employed by the Ritterschaft in his home town of Osnabrück before going on to become a leading parliamentarian.[108] But the tone of the legal profession was set by the bureaucracy, which provided employment for a majority of law graduates.

In contrast to the cameralist studies once popular among administrators, nineteenth-century legal education did not have much practical value. Indeed, in their nine years at a classical *Gymnasium* and three at the university, aspiring bureaucrats learned very little directly applicable to running a modern state. Instead of creating technically proficient experts, their legal training and fluency in ancient languages were supposed to foster a political élite, able to define and pursue the welfare of the state. The official's education was meant to train his mind, build his character, and encourage him to develop certain values. Often enough, the curricular substance was dull and uninspiring. Judging by the frequency with which their elders felt obliged to exhort students to apply themselves, it would seem that the young Bismarck's devotion to extracurricular matters was not unusual. But of course officials knew that the pleasures of student life were no less important for moulding civil servants than lectures and examinations. In the fraternities and beer halls of Heidelberg or Göttingen, the future leaders of the state acquired values and made contacts upon which they could depend throughout their careers.[109]

The process of socialization that began in the *Gymnasium* and continued at the university was intensified during the long apprenticeship through which all officials had to pass. In Prussia, for instance, a candidate for an élite administrative post spent from fifteen months to four years as a judicial clerk (*Auskultator*) and then served as an intern (*Referendar*) in a local government district. During this period, young men came into contact with the practical problems of law and administration and were also exposed to both the unwritten code and the formal regulations governing bureaucratic life. While they learned professional skills in law courts and bureaucratic offices, the apprentices' social life was apt to be spent in the company of their colleagues. As Rudolf von Delbrück recalled from his years as a junior official in Berlin during the 1840s, 'The bureaucratic circles, finding themselves between the

---

[108] Anderson, *Windthorst*, pp. 27 ff.
[109] Bleeck, *Kameralausbildung*; Wunder, *Privilegierung*.

tightly closed court society on the one hand and the bourgeois
community on the other, led a life of their own.' On duty and off,
the socialization of officials into the bureaucracy's distinctive
culture and corporate values continued.[110]

Considering the expensive education and the long, poorly paid
apprenticeship that a bureaucratic post demanded, only those with
some independent resources could hope to qualify. Candidates did
not have to be rich, but they could not be poor. In Prussia, for
example, the parents of aspirants were required to present a
financial statement demonstrating that their sons could support
themselves in a decent fashion during their internship. No less
important than financial backing, a would-be official needed the
social skills and cultural background most easily acquired at home.
It is understandable, therefore, why self-recruitment was so strong
in nineteenth-century bureaucracies. Nor is it surprising that in
Baden, the most highly bureaucratized of states, self-recruitment
was especially prevalent: as many as four-fifths of those holding an
important government post between 1815 and 1848 were the sons
of Badenese civil servants. Well versed in the corps' values and
assumptions, provided with the right sort of formal education, and
able to call on family friends and relations for aid along the way, the
product of a bureaucratic family had a number of obvious
advantages. Friedrich von Motz, for instance, who eventually
became Prussian Minister of Finance, was from a prominent family
of officials in Kassel, joined the Prussian service, married the
daughter of a *Landrat*, and, even before having passed his major
examination, was appointed as his father-in-law's successor. To an
unsympathetic observer like Friedrich von Blittersdorff, such
bureaucratic families seemed ready to become an official nobility
which treated the government like an entailed estate. Blittersdorff,
it will be recalled, was part of an older system of patronage,
controlled by noble kinship rather than official position.[111]

The bureaucracy's critics persistently accused it of being isolated
from society. Stein called officials 'salaried bookworms without
property or interests', Marwitz viewed them as 'the order of the
homeless', and the young Bismarck spoke of the 'bureaucratic

---

[110] Gillis, *Bureaucracy*, p. 33. See also Koselleck, *Preussen*, pp. 248 ff. Between
1820 and 1850 more than half of the bureaucrats studied by Henning married the
daughters of other bureaucrats: Henning, *Beamtenschaft*, p. 99.

[111] Bleeck, *Kameralausbildung*, pp. 123 ff.; Lee, *Politics*, p. 71 and Table 1, App. B,
p. 251; Petersdorff, *Motz*; Hippel, *Blittersdorff*, p. 12.

caste' in which individual opinion or behaviour was impossible. Significantly, the bureaucracy was similarly described by its most eloquent advocates, for whom its corporate values, social independence, and freedom from special interests formed the basis for its right to rule. Thus Hegel argued that the administration's position outside of 'civil society' made it a universal *Stand*, able to perceive and pursue the common good. Hegel favoured self-recruitment precisely because it insulated officials from the turmoil and temptations of ordinary social life and thus helped to ensure the bureaucracy's social neutrality.[112]

This neutrality was, of course, a myth. Far from being 'above' society—whatever that might mean—the bureaucracy was deeply engaged in the social process. To be sure, few acted for personal gain; most nineteenth-century bureaucrats were honest. But they all intervened in social life on behalf of interests, institutions, and individuals that represented their particular image of the common good. Because there was no unified bureaucratic social policy, no coherent vision of the common good shared by all, the character and direction of their interventions varied widely—from state to state, region to region, department to department, time to time. Some officials opposed industrial development, others backed it; some favoured free trade, others tariff protection, and so on. Officials' views on these matters were the result of a complex process, in which their values, interests, and experience all played a part.

Despite the bureaucracy's efforts to shape its members' values, interests, and experiences, officials were inevitably open to influences from the outside—from their families, friends, and neighbours. The boundaries between bureaucracy and society were always porous. In the eastern provinces of Prussia, the *Landrat* was necessarily a part of the local landed élite, upon which he depended for practical assistance as well as companionship. Officials in the Rhineland or Westphalia lived in a different social world, populated by merchants and industrialists. Among the German bureaucrats studied by Hansjoachim Henning, over half had wives from a bureaucratic family, but a substantial minority (16 per cent) married businessmen's daughters. As economic opportunities increased, some officials left government service and went into

---

[112] Wunder, *Privilegierung*, p. 18; Friedrich von Oertzen, *Die Junker: Preussischer Adel im Jahrhundert des Liberalismus* (Berlin, 1939), 68; Rothfels (ed.), *Bismarck*, p. 4. On Hegel's views, see above, Ch. 7, sect. iii.

business: for example, Hans Viktor von Unruh, a general's son
from east of the Elbe, took a job with the railroads after being
disappointed by the low pay and dull routine of the Prussian
administration. The bureaucracy, therefore, could not escape the
powerful social and economic forces at work in nineteenth-century
Europe. While civil servants surely represented a more cohesive
and self-conscious group than the economic élites, they were also
drawn towards a variety of competing allies and interests, ranging
from the traditional landed nobility to the most progressive
industrial entrepreneurs.[113]

Because the élites of property and education reflect the fluidity so
characteristic of mid-nineteenth century society, historians have
always had trouble finding a terminology supple enough to capture
the variety of social experience within the German middle strata.
Indeed, to use any singular noun in reference to these groups
distorts their diversity and imposes on them a spurious cohesion.
Many contemporaries found these social groups equally perplexing. Metternich, for example, warned Tsar Alexander about what
he called 'this intermediate class', which adopted 'all sorts of
disguises, uniting and subdividing as occasion offers, helping each
other in the hour of danger, and the next day depriving each other
of their conquests'. Goethe spoke of a 'Mittelstand' in which he
included a bewildering collection of people, including 'the inhabitants of small cities . . . officials and subaltern officials,
merchants, manufacturers, the wives and daughters of such
families, and rural clergymen . . .'. Without the legally imposed
cohesion of the traditional *Bürgertum* or the political self-consciousness of a class, the middle strata had no basis for a common life.
They are conceptually elusive because they were historically
disparate.[114]

'Upon the middle classes', Friedrich Harkort wrote in 1842, 'rest
the power and prestige of the state.' Harkort's use of the plural
Mittelklassen implied that he saw their diversity even while he
insisted on their centrality. For him, and for many of his fellow
liberals, the middle strata were the core of society, not merely its
intermediate ranks. They used terms like *Mittelstand, Mittelstände,
Mittelklasse, Mittelklassen*, sometimes *Bürgertum* to describe this
distinctive collection of social groups, and, while liberals might

---

[113] Henning, *Beamtenschaft*.

[114] Gay, *Experience*, i. 43–4; Sombart, *Volkswirtschaft*, p. 482. For more
examples, see Riedel's article in *GGB*, i. 689 ff.

have disagreed about who did and did not belong, they sought to present this amalgam of educated and propertied groups as the primary source of social progress, the location of rationality, and the expression of the common good. Throughout the rest of this book we shall consider various aspects of this attempt to create a 'universal class' out of the German middle strata.[115]

[115] Friedrich Harkort, *Schriften und Reden zu Volksschule und Volksbildung* (Paderborn, 1969), 5.

IX
The Cultural Establishment and its Critics

FRANZ KUGLER, a merchant's son from Stettin, established his scholarly reputation with influential works on Greek sculpture, European painting, and Prussian history. In 1835, when he was just twenty-seven, he became a professor at the Academy of Art in Berlin; eight years later he took charge of artistic affairs in the Prussian Ministry of Culture. In 1847 Kugler wrote an essay on art as an administrative concern in which he called for a series of state-initiated cultural programmes, including the creation of art schools, passage of copyright laws, establishment of awards for creative achievement, construction of museums and monuments, and the renovation or preservation of important historical buildings. 'Just as science is designed to make people spiritually free,' Kugler argued, 'art gives them the mark of spiritual nobility. Therefore since one of the government's duties is to further and direct the education of the *Volk*, this duty must include art as well as science.' But, while Kugler saw the need for state initiative in the promotion of art, he also recognized that another, no less powerful force was at work; in addition to being an object of 'administrative concern', art was also an object of what he called 'mercantile speculation'. Kugler found nothing wrong with this: 'a fresh, mobile commerce' belonged to a well-developed national existence and had its place in the realm of artistic production. But Kugler, like many German liberals, feared that commerce might lead to chaos and corruption, so he advocated a variety of governmental measures to preserve art's purity and honour from 'the remorseless drive of speculation'.[1]

The state and the market, the two fundamental forces at work in nineteenth-century social development, provided the institutional matrix for nineteenth-century culture. As patron, educator, and regulator, governments influenced what got built and produced, taught and studied, published and performed. Museum directors

[1] Franz Kugler, *Kleine Schriften und Studien zur Kunstgeschichte* (Stuttgart, 1854), iii. pp. 578, 582, 594. On Kugler's career, see Wilhelm Treue, 'Franz Theodor Kugler—Kulturhistoriker und Kulturpolitiker', *HZ* 170/3 (1953), 483–526.

and official architects, professors and researchers, censors and policemen, all attempted to shape citizens' tastes, values, and opinions. No nineteenth-century state, however, had either the ability or the will to control completely the production of art and ideas. In cultural life, as in economic affairs, government intervention was rarely as effective as its advocates claimed or as disruptive as its opponents feared. Even during the darkest days of restoration repression, subversive literature was written and read. Professors and teachers, as vulnerable as they often were to pressures for conformity, sometimes showed remarkable independence. A few artists and poets ignored directions from above and pursued their own distinctive vision. But those who bravely sought to act outside, and often against, the states' repressive pressures found themselves faced with another challenge to their autonomy. Without a patron's support or an official position, the artist was dependent on his clients, the writer on his readers, the publicist on his editor. The vagaries of public taste, the shifting currents of opinion, and the uncertain market for serious art and literature combined to limit the influence or undermine the independence of many creative Germans.

The following chapter begins with a discussion of the cultural institutions created by the states and ends with an analysis of intellectual disenchantment and cultural criticism. In between these extremes of conformity and alienation we will find a range of positions, created by the interplay of limits and opportunities, restraints and rewards within which nineteenth-century culture took shape.

i. PUBLIC CULTURE, PRIVATE TASTES

The least autonomous of the arts, architecture is always a social enterprise, shaped by politics, responsive to wealth, representative of cultural values. Whether they be pyramids, temples, cathedrals, or palaces, the characteristic buildings of an age reveal what people with power think should be celebrated, venerated, and preserved. In the nineteenth century, architectural talent and social resources were directed toward public buildings—those museums, theatres, libraries, railroad stations, and universities that still dominate the physiognomy of many European cities. These cultural institutions were 'public' in two senses of the term: they were usually sponsored by the state, and thus paid for with public funds, and they were, in theory at least, open to everyone in society, and thus directed toward a 'public'.

In the course of the nineteenth century, state institutions largely displaced the monarch and his court as patrons of the arts and arbiters of taste. Individual rulers, to be sure, patronized the arts, but they were rarely the focus of cultural activity. Neither in design nor in function did the royal residences built in the nineteenth century play the same role as the baroque palace; these residences, like other public buildings, did not centre around the royal person, just as the social and political order no longer revolved around the king. The same social and political forces that required the prince to exercise his authority within the confines of the constitution and by means of the bureaucratic apparatus, made it necessary for him to express his cultural authority by associating himself with the symbols and institutions of the state. In culture, as in politics, the monarch was supreme, but only as the state's first servant.[2]

The controversy over a proposed monument to Frederick the Great provides us with an early example of how abstract ideals of statehood could symbolically displace the personal authority of the monarch. Soon after the king's death in 1786, various artists and architects submitted plans for a memorial to his historic accomplishments. The most remarkable of these proposals was sketched in 1796 and 1797 by Friedrich Gilly, another of those extraordinary young people whose talent burned with brief intensity during the age of revolution and romanticism. Neo-classical in design, Gilly's conception was deeply romantic in mood and purpose. Like so many other artistic products of this time, it played with the limits of possibility, explored new forms, and sought to stir unprecedented emotions. With a temple-like mausoleum, sited above an area around Berlin's Leipzig Gate and approached along a path lined with trees, Gilly set out to create a sacred space, whose symbols transcended the career of any single person just as its scale transcended the dimensions of ordinary life. The king himself was the occasion rather than the subject for this monument, which aimed at evoking a sense of identification with the political community rather than the glories of a man or dynasty.[3]

[2] For an introduction to public culture, see Ulrich Scheuner, 'Die Kunst als Staatsaufgabe im 19. Jahrhundert', in Mai and Waetzoldt (eds.), Kunstverwaltung, pp. 13–46. Karl Ferdinand Werner (ed.), Hof, Kultur, und Politik im 19. Jahrhundert (Bonn, 1985), contains a number of essays on the monarch's changing political and cultural role. Throughout this section I am especially indebted to Beenken's remarkable book, Jahrhundert.

[3] Nipperdey, 'Nationalidee', pp. 137–8; Hubert Schrade, Das deutsche Nationaldenkmal. Idee, Geschichte, Aufgabe (Munich, 1934), 44 ff.

Gilly's monument was never built, but his aspirations, tamed and tailored to meet more restricted aesthetic and fiscal standards, were at the source of many new architectural projects after the turn of the century. In the wake of the upheavals that transformed central Europe during the revolutionary era, statesmen saw the need to create new political values and commitments to help consolidate the new states. In this enterprise, buildings and monuments could play an important part. 'It is our will', declared the king of Bavaria in 1808, 'that the beneficial influence of the fine arts be brought to bear on the entire nation more than in the past and that through this powerful educational instrument national talents be elevated.' Art could serve the nation as well as the state. As early as 1807, Bavaria's Crown Prince Ludwig began to make plans for a great national shrine which was eventually constructed as the Walhalla, built near Regensburg between 1830 and 1842. At the opening ceremonies, Ludwig expressed his hope that, in this structure, 'all Germans, from whatever clan, might always feel that they have a common fatherland'. Despite the uncertainty of its political implications and the shallowness of its symbolism, Walhalla represented a widespread sense that, in order to survive, political communities had to find new ways to bind their citizens, engage their loyalties, and harness their emotions. 'Large and useful buildings are . . . the clearest type with which the history of a people is written.'[4]

These goals were behind the great civic construction projects that transformed a number of central European capitals in the nineteenth century. Architects like Friedrich Weinbrenner in Karlsruhe, Georg Friedrich Laves in Hanover, Leo von Klenze in Munich, Karl Friedrich Schinkel in Berlin, and Gottfried Semper in Dresden searched for ways to reorganize public spaces, provide settings for political rituals, and mobilize patriotic sentiments. These architects usually worked under the patronage of a monarch, but their designs and plans were formulated in close consultation with administrative agencies and professional experts. No longer appendages of the courts, royal architects were employees of the state, devoted to creating structures through which the state's power could be expressed and magnified.[5]

[4] Friedrichs-Friedlaender, *Architektur*, p. 47. On Ludwig's role as patron of the arts, see Gollwitzer, *Ludwig I*.

[5] Herrmann, *Baukunst*, provides a useful introduction to the subject. The catalogue for the Dortmund Museum's exhibition, *Fünf Architekturen des Klassizismus in Deutschland* (Dortmund, 1977), has a rich collection of visual materials. The most recent account is David Watkin and Tilman Mellinghoff, *German Architecture and the Classical Ideal* (Cambridge, Mass., 1987).

Among this generation of architects and urban planners, the most prolific and influential was Karl Friedrich Schinkel. Born to a pastor's family in the Prussian garrison town of Neuruppin, Schinkel moved to Berlin and entered the Gymnasium zum grauen Kloster in 1792. After his passion for architecture was ignited by a visit to an exhibition of Gilly's sketches for the Frederick monument, he joined the workshop run by Gilly's father, David, an established figure in Berlin architectural circles. The following year David Gilly chose Schinkel to be a member of the first class in the new Bauakademie, where he worked with such luminaries as Heinrich Gentz, the designer of the Royal Mint in which the Bauakademie was housed, and Carl Gotthard Langhans, whose Brandenburg Gate is the era's best-known edifice. In 1803 Schinkel travelled to Italy in order to study the classical sites and develop his artistic skills. By the time he returned to Berlin two years later, the danger of war had brought public building to a halt. For the next decade, architectural work was almost impossible to find. David Gilly died penniless in 1808, while Schinkel supported himself with a variety of odd jobs such as designing stage sets. After Napoleon's defeat, however, a new era of public construction began in Berlin. Schinkel started work on the Neue Wache (New Guard House), his first important commission, in 1816; thereafter he was continually engaged in major building projects—the Schauspielhaus in the Gendarmenmarkt (1821), a renovation of Humboldt's villa at Tegel (1824), the Neue Pavillon at Charlottenburg (1825), the Crown Prince's palace of Charlottenhof (1827), what came to be called the Altes Museum (1830), the Royal Customs Warehouse (1832), and a new home for the Bauakademie (1836). In 1830 he was named *Geheimer Oberbaudirektor*, the highest architectural official in the kingdom. When Schinkel died in 1841, King Frederick William IV ordered the state to buy all of his drawings, paintings, and designs so that a permanent collection of his work might be established for the edification of future generations.[6]

The most conspicuous remains of Schinkel's legacy are the masterpieces still standing (or newly restored) in Berlin. These buildings suggest the range of his vision, from the monumental elegance of the Altes Museum to the restrained harmony of the Neue Pavillon, from the ornamental grandeur of the Schauspiel-haus to the clean-lined symmetry of the Neue Wache. While all

---

[6] Paul Ortwin Rave, *Karl Friedrich Schinkel* (Munich, 1953), is a good brief summary by the leading Schinkel scholar of his generation. Schinkel's own writings were published as *Aus Schinkels Nachlass* (4 vols.; Berlin, 1862–3).

these structures might be described as 'neo-classical', it is important not to overestimate the classical elements of Schinkel's sensibility. In his letters from Italy, for example, he showed less interest in the architectural achievements of the ancient world than in the feelings their ruins evoked: 'the sight of these works in their natural setting', he wrote from Sicily in 1804, 'holds a surprise which comes not only from their size, but also from their picturesque grouping.'[7] His paintings from this period are romantic in tone and disconcertingly gothic in appearance. Even at the highpoint of his neo-classical accomplishments, Schinkel continued to design gothic buildings and paint darkly romantic landscapes. What mattered to him was not the celebration of a particular style but rather the creation of a space conducive to certain emotions and activities. As a builder, an accomplished designer of theatrical scenery, and a creator of giant painted panoramas, Schinkel was interested in providing the setting, stage, and backdrop for the public and private ceremonies of his age: the appreciation of art in museums, the enjoyment of plays in the theatre, and the affirmation of state power in the capital's new civic spaces. To reach this goal, he was quite willing to use whatever style his patrons preferred.

The eclecticism characteristic of Schinkel's vision is even more apparent in the work of his Bavarian counterpart, Leo von Klenze, who for a time was his fellow pupil in David Gilly's Berlin atelier. The son of a Mecklenburg bureaucrat, Klenze studied in Berlin and Paris, managed to survive a brief stay in the ill-fated kingdom of Westphalia, and emerged from the Napoleonic years with a small fortune and a new patron, Crown Prince Ludwig of Bavaria. From 1817 until his death in 1864, Klenze served the Wittelsbachs as *Hofbauintendant*, built seventeen major public buildings and scores of smaller private ones, did archaeological research, travelled widely, and took a keen interest in canals and railroads. With Ludwig's advice and encouragement, he created the urban plan which determined Munich's development until well into the twentieth century. Even Heinrich Heine, whose experiences in the Bavarian capital had not been pleasant, praised 'the great master's joyful temples of art and noble palaces'.[8]

In theory, Klenze was committed to classicism. 'Greek architecture, developed from the necessity of things, serves human ends

---

[7] Hermann Pundt, *Schinkel's Berlin: A Study in Environmental Planning* (Cambridge, 1972), 80.
[8] On Klenze, see the fine treatment in Friedrichs-Friedlaender, *Architektur*, pp. 9 ff. The Heine quote is from Böhmer, *Welt*, p. 239.

like a second nature. Therefore it has become the architecture of every civilized people.'[9] But, while the Glyptothek, his first great building in Munich, is one of the century's most successful classical designs, its interior displays a variety of styles and modes of ornamentation. A number of Klenze's other projects had the same eclectic character, as can be seen in the various palaces he built for the Bavarian elite or in the Pinakothek which, despite its Grecian name, was done in the modified Renaissance style he thought most appropriate for housing a collection of great paintings.

For Klenze, as for many of his contemporaries, the history of architecture became a vast encyclopaedia in which one could search for an appropriate idea or style. 'Now that we have sought to appropriate Greek, Roman, and Byzantine architecture,' wrote a contributor to the periodical, *Museum*, in 1834, 'we should be allowed to employ other national styles as well.' A few years later the author of a training manual instructed young architects to examine 'Egyptian, old Indian, Persian, Roman, Byzantine, Arabic, the so-called Neo-gothic, and Neo-greco-roman' styles. The message was clear enough: every sort of design was potentially relevant, all had to be part of the modern builder's vocabulary, none was specially privileged or distinctively appropriate. The singularity of the nineteenth-century architectural revival, Peter Collins has written, 'was that it revived several kinds of architecture at the same time, and none of them was ever authoritative enough or fashionable enough to vanquish its competitors, or even to supersede the kind of architecture which had previously been built'.[10]

While some architects found nineteenth-century historicism boundlessly rich and exhilarating, others were overwhelmed by its variety and depressed by its derivative character. In a famous pamphlet of 1828, *In welchem Styl sollen wir bauen?*, Heinrich Hübsch condemned his contemporaries' mindless imitation of the past and demanded that they take into account the special needs, character, and techniques of the present.[11]

This criticism of historicism was taken up by Gottfried Semper, who became director of the architectural school at the Dresden Academy in 1834. Our cities, Semper declared in his inaugural

[9] Boehn, *Biedermeier*, p. 438.
[10] Klaus Döhmer, '*In welchem Style sollen wir bauen?*': *Architekturtheorie zwischen Klassizismus und Jugendstil* (Munich, 1976), 19; Peter Collins, *Changing Ideals in Modern Architecture, 1750–1950* (London, 1965), 62.
[11] See Beenken, *Jahrhundert*, especially pp. 69 ff.

lecture, 'bloom like the bouquet of a thousand flowers, with the essence of every time and place, so that we allow ourselves to be pleasantly deceived and forget to which century we belong'. Semper had little good to say about any of the public architects currently at work. He regarded the Karlsruhe school, for instance, as a sterile expression of 'the dreary impoverishment of the art forms helped on . . . by so-called connoisseurs and art patrons'. Nor were things better elsewhere in the other German states, which were 'so rich in artists and so poor in art'. Like his contemporary and sometime compatriot, Richard Wagner, Semper hoped for a new synthesis, in which the fragmentation of art would be overcome. But, while his own buildings show great energy and verve, Semper could not provide a compelling alternative to historicism. Klenze, who correctly saw himself as one of the chief targets of these barbed attacks, was surely right when he told Semper that, however depressing the present state of the art might be, 'there can be only one thing worse: trying to produce a new architecture out of abstraction and theory'. In the end, Semper was forced to recognize that architectural innovation would have to come from a political and cultural transformation, an enterprise to which he devoted himself with great courage but no success in 1848 and 1849.[12]

The eclectic historicism of central European architecture reached its culmination in the construction of Vienna's Ringstrasse, one of the century's last and greatest urban renewal projects. In the early 1850s, when the Austrian government decided to develop the area along the band of fortifications which had surrounded Vienna's urban core, a variety of public and private interests came into play. Significantly, the first edifice was the ornate Votivkirche, begun in 1856 to celebrate the emperor's escape from an assassination attempt and, by implication, the dynasty's triumph over the mid-century revolutions. A military museum and a carefully placed set of barracks also expressed the symbols and strategies of counter-revolution so important in the 1850s. But the aesthetic and social character of the Ringstrasse was established by a series of public buildings built for the urban élite: the Rathaus, whose Gothic design recalled the municipal liberties of the Middle Ages, a baroque theatre, neo-renaissance university, and the monumental neo-classical houses of parliament. Nearby were apartment houses that resembled the great palaces of the traditional Austrian

[12] Herrmann, *Baukunst*, pp. 153 ff.

aristocracy. With its distinctive blend of monarchical authority, state power, *bürgerlich* social and economic interests, and uninhibited architectural historicism, the Ringstrasse brought together many different elements in public culture. No wonder that it eventually provided the backdrop against which aesthetic alternatives to historicism were developed.[13]

In Vienna, as elsewhere in Europe, museums were usually an important element in mid-century urban reconstruction. Often created to house a particular collection, museums reflected the nineteenth century's conviction that works of art—like libraries, botanical gardens, and zoos—should no longer be monopolized by monarch and court, but should be open and available to the public. A museum, Klenze believed, must exist for 'all kinds of visitors' so that people would be able 'to divert art into life and mix it with life'. However, at the same time as museums brought art closer to people, they also severed it from those areas of life with which it had formerly been fused. A picture of the Madonna, which had once been a religious icon set in a context of ritual and belief, now became a *painting*, to be understood on its own terms. By separating works of art from the purposes for which they had been created, the museum reinforced the idea that art existed in an autonomous realm. No longer valuable as the representation of something sacred, art came to be sacred in itself. Thus Schinkel described his museum in Berlin as a 'Heiligtum', whose temple-like appearance proclaimed that it was a secular shrine in which visitors might worship beauty's sublime power. Often enough, the object of worship became not artistic beauty, but rather the expertise and social power of art's new political and academic guardians. Despite its public character, the nineteenth-century museum's atmosphere and organization ensured that it would be closed to the overwhelming majority of the population.[14]

---

[13] The basis for any study of the Ringstrasse is the multi-volume collection edited by Renate Wagner-Rieger, *Die Wiener Ringstrasse* (Vienna, 1969 ff.). My account owes a great deal to Schorske's brilliant essay in *Vienna*. See also Olsen, *City*, especially ch. 5. Eva Börsch-Supan, *Berliner Baukunst nach Schinkel, 1840–1870* (Munich, 1977), has some comparable material on Berlin.

[14] Klenze quoted in H. Seling, 'The Genesis of the Museum', *Architectural Review*, 141 (1967), 111–12. On museums, see Alma Wittlin, *The Museum: Its History and its Tasks in Education* (London, 1949); Volker Plagemann, *Das deutsche Kunstmuseum, 1790–1870: Lage, Baukörper, Raumorganisation, Bildprogramm* (Munich, 1969); Wolfgang Hardtwig, 'Kunst und Geschichte im Revolutionszeitalter. Historismus in der Kunst und der Historismusbegriff der Kunstwissenschaft', *AfK* 61/1 (1979), 154–90. For a contemporary response, see Fanny Lewald's account of her visit to the museum in Berlin; *Lebensgeschichte*, pp. 136–7.

Theatrical and musical performances, like art collections and libraries, moved into the public sphere during the first half of the nineteenth century. Patronage, of course, remained important, especially for composers: Wagner, Brahms, and even Richard Strauss were all dependent on a royal benefactor. But in the performing arts, as in architecture, the shift away from monarchical domination was unmistakable. No longer were opera houses built by royal command, staffed by court musicians, and attended by those with court connections. Increasingly, they became public or commercial enterprises, with their own professional staff and paid attendance. When the Hoftheater in Munich burned down in 1818, it was rebuilt and reopened as the 'Hof- und Nationaltheater', whose revised title suggested its new public role. Even more telling is the contrast between Langhans's Schauspielhaus, built in Berlin's Gendarmenmarkt at the end of the eighteenth century, and the replacement constructed by Schinkel three decades later. From the outside, Langhans' building looked more like a palace than a theatre; its most prominent feature was the king's ceremonial entrance. Schinkel, however, built a temple to the muse, a sacred but secular space comparable to the museum he would design for the Lustgarten a few years later. The interior design of theatres also changed: whereas the court theatre had been arranged to promote conviviality and display among the audience, the public theatre was oriented towards the stage, where highly trained actors and elaborate scenery were supposed to monopolize the ticket holders' attention. The characteristic music of the age was written to be performed in a similar setting. The symphony, unlike liturgical or chamber music, had no ancillary function; it had to be listened to on its own terms, without the distraction of religious rituals or courtly festivity.[15]

Many Germans were fascinated by the performing arts during the first half of the nineteenth century. While it was probably an exaggeration to claim, as did one contemporary, that the director of the Schauspielhaus was the second most important man in Berlin, there is no doubt that directors, actors, and dramatists had a special kind of glamour and fame. Nowhere was this more manifest than in Vienna, a city blessed with a variety of theatres, ranging from the well-established Burgtheater, founded by Joseph II in 1776, to a score of modest playhouses in which popular, often

[15] Henry Raynor, History, and The Orchestra: A History (New York and London, 1978); William Weber, Music and the Middle Class: The Social Structure of Concert Life in London, Paris, and Vienna (New York, 1976).

earthy dramas were performed. Throughout central Europe, actors and musicians were no longer servants of the court or wandering entertainers, but rather enjoyed the attention and adulation that we have come to associate with certain kinds of celebrity. The virtuoso violinist Nicolo Paganini, for instance, fascinated audiences, not merely because of his legendary skill on the G string, but also because of his extraordinary personal appearance and the rumours surrounding his private life. Fanny Elssler was famous for her interpretation of Spanish and Slavic dances, as well as for her love-affair with the ageing apostle of reaction, Friedrich Gentz. Henrietta Sontag, widely regarded as the most beautiful actress of her day, was regularly deluged with poems and letters from her stricken admirers. On one memorable occasion, a group of her fans from the University of Göttingen pushed a coach she had used into the river so that its cushions would not be profaned by the posteriors of lesser mortals.[16]

Nietzsche once complained that nineteenth-century culture isolated the spectators from one another at the same time as it alienated them from the creative process. He condemned 'the madness of art galleries and concert halls', which have accustomed people 'to enjoying the arts individually' rather than as part of the community's shared experience.[17] As was often the case, Nietzsche was remarkably insightful, but not altogether correct. Cultural institutions in the nineteenth century did encourage individual responses from their participants: in contrast to both popular and courtly cultures, conviviality was banned from theatres and museums, where the audience was limited to restrained and ritualized reactions to the performance or display. At the same time, however, public culture depended on a broad network of organizations, which people joined in order to support and take part in various artistic, literary, and musical enterprises. Berlin's Singakademie, for instance, which began as a singing school for fashionable young ladies, grew into a large and prestigious society with its own imposing building. The increasing popularity and professionalization of concert music encouraged the formation of choral associations, which brought together large numbers of performers or music lovers. *Kunstvereine*, devoted to supporting artistic endeavours and cultivating artistic tastes, began to appear at the end of the eighteenth century and eventually spread throughout central Europe. Together with publications such as the Stuttgart

---

[16] Böhmer, *Welt*, especially pp. 265 ff.; Hermann, *Biedermeier*, pp. 25 ff.
[17] Ronald Hayman, *Nietzsche: A Critical Life* (New York, 1980), 117.

Kunstblatt and other popular magazines, the *Kunstvereine* appealed to people eager to learn more about and, if possible, to acquire art. These societies, however, like the audience for public culture generally, were limited to those with the necessary educational and material resources. Public culture was open, but not everyone could enter.[18]

Choral associations and singing societies, like the reading and discussion groups so important for eighteenth-century *Öffentlichkeit*, were part of a complex system of *Vereine* designed to bring together like-minded people for a particular purpose. Some of these organizations were essentially convivial, such as the gourmet club in Nuremberg to which Gustav Blumröder delivered his famous essay on the culinary arts in 1838. Others combined sociability and culture or, as we shall see in the next chapter, sociability and politics. We get a graphic sense of the atmosphere in these clubs from W. F. Bendz's painting of 1828 entitled *Zusammenkunft der Raucher*, which shows a cheerful group of men smoking and playing music; their long pipes, which at first seem to be some sort of wind instrument, provide a symbol of contentment and leisure. Whatever its manifest purpose, the *Verein* was a place to be with people like oneself, to shed professional cares, and to enjoy a good time. In its membership, organization, and atmosphere, the *Verein* was at once a public and private institution, accessible but restricted, formally constituted but not official, convivial but not intimate. As such it served as an intermediary between the public and private spheres, the external world and the home, society and the family.[19]

In contrast to public culture, the private sphere was familiar rather than monumental, enclosed rather than open, inward-looking rather than expansive. For the private sphere, people wrote piano solos rather than symphonies, designed villas rather than public buildings, did family portraits rather than official statues. This was a domestic world, furnished with sideboards and comfortable chairs, filled with painted porcelain and hand

---

[18] Raynor, *History*, has material on choral societies; Elizabeth Holt (ed.), *The Triumph of Art for the Public* (Garden City, New York, 1979) discusses *Kunstvereine* on pp. 416–17.

[19] Bendz's painting is reproduced in Böhmer, *Welt*, p. 117. The best account of associations in the early nineteenth century is Nipperdey's classic essay, 'Verein'. For two local studies, see Heinz Schmitt, *Das Vereinsleben der Stadt Weinheim an der Bergstrasse: Volkskundliche Untersuchung zum kulturellen Leben einer Mittelstadt* (Weinheim, 1963) and Wolfgang Meyer, *Das Vereinswesen der Stadt Nürnberg im 19. Jahrhundert* (Nuremberg, 1970).

embroidery, ritualized in birthday celebrations and Christmas fêtes, idealized in sentimental songs and maudlin stories. We know a great deal about this world. It is portrayed in countless paintings and photographs and described in scores of novels and memoirs; its material remains are still around, some forgotten in our attics, others displayed as valuable antiques. But, despite this abundance of evidence, the domestic world of the mid-nineteenth century still seems remote, its style foreign, its emotional tone difficult to gauge.

Almost everything about this world is problematic, starting with the term conventionally used to describe it, *Biedermeier*. The word was coined in the 1850s, when Adolf Kussmaul and Ludwig Eichrodt discovered a book of verse which had been written and privately printed by an obscure village schoolmaster named Samuel Friedrich Sauter, who had died in 1846. Kussmaul and Eichrodt recognized the unintentionally comic quality of Sauter's poetry—which surely ranks among the worst written in any language—and published it over the name of 'Gottlieb Biedermaier' in the leading humour magazine of the day, *Fliegende Blätter*. Eventually people began to use the term, which combines the adjective *bieder*, once a positive, then a condescending designation of plainness, with the common surname *Meier*, to describe the visual style, literature, and values of the period as a whole. At first, *Biedermeier* retained the connotation given it by Kussmaul and Eichrodt and was used by those who wished to distance themselves from a culture they viewed with gentle irony. By the end of the nineteenth century, however, the term had lost its ironic overtones. *Biedermeier* style and values now became the objects of nostalgia, perhaps best illustrated by the work of Ludwig Richter, whose prints and paintings depict smiling children at play in a secure and happy time, untouched by social change or political upheaval. Moved by their longing for a simpler, more orderly age, people were now interested in preserving what they saw as the safe world of *Biedermeier* domesticity.[20]

Like the figures in Friedrich Amerling's portrait of the Arthaber family, *Biedermeier* culture turned inwards, away from state and market. At its core was the home, whose security and comfort was celebrated in poems such as Leopold Schefer's 'Hausreden':

[20] There is a great deal of information on *Biedermeier* culture in Böhmer, *Welt*; Boehn, *Biedermeier*; Hermann, *Biedermeier*; Geismeier, *Biedermeier*. The term itself is analysed in Hermand and Windfuhr (eds.), *Literatur*, pp. 18 ff. On Richter, see Otto von Simson, *Der Blick nach Innen: Vier Beiträge zur deutschen Malerei des 19. Jahrhunderts* (Berlin, 1986).

Drum ist das Haus der heiligste der Orte!
Der Liebe Altar und des Himmels Tempel
Auf schönsten Feier aller seiner Wunder,
Zum seligsten Genuss all seiner Zauber,
Und sei das Haus die ärmste kleinste Hütte.

Needless to say, the final line is an example of poetic licence: the *Biedermeier* ideal was not to be found in any sort of cottage. Its achievement required the well-ordered respectability of a *bürgerlich* house. Such a house—well-appointed but not grand, comfortable but not ostentatious—became the period's ideal dwelling. The Hohenzollern family quarters pictured in Mario Praz's *Illustrated History of Furnishing* suggest that even royalty sometimes sought to emulate such *bürgerlich* amenity; the rooms are clearly meant to be the setting for domestic sociability rather than for the expansive rituals of kingship. Similarly, Schinkel's Charlottenhof is luxurious but is in no way grand; it is a villa, not a baroque palace.[21]

If the core of *Biedermeier* culture was the house, the center of the house was the *Wohnzimmer*, the 'living room'. The term itself suggests that living must be a collective activity. Loneliness is a source of sorrow and dismay: as Sauter puts it in one of his inimitably inept verses, 'Einsam schlafen nichts daneben| Nichts von gleichem Fleisch und Bein| Traurig ist es, einsam sein.' Solitude was enjoyable only within a family setting, where the possibility of companionship was never far away. Thus the tranquil individuals in Georg Friedrich Kersting's paintings have nothing in common with the cosmically isolated figures in one of C. D. Friedrich's landscapes. Kersting's subjects are sometimes by themselves, but they do not seem lonely; they are part of a well-ordered, familiar environment, into which a spouse or child might walk at any moment.[22]

The *Wohnzimmer* was devoted to familial sociability. Here were to be found those practical objects and symbolic goods around which family life revolved. On the walls, portraits established the family's lineage, if only for a generation or two, while children's toys in the corner pointed towards the family's future. The furniture was usually free-standing, arranged to enhance social

---

[21] Amerling's painting is reproduced in Böhmer, *Welt*, p. 23; Schefer quoted in Sengle, *Biedermeierzeit*, i. 61. For more on domestic architecture, see the essays in Niethammer (ed.), *Wohnen*.

[22] Sauter quoted in Böhmer, *Welt*, p. 13. Some of Kersting's paintings are reproduced in Mario Praz, *An Illustrated History of Furnishing* (New York, 1964), 207 ff.

interaction rather than affirm architectural design. Except for comfortable chairs and upholstered sofas, the furnishings were made of wood: a writing desk for private—not business—correspondence, a vitrine in which to display the family's treasured ornaments, a table around which people might gather to talk, drink coffee, or play cards. Plants and flowers bespoke the love of nature as well as the power to domesticate it. Overall, this was an indoor world, which was often portrayed by contemporary artists in the evening, when the lamplight could be used to provide a warm, diffuse glow to people and things. The *Biedermeier* was a comfortable, cosy style, perhaps best captured in one of its characteristic terms, *Gemütlichkeit*, which J. P. Stern defines as a 'curious and unique configuration of time-honoured habits, rich meals, ancient or at least old-fashioned furniture, solid broadcloth and solid moral maxims . . .'.[23]

The centrality of the *Wohnzimmer* reminds us that for most *bürgerlich* families the household was now primarily an emotional and reproductive unit, rather than an economic and productive one. Although family members still lived and worked side by side with apprentices and servants on farms and in many artisanal enterprises and small shops, this blend of family and labour, life and work, was no longer the norm for many businessmen and most of the educated élite—civil servants, teachers, lawyers—who worked away from home. Of course, work still went on in the household. Women did an enormous amount of both necessary and symbolic labour: in the portraits from the period they are often shown pouring tea, sewing, or directing the children. Even when there was no economic and practical reason for it, women continued to produce much of what the household needed, from bakery goods to millinery, fruit preserves to children's clothes. In addition, every *bürgerlich* family depended on the labour of at least one servant, who cooked, cleaned, and cared for the children. But in contrast to the traditional household, where servants and apprentices were an unmistakable part of the family's collective life, in the nineteenth century they are apt to be virtually invisible, rarely shown in contemporary portraits, infrequently mentioned in novels and memoirs. Franz Grillparzer, for example, remembered the enormous social distance between himself and his parents' maid

[23] Stern, *Idylls*, p. 148; see also Georg Himmelheber, *Biedermeier Furniture* (London, 1974). A good illustration of a Biedermeier interior is F. W. Doppelmayr's painting, *The Artist's Family* (1831), reproduced in Geismeier, *Biedermeier*, p. 48.

who, together with her own child, 'seemed to us like the inhabitants of another world'.[24]

Biedermeier sociability was limited to members of the family and a few close friends, often regarded as almost like brothers and sisters, uncles and aunts. These people were the rightful denizens of the *Wohnzimmer* and the true guardians of the values it represented. Late nineteenth-century memoirs are filled with accounts of familial bliss—loving mothers, dutiful fathers, wise grandparents, kindly uncles. This is the intimate universe captured in paintings such as Richter's *Der Abend, das Beste*, celebrated in stories, and embellished in those treacle-like tunes so characteristic of the period: 'Schön ist die Jugend', 'Freut euch das Leben', and many more. The modern mode of celebrating Christmas, with its special foods and elaborate presents, was a *Biedermeier* invention that transformed the majesty of the Incarnation into an affirmation of domestic bliss. 'Stille Nacht', the most famous carol written during the first half of the century, evokes peace and tranquillity, just as popular presentations of the Nativity contrived to make even the Holy Family's manger seem *gemütlich*.[25]

In theory, the *Biedermeier* household was dominated by the eldest male. As husband and father, the man of the house continued to have special legal rights over his dependants' persons and properties. Furthermore, since the man was frequently the family's only participant in the public realm, he was its link to the world of politics and economics. Eventually, sons would follow their fathers into this world, where they too would find a place and eventually establish a household. In his *Philosophy of Right*, Hegel gave this prevailing view a characteristically complex and philosophically rich formulation:

man has his actual substantive life in the state, in learning, and so forth, as well as in labour and struggle with the external world and with himself so that it is only out of his diremption that he fights his way to self-subsistent unity with himself. In the family he has a tranquil intuition of this unity, and there he lives a subjective ethical life, on the plane of true feeling. Woman, on the other hand, has her substantive destiny in the family, and to be imbued with family piety is her ethical frame of mind.

In practice, of course, women often were not confined to the familial realm. A few exceptional women entered the public sphere

---

[24] Grillparzer, *Werke*, iv. 23.

[25] Geismeier, *Biedermeier*, p. 52; Ingeborg Weber-Kellermann, *Das Weihnachtsfest: Eine Kultur- und Sozialgeschichte der Weihnachtszeit* (Lucerne and Frankfurt, 1978).

as writers or political leaders and many more took part in economic life, either to replace or supplement the activities of husband or father. Nevertheless, the decline of the household as a productive unit and the growing privatization of family life did narrow the range of activities in which many women could engage.[26]

A great deal of contemporary art and literature was directed towards the promotion of domestic virtue among females. For example, the *Neuruppiner Bilderbogen*, published during the 1820s and 1830s by Gustav Kuhn, included 'Seven Requests by a Husband to his Wife' and 'Seven Requests by a Wife to her Husband', which were illustrated homilies admonishing men to be affectionate and understanding but insisting that women be industrious and obedient. 'Always let your husband have the last word,' wives are instructed, 'and the later he comes home, the friendlier you should be.' In the *Nürnberger Bilderbogen* from the 1830s, we find illustrated verses that convey moral lessons: in one, for instance, two young women are shown hard at work: 'Gar lieblich ist es anzuschauen,| Wenn waschen, bügeln, die Jung-frauen;| Die schönste Zierde, dass ihr wisst,| Ist, wenn das Mädchen reinlich ist.' Well-to-do young ladies did not have to wash and iron, but needlework of one kind or another was their constant companion. Even if it lacked an economic function, industriousness was an important social virtue, valuable for its own sake and also—as the verse just quoted not so subtly suggests—because it left no time for idleness and vice. In households where servants did all the work, too much leisure was a potential danger, the path to extravagance, disorder, and, worst of all, immodesty and impurity. As Hegel and many others pointed out, because a woman belonged to, and was confined in, the private sphere, her sexual honour was centrally important. Adultery was much more serious for women than for men, since when a woman had sexual relations outside marriage, she broke the rules of the only realm in which she could hope to realize her moral and social existence.[27]

Biedermeier culture was not very comfortable with the erotic aspects of life. For some, sex seemed impossible to domesticate. Franz Grillparzer, for instance, continually postponed his wedding

[26] Hegel, *Philosophy*, pp. 114–15. On the role of women, see Weber-Kellermann's various works, especially *Die deutsche Familie and Die Familie;* Frevert, *Frauen-Geschichte;* Gerhard, *Verhältnisse;* Hausen in Conze (ed.), *Sozialgeschichte;* Günther Häntzschel (ed.), *Bildung und Kultur bürgerlicher Frauen, 1850–1918 (Tübingen, 1986).*
[27] Böhmer, *Welt*, pp. 78, 110–11; Hegel, *Philosophy*, p. 263.

date because he felt his love for Katharina Fröhlich would not survive the physical intimacy of marriage; Katharina, after an engagement of almost fifty years, sensibly decided that marriage was no longer worth the effort. Most of Grillparzer's contemporaries, it is to be hoped, had better luck combining desire and domesticity. But, even within marriage, people seem to have believed that sexual urges had to be restrained. 'The grave-diggers of domestic bliss', Friedrich Jahn insisted, are 'a lack of moderation, deviation from nature, shamelessness, impurity of heart, and a loss of modesty through inhuman curiosity and animal tastelessness.' Should men find it impossible to overcome the urges leading to these deplorable conditions, there were brothels for every taste and pocketbook, and an army of desperate young women available for temporary liaisons or long-term exploitation. But like the realm of public and commercial life, this dark side of male eroticism had no place in the tranquil setting of the *bürgerlich* house. 'Please don't blame me, my beautiful child,' wrote Heinrich Heine to an abandoned love, 'And don't say hello when we meet.'[28]

Few Germans, to be sure, questioned the importance of sex. The philosopher Schopenhauer gave erotic drives a psychological primacy that anticipates Freud, while the poet Nikolaus Lenau called Don Juan the 'master of the world'. But official morality treated eroticism with deep distrust. Suggestive literature was swiftly repressed, as the young Karl Gutzkow discovered in 1835 when he reprinted Schleiermacher's letters on Schlegel's *Lucinde* and published his own *Wally, die Zweiflerin*.[29] *Biedermeier* culture sought to contain the passionate drives and energetic impulses that the romantics had found so fascinating. Those who set the norms for the world of *Biedermeier* domesticity wanted to tame eroticism with connubial affection, subsume isolation with familial sociability, and turn the forces of nature into a controlled landscape of gardens and household plants. At its most effective, *Biedermeier* took the fear and torment out of romanticism, leaving in its place only some vaguely menacing motifs and exciting titillation. In this regard, one of the era's most characteristic works is Carl Maria von Weber's *Der Freischütz*, which enjoyed extraordinary popularity when it opened in Schinkel's newly-completed Schauspielhaus in 1821. Like Weber's operatic protagonists, the makers of *Biedermeier*

---

[28] Böhmer, *Welt*, p. 113. There is a fine discussion of eroticism and literature in Sengle, *Biedermeierzeit*, i. 56 ff. See also Peter Borscheid, 'Geld und Liebe', in Borscheid and Teuteberg (eds.), *Ehe*, pp. 112 ff.; Schulte, *Sperrbezirke*, pp. 16–17.

[29] See below, sect. iv.

culture sought to master the powers of darkness or at least to establish a refuge where these powers had no place.

There were always those who found *Biedermeier* culture suffocating rather than sustaining, repressive rather than supportive, hypocritical rather than upright. Among the images of mid-nineteenth-century family life, Wilhelm Busch's vitriolic caricatures are as striking—and as misleading—as Ludwig Richter's affectionately sentimental pastels. Nor should we overlook the symptomatic significance of Heinrich Hoffmann's *Der Struwwelpeter*, an immensely popular and successful picture book for children first published in 1845. Through a series of economical drawings and clever verses, Hoffmann taught all the domestic virtues expounded by publications like the *Nürnberger Bilderbogen*, but he underscored his lessons with the threat of punishments both appallingly cruel and carefully described: finicky eaters starve, thumbsuckers are mutilated, the disobedient suffer unspeakable disaster. However light-hearted *Der Struwwelpeter* may have been intended to be, one cannot help but accept Peter Gay's assessment that it revealed a dark side of family life and contemporary culture.[30] Just as the monumental structures of public culture were not enough to compel obedience and intimidate political discontent, so the values of *Biedermeier* domesticity were unable to contain private conflicts and overcome personal frustrations.

ii. THE TRIUMPH OF HISTORY

Throughout the nineteenth century, Germans' public and private lives were filled with historical concerns; building styles and the subject matter of paintings, the formation of museums and the spread of antiquarian societies, the popularity of history books and the prominence of historians all point to the importance of the past for almost every facet of culture. Historical scholarship revolutionized theology, dominated philosophical enquiry, and became the basis for literary analysis. Even natural scientists took up historical methods in order to unlock the secrets of biological or geological evolution. Never before had educated people devoted themselves to the past with such fervour, never had they spent so much time and effort on the study of historical knowledge and objects.[31]

---

[30] Walter Arndt has made Busch's work accessible to English-speaking readers in *The Genius of Wilhelm Busch. The Comedy of Frustration* (Berkeley, 1982); Gay, *Experience*, i. 198.

[31] Two examples of history's centrality: on architecture, Olsen, *City*, p. 295; on

'History and the historical observation of the world', Jakob
Burckhardt told his students at Basel in 1851, permeates 'our entire
cultural formation [*Bildung*]. That this commitment to history
coincided with the wholesale destruction of traditional values and
institutions was, as Franz Schnabel once pointed out, a paradox
close to the core of nineteenth-century culture and society. Perhaps
historical studies were especially important in the German lands
because here the tension between preservation and destruction was
especially apparent.[32]

The roots of nineteenth-century historical consciousness are
deeply embedded in the rich cultural soil of the *Aufklärung*. It will
be recalled from our discussion in Chapter 3 that many eighteenth-
century German intellectuals were concerned with the past. In the
1760s Winckelmann had sought to recapture the classical world in
order to find standards of truth and beauty for modern men. Justus
Möser, from a quite different perspective, had pursued the history
of his native Osnabrück to combat the corrosive influence of
change. Herder, not much interested in historical details, had none
the less provided a powerful philosophical justification for history's
importance as a way of understanding thought and action. Lessing,
that prototypical Enlightenment figure, had spent the last productive years of his life writing *Die Erzeugung des Menschengeschlechts*, a
grand vision of history in which he demonstrated the waxing
power of reason over human affairs. In 1788, after he had
established his reputation as a dramatist and poet, · Schiller
published a history of the Netherlands that helped him to acquire
his professorship at Jena.

There is no one among you [he told those who crowded in to hear his
inaugural lecture], to whom history does not have something important to
say. However different the paths of your future vocations, somewhere
they will link up with history. But one vocation you have in common, the
task which you brought with you into the world, to cultivate yourselves as
men—and it is just to men that history speaks.[33]

the philosophical background, Schnädelbach, *Philosophy*, ch. 2. On the institutional
basis of historical study, see the essays in Hartmut Boockmann *et al.*, *Geschichtswissenschaft und Vereinswesen im 19. Jahrhundert. Beiträge zur Geschichte historischer
Forschung in Deutschland* (Göttingen, 1972).

[32] Burckhardt, *Studium*, p. 83; Franz Schnabel, 'Der Ursprung der vaterländischen Studien', *Blätter für deutsche Landesgeschichte*, NS 88/1 (1951), 24.
[33] F. Schiller, 'The Nature and Value of Universal History: An Inaugural Lecture
[1789]', *History and Theory*, 11/3 (1972), 322. On history in eighteenth-century
thought, see Meinecke, *Historicism*; Dilthey, 'Jahrhundert'; and the material cited
above, Ch. 3.

Germans' experiences after 1789 gave their historical awareness a new depth and urgency. 'Anyone who has lived through the revolution', Goethe wrote, 'feels impelled towards history. He sees the past in the present, and contemplates it with fresh eyes, which bring even the most distant objects into the picture.' For romantic poets, idealist philosophers, conservative theorists, and patriotic publicists, the past was of great significance as a source of inspiration and cosmic truth, political values and counter-revolutionary propaganda, national identity and social cohesion. Arnim and Brentano, Hegel and Schelling, Gentz and Müller, and Görres and Arndt turned to study historical developments so that they might understand and master contemporary problems. What Lord Acton wrote about the romantics applies, *mutatis mutandi*, to all these people, who 'relieved present need with all the abounding treasures of other times, subjecting thereby the will and the conscience of the living to the will and conscience of the dead'.[34]

As important as the intellectual stimulus given historical consciousness by the experience of revolution were the institutions created during the era of political reform and reorganization. Here too we must be careful not to overlook the continuity between the eighteenth and nineteenth centuries. Well before 1800 A. L. Schlözer had used his position as professor at Göttingen to support research based on self-consciously critical methods, while, in a variety of scientific academies and other learned societies, scholars gathered materials, evaluated sources, and published careful reconstructions of the past.[35] Nevertheless, the renewal of higher learning signalled by the foundation of the University of Berlin greatly strengthened the institutional basis for scholarship. During the first half of the century German universities became centres for research. Their seminars and their laboratories, the two characteristic pedagogical inventions from this period, were based on the conviction that teaching and research could and should be joined; in

[34] John Acton, 'German Schools of History', *Historical Essays and Studies* (London, 1919), 346. On the impact of the revolution, see Wolfgang Hardtwig, *Geschichtsschreibung zwischen Alt-Europa und moderner Welt: Jacob Burckhardt in seiner Zeit* (Göttingen, 1974), ch. 1.

[35] On these institutions, see Peter Hanns Reill, 'Die Geschichtswissenschaft um die Mitte des 18. Jahrhunderts', in R. Vierhaus (ed.), *Wissenschaften im Zeitalter der Aufklärung* (Göttingen, 1985) and *The German Enlightenment and the Rise of Historicism* (Berkeley and Los Angeles, 1975); Butterfield, *Man on his Past*; Andreas Kraus, *Vernunft und Geschichte: Die Bedeutung der deutschen Akademien für die Entwicklung der Geschichtswissenschaft im späten 18. Jahrhundert* (Freiburg, 1963); Notker Hammerstein, *Jus und Historie: Ein Beitrag zur Geschichte des historischen Denkens an den deutschen Universitäten im späten 17. und 18. Jahrhundert* (Göttingen, 1972).

both, the master–teacher directed his pupils in a research project to which all could contribute. The rise of what has been called the 'research imperative' had its base in the universities, but extended from them into separate disciplinary communities, composed of men sharing a common subject and mode of research, usually organized in a professional association, and communicating through one or more semi-official journals. History, together with philology, was the first discipline to take shape. No longer ancillary to established subjects like theology and law, history established itself as an autonomous field of enquiry, with its own curriculum, scholarly leaders, basic handbooks, and periodicals.[36]

An exemplary figure in the rise of nineteenth-century histori-ography was Barthold Georg Niebuhr, whose lectures on Roman history at the University of Berlin met with great popular success during the winter of 1810 and 1811. Like the romantics, Niebuhr belonged to the generation that had matured under the shadow of the revolution—an event he called the 'central experience of the last forty years, from which the whole era derives its epic unity'. Niebuhr believed that the study of the past necessarily draws its energy and inspiration from the present: 'true historical writing is only possible on the basis of what we have ourselves experienced; for in the past we can at best perceive what we have a certain impression of in the present . . .' Recalling the circumstances under which he lectured about Rome in 1810, Niebuhr wrote to a friend that 'we could do little more than ardently hope for better days and prepare for them. I went back to a great nation to strengthen my mind and that of my hearers. We felt like Tacitus.' Although sympathetic to the common folk, both in his own and former times, Niebuhr hated social unrest and political upheaval. Like many Germans, he was deeply shaken by the new wave of revolutions in 1830, which he feared would once again plunge Europe into the disorder he had experienced as a young man.[37]

[36] The best introduction to the 'research imperative' can be found in the works of R. Steven Turner: 'Growth', 'Reformers', and 'Professoriate'. On universities, see also McClelland, *State*. Alphons Lhotsky, 'Geschichtsforschung und Geschichts-schreibung in Österreich', *HZ* 189 (1959), 379–448, Josef Engel, 'Die deutschen Universitäten und die Geschichtswissenschaft', *HZ* 189 (1959), 223–378, discuss the impact of these developments on historical scholarship; Wolfgang Weber, *Priester der Klio: Historisch-sozialwissenschaftliche Studien zur Herkunft und Karriere deutscher Historiker und zur Geschichte der Geschichtswissenschaft, 1800–1970* (New York, 1984), analyses the profession itself.

[37] Reinhart Koselleck in *GGB* ii. 664; Christ, 'Niebuhr', p. 29; Gooch, *History*, p. 19. In addition to Christ's essay, see the brilliant treatment of Niebuhr's youth in Dilthey, 'Jahrhundert'.

While Niebuhr recognized the inevitable ties between present and past, he was committed to the search for historical truth. 'In laying down the pen, we must be able to say in the sight of God, "I have not knowingly . . . written anything which is not true."' Niebuhr realized that this would require a rigorous examination of the sources, to which the historian must bring the critical tools forged by students of classical languages and literature. Ancient history, he told his students, should be seen 'as a branch of philology, as a philological discipline, an instrument of interpretation and philological knowledge'. By studying the origins and usage of language, the historian can approach the contemporary meaning of his evidence and thus bridge the gap between himself and his subject. But this was only the first step: after weighing and interpreting each piece of evidence, the scholar must then search for a larger pattern, and thus 'create a complete picture from isolated remnants'.[38] Niebuhr's scrupulous commitment to each evidentiary fragment and his efforts to find broad patterns of change were shared by several generations of nineteenth-century German historians, who, like him, sought to combine critical concern for individual phenomena with an ambition to apprehend underlying structures of meaning.

Niebuhr was a popular writer and influential university teacher, but he was not what we would think of as a professional historian. His education had been uneven and eclectic; much of what he knew about the past he had taught himself in his father's well-stocked library. He wrote his first great work, a study of Roman agrarian policy, when he was a member of the Danish civil service. In 1806 he transferred to the Prussian administration, worked with Stein and the other reformers until 1810, was appointed the Hohenzollern's official historiographer, acted as the Prussian representative to the papacy from 1816 until 1823, and finally received a special appointment at the University of Bonn, where he taught and participated in a number of important research projects. Niebuhr, therefore, was a transitional figure, connected to, but not completely a part of, history as an academic discipline.

August Boeckh was closer to the new disciplinary norm than Niebuhr. After studying at Halle, Boeckh taught briefly at Heidelberg, where he knew Brentano and other romantics, and then moved to Berlin in 1811. Until his retirement more than five decades later, Boeckh wrote and taught about various aspects of

---

[38] Gooch, *History*, p. 19; Christ, 'Niebuhr', p. 28; Schulin, *Traditionskritik*, p. 25

Greek history and literature. His study of Athens's political economy, *Staatshaushaltung der Athener* was a pioneering examina tion of social and economic institutions which remained the standard work on the subject for several decades. The most important source of his influence, however, was his lecture course, delivered twenty-six times and posthumously published as the *Encyclopedie und Methodologie der philologischen Wissenschaften*. As the title suggests, Boeckh shared Niebuhr's conviction that philological methods were essential historiographical tools. Philology helped the historian learn what was once known; its purpose was not discovery but recovery, a process Boeckh called *anagignoskei*, which means both recognition and reading. When a historian reads philologically, he seeks to recapture an author's meaning by interpreting the language of the text within its original context. The goal of such a project is total knowledge of the past, a people's 'entire mental development, the history of all aspects of its culture'.[39]

While Niebuhr and Boeckh were breathing new life into the study of the ancient world, their contemporaries Karl Friedrich Eichhorn and Friedrich Karl von Savigny were consolidating a historical approach to law. Like the classical historians, Eichhorn and Savigny built upon the achievements of several generations of jurists and philologists to whose venerable endeavours they brought new energy and a heightened sense of political purpose. Deeply influenced by the ideas and spiritual ambitions of the romantics, the two men also shared the political hopes and national ideals generated during the Napoleonic wars. Contemporary politics, which was a leitmotif in the work of a scholar like Niebuhr, became the dominant theme in Eichhorn's and Savigny's search for a usable legal history.

Karl Eichhorn was born in 1781 and educated at Göttingen, where his father was a leading authority on the Old Testament. While a student, Eichhorn's interest in legal history was aroused by two well-known Göttingen scholars, Gustav Hugo and Johann Putter, who had pioneered the application of critical methods to the study of jurisprudence. In 1808, when he was only twenty-seven, Eichhorn published the first volume of his *Deutsche Staats- und*

---

[39] August Boeckh, *On Interpretation and Criticism*, trans. and ed. John Paul Pritchard (Norman, Oklahoma, 1968), 14; see also pp. 39 and 51. Gooch, *History*, pp. 28 ff., and Ulrich von Wilamowitz-Moellendorff, *History of Classical Scholarship* (1921; repr. London, 1982), 105 ff., both provide introductory accounts of Boeckh's achievements.

Rechtsgeschichte, one of the most influential studies of German law ever written. Surrounded by the devastation caused by foreign conquest and overwhelmed by the rapidity and scale of change, Eichhorn believed that 'it was more important than ever to turn our gaze to the past and become acquainted with the spirit of our former condition'. Like Fichte and so many other patriots, he wanted Germans to recognize their common past in the unbroken chain of law and language which joined them to their ancestors as well as to one another. Thus, while Eichhorn's approach was rigorously empirical, his respect for evidence obvious, and his research methods critical, his ultimate goal was to discover the true nature of the *Volk*, what Mack Walker called the 'central unity . . . at the heart of a bulb whose overlayers were the accidents and divisions that time had brought'.[40]

Karl Friedrich von Savigny devoted his life to a similar search for a central unity at the root of historical particularity. Born in 1779 into a well-established family of jurists and officials, Savigny spent part of his youth at Wetzlar, where he first learned about law amidst the decaying grandeur of the old regime. As was not uncommon in this age of intellectual opportunity, Savigny was a prodigy who established a major reputation at the age of twenty-one with a book on property rights. In 1810 he was among the first scholars called to join that firmament of academic stars assembled by Humboldt at Berlin. In addition to producing a series of important scholarly books, Savigny was a successful teacher, active participant in political affairs, and tireless academic polemicist. As the brother-in-law of Clemens, Bettina, and Christian Brentano, friend of Achim von Arnim, and mentor to the brothers Grimm, Savigny stood close to the heart of German cultural life during the first half of the nineteenth century. Intellectually, he was no more gifted or original than Eichhorn, but his personal connections, rhetorical skills, and physical vitality enabled him to serve as the chief spokesman for the historical school of jurisprudence.[41]

Savigny formulated his clearest programmatic statement on legal history in 1814, when he responded to A. J. Thibaut's plan to create

[40] Karl Friedrich Eichhorn, *Deutsche Staats- und Rechtsgeschichte* (5th edn.; Göttingen, 1843–4), i. p. xiii; Walker, *Home Towns*, p. 251. On Eichhorn, see Small, *Origins*, ch. 3.
[41] The standard biography is Adolf Stoll, *Friedrich Karl von Savigny* (3 vols.; Berlin, 1927–39). There is a good, brief treatment in Small, *Origins*, ch. 2. See also Donald R. Kelley, 'Gaius Noster: Substructures of Western Social Thought', *AHR* 84/3 (June 1979), 643 ff.

a new civil code for the German states. In an essay entitled 'Vom Beruf unserer Zeit für Gesetzgebung und Rechtswissenschaft', Savigny attacked Thibaut's assertion that government decrees could unify the diversity of German laws and institutions. The futility of such an enterprise could be seen in French efforts to impose the Code Napoleon, which 'still devoured German institutions like a cancer'. Instead, Savigny maintained, reformers had to acknowledge the political diversity in the German present and then search for a basis of communality in the German past.[42] To this task the *Zeitschrift für geschichtliche Rechtswissenschaft*, which Savigny and Eichhorn established in 1815, was primarily devoted. Its purpose, the editors wrote, was to 'seek in the multiplicity apparent in history a higher unity, a vital principle, through which specific phenomena can be explained'. This principle could only be pursued retrospectively, in a journey backwards 'through all its transmutations to its point of origin in the *Volk*'s nature, fate, and necessities'. Savigny's method was empirical, but the character of his enterprise rested upon his conviction that at the root of a nation's history was a discernible essence, 'a not merely accidental, but fundamental and necessary individuality'.[43]

Among Savigny's most appreciative students was Jacob Grimm, who first heard him lecture at Marburg, where Grimm was a reluctant law student and an enthusiastic literary intellectual. After leaving the university, Grimm finally found a position as librarian for King Jerome of Westphalia, who paid him well and left him ample time to begin his famous collection of folk tales, the first volume of which appeared in 1812. Over the next half century Jacob Grimm, sometimes alone, sometimes in collaboration with his brother Wilhelm, produced an enormous amount of work on folklore, mythology, law, and language. At the same time, he was actively involved in public life, attended the Congress of Vienna as a member of the Hessian delegation, was one of the famous 'Seven' dismissed from Göttingen in 1837, and served in the Frankfurt parliament. For Grimm, scholarship and politics were part of a single endeavour: gathering tales from the *Volk*, uncovering the origins of popular customs, and assembling a historical dictionary were as much a contribution to the search for national identity as political agitation and parliamentary debates. Like Eichhorn and

[42] Jacques Stern (ed.), *Thibaut und Savigny: Ihre programmatischen Schriften* (rev. edn.: Munich, 1973), 192.

[43] *Zeitschrift für geschichtliche Rechtswissenschaft* (1815), i. 395–6.

Savigny, he believed that the aim of historical study was to discover the hidden unities at the root of contemporary complexity. Grimm, therefore, approached language in the same way the legal historians approached law; he painstakingly gathered data on the varieties of current usage in order to penetrate backwards to the *Volksgeist*, that inexhaustible source from which linguistic practice, like legal institutions, ultimately flowed.[44]

We remain in the debt of those nineteenth-century German scholars who laid the foundation for our knowledge of Greek and Roman institutions, the evolution of European law, and the development of languages. At the same time, what Burckhardt called the 'historical observation of the world' affected many other disciplines. Geographers, for example, followed the lead of Karl Ritter's masterful *Erdkunde im Verhältnis zur Natur und Geschichte des Menschen* (1816). Franz Kugler, in his frequently-reprinted and extremely influential *Handbuch der Kunstgeschichte* of 1842, set out to establish a basis for the historical understanding of art throughout the world. In 1843 Wilhelm Roscher, then a professor at Göttingen, published his *Grundriss zu Vorlesungen über die Staatswirtschaft nach geschichtlicher Methode*, in which he hoped 'to accomplish for public economy what the Eichhorn–Savigny method did for jurisprudence'. Meanwhile, at Tübingen and other German universities, students of theology began to examine the scriptures through the lens of critically-informed historical research. Philosophers, often under the influence of Hegel's vision of the spirit's temporal journey, came to define their task in historical terms. As Acton wrote, 'History went on invading other provinces, resolving system into process, and getting the better of philosophy—for a whole generation.'[45]

The keystone in the arch of history's influence over German thought was the study of politics. There was, to be sure, nothing new about historians' interest in politics or statesmen's interest in the past—both go back to the very beginning of historical writing. In the eighteenth century, scholars like Justus Möser had helped to establish the genre called *Vaterlandsgeschichte*, while monarchs, including Frederick the Great, wrote or commissioned official accounts of their reigns. From a quite different perspective, men like Herder had tried to follow the *Volk*'s tracks in law, language,

[44] See Walker's comparison of Grimm and Eichhorn: *Home Towns*, p. 251; Rothacker, 'Savigny'. Ludwig Denecke, *Jacob Grimm und sein Bruder Wilhelm* (Stuttgart, 1971), provides a guide to the voluminous literature on the Grimms.
[45] Small, *Origins*, p. 155; Butterfield, *Man on his Past*; p. 98

and custom. Such historical projects continued to be written after 1800, but by the 1830s they had begun to be overshadowed by works devoted to the history of states. States offered historians fascinating subjects, inexhaustible sources of evidence, and powerful bases of institutional support. Grander and more compelling than the history of a particular city or a single monarch, the state's past was also more concrete and empirically accessible than the *Volksgeist*'s elusive residues. Of the many historians who were involved in establishing the state as a historiographical focus in between what Dilthey called the German inclination towards 'particularism' and 'universality', no one was more important than Leopold von Ranke, whose accomplishments opened a new chapter in the emergence of German historiography.

The Ranke family had long provided clergymen and lawyers for towns along Saxony's fertile Thuringian plain. Born in 1795, Leopold was a generation younger than the romantics and did not participate in the great events of the revolutionary era. While war raged across central Europe, he was learning ancient languages behind the Schulpforta's protective walls; in 1815, when his home passed from Saxony to Prussia, he was studying theology and philology at Leipzig. After he left the university, Ranke took a job as a *Gymnasium* teacher in Frankfurt-an-der-Oder, where he began work on his *Geschichten der romanischen und germanischen Völker, 1494–1514*, which, soon after its publication in 1824, established his reputation and led to his appointment at the University of Berlin. Ranke flourished in the Prussian capital; a frequent guest at the most fashionable salons and friend of the rich and powerful, he was patronized by Frederick William IV of Prussia and by Maximilian II of Bavaria, to whom he gave a private set of lectures. By mid-century Ranke was among the most famous historians in Europe. Through all of this time, he continued to work, despite public duties and private sorrows, in the face of heavy teaching burdens and the growing infirmities of age. Choosing his subjects from several centuries, moving his attention from one nation to another, he tirelessly practised his craft; his collected works number fifty-seven closely printed volumes. Appropriately enough, when he was ennobled in 1863, the motto he had inscribed upon his coat of arms was 'Labor ipse voluptas'.[46]

The phrase most often associated with Ranke appears in the

---

[46] Vierhaus's *Ranke* is an excellent account of the historian's family background. See also Von Laue, *Ranke*; Iggers's introduction to his edition of Ranke's works: *Theory*; Berding, 'Ranke'; Krieger, *Ranke*.

preface of his first book: 'To history has been given the function of judging the past, of instructing men for the profit of future years. The present attempt does not aspire to such a lofty undertaking. It merely wants to show how, essentially, things happened.' These words—'wie es eigentlich gewesen'—inspired generations of scholars to advocate archival research, textual criticism, and evidential rigour. Ranke's appendix to the *Geschichten*, in which he set out his 'method of research and critical results', became more famous than the book itself. Throughout his life he insisted on the importance of getting the facts right, of stripping away the distortions created by personal bias, both in contemporary sources and in the historian himself. Ranke rejected the romantic urge to introspection: 'I wanted to extinguish the self and let only the data speak and the powerful forces appear.' The truth was to be found outside, in the evidence left by real historical developments. Similarly, Ranke explicitly disassociated himself from Hegel and his followers, whom he found intellectually and personally uncongenial. Of the two schools, 'the historical and the philosophical', which he found upon his arrival in Berlin, he had no difficulty rejecting the latter in favour of the former.[47]

This image of Ranke as a scientific historian is accurate but incomplete. No less important for understanding his ideas and influence is a kinship with the romantics and the idealists that Ranke's positivist admirers often underestimated. For example, Ranke, like so many other turn-of-the-century German philosophers and poets, believed that there was a pattern of meaning behind events, a single source of coherence and understanding. He called this the 'Mar der Weltgeschichte', a divine order of things, 'which cannot be directly proved but can indeed be grasped. In this order, identical with the sequence of time, significant specificities have their place, and here must the historian apprehend them.' Like Niebuhr and Savigny, Ranke's belief in a larger order gave meaning to his fascination with particularity. Like Hegel and Schelling, he wished to explain God's ways to man—but by 'taking hold of situations' rather than 'speculative thoughts'. History, not philosophy or poetry, was best able to read the coded messages scattered by God through time. This was the historian's sacred calling, 'which can be compared to that of the priest'.[48]

---

[47] Ranke, *Theory*, p. 137; Vierhaus, 'Ranke', p. 29; Rothacker, 'Savigny', p. 418. For some wise reflections on Ranke's famous programmatic statement, see Felix Gilbert, 'What Ranke Meant', *American Scholar*, 56/3 (summer 1987).

[48] Vierhaus, 'Ranke', p. 29; Srbik, *Geist*, i. 242. Iggers convincingly shows the connections between Ranke and the idealists in *Conception*, pp. 63 ff.

Ranke's conception of nationality was also drawn from the cultural atmosphere of romanticism. 'Our fatherland', he wrote, 'is with us, in us. . . . We are rooted in it from the beginning, and we can never emancipate ourselves from it. This mysterious something that animates the lowliest as well as the greatest, this spiritual atmosphere in which we breathe, precedes every constitution.' In the modern world, Ranke recognized, nationality had great political power. 'What would become of our states', he asked in 1836, 'if they had not received new life from the national principle upon which they were based? It is inconceivable that any state could exist without it.' Yet he also saw that the relationship between nationality and politics was complex, especially in the German situation, where the political expression of nationhood was fundamentally obscure. 'Nations have a tendency to be states, but I do not know a single one which really is. . . . The sphere of the state is inherently far narrower than that of the nation. The state is a modification, not only of the human but also of the national existence.' Despite his emotional commitment to the *Volk*, therefore, Ranke was sceptical about the creation of a German nation-state and opposed to most suggestions for greater political unity in German Europe.[49]

For Ranke, the basis of public life was not the nation but the state. States are the true 'ideas of God', which moved through the historical order 'like celestial bodies, in their cycles, their mutual gravitations, their systems'. Divine in origin and cosmic in significance, states were also deeply individual in character. 'Every independent state has its own original life, which may have different stages and may perish like all living matter. But while it lives, it penetrates its entire environment, identical only with itself.' The primary task of every state is the defence of its individuality, the preservation of itself in the dangerous, violent world of international politics; to this struggle for self-preservation, all other political purposes must be subordinated. Through this blending of the sacred and the profane, Ranke gave historical meaning and political legitimacy to the state's quest for power and survival. Enlivened by his own deep attachment to Prussia and reaffirmed by the political experience of his age, Ranke's enshrinement of the *Machtstaat* as the historian's central subject was, as Helmut Berding

[49] Quotations from Ranke's 'Political Dialogue', as translated in Von Laue, *Ranke*, pp. 165 ff., and from Krieger, *Ranke*, p. 7. Rothacker, 'Savigny', gives an interesting comparative analysis of Ranke and the preceding generation.

has written, 'the decisive act' in the development of German historical thought.[50]

Ranke's influence extended well beyond the German-speaking world. 'We meet him at every step', wrote Lord Acton, who was by no means an uncritical admirer. 'He has done more for us than any other man.' Because his publications so beautifully combined empirical depth and stylistic grace, they found a wide audience, while his methodological prescriptions appealed to historians eager to establish a more 'scientific discipline'. Personally, Ranke touched several generations of young men who came to Berlin to be his pupils. 'I realized', Burckhardt wrote in 1840, 'that the same thing had befallen me as befell Don Quixote: I had loved my science as hearsay, and suddenly here it was appearing before me in gigantic proportions.' Forty-six years later, among those following Ranke's coffin down Berlin's Luisenstrasse was Friedrich Meinecke, who had passed his doctoral examination just three days earlier. Ranke had retired years before Meinecke began his studies, but the younger man saw him as his master and mourned his passing from the scene.[51] The brief coincidence of these two careers, the one reaching back to the Napoleonic era, the other stretching from Bismarck's Germany through Hitler's and beyond, suggests the links between Ranke and the historiographical currents of our own time. Scholarly disciplines, so extraordinarily effective as a means of creating new knowledge, are no less impressive as sources of continuity and protectors of corporate values.

By the time Ranke died in 1886 the German historical profession was closely tied to the status quo: its members tended to serve as well as to study the political life of the state. But in the century's middle decades, history had many uses and could be harnessed to support a range of political alternatives. Ranke was, by temperament and conviction, a conservative, at once fascinated by, and fearful of, change. For him, the past offered solace in an era of apparently accelerating transformation. Others drew quite different lessons from the past. The study of history could inspire rebellion as well as conformity, a celebration of freedom as well as obedience. To a new generation of radicals, therefore, the historical

---

[50] Quotations from 'The Great Powers' and 'Political Dialogue', translated in Von Laue, *Ranke*, pp. 217, 166; Ranke, 'Trennung', p. 172; Berding, 'Ranke', p. 7.

[51] Ranke, *Theory*, p. ix; Jacob Burckhardt, *Letters*, ed. Alexander Dru (London, 1955), 49; Friedrich Meinecke, *Erlebtes 1862–1901* (Leipzig, 1941), 125. For Ranke and Burckhardt, see F. Gilbert, 'Burckhardt's Student Years: The Road to Cultural History', *JHI* 47/2 (1986), 249–74.

observation of the world seemed to guarantee that the present order of things would not survive for long.

iii. RELIGION AND RADICALISM

. If Germans want to follow the French path to political emancipation, Heine wrote in 1833, they should begin by acquiring religious freedom; ten years later, Marx called the critique of religion the premises of all criticisms. In contrast to most historians, who view the nineteenth century as a resolutely secular age, most contemporaries regarded religion as a critically important cultural and political issue. Intellectuals passionately defended or attacked the role of religion in public and private life, while ordinary men and women continued to draw on their faith for personal satisfaction and social identity. Despite the undeniable power of secularization, nineteenth-century politics and culture remained permeated by religion.

Instead of destroying religious awareness, secularization turned religion into a problem to be debated, an issue to be resolved, a loyalty to be mobilized or manipulated. By undermining old certainties, history and science intensified the search for new foundations for faith. By challenging traditional institutions, the state raised questions about the church's internal governance and political responsibilities. By threatening established communities, social changes forced people to redefine or abandon their ties to the church. We shall consider the political dimensions of this process in the next two chapters; now we can focus on the cultural role of religion in an increasingly secular age.[52]

Let us begin with German Catholicism, which seemed to be the chief victim of secularization. As we have seen, the church's institutions were battered in the course of the revolutionary era. The destruction of the ecclesiastical states, the collapse of the imperial religious structure, and the wholesale transfer of Catholics into confessionally mixed polities—often with a Protestant majority—left the church politically vulnerable and culturally weakened. After 1815 Catholic leaders debated how they could best survive in this new environment. Some, following in the footsteps

[52] McLeod, *Religion*, and Chadwick, *Secularization*, are both well-informed, brief accounts of these issues. Nipperdey's *Geschichte* is especially good on religion, but the best single treatment remains the fourth volume of Schnabel, *Geschichte*. Richard Evans, 'Religion and Society in Germany', *Modern European Studies Review*, 22/3 (1982), 249–88, discusses the recent historical literature.

of the Catholic *Aufklärung*, continued to seek a common ground with the forces of modernity, while others argued that the only way to live in the modern world was to insulate the faithful from its corruptions by affirming ecclesiastical authority and doctrinal orthodoxy.[53]

Johann Michael Sailer was an important bridge between the ideals of the Enlightenment and the demands of the post-revolutionary age. Throughout his long career, Sailer suffered because of his reputation as a rationalist. In the 1790s his colleagues at the University of Dillingen secured his dismissal; two decades later his appointment as bishop of Augsburg was blocked by his enemies in Rome. But after 1800 Sailer's reputation for intellectual independence and tolerance made him attractive to the new reformist leaders of Bavaria, while his piety and personal integrity earned him the patronage of Crown Prince Ludwig. During the last decade of his life, Sailer occupied a number of important positions in the Bavarian church, which he used to spread his ideas about clerical reform, religious education, and pastoral care. Sailer was a reformer but not really a rationalist. Rather than bring the church up to date, he wanted to return to the authentic simplicities of early Christianity; he opposed what he considered the baroque's theatrical overindulgence as well as scholasticism's arid complexities. But he was also open to new ideas and eager for contacts with a variety of thinkers; among his friends and correspondents were many leading intellectuals, including the Brentano brothers, Bettina von Arnim, and Savigny.[54]

If Sailer personified Catholic efforts to create a tolerant, open institution, Georg Hermes best represented the attempt to find an intellectually coherent synthesis of theology and philosophy. Born in 1775, Hermes matured while Kant's influence was at its height; after undergoing a spiritual crisis provoked by reading Kant and Fichte, Hermes emerged convinced that reason and faith could live together. In 1819 he published his *Philosophische Einleitung in die Christkatholische Theologie*; the following year he was named to a professorship at Bonn, which became the centre of a 'Hermesian' school of rational theology. Like Kant, Hermes sought to move from doubt to certainty: throughout this book, he wrote in the *Einleitung*, 'I have been scrupulous in maintaining my resolution to doubt everything for as long as possible and to accept nothing as

[53] Reardon, *Religion*, provides an introduction to Catholic thought. See also Donald J. Dietrich, *The Goethezeit and the Metamorphosis of Catholic Theology in the Age of Idealism* (Bern, 1979).
[54] Schnabel, *Geschichte*, iv, ch. 3.

being determinately the case until I have been able to show the absolute rational necessity of admitting such determination.' We must be ready to follow the judgements of reason, he argued, 'regardless of their bearing on our settled opinions or religious beliefs'.[55] Hermes attracted many students and found some well-placed patrons in the German hierarchy; his ideas remained influential even after his sudden death in 1831. But Rome eventually rejected him, condemned his views, and in 1835 placed his books on the index of forbidden works. The same fate befell Hermes's Austrian contemporary, Anton Günther, whose theological project was the reconciliation of Hegelian thought and Catholic doctrine. Although Günther did not have an academic post, his books attracted a considerable following, including some important church leaders. During the 1840s Günther's influence surpassed that of Hermes—in part because the Prussian government advanced the careers of several of his disciples. However, Günther did not lack well-placed enemies, who eventually succeeded in having his works banned in 1857.[56]

An important source of intellectual vitality within German Catholicism was the University of Tübingen, where a group of scholars attempted to synthesize historical scholarship and theology. What came to be known as the 'Tübingen school' was founded by Johann Sebastian Drey, who viewed the evolution of Catholic doctrine in the light of the romantics' emphasis on organic growth and historical continuity. In order for the church to grow and remain healthy, Drey taught, her leaders had to distinguish authentic beliefs and institutions from illegitimate and accidental ideas and practices. Then Catholics would find 'a sagacious way of governing which does not frustrate new development and the church's proper investment, maintaining continuity, yet neither uprooting truth along with error nor confusing what is fundamental to the church with what is merely conventional'.[57]

Drey's work inspired Johann Adam Möhler, who brought to the study of religious history scientific rigour and scholarly commitment. Möhler found in the church's development evidence of divine inspiration as well as guidance for future decisions. When Möhler's well-placed enemies prevented him from getting a position at Tübingen, he went to Munich, where he helped to establish a new centre of Catholic intellectual life. Here the crucial

[55] Reardon, *Religion*, p. 120.
[56] Ibid. 126–30.
[57] On the Tübingen school, see James Burtschaell's chapter in Smart *et al.* (eds.), *Thought*, ii; the quotation in from p. 117.

figure was Ignaz von Döllinger, who, after his appointment as a twenty-seven-year-old professor in 1826, quickly became the most influential Catholic historian of the day. Döllinger's *Lehrbuch der Kirchengeschichte* (two volumes, 1836 and 1838) ranks with the other handbooks, whose appearance marked the emergence of scholarly disciplines—in art, literary history, philosophy, and the natural sciences. His three-volume collection of documents on the Reformation, published a decade later, was regarded as the Catholic answer to Ranke's *Deutsche Geschichte im Reformationszeitalter*.[58]

Church historians like Möhler and Döllinger were inevitably drawn into the debate over papal authority, perhaps the single most explosive issue confronting German Catholics in the nineteenth century. Their work, which often suggested that the historical grounds for papal supremacy were somewhat shaky, was quickly taken up by the defenders of local episcopal power against Rome. To the German advocates of ultramontanism, however, Möhler and Döllinger seemed to be spreading dangerous doubts about the very basis of the church's existence. The pope's partisans were convinced that a rigorous centralization of religious authority was the best means of protecting Catholic institutions from state interference and of preserving Catholic doctrine from secular infection.[59] Although the issue of papal authority was not finally decided until the declaration of the pope's infallibility in 1870, by the 1840s the balance of power within the German church had clearly begun to shift to the ultramontanes' favour. Even in the Habsburg lands, where opposition to Rome was deeply ingrained in the structure of religious life, statesmen worked out compromises with the papacy. For the first time since the reign of Joseph II, the Austrian government allowed priests to study in Rome, where they were exposed to the growing ultramontane movement. As ecclesiastical authority began to move from the German bishops to the Vatican, the focus of Catholic intellectual life shifted away from universities like Tübingen and Munich towards Mainz and other seminaries in which the clergy might be trained without being contaminated by secular ideas.[60]

These institutional changes in the church were accompanied by

[58] For a summary of Döllinger's career, see Stephen Tonsor, 'Lord Acton on Döllinger's Historical Theology', *JHI* 20/3 (1959). A basic source for Döllinger's life and thought is his *Briefwechsel, 1820–1890* (4 vols.; Munich, 1963).

[59] Weber, *Aufklärung*, is a good local study of religious ideas and institutions in the Rhineland.

[60] Alan Reinerman, *Austria and the Papacy in the Age of Metternich*, i. *Between Conflict and Co-operation, 1809–1830* (Washington, 1979), describes the diplomatic history of Austria's relationship with the Vatican.

equally important changes in the intellectual climate. With increasing vigour, ecclesiastical authorities now opposed efforts to
reconcile faith and enlightenment, suppressed philosophical differences within the church, and discouraged ecumenical co-öperation
with Protestants. This campaign against modernity, which would
culminate in the *Syllabus of Errors* promulgated by Pius IX in 1864,
put renewed emphasis on mystical dogmas, such as the Immaculate
Conception of the Virgin Mary, which were certain to widen the
gap between Catholics and other Christians. After mid-century,
conservative Catholics sought to revive scholasticism, whose
praises were sung by periodicals like *Der Katholik*, church leaders
like Archbishop Reisach of Munich and Cardinal Rauscher of
Vienna, and theologians like Joseph Kleutgen and Franz Jakob
Clemens. In short, the irenicist energies apparent in Catholic
thought and literature during the late eighteenth and early
nineteenth centuries had dissipated, giving way to an era of
intellectual retrenchment and cultural restoration. What Franz
Schnabel wrote about Catholic art could be applied to the church's
intellectual life as a whole: 'The Catholic movement was strong
enough to bring to life old forms and archaic values, but not to
create something new and great.'[61]

That the triumph of papal authority, scholastic philosophy, and
anti-modernism increased the cultural marginalization of German
Catholicism was of little concern to conservative churchmen. They
were not much interested in questions of art and philosophy; their
emphasis was on religious faith at the grass roots. To these
defenders of orthodoxy and authority, the most important task
facing the church was to provide leadership and spiritual guidance
for ordinary Catholics. They were practical men, involved in
everyday matters of organization and pedagogy: preparing new
catechisms to bring Catholic doctrine to the laity, reviving special
retreats, missions, and pilgrimages, and creating a web of
associations to supplement or replace the traditional parish. Among
their efforts were organizations, such as Adolf Kolping's *Gesellen-
verein*, designed to meet the material and spiritual needs of
particular social groups, for whom traditional modes of pastoral
care no longer sufficed.

There is some evidence that this campaign did help to revitalize
Catholicism by encouraging popular piety and fealty. For example,
Werner Blessing's study of Bavaria shows how the church, with
the active encouragement of Ludwig I's government, used missions, pilgrimages, and new liturgical forms to reverse a decline in

[61] Schnabel, *Geschichte*, iv. 249.

regular observance among its members. Jonathan Sperber's fine book on the Rhineland points to a comparable set of phenomena, although in this area a revival of popular religion was sometimes carried out by church officials acting independently of, and often enough in opposition to, state authority. We cannot be sure how typical these cases were. Nor can we measure the depth and consistency of ordinary people's religious belief: in parts of Bavaria where church attendance was extremely high, for example, the illegitimacy rate was also among the highest in Europe; pilgrimages could be expressions of devotion, but also the occasions for decidedly secular desires and activities. Regionally diverse, chronologically uneven, difficult to interpret and easy to distort, the evolution of popular religion will probably remain obscure, its precise character lost with the private feelings of men and women we cannot bring back to life. In the face of these evidentiary problems, it is not surprising that historians interpret the history of popular religion along ideological lines: those who identify with the Enlightenment regret the return of cults, pilgrimages, and popular superstitions, while those who remain sympathetic to ultramontane Catholicism view these phenomena as expressions of authentic belief and true community.[62]

However we interpret these developments, Hugh McLeod is correct to conclude that Catholics were much more successful than Protestants 'in developing forms of piety that were both popular and orthodox, and in keeping rival ideologies at bay'.[63] What data we have suggest that in the course of the century Protestant church membership declined sharply almost everywhere. As we should expect, this decline was especially apparent in cities, where an increasingly mobile population lost touch with old beliefs and established religious institutions. But there was no simple, straightforward connection between 'secularization' and urbanization; among the lowest figures of church attendance in any German land were those from three rural Mecklenburg parishes, where the traditional social structure seemed relatively untouched.[64]

[62] On popular religious practices, see Blessing, *Staat*; Sperber, *Catholicism*; Phayer, *Religion*; Wolfgang Schieder (ed.), *Volksreligiosität in der modernen Sozialgeschichte* (Göttingen, 1986); Wolfgang Schieder, 'Kirche und Revolution: Sozialgeschichtliche Aspekte der Trierer Wallfahrt von 1844', *Archiv für Sozialgeschichte*, 14 (1974), 419–54.

[63] McLeod, *Religion*, p. 47.

[64] Phayer, *Religion*, p. 75. See also Chadwick, *Secularization*, p. 75, and Rainer Marbach's careful study of a Hanoverian community, *Säkularisierung und sozialer Wandel im 19. Jahrhundert* (Göttingen, 1978).

Some Protestants responded to the manifest decline in religious observance by reasserting orthodoxy; like their Catholic counterparts, these conservative theologians rejected modernity in all its forms. For Protestants, however, this enterprise had quite different institutional implications. Catholics, as we know, always had a problematic relationship with their governments, even when, as in the case of Metternichian Austria, church and state shared a deep hostility to the forces of revolution. For Protestants, on the other hand, the state was a natural and necessary ally—natural because of the historic connections between Protestantism and secular authority, necessary because Protestantism had no centres of authority beyond the state. In most German lands, therefore, Protestants' struggles against modernity led to closer co-operation with, and greater dependence on, secular authorities. Only with the help of agents of state power—the censor, the policeman, and the school teacher—could the Protestant churches protect their congregations from evil influences and infectious opinions.

The most important example of this alliance between Protestant orthodoxy and political authority was Prussia, where, according to one visitor from abroad, religion had been converted into a 'state machine'. King Frederick William III was a deeply religious man, with a special interest in liturgical matters; a Calvinist like his forebears, he wanted to reconcile his own denomination with the Lutheran majority. This he effected with a decree of 1822 that merged Reformed and Lutheran churches into a strictly hierarchical, highly bureaucratized structure. Once these institutions were in place, leading Protestant conservatives could act against dissent of all sorts, including allegedly heretical theologians in the universities and recalcitrant sects like the so-called 'Old Lutherans' in Silesia. At the same time, E. W. Hengstenberg, a Berlin professor and editor of the *Evangelische Kirchenzeitung*, joined with other conservative theologians in efforts to repress heretical views. Under Frederick William IV, the defenders of orthodoxy increased their influence on government policy, which, as we shall see, resulted in heightened conflicts over the political structure and direction of Prussian Protestantism.[65]

Pietism, which had had such a powerful impact on eighteenth-century German culture, continued to be important during the first half of the nineteenth century. With its emphasis on a direct, emotionally charged relationship between the individual believer

---

[65] Laing, *Notes*, p. 194. On Prussian Protestantism, see Fischer, 'Protestantismus'; Bigler, *Politics*.

and God, pietism had never developed cohesive institutions of its own; it continued to be highly diverse, spread in a number of small communities throughout German Europe. There were pietists among peasants and craftsmen in Württemberg, in the patrician neighbourhoods of Hamburg, and in manufacturing towns in Westphalia. Some Prussian landowners were drawn to the movement, as we know from the example of the Thaddens, on whose Pomeranian estate the young Bismarck was exposed to a particularly potent blend of pietist religiosity and aristocratic sociability. In some places pietism inspired political opposition, but increasingly it became associated with theological and ideological conservatism. By the mid-1830s, many pietists in Prussia and elsewhere had made common cause with the orthodox establishment against the forces of rationalism and reform.[66]

Coexisting with orthodoxy and pietism was that tradition of enlightened Protestantism which had its roots in the eighteenth century and found its greatest theoretical exponents in Schleiermacher and Hegel. While both men agreed that it was possible to find a middle ground between theology and philosophy, they differed sharply on how this ground was to be defined. Schleiermacher, it will be recalled, combined an intense, emotive religious sensibility with a deep respect for the secular culture. He remained convinced that faith and reason could coexist, each with its own appropriate sphere of knowledge and understanding: Hegel, however, had tried to resolve the problematic relationship between faith and reason by demonstrating that they were both part of mankind's search for knowledge. 'The object of religion as well as of philosophy is eternal truth in its objectivity, God and nothing but God,' he told his students in Berlin, 'Philosophy explicates itself when it explicates religion, and in explicating itself it explicates religion . . .' Although the orthodoxy of Hegel's own views remains questionable, during the 1820s, while he was delivering his influential lectures at Berlin, his synthesis of faith and reason seemed compatible with conventional Christian belief. For a brief moment Hegel brought together orthodox belief and enlightened rationality, historical particularity and eternal truth, sacred scripture and profane analysis.[67]

As Hegel's influence spread, the countervailing pressures within his system increased, and erstwhile Hegelians started to quarrel

---

[66] Engelberg's *Bismarck* has a good account of pietism among the Junkers.
[67] On Hegel and religion, see Reardon, *Religion*, ch. 3; the quotation is from p. 82.

over the true meaning of their master's achievement. After the philosopher's death in 1831, these centripetal forces within Hegelianism intensified when his chair was given to Georg Gabler, one of his least talented followers. On the one hand, conservative Hegelians were pulled into the growing movement on the right that emphasized the orthodox, conservative aspects in Hegel's ideas. On the other hand, another group began to develop the subversive potential in Hegelian thought, turning his defence of religion and the state into a radical critique of orthodoxy and order. There were, to be sure, still a number of philosophers who tried to protect Hegelianism's essentially synthetic character, but their position was eroded by defections to the left and pressures from the orthodox right. To those on both extremes, the time for compromise had passed, the common ground between faith and reason seemed untenable.

Two peoples exist in the body of our time and only two [wrote Hengstenberg with great satisfaction in 1836], Their opposition to one another will become increasingly intense and exclusive. Infidelity will gradually divest itself of any remnants of faith, just as faith will purge the remnants of infidelity from itself.[68]

An important stage in the crystallization of the conflicts among Hegel's heirs was the appearance in 1835 of *The Life of Jesus*, by David Friedrich Strauss. Like Hegel, Strauss was a product of the Tübingen *Stift*, where he had experienced an emotionally charged conversion to Hegelianism. In 1831 he went to Berlin to seek Hegel's help in creating his own synthesis of Christian faith and philosophy. As it turned out, Strauss spoke with Hegel only once, when the two drank some tea and exchanged an hour of Swabian gossip just a few days before the philosopher's sudden death. After a year in Berlin, Strauss returned to teach in Tübingen, where he wrote the book that would make him 'the most notorious' theologian of his time. Although Strauss concluded *The Life of Jesus* by assuring his readers that 'the supernatural birth of Christ, his miracles, his resurrection and ascension, remain eternal truths, whatever doubts may be cast on their reality as historical facts', no one could avoid the implications of his attempt to analyse the Gospels by setting their stories within the context of contemporary

[68] Toews, *Hegelianism*, p. 250. Toews's brilliant book is the best single account of the divisions among Hegel's followers. See also Harold Mah, *The End of Philosophy: The Origin of 'Ideology': Karl Marx and the Crisis of the Young Hegelians* (Berkeley, Los Angeles, and London, 1987); Brazill, *Hegelians*.

mythology. It was clear to defenders and critics of religion that, if the story of Jesus was explicable in human terms, then the divine foundations of Christianity could be kicked away.[69]

The particular power of Strauss's work came from the way he combined a number of contemporary intellectual currents: Hegelianism, historicism, the canons of biblical scholarship, and philological analysis. As his former teacher, Ferdinand Christian Baur, put it, 'Strauss was hated because the spirit of the age could not endure its own image which he held up before it in sharply profiled form.' Hated he certainly was: after being bitterly attacked by both the Hegelian and the orthodox theological establishments, he was removed from the seminary and eventually forced out of teaching altogether. When his efforts to soften and qualify his position failed to win over critics, he suffered a severe personal and intellectual crisis from which he emerged with the conviction that Hegelian philosophy and Christian faith were irreconcilable. 'No peace will be found', he wrote, 'until eternity is fully absorbed into time, piety has been completely taken up into mortality, and the church has been absorbed into the state.'[70]

In 1841, the year in which these words appeared in the second volume of Strauss's *Die christliche Glaubenslehre in ihrer geschichtlichen Entwicklung und im Kampfe mit der modernen Wissenschaft*, Bruno Bauer published his *Kritik der evangelischen Geschichte der Synoptiker*, which also turned Hegelian methods against traditional belief. Bauer was a craftsman's son who had used the study of theology as an avenue of upward social mobility. Even after his conversion to Hegelianism, Bauer had retained a deep commitment to Christianity. 'If contemporary developments are led by science [*Wissenschaft*]', he had assured the Prussian Minister of Culture in 1836, 'they will progress towards a recognition of the absolute truth of the orthodox faith.' On the basis of this conviction, Bauer joined in the chorus of voices attacking Strauss's apparent renunciation of religion's harmony with reason. But, within the intellectually and politically turbulent climate of the 1830s, Bauer's own work came under assault from the defenders of orthodoxy, who condemned his views and frustrated his efforts to find a permanent academic appointment. Slowly and reluctantly, he came

---

[69] Horton Harris, *David Friedrich Strauss and his Theology* (Cambridge, 1973), 47. In addition to Harris's monograph, see Hans Frei's chapter on Strauss in Smart *et al.* (eds.), *Thought*, i; Marilyn Chapin Massey, *Christ Unmasked: The Meaning of the Life of Jesus in German Politics* (Chapel Hill and London, 1983).

[70] Baur quoted by R. Morgan in Smart *et al.* (eds.), *Thought*, i. 263; Toews, *Hegelianism*, p. 285.

to realize that the ties between philosophy and faith had to be severed. 'Wissenschaft', he told his friend and sometime collaborator Arnold Ruge in 1841, 'must make sure that its categories and evolution are kept free of any infection from earlier representations. The break must be clean and absolute.' That year he published a satirical pamphlet entitled *Die Posaune des jüngsten Gerichts über Hegel den Atheisten und Antichristen*, in which he revealed the essentially subversive character of Hegel's historical vision. By this time, the demise of Bauer's hopes for an academic career left him free to advertise his atheism. He now believed that the shell of religious dogma had to be shattered if a new human nature was to be born. Philosophy, therefore, was the sworn enemy of religion, against whose debilitating illusions what he once called 'the terrorism of pure theory' must prevail.[71]

The most important publication in 1841 was Ludwig Feuerbach's *Essence of Christianity*. Born in 1804, Feuerbach belonged to one of those extraordinarily talented families whose members excelled in a variety of subjects; his father was a well-known jurist and advocate of legal reform, his brothers were famous for their work in law, mathematics, and philology, and his nephew was an important painter. Feuerbach's youth was clouded by the disintegration of his parent's marriage, from which he sought refuge in religion and romanticism. He began to study theology, but, after having been influenced by one of Hegel's students, he went to Berlin where he experienced the full force of a conversion to Hegelianism. Here, in what he called 'the Bethlehem of a new world', Feuerbach turned from theology to philosophy. He realized more swiftly than most of his contemporaries that Christianity could not survive the analytical implications of the Hegelian method. In 1830, after having been revealed as the author of a work denying personal immortality, Feuerbach's academic career came to an abrupt end. There followed a long and painful process of self-criticism and intellectual growth, through which Feuerbach, usually alone and often in difficult personal circumstances, struggled with Hegel's legacy: 'It was under his influence that I came to self-consciousness and world consciousness. It was he who was my second father, as Berlin became my spiritual birthplace. . . .' Eventually Feuerbach married a woman with enough property to support him in some comfort; from 1837 on he rarely was drawn from the security of his wife's home. But with the publication of *The Essence of Christianity*,

---

[71] Toews, *Hegelianism*, ch. 9, has a good account of Bauer; the quotations are from pp. 297, 317.

his influence spread throughout the growing community of left-wing Hegelians and then to free-thinkers everywhere in Europe. When he and his friends read this book, Friedrich Engels recalled later, 'we all at once became Feuerbachians'.[72]

In *The Essence* Feuerbach completes the process of philosophical inversion on which the left Hegelian project depended. His point of departure is bold yet breathtakingly simple: since religion is 'the dream of the human mind', it is to be studied, not 'in the emptiness of Heaven', but in its true setting, here on earth, in the realm of historical reality. Whereas Hegel had argued that human experience could only be understood in terms of a divine order, Feuerbach insisted that the evolution of the divine must be seen as part of human history. God did not will history as part of *His* self-realization; rather human beings have created God from *their* own self-knowledge. Because the mysteries of religion are 'native mysteries, the mysteries of human nature', we must seek to understand how cultural values and social needs shaped the characteristics men gave to their divinities. 'The personality of God is thus the means by which man converts the qualities of his own nature into the qualities of another being—of a being external to himself. The personality of God is nothing else than the projected personality of man.'[73]

Feuerbach's purpose is not to denigrate religion but to elevate humanity, or, as he put it, 'to exalt anthropology into theology'. By following the roots of religious dogmas and rituals into the rich loam of human consciousness, Feuerbach believed that he had discovered the source of our true nature, those qualities of will, thought, and affection which make us what we are. 'Religion', he wrote in the first sentence of Chapter 1, 'has its basis in the essential difference between the man and the brute—the brutes have no religion.' But, because religion directs these essential human feelings outside the human realm, it alienates us from the best we have in us. 'To know God and not oneself to be God, to know blessedness and not oneself to enjoy it, is a state of disunity, of unhappiness.' Like so many German intellectuals, Feuerbach wanted to restore unity to human life, to lead people back to themselves; to do this he called upon men to reject the spirit, overcome the illusion of heaven, and become reconciled with the realities of earth. This will transform 'the friends of God into the

---

[72] Ibid. 183; Brazill, *Hegelians*, p. 145. For a fine introduction to Feuerbach's thought, see Van Harvey's chapter in Smart *et al.* (eds)., *Thought*, i.
[73] Feuerbach, *Essence*, pp. xxxviii–xxxix, 226.

friends of man, believers into thinkers, worshippers into workers, candidates for the other world into students of this world, Christians, who on their own confession are half-animal and half-angel, into whole men'. To create 'whole men'—the goal of romantic poets and idealist philosophers—remained Feuerbach's ambition for the rest of his life.[74]

During the late 1830s a number of young men followed the same path from orthodoxy to criticism taken by Strauss, Bauer, and Feuerbach. They were to be found throughout German Europe, but especially in a few academic centres of Hegelianism, such as Berlin, Halle, and Tübingen. In 1838 Arnold Ruge established a new journal, the *Hallische Jahrbücher*, which he hoped would provide an alternative to the increasingly arid and intolerant *Jahrbücher für wissenschaftliche Kritik*, the semi-official organ of Hegelianism founded in 1827. At first Ruge and his collaborators did not expect the left to monopolize their journal, but the cohesion and radicalism of the *Hallische Jahrbücher* group increased as attacks from the right intensified. After King Frederick William III and his Minister of Culture von Altenstein died in 1840, Prussian cultural policies became hostile to Hegelianism of all sorts, censorship was tightened, and the demands for orthodoxy heightened. In what amounted to a posthumous insult to Hegel, his old enemy Schelling was appointed to his chair, in order, as King Frederick William IV said, 'to root out the Dragon seed of Hegelianism'. With the Prussian educational establishment now in enemy hands, academic careers were closed to young Hegelians.[75] Among those affected was Karl Marx, a twenty-three-year-old philosophy student whose dissertation had been accepted by the University of Jena in the spring of 1841.

Marx was born and reared in Trier, an ancient city in the Mosel valley. Once an ecclesiastical state, then conquered by France in the 1790s, and eventually annexed by Prussia in 1815, Trier's recent past mirrored the turmoil and uncertainty of the revolutionary age. Although descended from a distinguished line of rabbis, Karl's father had become a Protestant so that he could practice law under Prussian rule; to a man of the Enlightenment like Heinrich Marx, there did not seem much difference between being a non-practising Jew and 'a Protestant à la Lessing'. Karl grew up in a secular,

---

[74] Ibid. 1, 18, xi.
[75] McLellan, *Marx*, p. 41. Toews, *Hegelianism*, pp. 233 ff., correctly argues that one should not overestimate the coherence of the 'left Hegelians'; they remained a diverse and contentious group of thinkers.

enlightened family, materially comfortable and upwardly mobile. From his neighbour and family friend, Baron von Westphalen, the young man learned about the romantic poets, Homer, and Shakespeare, whose literary achievements he admired and hoped to emulate. Sent by his father to study law in Bonn in 1835, Marx spent most of his time writing verse, drinking, duelling, and carousing. He was better known in the Trier tavern club than in lecture halls and library. This was certainly not what Heinrich had in mind for his promising offspring. After a year, he paid the young man's debts and sent him off to what he hoped would be the more bracing intellectual climate of Berlin. Karl arrived there in October 1836, having been admonished by his father to live within his allowance, stay away from bad companions, and devote himself to becoming an important lawyer rather than a minor poet.[76]

Although Marx did find time for academic pursuits in Berlin, the turning-point in his intellectual development came not in a university classroom but in the nearby village of Stralow, where he spent the autumn of 1837 recovering from a lung infection. Here he found himself at one of those moments in life 'which are like frontier posts marking the completion of a period but at the same time clearly indicating a new direction'. As we can see in the remarkable letter that he wrote to his father just before dawn on 11 November 1837, Marx was in the throes of a conversion experience, common enough among the young men who fell under the spell of Hegelianism: 'For some days my vexation made me quite incapable of thinking; I ran about madly in the garden by the dirty water of the Spree . . . even joined my landlord in a hunting excursion, rushed off to Berlin and wanted to embrace every street corner loafer.' In the end, Marx found peace by accepting those ideas whose 'grotesque craggy melody' had once repelled him. The emotional intensity of Marx's commitment to Hegelianism suggests that there was more at stake here than speculative perplexity: by embracing Hegel, he had apparently resolved a nest of psychological and practical as well as philosophical conflicts— between poetry and law, romanticism and reason, his father's ambitions and his own sensibility. To become a philosopher indentured to the great truths of the Hegelian system offered Marx the promise of both career and cause; furthermore, in the 'Doctors' Club', the discussion group of which he quickly became a leading

---

[76] McLellan's *Marx* is a reliable biographical account. Kolakowski, *Main Currents of Marxism*, i. *The Founders*, provides a richly evocative analysis of Marx's place in western thought.

member, the new Hegelian discovered a supportive intellectual community of talented young men with common values and similar goals.[77]

There was, unfortunately, no market for Hegelians. After finishing his dissertation and working for a time at Bonn with his friend and former teacher, Bruno Bauer, Marx gradually and reluctantly realized that he would not find an academic post. In early 1841 he still seems to have hoped he could curry favour with the new Cultural Minister Eichhorn, but by the end of the year, after Bauer had been fired and the *Hallische Jahrbücher* could no longer be published in Prussia, the grim truth was unmistakable. Meanwhile, Marx's personal situation had become more difficult. His father had died in 1838, leaving the family finances diminished and in the hands of Marx's mother, who had little sympathy for her son's philosophical ambitions. She saw no reason why someone as gifted and energetic as her Karl could not go out and get a decent job in some respectable profession. By the summer of 1842 she had cut off his allowance and blocked his way to his father's legacy. As a result, Karl's marriage to Jenny von Westphalen had to be postponed, thus further prolonging what was already a painfully protracted courtship.

In 1842 Marx took an editorial post on the *Rheinische Zeitung*, a newspaper financed by wealthy Rhenish liberals but run by young radicals. Under Marx's inspired leadership, the paper's circulation doubled and its reputation for incisive analysis spread throughout central Europe. For the young philosopher himself, fresh from a learned thesis on Democritus and Epicurus, journalism involved a direct confrontation with contemporary affairs. Censorship, communal reform, divorce legislation, representative institutions, rural poverty—the pressing social, economic, and political issues of the day occupied his attention and became the subject matter for his sharp, critical essays. In his last important series for the *Rheinische Zeitung*, Marx dealt with the problem of illegal firewood gathering, an issue that brought together questions about a community's traditional rights, the demands of the market, and the privation of the peasantry. These articles were more than the Prussian censor was prepared to accept; already alarmed by the newspaper's increasing success, the authorities banned its further publication and left its editor once again without a job. There was, Marx realized, no place for him in a state like this. 'In Germany', he wrote to Ruge, 'I cannot start anything fresh; here you are obliged

[77] Marx and Engels, *Works*, i. 10 ff.

to falsify yourself.' After accepting a position with a periodical to be published in Strasburg, Marx married Jenny von Westphalen in June 1843 and prepared for a new life abroad.

Before leaving German soil, Marx began a four-year process of intellectual self-criticism from which he would emerge as a 'Marxist'. In a series of essays and short books, some published, many unknown until they were rediscovered by scholars in the twentieth century, Marx came to terms with his own Hegelianism and then with his former allies among the young Hegelians. Beginning with an analysis of Hegel's *Rechtsphilosophie* and ending with a polemic against the 'German ideology', these writings trace his slow, painful, and psychologically difficult campaign to turn what he had learned from Hegel into an instrument for political and cultural renewal. This enterprise, it should be noted, remained very much within the left-wing Hegelian mode: 'Our programme', he told Ruge in September 1843, is a 'reform of consciousness, not through dogmas but by analysing mystical consciousness obscure to itself.'[78]

Fully committed to what he called 'the self-clarification of the struggles and wishes of the age', Marx moved with his pregnant wife to Paris. Here, in late 1843 and 1844, he began to sever his ties with the Hegelian left. In an article 'On the Jewish Question', written for the *Deutsch-Französische Jahrbücher*, he bitterly attacked Bruno Bauer's conception of Jewish emancipation 'within the prevailing scheme of things'. Real emancipation, Marx now insisted, was not primarily political or cultural; it had to take place in civil society, the realm of productive relations where men and women had their real existence. In a second essay for the *Jahrbücher*, 'An Introduction to the Critique of Hegel's *Rechtsphilosophie*', we get a glimpse of how emancipation could occur: through the formation of 'a class with radical chains, a class of civil society which is not a class of civil society, a class which is the dissolution of all classes, a sphere which has a universal character because of its universal suffering . . .' With the appearance of this class, the proletariat, the essential elements in Marx's inversion of the Hegelian political order were in place. For Hegel, universality had been most fully realized in the state, whose servants, standing above civil society, could use their reason to plot the common good; for Marx, universality would be realized by the proletariat, whose radical exploitation expelled them from civil society and

[78] Marx, *Writings*, p. 209.

thus made them the true expression of human values and the historical instrument of revolutionary change.[79]

One day during the summer of 1844 Marx was introduced to Friedrich Engels at the Café de la Régence in Paris and thus found the man who would remain his companion, patron, and collaborator for the next four decades. Marx was twenty-five in 1844, Engels twenty-three; both came from the German west, had disappointed their practically minded fathers with youthful literary enthusiasms and left-wing Hegelianism, and were now becoming more and more interested in social problems.[80] So immediate and complete was their initial rapport that the two men spent ten days in non-stop discussion, after which they determined to write a joint work attacking Bauer and, by implication, their own intellectual origins. This turned out to be a three-hundred page polemic published in 1845 under the title *Die heilige Familie, oder Kritik der kritischen Kritik*. Marx continued this project alone with his unpublished 'Theses on Feuerbach', and then, again with Engels, in *Die deutsche Ideologie*. Taken together, these works completed what Marx called a 'settling of accounts with our erstwhile philosophical consciousness'.[81] By consolidating his alliance with Engels, and breaking with Feuerbach, the left Hegelian for whom his sympathies ran deepest and lasted longest, Marx was ready to make a lifetime commitment to the political movement with which his name will be irrevocably connected. In these writings of 1844 and 1845 we find for the first time a clear and straightforward statement about Communism's role as the essential clue to history's riddle and the ultimate product of history's revolutionary course.

'The philosophers have only *interpreted* the world,' Marx wrote in his final thesis on Feuerbach; 'the point is to *change* it.'[82] This remark, so often quoted by Marx's admirers, is characteristically unfair: most German philosophers had wanted both to interpret and to change the world. What set Marx apart from these thinkers was not his desire for change but his ideas about how change could be achieved. In contrast to several generations of writers, from Lessing through Kant, Hegel, and Feuerbach, Marx did not believe that spiritual enlightenment and moral reform preceded social change. For him, a new moral system could come only from social transformation. Within the context of German intellectual history,

[79] Ibid. 221, 234, 256. On Hegel's view of 'civil society', see above, Ch. 7, sect. iii.
[80] Gustav Mayer, *Friedrich Engels. Eine Biographie* (2 vols.; The Hague, 1934).
[81] McLellan, *Marx*, p. 140.
[82] Marx, *Writings*, p. 423.

therefore, Marx's attack on the primacy of spiritual reform represented a sharp break with the entire tradition of *Bildung*. Nevertheless, as Marx was sometimes willing to admit, this break with his intellectual ancestors was qualified in two important ways. First, his mode of analysis remained Hegelian; like Hegel, he viewed history as a unified, purposeful process, which had to be understood dialectically. Marx may have turned over the Hegelian relationship between idea and reality, but he did not doubt that the philosopher's task was to dive beneath the confusing phenomena on the surface of history and find the hidden source of change. Second, Marx's conception of humanity's ultimate goal remained firmly anchored in German culture. Like Hegel and so many other philosophers and poets, Marx set out to overcome humanity's alienation by bringing men and women home from their historic exile and creating that 'whole man' for whom so many German thinkers had fervently searched.

iv. THE LITERATURE OF ALIENATION AND COMMITMENT

Left-wing Hegelianism was just one of several forms of cultural criticism produced after 1830 by political unrest, a growing sense of social crisis, and a profound shift in generational self-awareness among German intellectuals. Alienation and exile, the fate of many radical Hegelians, also befell a number of their literary contemporaries, who found the status quo no less spiritually suffocating and politically repressive. 'Life, reality, and time [*Leben, Wirklichkeit, und Zeit*]—the three terms that Jeffrey Sammons identified with the 'Young Germans'—were also a part of the Young Hegelians' vocabulary. Both groups sought to reject worn-out ideals in favour of life, bring the world of the spirit closer to reality, and create a culture appropriate for the time. 'The new age will give birth to a new art in enthusiastic harmony with itself,' Heine wrote in 1831, 'an art which will not have to unearth its symbolism from the past, and which will even bring forth a new, unprecedented technique.'[83]

Perhaps the most important date in the history of nineteenth-century German literature was 22 March 1832, the day when death removed the man who had been a major force in European cultural life since the publication of *Götz* and *Werther* in the early 1770s.

[83] Koopmann, *Deutschland*. The basic source on German literature during this period is Sengle, *Biedermeierzeit*.

Although Goethe's reputation had fluctuated and he had never lacked detractors, the scale of his achievement was undeniable: no other German writer had produced a body of work of comparable size, range, and quality. By the early 1800s his fame was sufficient to paralyse even so sensible a visitor as Henry Crabb Robinson, who recorded in his diary that, 'had the opportunity offered, I think I should have been incapable of entering into conversation with him; but as it was, I was allowed to gaze on him in silence'.[84] During the last three decades of his life, Goethe wrote what we now recognize as some of his greatest books: *Der westöstliche Divan*, *Wilhelm Meisters Wanderjahre*, and especially the second part of *Faust*, which brought to a glorious conclusion the project on which he had laboured for so long. At the same time, Goethe carefully prepared the foundation for his historical reputation by publishing his autobiography, records of his Italian journey and the French campaign, and his correspondence with Schiller. 'I am bound to confess', he wrote, 'that in old age, life becomes for me more and more a matter of history. . . . In fact, I am growing more and more historical in my own eyes'. After his death, the task of converting his prodigiously complex and not wholly admirable life into a smooth historical monument was carried on by an army of admirers, who produced a sizable number of uninspired hagiographies, as well as two works of enduring literary interest— Bettina von Arnim's *Goethes Briefwechsel mit einem Kind* (1835) and Eckermann's *Conversations* (1836).[85]

Against this chorus of admiring voices a few dissenters could be heard. Conservatives like the theologian Hengstenberg objected to Goethe's unconcealed paganism, while patriotic publicists like Wolfgang Menzel condemned his manifest lack of nationalist enthusiasm. More interesting for our purposes was the hostility expressed by young, liberal writers, who acknowledged the magnitude of Goethe's talent but decried the ways he had chosen to use it. Most outspoken among this group of critics was Ludwig Börne, a literary journalist and political commentator who continually attacked Goethe's personal detachment, public conformity, and stylistic restraint: 'Heaven has given you a tongue of fire, but have you ever defended justice?' he wrote, 'You had a good sword,

[84] Henry Crabb Robinson, *Diary, Reminiscences, and Correspondence* (London, 1869), i. 110. For more on Goethe's English admirers, see Rosemary Ashton, *The German Idea: Four English Writers and the Reception of German Thought, 1800–1860* (Cambridge, 1980).

[85] Leppmann, *Image*, p. 66; this is an excellent source for contemporary attitudes about Goethe. On Bettina von Arnim, see Craig, *End*.

but you were always only your own guardian.' As a result of this selfishness, Börne believed, Goethe's art lacked life and energy: 'Goethe only understood what was dead, and therefore killed every living thing in order to understand it.' Heine, who was much less obsessive and consistent about the subject than Börne, agreed that Goethe's writing was too cool. In 1830, for example, Heine compared Goethe's recent output to the statues in the Louvre, 'that cannot suffer and rejoice with us, that are not men but halfcasts of divinity and stone'. But even those who liked him least recognized that his passing marked a cultural watershed, the end of an era that would be forever inseparable from this name: 'This literary period', concluded Theodore Mundt in 1833, 'lies behind us'.[86]

During the 1830s many European intellectuals sensed that they belonged to a successor generation that stood at the end of one era and before the beginning of another. Such feelings are common enough; young people often regard their elders' world as peculiarly out of date. But it can happen, as Heinrich Laube wrote in 1840,

that one epoch puts greater pressure on its youth than the others, thus making *youth* a decisive word. During the 1830s this happened in political and literary affairs throughout Europe. *Jeune, giovane, jung* became the slogans that helped to characterize a good deal of immaturity but also grasped the most vital pulse of the age.[87]

In some ways, the generation of the 1830s reminds us of the young romantics forty years earlier: we find among them the same ambitions, restlessness, and energy. But there had been among most romantics a purity of hope and boundlessness of vision one rarely sees in those who came of age after 1830. In a fashion now familiar to modern sensibilities, the members of this generation self-consciously carried the burdens of their elders' failures and achievements. They always wondered if they would ever reach the end of the long shadows cast over them by the giants of the past.

One of the books that best captured this mood was Karl Immermann's *Die Epigonen* (1836). At first glance, Immermann seems an unlikely spokesman for intellectuals often regarded as enemies of the established order. A veteran of Waterloo, a patriot, and a conservative by temperament and conviction, Immermann remained a loyal servant of the Prussian state until his death, at the age of forty-four, in 1840. But he was also a prolific writer, a gifted theatrical director, a friend of Heine and defender of censorship's

[86] Sammons, *Heine*, p. 101; Koopmann, *Deutschland*, pp. 120, 128.
[87] Koopmann, *Deutschland*, pp. 7–8.

victims, and an astute observer of the political and cultural scene. The full title of his novel suggests its subject and intent: *Die Epigonen. Familienmemoiren in neun Büchern, 1823–1835* is the personal story of an epigonal generation, seen from a familial perspective, and set in a specific time. At the centre of the plot are a series of legacies—biological, social, and spiritual—with which the characters must come to terms. While the novel concludes with the creation of a Utopian community in which past and present are reconciled, the overall tone is one of tension, unease, and excess— what one character refers to as

a desolate irresolution and perturbation, a ridiculous quest for security, a distractedness, a chasing after one knows not what, a fear of terrors that are the more uncanny for having no form! It is as if mankind, cast about in its boat on an overpowering sea, is suffering from a moral seasickness whose end can hardly be conceived.

In 1830, five years before he finished the novel, Immermann explained its title to his brother by saying that 'our age, which has raised itself on the shoulders of our elders' efforts and industry, suffers from a certain spiritual surplus. We have a ready access to the remains of their accomplishments; in this sense we are epigoni. From this a quite peculiar malady has arisen . . .' As if to illustrate this theme, Immermann himself borrowed heavily from Goethe's *Wilhelm Meister*, whose influence is everywhere apparent in the novel's structure and substance.[88]

Generational self-awareness among young Germans in the 1830s was not merely a matter of mood and sensibility. Equally important were changes in the social and political conditions of intellectual life that significantly narrowed the opportunities for a stable career. We have already had occasion to note the growing importance of the university as site of, and source of support for, cultural activity: by 1816, Hegel wrote to a friend, a university appointment was 'an almost indispensable condition' for philosophical influence. After a brief expansionary period, however, it became increasingly difficult to find an academic job; enrolments, in both the *Gymnasium* and the university, peaked at the end of the 1820s and then declined, as parents decided that higher education was no longer a sensible investment. Government service, the church, and the legal profession were all inundated with applicants, whose prospects were dampened by what Lenore O'Boyle has

[88] Glaser, *Mind*, p. 144; Rürup, *Deutschland*, p. 153. See Benno von Wiese, *Karl Immermann: Sein Werk und sein Leben* (Bad Homburg, 1969).

called a European-wide 'excess of educated men'. According to one contemporary statistician, during the early 1830s there were 262 candidates for every 100 clerical positions, 230 for every 100 bureaucratic posts. In the 1840s Samuel Laing was struck by the oversupply of qualified personnel, whose numbers were 'far too great for the natural demand, or for the real benefit of the country, the unemployed surplus being, in fact, literary idlers abstracted from the paths of productive employment, and hanging on in expectation of preferment to office'.[89]

Except for those with private means, unattached intellectuals had to support themselves with the proceeds from their writing or the charity of their friends—in fact, most required some combination of the two. The lives of those whom Laing called 'literary idlers' were not easy. Although book production greatly increased in the early nineteenth century, it was still difficult to earn much money from serious literary efforts. Editions remained small, royalties low, and circulation limited. Copyright laws were not introduced until the late 1830s, so even successful writers rarely realized the full benefits of their work; if a book became popular, pirate publishers flooded the market with cheap copies. Moreover, censorship, at once pervasive and unpredictable, could cut an author off from a large sector of his potential public. Only a few authors, therefore, made a comfortable living from their writing alone. To do so they had to be willing to write constantly, on a variety of subjects, and in a way guaranteed to please the most banal taste. Theodor Mundt's wife, for instance, produced over 250 volumes of what Jeffrey Sammons has described as 'irredeemably trivial historical novels'. Those who took their work seriously had to resist a system in which, according to Heine, 'even the Muse is a cow milked for an honorarium until it gives pure water'. Heine himself, a famous and relatively popular author, never achieved financial independence. He badly needed an allowance from his family and was bitterly disappointed when his mythically rich uncle did not leave him a substantial legacy. For a time, Heine, surely one of the least professorial personalities of his generation, hoped for the security of an academic appointment at the University of Munich. In 1844, when the poet Freiligrath renounced his government pension for political reasons, his friend, the erstwhile democrat Friedrich Dingelstedt, was appalled: 'To fling away a royal pension so that

---

[89] Hegel quoted in Toews, *Hegelianism*, p. 75, and Laing in O'Boyle, 'Problem', p. 473, both of whom have additional material on this issue. See also Ringer, *Education*, pp. 46 ff.

the liberal rabble, with its importunate collections and subscriptions, may bring you its public offerings with peasant pride? Good heavens, Freiligrath, not that!'[90]

With few exceptions, the radical intellectuals of the 1830s and 1840s suffered from financial insecurity and social marginality. In the preceding section we saw examples of this among the left-wing Hegelians, none of whom found regular employment: Strauss, who had been trained from boyhood for the ministry, was fired from his job in the Tübingen seminary and finally had to give up teaching altogether; Bruno Bauer hung around Berlin as an unsalaried *Privat Docent* for almost a decade, finally got a temporary appointment at Bonn, but eventually had to abandon his hopes for anything permanent; Feuerbach also lost his teaching position, and had to depend on his family and then his wife for financial support; Marx, destined for a legal career before aspiring to an academic position, ended up living the uncertain life of a political journalist. Most of the writers with whom the present section is concerned had similarly unsettled lives. Heine, who, like Marx, had been reared for a career in the law, also ended up in exile, trying to make a living with his pen. Karl Gutzkow, after abandoning theology for literature, had frequent run-ins with the censors and, despite having produced more than fifty plays, was only modestly successful; in 1846 he became resident dramatist at the court theatre in Saxony. Georg Herwegh and Friedrich Freiligrath, like Heine and Börne, lived in exile. Christian Dietrich Grabbe practised law intermittently, but devoted most of his brief life to unrewarding literary pursuits; only one of his plays was performed during his lifetime. Finally Georg Büchner, whose work recorded with precocious modernity the restless anxiety of the time, tried and abandoned several careers before his death, at the age of twenty-three, in 1837.

Büchner's story 'Lenz' is a powerful artistic projection of the unattached intellectual's spiritual situation. Its recurrent theme is the hero's separation—from society, family, friends, and finally from the natural and divine order. In the opening scene, Lenz stands on a mountain, where he 'experienced a feeling of terrible loneliness, he was alone, quite alone'. There follows a series of painful encounters in which he fails to connect and is left bereft of feelings and faith. 'There was', Büchner tells us, 'a terrible emptiness inside him, he no longer felt any fear, any desire, his

[90] Sammons, *Heine*, p. 114; Bramstedt, *Aristocracy*, p. 284. See also O'Boyle, 'Image', for some interesting comparative material.

existence was a burden to him, a burden he must bear.' Historically, Büchner's tale stands midway in a lineage that begins with J.
M. Lenz's own works during the *Sturm-und-Drang* era and extends
forward to Brecht, who used Lenz's *Der Hofmeister* as the basis for
one of his own plays. But more important, Büchner's 'Lenz' is
what J. P. Stern called 'an act of imaginative self-identification',
written by someone who knew what it was like to struggle against
loneliness and despair, and who, like his protagonist, lived on the
edge of sanity, always fearful of the abyss.[91]

Like many of his contemporaries, Büchner sought to overcome
isolation. As scientist, writer, and political activist, he wanted to
establish connections with life: 'The feeling that there's life in the
things created', he has Lenz exclaim, 'is much more important than
considerations of beauty and ugliness; it's the sole criterion in
matters of art.' Georg Herwegh shared this commitment to life,
which he identified with a politically-engaged poetry. 'The inner
and outer worlds cannot remain separated from one another any
longer,' he wrote in 1839; 'each must be thought of in relation to
the other, each must be explained in terms of the other.' That same
year, in a youthful poem entitled 'Book Wisdom', Friedrich Engels
wrote: 'He is not wise who from his reading draws| Nothing but
floods of useless erudition| For all his learning, life's mysterious
laws| Are a closed book beyond his comprehension.' Such
convictions were, as we know, common among the left Hegelians,
who sought to bring philosophy down to earth, and were shared
by Heine, who ridiculed his fellow countrymen for their contented
dominion over 'the airy world of dreams'. Georg Gervinus, in a
famous passage from the final volume of his history of German
literature, published in 1842, declared that, since 'the campaign of
art is completed', the time had come for Germans to devote their
energies to political action. But few writers went that far: as
Ludolph Wienbarg wrote in his *Aesthetische Feldzüge* of 1834, 'The
poets and writers of fine prose no longer serve the Muses alone, but
the Fatherland; let them be allies in the great causes of our time.'
Wienbarg, like Herwegh and many others, wanted to combine art
and life, literature and action, poetry and politics.[92]

Such combinations were not easy to achieve in Metternich's

[91] Büchner, *Leonce and Lena. Lenz. Woyzeck*, pp. 38–62; Stern, *Re-Interpretations*,
p. 133.
    [92] Büchner, pp. 45–6. Brazill, 'Herwegh', p. 117; Marx and Engels, *Works*, ii. 6;
Hohendahl, *Kultur*, p. 161; Sagarra, *Tradition*, p. 126.

Europe, where policeman and censor viewed with suspicion any book with a contemporary setting or potentially controversial subject. This kind of repressive pressure, which we have already seen at work in the lives of the young Hegelians, was another important source of generational identity. Appropriately enough, therefore, it was the authorities who gave the so-called 'young German' writers their collective identity when, following the publication of Karl Gutzkow's *Wally* in 1835, a series of laws, culminating in an edict from the Confederation, banned the works of Gutzkow, Heine, Heinrich Laube, Ludolph Wienbarg, and Theodor Mundt, prohibited their circulation in any form, and instructed the city government of Hamburg to move against the publishing firm of Hoffmann and Campe. This 'literary school', the edict declared, 'openly attempted, in belletristic works accessible to all classes of readers, to attack the Christian religion, undermine the existing social order, and destroy all discipline and morality.'[93]

Gutzkow was a twenty-four-year-old journalist when, after three weeks of intense work, he threatened the existing moral and political order with *Wally, die Zweiflerin*. A young man of extraordinary energy and drive, Gutzkow came from an impoverished family—his father was a groom in the royal stables—studied theology, then devoted himself to journalism and literature. After a brief and stormy apprenticeship with Wolfgang Menzel on the influential *Morgenblatt*, Gutzkow became literary editor of the *Phönix* in 1834. Following the Confederation's proscription of *Wally*, he served several months in prison, and continued to be harassed by the censors even after he had signed a 'loyalty oath' in 1843. Throughout his life Gutzkow overcame many obstacles, worked extremely hard, and suffered a great deal. But he lacked those qualities of mind and spirit necessary for literary greatness. There is, as E. M. Butler once noted, a special sort of poignancy in the fact that 'a man should undergo all the worst tortures of the unknown great . . . that he should be their blood brother in sorrow, yet not their fellow in joy; and akin to them by temperament should not rank with them by achievement'.[94]

Most twentieth-century readers will have difficulty understanding how *Wally* could have provoked Wolfgang Menzel into

[93] Huber, *Dokumente*, i. 137.
[94] Butler, *Religion*, p. 258. On Gutzkow, see Leo Löwenthal, *Erzählkunst und Gesellschaft: Die Gesellschaftsproblematik in der deutschen Literatur des 19. Jahrhunderts* (Neuwied and Berlin, 1971), ch. 4; Sammons, *Essays*.

accusing his former colleague of seeking to create 'a religion of lust', to be celebrated in brothels by young Germanys' 'sick, enervated priesthood'. The book's supposedly erotic passages are tepid enough, and not simply when judged by our own incendiary standards. Moreover, the novel hardly qualifies as a defence of scepticism, since the absence of belief turns out to have terrible consequences for the heroine, who comes to the 'deep conviction that without religion the life of a human being is desolate'. But when set against the values of *Biedermeier* domesticity, *Wally* must have seemed subversive indeed. Moved by passion, intolerant of hypocrisy, unsatisfied with political platitudes and cultural clichés, 'Wally the sceptic' represented everything a modest, pious, and compliant wife was not supposed to be. In her restlessness, nervous energy, and spiritual turbulence, she stands directly opposed to *Biedermeier* culture's celebration of calmness and cohesion. As Sammons writes, because the novel presented 'an outcry of pain and bewilderment at the alienation of the individual and the erosion of sustaining values in society, it is a symptomatic event of this turbulent year of 1835'. It is still, despite its irritating style and simple-minded plot, a strangely moving book.[95]

The men whom the federal authorities associated with Gutzkow made up a motley collection. Ludolph Wienbarg, who had first used the term 'young Germany' in his *Aesthetische Feldzüge*, was a prolific but not especially talented writer, whose run-in with the authorities in 1835 helped push him along a destructive path that would end in alcoholism and mental collapse. Theodor Mundt vigorously denied any connection with 'young German' writers, and especially with Gutzkow, whose work he deplored. He was nevertheless denied a university appointment and made to suffer various indignities until, with great relief and enthusiasm, he accepted the offer to swear his loyalty to the Confederation. Heinrich Laube, who had been imprisoned for seditious writing in July 1834, also persistently repudiated the 'young Germans'—even while he was being persecuted for his alleged sympathies with them. Like Mundt, Laube eventually made his peace with the authorities and spent the last eighteen years of his life as artistic director of the Vienna Burgtheater.

Although they were different in temperament, character, and fate, the 'young Germans'—together with a score of other writers who are sometimes associated with them—shared a set of historical experiences which gave their work from the mid-1830s (Gutzkow's

[95] Gutzkow, *Wally*, pp. 107–8; Sammons, *Essays*, p. 51.

Wally, Wienbarg's *Feldzüge*, Mundt's *Moderne Lebenswirren* and *Madonna*, Laube's *Das neue Jahrhundert* and *Das junge Europa*) a similar emotional tone and critical inclination. Never a school or even a movement, the 'young Germans' belonged together because of their common discomfort with traditional culture and existing social values. Moreover, with one central exception, all of the 'young Germans' failed to create major literary works. 'I find in the products by the best of them', Karl Immermann wrote a few years after 1835, 'hints of much that is good, even great. . . . However I am afraid that, despite all the talent they doubtlessly possess, their impact will be ephemeral.' Sammons's recent assessment is strikingly similar: 'That young Germany was a failure in every conceivable respect, no one will deny. . . . Their realistic impulses turned to triteness, their idealism to resignation.'[96]

The single exception to this record of artistic underachievement is the one truly great figure associated with the 'young Germans', Heinrich Heine. When his works were banned by the Confederation in 1835, Heine was thirty-nine and had been living in Paris for almost five years. A Jew from the German west, Heine was born in Düsseldorf where his father was a merchant. His own commercial efforts were brief and unsuccessful, despite his rich uncle Salomon's patronage. In 1819 he went to study law, first at Bonn, then Göttingen, and finally Berlin. In 1825 he was baptized, discreetly and without conviction, evidently so that he could begin a legal career. But by this time Heine's commitment to literature was irreversible. As a student in Bonn his poetry had attracted the sympathetic attention of August Wilhelm Schlegel, and thereafter he began to achieve a modest but steadily growing reputation as a lyricist. His contacts with the literary life increased during his time in Berlin, where he frequented the Varnhagen salon, began a lifelong friendship with Immermann, and published essays and articles on contemporary affairs. In 1827 he entered into an agreement with the Hamburg publisher Julius Campe, who brought out an edition of his poems and the full text of his *Harzreise*, the first of his great travel books. The following year Heine went to Munich, contracted to do some journalistic work for the important publishing house of Cotta, and attempted to get himself a post at the university. Although he continued to produce notable work, including a remarkable, three-part record of his trip to Italy in 1828–9, Heine was constantly in need of money and forced to depend on reluctantly given subsidies from his rich

[96] Sengle, *Biedermeierzeit*, i. 155; Sammons, *Essays*, p. 23.

relations. In 1831, frustrated in his efforts to find financial security, irritated by his uncle's niggardliness, and increasingly at odds with the Prussian censors, Heine left for Paris, where he remained until his death a quarter of a century later.[97]

Heine's poetry treats the familiar themes of love and nature; his essays include descriptions of people and places as well as reflections on religion, culture, and literature. Yet through this wide range of subjects the one matter of enduring interest in Heine's work is himself. However much Heine may have differed from the romantics, like them he placed his own feelings at the centre of his art. Either directly or as an elusive *Doppelgänger*, Heine's persona shadows much of what he wrote; ironically or poignantly, with playful distance or disconcerting candour, he used his own character and experience as his principal source and subject. Nowhere is this more evident than in his final poems, which create from the experience of his last, lingering illness a lyrical celebration of life's power and death's pain. 'Out of his opium dreams and nocturnal visions,' S. S. Prawer writes, 'out of his apprehension of death and memories of life, out of his physical pain, mental anguish and spiritual resurgence, Heine fashioned his greatest and truest poetry.'[98]

So thin is the membrane separating Heine's life and art that even the most skilful biographer can have trouble telling where each begins and ends. Despite—or more likely precisely because of—his capacity for self-disclosure, much about Heine's life remains obscure. Even the year of his birth is a matter of uncertainty and scholarly debate. Moreover, his incessant autobiographical impulse makes Heine's work difficult to categorize. Few of his prose pieces are quite what they seem to be. 'Nothing could be more misleading than Heine's titles,' E. M. Butler warns us, 'nothing more bewildering than his technique. Biography slides into auto-biography, resolves itself into recriminations and finally melts into mythology. Lampoons may flare up into visions.' The only unity in this unstable and fragmentary œuvre is what Butler calls the 'great edition of the conflict between poetry and life', the endlessly fascinating spectacle of Heine's confrontation with his social environment, historical situation, and inner being.[99]

[97] Sammons, *Heine*, is a good biographical introduction. Barker Fairley, *Heine: An Interpretation* (Oxford, 1954), and Prawer, *Heine*, are both worth reading on his poetry.

[98] Prawer, *Heine*, p. 269.

[99] Butler, *Tyranny*, pp. 244–5.

Soon after moving to Paris, Heine became a well-known figure, part of the international literary élite then assembled in the city Arnold Ruge called 'the cradle of the new Europe, the great laboratory where world history is formed. . . .' In his *Florentinsche Nächte*, Heine spoke of Paris's 'rosy light', which softens tragedies, dulls suffering, heals wounds. Ask a fish in the water how it feels, Heine wrote to a friend, and it will reply, 'Like Heine in Paris.' But he always felt the pain of separation—from his family, the scenes of his childhood, and, most important, his language. In his poem 'Anno 1839', the anguish of exile clearly shows through the irony in which he so characteristically wrapped it:

> Oh, Deutschland, meine ferne Liebe,
> Gedenk ich deiner, wein ich fast!
> Das muntre Frankreich scheint mir trübe,
> Das leichte Volk wird mir zur Last.
>
> Nur der Verstand, so kalt und trocken,
> Herrscht in dem witzigen Paris——
> Oh, Narrheitsglöcklein, Glaubensglocken,
> Wie klingelt ihr daheim so süss.

However much he may have felt at home in France, the best of what he wrote was in German and about the German situation.[100]

During the mid-1830s, while the 'young Germans' were writing the books that would bring upon them the authorities' wrath, Heine was at work on two connected essays with which he intended to explain German culture to the French and to the Germans themselves. 'The Romantic School' and 'On the History of Religion and Philosophy in Germany' were published separately in German, but appeared together in French under the title, *De l'Allemagne*, which was meant to evoke de Staël's famous work of 1810. In contrast to de Staël—'Staëlschen' as Heine condescendingly called her—he viewed romanticism as an unfortunate return to outdated beliefs, an illusory flight to the past by men who hated the present and feared the future. For Heine, the characteristic romantic was August Wilhelm Schlegel, his one time teacher and benefactor, whose thought and character he singled out for especially savage treatment. Like the young Hegelians, Heine identified Germans' cultural anachronism with their historical backwardness. For the French, medievalism was a fad and affectation, but to Germans, the Middle Ages were not dead and buried and so could be 'brought to

[100] Sammons, *Heine*, p. 168.

life by an evil spirit, which walks about in the broad daylight and sucks the red blood from our breasts'.[101]

In his essay on religion and philosophy, Heine displayed a different side of German culture: whereas romanticism was the reactionary, irrational symptom of German backwardness, the philosophical tradition culminating in Hegel and the idealists was powerfully progressive and potentially revolutionary. If understood correctly, this tradition could make possible a definitive break with Christian belief by creating the basis for what Heine vaguely described as a new pantheistic religion. Once again, Heine reminds us of the young Hegelians, who also turned Hegel from a defender into an enemy of orthodoxy. Moreover, like the Hegelian left, Heine argued that Germany's philosophical revolution was no less earthshaking than the political revolution in France. Eventually, Germans would move from the realm of the spirit to the world of action: 'The thought comes before the deed, like lightning before thunder.' And, however slowly the German thunder might travel, its arrival would be unmistakable. 'Eagles will fall dead from the sky, and in the farthest deserts of Africa lions will lower their tails and seek refuge in their royal lair.' What follows, Heine warned his French readers, will make your revolution seem like 'a harmless idyll'.[102]

After 1840 Heine became more radical and more committed to political action. At about the same time that Marx told German philosophers that their task was to change the world, Heine delivered a similar message to German poets:

> Deutscher Sänger! sing und preise
> Deutsche Freiheit, dass dein Lied
> Unsrer Seelen sich bemeistre
> Und zu Taten uns begeistre
> In Marseillerhymnenweise.
>
> Girre nicht mehr wie ein Werther,
> Welche nur fur Lotten glüht——
> Was die Glocke hat geschlagen,
> Sollst du deinem Volke sagen,
> Rede Dolche, rede Schwerter!

Heine and Marx met just before Christmas 1843, saw a good deal of each other in the following months, and for a time even seemed embarked on a common political course. Heine's poem on the

---

[101] Heine, 'Schule', p. 228.
[102] Heine, 'Geschichte, p. 109.

Silesian weavers, which will be quoted in the next chapter, expressed the same sense of impending social collapse that would later inform the *Communist Manifesto*.[103] But Heine's political commitment was inconstant and unreliable. He could be as brutally critical of allies like Ludwig Börne as he was of antagonists like Schlegel. Towards politically engaged poets like Georg Herwegh he was unfailingly hostile. 'Artists who choose as their subject liberty and liberation are usually men of limited, inhibited understanding, unfree at heart,' he wrote in the *Augsburger Allgemeine Zeitung* in March 1843. 'The boldest, the most unbridled singers of liberty turn out to be, on closer inspection, nothing but narrow-minded Philistines . . .'[104] That same year he published his mock epic 'Atta Troll', a scalpel-sharp satire of contemporary politics and poetry, from which Heine characteristically does not spare himself. But in 'Deutschland, ein Wintermärchen', published in 1844, he once again made fun of Germans' reluctance to act:

> Man schläft sehr gut und träumt auch gut
> In unsern Federbetten.
> Hier fühlt die deutsche Seele sich frei
> Von allen Erdenketten.

And, albeit not without a certain ironic reserve, he identified himself with the radical left:

> Ich bin kein Schaf, ich bin kein Hund,
> Kein Hofrat und kein Schellfisch—
> Ich bin ein Wolf geblieben, mein Herz
> Und meine Zähne sind wölfisch.

Heine was ambivalent about his public role and uncertain about his political sympathies. To be sure, he remained a consistent opponent of the status quo; in his opposition to censorship and repression, chauvinism and intolerance, hypocrisy and pretension, he never wavered. Nor did he ever give up his hatred of the philistines, those shallow, money-grubbing burghers whose weaknesses are personified by the banker Gumpel in *Die Bäder von Lucca*. But Heine's positive views are less easily defined. An admirer of Napoleon and Rousseau, fellow-traveller of the Saint-Simonians and the young Hegelians, friend of democrats and revolutionaries, he was never entirely comfortable with any party or movement. Heine's politics, like everything else about him, was a product of

[103] The poem is 'Die Tendenz' of 1842, in *Schriften*, iv. 422–3. On Marx and Heine, see Reeves, 'Heine'.

[104] Prawer, *Heine*, p. 61.

his own intensely personal interaction with the world. On the shifting ground of his private frustrations and antagonisms, he could erect an impressive critique of existing institutions, but not a persuasive alternative to them. Without doubt this critique is brilliant, but its brilliance—to borrow one of his own images—served to display the surrounding darkness rather than illuminate a path towards the light.[105]

Heine's political views were characteristic of people cut off from the world of action; his was a politics of exile and alienation. Like so many of those forced to emigrate or be silent, Heine remained on the periphery of public discourse, without the responsibilities of action and the burdens of compromise. No wonder that he could change his mind so easily and express his personal antagonisms with such abandon, and no wonder that he wavered between admiration and contempt for those who tried to find a means to act. In contrast to Marx, who extended his German experiences to embrace international loyalties and ambitions, Heine remained too closely tied to a nation that would never be his. 'The French adopted him, but he did not adopt them,' Sammons writes, 'the Germans cast him out, but he remained German to the end.'[106]

Heine, the quintessential exile, is an extreme case of the writer's estrangement from his society. According to Robert Minder, this estrangement was especially common in Germany, whose poets tend to be 'citizens of another world' rather than participants in their own society. In this regard, Minder argues, the ageing Goethe, extravagantly praised but universally misunderstood, had much in common with his harshest critics among the 'young Germans'. At the outset of his own career, Heine addressed the peculiar problems of German authors by contrasting them with their counterparts in England and France. English writers, he maintained, can travel in style through their land, observing the customs, passions, and actions of their fellow men. The French writer 'lives constantly in society, indeed in high society, no matter how needy and obscure he might be'. The German writer, however, is too poor to travel and too humble to be accepted in society, and so must remain in his lonely garret. As a result, whereas English and French literature is devoted to outside reality, German books turn inwards towards a private, fantastic world of

---

[105] 'Es herrscht im ungeheuren Raum| Nur Tod und Nacht und Schweigen;| Es brannten Ampeln hie und da,| Um die Dunkelheit recht zu zeigen': *Deutschland: Ein Wintermärchen.*
[106] Sammons, *Heine*, p. 171.

the author's own creation. 'Among all nations,' Heine laments, 'we Germans are most receptive to mysticism, secret societies, natural philosophy, spiritualism, love, nonsense, and—poetry.' However deficient it might be as a description of culture and society in the three nations—counter-examples from all three come readily to mind—Heine's statement reflected a deeply felt sense of literature's social isolation against which he himself and many of his contemporaries struggled, persistently but without success.[107]

[107] Minder, *Kultur*, pp. 11 ff.; Heine, 'Briefe aus Berlin', *Schriften*, ii. 68.

X

The Growth Of Participatory Politics, 1830–1848

I N HIS introductory essay to the first edition of the *Staatslexikon* (1834), Theodor Welcker described the contemporary period as a distinctively 'political era'. Never before, he argued, had the ambitions of individuals and nations taken such a manifestly political form, never had the clash of parties so dominated people's thought and action. Welcker was surely correct. During the 1830s and 1840s Germans' interest in public affairs steadily increased. Political news, diluted but not destroyed by the censors, found its way into the daily Press; theories and opinions on political matters were expressed in lexicons and lecture halls, periodicals and public meetings. The social, literary, and scholarly institutions that sustained the public sphere extended their reach, diversified their functions, and deepened their social base. 'All of human reality', Julius Froebel believed, 'is subsumed under the unity of politics'. Politics even threatened to permeate the private space of *Biedermeier* sociability: as one hostess complained in the 1830s, 'The affliction of political conversation was no longer to be excluded from the drawing room'.[1]

The growth of participatory politics in the German states was part of the historical process set in motion by the great revolutionary upheavals of the late eighteenth century and furthered by the social, economic, and cultural developments we have considered in the preceding chapters. More and more Germans felt themselves to be part of this process, which brought to some the hope of emancipation and progress, to others the fear of chaos and destruction. But in addition to the grand drama of revolutionary change being played out on the European stage, everyday considerations also drew Germans towards public affairs. The growing involvement of the state in social life—as tax collector and policy-maker, educator and employer, regulator and patron— evoked a complex set of political aspirations and frustrations from a variety of groups. Businessmen eager to open a new rail line,

---

[1] *StL* (1st edn.), i. 3–4; Koch, *Demokratie*, p. 93; Georg Steinhausen, *Häusliches und gesellschaftliches Leben im 19. Jahrhundert* (Berlin, 1898), 147.

teachers anxious about their occupational status, craftsmen threatened by technological change, all confronted their governments with demands for help. Individual ambitions and social antagonisms thus became the source of political passions and alignments.[2]

To think and act politically people have to make a connection between their personal condition and their public affairs. This connection is at once intellectual and institutional. It requires a set of ideas through which men and women can see how the immediate realities of their lives fit into a larger world, and a set of institutions with which they can co-ordinate and sustain their efforts to influence this world. As we have seen, it was by no means easy for Germans to acquire either the ideas or the institutions necessary for effective political action. Throughout the first half of the century, the forces of repression remained strong, habits of deference hard to break. But slowly, and often at considerable cost, Germans created the intellectual systems and associational networks upon which participatory politics could be based. As a result, the character of public life was fundamentally altered. No longer did politics revolve around the relationship between *Herrschaft* and *Verwaltung*, no longer was the political realm restricted to men from landed or bureaucratic élites, no longer was popular action limited to isolated protests or indirect persuasion. New sorts of organizations, issues, and élites provided Germans with a new sense of movement and possibility. In this chapter we will begin by considering the formulation of ideological alternatives, and then trace the rising wave of organized political action between the revolutions of 1830 and 1848.

i. CONSERVATISM AND LIBERALISM

Ideologies, Clifford Geertz has written, are cognitive maps 'of problematic social reality'. This cartographical metaphor seems especially appropriate to describe the alternative visions of the world that Germans began to sketch during the first decades of the nineteenth century. Ideologies, like maps, represent the historical landscape in different ways, for various purposes, and with greater or less precision. These representations can be accurate, but ideologies—again like maps—are always incomplete, abbreviated, and encoded. By emphasizing some features and neglecting others, ideologies simultaneously chart a terrain and shape the way people perceive it. Moreover, formulation of ideologies, like the making

---

[2] For an introduction to these issues, see the essays in Steinbach (ed.), *Probleme*.

of maps, presupposes a certain estrangement between people and their environment. For the cartographer, this estrangement comes from movement, for the ideologist from change. One does not draw maps of one's village or create an ideological picture of a static society. Maps imply travel, ideologies historical transformation.[3]

We have already seen in some detail the historical transformations to which German ideologists had to respond: the slow dissolution of the old regime during the second half of the eighteenth century, the trauma of war, defeat, and territorial reorganization, the challenge of reform and social reconstruction, and, finally, the failure of the restoration to halt the forces of political, economic, and cultural innovation. However much some of them might have wished to do so, most politically conscious Germans realized that there was no way to avoid the historic journey upon which they had embarked. Those who wished to recreate the past and those who sought to embrace the future had at least one thing in common—the belief that change was inevitable. Standing still was not an option.

In the face of this conviction, the ideas and attitudes prevalent in the eighteenth-century public seemed insufficient. Constitutional issues, which had not made much sense to pre-revolutionary theorists, now seemed inescapable. Similarly, the clarification of political alternatives, which had often been obscured by the rhetoric of moral reform, now seemed essential. Of course the legacy of eighteenth-century political discourse remained important even after its political world had disappeared. The ideas of cameralists like Justi, defenders of the old order like Möser, and moral reformers like Lessing continued to reverberate in nineteenth-century political thought. How could it have been otherwise? After all, most of the thinkers who created the new century's ideological alternatives came from the same social groups, participated in the same kind of associations, and were heirs to the same cultural traditions as their predecessors.

Ideologies characteristically fuse people's moral values, material interests, and political convictions into a system of ideas that can explain historical change, guide present actions, and point towards future achievements. Conservatism, for example, as it was defined

---

[3] Clifford Geertz, 'Ideology as a Cultural System', *The Interpretation of Cultures: Selected Essays* (New York, 1973), especially pp. 218 ff. On the changing historical meaning of the term, see *GGB* iii. 131–69. Harold Mah's *The End of Philosophy, the Origins of 'Ideology': Karl Marx and the Crisis of the Young Hegelians* (Berkeley, Los Angeles, and London, 1987) examines the term in its German context.

in the ideas of Gentz and Müller, created a view of the world woven from romantic sensibilities, religious beliefs, aristocratic interests, and personal ties to the old regime. With this ideology, conservatives could seek to understand the direction of events and justify their claims against both democratic revolutionaries and bureaucratic reformers. Well before the term *conservatism* was given its specific political meaning in Chateaubriand's *Le Conservateur*, the ideology was at work in German political theory and practice.[4]

The most important conservative thinker in the years immediately after 1815 was Carl Ludwig von Haller. Like Gentz and Müller, Haller fashioned his views in opposition to the French revolution, but he brought to the conservative cause a very different set of experiences and convictions. Born in 1768 into a family long prominent in the Bern patriciate, Haller entered his city's civil service when he was eighteen. While still in his twenties, he played a prominent role in Bern's desperate struggle to survive the perils of war and revolution. When the French conquest of Switzerland brought his career to an end, he worked with a circle of counter-revolutionary publicists; eventually he returned to Bern, but was again forced to leave when his conversion to Catholicism became known. After brief service in the ill-fated regime of the last Bourbon king of France, he spent the remainder of his life as a private scholar.[5]

Haller's reputation and influence rested upon his six-volume work, *Die Restauration der Staatswissenschaften* (1816–1822), which lent its title to the age. With this treatise Haller wanted to give political thought an intellectual foundation to replace the revolutionaries' social contract theory, that 'false, impossible, self-contradictory caprice' which he held responsible for his contemporaries' philosophical errors and political excesses. In the course of his restorative efforts, Haller often invoked God, but only as the author of a natural order to which we must turn for the answers to our political perplexities. In comparison to Müller, Haller was cool, rational, and scientific; he wanted to erect a system

---

[4] On the changing meaning of *Conservatism* see *GGB* iii. 531 ff. Epstein, *Genesis*, remains a basic source for the movement's ideological origins. Unfortunately, Robert Berdahl's excellent book *The Politics of the Prussian Nobility: The Development of a Conservative Ideology, 1770–1848* (Princeton, 1988), appeared too late to be used for this chapter.

[5] Guggisberg, *Haller*, provides the necessary biographical information. On Haller's significance see H. Diwald's introduction to Gerlach, *Revolution*, p. 28; Grosser, *Grundlagen*, pp. 3 ff.

that would appeal to his readers' 'reason and experience' rather than to their faith and emotions.

Haller grounded his premiss that all social relationships are fundamentally unequal on empirical evidence, things 'we see everyday with our own eyes'. Inequality exists throughout the social order because everywhere the weak are dependent on the strong. In the state, Haller insisted, subjects are dependent on the prince, whose independence is 'the highest source of human happiness, the natural product of relative power'. The prince's authority, therefore, was inalienable—it belonged to him and was no more subject to contractual limits than the authority of a father over his children. Indeed at one point Haller declared that the essential character of the state was like a private association, a *Hauswesen* or *magna familia*.[6]

Haller left an ambiguous ideological legacy Like other conservatives, he opposed the secular abstractions of Enlightenment political theories. His own conversion and his personal ties to the French legitimists maintained the historical association between Catholicism and conservatism. But to some of his contemporaries, Haller's thought seemed too rational and naturalistic. 'He is totally without a trace of Christian sensibility', wrote Otto von Gerlach after reading the fourth volume of *Die Restauration* in 1820. Moreover, Haller's defence of political authority was not unconditional. To be sure, he insisted that the ruler's power was natural and essential. But he did not regard the state as a sacred community, different in kind from other social institutions; the rights and powers of the state were based on the same principles as those of families, corporations, and communities. Nor did Haller exclude the possibility of resistance to unjust rule, a position that earned him the lasting distrust of the Austrian government. As a proud citizen of Bern, he cherished a vision of small, independent polities from a pre-absolutist era. 'Smaller states', he once wrote, 'are the true, simple order of nature, and one way or another she will always return to them eventually.' Like Rousseau's image of democracy, Haller's conception of the patrimonial state was easily distorted once it was detached from the small-scale institutions for which it had originally been intended.[7]

As Alfred von Martin has written, the distinctive feature of early nineteenth-century German conservatism was its 'Janus-like' opposition to both bureaucratic absolutism and radical democracy,

---

[6] The quotations are from the second edition of 1820: i, pp. xlviii, 515.
[7] Guggisberg, *Haller*, p. 117; Meinecke, *Cosmopolitanism*, p. 165.

which conservatives regarded as parallel threats to religious orthodoxy, local autonomy, and traditional social institutions. Bureaucrats and democrats, they believed, advocated an abstract, universal notion of freedom behind which despotism inevitably loomed; both sought a legal and social equality through which society's organic cohesion and essential diversity would be destroyed. Conservatives insisted that they were in favour of liberty, but the liberty they desired had little to do with the emancipation promised by the *Aufklärung*; instead it was the *Libertät* so essential to the world of *Herrschaft*, a set of rights and privileges defined and protected by custom and sustained by a complex net of small-scale, face-to-face relationships. Yet by the time conservatism began to take shape, only the tattered remnants of these liberties remained—in guilds desperate to find a way of surviving, landed élites eager to defend what was left of their privileges, and corporate representative institutions vainly attempting to remain free of bureaucratic influence and untainted by political agitation. No wonder that some conservatives looked backward, beyond the age of absolutism and revolution, and took their ideals from a mythically reconstituted past. Yet neither as theorists nor as practical politicians could conservatives evade the forces at work in nineteenth century politics. In time, conservatives—no less than liberals and socialists—felt the theoretical and practical pull of both bureaucracy and democracy. An important moment in this process of ideological adjustment can be seen in the work of Friedrich Julius Stahl.

Stahl belonged to a different generation and grew up in a different world form that of Gentz, Müller, and Haller. He was born in 1802, too late to experience the revolution first hand; his grandfather, who reared him, was the elder of Munich's small Jewish community. At seventeen, Stahl converted to Protestantism, changed his name, and embraced the patriotic ideals then sweeping through German universities. As a teacher of law at Munich in the late 1820s, Stahl came into contact with Schelling and other romantic thinkers, who strengthened his commitment to religious orthodoxy and conservative politics. In 1832 he moved to the University of Erlangen, where he published treatises on legal theory and served as the university's delegate to the Bavarian *Landtag*. During the 1840s he was among those right-wing intellectuals brought to Berlin by Frederick William IV to combat Hegelian subversion by upholding Christian dogma. A friend of the Gerlach brothers and other aristocratic political leaders, Stahl helped to formulate the first Protestant version of conservative ideology.[8]

Christianity provided the foundation for Stahl's life and thought. His conversion, unlike Heinrich Marx's or Heinrich Heine's, had not been a matter of convenience or opportunism; it was done at some personal cost and brought him not only a new set of beliefs but also a new personal identity and access to a new political community. Politics and religion, he was convinced, were inseparable; to be politically conservative required religious orthodoxy; indeed without Christianity conservatism was no more than a *vis inertiae*. Throughout his life, Stahl tried to reconcile power and revelation, ideology and belief, state and church by creating 'a doctrine of law and politics based on a Christian world view'. While he was sympathetic to certain aspects of Catholicism, Stahl's Christianity was resolutely Protestant. 'Evangelical freedom', he wrote, 'unconditionally binds a person to God's law, but it frees him in that, through grace, obedience to the law is a product of his own will and being.' Protestant freedom, therefore, rests on 'the free obedience of the Volk . . . [T]he priesthood of all believers corresponds to universal citizenship.'[9]

Despite the centrality of his religious convictions, Stahl acknowledged that politics was a human activity, created through a divinely inspired but secularly based historical process. He also recognized the need to take into account existing realities and historical trends: 'We must keep in mind not only what should happen but also what will happen.' Change, often painful and sometimes dangerous, was necessary, perhaps inevitable. The past, despite its many attractions, could not be reclaimed. He was persuaded, he wrote to a friend in 1834, that 'medieval principles and liberalism both have some truth in them, and in my concept of the state, I have tried to weave them together'.[10]

Stahl's most influential attempt to construct such a synthesis was his brief pamphlet, *Das monarchische Princip*, published in 1845. In contrast to Haller, who began his *Restauration* with a statement about the nature of the social order, Stahl opened his work with a historical assessment of what he called 'the innermost drive of the age. . . . the progress from corporate particularism to national

---

[8] Masur, *Stahl*, is still the best account of his youth. Grosser, *Grundlagen*, gives a useful summary of his ideas. See also Stahl's *Briefe*, edited and with an introduction by Olaf Koglin (Kiel, 1975).

[9] Martin, 'Motive', p. 362; Grosser, *Grundlagen*, pp. 19-20.

[10] Gerlach, *Revolution*, p. 31; Martin, 'Motive', p. 365, n. 2.

unity, from a patriarchal to a statist or constituional system'. This movement, Stahl argued, was irreversible. 'In our time, every healthy representative institution must represent both national unity and corporate hierarchy . . . the *Land* and the *Volk*.' The question confronting conservatives, therefore, was how to prevent these developments from leading to revolutionary upheaval or parliamentary hegemony. Stahl's response was concerned less with sovereignty—the legally defined locus of authority—than with the reality of power. As he presented it, the 'monarchical principle' was not so much a doctrine as a description of the conditions in which 'the prince himself has the right and power to govern'. There was a place here for representative institutions and constitutional government: 'the prince must heed the estates, just as they must heed the prince; they are two independent but different centres of power.' However, since the prince should not be dependent on the parliament, he had to be free to choose his ministers, initiate legislation, and determine the details of his budget. Although Stahl recognized the importance of constitutions, he knew that maintaining monarchical authority was not merely a matter of constitutional form. To defend himself, Stahl insisted, the king needed a cohesive administrative system. Indeed, one reason why the monarchical principle was both necessary and possible in Germany was the existence of an 'intelligent, honourable, and irreplaceable bureaucracy'. No wonder that Stahl's ideas would find particular resonance in the 1850s when bureaucratic repression replaced revolutionary fervour.[11]

Stahl differed from Müller and Haller in style and substance, in the questions he asked and the answers he proposed. He shared neither the former's romantic pathos nor the latter's systematic rationality—in fact, his clear-sighted calculations of what was necessary and possible remind us of the coming age of '*Realpolitik*.' Moreover, by setting the monarchical principle in the realm of constitutions, parliaments, and administration, he substantially broadened the range of conservative discourse and heightened its relevance to the contemporary world. But in two important ways Stahl remained close to the source of traditional conservatism. First, the powerful religious current in his thought kept him close to the pious circle of advisers around Frederick William IV. Second, like the other conservative ideologists we have considered, Stahl saw his primary task as the struggle against what he regarded

[11] Stahl, *Prinzip*, pp. v, viii, 18, 24, 27, 39.

as the party of rebellion and unbelief, a subversive coalition that embraced liberal constitutionalists and radical democrats, moderate reformers and violent revolutionaries. From this belief that there was but one fundamental cleavage in society—between the friends and enemies of religion, the forces of order and disruption, the defenders of truth and error—all conservatives drew their sense of purpose and identity.

Like their conservative rivals, liberals also had a dichotomous vision: they presented themselves as the party of movement, progress, and the future, locked in a historic struggle with the forces of order, reaction, and the past. However, liberals' relationship to revolutionary change was more complex than the conservatives'. Liberals could not deny the revolution's emancipatory purpose; they too stood for liberty, equality, and fraternity. But few liberals had much sympathy for revolutionary violence or democratic agitation. They hated and feared Jacobin terror no less than the staunchest conservative. This ambivalence about revolutionary democracy matched with the liberal movement's ambivalence about bureaucratic absolutism. On the one hand, liberals—like conservatives—condemned state despotism, arbitrary authority, and excessive administrative interference in private affairs. On the other hand, however, liberals acknowledged that the bureaucratic state had often been the instrument of progress and enlightenment in social, cultural, and legal affairs. Well before conservatives and socialists, liberal ideologues felt the magnetic pull of the state, whose power they hoped to use on behalf of their own interests and ideals.[12]

From the start, liberalism embraced a number of potentially divisive elements. Liberals were never entirely sure about the boundaries of their own movement, never confident that they knew who belonged and who did not. The problem of defining liberalism, which has always perplexed the movement's historians, was no less troubling to the liberals themselves. Of course, all liberals believed in liberty—'domestic freedom and foreign political independence' were the words that Paul Pfizer used to summarize 'Liberal Goals and Tasks' in an essay of 1832. What this

[12] For an introduction to liberalism, see the essays in Lothar Gall (ed.), *Liberalismus* (Cologne, 1976); Dieter Langewiesche, *Liberalismus in Deutschland* (Frankfurt, 1988); Jürgen Hess, *Bibliographie zum deutschen Liberalismus* (Göttingen, 1981). For a more extended version of the analysis given here, see Sheehan, *Liberalism*. Michael Neumüller, *Liberalismus und Revolution. Das Problem der Revolution in der deutschen liberalen Geschichtsschreibung des neunzehnten Jahrhunderts* (Düsseldorf, 1973), examines liberal attitudes towards revolution.

meant was easy enough to express negatively: most liberals agreed that freedom required an end to censorship and political oppression, outworn privilege and harmful social restraint, despotism and superstition. But while they were more or less agreed about what to oppose, liberals were deeply divided about freedom's scope, character, and implications. Many favoured economic freedom, some did not; a few advocated an extension of political liberties to all male citizens, most feared such democratization; some advocated corporate representation, others demanded western-style parliaments; some associated freedom with a strong administration, others wishes to curtail bureaucratic authority. In short, the freedom for which liberals fought had many sources, took many forms, and appealed to various groups for quite different reasons. This multiplicity was a reason for liberalism's rapid rise and impressive strength as well as for its internal conflicts and eventual decline.[13]

At the centre of liberal ideology was the *Volk*. In contrast to conservatives, who still talked about regional traditions, special privileges, and corporate distinctions, liberals spoke to and for a universal entity, the nation as a whole. The genealogy of liberal ideas about the *Volk* reaches back to the eighteenth-century concept of national culture that we considered in Chapter 3. But in contrast to men like Lessing and Herder, liberal theorists gave the *Volk* a constitutional function: within the context of their ideology, the *Volk* became the focus of their efforts, the foundation of their movement, and the source of their claim to set the course for the German future. As Pfizer put it, liberals would lead the state towards what 'the collectivity in its rational interests wants or must want'. In this sense, liberalism was not *an* opinion, but *the* only rational opinion, not *a* party, but *the* party representing the whole, the common good, the 'real' *Volk*.[14]

Unlike the grateful recipients of state support whom we found in cameralist thought, the liberal *Volk* was not passive. Every liberal believed in some measure of political participation and in some sort of representative government. Friedrich Dahlmann, for example, wrote in his influential *Politik* that one man should be born to rule, but no one should be born to serve; the public sphere should be open to all. Similarly, Carl von Rotteck defined the purpose of the *Staatslexikon* as 'the broadest possible dissemination of healthy political opinions among all classes of society . . .'. Yet most liberals qualified their belief in the *Volk's* potential universality with a series of practical restrictions. Thus David Hansemann advocated majority rule but did not believe it could be achieved by counting heads; only those with education and property, what he called 'the real power of the nation', could be expected to have the skills and interests necessary to govern. Versions of Hansemann's phrase 'die eigentliche Kraft der Nation' appear again and again in liberal discussions of politics and society. The term *eigentlich* suggests that there is a *Volk* more 'real' than the masses, whom liberals viewed with a mixture of fear and condescension.[15]

Most liberals would have agreed that the 'real' *Volk* corresponded to the *Mittelstand* or *Mittelklasse*, which Dahlmann once called 'the core of the population'. This was the social group, Dahlmann went on, to which every government had to pay attention: 'Since now it represents the political centre of gravity, the whole society follows its movement.' To belong to the Mittelstand required 'independence', which, everyone recognized, demanded a certain amount of financial security and social autonomy. No less important, however, was the independence of spirit, rationality, and disinterestedness necessary for proper participation in public affairs.

Like so much liberal vocabulary, *Mittelstand* fused economic, social, and moral categories. The middle groups in society were somehow 'in-between' the very rich and the very poor, the aristocracy and the masses, but they were also morally central to the entire social order, at once the heart and instrument of the common good. As a moral category, the *Mittelstand*, like the *Volk*, was potentially universal, even though in practice its advocates realized that membership would have to be limited to men with property and education. Just as the *Volk* might degenerate into a mob, so the *Mittelstand* could lose its claim to moral superiority if, as Dahlmann warned, it acted like a mass and thus was transformed into a 'bildungs- und vermögensloser Pöbel', a *canaille* without cultivation or property.[16]

Who should be active participants in public life and who should

[15] Dahlmann, *Politik*, p. 231; *StL*, quoted in Haltern, 'Bildung', p. 76; Hansen, *Briefe*, i. 17.

[16] Dahlmann, *Politik*, p. 200. For an excellent analysis of how these terms are used in the *Staatslexikon*, see Martin Schumacher, 'Gesellschafts- und Ständebegriff um 1846. Ein Beitrag zum sozialen Bild des süddeutschen Liberalismus nach dem Rotteck-Welckerschen Staatslexikon', unpublished dissertation (Göttingen, 1956), especially fos. 211 ff.

be content with passivity? Very few liberals believed that women, children, or servants were sufficiently independent to act politically; others would have extended this list to include wage labourers, apprentices, small farmers, and shopkeepers. Often enough liberals could conceal their uncertainties and division on this issue behind a cloud of moral rhetoric, but on questions like the suffrage, evasion was impossible. No wonder that Rotteck viewed voting rights as the single most difficult constitutional question which liberals would have to face. In his article in the *Staatslexikon* on 'Census, insbesondere Wahlcensus', Rotteck wrestled with how to limit political rights to those who would use them wisely. It could not be done, he realized, on an individual basis; only groups can be included and excluded. Rotteck drew his line along the social frontier between those with and without the ability to support themslves—what he calls 'Selbständigkeit des Lebensunterhaltes'. Other, less democratically inclined liberals were quite prepared to set rather high economic requirements for voting and to advocate indirect voting and various pre-conditions for office-holding in order to ensure that political power did not pass into unworthy hands. As we shall see, liberals remained divided on the suffrage question, which often brought to the surface disagreements and self-doubts about their relationship to the *Volk* for whom they claimed to speak.[17]

Liberals were also divided on the question of the *Volk's* relationship with the state. Almost every liberal believed in a constitution through which the power of the state could be legally limited and politically directed towards progressive ends. For example, here is how Theodor Welcker described 'the concept of the state' in the *Staatslexikon*:

The state is the sovereign, moral, personally and vitally free social association of a *Volk*, which, under a collective constitution, in freely constituted popular assemblies and led by a constitutionally independent government, strives for just freedom . . . and the happiness of all its members.

Represer.tation was an essential element in liberal political theory. To earn the right to call itself free, Heinrich von Gagern believed, a *Volk* had to be able to make its own laws 'by means of representatives in agreement with the government'. Such a system would enable what Rotteck called the *Gesamtwille* to be realized.

---

[17] *StL* (1st edn.), iii. 376–7. On the suffrage issue, see Boberach, *Wahlrechtsfrage*; Gagel, *Wahlrechtsfrage*.

But virtually no liberals, including Rotteck, believed that the *Volk's* representatives should be able to dictate the character and course of the government. When liberals talked about 'ministerial responsibility', they almost always had in mind the government's juridical responsibility to act legally, not its political responsibility to follow the will of the majority. Their assumption, as we can see in both Welcker's and Gagern's formulation, was that the people's representatives and the government would act harmoniously on the basis of a shared vision of political rationality and social well-being. About what would happen if this harmony broke down, liberals were uncertain. Even Rotteck, who professed to believe that a republic was the best governmental form, maintained that, if the executive did not retain 'a certain independence' from the legislature, republican institutions would remain 'dangerous and unstable'. Most liberals were more insistent that the ultimate authority should not reside in the *Volk* or the *Volk's* representatives. For example, Droysen, who represented the more conservative brand of north German liberalism, explicitly condemned the separation of powers ('inherently senseless and illusory in practice') as well as the idea of a contract between monarch and people.[18]

German liberals' constitutional theory was greatly complicated by the fact that it had to have both a domestic and a foreign political dimension. Pfizer's innocuous phrase about 'domestic freedom and foreign political independence' concealed a nest of questions concerning the nation's geographical shape as well as its institutional character. For most liberals, domestic and foreign policy were inseparable elements in a single enterprise. Domestic reform, they believed, was essential for national power, just as national renewal would inevitably bring about domestic progress. At the root of domestic and foreign policy was the same *Volk,* which justified liberals' claims to power at home and Germans' claims to nationhood on the international scene. By setting the German struggle for national identity in an ideological context, liberals were able to give it a new sense of political direction and significance.

Almost no liberals imagined a popular nationalism that would wipe away the existing structure of states—even though some regarded the smaller members of the Confederation as expendable. Instead, a majority looked to a national dualism of states and nation comparable to the constitutional dualism of monarch and parliament. Welcker, for example, proposed that Germans create a

[18] *StL* (1st edn.), xv. 66–7; Gagern, *Liberalismus*, p. 124; Schib, *Grundlagen*, pp. 59, 62; Droysen, *Schriften*, p. 114. See also Angermann, *Mohl*, pp. 402 ff.

national parliament and army to supplement the Confederation's diet as instruments of unity. A few liberals recognized that the nation might have to be created from above, by a state. Pfizer believed that it would be much easier to go from a united, authoritarian nation to a liberal one than from a collection of liberal polities to a single nation. 'It is doubtful', he wrote, 'whether great personal freedom in the constitutional states would lead us to unity. On the other hand, it is not to be doubted that once unity had been obtained, freedom . . . cannot but be at hand.'[19] As Pfizer recognized, this position had a clear and necessary tactical corollary: the best hope for a united Germany was Prussia, the only state potentially in a position to impose a national solution on central Europe. Among those who read Pfizer's work with approval was the young Johann Gustav Droysen, whose importance for the evolution of German historiography will be considered in Chapter 13. Like Pfizer, Droysen regarded a reformed Hohenzollern monarchy as the natural centre for a new German nation. Neither man, however, saw this as a move towards Prussian hegemony since both envisioned a dissolution of Prussia into provinces, which would then be joined with the other German states as component parts of what Droysen called the 'Prussian empire'.[20]

Few liberals in the 1830s and 1840s realized that they might have to choose between Austria and Prussia, and no one thought they would have to choose between unity and freedom. Just as they believed in an ultimate harmony of state and *Volk*, so they were confident in the emergence of a balance between particularism and unity. 'Freedom', Pfizer wrote, 'has now become a necessity, and no earthly power may hope to deflect these world-shaking ideas, which will find their way through every limit and inhibition until they follow that course set for them by a higher power.' Liberalism's triumph was woven into the pattern of the age. Time was on their side: as one of them remarked, 'We are the times.'[21]

But with this profound belief that they represented the wave of the future went an unmistakable undercurrent of uneasiness— about the reliability of the *Volk*, the possibilities of political action, the dangers of revolution, and, ultimately, the legitimacy of their own claims. Liberals rarely believed in the right of rebellion; most distrusted democracy; almost all condemned the mob, which

[19] Pfizer, 'Gedanken', pp. 337–8.
[20] On Droysen's early views of the German question, see Gilbert, *Droysen*.
[21] *StL* (1st edn.), ix. 730.

Welcker regarded as 'a more savage enemy of the common good than any other'. This lingering uneasiness is shown in Pfizer's insistence that the monarch had to be strong enough to 'grasp or pull in the reigns every time the *Volk* lacks the decisive will, or because of factionalism or flaccidity, approaches the dangers of dissolution'. Liberals, Pfizer went on, cannot demand more freedom than state or society is prepared to absorb: 'Slow progress is a characteristic of freedom.' At the heart of the liberal vision of the *Volk*, therefore, was a distinctive mixture of self-confidence and anxiety, faith and fear, theoretical reliance and practical abhorrence.[22]

To the liberals' left, the ideological spectrum was marked by a steadily increasing commitment to the *Volk* and a corresponding reluctance to work with and within the existing states. Democrats like Julius Fröbel, for example, tried to strip away the ambiguities and ambivalence with which liberals surrounded the relationship of *Volk* and state. 'The movement of our time', he wrote in 1843, 'points towards the more and more decisive realization of true Democracy.' Democracy, therefore, is the political side of the contemporary revolution, 'the true state'. In fact, Fröbel viewed 'state and democracy' as 'interchangeable concepts'. He wanted to put the *Volk* at the institutional centre of the state; for him it was to be the practical as well as the symbolic source of legitimate power. The ideal polity must be some kind of republic. The democratic left also defined the *Volk* more generously than most liberals. When Robert Blum talked about the 'real' *Volk*, he meant 'citizens, craftsmen, and workers'. Most democrats, therefore, favoured some form of universal manhood suffrage. From this ideological radicalism about state and *Volk* flowed a strategy of direct action and political confrontation. In comparison to liberals, democrats were less likely to think that states could be turned into reliable instruments of reform or that the Confederation could be reconstructed as a basis for national unity. Democrats were prepared to start again with a new, radically different political order.[23]

While we can find the roots of later ideological divisions between liberals and democrats in *Vormärz* political thought, it is important

[22] Gall, *Constant*, p. 90; *StL* (1st edn.), ix. 721.
[23] Koch, *Demokratie*, pp. 17, 102; Schmidt, *Blum*, pp. 73–4. There is a good introduction to the problem of German democracy in Langewiesche, *Liberalismus*. See also Snell, *Movement*; Lenore O'Boyle, 'The Democratic Left in Germany, 1848', *JMH* 32/4 (1961), 374–83. Only a few democrats considered extending political rights to women as well as men: on the beginning of political feminism, see the material in Mohrmann (ed.), *Frauenemanzipation*.

to realize that few contemporaries saw these divisions as clearly as we do. At least until the mid-1840s, the political opposition—which ranged from moderate liberals to radical democrats—shared a common antagonism to the status quo and often suffered from the same kind of repressive measures. Government repression also interfered with the creation of national participatory institutions and inhibited the free flow of ideas, thereby further limiting people's ability to exchange and clarify their political views. After 1830 the level of political involvement certainly increased, but its loci were usually fragmented institutions, closely tied to a particular region or limited to a distinctive purpose. The principal means of communication across the German states were publications like the *Staatslexikon* or theoretical tracts like Dahlmann's *Politik*, in which abstract and moral categories frequently concealed fundamental sources of division and uncertainty. This should not surprise us: in itself, political language is always ambiguous enough to invite misunderstanding; ideological alignments and implications are usually clarified by action, not theoretical debates or scholarly disputations.

The political opposition's self-image reflected a world in which the formulation of ideas had a particular primacy over the execution of policy. For most liberals, belonging to a party was a question of opinion and sensibility, not organization and action: 'I don't deny being a party man', wrote Heinrich von Gagern, 'what else does that mean besides having an opinion and seeking to realize it.' Similarly, Rotteck distinguished between *party* and *faction*, with the former defined only through what he called a 'sensibility' (*Gesinnung*). Even in Baden, where public life was unusually free and political debate exceptionally vigorous, political organizations and alignments emerged slowly and unevenly. As one liberal parliamentarian described the situation at the end of the 1830s, 'differences of opinion . . . can often split us into parties. But how often, indeed I would say always, unanimity reigned in all important questions touching the entire fatherland. . . .' This image of a single movement, sharing a commitment to the common good and inspired by the same, independent spirit, would gradually dissolve as liberals sought to test their ideological maps against the obdurate realities of the terrain through which they sought to move.[24]

---

[24] Gagern, *Liberalismus*, p. 133; Gall, 'Problem', p. 168; Conze, in Conze (ed.), *Staat*, p. 232.

ii. CRACKS IN THE DAM: GERMANS AND THE REVOLUTION OF 1830

The revolution of 1830 marked a significant turning-point in the evolution of German political life. In contrast to 1789, when most Germans viewed the news from Paris with unconcern or incomprehension, in 1830 the fall of the Bourbons had an immediate impact.[25] Metternich, summoned home from the elegant pleasures of his country estate, regarded the revolution 'as the collapse of the dam in Europe'. Hegel spoke of 'a crisis in which everything that was formerly valid seems to have become problematical'. But to progressives, the revolution and its aftermath were a welcome sign that the arid era of reaction might be coming to an end. Rotteck, who had already established himself as a leader of the Baden opposition, believed that there had never been a year 'of such immeasurable and consequential importance'. The young historian Georg Gervinus felt the world open up around him. In words that nicely illustrate contemporary liberal rhetoric, Gervinus rejoiced that 'slowly but surely maturing *Bildung* bears fruit in Europe [and] spiritual endeavour penetrates and permeates the status quo'. Under the weight of history and experience, 'despotism and obscurantism' would have to bow their heads. The days of the 'ultras' had passed, wrote the radical poet Graf von Platen,

> Du rühmst die Zeit, in welcher deine Kaste
> Genoss ein ruhig Glück?
> Was aber, ausser einer Puderquaste,
> Liess jene goldne Zeit zurück?

There was more than enough going on in 1830 and 1831 to feed reactionary fears and liberal hopes. From the Iberian peninsula to the Russian frontier, social conflicts and political demonstrations threatened public order. In the Low Countries, where Belgians fought for independence from the Dutch, and in Congress Poland, where Polish nationalists rebelled against Russia, the international settlement so painstakingly created in 1815 came under direct attack.[26]

Few German states escaped some measure of unrest, which ranged in severity from minor clashes with the police to full-scale rebellion. In Aachen, for example, citizens put on the *tricolore* to

---

[25] On the impact of 1830, see Wirtz, '*Widersetzlichkeiten*', and the essays in Schieder (ed.), *Liberalismus*.

[26] Srbik, *Metternich*, i. 647; Toews, *Hegelianism*, p. 218; Carl von Rotteck, 'Das Jahr 1830', in his *Schriften*, i. 286; Gervinus, *Leben*, pp. 238–9.

express their solidarity with the French. Resentment of Prussia, distress caused by falling wages and rising prices, and a variety of other discontents created an atmosphere of anticipation and unrest. Early in September, crowds of craftsmen and workers gathered, defied the authorities, and eventually turned their anger against the property of some unpopular manufacturers. Only the arrival of two thousand combat-ready Prussian troops restored order. Comparable events shook the establishment in Cologne, Elberfeld, Frankfurt, Munich, Chemnitz, Leipzig, and many other urban centres. There were bread riots in Kassel and unrest throughout the Hessian countryside where peasants burned manorial records and attacked customs stations. Even in Vienna and Berlin, minor disturbances occurred, although in these capitals the forces of order were powerful enough to prevent any serious trouble.[27]

As is almost always the case in revolutionary situations, the more closely we examine the course of events, the more we become aware of the importance of local conditions, particular incidents, and the actions of a few individuals. This may have been particularly true in the disorders of 1830, where a variety of motives pushed men and women over the brink of rebellion. In Leipzig, for example, trouble started on 2 September after apprentice blacksmiths gathered to protest a fellow artisan's arrest. Other currents of discontent swiftly raised the level of violence: on 4 September angry journeymen attacked the Brockhaus printing firm and threatened to destroy the machines they feared would put them out of work. Elsewhere in the city, people had their own scores to settle. Wilhelm Weitling, a future radical leader who was by no means an unsympathetic observer, has left us an account of his observations of crowds that roamed Leipzig's streets during those late summer nights:

In one night the people were masters of the city and its environs. Because they did not know what else to do, they set about to destroy a dozen houses. Everyone sought to express his anger in his own way: some [attacked] the villa of a merchant who had employed locksmiths from outside the city and thus deprived citizens of their proper work, others broke up the furniture of an unpopular lawyer, while some apprentices demolished the house and furniture of an official employed in the passport office and hated for his harshness.

We can see here the energy of the crowd, as well as its lack of social direction. The rebels' goals were revenge on particular individuals and the satisfaction of immediate demands rather that the creation

[27] Husung, 'Gewaltprotest'; Bock, *Illusion*.

of a new social order. Not surprisingly, in Leipzig, as in every other German city, rebellion was easily repressed.[28]

Few liberals took part in these social protests; most opposed what Rotteck called 'crimes against the community without concern for the fatherland and constitution—which have as their impulse and expression the mob's personal passions, crude energy, irrationality, and larcenous desires'.[29] In some places, however, local liberal leaders were able to take advantage of the social unrest and extract reforms from frightened governments. This 'alliance' between the political and social opposition, often accidental in origin and always attenuated by deep distrust, produced some important political changes in 1830 and foreshadowed the constellation of forces which would lead to the liberals' brief triumph in 1848.

In Brunswick, where the level of both social and political discontent was high, a group of notables led by an official named Wilhelm Bode became involved in a complex series of negotiations to replace the discredited ruler, Duke Carl, with his brother William. These negotiations succeeded because of Bode's skilful legal manœuvres and because both sides feared a massive popular uprising. Eventually, the principle of legitimacy was sacrificed, Carl was deposed, William became duke. In 1832 he agreed to replace the traditional corporate order with a representative constitution on the south German model.

Hesse-Kassel also emerged from the disorders of 1830 with a new constitution. Like many of his fellow rulers, Elector William II had to confront angry crowds in his capital—rebellious peasants and an imposing collection of educated and propertied men, who were appalled by his embarrassing efforts to make his mistress a princess. The *Landtag*, whose progressive forces were led by the Marburg jurist Sylvester Jordan, was able to force William to accept an extremely progressive constitution that established a unicameral legislature with clearly defined powers, including the right to take legal action against the ruler's ministers. Although it did not abandon the principle of the ruler's sovereign power, the constitution did represent the clearest and most forceful expression of the *Rechtsstaat*, both as an instrument for protecting individual

---

[28] Bock, *Illusion*, p. 76. See also Bazillion, 'Violence'.
[29] Quoted in Rudolf Muhs, 'Zwischen Staatsreform und politischem Protest. Liberalismus in Sachsen zur Zeit des Hambacher Festes', in Schieder (ed.), *Liberalismus*, p. 213.

rights and as a means of preventing irresponsible governmental action.[30]

In comparison to Brunswick and Hesse, Hanover had been fairly quiet during the summer of 1830. In January 1831, however, the university town of Göttingen was the scene of a miniature revolution by students and citizens. Even though the insurrection collapsed after three exciting days, it did help to encourage a series of governmental reforms that culminated in the promulgation of a new constitution, which finally went into effect in September 1833. As we shall see presently, this constitution was abrogated just four years later.

The same wave of disorder that drove the rulers of Brunswick, Hesse and Hanover to compromise also compelled the king of Saxony to grant his state a written constitution. In 1830 the situation in Saxony was among the most volatile in Europe. At the Congress of Vienna the state had lost two-fifths of its territory and much of its foreign political significance. Largely untouched by the era of reforms, it retained an antiquated set of estates that were dominated by the aristocracy, a poorly integrated administration, and a repressive seigniorial system. Its ruler in 1830 was elderly, inexperienced, and unpopular. Coexisting with these stagnant political institutions was a dynamic economy, centred in Leipzig and fed by an active industrial sector in the countryside. When the troubles started in 1830, first in Leipzig, then in other towns and villages throughout the state, a group of progressive civil servants realized that reform was necessary if the dynasty was to survive. Using the dangers of social upheaval as their lever, these men were able to force out of office the king's most reactionary advisers, establish a co-regency with the popular young prince, Frederick August, and begin work on a constitution. After some painfully achieved compromises with the old nobility, the reformers were finally able to promulgate a constitution in September 1831.[31]

At the same time that the old order seemed to be collapsing in these northern and central states, the events of 1830 injected new vitality into the public life of the constitutional states in the south and west. This was most obviously the case in Baden, where the year began with the reign of a new ruler, Duke Leopold, who was sympathetic to progressive ideas and closely associated with liberal

[30] Bullik, Staat.
[31] See the essay by Muhs cited in n. 29 and Gerhard Schmidt, Die Staatsreform in Sachsen in der ersten Hälfte des 19. Jahrhunderts (Weimar, 1966).

members of the bureaucracy like Ludwig Winter. In the *Landtag* elections held during the autumn of 1830, liberal candidates did extremely well, so that, when the parliament met early the following year, it was filled with men who wanted to abolish restrictions on public debate, clarify the powers of the legislature, and increase social and economic freedom. One of the first results of this new spirit was a reformed press law that defied the Confederation's endorsement of censorship and guaranteed freedom to express political opinion. Newspapers, usually with a liberal political orientation, began to appear in cities throughout the state.[32]

Although the king of Württemberg resisted pressures for reform throughout 1830, he could not dampen the spread of political agitation among his subjects. During the *Landtag* election campaign, people formed committees in which they discussed the political opinions of candidates and sought to influence the outcome of the voting, while the *Hochwächter*, a politically engaged liberal newspaper, mobilized progressive voters. When the new *Landtag* convened at the end of 1831, it contained a substantial liberal minority. From 1831 to 1833, parliamentarians such as Paul Pfizer, a lawyer and former civil servant, and Friedrich Römer, a judicial official, struggled to make the government 'pay attention to the judgement of the public and take into account the mood of the *Volk*'.[33]

In Bavaria, new elections also returned a large number of liberal sympathizers, much to the displeasure of King Ludwig, who had appointed Eduard von Schenk to head a politically and religiously conservative government. When students at the University of Munich celebrated Christmas 1830 with a political demonstration, the king decided to exert his authority by decreeing a repressive press law. This was strongly opposed by the new *Landtag* when it met in February 1831. For the next several months the *Landtag* fought with the government, first over the press law, then over a series of other issues. For a while the progressives won some astonishing victories: in May they forced Schenk's resignation and in June passed a new press ordinance. But by December the king had had enough. After closing the *Landtag*, he appointed a new ministry under Prince Wrede, a tough, conservative soldier who

---

[32] Lee, *Politics*, pp. 133 ff. See also Hans Fenske, *Der liberale Südwesten. Freiheitliche und demokratische Traditionen in Baden und Württemberg, 1790–1933* (Stuttgart, 1981).

[33] Brandt, 'Gesellschaft', p. 115. See also Müth, *Emanzipation*; Brandt, *Parlamentarismus*.

was ready to restore royal authority. At that point, the focus of political activity shifted from the parliament to popular protests and from Munich to the Palatinate.[34]

There were several reasons why this region became the most politically dynamic German area during the final stage of the revolutionary upheavals of 1830–2. Like many areas that developed strong opposition movements in the *Vormärz*, the Palatinate had had a turbulent history during the Napoleonic era before it ended up as part of Bavaria, a state for which its inhabitants felt little loyalty or affection. Dismayed by the severing of their traditional ties and resentful about their annexation by an essentially foreign regime, many inhabitants of the Palatinate were prepared to think of alternatives to the status quo. Moreover, the region's social and economic condition was adversely affected, first by an unfavourable commercial agreement signed by Prussia, Hesse, Württemberg, and Bavaria in 1829, and then by a disastrously poor harvest in 1831. Finally, because censorship was more lenient here than in the core provinces of Bavaria, the Palatinate seemed to be a natural refuge for liberal journalists driven north by the new reactionary turn in government policy. Chief among them was Johann Georg August Wirth, the thirty-three-year-old editor of *Die Tribune* who became the personification of the Palatinate's protest movement.[35]

In January 1832 Wirth established the *Pressverein* to support the propagation of liberal ideals throughout German Europe. The *Pressverein* grew with astonishing speed: between February and September 1832 it attracted five thousand members, about half from the Palatinate, another third from the rest of Bavaria, and the remainder from other German states. These people were drawn from throughout the middle strata of society—craftsmen, shopkeepers, and other small businessmen, as well as students, lawyers, journalists, and academics. Since its leaders wanted an organization that would be more broadly based than the usual Verein, they set up over a hundred branches in the course of 1832. But they were not able to co-ordinate their activities or settle their recurrent internal conflicts. Moreover, while the *Pressverein* was an explicitly political organization, devoted to mobilizing support behind a specific programme, its leaders were most comfortable with the sort of educational efforts so characteristic of German public life. Both organizationally and tactically, therefore, the *Pressverein*

---

[34] Schieder, 'Liberalismus'.
[35] In addition to Schieder's essay cited in n. 34, see the essays by Foerster and Wegert in Schieder (ed.), *Liberalismus*.

represented a transitional phase between the traditional political public and the participatory institutions that would begin to emerge in the 1840s.[36]

Members of the *Pressverein* were active in planning what is usually seen as the highpoint of early German liberalism, the great popular festival held in May 1832 at the old castle ruins near the town of Hambach. Festivals to celebrate an event or an individual had, of course, been part of European life for centuries. In the 1790s the French revolutionaries had transformed such festivals from expressions of religious devotion or traditional deference into demonstrations of secular faith and political solidarity. As we have seen, the Wartburg meeting of 1817 was meant to be a German version of these revolutionary fetes, a celebration of the *Volk* and an inspiration for future action. After 1830 political festivals again became popular, usually in the form of public banquets similar to those which had helped marshal French opposition to the Bourbons. The Hambach gathering was an extension of these liberal festivities, a *Konstitutionsfest* led by representatives of the *Volk*. Larger, more socially diverse, and more politically informed than the Wartburg meeting, the Hambacher Fest was meant to honor and inspire the new political spirit of the age. Heine, working from an account provided by Ludwig Börne, wrote that it 'shouted the sunrise songs for modern times. . . . [Even if] unreasonable things were often said there, none the less the ultimate authority of reason was recognized. . . .'[37]

On the morning of 27 May, between twenty thousand and thirty thousand people gathered at the Schiesshaus at Neustadt and marched, with flags of black-red-gold and a banner proclaiming 'Deutschlands Wiedergeburt', to the castle ruins. Biographical information on 187 participants from the Palatinate itself yields the data shown in table 10.1 on the festival's social character.

Wirth gave the keynote address, whose tone and content suggest both the rhetorical range and underlying assumptions of the early opposition movement. Germans, Wirth insisted, had to work for their own freedom; foreign intervention from nearby France was to be resisted. The best instrument of liberation was 'an alliance of patriots with the purpose of teaching the entire *Volk* about the kind

[36] Cornelia Foerster, *Der Press- und Vaterlandsverein von 1832/33: Sozialstruktur und Organisationsformen der bürgerlichen Bewegung in der Zeit des Hambacher Festes* (Trier, 1982).

[37] Heine, 'Über Ludwig Börne', in his *Werke*, ii. 747 ff. On the Fest, see the works by Foerster, Wegert, and Schieder just cited and the valuable documents in Valentin, *Fest*.

TABLE 10.1. *Residents of the Palatinate at the Hambacher Fest, 1832* [a]

Academically-trained Professionals	29
Businessmen and Merchants	36
Farmers	6
Foresters	1
Printers and Booksellers	10
Craftsmen	34
Farmworkers	4
Employees, Wage-labourers	10
Students	57

Note: [a] Based on a list of subversives compiled by the Bavarian government.

Source: Süss, *Pfälzer*, p. 152.

of reforms necessary for Germany'. Confusion, division, and organizational diversity can defeat the opposition, he warned, but clarity and unity will render it invincible. If only

the purest, most able, and courageous patriots could agree . . . if only twenty such men, bound together by a common cause and led by a man they trusted . . . tirelessly pursued their mission . . . then the great work must succeed and the forces of treason would sink into the dust before the power of patriotic love and the omnipotence of public opinion.

To Wirth, political action was a matter of education rather than power. In order to further the cause of reform, one had to tell the *Volk* the truth, make them aware of what was needed, lead them to enlightenment. Once that was done, the inherent power of public opinion would do the rest. There was no need for violence or bloodshed.[38]

The Hambach gathering was also addressed by Philipp Jakob Siebenpfeiffer, a tailor's son who had managed to become a civil servant, Daniel Ludwig Pistor, a radical lawyer and member of the Munich *Pressverein*, Karl Heinrich Brüggemann, a law student and representative of the secret *Burschenschaften*, and many others. The speakers represented different viewpoints and political strategies, but all emphasized the great goals of German rebirth 'in Einheit and Freiheit', popular sovereignty, and economic freedom. Speaking for the radical left, Brüggemann threatened rebellion if the

[38] Mommsen, *Parteiprogramme*, pp. 117 ff.

governments ignored the law, but even he recognized that the time for 'Losschlagen' had not yet come. Surely the respectable, solid citizens who made up the majority of his audience must have agreed; only a few wanted to turn the festival into a direct confrontation with the German Confederation. In the end, therefore, the result of the Hambach meeting was a reorganization of the *Pressverein* into a *Reformverein* and the resolution of some differences among rival journalists. The men at Hambach wanted to found newspapers not build barricades. That they sought to convert rather than destroy their enemies is suggested by a contemporary lithograph that shows reactionaries being dragged to the temple of enlightenment—there is no guillotine in sight.[39]

For Metternich, the Hambach meeting was just one more in a series of disturbing events, all of which seemed to be contrary to Austrian interests. In 1830 he had been shaken by the Belgian and Polish rebellions and had sent Austrian troops to help restore order in central Italy. The following year he had had to use all his diplomatic skills to torpedo moves towards closer military co-operation between Prussia and the south German states during a brief 'war scare' on the French border.[40] In 1832 he viewed the persistence of agitation in the Palatinate as a sign of the Bavarian government's apparent inability to stem the tide of radicalism within its frontiers. Since this could expose the Confederation's western flank to the unwholesome influence of liberal ideas, it was time to act.

Despite its orderly character and modest results, Hambach presented Metternich with a perfect excuse to rally the reactionary forces within the Confederation. 'Le libéralisme a cédé la place au radicalisme,' he told his ambassador to Berlin on 10 June. Because 'les questions simples ont toujours un grand avantage sur celles compliquées', he much preferred dealing with affairs like the Hambach Fest rather than with the debates that took place in various German *Landtage*; in the former, the subversive forces were open, in the latter shrouded by hypocrisy. Over the next few weeks Metternich sought to use Hambach—as he had once used the murder of Kotzebue—to rally his supporters and bully his opponents among the German states. On 28 June the diet passed the so-called 'Six Articles', which began by expressing the German states' 'grateful recognition' of Prussia's and Austria's efforts for

[39] Valentin, *Fest*, p. 48.
[40] Robert Billinger, 'The War Scare of 1831 and Prussian-South German Plans for the End of Austrian Dominance in Germany', *CEH* 9/3 (1976), 203–19.

the 'common good of the German fatherland'. The rest of the document reaffirmed the principle of monarchical authority and established a commission to ensure that the German states would conform. On 5 July the diet voted for the 'Ten Articles', which underscored existing rules on censorship, political organizations, and other forms of public activity; the member states promised to send military assistance to any government threatened by unrest.[41]

Metternich's counter-offensive against the revolution continued for the next two years. In June 1833 the Confederation formed a Central Bureau of Political Investigation, which would examine more than two thousand suspicious individuals during its nine-year history. In September, the chancellor brought together the rulers of Austria, Prussia, and Russia at Münchengrätz, where they pledged to stand firm against revolutionary change and to act together to solve the questions arising from the Ottoman Empire's continued decline. Fortified with this new version of the 'Holy Alliance', Metternich convened a ministerial conference at Vienna from January to June 1834, which issued a long memorandum (the 'Sixty Articles') on monarchical authority and the need for total control over dissent. While this document masked the threat of intervention with offers of assistance, its message to the more tolerant governments was clear enough: get your houses in order or risk reprisals from a reactionary coalition led by the two great powers.

Most rulers were only too glad to follow Metternich's lead. King Ludwig of Bavaria, who had been on an extended visit to Italy during the first half of 1832, returned to his capital on 18 June and appointed Prince Wrede *ausserordentlicher Hofkommissar* for the Palatinate. With 8,500 men—almost half the total Bavarian army— at his disposal, Wrede established martial law in the restless province. Wirth, Siebenpfeiffer, and several other Hambach speakers were tried, found guilty, and sent to prison. Brüggemann, twice arrested by the authorities in Baden, was finally deported to Prussia, where he was condemned to death but eventually pardoned. Pistor and a few others fled across the frontier to France.

A similar pattern was repeated throughout the Confederation. Even before the Hambacher Fest, the king of Württemberg had issued a decree outlawing all *Vereine* that 'were concerned with parliamentary affairs or were designed to instruct parliamentary delegates'. Early in 1833 he prohibited the Press from mentioning anything having to do with *Landtag* elections. In Baden, pressure

---

[41] Metternich quoted in Valentin, *Fest*, pp. 13–40. On the Confederation's reaction, see Huber, ii. 151 ff.; and Huber, *Dokumente*, i. 119 ff.

from the Confederation was necessary before the government would take extreme measures against the liberal opposition. In the summer of 1832 the diet declared Baden's press law to be null and void and at the same time put Rotteck and Welcker, Baden's two most prominent liberals, on its list of wanted subversives. The duke, whose own impatience with the *Landtag* had been growing steadily, now took action. The government vetoed Rotteck's election as mayor of Freiburg and began to move against disloyal civil servants in the parliament.

The force of reaction was felt even more sharply in Hesse-Kassel, Hanover, and Saxony, where constitutional regimes had just recently been established. In Hesse, the new elector began a prolonged campaign against his *Landtag* which eventually resulted in the arrest and conviction of its spokesman, Sylvester Jordan. The Saxon government also turned against reform, repressed political agitation, and converted the *Landtag* into what one observer called 'as rare a spectacle of decorum and pliability as the heart of man need desire'.[42]

The reactionary shift in 1832 was greeted by protests, especially in the Palatinate, where people signed petitions and newspaper announcements condemning the government for violating the rights of its citizens. But only a few Germans were willing to take more drastic steps. In Frankfurt, a handful of old *Burschenschaftler* formed an underground organization that they hoped would spark a new wave of rebellion. But when these woefully incompetent conspirators seized the Frankfurt police station in April 1833, they were swiftly overpowered by the authorities.[43] Neither peaceful protests nor abortive rebellions deterred the governments from their counter-revolutionary course. Wrede's troops pacified the Palatinate, political organizations were dissolved, and more pliable men once again set the tone for parliamentary life. The forces of reform, which had once seemed so formidable, crumbled when confronted by the armed might of the states. The same political fragmentation that had enabled liberals to push individual governments towards compromise now made it possible for the forces of order to isolate and defeat the opposition.

But in comparison to the repressive tranquillity that followed the

[42] G. R. Gleig, *Germany, Bohemia, and Hungary Visited in 1837* (London, 1839), i. 193–4.

[43] On the background of this affair, see Wolfgang Hardtwig, 'Protestformen und Organisationsstrukturen der deutschen Burschenschaft, 1815–1833', in H. Reinalter (ed.), *Demokratische und soziale Protestbewegungen in Mitteleuropa, 1815–1848/49* (Frankfurt, 1986), 37–75.

Karlsbad Decrees of 1819, the reactionary triumphs of the early 1830s were incomplete and short-lived. Despite Metternich's mobilization of the Confederation and the return of reactionary governments in most states, political ferment continued throughout the German lands. Censors lacked the means, and sometimes the desire, to stop the flood of liberal books, periodicals, and even newspapers th. ι spread across German Europe. Social clubs and and cultural organizations became the forums for political discussions. Scholarly publications like the famous multi-volume *Staatslexikon*, which began to appear in 1834, became a basic reference work for the political opposition. As the intense debates provoked by the creation of the *Zollverein* demonstrated, more and more Germans now took an active interest in public affairs, which they no longer regarded as the exclusive concern of statesmen. By the 1830s the loyalties and institutions upon which the old régime had rested were manifestly in decline; no longer were passivity and deference the characteristic posture for most men and women.[44]

The primary target of political protest during these years was the bureaucracy, whose growing influence over German life was examined in Chapter 7. For many people, bureaucratic institutions were a persistent source of frustration and resentment: censors limited the spread of enlightened opinions and necessary knowledge, policemen harassed innocent travellers, officials inhibited trade or restrained enterprise, soldiers wasted funds better spent on education or economic development. 'Excessive government or the interference of the administration in too many affairs has become the rule,' David Hansemann complained in 1840, 'Unconsciously, officials have taken upon themselves the most varied matters that could be left to private individuals or organizations.' A few years later Robert von Mohl wrote that 'we can no longer see reality amid the floods of paper, and if someone promises to simplify administrative business, the result is merely a dozen more unnecessary reports and decrees'. Otto Camphausen noted with alarm what he regarded as a 'fanatical' hostility to the bureaucracy. Camphausen, a Prussian civil servant with close ties to the Rhenish business élite, was in an especially good position to observe anti-bureaucratic opinion, since in the Rhineland, as in many other areas

---

[44] On the debate over tariff policy, see Hans-Werner Hahn's article in Schieder (ed.), *Liberalismus*, and the opening sections of Heinrich Best, *Interessenpolitik und nationale Integration, 1848/49. Handelspolitische Konflikte im frühindustriellen Deutschland* (Göttingen, 1980).

that had changed hands during the post-revolutionary settlement, opposition to the administration was fed by regional antagonisms, economic rivalries, and religious divisions.[45]

Throughout German Europe the political opposition sought to curb excessive bureaucratic power and subject governments to the rule of law. 'It is a fundamental truth', declared a liberal member of the Baden parliament in 1831, 'that the government should not be allowed unilateral authority over private legal conditions, and has no right to limit the free use of its citizens' physical and intellectual resources'.[46] Liberals regarded constitutions not merely as a way to regulate the distribution of power but also as a means to define the proper uses of power and to prevent its abuse. Similarly, the liberal concept of the *Rechtsstaat*, which was of great importance to theorists like Mohl, was an effort to protect persons and property from unreasonable regulations and arbitrary interference.

During the 1830s liberals' commitment to constitutional government and the rule of law was most dramatically expressed by the conflict of the so-called 'Göttingen Seven' with the Hanoverian government. As the reader will recall, Hanover's constitutional settlement of 1833 was one of the revolution's belated political by-products. Four years later, the century-old personal union between England and Hanover was broken when Victoria became queen and, according to the provisions of Salic law, the Hanoverian crown passed to her uncle, Ernest August, duke of Cumberland. The new monarch immediately abrogated the constitution of 1833 and demanded an oath of allegiance from all state employees. Seven members of the Göttingen faculty—the historians Dahlmann and Gervinus, the jurist Wilhelm Albrecht, the philologist Heinrich Ewald, the physicist Wilhelm Weber, and the literary scholars Jacob and Wilhelm Grimm—refused to obey the royal command on the grounds that it violated the oath they had already taken to the constitution. As Dahlmann put it, 'I fight for the immortal king, the legal will of the government, when—with legal weapons—I resist what the mortal king does in violation of existing laws.' Despite the Seven's opposition, Ernest August's will prevailed: the constitution was revoked, the protesters were removed from their positions, and three of them forced into exile.

---

[45] Hansen, *Briefe*, i. 197; Angermann, *Mohl*, pp. 51–2; Hansen, *Briefe*; ii. 55. For more on the Rhineland, see Droz, *Libéralisme*; Fehrenbach, 'Problematik'; and Schütz, *Preussen*.

[46] Gall, *Constant*, pp. 135–6.

But everywhere the Seven found supporters among German liberals, who applauded their insistence that the state and its laws were not subject to the whim of an individual ruler.[47]

In 1837, the same year as the Hanoverian *Staatsstreich*, another kind of protest against the misuse of state power erupted in the Rhineland. Ever since this region had become part of the Hohenzollern monarchy, relations between Prussian authorities and the Catholic Church had been strained. However, as long as Count Ferdinand August von Spiegel remained archbishop of Cologne, compromise between ecclesiastical and secular authorities was possible: for instance, Spiegel was party to a complex series of negotiations on the vexing question of how the children of mixed marriages were to be educated, which was eventually settled in a confidential agreement of 1834. After Spiegel's death in 1835, the situation deteriorated. The new archbishop, Clemens August Freiherr von Droste-Vischering, eventually denounced the agreement of 1834 and adhered instead to the papacy's much tougher line on the mixed-marriage question. At the same time, Droste entered into the controversy surrounding the followers of Georg Hermes at the University of Bonn. Ignoring government efforts to protect the Hermesians, the archbishop prohibited seminarians from attending their lectures and demanded that all candidates for the priesthood accept a declaration condemning Hermes's ideas. Berlin promptly responded by imprisoning Droste on treason charges and taking over the administration of the archdiocese. German Catholics were slow to react. Droste was not a popular man and there were some who thought he got what he deserved. 'Despite their piety', reported Annette von Droste-Hülshoff to her mother, 'the citizens of Cologne are so glad to be rid of him that not a mouse has stirred . . .' Gradually, however, opposition to the government gathered momentum. First in Koblenz, then in Paderborn, then in an increasing number of Rhenish cities and towns, clergy and laymen gathered to protest against the archbishop's arrest. When the archbishop of Posen also defied the government, he too was arrested. Eventually a flood of polemical books and pamphlets appeared: Joseph Görres, for example, who had moved to the right since his days as a patriotic publicist, wrote a famous anti-Prussian diatribe entitled *Athanasius*, which quickly sold over seven thousand copies after its publication in January 1838. The conflict dragged on for three years until, under the reign of Frederick

[47] Huber, ii. 91 ff.; and *Dokumente*, i. 248 ff.

William IV, it was settled through a compromise that largely accepted the church's position.[48]

Although the matter of mixed marriages was not without practical significance—especially in the Rhineland where unions between Catholics and Protestants were rather common—the broad and lasting impact of the 'Kölner Wirren' came from the way in which this issue brought to the surface a range of other conflicts—between church and state, Catholics and Protestants, the proponents and critics of papal authority, and perhaps most of all, the Hohenzollern monarchy and the inhabitants of its new territories. To those who resented the heavy hand of Prussian power, the imprisoned bishop was a martyr, the personification of courageous resistance to unjust authority.

Elsewhere in German Europe, Prussia's rivals rushed to use the conflict for their own ends. The centre of these efforts was Munich, where King Ludwig tried to develop a Catholic counterpoise to Berlin. The ministry of Karl von Abel, which had been formed just before the Cologne crisis, adopted a staunchly pro-Catholic policy that eventually alienated Bavaria's Protestant minority. In 1838 religious antagonisms in the kingdom intensified when the king issued an order requiring both Protestant and Catholic soldiers to kneel when the Blessed Sacrament was carried by. Once again, we are struck by the symbolic character of the issue, which drew its significance from a complex set of religious, regional, and political fissures. In essence, Ludwig, like Prussia's Frederick William III, wanted to create a Christian state in which religion could be harnessed in defence of the established order. But as both the Wittelsbachs and Hohenzollern would eventually learn, such an enterprise was a recipe for conflict rather than consolidation.[49]

Religious issues were also of considerable importance for many members of the liberal opposition. Rotteck wrote a pamphlet in 1837 condemning Prussian policies towards the church, while Heinrich von Gagern, himself the product of a mixed marriage, contrasted Catholics' willingness to resist tyranny with what he called 'the servile *Staatsdienerei*' of German Protestantism. Most liberals, however, were uncomfortable allies of Catholic leaders

[48] The quotation is from Weber, *Aufklärung*, p. 79. The latest survey of these developments is Karl-Egon Lönne, *Politischer Katholizismus im 19. und 20. Jahrhundert* (Frankfurt, 1986), 51 ff. See also Schnabel, *Geschichte*, iv, especially pp. 106 ff.

[49] Gollwitzer, *Ludwig I.*, chs. 15, 16, 17.

like Droste, whom they saw as the defenders of an intolerant, rigid orthodoxy. Liberals also condemned the growing authority of the papacy, with which Droste was identified, not only because the pope was an outspoken enemy of progressive ideas but also because he personified the unwholesome influence of foreign forces on 'German' affairs. Finally, and perhaps most important, liberals viewed the state as a necessary ally against the cultural and political power of the Church. In specific terms, this meant that liberals supported state control over educational institutions in order to guarantee the 'independence' of the schools from the churches.[50] A similar sort of ambivalence can be found among liberal advocates of Jewish rights, who condemned the state's role in restricting Jews' freedom at the same time as they displayed what Reinhard Rürup has called 'an astonishing confidence in the state's potential and ability' to fulfil the promise of emancipation.[51]

Businessmen were also uncertain about their relationship to the state. Everywhere they complained bitterly about what they regarded as the unjust and unproductive restraints put on their activities by the state. Manufacturers accused officials of favouring agriculture, bankers complained about harmful regulations, merchants demanded freer access to larger markets. When one Prussian official told a delegation of economic leaders from Barmen that industry was a 'cancer' in society, he conformed to the stereotype of the anti-business, doctrinaire bureaucrat prevalent among many German entrepreneurs. But with this natural hostility between the self-proclaimed representatives of practical affairs and those whom one businessman contemptuously called 'examination-passers without property' went a no less powerful urge to co-operate. Businessmen, like the advocates of educational reform and Jewish emancipation, needed the state to provide resources, remove old barriers, and combat rival institutions. As frustrating as it might sometimes be, co-operation between businessmen and the state was essential, particularly in major projects such as railroad construction which required both large capital investment and complex jurisdictional arrangements. Rhenish capitalists like Gustav Mevissen and David Hansemann, therefore, were grateful recipients of

[50] Frank Eyck, 'Liberalismus und Katholizismus in der Zeit des deutschen Vormärz', in Schieder (ed.), *Liberalismus*, p. 142.

[51] Rürup, *Emanzipation*, p. 23. For an example of liberal views of the state and education, see Friedrich Harkort, *Schriften und Reden zu Volksschule und Volksbildung* (Paderborn, 1969), especially pp. 16 ff. This argument is developed at greater length in Sheehan, *Liberalism*, chs. 2, 3.

governmental support as well as bitter critics of governmental hostility.[52]

Liberals' ambivalence about the state was built into the social composition of the political opposition, whose leadership continued to be drawn from men with government positions. As we have seen, from its beginnings in the eighteenth century, the German political public was heavily dependent on and influenced by civil servants. Their political importance continued in the representative institutions created during the era of reform: thus administrative and judicial officials were usually the largest single occupational group in the Badenese *Landtag*, where they provided leaders for both government and opposition. To many Germans, it seemed natural enough that civil servants should represent their views, after all, they were supposed to stand for the common good. Moreover, in a society where communications were still uneven and national institutions weak, officials had greater visibility and wider connections than most other élites. Finally, bureaucrats had certain practical advantages; they could, for example, combine service in parliament with their careers more easily than most businessmen, who were tied down by the constant demands of their firms. Needless to say, many governments viewed bureaucratic parliamentarians with considerable misgivings; by the 1830s conservatives frequently demanded that they be disciplined for disloyalty or prosecuted for subversion. Nevertheless, as paradoxical as it might at first appear, the major role played by officials in movements opposing the governments of which they were a part is further indication of the bureaucracy's central significance for German public life.[53]

In comparison to political life in England or France during the 1830s German participatory politics was still backward, but in comparison to the German situation around the turn of the century, extraordinary changes had taken place. While the major reforms of the early 1800s had been carried out without much public involvement, Germans now regarded what governments did in the realm of politics, religion, or economics as something they had a right to know about and to influence. Against these pressures for

[52] Köllmann, *Sozialgeschichte*, pp. 42 ff.; Friedrich Zunkel, *Unternehmer*, pp. 87 ff., and 'Beamtenschaft und Unternehmertum beim Aufbau der Ruhrindustrie', *Tradition*, 9/6 (1964), 261–77.

[53] On the political role of civil servants, see Conze in Conze (ed.), *Staat*, pp. 228 ff.; Bleeck, *Kameralausbildung*. For a striking example, see Lee, *Politics*, pp. 132 ff., and the table on p. 252, which gives data on Baden.

knowledge and influence, governmental repression was only sporadically successful—in fact, as the Prussian authorities found when they arrested Archbishop Droste, repression sometimes evoked powerful counter-movements. After 1830 political energies could be frustrated, inhibited, or displaced, but they could not be destroyed.

In a *Volk* as dynamic as the Germans in the first half of the nineteenth century [Johann Caspar Bluntschli wrote], if the impulse to form political parties is suppressed through punishments and prohibitions, this impulse flees into the realm of religious or confessional policies or sharpens conflicts in the realm of scholarship, art or society. Between these political and unpolitical parties a certain affinity develops, so that for a time one can be the surrogate for the other.[54]

As we shall see in the following two sections of this chapter, during the 1840s what Bluntschli called the *Wahlverwandtschaft* between political and nonpolitical alignments intensified, as an increasing number of Germans sought answers to a deepening crisis in state and society.

iii. THE GROWTH OF POLITICAL OPPOSITION

Frederick William III, who had ruled Prussia since 1797, died in June 1840. As frequently happens at the end of a long, oppressive reign, people placed great hopes in their new king, Frederick William IV, whose intellect and style made him seem so different from his phlegmatic father. When Frederick William pardoned political offenders, restored Ernst Moritz Arndt to his teaching post, and appointed old Hermann von Boyen, one of Scharnhorst's former protégés, Minister of War, many expected that a new era of reform was about to begin. 'After a long series of dark, disappointing years', wrote Ernst Dronke, 'a breathtaking movement arose from the heart of Prussia at the beginning of June 1840.'[55]

The hopeful excitement that surrounded the opening of Frederick William's reign was intensified by an international crisis in the eastern Mediterranean. In 1839 Mehemet Ali, the energetic and ambitious pasha of Egypt, once again threatened the integrity of the Ottoman Empire. Britain, Russia, Austria, and Prussia acted together in support of the Turks, whereas France looked upon Mehemet Ali with some sympathy. In the summer of 1840, when

[54] Graf, *Politisierung*, p. 23.
[55] Ernst Dronke, *Berlin* (Frankfurt, 1846), i. 177.

the crisis was at its height, the French government refused to join the other great powers' efforts to rein in Mehemet Ali and French opinion became violently anti-British and anti-German. In some circles there was even talk about reclaiming France's 'natural borders' on the Rhine. The result was an outburst of national enthusiasm among many Germans, especially those living in the west. Newspapers like Cotta's *Allgemeine Zeitung* carried patriotic articles, songs like Schneckenburger's 'Wacht am Rhein' and Hoffmann von Fallersleben's 'Deutschland, Deutschland über alles' celebrated the German cause, and businessmen like Ludolf Camphausen underscored the national significance of steamer traffic on the Rhine. The opening of Mannheim's new port facilities in October 1840 turned into a great patriotic celebration, at which Camphausen quoted from Nikolaus Becker's 'Der deutsche Rhein':

> Sie sollen ihn nicht haben
> Den freien deutschen Rhein,
> Bis seine Flut begraben
> Des letzten Mann's Gebein!

Against this background of nationalistic pathos, statesmen moved to stabilize the Middle Eastern situation and to contain French ambitions with quiet diplomacy. The crisis eventually passed, leaving in its wake a few songs and the growing conviction among many patriots that German national interests needed a new institutional base.[56]

Both the dynastic and diplomatic events of 1840 underscored the particular position Prussia occupied in the minds of many German patriots. Those who looked to Berlin for national leadership were naturally encouraged by the new monarch's apparently progressive policies and by his half-hearted efforts to reform the Confederation's military institutions. Moreover, in 1840 Metternich had once again demonstrated Austria's apparent inability or unwillingness to work with the national movement. 'Germany's hope', wrote a contributor to the *Badische Zeitung* in May 1841, 'rests on Prussia'. But, to fulfil these hopes, Prussia would have to join the ranks of the constitutional states and thus begin, once again, to move along the path laid out during the great era of reform.[57]

Considering the role the reform era played in the minds of Prussia's admirers, it was highly appropriate that one of the first attempts to persuade King Frederick William to adopt progressive

---

[56] Gruner, *Frage*, p. 82.

[57] Irmline Veit-Brause, *Die deutsch-französische Krise von 1840* (Cologne, 1967), 262.

policies should have been made by Theodor von Schön, a former collaborator of Stein's and thus a living link to that heroic age. In 1840 Schön was President of the Provincial Administration in East Prussia, close friend of the new monarch, and the spokesman for a group of liberal nobles that included Rudolf von Auerswald, the Lord Mayor of Königsberg, his brother Alfred, Ernst von Saucken-Tarputschen, and several others. Shortly after Frederick William became king, Schön presented him with a small, privately printed pamphlet entitled 'Woher und Wohin', which respectfully requested that he fulfil the constitutional promises his father had made twenty-five years before. 'Only with national representative institutions', Schön was convinced, 'can public life begin and develop in our state.' Frederick William's answer was sharp and negative. In words which would appear again and again in his public remarks, he firmly rejected putting a 'piece of paper' between himself and his subjects; it was 'the natural duty of a German prince' to maintain 'a patriarchical regime', for which no constitutional guarantees or artificial representation was necessary. In 1842, when Schön's pamphlet fell into the hands of a liberal publisher and was printed without his permission, he was forced to resign.[58]

By this time, Frederick William's subjects had begun to realize that what had seemed like goodwill and progressive sympathies was actually rhetorical confusion and political uncertainty. Far from initiating a new era of reform, Frederick William was even more unyielding than his father. Liberals viewed him with disappointment, radicals with anger and contempt. The young Marx, driven into exile by his experience with the king's censors, called Prussia a 'ship of fools' driven by historical winds towards revolutionary destruction. In a poem entitled 'Der neue Alexander', Heine provided a classic formulation of the king's divided nature:

> Ich ward ein Zwitter, ein Mittelding
> Das weder Fleisch noch Fisch ist,
> Das von den Extremen unsrer Zeit
> Ein närrisches Gemisch ist.

> Ich bin nicht schlecht, ich bin nicht gut,
> Nicht dumm und nicht gescheute,
> Und wenn ich gestern vorwärts ging,
> So geh ich rückwärts heute.

---

[58] Huber, ii. 486–7. See Gerhard Krüger, . . . *Gründeten auch unsere Freiheit* . . . *Der Kampf Theodor von Schöns gegen die Reaktion* (Hamburg, 1978).

Closer to home, the citizens of Frederick William's capital described him with the biting humour so characteristic of Berlin: 'The ghost of Frederick the Great is moving around the Palace of Sanssouci,' they joked, 'but without its head.'[59]

Popular disenchantment quickly led to new expressions of discontent, such as Johann Jacoby's pamphlet, 'Vier Fragen, beantwortet von einem Ostpreussen', that caused an immediate sensation when it was published in February 1841. The son of a businessman just prosperous enough to send him to Königsberg's famous Friedrichs-Kollegium and to support his medical studies, Jacoby was active in public health issues and a leading member of the local political club that gathered once a week at Siegel's *Konditorei*. Like many of his younger colleagues in the medical profession, Jacoby was drawn to politics by his everyday contacts with poverty and administrative inefficiency. His experiences fighting cholera, for instance, convinced him that such epidemics could never be defeated until people were liberated from the fear, ignorance and repression which made them susceptible to disease. Moreover, Jacoby was a Jew and thus particularly sensitive to changes in the political climate; he knew that reaction and anti-Semitism were often linked, just as were reform and emancipation. But the triumph of freedom in society would benefit everyone because, as Jacoby wrote to a Christian friend, 'we are all together in the same prison—you are free to move around inside while we [Jews] must wear heavy chains'.[60]

Jacoby's 'Vier Fragen' was moderate in tone, but unambiguous in its demand that 'independent citizens [*selbständige Bürger*]' be given the opportunity for 'lawful participation in the affairs of state'. What the *Stände* had once 'requested as a favour', they must now demand as 'an inalienable right'.[61] Frederick William's government could not allow this challenge to go unanswered. Jacoby's work was banned—although it continued to circulate illegally—and he himself was arrested for treason. A series of trials followed, in the course of which Jacoby's fame spread throughout German Europe; he became a liberal hero, praised and encouraged by men from every sector of the opposition. Finally acquitted by an appeals court, he had the added satisfaction of enjoying a martyr's status without suffering martyrdom's pains.

---

[59] Heine, *Schriften*, iv. 458; Böhmer, *Welt*, p. 338.

[60] Sterling, *Judenhass*, p. 41. Silberner, *Jacoby*, is the definitive biography. For more on Jews and politics, see Jacob Toury, *Die politischen Orientierungen der Juden in Deutschland von Jena bis Weimar* (Tübingen, 1966).

[61] Jacoby, *Fragen*.

Jacoby represented a sector of the Prussian opposition very different from the progressive Junkers around President von Schön. But perhaps even more important than their ideological differences was the difference between their social positions: Schön, after all, came from an élite long dominant in Prussian affairs, whereas Jacoby was a 'new man', whose entrance into public life would have been unthinkable a generation earlier. That Jacoby could choose politics to fulfil what he called 'my hunger for life' exemplifies the widening circle of social responsibility and personal ambition that was transforming German politics in the 1830s and 1840s. As Jacoby knew well, political engagement could be a hazardous enterprise. But for those brave and strong enough, the possibilities for participation were there—in informal meeting places like Siegel's *Konditorei*, in parliaments and local representative assemblies, in professional societies and economic interest groups.

The excitement that greeted the protests of men like Jacoby reflected a new vigour in Prussian public life. After 1840 the Press became more politically engaged, new journals were established, and political pamphlets appeared with greater frequency—activities that can be measured in the increasing burdens born by the royal censors, whose caseload substantially grew from what it had been a few years before. Characteristically, a great deal of this political energy found its outlet in local clubs and associations, such as the *Donnerstag Gesellschaft*, which was founded on the basis of Jacoby's old Siegel group, or the *Bürgergesellschaft* established in Magdeburg, or the *Ressource* in Breslau. As usual, political agitation was often hidden behind cultural façades. According to government sources, for instance, the *Verein der Dombaufreunde* in Cologne was a 'gathering place for the discussion of political matters'. Similarly, the hundreds of people who came to Halle's wine gardens to hear visiting lecturers were obviously using this occasion to discuss the burning issues of the day.[62]

Throughout the 1840s religious issues continued to spark political agitation. Thus the renewed pressures for orthodoxy applied by Frederick William IV evoked a strong response among liberal Protestants. In 1841 a group of progressive theologians met to protest government policies; they quickly found support among the laity, who joined with them to form the so-called *Lichtfreunde*, 'friends of light'. Within a few years this movement had spread to a

---

[62] There are some examples in Obermann, 'Volksbewegung'. On censorship and publications, see Koszyk, *Geschichte*, p. 89.

number of Prussian cities, in which a diverse collection of groups gathered in 'Free Congregations' devoted to liberal theology and greater democracy within the church. As both the *Lichtfreunde* and their orthodox enemies realized, these religious attitudes and institutions had clear political implications. 'The agitation for a free organization of church life', Rudolf Haym wrote, 'served at the same time to prepare the ground for participation in public affairs as a whole. Liberalism in the church was the training school for political liberalism.'[63]

The Catholic equivalent of the *Lichtfreunde* and the Free Congregations was the 'German Catholic' movement, which coalesced in 1844 in response to the pilgrimages organized by the bishop of Trier to venerate the relic reputed to be Christ's 'Holy Robe'. Enlightened Catholics viewed these devotions as medieval residues, designed to preserve the faithful's ignorant obedience to authority. Under the leadership of former clergymen and liberal laymen, the German Catholics established over two hundred congregations, with some 70,000 members. They advocated religious toleration, institutional reform, and independence from Rome. Like the liberal Protestants, they knew religion and politics were inseparable. In our time, Robert Blum wrote, 'the enemies of enlightenment in church and state work hand in hand to enslave the spirit'. Just as a progressive physician like Johann Jacoby did not draw a line between improvements in public health and political reform, so these advocates of progressive Christianity recognized that to have a free church it would be necessary to have a free state. Progress, freedom, and enlightenment were indivisible, applicable to all aspects of life and opposed by a united front of reactionaries, tyrants, and obscurantists.[64]

As the level of political interest rose throughout Prussian society, local representative institutions became politically engaged for the first time. Until the 1840s most of the city parliaments set up by Stein's *Städeordnung* had been filled with the ineffective representatives of an apathetic electorate—in Berlin, where tired councilmen often dozed off during early morning sessions, one wit announced that 'sleeping space could be rented at the City Hall in Breitenstrasse'. During the 1840s organs of municipal self-government became forums for political debate and instruments for political action, first in large eastern cities like Königsberg and Breslau, and

---

[63] Haym, *Leben*, p. 167. See Brederlow, *'Lichtfreunde'*; Bigler, *Politics*, pp. 187 ff.

[64] Schmidt, *Blum*, p. 85. See Graf, *Politisierung*; Frank Eyck's essay in Schieder (ed.), *Liberalismus*.

then throughout the kingdom. City governments petitioned the king to grant a constituent assembly, protested reactionary policies, and organized celebrations for liberal notables. Equally important, the councils, like *Vereine* and religious organizations, provided settings in which people could get to know one another, identify effective leaders, and begin the long process of clarifying the issues they confronted. They became, as Eduard von Simson noted, 'elementary schools for parliamentary life'.[65]

Political activity was particularly intense in Prussia's western provinces, where regional loyalties, lingering confessional antagonisms, and popular hostility to official economic policies combined to feed a broad opposition movement. The *Regierungspräsident* of Cologne, who understandably tried to play down the troubles in his district, was forced to admit to his superiors in November 1842 that 'here too more and more people indicate their desire to participate as much as possible in legislation and administration'. Local elections in 1846 showed the degree to which oppositional groups had penetrated Rhenish affairs: thereafter, city councils through the Rhineland and Westphalia lost no opportunity to take stands on national issues and to mobilize opposition to government policy. As Friedrich Kapp, a young civil servant devoted to the liberal cause, proudly announced from the city of Hamm, 'Here in Westphalia, a new spirit is active on all sides.'[66]

In February 1847 Frederick William attempted to defuse the growing discontent in his realm by calling a combined meeting of the provincial *Landtage*, which was supposed to approve loans to support railroad construction in the eastern provinces. The result was a brief replay of that cycle of hope and disappointment that had attended Frederick William's succession to the throne.

Although the king's decree summoning the so-called United *Landtag* carefully avoided any reference to the famous constitutional promises of the reform era, he obviously hoped that this corporately organized, highly restricted representative institution would satisfy the liberal opposition. When they gathered in Berlin in April, some *Landtag* members formed loose political alliances, even though the king had insisted that he had no intention of

[65] Heinrich Eduard Kochhann, *Auszüge aus seinen Tagebüchern* (Berlin, 1906), 2; Simson, *Erinnerungen*, p. 94. Other examples can be found in Gause, *Stadt Königsberg* ii. 507 ff.; Dora Meyer, *Das öffentliche Leben in Berlin im Jahre vor der Märzrevolution* (Berlin, 1912).
[66] Hansen, *Briefe*, i. 372; Kapp, *Frühsozialisten*, p. 46.

presiding over a parliament in which 'opinions were represented'. No power on earth, he assured the delegates, would force him 'to change the natural and especially for us inherently true relationship between Prince and people into something conventional and constitutional . . .'[67]

The king gravely disappointed those who had hoped that the United *Landtag* might be the prelude to real reforms. Wilhelm von Kügelgen, a conservative admirer of Prussia and no great friend of liberalism, was convinced that Frederick William had made a serious tactical mistake. If I were a revolutionary, Kügelgen wrote on 21 April, I would be delighted, 'as are many who see the only salvation for Germany's political decline in a mobilization of the nation'. In fact, the more progressive delegates, together with moderate opinion throughout the state, expressed their outrage at the government's insensitivity to the needs for constitutional reform. When their request for regularly scheduled meetings was rejected, a majority of the *Landtag* refused to vote for tax reform or new loans. The level of political frustration remained high for the rest of the year: for example, in December, after Prussia's city councils had received the right to hold public sessions, liberals and their supporters crowded into the council chambers, ignored the ban on political agitation, and used the occasion to circulate petitions demanding reform.[68]

Metternich watched developments in Prussia with great concern. He had warned Frederick William about the dangers of calling the United *Landtag*: 'Your majesty will bring together eight separate representative bodies and they will return home as a national parliament.'[69] The results had been even worse than he expected. Moreover, by 1847, Metternich's anxieties were intensified by the powerful pressures for change he confronted within the Habsburg monarchy itself. Both of the great powers, whose conservative solidarity had guaranteed the victory of reaction in 1819 and 1830, were now in danger.

In Austria, as in Prussia, political opposition was encouraged by the character of the monarch. The difference was that, while Frederick William was a disappointment, Ferdinand, the mentally deficient heir to the Habsburg crown, was a disaster, whose

---

[67] Koselleck, *Preussen*, pp. 367 ff. The most complete account is Obenaus, *Anfänge*.

[68] Kügelgen, *Lebenserinnerungen*, p. 115. On the city councils, see Falkson, *Bewegung*, pp. 145 ff.

[69] Valentin, *Geschichte*, i. 76.

presence on the throne seemed both symptom and source of the empire's maladies. That Ferdinand had been allowed to succeed his father demonstrated just how much the monarchy feared change; his total incapacity as a ruler—he could do no more than sign his name, and that with difficulty—underscored the price of dynastic immobility. To operate an absolute monarchy without a monarch is a difficult task under the best of circumstances; in the Habsburg empire, where the dynasty had traditionally proclaimed itself the single most important cohesive force, such a situation was perilous indeed. In fact, the vacuum at the centre of power enabled various groups to struggle for control over the cumbersome machinery of state. Within the *Staatskonferenz*, a kind of regency council made up of the emperor's brothers and main advisers, Metternich battled with his rival Count Kolowrat. Meanwhile, the government's chronic fiscal problems became worse, economic dislocation increased, and social conflicts intensified.[70]

Political discontent in Austria built slowly following Ferdinand's succession in 1835. Poets and pamphleteers proclaimed the need for freedom while they tried to evade the censor and avoid arrest. By the 1840s censorship was still a source of frustration, but it could no longer inhibit the circulation of subversive literature. More and more educated Austrians had come to believe that, without reform, the monarchy was doomed: 'Flicke, flicke, flicke zu,' went Grillparzer's bitter lyric, 'aus dem Stiefel ward ein Schuh, willst du nicht nach neuem Leder sehen, müsst ihr endlich barfuss gehen.' The mood in Austria seemed to have changed. People have become serious, wrote one observer in 1843; 'They no longer believe in the authorities' infallibility; they think, count, compare.' Two years later a petition signed by ninety-nine writers and scholars— including almost all the great names of Austrian culture—asked the government for a modification of the censorship laws. Against this rising tide of criticism, the defenders of the system were clearly in disarray. A pamphlet written at Metternich's request by Freiherr von Hügel tried to justify the state's power to control dangerous ideas, but it was largely ignored.[71]

Perhaps the most influential political work from this period was *Österreich und dessen Zukunft*, published in 1841 by Freiherr

---

[70] On Austria in the 1840s, see the opening sections of Brandt, *Neoabsolutismus*, i; Springer, *Geschichte*.
[71] Bibl, *Zerfall*, ii. 64–5; Srbik, *Metternich*, ii. 212–13, 225. For an introduction to Austrian liberalism, see Franz, *Liberalismus*; Winter, *Frühliberalismus*. Kann, *Empire*, i., summarizes various reform proposals.

Andrian-Werburg, a twenty-eight-year-old civil servant, who, like Schön and Jacoby in Prussia, was convinced that the time had come for fundamental change. 'We stand', his book begins, 'on the eve of great events.' All around him Andrian-Werburg saw a process of dissolution at work—in the various nationalities that made up the Reich, among the élites, and in the lower orders. What did Austria have to set against this process? It was 'a purely imaginary name, which signifies no solid *Volk*, no land, no nation'. Its bureaucracy, upon which the existing order rested, was corrupt and debilitating, a source of the problem, not its solution. There was only one way out, Andrian-Weburg believed, and that was the creation of a 'Gemeinsinn', a 'public spirit' that he found exemplified in England, 'the best of all existing constitutional orders'. In Austria, as in England, public spirit would be the product of freedom and the right to participate in a variety of representative institutions ranging from local assemblies to a state parliament.[72]

Andrian-Werburg's dislike of the bureaucracy, admiration for England, and faith in representative institutions reflected views current among the liberal nobility of the Lower Austrian *Stände*. Under the leadership of aristocrats with venerable names like von Schmerling and von Doblhoff, the *Stände* pressed the government in Vienna for agrarian reforms, an extension of representation to other social groups, and the formation of a state parliament. In a memorandum prepared by Baron Doblhoff, Baron Tinti, and Count Breuner, the need for reform was justified on the grounds that the state simply could not survive much longer in its present condition. The alternative to reform was revolution.

The *Stände* had ties to educated people throughout the monarchy, who read reports of its deliberations in the *Grenzboten*, a periodical edited by an Austrian exile and printed in Leipzig. Aristocratic liberals were also active in the opinion-forming organizations that developed during the 1840s. The *Gewerbeverein*, for instance, brought together active citizens from both nobility and *Bürgertum*, who co-operated to encourage economic growth as well as political reform. The same social mixture was present in the Legal Reading Club (*Juristischer Leseverein*), which attracted some of the most prominent men in the monarchy. Behind a façade of sociability and cultural involvement, the *Leseverein* served as a centre for political dissent; as one outraged official warned his superiors in 1846, the organization was a 'seedbed for the spread of propaganda'.[73]

[72] Andrian-Werburg, *Österreich*, i. 2, 8, 11, 180.
[73] Franz, *Liberalismus*, pp. 32 ff.

While the Austrian opposition was surely weaker than in many German states, the range of its views and its institutional setting were similar to those in most of German-speaking Europe. Not surprisingly, an Austrian liberal like Andrian-Werburg felt a kinship with events across the frontier: 'Every word spoken in Germany, every movement forward and backward finds in Austria a thousand-fold resonance and reflection.' Similarly, liberals in other states began to take greater interest in events within the Habsburg monarchy: 'German liberals', wrote a contributor to the *Deutsche Monatsschrift* in 1844, 'came close to throwing Austrian Germans overboard, until the appearance of these new symptoms of renewed liberal spirit . . . turned people's attention back towards Austria.' In retrospect, of course, we can see that the Austrians were not only part of a German liberal movement but also had to coexist with a variety of other national movements in the monarchy, each with its own political agenda. At the time, however, most German liberals in Austria believed that their goals could be achieved without disrupting the basic character of the Habsburg system. Only a small minority imagined a situation in which they would have to choose between being part of a united Germany and remaining Austrians.[74]

Every aspect of the political crisis in Austria got worse in 1846–7: social conflicts erupted in cities and villages across the empire, a full-scale peasant revolt raged in Galicia, and increasingly bitter political opposition spread among the educated public. At court, the Archduchess Sophie, the emperor's ambitious and tough-minded sister-in-law, conspired to bring her son, the future emperor Francis Joseph, to the throne. Andrian-Werburg, who had quit the bureaucracy to work full-time for the *Stände*, published a second volume of his *Österreich und dessen Zukunft* in which he warned 'we are now where France was in 1788'. Kübeck, who was close enough to the centre of power to appreciate fully how much the government suffered from its leaders' rivalries, uncertainties, and incompetence, wrote in his diary on 30 August 1847: 'A feeling of hopelessness and spiritual distress. Ah, how the weakness of the government upsets and troubles me!'[75]

The political climate in Munich was as threatening as it was in Vienna or Berlin. Here too dynastic accident had helped to turn a difficult situation into a crisis threatening the existence of the regime. Bavaria's King Ludwig, like Prussia's Frederick William,

[74] Andrian-Werburg, *Österreich*, i. 154–5; Altgeld, *Italienbild*, p. 269.
[75] Andrian-Werburg, *Österreich*, ii. 7; Winter, *Frühliberalismus*, p. 134.

was talented and interesting, but without political instincts and personal self-control. Ludwig had great cultural ambitions, which resulted in the architectural grandeur still evident in his capital city. But after the uprisings of the early 1830s, he combined this urge for cultural aggrandizement with an unwavering commitment to political reaction. Ludwig wanted to undo decades of political development by restoring monarchical absolutism; in 1836, for example, he directed that reference no longer be made to the *Staatsregierung*, but rather to the *Regierung des Königs*, and to *Untertan* rather than *Staatsbürger*. In fact, Ludwig had neither the strengths nor the weaknesses of a tyrant. After 1837 he left the running of the state to Karl von Abel, a professional bureaucrat who devoted himself to furthering the interests of the Catholic Church. By the mid-1840s, the Abel regime's unlikely blend of bureaucratic authority and clerical domination had managed to alienate progressive elements throughout Bavarian society.

In 1846 Bavarian public life was transformed by the arrival of a woman calling herself Lola Montez, a dancer of great beauty and shady origins, who captured the king's affection and eventually became his obsession. Fortunately, we need not deliver a final verdict on the much-debated question of whether Ludwig's and Lola's relationship was as chaste as both maintained. What matters to us are the affair's political consequences, which were calamitous. In the first place, Lola's presence did not please Bavaria's Catholic establishment, especially when she found allies among anti-clericals at court and in society. Second, the king's increasingly eccentric behaviour, not to mention the fortune he spent gratifying Lola's every whim, made him an object of ridicule or contempt among many of his subjects. The sort of liberties a rococo prince might allow himself were no longer acceptable to an age which demanded, if not chastity, at least discretion. As Veit Valentin wrote, 'Ludwig forgot who he was and what century he lived in.'[76]

By February 1847 Abel was no longer willing to preside over the king's government. In his letter of resignation, the minister warned Ludwig that

not only Your Majesty's happiness and glory is at stake, but also the fate of the kingdom. That is why all those who plot rebellion rejoice. . . . In the long run, it will be beyond human power to prevent these events from having an impact on the armed forces, and if this incredible evil occurs and this bulwark is shaken, where will help come from?

[76] There is a good summary of the situation in Valentin, *Geschichte*, i. 108 ff. See also Gollwitzer, *Ludwig I.*, chs. 20, 21.

Abel's letter deserves a special place among the jeremiads this unhappy year produced in such large number because it underscores two basic facts of political life on the eve of the revolution: the growing power of public opinion and the essential role of the army as a foundation for the existing order.[77]

While no other German state could match Bavaria's extraordinary mixture of tragedy and farce, social unrest and political tension could be found almost everywhere. Württemberg's King William, like his Bavarian neighbour, had tried to realize his absolutist ambitions by circumventing the constitution and repressing public criticism. When economic hardship helped to spark rioting in Ulm and Stuttgart in May 1847, the king blamed outside agitators and ignored demands for reform. By the end of the year, an active opposition under the leadership of Friedrich Römer commanded the loyalties of progressive groups throughout the state. In Hesse-Darmstadt, a well established liberal movement led by Heinrich von Gagern won impressive victories in the *Landtag* elections of September 1847. Protracted debates over a new civil code helped to mobilize opposition and intensify conflicts between the government and its critics. Hesse-Kassel, on the other hand, had never reaped the benefits of its model constitution, which had been undermined from the start by the regent and his reactionary advisers. 'Vertagungen, Auflösungen, Protestationen, Reserven, Aufklagen, Prinzipienerklärungen'—this was the litany of political crises with which the Prussian ambassador summarized fifteen years of Hesse's constitutional development. In 1847 people feared that a new wave of crises would follow the death of the exiled elector, since the regent had often threatened to revise the constitution once he succeeded his father. As we have seen, in 1837 King Ernest Augustus of Hanover had done what the Hessian elector long threatened to do. But King Ernest Augustus had not enjoyed his absolute power; as he grew old and tired, his attention to the affairs of state drifted and opposition to his rule increased.[78]

Although social, constitutional, and dynastic issues helped to engender political unrest everywhere, it was especially vigorous in Baden, which continued to have the best developed and most clearly articulated public life in German Europe. In 1839 the reactionary ministry of Freiherr von Bittersdorff attempted to

[77] Quoted in Valentin, *Geschichte*, i. 119.

[78] Huber, ii. 435 ff., surveys these developments. On Württemberg, see Langewiesche, *Liberalismus*, pp. 80 ff.; on Electoral Hesse, Bullik, *Staat*, pp. 381 ff. The quotation is from Valentin, *Geschichte*, i. 185.

purge the Baden *Landtag* of its most influential liberals by denying certain civil servants the leave time they needed in order to pursue a parliamentary career. This provoked the so-called *Urlaubsstreit*, in which liberal bureaucrats throughout the state mobilized public opinion against the government. The elections of 1843 were contested along relatively well-defined political lines; electoral meetings were held and in many places candidates were asked to commit themselves to a liberal programme. Within the new *Landtag*, liberal delegates decided to sit together and thus to express formally their intention to co-operate. As Robert von Mohl recognized, this unprecedented action introduced a new level of commitment and communality into German parliamentary life:

Merely a turn of the body or a look can be a challenge and provoke a storm. By taking his place in the assembly a member makes a political statement. . . . To change one's place is a kind of apostasy . . . Finally, it will be easy for weaker characters to be dominated by their companions and to follow their lead, not because they agree but because they sit with them.

When Badenese liberals won a stunning electoral victory in 1846, Grand Duke Leopold was forced to appoint a moderate liberal bureaucrat, Johann Baptist Bekk, to head a new ministry and to offer a series of accommodations to the opposition.[79]

In most of the German lands, political activity remained within state and local institutions, but in some places opposition leaders created wider organizational connections. Both the *Lichtfreunde* and the German Catholics, for example, developed supralocal institutions. Scholarly and professional organizations also became larger and better organized. The *Deutsche Zeitung*, edited in Heidelberg by Georg Gervinus, was supported by Prussian and south German liberals who shared a common commitment to the creation of a 'free national unity'. By the mid-1840s there were even a few explicitly political associations that extended beyond local *Vereine* or parliamentary associations. Most of these were informal and irregular—little more than a network of correspondents or an occasional meeting among men who had heard of one another's political views and accomplishments, such as the gathering of men from different states held under the leadership of Adam von Itzstein at his country house in Hallgarten.[80]

Some contemporaries were astute enough to notice that the intensification of political activity was attended by an increase in

[79] Kramer, *Fraktionsbindungen*, pp. 51–2. On Baden, see Gall, *Liberalismus*, ch. 3.
[80] Schmidt, *Blum*, pp. 58 ff.

political divisiveness. According to a contributor to the *Mannheimer Abendzeitung* in December 1846, 'The different sides of our political life have finally begun to develop more sharply and present themselves more clearly . . . [T]he old labels of 'liberal', and 'servile', 'right' and 'left' have proved to be too general. Many divisions have emerged . . . and one can clearly distinguish parties within parties.'[81] Baden was an especially good place to observe this process because, after the liberals' victory in 1846, the opposition had split between those eager to accept the grand duke's offer of co-operation and those committed to radical change. In the course of 1847, 'parties within parties' had begun to emerge in other states as well, where divisions about goals and strategies could no longer be concealed behind programmatic generalities.

Divisive pressures within the opposition came from both left and right. Men on the democratic end of the opposition were increasingly frustrated by the lack of real progress on political issues and increasingly concerned by the social problems they saw around them. These people—journalists, unemployed academics, lawyers, physicians—began to believe that moderation would never achieve their ideals. 'The whole world has had enough of beautiful speeches and tired clichés; it yearns for action from the liberal party,' declared Ruge as early as 1843. Hoffmann von Fallersleben, in a poem entitled 'Der gute Wille', linked liberal impotence with its excessive dependence on bureaucratic leaders:

> Gern will ich sein ein Rater
> Verlangt nur keine Tat—
> Ich bin Familienvater
> Und auch Geheimrat.
>
> Ja freilich, beides bin ich,
> Das macht mir viele Pein
> Ich bin gewiss freisinnig,
> Wie's einer nur kann sein.

Gustav von Struve, who, as leader of Baden's radicals knew a great deal about liberal *Geheimräte*, referred to them as 'parliamentary mandarins, parade heroes, big mouth liberals', and contemptuously dismissed the Chamber of Deputies as the 'sixty-three rabbits'. Struve, together with Robert Blum from Saxony and Johann Jacoby from Prussia, demanded a more rigorous pursuit of universal suffrage, the creation of a militia, equalization of educational opportunity, reform of the tax system, an end to social

[81] Koszyk, *Geschichte*, p. 104.

privilege, and the structural transformation of the civil service.[82]

These radical goals threatened moderates' interests and values. Liberal civil servants wanted an enlightened political system, but they did not favour dismantling the bureaucracy; liberal business-men wanted more freedom, but not social and economic equality. Moreover, liberals everywhere were willing to co-operate with the government when such co-operation served their interests; both in theory and in practice, their ideal was a union of *Volk* and *Staat*, joined in the pursuit of enlightened policies. Indeed, when they observed the turmoil in their society, the urge to act with rather than against the state increased. As a Württemberg newspaper put the matter in November 1847, the 'political ascension of the *Bürgertum* and the fusion of its interests with the interests of the government provide the best and most secure defence against the proletariat'.[83]

In the autumn of 1847 various radicals and moderate groups tried to define programmes around which they could rally support. On 10 September the left wing of the Baden opposition met in Offenburg with delegates from nearby states. They agreed to a thirteen-point statement that called for a variety of reforms, including 'popular representation in the Confederation: Germans want a fatherland and a voice in its affairs'. A month later a group of moderates gathered in Heppenheim to endorse a set of reforms based on the *Zollverein*, which was to be given wider political powers and representative institutions. Through such changes, 'the German *Verein* would become irresistibly attractive to other German states, and finally lead to the inclusion of the Austrian lands within the Confederation and thus found a true German power'.[84]

We should keep in mind that divisions within the opposition are clearer in retrospect than they were at the time. The phrasing of the Offenburg and Heppenheim programmes was vague enough to conceal important differences. In most states, parliamentary align-ments were still obscured by legal restrictions, well-established habits of mind, and the need to stand firm against reaction. Even in Baden, where moderates and radicals had begun to compete openly for popular support, government repression could bring them together again. Elsewhere, many liberals still talked about a

---

[82] A. Ruge, 'Selbstkritik des Liberalismus' (1843), in *Sämtliche Werke* (Mannheim, 1847), iv. 80; Böhmer, *Welt*, p. 336; Valentin, *Geschichte*, i. 160.

[83] Langewiesche, *Liberalismus*, p. 93.

[84] Huber, *Dokumente*, i. 261–4.

common *Gesinnung* and did not seek to clarify the issues that divided them. Some of those most clearly aware of these divisions argued that they should be subordinated to the immediate needs of a common struggle. Thus Otto Lüning, who acknowledged the existence of two 'vital, dynamic, reasonable parties' in 1847, also maintained that, because they had common enemies, they should march together.[85] But, while we should not overestimate the clarity or consistency of the divisions between radicals and moderates in the 1840s, it is worth noting that, even before the revolution, political lines had begun to be drawn. The better organized people became, the closer their ties and the clearer their programmes, the more they tended to divide into separate, competing groups.

iv. SOCIAL CRISIS

The political opposition, one of its members wrote, included 'everyone with talent, all free and independent spirits, in short, the entire third estate'. C. H. Pagenstecher's characteristic combination of social and moral categories expressed a widespread conviction among liberals that they spoke for society as a whole. By the 1840s the ranks of the opposition were indeed filled with energetic and able people from a variety of social groups: businessmen like David Hansemann and Ludolf Camphausen, physicians like Carl d'Ester and Johann Jacoby, professors like Robert von Mohl and Carl Biedermann, and many others from throughout the educated and propertied middle strata of *Vormärz* society. Moreover, the opposition attracted shopkeepers and craftsmen, small landowners and schoolteachers, petty officials and even some skilled workmen—people from rather modest backgrounds who supported religious reform in the Free Congregations and German Catholic movement, signed petitions in support of constitutional government, and participated in festivals to celebrate national heroes like Schiller and Dürer.[86]

The opposition could plausibly claim to represent a clear majority of those engaged in political life. But, since most Germans remained untouched by political issues and appeals, the opposition was a small minority within the population as a whole. The Free Congregations and German Catholics, for example, had rather

[85] Obermann, 'Volksbewegung', pp. 506 ff.
[86] Pagenstecher, *Lebenserinnerungen*, iii. 25. On the social composition of the political opposition, see Sheehan, 'Liberalism', and *Liberalism*, ch. 2.

quickly reached the limits of their strength; the vast majority of German Protestants and Catholics did not respond to the call for theological renewal and ecclesiastical reform. Similarly, the opposition's political demands were supported by an active but small proportion of the population. The citizens of Königsberg who refused to accept free copies of Jacoby's 'Vier Fragen' were more representative of the *Volk* than those who demonstrated in favour of his freedom of speech.

Although only a minority of Germans understood the political issues that drove men like Jacoby, many more were stirred by the social crisis that gripped most of German Europe during the 1840s. To those without work, shelter, or food—and to the larger number who feared such privations—constitutional revisions and church politics were of marginal interest. What mattered was the creation of a social order that would allow them and their children to live with some measure of dignity and security. These social discontents and aspirations fed a large, inchoate movement that ranged from moderate self-help associations to revolutionary bands. To the political opposition, this movement was a source of hope and fear: it gave their reformist programmes a particular urgency and potential power at the same time as it evoked images of uncontrollable violence and political chaos.[87]

The social crisis of the 1840s was essentially an intensification of the problem that had been plaguing much of Europe for decades: productive capacities simply could not grow quickly or evenly enough to provide for an expanding population. Despite regional pockets of prosperity, the remarkable dynamism of certain industries, and aggregate economic growth, this basic discrepancy between development and demography had produced a situation in which a substantial minority of Germans was permanently destitute, a large number lived on the edge of subsistence, and millions more felt severely threatened. After several lean years, things came to a head in 1846–7, when a downturn in the trade cycle cut the demand for goods, increased unemployment, and forced many marginal enterprises out of business. In Cologne, for example, the number of bankruptcies—most of them taverns, printing shops, and other small firms—went from forty-five in 1845–6 to seventy in 1846–7. At the same time as profits and wages fell, food prices soared—in some places by as much as 400 per cent. A potato blight struck at the supply of what had become an important part of many

---

[87] For an introduction to the social crisis of the 1840s, see Abel, *Massenarmut*; Fischer and Bajor, *Frage*; and Jantke and Hilger (eds.), *Eigentumslosen*.

people's diet during the first half of the century; grain harvests were off by a third, which directly affected the price of bread. In short, Europe faced what Eric Hobsbawm called 'an old style agrarian-dominated depression . . . the last, and perhaps the worst, economic breakdown of the ancien regime'.[88]

Even at its worst, the depression did not hurt everyone. Some industries and enterprises continued to thrive: in both Austria and Prussia, for example, the production of coal and iron increased significantly throughout the 1840s as mining was transformed, in part by the introduction of new technology (especially the steam engine), in part by the demands of new customers like the railroads. Moreover, those who were hurt by the depression were hurt unequally: people connected with the manufacturing of cotton cloth, for example, did much better than those who worked with linen. But the unevenness of the crisis did nothing to soften its social impact. If anything, the presence of prosperous sectors increased the level of discontent, not simply by generating conflicts between the haves and the have-nots, but also by intensifying competition for scarce goods. In this way, even the growth of capital industries like the railroads had a destabilizing effect on the economy as a whole.

The crisis was, of course, especially painful for those on the margins of society. Even in the best of times, the poorest families spent most of their income on food; when prices rose, they bought less, ate less, and became susceptible to typhus, typhoid, and the other infections that raged throughout these years. As many as 50,000 died from famine-related diseases in upper Silesia, which was one of the hardest-hit regions. The number of those living on some form of charity greatly increased, reaching 10 per cent in Hamburg, nearly 20 per cent in Cologne. In the regions of upper Hesse that Bruno Hildebrand studied in 1846–47, officials organized beggars in processions that marched through more prosperous neighbourhoods. Almost one-third of the people of this area, which was composed largely of crowded farms and depressed crafts, were unable to support themselves. To those who were just getting by, the swelling ranks of the indigent represented a

[88] Hobsbawm, Age, p. 169. Data from Obermann, 'Wirtschafts- und sozial-politische Aspekte'. Dieter Dowe, 'Methodologische überlegungen zum Problem des Hungers in der ersten Hälfte des 19. Jahrhunderts', in Conze and Engelhardt (eds.), Arbeiterexistenz, provides a critical analysis of the literature on hunger and nutrition. The best introduction to the agrarian situation is the work of Abel: Fluctuations, Massenarmut, and Geschichte.

perpetual threat that for some would become a terrible reality. In his report on conditions in Cologne from the turn of the year 1845–6, a government official noted that 'part of the class of wage earners and poor inhabitants is already in real need'. Six months later, as prices continued to rise, he reported that 'families from the lower ranks of the artisanate are being forced to sell their possessions'.[89]

On the fringes of society, among those without enough work, savings, or marketable skills, the choice was often between stealing, begging, or starving. Dirk Blasius, who has studied the problem of crime during this period, has provided us with a graph tracing the incidence of theft and the price of rye: as we should expect, the lines plot a similar course, both reaching a peak in 1846–7. Contemporaries did not fail to make the link between poverty and criminality. In a book entitled *Diebe in Berlin*, written between 1844 and 1846 and published, after great difficulty, in 1847, Zimmermann described how the 'pressure' of pauperism necessarily led to 'demoralization, crime, and prostitution'. Ernst Dronke, whose portrait of Berlin remains one of the finest social analyses of the age, estimated that almost one quarter of the city's population was potentially a part of that 'proletariat' among whom crime and prostitution flourished.[90]

Many of the vagrants, highwaymen, and prostitutes who prowl through the pages of popular literature and haunted the imaginations of their respectable contemporaries had no choice but to wander outside the established order. Such people had always been present in European society; undoubtedly their numbers increased during the 1840s as the margins of privation widened. But not all vagrants and mendicants were social outcasts. Among what one observer called the 'the columns of beggars which pass through our cities everyday', there were often entire families, from grand-parents to infants in arms, who begged together and returned home to share what they had managed to acquire. Wood stealing, poaching, and crop-robbing were not the work of professional criminals but of men and women with hearths and stoves, dependants to warm and feed, homes to protect. For such people begging and theft were a last resort, a final, desperate effort to keep going. When they broke the law or violated the code of respectability, they usually did so in order to keep their place in a

[89] Werner Conze in *HWSG* ii. 441; Abel, *Fluctuations*, pp. 242 f.; Obermann, 'Wirtschafts- und sozialpolitische Aspekte', pp. 144, 166.
[90] Blasius, *Kriminalität*, p. 48; C. W. Zimmermann, *Die Diebe in Berlin* (1847; repr. Berlin, 1979), 1; Ernst Dronke, *Berlin* (Frankfurt, 1846), ii. 56–8.

community, which often acknowledged their right to take extreme measures in order to survive.[91]

To most law-abiding citizens, the fear of criminality was associated with fear of the mob, which they saw as an anarchic collection of the alienated and uprooted, a random gathering of those brutal elements found in every urban slum and along every rural highway. Wild-eyed and dishevelled, morally corrupt and physically dangerous, this mob appears in the pages of anti-revolutionary tracts, in popular novels, and in the nightmares of the well-to-do. It is difficult, however, to find evidence of such mobs in what we know about the social reality of mid-nineteenth-century Europe. In fact, most collective action was not carried on by the socially marginal. 'Mobs' were usually composed of people who knew one another and were acting together in the pursuit of particular goals and according to socially-accepted norms. Those who took to the street to demand lower prices, protest against government policies, or attack an unpopular official did so within, and on behalf of, a particular community, whose existence provided both the practical basis and moral justification for what they did. Significantly, most of the mob's targets were people who seemed to be outsiders or their agents—tax-collectors, bailiffs, merchants, gamekeepers, foreigners, Jews. Members of a guild, parish, or village often saw these outsiders as the source of their discontent, violators of privileged territory, breakers of traditional codes, disrupters of what Edward Thompson has called the 'moral economy' on which local life was based.[92]

The incidence of collective violence increased steadily throughout the 1840s and reached its pre-revolutionary peak in 1846–7. Not surprisingly, a line tracing this incidence coincides with the lines measuring food prices and criminality. Frequently, riots were the direct result of what consumers regarded as an unfair and unacceptable increase in the cost of basic commodities. For instance, in Bavaria, where beer was a source of nutrition as well as a lubricant for social interaction, price increases had triggered angry demonstrations and sometimes full-scale attacks on breweries or taverns. During the spring and early summer of 1847 this kind of protest became common throughout Europe when the full impact of the poor harvest was felt. In April the local garrison had to be called out in Berlin to quell the disorders caused by a violent confrontation between potato dealers and their customers. Two months later a crowd, largely composed of women shoppers and their children, broke into bakeries in Hamburg, smashed furniture, slashed flour sacks, and demanded bread at a price they could afford. About the same time, people living in the port cities along the Elbe demonstrated against grain merchants whose storehouses were thought to be full of produce destined for foreign markets. The common thread running through all these incidents—and the scores of others like them—was the popular belief that there was a fair price for basic goods, a price determined, not by supply and demand or commercial opportunities, but rather by an individual's right to just compensation and a community's right to buy the commodities its members needed to survive.[93]

In addition to these consumer protests, there was a good deal of labour unrest during the Vormärz. Some of it was caused by such 'modern' issues as wages, hours, and security of employment. Railroad workers, for instance, who were well paid when they worked, sometimes rioted when they suddenly found themselves without a job after a particular line had been laid. Other labour disputes were created within traditional enterprises by over-crowding, economic depression, or the competition of newer enterprises. If craftsmen were unable to impose the monopoly granted them by the guilds, they might resort to threats or acts of violence in order to assert their traditional authority. When work was scarce, apprentices saw the journeymen from other towns as unwelcome and unfair competition; pitched battles between such groups were sometimes the result.[94]

Religion, whose centrality to Vormärz culture we have already noted, could also be a source of conflict and disorder. Here too a community often struggled against apparent outsiders: Catholic parishes against the agents of a secular state, Protestant villages against Jews, the defenders of traditional piety against would-be reformers. Religious antagonisms were most serious if they coincided with political, social, or economic dissension and discontent. This was evidently what happened in Leipzig during the summer of 1845, when a crowd gathered to demonstrate

---

[93] Tilly, 'Disorders', p. 12; Werner K. Blessing, 'Theuerungsexcesse', in Conze and Engelhardt (eds.), Arbeiterexistenz; Valentin, Geschichte, i. 83; Husung, 'Gewaltprotest', p. 58.

[94] For some examples, see Husung, 'Gewaltprotest'.

against the crown prince, whose unpopularity made him a target of both religious and political animosity. A similar combination seems to have been at work in Cologne, where the police arrested several young people for setting off fireworks during the *Martins-kirchmesse* of 1846. To the angry crowd that swiftly gathered, these arrests were yet another example of the authorities' contempt for local tradition and religious ceremony.[95]

In both Leipzig and Cologne the disorders of 1845 and 1846 followed a similar pattern: after long-term animosities had been intensified and then ignited by a single incident, a demonstration was held by a large and spontaneously formed crowd, which then provoked large-scale repression by the armed forces. As a rule, most of the violence was caused by the forces of the state. While crowds destroyed property, threatened and occasionally assaulted their enemies, it was soldiers who did the killing. This is not surprising when we consider the institutional realities of the *Vormärz*. Everywhere police forces were weak—adequate for arresting vagrants, clearing the streets of drunks, and pursuing thieves, but impotent when confronted by an angry crowd. Once the civil authorities realized that they could not preserve order, they had only one place to turn, the army. By the time the troops arrived, the demonstrators had often begun to feel their own power; their painless triumph over the authorities seemed to reaffirm their belief in the justice of their cause. Thus the soldiers, untrained in riot control and led by officers who had only contempt for civilians, had to face an aroused and confident crowd. At this point, a few stones or an accidental shot could provoke a bloodbath in which several people—inevitably including bystanders and passers-by—were killed or seriously injured. The restoration of order, therefore, was a costly affair in both human and political terms. As we shall see, the mutual antagonism between the military and society would play an important part in the revolutionary crisis of 1848.

Many characteristics of *Vormärz* social protest can be found in one of its most famous expressions, the so-called 'revolt' of the Silesian weavers during the early summer of 1844. The setting of the uprising was an area blighted by unemployment, hunger, and disease, but the weavers were by no means the worst off of Silesia's inhabitants. Their suffering was socially volatile because they had once been rather prosperous, independent craftsmen. In the early 1840s however, the weavers' economic position deteriorated

[95] Valentin, *Geschichte*, i. 60–1, 222 ff.

because of declining demand and increasing competition from more technologically advanced enterprises. As a result, they became increasingly dependent on the merchants who provided their raw material and marketed their finished products. Some of these merchants used their economic leverage to depress the weavers' earnings to near starvation levels. As distress spread through the large weaving villages of Langenbielau, Peterswaldau, and Arnsdorf, incidents of violence and collective protests became more frequent. Efforts by the police to arrest agitators were sometimes frustrated by the community. Anger and resentment towards the merchants grew as tales of their wealth and chicanery spread among the population.

On 4 June a crowd advanced on the house of the Zwanzigers, a rich and especially unpopular family. Weavers demanded higher pay and, echoing protests from another era, a present to compensate them for their suffering. When their requests were refused, they attacked and badly damaged the Zwanzigers' palatial home. The next day the protests continued despite the police's futile efforts to restore order. As the crowd lined up to receive money from one frightened merchant, troops arrived and the balance of power suddenly shifted against the protesters. A squad of riflemen, either frightened or provoked into action, fired on the crowd, killing eleven and seriously wounding many more.[96]

This event illustrates the transitional condition that was characteristic of so much social thought and action during the *Vormärz*. The weavers acted as workers, not as consumers or guildsmen; they demanded better compensation for their labour, not 'just prices' or traditional rights. Nevertheless, they were not acting as members of a class. As contemporary descriptions make clear, the weavers operated within their community, joining with friends and neighbours against hostile outsiders. Nor did they see these enemies as a class; their anger was directed against individuals who had violated the 'moral economy' of their relationships. Once they were compensated for this violation, the weavers were prepared to stop. There is no evidence that they had an alternative vision of the social order; they wanted the old order to work and to fulfil what they saw as their just expectations.

The weavers were significant more as a symbol than as a social force. To many contemporaries, their bloody struggle seemed to foreshadow future catastrophes. No one put this better than

---

[96] See the contemporary description by Wilhelm Wolf, repr. in Eyck (ed.), *Revolutions*, pp. 20-3.

Heinrich Heine, whose great poem associates the rhythms of the weavers' work with the historical necessity of social revolution:

> Im düstern Auge keine Träne,
> Sie sitzen am Webstuhl und fletschen die Zähne:
> Deutschland, wir weben dein Leichentuch,
> Wir weben hinein den dreifachen Fluch—
> Wir weben, wir weben!
>
> Ein Fluch dem Gotte, zu dem wir gebeten . . .
> Ein Fluch dem König, dem König der Reichen . . .
> Ein Fluch dem falschen Vaterlande . . .
>
> Das Schiffchen fliegt, der Webstuhl kracht,
> Wir weben emsig Tag und Nacht—
> Altdeutschland, wir weben dein Leichentuch,
> Wir weben hinein den dreifachen Fluch,
> Wir weben, wir weben!

The Provincial President of Silesia had a less poetic but similar response to the weavers' revolt: it was, he wrote on 9 June, part of a 'universal assault of the poor against the rich'.[97]

The same year that informed public opinion was shaken by the events in Silesia. August Brass published his *Mysterieen von Berlin*, one of the many imitations of Suë's famous novel about the Paris underworld, which was, in the opinion of one contemporary, the most influential book to appear in Germany since Goethe's *Werther*. Suë, Brass wrote, did not intend his 'mysteries' to be secrets locked away from our experience; these mysteries were events everyone could observe 'if we took the trouble to cast off the convenient veil of selfish comforts and turned our gaze outside our usual circles'. By playing on people's fascination with criminality and urban low life, Brass wanted to show his fellow citizens the hidden aspects of their world, to force them to confront the suffering and privation from which they usually turned away. Other writers pointed to future dangers by calling attention to social problems in more advanced states like England and France. Some used traditional Christian compassion for the poor as a way to engage people's sympathy and concern. But whatever their specific subject, more and more commentators in the 1840s insisted that the mysteries of contemporary society could not remain hidden. Too long, wrote the author of an essay on the 'Verbreitung des Pauperismus', have we denied this 'cancerous growth in civilized society', too long have

---

[97] Heine, *Schriften*, iv. 455; Obermann, 'Volksbewegung', p. 504.

we sought to evade the necessity of finding effective solutions. But 'facts are facts' and will soon be unmistakable even to the most insensitive observer.[98]

Interpretations of these social 'facts' varied enormously. Conservatives and radicals, Christians and atheists, educational reformers and political agitators, intellectuals and entrepreneurs all found different ways of coming to grips with the apparently unstable world around them. Social thought in the 1840s therefore, was extremely diverse, its vocabulary uncertain and fluid, its proposals for reform inchoate and ambiguous. The pace of change, wrote W. H. Riehl, produces innovation everyday and with these innovations come 'new words' or old words quickly turned to new uses. But behind this 'Begriffsverwirrung' was the shared conviction that the modern world had entered a new and dangerous stage of development in which civilization was threatened by forces that had to be harnessed or subdued.[99]

The words that appear again and again in contemporaries' efforts to understand these forces are *pauperism* and *proletariat*. The former, according to the Brockhaus *Real-Encyklopädie* of 1846, was a newly minted term for a

new and extremely unhealthy phenomenon . . . it has not to do with natural poverty, such as might befall anyone as the result of physical, spiritual, or moral breakdowns or accidental misfortune. . . . Pauperism occurs when a large class can subsist only as the result of the most intensive labour . . . and in the process becomes larger and larger with increasing speed.

In other words, pauperism was caused by a structural crisis that threatened the social order as a whole rather than unfortunate individuals. If it were not stopped, it would engulf more and more of the population, driving them to misery and perhaps revolt.[100]

As early as 1835 Franz von Baader referred to those threatened by pauperism as the *proletariat*, a term that evoked memories of the destructive mobs of ancient Rome. Five years later, in his memorandum on political reform, Theodor von Schön used *proletariat* as a synonym for 'people without home or property'—a broad and diffuse meaning that was retained in most definitions of the term. Thus in *Die Proletarier*, published in 1847, H. W. Bensen distinguished seven different elements ranging from factory

---

[98] Edler, *Anfänge* and *Sue*; Rohr, *Origins*, p. 52.
[99] Jantke and Hilger (eds.), *Eigentumslosen*, pp. 394, 400.
[100] Abel, *Massenarmut*, pp. 60–1.

workers to criminals, prostitutes, and those living from public assistance. Behind their diverse material conditions the groups within the proletariat shared certain moral and psychological characteristics: they were, for example, rootless, without property and therefore without a stake in the social order; they were dependent—on wages, public welfare, or individual charity—and therefore unreliable and easy to manipulat Moreover, the proletariat was conscious of its condition: unlike the traditional poor and down trodden, the proletariat 'felt the lament and poverty of its condition and wished to overcome it at any price'. Impoverished, unskilled, politically and socially volatile, the proletariat was ready for anything—the raw material of outlaw bands, urban mobs, and revolutionary movements.[101]

Robert von Mohl was one of the first German theorists to associate the proletariat's material and moral condition with industrialization. In an essay on the 'Nachteile' of the factory system which he published in 1835, Mohl pointed out that the factory worker, unlike the apprentice, cannot even hope to become a master and is therefore destined to remain a 'serf, chained like Ixion to his wheel'. Since he is forced to rely on his employer for work and wages, the worker's person 'is like the machinery that belongs to a third party'. Without this machinery, he is powerless, unable to work or to live, an 'absolute nothing'. Understandably this situation encourages hatred, envy, and aggression—'every sort of immorality'. Moreover, not only the workers themselves must suffer; the factory destroys family life by taking men from their homes and by employing their wives and children as well. 'Wherever all the ties of family life are severed and its habits and customs no longer support morality, the worst savagery must occur.'

In order to combat this 'Verwilderung' of society, Mohl proposed a series of measures aimed at improving workers' material and spiritual life. Everything possible, he argued, should be done to restore an atmosphere of trust between workers and employers. Legislation was necessary to protect workers and their families from the worst abuses of the factory system. In addition to helping the workers as workers, Mohl wanted to help some of them to escape from the factory. He believed, therefore, that co-operatives and savings associations should be used to develop in

---

[101] Jantke, *Stand*, p. 26; Jantke and Hilger (eds.), *Eigentumslosen*, pp. 426 ff. On this issue, see especially Werner Conze's classic article, ' "Pöbel" '.

the new kind of worker hope and expectation of a gradually improving condition, that is, personal independence'. Mohl wanted to accomplish all of these things within the framework of a liberal social order, but in the 1840s as the dangers of pauperism and the proletariat manifestly increased, he began to consider more drastic means to protect society from the dangers of savagery. At one point, for example, he argued that to combat overpopulation it might be necessary to force emigration or to limit people's right to marry. Mohl feared that without firm action by the state society might not survive.[102]

But Mohl, like most social reformers, was convinced that state action would not be sufficient to overcome the growing fragmentation in modern society. In order to become independent citizens, the proletariat needed new forms of cohesion: as one observer put it in 1845, 'association and love' had to replace 'disunity and hate'. The best way to do this was through some form of organization— co-operatives, educational societies, self-help associations. Such organizations would have both material and moral impact; they would help people pool their resources, improve their skills, save their money, and at the same time teach them discipline, co-operation, and restraint. 'The Vereinswesen', wrote J. Fallat, 'is the true school of community, the healing measure given us by history to improve the disorders of our age, to fill the gaps from which our social organization has suffered.' In all of its different formulations, the association was meant to reconstruct the bonds uniting people to one another and to society, to counter alienation, and to promote community. Like the corporate institutions of traditional society, these new forms of organization were supposed to give people a place and therefore a stake in the social order.[103]

The most common organizations devoted to the lower orders in the *Vormärz* were connected to a particular trade or a specific firm. Most of these were locally based and practically oriented, designed to perform some of the functions of a guild plus meet the needs of new social groups. They provided various kinds of accident or burial insurance, support during times of unemployment, and banks in which savings could be pooled. Some of these organizations were sponsored by employers, some by local authorities or

[102] Jantke and Hilger (eds.), *Eigentumslosen*, pp. 294 ff.; Angermann, *Mohl*, especially pp. 211 ff.

[103] Stein, 'Pauperismus', pp. 22–3. For another example, see Erich Angermann, 'Karl Mathy als Sozial- und Wirtschaftspolitiker (1842–1848)', *ZGO* NS 64/2 (1955), 521.

charitable institutions. Everywhere they were regarded with suspicion and carefully regulated by the state.[104]

Another sort of organization had more general purposes and appeals: these educational or self-help societies, directed to workers and craftsmen from a variety of firms and trades, sought, according to the statutes of a *Bildungsverein* founded in Cologne in 1844, 'ways of collectively promoting as high a degree of welfare and education as an individual is capable of, and especially to counter the spiritual and corporeal privation of those who work with their hands'. When public awareness of social problems grew in the 1840s the number of these *Bildungsvereine* increased. In Saxony, for instance, the *Verein für Verbreitung von Volksschriften*, which provided educational lectures and inspirational reading for upwardly mobile working men, had almost 250 branches with over 7,500 members. The *Verein für die deutsche Volksschule und für Verbreitung gemeinnütziger Kenntnisse im Leben* performed similar functions in Prussia's western provinces. The *Centralverein für das Wohl der arbeitenden Klassen*, founded in Berlin in 1845, had a smaller and more limited membership, but was also devoted to discussing solutions to the social question.[105]

In both theory and practice, the *Bildungsvereine* wanted to encourage the lower orders to learn from and be inspired by their betters. To the educated and propertied elements in the *Vereine*, this did not require a democratic organization. One Rhenish business-man, for instance, was scandalized by the fact that in his *Verein* any *Lump* who could pay his dues might be elected to the executive committee—'no, this is not how participation is to be understood! The proletarians should have our trust . . . but not a say in how things are run.' In fact, not many *Lumpen*—the poorest and most oppressed members of society—were willing or able to join these *Vereine*, whose membership tended to be drawn from a fairly broad range of the middle strata. Among the first 168 members of the *Verein für Handel und Gewerbe*, founded in Saxony in 1843, there were 73 merchants, 52 master craftsmen, 16 manufacturers, 14 brewers and distillers, 3 pharmacists, and a few officials and academi.ians. The intense organizational activities of the 1840s therefore, usually managed to extend and reinforce relationships among various elements within the *Mittelstand* without doing much

---

[104] For an introduction to the origins of labour organizations, see Kocka, *Lohnarbeit*.

[105] Birker, *Arbeiterbildungsvereine*, pp. 30 ff.; Hansen, *Briefe*, i. 689–90. See also Balser, *Anfänge*.

to improve the economic or spiritual condition of those hardest hit by the contemporary social crisis.[106]

Despite close scrutiny by the authorities, some of these *Vereine* did become centres of political activity in the 1840s. As a sense of social crisis spread across central Europe, the workers and craftsmen who co-operated in the various *Hilfsvereine* were naturally drawn to politics. In the *Bildungsvereine*, men from different trades became acquainted with one another as well as with the major issues of the day. The Berlin *Handwerkerverein*, for example, which had a membership of 3,000 by 1847, was ostensibly devoted to edifying lectures and uplifting entertainments. Its sponsors, largely moderate businessmen and progressive officials, would have been scandalized to learn that the *Handwerkerverein* was also functioning as what Stephen Born called a 'training ground for up and coming revolutionaries', in which people acquired a sense of social solidarity and political direction. [107]

The radical politics that were necessarily latent in the educational societies were clearly manifest in the associations of German craftsmen and intellectuals that existed outside the boundaries of the Confederation. Taking advantage of the more permissive atmosphere in France, Belgium, and England, these associations brought together journeymen, workers, and exiled intellectuals. Even the most famous of these groups, however, such as the Bund der Gerechten, founded in Paris in 1836, was quite small, numbering no more than a hundred or so. Like the *Bildungsvereine* within the German states, these exile organizations often combined politics and education—they shared the characteristic *Vormärz* conviction that the transformation of public life was essentially a spiritual process. Nevertheless, these organizations provided the forums within which many future labour leaders first formulated and refined their ideas about political action and class consciousness.[108]

In different ways and with differing intensity, almost all *Vormärz* organizations encouraged craftsmen and wage-earners to develop a sense of their common interests. Slowly and unevenly, a few participants in these organizations began to see themselves as *workers*, rather than as members of a trade, masters, apprentices, or employees of a particular firm. As workers, they shared a common plight; their interests and their enemies were the same.

[106] Hansen, *Briefe*, i. 698; Obermann, *Arbeiter*, p. 45.
[107] Born, *Erinnerungen*, pp. 23–4.
[108] Schieder, *Anfänge*.

What we hardly dared to think while alone at home [a railroad worker told Wilhelm Wolff in 1844], we now speak out openly among ourselves . . . we're the real support of the rich, and if we only want it strongly enough, the rich will have to work for their bread, beg it from us, or starve. You may believe me when I say that if the weavers had held out a bit longer, there would have been trouble and unrest among us very soon. The weavers' problems are our problems too.

Such feelings of class solidarity were surely rare. Even in the large cities, old loyalties continued to operate and to inhibit collective loyalties and action. As Stephen Born recalled the world of the *Vormärz*, 'The phrase, "the antithesis of classes" had then, measured by the actual conditions of Germany, scarcely any justification. . . . [there were] employers and employees but the master as a rule was nothing more than a former journeyman. There were two age levels, not two classes.'[109]

The career of Wilhelm Weitling illustrates the fluidity that persisted in the theory and practice of the German labour movement throughout the first half of the century. Born in 1808, Weitling was a journeyman tailor who failed to become a master. After wandering around central Europe for several years, he went to France to look for work but instead found radical politics. In 1837 he joined the *Bund der Gerechten*, for which he prepared his first and most famous work, *Die Menschheit, wie sie ist und wie sie sein sollte*. A revolutionary and a socialist, Weitling regarded the destruction of private property as 'humanity's means of salvation'. When he spoke on behalf of this salvation, his words were charged with a pathos drawn from direct experience. Unlike many early socialists, he could identify with 'the *Volk* in workers' blouses, jackets, aprons, and caps . . . the most numerous, useful, and powerful people in God's wide world'. Weitling was both a pioneer and a transitional figure, whose thought and experience were deeply rooted in traditional culture and society. A spokesman for French radicalism, he was also inspired by the gospels and evangelical Christianity; a self-proclaimed revolutionary, he often spoke of spiritual renewal and Utopian contentment; an early advocate of class consciousness among workers, he continued to view the world in terms of his own artisanal origins and had little understanding for industrial labour.[110]

[109] Tilly, 'Disorders', p. 18; Noyes, *Organization*, p. 150. On the problem of class formation, see Kocka, *Lohnarbeit*; Marquardt, 'Class' and 'Aufstieg'; Zwahr, *Konstituierung*.
[110] Balser, *Anfänge*, p. 100. On Weitling, see Schraepler, *Handwerkerbünde*, especially pp. 58 ff.; Kolakowski, *Main Currents of Marxism*, i. 211 ff.

Two chapters in the history of the German labour movement briefly overlapped when Weitling met Marx at the latter's house outside Brussels early in 1846. The meeting did not go well: as Marx and his friends listened with growing discomfort, Weitling delivered a passionate speech on the need to combat poverty. Marx regarded such flights of Utopian fancy and diffuse enthusiasm as the most dangerous sort of nonsense. The purpose of the radical intellectual was not to provide eloquent descriptions of social affliction but rather to develop a science of social action that could guide the working class to victory. 'Ignorance', he finally shouted at Weitling, 'never yet helped anybody.'[111]

By 1846 Marx was becoming a formidable intellectual presence on the European left. After having come to terms with his Hegelian origins and his left-Hegelian compatriots, he had devoted himself to cleansing socialism of its Utopian and unscientific ingredients. Once more, this required abandoning his own earlier opinions; as usual, Marx discharged his debts by dissolving his personal and philosophical ties to those who had influenced him. His polemical style was bitter and brilliant; none of his opponents' errors was left unchallenged, no personal weakness unexploited. His targets ranged from obscure left-wing journalists like Hermann Kriege— against whom Marx directed an attack so vitriolic that it made Weitling physically ill—to the star of French socialism, Pierre Proudhon.

While Marx was in the process of purifying socialist theory, he searched for an appropriate basis for action. In 1846 he made contact with a small but well-established group of German exiles in London who had constituted themselves as the Communist League; shortly thereafter he formed an affiliated branch in Brussels. After attending the League's second general meeting in November 1847, Marx returned home to prepare a statement of goals and strategy. The result, hurriedly written from various drafts prepared by other League members, including an important version by Engels, was sent to the printers early in 1848 and appeared in March just as the revolutionary movement began.

Although it had virtually no immediate impact, the *Communist Manifesto* turned out to be one of the most influential pamphlets ever written. Like most extraordinarily influential works, the *Manifesto* is not especially original; its key theoretical insights had been elaborated by Marx and Engels over the past several years; many of the ideas, as well as some of its most famous turns of

[111] McLellan, *Marx*, pp. 155 ff.

phrase, were taken from other works, making it what S. S. Prawer calls a 'palimpsest' of references to literature, theory, and contemporary journalism. But if the *Manifesto* is a synthesis, it is a synthesis of great genius, put together with remarkable intellectual power and stylistic energy. At once a theory of history, a description of contemporary society, an image of the future, a strategy of political change, and a critique of competing theories, it is also—perhaps most of all—an expression of moral outrage and political passion. Like Suë and the other students of the social question, Marx set out to reveal the mysteries of the modern condition by giving flesh and blood to the spectre haunting Europe. But his purpose was more than revelatory. By showing the proletariat their true interests, he wanted to give them the intellectual weapons necessary to construct a new social order. That great moment was nearly at hand: 'we traced the more or less veiled civil war, raging within existing society, up to the point where the war breaks out into open revolution, and where the violent overthrow of the bourgeoisie lays the foundation for the sway of the proletariat.'[112]

Marx dealt with the German situation in the closing passages of the *Manifesto*. In the German states, he argued, the course of the revolution would be of particular interest to communists because here it would take place under uniquely advanced conditions. Unlike their counterparts in seventeenth-century England or eighteenth-century France, the German bourgeoisie would rise against the old order while a proletariat was waiting in the wings. As a result, the bourgeois revolution in Germany 'will be but a prelude to an immediately following proletarian revolution'. Marx turned out to be a shrewder analyst than prophet. He grasped with uncanny prescience the peculiarly volatile blend of social and political tensions that would make German Europe the heartland of the mid-century revolutions. But these tensions did not produce the sort of revolution Marx expected. From the start, the German bourgeoisie and proletariat failed to behave as he had predicted; after the last flames of revolt had been extinguished, neither of them had won.

[112] For a brilliant analysis of the *Manifesto's* sources, see S. S. Prawer, *Karl Marx and World Literature* (Oxford 1978), 138 ff.

PART FOUR

Towards a New Order, 1848–1866

XI
Revolution and Reaction

WHY DO people rebel? Our instinctive answer is, because they find their lives intolerable. But this is obviously no answer at all: not only is it circular, it ignores the unhappy truth that, while intolerable conditions are common, rebellions are rare. Suffering alone is not enough; it is a necessary but not a sufficient cause for revolution. Before they rebel, those who suffer must believe, if only for a short time, that their rebellion will lead to a better life for themselves or their communities. Only in this belief can people find the courage to act, the strength to break the bonds of habit and run the risks rebellion inevitably involves. By itself, suffering will not provide this strength and courage; indeed, suffering is more likely to weaken and demoralize than to incite and inspire. Revolutions are rare because they require an unusual conjunction of suffering and hope, a sense of outrage and an act of faith.[1]

To understand the great mid-century revolutions, therefore, we must bear in mind not only the social and political crises that inflicted hardships on so many during the 1840s but also the sense of hope and possibility that simultaneously reverberated throughout Europe. Everywhere we look in 1846 and 1847 we find expressions of faith—in the special parliaments summoned by the kings of Württemberg, Prussia, and Saxony, in the meetings of professional groups and scholarly societies, in cafés and taverns, city halls and bureaucratic offices, lecture halls and students' rooms. As Richard Wagner told a friend in the autumn of 1846, a revolution had already occurred in people's minds, so that 'the new Germany is ready, like a bronze statue which requires only a single

[1] Charles Tilly, *From Mobilization to Revolutions* (Reading, Mass., 1978), is a good introduction to the theoretical literature on revolutionary movements. For the historiography of 1848 in German Europe, see Theodore S. Hamerow, 'History and the German Revolution of 1848', *AHR* 60/1 (Oct. 1954); Donald Mattheisen, 'History as Current Events: Recent Work on the German Revolution of 1848', *AHR* 88/5 (1985). Some representative recent scholarship can be found in Baumgart, *Revolution*; Langewiesche (ed.), *Revolution*; Siemann, *Revolution*. Valentin, *Geschichte*, remains worth reading for the richness and colour of its detail. There is a guide to the contemporary literature in Paul Wentzcke, *Kritische Bibliographie der Flugschriften zur deutschen Verfassungsfrage, 1848–1851* (Halle, 1911).

blow from a hammer in order to emerge from its mould'. Gustav Freytag was just one of many contemporaries who compared the pre-revolutionary political climate to an impending natural catastrophe. 'We lived then', he recalled, 'like people who feel under their feet the pressures of an earthquake. Everything in the German situation seemed loose and unstable, and everyone declared that things could not remain as they were.'[2]

The same ferment that evoked hope among young radicals terrified members of the ruling elite, who also felt the forces of change pressing against the limits of the old order. Thus Wilhelm von Kügelgen wrote in February 1847 that the nation was racing towards a terrible abyss: 'In the end God will lead us where he will, but it is frightful when an entire society, wide-awake and with its eyes open, gallops towards the edge and the coachman seems to crack the whip.' A few months later, as he strolled through his villa's stately rooms, Metternich expressed his own fears about the future. 'I am not a prophet', he told a visiting diplomat, 'and I don't know what will happen, but I am an old physician and can distinguish between temporary and fatal diseases. We now face one of the latter. We'll hold on as long as we can, but I have doubts about the outcome.' Such images of headlong flight and terminal illness capture the fatalism that gripped many of those in authority. Confronted by an apparently limitless reservoir of discontent, they had begun to doubt their own right and ability to rule. As significant as the waxing hope among the opposition, this waning confidence among the establishment was an essential element in the revolution's outbreak and initial triumph.[3]

i. THE OUTBREAK OF THE REVOLUTION

Despite the hopes and fears expressed by many Europeans during the late 1840s, revolution was not inevitable in 1848. Ever since the terrible surprise of 1789, people had anticipated the outbreak of revolution whenever there was a serious crisis; they were more often wrong than right. In fact, at the turn of the year 1847–8 things seemed to be getting better: the price of food was lower, the incidence of collective violence decreased, and the pace of political activity slowed. In January 1848 the citizens of Cologne celebrated

---

[2] M. Gregor Dellin, *Richard Wagner* (Munich, 1962), 207; Böhmer, *Welt*, p. 351. Another example of this can be seen in the anonymous article on 'Deutschland in 1847', *Grenzboten*, 7 (1847), 24 ff.

[3] Kügelgen, *Lebenserinnerungen*, p. 111; Srbik, *Metternich*, ii. 242.

Carnival with unprecedented gaiety and spirit; Gustav Mevissen complained that the political climate was '*stumpf*' and apathetic. Within a few weeks, however, the German situation was transformed by news from abroad. The troubles in Italy, which had begun with an insurrection in Palermo on 12 January, slowly spread northwards, threatening governments all along the peninsula. On 27 January Tocqueville described to the French Chamber of Deputies 'that feeling or instinct of instability . . . which precedes revolutions, which always proclaims them, which sometimes gives rise to them'. Three weeks later, on 22 February, the streets of Paris were filled with anti-government demonstrators; the next day they built barricades and fought with royal troops; on the day after that King Louis Philippe fled. Few people could now doubt that a great historical moment had arrived. For the third—and as it turned out, the last—time, events in France signalled revolution in Europe.[4]

Beginning in the south-west at the end of February, a wave of unrest spread through the German states until it reached the Russian frontier. In hundreds of cities, towns, and villages, people demanded political reform, social justice, and relief from misery and servitude. In petitions and parliamentary debates, demonstrations and strikes, and sometimes even armed insurrection against regular troops, Germans joined a national struggle for a new and better world. With the possible exception of the months immediately after the First World War, there is no other period in German history so full of spontaneous social action and dramatic political possibilities. As we try to understand this unfolding revolutionary drama, it is difficult not to speak of *the* Revolution of 1848: common usage tempts us to turn *it* into a singular movement, a cohesive and coherent process of change. Of course this was not so; there were many different revolutions in 1848, carried out in various places by diverse groups with incompatible objectives. Naturally enough, these revolutions were connected; their coincidence in time allowed them to exert great pressure against the defenders of the status quo. But, from the start, the upheavals of 1848 were a cluster of separate phenomena, combining to make up what Mack Walker called a 'revolution of conflicting expectations'. We must not lose sight of this essential multiplicity if we are to understand the reasons for the revolutionaries' initial successes and for their ultimate defeat.

---

[4] Repgen, *Märzbewegung*, p. 3; Mack Walker (ed.), *Metternich's Europe, 1813–1848* (New York, 1968), 342 ff.

During March a variety of groups acted together—or, to put the matter more precisely, acted at the same time—because they shared a common hostility to the established order. The members of this negative coalition were roughly comparable to the various elements in the pre-March opposition. First, there was a political movement, which ranged from moderate liberals, who wanted limited reform, to radical democrats, who wanted a totally new constitutional system. Relationships within the political opposition remained fluid throughout the spring of 1848, but centrifugal pressures steadily increased as moderates were drawn into co-operation with the governments and radicals were pulled towards more decisive expressions of their discontent. In addition to the political opposition, there was a broader and more diverse collection of groups for whom Germany's problems were social and economic rather than legal or constitutional. This wing of the revolutionary coalition was diffuse and spontaneous; it reflected the complex strains and conflicts within *Vormärz* society, which were now activated and intensified by the revolutionary situation. Throughout the spring and summer of 1848 a variety of social confrontations took place in the German lands—between workers and employers, townsmen and farmers, masters and journeymen, communities and outsiders, students and teachers, landowners and peasants, Christians and Jews. Some of these conflicts seem like modern labour disputes, others recall traditional battles over community rights and corporate identity.[5]

The multiplicity of forces at work in 1848 can be seen in Baden, where the revolutionaries gained one of their first important victories. On 12 February, even before the Paris uprising, Friedrich Bassermann, a prominent spokesman for south German liberals, formulated the goals of the moderate opposition in a widely-quoted speech to the *Landtag*. Two weeks later, when the news from France crossed the frontier, demonstrators took to the streets, first in Mannheim, then in Heidelberg and other Badenese cities. In this initial expression of political enthusiasm, people from many social groups and with quite different ideological positions worked

---

[5] 'The social crisis', Koselleck pointed out, 'gave the constitutional movement its essential impetus but at the same time prevented it from achieving its goal': *Preussen*, p. 620. For some examples of social conflicts, see Repgen's description of urban unrest in the Rhineland in *Märzbewegung*. A good recent summary can be found in Wolfram Siemann, 'Soziale Protestbewegungen in der deutschen Revolution von 1848/49', in H. Reinalter (ed.), *Demokratische and Soziale Protestbewegungen in Mitteleuropa, 1815–1848/49* (Frankfurt, 1986). On rural protests, Koch, 'Agrarrevolution'.

together, united behind a general programme that called for constitutional reform in Baden and a restructured federation in Germany. The main spokesmen for the political establishment—businessmen, civil servants, and academics—hoped that the events of 1848—just as they had hoped of the events of 1830—would enable them to extract constitutional concessions from the government. Their co-operation with the popular movement was instrumental and conditional, their practical aims limited, their willingness to act with the government readily apparent. As one observer reported, 'intelligent and prosperous citizens realized that now order and decorum are necessary or else their existence will be threatened'. Dignified processions, carefully drafted petitions, respectful audiences with the ruler, and moderate political change—these were the means and ends that appealed to those who acted from within Baden's political and social structure.[6]

Left-wing leaders like the radical lawyers Friedrich Hecker and Gustav von Struve, who viewed events from the fringes of Baden's establishment, had a different image of the revolution's proper course and destination. Although they had stood with the moderates during the first great demonstrations, Struve and Hecker were soon ready to set out on an independent path. By early March, when the petitions gathered during the previous week were presented to the *Landtag* in Karlsruhe, the capital was full of excited citizens, many of them recently arrived by railroad from neighbouring regions. Crowds threatened both the parliament and the palace; full-scale civil war seemed imminent. Within this overheated atmosphere, the left greatly overestimated its strength. When Hecker spoke to his colleagues in the *Landtag*, he sounded like a 'conqueror addressing his defeated foes'. With some difficulty, the moderate majority managed to refer proposals for reform to a committee, which set to work on a new constitutional order for the state. Meanwhile, the grand-duke, after having considered the possibility of a counter-revolutionary coup, accepted the moderate programme, appointed a liberal ministry, and committed himself to constitutional reform. For a time at least, the capital was quiet, the crowds eventually dispersed, and the immediate danger of violence passed. But the split between left and right steadily widened as men on each side recognized they might have to use force against the other.

[6] Valentin, *Geschichte*, i. 340 ff.; Botzenhart, *Parlamentarismus*, pp. 91–2; Wirtz, '*Widersetzlichkeiten*'.

While these conflicts over political ends and means were manifesting themselves within Baden's political opposition, another sort of revolution was going on in the countryside. At first peasants in the south-west had seemed immune to the political agitation unleashed by the fall of the July Monarchy. By the second week of March, however, unrest spread throughout the region and contemporaries began to talk about a 'new version of the peasant wars'. One centre of revolutionary activity was the Odenwald, an area dominated by the great estates of the *Standesherren*, whose peasants had to bear the burdens of seigneurial obligation as well as the taxes imposed by the state. The Odenwald peasants were not uninformed about politics; they had heard of Hecker, Struve, Mathy, and other parliamentary notables. But to the rural masses, freedom of the Press meant less than freedom from the oppressive control of the estate agent and the tax collector. When they decided to rid themselves of these burdens, they acted in the traditional manner, as a community, confronting the agents of their absentee landlords and the Jewish middlemen whom they held responsible for their poverty and oppression. When they met resistance, the peasants resorted to violence, sometimes against individuals, more often against the documents that recorded their obligations or against the property of their oppressors.[7]

In almost every German state, the same volatile blend of political agitation and social unrest forced concessions from the government. Although the details varied greatly, everywhere a similar pattern emerged: reports from France produced widespread expressions of discontent, usually led by the *Vormärz* opposition but quickly joined by more radical groups and reinforced by collective action among urban working people and peasants; confronted with this movement for change, rulers were at first uncertain and divided, then persuaded that some form of compromise was unavoidable. In the end, only one monarch was driven from his throne—Ludwig of Bavaria, his reign hopelessly damaged by his relationship to Lola Montez, had to abdicate in favour of his son, Maximilian II—but almost everywhere reactionary ministers were forced to resign and were replaced by members of the moderate opposition. These new ministries then proceeded to abolish censorship, lift restrictions on political organizations, and promise far-reaching constitutional reforms. With extraordinary speed and

[7] Gailus, 'Politisierung', especially pp. 91 ff.; Wirtz, '*Widersetzlichkeiten*', pp. 169 ff.; Rürup, *Emanzipation*, pp. 65 ff.

incredible ubiquity, a new political order had apparently been created.[8]

In late February and early March, before government concessions had reached epidemic proportions, some rulers had considered fighting to preserve the old order. King William of Württemberg, for instance, was an old soldier with happy memories of his campaigns against Napoleon. When first confronted with demands for reform, his initial response had been defiance. We are not alone, he told one liberal delegation, because Prussia, Austria, and Russia will stand with us against disorder. As the Russian ambassador reported from Stuttgart, 'Here one looks to an *entente* of conservative states for salvation.'[9] And why not? Had not such a conservative alliance defeated the great revolution and its Napoleonic heirs? Had not Austria and Prussia underwritten the restoration in 1815 and the counter-revolution after 1830? During the early spring of 1848 there must have been many minor princes who hoped that the great powers would once again save them from the rabble. But in 1848 the situation was different: this time, the lands of the Habsburgs and Hohenzollern did not remain immune to revolutionary infection. By the middle of March it was not at all clear that the rulers of Austria and Prussia could save themselves, let alone come to the aid of their brother monarchs.

Reports of the revolution in Paris reached Vienna on 29 February. When Metternich received word of the July Monarchy's collapse from one of the Rothschilds' agents, he is supposed to have said, 'Eh bien, mon cher, tout est fini.' Many of the prince's fellow citizens shared his sense of impending doom; within hours, long lines appeared outside of Vienna's banks as depositors rushed to convert paper money into silver; some merchants refused to accept notes and the price of foodstuffs rose sharply. While people thus demonstrated their lack of faith in the government, the *Vormärz* opposition asserted the need for fundamental change in the political system. On 3 March Louis Kossuth delivered a biting attack on the regime in a speech to the Hungarian Diet at Pressburg: 'A pestilent breeze', he declared, 'blows from the charnel house of the Vienna system, paralysing our nerve, impeding our spirit.' By the following evening a German translation of Kossuth's speech was being circulated in Vienna, where members of the *Juristischer Leseverein* were busy formulating petitions and mobilizing opinion. Ferment quickly spread from these established centres of

---

[8] The best narrative of these events remains Valentin, *Geschichte*, i.
[9] Ibid. i. 349–50.

dissent to other groups, especially university students and working people in the industrial suburbs.[10]

The imperial government watched the growth of political agitation with alarm and dismay. On 6 March Joseph Maria von Radowitz reported from Vienna to King Frederick William that the authorities were 'deeply shaken and confused'. Radowitz was scandalized to discover that 'many have the growing feeling that any struggle against the impending doom will be in vain'.[11] Even Metternich, who had recovered from his initial shock and was trying to build a reactionary coalition, seemed incapable of responding to the deepening crisis. Meanwhile, the chancellor's enemies at court seized the opportunity to intensify their intrigues against him. Kolowrat, Metternich's chief rival and the self-appointed champion of reform within the government, continued to woo the liberals but could not effect any changes in policy. A resolute minority was in favour of resistance, but they could not formulate a coherent strategy of self-defence. In retrospect, it seems likely that, if the government had had the will, it could have defeated any popular movement. But this would have required a willingness to risk civil war through a quick and decisive use of the army; neither the police force nor the largely ceremonial Civil Guard was sufficient to maintain order.

While the imperial government struggled to overcome its internal weakness and division, support for the political opposition grew. On 13 March a large and well-planned demonstration was held outside the Landhaus, where the Lower Austrian *Stände* had convened. The day was warm, and the crowd, mostly well-dressed and respectable citizens, students, and some artisans, must have felt that sense of excitement and anticipation that frequently attends the first, innocent acts of a revolutionary drama. Spontaneously, speakers addressed the throng, someone read Kossuth's speech, people cheered their alleged champions at court and demanded Metternich's resignation. After the Grand Marshal of the *Stände* emerged to announce his colleagues' sympathy for reform, a

---

[10] Srbik, *Metternich*, ii. 247; Jessen (ed.), *Revolution*, p. 48. For the background to Kossuth's speech, see Deak, *Revolution*, pp. 66 ff. On the Austrian revolution as a whole, see Rath, *Revolution*; Brandt, *Neoabsolutismus*, i. ch. 2; Josef Polisensky, *Aristocrats and the Crowd in the Revolutionary Year 1848. A Contribution to the History of the Revolution and Counter-Revolution in Austria* (Albany, 1980). Kudlich, *Rückblicke*, is an eyewitness account from a left-wing perspective. Heinrich Friedjung's *Österreich von 1848 bis 1860* (2 vols., Stuttgart and Berlin, 1908) is still worth reading.

[11] Radowitz, *Briefe*, pp. 12–14.

delegation left for the palace. As the day wore on, the crowd continued to grow in size and self-confidence, but not in organization or direction. Throughout the city, skirmishes between demonstrators and the army took place. As so often happened when soldiers were employed to quell unrest, they overreacted and responded to peaceful protests with excessive force. But this time, instead of melting away, the crowds fought back or regrouped elsewhere. Outside the walls, in the crowded and depressed suburbs that encircled the city, workers and artisans settled old scores against unpopular landlords and factory owners, tax collectors and government officials. By nightfall, the sky was illuminated by the flames of burning buildings and the flickering light from gas mains that had been broken and ignited.[12]

To the frightened and exhausted men meeting in the Hofburg, the sights and sounds that filled the streets must have seemed like a nightmare come to life. All day the archdukes and their closest advisers met delegations, heard petitions, and debated what to do. They had to decide by nine o'clock, the deadline set late that afternoon, when the officers of the Civil Guard had met to demand that Metternich resign and that they be issued weapons. Just before nine, the last advocates of armed resistance agreed to a compromise settlement. Metternich wrote a brief letter relinquishing all his posts; twenty-four hours later, in disguise and with money borrowed from the Rothschilds, he left the city to begin a long and circuitous passage to England, where he joined other casualties of the revolution such as Louis Philippe, Guizot, Prince William of Prussia, and Lola Montez. In fact, the Austrian prince and Lola, a newly-minted Bavarian countess, almost crossed the Channel on the same ship—a coincidence of fate that might have amused the lady but that could only have added one more indignity to the statesman's journey. Franz Grillparzer, a victim of reaction but no friend of the revolution, marked Metternich's fall with the following bitter epitaph:

> Hier liegt, für seinen Ruhm zu spät,
> Der Don Quijote der Legitimität,
> Der Falsch und Wahr nach seinem Sinne bog,
> Zuerst die andern, dann sich selbst belog;
> Vom Schelm zum Toren ward bei grauem Haupte,
> Weil er zuletzt die eignen Lügen glaubte.[13]

[12] Häusler, *Massenarmut*, pp. 145 ff.
[13] Jessen (ed.), *Revolution*, p. 64.

Metternich's departure seemed to signal the end of the regime he had personified. But what would take its place? Austrian moderates had reason to hope that the final victory would be theirs. Surely they were the 'genuine, enlightened representatives of the people', who could now lead the nation to a more progressive future. Moderate opinion was delighted by the emperor's proclamation of 15 March which abolished censorship, acknowledged the importance of the Civil Guard, and promised to convene a constitutional assembly as soon as possible. But in order to enjoy these newly won achievements, it would be necessary to have peace and domestic tranquillity. The violence, which the moderates had used for their own ends on 13 March, had to stop. Count Hoyos, the new commander of the Civil Guard, called upon responsible people to join his fight against 'the wild, criminal impulses of the proletariat . . . who believe they will profit from an upheaval in the entire social order'.[14] During the next few days the authorities were able to restore a fragile peace to the capital, but disorder continued in the countryside and the forces of discontent grew stronger throughout the Habsburgs' scattered lands.

Most observers recognized that the Austrian government's defeat on 13 March would have major implications for Prussia. Radowitz, for example, feared that the events in Vienna had broken 'the most secure dam against the revolutionary tide'. Writing to his wife from the Austrian capital on 15 March, he expressed his concern that even now, as 'I direct these troubled words to you, perhaps the same tumult will be taking place under the palace windows in Berlin'. The next day, in an official dispatch to the king, Radowitz urged Frederick William to stand firm and defend his historic rights, even if that meant temporarily abandoning Berlin for a more defensible position elsewhere in Prussia. Radowitz was not opposed to reform, but he believed that it should come as a gift from the throne, not as a prize won by popular action: 'It is only acts of free will that can save the essence of monarchy and perhaps contain within themselves the germ of legal development. . . . The same measures, if obtained by force during an attempt at rebellion, would lead to the abyss of revolution.'[15]

By mid-March there was good reason to be worried about Prussia's fate. People in the kingdom's western provinces, like Germans all along the border with France, had reacted to the news from Paris with speed and sympathy. For instance, on 3 March a

[14] Häusler, *Massenarmut*, p. 154.
[15] Radowitz, *Briefe*, pp. 32–3.

large but orderly crowd gathered in Cologne; their leader, a radical public health official named Andreas Gottschalk, demanded political equality, freedom of the Press, and a Civil Guard. When the city council was unable to deflect popular protests with promises of reform, troops were called to disperse the crowd and arrest its leaders, including Gottschalk and several others. The town fathers then established their own guard to keep order while they joined with other Rhenish liberals to petition the government for moderate reforms. Although things remained relatively quiet in Cologne after the demonstrations of early March, these first spontaneous expressions of popular political action, together with the revolutionary activity apparent elsewhere in the German west, were enough to frighten many members of the *Bürgertum*. 'We are approaching anarchy with rapid steps', wrote Camphausen on 15 March. Unless the king 'acts at once', the Rhine provinces might easily be drawn away from Prussia into some kind of western confederation of revolutionary states.[16]

As we have seen, the ability to 'act at once' was not among Frederick William's most prominent characteristics. Even while dispatches arrived daily bearing news of turmoil throughout the German lands and the citizens of Berlin were growing more and more restless, the king hesitated. When the weather turned unseasonably warm in mid-March, crowds gathered every day on the Zelten, north of the Tiergarten, where they listened to speeches, read the broadsides being produced in great quantity, and signed petitions demanding political change and increased public assistance for the unemployed and distressed. Something had to be done. The Berlin court, like its counterpart in Vienna, was divided between those who wanted to defy the opposition and those who were prepared to make compromises in order to avoid bloodshed. Yet neither side could say for sure what its strategy might entail. How much violence would be needed to quell the crowds? How far would the reformers have to go in order to satisfy the discontented? Faced with such persistent uncertainties, the king followed his instincts and did nothing.

Finally, on the evening of 17 March, Frederick William approved plans that met some of the moderates' most important demands: immediate recall of the United *Landtag*, a constitution for Prussia, initiatives to reform the Confederation, and freedom of the Press. On the morning of the 18th, however, the king appointed General

---

[16] Repgen, *Märzbewegung*, p. 45.

von Prittwitz, a hard-liner, as military commander of Berlin. Prittwitz's troops, apparently frightened by the presence of a large and peaceful gathering in front of the royal palace, fired into the crowd, killing several civilians. People reacted furiously. Even moderate and respectable Berliners felt that they had been betrayed by the king and callously assaulted by his soldiers. Throughout the city, men and women built barricades and prepared to fight to obtain what they thought they had been given. Thus the day that had begun as a celebration of the king's goodwill ended with a broadly based insurrection against the established order. We do not know the social position of those who fought against the king's soldiers through the afternoon and into the night of 18 March, but we do know the identities of many who died in the fighting. Most of them were males—only eleven of the three hundred *Märzge-fallenen* were women—between the ages of twenty and thirty-five; they included a few members of the *Bürgertum* (an official, a manufacturer, two students) and some manual workers, but the overwhelming majority consisted of craftsmen, usually journey-men—butchers, smiths, printers, saddlers, masons, shoemakers, mechanics, and bakers. For some reason, tailors (with eleven) and cabinet-makers (with twenty-three) were most numerous.[17]

While there may seem to be something contingent, even accidental, about the way the shooting started on the Schlossplatz, there was nothing contingent or accidental about the conflicts which these events brought to a head. Political frustrations and social discontents were deeply rooted in Prussia, whose citizens remembered how often their monarchs had reneged on promised reforms. More immediately, relations between civilians and soldiers were chronically tense. The officer corps, staffed by the sons of the landed nobility, viewed townsmen with contempt and regarded any crowd of civilians as little better than a rabble, waiting to be taught a lesson by their betters. Civilians, on the other hand, viewed the army as both symbol and instrument of reaction. Among those gathered on the Schlossplatz there were surely some who had suffered from the arrogance of the military élite and many more who had seen soldiers used against demon-strators. When the crowd chanted, 'Militär zurück!', they were calling not just for the removal of an immediate threat but also for what they recognized was a necessary prerequisite for meaningful reform. If political change in Prussia were to be a reality, the officer

---

[17] Jürgen Kuczynski and Ruth Hoppe, 'Eine Beruf- bzw. auch Klassen- und Schichtenanalyse der Märzgefallenen 1848 in Berlin', *JbW* 4 (1964), 200–77.

corps would have to be reformed and the repressive power of the army controlled.[18]

The bloody events of 18 March made a shambles out of Frederick William's attempt to channel the opposition into a moderate course. That evening he faced in stark and unyielding terms what he had been trying to avoid for a fortnight—the choice between determined resistance or unambiguous surrender to popular demands. After being told by Prittwitz that the city could be pacified only with difficulty and considerable loss of life, the king decided to give in to the reformers and put his fate in the hands of his subjects. Early in the morning of 19 March, he wrote his famous proclamation 'An meine lieben Berliner!'—an extra-ordinary mixture of pathos and recrimination, which accepted the insurgents' key demand by promising to withdraw the troops. Theodor Fontane, who had spent the evening crouched on a barricade in Alexanderplatz armed with a useless carbine, recalled the feelings of joy and exultation with which he and his comrades learned of the king's decision. Victory was theirs—but, as Fontane recognized, the revolution's triumph had been given them as a gift and could just as easily be taken back.[19]

On 19 March Frederick William had to participate in a ritualized expression of his subordination to the popular will by standing, in respectful silence, as the bloody bodies of the revolution's victims were carried by. Over the next few days the king summoned the United *Landtag*, issued an address 'An mein Volk und an die deutsche Nation,' which seemed to promise Prussian leadership for a movement of national unification, and appointed a new ministry including the Rhenish liberals Camphausen and Hansemann.[20] Meanwhile, Prussian liberals joined representatives from other states to plan for a national German parliament, which was to prepare a new constitutional order for central Europe.

The appointment of the liberal March ministries—Camphausen in Prussia, Bekk in Baden, Römer and Pfizer in Württemberg, Stüve in Hanover—was a major triumph for the moderate opposition. Their revolution was now essentially over; once the leadership and conditions of public life had been transformed, these men thought the time had come to consolidate their gains, draft

---

[18] Craig, *Politics*, pp. 92 ff., has an excellent account of the army's role in 1848.

[19] Fontane, *Zwanzig*, pp. 327 ff.

[20] Huber, *Dokumente*, i. 262 ff. For a description of the king viewing the corpses, a scene grotesque enough to be the subject of a Goya painting, see Bettina von Arnim's account, reprinted in Jessen (ed.), *Revolution*, pp. 90–1.

new constitutional documents, and get back to the pressing business of everyday life.

The vast majority of Germans, however, still confronted the same problems which had pushed them over the brink of revolution. To them, the formation of the March ministries and the promise of constitutional reform seemed to make little difference. In fact, as Richard Tilly has shown, the incidence of violence increased after the liberals' victory: from 1 April to 1 June there were fifty-two outbreaks of violence as compared to forty-three during the preceding three months. Writing at the end of March from his headquarters at Koblenz, the chief of staff of the Prussian Eighth Corps told his superiors that everywhere in the Rhineland there was 'resistance against the authorities, lawlessness, and open unrest'. The same could certainly have been said about Silesia—where peasants began to attack manor houses and tax offices on 22 March—and about many other rural areas where peasant protests continued despite ministerial changes and constitutional promises. In large cities like Vienna, Berlin, and Cologne, poor people still faced the grim realities of hunger, crowded housing, and unemployment. In the words of one worker at a mass meeting in Elberfeld, these people wanted *Fressfreiheit*, not *Pressfreiheit*, 'freedom to feed', not 'freedom to read'.[21]

For some, the revolutionary situation had brought a new sense of common purpose and social identity. 'After March', Stephen Born recalled, 'the individual immediately felt part of a great and important political movement, and various groups sought and soon found a basis for co-operation.' As we shall see, the events of 1848 and 1849 encouraged the rise of new political leaders and the spread of a variety of new participatory institutions. Many of these leaders and institutions did not last long. In Königsberg, for instance, a group of radicals formed an *Arbeiterverein* on 16 April but could not control the unruly throng who shouted down their speeches and demanded immediate action. The revolutionary era was filled with short-lived organizations and popular agitators with careers of meteoric brevity and brightness. It was easier to gather a crowd than to channel its energies.[22]

The lower orders' persistent restlessness frightened and infuriated the moderate opposition. As early as 28 February the Rhenish

[21] Tilly *et al.*, (eds.), *Century*, p. 221; Schraepler, *Handwerkerbünde*, p. 247; Orr, 'Prussia'; Gailus, 'Politisierung', pp. 96 ff.; Repgen, *Märzbewegung*, p. 53.

[22] Born, *Erinnerungen*, p. 65. On the ebb and flow of organizational energies during the revolution, see Noyes, *Organization*.

liberal Gustav Mevissen had written that it would soon be necessary to support the government in an effort to defeat the 'Wühlereien der Kommunistencliquen'. A few days later, as the first wave of unrest was beginning to manifest itself, Robert von Mohl spoke of a new barbarism, whose threat to civilization was comparable to the invaders who destroyed Rome in the fifth century. Even those who had been prepared to use unrest to lever concessions from the government demanded law and order as soon as they got what they wanted. Thus in late March, the left-wing liberal Rudolf Virchow sadly reported from Berlin that a reaction against the lower classes had already begun; 'once again there is talk of the rabble.' Of course the same social unrest that pushed moderates to the right encouraged a greater militancy among the left-wing of the political opposition and thus undermined the co-operation of moderates and radicals. Once the initial victory over the old order had been won, the victors started to fight among themselves about whose image of the future should triumph.[23]

Events in Saxony provide a good illustration of this process. The Saxon revolution began in Leipzig almost as soon as the news from France arrived. The prime mover was Karl Biedermann, a moderate publicist with good connections to the city's intellectual and commercial élite. Robert Blum, the most influential leader of the Leipzig left, supported Biedermann's original petition to the king, even though it did not provide a 'clear, decisive expression' of the popular will. The moderates, for their part, were uneasy about the mass demonstrations that Blum organized in support of reform. Nevertheless, on 12 March the two groups were able to draft a programme which stated their common opposition to the status quo and concealed their differences behind vague generalities. With the formation of the Saxon reform ministry, however, relations between moderates and radicals entered a new phase. On 28 March Blum and the other left-wing leaders began to establish *Vaterlandsvereine*, into which only 'determined, progressive men' would be welcomed. By the end of April there were fifty-nine of these associations throughout the kingdom. Two days after the first *Vaterlandverein* was established, Leipzig liberals formed a *Deutscher Verein*, which soon had over forty branches. The two organizations were still united by their commitment to reform and

[23] Repgen, *Märzbewegung*, p. 16; Angermann, *Mohl*, p. 59; Virchow, *Briefe*, pp. 139–40. See also Fanny Lewald's comparison of the public mood in Paris and Berlin: *Erinnerungen aus dem Jahre 1848* (1850; repr. Frankfurt, 1969), 74–5.

their hostility to reaction, but institutionally, socially, and ideologically the cleavage between Saxony's moderates and leftists was unmistakable.[24]

In Württemberg, liberals and democrats remained institutionally united until the summer of 1848, but here too strains within the coalition gradually became apparent. The first indication of disagreement came with the formation of the Römer ministry, which was accompanied by a declaration calling for 'Ruhe and Ordnung' so that the future might be prepared with 'Vernunft und Mässigung'. But the Württemberg left could not remain idle as unrest spread in the countryside and the forces of reaction seemed to be in such disarray. Surely, radicals believed, it would now be possible to preserve the momentum for change, move with the times, and create a new political order. While the reform ministry urged caution, the left began to demand a greater say in the conduct of affairs. As one radical journalist put the matter early in April, 'The hour of privilege has passed . . . we no more want to be ruled by the liberal plutocrats than we did by the old reactionary system.' This statement went to the heart of their differences: in the view of an increasing number on the left, the moderates had joined the other side, taking the place of the enemies against whom they had once waged a common struggle.[25]

The deepest and most consequential break between moderates and radicals occurred in Baden, where political antagonisms had steadily increased after the appointment of a liberal ministry in mid-March. Baden's proximity to both France and Switzerland opened the state to foreign influences and, potentially at least, to armed intervention. Furthermore, Baden's radical leaders, Hecker and Struve, were deeply suspicious of the new government and, impressed by the level of popular unrest they saw throughout the south-west, confident that they could lead a successful rebellion of the *Volk*. To the Badenese radicals, liberal efforts to work within the existing order betrayed the essential meaning of the revolution, which, as Struve declared at the end of March, 'had dissolved all the bonds connecting the German *Volk* to the so-called existing order of things'. After Hecker's and Struve's efforts to mobilize a national movement behind their radical programme were frustrated by their liberal antagonists in Baden and at the Frankfurt *Vorparlament*,

---

[24] Weber, *Revolution*, pp. 24 ff. There is a good firsthand account in Biedermann, *Leben*, i. 244 ff.

[25] Langewiesche, *Liberalismus*, pp. 127 ff.

they proclaimed a republic and called for an armed rising of the *Volk*. Several thousand people answered this call for rebellion, including a detachment of German craftsmen and students mobilized by the poet Georg Herwegh in France. The rebels fought bravely, but they were poorly led, ill-equipped, and badly outnumbered. By the end of the month, the rebellion was totally defeated, its leaders either in prison or in exile.[26]

At least in retrospect, the outcome of the Badenese rebellion demonstrates that the radicals, despite their apparent popularity and the persistence of social unrest, were not in a position to impose a political solution. Popular violence could still disrupt local institutions, force concessions, and create disorder, but it could not provide the basis for a new social or political order. Moreover, as became clear when the Confederation's troops soundly defeated the Badenese rebels, the governments retained instruments of effective force. The institutions of the old regime, despite their failures in March, were a good deal stronger than they appeared. Yet the conservatives, like the radicals, could not impose their own social and political solution: strong enough to defeat the revolutionaries, the forces of order were not strong enough to turn the clock back to the days before March. Given this constellation of forces, the outcome of the revolution depended on those occupying the middle ground, the moderate leaders of the political opposition who seemed to have emerged victorious from the first phase of the revolution. In the next two sections, we will follow the moderates' efforts to come to terms with radical and reactionary pressures, first on the newly created level of national politics, then in the various states, where the essential political contests were to be won and lost.

ii. THE FRANKFURT PARLIAMENT AND THE GERMAN QUESTION

From Friedrich Bassermann's speech to the Baden *Landtag* on 12 February 1848 until the triumph of reaction eighteen months later, national issues and aspirations played a central role in the revolution. Liberals and radicals were convinced that the existing political order in central Europe was intolerable; both groups believed that Metternich's Confederation was an inadequate foundation for German public life. But on the national question, as on most other issues, the political opposition was divided over means

[26] Mommsen, *Parteiprogramme*, pp. 125 ff.

and ends: at one end of the spectrum were those like Hecker and Struve, who wanted to use a mass insurrection to create a German republic, while at the other were people like Hansemann and Camphausen, who would have been satisfied with a reformed version of the Confederation. As we should expect, most Germans took a position somewhere between these extremes, committed in some ill-defined way to a combination of innovation and continuity. Moreover, during the revolution's first stage, few realized the full extent of their disagreements, which seemed much less important than a common commitment to finding a more powerful and cohesive basis for national life.[27]

Members of the political opposition were not alone in their dissatisfaction with the Confederation. In the autumn of 1847 Joseph Maria von Radowitz, the Prussian attaché to the diet, managed to convince King Frederick William IV that a congress of German princes should assemble to consider federal reform. Metternich, however, firmly opposed Radowitz's plan, since he recognized that strengthening the Confederation would most probably also strengthen Prussian influence at Austria's expense. Radowitz was still seeking some form of an Austro-Prussian agreement in March 1848 when the pressure of events rendered his plan obsolete. Meanwhile, in Frankfurt a reform movement was under way within the federal diet itself. On 3 March, as the wave of unrest was just beginning to spread eastwards, the diet acknowledged the bankruptcy of its reactionary policies by granting each state the right to revoke the repressive laws of 1819. Six days later it embraced the symbols of nationalism by adopting Black-Red-Gold as the Confederation's official colours. Finally, on 10 March, a majority of the diet's membership—some acting without instructions from their governments—called upon the various German states to send 'men trusted by the public' to Frankfurt in order to draft a new federal constitution. 'Männer des öffentlichen Vertrauens'—the phrase underscored the dramatic shift in the nature of German politics which had taken place during the first week of March. Political legitimacy required more than the traditional support of aristocracy or state; power now seemed to flow from the

[27] For an introduction to the literature on the 'German question', see Werner Conze, *The Shaping of the German Nation* (New York, 1979); Hagen Schulze, *Der Weg zum Nationalstaat. Die deutsche Nationalbewegung vom 18. Jahrhundert bis zur Reichsgründung* (Munich, 1985); Gruner, *Frage*; Erich Angermann, 'Die deutsche Frage, 1806–1866', in Theodor Schieder and Ernst Deuerlein (eds.), *Reichsgründung 1870/71* (Stuttgart, 1970), 9–32. The literature on nationalism is cited above, Ch. 6, sect. iv, n. 78.

'public', whose spokesmen suddenly found themselves at the centre of events.[28]

On 5 March, while Radowitz and Metternich were negotiating in Vienna and members of the diet were making their first concessions to the national movement, fifty-one self-selected leaders of the public met in Heidelberg to discuss Germany's future. Most of these men held some elective office, usually in one of the western *Landtage*, but as a group they had no legal standing. Except for a minority on the far left, those meeting at Heidelberg wanted to take advantage of the opportunities at hand without directly challenging either the states or the Confederation. Even at the peak of their power, when one state after another was bowing to their will, liberals were reluctant to set out on their own, to speak and act for the *Volk*. They wanted to work with, not against, the states, 'as long as a solution was possible along this path'. They saw themselves not as the vanguard of a new order, but as a source of encouragement and advice for the established authorities. In the end, therefore, the Heidelberg meeting left open the question of how Germany's future was to be defined. Instead it established a committee that was to summon a larger meeting of 'Vertrauens-männer aller deutschen Volksstämmer.' This body would then co-operate with 'the Vaterland as well as the governments' to prepare an elected national parliament. But even some of those who had agreed to the call for a national parliament hoped that the German question could be resolved by federal reform or the independent action of the major states.[29]

The so-called *Vorparlament*, convened by the committee established at Heidelberg, met in Frankfurt on 31 March. Five hundred and seventy-four men attended; they came from virtually every German state and represented the full spectrum of opinion among the political opposition. Most were members of a state or local representative institution. When they marched through the decorated streets of the old imperial city and gathered in the hall where the German emperors had once been crowned, the members of the *Vorparlament* must have felt that they were witnessing the passage from one era to another. As they became caught up in the celebrations of this *Freiheitsfest*, they must have hoped that the future—their future—was at hand. Once their deliberations had

[28] Radowitz, *Briefe*, pp. 8 ff.; Huber, ii. 588; Huber, *Dokumente*, i. 268–9.
[29] Huber, *Dokumente*, i. 265. On the pervasive uncertainties among the opposition, see Boldt, 'Monarchie'.

begun, however, the deep divisions in their ranks became unmistakable.

The *Vorparlament*'s first important order of business was to reject decisively Struve's call for a radical break with the present system, thus provoking the April rising discussed in the preceding section. Most of the *Vorparlament*, like the majority at the Heidelberg gathering, wanted to reform, not destroy the political order, Nevertheless, it was clearer now than it had been three weeks earlier that some kind of national parliament was unavoidable. The *Vorparlament*, therefore, voted in favour of elections for a constituent assembly and established a committee of fifty to help administer them. In the meantime, the Confederation and the states were to remain the only legitimate instruments of political authority. Even so, some moderates thought the *Vorparlament* had gone too far: the chances for change without revolution are diminishing, Droysen wrote on 5 April, 'people are boring holes in the barrel into which the water should be poured'.[30]

After the diet, which now represented the views of the new liberal 'March ministries', accepted the *Vorparlament*'s proposals, preparations for Germany's first national elections got under way. While these elections opened a new era in the history of German politics, their administration was a reminder that the everyday conduct of public life remained in the hands of the states, which were, by necessity, responsible for carrying out the *Vorparlament*'s decision. The ability of individual governments to control the elections was increased by the imprecision of the *Vorparlament*'s suffrage regulations. In the first place, these regulations did not make clear whether the voting should be direct or indirect, open or secret. With few exceptions (Württemberg, Hesse-Kassel, Schleswig-Holstein, Frankfurt, Hamburg, and Bremen), the states established a two-step ballot in which the final selection of a candidate was left in the hands of a college of electors. In some places, voting was public and, in a few, signed ballots were required. Second, while the *Vorparlament* specifically outlawed limiting the franchise on religious or financial grounds, it did say that only 'mature, independent' citizens (and this meant *male* citizens) could vote or be elected to office. No one was quite sure how the words 'volljährige, selbständige' got into the statement and no one was sure what they should mean. In some states, however, the authorities used this term to exclude the lower

---

[30] Droysen, *Briefwechsel*. i. 401.

orders. In Bavaria and Oldenburg, for instance, 'independence' was defined as the obligation to pay a direct tax; anyone whose income was too low to be taxable could not vote. Almost everywhere, the indigent were excluded and, somewhat less frequently, those without households of their own. All of these considerations meant that, despite the *Vorparlament*'s call for national elections on the basis of a unified and unrestricted suffrage, the actual electoral process varied enormously—at least from state to state and often from one community to the next, since local authorities might interpret the rules according to their own notions of what should be done.[31]

As important as the formal rules governing the elections were the institutional and attitudinal limitations on political participation that persisted throughout the German lands. Despite the powerful mobilizing experience of the past two months, most people approached the elections of May 1848 without a very clear idea about what was at stake. Only in a few places, such as the largest cities, were there political organizations to educate voters and shape their opinions. In the time available, it was impossible to build the lines of communication and bonds of allegiance on which effective participatory institutions must depend. Instead, the elections of 1848 had to draw on the same resources that had sustained German public life before the revolution: loose and informal groups of local notables, social and cultural organizations with latent political objectives, and a small, imperfectly defined national élite whose prominence rested on their reputation as publicists or state parliamentarians.[32]

Considering the diversity of suffrage regulations and the fragmented character of public life, it might seem remarkable that the elections of 1848 produced such a socially homogeneous parliament. As the data in table 11.1 suggest, the members of the Frankfurt parliament were from the same social groups that had comprised the German public since its first appearance in the last third of the eighteenth century. The overwhelming majority had attended a *Gymnasium*; at least 80 per cent held university degrees. Jurists were the largest single group, state employment the characteristic occupation. Some of these men had close ties to their voters, often as locally prominent bureaucrats or well-known

---

[31] Hamerow, 'Elections'.

[32] For some examples of local electoral activity, see Repgen, *Märzbewegung*; Köllmann, *Sozialgeschichte*, pp. 224 ff.; Nickel, *Revolution*, pp. 63 ff.; Fontane, *Zwanzig*, pp. 354–9 [on Berlin]; Sperber, *Catholicism*, pp. 47 ff.

TABLE 11.1. *Social composition of the Frankfurt parliament*

	Number	%
Administrative officials (in state and local government)	157	19.7
Judicial officials	119	14.9
University or Schoolteachers	123	15.4
Lawyers	130	16.3
Businessmen	75	9.4
Landowners	68	8.5
Clergy	45	5.6
Writers, Journalists	36	4.5
Physicians	25	3.1
Officers	15	1.9
Unknown	6	0.7
TOTAL	799	100

Source: Eyck, *Parliament*, p. 95.

public figures. Others were elected by men they did not know and from districts they had never visited; this group included 'celebrities' like Bassermann or Radowitz, as well as urban notables who were adopted by the electoral colleges in nearby rural communities. What seems to have mattered to many voters was that the candidate be a 'mover and doer', able to operate on a terrain beyond the local world. That most of these men considered themselves 'liberals' may tell us more about the political orientation of this national élite than it does about the political values of the electorate.[33]

On 18 May the newly elected members of the Frankfurt parliament assembled in the Römersaal, under the portraits of the Holy Roman Emperors, and then marched in formal procession to the Paulskirche, which would remain the site of their deliberations for most of the next eleven months. If the choice of Frankfurt as a meeting place underscored the lines of continuity liberals wished to draw between their enterprise and the Confederation, the selection

[33] Eyck, *Parliament*, pp. 62 ff.; Walker, *Home Towns*, pp. 366 ff. Wolfram Siemann has some interesting reflections on the significance of the parliament's social composition; *Die Frankfurter Nationalversammlung 1848/49 zwischen demokratischem Liberalismus und konservativer Reform. Die Bedeutung der Juristendominanz in den Verfassungsverhandlungen des Paulskirchenparlaments* (Bern, 1976).

of the Paulskirche as a meeting place suggested how they defined their task. The church was large enough to hold all of the delegates, representatives of the Press, and a substantial number of spectators. Speakers addressed their audience individually, from the pulpit. Debate from the floor was nearly impossible; there were no facilities for committees or caucuses. Apparently, the parliament's work was to be done in the plenum, which would respond to the reasoned eloquence of each speaker and, under the respectful scrutiny of the *Volk*, come to a collective decision. The opening session showed how unrealistic these expectations were. When the first chairman, who had been selected because of his seniority, proved incapable of maintaining order, the proceedings quickly deteriorated into chaos, as various speakers competed for attention with one another and with the noisy galleries.[34]

Things improved somewhat after the delegates elected Heinrich von Gagern as their first permanent president. Born in 1799, a veteran of Waterloo, *Burschenschaftler*, one-time civil servant, successful landowner, leader of the *Vormärz* opposition in Hesse, and an eloquent spokesman for the majority at the *Vorparlament*, Gagern personified moderate liberalism. Moreover, in his character and personality, he stood for the qualities liberals most admired: he was passionate but restrained, idealistic but not doctrinaire, committed but dignified. Gustav Freytag spoke of the 'purity and innocence', of his idealism, his 'great trust in the goodness of the national character, honest loyalty, and proud, moral force'—a description which reminds us once again how easily German liberals blended ethical and political categories.[35]

Under Gagern's leadership, the parliament gradually evolved rules and procedures which enabled its members to limit debate and come to decisions on major issues. Nevertheless, throughout its life the *Nationalversammlung* would be marked by what one participant called the professors' 'Sprechsucht'—an insatiable appetite for words (preferably their own)—and the lawyers' 'Klauben und Makeln' about every detail. On important questions, such as the definition of the executive, as many as one hundred men felt obliged to speak, many of them inevitably repeating what had already been said. It has long been fashionable to attack the men at Frankfurt for their loquacity—as early as the autumn of 1848 Georg Herwegh mocked the 'Parla- Parla- Parlament'. Of course,

[34] For a description of Paulskirche, see Jessen (ed.), *Revolution*, pp. 131 ff.; Helmut Heiber, 'Die Rhetorik der Paulskirche', unpublished diss. (Berlin, 1953).
[35] Hock, *Denken*, p. 83. See also Gagern, *Liberalismus*.

language had always been of crucial importance for the leaders of the German political public. As members of the clerisy and participants in literary culture, the parliamentarians brought with them to Frankfurt a profound faith in the power of words to express and resolve political issues. Moreover, we should not overlook the function this speechifying performed. Most members of the national assembly had little experience with the kind of issues they faced; they had neither formal organizations to guide them nor established relationships upon which they could rely. What else could they do but state their own opinions, listen carefully for potential allies, and slowly distance themselves from apparent enemies?[36]

During the first weeks of May, when the parliamentarians began to arrive in Frankfurt, their initial task, after finding a place to live, was to locate people who shared their views. This was not easy. Most did not know one another personally; few had the kind of organizational connections that could help them identify like-minded men. Moreover, many liberals distrusted formally defined factions. Robert von Mohl, for example, believed that parties were a sign of 'unfinished political education'. But some form of collective action turned out to be unavoidable. By the middle of June political groups had begun to coalesce, taking their names from the hotels and restaurants in which they met; the conservatives gathered at the Café Milani, the liberals at the Landsberg, Augsburger Hof, Württemberger Hof, and Westendhall, and the democrats at the Deutscher Hof and Donnersberg. Initially, these groups resembled the informally organized, socially oriented associations so characteristic of *Vormärz* public life. Eventually, however, they drafted rules to govern their activites and programmes to define the basis for membership.[37]

Too much should not be made of these factions. A sizeable minority, perhaps as large as 25 per cent of the membership, never joined one. Others moved from one group to another, and sometimes back again. Not surprisingly, therefore, various calculations of the size of the factions vary widely. Nevertheless, for most parliamentarians, membership in a faction eventually became

[36] Jessen (ed.), *Revolution*, pp. 138–9. See also Eyck, *Parliament*, pp. 150 ff.; Ziebura, 'Anfänge'.

[37] Eyck, *Parliament*, p. 198, gives the following summary of political alignments as of June 1848: Right 43 (7.5%), Right Centre 156 (27%), Left Centre 121 (21%), Left 55 (9.5%), Extreme Left 46 (8%), No Party 155 (27%), Total 576. For other assessments, see Boldt, *Anfänge*, pp. 68 ff.; Botzenhart, *Parlamentarismus*, pp. 415 ff.; Kramer, *Fraktionsbindungen*, pp. 74 ff.

a prerequisite for influence. More and more of the most significant issues were debated and decided outside the plenum, at late-night meetings in smoke-filled rooms. In the words of one observer, 'the decisions were taken in the clubs and thereafter the final result was voted on—the great speakers at the podium could say what they wanted'.[38]

The first major issue around which the factions took shape was the same one that had plagued the liberal revolutionaries when they met in Heidelberg in early March: what was their relationship to the existing order? How did their authority relate to the authority of the states? The very act of posing these questions shows that, even after their political legitimacy had been validated by national elections, many delegates at Frankfurt were uncertain if they could or should speak for the *Volk*.

In his opening address as president, Gagern, who had accepted the idea of a national assembly with great reluctance, seemed to take an equivocal view of the parliament's power and responsibility. 'We want to create a constitution for Germany', he said. 'The obligation and power for this creation lies in the sovereignty of the nation.' But what did this mean in practice? For instance, did the Frankfurt assembly, as the expression of national sovereignty, take precedence over all other German political institutions? Franz Raveaux, a radical delegate from Cologne, tried to establish the legal basis for such precedence with a resolution calling for the adjournment of other legislative bodies while the national parliament was at work. Raveaux's motion met bitter opposition from Gagern and the other moderates. The end result was a compromise resolution that proclaimed the principle of Frankfurt's sovereignty, but refrained from questioning the authority of the states to carry on business as usual. As would often happen during the following months, the parliamentarians achieved a kind of consensus by joining a clear statement of principle with an ambiguous set of practical limits and qualifications.[39]

A similar pattern emerged a month later when the parliament considered the establishment of a temporary executive. Most delegates were convinced that they needed some executive power to defend themselves against their enemies at home and abroad. But there was considerable disagreement about this executive's institutional character and its relationship to the existing authorities

---

[38] Max Schwarz, *MdR: Biographisches Handbuch der Reichstage* (Hanover, 1965), 11.

[39] Huber, ii. 621.

in the states and Confederation. The special committee selected to consider the matter produced a divided report that touched off a bitter debate in the plenum. After six days of prolonged discussion, with no consensus in sight, Heinrich von Gagern left his place as chairman to address the assembly. He proposed what he called a 'kühner Griff', which was actually a skilful compromise: the parliament was to establish an executive on its own, without reference to existing authorities, but the executive's formal head, the so-called *Reichsverweser*, or Imperial Vicar, would be a Habsburg, Archduke John, and would not be responsible to the parliament that had appointed him. A conservative like Radowitz, who had opposed the notion of an independent executive, accepted Gagern's proposal as a reasonable compromise, but Georg Herwegh, writing from exile, regarded the appointment of a Habsburg prince as one more sign that the revolution had sold its soul:

> Glocken tönt! Kanonen donnert! Schmeichte, schmeichte, feiles Erz!
> Geht ein jeder Schuss doch mitten durch der jungen Freiheit Herz.[40].

The ministry appointed by the Imperial Vicar did nothing to assuage radicals' sense of betrayal: Prince Karl Leiningen became Minister President; Eduard von Peucker, a Prussian general, Minister of War; Hermann von Beckerath, a Rhenish businessman and moderate liberal, Minister of Finance, Anton von Schmerling, an advocate of Austrian interests, Minister of the Interior, Johann Gustav Heckscher, a lawyer from Hamburg, Foreign Minister, Arnold Duckwitz, a merchant from Bremen, Minister of Commerce, and Robert von Mohl, Minister of Justice. Although the ministers were an impressive group, who brought to their tasks considerable talent and goodwill, they were not the sort of men to mobilize the *Volk* behind a revolutionary movement. Had they had a state to serve, the Frankfurt executive would have served it well; but while the parliament could claim to represent the German nation, its executive could hardly pretend to be a state. Legally, it continued to face competing sources of power, both in the Confederation and, much more important, in the various state governments. Practically, the Frankfurt executive continued to be without those instruments of effective force upon which all politics ultimately must depend. Less than three months after its creation, the fragility of the national executive's authority became painfully

---

[40] Jessen (ed.), *Revolution*, p. 163. On this debate, see Eyck, *Parliament*, pp. 166 ff.

clear when a series of crises threatened the very existence of the liberal revolution.

The so-called 'September crisis' was triggered by events in Schleswig-Holstein, whose complicated constitutional status produced a series of disruptions on the northern fringes of German Europe. The duchies were ruled by the king of Denmark; they were legally inseparable, but only Holstein belonged to the German Confederation. Moreover, they were governed under Salic Law, which stipulated that their sovereign must be a male. Since the male line of the Danish royal house was about to die out, the duchies' future was in doubt. Although they were linguistically mixed— German in the south, heavily Danish in the north—German nationalists hoped to use the impending constitutional crisis to unhitch the duchies from Denmark and turn them into a German state. Since several of the most prominent liberal leaders, including Dahlmann, Droysen, and Georg Beseler, had close ties to the duchies, this agitation had a considerable impact on the national movement as a whole. However, the new Danish government, which had no intention of abandoning the duchies, annexed Schleswig on 21 March. The Germans in the south rebelled and established their own provisional government. When the Danes sent troops to back up their claims, the Germans sought support from Prussia and a few smaller states.

As was true of everything to do with Schleswig and Holstein, the military and diplomatic developments during the summer of 1848 were excruciatingly complex. The German troops did well on land, but were restrained from final victory both by the Danes' naval superiority and the great powers' determination that Denmark should not be allowed to suffer a humiliating defeat. Finally, on 26 August, the Prussians and the Danes signed an armistice at Malmö, which called for a mutual evacuation of troops and new efforts to reach a political solution. Prussia acted for itself and for the Confederation, but said nothing about the Frankfurt parliament, on whose behalf it was supposed to be at war. In Frankfurt, the Holstein lobby, led by Dahlmann, was outraged. On 5 September the delegates voted 238 to 221 to inhibit the execution of the armistice; the Leiningen government, accepting responsibility for the débâcle, resigned. Now what? While Dahlmann tried without success to find majority support for a new ministry, it became increasingly clear that the assembly had little purchase on Prussia and virtually no control over the situation in the north. On 16 September the parliament reversed itself and accepted the Malmö agreement, thus acknowledging its military and diplomatic impotence. As if this were not enough, the parliament's humiliation continued over the next week when angry crowds attacked delegates, killed two right-wing representatives, and threatened the Paulskirche itself. Only the intervention of federal troops restored order.[41]

In the September crisis we catch a glimpse of those forces that would ultimately defeat the liberal revolution: the Prussian government's disdain foreshadows the parliament's failure to control the states, just as the Frankfurt populace's hostility foreshadows its failure to mobilize the *Volk*. After September, as we shall see, anti-liberal forces grew steadily stronger—both in the major state governments and in popular organizations throughout the German lands. In retrospect, therefore, it seems clear that, during the autumn of 1848, the tide turned against the liberals. Whatever the men at Frankfurt did, however swiftly and creatively they settled the questions before them, their efforts may well have been doomed to fail. But while the most perceptive parliamentarians sometimes must have sensed the weakness of their position, few gave up hope that they might fashion a nation according to their own ideals. Their faith in the power of their words which was the basis of their faith in themselves and in their claim to represent the real *Volk*, was shaken but not destroyed by the September crisis in Frankfurt and the restoration of monarchical authority in Vienna and Berlin that occurred a few weeks later. This faith sustained the parliamentarians during the long, exhausting debates that captivated them from May 1848 until the following March.

On 24 May, in one of their first moves to impose order on the proceedings, the delegates had elected a Constitutional Committee, composed of thirty of the assembly's best-known and most effective members, who were charged with drafting proposals for the plenum's consideration. Two days after its creation, the Constitutional Committee decided to begin its deliberations with a discussion of the basic rights—*Grundrechte*—to be guaranteed by the new constitution. Everyone at Frankfurt recognized that some statement about basic rights would be a necessary part of any constitutional document. Moreover, there seemed to be some good reasons to deal with these matters before turning to the definition of sovereignty, which many believed would be a much more difficult and divisive problem. Agreement on basic rights, it was

---

[41] See the contemporary views reprinted in Jessen (ed.), *Revolution*, pp. 223 ff. Sharlin, 'Structure', ch. 6, has an analysis of the demonstrators.

hoped, could easily be attained and thus might lubricate the assembly's decision-making mechanisms. Some also believed that a clear statement of rights would have a soothing impact on those social groups whose organized discontent continued to disturb liberals. Such calculations reveal delegates' touching confidence in the universality of their ideals and in the ease with which they could be defined and applied. But in fact the debate over the *Grundrechte* was long and gruelling—it lasted from July to October and was forced to leave several important issues unresolved. Furthermore, neither the debate nor its outcome did much to win the allegiance of discontented elements in German society. On the contrary, as the parliamentarians' goals became apparent, many Germans turned away in anger.[42]

The least controversial issue in the debate on basic rights was the section guaranteeing freedom of speech. In a series of articles, the parliament effectively dismantled the institutions of Metternichian reaction: every German was guaranteed the right 'freely to express his opinion in words, writing, print, and pictures', to assemble and to form organizations, and to be free from unauthorized searches and arbitrary arrest. The basis for an informed public, nourished by the unimpeded flow of ideas and opinions, was thus firmly established.

The delegates also agreed on a series of provisions establishing civil equality. In the first place, they passed a surprisingly tough set of provisions limiting the privileges and power of the nobility. To be sure, the left's demand that the aristocracy be totally abolished was rejected by a healthy majority. But the parliament voted to dissolve the nobility 'as a Stand'—a legal status group—and to destroy all 'Standesvorrechte'. Furthermore, the provisions on rural society took away the power of noble landlords over their tenants; patrimonial justice and police authority, labour services and seignioreul dues, hunting rights and other special privileges were all explicitly outlawed. Other provisions granted full equality to all religious groups, including Jews; the provisions on religion gave 'every German' complete religious freedom, removed all

---

[42] Eyck, *Parliament*, ch. 6, is a useful guide to the debate; Huber, *Dokumente*, i. 318–23, reprints the final version. Droysen, who was involved with constitutional issues throughout the life of the parliament, published the *Verhandlungen des Verfassungsausschusses der deutschen Nationalversammlung* (Leipzig, 1849). Also of value is Droysen, *Aktenstücke und Aufzeichnungen zur Geschichte der Frankfurter National-versammlung*, ed. R. Hübner (1924; repr. Osnabrück, 1967).

compulsion to reveal one's religion, and explicitly stated that civil or political rights could not be abridged on religious grounds.[43]

But while the liberal parliamentarians had relatively little difficulty abolishing limitations on free speech and dismantling social privileges and religious restrictions, they were hard pressed to agree on the positive meaning of freedom and equality. The most controversial elements in the debate over basic rights, therefore, were not the provisions against repression and inequality, but rather those in favour of political and social liberty. A good illustration of this was the conflict over church-state relations. Most liberals were convinced that no denomination should have particular privileges or a special place in the political system. But they were much less certain about the state's proper role in religious life. Many on the movement's left wanted to use political power to limit the churches' authority and to encourage secular ideals. Moderates, however, were reluctant to do anything that might undermine popular religious beliefs and were thus prepared to defend the churches' autonomy, even if that meant increasing clerical power. Once they had moved beyond a declaration of 'Glaubens- und Gewissensfreiheit', the delegates found themselves locked in a heated conflict over freedom's institutional meaning. The final wording of the provision on church and state expressed rather than resolved this perplexity: 'Every religious community orders and administers its affairs independently, but remains subordinated to the state's general laws.' Not surprisingly, many Catholics, who had originally looked to the liberal movement as an ally against the excessive power of the state, viewed this statement as an excuse for political subjection rather than as a guarantee of independence and autonomy.[44]

The delegates confronted a similar set of conflicts in their discussion of citizenship rights and community autonomy. Freedom to live where one wished and to practise any trade were fundamental liberal convictions, no less important than a commitment to freedom of belief. If Germany were to be a unified nation, citizenship must be universal and universally applicable. Thus the *Grundrechte* began by conferring national citizenship on every German. But to enforce this meant abridging another liberal tenet, the right of local self-government, which to many communities

---

[43] Rürup, *Emanzipation*, pp. 32–3. See also the essays in Mosse *et al.* (eds.), *Revolution*.

[44] Lempp, *Frage*; the documents in Huber and Huber (eds.), *Staat*, ii.

necessarily included the right to control who could belong and who could not. Considering the kind of men who set the tone in Frankfurt, there was never any doubt that national interests would prevail. Nevertheless, the final formulation of the citizenship provisions did promise legislation (entitled, significantly, a *Heimatsgesetz*) to regulate the question of residence and settlement.[45]

Even after the Constitutional Committee and the plenum had turned their attention to other constitutional issues, the problem of giving positive content to liberal promises of freedom and equality continued to plague the Economics Committee, which had been established in May to guide the parliament's consideration of economic and social questions. The Economics Committee was one of the hardest working groups at Frankfurt; for several months its members devoted a considerable part of their time to gathering data, holding hearings, and receiving delegations. In addition, they received and catalogued hundreds of petitions sent by craftsmen, apprentices, factory workers, farmers, and businessmen. From all sides they heard pleas for help, demands that the new central power end economic privation and create social stability. But despite its best efforts, the Economics Committee could do little to respond to these expressions of suffering and hope. When a minority in the committee proposed adding a guarantee of work to the basic rights, their motion was firmly rejected by the parliament. Efforts to draft a new Industrial Ordinance, which dragged on for months as the committee sought a compromise between what one member called 'the exclusiveness of privilege and the unbridled anarchy of *laissez-faire*', finally produced a document that the plenum briefly considered and then shelved. Nowhere is Frankfurt's failure to answer the needs of a broad majority of the population so apparent as it was in the Economics Committee's fruitless labour.[46]

In seeking to understand why the committee failed, we certainly should not underestimate the complexity of its task. The vast quantity of information the committee gathered provided unmistakable evidence of social discontent, but no clear indication of how this discontent might be alleviated. Indeed, it is difficult to see how any remedy could have avoided alienating some groups at the same time that it satisfied others. Moreover, however sympathetic some members of the Economics Committee might have been to the distress they observed, their interests and experience created a wide gulf between them and most of those who sought their aid. As

---

[45] Walker, *Home Towns*, ch. 11; Koch, 'Staat'.

[46] On the Economics Committee, see Noyes, *Organization*, pp. 221 ff., 322 ff.

businessmen, civil servants, and academicians, committee members thought in terms of national issues and long-term development rather than the special needs of embattled communities and trades. Finally, the men on the Economics Committee—and to an even greater degree, the parliament as a whole—were persuaded that their primary task was to write a constitution and thus provide the political context within which future problems could be faced. In the light of this conviction, they were quite prepared to push aside the complex problem of an Industrial Ordinance so that the parliament could proceed with its constitutional agenda.

This agenda consisted of two distinct but ultimately inseparable sets of questions. The first revolved around the problem of sovereignty: how should authority be defined, who should participate in public affairs, and what should be the relationship among the different institutions of the state? Although difficult and deeply divisive, for several decades these matters had been the subjects of intense theoretical debate and occasional practical application. The second set of questions, which concerned the definition of the nation itself, had generated little theory and less practice—which is perhaps why so few parliamentarians realized just how hard it would be to draw boundaries for the nation and thus lead Germany out of what Georg Waitz called its current 'unclear, problematic, completely untenable situation'. As the men at Frankfurt swiftly learned, Arndt's famous declaration that the fatherland extended 'soweit die deutsche Zunge klingt' was stirring poetry but woefully inadequate political geography.[47]

Clear boundaries were difficult to draw at every point of the compass—Limburg in the west, Schleswig-Holstein in the north, Posen in the east, and the Tirol in the south all posed complex questions of national identity. We have already seen how conflicts with Denmark had created the parliament's first great crisis in September 1848. The problem of Posen was no less vexing. A Prussian province, but not part of the German Confederation, Posen was linguistically mixed (with roughly 400,000 German-speakers and 800,000 thousand Polish) and ethnically entangled. Posen's German inhabitants saw the revolution as an opportunity to consolidate their own position by having the province annexed to a new German state; the Poles wanted a chance to recreate their long-divided fatherland. The matter came before the delegates at Frankfurt in July, when they

---

[47] Emil Meynen, *Deutschland und Deutsches Reich. Sprachgebrauch und Begriffs-wesenheit des Wortes Deutschland* (Leipzig, 1935), 61.

were asked to absorb Posen into the Confederation and thus pave the way for its inclusion in the future nation. During the debate on this motion, a variety of opinions were expressed, ranging from support for a reunited Poland to demands for German hegemony over a culturally inferior people. Wilhelm Jordan, a left-wing delegate from Prussia, defended the latter viewpoint with the oft-quoted claim that 'the superiority of the German peoples over the Slavs—with the possible exception of the Russians—is a fact . . . and against such, I would say, facts of natural history, decrees issued in the name of cosmopolitan righteousness will have little impact.' Although greeted with prolonged applause, Jordan's position was probably not shared by most delegates, whose nationalism was less obviously permeated by ethnic aggression. In the end, a majority voted to annex the German parts of Posen, according to a line of demarcation to be determined after the necessary data had been gathered. Once again, the parliamentarians agreed on principles while postponing their practical application. That the delegates had no way of imposing their decisions made such postponements all the easier. Everyone recognized that the final definition of national boundaries would have to be settled by the new Germany.[48]

The problems of German nationhood could be raised at the periphery, but would have to be resolved at the centre. Here the critical issue was the relationship between the two major German powers, Austria and Prussia. During the opening stages of the revolution there had been a great deal of enthusiasm among Austrians for the German cause. In Vienna, nationalistic students had raised the German colours above St Stephens to indicate their solidarity with patriots throughout the fatherland. On the other hand, Austrian Germans did not anticipate that joining the nation would require that they abandon their old allegiances or give up their special position in the Habsburg Reich. They wished, as Friedrich Hebbel put it in April 1849, 'to unite with Germany without joining it', which is like 'two people [who] want to kiss with their backs turned to one another'. In fact, Austrians were significantly underrepresented in the institutions that prepared the way from the Frankfurt parliament and they had less than their share of leading positions when the proceedings began. Nevertheless, few people could imagine a Germany without Austria, which was not only an integral part of the nation but also a necessary counterweight to Prussia, whose political institutions and Protestant

<hr>

[48] Wollstein, 'Grossdeutschland', p. 146.

traditions seemed alien to many inhabitants of the smaller German states.[49]

For some liberals, however, Prussia was the natural leader of a German nation. These men were usually Protestants and northerners, to whom the Hohenzollern's state seemed much more progressive and effective than the Habsburgs'. Prussia's advocates were greatly encouraged by Frederick William's declaration of 21 March 'An mein Volk und an die deutsche Nation', in which he seemed to commit himself to the national cause. At first, however, only a few liberals imagined a *Kleindeutschland*—a Germany without Austria. To the majority at Frankfurt, this remained a last resort, to be accepted reluctantly, after all else had failed.

In late October the plenum adopted Articles Two and Three of the draft constitution, which called for a nation composed exclusively of German states. German princes might still rule non-German territories, but these could only be joined to the nation through the personal rule of the sovereign. Most of those who voted in favour of these articles regarded them as the basis for a Germany that would include a reconstituted Austria. The government in Vienna, however, made clear that the Habsburg monarchy would make no accommodations to German national aspirations. Prince Schwarzenberg, the newly installed leader of the Austrian counter-revolution, called 'the maintenance of Austria's political unity a German and a European necessity'. Although he left open the possibility of some further developments in 'a process of change as yet incomplete', Schwarzenberg announced that in the meantime Austria would continue 'faithfully to fulfill her obligations to the Confederation'. In effect, this statement cut the ground out from under the advocates of a *Grossdeutschland*—a Germany including German-speaking Austria. Schmerling, the Austrian who had replaced Leiningen as President of the Frankfurt ministry, resigned his post in mid-December and was replaced by Gagern, a leader of the Prussian party.[50]

Since October, Gagern had been seeking support for a plan to create a Germany ruled by the Hohenzollern, but joined in a special relationship to a unified Habsburg Reich. On 13 January he was able to gather a narrow majority behind this definition of the nation. The

[49] Srbik, *Metternich*, i. 324. See also Rath, *Revolution*; Wollstein, '*Grossdeutschland*'. Sixty Austrian electoral districts (most of them in Bohemia) were not represented at Frankfurt, either because no elections were held there or because the elected delegate did not show up.

[50] Huber, ii. 799. Demeter, *Stimmen*, surveys *grossdeutsch* opinion. On the Austrian situation, see below, sect. iii.

core of his support came from moderate and right-wing liberals; most leftists voted against him. But the clearest divisions were religious and regional rather than ideological, with Protestants and Prussians favouring Gagern, Catholics and Austrians overwhelmingly opposed. Ten days after his initial victory, Gagern's majority collapsed when a negative coalition of leftists and advocates of *Grossdeutschland* defeated a proposal to create a hereditary monarchy. At this point, the proceedings in Frankfurt were near stalemate: Gagern's support was too narrow and shaky to hold the weight of the constitution, but his opponents, however formidable in opposition, were incapable of agreeing upon an alternative solution. In early March the parliament was still deadlocked when the Austrian government issued the Kremsier constitution, which effectively foreclosed a *grossdeutsch* solution; as a result, the pro-Austrian faction began to unravel and some of its leading members resigned their seats.

The leaders of the *kleindeutsch* party now had only one course of action: they had to gather support for the national dimensions of their proposal by winning over left-wing delegates with concessions on other issues. At the end of March the moderates agreed to a weaker definition of monarchical power (the monarch was to have a suspensive rather than absolute veto over legislation) and a more democratic suffrage law, and thereby attracted enough votes to create a small majority (267 to 263) in favour of a hereditary emperor. Frederick William was then elected 'Kaiser der Deutschen', with 290 in favour and 248 abstentions. Essentially, the alignment of forces had not changed much since January: Prussians, Protestants, and northerners supported Frederick William, Austrians, Catholics, and southerners did not.[51]

In its final form, the constitution of 1849 gathered the various German states into a constitutional monarchy with a potentially powerful and democratically based representative institution. Theoretically, the constitution was a formidable achievement, which reflected many of the liberals' most important aspirations. But the constitution also reflected German liberalism's uncertainties and divisions—about the proper balance of freedom and restraint, central power and state autonomy, monarchical authority and parliamentary control. Furthermore, the constitution was full of unresolved questions: What changes would a new law on citizenship and a new industrial ordinance have made in the definition of basic rights? How would the Reich have coexisted with the states? What did it mean for the executive to be 'responsible'? As is always the case when

[51] Eyck, *Parliament*, pp. 349 ff., analyses the vote.

constitutional provisions are translated into institutional action, such questions could only have been settled in the day-to-day conduct of public affairs, that crucible of practice where all theoretical statements and constitutional pronouncements must harden or dissolve.[52]

Once the Frankfurt parliament had accepted the constitution, the liberal revolution's fate depended on whether Frederick William IV would accept the crown. Although the signals coming from Berlin were not encouraging, a delegation, led by the President of the Assembly, Eduard von Simson, set off for the Prussian capital. The king received them on 3 April. He was cordial and polite, but made clear that he would not recognize the parliament's right to name him king. Germany's cause could not be served, he said, if he were to violate his 'heilige Rechte' without the prior agreement of his fellow monarchs, princes, and governments of the free cities. In private, his view of the delegation's offer was much harsher: 'This so-called crown', he wrote to Ernest Augustus of Hanover, 'is not really a crown at all, but actually a dog-collar, with which they want to leash me to the revolution of 1848.'[53] The king's decision had a devastating impact on the liberal revolutionaries, who now confronted a direct denial of their own legitimacy from the one authority powerful enough to help them realize their goals. Within a few days, the Frankfurt parliament began a painful process of disintegration, and the revolution entered a new phase. Before describing this unhappy coda, we must turn back and follow the evolution of public life in the various German states between the national elections of May 1848 and Frederick William's fateful decision eleven months later.

iii. THE DEFEAT OF THE REVOLUTION: POLITICS IN THE STATES

In the spring of 1848 moderate liberals had good reason to believe that the future belonged to them: their friends and allies occupied ministerial positions in almost every important capital, their candidates had triumphed in Germany's first national elections, their once powerful opponents were silent or in obvious disarray. During the second half of 1848, however, liberalism's enemies gradually recovered their strength, while the basis of liberal support narrowed, both in the governments and on the streets. As

---

[52] Boldt, 'Monarchie'; Rose, 'Issue'; Schilfert, *Sieg.*
[53] Simson, *Erinnerungen*, pp. 174 ff.

the men at Frankfurt turned their attention to the task at hand, the world around them changed, leaving them more and more isolated and exposed. The *Schlesische Zeitung*, therefore, was cruel but not inaccurate when it compared the national parliament to Faust, who had flown over the German landscape 'without giving thought to the solid ground on which he would be able to set foot'.[54] Could the liberals have found the solid ground upon which to build their future? Perhaps not. Even in the spring of 1848 they were much weaker than they seemed to be—their alliance with the governments more tenuous than it appeared, their support in the *Volk* shallower, their enemies stronger. Nor should we underestimate the intrinsic difficulties in their position during the following months, when social and political divisions among the opposition deepened at the same time as the reactionaries' cohesion and confidence returned. Yet it is also true that the liberals did not fully exploit the opportunities open to them. They sometimes gave in too easily to their opponents on the right and did not try hard enough to achieve a united front with possible allies on the left. By not making better use of their position in the middle of the political spectrum, liberals opened themselves to attack from both directions, thus allowing a source of potential strength to become a source of fatal weakness.

In the German states, as in the rest of Europe, most liberals were reluctant to realize that, if they were to have any chance of influencing the future, they would have to find ways of sustaining and expanding their popular support. As we should expect, this reluctance was especially apparent among moderates, many of whom had established social positions and considerable local prestige, and saw no need to curry favour with the masses. During the early stages of the revolution, therefore, moderates remained true to the style of politics they had employed in the *Vormärz* and continued to act within their usual institutional settings—local *Vereine*, municipal representative assemblies, and various community organizations. Few thought that it would be necessary to knit these institutions into a national movement; most were confident that national politics would be created by a constitution and unified representative institutions, not by the mobilization of popular forces.

Only gradually did some liberals come to see that more had to be done. Liberal delegates at Frankfurt slowly evolved links to their constituencies. Moreover, persistent pressures from their political

[54] Jessen (ed.), *Revolution*, pp. 313–14.

opponents, especially on the left, forced liberals to build better organizations, both within their communities and across local lines. Thus in November 1848 liberals meeting in Kassel established the *Nationaler Verein* to co-ordinate their political activities throughout Germany. But, despite these efforts, liberal organizations remained weak, regionally dispersed, and institutionally fragile.[55]

Both necessity and conviction spurred the left wing of the political opposition to greater organizational efforts. Unlike the moderates, the left usually could not count on the support of local notables with secure positions in *Vormärz* politics and society; their spokesmen tended to be lower-ranking civil servants, intellectuals without a fixed place, craftsmen, teachers, and the like. Practically, these men needed the material support of the organized masses; ideologically, they were committed to a democratization of politics. 'To secure the revolution and to fulfil its promise', wrote one democratic leader, 'it is essential to form a political club, so that the fighters for freedom do not waste their efforts individually as they once did, but rather get to know one another and strive in unity and strength for the same goals.' Members of the left also realized that local institutions would not be enough; in May 1848 the *Democratischer Verein* in Marburg sent out a call for collaboration on the national level.[56]

Growing fears of reaction and declining confidence in the national parliament led the left to increase its efforts at mobilizing the masses. In the summer and autumn of 1848 Democratic Congresses were held to coordinate local agitation; in November leading delegates from the left-wing faction at Frankfurt formed the *Centralmärzverein*, which eventually had 950 branches with over half a million members. By the spring of 1849 the left had built an impressive institutional base, far larger and more cohesive than their moderate rivals. Nevertheless, the left was also weakened by problems of co-ordination and control. More important, the organizations of the left were unable to harness the social discontents that had helped to make the revolution so powerful in its opening phase. Throughout 1848 and 1849 there remained what Stephen Born called 'two parties within the democratic camp . . . the purely political and the social'.[57]

[55] Langewiesche's 'Anfänge' is an excellent survey of party organization during the revolution. See also Botzenhart, *Parlamentarismus*; Boldt, *Anfänge*; Gebhardt, *Revolution*.

[56] Fricke, *et al.* (ed.), *Parteien*, i. 227–35, summarizes the development of democratic party organization. See also Paschen, *Vereine*.

[57] Noyes, *Organization*, p. 277.

The division between these two 'parties' significantly weakened the political left by cutting it off from a large and potentially powerful source of support. But this division had equally deleterious effects on the social movements, which remained without the political organization and direction necessary to overcome their special interests and co-ordinate their specific goals.

As soon as the new liberal government granted freedom of association in the spring of 1848, organizations of craftsmen, journeymen, and workers spread across the German lands. Their variety defies summary: they ranged from small local gatherings of a particular craft to the nationally based *Verbrüderung*, from communist revolutionaries to traditionalist advocates of guild restrictions, from trade unions to conspiratorial cells. Some wanted free trade and broader economic opportunities, others, protectionism and restraint; some demanded higher wages, others, government control of competition; some fought for limited, pragmatic ends, others, for a new social and economic order. There is nothing surprising about this variety, which reflected the character of German society at mid-century when, as we have seen, economic enterprises and social institutions of all sorts existed next to one another. Within the revolutionary setting, however, this variety produced a diversity of organized action and a diffusion of popular energies that inevitably worked to the advantage of the established order.[58]

In addition to the parties and associations devoted to social issues, the most popular organizations to emerge in 1848 were formed by Catholics to defend the interests of their church. At the end of March, priests and laymen in Mainz established the first *Piusvereine für religiöse Freiheit*, which quickly spread to other Catholic regions. In October, the participants in a *Katholikentag* held in Mainz created the German Catholic Verein. Two weeks later, the first German bishops' conference in over thirty years convened in Würzburg. This impressive display of organizational energy and institutional cohesion foreshadowed the extraordinarily important political role Catholicism would play later in the century. At the same time, however, we can already see some of Catholicism's persistent weaknesses as a political force. No less than moderates, left-wing opposition, and labour movement, Catholics were divided by their differences over strategy and goals.

---

[58] Noyes, *Organization* discusses these various institutions. For some examples of the different interests at work among craftsmen, see Walker, *Home Towns*, pp. 364–6.

Some Catholics, especially those in the Prussian west, wanted to use their influence for political ends; the *Piusverein* in Cologne, for instance, declared that it would deal with 'social and political questions from a Catholic perspective'. Others took a much narrower view of their purpose: a majority at the meeting of the Catholic *Verein* in October 1849 put the interests of the church first and disavowed any interest in what they called 'ordinary politics'.[59]

Seen together, these various participatory institutions represented an unprecedented amount of political mobilization throughout the German states. Although comparative analyses are not available, it is difficult to believe that the level of participation was any higher in the rest of western Europe. The usual clichés about Germans' political apathy, therefore, seem particularly inappropriate in the light of our evidence about 1848–9. The problem was not passivity but fragmentation. Many Germans were ready and willing to act politically, even at considerable risk, but they could not find ways of channelling their activities into organizations powerful enough to win decisive victories over the existing order. Political debates about goals and strategies, social conflicts, religious and regional differences fractured popular forces into competing groups. Moreover, these divisions coexisted with, and were often reinforced by, the divisions created by diverse patterns of political life within the various states.

As the reader will remember, during the first stage of the revolution politics in the German states seemed to have a similar structure: almost everywhere broadly based movements for reform forced concessions from the governments, new ministers were installed, censorship was ended, and political freedoms guaranteed. Once these changes had taken place, most states set about creating the basis for a new public life by considering constitutional revisions, suffrage reform, and various other items from the political opposition's agenda. Gradually, however, this apparent similarity in political development gave way to new and more deeply rooted diversity. Because the character and quality of the 'March ministries', the strength and cohesion of the opposition, and the constellation of counter-revolutionary forces varied so

---

[59] Botzenhart, *Parlamentarismus*, pp. 335, 338. Among the 2,000 petitions sent to the Frankfurt parliament, there were 163,000 signatures on issues relating to church-state relations as compared to 54,000 on economic and 20,000 on political issues: Langewiesche, 'Anfänge', pp. 347–8. For more on Catholic associations during the revolution, see Sperber, *Catholicism*; Konrad Repgen, 'Klerus und Politik 1848', *Aus Geschichte und Landeskunde: Festschrift für Franz Steinbach* (Bonn, 1960), 133–65.

greatly from state to state, quite distinctive political patterns began to emerge.

In every German state, the revolution mobilized public opinion and expanded the possibilities of political participation. But the timing, rules, and style of electoral politics differed. In Baden, for example, there were no new elections in 1848, largely because the liberal majority of the *Landtag* feared the growing power of their radical rivals. In Württemberg, on the other hand, a *Landtag* was elected in May 1848 according to the old suffrage law, but the king managed to delay calling it into session until the following September, thereby weakening its influence during the high point of reform. Saxony, Bavaria, and Hanover all held elections late in 1848, after counter-revolutionary victories in Austria and Prussia; as a result, moderate reformers lost majority support in all three states.[60]

Although it is always a mistake to lose sight of how differently things worked out in the various states, the fate of the revolution was not decided in Stuttgart, Karlsruhe, or Munich, but rather in Vienna and Berlin. Ultimately, only the two major powers were in a position to determine Germany's future. If Austria and Prussia were willing and able to resist the forces of movement, as they had done in 1830, then the revolution was doomed. If they could not or would not do so, then a range of new possibilities existed.

In the spring of 1848 it would have been difficult to predict that the Habsburg empire would ever again be able to impose its will on central Europe. Rebellion stirred in every corner of the monarchy, while, at the centre, chaos reigned. On 25 April, in a desperate attempt to create the basis for a stable government, the government issued a constitution that proclaimed 'all lands belonging to the Austrian imperial state form an indivisible constitutional monarchy'. The non–German nationalities were not satisfied by this document's vague promises of protection, while the radical forces in Vienna objected to its provisions guaranteeing imperial authority. On 11 May, when the laws governing elections to the new *Reichstag* were announced, a band of armed students, the so-called Academic Legion, supported by workers, took to the streets and forced the government to issue a new, more democratic franchise. A few days later the emperor's entourage decided that he was no longer safe in his capital; accompanied by a few family members

---

[60] Schilfert, *Sieg*, pp. 131 ff., surveys state suffrage laws. There is a summary of political activities in Botzenhart, *Parlamentarismus*. The best single account of a state during the revolution is Langewiesche, *Liberalismus*.

and retainers, Ferdinand was secretly transported to Innsbruck. Shocked by the court's removal and frightened by the continued disorder in their streets, many Viennese were ready to welcome a return to law and order. But the authorities were unable to prevail over the revolutionary movement. On 26 May the government provoked but could not defeat a new wave of demonstrations by students and workers, who once again took control of Vienna's streets. At this point, the forces of nationalism and liberalism seemed ascendant throughout the Habsburgs' far-flung lands. Against these forces, an incompetent sovereign, surrounded by frightened courtiers, uncertain ministers, and discouraged generals, was apparently powerless.[61]

The reassertion of political authority began at the periphery. In June an army commanded by Prince Windischgrätz defeated the Czech rebels after six days of bloody street fighting. A month later General Jellacic, ignoring his superiors' orders to withdraw, pressed the war against the Hungarians. Finally and most dramatically, Radetzky, the eighty-one-year-old commander of the Austrian army in Italy, led a multinational force to a series of victories, culminating in a decisive engagement against the Piedmontese at Custozza on 25 July. Radetzky's triumphs encouraged frightened reactionaries all over Europe. To the Baroness Blaze de Bury, Custozza was 'le prémier coup de cloche', the first clear sign that the revolutionaries were vulnerable. In Vienna, Johann Strauss celebrated the occasion with the great march which would keep Radetzky's name alive in the world of music long after it had disappeared from the annals of war. A month earlier, when the old field marshal had just begun to reassert Austrian power south of the Alps, Grillparzer had celebrated him as the new saviour and personification of the monarchy:

> Glück auf, mein Feldherr, führe den Streich!
> Nicht bloss um Ruhmesschimmer,
> In deinem Lager ist Österreich,
> Wir andre sind einzelne Trümmer.

Grillparzer's line that Austria was in Radetzky's camp should not be read merely as poetic hyperbole. Disgusted by the revolution and dismayed by the impotence of the government, many Austrians now came to believe that the monarchy's future depended on the army. Over the next several months, when officers rode into battle with W–J–R—Windischgrätz, Jellacic,

[61] The literature on the Austrian revolution is given above, sect. i, n. 10.

Radetzky—inscribed on their sabres, they were expressing a basic shift in the symbolic and institutional basis of Habsburg rule. Not the dynasty or the empire, but the state and its army had become the primary loyalty for many of those who struggled to defeat the revolution. 'Above all,' Jellacic proclaimed in the autumn of 1848, 'we remain Austrians. If there were to be no Austria, then now we must create it.'[62]

Despite the victories won by the emperor's armies in Bohemia and Italy, his capital remained in the hands of the revolutionaries. Richard Wagner, who went there briefly in early July, found that the sights and sounds of radical Vienna had an operatic splendour: 'The Civil Guard, rather military in their dress, with broad silk sashes in the national colours, students in old Germanic garb, wearing feathered hats and carrying long rifles with bayonets, are standing guard. I saw beautiful people everywhere. Ah, this richness, this life.'[63] But behind such picturesque scenes stood the grim realities of economic depression and social conflict. The revolution had attracted to Vienna large numbers of people looking for work or public assistance; it had also disrupted the city's manufacturing enterprises and come close to paralysing its commerce. As the demand for luxury goods declined, the ranks of the unemployed increased; at the same time, food supplies dwindled and prices rose. The rich fled or locked themselves in their houses, while the respectable middle strata were frustrated and frightened. With more and more people worried about their property and livelihoods, support for the revolution ebbed. In late August, when workers demonstrated against legislation that reduced their wages, the Civil Guard responded swiftly and violently. The students, to whose aid the workers had rushed three months earlier, did nothing. The revolutionary coalition was coming unstuck.

Meanwhile, the Austrian *Reichstag* had begun its deliberations. This body was unlike any other elected during the revolutionary year: in the first place, less than half of its 383 delegates were German, the rest were Slavs, Italians, or members of some smaller national minority; second, almost one-quarter were peasants, many of them well-to-do Poles who voted with the right on most issues; and, third, the radicals were relatively weak—even in Vienna, where the left had campaigned vigorously, they had been able to

[62] Sked, *Survival*, p. x; Herre, *Franz Joseph*, p. 66; Jessen (ed.), *Revolution*, p. 268. For the resurgence of Habsburg military power, see, in addition to Sked, Rothenberg, *Army*. The best account of events in Hungary is Deak, *Revolution*.
[63] Herre, *Franz Joseph*, pp. 66–7.

elect no more than a third of their candidates. Almost entirely
without parliamentary experience, lacking a common language,
and deeply divided on every important matter, the Austrian
Reichstag frittered away its time with ill-tempered debates and arid
procedural squabbles. It did, however, achieve one major, lasting
reform, perhaps the most impressive piece of legislation passed by
any German parliament in 1848–9: after prolonged and complex
discussion, the Reichstag approved a series of laws ending serfdom
throughout the monarchy and regulating the compensation to be
paid to landlords for the dues and services they would lose.[64]

While the *Reichstag* carried on its stormy proceedings in the
inappropriately elegant quarters of the Court Riding School, the
social and political situation in Vienna continued to deteriorate.
The showdown came in October when the Richter Battalion, a unit
with close ties to the radicals, refused to assemble for deployment
against the Hungarian rebellion. After loyal troops failed to restore
order, fighting broke out in various parts of the city; the court,
which had returned two months earlier, once again had to flee for
safety. On 20 October Robert Blum, who had hurried to Vienna
from Frankfurt and was soon to be the rebellion's most famous
martyr, wrote to his wife that the future was at stake: 'If the
revolution is victorious here, it can regain its momentum, but if the
revolution is defeated, then Germany will be, at least for a time, as
quiet as a tomb.'[65] The revolutionaries remained divided and
uncertain. Competing authorities issued commands and counter-
commands, made badly drawn and incompletely executed plans,
and neglected obvious measures, such as the destruction of the
railroad lines leading into the city. On the barricades and in the
streets, people fought with great courage, but the issue was never
in doubt. By 23 October Windischgrätz surrounded the city with
60,000 troops; on the morning of the 28th he began an artillery
bombardment; three days later the imperial flag flew from St
Stephen's once again.

Even before the reconquest of the capital, a new government had
secretly been formed. At its head was Prinz Felix zu Schwarzenberg, who was to guide the monarchy into a new historical era.
Born in 1800, Schwarzenberg belonged to a family of imperial
nobles with great estates in Bohemia. Like the Stadions and the
Metternichs, the Schwarzenbergs combined the trappings of

[64] Blum, *End*, pp. 370–1.
[65] Jessen (ed.), *Revolution*, p. 244. Blum was executed after the military
recaptured Vienna.

independence with service to the Habsburgs. At eighteen, Felix joined a cavalry regiment commanded by Windischgrätz, his brother-in-law, and for the next three decades enjoyed the opportunities for pleasure and advancement open to a talented, charming, and well-connected young man. When the revolution began, he was stationed at the Austrian embassy in Naples, but managed to get command of a brigade that went into action under Radetzky; soon he became the field marshal's liaison with the court. In October, Schwarzenberg appeared to be an ideal candidate to take over the reigns of government: with family ties to Windischgrätz and recent service under Radetzky, he was close to the most powerful men in the monarchy. Moreover, his extensive political and military service had been outside the capital, which left him unencumbered by court intrigues and unblemished by responsibility for recent disasters.[66]

Schwarzenberg was a nobleman and a faithful servant of the Habsburgs, but his fundamental loyalties were to the state, not to the nobility or the dynasty. He had little confidence in the ability and will of his fellow aristocrats: 'I know of not a dozen men of our class', he wrote to Windischgrätz, 'with sufficient political wisdom or the necessary experience to whom an important share of power could be entrusted. . . . To rely on an ally as weak as our aristocracy unfortunately is, would be to damage our cause more than to help it.' For his cabinet, therefore, Schwarzenberg chose men of talent without regard to rank: a reform-minded noble, Count Franz Stadion, served with Karl von Bruck, a craftsman's son from Elberfeld who had made his fortune in shipping, and with Alexander Bach, a liberal holdover from the preceding administration, who remained as Minister of Justice. Furthermore, the new Minister President felt none of the dynastic scruples that had kept the unfortunate Ferdinand on the throne, but rather insisted that the emperor abdicate in favour of his nephew, Francis Joseph.[67]

Francis Joseph, who would live long enough to become 'the last true king in history', was only eighteen when he inherited his war-torn and restless realm.[68] His mother, the Archduchess Sophie, daughter of the king of Bavaria, had married the lacklustre brother

---

[66] Kiszling, *Schwarzenberg*.

[67] Sked, *Survival*, p. 208. On the cabinet, see Brandt, *Neoabsolutismus*, i. 247 ff.

[68] Tapie, *Rise*, p. 284. The standard English work on Francis Joseph remains Redlich, *Francis Joseph*; the most recent biography is Herre's readable but uncritical account: *Franz Joseph*. Heinrich Ritter von Srbik, 'Franz Joseph I. Charakter und Regierungsgrundsätze', *HZ* 144/3 (1931), is a brilliant brief characterization.

of the Habsburg heir in the hope that he would be chosen to take Ferdinand's place as emperor. When that hope was thwarted, she devoted her formidable talent for intrigue to furthering the career of her eldest son. Reared by carefully selected tutors, schooled in family traditions, and imbued with religious orthodoxy, Francis Joseph had been shielded from the symptoms of unrest and dissatisfaction that abounded in the Austrian *Vormärz*. He was understandably shocked by the outbreak of the revolution and the government's apparent collapse. In April, dressed as a subaltern in the imperial Hussars, he had made his way to Radetzky's forces in Italy, where he displayed great courage and developed a deep commitment to the army, which he, like many of his subjects, came to see as the ultimate basis for the state.

By insisting that the new emperor use both his names, Schwarzenberg wanted to underscore the dual character of the Habsburg legacy, in which the progressive impulses personified by Joseph II coexisted with Francis's relentless conservatism. In order to survive, Schwarzenberg realized, the monarchy would have to be both flexible and tough, ready to compromise if necessary, prepared to fight if violence was unavoidable. There were even signs that Schwarzenberg was willing to consider granting a constitution to the monarchy. When the *Reichstag*, which had been disbanded by Windischgrätz's soldiers in October, reconvened at Kremsier later the following month, Schwarzenberg told its members that he favoured a settlement that would 'unite all the lands and peoples of the monarchy into one great state'. He did not, to be sure, show much interest in the *Reichstag*'s own efforts, but rather issued a constitution by imperial decree in March 1849. Whether Schwarzenberg saw this document as anything other than an expedient—against the Frankfurt parliament and the Hungarian rebellion—is uncertain; his remarks on the subject are contradictory and inconclusive. But whatever he intended to do with his constitution, there is no doubt that Schwarzenberg's major commitment was to preserve the integrity of the Habsburg realm and the authority of the Austrian government. By the early spring of 1849 he was well on his way to achieving these goals.[69]

In defeat, as in victory, the Prussian revolution followed the Austrian example: just as Metternich's fall in March 1848 had encouraged popular forces in Berlin, so Windischgrätz's reconquest

---

[69] Kiszling, *Schwarzenberg*, p. 52. On the constitution, see Kann, *Empire*, ii. 21 ff.; on the fate of the Reichstag, Botzenhart, *Parlamentarismus*, pp. 636 ff.

of Vienna strengthened the resolve of the Prussian counter-revolution. Despite these parallels and connections, however, the revolutions in Austria and Prussia had different trajectories and significance. Unlike the Habsburgs, the Hohenzollern were never in mortal danger; their authority was disputed but did not come close to disintegration; they faced angry crowds and street barricades, not rebellious armies and full-scale battles. Because neither the revolution nor the counter-revolution was as violent in Prussia as in Austria, the lines of continuity linking the revolution to its aftermath remained much stronger in the Hohenzollern's realm than in the Habsburgs'.

The Hohenzollern's relative strength, however, was not immediately apparent in March 1848. Berlin, like Vienna, seemed to belong to the revolutionaries. A reformist ministry directed affairs of state, irregular troops stood guard at the old monuments, the dynasty capitulated and then withdrew, and preparations were made for an elected assembly that would determine the future. No wonder that unreconstructed reactionaries like the young Otto von Bismarck were close to despair, while Albrecht von Roon placed all his faith in the army, which is now, he wrote, 'our fatherland, for there alone have the unclean and violent elements who put everything into turmoil failed to penetrate'.[70]

Prussians elected a constituent assembly at the same time, and under the same suffrage law, as they voted for delegates to the Frankfurt parliament. But despite their common origins, the two institutions had quite different social and political characters. It was apparently easier for men of modest means to go to Berlin as delegates; for most Prussians, the Frankfurt parliament seemed farther away, its task more broadly drawn, its duration more uncertain. Furthermore, voters sensed that the national parliament might require wider experience in the great world, so they turned to people with prestigious jobs and big reputations; the Prussian assembly, on the other hand, would deal with more down-to-earth, practical matters. For the former, as one contemporary put it, 'one looked more at a candidate's head', for the latter, at his 'heart and kidneys'. Like the social groups to which they belonged, the delegates in Berlin were ideologically to the left of their Frankfurt colleagues; a majority thought of themselves as radicals, only a few were conservative defenders of the old order.[71]

[70] Craig, *Politics*, p. 107.
[71] Hans Viktor von Unruh, *Erfahrungen aus den letzten drei Jahren* (Magdeburg, 1851), 22. See also Repgen, *Märzbewegung*, pp. 235 ff.

When the Berlin parliament gathered on 22 May, most of its members wanted to create a new basis for Prussian public life. Frederick William seemed to agree. When he established the assembly, he had spoken of a *Vereinbarung*, a collaboration between monarch and parliament on the constitution. This formulation suited most liberals, for whom, as we know, continuity and co-operation with the old regime were of great importance. The left, however, believed that the revolution had affirmed the political primacy of the *Volk* and its representatives. In early June, when some delegates tried to establish this point with a resolution honouring the heroes of the March uprising, they met bitter opposition from the moderates. Eventually, the Camphausen ministry resigned, the king's hatred of the revolution deepened, and a rift within the assembly itself began to emerge. The debate ended with a compromise statement that once again shrouded the question of sovereignty in vague pronouncements about co-operation. However, the basic issue was merely pushed to one side while the delegates tried to reach agreement on how best to respond to the government's proposed constitution.[72]

In the course of the summer, as the parliament debated Prussia's future, the actual balance of political forces slowly shifted in favour of the right. Once they had recovered from the shock and humiliation of March, counter-revolutionary groups became active on a variety of fronts: at court, a camarilla led by Leopold von Gerlach struggled to influence the king; in the army, some officers began to publish the *Deutsche-Wehrzeitung* as part of the fight against the 'demon of revolution'; in the arena of public opinion, the conservative *Kreuzzeitung* began its long career in July and the so-called Junker parliament gathered in August to defend the interests of the landowning élite. These pressures from the right frightened the left, whose impatience with parliamentary deliberations—both in Frankfurt and Berlin—increased. Many moderates, on the other hand, tended to be drawn in the other direction. Frightened by continued violence, such as the storming of the Berlin Armoury on 14 June, people who had once been mildly sympathetic to reform now longed for law and order.[73]

---

[72] Kramer, *Fraktionsbindungen*, pp. 233 ff. surveys parties in the Prussian assembly. See also Sigrid Weigel's useful analysis of the contemporary literature: *Flugschriftenliteratur 1848 in Berlin: Geschichte und Öffentlichkeit einer volkstümlichen Gattung* (Stuttgart, 1979).

[73] Craig, *Politics*, has a good account of the military aspect of this development. Gerlach, *Denkwürdigkeiten*, is a basic source.

On 10 September the Auerswald–Hansemann ministry, exhausted by three months of manœuvring between left and right, was replaced by a cabinet dominated by moderate civil servants. The new Minister President was General Ernst von Pfuel, a military reformer of the old school, who continued to search for a way of accommodating both court and parliament. The chances of accommodation, however, were slim. The camarilla's influence on the king, which had been increasing all summer, was greatly strengthened when the assembly released its constitutional draft. Although surprisingly moderate in many respects, the proposed constitution contained a number of provisions on civil rights, military institutions, and parliamentary authority that Frederick William found abhorrent. On 2 November the king announced the formation of a new ministry to be led by Count Brandenburg, a career officer with impeccable conservative credentials. A week later, when General von Wrangel entered the capital with 13,000 troops, he met no resistance, either from the Civil Guard, who were understandably reluctant to fight against professionals, or from the population, many of whom greeted the soldiers with enthusiasm. While Wrangel sat calmly in the Gendarmenmarkt, the parliament met in the Schauspielhaus and voted to accept his order to disband. In the days thereafter, the rich array of institutions that had marked the awakening of Prussian public life were repressed. Efforts to organize a tax boycott, bravely adopted by some on the left, failed to gather enough support to shake the government. Throughout Europe, conservatives breathed a sigh of relief that order had been restored in Berlin. Wilhelm von Kügelgen, for instance, who had sought refuge from local unrest on Prussian territory, expressed his delight about the coup in a letter of 18 November; his only worry was that the king's resolve would fail and that he would not go far enough.[74]

In fact, the king's mood had shifted. Encouraged by Wrangel's bloodless triumph, he was ready to reclaim everything he had once given away. But Brandenburg was clever enough to see that it was neither necessary nor possible to return to pre-revolutionary conditions. Instead, he managed to persuade the king that a constitution, granted by the crown, would split the opposition, isolate the radical left, and consolidate monarchical authority. On 5 December, therefore, the Prussian parliament was dissolved and a consitution was decreed. Formally, the new constitution re-sembled the Belgian constitution of 1830, but its provisions for a

[74] Kügelgen, *Lebenserinnerungen*, pp. 139 ff.

democratically elected lower house reflected the democratic pressures of 1848, while its clear-cut definition of monarchical
sovereignty and ample emergency powers for the executive
underscored its conservative origins and intention.[75]

New elections were held in late January and early February 1849.
The upper house of the bicameral legislature was chosen according
to a restricted suffrage, the lower house by virtually all adult males.
As we should expect, these elections produced a more conservative
group of delegates; the number of high-ranking officials and estate
owners increased, thereby strengthening the assembly's right
wing. However, the swing to the right was by no means
overwhelming. Despite governmental interference and restrictions,
the radical left triumphed in many areas, including Berlin.
Moreover, the political implications of the electoral process
continued to be obscure. Outside the big cities, local notables and
regional issues remained important, party activity infrequent and ill
organized. Even well-informed contemporaries, therefore, had
trouble interpreting the meaning of a particular election and
predicting the victor's political preferences.[76]

When it met for the first time on 26 February 1849, the Prussian
parliament's main order of business was to respond to the royal
coup of 5 December. A left-wing resolution declaring the new
constitution invalid until it had been accepted by the parliament
failed by a wide margin (255–62); the moderates' qualified
endorsement of the new order passed by a narrow majority. Within
a few weeks, the delegates' attention was absorbed by the final
stages of the constitutional debate in Frankfurt and the election of
Frederick William as German emperor. A clear majority of the
lower house supported the national parliament and opposed the
king's reluctance to accept the crown. But this was of little
consequence to Frederick William and his ministers, who pursued
their own German policy and, as soon as they could, simply
dissolved the Chamber of Deputies and adjourned the upper house.

Frederick William's rejection of the imperial crown marked the
beginning of the end of the moderate revolution, in Prussia and
throughout the German lands. Gradually, the moderates had to
abandon their hope that fundamental reforms could be achieved

[75] Huber, *Dokumente*, i. 385 ff., reprints the constitution. See the analysis in
Grünthal, *Parlamentarismus*, ch. 1.
[76] Botzenhart, *Parlamentarismus*, p. 608, gives the *Landtag's* composition. For a
satirical description of government interference, see Adolf Glassbrenner's 'Eine
Urwählerversammlung unter Wrangel', in his *Unterrichtung*, iii.

with, rather than against, the states. Throughout most of April liberals tried to find ways of keeping this hope alive; in many states there was a new round of petitions, demonstrations, and parliamentary resolutions, which called for the ratification of the Frankfurt constitution. But Frederick William, supported by the rulers of the most important states, remained obdurate. If there was to be reform, it would be on his terms—not those of the people's representatives. By the end of the month, liberals faced a clear choice between acquiescence and rebellion, between accepting monarchical authority or joining a civil war against the states.

Nowhere was this choice more destructive and debilitating than in Frankfurt, where delegates had to come to terms with the fact that their hard-won constitutional compromise had not brought them the power necessary to make it work. Gagern, the key figure in the formulation of the majority programme, struggled desperately to gather support among the states. Eventually, twenty-nine governments, mostly of small states, ratified the constitution, but they could not prevail against Prussian opposition. When they saw that there was no legal basis for action, many moderate delegates simply went home. Some, like Gustav Rümelin, were not sorry to see their political ambitions laid to rest: 'Oddly enough,' he wrote in mid-May, 'we are pleased and relieved that we no longer are a majority and no longer must bear responsibility.' Those who remained in Frankfurt seemed paralysed by the hopelessness of their situation. The parliament's sessions were like a wake, one participant recalled, 'a sad spectacle of inconsolable confusion, uncertainty, and depression'. Eventually, with only a divided and dispirited minority remaining, the parliament adjourned and moved to Stuttgart, where a rump session sought refuge from the threat of Prussian military action.[77]

By this time the struggle over the German constitution had produced a series of violent confrontations between protesters and the authorities. Popular disappointment over the constitution's failure provided the immediate cause for this new wave of revolutionary unrest, but the violence of April and May 1849, like the turmoil of March and April 1848, had deeper roots. Religious and regional antagonisms, social and economic discontents, long-standing political frustrations all resurfaced to push the revolution into a new, radical phase. As in 1848, the variety of those involved makes any facile generalizations about the social basis of the

[77] *Bergsträsser (ed.), Parlament*, p. 131; Jessen (ed.), *Revolution*, p. 321. For the evolution of Rümelin's views, see *Aus der Paulskirche: Berichte an den Schwäbischen Merkur aus den Jahren 1848 und 1849* (Stuttgart, 1892).

revolution impossible. However, as Christoph Klessmann has argued, 'when the political situation became more precarious and demonstrations and petitions gave way to bloody struggles, the weight of active participation shifted from the top of the social pyramid to its broad base.' The overwhelming majority of those killed on the barricades and in the streets were working people— wage labourers, craftsmen, and apprentices.[78]

In 1848 the revolution's social diversity and geographical dispersal made it seem invincible; both revolutionaries and their opponents had the impression that everywhere the social order was coming unglued. In 1849, however, diversity and dispersal were sources of weakness, not strength. Revolutionaries felt isolated, both socially and geographically, while reactionaries could bide their time, moving from one pocket of unrest to the next. In areas where the government controlled the means of effective force, protest never got beyond a few scattered riots and demonstrations. Most of the northern states—Hanover, Oldenburg, Brunswick— were able to weather the storm without serious disorder. Except for a major uprising in Breslau, the Prussian east was also quiet. Berlin remained tightly sealed by Wrangel's troops. Only in Prussia's western provinces, where regional loyalties joined with social discontent and political ambitions, were there pitched battles between regular troops and mutinous *Landwehr* units or rebellious workers. But the ability of the Prussian state to defend itself was never in doubt; even the most serious conflicts were immediately isolated and easily repressed. In Saxony, Baden, and the Bavarian Palatinate, however, revolutionary forces were strong enough to defeat divided governments and, for a brief period, to raise the spectre of full-scale civil war.

In April 1849 a majority of the Saxon *Landtag* sought to compel the government to accept the Frankfurt constitution, while the far left, increasingly disenchanted with parliamentary politics, moved towards revolution. On 30 April King Frederick Augustus II, confident that Prussia would come to his aid, defied the opposition and closed the *Landtag*. The next few days were hot and humid, what the *Dresdener Zeitung* called 'Barrikadenwetter und Revolutionshimmel'. In hurriedly called meetings of political organizations and on street corners throughout the capital, angry young men like Richard Wagner and Gottfried Semper joined professional

[78] Klessmann, 'Sozialgeschichte', p. 333; this is the best short account of the 1849 uprising. See also Bernhard Mann, 'Das Ende der deutschen Nationalversammlung im Jahre 1849', *HZ* 214/2 (1972), 265–309, which is especially good for events in Württemberg.

revolutionaries like Michael Bakunin in calling for an uprising to inspire revolutionary forces throughout Europe. Full-scale rebellion broke out when soldiers fired on a crowd of demonstrators in front of the Dresden arsenal; barricades sprang up, a provisional government was formed. But the Saxon army remained loyal, and the effectiveness of the revolutionaries was undermined by their own divisions. The arrival of Prussian troops decided the issue; Dresden was recaptured on 9 May. Of the 250 Saxons killed in the fighting and the roughly 10,000 investigated by the police thereafter, the overwhelming majority were from the lower strata of society.[79]

In Baden, as in Saxony, political unrest was fed by continued social discontent. Indeed, the Badenese government had been even more battered by revolutionary turmoil than its Saxon counterpart; dynastic authority was weak, the loyalty of the armed forces uncertain, fear of domestic subversion and foreign aggression pervasive. In an effort to stabilize the situation, the authorities had accepted the Frankfurt constitution, but this had not quieted popular agitation for a democratic nation-state. On 12 May mutinous troops at Rastatt demanded reform and the release of political prisoners. The next day, 40,000 people gathered in Offenburg to hear radical speeches on social change and political transformation. Lorenz Brentano, a lawyer from Mannheim, emerged as the most prominent spokesman for the new movement; when the grand duke fled on 14 May, Brentano became the chief of a provisional government, which set about organizing military resistance to the counter-revolution. For the next four weeks, fighting continued between rebel troops, skilfully led by radical ex-officers from throughout central Europe, and the regular armies of various states. On 15 June the Prussians captured Mannheim; six days later, at Waghausel, the rebels were definitively defeated. Meanwhile, the Frankfurt parliament's final remnants, who had sought sanctuary in Stuttgart, were disbanded by a handful of soldiers. Only the garrison at Rastatt kept the revolutionary cause alive; it surrendered on 23 July. By then, the German revolution was over.[80]

The revolution's unpredictable course and violent demise turned many liberals away from politics. Consider, for example, the case of Dr C. H. A. Pagenstecher, former *Burschenschaftler*, local notable, and delegate to the *Nationalversammlung*, who had grown

---

[79] Rupieper, 'Sozialstruktur'. See also the data in Klessmann, 'Sozialgeschichte', pp. 294–5.
[80] Klessmann, 'Sozialgeschichte', pp. 326–7.

increasingly restive in Frankfurt and was, by the spring of 1849, disenchanted with public life in general. 'Now is the time', he wrote, 'to establish a worthy life, to cultivate intellectual concerns, to educate one's family and to make them happy. . . . in short, now is the time to lead a purely human existence.' About the same time, Friedrich Hammacher wrote to his wife that it would be necessary 'temporarily to become a philistine' and devote his energy to private affairs. These remarks remind us of Heine's poem, 'Im Oktober 1849':

> Wir treiben jetzt Familienglück—
> Was höher lockt, das ist von Übel—
> Die Friedensschwalbe kehrt zurück,
> Die einst genistet in des Hauses Giebel
>
> Gemütlich ruhen Wald und Fluss,
> Von sanftem Mondlicht übergossen;
> Nur manchmal knallts—Ist das ein Schuss?
> Es ist vielleicht ein Freund, den man erschossen.[81]

Born in an atmosphere of euphoria, nourished by inflated hopes and misplaced confidence, then abandoned by the *Volk* it sought to represent and repressed by the states it sought to preserve, the liberals' revolution collapsed in a spasm of violence and despair. Measured against the expectations with which it began, the revolution fell far short of success. By the time the last rebels were disarmed in the summer of 1849, representatives of the old order had resumed their hold over German public life. But we should not underestimate the revolution's historical significance. The Prussian constitution, the emancipation of the Austrian peasantry, and many lesser accomplishments had a profound impact on politics and society. While the revolution did less than many of its advocates had hoped, it was not 'a turning-point at which history did not turn', an episode to be dismissed with that easy irony so often evoked by an abridgement of other people's hopes. Nor should we overestimate the depth and persistence of the disillusionment caused by the liberals' defeat. Certainly some Germans lost their taste for politics and their faith in themselves. But many more eventually recovered from the shock of defeat and were ready to fight again for their ideals. Let us, therefore, give the last word to a liberal delegate to the Württemberg *Landtag*, who told his friends and enemies on the day the Frankfurt parliament was closed that, while 'the national enterprise will perhaps sink into the dust for a

[81] Pagenstecher, *Lebenserinnerungen*, iii. 102; Alex Bein and Hans Goldschmidt, *Friedrich Hammacher* (Berlin, 1932), 28; Heine, *Schriften*, vi. pt. 1, p. 116.

short time, the spirit, my dear ministers, will not be so easily
buried, and, despite all your bayonets, this spirit will once again
emerge'.[82]

iv. THE NEW FACE OF REACTION

Writing in 1853, the conservative historian Hermann Meynert
described the 'March days' as a pantomime battle in which one side
pretended to lose, without actually having been defeated, while the
other acted as if it had won, without really being victorious. But
Meynert went on to warn his readers that this 'struggle of shadows
and illusions' is imperceptibly becoming more and more real; 'the
weapons on both sides grow sharper and sharper as they strike
against one another, the gesturing puppets are coming to life, and
pantomime is turning into an actual battle.' Meynert's metaphor
captures the mixture of contempt and anxiety with which many
German conservatives viewed the events of 1848 and 1849; once it
had been safely defeated, the revolution might appear to have been
a pathetic episode, but it was none the less part of a dangerous
historical process deeply rooted in nineteenth-century life. The
conservatives seemed to have won, but most of them believed that
they would have to fight again. Their victory in 1849 was not,
therefore, attended by those inflated hopes and bold ambitions that
had been so apparent in 1815. After this revolution, there were no
'Holy Alliance', no Gothic posturing or talk of restoration. 'The
old times are gone and cannot return,' declared the Prussian
minister Manteuffel in 1849. 'To return to the decaying conditions
of the past is like scooping water with a sieve.'[83]

As they planned for the next round in the struggle against
revolution, the men of the fifties proved to be more flexible and
broad-minded than the generation that had tried to recreate the old
order after Waterloo. Schwarzenberg and Brandenburg, like Louis

[82] Valentin, *Geschichte*, ii. 506. After 1866, divisions within liberalism, the rise of
anti-liberal movements, and the consolidation of the Bismarckian state provided a
historical perspective quite different from that of the 1850s and early 1860s. When
reading the histories—and even the memoirs—of the revolution written in the new
Germany, it is important to be sensitive to the way in which people read back into
1848 later developments. In a sense, the revolution eventually became what Erik
Erikson calls a 'cover memory', that is, 'the condensation and projection of
pervasive conflict on one dramatized scene': *Gandhi's Truth* (New York, 1969), 128.

[83] Häusler, *Massenarmut*, p. 156; Gillis, *Bureaucracy*, p. 121. For a subtle analysis
of the revolution's impact on a graphic artist, see Peter Paret, 'The German
Revolution of 1848 and Rethel's *Dance of Death*', *Journal of Interdisciplinary History*,
17/1 (1986), 233–55.

Napoleon and Cavour, realized that a successful defence of the old order required new ideas and institutions, some of which might have to come from the arsenals of their enemies. The hallmark of post-revolutionary conservatism, therefore, was its growing association with the most powerful forces of the age: bureaucratization, constitutionalism, nationalism, and economic development.

Among the first German conservatives to see that the old order would have to compromise with the new was Joseph Maria von Radowitz, whom we have already encountered as Frederick William's envoy to Vienna during the early stages of the revolution. Born in 1797 to a family of Hungarian nobles living in northern Germany, Radowitz was educated in France, fought in the Westphalian contingent of Napoleon's forces, was wounded at Leipzig, and finally took an officer's commission in the small army of Hesse Kassel. In 1823 Radowitz moved to Prussia, where, like many other talented outsiders, he found an appropriate focus for his loyalty and an adequate theatre for his ambitions. After marrying into an old Prussian family, he became part of the court circle around the crown prince, the future Frederick William IV, whose brand of romantic, intensely religious conservatism he seemed to share. When Radowitz was appointed Prussia's military representative to the federal diet in 1836, his interest in German affairs increased. Appalled by the selfishness and superficiality he found at Frankfurt and concerned by the signs of unrest he saw all around him, Radowitz searched for ways to strengthen the Confederation by deepening its support among German nationalists. As we have seen, in March 1848 Radowitz was still trying to sell his plan to a reluctant Metternich when his efforts to use 'revolutionary tendencies and forces for the renewal of the state' were overtaken by events.[84]

A year later, Radowitz was prepared to try again. After serving in the Frankfurt parliament as a spokesman for Catholic interests and conservative values, he abandoned his colleagues on the right to support Gagern's *kleindeutsch* solution. When Frederick William refused the parliamentary crown, Radowitz hoped to attain Gagern's end with other means. 'The roles must now be reversed,' he wrote to his wife on 3 May. The government must draft a constitution to fulfil 'the authentic needs and just demands of the nation'.[85] By employing all his skills as a courtier and exploiting to the fullest his old friendship with the king, he managed to persuade

[84] Radowitz, *Briefe*, p. 21. See Meinecke, *Radowitz*, ch. 1.
[85] Radowitz, *Briefe*, p. 89.

Frederick William to take a leading role in this process of nation-building from above. Thus, while Prussian troops were repressing the last outbursts of revolutionary violence, Prussian diplomats were engaged in a campaign to mobilize the various states behind a *kleindeutsch* nation which would be, as in Gagern's plan, linked in some larger union with Austria.

Despite his success in gaining Frederick William's support, Radowitz faced formidable opposition at home and abroad. Many of his old cronies among the king's advisers viewed him as an unwitting ally of the revolution, a tempter whose promise of expanded power would lead Prussia into the abyss. Nor could he count on the support of most ministers, who resented his personal ties to the king and questioned his credentials as a diplomat. Outside Prussia, Radowitz's campaign had a mixed reception. As was to be expected, the response in Vienna was negative; Schwarzenberg recognized that a monarchically sponsored *Kleindeutschland* was no less antithetical to Austrian interests than its parliamentary predecessor. Among the rulers of the smaller German states, there were some who admired Prussia and welcomed its leadership and protection, while many others saw it as a threat to their own sovereignty and independence. But in the late spring of 1849 even Prussia's enemies had to move with caution. As long as Austria was still locked in a bitter war with the Hungarian rebels, Prussian power was indispensable to liquidate the last round of revolutionary disorder. Few German governments, therefore, were prepared to risk the potential costs of opposition to Berlin.

On 17 May 1849 representatives of the five German monarchies— Prussia, Hanover, Saxony, Württemberg, and Bavaria—met to consider Radowitz's plan. Ten days later, after the defection of the two southern states, the Prussians, Hanoverians, and Saxons formed the *Dreikönigsbund*, an alliance pledged to the creation of a German Union without Austria. A constitution for this new union was issued on 28 May: although it closely followed Frankfurt's stillborn document, the so-called *Unionsverfassung* substituted an indirect, class-based suffrage for the parliament's democratic franchise and gave the chief executive (who did not have the title of emperor) absolute veto power. On 11 June the three kings invited all the German states to participate in elections for a union parliament, which was supposed to debate and eventually to ratify the constitution.[86]

---

[86] Huber, ii. 885ff., Huber *Dokumente*, i. 434 ff.

Like the leaders of the liberal revolution, Radowitz hoped for an alliance between the *Volk* and the states, both to create and to govern the new Germany. But he wanted the terms of this alliance to be set by the Prussian state rather than the German *Volk*. In contrast to the national parliament, the new *Reichstag* was little more than the recipient of a constitution, whose origins and final formulation remained under government control. Not surprisingly, the democratic left responded to these proposals with anger and contempt. To the moderate supporters of a *Kleindeutschland*, however, Radowitz's union seemed, despite its provenance, very attractive indeed. These men had, after all, always favoured a strong executive and had accepted the democratic suffrage with great reluctance. In June, 150 former Frankfurt delegates, including most of the old moderate stalwarts, congregated at Gotha; 130 signed a declaration in favour of the Prussian plan. The goals of the original constitution, they argued, were more important than 'a stubborn commitment to the means with which one seeks these goals'.[87]

Throughout the second half of 1849 Radowitz attempted to consolidate support among the states. But as Austria's position improved—most significantly because of its victory over the Hungarians in August—opposition to Prussian leadership increased. During the summer, Bavaria, always suspicious of the Protestant superpower in the north, rejected Radowitz's plan, as did Württemberg and six smaller states. By the end of the year, when the election campaign for the Union parliament began, ten states—including both of Prussia's original allies, Saxony and Hanover—remained outside the Union, while twenty-six belonged. The *Reichstag*, elected in January and convened in Erfurt in March 1850, was dominated by the 'Gotha' party, which was composed of liberal leaders who now found themselves in the paradoxical position of defending Frederick William from attacks by his own conservative friends and allies. Since the left was virtually unrepresented at Erfurt, the 'opposition' was provided by Prussian reactionaries, who saw Radowit's scheme as the ruination of everything they held sacred.

While Radowitz and his erstwhile liberal partners were debating the constitution at Erfurt, Schwarzenberg was busy organizing an Austrian counter-offensive. First, he secured the support of Russia, thus depriving Berlin of a critically important European ally. Then he began to gather the German states into an anti-Prussian alliance;

[87] Botzenhart, *Parlamentarismus*, p. 723.

in February 1850 the kings of Bavaria, Hanover, Württemberg, and Saxony declared their support for a reconstituted German Confederation that would include the entire Habsburg monarchy. These kingdoms, together with six smaller states, attended a rump session of the Confederation convened by Austria early in May. At the same time, Prussia and its allies gathered in Berlin. By the summer, with trouble brewing in Schleswig-Holstein and a serious constitutional crisis under way in Hesse-Kassel, the German question seemed about to ignite into full-scale civil war. At the end of July, during what he regarded an 'uncanny calm, which seems to come before a storm', Count Vitzthum wrote that Prussia would either have to give way to Austrian pressures or fight on behalf of its national ambitions.[88]

The crisis came to a head because of the situation in Hesse, whose ruler, Frederick William, was busy liquidating the revolution. Hessian domestic politics became enmeshed with larger German issues after the newly reappointed minister Hassenpflug, a most unpopular relic from the Metternichian era, withdrew from the Prussian Union at the same time as he introduced reactionary measures in defiance of the Hessian *Landtag*. When important elements in both the army and the civil service supported the *Landtag* against the ministry, Frederick William sought aid from the Confederation. The diet, following Austria's lead, promised to support the elector against his rebellious subjects. This was a direct challenge to the Prussian Union, as well as to Prussia's strategic position, since two important military roads linking her eastern and western provinces ran through Hessian territory.[89]

During the autumn of 1850, war between Prussia and the Austrian-led rump Confederation seemed likely. Prussia began to mobilize its troops, while General Radetzky, fresh from new victories in Italy, waited in Vienna to take command of the Habsburgs' army. In October, Austria, Bavaria, and Württemberg signed a treating supporting the Confederation's position against Prussia. Despite efforts by the tsar to mediate a solution, matters continued to deteriorate after federal troops moved into Hesse and, in response, Prussian units occupied strategically vital parts of the electorate. At one point, shots were exchanged between federal and Prussian forces. But at the last minute, Prussia drew back. Radowitz's opponents in the ministries and at the Hohenzollern court, appalled by the prospect of fighting both Austria and Russia

---

[88] Jessen (ed.), *Revolution*, p. 355.
[89] On the Hessian crisis, see Huber, ii. 908 ff.

for a cause in which they did not believe, finally prevailed. Radowitz, who had resigned as Foreign Minister even before the highpoint of the crisis, now lost all influence on the king. Manteuffel, who became Minister President following Brandenburg's sudden death on 6 November, accepted Schwarzenberg's demand that he withdraw Prussian forces from Hesse. On 29 November the two statesmen met in the Austrian town of Olmütz, from where they issued a joint proclamation that effectively killed the Union, provided for joint action in Hesse and Schleswig, and called for a conference to decide Germany's future.

Like the Frankfurt liberals, Radowitz had tried to effect a radical reorganization of German affairs with a moderate strategy—both efforts failed because of this discrepancy between ends and means. To Radowitz's supporters in the Gotha party—and to the generations of *kleindeutsch* historians who told the story from their point of view—Olmütz was a humiliation, a blot on Prussia's honour which would have to be revenged. Most Prussian conservatives, on the other hand, saw the Olmütz agreement as a relatively painless way of getting rid of Radowitz and avoiding a war that might have once again unleashed the forces of disorder and unrest. Otto von Bismarck, who gave his first important speech in the *Landtag* a few days after Olmütz, declared that he saw nothing dishonourable about not wanting to play quixotic games on behalf of 'gekränkte Kammerzelebritäten'. He did not understand how Austria could be regarded as a foreign power, nor how the cause of German unity could be furthered by encouraging northerners and southerners to kill one another.[90]

Schwarzenberg succeeded in stopping Radowitz's attempt to redefine the political basis for German politics, but his own alternative vision of a federation of German states tied to a unified Habsburg monarchy turned out to be no less unworkable—as Schwarzenberg himself may well have known all along. When the conference on German affairs which met in Dresden from 3 December 1850 until 15 May 1851 could not come up with a satisfactory formula for redistributing political authority between the two superpowers or for reconciling their interests with those of the smaller states, Metternich's old federal structure turned out to be the solution that divided German statesmen least. Three years after it had been declared a corpse by the optimistic men of March 1848, the Confederation once again provided the official centre for German public life. Among its first acts was the so-called

---

[90] Bismarck, *Werke*, x. 105, 108.

Bundesreaktionsbeschluss of August 1851, a measure jointly sponsored by Austria and Prussia, which reaffirmed the anti-revolutionary legislation of 1819 and 1830–4.[91]

Even before the Confederation had reminded governments of their repressive obligations, most German states had begun to reverse the reformist course set in the spring of 1848. In one capital after another, the 'March ministries' were replaced by men willing and able to revoke liberal legislation, defy parliamentary majorities, and crush popular dissent. In Baden, for instance, Grand Duke Leopold appointed a conservative ministry as soon as Prussian troops had restored order. Acting through a series of emergency decrees, this government dismantled the progressive accomplishments of its predecessors. Saxony, another centre of unrest in 1849, was also put under military rule; after a series of confrontations with the parliament, the king finally violated the constitution, unilaterally issued a new suffrage law, and revoked most of the political freedoms he had granted two years before. In Württemberg reaction took place in stages: the king replaced Römer with a moderate ministry in October 1849; four months later, he appointed the reactionary Freiherr von Linden, who attacked the *Landtag*, altered the suffrage, and restored the constitution of 1819. The Hanoverian reaction also came in instalments: the Stüve ministry fell in October 1850; it was replaced first by a government under Baron Alexander von Münchhausen, and then, after George V became king in 1851, by a moderate conservative coalition under Baron von Schele (the son of the man responsible for the revocation of the constitution in 1837). Finally, in 1855, King George set aside the constitution and installed a reactionary ministry led by Count Wilhelm Friedrich von Borries, who remained in office until 1862. Reinhard Freiherr von Dalwigk began his long tenure as Minister President of Hesse-Darmstadt in late 1850 when he abandoned the Prussian Union and pushed through a series of constitutional revisions. Among the *Mittelstaaten*, only Bavaria tried to retain a more moderate course: under von der Pfordten, the Munich government continued to co-operate with the parliament until the mid-1850s.[92]

[91] For the conventional view of Schwarzenberg's plans in 1850, see Kann, *Empire*, ii. 71 ff.; Srbik, *Metternich*, ii. 92 ff. All emphasize the significance of his efforts to join the German states and the monarchy. My account is based on Austensen's critique of this position in 'Austria'. On the shifting positions of the states, see Rumpler, *Politik*, which analyses Saxon foreign policy under Count Beust.

[92] See below, Ch. 14 sec. i, for more on German politics in the 1850s. Huber, iii. 182 ff. surveys the most important constitutional revisions.

Like reform, reaction varied from state to state in intensity, scope, and spirit. In some places, the governments managed to act legally, elsewhere they had to resort to a *coup d'état*. The reaction in Baden was relatively mild, especially after Leopold's death in 1852; in Saxony, on the other hand, the political atmosphere was poisoned by chronic hostility between government and opposition. Generally speaking, the bureaucracy was the chief instrument of reaction in the southern states, just as it had been the instrument of reform two generations before. In the north, the landed élite was also important, both in the new reactionary ministries and in representative institutions. As in the first half of the century, aristocratic hegemony was most apparent in the Mecklenburgs, whose *Stände* returned to the dominant position that they would be able to defend until 1918.

Except for the Mecklenburgs, however, none of the small or middle-sized German states completely abandoned constitutional government. Even where reactionary policies were harshest, monarchs and ministers seem to have sensed some limitations on what they could do. With varying degrees of reluctance and self-consciousness, many German conservatives had come to accept the fact that constitutions and parliaments were here to stay. They made sure that the constitution contained safeguards against revolutionary upheavals and that the parliament was arranged in ways that would further their own interests, but they did not feel strong enough to do without constitutions or to destroy representative institutions. As difficult as it may be to see amid the turmoil of political conflict and the pains of political repression, by the 1850s a fragile, tension-filled consensus about the nature of politics had begun to emerge in many of the smaller and middle-sized German states: liberals, although eager for reform and dissatisfied with the status quo, none the less recognized the necessity for state authority, just as conservatives, hostile to liberalism and fearful of unrest, acknowledged the inevitability of constitutional and representative government. How long this consensus would last and how far it would spread depended in large measure on the political course set by the two German superpowers.

The Prussian constitution, issued by decree at the end of 1848, was supposed to have been ratified by the *Landtag*, but, because the Brandenburg government had little or no interest in parliamentary collaboration, the king dissolved the lower house in April 1849. In order to avoid having to deal with another hostile majority, Frederick William replaced the democratic suffrage guaranteed by the constitution with the so-called Three Class suffrage system, which was based on the franchise for local representative institutions in the Rhineland. Under this system, virtually all adult males could vote for a group of electors, who in turn chose the delegates. But, while most males might be able to vote, the weight of their votes was unequal since they were divided into three groups according to their tax obligations; each of these groups selected one third of the electors. In the summer of 1849, for example, the first group, composed of less than 5 per cent of the electorate, chose as many electors as the second group (to which 12.6 per cent belonged) or the third (with 82.7 per cent). Moreover, the influence of what one conservative called the 'natural authorities' in society was increased by the way the voting was done: each class voted separately and publicly, the third went first, in the presence of the other two, and then left the polling place. This suffrage system is of interest not simply because it regulated Prussian elections until the end of the monarchy, but also because it so accurately reflects the combination of forces at work in the Prussian reaction: a bureaucratic preference for legal equality, an implicit faith in the conservative influence of property, and a desire to preserve the power of traditional deference communities.[93]

The first elections under the new suffrage law were held in July. The left, outraged by the king's unilateral actions, disadvantaged by the franchise, and harassed by the authorities, did not take part. Some liberals, however, were prepared to go along with the government at home just as they were ready to support Radowitz's plans for a new Germany. A group of men who referred to themselves as 'Conservative-liberals' declared that they would rather come to terms with a *coup d'état* than with a revolution from below: 'We can again and again win just power and authority for freedom's cause, but from the absolutism of doctrinaire revolution we will not be able to return to order and freedom.' For these liberals, at least, the state remained a more reliable ally than the *Volk*.[94]

In the summer of 1849 the level of popular participation in Prussian politics was low: as a contributor to the *Grenzboten* noted,

[93] Huber, *Dokumente*, i. 398 ff., reprints the relevant materials on the new suffrage. See also Jacques Droz, 'Liberale Anschauungen zur Wahlrechtsfrage und das preussische Dreiklassenwahlrecht', in Böckenförde (ed.), *Verfassungsgeschichte*, pp. 195–214; Schilfert, *Sieg*.

[94] Grünthal, *Parlamentarismus*, p. 101. This is the best account of Prussian politics in the 1850s.

'no trace exists of dramatic political vitality'. Nor was there much excitement apparent among the newly elected delegates, many of whom eschewed all formal party alignment. The chamber was dominated by a right-wing group under Adolf Heinrich von Arnim Boytzenburg, against which a divided and uncertain collection of liberals tried to carry on half-hearted opposition. After a somewhat desultory series of debates, the *Landtag* presented a slightly revised version of the constitution to the king in January 1850. There was a flurry of activity at court when Frederick William wanted to reopen the whole constitutional question, but finally Radowitz—for whose diplomatic offensive the constitution was essential—prevailed upon him to swear an oath of loyalty to the new order. Many moderate liberals, who had been advocating some kind of constitutional settlement for more than a decade, were satisfied but not elated by the final outcome: 'the bird is in the cage', Camphausen wrote on 1 February 1850, 'and that's the main thing.'[95]

As long as Radowitz was trying to win the constitutional *Mittelstaaten* for his Union plan, diplomatic considerations inhibited those who hoped to push Frederick William further along the path of reaction. Radowitz's fall and the Olmütz agreements opened the way for a new anti-constitutional offensive, led by the old court camarilla and most forcefully articulated in the pages of the *Kreuzzeitung*. In the summer of 1851 the king, acting in clear violation of the constitution, issued a decree reinstating the district and provincial *Stände*, which some conservatives hoped would undermine the *Landtag*'s position. The camarilla's influence was also apparent in the newly constituted upper chamber of the *Landtag* (which came to be called the *Herrenhaus*): according to a law of October 1854, this body was dominated by the nobility, who held at least three-quarters of the seats either through office or inheritance. On several occasions during the early 1850s, therefore, there seemed to be grounds for Leopold von Gerlach's hope that the consitution would 'die a natural death'.[96]

But despite the growing strength of the reactionary party, the enemies of the constitution did not prevail, in part because of their own divisions and self-doubt, in part because of the king's characteristic refusal to take decisive action, but most of all because of the bureaucracy's unwillingness to support a resolute assault on

[95] Ibid. 107, 174.
[96] Grünthal, 'Konstitutionalismus', p. 150. On the provincial *Landtage* and the *Herrenhaus*, see Heffter, *Selbstverwaltung*, pp. 329 ff.; Huber, iii. 81 ff.

the constitution. Manteuffel, for example, was a deeply conservative man and an unyielding enemy of the left, but he was none the less convinced that that a government could 'durchaus regieren' with the constitution. In the first place, the constitution protected monarchical power and preserved the monarch's right to act in times of danger. Second, by defining and guaranteeing the rights of bureaucrats, the constitution consolidated the administration's position in the centre of the political system. Finally, the Minister President believed that Prussia was better able to live with a constitution than many other states, because the Hohenzollern monarchy was not really a 'nation', but rather an administrative structure, in which constitutional developments—and especially their most harmful by-product, parliamentarism—would not deeply penetrate. For the same reason, he did not believe in the medieval fantasies prevalent among some of the king's advisers: 'The Prussian state cannot be based on corporate institutions,' Manteuffel wrote in December 1850; 'it is essentially a bureaucratic and military system.'[97]

In order for that system to work, the bureaucracy had to be free—not simply from parliamentary influence but also from the interference of royal cronies, whose intrigues spread across Frederick William's court like a spider's web. Throughout the early 1850s Manteuffel sought ways to co-ordinate and direct the Ministry of State, most notably in the cabinet order of September 1852, which seemed to affirm the Minister President's primacy. At the same time, the bureaucracy had to protect itself from subversive forces, within its own ranks and in society at large. A disciplinary order, first issued in July 1849 and then reaffirmed three years later, strengthened ministerial authority over both judicial and administrative personnel by establishing a category of 'political official' from whom conformity to government policy was to be expected. As the original order put it, 'An effective government [can] not allow that an official interfere with the proper conduct of his duties through the inappropriate expression of oppositional private opinions.' Behind the tortured bureaucratic prose the message was clear: conform or face the consequences. Nor was conformity enough; throughout the 1850s the Ministry of the Interior called upon local officials to use their influence to ensure the election of pro-government candidates, who were often

[97] Grünthal, *Parlamentarismus*, pp. 216–17; Gillis, *Bureaucracy*, p. 132.

government employees. In the *Landtag* of 1855, for example, half of the delegates held some kind of official position.[98]

At the same time as it increased its control over its own ranks, the bureaucracy also tightened its hold on Prussian society. The municipal ordinances of 1853 and 1856 strengthened the local bureaucracy's role within, and the central administration's authority over, urban affairs. Official influences over educational and religious institutions also increased; the authorities made a greater effort to impose political conformity on school teachers, while in Catholic areas officials co-operated with ecclesiastical institutions against subversion. The regulatory power of the state also grew in the areas of public health and worker protection: for example, a law of May 1853 prohibited the employment of children under twelve and established special rules for those between twelve and fourteen, including a limitation on their work day to seven hours. Much more important, the government expanded the size of the bureaucracy, especially those branches in charge of keeping order. Under its new chief, Carl von Hinckeldey, the Berlin police, which had been a self-consciously civilian and relatively innocuous organization, was reorganized and expanded. Its uniform branch, now under military discipline, scrutinized the details of social and political life in the capital, while its undercover agents watched for the faintest signs of unrest. The *Landgendarmen* and border guards also increased in number, from 1,500 in 1840 to 2,500 in 1855. By that time, the Ministry of the Interior was spending two million talers a year more than it had ten years earlier, most of it on public security. It was now no longer necessary to call for the army whenever a strike or demonstration threatened to get out of hand.[99]

We should not overestimate the extent or effectiveness of bureaucratic power after 1850. Despite Manteuffel's efforts, the

---

[98] Grünthal, *Parlamentarismus*, pp. 106–7; Huber, iii. 65. There is an example of officials' electoral activity in Otto Röttges, *Die politischen Wahlen in den links-rheinischen Kreisen des Regierungsbezirkes Düsseldorf, 1848–1867* (Kempen-Niederrhein, 1964), 180.

[99] Heffter, *Selbstverwaltung*, pp. 331 ff.; Tilly *et al.* (eds.), *Century*, pp. 220–1; Berthold Schulze, 'Polizeipräsident Carl von Hinckeldey', *JbGMO* 4 (1955). For a local study of these developments, see Elaine Glovka Spencer, 'State Power and Local Interests in Prussian Cities. Police in the Düsseldorf District, 1848–1914', *CEH* 19/3 (1986). The role of the political police expanded throughout German Europe; in early 1851 several states formed the so-called *Polizeiverein* to co-ordinate the battle against subversion. On this organization, see Wolfram Siemann, *'Deutschlands Ruhe, Sicherheit und Ordnung': Die Anfänge der politischen Polizei, 1806–1866* (Tübingen, 1985).

king and his cronies continued to play one minister off against another. Moreover, while some politically unreliable officials were removed and the pressure for conformity did increase, a significant number of civil servants still supported the liberal opposition. Finally, as impressive as the new security forces were in comparison to their predecessors, the state apparatus remained relatively small and its capacity for social control was still limited. Nevertheless, it is important to note how the achievement of constitutional government in Prussia was accompanied by an expansion of bureaucratic institutions. In Prussia, as in the constitutional states of the south-west, *Verfassung* and *Verwaltung* were densely interwoven.

The Austrian constitution, like its Prussian counterpart, can be seen as an attempt to consolidate governmental authority by means of a carefully designed compromise with the moderate opposition. Throughout 1850 and 1851 the terms of this compromise were debated in Vienna, just as they were in Berlin, and in both capitals this debate was influenced by foreign and domestic considerations. But the outcome of the debate was different in the Habsburg realm; as soon as he felt strong enough, Francis Joseph freed himself from constitutional restraints and set out to create his own version of absolutist rule. It was of great significance for the future course of German developments that, at this critical moment, the Habsburg monarchy did not join the broad movement towards constitutionalism.[100]

As early as the autumn of 1850 the emperor began to prepare for a regime without the constitution. At the end of the year he enlisted an important ally in the person of Metternich's old associate, Baron Kübeck, who became president of the newly created *Reichsrat*, an advisory organ designed to strengthen the sovereign's hand against both the Council of Ministers and the parliament. Throughout 1851 Kübeck, acting under Francis Joseph's orders, steadily worked to undermine the constitution. Important members of Schwarzenberg's original cabinet, among them Bruck and Schmerling, resigned their posts as more and more power shifted to the *Reichsrat*. In August a series of proclamations ended ministerial responsibility, confirmed the *Reichsrat*'s position as the emperor's paramount advisory council, and directed Schwarzenberg and Kübeck to prepare a report on the constitution's future. 'We have

[100] The best account of Austrian history in the 1850s is Brandt, *Neoabsolutismus*. There is a great deal of valuable information in Karl Czoernig von Czernhausen, *Österreichs Neugestaltung, 1848–1858* (Stuttgart, 1858).

thrown the constitution overboard,' Francis Joseph wrote in a exuberant letter to his mother, 'and Austria has now only one master.' On New Year's Eve 1851 the final blow fell. Inspired by Napoleon's coup in Paris and encouraged by the successful conclusion of the ministerial conference in Dresden, the emperor issued the so-called 'Sylvester Patent'—actually three separate declarations in which he instructed Schwarzenberg to revoke the constitution of March 1849 (except for the guarantees of equal rights and the emancipation of the serfs), to abandon, with a few exceptions, the *Grundrechte* granted earlier, and to cancel every political reform that could be discovered in law or administrative practice. Gone were the elaborate array of representative institutions, the separation of judicial and administrative bureaucracies, the promise of national autonomy and linguistic equality, jury trials, and much else that Stadion, Schmerling, and the other reformers had tried to create. In their place came a system that, one critic declared, was run by 'a standing army of soldiers, a sitting army of officials, a kneeling army of priests, and a creeping army of denunciators'.[101]

Even before the revocation of the constitution some Austrians began to talk about the return of a Metternichian age. A writer in the liberal *Grenzboten*, for instance, called the post-revolutionary period a 'second edition of the Metternichian system, on cheaper paper and with worse type'. The old chancellor himself moved back to the Austrian capital in September 1851, took up residence in a palace on the Rennweg, and proceeded to receive distinguished visitors and dispense unsolicited advice. But the Austrian reaction was not simply a return to the *Vormärz*. In the first place, neo-absolutism was tougher than its predecessor—more centralized, efficient, and effective. Moreover, there was a modernizing impulse in neo-absolutism, which took steps to encourage economic growth and social emancipation. In 1851, for example, the government established a customs union for the monarchy, two years later it signed a tariff agreement with the *Zollverein*, and, most important, in 1859 it issued a liberal industrial code. In the words of Freiherr von Bruck, there would be no return to the dark days of 1848, 'because the situation of material life, money, capital the economy, and a strengthened peasantry and *Bürgertum* would not allow it'.[102]

---

[101] Kiszling, *Schwarzenberg*, pp. 189–90; Jászi, *Dissolution*, p. 102.

[102] Bibl, *Zerfall*, i. 195; Rosenberg, *Weltwirtschaftskrise*, p. 17. For a survey of the literature on neo-absolutism, see Brandt, *Neoabsolutismus*, i. 246, n. 1.

At the head of the neo-absolutist regime stood its chief architect and instrument, the Emperor Francis Joseph, who was now free from constitutional limits, ministerial responsibility, and parliamentary supervision. When Schwarzenberg died suddenly in April 1852, his sovereign mourned but did not replace him. The new Foreign Minister, Count Buol Schauenstein, lacked both the formal position and the personal qualities necessary to control the government or provide direction for public affairs. Instead, Francis Joseph sought to be both the practical and the symbolic centre of the state. Wholly devoted to his duties, rigidly insistent upon his supreme power, and almost pathologically concerned with ceremonial correctness, the emperor tried to turn politics into an expression of his personality and an act of individual will. 'The master would be a marvellous minister of police,' his military adjutant once said, 'because he sees and knows everything.' That this was meant as a compliment is a sad commentary on the Austrian situation.[103]

At the end of 1849 Kübeck had written that the counter-revolution brought to power the army, the church, and the bureaucracy, which would be 'three great instruments of monarchical authority, if they were firmly grasped and wisely used'. In fact, the army, church, and bureaucracy were neo-absolutism's chief instruments, but none was merely a pliable tool of the monarch's will. The army, which emerged from its successful campaigns against the rebels as the acknowledged saviour of the state, fought for its independence against civilian interference. In May 1853 authority over military affairs was transferred from the Ministry of War to a supreme army command, which defended its institutional self-interest even when it could not master the complex forces under its control. The church, traditionally subordinated to the administration, also increased its autonomy after the revolution. Personally pious and convinced that religion was a powerful antidote to revolution, the emperor signed a concordat with the papacy in 1855, through which Austrian Catholicism regained an important measure of independence. Perhaps most important of all, the bureaucracy resisted monarchical domination. To be sure, Francis Joseph could try to balance the competing elements in his government, but he was no more able than his predecessors to bring order and direction to the complex business of running the Habsburg lands. At the centre of policy-making, therefore, the fragmentation so long characteristic of the Austrian system

[103] Herre, *Franz Joseph*, p. 104.

continued under neo-absolutism—indeed, by demolishing the constitution, the emperor had helped to make this fragmentation worse.[104]

The strength of the system was not at its core but rather in the extended network of officials upon whose diligence, efficiency, and relative honesty the monarchy ultimately had to depend. After 1850 the bureaucracy significantly expanded: between 1847 and 1856 public expenditures on political and judicial administration increased by as much as 873 per cent in some parts of the monarchy. Furthermore, under the direction of Bach, who remained as Minister of the Interior, administrative institutions were centralized, with a chain of command reaching from the capital to small communities. As had always been true in the monarchy, centralization meant Germanization; although officials were supposed to use local languages in dealing with the population, the 'internal language' of the bureaucratic apparatus itself was German. In addition to the so-called 'Bach hussars', who represented state power in the far corners of the realm, the chief instrument of the new regime was the *Gendarmerie*, a paramilitary police force which Francis Joseph removed from the control of the Ministry of the Interior and put under the command of a former general, Freiherr von Kempen. Like Hinckeldey's police in Prussia, Kempen's *Gendarmes* represented the state's new commitment to internal security, public order, and political repression.[105]

Kempen and Hinckeldey, together with Bach and Manteuffel, best personify the politics of the 1850s. While its features differed from state to state, the new face of reaction was essentially bureaucratic. Almost everywhere in German Europe the administrative apparatus became larger, more effective, and more ambitious. Bureaucratic growth was not simply a response to revolutionary dangers, rather it was part of a broader pattern of change which required that the states accept new tasks: to regulate and direct economic activity, to channel and distribute social resources, to

[104] Walter, *Verfassungs- und verwaltungsgeschichte*, p. 169. On the army, see Brandt, *Neoabsolutismus*, i. 264 ff.; Rothenberg, *Army*, pp. 36 ff.; on the Concordat, see Hantsch, *Geschichte*, ii. 371 ff.

[105] Brandt, *Neoabsolutismus*, ii. 1095 surveys administrative costs; on bureaucratic structure, see Walter Goldinger in Wandruszka and Urbanitsch (eds.), *Habsburgermonarchie*, ii; the documents in Helmut Rumpler (ed.), *Die Protokolle des Österreichischen Ministerrates, 1848–1867* (Vienna, 1970 ff.). Also of interest is Johann Freiherr von Kempen, *Das Tagebuch des Polizeiministers Kempen von 1848 bis 1859*, ed. J. K. Mayr (Vienna and Leipzig, 1931). According to Robert Kann's calculations, in 1914 4,772 of the 6,293 members of the monarchy's central bureaucracy were Germans: *Empire*, ii, app. V.

mobilize and exert political authority. Bureaucratization and modernization, some observers recognized, were two facets of the same process.

> With the tighter unity and uniformity of the modern state [wrote Ludwig Häusser in 1851], there naturally developed that form of administration which we call bureaucratic. The advantage of greater unity and order that permeates modern politics is also a characteristic of the bureaucracy, indeed the bureaucracy is actually the uniformity and mechanical equality of the state carried to the extreme.

Twelve years later, the economist Adolf Wagner formulated his 'law on the expansion of public, especially state activities', with which he tried to measure the inevitable growth of the state's role in social and economic life.[106]

Traditional conservatives viewed this expansion of bureaucratic authority with distaste and alarm. The young Bismarck, for instance, found Hinckeldey's police 'unnötig barsch' and ridiculed their alleged attempt to regulate the height ladies might lift their skirts to avoid puddles. To this Pomeranian squire, the bureaucracy was much more dangerous than a few parliamentary gossips. 'Cancerous in its brain and limbs,' he wrote in 1850, 'only its stomach is healthy.' Like many of his fellow Junkers, Bismarck viewed bureaucrats as social upstarts, ever ready to interfere with the treasured rights and privileges of the landed élite. Driven by the officials' personal ambitions and doctrinaire commitments to uniform regulations, the Beamtenstaat was as much a threat to the traditional order as the worst rabble-rousers. Indeed, to someone like Leopold von Gerlach, 'absolutism is the revolution'.[107]

Gerlach, together with his younger brother Ludwig, was one of the most influential advocates of anti-statist conservatism in the 1840s and 1850s. Born in 1790 and 1795, the two Gerlachs had fought with distinction in the Napoleonic wars and continued to serve the Prussian state, Leopold as an officer, Ludwig as an official. They owed their prominence, however, to their place in the court circle around Frederick William, who shared their intense Protestant piety and profound distaste for modern political life. To them, the state was not primarily a source of power; it was, above all, 'the realm of divine law in human affairs'. They had no doubt that God favoured royal authority, corporate institutions, and a hierarchical social order. After the trauma of 1848, the Gerlachs

---

[106] Rudolf Vierhaus, 'Liberalismus, Beamtenstand und konstitutionelles System', Schieder (ed.), Liberalismus, p. 39; Fischer, et al., Arbeitsbuch, p. 191.

[107] Rothfels, ed., Bismarck, p. 25; Ludwig von Gerlach, Revolution, p. 36.

became leading members of the camarilla that encouraged the king's counter-revolutionary sympathies. They had not favoured the constitutional decree, but, once the king had sworn allegiance to it, they set about trying to strengthen the role of the *Stände* at the expense of both *Landtag* and administration. As the direction of social and political change after 1850 rendered the Gerlachs' brand of conservatism increasingly obsolete, they stubbornly restated their views, harshly condemning those who seemed prepared to compromise with the new state and society.[108]

In contrast to the Gerlachs, the experience of revolution led Leopold von Ranke to seek a more secure footing for conservative values than the vanishing world of the *Stände*. Ranke was appalled by the spectacle of revolution: 'The whole order of things on which the further development of mankind depends', he wrote in March 1848, 'is threatened by anarchic powers.' From October 1848 until 1851, Ranke had prepared a series of memoranda for his friend, Erwin von Manteuffel, newly appointed adjutant to King Frederick William IV. In these documents Ranke had tried to understand the revolution in its historical context and to grope towards ways of saving the existing order from the pestilence of unrest. Like the bureaucrats who took over the major states in late 1848 and 1849, Ranke saw there was no turning back: 'The storms of today must be met with the institutions of today.' This meant, first of all, a willingness to accept constitutional government, not from affection or conviction, but because this was the kind of state in which men now expected to live. Moreover, Ranke believed that the old federative mode of organizing German affairs was doomed. Instead, Prussia must take the lead in imposing a new German order on the smaller states. The strong, Ranke argued, must dictate to the weak and only Prussia, with its firmly established monarchical and military institutions, was strong enough to dominate German politics and defeat the forces of revolution. Tactical compromise on the domestic front, increased vigour in international affairs, and a growing concern for power as the basis of statecraft—these essential elements in Bismarckian conservatism are already clearly adumbrated in Ranke's private reflections on the revolution.[109]

[108] Schoeps, *Preussen,* p. 9. On the Gerlachs, see Ludwig's *Revolution,* and Leopold's *Denkwürdigkeiten* (2 vols.; 1891–92). Sigmund Neumann, *Die Stufen des preussischen Konservatismus. Ein Beitrag zum Staats- und Gesellschaftsbild Deutschlands im 19. Jahrhundert* (Berlin, 1930) is a good summary of conservatism.

[109] Krieger, *Ranke,* pp. 210 ff. On Ranke, see above, Ch. 9, sect. ii.

Lorenz von Stein approached the post-revolutionary state as a social theorist rather than a historian of statecraft. Born in 1815, the illegitimate son of a nobleman recently dismissed from the Danish army, Stein was reared in an orphanage, studied as a scholarship student at the University of Kiel, and made his reputation with a book on French socialism published in 1842. As one of the first and most perceptive analysts of the social crisis that gripped Europe in the 1840s, Stein was acutely aware of the dangers of revolution. After his experiences in Schleswig-Holstein during 1848 had left him disappointed with the possibilities of liberal reform, he became convinced that the only bulwark against the disorder inherent in modern society was the monarchical state. Society, driven by self-interest, was creative but potentially chaotic, whereas the state, which transcended the will of any single individual, was a source of order, cohesion, and unity. Like Ranke, Stein viewed Prussia as a paradigmatic monarchical state. But for him the monarchy's primary function was to be a source of social regulation and stability rather than an expression of diplomatic and military power.[110]

Behind the varieties of conservatism in the 1850s was one common conviction: the principal danger confronting European society was revolution. The revolutionary disease from which Germany suffers, wrote Tocqueville in 1851, 'may be temporarily arrested but . . . cannot be cured'. Like their contemporaries on the left, conservatives believed that the revolution was part of modern life, a historical force of limitless potential. In a variety of ways— from the Gerlachs' idealistic corporatism to Stein's monarchical social reform—conservatives searched for an antidote to this infection, a new source of order, a new foundation for legitimacy.[111]

The voices proclaiming the fragility of the existing order are so loud and eloquent that we sometimes overlook the fact that they were wrong. Despite repeated predictions, expressed with fear on the right and hopeful expectation on the left, revolution did not return to western Europe, at least not in its mid-century form. The apparent sequence 1789–1830–1848 was broken; the Paris commune of 1871 was isolated and easily repressed, the great wave of revolutions in 1918–19 was the product of war and defeat. What

[110] There is a good introduction to Stein's life and thought in Dirk Blasius and Eckart Pankoke, *Lorenz von Stein* (Darmstadt, 1977). See also Ernst Forsthoff (ed.), *Lorenz von Stein: Gesellschaft. Staat. Recht* (Frankfurt, 1972); Roman Schnur (ed.), *Staat und Gesellschaft: Studien über Lorenz von Stein* (Berlin, 1978).

[111] Alexis de Tocqueville, *Recollections* (New York, 1970), 279–80.

had changed to make the existing order, apparently so fragile in 1848, increasingly resistant to upheavals from below? We have already seen an important part of the answer: the growth and increasing effectiveness of the security forces available to every European government. In the following chapters, we will touch upon other social, cultural, and political developments that strengthened the forces of order at the same time that they undermined those traditional communities upon which collective action had characteristically been based.

XII
Society in the Age of the
Bürgertum

GERMANS do not have a theory of society, Lorenz von Stein wrote in 1842, because in Germany 'the life of society and the struggle of its elements have not yet begun to develop independently'. Shortly thereafter Karl Marx made the same point when he explained German 'ideology' in terms of his society's fundamental backwardness. But even as these theorists noted German underdevelopment, the social order was in the process of transformation. By the 1850s the concept of society—and the fact of social change—were part of the German scene. In 1851, for example, Robert von Mohl insisted that the autonomy of social forces made it necessary to study them outside the political realm. That same year Wilhelm Heinrich Riehl described 'the emancipation of the idea of society from the despotism of the idea of the state' as 'the most genuine property of the present age, the source of a thousand conflicts and discontents, but also the hope of our political future'. This viewpoint was not universally accepted: political theorists like Heinrich von Treitschke regarded any effort to separate state and society as intellectually flawed and politically dangerous. Nevertheless, to radicals like Marx, liberals like Mohl, and conservatives like Riehl, the centrality of social forces was an inescapable fact of life.[1]

Some contemporaries and, following them, many historians viewed this 'discovery of society' as a response to the failure of politics in 1848–9. Ludwig Bamberger, for instance, recalled how he read with admiration the classical economist Frédéric Bastiat while he was fleeing westwards to avoid prosecution for his part in the 1849 uprisings; during the next decade Bamberger devoted himself to making money in the banking business. Hermann von Schulze-Delitzsch wrote in 1850 that 'after the general defeat of the political movement in our day, it has returned to its real point of

---

[1] Sombart, *Volkswirtschaft*, p. 482; Riehl, *Gesellschaft*, p. 4; Robert von Mohl, 'Die Staatswissenschaften und die Gesellschaftswissenschaften', *Die Geschichte und Literatur der Staatswissenschaften* (Erlangen, 1855). On social thought in this period, see Pankoke, *'Bewegung'*.

departure, the social realm'. A contributor to the liberal *National-zeitung* put the matter more positively when he proclaimed in 1856 that 'what idealistic efforts strove in vain to do, materialism has accomplished in a few months'. To many disappointed participants in the revolution, it seemed that economic growth and social progress, not political agitation and parliamentary debates, would be the true source of freedom and unity.[2]

Like most efforts to impose a political framework on social and economic developments, this tendency to view social theory and practice as a result of the revolution's failure does not work very well. There is good evidence that the economy had begun to grow in the 1840s and that its expansion after mid-century was part of a European-wide process. The same thing is true of social changes such as the emergence of new forms of production, the structural decline of certain handicrafts, and the development of an industrial working class. Even the emancipation of the peasantry in the Habsburg monarchy, perhaps the revolution's single most dramatic social reform, was the culmination of a process that had been transforming the rural order for decades. This does not mean that the revolution was unimportant, only that its importance came from the way in which it intensified or accelerated forces already at work in German Europe.

The following chapter brings together a number of the themes from our earlier discussions of social and economic developments. After analysing the problem of economic growth, we shall turn to the changes in the composition and relationship of social groups, first in the countryside, then in cities and industrial areas. The chapter concludes with a general analysis of German society in the second half of the nineteenth century, with particular emphasis on what many observers agreed were the chief characteristics of the new social order—its increasing freedom, equality, and mobility.

i. ECONOMIIC GROWTH

No aspect of nineteenth-century German history is more important than the economic expansion that took place during the century's middle decades. Through a complex combination of physical resources and social institutions, Germans were able to develop the productive capacities of both industry and agriculture, assume the lead in a number of key industries, and, later on, challenge Britain's

[2] Ludwig Bamberger, *Erinnerungen* (Berlin, 1899), 214 ff.; Schulze-Delitzsch, *Schriften* i. 1; Krieger, *Idea*, p. 346.

economic hegemony. This economic growth touched every facet of life, from the conduct of war to the character of sexual relations, from the organization of the state to patterns of recreation, from what people believed to what they wore. The nature and rhythm of work changed with the spread of machines, the meaning of time and space was altered by new forms of communication, the length as well as the quality of life was affected by the availability of new commodities and modes of production. While many of the most significant changes in the economy occurred after the period covered by this book, German economic power first became apparent in the 1850s and 1860s, and it is to these decades that we must look for the roots of future growth.[3]

Like Britain and the rest of western Europe—and unlike most other parts of the world—the German lands developed economically by releasing and co-ordinating their productive potential rather than by being forced to create or import it. It is worthwhile, therefore, to begin our account of economic growth by recalling the advantages Germans enjoyed at mid-century. By then most of them lived in relatively cohesive, well-organized states that had what Max Weber called 'the calculability and reliability in the functioning of the legal order and the administrative system [that] is vital to rational capitalism'.[4] Compared to their contemporaries in southern and eastern Europe, Germans were reasonably well off and well educated. In their workshops, a skilled, disciplined labour force was starting to take shape; in their cities, merchants and bankers experimented with new forms of enterprise and adopted the latest techniques of production; and alongside their rich deposits of coal and iron, the first great industrial complexes had begun to appear. The development of an effective system of communication helped bring together these scattered pockets of economic strength and natural endowment: roads, canals, steamships, and especially railroads gave people the means to overcome barriers imposed by politics and geography, create wider markets for their goods, and draw upon new sources of skilled labour and investment capital.

---

[3] On the historiography of German economic development, see Otto Büsch (ed.), *Industrialisierung und Geschichtswissenschaft* (2nd edn., Berlin, 1979); Karl W. Hardach, 'Some Remarks on German Economic Historiography and its Understanding of the Industrial Revolution in Germany', *Journal of European Economic History*, i (1972); Richard Tilly, 'Renaissance der Konjunkturgeschichte', *GuG* 6/2 (1980). Reinhard Spree's *Die Wachstumszyklen der deutschen Wirtschaft von 1840 bis 1880* (Berlin and Munich, 1977) has a well-informed quantitative analysis. Wehler, *Gesellschaftsgeschichte*, ii, is especially good on economic history.

[4] Weber, *Economy*, i. 296.

Seen in the aggregate, the economy showed some significant signs of expansion in the 1840s, largely because investment in railroads stimulated a variety of activities, especially coal-mining, iron and steel production, and machine works. Railroad construction and maintenance provided contracts for firms and jobs for skilled workers, created a demand for raw materials, and encouraged a number of ancillary enterprises, from the building trades to the manufacture of telegraph apparatus. At the same time, the creation of a rail network lowered some production costs and facilitated trade. Unfortunately, the possible benefits of these developments were offset by the recurrent social crises that culminated in the revolutions of 1848. Indeed, as we saw in Chapter 10, the presence of dynamic sectors in the economy intensified strains within society and raised the level of social discontent.

During the 1850s, when harvests were better, the international economy healthier, and the forces of order more secure, Germans became increasingly aware of economic progress. 'At the present time', wrote the Prussian statistician Dieterici in 1855, 'industry is penetrating human affairs with such power and significance that a comparison with earlier conditions is scarcely possible.' Three years later, the Austrian economist Carl Freiherr von Czoernig commented that so much had changed over the past decade that 'conditions in 1847 seem much closer to 1758 than to 1858'.[5] In popular periodicals and scholarly publications, parliamentary debates and bureaucratic reports, the economy became a matter of great concern. Popular encyclopaedias, whose leather bindings filled the shelves of educated families throughout central Europe, devoted much more attention to economic matters than had their *Vormärz* counterparts; even the third edition of the *Staatslexikon* followed this trend—its editors, for instance, replaced an article on 'Secret Societies' with one on 'Joint Stock Companies'. When repressive measures eased towards the end of the decade, among the first participatory institutions to emerge were those devoted to the discussion of economic issues or the defence of specific economic interests.

To much of the educated public, commercial expansion, industrial growth, and increasing prosperity seemed to demonstrate the efficacy of economic freedom. Throughout the late 1850s and early 1860s one German government after another dismantled restrictions on economic activity, weakened still further the

---

[5] Abraham, *Strukturwandel*, p. 96; Matis, *Wirtschaft*, pp. 85–6.

residual power of guilds, and signed commercial agreements with its neighbours. Even Austria joined this trend by establishing a customs union within the entire Habsburg realm, issuing a liberal enterprise law in 1859, and making a series of tariff agreements with other nations.

The post-revolutionary period, therefore, was the great age of free trade and freedom of enterprise—*Handelsfreiheit* and *Gewerbefreiheit*—which were celebrated in the urgent prose of pressure group petitions and scientifically affirmed by the cooler calculations of economic theorists. John Prince Smith, born and educated in England but now a Prussian subject, found an increasing corps of admirers for his attempt to bring classical British economic thought to the German public. In opposition to national economists like List, Prince Smith insisted that there was a uniform set of economic laws applicable to all societies. The same liberties that had produced Britain's economic power would do the same for the German states. Indeed, to economists like Prince Smith politics had little relevance: 'The solution of political conflicts, as well as the alleviation of material want, can only be achieved with a healthy economic policy.'[6]

These free-trade ideals were given institutional support in the *Kongress deutscher Volkswirte*, which was founded by a group of businessmen, publicists, and academicians in 1857. Designed to bring 'all friends of economic progress' into 'an earnest alliance with the power of public opinion and national conviction', the *Kongress* held annual meetings on the leading issues of the day. In many ways, the *Kongress* was more like a traditional *Verein* than a modern interest group; its methods were educational, its meetings open, and its membership drawn from the élites of property and education. But its emphasis reflected the importance now given to economic matters, even among academicians.

Many believe [wrote the *Bremer Handelsblatt* after the *Kongress's* first general meeting in 1858] that a new German economic party must emerge from the ruins of the old parties and over the grave of disappointed political hopes. Above all, this party must work towards the solution of important social questions, so that our *Volk* can strive for the fulfilment of its national

---

[6] Sheehan, *Liberalism*, p. 85. See W. O. Henderson, 'Prince Smith and Free Trade in Germany', *Economic History Review*, 2nd Ser., 2/3 (1950); John Prince Smith's *Gesammelte Schriften* (3 vols., Berlin, 1877–80). There are other examples of contemporary support for economic liberalism in Hamerow, *Foundations*, i. 95 ff. On the changing legal environment, see Harald Steindl, 'Die Einführung der Gewerbefreiheit', *Handbuch der Quellen und Literatur der neueren europäischen Privatrechtsgeschichte* (Munich, 1986), 3, pt. 3, 3527–628.

goals on a healthy social basis and armed with a clear knowledge of its essential interests.[7]

The early 1850s were a time of rapid expansion throughout the European economy. An upswing in world trade, in part stimulated by an influx of gold from California and Australia, encouraged firms to expand and investors to put their money into commercial and industrial enterprises. According to one estimate, the *Zollverein's* exports and imports increased from 511.7 million talers in 1850 to 995.5 million in 1857, Austria's from 175.8 million to 354.2 million. Between 1850 and 1856 imports passing through the port of Hamburg increased in value from 353,136 million to 654,872 million Bankomarks, exports from 313,829 to 613,434. As the volume of commercial activity grew, so did the capacity of individual enterprises. Although most German firms were still small, locally based, and run by a single proprietor and his family, some expanded in size, extended their operations across regional boundaries, and developed more complicated institutional structures. At the same time, joint stock companies became more popular: in the 1850s and 1860s almost three hundred were formed, with a total capital of 2,404 million marks. Investors, who had once been inclined to put their capital in land or government securities, now directed it towards innovative and speculative enterprises. Thus in 1856, Gustav Mevissen, a leading organizer of these new forms of capital investment, could point with obvious pride to the 'industrial sector's unification of capital and spiritual forces in the form of joint stock companies'.[8]

Mevissen was also involved in the creation of banks to meet the new demand for investment capital. The Schaaffhausen bank of Cologne, for instance, which had itself become a joint stock company in 1848, actively supported iron and steel firms in the Ruhr. The Darmstädter Bank für Handel und Industrie, founded at Mevissen's suggestion by the Cologne financier Oppenheim in 1854 and modelled on the Crédit Mobilier of Paris, sought to 'orient the spirit of enterprise and German capital towards the real needs of the moment—the development of German industry'. To do this, the bank was prepared not only to make short-term loans, but also to participate in the formation and direction of corporations. By 1857 there were six banks of this sort in the German

---

[7] On the *Kongress*, see Volker Hentschel, *Die deutschen Freihändler und der volkswirtschaftliche Kongress, 1858 bis 1885* (Stuttgart, 1975); the quotation is from p. 53.

[8] Rosenberg, *Weltwirtschaftskrise*, pp. 52, 85–6.

states: Schaaffhausen, the Darmstädter, Disconto Gesellschaft, Berliner Bank, Credit Anstalt in Leipzig, and Credit Anstalt in Vienna. Altogether, the five banks within the *Zollverein* contributed between twenty million and twenty-five million talers to industrial enterprises. In addition to these large investment houses, a variety of other financial institutions were founded: in Prussia, the total number of banks increased from 424 in 1843 to 642 in 1861; in the *Zollverein* as a whole, the quantity of bank notes in circulation rose from six million taler in 1845 to three hundred million twenty years later. Obviously, these changes had broad implications for German businesses, which now became less dependent on personal ties and familial bonds for credit and investment capital. As firms' capital requirements increased, they had no choice but to bring in outside investors, whose influence changed both the structure and style of their organizations.[9]

In the 1850s the German economy benefited from, but also became more vulnerable to, changes in the international economy. Throughout the first half of the decade, rapid growth had occasionally disturbed financial markets in various parts of the world. In 1856 signs of more serious trouble began to appear; interest rates rose, sources of credit dried up, share prices declined. Between mid–1856 and mid–1857 the value of the Vienna Credit Anstalt's stock dropped more than 50 per cent. The situation worsened in 1857, when unusually bountiful harvests depressed agricultural prices in Europe and the United States. That autumn several American stock markets suffered serious losses, some banks began to fail, and financial panic swiftly spread from New York to London. Except in Hamburg, whose financial institutions were closely tied to Britain's, no German banks faced insolvency. But everywhere financial markets were disrupted, commercial transactions slowed, and prices fell. In the *Zollverein* states, imports and exports declined from 962.7 million talers in 1856 to 886.8 three years later, the average price of goods (indexed with 1913 as a base) fell from 109.9 to 86.

The worldwide depression of 1857–9, unlike the crises of the late 1840s, was not caused by locally severe crop failures and food shortages, but rather by financial panic and overproduction in the world economy. As they struggled to understand these forces, Germans were compelled to recognize how much their prosperity depended on a global market. 'The world is one,' wrote the

---

[9] Riesser, *Banks*, especially pp. 46 ff.; Tilly, *Institutions*, and the essays in *Kapital*.

Elberfeld Chamber of Commerce in its annual report for 1857; 'trade and industry have made it so.'[10]

The depression's impact on the German lands was uneven. Hardest hit was the Austrian economy, which was rocked first by the depression, then by the military defeats and political crises that we will consider in Chapter 14. According to Alexander von Peez, a well-informed contemporary, the years from 1860 to 1866 were 'among the least favourable in all of Austrian economic history'. In most of the other German states, however, the overall effect of the depression was not severe. By 1860 the *Zollverein's* imports and exports were 1,006.3 million talers. Thereafter economic growth continued until the next and much more severe cyclical downturn came in 1873.[11]

Seen as a totality, the record growth in the 1850s and 1860s was impressive in every respect: production, income, and investment all substantially increased. We can measure these trends with the statistical data gathered by W. G. Hoffmann. The data are highly approximate and, unfortunately for our purposes, they are aggregated for the area that formed part of the German empire of 1871; nevertheless, they suggest the shape and direction of economic development. Between 1850 and 1866 the net social product increased from 9.4 million to 13.16 million marks, that is, from 268 to 333 marks per capita; national income went from 9.1 million to 12.42 million marks, 256 to 314 marks per capita; total investments were 890 million marks in the early 1850s, fell back to 776 million during the second half of the decade, then increased to 1538 million from 1861 to 1864.[12]

When we try to consider the meaning of these numbers, it is useful to remember that an economy can expand in two ways: first, through a growth in the 'factors of production', that is, labour and capital (including, of course, land), and, second, through an increase in the productivity of these factors, which usually means improvements in the techniques and organization of production. That the factors of production grew in the 1850s and 1860s is relatively clear and easy to measure: between 1852 and 1867 the 'German' work-force increased from 15 million to 16.17 million; the value of all capital goods was 48.5 million marks in the early 1850s and 66.31 million in the late 1860s.[13] Although more difficult

[10] Rosenberg, *Weltwirtschaftskrise*, pp. 136, 142, 156.

[11] Matis, *Wirtschaft*, p. 128; Rosenberg, *Weltwirtschaftskrise*, p. 156.

[12] Fischer *et al.*, *Arbeitsbuch*, pp. 52, 101, 119; Hoffmann, *Wachstum*, p. 143.

[13] Fischer *et al.*, *Arbeitsbuch*, p. 52; Hoffmann, *Wachstum*, p. 44. See the general observations in Borchardt, 'Revolution', pp. 116 ff.

to measure quantitatively, technological advances also occurred in a number of key areas. To some extent these advances were connected to the scientific and educational achievements which we will examine later on; after mid-century, scientific research in German universities flourished, the supply of technically trained individuals expanded, and an increasing number of institutions devoted themselves to spreading technological information. In our period, however, most technical advances in production were made by men without formal training, who were trying to solve particular, practical problems.[14]

While the entire economy grew after mid-century, there was a small but not insignificant decline in agriculture's relative position. The agrarian sector's share in the 'German' net social product was 46.5 per cent in 1850, 44.4 per cent in 1858, and 41.6 per cent in 1867; at the same time, the percentage of agricultural employees in the total work-force slipped from 56 to 51.3. Capital investment in agriculture made up 25.3 per cent of the total in the early 1850s, increased to 37.5 in the early 1860s, then fell to 21.8 per cent at the end of the decade. Over that period, the agrarian component in the value of all capital goods went from 51 per cent to 46 per cent. By 1866, therefore, the momentous transformation from an agricultural to an industrial economy was clearly under way in the *Zollverein* states. In Austria, however, the movement from agriculture to industry was much slower: in 1850, 71 per cent of the Austrian labour force was still employed in agriculture, in 1869, almost 64 per cent, and even in 1910 over 50 per cent.[15]

Between 1852 and 1867 the number of those employed in the 'German' service sector increased from 2.97 million to 3.45 million, their share in the total labour force from 19.8 per cent to 21.4 per cent. Because this sector of the economy is a residual category, composed of those who do not fit into agriculture or industry, it is made up of an extraordinarily broad and diverse range of occupations, including those who work in transportation, education and the arts, finance and commerce, government and religion, law and recreation, innkeeping and domestic service. In our period, domestic service remained the largest single component of this sector; in absolute terms it had changed rather little in the 1850s and 1860s. According to Hoffmann's calculations, there were 1.36 million servants in 1852, 1.59 in 1861, and 1.42 in 1867. Most of the rest of the service sector, including government employment

[14] Pollard, *Conquest*, pp. 143 ff.; Milward and Saul, *Development*, pp. 181 ff.
[15] Fischer *et al.*, *Arbeitsbuch*, pp. 52, 101; Hoffmann, *Wachstum*, pp. 44, 143.

and wholesale and retail trade, grew at roughly the same rate as the work force as a whole. Only the number of employees in the field of communications increased substantially—from 158,000 in 1852 to approximately 271,000 in 1867. Here, as we should expect, the growth of full-time railroad workers was especially significant: there were just 7,000 of them in 1846, 17,000 in 1852, and 74,000 in 1867.[16]

The aggregate growth of the industrial sector (which includes manufacturing of all sorts as well as mining and construction) was modest in the 1850s and 1860s: its share of the net social product went from 22 per cent in 1849 to 25 per cent in 1871, its share of the work-force from 25 per cent to 28 per cent—on the eve of the First World war, these figures were 45 per cent and 38 per cent. When we look at individual branches and regions, however, the rate of industrial growth is much more impressive.[17]

Textiles remained the largest single component of the industrial sector. Between 1846 and 1861 'German' textile manufacturing employed 20 per cent of those working in the industrial sector—more than twice the number in metal production or the building trades, and only slightly less than the number of those working in garment and leather production. The output of German textile firms increased significantly: indexed with 1913 at a base of 100, production went from 17.7 in 1850, to 25.7 in 1860, and 27.1 in 1865. In many places, firms engaged in textile production became larger and more mechanized. Badenese mills, for instance, had an average of 73 employees in 1849, but 110 only twelve years later; over roughly the same period the number of steam-engines used by Baden's cotton manufacturers increased from 2 to 46. But these technological advances were unevenly distributed: mechanization was more common in spinning than in weaving; cotton manufacturing was more technically advanced—and faster growing—than linen or wool.[18]

While substantially smaller than textile production, mining and metal manufacturing grew at an even faster rate: once again using 1913 as our index year, mining increased from 3.3 in 1850 to 6.9 in 1860 and 11.6 in 1865, metal production from 1.5 to 3.2 to 5.4, and metalworking from 2.6 to 4.3 to 7.[19] Most of this growth occurred in the coalfields, where 60 per cent of the total work-force in

[16] Hoffmann, *Wachstum*, pp. 200 ff.
[17] Wolfram Fischer in *HWSG* ii. 528.
[18] Wolfram Fischer in *HWSG* ii. 535, 538; Landes, *Prometheus* p. 167.
[19] Wolfram Fischer in *HWSG* ii. 538.

mining was employed by 1861. Between 1850 and 1869 coal production increased fivefold, from 5,100,000 to 26,774,000 metric tons. Equally important were the organizational changes that transformed the structure of mining enterprises. The government's role as mine owner and operator—but not as regulator—declined after 1850; private companies, often led by a new, aggressive generation of entrepreneurs, rushed to fill the expanding demand for coal and iron.[20] Moreover, the size of mining enterprises grew, as new technologies demanded larger concentration of capital and made possible more extensive exploitation of mineral resources. As the data in table 12.1 suggest, this process of expansion and concentration was particularly evident in the Ruhr.

TABLE 12.1. *Size of coal-mines in the Ruhr, 1850–1870*

	Mining enterprises	Employees	Employees/mine
1850	198	12,741	64
1855	234	23,474	100
1860	277	28,657	103
1865	234	42,450	181
1870	215	50,749	236

Source: Wolfram Fischer in *HWSG* ii. 545.

The growth of coal production was closely connected to developments in metallurgy, especially refining processes and machine building. The production of both pig iron and iron ore grew markedly in the 1850s and 1860s: the former from 217,000 to 1,391,000 tons between 1850 and 1870, the latter from 851,000 to 3,839,000. Both coal and iron production in Austria also increased after 1850, but the rate and magnitude of growth were substantially below those of the *Zollverein*. In large measure this was because Austria had fewer natural resources, and what it had were less well located. Many traditional centres of industrial growth, such as the Vienna basin, were without coal; elsewhere, coal and iron deposits were far apart.[21]

Railroads continued to play a central role in economic development and especially in the growth of mining and metalworking. As

[20] Landes, *Prometheus*, p. 194.
[21] Matis, *Wirtschaft*, pp. 91 ff. For more on Austrian economic development, see the works listed below, n.30.

the rail network expanded, it integrated and connected regional economies, stimulated demand for labour and raw materials, and supported a large infrastructure of stations, maintenance yards, and administrative organizations. In the *Zollverein*, rail lines increased from 3,639 statute miles in 1850 to 10,834 in 1869. Between 1850 and 1869 the number of locomotives in Prussia went from 528 to 2,021; their average horsepower, from 157 to 256. Almost all of these machines were now manufactured by German firms, most of them by Borsig's in Berlin. Net investment in railroad construction represented over 10 per cent of all German investments in the 1850s and early 1860s then grew to 17.5 per cent between 1865 and 1869. Railroads were also crucial for the Austrian economy's rapid expansion in the 1850s, when they drew over a fifth of total investment. Between 1851 and 1860 the rail network in the monarchy expanded from 2,345 to 5,393 kilometres, with much of this growth financed and operated by private companies instead of the state. The sharp decline in new construction caused by the military and political crises of the early 1860s had a range of unfortunate consequences for Austrian mining and metal production.[22]

In the 1850s and 1860s many of the industries that we associate with Germany's great economic strength had only begun to establish themselves. Chemical production, for instance, still lagged behind Britain and France; at mid-century, firms making chemical products employed only about 30,000 workers. But some important developments were under way. After its first use in 1863, the Solvay process for the production of soda ash was quickly adopted by German chemical companies. The discovery of extensive potash deposits in Saxony eventually enabled German entrepreneurs to take the lead in the production of artificial fertilizers. Aniline dyes, first discovered by an English chemist in 1856 and then developed by a number of English and German researchers in the 1860s and 1870s, became a mainstay of Germany's achievements in the industrial application of organic chemistry. Similarly, we can see the origins of later accomplishments in the manufacturing of electrical apparatus, precision instruments, optical equipment, and the like.[23]

Although the aggregate weight of the economy had begun to shift towards larger, technologically innovative forms of production, most enterprises remained small and traditionally organized.

---

[22] Fremdling, *Eisenbahnen*, pp. 34, 48–9, 76; Matis, *Wirtschaft*, p. 107.

[23] Pounds, *Geography . . . 1800–1914*, pp. 345 ff.; Landes, *Prometheus*, pp. 186–7.

As we shall see in the next two sections, agricultural activities and craft manufacturing continued to employ a majority of Germans. Moreover, rapid growth was concentrated in a few regions, whose location, resources, and social structure helped to stimulate and sustain innovation. When we borrow the metaphor of 'growth' from biology, therefore, we must not lose sight of the fact that the economy is not an organism but an arbitrarily defined aggregate of various firms, branches, sectors, and regions which 'grow' at different rates and in diverse directions.[24]

After mid-century, the geographical centre of economic growth was located in a series of interconnected regions stretching from the Ruhr valley to the industrialized Rhineland, through central Belgium to the Pas de Calais. As E. A. Wrigley has convincingly demonstrated, this industrial landscape displayed common economic, social, and demographic characteristics that transcended political frontiers.[25] Parts of this area had been economically active since the eighteenth century, but the exploitation of its coal resources after 1850 provided the principal impetus for growth. At first, coal was discovered and mined at a series of points scattered across the north-west; then mining intensified— and attracted other industrial enterprises—so that these points were joined in an expanding network. By far the richest area, with almost 90 per cent of the total coal resources in the north-west, was in the hills to the south of the Ruhr River; this area contained thick seams of some of Europe's best coking coal. Between 1850 and 1870 coal production here increased from 1.7 million to 11.6 million tons. At the same time, firms began to exploit the region's rich iron ore and, after a series of failures, learned to use Ruhr coal in the smelting process. Friedrich and Alfred Krupp in Essen and Jacob Mayer in Bochum helped to perfect steel making, which was a heavy user of coal and a critical element in the region's economic expansion. At the same time, rail lines and an improved system of canals enabled businesses to move the Ruhr's coal, iron, and steel to their customers throughout Europe.[26]

Silesia also had abundant coal deposits: during the 1850s and 1860s the output of Silesian mines went from 975,000 tons to 5.8 million tons. In addition, the region produced zinc and pig iron, and, after 1870, began to use the latest technique for smelting and

[24] The literature on the role of region in economic development is given above, Ch. 8, sect. iii, n. 72.

[25] Wrigley, *Growth*.

[26] Pollard, *Conquest*, pp. 99 ff.; Pounds, *Geography . . . 1800–1914*, pp. 357 ff.

refining. But in comparison to the west, Silesia's local markets were less dynamic, its links to central markets weaker, its access to skilled labour more difficult. Whereas the Ruhr was on the fringe of regions with a highly developed textile industry and traditionally important metallurgy, Silesia was part of a rural, more traditional area. Moreover, Silesia did not develop the large, heavily capitalized, and aggressive enterprises that characterized the Ruhr's expansion. Instead, smaller, more traditional firms, often run by local landowning families, continued to be important until the last decades of the nineteenth century.[27]

The presence of natural resources, the availability of capital and labour, and the accessibility of markets shaped the expansion and contraction of regional economies across central Europe. In Austria, for instance, industrial activity concentrated around Vienna, Styria, the Vorarlberg, and especially Bohemia. Among the *Zollverein* states, Saxony, once the most industrially advanced of the German lands, remained a textile centre but fell behind the Ruhr. In the Saarland, a small but thriving mining industry developed. Textile production increased in the south-west. Railroad construction and maintenance continued to support engineering firms and repair yards in various state capitals. Elsewhere, firms and regions declined as their techniques became outmoded or their resources dried up. The advantage of water power shrank as steam-engines spread; coking coal became substantially more desirable than other kinds; new processes drove traditional forms of smelting and refining out of business.

While the economy remained regionally diverse after mid-century, the web of connections within and between regions widened and thickened. Once again, the key element in this process was the railroad. According to one estimate, in 1860 50 per cent of the German goods not shipped by road went by train, as compared with 14 per cent by sea, and 36 per cent by an inland waterway; ten years later, the railroad's share was 70 per cent. Coal shipments, such as those moving along the heavily travelled Cologne–Minden–Berlin and Saargebiet–Ludwigshafen lines, made up a significant part of this traffic, but grain and other agrarian products were also important since the heavily industrialized regions of the north-west had to bring in an increasingly large part of their food. Wood came by ship from Scandinavia or by rail from the Bavarian forests to the minefields and fast-growing industrial villages of the Ruhr. Capital

[27] Pollard, *Conquest*, p. 104.

and labour moved ever greater distances, pulled by the attraction of industrial development, pushed by regional declines in interest rates or wages. As the economy became more integrated, other forms of communication increased. The postal service, for example, steadily improved, mailboxes came into use, costs declined, and volume expanded. Between 1850 and 1860 the number of letters posted annually in Prussia increased from 62.7 to 135.3 million, the number of telegrams from 35,000 to 384,000. From 1850 on, the *Zollverein* and Austria belonged to a postal association designed to encourage more uniform, reliable service.[28]

Economic and social integration brought regions closer together but did not make them more alike. As transportation costs declined, the comparative advantage of local enterprises decreased; even after paying its shipping bills, a modern mine, steel mill, or textile factory could sell its products more cheaply than an inefficient local enterprise. Similarly, farmers could ship their goods greater distances and compete successfully with marginally less profitable agricultural units in industrialized areas. Thus some areas became more intensely industrialized while others became more agricultural. After mid-century, therefore, areas like the Ruhr lost more and more of their agrarian sector; parts of eastern Prussia, southern Bavaria, and eastern Westphalia became increasingly agrarian. Because the more advanced areas could drain capital and labour from their backward trading partners, regional specialization was often attended by regional inequalities. Sustained economic growth narrowed but did not destroy these pockets of backwardness: in Frank Tipton's summary phrase, by the 1880s Germany had gone from being 'a backward country with a few advanced regions . . .[to] an advanced country with important backward regions'.[29]

For many historians, the unevenness of regional development within German Europe has been overshadowed by the more compelling contrast between the *Zollverein* and the Habsburg monarchy. As we have seen, those working within the framework of *kleindeutsch* historiography have usually viewed the *Zollverein* as an important step in Prussia's rise to hegemony over Germany. Austria's failure to create a central European customs area in 1850 and its ill-fated attempts at tariff negotiations in the early 1860s

---

[28] Zorn, 'Integration'; H. von Stephen and K. Sautter, *Geschichte der preussischen Post* (Berlin, 1928), 716; Schmoller, *Geschichte*, p. 171.

[29] Tipton, *Variations*, p. 39. See also his article on 'Labour'.

seemed like the economic preparation for, and equivalent to, its military defeat at Königgrätz. According to many scholars, extrusion from the *Zollverein* helped ensure Austria's alleged backwardness, which seemed to contrast so sharply with the rest of Germany's meteoric economic development.

While there is no doubt that the failure of Austrian efforts to join the *Zollverein* had some important political consequences, its economic implications are by no means clear. In the first place, historians have recently revised their gloomy estimates of Austrian economic growth. According to the latest views on the subject, the western half of the monarchy grew vigorously from the early 1840s until 1856–7 and again after 1867. Moreover, just as there is little evidence that the creation of the *Zollverein* had a dramatically positive impact on its members' economies, so there is no reason to believe that being outside had dramatically negative effects on Austria. As Thomas Huertas has shown, the most serious impediments to Austrian economic growth in the late 1850s and early 1860s came from military disasters and ill-conceived financial policies, not commercial isolation. In any event, Austria's economic relationship to her neighbours cannot be subordinated to her political conflict with Prussia. The economic geography of central Europe was never simply a field on which these two states carried on their struggle for supremacy.[30]

Any attempt to understand the central European economy is complicated by the fact that statisticians have retrospectively imposed the political divisions of 1866 and 1871: Hoffmann's influential compendium, for instance, is based on the Kaiserreich. As a result, we tend to think of the 'German' and Austrian economies as two separate, national entities. In fact, economic ties between the Habsburg monarchy and the *Zollverein* were extensive. The postal union of 1850, the tariff treaty of 1853, and the monetary convention

---

[30] As its title suggests, Eugen Franz's *Der Entscheidungskampf um die wirtschafts-politische Führung Deutschlands (1856–1867)* (Munich, 1933) views economic development in terms of political conflict. 'Through the actions of far-sighted statesmen,' Franz argues, 'the German economy became the platform for the new Reich. . . .' (p. 436). Böhme's *Deutschlands Weg* builds on Franz's interpretation but reverses its ideological direction.

For some new and more positive interpretations of Austrian economic development, see Good, *Rise*; Komlos, *Monarchy*; Thomas Huerta, *Economic Growth and Economic Policy in a Multinational Setting: The Habsburg Monarchy, 1841–1865* (New York, 1977). These interpretations are analysed in Richard Tilly's useful bibliographical essay, 'Entwicklung an der Donau. Neuere Beiträge zur Wirtschaftsgeschichte der Habsburger Monarchie', *GuG* (forthcoming in 1989).

of 1857 were all designed to ease commercial contacts. Even though a majority of Austrian businessmen wanted to remain outside the *Zollverein* and thus retain a degree of tariff protection, many of them were dependent on German markets. Between 1851 and 1864 imports into Austria from the *Zollverein* went from 17 to 34 per cent; exports, from 29 to 32 per cent of the monarchy's total trade. Hungarian grain, its movement facilitated by the opening of the Budapest–Vienna–Munich rail line in 1860, was marketed throughout the west. Austrians also traded other agrarian products—cereals, wool, timber, livestock—on German markets, where they bought cotton yarn, machines, metal products, and textiles. Capital from German sources was important for a number of Austrian enterprises; among the 65 million gulden raised in 1856 to finance the Vienna–Salzburg–Linz–Passau railroad were funds from bankers in Cologne, Breslau, and Hamburg. Along Austria's western borders, some enterprises were joined in regional patterns transcending political divisions: the Vorarlberg, for instance, was closely linked to Swiss and Swabian textile industries. Certainly the removal of the tariff barrier would have made many of these various connections easier, but it is not clear that this would have been decisive, either for the 'German question' or for Austrian economic development.[31]

If we take away the political categories imposed by *kleindeutsch* historiography, the economic geography of German Europe can be seen as a series of regional units, created by concentrations of natural resources, market relations, and local social structures. By mid-century, all of these regions were linked to an international economy, but in different ways. In some, firms operated in markets still dominated by Britain: Rhenish textile makers, for instance, might buy their thread from British spinning mills and then sell finished products domestically. Elsewhere, industries sold their products in less developed regions to the east or south. Of course, in many areas the mainstay of trade remained agricultural products that were shipped westwards, to Britain or to the industrialized parts of the German west. From this perspective, the contrast between the *Zollverein* and Austria seems less impressive than that between highly dynamic regions, such as the Ruhr, and backward ones, such as parts of the eastern provinces of Prussia or some areas in southern Bavaria. Prussia was extremely fortunate that among the territories that it had reluctantly acquired in 1815

---

[31] Pollard, *Conquest*, p. 77; Katzenstein, *Partners*.

were some of the most dynamic in Europe. But, while her possession of these territories would have profound political consequences, the causes of Prussia's economic superiority had more to do with the location of coking coal than with tariff boundaries and political institutions.

ii. RURAL SOCIETY IN AN INDUSTRIAL AGE

In 1870, six million Prussians, over two million Bavarians, and almost half a million Saxons earned their livelihoods from agriculture. In German Europe as a whole, more than half the work-force was employed in the agrarian sector, and in some areas—the Prussian province of Posen, for example, or the Karpatenländer of the Habsburg monarchy—agriculture accounted for up to three-quarters of all employment. Even when they did not earn their living directly from agriculture, most Germans worked in a rural setting, close to and dependent on the land. As late as the 1870s, over 60 per cent of the Prussian and over 70 per cent of the Austrian populations resided in communities with less than two thousand inhabitants. On prosperous northern dairy farms and in isolated Alpine meadows, in vineyards terraced along the Rhine's steep banks and on Junker estates east of the Elbe, people still conformed to the land's demands, their nourishment remained dependent on its uncertain bounties, their lives were set by its seasonal rhythms. Even in cities, rural life continued to intrude; peasants drove their animals through city streets for sale or slaughter and brought their produce to city markets. And of course, many city-dwellers were bound to the land through family ties and childhood memories.[32]

W. H. Riehl, who devoted the first section of his *Die bürgerliche Gesellschaft* (1851) to rural society, regarded the continued importance of agriculture as the best hope for Germany's future. 'There is one invincible conservative power in the German nation,' Riehl wrote, 'a solid and, despite all its changes, persistent core—and that is our peasantry. It is a true original, which no other nation can match.' To Riehl, the peasantry provided both stability and renewal; it was a barrier against revolutionary chaos and a source of 'refreshment and rejuvenation'. Riehl recognized that rural society was now under siege. Cancer-like, the market was spreading its

[32] Helling, 'Entwicklung'; Hoffmann, *Wachstum*, p. 178; Bolognese-Leuchtenmüller, *Bevölkerungsentwicklung*, p. 40.

influence through the countryside, where it could destroy the healthy tissues of community life. With the market came the influence of big cities, those 'monstrosities' that had infected all of Europe. This hegemony of city over the countryside, 'the essential social question of our time', was an unhappy reality in France and England and a 'dark ghost in Germany's social future'.[33]

Around mid-century many Germans shared Riehl's fear that rural society's distinctive virtues were being undermined by commercial values and urban institutions. Jeremias Gotthelf's village stories, which often depicted a sturdy farmer's struggle to preserve his way of life in the face of relentless outside pressures, became a popular literary genre in the 1840s and 1850s. At the same time, folklore experts collected information about peasant life with an urgency born of admiration and anxiety. In 1865, for instance, Wilhelm Mannhardt sent out thousands of questionnaires in a desperate attempt to gather material on harvesting customs before they slipped into historical oblivion. The world of peasant farm and rural village seemed all the more precious to whose who realized that it was imperilled by the spread of factory and town.[34]

While rural society's conservative admirers lamented its passing, many liberal and radical observers celebrated the impending demise of what Marx called 'the idiocy of rural life'. Georg Siemens believed that 'agriculture and slavery always go hand in hand, as we can see in the American south and in Russia. Freedom is possible only in industrial—not commercial—states.'[35] But whether they saw it as victim or villain, conservatives and progressives both tended to see the agrarian sector as a backdrop against which the powerful drama of social change—tragedy for some, progress for others—was unfolding. For different reasons and usually with the opposite ideological charge, contemporaries contrasted the stability of rural society with the dynamism of industrialism and urbanization. Explicitly or implicitly, this same image has been absorbed by many modern scholars who persistently make the mistake of associating 'growth' with industrialism.[36]

There is no question that after 1850 the agrarian sector did grow

---

[33] Riehl, *Gesellschaft*, p. 41.

[34] Weber-Kellermann used Mannhardt's data as the basis for her *Erntebrauch in der ländlichen Arbeitswelt des 19. Jahrhunderts. Auf Grund des Mannhardtmaterials von 1865* (Marburg, 1965).

[35] Ludwig Maenner, 'Deutschlands Wirtschaft und Liberalismus in der Krise von 1879', *Archiv für Politik und Geschichte*, 9/11 (1927), 356–7.

[36] See Ian Farr's critical analysis of the historiography in Evans and Lee (eds.), *Peasantry*.

more slowly than the most dynamic industries; as the century progressed, the difference between their growth rates became more pronounced. What von der Goltz called 'the constant, conservative character of agriculture' proved far more resistant to change than did most kinds of manufacturing.[37] There were no technological breakthroughs in farming to compare with the railroads, no regional transformations as swift as the industrialization of the Ruhr. Set against the rapid rise of towns like Essen or Ludwigshafen, the landscape and social institutions of most farming districts appeared unchanged—especially when viewed from behind a desk or through the window of a passing train. But while the tempo of change was slower in the countryside, rural society was anything but stagnant during the second half of the nineteenth century. The same forces that were at work in German cities and industrial settlements can be found in German villages and farms, where they altered fundamentally the lives of those who still lived on, and from, the land.

As will be recalled from our discussion of rural society in Chapters 2 and 8, changes in agriculture and manufacturing had always been connected. The industrial revolution depended upon, and in many ways presupposed, an agricultural revolution; without the surplus capital, labour, and commodities created by increased agricultural productivity, societies would not have been able to sustain growth in the industrial sector. Thus joined at the root, industrial and agricultural development continued to be entwined throughout the nineteenth century. Improvements in transportation, for example, helped to create an international market for both industrial and agricultural products, encouraged regional specialization, and opened rural society to an influx of manufactured goods. As a result of these changes, the interdependence of industry and agriculture became more apparent: since cities and industrial regions could no longer feed their population with locally grown products, they became increasingly dependent on agricultural areas, while agricultural regions became more and more dependent on railroads, chemical fertilizers, and a variety of machines.[38]

With the help of these technological innovations, German farmers significantly increased their productivity. Norman Pounds estimates that the cereal supply increased threefold in the course of

[37] Goltz, *Geschichte*, i. 10.
[38] Haines, 'Agriculture', provides a good local study of this process.

the nineteenth century, the food supply as a whole somewhere between four- and fivefold. According to Wilhelm Abel's calculations of a 'grain value' index, based on the nutritional content of agricultural products, there was a net per capita growth from 5.6 to 8.1 between 1800 and 1900. More impressive than these highly aggregated and therefore rather abstract numbers are data on local productivity. For example, in the Oppeln district of Silesia the total average annual output of cereals grew by 3.39 per cent between 1846–50 and 1861–5. In Westphalia, the output of the four major cereals went from 498,600 tons in 1852 to 673,000 tons in 1864; the potato crop grew from 463,800 to 471,000 tons and sugar beets from 495,100 to 660,100. On the east Elbian domains of Count Stolberg, the production of wheat increased from 11.5 scheffel per morgen in 1850 to 15.1 scheffel in 1882; on another estate, the average annual yield of wheat was 8.9 zentner per morgen in the early 1850s and 10.77 a decade later. As J. A. Perkins writes in his summary analysis of 'The Agricultural Revolution in Germany', the outstanding characteristic of late nineteenth-century German agriculture was 'the intensification of production, which in essence involved increasing inputs of capital and entrepreneurial skill—and also labour in terms of efficiency more than in terms of quantity—to a more or less fixed area of production'.[39]

The application of new knowledge, techniques, and equipment changed the face of German agriculture. More and more farmers began to buy fertilizers to enrich their soil: in Saxony, for example, the use of guano, most of it imported from Chile, went from 5 zentner in 1843 to 20,000 in 1847 and 124,000 in 1854. Elsewhere, bones gathered from the sites of slaughterhouses and battlefields were added to provide phosphate to the earth. Increasingly, artificial fertilizers, mined and manufactured domestically or imported from abroad, became the chief source of soil enrichment. At the same time, farmers learned to use other additives, such as lime and marl, which balanced acidity and lightened heavy soils. Drilling machines made planting more efficient by improving crop–seed ratios, scythes continued to replace sickles at harvest time, and—more slowly—mechanical threshers began to be used instead of the time-honoured method of flailing. In the 1860s the steam-plough made its first appearance. Since it was expensive to buy and maintain, the steam plough was limited to large farms,

[39] Pounds, *Geography . . . 1800–1914*, p. 246; Abel, *Geschichte*, p. 276; Haines, 'Agriculture', p. 360; Teuteberg, 'Einfluss', pp. 250–1; Goltz, *Geschichte*, ii. 341; Perkins, 'Revolution', p. 75.

where it was especially useful in the cultivation of root crops. Taken together, these various improvements greatly increased labour productivity, which, according to an index compiled by Paul Bairoch, almost doubled between 1840 and 1880. By the end of the century, German agriculture had become one of the most advanced in the world.[40]

In agriculture, as in manufacturing, Germans began by importing new techniques and technology from the more advanced regions of the west. The steam-plough, for instance, was a British invention, popularized on the Continent by Max Eyth, a German engineer working for a manufacturer in Leeds. Similarly, the use of drainage systems to reclaim or improve water-logged lands was widely used in the Netherlands and was perfected by British landowners before being adopted on the Continent. Gradually, however, German agronomists, like their counterparts in industry, developed their own innovations. Sometimes this was done by practical men like Hermann von Nathusius, who did some basic work on animal breeding during the 1850s and 1860s. Increasingly, however, German farming came under the influence of academic science. In agriculture, as in so many other aspects of life, universities, and special schools helped to institutionalize research, the results of which were disseminated in journals and the meetings of professional organizations. Word of these innovations then spread among practising agriculturists, who began to use chemicals and machines, drainage pipes and breeding techniques. In the countryside, as in the city, no innovation was more important than the widespread acceptance of innovation as a necessary part of life.[41]

The introduction of new techniques and machines changed the way Germans worked their land. In the first place, the amount of usable land continued to increase: for example, agricultural land in Prussia's eastern provinces expanded by almost 70 per cent during the nineteenth century, land under cultivation by between 30 and 50 per cent. Large areas in the east remained forested (up to thirty per cent of Brandenburg), but in more densely settled areas forests continued to be cut down, their products used for fuel or construction, and the soil then cultivated to meet local needs. Fertilizers and new methods of crop rotation made it possible to do away with fallow fields and to work formerly wasted terrain; in

---

[40] Paul Bairoch in Cipolla (ed.), *History*, iii. 472. In addition to the works cited in n. 39, see Haushofer, *Landwirtschaft*.

[41] There is a good account of these developments in Goltz, *Geschichte*, ii.

Westphalia, the amount of fallow declined from 40 per cent in 1800 to 5 per cent sixty years later. But, while the quantity of cultivated land was thereby increased, the supply of grazing land declined. As a result, it became less common to raise animals extensively and the use of fodder feeds grew. The impact of this trend can be most clearly seen in the decline of the sheep population; by the 1880s central Europe had changed from being a leading supplier to a heavy importer of wool products. On the other hand, the number of animals raised on fodder steadily increased. Throughout the century, the demand for horses remained surprisingly high. Between 1850 and 1900 the number of horses in the German states went from 2.73 million to 4.19 million. At the same time, increasing prosperity stimulated demand for meat and dairy products. In the 1850s and 1860s annual consumption of meat rose from 19.9 to 25.9 kilograms per capita—by 1910, it was 43.2 kilograms.[42]

The pattern of land use reflected the growth of specialized production throughout the agrarian sector. Now that they were not dependent on animals for manure, some farmers could cultivate lands formerly needed for pasture. When climate and soil were appropriate, growers could concentrate on commercially valuable products like hops, which could be moved by train to meet the breweries' growing demand. On the other hand, some had to abandon crops that could be grown more economically elsewhere: for instance, the acreage devoted to vineyards declined after mid-century, as the wine producers in south and east, who had once been able to depend on local markets, lost out to their competitors along the Rhine and Mosel.

The most important form of specialized agriculture was the production of root crops—potatoes, particularly popular in the sandy soils of the east, and sugar-beets, most often found in parts of the Rhineland, Prussian Saxony, and Silesia. Especially impressive is the expansion of sugar-beet production, which increased as much as twenty-five times in the second half of the century. In 1851–2 the *Zollverein's* 234 refineries produced 63,068 tons of raw sugar; in 1871–2 the Kaiserreich had 311 refineries with an output of 186,442 tons. Beets and potatoes significantly added to overall agricultural productivity since they played a crucial role in new forms of crop rotation. Moreover, these root crops provided an important link

---

[42] Berthold, 'Veränderungen'; Teuteberg, 'Einfluss', p. 270; Fischer *et al.*, *Arbeitsbuch*, pp. 58–61.

between industry and agriculture, both because they were best cultivated intensively with chemical fertilizers and because they were used as raw materials for industrial products such as starch, alcohol, and sugar.[43]

In his *Geschichte der deutschen Landwirtschaft*, first published in 1903, Theodor von der Goltz called the years between 1850 and 1880 'the happiest period that German agriculture has ever experienced'. After the serious crop failures and turmoil of the 1840s, the 1850s and 1860s were a time of remarkable prosperity for many German farmers. The weight of foreign competition, which was to threaten parts of the agrarian sector towards the end of the century, had not yet been fully felt. Grain exporters, especially in the east, took advantage of lower tariffs to sell their produce on world markets. Similarly, German industry had not yet begun to threaten the supply of rural labour but rather had helped sustain the domestic market for agricultural goods. As a result, farm prices increased after mid-century: according to Goltz, the average price of a zentner of rye was 6.18 marks in the 1840s, 8.02 in the 1850s, 7.78 in the 1860s, and 8.16 in the 1870s, over this same period butter went from 0.6 marks to 0.73 to 1.12 marks per pound, beef from 0.28 to 0.35 to 0.55. Rents and land values followed this upward trend; the average rent for a Prussian farm more than doubled between 1849 and 1869; sales prices increased at least as much. According to one careful case study of a Prussian, in the course of the nineteenth century the value of the property grew from 70,000 to 320,000 taler, the value of its rents from 4,000 to 21,000 taler.[44]

Some people made a great deal of money in farming. The Nagel brothers, for instance, left their work as stonemasons during the 1840s and bought 100 hectares of land near Halle, which they planted with sugar-beets. With the profits from their crop they built a brickworks, a sugar mill, a flour mill, and a distillery. By the 1880s the family controlled over 1,400 hectares of prime land. Enterprising estate owners east of the Elbe also flourished: as grain prices rose, they sold their crops at good profit, settled their debts, and invested in more land or in some sort of industrial firm. When Leopold von Hoverbeck took over his father's estate at Nickelsdorf in 1856, he swiftly established a thriving agricultural concern which

---

[43] Pounds, *Geography . . . 1800–1914*, p. 237; Goltz, *Geschichte*, ii. 338. Perkins, 'Revolution', emphasizes the importance of root crops as a force for change in the agricultural sector.

[44] Goltz, *Geschichte*, ii. 345–6, 350; Abel, *Geschichte*, pp. 280 ff.

earned him a fine income and considerable political influence. In Hanna Schissler's opinion, it was during the 1850s and 1860s that 'the Junkers attained the historical peak of their economic power'.[45]

Of course not everyone benefited. Some landed families were too deeply in debt, too incompetent, or too distracted by other interests to take advantage of the opportunities agriculture offered them. At best, these families were able to liquidate their heavily mortgaged estates and live from the proceeds. Sometimes they sold their land but tried to save their house and garden, thus creating *Rittergüter* of a hectare or less. The turnover in landed properties continued to be high: of the 355 Silesian estates studied by Johannes Ziekursch, only fifty-nine had been in the same family for more than forty years. Among the buyers were new men who acquired land because they wanted a place to retire, a good investment, or a base from which to launch a political career. By the 1880s almost two-thirds of all estate owners in Prussia's eastern provinces were commoners. Georg Siemens, who purchased an estate in 1858, concluded that land had become a commodity like any other: 'As soon as it was permissible for a commoner to own an estate, it no longer meant anything to have one.'[46]

But Siemens well knew that it did mean something to own an estate—one of the reasons he bought his was because he imagined himself serving as *Landrat* and perhaps representing his district in the *Landtag*. Such hopes were not unrealistic: for instance, almost as soon as he established himself at Nickelsdorf, Hoverbeck became a member of the district assembly (*Kreistag*) and soon parlayed his local standing into a national political career. Thus, despite its ever-changing social composition, the landed élite still clung to its special status. Although most formal privileges and power were gone—even landowners' cherished hunting rights had been abolished during the revolution—informal authority, traditional prestige, and lasting political connections continued to play an important role. No longer *Herr* in the traditional sense, the German nobles remained privileged and powerful enough to evoke anger and antagonism among their progressive contemporaries. In fact, an anonymous contributor to the *Grenzboten* wrote in 1858 that 'the conflict between aristocracy and democracy, i.e. between nobility and *Bürgertum*, is sharper today than ten years ago'. If it came to a

---

[45] Perkins, 'Revolution'; Parisius, *Hoverbeck*, i. 142 ff.; Hanna Schissler in Moeller (ed.), *Peasants*, p. 34.

[46] Ziekursch, *Jahre,* p. 385; Sombart, *Volkswirtschaft*, p. 357; Helfferich, *Siemens*, i. 26.

showdown, this writer was convinced, 'the productive forces' of the present would win over 'the residual memories of the past'. But, like most of the nobility's liberal critics, he hoped it would not come to that. Rather than a democratic society on the American model, he preferred a reconstituted aristocracy that would be ready and willing to find a place in a modern social world. An open, progressive, patriotic, and disinterested élite—similar to what many contemporaries thought existed in England—was the liberal ideal of a reformed nobility.[47]

Against the mythical ideal of the English gentry, German liberals set the all-too-real presence of the Prussian Junkers, whose social position and political values continued to confound progressives everywhere. During the revolution of 1848, liberals had reason to hope that history had finally caught up with the Prussian aristocracy. Even the revised constitution, finally accepted by King Frederick William at the end of January 1850, retained most of the emancipatory measures written into the liberals' draft two years earlier. Article forty-two formally abolished the final remnants of *Herrschaft:* restrictions on the exchange of landed property, patrimonial courts and police power, and the remaining services owed by peasants to their lords. These principles were affirmed by an edict issued in March 1850, which superseded the thirty-odd laws with which the government had tried to regulate rural government since the era of reforms. According to Georg von Viebahn's contemporary calculation, in the course of the 1860s Prussian peasants paid their lords compensation for over 6.3 million days of *Spanndienst*, that is, service with a team of draft animals, and 23.44 million days of hand labour.[48]

Nevertheless, the Junkers survived. In 1860 *Rittergüter* continued to make up 26 per cent of the land in the province of Saxony, 45 per cent in Brandenburg, and 58 per cent in Pomerania. Until 1861 all of this property was exempted from taxation. In much of the east, the average size of an estate increased between 1837 and 1858. Everywhere, most of the largest estates, and especially those protected by entail, remained in the hands of noble families, who continued to set the social and political tone. Even though most of their legal authority was gone, they managed to regain their police powers. At court, in the bureaucracy, and in the officer corps, aristocrats continued to be important. Here, as in the countryside,

---

[47] *Grenzboten*, 17/2 (1858), 479–80.
[48] Blum, *End*, p. 383; Rosenberg, *Probleme*, pp. 18–19.

their power was enhanced by their ability to exert influence on men from other social backgrounds. This influence increased after mid-century, as the reactionary regime applied pressure for conformity throughout the state apparatus.[49]

In the Habsburg lands, the revolution of 1848 completed the process of peasant emancipation begun by Joseph II and long delayed by the inertia and uncertainty so characteristic of Austrian absolutism. We have already seen how the only great accomplishment of the revolutionary *Reichstag* was its decree of 7 September 1848, which abolished serfdom, seigneurial authority, and peasant services. Since Schwarzenberg realized that the rural old regime could not be saved, emancipation survived the revolution's defeat. In the course of the 1850s, therefore, 29.4 million days of *Spanndienst* and 38.6 million days of regular labour were either removed or converted into cash. Overall, in the western half of the monarchy, the schedule of compensation was less favourable to the nobility than it had been in the Hohenzollern lands. Large landholders, however, did substantially better than those with smaller estates: the Schwarzenberg family, for instance, received compensation totaling 1.87 million gulden, whereas the average compensation paid was 22,000.[50]

Rural reform, often reduced by German historians to a political process of emancipation, actually involved long-term social and economic developments as well as administrative action and parliamentary legislation. Indeed, scholars have recently begun to downplay the significance of these political changes: John Komlos, for example, believes that formal emancipation in Austria had relatively little significance. Whatever the government did or did not do, he writes, 'the market would undoubtedly have replaced the lord–peasant relationship . . . by a more impersonal one, based on cash'. Furthermore Komlos did not find much of an impact on rates of agricultural productivity, which seem to have remained relatively constant. It seems likely that by mid-century, economic pressures for change within German agriculture were more powerful and important than political interventions. The introduction of new crops, increased mechanization, shifts in market demand and labour supply made traditional rural relationships obsolete. As one Austrian writer put it in 1848, 'The cultivation of

---

[49] Berthold, 'Veränderungen', pp. 31 ff., 49.
[50] Blum, *End*, pp. 389 ff.; Matis, *Wirtschaft*, pp. 38 ff.; Pollard, *Conquest*, p. 198.

the sugar-beet is incompatible with labour services; instead it demands free labourers'.[51]

Of course, for many peasants, being 'free' meant trading one sort of dependence for another. They were free from the coils of the seigneurial system—a freedom we would do well not to underestimate—but they were still exposed to their lords' political, social, and economic power as well as to unrestrained market forces. As we should expect, the degree of a peasant's vulnerability was usually determined by the amount of land he controlled. Those with marginal holdings were often put out of business by the emancipation process, in part because they had trouble making compensation payments, in part because they could not do without the common lands usually taken over by the lord. These peasants had to enter into some kind of tenancy agreements with an estate owner, who paid them a wage and allowed them to work a small portion of land.

Conservative theorists viewed the commercialization of rural social relations with alarm. Riehl believed that, however much noble landowners might have gained materially by their economic ventures, they lost a great deal morally and spiritually; by becoming agrarian capitalists, aristocrats gave up their special character and purpose. Wilhelm von Kügelgen came away from reading Riehl in 1857 with the sad knowledge that 'our nobility is no longer a nobility, our peasants are no longer peasants, and our *Bürger* are nowhere to be found.' Ten years later, Leopold von Ranke told his students that 'the warm comfort [*Gemütlichkeit*] of patriarchical conditions is gone; the power of money has achieved equality with the inherited authority of blood.'[52]

After mid-century, changes in rural society extended far beyond those estates which were affected by emancipation decrees. As the reader will recall from our discussion in Chapter 8, any innovation was likely to have implications for the entire social system in the countryside: a different crop, a new machine, a reorganization of the fields will effect the structure of social relations at work, in the household, and in the community. Root crops, for instance, require a quite different sort of care than cereals, so their introduction inevitably altered the character and rhythm of farm

[51] Komlos, *Monarchy*, p. 12; Perkins, 'Revolution', p. 101. See also Good, *Rise*, ch. 3,.
[52] Riehl, *Gesellschaft*, pt. 2; Kügelgen, *Lebenserinnerungen*, p. 263; Vierhaus, *Ranke*, p. 112.

labour. Moreover, because growers wanted to take full advantage of the profits to be made from root crops, they often enclosed their fields, cultivated waste areas, and tried to divide common lands. Farmers also tended to give up some of their animals because root crops do not permit late summer grazing. Similarly, the adoption of threshing machines not only reduced the amount of labour needed after the harvest—and thus pushed some people below the margin of subsistence—it also effected new modes of compensation. When the job had been done by hand, it made sense to encourage quality work by giving threshers a share in their product. Machines did not require such incentives.

While making generalizations about rural society is always hazardous, it does seem that, after mid-century, an increasing proportion of agricultural labour was done for wages. Most full-time workers still received some of their compensation in kind— *Gesinde* got an annual cash payment plus room and board, wage labourers with a family usually had the right to work a small plot of land—but the shift towards cash is unmistakable. Between 1849 and 1873 money payments increased by 10.8 to 13.5 per cent of total compensation in the province of East Prussia, from 23.8 to 28.3 per cent in Brandenburg, and from 64.4 to 82 per cent in Prussian Saxony. The movement to wage labour was greater in more developed regions; cash crops, such as sugar-beets, were more appropriately cultivated by wage-earners than cereals, which could be used directly as food. As we should expect, wages for farm work improved as the competition for labour increased. Where alternative sources of employment were not readily at hand, compensation was low. In the 1860s farmworkers earned between 55 and 75 marks per year in parts of Prussia, up to 135 marks in Saxony and the developed regions of Brandenburg, and even more around Cologne and in the Saar. But almost everywhere wages seem to have risen after mid-century, according to von der Goltz, by as much as 50 per cent for workers and 100 per cent for *Gesinde*.[53]

As farmers' labour costs grew, so did their willingness to invest in machines that could cut down on the size of the work-force. This was, for example, the primary advantage of steam-threshers and ploughs. Moreover, rising labour costs also encouraged farmers to use seasonal workers whenever possible. By the 1840s the movement of people into Saxony in order to harvest sugar-beets

[53] Max Rolfes in *HWSG* ii. 508–9; Goltz, *Geschichte*, ii. 347.

was called *Sachsengängerei*, a term eventually applied to migratory labour in general. For some, this demanding and poorly paid occupation became a way of life. Because they moved, frequently in groups, from one area to the next, following the crops and the seasons, these people no longer belonged to a community, their villages became no more than a place to spend the winter.[54]

When opportunities for regular agricultural employment declined—at the same time as the population as a whole increased—more and more men and women were forced out of rural communities. Some left for good, either overseas or to an urban area. Where as this permanent flight from the land became increasingly common in the final decades of the century, in our period people's movement away from their communities was often tentative and reversible. For example, the number of full-time agricultural employees in Prussia's eastern provinces fluctuated significantly during the 1860s: after opportunities in the textile industry drew many workers away from farming early in the decade, a downturn in 1867 drove them back again to agriculture, which they once more abandoned as the economic situation improved in 1871.[55]

Even when they could no longer subsist as farmers, families with a house and a small piece of land were understandably reluctant to cut their ties with rural society. Sometimes they could stay on by working for another farmer. Or, if they were fortunate, they might find a source of income close by, perhaps working on construction jobs or in a neighbouring factory. More often, they tried to sustain themselves through some combination of domestic manufacturing and agriculture. Frequently enough, the result of this was similar to the situation of the linen weavers in Württemberg, who moved along 'an obviously dead-end street . . . so narrow and confining that they could neither escape nor retreat'.[56] Unwilling to leave the village but unable to make a living there, these survivors of the protoindustrial system could do no more than postpone the day when they would be forced into the ranks of landless labourers.

Kaschuba's and Lipp's study of the Württemberg village of Kiebingen illustrates what these changes might mean for a rural community's social composition. As the data in table 12.2 show, the circle of peasant proprietors with enough land to make a full-time living from farming steadily contracted. Those who survived

---

[54] Plaul, 'Proletariat'.
[55] Tipton, 'Labour', pp. 958, 974 ff.
[56] Kaschuba and Lipp, *Überleben*, p. 32.

TABLE 12.2. *Occupational structure of Kiebingen,*
1823–1864 (% of total)

	1823	1844	1864
Farmers	34.3	30.3	24.2
Day-labourers	14.7	11.9	9.5
Weavers	14.0	10.9	9.5
Craftsmen	16.8	20.4	19.9
Village employees	4.2	3.0	2.4
Construction workers	10.5	17.9	25.6
Others	5.5	6.6	0.9

Source: Kaschuba and Lipp, *Überleben*, p. 120.

frequently flourished, expanding their fields by enclosing common
lands or buying out their less productive neighbours. But everywhere independent peasant proprietors represented a minority—
and usually a shrinking minority. Most people in the countryside
were dependent for their livelihoods on someone else. As farm
labourers (with or without a little land), domestic servants, rural
craftsmen or manufacturers, migrant workers or commuters, these
various groups lived and worked on the margin of what Kaschuba
and Lipp call 'das Dorf im Dorf', the village within the village. In
the course of the nineteenth century most people's material
condition may have improved, but the social, economic, and
cultural divisions within the community almost certainly
increased.[57]

For peasant proprietors, the essential productive unit remained
the household—indeed, increased labour costs made the use of
family members more economical. As in traditional society, most
peasant families were dominated by the eldest male. It was
exceptional for a woman to run a farm on her own. In the kingdom
of Saxony, for example, there were only 1,900 women among the
41,000 people listed as 'Gutsbesitzer, Pächter, and Weinbauer' in
the census of 1861. Nevertheless, peasants' wives remained
essential to the successful operation of a farm; they continued to
have primary responsibility for running the house, preparing the
meals, rearing the children, and performing certain agricultural
tasks, as well as planting and harvesting during these critical times

[57] See also Hainer Plaul on Magdeburg and Cathleen Catt on the Bavarian
Palatinate, both in Evans and Lee (eds.), *Peasantry*; Solta, *Bauern*.

in the agricultural cycle. Sometimes, changes in the mode or organization of production forced rearrangements in household organization: women's economic responsibilities might increase, for example, if dairy farming became the principal source of income. Never equal in power or status, rural women usually did more than their share of the work.[58]

Despite the extraordinary burdens a farmer's wife had to carry, marriage and a family remained the chief aspiration of most rural women. The only alternative was some sort of dependent status, as either a wage-earner or a domestic servant. Thus while only one out of two hundred Saxon proprietors was a female in 1861, women accounted for 92,983 of the 163,828 'Gesinde and Gehilfen'. Among the 1.91 million women in the Prussian work force in 1861, half a million were listed as agricultural 'maids or servants' and half a million as agricultural workers—as compared to just over 90,000 factory workers. Most of these servants were the daughters of labourers or small farmers, who usually began work when they were thirteen or fourteen, taking care of a variety of chores in return for food, lodging, a small salary, and some payment in kind, usually wool, flax, or yarn. After ten or fifteen years of such work, these women hoped to have money for a dowry and the clothes and linen for a trousseau so that they might marry some established member of rural society. Of course, such hopes could easily be undermined by any number of misfortunes, such as a sickness or injury, an ill-timed pregnancy, or petty criminal offence.[59]

In most of the German lands, there was a trend away from employing *Gesinde* of either sex. Wage earners, tenants, family members, or migrant workers all seemed to provide more flexible, efficient sorts of labour. Nevertheless, around 3.5 per cent of the Kaiserreich's total population were employed as farm servants in 1882; in some places, such as Bavaria, they made up one-third of all those employed in agriculture. Relations between servant and master continued to be governed by regulations with strong patriarchical residues: in Prussia, for instance, the *Gesindeordnung* of 1810, which remained in effect until the end of the monarchy,

[58] Hubert Kiesewetter, 'Agrarreform, landwirtschaftliche Produktion und Industrialisierung im Königreich Sachsen, 1832–61', in Blaich (ed.), *Entwicklungsprobleme*, p. 130; on women's work, see Roman Sandgruber's essay in Borscheid and Teuteberg (eds.), *Ehe*, pp. 138 ff.

[59] On female farm servants, see Regina Schulte in Evans and Lee (eds.), *Peasantry*. The data are from Frevert, *Frauen-Geschichte*, p. 82.

denied servants many of the contractual rights granted to wage labourers. Sometimes, what Ranke called the 'Gemütlichkeit' of patriarchy also remained: on many small farms, for instance, servants continued to eat and live with their employers. Elsewhere, however, family and servants no longer shared the same table or lived in the same domestic spaces. Here too we get a sense that the divisions within the rural social order were hardening.[60]

Perhaps we can best appreciate the magnitude of rural society's transformation if we compare agriculture after 1850 with its situation under the old regime, rather than with the burgeoning industrial sector. From this perspective we can see that German farmers had finally succeeded in shaking off the limits within which they had operated throughout most of European history. Slowly, the painful cycle so well described by Malthus and Ricardo was broken; no longer did increases in population necessarily lead to privation and crisis, no longer did an inelastic food supply set limits on the growth of real wages. There were, to be sure, still agricultural crises after 1850, but they were briefer and significantly less severe than the subsistence crisis following the Napoleonic wars or the terrible dislocations of the hungry 1840s. Of course poverty and privation remained a part of many people's lives, but the threat of starvation, ever present in traditional society, began to fade. Against famine the expanding economies of the nineteenth century scored a victory whose importance should not be overlooked.[61]

This triumph was in fact a composite of thousands of small victories—over exhausted soil and flooded fields, plant blights and animal epidemics, unfavourable yield ratios and inefficient crop rotations. Needless to say, farmers remained dependent on the weather (which does seem to have improved after mid-century) as well as a variety of other, no less implacable natural forces. Compared to their ancestors, however, farmers in the late nineteenth century were in a much better position to understand and control their worlds. Moreover, they had begun to organize themselves in new ways. Between 1850 and 1870 the number of agrarian associations in Prussia grew from 313 to 865; most of these were general purpose organizations devoted to promoting agricultural knowledge and interests, although an increasingly large minority served a more specialized agrarian activity such as horse breeding, cereal growing, and the like. Around mid-century, Friedrich Wilhelm Raiffeisen formed the first of a series of

[60] Tipton, 'Labour'; Hainer Plaul in Evans and Lee (eds.), *Peasantry*, pp. 116 ff.
[61] Abel, *Fluctuations*, pt. 4.

co-operatives designed to provide credit, investment capital, and other forms of support for Prussian farmers. Raiffeisen's efforts and others like them eventually spread throughout German Europe.

In the industrial era, farmers' primordial struggle to coax a living from the land was carried on with greater knowledge and better tools. Equally important, it took place within an expanding network of relations through which farmers were joined to, and dependent upon, a variety of forces far beyond their immediate environments. The size of the harvest in the American mid-west, the price of guano in Chile, the condition of credit markets in distant cities all touched the lives of men and women in the far corners of the countryside. As German farmers slowly began to recognize, their inevitable involvement in this wider world brought them a complex range of new opportunities and new dangers.

iii. CITIES, ENTREPRENEURS, AND WORKERS

During the first half of the nineteenth century, most German cities had not grown much faster than the population as a whole. In Prussia, for instance, there were eighteen cities with a population of more than 20,000 in 1837 and only twenty a decade later; in 1849, 4.8 per cent of the population lived in cities larger than 20,000 but smaller than 100,000, while 3.3 per cent lived in Berlin and Breslau, the only Prussian cities with more than 100,000 inhabitants. After mid-century, however, this situation began to change dramatically. By 1864 thirty Prussian cities had more than 20,000 inhabitants— their total population was over two million, roughly 10 per cent of the state's total. In some regions, urbanization was especially rapid: in the Prussian Administrative District of Düsseldorf, for instance, the percentage of people living in cities went from 41.8 to 57.6 between 1850 and 1870; by then over 30 per cent of the population were in towns with more than 20,000 inhabitants. Berlin continued to expand at a remarkable rate: between 1838 and 1858 the population of Prussian capital had increased by an average of 8,381 per annum, whereas between 1856 and 1880 the average increase was 27,273. In 1861 Brandenburg, which was dominated by Berlin and its suburbs, became the first German region to have more than 10 per cent of its inhabitants in cities of over 50,000.[62]

[62] Horst Matzerath in Rausch (ed.), *Städte . . .im 19.Jahrhundert*, p. 28. The bibliography on German cities is given above, Ch. 2, sect. iii, n. 56 and Ch. 8, sect. iii, n. 55.

Since urban mortality rates remained high, most of this growth came from migration rather than natural increase. Between 1856 and 1880, for instance, Berlin's average annual growth was composed of 19,917 new arrivals and 7,340 surplus births. As we should expect, migration was extremely important in the new industrial towns of the west, which went from being villages to sprawling settlements in the course of a few decades. For instance, only a third of Bochum's population in 1871 had been born in the city: about 50 per cent came from Westphalia or the Rhineland, 15 per cent from elsewhere in central Europe. Of course, this static breakdown greatly understates the rate of population movement over the course of a year since a significant number of people moved in and out again. According to David Crew's calculations, the net volume of turnover in Bochum during the last two decades of the nineteenth century was as much as thirteen times the total population.[63]

'Industrial society', Wolfgang Köllman has written, 'was created by migration.'[64] After 1850 this migration was in large measure from the countryside to the cities, and from one city to another. Cities became the principal destinations for internal migration because the jobs were there—or so people hoped. Domestic manufacturing and rural industry were increasingly unable to absorb the countryside's excess population. More and more manufacturing now had an urban base. In part this was because factories no longer had to depend on water power, in part because the railroads facilitated the movement of raw materials and finished goods to and from cities.

The urbanization of German Europe, therefore, paralleled the process of economic growth outlined at the beginning of this chapter: in both, we find a quickening of the pace in the 1840s, a substantial increase between 1850 and 1870, and then a major upswing that lasted, with some interruptions, until the second decade of the twentieth century. Between 1871 and 1910 the urban population of the German Reich grew from 36.1 to 60 percent; the greatest increase was in cities with over 100,000 inhabitants, which had less than 5 per cent of the total German population in 1871 but more than 20 per cent four decades later. The following examples suggest what this trend meant for particular cities: in the course of the nineteenth century the population of Hamburg grew from

---

[63] Reulecke, *Geschichte*, pp. 41–3; DeVries, *Urbanization*, p. 236; Crew, *Town*, pp. 60–1. For another example, see Lenger, *Kleinbürgertum*, p. 84, on Düsseldorf.

[64] Köllmann, *Bevölkerung*, p. 141.

132,000 to 768,000, of Munich from 45,000 to 422,000, of Frankfurt from 40,000 to 422,000, and of Hanover from 23,000 to 235,000. Taken together, these figures reveal a fundamental change in the pattern of European urbanization, which now shifted from the Atlantic to the Continent, at whose vital centre was the extraordinarily expansive power of German economic development.[65]

Within the German lands, urban growth produced a significant series of changes in the relationship between cities and their environs. Of course, cities had never been completely cut off from their surroundings; even when townsmen defended their precious autonomy with stone walls and legal restrictions, they had been linked to the countryside by a complex mix of interdependent relationships. In many ways modern cities were less independent than their traditional counterparts. More than ever before, cities needed to import food to feed their populations and fuel and raw materials to supply their factories. To pay for these necessities, urban economies had to make their goods and services available to a growing body of consumers. Even the new towns along the Ruhr, which were literally on top of their raw materials, lived in an expanding economic and social network through which labour, capital, consumer goods, and finished products moved over increasingly large distances.

As German cities grew in size and importance, they extended their reach into the countryside. Cities had once been islands in a rural sea, confined by poor communications, threatened by the power of rural élites, restrained by the weakness of their own economies. But the coming of the railroad, the rise of new economic and cultural élites, and the expansion of industry enabled cities to exert greater influence over society as a whole. For more and more Germans, the city became the source of new ideas, commodities, fashions, manners, and opinions. Gradually and unevenly, men and women gave up or supplemented local customs and handmade objects with what they saw advertised in magazines and could find in the stores of nearby cities. Tools for planting and harvesting, Sunday suits and special dresses, prepared foods and household ornaments, family photographs and pocket-watches, colloquial expressions and table manners—all these products of the urban world slowly seeped into German towns and villages. Urbanization, therefore, was not just a demographic phenomenon

---

[65] Karl Bosl in Rausch (ed.), *Städte . . . im 19. Jahrhundert*, p. 7.

to be measured by data on population growth and distribution, it was also a cultural and political process that eventually affected every aspect of life.[66]

But there was another side to this process of urbanization: as urban habits and values spread through society as a whole, cities seemed to become less distinctive, individual, and independent. Spatially, the expansion of cities, either through the growth of suburbs or the absorption of surrounding communities, blurred the physical distinction between town and country. In some areas, settlements that were more than large enough to be cities lacked an urban core or historic identity. Without signs to inform them, people travelling through the Ruhr or in the suburbs of Berlin would have had trouble knowing when they had passed the 'city limits'—such signs would rarely have been necessary in traditional society, where the physical separation of cities from their surroundings was unmistakable. In 1860 even Hamburg, that jealous guardian of urban autonomy, stopped locking its gates each night.

After 1850 the legal separation of city and countryside also decreased, thus continuing a process which we have observed at work throughout the era of bureaucratic consolidation and reform. The central government's influence over urban affairs increased almost everywhere in German Europe; the Prussian Poor Laws of 1842, 1843, and 1855, for instance, severely limited a city's right to refuse welfare support. Other laws on local government undermined the time-honoured distinction between urban and rural institutions, and erased special categories of citizenship within the cities themselves.[67] The one exception to this trend was the Habsburg monarchy, where a new local government law passed in 1860 transferred to each local authority 'everything that touched the vital interest of the community and could be accomplished within its boundaries by its own resources'. Although in practice local autonomy did not live up to this promise, the centralization characteristic of Habsburg rule was temporarily reversed.[68] Elsewhere in the German lands, however, the reduction of cities to quantitatively defined administrative units continued. Thus at the

---

[66] There is a discussion of consumption in Walter Minchinton, 'Patterns of Demand', in Cipolla (ed.), *History*, iii. On the spread of urban values and habits, see Sandgruber, *Anfänge*, pp. 268 ff.; Hohenberg and Lees, *Making*, p. 178.

[67] Reulecke, *Geschichte*, pp. 37 ff.; Matzerath, 'Stadt'; Heffter, *Selbstverwaltung*, chs. 6 and 7.

[68] William Hubbard, 'Politics and Society in the Central European City: Graz, Austria, 1861–1918', *Canadian Journal of History*, 5/1 (Mar. 1970), 33–4.

end of the 1860s it became a statistical convention to list as *Städte* all settlements with over two thousand inhabitants. The era of the city as a legally defined, corporately privileged community was clearly coming to an end.

As critics of urbanism frequently observed, modern cities even began to look alike. W. H. Riehl, for example, lamented that communities no longer took pride in what made them different; now every new metropolis wanted to be like all the rest. Although characteristically hyperbolic, Riehl's comment is not without some foundation. It is difficult to find much regional personality or historical identity in those pseudo-Gothic *Rathäuser* with which many German cities sought to evoke the vanished glories of medieval urbanism. Railroad stations, which we have already identified as one of the emblematic public structures in the nineteenth-century city, were built and ornamented in an international style.

In almost every city, private and public spaces became more sharply separated. Fewer households now combined both a dwelling place and a workshop; the domestic apartment or detached villa became the ideal urban home. At the same time, the rules governing public spaces were recast; some areas were set aside for recreation, others for commerce. Retailing became a specialized and stable occupation; peddlers and vendors lost ground to covered market stalls and established shops, which sometimes used elaborate displays to entice the customer inside. Traditionally, urban consumption had been limited to basic necessities or elaborate luxuries; after mid-century the variety of goods available significantly increased and sellers began regularly to advertise their wares with printed announcements, handbills, and rudimentary placards. To be sure, specialized craftsmen still produced precious objects for the very rich, but now there were things to buy for every taste and pocket-book.[69]

The physical appearance and social dynamics of German cities were shaped by common problems, to which urban leaders applied a widely shared set of solutions. For example, every city eventually had to adopt some form of mass transport: the omnibus was first used in Hamburg in 1843, Berlin in 1846, Munich in 1854, and Breslau in 1862. Gas street lights were erected in Berlin as early as 1816; by mid-century, thirty-four cities had similar systems, and

---

[69] Sandgruber, *Anfänge*. Bähr, *Stadt*, pp. 93 ff., has some interesting observations on retailing.

by 1860, after the railroad network had made the delivery of fuel relatively inexpensive, 250 others had some form of illumination.[70] Improvements in water supply and sanitation also occurred, albeit slowly and unevenly. Berlin, for instance, acquired a much-publicized municipal water system in the 1850s, but it took several decades before most Berliners had access to relatively clean water in their houses. Until the 1870s Berlin's sewerage was carried by open pipes and released into public water. Nor were things better elsewhere: as late as the 1890s fewer than half of Prussia's cities and towns had a central water supply. It is hardly surprising, therefore, that big cities continued to have higher than average mortality rates, especially among the very poor and the very young. In the late 1860s, for example, infant mortality was 162 per mille in the Rhineland and 315 per mille in Berlin.[71]

In fast-growing cities, housing was a major problem, especially for the working poor, who had to spend a growing proportion of their wages for small, unsanitary quarters. In Vienna, for example, where the population grew from 356,900 in 1840 to 595,700 in 1866, the average rent went from 151.3 to 281.8 florins (that is, 34.4 to 54.1 florins per capita), while the average number of people per dwelling rose from 4.4 to 5.2. Just over half the city's population could afford to live independently; one fifth continued to reside with their employers, while almost one quarter subsisted as lodgers, most often *Bettgeher*, whose living space was limited to a bed, or part of a bed, in someone else's crowded apartment. 'The housing shortage in Vienna', wrote Emil Sax in 1869, 'has become a persistent calamity. . . . For years, indeed for decades, people speak of it as though it were self-evident, something inseparable from big city life.'[72]

The housing problem in Berlin may have been even worse. Since real estate was expensive and building costs high, Berlin suffered from a chronic inability to provide decent shelter for its growing population. Between 1850 and 1870 the average rent increased from 295 to 451 marks per year. The supply of cheap housing declined sharply. Perhaps as many as one fifth of the city's inhabitants were forced into overcrowded, filthy dwellings—cold attics, damp cellars, poorly ventilated inner rooms. In 1875 about 40 per cent of

[70] Sombart, *Volkswirtschaft*, p. 19; Pounds, *Geography . . . 1800–1914*, pp. 146 ff.; Reulecke, *Geschichte*, pp. 56–62.

[71] Spree, *Ungleichheit*, pp. 34, 118 ff. Evans, *Death*, ch. 2, gives a grim account of public health in Hamburg.

[72] Sandgruber, *Anfänge*, pp. 347, 352, 366. For more on housing, see the essays in Niethammer (ed.), *Wohnen*.

all households lived in one heatable room, another 26.6 per cent in two rooms. More and more of these cramped dwellings were in huge tenements—*Mietskasernen* or rental barracks—which became the characteristic residential environment for the urban poor in many German cities. The average number of residents per building site increased in Berlin from thirty in 1815 to forty-eight in 1861, whereas during the 1860s the number of buildings large enough to hold twenty or more households went from 815 to 2,352. By the 1850s the authorities began to make a few, extremely modest efforts to regulate housing: for instance, in 1853 the municipal government issued a construction code that required builders to leave enough space—about five metres square—for the fire brigade to turn its equipment; seven years later, a minimum ceiling height was established for rooms in which people lived.[73]

As bad as the housing situation might be in cities like Vienna and Berlin, such well-established urban centres did have a variety of public spaces and recreational opportunities that were available to everyone. These amenities were hard to find in the new towns that had spread out around the old textile centres of the Rhine or had mushroomed along the coal deposits of the Ruhr. Occasionally, an employer like Krupp, whose factories played an important role in the economic and social life of Essen, would try to play a patriarchical role and provide his workers with parks and play areas. More often, however, these industrial towns were no more than concentrations of workers clustered around a factory or mine. As we can see in Erhard Lucas's comparative study of Remscheid, an established metalworking centre, and Hamborn, a new settlement surrounding the Thyssen works, education, recreation, sexual behavior, and political organization had a distinctive shape in these rapidly growing, largely traditionless conglomerations, where social life was stripped to its bare essentials and carried out in an environment scarred by ugliness and exploitation. Even before mid-century one visitor was shocked by the condition of the Wupper River, which had become 'an open receptacle for all sewers, disguising the various tinctures contributed from the dyeing establishments in one murky, impenetrable hue that makes the strangers shudder on beholding'. In the following decades,

[73] Nicholas Bullock and James Read, *The Movement for Housing in Germany and France, 1840–1914* (Cambridge, 1984), 37ff.; Fischer *et al.*, *Arbeitsbuch*, p. 183; A. Sutcliffe, *Towards the Planned City: Germany, Britain, the United States and France, 1780–1914* (Oxford, 1981), 15; Walter Minchinton in Cipolla (ed.), *History*, iii. 148–9; Reulecke, *Geschichte*, p. 52. For another example, see James Jackson's essay in Evans and Lee (eds.), *Family*.

more and more of the delicate landscape in the river valleys of the west would yield to the advance of 'progress', which covered the terrain with ugly buildings, filled the water with effluent, and darkened the air with vile-smelling smoke.[74]

Of course not all German cities were physically and socially transformed during the second half of the century. Trier, for instance, which had been an important urban centre at the end of the old regime, changed rather little in the nineteenth century, because the social, economic, and political power of the Rhineland had shifted in another direction. Only in 1860, when Trier joined the western rail complex, did the city begin to grow and prosper. Arnsberg, which was on the edge of Westphalia's industrial zone, owed its slow, even growth to the fact that it was made the district capital by the new Prussian administration in 1816: over the century Arnsberg's population went from about 2,000 to 8,500. Even in this age of rapid urbanization, therefore, some cities— agricultural market towns in the east, former home-town communities in the less developed parts of the south-west, small ports along the Baltic coast—stayed within their old boundaries, preserved their traditional character, and responded slowly, if at all, to the pressures of population growth and industrial development.[75]

The nineteenth-century urban world was extraordinarily diverse. Cities grew at different rates and for different reasons. Some, like the mining towns of the Ruhr, depended on a single industry; others, like Frankfurt and Cologne, combined commerce and manufacturing into a more balanced economic system. Hamburg continued to provide a crucial link between the inland economy and the sea; Leipzig still benefited from its location on trade routes to the east. The central districts of Vienna remained dominated by court, aristocracy, and government, while the suburbs expanded with new industries and blocks of workers' tenements. On a much smaller scale, a town like Koblenz was an important military and administrative centre, as well as being a secondary Rhenish port. Perhaps, as Riehl complained, nineteenth-century cities were losing their specific personalities, but the structure of their societies and the character of their public lives still varied enormously.

[74] Pounds, *Geography . . . 1800–1914*, p. 356. Hamborn grew from a village of 2,000 in 1870 to a city of 100,000 in 1910: Erhard Lucas, *Zwei Formen von Radikalismus in der deutschen Arbeiterbewegung* (Frankfurt, 1976). On these new cities, see Reulecke, *Geschichte*, p. 45.

[75] Kohl, *Familie*; on Arnsberg, Christian Engeli in Rausche (ed.), *Städte . . . im 19.Jahrhundert*, pp. 53 ff.

Except in the newest industrial towns, at mid-century servants remained the largest single occupational group in most German cities. In 1861, for instance, the workforce of Barmen, which numbered about 24,000, contained 1,854 domestic servants (plus another 2,048 household employees, *Gesinde*). Servants made up 11.6 per cent of the population in Hamburg in 1846, 7.5 per cent in 1871. Almost one-fifth of the households in Hamburg, and almost one-quarter of those in Bremen, had a servant. Since servants were cheap and plentiful, they seemed indispensable for carrying on a proper *bürgerlich* existence: in Bremen, as someone remarked in 1850, 'no teacher's family is complete without a serving girl'. Over the following decades, however, servants' relative position in the work-force steadily declined: for example, by 1910 there were only 1,614 servants among the 72,469 people employed in Barmen. By the turn of the century, just 12 per cent of Hamburg's households and 14 per cent of Bremen's had one or more domestics. The reasons for this trend are obvious enough: because of growing forms of alternative employment, labour costs grew and the supply of servants dwindled; at the same time, labour-saving devices, prepared food, and a growing service sector made domestic help less essential. The number of male servants shrank more swiftly than that of their female counterparts, in part because the cost of their labour grew faster, in part because some of what they did was no longer necessary—the telegram and telephone, for instance, often put private messengers out of a job—and in part because certain kinds of domestic work were now thought of as being exclusively female.[76]

In contrast to domestic servants, whose social decline went unmourned by most social theorists, German craftsmen were the object of constant attention from those who viewed their condition with compassion and alarm. 'No stratum', declared a contributor to the *Grenzboten* in 1855, 'finds itself in such a precarious and uncertain economic position as the artisans.'[77] Again and again, political movements claiming to speak to or for craftsmen announced that, unless drastic measures were taken, these groups would be crushed beneath the wheels of industrialism, thus removing an essential source of social stability and national values. But, despite frequent proclamations about their imminent demise, the crafts lasted—always dying, never dead—throughout the

[76] Köllmann, *Sozialgeschichte*, p. 104; Engelsing, *Sozialgeschichte*, pp. 239–40 and 249.
[77] Anon., 'Zukunft des Handwerks', *Grenzboten*, 14 (1855), 321–2.

nineteenth and well into the twentieth century. Only recently have some historians noted this longevity and begun to see the decline of the *Handwerkerstand* in a more nuanced and critical fashion.[78]

When they wrote about artisanal decline, most nineteenth-century observers had in mind the proprietors of small, familial enterprises, where the mode of production was not mechanized and the organization of work was governed by the guilds. Here, in Gustav Schmoller's view, could be found 'the social equality of employer and worker, the fusion of work and education, and of technical and human training.' As we have seen, threats to this mode of production were nothing new. By the eighteenth century a growing number of alternatives to the guilds had already begun to develop: *Manufakturen*, in which a large number of craftsmen worked together in a complicated productive process, and various 'protoindustrial' enterprises, in which production was carried on outside the old guild structure. At the same time that these institutions had undermined the guilds' economic primacy, the latter's institutional autonomy had come under attack from the bureaucrats, who wanted to take over the guild's authority over the local economy and their own members. By the middle of the nineteenth century every German polity had taken steps to limit the corporate rights of craftsmen; in the most highly centralized states, guilds had become little more than governmental agencies or economic interest groups. The decline—even the crisis—of German craftsmen, therefore, began well before the arrival of industrialism; indeed, it is difficult to find a time when someone was not lamenting some sort of declension.[79]

In the years immediately after the revolution of 1848, a few states made tentative efforts to restore the authority of the guilds. Hesse-Darmstadt, Hanover, Baden, Württemberg, Bavaria, and Saxony all passed laws that seemed to favour traditional corporate institutions. In the late 1850s, however, this process began to be reversed almost everywhere; *Gewerbefreiheit* was embraced as the governing principle for economic activity. 'We may expect', the Saxon ministry announced in 1861, 'that the achievement of greater uniformity in economic legislation will be followed by a growing effort by the German nation for freer exchange among the elements of the population.' In 1862 Württemberg passed a new Commercial

[78] The literature on craftsmen is given above, Ch. 2, sec. iii, n. 60 and Ch. 8, sec. iii, n. 65. See also Angel-Volkov, 'Decline'.

[79] Schmoller, *Geschichte*, p. 327. On contemporary views of *Mittelstand's* decline, see Blackbourn, '*Mittelstand*'; Winkler, *Mittelstand*, pp. 21 ff.

Code that abolished restraints on trade and occupational mobility; in Stuttgart alone, over four hundred new firms registered during the next ten months. That same year Hamburg and Baden passed similar laws; Frankfurt followed two years later. '*Gewerbefreiheit*,' Schmoller somewhat reluctantly acknowledged, 'is now unavoidable, because the old divisions among the branches of labour have become impossible.'[80]

In fact, the legal environment probably had less effect on the condition of the crafts than either the advocates or the opponents of *Gewerbefreiheit* realized. In some areas and in some trades, traditional values and modes of organization seem to have persisted despite their formal abolition, while in others even the most restrictive legislation could not prevent disruption and decline. In most cases, the character and condition of a craft were determined by economic forces; trades that could not compete with new forms of production had to reorganize or decline, while others could benefit from industrial development and urban growth. Therefore, no single summary statement can be made to fit the evolution of nailmakers and carpenters, silk weavers and barbers, mechanics and tailors, brewers and blacksmiths, and the hundreds of other crafts that continued to produce goods and provide services. If we must generalize about such a diverse sector, it is better to speak of polarization rather than decline: the practitioners of some crafts were forced out of business or into positions of painful marginality, others became flourishing small businessmen or well-paid skilled employees. In contrast to the image presented by their political spokesmen, craftsmen were not a cohesive *Mittelstand*, but rather a highly mobile and extremely disparate collection of different branches and firms.[81] Overall, craftsmen continued to play an important role in most kinds of manufacturing throughout the 1850s and 1860s. In absolute terms, their numbers increased almost everywhere: between 1816 and 1861, for example, the number of Prussian artisans went from 404,400 to 1,092,900.[82] Only in a few highly-industrial cities were there more factory workers than craftsmen (see table 12.3).

These data, of course, are necessarily tentative because the definitions of 'worker' and craftsmen' are porous and imprecise.

[80] Walker, *Home Towns*, p. 412; Langewiesche, *Liberalismus*, p. 60; Schmoller, *Geschichte*, p. 154.

[81] For some examples, see Engelhardt (ed.), *Handwerker*.

[82] Köllmann, *Bevölkerung*, p. 80.

TABLE 12.3. *Craftsmen and workers in five Prussian cities, 1861*

	Population	% of total population	
		Craftsmen	Factory workers
Königsberg	94,579	10.34	2.76
Berlin	547,571	12.64	7.06
Cologne	120,568	9.83	5.79
Essen	20,811	7.68	13.41
Bremen	49,787	7.5	27.79

Source: Schmoller, *Geschichte*, p. 281.

Throughout the second half of the century, the practical and conceptual differences between most 'factories' and workshops were unclear. Moreover, the social and economic lives of 'workers' and craftsmen frequently overlapped, since both groups lived in the same neighbourhoods, participated in the same clubs and associations, and supported the same political organizations. Even in the workplace, their roles are not easy to disentangle. Domestic workers, who laboured for wages but within a household, remained important in textiles, as well as in tobacco and other forms of manufacturing. Apprentices in trades where guild customs and values had virtually disappeared were often no more than wage earners, whose standard and style of life were hardly distinguishable from that of factory workers. At the same time, skilled workers employed by large enterprises—machinists, plumbers, carpenters—thought of themselves as craftsmen, clearly different from those who performed routine, unskilled tasks. For many contemporaries, the term *Arbeiter* continued to cover a broad range of meanings; only gradually did its usage narrow and become identified with factory labour.

In our period there were not many large factories. At the end of the 1850s only about 2,000 Prussian enterprises had more than fifty employees—and of course not all of them were what we would regard as factories. These large enterprises were, as we should expect, unevenly distributed across the German lands: in the provinces of East Prussian and West Prussia, for example, about 2.6 per cent of the industrial work force was employed in firms with fifty or more workers, while in the Rhineland almost one-quarter worked in such establishments. Nevertheless, by the middle decades of the century the relative economic importance of factories was growing rapidly, as was their place in people's imagination. Franz Louis Fischer, who went to work in a textile mill at the age of fourteen, never forgot the impression created by the 'loud noise of the gears, the narrow passages through the machines, the stench of oil and grease, the dust of the wool, and the heat'.[83] Always unpleasant, often unhealthy, sometimes dangerous, the nineteenth-century factory seemed to be the antithesis of the craftsman's workshop: its scale and setting were completely divorced from the household, its rhythms conformed to the demands of machines, its organization was stripped of all familial and customary restraints. The sounds, sights, and smells of the factory now belonged to a new social order.

Because factories were so different from traditional workplaces, factory labour had to be trained and disciplined in new ways. The best guide to this process of socialization are the 'Factory Rules', which one historian has called 'a largely unfiltered expression of the authorities' interest in how labour was to be used'. In the first place, Factory Rules had to do with time—when work began and ended, when workers could rest, under what conditions they might enter or leave the building. Second, the rules governed social interaction in the factory—conversations were limited, smoking and drinking prohibited, standards of personal hygiene upheld. Third, the rules established a clear chain of command from foreman to manager, and the particular duties of each were defined. No longer could men and women work at their own pace, combine work and recreation, and share tasks as they wished. 'In every large works, and in the co-ordination of any large number of workmen, good order and harmony must be looked upon as the fundamentals of success. . . .' In economic enterprises, as in many other public and private institutions, changes in scale demanded clearly articulated, carefully co-ordinated regulations.[84]

Traditional forms of authority—which were, in their own way, every bit as restrictive as the harshest Factory Rules—presupposed a relatively stable situation in which people could slowly learn customary habits and procedures. In most factories, however, both the organization of production and the work-force were in constant

---

[83] Fischer *et al.*, *Arbeitsbuch*, p. 57; Tipton, *Variations*, p. 28; Kaelble, 'Aufstieg', p. 46; Scholz, *Arbeiterselbstbild*, p. 31.

[84] Flohr, *Arbeiter*, p. 72; Pollard and Holmes (eds.), *Documents*, p. 534; Peter Borscheid, *Textilarbeiterschaft in der Industrialisierung: Soziale Lage und Mobilität in Württemberg (19. Jahrhundert)* (Stuttgart, 1978), 360 ff. For a richly illustrated history of the factory, see Wolfgang Ruppert, *Die Fabrik: Geschichte von Arbeit und Industrialisierung in Deutschland* (Munich, 1983).

flux. We have already mentioned the demographic sources that fed the increasing streams of factory workers—men and women from the overcrowded agricultural areas of the south-west, landless farmworkers from the east, dispossessed domestic workers from stagnant protoindustries, apprentices from declining trades. A few of these people were drawn by the promise of a brighter future, but most were driven by the realities of a hopeless present. Besides this migration *into* the workforce, there was a considerable amount of mobility *within* the industrial sector itself. Skilled workers moved in order to take advantage of the high demand for their services; less fortunate workers moved when they were laid off or dismissed. In many establishments, the annual turnover of the work-force might exceed 100 percent: in 1857 the Augsburg machine works studied by Hermann-Joseph Rupieper hired 369 new employees in order to maintain a work-force of 269. Most of those who moved were people with the fewest ties to firm or region— young, unmarried, unskilled workers in search of higher wages or greater security. Restless and unsettled, these people drifted from job to job, town to town, furnished room to furnished room.[85]

TABLE 12.4. *Real wages in Germany,[a] 1850–1865*

	Absolute (marks)	Index of real income[b]
1850	313	64
1855	348	43
1860	396	60
1865	414	63

Note: [a] Boundaries of 1914.   [b] 1913 = 100
Source: Fischer *et al.*, *Arbeitsbuch*, pp. 155–6.

Seen as an aggregate, German workers did not benefit from the economic growth of the 1850s and 1860s. To be sure, national income increased: in Prussia from 248 marks per capita in 1851 to 304 marks per capita fifteen years later. According to Rainer Gömmel's calculations, the average wage for employees went from 313 marks in 1851 to 434 in 1866, a climb from 29 to 40 if indexed on the basis of 1913. The real wage index, however, rose less evenly, in large part because higher food prices eroded gains in

[85] Hermann-Josef Rupieper in Werner Conze and Ulrich Engelhardt (eds.), *Arbeiter im Industrialisierungsprozess (Stuttgart, 1979)*, 105. See also the essays in this volume by Langewiesche and Schomerus.

nominal income (see table 12.4). Heilwig Schomerus's study of a machine works in Esslingen, for example, shows that, while a worker's average wage went from 491 to 735 marks between 1850 and 1866, his real wage declined from 556 to 467. Managerial employees suffered roughly the same fate: their take-home pay went from 1,451 to 1,969 marks, their real income from 1,665 to 1,247.[86]

From the outside, the workers' world often seemed uniformly bleak and bleakly uniform. In fact, industrial labour was extremely diverse. Jobs that required considerable skill or produced precise, highly finished commodities had more prestige than rougher, less difficult ones. Most factories, therefore, had a clear hierarchy, structured around differences in skill, authority, and compensation. Workers in some industries—railroads and mining, for instance—tended to earn more than those in most textile trades. Wages were higher in fast-growing, competitive regions than in more backward areas. Men earned more than women, adults more than children. Even in a single firm, wages might vary greatly; sometimes the best paid worker would earn eight, even twelve times more than the worst paid. On top of these social and economic differences were the no less powerful divisions created by religion, region, and politics.[87]

When we consider the diversity among industrial workers, we see how misleading it is to think of class consciousness as a natural product of their condition. Stevedores and miners, cigar makers and machine minders, weavers and foundrymen were all 'workers', but the nature of their work and of the social life around it was very different. These people did not have a common identity of which they could 'become' conscious. When, how, and if they developed a sense of identity with other workers depended on a long, difficult, uneven, and always imperfect historical process. The timing, location, and character of this process varied from place to place and industry to industry. Sometimes it began in the workplace, perhaps as the result of a struggle over wages and working conditions. Sometimes its site was an urban neighbourhood, where workers from various firms sought new forms of recreation and sociability. Clearly, the process took a different

---

[86] This research is summarized in Fischer *et al.*, *Arbeitsbuch*, pp. 149 ff. See also Walter Hoffmann *et al.*, *Das deutsche Volkseinkommen, 1851–1957* (Tübingen, 1959); Sandgruber, *Anfänge*, pp. 114–15; Lothar Schneider, *Der Arbeiterhaushalt im 18. und 19. Jahrhundert dargestellt am Beispiel des Heim-und Fabrikarbeiters* (Berlin, 1967).

[87] Fisher, *Wirtschaft*, pp. 251 ff.; Scholz, *Arbeiterselbstbild*, ch. 4; Köllmann, *Sozialgeschichte*, pp. 131–54.

form in a town like Krefeld, where craft traditions were strong, than it did in an industrial village on the Ruhr, which was filled with first-generation workers. The state of the labour market and the character of production, the political climate and religious composition of a region—all these variables helped or hindered working people's ability to understand and act on their common concerns. By the 1860s we can speak of 'working classes' in some places—Leipzig's industrial suburbs, parts of Berlin, a few places in the west—but in most of the German lands working men's and women's social relations remained fluid and diffuse, their social identity diverse and uncertain.[88]

We find the same fluidity and diffusion, diversity and uncertainty when we turn to the social identity of German businessmen. Employers, like their employees, were divided from one another by countless differences in wealth, status, market position, education, religion, regional tradition, and political persuasion.[89]

'Money', wrote a Rhenish businessman around mid-century, 'plays such an important role in recent times that possessing some is an absolute necessity for anyone who wants to make his way in life.' Many contemporaries agreed with this assessment during the 1850s and 1860s, when economic growth seemed to create unlimited opportunities for acquiring wealth. Between 1848–9 and 1856–7 the income of Prussia's highest taxpayers grew by 142 per cent, that of the lowest by 7 per cent. Successful bankers, speculators, and entrepreneurs amassed fortunes, built stately villas, and moved easily in the highest circles of society. The owners and managers of mines and factories controlled enormous resources, wielded authority over an army of employees, and made decisions affecting the lives of entire communities. In comparison to this new generation of economic leaders, businessmen in the first half of the century seem to have had less money and to have lived less grandly. Contemporaries, therefore, frequently contrasted the traditional merchant, who worked hard and lived frugally in an apartment above his firm, with the modern capitalist, who commanded a carriage to bring him into town from his suburban villa. The nostalgia for the comfortable sobriety of this traditional commercial élite had become commonplace decades before

---

[88] See the material cited above, Ch. 8, sect. iii, n. 69. On workers' culture, see the essays and bibliography in Gerhard A. Ritter (ed.), *Arbeiterkultur* (Meisenheim, 1979).

[89] See the material cited above, Ch. 8, sect. iv, n. 98.

Thomas Mann provided its greatest literary expression in *Budden-brooks*.[90]

But the new, flamboyant type of capitalist did not replace traditional businessmen. Rather the two types coexisted, thus extending the economic scale and diversifying the social world of the commercial élite. Throughout our period most businesses, even in mining and manufacturing, remained small and personal, consisting of the owner, perhaps a clerk or two, and a handful of workers. Clearly, the nature of labour relations, the mode of authority, and the style of organization in these firms differed from their larger counterparts, which employed scores, sometimes hundreds of workers in a bureaucratically structured corporation, run by managers who were responsible to stock holders. In towns like Lübeck, which were off the main track, in industries like silk, where technological innovation came late, and in luxury trades like jewellery-making and custom tailoring, the pace of change was relatively slow and the position of established groups relatively strong. The situation was very different in the fast-growing towns of the Ruhr or in industries like machine-making and chemicals. To make one's way here often required special skills and training, a capacity for innovation, and a ruthless dedication to success.

At the same time that the business élite was becoming more diverse, its elements were drawn into closer contact with other social groups. In exceptional cases, successful businessmen moved into the nobility—this was, as we have seen, always a rare but highly valued avenue of upward mobility. After mid-century, and more prominently after 1866, commercial and industrial leaders joined the world of traditional élites through informal social contacts, intermarriage, and a range of honorific titles and awards granted by the state. In the 1850s and 1860s businessmen also established closer relations to educated élites. Officials and other academically trained groups participated in business as shareholders and advisers. In mining, government employment was seen as excellent preparation for a managerial career; no other qualification for an executive position was as highly regarded as the title of 'Bergassessor a.D.'. There was movement in the other direction as well, as businessmen's sons sought university degrees or chose

---

[90] Zunkel, *Unternehmer*, p. 100; Rosenberg, *Weltwirtschaftskrise*, p. 76. See also the data in Riesser, *Banks*, pp. 97–8. In addition to Zunkel's study of the Rhineland, information about changing values among German businessmen can be found in Henning, *Bürgertum*; Böhme, *Deutschlands Weg*; and Schramm, *Hamburg*.

their wives from among the daughters of professors and civil servants. According to Helmuth Croon's careful studies of the western business élite, between the 1840s and the 1860s, 'a *Bürgertum*, defined through property and education, developed from old burgher families, newly successful entrepreneurs, and the officials and professionals who came from these circles'.[91]

In 1864 Gustav Schmoller warned his contemporaries that 'social egotism, irreconcilable conflicts between social classes, and the exploitation of the lower by the upper orders' had destroyed earlier civilizations. Unless we find the 'ethical strength' to overcome these tendencies, Schmoller wrote, they will destroy our civilization as well.[92] Schmoller, like Karl Marx and scores of others at various points on the political spectrum, perceived a growing polarization of society, a hardening of the divisions between rich and poor, a steadily expanding potential for social conflict. But, as interesting as these perceptions might be for a study of social attitudes, they are an imperfect guide to social realities. During the middle decades of the nineteenth century the German social order did not become simpler or more uniform. The *Mittelstand* did not disappear; a mass of unskilled workers did not confront a shrinking capitalist élite. Both workers and capitalists belonged to highly diversified groups, each connected to other elements in society. Few on either side thought of themselves as a 'class' locked in irreconcilable conflict with the rest of society. The fault lines that would eventually cleave the German social order had only begun to emerge.

iv. SOME CHARACTERISTICS OF THE MODERN SOCIAL ORDER

In an essay published in 1860 Wilhelm Kiesselbach used his family's history to measure the intensification of social change during the preceding century. Life in his grandfather's day, Kiesselbach maintained, was simple, cohesive, and slow; his father's world had begun to be transformed by economic development and political unrest. Now the full force of change was unmistakable: 'Only with the astonishing division of labour in our time have the conditions of everyday existence become completely different, both for states and for individuals.' Much the same sentiment can be found in Otto Bähr's evocative portrait of Kassel in the early nineteenth

---

[91] Croon, 'Einwirkungen', p. 20. See also Henning, 'Verflechtungen'.
[92] Gustav Schmoller, 'Die Arbeiterfrage', *Preussische Jahrbücher*, 14/4 (1864), 422.

century, when people still heard the 'cheerful sound of the post horn' rather than the 'locomotive's shrill whistle', and in W. H. Riehl's ethnographic studies of a vanishing rural society. These testimonies to the social transformations in the 1850s and 1860s carry such conviction that we would be inclined to accept them without question if it were not for the fact that we can find similar statements from every decade between the end of the eighteenth century and the First World War. One of the characteristics of the modern condition seems to be each generation's belief that it stands just on the other side of a great divide between tradition and modernity. As Stadelmann and Fischer have pointed out, 'every alert contemporary has had the impression that he lived at a crucial turning point'.[93]

While nostalgia doubtlessly plays a part in these perceptions, there is more at work here than that familiar inclination to think of one's own youth as 'the good old days'. These recurring proclamations of modernity's arrival remind us that the erosion of the traditional social order was slow, complex, and uneven. Throughout the nineteenth century, residues of the past were everywhere apparent—in landscapes as yet untouched by economic development, in trades immune to technological transformation, and most of all, in the language with which people spoke and thought about their social world. When change did come, it affected various groups and regions at different times and in different ways. What we usually think of as 'modernization' was not a single process but rather an enormously complicated aggregate of developments, vastly extended over time and space.[94]

We can get a sense of modernization's multiplicity if we consider the varieties of social time that coexisted during the middle decades of the century. In the countryside, as we have seen, men and women still worked and lived as they always had, according to the rhythms of the agricultural year. For them, sun and seasons meant more than any artificial measurement of time's passing. But if they wished to ship their goods or travel by train, farmers had to submit to the uniform and precise schedule followed by the railroad. Trains not only moved faster than traditional forms of transport, they moved within a different temporal realm. Factories also existed in a temporal realm that was sharply different from that of

---

[93] Wilhelm Kiesselbach, 'Drei Generationen', *DV* 23/3 (1860), 7; Bähr, *Stadt*, p. 86; Stadelmann and Fischer, *Bildungswelt*, p. 59.

[94] Koselleck (ed.), *Studien*, brings together some interesting essays on problems of social change and modernization.

the workshop or farm. In factories people had to work according to an unyielding schedule; factory discipline meant, above all else, making people conform to the rhythm of the machines. The loose, open-ended—and frequently no less exploitative—hours worked by craftsmen and peasants were obviously inappropriate for complex, interdependent productive processes. Moreover, factory labour encouraged another kind of temporal division, that between work and leisure, company time and private time. On the playing field, in the park, or at the pub, time was measured in different ways—indeed it seemed to pass at a different rate—from in the workplace. Political, religious, and educational institutions also had their own calendars and schedules—elections, feast days, examination dates—which people had to learn and follow. While such temporal multiplicity can be found in every social order, it seems especially apparent during periods of transition, when the dominant institutions are not yet strong enough to impose consistency and create what Gurvitch calls 'a unifying hierarchy of social time'.[95]

During the middle decades of the century there was no unifying hierarchy of time in the German lands because there was no single cohesive order, no unified social realm. Yet, if we compare the German situation in the 1860s with that of a hundred years earlier, we cannot fail to detect how the expansion of bureaucratic authority and economic development—the growth of the state and the market—had begun to create a new kind of society. This chapter would not be complete without a tentative attempt to plot the historical distance between the traditional social order with which we began and the new one that was taking shape as our story draws to a close.

We have already come upon one of the most important characteristics of this new order—the transformation in scale that affected a wide range of social, economic, and political institutions in the course of the nineteenth century. Individual enterprises and market relationships, bureaucratic organizations and political alignments, universities and professional associations all became larger and more highly organized. With these alterations in scale went improvements in performance which enabled men and women to produce more goods and travel more swiftly than their grandparents would have thought possible. The most obvious sources of these improvements were the technological innovations

---

[95] G. Gurvitch, *The Spectrum of Social Time* (Dordrecht, 1964), 13. See also Nahrstedt, *Entstehung*.

THE AGE OF THE *BÜRGERTUM*: SOCIETY

that, for the first time in human history, freed people from the limitations imposed by nature. But equally important were new techniques for gathering, storing, and transmitting information. In administrative files and scholarly publications, telegrams and professional meetings, military maps and statistical surveys, Germans now had available to them vast quantities of data about their world. Combined with the new machinery of production, communication, and control, these new sources of knowledge enhanced the power of entrepreneurs and diplomats, physicians and strategists, journalists and policemen.[96]

As the scale and capacity of institutions changed, so too did their internal organization. The tendency towards formulating uniform procedures and regulations, whose roots we uncovered in the early stages of political bureaucratization, spread throughout the social order. Factories posted rules, political groups published programmes, schools established set curricula, and everywhere governments formulated laws, statutes, and policies. To be sure, the weight of custom, habit, and tradition continued to be felt in most people's lives, but these ingrained assumptions were qualified or overcome by articulated norms and codes of behaviour.

The articulation of institutional procedures was connected to an articulation of institutional boundaries. In the traditional world of *Herrschaft*, forms of authority and spheres of influence were often— by our standards—fluid and ill-defined. The rule of a seigneur over his peasants, of a master over his apprentices, and of a father over those in his household was a diffuse blend of what we would regard as political, economic, and familial power. Increasingly, however, jurisdictional lines between these forms of authority were clarified. Lawyers, politicians, and social theorists came to regard the state, civil society, and family as separate if mutually dependent realms. Among the central questions people then had to confront was how these various realms should interact. What was the proper role of the state in social life? How were social interests to find political expression? To what degree should the family be subject to social forces or political authority?

For over a century, from the great codification projects undertaken by the absolutist states in the 1780s and 1790s to the civil law reforms passed by parliaments a hundred years later, legislators tried to frame answers to these questions. In the first place, they

---

[96] See above, Ch. 8, sect. i. It should be emphasized that I am using the concept of 'performance' as a measure of how well an institution fulfils its task, not how well it serves some larger human purpose.

sought to designate a distinctively political sphere, constitutionally defined as separate from—and superior to—other institutional arrangements. At the same time, however, they created quasi-autonomous spheres of social and family life, which were not simply freed from the traditional restraints of corporate society but were also supposed to be insulated from illegitimate interference by the state itself. These realms were to be governed by principles of freedom and equality which were totally foreign to the old order. The cherished 'liberties' of privileged individuals and groups had been replaced by the principle of 'Liberty', supposedly possessed by everyone; the special rights and separate status that had once divided society were levelled by the principle of legal equality. At least in theory, the state protected everyone's rights, including the right to engage in a productive enterprise, be party to a contract, and establish a household.[97]

Of course the movement to freedom and equality was incomplete. Systematic restrictions and structural inequities retained their legal sanctions until well into the twentieth century—most dramatically at the expense of women, who were persistently denied legal, economic, and political equality. Moreover, inherent in the social order's new freedom and equality was the potential for new kinds of repression and injustice.

A legal order which contains ever so few mandatory and prohibitory norms and ever so many freedoms and improvements [Max Weber noted] can none the less in its practical effects facilitate a quantitative and qualitative increase not only of coercion in general but quite specifically of authoritarian coercion.[98]

The changing position of the family provides us with a useful vantage point from which to view the social meaning of freedom. In traditional society, as we have seen, people's freedom to marry was subject to a variety of formal and informal constraints that could be imposed by their community, guild, church, or local authorities. The force of these constraints came from the fact that family life was embedded in a dense network of other relationships. Gradually these relationships between the family and the outer

---

[97] On the changing meaning of freedom, see the essays in Günther Birtsch, (ed.), *Grund-und Freiheitsrechte im Wandel von Gesellschaft und Geschichte* (Göttingen, 1981); Rolf Grawert's essay in Koselleck (ed.), *Studien*.

[98] Weber, *Economy*, ii. 731. Frevert, *Frauen-Geschichte*, p. 9, makes a strong case for the deterioration of women's social position in the course of the nineteenth century. A good example of what Dieter Grimm has called 'enclaves of inequality' in the German legal system is the Prussian *Gesindeordnung* of 1810, which remained in effect through the century: see Gerhard, *Verhältnisse*, pp. 261 ff.

world began to change; state power and economic development limited the control that the village, church, guild, and landlord had once exerted over people's lives. By mid-century, the decision to establish a family had become a matter of legal requirements and economic opportunities. More and more individuals were free to marry, or at least to live together as man and wife, without the consent of intermediate institutions. No longer the keystone in an arch between individual and community, the family increasingly functioned as an autonomous unit. But this autonomy came at a price since the destruction of intermediate institutions left the family exposed both to state regulation and to the free play of the market.[99]

On the open terrain left by the decline of traditional institutions, states constructed laws governing marriage and child-rearing. During the first half of the century some governments had tried to impose their own restrictions on marriage in an attempt to slow demographic growth; eventually, however, most recognized that such restrictions were difficult to apply and largely ineffective. Their principal result seems to have been a rise in the number of illegitimate births rather than a decline in the birth rate. By the 1860s, therefore, marriage laws—like so many other social and economic regulations—were liberalized: individual freedom became the basis for family law.

Even the most liberal states, however, did not view the family as a purely contractual unit. 'Marriage', wrote the jurist Emil Friedberg in 1865, 'is the foundation of the family and therefore of the state; it is the most important institution which the state has to regulate and supervise.'[100] The husband's superior rights over his wife's property and children's education were everywhere acknowledged; the right to dissolve the marriage contract through divorce was limited; religious influences were reduced but not totally removed. Moreover, the state intervened directly in the relationship between parents and their children. Adult status was now a matter of legal definition rather than custom or communal rite. When and how long children could work was subject to legislative controls, which might strike us as outrageously insufficient (according to a Prussian law of 1839, for instance, children

[99] See Conze (ed.), *Sozialgeschichte*; Mitterauer and Sieder, *Family*; Hubbard, *Familiengeschichte*; Dirk Blasius, *Ehescheidung in Deutschland, 1794–1945. Scheidung und Scheidungsrecht in historischer Perspektive* (Göttingen, 1987); Dieter Schwab, *Grundlagen und Gestalt der staatlichen Ehegetzgebung in der Neuzeit bis zum Beginn des 19. Jahrhunderts* (Bielefeld, 1967).

[100] Hubbard, *Familiengeschichte*, p. 37.

under nine could not work in factories, those from nine to sixteen could work no more than ten hours a day) but at the time seemed to be an extraordinary intervention by the state into the household's economic activities.[101]

The state also intervened in familial relationships by insisting that young people spend a certain amount of time in school. Long a goal of state-builders, compulsory education became a reality when states acquired the resources necessary to put legal compulsion into practice. By thus taking over an important part of the socialization process from family, community, and church, the state was in a position to influence its citizens at a critical stage in their lives. In addition to schools, other public institutions—prisons, hospitals, and asylums—now performed tasks once left to · family or community. Slowly, reluctantly, and with uneven effectiveness, governments assumed responsibility for keeping public order, treating the sick, and taking care of the insane.[102]

Despite the importance of the state as a source of regulation and support, the everyday life of most families was determined by economic rather than political forces. In the autonomous realm of civil society—*bürgerliche Gesellschaft*—men and women had to acquire the resources necessary to survive and reproduce. This realm was not, to be sure, as autonomous as its admirers sometimes supposed. The legal foundations of *bürgerliche Gesellschaft* had been created and had to be sustained by political power. Moreover, political authorities intervened in the social realm, usually to the advantage of certain groups—men as opposed to women, masters as opposed to servants, estate owners as opposed to peasant proprietors. Nevertheless, private law presumed that civil society was shaped by contractual relationships freely formed by equal partners. The great liberal legislative achievements of the 1850s and 1860s rested on the assumption that from a sum of these relationships the common good would flow.

But when the parties to a contract are unequally endowed with resources, freedom can easily become no more than an opportunity for exploitation. Workers, Heinrich von Treitschke wrote in 1876, exist 'in a persistent sharp contradiction' because 'their formal

---

[101] Gerhard, *Verhältnisse*; Mitterauer, *Sozialgeschichte der Jugend*; Andreas Gestrich, *Traditionelle Jugendkultur und Industrialisierung. Sozialgeschichte der Jugend in einer ländlichen Arbeitergemeinde Württembergs, 1800–1920* (Göttingen, 1986).

[102] Gerhard A. Ritter, 'Entstehung und Entwicklung des Sozialstaates in vergleichender Perspektive', *HZ* 243/1 (1986), discusses the development of the state's social functions in a broad comparative perspective. For more on these institutions, see below, Ch. 13, sect. i.

freedom stands in clear contrast to their material bondedness [*Gebundenheit*]'. Max Weber, who saw the paradoxes of liberal freedom with uncommon clarity, realized that formal equality and abstract rights do not necessarily enhance 'the individual's freedom to shape the conditions of his own life'. The potential advantages of civil society are not available to everyone: 'Such availability is prevented above all by the differences in the distribution of property as guaranteed by law.'[103]

In the last third of the century the distribution of property became the single most important element in the social order. This is not to say that traditional status was no longer important—we have seen how aristocratic élites managed to hold on to a great deal of symbolic and substantial power. Nor is the social importance of property distinctively modern: throughout European history, wealth in all forms was always both the source of, and the reward for, power and status. In the nineteenth century, however, the relative weight and symbolic significance of property did increase significantly. 'Between masters and apprentices', wrote one observer in the 1860s, 'only a money economy exists . . . apprentices no longer reside and eat with their masters . . . the old patriarchical custom that viewed workers as members of the household has disappeared practically everywhere.' No longer limited by customary restraints, confined by special rights and obligations, or wrapped in traditional values, the role of wealth in society was revealed with stark clarity. In a sense, therefore, the achievement of legal equality made the existence of economic inequality especially apparent and particularly significant: both were essential elements in the *bürgerlich* legal order. Civil law, Lorenz von Stein wrote, 'sanctifies everything that flows from inequality just as it defends the essential equality of all persons; it outlaws every attack on both. . . .'[104]

There is no better example of this combination of equality and inequality than the Prussian Three Class suffrage system, which gave every—that is, every male—citizen an equal opportunity to participate in political affairs, but weighed this participation according to the voter's economic position. Although we sometimes associate this system with reactionary Junkers, it was *bürgerlich* in origin—it had been first used in the Rhenish local

---

[103] Nahrstedt, *Entstehung*, p. 261; Weber, *Economy*, ii. 729.
[104] Lenger, *Kleinbürgertum*, p. 119; Blasius, 'Recht', p. 224. See also Grimm's essay in Kocka (ed.), *Bürger*, pp. 149–89; Franz Wieacker, *Privatrechtsgechichte der Neuzeit* (Göttingen, 1967).

government law of 1845—and *bürgerlich* in spirit. We need only compare this arrangement to the definition of participation upon which the traditional *Stände* had been based in order to see the distance we have travelled from the old regime: not birth, occupation, or status, only how much tax one paid was what counted. 'There are no more clearly defined status groups, no more restricted activities', wrote a contributor to the *Westfälische Zeitung* in the 1850s, adding regretfully that nowadays only money seems to matter.[105]

It is not true that only money mattered; property was the most important, but not the only legitimate agent of stratification recognized by the new social order. Overlapping but not coinciding with the economic hierarchy was one based on office and profession. In this hierarchy, the source and measure of one's position was education, which one contemporary called 'the modern equivalent of ennoblement'. Here too we are struck by a characteristic blend of equality and inequality. Many of the formal restrictions that had once limited access to education were removed, at least for men. Women had much more trouble getting on the educational ladder; the first, quite limited and always exceptional steps in this direction were taken in the 1860s.[106] But even for men, formal guarantees of educational opportunities left many inequalities within the educational hierarchy intact. Indeed some of these inequalities may have increased after mid-century. Among civil servants, teachers, and many other professionals, the lines between the ranks tended to be clarified. Subaltern officials, for instance, were separated from their superiors by background, training, and function as well as by pay and prestige. Similarly, university-trained physicians were able to relegate other medical personnel to ancillary or subordinate status. In time, equivalent distinctions began to intrude among engineers, architects, and a variety of other would-be professionals. Thus, clearly defined status groups and restricted activities remained in modern society, but the nature of their definition and the instruments of restriction changed: educational achievements, professional standing, and,

---

[105] Zunkel, *Unternehmer*, p. 52.

[106] Quote from A. Schäffle's 1856 essay, 'Der moderne Adelsbegriff', in Hans Weil, *Die Entstehung des deutschen Bildungsprinzips* (Bonn, 1930), 149. James Albisetti's essay on 'Women and the Professions', in Joeres and Maynes (eds.), *Women*, describes women's long, difficult struggle to gain access to careers in medicine, law, and education.

above all, accreditation by the state replaced the old barriers of birth, custom, and corporate control.[107]

That property and education—what Pierre Bourdieu calls economic and cultural capital—were unequally distributed in our period will come as no surprise. But it is well to bear in mind the full implications of this inequality, which we can see in contemporary descriptions of urban slums and rural privation, statistical portraits of income distribution, and scattered evidence on nutrition and public health. While we know less than we would like about these aspects of nineteenth-century society, what we do know reveals with painful clarity the sufferings endured by those without property and education. Things were worse—as they always had been—on the fringes of society. In the 1870s, for example, mortality among illegitimate infants was almost twice as high as among those born legitimately. Half of the illegitimate infants born in Berlin did not reach their first birthday. The elderly, the sick, and the powerless were forced to live from private charity or meagre state subsidies. In Berlin during the 1860s, two-thirds of those receiving poor relief were widows or abandoned women. Mortality rates also varied dramatically by social group: almost 30 per cent of the babies born to servants did not live a year, as opposed to less than 20 per cent of those born into civil servants' families. When Ernst Engel studied 17,625 people who died in Berlin between 1855 and 1860, he found that teachers, officials, and clerks reached an average age of fifty-four, wage earners forty-two. Other data suggest that, while the mortality rate for all social groups declined in the late nineteenth and early twentieth centuries, the differences among rates for various groups significantly increased.[108]

The defenders of the new order recognized its inherent inequality, but maintained that greater social mobility would increase individual opportunity as well as collective well-being. Here too the forces of state-building and economic development worked in tandem to undermine legal and practical restrictions on movement and to encourage, perhaps even to compel, men and women to move from the communities in which they had traditionally sought

[107] See McClelland's essay in Conze and Kocka (eds.), *Bildungsbürgertum*, pp. 233 ff. Henning, *Beamtenschaft*.

[108] Marschalck, *Bevölkerungsgeschichte*, p. 167; Jutta Wietog, in Conze (ed.) *Sozialgeschichte*, p. 127; Spree, *Ungleichheit*, p. 59; Fischer *et al.*, *Arbeitsbuch*, pp. 145–146. See also Imhof, *Jahre*, especially pp. 118–19; Frevert, *Krankheit*, pp. 222 ff.

refuge. Of course people had also moved during the old regime, but the social and legal presumptions of the two social orders were different: traditional society, Ernest Gellner has written, 'wills itself to be stable', whereas modern society 'wills itself to be mobile'.[109]

A good illustration of this mobility can be found in the social and cultural history of German Jews. As we have seen, in traditional central Europe the overwhelming majority of Jews lived in small towns and villages, mostly in the eastern provinces of Prussia, Hesse, Franconia, and a few other regions. Everywhere, they were denied political rights, limited to certain occupations, and restricted in various other ways. As these restraints were gradually removed, Jews began to move out of their traditional communities. Some left physically, migrating towards large cities, especially Berlin, where the number of Jewish inhabitants went from 3,373 in 1816 to 9,595 in 1849 and 36,015 in 1871. But even those who remained in the countryside took advantage of new opportunities for education and economic improvement. More and more Jews adopted German as their first language, sent their children to German schools, and tried to participate in German public life. A minority was able to move into the ranks of the educated *Bürgertum*; by mid-century 6 per cent of Berlin's Jews were academically trained. Despite these significant achievements, however, the potential mobility of German Jews was limited in some important ways. First of all, emancipation removed many but by no means all restrictions on their rights. In some states, Jews were still forbidden to settle in certain areas; in most, they were banned from the army and civil service. Moreover, Jews continued to be divided from their fellow countrymen not only by the persistence of traditional anti-Jewish feeling—what one contemporary called 'the abyss of barbarism behind the veneer of civilization'—but also by the emergence of yet more poisonous notions of racial superiority. In the last decades of the nineteenth century, therefore, Jews remained what they had been since the 1780s, a test case for the power and limitations of social emancipation as ideal and reality.[110]

There is no doubt that, to some Germans, social mobility meant a chance for a better life—higher pay, more comfortable housing, greater security for themselves, better opportunities for their

---

[109] Ernest Gellner, *Nations and Nationalism* (Ithaca and London, 1983), 25.

[110] In addition to the material on Jews cited above, Ch. 2, sect. iii, n. 70 see Steven Lowenstein, 'The Rural Community and the Urbanization of German Jewry', *CEH* 13/3 (1980), 218–36; Monika Richarz, *Der Eintritt der Juden in die akademischen Berufe: Jüdische Studenten und Akademiker in Deutschland, 1678–1848* (Tübingen, 1974). The quotation is by a Bavarian civil servant in 1861, from Rürup, *Emanzipation*, p. 30.

children. Since such improvements were usually marginal, they often left few traces in the historical record—they were movements within a particular social and economic category. Dramatic improvements—involving movement between categories—were certainly rare; the greater the movement, the more unusual it was. A few workers got to be foremen or clerks, almost none got to be managers; some craftsmen built successful small businesses, almost none became powerful entrepreneurs.[111] In the educational hierarchy, upward mobility was most often a matter of two or more generations: craftsmen's sons became teachers, teachers' sons, pastors, jurists, or physicians. The number of those from workers' families at German universities was minuscule. Of the educated professions, only the Catholic priesthood drew a substantial part of its members from artisanal or peasant backgrounds. Furthermore, even after the best case possible has been made for the existence of upward mobility, there is every reason to believe that it was more than balanced by movements in the other direction.[112]

Only a minority could take advantage of the opportunities offered by *bürgerlich* society. Most men and women still found their way to a better life blocked by powerful barriers, hardly less formidable than the formal restrictions imposed during the old regime. The essential difference was that now the barriers were often more difficult to see. As Walther Rathenau once wrote, the divisions in modern society resembled glass walls because they were 'transparent but insurmountable, and just beyond them was freedom, self-determination, prosperity, and power'. The keys to this forbidden terrain, Rathenau continued, were wealth and education, both of which were hereditary.[113] To a great extent, Rathenau was right; few passed through the barriers of poverty and ignorance without their families' support. Even though personal status was no longer determined by birth, the family remained the chief source of those material and cultural advantages upon which an individual's social position usually had to depend. The character and legal definition of status might have changed; its essentially hereditary nature did not.

By the 1860s German society had achieved a level of productivity

---

[111] For a guide to the literature, see Kaelble, *Research*: Kocka, 'Study'. Three good local studies: Crew, *Town*; Sharlin, 'Study'; Jürgen Kocka *et al.*, *Familie und soziale Plazierung. Studien zum Verhältnis von Familie, sozialer Mobilität und Heiratsverhalten an westfälischen Beispielen im späten 18. und 19. Jahrhundert* (Opladen, 1980).

[112] Kaelble, 'Aufstieg', p. 35; Ringer, *Education*, p. 88. For a useful local study, see Maynes, *Schooling*, ch. 7, on Baden.

[113] Jeismann, *Gymnasium*, p. 25.

and a trajectory of growth which would have been impossible to imagine a century earlier. As we try to reach some final assessment of the new social order's meaning in human terms, we should not lose sight of these material achievements, however unevenly distributed they may have been. Nor should we condemn the new social order by comparing it to some idealized vision of traditional society. For most people, life in the old regime had been harsh, painful, and short. Those supportive institutions so dear to the heart of conservative theorists had demanded conformity, smothered initiative, and often had failed to give much in return. As the population expanded, the number of those outside these institutions grew, the competition for a place became more intense, the consequences of homelessness more terrible. If we measure the new social order against these grim realities of life under the old regime, we can find some signs of progress, some glimmer of hope. But if we measure this new order according to its own ideals, then we must be struck by how far it was from fulfilling the promise of freedom and equality. From this tension between promise and accomplishment would spring many of the political and social conflicts which continue to beset modern society.

XIII
Culture in the Age of the *Bürgertum*

'I N OUR day', wrote Wilhelm Heinrich Riehl in 1851, 'the *Bürgertum* unquestionably possesses overwhelming moral and material power. Our entire era has a *bürgerlich* character.' Riehl believed that the *Bürgertum* was the epitome of modern society; other groups were no more than ruined residues of a bygone age. And he knew that, as usual, this social fact was reflected in the way people talked about their world. 'Now we speak of *bürgerlich* honour, *bürgerlich* death, where once we had spoken more generally of social honour, social or political death. Instead of speaking of members of the state, current usage takes the most significant part for the whole and refers to *Staatsbürger*.' Riehl himself acknowledged the *Bürgertum*'s universal significance when he entitled his study of contemporary society *Die bürgerliche Gesellschaft*.[1]

Riehl's perceptions cut against the grain of conventional historiography, which emphasizes how the political failure of German liberalism was connected to the social and cultural failure of the German *Bürgertum*. According to this view of the nineteenth century, *bürgerlich* elements in the German lands were either too weak or too self-serving to assert themselves against the forces of reaction. Since the German variant of modernization was flawed, elements of the old regime persisted, thus creating a set of fatal tensions at the heart of the political and social order. Now it is certainly clear enough that liberals did not succeed in assuming political hegemony: as we saw in Chapter 11 and will see again in Chapter 14 illiberal political forces remained powerful in almost every German state. It is much less obvious, however, that the strength of illiberalism in the political sphere reflected the *Bürgertum*'s weakness in culture and society. Indeed, some historians have recently begun to argue that, despite liberalism's constitutional defeats, a successful 'bourgeois revolution' did occur in German

---

[1] Riehl, *Gesellschaft*, pp. 153–4. Cf. Treitschke's comment that 'The middle strata of society among which this new culture sprang to life came to such an extent to occupy the foreground of the national life that Germany, more than any other country, became a land of the middle class; the moral judgments and the artistic taste of the middle class were the determinants of public opinion': *History*, i. 102.

economic, cultural, and legal institutions. This revolution created a kind of bourgeois dominance that was, as David Blackbourn has written, 'most effective where it was most silent and anonymous, where its forms and institutions came to seem most natural'.[2]

In the preceding chapter we saw the material basis of this revolution in the growing strength of the German economy, the movement of technological and commercial innovations into the countryside, the expansion of cities and the spread of urban values, and the triumph of legal equality and contractual freedom. Driven by forces in both the economy and the state, these developments created what Riehl regarded as the essential elements of a *bürgerliche Gesellschaft*. This chapter begins with a general analysis of social mores, which will test the extent and limits of Riehl's claim that the *Bürgertum* had become the universal source of values and behaviour. Then we turn to three aspects of modern culture which are characteristically associated with the *Bürgertum*: natural science, literary realism, and national consciousness.

i. THE CULTURE OF *BÜRGERLICHKEIT*: FASHIONS, MANNERS, VALUES

The invention of photography gave ordinary people what had once been reserved for the rich and powerful. First the daguerreotype and then, after 1850, the cheaper and more versatile collodion print made it possible for millions of Europeans to possess a visual affirmation of their existence, the democratic equivalent of an oil painting or marble bust. By the end of the century, making a photograph had become the accepted way to register happiness, achievement, or grief. The camera was an important part of weddings, anniversaries, school graduations, and even funerals; the album often replaced inscriptions in the family bible as the most important record of people's lives. Until well into the twentieth century, these images of the past retained their symbolic power as treasures to be carefully preserved and transmitted from one generation to the next.[3]

Nineteenth-century photography enables us, for the first time in history, to see what a large number of people in the past looked like. Fortunately for us, some photographers, moved by that urge

---

[2] Blackbourn and Eley, *Peculiarities*, p. 204.

[3] For a representative collection of early German photographs, see the publication of an exhibition at the Cologne City Museum, *'In unnachahmlicher Treue': Photographie im 19. Jahrhundert* (Cologne, 1979).

to record and classify so characteristic of the age, made pictures of 'typical' figures from various occupations and particular regions. Moreover, quite early in its history, photography was drawn towards the quaint, exotic, or grotesque. But most of those who paid to have their pictures taken presented themselves as individuals, couples, or families, not as members of a social group or as representatives of a regional type. Standing before the camera, often looking somewhat ill at ease in their Sunday best, these men and women dressed according to the universal logic of fashion rather than the specific dictates of class or community. Their appearance, therefore, strikes us as oddly uniform—the men in dark suits and stiff collars, the women in whatever dress the current mode dictated. But behind these apparent uniformities were scores of subtle differences in style and quality. In the old regime, people's manner of dressing marked their place in the social order; in the nineteenth century it expressed a more complicated set of distinctions based on wealth, taste, and fashion. Clothing had become an example of a process Norbert Elias believes is characteristic of modernity: 'The contrasts in conduct between upper and lower groups are reduced with the spread of civilization; the varieties or nuances of civilized conduct are increased.' However indistinct these varieties and nuances in dress may seem to us as we look at old photographs, no alert contemporary would have missed them.[4]

By our standards, most Germans in the last third of the nineteenth century owned very little. Those who did possess some dishes or ornaments were inclined to display them, as can be seen in contemporary pictures of object-laden *Biedermeier* interiors; not until quite recently has the possession of things become common enough to allow the rich to indulge a taste for conspicuous simplicity. Nevertheless, the slowly rising standard of living and the availability of cheap consumer goods did make it possible for many people to acquire more possessions than their ancestors: some articles of clothing, much of it now manufactured and purchased rather than made by hand and at home, linens and kitchen utensils, photographs and cheap engravings, perhaps even a few books. Coffee, sugar, together with various prepared foods—bakery goods, sausages, cheeses, and preserves—could be found in an increasing number of German households, at least on special occasions. By mid-century these various commodities had become essential parts of bürgerlich domesticity, an ideal of private life

[4] Elias, *Process*, ii. 255. On fashion, see Böhmer, *Welt*, pp. 153 ff.; Bausinger's essay in Kocka (ed.), *Bürger*.

promoted in popular periodicals, exploited by commercial advertisers, and extolled by social reformers.

Like many revolutionary transformations in everyday life, the spread of this *bürgerlich* ideal was silent and largely unrecorded. We can find traces of its progress in the popularity of books about child care and *bürgerliche Küche*, as well as in changing attitudes towards nutrition and manners, personal hygiene and household management. More and more people hoped to be able to afford the proper setting for a *bürgerlich* existence, complete with a living room for conviviality and separate spaces for the secret intimacies of family life. Within such a setting, those who aspired to *Bürgerlichkeit* could teach their children its complicated values and habits: how to cook and eat their food, how to dress and behave, how to work and relax, how to express or conceal love and hate.[5]

The spread of *bürgerlich* domesticity, with its emphasis on decorum, modesty, and manners, was part of a broader redefinition of private and public deportment. For example, there was a marked decline in the overt violence and cruelty that had been such an essential part of popular entertainments during the old regime. The authorities subjected festivals like the Cologne Carnival to new regulations designed to make them safer and more respectable. At the same time, public floggings, executions, and judicial tortures, which had once been expressions of state power and occasions for popular festivity, were gradually abandoned. The last public hanging in Vienna took place, with all the usual attendant merrymaking, in 1868. Unnecessarily demeaning to the criminal and disturbing to the onlooker, ritualized brutality seemed out of place in the new social world of the nineteenth century. Punishment was something best left to experts, who did their job away from public scrutiny. Indeed, most overt violence began to disappear from people's lives; it was, as Elias puts it, 'confined to barracks' from which it could be released in extreme cases. The sporadic outbursts of terror with which traditional authorities kept order now gave way to more subtle, pervasive forms of discipline and persuasion. The modern state exerted 'a continuous, uniform pressure . . . on individual life by the physical violence stored behind the scenes of everyday life, a pressure totally familiar and hardly perceived.'[6]

The treatment of animals provides another example of changing

---

[5] On nutrition, table manners, and cuisine, see the pioneering work by Teuteberg and Wiegelmann, *Wandel*; Teuteberg and Bernhard, 'Wandel'.

[6] Elias, *Process*, ii. 238–40; Anton Fahne, *Der Carnival mit Rücksicht auf verwandte*

standards of taste and deportment. Under the old regime, spectacles featuring bear-baiting, dog fights, and other blood sports were popular entertainments. In the nineteenth century, such practices were banned, not simply because they caused unnecessary pain to the animals, but also because they evoked barbaric urges among the spectators. Instead, people were encouraged to go to zoological gardens, where animals were treated in a supposedly civilized manner and displayed for educational purposes. In the old spectacles, the onlookers had been thrilled by the sight of animals' ferocity, power, and anguish, now they were invited to admire animals' beauty, grace, and containment. Zoos were run by experts, who were in charge of the animals' well-being, and staffed by uniformed guards, who guaranteed decorous behaviour among the visitors. Perhaps equally important, the bars separating humans and beasts symbolically affirmed the basic message of what Elias calls the 'civilizing process', that is, people's effort 'to suppress in themselves every characteristic that they feel to be "animal" '.[7]

Nowhere was such suppression more difficult and more necessary than in the realm of sexual relations. To quote Elias again, 'In the civilizing process, sexuality too is increasingly removed behind the scenes of social life. . . . Likewise, the relations between the sexes are isolated, placed behind walls in consciousness.' *Bürgerlichkeit* extended the double standard of sexual behaviour characteristic of *Biedermeier* morality: men might indulge themselves with prostitution or pornography, but their private, family life had to be kept free from the dangerous interplay of passion and excess. Even those who enjoyed marital sexuality agreed that it had to be hidden and contained. Almost everyone believed that children should be kept innocent and pure for as long as possible, while some held that girls should be insulated from sexual knowledge throughout adolescence. Karl von Raumer, for instance, cautioned mothers against satisfying their daughters' curiosity about reproduction: 'A mother . . . ought only once to say seriously: "It would not be

Erscheinungen (Cologne and Bonn, 1854), 166 ff. On crime and punishment, see Richard von Dülmen, *Theater des Schreckens. Gerichtspraxis und Strafrituale in der frühen Neuzeit* (Munich, 1985); Friedrich Hartl, *Das Wiener Kriminalgericht: Strafrechtspflege vom Zeitalter der Aufklärung bis zur österreichischen Revolution* (Vienna, 1973); Blasius, *Gesellschaft*, and *Kriminalität*.

[7] Elias, *Process*, i. 120. On the cultural meaning of zoos, see H. F. Ellenberger, 'The Mental Hospital and the Zoological Garden', in J. and B. Klaits (eds.), *Animals and Man in Historical Perspective* (New York, 1974). It would be useful to have a book on the role of animals in German culture comparable to Harriet Ritvo's *The Animal Estate: The English and Other Creatures in the Victorian Age* (Cambridge, 1987).

good for you to know such a thing, and you should take care not to listen to anything said about it." A truly well-brought-up girl will from then on feel shame at hearing things of this kind spoken of.' Peter Gay is right to warn us against taking such prescriptive statements too literally; many women must have been sensible enough to ignore 'experts' like Raumer, but others probably did participate in a conspiracy of silence that left their daughters woefully unprepared for the realities of married life. As Fanny Lewald, who was among the first and most eloquent opponents of these limitations, once lamented about women, 'the sex best suited for love, is not allowed to love, but above all things must marry.'[8]

The ideal of *bürgerlich* marriage was based upon a belief in the fundamental inequality of the sexes. Most social theorists maintained that women were naturally more emotional, modest, receptive, nurturing, gentle, and affectionate than men, who were more courageous, energetic, vigorous, rational, ambitious, and aggressive. So great were the 'diverse inequalities between men and women, and the enormous difference between their functions and powers' that even so progressive a thinker as Theodor Welcker was inclined to wonder if civil equality for the sexes would ever be possible. On that issue a conservative like Riehl had no doubts: 'The contrast between men and women', he wrote in 1854, 'reveals that social inequality is the only natural law of human life.' Against these pervasive stereotypes only a few voices were raised, usually by a small but courageous group of women who demanded legal equality and broader opportunities for self-fulfilment.[9]

Most people assumed that only men could be full members of *bürgerlich* society. Here, in the public world of work, politics, and culture, their achievements were measured by how much they earned, how high their rank, how broad their power. What a man might be able to achieve would undoubtedly vary, but every man should strive for independence, that is, the ability to act and think for himself. *Selbstständigkeit*, which was, as we have seen, the liberals' favourite criterion for active political participation, was both a material and a spiritual condition: it required sufficient property to be free from social constrains and financial dependence,

---

[8] Elias, *Process*, i. 179–80; Mohrmann, *Frauenemanzipation*, p. 121. Gay, *Experience*, argues persuasively that we should not overestimate Victorian prudery. On the double standard, see Regina Schulte, *Sperrbezirke, Tugendhaftigkeit und Prostitution in der bürgerlichen Welt* (Frankfurt, 1979).

[9] Hausen in Conze (ed.), *Sozialgeschichte*, p. 375; Riehl, introduction to the 1854 edition of *Die Familie* (Stuttgart and Augsburg, 1854), p. vi. On these matters, see Rosenbaum, *Formen*; Frevert, *Frauen-Geschichte* (1986).

as well as sufficient moral substance to be free from irrational desire and unwholesome drives. But independence was only one side of the *bürgerlich* social ideal. No less important was a man's willingness to subject himself to social discipline, obey legitimate authority, and adopt sensible opinions. In the culture of *Bürgerlichkeit*, the ideal self was supposed to be autonomous but not autarkic, free but not isolated, independent but not without sustaining bonds.

Perhaps because it so nicely captures this blend of autonomy and discipline, the pocket-watch seems to be the perfect emblem of selfhood in a *bürgerlich* society. Like photography, the mass-produced timepiece was a product of nineteenth-century technical progress. Watches had once been toys or ornaments for the rich, but by the 1850s millions of men could proudly display a watch-chain across their chests. Owning a watch was a sign of autonomy since it implied a kind of power over time that dependent people could not enjoy, but it also suggested the owner's voluntary conformity to the authority of schedules and timetables. To be on time, to save time, and to spend it wisely were all important *bürgerlich* virtues.[10]

These virtues were no less apparent in people's attitudes towards *Freizeit*—free time—a *bürgerlich* neologism that directs us to a new set of social attitudes and institutions. No longer defined by church or custom, free time was supposed to belong to every man, who earned the right to rest and recreate as he saw fit. But free time was not wholly free; it had to be limited, regularized, and properly subordinated to the demands of economic productivity. Throughout the late eighteenth and early nineteenth centuries, the authorities steadily cut back on the number of holidays that had filled Europe's sacred calendar and did their best to ban informal celebrations, such as those 'blue Mondays' that had once broken the demanding rhythms of traditional labour. Moreover, the character of leisure activity reflected dominant *bürgerlich* values. Organized sports, with their rules, records, and discipline, reaffirmed the emphasis on achievement and organization to be found in school and workplace. Against harmful leisure activities, especially the excessive use of alcohol, reformers persistently struggled. Socially dangerous, economically wasteful, and morally destructive, drunkenness was the antithesis of the *bürgerlich* ideal. Instead, people should take advantage of museums, zoos, botanical gardens,

[10] David S. Landes, *Revolution in Time. Clocks and the Making of the Modern World* (Cambridge and London, 1983), relates the history of the watch.

lending libraries, and educational societies, which were designed to make free time a time for self-education and self-improvement.[11]

In the course of the nineteenth century, the urge to improve began to affect conditions that had once been accepted as inevitable facts of life. Mental illness, for example, had traditionally been treated with a characteristic mixture of tolerance and brutality. If the insane were harmless, they could usually remain on the fringes of community life, the object of private charity and public ridicule; but if they became a danger or a burden, they would be locked away in some dreadful place and left to die. Gradually, the situation of the insane became better regulated and, in a sense, more humane. States passed laws defining mental illness and controlling its treatment. Asylums, such as the model institution constructed at Illenau between 1837 and 1842, began to emphasize therapy rather than just confinement.[12]

More slowly and with greater reluctance, some people also began to apply the ideal of improvement to criminals. Under the old regime, crime, like insanity, was seen as an inexorable part of life, not as a problem to be measured, studied, and combated. Prisons were places to store wrongdoers while they were awaiting punishment. Now some reformers insisted that prisons should become 'correctional institutions' designed to turn criminals into productive citizens. 'What is the purpose of cruel penalties?' asked one advocate of penal reform in the 1820s. 'Will they improve the person punished? Is not improvement . . . the highest purpose of punishment?'[13] Asylums and prisons, like schools, co-operatives,

---

[11] On the concept of 'free time', see Nahrstedt, *Entstehung*. On sport, see Henning Eichberg, 'Zivilisation und Breitensport: Die Veränderung des Sports ist gesellschaftlich', in Huck (ed.), *Sozialgeschichte*. For more on the social history of leisure, see Reulecke and Weber (eds.), *Fabrik*; Jürgen Reulecke, 'Vom blauen Montag zum Arbeiterurlaub', *AfS* 16 (1976), 205–48; the essays in Huck (ed.), *Sozialgeschichte*. James S. Roberts, *Drink, Temperance and the Working Class in Nineteenth-Century Germany* (Boston, 1984), discusses the social role of alcohol and the origins of the temperance movement.

[12] Friedrich Panse, *Das psychiatrische Krankenhauswesen* (Stuttgart, 1964), is a good introduction to the development of mental hospitals. Theodor Kirchhoff, *Geschichte der Psychiatrie. Handbuch der Psychiatrie*, ed. G. Aschaffenburg (Leipzig and Vienna, 1912), pt. 4, pp. 5–48, gives a graphic account of how the mentally ill were treated in traditional society. The best brief introduction to the larger issues involved is Blasius, 'Gesellschaft'. Klaus Doerner, *Madmen and the Bourgeoisie: A Social History of Insanity and Psychiatry* (Oxford, 1981), is stimulating if not always convincing.

[13] Blasius, *Gesellschaft*, p. 103. The scholarship on German crime and prisons is sparse and often tendentious: Thomas Berger, *Die konstante Repression: Zur Geschichte des Strafvollzugs in Preussen nach 1850* (Frankfurt, 1974); Gerhard Deimling, *Erziehung und Bildung im Freiheitsentzug* (Frankfurt, 1980); Sigrid Weigel, 'Und selbst im Kerker frei . . .!' *Schreiben im Gefängnis: Zur Theorie und Gattungsgeschichte der Gefängnisliteratur (1750–1933)* (Marburg, 1982).

and a vast array of other institutions devoted to improvement, aimed at instilling the basic virtues of *Bürgerlichkeit*: independence and discipline—sometimes fused as 'self-discipline'.

Although some of its elements have ancient roots, the culture of *Bürgerlichkeit* took on its distinctive modern form during the age of Enlightenment. Here, among the new élites of property and education, we find the first clear expression of *bürgerlich* symbols and values, habits and norms, tastes and manners. From the life experience of businessmen and bureaucrats, teachers and pastors, ambitious craftsmen and enlightened landlords came the essential ingredients in the *bürgerlich* image of selfhood and society. From the start, *Bürgerlichkeit* was inseparable from what we have called literary culture. *Bürgerlich* values were expressed in a variety of written forms: novels and poems, cookbooks and guides to proper deportment, periodicals and pamphlets, train schedules and factory rules. Better schools and new, cheaper methods of printing meant that the impact of literary culture was felt throughout the social order.[14]

Like literary culture, *Bürgerlichkeit* aspired to a sort of universality. Its advocates wanted to define the form and content of culture for everyone; they wanted to establish one way to dress, rear children, express affection, measure success, and enjoy leisure. These norms and habits were no longer to be limited to a particular group or region, their expansion was not restricted by impenetrable boundaries of custom, heredity, or dialect. In this conception, culture should become what Ernest Gellner has called 'the necessarily shared medium, the life-blood or perhaps rather the minimal shared atmosphere with which alone the members of the society can breathe and survive and produce'. This meant, of course, that to control the media of cultural exchange would be to gain access to enormous potential power—which is why Gellner believed that, in a modern society, 'the monopoly of legitimate education is now more important, more central than the monopoly of legitimate violence.'[15] Certainly those liberals and Catholics who struggled with each other for control over German schools would have been inclined to agree.

The universal aspirations of *bürgerlich* culture were never

[14] Paul Münch, *Ordnung, Fleiss und Sparsamkeit: Texte und Dokumente zur Entstehung der 'bürgerlichen Tugenden'* (Munich, 1974), shows that what we consider *bürgerlich* virtues date from the sixteenth century. Nevertheless, I would argue that the culture of *Bürgerlichkeit* requires the social, economic, and political changes described above, especially in Ch. 2, sect. iv, and Ch. 3, sect. i.

[15] Ernest Gellner, *Nations and Nationalism* (Ithaca and London, 1983), 34, 37–8.

fulfilled. Despite the growth of schools and the dissemination of books and periodicals, millions of Germans still had no real access to the printed word.[16] Moreover, a large section of the population was cut off from the fashions, manners, and values of *Bürgerlichkeit* by persistent barriers of poverty and powerlessness. How, for example, could the ideal of *bürgerlich* domesticity be made to fit the experience of a farm labourer without the means to marry or of a factory worker unable to afford more than part of a bed in someone's crowded flat? What sense could the *bürgerlich* ideal of womanhood have for the millions of women who toiled in factories or fields all over central Europe? What chance did landless peasants, underemployed artisans, or marginal workers have of becoming spiritually and materially 'independent'?[17]

Bürgerlichkeit claimed universality but, like every culture, it created divisions. Indeed, the very scope of its aspirations and the magnitude of its power invited protest and encouraged disenchantment. By the end of the century, *bürgerlich* culture was under attack both from those who felt they had been denied access to its accomplishments and from those who viewed these accomplishments as hollow and unsatisfying. In the German lands, as in the rest of Europe, most of what we have come to think of as 'modernism' was defined in opposition to *bürgerlich* ideals. Nevertheless, even after the power of these ideals had begun to fade in the realm of high culture, *bürgerlich* fashions, manners, and values continued to shape the way an increasing number of ordinary people ordered their lives.

ii. THE RISE OF GERMAN SCIENCE

'The age of systems is passed . . . system is the childhood of philosophy; the manhood of philosophy is investigation.' George Eliot chose these lines from Otto Friedrich Gruppe's *Gegenwart und*

---

[16] The basic work on the spread of literacy and its social significance is by Rolf Engelsing and Rudolf Schenda: see Engelsing's essays in his *Sozialgeschichte, Massenpublikum und Journalistentum im 19. Jahrhundert in Nordwestdeutschland* (Berlin, 1966), and *Analphabetentum und Lektüre. Zur Sozialgeschichte des Lesens in Deutschland* (Stuttgart, 1973); and Schenda's pioneering *Volk*, and *Die Lesestoffe der kleinen Leute: Studien zur populären Literatur im 19. und 20. Jahrhundert* (Munich, 1976). There is a sharp analysis of these issues in Hohendahl, *Kultur*. Also of interest in Ilsedore Rarisch's study of *Industrialisierung und Literatur: Buchproduktion, Verlagswesen und Buchhandel in Deutschland im 19. Jahrhundert in ihrem statistischen Zusammenhang* (Berlin, 1976).

[17] On the housing shortage in German cities, see the material cited above, Ch. 12, sect. iii, nn. 72, 73. On working women, see Frevert, *Frauen-Geschichte*.

Zukunft der Philosophie in Deutschland to characterize the intellectual climate she found in Berlin during the mid-1850s. Many contemporaries agreed that the future belonged to 'investigation', by which they meant empiricism as opposed to idealism. Rudolf Haym, whose new biography of Hegel marked a milestone in the historical reassessment of systematic philosophy's last giant, spoke of the 1850s as a period 'which has learned to renounce poetic illusions and romantic confusions' and 'sees itself surrounded by unresolved contradictions and complicated practical tasks'. At such a time, Haym believed, men had to turn from the realm of abstractions to the hard realities of human history. We must, Max Duncker told J. G. Droysen, 'replace the imaginary idealism of philosophy with the realistic idealism of history'.[18]

This change in intellectual climate may have been caused in part by the failure of revolutionary ideals, but it was much more clearly the result of those social and economic accomplishments that were described in the preceding chapter. The expanding rail network, the growth of large cities, and the spread of factories all seemed to be creating a distinctively materialistic society. No less important were the cultural changes to which we turn in this section and the one following: the increasing importance of natural science and the emergence of literary realism.

In the middle decades of the nineteenth century, German science, which had traditionally been on the periphery of European developments, moved into a position of unquestioned creative leadership. In one field of enquiry after another, German researchers established their pre-eminence and retained it with awesome persistence. German universities and technical schools, hospitals and private laboratories became objects of envy and emulation throughout the world. We can get a sense of the timing and scale of German scientific supremacy in comparative data compiled by Joseph Ben-David: (table 13.1). German science continued to build on these accomplishments until well into the twentieth century: between 1901 and 1930, Germans won twenty-six Nobel Prizes in Chemistry, Physics, and Medicine—a substantially greater number than those won by any other single nation and more than one-quarter of the total prizes awarded.[19]

In the natural sciences, as in the fields of history and philology

[18] Rosemary Ashton, *The German Idea: Four English Writers and the Reception of German Thought, 1800–1860* (Cambridge, 1980), 150–1; Lees, *Revolution*, p. 38; Duncker, letter of 12 Dec. 1853, in Droysen, *Briefwechsel*, ii. 201.

[19] Nipperdey, *Geschichte*, and Schnabel, *Geschichte*, iii, have good general

TABLE 13.1. *Scientific discoveries in Germany, France, and England, 1800–1870*

a. Physiology

	Germany	France	England
1800–09	5	5	8
1810–19	12	15	6
1820–29	29	17	6
1830–39	46	16	9
1840–49	91	22	13
1850–59	126	37	8
1860–69	171	16	2

b. Medical sciences

	Germany	France	England
1800–09	5	9	8
1810–19	6	19	14
1820–29	12	26	12
1830–39	25	18	20
1840–49	28	13	14
1850–59	32	11	12
1860–69	33	10	5

c. Heat, light, electricity, magnetism

	Germany	France	England
1801–10	37	30	49
1811–20	27	91	39
1821–30	54	91	54
1831–40	90	69	99
1841–50	138	166	93
1851–60	223	117	99
1861–70	245	124	69

Source: Ben-David, *Scientist's Role*, pp. 188–9, 192.

accounts of German science. On scientific institutions, see Ben-David, *Scientist's Role*, who cites the data about Nobel Prize winners on p. 193. There are useful essays on the various disciplines in Wilhelm Treue and Kurt Mauel (eds.), *Naturwissenschaft, Technik und Wirtschaft im 19. Jahrhundert* (2 vols.; Göttingen, 1976). The *DSB* has excellent articles on individual scientists.

we considered in Chapter 9, these nineteenth-century triumphs would not have been possible without a variety of eighteenth-century achievements. Throughout the eighteenth century, scores of physicians, pharmacists, opticians, mining engineers, and assorted amateurs had patiently gathered information about the world of nature. At a few universities, professors had actively pursued research. More and more periodicals—such· as Lorenz Crell's *Chemische Journal für die Freunde der Naturlehre, Arzneygelahrtheit, Haushaltungskunst und Manufacturen*, first published in 1778—brought news of scientific discoveries to a broad sector of the educated public, for whom science was a subject of enormous interest and importance. In Alexander von Humboldt, Germans had a scientific leader of European stature. An explorer, indefatigable public speaker and correspondent, member of numerous academies, and patron of promising young researchers, Humboldt helped lay the foundations for the study of natural history. Less well known than Humboldt but more significant for the history of several disciplines was Carl Friedrich Gauss, who established his reputation with his *Disquisitiones arithmeticae* in 1801 and then went on to make a series of fundamental contributions to number theory, algebra, geometry, statistics, geodesy, geomagnetism, mechanics, dioptics, and physics—all while serving as the director of the Göttingen observatory.[20]

But despite the extraordinary work of men like Humboldt and Gauss, until the early nineteenth century German science lacked the social basis and institutional connections necessary for widespread, self-sustained growth. By the 1820s, however, the situation had begun to change: in former times, a speaker told a meeting of the Gesellschaft Deutscher Naturforscher und Ärtze at the end of the decade,

men regarded the inquisition of nature as a pleasant but useless employment . . . [but] they have, of late years, become every day more and more convinced of its influence upon the civilization and welfare of nations, and the leaders of the people are everywhere bestirring themselves for the erection of establishments to promote its advancement and extension.

It took time to create such establishments. Even in the 1830s and 1840s Robert Mayer and Georg Ohm could make fundamentally important discoveries that were virtually ignored by the scientific community. Mayer was apparently driven insane by his failure to

---

[20] Karl Hufbauer, *The Formation of the German Chemical Community, 1720–1795* (Berkeley, 1982), discusses Crell. On Gauss, see *DSB* v. 298–315.

gain recognition for his theory on heat and motion, while Ohm, despite his accomplishments, had a restless and uncertain career until he finally received a university chair just two years before his death. However, by mid-century the isolation that so often hindered the work of early scientists gave way to a dense, self-perpetuating set of institutional connections through which knowledge was created, tested, and communicated. In 1862 Hermann von Helmholtz, who was one of the first major beneficiaries of these new institutions, described in glowing terms 'the division of labour and improved organization among scientific workers'. Scientists, he continued, now resembled 'an organized army, labouring on behalf of the whole nation, and generally under its direction and at its expense'.[21]

Helmholtz's confident sense of community and purpose reflected the successful professionalization of German science during the century's middle decades. In these years, scientific and mathematical endeavours acquired a research agenda based upon a body of shared information about past discoveries and a mix of theories and hypotheses to guide future enquiry. Characteristically, these data, theories, and hypotheses were incorporated in a handbook—usually a multi-volume work produced by a leading scholar in order to consolidate a particular discipline. Researchers reported new findings and carried on scholarly controversies in one of the specialized journals that proliferated during this same period. Around this empirical and theoretical core scientists established formal and informal institutions to perform the essential tasks of every profession: recruiting, training, and accrediting new members, evaluating professional performance, rewarding those who met the profession's goals and cherished its values, and finally—and perhaps most important—protecting the profession's boundaries from 'unqualified' outsiders. As a result of this process, the disciplinary communities that formed the basic social and epistemological units for modern scientific research came into existence.[22]

The creation of scientific disciplines involved new sources of division as well as new centres of community. By mid-century, the powerful process of specialization—what Helmholtz called the 'division of labour'—had begun to separate researchers into independent fields. As disciplinary lines hardened and the material to be mastered proliferated, the range and variety that had

[21] Mendelsohn, 'Emergence', p. 23; Helmholtz, 'Relation', p. 28.
[22] The best introduction to these issues is the work of R. Steven Turner: 'Growth', 'Reformers', 'Professoriate', 'Helmholtz'.

characterized the work of many early scientists became impossible. No longer could a man like Karl Gottfried Hagen make his fortune as a pharmacist and then lecture and do research in pharmacy, chemistry, physics, mineralogy, botany, and zoology.[23] Journals devoted to general scientific issues continued to be published, but they were joined by an ever-increasing number of specialized publications written by and for the practitioners of a particular discipline or subdiscipline. The Gesellschaft Deutscher Natur-forscher und Ärtze, founded in the early 1820s to promote a unified vision of scientific work, eventually had to break up into separate sections devoted to special fields. The dream of a unified theory about the natural world still inspired the most ambitious scientists, but in practice it became more and more difficult to move—or even communicate—across the disciplines' intellectual and institutional boundaries.

The most important institution for the rise of German science was the university, which became the location for research, agent of professional development, and major beneficiary of science's growing claims on social resources. Two elements in the mutually advantageous relationship between science and academia were of particular significance. First, the subtle transformation of Hum-boldt's ideal of *Bildung* into what Steven Turner calls a 'research imperative' proved to be of immense value to the natural sciences during their formative years. Since this imperative made the creation of new knowledge part of the university's central mission, it helped to free scientists from the practical burdens of excessive teaching as well as from the intellectual burdens of traditional erudition. The research imperative made innovation—in the natural sciences, as in the humanities—a primary value, for the individual and for his institution. Second, the close connection between universities and states gave scientists an opportunity to mobilize public resources in support of their research. As long as this research was relatively inexpensive, Germans' political frag-mentation was not a disadvantage; in fact, enterprising researchers could play one government off against another in order to win the best conditions under which to work.[24]

When the university became the disciplines' primary setting, the career patterns of German scientists changed. The relative import-ance of affluent amateurs like Goethe and Humboldt decreased, as

[23] Silberner, *Jacoby*, p. 22.
[24] See Turner's articles cited in n. 22. For some useful comparative material, see Coleman, *Biology*.

did the number of skilled artisans who combined scientific research with a craft such as pharmacy or lens grinding. Increasingly, the right to do serious, professional research required academic credentials—a doctorate, published research in an approved forum, a position in the academic hierarchy. Kenneth Caneva's study of two generations of German physicists illustrates this shift very clearly. Among those born in the 1770s, none received specialized training in physics, most studied medicine, some did not attend a university at all. Moreover, no member of this generation made his living as a physicist; those who were not financially independent had to practise medicine or combine an academic position with some other occupation. Physicists born around the turn of the century, on the other hand, all went to a university and, with few exceptions, earned a doctorate, sometimes in physics, sometimes in another scientific discipline; most of these men then acquired university positions in which they were able to devote themselves to full-time teaching and research.[25]

Justus Liebig, long-time Professor of Chemistry at Giessen, is an exemplary figure in this process of scientific professionalization. Born in 1803, Liebig was apprenticed to an apothecary so that he might emulate his father, who was both a chemist and a pharmacist. But Justus recognized that chemistry was no longer a craft and now required academic training. He managed to study at Bonn, and then went to Paris, which was still regarded as the capital of European science. Here he was fortunate enough to come to the attention of Alexander von Humboldt, who arranged a job for him at Giessen. Liebig brought to his research the meticulous methods of observation and experimentation he had learned in France; by carefully studying the physiology of respiration, nutrition, and excretion he was able to identify some of the essential principles of biochemistry. In his great work, *Die organische Chemie in ihrer Anwendung auf Physiologie und Pathologie*, first published in 1842, he looked forward to the eventual fusion of chemistry and physiology. Liebig also did basic research in several other fields, helped to introduce new methods into German agriculture, influenced the emerging dye industry, and spread scientific knowledge and values to the public at large.

[25] Kenneth Caneva, 'From Galvanism to Electrodynamics: The Transformation of German Physics and its Social Context', *Historical Studies in the Physical Sciences*, 9 (1978), 131 ff. For some examples of generational conflicts in the biological sciences, see Timothy Lenoir, *The Strategy of Life: Theology, Mechanics and the Development of Nineteenth Century German Biology* (Dordrecht, 1982).

As impressive as they were, none of Liebig's achievements was more important than his role in the promotion of the modern research laboratory. Of course, scientists had always had workrooms—usually in their own or their patrons' homes. The teaching of science, however, was done in regular classrooms, where students heard lectures about the natural world. Liebig's contribution was to bring teaching and research together; using his own funds to remodel a deserted army barracks, he created a new way of training scientists. The process, so familiar to us, was a revolutionary departure from traditional methods: beginners were given instruction by advanced students, who were themselves expected to work independently. Except for twice-weekly summaries and reviews of the research, Liebig himself did no formal teaching. 'The progress of my special students', he wrote, 'depended on themselves. I gave the task and supervised the carrying out. . . . Everyone was obligated to follow his own course.' In effect, the laboratory institutionalized the research imperative by turning teaching and learning away from the acquisition of established truths and towards the creation of new knowledge.[26]

The laboratory soon became both instrument and expression of science as a profession. It was a perfect means to propagate and test a discipline's central intellectual core, whose problems thus became the subject of intense scrutiny by talented young men eager to make their reputations. Furthermore, the laboratory was a powerful instrument of socialization, through which apprentice scientists learned the formal rules and the hidden culture of their profession. Not surprisingly, the Giessen model was quickly taken up elsewhere. Within a generation, laboratories existed at every major university, where they generated vast quantities of scientific knowledge and trained a corps of committed researchers.

To the new generation of professionals, the rise of the laboratory appeared to be a triumph of modernity over tradition, careful observation over blind faith, experimental rigour over irrational assumptions. Liebig and his colleagues defined their own self-image against what they saw as the absurdities of romantic science and natural philosophy, which they viewed as a 'pestilence of our time', nurturing superstition and hindering progress. No doubt a great deal of what passed for science in the eighteenth and early nineteenth century deserved the professionals' contempt. The era was full of eccentric theories and fashionable fakery, such as Franz

[26] Mendelsohn, 'Emergence', p. 20. On Liebig, see F. L. Holmes's article in *DSB* viii; Smith, *Problem*, especially p. 199.

Joseph Gall's phrenological research. Philosophers like Schelling vainly searched for hidden unities that would reduce human experience to a single principle. However, romantic science and natural philosophy were not merely impediments to progress; the line between speculation and observation is often harder to draw than later generations liked to insist. Moreover, the ambitions of earlier scientists to unify diverse phenomena and uncover fundamental principles helped inspire the professionals' empirically based theory-building. Stripped of its mystical overtones and speculative pretensions, natural philosophy could encourage what Alexander von Humboldt called 'the noble effort to link together observations, and to dominate empirical data with ideas'.[27]

A good example of the complex relationship between romantic aspirations and professional accomplishments can be found in the career of Johannes Müller, one of the founders of modern German biology. Müller was born in 1801, the son of a craftsman who was financially successful enough to send him to the university to study medicine. After deciding to devote himself to scientific research, he taught at the University of Bonn before moving to Berlin in 1833. An extraordinarily productive scholar, Müller was able to do important work in physiology, comparative anatomy, and zoology. In all these subjects, his achievement was an uncompromising commitment to exact observation in both teaching and research; he had caused a sensation by bringing a microscope into the lecture hall. But to his empirical convictions Müller added a belief in a *Lebenskraft*, a life force, which remained from his youthful adherence to natural philosophy. Thus he devoted a long chapter in his *Handbuch der Physiologie* (1833–40) to questions about the nature, location, and divisibility of the soul. As his student Helmholtz put it, Müller 'still struggled between the older—essentially metaphysical—view and the naturalistic one'. Moreover, Helmholtz astutely noted, 'it may be that his influence over his students was the greater because he still so struggled'.[28]

Among Müller's students, Rudolf Virchow best personified the demystification of biology. Twenty years younger than his teacher, Virchow began to study science after disciplinary communities had begun to form. Since he was poor, he too had started out by

---

[27] Schnabel, *Geschichte*, iii. 202. Schnabel has some examples of scientific eccentricities on pp. 171 ff. For a largely positive interpretation of natural philosophy, see M. Heidelberger, 'Some Patterns of Change in the Baconian Sciences of Early 19th Century Germany', in Jahnke and Otte (eds.), *Problems*.

[28] Helmholtz, 'Autobiographical Sketch', p. 275. On Müller, see Johannes Stendel's article in *DSB* ix.

studying medicine—at the Friedrich Wilhelm Institute in Berlin, where scholarships were available—but he quickly made the shift to basic research, first in Würzburg and then in Berlin, where a Pathological Institute was specially constructed to house his laboratory. A man of quite remarkable energy and intellectual power, Virchow established the principles of modern pathology, discovered the embolism, clarified the process of thrombosis, linked leukemia to cellular disorders, did significant research in epidemiology, contributed to the development of physical anthropology, advocated medical reform, and participated in politics. Virchow's most impressive scientific achievement came in 1855, when he published his clarification and emendation of the cell theory advanced by Schleiden and Schwann fifteen years earlier. Cells, Virchow maintained, were the basis of life—in his famous phrase, 'omnis cellula a cellula'. He described their organization in terms that unmistakably reflect the images of society popular in the 1850s: cellular pathology, he wrote, 'showed the body to be a free state of equal individuals, a federation of cells, a democratic cell state'.[29]

Virchow was a self-consciously secular person who is best known to historians of German politics for coining the term *Kulturkampf* during the struggle between liberals and Catholics in the 1870s. His faith was in science itself: 'We confined ourselves to the investigation of isolated problems completely confident that every new fact would necessarily spread light in fields as yet dark.' Virchow retained a belief in the unity of phenomena: 'I have never,' he wrote in 1849, 'not at the dissection table or in front of the microscope, at a patient's bedside or in public life, forgotten the search for higher, unifying principles behind the multiplicity of individual phenomena.' Yet his search was secularized, without a spiritual dimension. Life, for Virchow, was merely a complicated form of 'Mechanik'.[30]

Many of Virchow's contemporaries among the first generation of professional scientists shared his faith that they could establish an empirically based theory to explain the mysteries of nature. Hermann von Helmholtz seemed to take an important step in this direction with the paper 'Über die Erhaltung der Kraft', which he

---

[29] Ackerknecht, *Virchow*, p. 45. The range and volume of Virchow's accomplishments can be seen in J. Schwalbe's *Virchow-Bibliographie, 1843–1901* (Berlin, 1901), which runs to 118 pages. Coleman, *Biology*, puts his work into its historical context.

[30] Mendelsohn, 'Emergence', p. 43; Virchow, 'Einheitsbestrebungen', quoted in E. Schmidt-Weissenfels, *Preussische Landtagsmänner* (Breslau, 1862), 67.

read to the Berlin Physikalische Gesellschaft in the summer of 1847. Born in 1821, Helmholtz was Virchow's exact contemporary and like him attended the Friedrich Wilhelm Institute on a government scholarship. He came to his theory about the conservation of energy in the course of research on animal heat and muscle contraction—at about the same time as twelve other researchers independently formulated various versions of the concept. To Helmholtz, the theory indicated that nature was a closed system, with eternal but interchangeable elements. This meant that it was absurd to look for some special 'vital force' to explain the phenomena of life; living organisms were subject to the same laws as the rest of the universe.[31]

Emil DuBois-Reymond, Helmholtz's fellow student and friend, recognized immediately that 'Über die Erhaltung der Kraft' opened the way for biology to merge with physics. As he wrote to a colleague in early 1848, Helmholtz's paper provided physics with a goal worthy of its status as a science. DuBois-Reymond's *Untersuchungen über thierische Elektrizität*, published later that year, attempted to move towards this goal:

If one observes the development of our science one cannot fail to note . . . how new areas are increasingly brought under the dominion of physical and chemical forces. . . . [I]t cannot fail that physiology, giving up its special interest, will one day be absorbed into the great unity of the physical sciences; [physiology] will in fact dissolve into organic physics and chemistry.[32]

Both Helmholtz and DuBois-Reymond had long, productive careers. Helmholtz taught at Königsberg, Bonn, and Heidelberg before moving to Berlin in 1871, when his arrival was heralded as another indication of Prussian hegemony. For quarter of a century he presided over a thriving research institute, trained generations of students, and served as president of the Physikalish-technische Reichsanstalt, a privately endowed foundation established to support German science. DuBois-Reymond began studying in Berlin, where he supported himself by teaching anatomy to artists until Müller took him on as an assistant in 1854. When Müller died four years later, his position was divided into two, a chair in

---

[31] In addition to Helmholtz's 'Autobiographical Sketch', see *DSB* vi. 241–53. See also Thomas S. Kuhn, 'Energy Conservation as an Example of Simultaneous Discovery', in Clagett (ed.), *Problems*, pp. 321–56.

[32] Emil DuBois-Reymond and Carl Ludwig, *Two Great Scientists of the Nineteenth Century: Correspondence*, ed. Paul Diepgen (Baltimore and London, 1982), 6; Coleman, *Biology*, p. 151.

anatomy and one in physiology. DuBois-Reymond occupied the latter, from which he directed an institute for physiological research. Internationally known for their work, laden with honours, and extremely influential in academic affairs, Helmholtz and Dubois-Reymond personify the rise of German science in the nineteenth century.

Those scientists who hoped that their methods would have universal validity were greatly encouraged by the development of German psychology after mid-century. Helmholtz's studies of the physiology of perception, culminating in the publication of his *Handbuch der physiologischen Optik* in 1856, provided what one admirer called a 'bridge between physiology and psychology on which thousands of workers today [1895] go back and forth'.[33]

Another bridge-builder was Gustav Theodor Fechner, whose *Elemente der Psychophysik* of 1860 was also important for the emergence of scientific psychology. Fechner, a contemporary of Virchow and Helmholtz, seemed destined to enjoy a similarly successful and rewarding position in the front ranks of the new scientific profession. When his promising career as a physicist was cut short by an eye disease, he was forced into semi-retirement. For two decades he contemplated the relationship between the inner world of mental activity, in which he was forced to dwell, and the outer world of sensation from which his semi-blindness all but excluded him. His formulation of this relationship clearly parallels the theories unifying force and matter so popular among his contemporaries: the mental and material realms, he argued, are like the concave and convex sides of a curve, that is, they are the same thing seen from different perspectives. The aim of psychophysics was to discover the laws which govern both mind and matter and thus to transform psychology from being the occasion for poetic introspection and philosophical speculation into the subject of rigorous scientific research. Needless to say, poets and philosophers did not stop considering the human mind, but in the course of the nineteenth century they had to contend with a new set of competitors, inspired by Helmholtz and Fechner to create a science of the spirit that could join with physics and biology in the search for universal laws.[34]

The growth and intellectual vitality of the natural sciences during

---

[33] Quoted in Turner, 'Helmholtz', p. 148. The classic work on the subject is Edwin Boring, *A History of Experimental Psychology* (2nd edn., New York, 1950).

[34] See Marilyn Marshall, 'Physics, Metaphysics, and Fechner's Psychophysics', in Ash and Woodward (eds.), *Science*.

the 1840s and 1850s attracted considerable attention among educated Germans, who read accounts of the new research in general periodicals like the *Grenzboten* and tried to grasp the implications of scientific progress for politics and culture. Liebig's 'Chemische Briefe', which began to appear in the *Allgemeine Zeitung* in 1842, were widely read and frequently reprinted in book form. In the early 1850s several journals catered to the popular taste for information about science and its implications. *Die Natur*, for example, commenced publication in 1852; its subtitle, *Zeitung zur Verbreitung naturwissenschaftlicher Kenntniss and Naturanschauung für Leser aller Stände*, expressed the essential purpose its editors pursued for almost fifty years.[35]

Some writers tried to use this new interest in science to attack religion in the name of philosophical materialism. Among them, one of the most influential was Jacob Moleschott (1822–93), who studied new trends in academic science as well as the ideas of Strauss and Feuerbach. While a student at Heidelberg in 1850, Moleschott published his first important work, *Die Lehre der Nährungsmittel*, which he wrote in both an extended and a popular version. Like so many of his contemporaries, he believed that nature, including living organisms, was composed of interchangeable elements: 'Therefore I have been able to derive all life from the bonding and breaking up of the matter of our body. Life is an exchange of matter [*Stoffwechsel*].' Feuerbach, to whom Moleschott sent a copy of *Die Lehre*, embraced his ideas without qualification; Feuerbach's oft-quoted (and rather uncharacteristic) reductionist line, 'Der Mensch ist was er isst', appeared at the end of an essay in praise of the book.

Moleschott's efforts to link scientific methods and philosophical materialism found their fullest and most influential expression in *Der Kreislauf des Lebens*, published in 1852. Here Moleschott argued that, since there was no knowledge other than perception, there could be no existence beyond the world of force and matter. 'The motion of the elements, combination and separation, assimilation and excretion, that is the essence of all activity on earth.' We must find meaning and consolation, not in some mythic vision of an after life, but in the remorseless cycle of nature: 'There is death in life and life in death. This death is not black and horrible. For swaying in the air and resting in the mould are the eternally smouldering seeds of blossoms.' This sort of language gained Moleschott great

---

[35] Gregory, *Materialism*, discusses the popularization of science. For an example, see 'Die Naturwissenschaft und die Gegenwart', *Grenzboten*, 14/1 (1855), 281–7.

popularity in some circles, but it did not please the authorities. After having been warned by his superiors to stop corrupting the young, he resigned from Heidelberg; eventually he taught for several years at Zurich before moving to Turin and finally to Rome. Although he lived until 1893, his fame rested on the work he did in the early 1850s.[36]

Ludwig Büchner also tried to fashion a philosophy of life from the accomplishments of mid-century science. Like Moleschott, Büchner was a physician's son; born in 1824, he had been a schoolboy when his elder brother Georg's meteoric career ended in his early death. After a somewhat restless youth, Ludwig settled down in 1852 as an assistant to a Professor of Medicine in Tübingen. Here, working in his spare time, he wrote *Kraft und Stoff*, which went through sixteen editions between 1855 and 1889. As is often the case with widely influential works, *Kraft und Stoff* owed its success to its author's synthetic skills rather than his originality. Drawing on the work of Moleschott and other contemporaries, Büchner provided a lucid, forceful, and highly accessible version of the new, scientifically based materialism. Since *Kraft* and *Stoff*—energy and matter—were eternal, he argued, the world could not have been created. 'How can anyone deny the axiom, that out of nothing, nothing can arise.' What we take to be spiritual is produced by complex material phenomena: our brains generate thought, he says at one point, just as a steam-engine produces motion. All true knowledge, therefore, is scientific knowledge, the empirically based data we gather about the only world that exists. Büchner, like Moleschott, lived into the 1890s, but he too never repeated his youthful success; he remained primarily known as the author of *Kraft und Stoff*, the object of the admiration or acrimony this book continued to generate.[37]

Soon after Darwin's *Origin of Species* was published in 1859, German materialists recognized it as a key text to support their campaign against theology and idealism. Even though the first translation of the book, by the paleontologist Heinrich Bronn, was both inaccurate and unsympathetic, Darwinian ideas swiftly found defenders among German scientists and, more important, among scientific popularizers. Ernst Haeckel, the young zoologist who would become the most persistent and influential German Darwinian, told the 1863 meeting of the Gesellschaft Deutscher Naturforscher und Ärtze that evolution equalled progress, 'a natural law

---

[36] Gregory, *Materialism*, pp. 89, 91–3, 96.
[37] Binkley, *Realism*, p. 8. On Büchner, see Gregory, *Materialism*, pp. 100 ff.

that no human power, neither the weapons of tyrants nor the curses of priests, can ever succeed in suppressing'. That year Carl Vogt, whose materialist views were cut from the same cloth as Moleschott's and Büchner's, incorporated evolutionary ideas into his *Vorlesungen über den Menschen*. In 1868 Büchner himself embraced Darwin, whom he praised for reuniting biology and philosophy without falling into the empty verbiage of traditional natural philosophy. By the time a revised and complete translation of Darwin's works was published in 1875, his ideas had passed into the mainstream of German culture. Eventually, his influence was probably greater in Germany than anywhere else in Europe, including Britain.[38]

This receptivity to Darwin, as well as the persistent popularity of men like Vogt, Moleschott, and Büchner, underscore the fascination that science held for many educated Germans. Perhaps this fascination was in some way connected to the decline of political ideals following the liberal defeats in 1848. Certainly there were people who, as Büchner put it in 1855, turned 'to the powerfully unfolding researches of natural science, in which . . . [they] see a new kind of opposition against the triumphant reaction'.[39] But science's impact on culture had deeper roots than this and lasted even when the political climate changed again at the end of the 1850s. As a source of values and explanation of the world, science was both cause and reflection of the secularization of culture that occurred everywhere in nineteenth-century Europe. Moreover, scientific values and modes of thinking were obviously sustained by the unmistakable changes taking place in medicine and public health, transportation and communication, production and distribution. Every inoculation, train ride, or telegram seemed to underscore the role science played in the conduct of human affairs.

A belief in the power of scientific knowledge and the importance of scientific achievements made it easier for some people to embrace philosophical materialism. But many scientists continued to have rather conventional theological views. Liebig, for example, argued in his 'Chemische Briefe' that science was not incompatible with revelation and could, if properly viewed, lead its practitioners closer to God. While Fechner rejected that 'unedifying scaffolding which theologians generally build around Christianity', he wrote at

---

[38] Kelly, *Descent*, p. 22. In addition to Kelly's book, see Montgomery, 'Germany', which emphasizes Darwin's impact on German biology.

[39] Kelly, *Descent*, p. 19.

length about God and the soul, which he took to be quite compatible with his psychophysical theories.[40]

Fechner's student, Rudolf Hermann Lotze, also tried to combine science and religion. But, despite his repeated efforts to create a unified philosophy that would bring together his faith in a personal God and his commitment to scientific knowledge, Lotze was forced into a dualistic view of the world which anticipates neo-Kantianism. Human thought, he concluded, could not arrive at final answers; it 'is tentative, and is debarred by the frailty of human knowledge from the possibility of arriving at absolute certainty'. We can, therefore, grasp the mechanical order which governs the world of things and can try to understand the ideal order which governs the world of values, but the ultimate connection between the two will always elude us. Virtually forgotten today, Lotze was extremely influential throughout the second half of the nineteenth century, both in Germany, where he taught at Göttingen and Berlin, and in Britain and the United States. George Santayana, for example, chose Lotze's ideas as the subject of the dissertation he wrote for Josiah Royce at Harvard in the 1880s.[41]

Friedrich Albert Lange, like Lotze, tried to find a place to attack materialistic reductionism without rejecting science or falling into mysticism. Lange's three-volume *History of Materialism* examined the evolution of materialism from ancient times to the present age, in which he found 'a general enfeeblement of philosophical effort' and 'a retrogression of ideas'. Now, Lange went on, 'the perishable material to which our forefathers gave the stamp of the sublime and divine . . . is devoured by the flames of criticism'. However, he remained optimistic. In words that reflect the scientific idiom of his age, Lange declared that, 'as in the circuit of nature from the decay of lower materials new life struggles into being and higher phenomena appear when the old have disappeared, so we may expect a new impulse of ideas will advance humanity another stage.' These ideas will come neither from orthodox religion nor from materialist science; both ways of thinking have their uses, but they promise certainties that they cannot deliver. The new ideal must be based on ethical imperatives that take into account our epistemological limitations. Nietzsche, who was much taken by

[40] Harold Höffding, *A History of Modern Philosophy* (2 vols.; London, 1908), 528.
[41] Thomas Willey, *Back to Kant: The Revival of Kantianism in German Social and Historical Thought, 1860–1914* (Detroit, 1978), 49.

Lange's book soon after it appeared in 1866, called it a 'an outstanding and instructive work' by a 'highly enlightened Kantian and natural scientist'. Unfortunately, Lange was never able to develop his ideas: politically active in the 1860s he went into exile after the liberal defeat in 1866, and did not return to academic life until he was given a university position at Marburg just three years before his early death in 1875.[42]

No compelling synthesis united German philosophers during the second half of the century. The fragmentation of philosophy, already apparent in the decades after Hegel's death, persisted. Moreover, the scope of philosophical enquiry seemed to narrow as the impulse to create an ordering synthesis declined. Some thinkers, like Lotze and Lange, focused their attention on epistemology, through which they tested the nature and limits of scientific knowledge. Others gave philosophy a psychological thrust, following, like Nietzsche, the path taken by Schopenhauer, whose influence steadily increased after 1850. Finally, some academic philosophy became essentially historical, devoting itself to the recovery and transmission of ideas from the past. To this historical tradition we owe the great works on the Greeks by Eduard Zeller and the impressive syntheses of philosophical development by Wilhelm Windelband.[43]

Despite the extraordinary intellectual and material power of science, scientific methods were no more able to provide the basis for a new philosophical synthesis than idealism had been two generations earlier. Nor did science triumph in other disciplines. Except for empirical psychology, most of what Germans called the 'human sciences' preserved their intellectual and institutional independence. Historians, philosophers, philologists, and literary scholars insisted that their *Wissenschaft*—significantly, the German term for 'science' is not limited to the natural sciences—had distinctive methods appropriate to their own subject matter and purpose. Moreover, these humanistic disciplines were no less professionalized than their scientific counterparts. As we saw in Chapter 9, the German university had sustained the growth of professional research in philology and history two decades before most scientific disciplines were formed.

During the 1850s and 1860s Johann Gustav Droysen attempted

---

[42] Lange, *History*, iii. 359–60; Nietzsche, *Briefwechsel* pt. 1, vol. ii, p. 159. On Lange, see the book by Thomas Willey cited in n. 41, pp. 83 ff.

[43] There is a summary of these developments in Schädelbach, *Philosophy*. See also Martini, *Literatur*, pp. 25 ff.

to define a distinctive method for the human sciences. Whereas philosophers like Lotze and Lange went back to Kant to set limits on the natural sciences' claim to truth, Droysen adapted the historical methods of Herder and Wilhelm von Humboldt. Droysen was not opposed to science or the scientific method. 'We must,' he wrote, 'without envy, give the prize to the natural sciences for what they accomplish' in the promotion of freedom and practical progress. Moreover, we should note carefully why science is so successful:

The energy of these branches of learning comes from their having a completely clear consciousness of their problems, their means, their methods, and from the fact that they consider the things which they draw into the compass of their investigations under those points of view, and those only, upon which their method is based.

This self-consciousness about the necessary relationship between method and subject-matter is precisely what those who would apply scientific procedures to the study of human affairs lack. In Droysen's view, they fail to see that the human world, unlike the world of nature, is a realm of freedom, of purpose, and, above all, of history. 'Man's essential concept of humanity is history, the common life and creation in this great continuity, this collective and progressive labour of humanity.' The world of history, Droysen insisted, is *our* world. In contrast to the world of animals and things, which is inevitably alien to us, we share a common humanity with the subject-matter of historical investigation. This community of observer and subject establishes the basis for the historian's method: 'The possibility of understanding assumes that in us, the observers, can be found the same ethical and intellectual categories that are expressed in those we are trying to understand.' In a series of lectures, conventionally called the *Historik*, which he began to deliver at the University of Berlin in 1857, Droysen spelled out the peculiar problems and possibilities in this mode of understanding, *Verstehen*, which he believed would provide know-ledge about historical individuals and about the historical process itself. Droysen, therefore, shared the optimism and ambition of his scientific contemporaries, even when he questioned the relevance of their methods to his own discipline. Historical *Verstehen* was different from, but in no sense inferior to, the scientists' modes of analysis.[44]

The resistance to the scientific study of human behaviour, so

[44] Johann Gustav Droysen, *Outline of the Principles of History* (Boston, 1893), 61,

powerfully exemplified by Droysen, inhibited the growth of the new positivist social sciences in most of German Europe. Even economics, in some ways the subject most amenable to abstract analysis and quantifiable investigation, remained closer to history than to mathematics. The new social sciences, such as anthropology or sociology, were slow to develop in the German academic environment. During the middle decades of the century, this resistance to the social sciences often made some German scholarship seem parochial and isolated, cut off from the main currents of contemporary thought. But towards the end of the century, when a widespread reaction against positivism's approach to the study of human affairs set in, a number of German thinkers swiftly moved into positions of European pre-eminence.

iii. THE PROBLEM OF LITERARY REALISM

'Literary realism' is an oxymoron, a contradiction in terms. As Nietzsche once observed, 'all good artists imagined they were realistic', just as all artists must, by definition, create a world of artifice and contrivance. Art must be a mixture of truth and falsehood, reality and illusion. The interesting question to ask about those who called themselves 'realists' is not why they suddenly began to deal with 'reality'—artists have never done anything else—but rather why they felt it necessary to announce that that was what they were about. *Realism*, therefore, may not be a very helpful term to describe what mid-century artists and writers were actually doing, but its use does raise questions about how they tried to understand and justify their work.[45]

In the 1840s the term *realism* made its way from France into the discussions of contemporary issues held by young artists and writers in Dresden and Berlin. After mid-century the capital of German realism became Leipzig, German Europe's publishing centre and the home of the *Grenzboten*, a periodical edited by Julian Schmidt and Gustav Freytag, who were both tireless defenders of the new style. For them, realism was, most of all, a break with the

and *Historik*, p. 17. There is a good, brief treatment of Droysen in Iggers, *Conception*, and Schnädelbach, *Philosophy*, ch. 4. On his political views, see below, sect. iv.

[45] On German literature during this period, see Martini, *Literatur*, the sources edited by Bücher *et al.*, *Realismus*; and the essays by J. P. Stern published in *Re-Interpretations* and *Idylls*.

past and especially with romanticism, which Schmidt regarded as an alienated and alienating artistic mode, without content, principle, or form. Romanticism was medieval and Catholic, realism enlightened and Protestant; romanticism was sick and self-indulgent, realism was healthy and socially useful; romanticism fostered illusion and evasion, realism confronted the world as it is. As befitted a contemporary of Virchow and Helmholtz, Schmidt urged German writers and artists to base their work on observation and experience, not tradition and speculation. Only then could they establish what he regarded as the 'foundation for a great and genuine literature . . . the expansion and penetration of moral ideas into the details of real life'. Freytag believed that realism 'in art, science, religion, and politics is nothing other than the first cultural stage of a new generation, which seeks to spiritualize every aspect of contemporary life in order to give new content to sensibilities'.[46]

Many literary theorists were convinced that the novel was the most appropriate genre with which to fulfil the realist mission. The novel, according to the critic Robert Prutz, was the 'the most genuine expression of our highly mobile, intertwined, and confusing modern life'. Friedrich Spielhagen called it a declaration of faith in the reality of life as 'the source from which our joys and sorrows flow'. Hegel, in a famous phrase, had defined the novel 'as the epic of the bourgeois age', because, like the epic, the novel tried to evoke a total world, but a world without poetic universality, a world of individualism and prose. During the 1850s Theodor Vischer developed Hegel's analysis in a number of influential works on aesthetics. For Vischer, the bourgeois novel was 'the genuine normal species', the perfect reflection of a secular, empirical, disenchanted society. The novel's central theme was the struggle between personal ambition and desire, between social values and constraints, between individual irrationality and social rationality, between what Hegel called 'the heart's poetry and the external world's contrasting prose'.[47]

One of the first important novels to appear in Germany in the 1850s was Karl Gutzkow's *Die Ritter vom Geiste*. Written in the wake of the revolution's defeat and published in 1850 and 1851, *Die Ritter* was monumental in both size (it ran to well over four thousand pages in nine volumes) and ambition. In it, Gutzkow intended to present a portrait of his entire society, a vast canvas on

---

[46] Bücher *et al.*, (eds.), *Realismus*, i. 41, ii. 78; Freytag, *Bilder*, iv. 2–3. There is a stimulating analysis of these theories of realism in Berman, *Rise*, ch. 4.

[47] Martini, *Literatur*, pp. 390 ff.

which every group and contemporary issue would find its place. The result, he hoped, would be a novel of *Nebeneinanders*—the term Lessing had used for representation in the visual arts—showing the inherent interconnectedness of individuals and classes. In fact, Gutzkow did succeed in achieving some striking descriptions of contemporary society, as well as a sustained critique of the emptiness of post-revolutionary public life. But the book as a whole lacks stylistic coherence and structural cohesion; what the author intended to be complexity often becomes merely confusion or contrived connection. More important, the political conspiracy that gives the book its title is peculiarly vague and uncertain—what exactly the 'Ritter vom Geiste' want and how they will get it are left very much up in the air. Nor was Gutzkow's message helped along by events in the real world: no sooner had he sent his fictional conspirators across the border into the progressive west than Louis Napoleon destroyed the French republic and laid the basis for his authoritarian regime.[48]

Gutzkow's novel was, however, a popular success. The dramatist Friedrich Hebbel admired it as a 'historical daguerreotype' and Theodor Storm wrote that it was 'really a deed, this book, such as the times demand'. Some spokesmen for realistic literature, however, were appalled by *Die Ritter vom Geiste*. They were offended by its critical stance towards society, scandalized by the thinly disguised portraits of important contemporaries, and dismayed by the persistent idealism of its politics. Julian Schmidt's hostile review in *Grenzboten* set off one of the great literary feuds of the decade. One would like to admire Gutzkow, Schmidt concluded, but 'the pretensions that the writer assumes are so great and what he has accomplished so meagre, that the critic would not be doing his duty if he did not accurately assess the book'.[49]

Much closer to Schmidt's notion of what realistic fiction ought to be was *Soll und Haben*, the phenomenally successful novel published in 1855 by his friend and collaborator, Gustav Freytag. Freytag was almost forty when *Soll und Haben* appeared; after a brief academic career, he had worked as a writer and critic and, since 1848, as co-editor of the *Grenzboten*. Freytag turned to fiction in order to advance the values he believed should guide the social

---

[48] On Gutzkow's early career, see above, ch. 9. sect. iv. Gutzkow stated his aspirations in the introduction to his novel, which is reprinted in Bücher *et al.* (eds.), *Realismus*, ii. 312 ff.

[49] Herbert Kaiser, *Studien zum deutschen Roman nach 1848* (Duisberg, 1977), 9; Martini, *Literatur*, p. 413; Bücher *et al.* (eds.), *Realismus*, ii. 314 ff.

and political world: Prussian supremacy in a unified nation, moderate liberal constitutionalism, stable *bürgerlich* virtues, and enlightened Protestantism. The best place to discover and display these values, he believed, was 'in our offices, our workrooms, and our fields. . . . The German is at his greatest and most beautiful when he is at work.' As its title suggests, *Soll und Haben*—debit and credit—is a novel about commerce. Within its first few pages, the novel's hero, Anton Wohlfart, agrees to follow his father's advice and become a merchant. Eight hundred pages and innumerable adventures later, Anton becomes the proprietor of a fine old firm, whose fortunes have been valiantly protected by his bride-to-be, the beauteous but businesslike Sabine.

Soll und Haben went through six printings in two years, thirty in the next fifteen; its popularity persisted well into the twentieth century. Freytag's contemporaries obviously were charmed by Anton's strenuous journey from his father's modest house in Ostrau—'a small county town near the Oder, known as far as the Polish frontier for its *Gymnasium* and sweet *Pfefferkuchen*'—to the director's office of T. O. Schröter in Breslau. Moreover, they must have found something inspiring and comforting in the alleged portrait of themselves that Freytag offered: Anton is virtuous in every important way, thrifty, honest, and kind; he triumphs over his enemies and overcomes the temptations offered him by the conniving Jew, Veitel Itzig, and the decadent noble, Baron Rothsattel. In the end, Freytag assures us, the dreams that he 'nourished under the blessings of his good parents' were honest dreams, uncorrupted by false ambitions and excessive passion. Like Gutzkow's *Ritter*, this is a post-revolutionary novel, but the message it offers is quite different from Gutzkow's vague Utopia. Instead Freytag provides the impressive but not extravagant rewards of probity and diligence: a thriving business, an affectionate family, a secure place in the social order. After what Freytag called the 'confusions of the past years', which have been filled with 'national anxiety and exhaustion', it is the poet's duty to offer the nation a 'mirror of its *Tüchtigkeit*' for pleasure and inspiration.[50]

Like *Soll und Haben*, Wilhelm Raabe's *Der Hungerpastor* begins by describing the secure comforts of home. Raabe's hero, Hans Unwirrsch, is the long-awaited son of a shoemaker, whose craft is

---

[50] Quotations from Bücher *et al.* (eds.), *Realismus*, ii. 73; Freytag, *Soll und Haben* (Munich and Vienna, 1977), 836, and the dedication to Duke Ernst of Coburg on p. 9. T. E. Carter, 'Freytag's *Soll und Haben*. A Liberal National Manifesto as Best Seller', *German Life and Letters*, 21/4 (July 1968), has data on the novel's popularity.

THE AGE OF THE *BÜRGERTUM*: CULTURE

lovingly rendered in the novel's first chapter. But his father dies
early, and among the things for which Hans hungers is a family's
warmth and protection. As a precocious schoolboy, theology
student, and private tutor, Hans goes his innocent way, propelled
by an appetite for love, knowledge, and enlightenment. He finally
finds satisfaction within himself, in a modest world of domesticity
and public service as the pastor of an isolated Baltic village.
Interwoven with Hans's story is that of his *alter ego*, Moses
Freudenstein, who ruthlessly pursues fame and fortune as a student
of philosophy, writer, *émigré* intellectual, police spy, and finally
privy councillor. Moses's external success in the great world of
politics is accompanied by his internal corruption and social
alienation. Freudenstein was, Raabe tells us, 'despised by those
who used him, and despised by those against whom he was used.
. . . [he was] socially dead in the most frightful sense of the
word.'[51] *Der Hungerpastor* is filled with comments critical of
thoughtless anti-Semitism, but Raabe's contrast between the
virtuous Hans and the malevolent Moses deepened that stereo-
typical view of German and Jew that we saw in Freytag's portrait of
Anton and Veitel. Although Raabe continued to write until the end
of the century, none of his books was as popular as *Der
Hungerpastor*, whose celebration of innocence, modesty, and self-
sacrifice illuminates an important facet of the German *Bürgertum*'s
idealized self-image.

The publication of Friedrich Spielhagen's *Problematische Naturen*
(1861–2) established his place among the foremost spokesman for
the post-revolutionary *Bürgertum*. Fritz Martini has called the novel
a 'Stimmungsgeschichte of Vormärz', a sustained account of the
author's search for an intellectual, social, and political position.
Spielhagen pursues this larger purpose within the context of a
characteristically nineteenth-century story of family fortunes and
individual careers, intrigues and ambitions, temporary failures and
eventual success. His hero, Dr Oswald Stein, appears as a tutor to a
noble family, one of a long literary line of young men forced to
undergo the psychological and practical pressures of dependence.
But Dr Stein is not an unmanned victim like Lenz's tragic
Hofmeister; intelligent, well-mannered, and strong, he wins the
friendship of an enlightened aristocrat with whom he joins in a
struggle against the unearned and outmoded privileges of the feudal
caste. In its sharp attacks on the nobility, as well as in the latent

---

[51] Raabe, *Der Hungerpastor*, p. 461. See Barker Fairley, *Wilhelm Raabe: An
Introduction to his Novels* (Oxford, 1961).

desire for social reconciliation it reflects, Spielhagen's novel beautifully captures the ambivalence many German burghers felt towards the traditional élite.[52]

Despite the accomplishments and success of Gutzkow, Freytag, Raabe, and Spielhagen, the best German writers in the 1850s and 1860s were more comfortable with, and productive in, the novella rather than the novel. The difference between the two genres is not simply length: unlike the novel, the novella does not seek to create a unified world, but rather concentrates on a single event or character, usually seen in one place and often within a limited period of time. As Vischer put it, 'The novella is to the novel what a ray is to a mass of light.' Instead of presenting a comprehensive picture of the world, the novella concentrates with great intensity on a slender segment of reality. Delicately crafted, deceptively modest in theme and style, and lyrically evocative of a particular region or village, the novellas produced by Adalbert Stifter, Gottfried Keller, and Theodor Storm rank with the finest examples of this literary form.[53]

In both their novels and novellas, realist writers chose natural settings that contrasted sharply with the romantics' imaginary landscapes. For most realists, nature was not an occasion for introspection. Even poets like Droste or Mörike, who were deeply concerned with emotional states, give us clear and concrete pictures of the world outside themselves. Stifter, who had had ambitions to be a painter, carefully reproduced the fields, forests, and gardens within which his characters move. Furthermore, the realists' landscape is apt to be pastoral rather than primitive, a landscape of ploughed fields rather than trackless forests, carefully tended cottages rather than abandoned ruins, fenced-in gardens rather than open spaces. This is the landscape that appears in the painter Ludwig Richter's pastoral scenes, such as his *Spring Evening* of 1844, in which two lovers sit together, joined through affection rather than passion, in a benign natural world under a cloudless sky.[54]

The harmonious interplay between man and nature, which provides the setting and theme for a great deal of realist literature, was not to be found in big cities. Few mid-century German writers—or their literary creations—felt comfortable in an urban

---

[52] Martini, *Literatur*, p. 427. Bramstedt, *Aristocracy*, ch. 4, analyses Spielhagen in the context of contemporary attitudes towards the aristocracy.

[53] Bücher *et al.*, (eds.), *Realismus*, ii. 363. For an introduction to the genre, see Martin Swales, *The German Novelle* (Princeton, 1977).

[54] See Prawer's discussion of poetic realism in *Poetry*, ch. 9.

environment. Unlike his French counterpart, the German novel's young man from the provinces does not treat the city as a mistress to be won or an enemy to be conquered; instead, the urban world is a source of isolation and estrangement. Vienna, wrote Stifter in 1844, is a 'colossal wilderness of walls and roofs, countless crowds of human beings, all strangers to one another as they hurry past'. Wilhelm Raabe described this same sense of loneliness when he recalled his arrival in Berlin a decade later: 'Without acquaintances or friends in the big city, I was thrown back on myself and had to imagine my own world. . . .' Raabe used this experience as the basis for his first novel, *Chronik der Sperlingsgasse*, which describes life on the street (actually Spreegasse) where he lived from 1854 to 1856. Essentially, Raabe tells the story of Sperlingsgasse as though it were a village; in the course of the book we get to know in dense detail the life within its confines, but the world beyond, in the nameless city, is left vague, uncertain, and contingent. In *Der Hungerpastor* the hero must flee from the city to find himself, while the villain flourishes there like a green bay tree.[55]

A characteristic setting for German realistic fiction was the village, which became the basis for a special genre after the publication of Berthold Auerbach's *Schwarzwälder Dorfgeschichte* in 1843. The son of a Jewish family from a Black Forest village, student of Hebrew theology and then secular philosophy, liberal activist and professional writer, Auerbach viewed rural life with affectionate detachment. Like his contemporary 'Jeremias Gotthelf', the pseudonym of the Swiss clergyman who wrote a series of popular novels set in the rural parish where he lived from 1831 to 1854, Auerbach hoped that his celebration of farming and village society would be read for entertainment and enlightenment by the people he described. Instead, Auerbach and Gotthelf found their audience among members of the urban middle strata who were fascinated by and often nostalgic for a vanishing social world. After mid-century, writers such as Theodor Storm, Stifter, and Keller extended and enriched the conventions and tone of the *Dorfgeschichte*, which, as F. T. Vischer pointed out in 1857, became the modern equivalent of the classical Idyll, a 'Sittenbildchen' with an expanded plot designed to meet the prevailing taste for narrative.[56]

---

[55] Sagarra, *Tradition*, p. 226; Volker Klotz, *Die erzählte Stadt. Ein Sujet als Herausforderung des Romans von Lessing bis Döblin* (Munich, 1969), 167. Klotz has a fine analysis of the image of the city in Raabe's novel.

[56] Bücher *et al.* (eds.), *Realismus*, ii. 189. On Gotthelf, see Pascal, *Novel*, pp. 101–45.

Another popular setting for mid-century fiction was the small town: 'eine mittlere Stadt', as Friedrich Hebbel tersely describes the place where his tragedy, *Maria Magdalene*, occurs. Without the dynamism and anonymity of the big city, the town had a greater social range than the village. In addition to craftsmen and peasants from the surrounding countryside, merchants, civil servants, even the occasional *Bildungsbürger* move through its streets. Perhaps the classic realist town is Keller's Seldwyla, the location of his two great volumes of collected novellas published in 1856 and 1874. Seldwyla, which lies 'somewhere in Switzerland', is still 'surrounded by the same old walls and towers as three centuries ago and thus is still the same nest . . . beautifully set amid green mountains, open on the midday side so that the sun might enter but not a harsh wind'. Unlike many fictional towns, Keller's has an intense political life—inhabitants are 'passionate partisans, constitutional critics, and motion makers'—but the scale of Seldwyla's politics is too small to be threatening; disagreements that might be dangerous in Berlin or Vienna can here be treated with gentle irony. The townspeople, after all, know that they must live with one another.[57]

Often the realist's village or town has a strong regional character. This was most obviously true in the works of dialect writers like John Brinckman and Fritz Reuter, whose tales of local life and characters take on a special charm because of the idiom in which they appear. But the distinctive character of a region, that blend of natural conditions and human customs which Germans began to call their *Heimat*, was important to many writers in the 1850s and 1860s. Keller's and Gotthelf's characters are manifestly Swiss, just as Storm's are shaped by the very different environment of Holstein. Stifter, although he lived in Vienna and Linz, spiritually stayed close to the Bohemian forests in which he was reared.

Whatever its regional or social setting, the central institution in realist fiction was the family. Characteristically, the narrative begins by evoking the fragile innocence and security of childhood and ends happily in marriage or tragically in familial dissolution. Often the dramatic turning-points are leave-takings or home-comings, the abandonment or recapturing of the family's material support and emotional sustenance. Life outside the family is difficult, perhaps even impossible to imagine. In Hebbel's *Maria Magdalena*, for example, the heroine, seduced and then abandoned

---

[57] Keller, *Leute*, pp. 7, 9. For a sophisticated psychological and social analysis of Keller's work, see Kaiser, *Keller*.

by a man she does not love, sees no choice but death; within the confines of her world, saturated with Christian morals and *bürgerlich* values, there is no middle way. Even more striking is the case of Keller's Romeo and Juliet, who have a chance to join a group of vagabonds and nurture their love in the forest, beyond social bonds. But, Keller tells us, 'the feeling that it was possible to be happy in the social world only in an honest and moral marriage' was strong in both the lovers. Since such a marriage was out of the question, death was their only alternative.[58]

Much of the emotional energy that these writers pumped into their portraits of family happiness and misery was drawn from their own, often turbulent domestic situations. Hebbel wrote *Maria Magdalena* while he was trying to end a long, painful relationship with a woman who had supported him and borne his children. The play was first performed the year he married someone else, the actress upon whose income he was to depend for several years. Keller never married; until his late twenties he was the guilty recipient of aid from his widowed mother; after her death, his sister became the most important woman in his life. Not surprisingly, Keller's *Grüne Heinrich* is loaded with familial longings and frustrations: it is, as one critic wrote, a 'novel of mother–son guilt about a lost father', which ends when the hero returns to his mother's grave.[59] Adalbert Stifter endured a long, loveless marriage, tormented by childlessness. He tried to conceal or transform imaginatively the emotional emptiness of his married life with a remarkable series of affectionate letters to his wife— another example of that mysterious interpenetration of art and life.

Many realists depicted all social relationships within a familial mode and from a domestic perspective. The characteristic professions—especially of the heroes—in the novels and stories of the 1850s and 1860s are those in which economic activities take place at home, in a domestic setting. The commercial establishment described in Freytag's *Soll und Haben* is clearly patriarchal; the proprietor lives where he works and treats his employees with a father's firm authority. The shoemaker, so carefully described in *Der Hungerpastor*'s opening chapter, practises his craft a few steps away from wife and child. Keller's Romeo and Juliet play together as children while their fathers plough the field whose contested ownership will eventually destroy them. Work and family blend into one another, concern the same people, and are governed by the

---

[58] Keller, *Leute*, p. 140.
[59] Kaiser, *Keller*, p. 42.

same rules. Together, they form the world in which most narratives unfold.

Because this fictional world unites the realms of love and work, it is at once cohesive and vulnerable. Success brings both material and emotional rewards—at the end of his story, Anton Wohlfart can look forward to a flourishing family and firm. But the threat of failure is everywhere present, in the private as well as the public realm, in uncontrolled desire and unreasonable ambition, faithless lovers and dishonest employees, seduction and bankruptcy. Klara in Hebbel's *Maria Magdalena* is undone by an interconnected set of mistakes, including her own weakness and her father's miscalculations. Behind the particular fate of individuals lie great dangers, threats to the entire social world of village and town, peasant and craftsman, merchant and pastor. Writers and readers of mid-century fiction knew that these worlds were at risk, undermined by powerful cultural and economic forces. Writers and readers shared the knowledge that someday soon Seldwyla would become like any other town, expanding beyond its walls, enveloping the surrounding countryside, sacrificing its own special qualities. This knowledge could easily lead to sentimentality or shallow nostalgia, but in the best writing of the age—in some of Stifter, Keller, and Mörike, for example—it could become a moving evocation of lost innocence and fading beauty.

Even though his plots sometimes seem almost static, no mid-century writer was more aware of the power of change than Adalbert Stifter. Like many of those whose work we have mentioned, Stifter came from the periphery: he was born in 1805, in a small Bohemian town, then studied law in Vienna, where he lived in poverty after his father's death. Until well into his thirties he had to support himself as a tutor to noble families, among them the Metternichs. Stifter began writing and painting while still living in the capital, recreating in both media portraits of the world he had left behind—pastoral, childlike, secure. When the revolution began, Stifter was initially enthusiastic; he had seen enough of the Austrian élite to know that much needed to be changed. Within a few weeks, however, he was frightened and disillusioned by the violence, the potential chaos, and the absence of immediate reform. In 1849 he finally succeeded in gaining an official position as school inspector at Linz, where he spent almost twenty years, attending to petty bureaucratic tasks, dealing with his quarrelsome wife, eating too much rich food, and coping with an increasing array of ailments, both mental and physical. He also continued to write essays, stories, and two novels, one of which, *Der Nachsommer*, is widely regarded as a major contribution to that characteristically German genre, the *Bildungsroman*.[60]

Der Nachsommer begins where *Soll und Haben* ends. 'My father', the hero, Heinrich Drendorf, tells us, 'was a merchant'. At home, Heinrich learns about property, culture, and nature; his father is interested in all three, although he must deal with them separately, in his office, library and picture room, and garden. After swiftly achieving a degree of financial independence, Heinrich devotes himself to natural history, the careful collection and description of flora and fauna from the surrounding area. To do this, he must wander farther and farther from home—and from his father's world. On one of these journeys he comes upon Rosenhaus, the estate of a retired civil servant, Baron von Risach, who soon becomes Heinrich's second father and educator. Heinrich's *Bildung* is a gradual, indirect process; he does not learn by confronting crises or dramatic events (of which Stifter's plot is totally devoid), nor does he gain much explicit instruction from Risach. Instead, the hero is slowly absorbed into Rosenhaus and the social and moral order it represents. Eventually, he sees that, just as Rosenhaus's beauty comes from its integration into its natural setting, so Risach's moral strength comes from his harmonious relationship to the external world. In art and in life, one must seek to avoid the dislocations that can be caused by unbridled passions and excessive spontaneity. Stifter's style seems to replicate the moral lesson he wants his hero—and his readers—to learn; he writes without passion or spontaneity, self-consciously submitting to the material he describes, depicting in painstaking detail the cohesive universe of which he wishes us to be a part. In *Der Nachsommer*, Stifter once wrote, 'I wanted to counterpoise a great simple ethical force against the wretched degeneration [of the times]'. This force must impress itself on the individual spirit and can best express itself within the small community of family and estate. Here Stifter found his instruments and models, the means and end of regeneration.[61]

Certainly some German writers in the 1850s and 1860s had a better sense of social reality than Stifter. Freytag, Raabe, Hebbel,

[60] There are good analyses of Stifter in Stern, *Idylls*, pp. 97 ff.; Berman, *Rise*, ch. 5. For an introduction to the *Bildungsroman*, see Bruford, *Tradition*; Swales, *Bildungsroman*.

[61] Schorske, *Vienna*, p. 283. My treatment of *Der Nachsommer* owes a great deal to Schorske's analysis.

and even Keller recognized the essential interplay of individuals and the larger social world, as well as the determinate relationship between spiritual states and material conditions. But, like Stifter, these writers also feared the excesses of individualism and mourned the passing of a more integrated world; and, like him, they hoped their writing might point the way to new sources of harmony and commitment.

There is, to be sure, nothing especially new or particularly German about this search for harmony and commitment. Since the eighteenth century, every generation of European writers had tried, each in its own way, to reconcile inner drives and external necessities, individual ambition and social possibility. The distinctive feature of this enterprise among the German realists was their emphasis on the need for self-mastery and compromise, restraint and renunciation. Once again, Stifter gives us the most explicit statement of this theme: freedom, he argued, 'demands the most self-control, the most constraint of one's desires'. The enemies of freedom 'are all those people who are possessed by powerful desires and urges, which they wish to gratify by any means'.[62] Such urges have been banished from Rosenhaus. Its owner enjoys the chaste companionship of a woman with whom he was once passionately in love—their summer of desire ended badly, their autumnal friendship is a source of great contentment. In Hebbel's *Judith*, the biblical heroine is seen as the victim of her own desires and frustrations, which lead her to murder and self-destruction. Not accidentally, Judith is the name Keller gave to the sensual woman in his green Heinrich's early life; in the second version of the novel, Judith and Heinrich are reunited, but as friends, not lovers. Even Mörike, for whom love is often a central theme, eschews the romantics' burning passions and bright desire; he is given to more muted feelings, memories and expectations, ambivalent expressions of *Schmerzensglück* suitable for those moments of dawn or twilight in which so many of his poems are set. In 'Mein Fluss', Mörike's feelings are as cool as the poem's central image—water and refreshment, not fire and consumption, are his symbols for love.[63]

The social equivalents of moral restraint are resignation and withdrawal. Risach's Rosenhaus, like *Der Hungerpastor*'s seaside village, is a retreat, a world of its own set apart from external dangers and demands. There is a chance for solitude in these

[62] Schorske, *Vienna*, p. 281.
[63] On Mörike, see Stern, *Idylls*, pp. 76 ff.

retreats, a solitude which, in a writer like Stifter, seems so natural that man's 'social condition comes to be seen as derivative and his everyday world as provisional'. In the solitary, usually pastoral refuges to which so many German realists were drawn, we can find the mid-century equivalents of what Robert Minder has identified as a central topos in German literature: 'the world outside is barren, while within is the protective circle of the house . . . the basic unit of community, behind which is the victorious inner realm.' Like the children in Stifter's 'Bergkristall', who find refuge in a cave, the characters in mid-century fiction often escape a world filled with disorder, dangerous ambitions, and destructive passions.[64]

This was not a climate in which drama could flourish. Of course Germans remained enthusiastic theatregoers, but they were most apt to see classic revivals, imported pieces, or lightweight comedy and melodrama. Prutz was not surprised by the dismal condition of German drama in the 1850s. 'Where can we find the strength, where should we take the courage for a literary form whose essence is action, action which embodies and culminates in vital, vigorous elements?'[65] Indeed, the two greatest German dramatists at mid-century both wrote plays in which the price of action is usually terrible and swift.

Franz Grillparzer, whose troubles with the Austrian censor we observed in Chapter 7, by the 1840s no longer tried to have his work performed. After having been briefly inspired by the promise of change in 1848, he sank further into disillusionment and political passivity. 'The horrors of the last three years and the foolishness of the last twenty or thirty', he wrote in his diary in 1851, 'have produced the conviction in every honest man that he has to support the government and not just as is the duty of honest men in normal times but in a more definite, decisive way.' His last great play, *Ein Bruderzwist in Habsburg*, confronts politics directly, but ends in total despair. The characters, unable to change or to be reconciled with their social order, find all action meaningless.[66]

Friedrich Hebbel, perhaps the last major representative of the classical tradition in German drama, was born in 1813 in Holstein. His family was poor and, despite the help of a series of patrons, Hebbel's own life was blighted by want and uncertainty until he married a well-known Viennese actress in 1846. An extraordinarily

---

[64] Stern, *Idylls*, p. 97; Minder, *Kultur*, pp. 8–9.
[65] Martini, *Literatur*, p. 117.
[66] Grillparzer, *Werke*, iv. 720. See W. E. Yates, *Grillparzer: A Critical Introduction* (Cambridge, 1972).

prolific writer of poetry, essays, and dramas, Hebbel enjoyed a moderate amount of success in the 1850s, when, partly because of his plays, partly because of his wife's position, he became an accepted member of the Viennese theatrical establishment. From his first drama, *Judith*, written and produced in 1840, until *Die Nibelungen* of 1860–1, Hebbel was concerned with the tragic interaction of individual will and social forces. His central figures often suffer from their virtues rather than their vices; because they are strong, beautiful, or patriotic, they set into motion processes that destroy them.[67]

Adalbert Stifter regarded Hebbel as 'grotesque, morally distorted, and unnatural in the extreme' and took some consolation from the fact that, while he worked in Vienna, he was not an Austrian. To Stifter and to most of his contemporaries, good and evil, fate and fortune, suffering and triumph should not be shown through the action of the extraordinary men and women who move across the stage in Hebbel's dramas. Stifter, in the preface to his collection of novellas entitled *Bunte Steine*, denied that greatness was the work of heroes on some epic quest, of warriors or kings; greatness is 'a lifetime full of justice, simplicity, self-satisfaction, moderation, effectiveness in one's own circle, admiration for what is beautiful, bound with a joyfully accepted death'.[68] Even tragedy should be no larger than everyday life. When Gottfried Keller retold the story of Romeo and Juliet, he made the lovers peasants whose fate is sealed by their fathers' foolish fight over a small patch of land. In Keller's version, the unhappy pair's tragic end moves us, not because they are so beautiful and passionate, but because they are so ordinary— except in their commitment to the code that eventually destroys them.

When German writers moved away from the smaller world of domesticity, their writing was likely to become vague and uncertain. Just as Raabe's Sperlingsgasse seems to float in an uncharted urban sea, so Freytag's firm, Stifter's villages, and Keller's town lack clear connections to an extended network of social and political relationships. The sense of a civic world of political action, so powerfully present in a writer like Trollope, is entirely missing from the work of these writers. The portrayal of a spacious social landscape, essential to Balzac and Dickens, is very rare among German realists. Nor can we find many examples of

---

[67] For an introduction to Hebbel, see Edna Purdie, *Friedrich Hebbel. A Study of his Life and Work* (Oxford, 1932).

[68] Bruford, *Tradition*, p. 130; Stifter, *Bunte Steine* (1852; repr. Munich, 1971), 7.

that sure grasp of historical location which distinguishes Eliot or Flaubert; most German fiction is set in some vague present or unspecified past. Again and again, the larger world is subordinated to the smaller one, the public to the private, the outer to the inner. As Roy Pascal has noted, in German literature 'the struggle between personal and social values, which forms the theme of so many European novels, tends to take the form of a struggle between the claims of inner, transcendental values and outer social reality.'[69] In this struggle, both for the author and his creations, the former almost always prevails.

Perhaps because German writers did not feel at home with what J. P. Stern has called 'the common social certainties and *données*' of the age, they could not create a great realistic literature. G. H. Lewes, an avid admirer of all things German, was forced to admit that 'the novels of Germany are singularly inferior to those of France and England. . . . Fiction seems but little suited to the German genius, and novels of real life almost altogether beyond its range.' *Soll und Haben*, Lewes argued, would have been read with appreciation in the west but hardly with the sort of unqualified admiration it found among German readers; it is simply not a distinguished book. Eighty years later, in a lecture on 'The Art of the Novel', Thomas Mann told an audience at Princeton that the 'social novels of Dickens, Thackeray, Tolstoi, Dostoevsky, Balzac, Zola, Proust are the great artistic monuments of the nineteenth century. These are English, Russian, French names—why are the Germans missing?'[70]

Why indeed? Part of the answer may be found in the literary traditions within which German writers had to operate. Since the eighteenth century, German poets and writers had excelled at creating an idiom to explore the depths of their feeling and sensibility, the universal realm of value, and the external world of nature; characteristically, they were much less interested in historical settings, political conditions, or the specifics of a social situation. That web of intermediate connections that exists between the private lives of individuals and their historical, political, and social circumstances was conspicuously neglected by the great figures who established the canons of German literary language, taste, and sensibility.[71]

[69] Pascal, *Novel*, p. 297.

[70] Stern, *Idylls*, p. 7; G. H. Lewes, 'Realism in Art: Modern German Fiction', *Westminster Review*, 70 (Oct. 1858), 491; Hans Mayer, 'Der deutsche Roman des 19. Jahrhunderts', *Deutsche Literatur und Weltliteratur: Aufsätze* (Berlin, 1955), 271.

[71] Stern makes this point in *Re-Interpretations*, ch. 1.

No less important than this literary tradition were the conditions under which German writers had to work. We have already mentioned the censorship that still plagued literary production. Moreover, even after governmental pressures eased in the late 1850s and 1860s, the men running the periodicals that provided the largest market for German fiction discouraged their authors from treating themes and subjects that might disturb the alleged tranquillity of the *Biedermeier* family. The *Gartenlaube*—even the title points to a special kind of literary taste and audience—declared itself to be 'A magazine for house and family . . . a book for large and small . . . far from all political, religious, and other controversies, we want to take you by means of truly good stories into the history of the human heart.' While they were by no means as nonpartisan and unpolitical as they pretended, *Die Gartenlaube* and its counterparts did nourish a literature of domesticity and sentimentality in which political conflicts and social institutions play a subordinate role.[72]

Even those writers who were able to extend the range of literary language and transcend the limitations of *Biedermeier* taste had trouble with that social realm that Europe realists claimed as their own. Most of the writers whose work we have considered remained on the periphery of German society. 'They all come from Nippenburg, whatever its name might be,' Raabe once wrote about the great figures in German literature, 'and they are in no way ashamed of their origins.' Many of those who, like Raabe himself, moved to a big city, fled from it as soon as they could, back to the small, manageable worlds from which they came. 'Dickens had the good fortune to be English,' Berthold Auerbach lamented, 'What are we? Ever and always provincial people. We have no centre that everyone knows, we have no national types. . . . What has Freytag, and what have I done? Only provincial life.'[73] Most European writers had a tense and problematic relationship to their societies, but this conviction of invincible provincialism seems to be distinctly German. From it came a lack of certainty about what social, political, and historical *données* writer and reader share, a basic insecurity about what aspects of life the writer can assume or communicate.

[72] J. M. Ritchie, 'The Ambivalence of "Realism" in German Literature, 1830–1880', *Orbis Litterarum*, 15 (1961), 208. On the position of the writer in this period, see Martini, *Literatur*, especially pp. 82 ff.; Hohendahl, *Kultur*.

[73] H. R. Klieneberger, *The Novel in England and Germany: A Comparative Study* (London, 1981), 110. See Kermit and Kate Champa, *German Painting of the Nineteenth Century* (New Haven, 1970), for a discussion of the impact of this situation on the visual arts.

'To believe that your impressions hold good for others', Virginia Woolf once remarked, 'is to be released from the cramp and confinement of personality.'[74] Because German writers rarely had such a belief, they rarely found such release; instead, they were drawn back, again and again, into the isolated personality of their characters and of themselves. After 1871 German realism would have a brilliant if belated flowering in the novels of Fontane and the paintings of Menzel, Liebermann, Corinth, and Slevogt. But it was not until the turn of the century, when the great age of European realism had passed, that Germans regained their place on the creative edge of cultural achievement. By then most writers came to fear what the Germans seemed to have sensed all along—that their impressions might not hold good for their readers, that their social world was fragmentary, and that their grasp of politics and history uncertain. At this point, 'the cramp and confinement of personality' became the central theme for European art and literature.

iv. THE SEARCH FOR NATIONAL IDENTITY

In an article that he wrote for the *Grenzboten* in 1852, Julian Schmidt tried to explain why there were so few 'patriotic novels' in Germany. The reason, Schmidt argued, was that our 'vital national consciousness does not have a precise focus'. Neither the present nor the past offers much chance to provide such a focus, he continued, 'not because our past lacks historical life . . . but because it is fragmented into small parcels, none of which is strong enough to nourish a living tradition'.[75] Schmidt's assessment of the German condition was just the most recent in a familiar series of patriotic laments. Despite the intellectual foundation laid by Herder and his contemporaries, despite the emotionally charged experiences of the 'national liberation' celebrated by Fichte and Arndt, and despite the struggles of *Burschenschaften*, *Vormärz* liberals, and Frankfurt parliamentarians, the national question remained open, the problem of German identity unsolved. There was no shortage of national consciousness—at least among the readers of the *Grenzboten*—but Germans remained without a way to order their past and control their present.

In the wake of the revolution's collapse, some Germans once

[74] David Daiches, *The Novel and the Modern World* (Chicago and London, 1960), 3.

[75] Bücher *et al.* (eds.), *Realismus*, ii. 278.

again looked to the *Volk* as a source of identity and continuity. For example, in the first volume of his extremely popular *Bilder aus der deutschen Vergangenheit*, Gustav Freytag argued that every *Volk*, like every individual, 'develops spiritually over the course of time . . . [and is] original, characteristic, unique'. Language and mores are not the product or possession of individuals; they are created by and for the *Volk*. 'Without meaning anything mystical,' Freytag concluded, 'one can safely speak of a national soul.' The appeal of this notion to Freytag and his contemporaries is understandable enough; in the absence of political unity or social integration, the *Volksseele* remained, as it had been for Herder, the surest source of national identity. 'After all,' as Jacob Grimm pointed out in the preface to the 1854 edition of his dictionary, 'what else have we in common apart from our language and literature.'[76]

A few years earlier, Richard Wagner had drawn upon these same national traditions when, in an early draft of the concluding chorus for *Die Meistersinger*, he has Hans Sachs and the assembled '*Volk*' exclaim:

> Ehrt Eure deutschen Meister!
> Dann bannt ihr gute Geister!
> Und gebt Ihr ihrem Wirken Gunst,
> Zerging in Dunst
> Das heil'ge röm'sche Reich,
> Uns bliebe gleich
> Die heil'ge deutsche Kunst!

We have already caught glimpses of Richard Wagner at various points in our narrative. Born in 1813, left fatherless by the epidemic following the battle of Leipzig, he had a restless childhood and troubled youth. Despite talent, ambition, and a sure sense of his own destiny, Wagner's early musical career brought him no more than occasional success. Like so many contemporary artists and intellectuals, he prowled the fringes of *Vormärz* society in flight from persistent creditors or in pursuit of elusive opportunities. When he finally was named musical director of the Dresden Opera in 1843, he found some measure of security, but neither the salary necessary to meet his financial needs nor a podium high enough to satisfy his appetite for fame. It is not surprising, therefore, that he was drawn to radical politics. On the eve of the revolution, he proclaimed a new age of destruction and rebirth: 'Denn über allen

---

[76] Freytag, *Bilder*, i. 22–3; Stern, *Idylls*, p. 12. Another example: Böckh, *Volkszahl*, p. 1.

Trummerstätten,' he wrote in February 1848, 'blüht auf des Lebens Glück| Es blieb die Menschheit, frei von Ketten| und die Natur zurück.' A year and a half later, when his revolutionary dreams were in shambles, Wagner fled into exile.[77]

Wagner's main chance came from royal patronage rather than revolutionary transformation. In May 1864 Ludwig II, newly crowned king of Bavaria and a passionate admirer of Wagner's music, summoned the composer to Munich with promises of support for a vast new artistic enterprise. Wagner set out at once to create secure foundations for his music and his own financial future. Wagner's grandiose projects and his immediate needs went naturally together; he never distinguished between his personal interests, his artistic creations, and his increasingly eccentric views about politics and society. Each one blended with and reaffirmed the other. The result of this intermingling of personality, attitudes, and art was most unfortunate because, from the 1860s until the present, writers about Wagner have often concentrated on his character, which was frequently tawdry and devious, or his ideas, which were unfailingly shallow and derivative, at the expense of his music, which is almost always glorious and original.

At one time or another, Wagner's path crossed with some of Europe's most interesting intellectuals—Heine, Nietzsche, Gottfried Keller, Bakunin, Georg Herwegh, and Franz Lizst. He was curious and quick enough to learn something from most of these people. But from his childhood until his death, Wagner was most persistently drawn to and most deeply moved by some form of romanticism. As a boy, he had delighted in the *Biedermeier* mysticism of Weber's *Freischutz*; throughout his life he idolized E. T. A. Hoffmann; in the late 1830s and 1840s he was taken by the political romanticism of the young Germans; and after reading *Die Welt als Wille und Vorstellung* in October 1854, he immediately absorbed Schopenhauer's dark psychological insights. Many aspects of the romantics' vision—their introspective impulses, their fascination with emotion, mystery and myth, their search for new and higher forms of synthesis—corresponded to Wagner's personality and values. Most important, he shared their belief in the prime importance of art as a source of personal meaning, cultural renewal, and political regeneration. Whether as an expression of revolutionary energy or as an instrument of monarchical power, art for

[77] Martin Gregor-Dellin, *Richard Wagner* (Munich, 1962), 256–7; this is a thoughtful, beautifully written biography.

Wagner was the only way to restore that wholeness so painfully absent from the human condition.[78]

Like many romantics, Wagner believed that the Germans had a special role to play in the restoration of wholeness to contemporary culture. As early as his essay on 'Die deutsche Oper', first published in 1834, Wagner pointed to the profound forces at work within the German *Volk*, which he contrasted to the superficial intellectualism of western Europe. At its best—in Bach, for example—German art touched the deepest roots of spiritual and social vitality. Wagner believed that his own work would draw from, and contribute to, this great national mission by helping to bring Germans a new sense of identity and purpose. There were, of course, enemies to be overcome. Just as eighteenth-century courtiers had ignored Bach in favour of French and Italian entertainers, so many of Wagner's contemporary critics praised inferior foreign products at his expense. Moreover, Wagner gradually came to realize that some groups would never be part of the *Volk*. In 'Das Judentum in der Musik', written in 1850, he argued that Jews were permanent aliens and thus inclined to conspire against the *Volk*'s true paladins. When things went wrong, Wagner was quick to put the blame on a conspiracy of the Jewish politicians, bankers, and critics who were allied against him.[79]

Thomas Mann once spoke of 'the romantic purity' of Wagner's nationalism; Wagner, Mann maintained, expressed nationalism 'in its heroic, historically legitimate epoch'.[80] Quite the opposite is true. There is nothing pure or heroic about Wagner's efforts to define German nationality through the creation of negative stereotypes. Like Freytag and Raabe, Wagner anticipates a sinister turn in national consciousness, a movement from the liberal nationalism of *Vormärz* to the xenophobia of the late nineteenth century. Far from nourishing a new, vital culture, the political values in Wagner's art actually encouraged the worst characteristics of those philistines he himself pretended to despise.

One of Wagner's most persistent critics was Wilhelm Heinrich Riehl, who, in addition to being an important social theorist, was also active as a journalist, fiction writer, music critic, and sometime

---

[78] On Wagner's development, see Carl E. Schorske, 'The Quest for the Grail: Wagner and Morris', in K. Wolff and B. Moore (eds.), *The Critical Spirit: Essays in Honor of Herbert Marcuse* (Boston, 1967), 216–32.

[79] Wagner, *Schriften*, vii. 7–10, xiii. 7–28, 158–73.

[80] Thomas Mann, 'Sufferings and Greatness of Richard Wagner', in *Essays of Three Decades* (New York, 1965), 346.

professor at the University of Munich. The reasons for Riehl's animosity to Wagner are not difficult to uncover. A conservative who had mounted a bitter journalistic attack on the revolution of 1848, Riehl was suspicious of Wagner's radical past. 'I am among Wagner's oldest enemies,' he told one of the composer's aristocratic admirers; 'I was already opposed to him when the Royal Saxon Court Conductor stood behind the barricades in Dresden.' Furthermore, as a leading member of King Maximilian of Bavaria's intellectual entourage, Riehl could not help but view Wagner's influence over King Ludwig with a mixture of outrage and envy. How far the new monarch's expensive duets with his favourite must have seemed from the frugal seriousness of the discussions at Maximilian's *Tafelrunde*. Finally and perhaps most important, Riehl was offended by Wagner's claim to speak for the *Volk*: the Germany of Wagnerian opera was not the Germany Riehl knew and loved.[81]

By experience and often by necessity, Wagner was a European intellectual, who had moved often and spent many years abroad. However passionate he might have been about the *Volk* in the abstract, he had little interest in, or affection for, his homeland. For instance, he scornfully dismissed his fellow Saxons as 'dirty, fat, lazy, and crude'. When he returned from exile in 1860, therefore, he was not especially moved: 'Unfortunately, I felt not the slightest emotion when I once again stepped on German soil.'[82] Riehl, on the other hand, was devoted to the natural beauty and historical character of his *Heimat*, Biebrich-am-Rhein, where he was born and reared. Throughout his life Riehl learned about the *Volk* by walking along country roads, stopping to chat with passers-by, and spending the night in village inns. From this perspective, the notion that Wagner's complex melodies were 'German music' seemed grotesque. The origin of all national music, Riehl argued, was the folk-song and, among all folk-music, the German is distinguished by being 'simple, fresh, tender, and deep'. Real German music 'flees from what [Wagner's] 'German music' eagerly seeks, and already possesses that from which this new music flees'.[83]

Like the great eighteenth-century inventors of the *Volk*, Riehl

[81] Riehl, *Charakterköpfe*, p. 446. For Wagner's view of Riehl, see *Schriften*, xiii. 70 ff. There is a good account of Riehl in Lees, *Revolution*, pp. 147 ff. See also George Eliot's analysis reprinted in *Essays*, pp. 266–99, and Wolf Lepenies's reflections on Riehl's place in German social thought, *Die drei Kulturen: Soziologie zwischen Literatur und Wissenschaft* (Munich and Vienna, 1985), 239–43.

[82] Gregor-Dellin, *Richard Wagner* (Munich, 1962), 169, 464.

[83] *Charakterköpfe*, pp. 514–15.

began with the conviction that it was part of the natural order of things. Nations, he wrote, do not arise through 'the voluntary collaboration' of men but rather they exist 'under necessity's iron hand, under the hand of divine providence'. A *Volk* can and should have a political expression, but its essence is to be found in the four great S's: *Sprache, Sitte, Stamm*, and *Siedlung*—language, mores, tribe, and settlement—which provide the 'foundation of all vital life, an elementary basis, which lasts well beyond transitory national politics and collapses only with the nation's last breath'. The unity of the *Volk* is not to be found in the centralizing forces of a bureaucratic state nor in the levelling tendencies of modern social and economic life, but rather in the diversity of the historical landscape, the peculiarities of the village, the special qualities of the region—what Riehl called the 'rich multiplicity' of German life.[84]

Although many contemporaries found Riehl's theoretical and ethnographic evocations of German multiplicity appealing, some of them wanted firmer foundations for national identity. Heinrich von Treitschke, for example, praised Riehl's *Naturgeschichte des Volkes* as a 'fresh and colourful' collection of facts, but rejected his claims to having established a science of the *Volk*. Treitschke objected to the way Riehl subordinated politics to society—the *Staat* to the *Volk*—because the two were inseparable, the one inevitably influencing and influenced by the other. In the modern era, Treitschke believed, the cohesive power of the state has increased; eventually, the state will not stand in opposition to the *Volk*, nor will it endanger the rich diversity of local life, but rather will become the true source of national unity, the final expression of the *Volk*'s identity. As Treitschke's fellow historian, Georg Waitz, put it in 1862, 'the natural cohesion of the *Volk* is fulfilled when it becomes political'. Gustav Freytag, in the volume of his *Bilder aus der deutschen Vergangenheit* that appeared in 1866, argued that 'the political construction of the individual and the *Volk* by the state' was the final precondition of 'all other achievements'.[85]

By moving the question of national identity into the political realm, Treitschke and his colleagues proclaimed a political goal but also posed a historiographical problem. If one shared Riehl's belief that the *Volk* was a cultural and social entity, then its history was to

[84] Riehl, *Kulturstudien*, pp. 243 ff.; Viktor Ritter von Geramb, *Wilhelm Heinrich Riehl* (Salzburg, 1954), 319, 121.

[85] Heinrich von Treitschke, *Die Gesellschaftswissenschaft: Ein kritischer Versuch* (1858; repr. Halle/Saale, 1927), 69; Böckenförde, 'Einheit', p. 35, n. 10; Freytag, *Bilder*, iv. 1.

be found in the evolution of language, customs, and mores. But if Germanness was essentially political, then where was the national past? Was it contained in all the scattered German polities of central Europe with their tangle of interlocking histories? Or in some particular German form of public life, a mode of political action shared by these states and by the institutions that had sought to unite them? Or was there some representative German state whose history might be taken as the taproot from which a larger national past might grow? During the middle decades of the century, as the political struggle for national identity entered its decisive phase, these historiographical questions became unavoidable. The most coherent—and ultimately, of course, the triumphant—answer was offered by the so-called *kleindeutsch* school, whose emergence can best be observed by considering the career of its founder and greatest exponent, Johann Gustav Droysen.[86]

A pastor's son from Pomerania, Droysen studied at the University of Berlin, where he attended Hegel's lectures and became fascinated by the methods and subject-matter in Boeckh's courses on the ancient world. Droysen's first major works, a biography of Alexander the Great and a two-volume study of the Hellenistic era, were milestones in the evolution of classical scholarship; instead of mournfully marking the decline of the *Polis*, Droysen emphasized the vitality and energy of the Hellenistic world and presented Alexander as a true personification of the Hegelian world spirit. After teaching in a *Gymnasium* and serving as a *Privat Docent* at Berlin, Droysen was appointed to a chair at Kiel in 1840. Here he became actively involved in the campaign against the Danes' drive to annex Holstein and, as a result, turned from ancient to modern history.[87]

In 1842–3, Droysen delivered a series of lectures on the 'Zeitalter der Freiheitskriege', which he published in book form three years later. Although he covered the entire period from 1770 to 1815, the highpoint of his narrative were those 'unforgettable years . . . in which, for the the first time in centuries, the German *Volk* united and in full consciousness of its unity fought and was victorious'. It was not only the mobilization of the *Volk* that gave this period its

---

[86] See Sheehan, 'Problem'; Hardtwig, 'Aufgabe'; List, 'Theorie'; Iggers, *Conception*; Manfred Asendorf, *Geschichte und Parteilichkeit* (Berlin, 1984).

[87] There is an excellent account of Droysen in Srbik's *Geist*, i. Gilbert, *Droysen*, is still unsurpassed for his early career. Günter Birtsch, *Die Nation als sittliche Idee. Der Nationalstaatsbegriff in Geschichtsschreibung und politischer Gedankenwelt Johann Gustav Droysens* (Cologne and Graz, 1964), has a good treatment of his political development.

great historical and political significance; no less important was the fact that the 'wars of liberation' represented a partnership between the German *Volk* and the Prussian state, a partnership rooted in the era of reforms and then gloriously triumphant on the field of battle. 'From then on,' Droysen wrote, 'it belonged to the true nature of the state to be national, and to the true nature of the *Volk* to have a state'—a concise summary of the relationship between state and nation which stood at the centre of the *kleindeutsch* solution to the question of German identity.[88]

The problem, of course, was that in the 1840s and 1850s the Prussian state did not become national and the German *Volk* did not achieve its state. Droysen and the other advocates of Prussian leadership had to come to terms with the sad fact that *Volk* and *Staat* were not so easily reconciled—politically, ideologically, or historiographically. Droysen's own response to this was clear and exemplary. He remained politically liberal, with a deep commitment to the *Volk* as a 'natural community' and as a source of political value. But he also recognized that *Volk* and *Staat* rarely coincided. In his lectures of 1857 he pointed out that the 'history of peoples' would almost always be different from the 'history of states'. Much of the 'vital movement' in the past comes from this lack of symmetry, which forces people and state to seek each other, the one eager for its 'power base', the other anxious to turn its subjects into a *Volk*, that is, 'a substantive community'. In practice, Droysen became increasingly concerned with the state. From the 1850s until his death in 1884 he devoted himself to a history of Prussia, a multi-volume monument to the state that gave 'the one side of our national life its expression, representation, and weight'. Eventually Droysen came to see the state as a community with a life of its own: 'The state is not the sum of the individuals living in it, nor does it originate from their will, nor does it exist for them.'[89]

Droysen's scholarly efforts to define a national past were inseparable from his political commitment to a Prussian-led Germany. He was, he proclaimed, 'neither liberal nor conservative, but Prussian, that is German, and German, that is Prussian'. While he shared Ranke's commitment to critical rigour in the use of sources, he did not embrace the ideological austerity and selflessness these methods sometimes seem to imply. Indeed he worried that an excessive concern for historical method might turn scholars into 'factory workers', whose scope would be narrowed by a

---

[88] Droysen, *Vorlesungen,* i. 3, ii. 457.
[89] Droysen, *Historik*, pp. 307, 441, *Geschichte*, i. 4.

senseless quest for 'eunuch-like objectivity'. History, he believed, was always joined to politics, knowledge linked to power. 'Only a genuinely historical point of view', he wrote in 1843, 'will be able to remedy the sad derangement of our political and social affairs and indicate the right course to a happier future'.[90]

Ludwig Häusser, who advanced the ideas of the *kleindeutsch* school from an influential academic position at Heidelberg, was also convinced that history was a proper instrument of politics. 'Should our German historiography march in step with the needs of the nation,' he asked in 1841, 'or should they be separate, the nation and the scholars, should the latter write for themselves and the former look elsewhere for instruction?' Häusser had no doubts about the correct answer to this question: his ideal was what he called the 'historian of life', who combined scholarship and commitment, objectivity and engagement. Häusser's *Deutsche Geschichte vom Tode Friedrichs des Grossen bis zur Gründung des Deutschen Bundes* was one of the major historical works to be published during the 1850s. Like Droysen and many others, Häusser presented the era of reform and liberation as a time when Prussian and German history were dramatically connected. By taking the lead in the national battle against the French, Prussia at once anticipated and legitimized her eventual domination of German Europe. This image, expressed in history books as well as paintings and novels, became one of *Kleindeutschland's* formative myths.[91]

There are no more 'non-partisan, blood- and nerveless historians', Heinrich von Sybel wrote in 1856, and that is 'a very significant advance'. Born in 1817, reared in a prosperous family with links to both the Prussian bureaucracy and the Rhenish economic élite, Sybel studied with Ranke, taught at Bonn, and in 1856 was called to Munich as part of King Maximilian's efforts to revitalize Bavarian scholarship. During his five years in Munich, Sybel helped to organize the university's historical seminar and the Bavarian Historical Commission, as well as to establish the *Historische Zeitschrift*, which soon became the German historical profession's most important journal. In his 'Preface' to the first issue, Sybel captured that distinctive blend of historiography and politics shared by many of his collaborators: 'The journal should

---

[90] Srbik, *Geist*, i. 377; Robert Southard, 'Theology in Droysen's Early Political Historiography: Free Will, Necessity, and the Historian', *History and Theory*, 18/3 (1979), 379–80.

[91] List, 'Theorie', pp. 38–9.

above all be scholarly. Its first task, therefore, is to represent true research methods and uncover deviations from them.' At the same time, however, the *Zeitschrift* had a national mission: the life of the *Volk* appears to the historian 'as the natural and individual development that necessarily nourishes the form of states and culture. . . .' For this reason, Sybel insisted, three political positions are historically illegitimate: feudalism, because it hinders progress, radicalism, because it favours subjective caprice over organic development, and ultramontanism, because it subjects national interests to a foreign authority. Thus his commitment to scholarly objectivity and critical historiography was not unqualified; people and positions outside the range of his own moderate liberalism could be excluded from both the journal and serious political consideration.[92]

Sybel was only nine years younger than Droysen, but he none the less belonged to an intellectual generation that was more clearly political, unambiguously partisan, and self-consciously 'realistic'. Unlike Droysen, who continued to cherish an eighteenth-century view of the *Volk*, Sybel's primary commitment was to the state, which he called the 'realization of freedom through the power of the community'.[93] In fact, when Sybel became engaged with the German question after 1848, he tended to transform questions of national identity into practical problems of state-building. His ideal was not a union of *Volk* and *Staat* but rather a triumph of the Prussian state over German Europe. As long-time editor of the *Historische Zeitschrift*, director of the Prussian State Archives, National Liberal parliamentarian, and author of the *Begründung des Deutschen Reiches durch Wilhelm I* (1889–94), he became the semi-official chronicler of this triumph.

Among the historians advocating a *kleindeutsch* Germany during the late 1850s and 1860s the youngest and one of the most brilliant was Heinrich von Treitschke. A Saxon whose path to Prussia had led him away from his family's values and traditions, Treitschke approached national questions with a convert's zeal and a young man's contempt for his elders' failings. Treitschke had even less patience with residual romanticism than did Sybel. He dismissed without ado that long, rich tradition of historical thought that

[92] Quotations are from Albert Wucher, *Theodor Mommsen: Geschichtsschreibung und Politik* (Göttingen, 1956); Dotterweich, *Sybel*, pp. 326, 330. Dotterweich's book is the fullest account of Sybel's early career.

[93] Hellmut Seier, *Die Staatsidee Heinrich von Sybels in den Wandlungen der Reichsgründungszeit, 1862/71* (Lübeck and Hamburg, 1961), 31–2. See also Dotterweich, *Sybel*, pp. 187 ff.

insisted on the organic evolution of the *Volk*. 'Ultimately we realize', he wrote in 1864, 'that this unfortunate word *organic* engages politics where thought is absent.' With Treitschke we enter a world of action and power. There is nothing necessary about a nation's existence: 'What later generations call historical necessity was always no more than a possibility that was made into a reality by the will and force of the nation.' It is hardly surprising, therefore, that Treitschke distrusted Riehl's lyrical defence of the *Volk*'s rich diversity. Instead, he wanted a unified state, which would dissolve the 'fairy-tale world of particularism' and provide the basis for a free and powerful Germany. Posed in this way, there was really only one answer to the German question: the conquest of the small states by Prussia. As a historian, Treitschke saw the German past from this Prussocentric perspective. In 1866, when he moved to Berlin following the Prussian victory, he expressed the primary assumption to which he would devote the remaining three decades of his life: 'Prussian and German history must be joined in a single enterprise.'[94]

The conviction that the state was the essential expression of national identity, advanced tentatively by Droysen and enthusiastically by Sybel and Treitschke, spread to historians not directly concerned with contemporary German affairs. This primacy of the state, for example, is the ordering assumption behind Theodor Mommsen's *Römische Geschichte*, whose appearance in 1854 established his reputation as Niebuhr's legitimate heir. Mommsen presented the emergence of Rome as a process of national unification, the long and painful triumph of cohesion over particularism. In this process Mommsen viewed the nation-state as normative in two senses of the word—it is the normal political condition towards which men strive and it provides the standards according to which their efforts can be judged. Mommsen, therefore, praised Caesar as the state's personification and saviour, who drew his legitimacy from his ability to restore order amid the chaos of the republic's decline. Like Treitschke, Mommsen was convinced that the power and persistence of the state were ends in themselves. Mommsen's *Römische Geschichte*, wrote Wilhelm Dilthey, reflected contemporary politics more accurately than any other work; for him, 'it was not speeches, critical thought, inner nobility or spiritual ascendance that drove historical mechanisms, but rather power alone'.[95]

---

[94] Treitschke, 'Bundesstaat', pp. 11, 13; Schulin, *Traditionskritik*, p. 82. A good introduction to Treitschke's life and thought is Andreas Dorpalen, *Heinrich von Treitschke* (New Haven, 1957).

[95] The fullest treatment of Mommsen's career is Wickert, *Mommsen*. Alfred

Prussia's opponents recognized that the growing prominence of *kleindeutsch* historiography was a political force to be reckoned with. For instance, when he was the Austrian delegate to the federal diet, Count Rechberg wrote to his superiors in Vienna that Prussia's scholarly advocates were taking over throughout the German lands—in Göttingen, Weimar, Heidelberg, and Munich, as well as Berlin, Königsberg, and Kiel. He was alarmed by the impending publication of Sybel's *Historische Zeitschrift*, which would further extend the influence of this group over the educated public. Five years later, the great church historian Ignaz von Döllinger warned King Maximilian about the historical movement he was apparently encouraging in Munich. Men like Droysen, Häusser, and Sybel, Döllinger argued, consider 'the supremacy of Prussia, the gradual and peaceful or abrupt and violent absorption of the other German states and the expropriation of other German dynasties as the final goal of the entire German past, as a necessity emerging from the whole course of Germany's historical development. . . .'[96] Only an alternative vision of the German past, another set of necessities, could counter Prussia's historiographical offensive.

For no polity was this search more pressing—or more difficult— than it was for Austria. In 1853 Joseph Alexander von Helfert tried to establish an Austrian national history with his *Über National-geschichte und den gegenwärtigen Stand ihrer Pflege in Österreich*. But, while Helfert hoped that his book would help create an Austrian national past, he knew this past could not be confined to a single ethnic group. What Helfert called *Gross-Österreich* was a 'provid-ential necessity' for all of Europe.[97] Some Austrians also tried to build an institutional base for historical research. Count Thun, for example, established an historical institute in Vienna in 1854 as part of a general overhaul of the educational system. Nevertheless, most Austrian historians lacked the cohesion and self-confidence dis-played by their Prussian counterparts. Compared to most other

Heuss's *Theodor Mommsen und das 19. Jahrhundert* (Kiel, 1956) places his life and work in their historical context. Dilthey is quoted by Karl Christ in his essay published with the new edition of Mommsen's *Römische Geschichte* (Nördlingen, 1976), viii. 27. Mommsen's treatment of Caesar is in vol. iii, ch. 11.

[96] A. O. Meyer, 'Graf Rechberg über die kleindeutsche Geschichtsschreibung', *HZ* 133 (1926), 259–61; Hans Rall, 'Geschichtswissenschaftlicher Fortschritt in München vor 100 Jahren: Gedanken zu zwei neuen Büchern', *ZBL*, 22/1 (1959), 150. Compare Ketteler's definition of '*Borussianismus*', quoted in Hardtwig, 'Aufgabe', p. 265.

[97] Joseph Alexander von Helfert, *Über Nationalgeschichte und den gegenwärtigen Stand ihrer Pflege in Österreich* (Prague, 1853), 53.

German states, academic history in Austria was weak, archival research suffered from political interference, and professional standards were low. The best Austrian history, therefore, continued to be written outside universities. Helfert, for instance, was a former professor of law, who held a post in the Ministry of Education when he wrote his call for national historiography. Alfred von Arneth, whose three-volume biography of Eugen of Savoy was one of the great works of the late 1850s, was also a bureaucrat; his appointment as vice-director of the Staatsarchiv in 1860 represented an important step towards increasing scholarly access to the Habsburg documents. And Anton Springer, the author of a fine history of Austria from 1815 to 1850, had been forced from his job in Prague and taught History of Art in Bonn.[98]

The most vigorous opponents of the *kleindeutsch* version of German identity came from the smaller states. Onno Klopp, for instance, was a school official in Osnabrück when his *Geschichte Ostfrieslands* attracted attention because of its outspoken opposition to Prussia. In 1861 he was hired by King George of Hanover, first to edit the Leibniz papers and then to oversee the royal archives. From this position, Klopp delivered a series of attacks on the Prussian past and present which amused Berlin's enemies and outraged its partisans. His biography of Frederick the Great, published in 1861, sought to demonstrate that each of that monarch's victories was 'a new assault on the moral laws which are inscribed on the human heart'. For Klopp, it was not the liberal reformers, so beloved by Droysen, nor the clear-sighted statesmen praised by Sybel and Treitschke, but the aggressive, repressive absolutist monarch who best represented the essence of Prussia, a predatory state out for its own interests at the expense of its neighbours. Klopp would have agreed with the assessment offered by another of Prussia's opponents, Edmund Jörg, who wrote that Prussia had 'only a stomach for Germany, never a heart'.[99]

Klopp believed that Germans' historical identity was tied to their diversity, which required 'a federative system with our fatherland, a defensive posture towards the outside'. Klopp knew that this situation had obvious disadvantages, not least among them a vulnerability to expansionist states such as Prussia. But it was also 'the basic pre-condition for the rich development of our cultural

[98] See Heinrich Friedjung, *Historische Aufsätze* (Stuttgart and Berlin, 1919); Alphons Lhotsky, 'Geschichtsforschung und Geschichtsschreibung in Österreich', *HZ* 189 (1959); Heer, *Kampf*, especially p. 265.
[99] Klopp, *Friedrich II.* pp. 542–3; Heer, *Kampf*, p. 218.

life, which has consistently made us the first nation in Europe'. What, he wondered, will defend German federalism and particularism in these dangerous times? His answer: a feeling for the law, which is inseparable from the German national character and 'the source of our hopes for the creation of the nation'. [100]

A similar vision of German history and character appears in the work of Constantin Frantz. Born near Halberstadt in 1817, a pastor's son, Frantz belonged to the same restless and creative generation as Marx. Like Marx, he embraced then rejected Hegelianism; but whereas Marx turned left, towards Feuerbach and radicalism, Frantz turned right, towards the later Schelling and conservatism. After a few years in the Prussian Civil Service, Frantz became an independent writer, flooding the market with his views on contemporary social and political issues. [101]

Like most of his contemporaries, Frantz believed the answers to political questions were primarily historical: 'We can understand something only in so far as we know its origins. . . .' The origins of German politics were to be found in the Holy Roman Empire, the great expression of European federalism which was Germany's gift to western culture and the key to what Frantz calls Germany's 'historical vocation'. 'Universality' is the Germans' inalienable national character, demonstrated again and again at the decisive moments in the nation's history. Since Europe was affected by the collapse of the medieval empire, Europe was involved in the re-emergence of the imperial ideal out of the wreckage of the old. But the Reich is gone, as is the European Concert which took its place. Germans, therefore, must once again face their historical mission and lead Europe back to equilibrium and peace. This can be accomplished, Frantz believes, if Austria and Prussia abandon their self-defeating efforts to be independent great powers and act through and within the German Confederation, thereby making it a model for European international relations as a whole, an ideal of co-operation and federation towards which all states must strive. [102]

When the events of the 1850s and 1860s—the Crimean War, Italian unification, and the three wars of German unification—confounded Frantz, his writing became more shrill, his ideas more extreme. Increasingly, he saw the triumph of the nation-state as

---

[100] Klopp, *Friedrich II.* p. 594.

[101] A good source for Frantz's career is the collection of his *Briefe*, edited by Udo Sauter and Hans Onnau (Wiesbaden, 1974).

[102] Constantin Frantz, *Untersuchungen über das europäische Gleichgewicht* (1859; repr. Osnabrück, 1968), 353; for Frantz's account of Germany's vocation, see pp. 399–400, 415–16.

part of a Jewish conspiracy, linked to the spread of liberalism and materialism throughout modern society. When he died in 1891, he was isolated and nearly forgotten.

Although charged with very different political values, Georg Gervinus's conception of Germans' national identity was strikingly similar to Klopp's and Frantz's. The nation, he wrote, has always been characterized by its 'individualistic drive . . . in which everything strives for the independence and self-government of the natural states, for regionalism, for small territorial states, and in its highest form, when great nationalities inhabit a single state, for federative unity'. Unlike most moderate liberals, Gervinus's experiences in 1848–9 had driven him to republicanism. His *Einleitung in die Geschichte des neunzehnten Jahrhunderts*, which caused him to lose his teaching position and to be tried for high treason, argued that only a democratic Germany—a Germany which trusted the 'zahen und gesunden Volksnatur'—could play a leading role in Europe. The goal of German politics should be to dissolve 'the dangerous unified great states' into federations, which would combine the advantages of great and small states and offer the best protection for 'universal freedom and the peaceful dissemination of every sort of culture'.[103]

The most direct confrontation over the problem of Germany's historical identity was the polemic touched off by the publication of Wilhelm Giesebrecht's *Geschichte der deutschen Kaiserzeit*. Giesebrecht, a student of Ranke, taught in Berlin's famous Joachimsthaler Gymnasium before moving to the University of Königsberg and then to Munich. He viewed the medieval Ottonian empire as the time when 'the German *Volk*, strong in its unity, had reached the fullest expansion of its power . . . [and] when Germans counted for most in the world and the German name had the greatest resonance'. In a much publicized *Festrede* of 1859, Heinrich von Sybel accused Giesebrecht of being naive and anachronistic. Two years later, Sybel was attacked by Julius Ficker, a Catholic from Westphalia who taught medieval history in the Tyrol. Ficker combined technical expertise with a deep commitment to the medieval empire, whose religious foundations and universalist appeal provided cohesion without damaging independence, unity

---

[103] Gervinus, *Einleitung*. p. 178; Schieder, in Conze (ed.), *Staat*, p. 29. On Gervinus, see Rosenberg's essay in *Denkströmungen*; Jonathan Wagner, 'Georg Gottfried Gervinus: The Tribulations of a Liberal Federalist', *CEH* 4/4 (Dec. 1971); Charles E. McClelland, 'History in the Science of Politics: A Reassessment of G. G. Gervinus', *CEH* 4/4 (Dec. 1971).

without destroying particularity. He especially admired the way in which the empire had had no interest in expanding its own control over its subjects but rather had 'left the most important duties of the state to local authorities or communities'.[104]

While Sybel and Ficker fought with the weapons of scholarship, their battlefield was contemporary and their goals political. Behind their versions of medieval politics were different images of the German past and competing agenda for the German future. The confrontation between *Reich* and *Staat*, Catholic and Protestant, centralizer and particularist corresponded to the political struggles going on around them. 'During these fertile times,' Sybel wrote, historiography 'became a mirror of the currents within the *Volk*'. As the conflict between Austria and Prussia intensified, both states turned to the past for weapons against the other.[105]

In this struggle over German national identity, the *kleindeutsch* school had the great advantage of being relatively cohesive. The *kleindeutsch* allegiance to Prussia gave its adherents a focus conspicuously absent among those who favoured Austria or some brand of federalism. Similarly, the most articulate spokesmen for *Kleindeutschland* were moderate liberals, while their enemies were scattered all along the political spectrum. It is, however, by no means clear that the *kleindeutsch* answer to national identity was either the most popular or the most cogent in the 1850s and 1860s. To choose the Prussian state as the demiurge of nationhood, as did Droysen and his colleagues, required that one ignore or repress persistently important aspects of the national experience. On the other hand, to build a vision of the future on the old Reich and its defence of particularism, as did Frantz and the other federalists, required that one overlook the powerful forces of centralization that had been at work in the German lands for a century or more. In fact, German history could not yield a single, satisfying answer to the German question because, despite what the various contesting versions of German identity might claim, the German past included both the forces of centralization and the persistence of particularism, Catholics and Protestants, Austrians and Prussians.

The *kleindeutsch* version of German identity—that fusion of the Prussian and German pasts for which Treitschke yearned—became

---

[104] Srbik, *Geist.* ii. 33–4. On the debate, see Gottfried Koch's essay 'Der Streit zwischen Sybel und Ficker un die Einschätzung der mittelalterlichen Kaiserpolitik in der modernen Historiographie', in Streisand (ed.), *Studien*, i. 311 ff.

[105] Srbik, *Geist*, i. 355.

the answer to the German question retrospectively, after the issue was decided politically and militarily. Then and only then did *Kleindeutschland* become so obvious, necessary, and unavoidable. Droysen, Sybel, and Treitschke were the beneficiaries as well as the advocates of German nation-building. Their answer to the German question triumphed not because of its inherent superiority or their own fervour and eloquence; it triumphed because after 1866 it was backed by the undeniable logic of events and the formidable power of a modern state.

XIV
Political Opportunities and Alternatives

'THE discussion of the question, who should rule . . . belongs in the realm of philosophical speculation; the practical question only has to do with the simple fact that it is power alone which can rule.' These lines from the opening pages of Ludwig August von Rochau's *Grundsätze der Realpolitik* are often taken as a kind of epigraph for the post-revolutionary era, just as Rochau's personal evolution from student rebel to political exile to enthusiastic advocate of the Bismarckian Reich apparently illustrates a generational shift from opposition to reconciliation. Like so many contemporary philosophers, scientists, and writers, Rochau based his view of the world on a new appreciation of the importance of facts:

It is certain that the spoken and written word can accomplish nothing in the face of physical facts and that facts can only give way to other facts, and it is equally certain that the fragmented German powers will not be united by a principle, an idea, or a treaty, but only by an overwhelming power that will subdue the rest.[1]

When it appeared in 1853, Rochau's book enjoyed considerable success. The young Heinrich von Treitschke, for example, believed that it contained 'more that was useful for scholarship than a thick textbook on politics'.[2] But, despite its supposedly exemplary character, Rochau's *Grundsätze der Realpolitik* is an ambiguous and problematic document. As a description of political behaviour, the concept of *Realpolitik* involves difficulties similar to those we encountered when we tried to apply 'realism' to literary works. Just as literature is at once an expression of truth and an exercise in contrivance, so politics is always based on perceptions of reality and judgements about value. These perceptions and judgements change, but some blend of the two is always present. *Vormärz*

---

[1] Rochau, *Grundsätze der Realpolitik* (first pub. 1853–69, new edn. by Hans-Ulrich Wehler, Frankfurt, Berlin, and Vienna, 1972), 25 and 191. For a good introduction to Rochau's ideas, see Lees, *Revolution*, pp. 107 ff.
[2] Quoted in Wehler's introduction to the *Grundsätze*, p. 9.

conservatives like Metternich and Gentz were no more 'idealistic' than their counterparts in the 1850s and 1860s; liberals like Hansemann and Mohl were as concerned about the real world as Bennigsen or Lasker. Even Bismarck, for all his talk about the centrality of power, was driven by deeply felt loyalties and values.

In politics, as in art, those who talked about the importance of 'realism' did so in order to distinguish themselves from an earlier generation. To Rochau, *Realpolitik* was primarily an antidote to the illusions that had proved so debilitating to an earlier generation of German liberals. 'The castles that they built in the air have evaporated, the defenceless rights, whose theoretical recognition they achieved, have no more than an apparent effect on practice.' Rochau spoke to and for a generation that did not want to follow its elders along the road to humiliation and defeat. Nevertheless, Rochau's break with the past was not clear-cut. He continued to pursue liberalism's characteristic goals—representative institutions, constitutional government, and a social order based on the *Mittelstand*. Moreover, he did not ignore the importance of ideas and spiritual forces. 'Under all circumstances', he wrote, 'the spirit of the times has the most decisive influence on the general direction of politics.'[3]

Rochau deserves his exemplary status not because his ideas mark a totally new era but rather because they combine the heritage of the *Vormärz* with the insistent demands of the new, post-revolutionary age. To understand Rochau—and to understand the the political world of the 1850s and 1860s—we must grasp the interplay between the ideas and institutions of the past and the opportunities and alternatives of the present. In this chapter, we will examine this interplay at work in three familiar aspects of German public life: the continued expansion of participatory politics, the persistent problems of political opposition, and the increasingly insistent conflict over Germans' national identity and organization.

i. THE RE-EMERGENCE OF THE GERMAN QUESTION

In his 'Politisches Gespräch', first published in 1836, Leopold von Ranke wrote that 'a state owes its position in the world to the degree of its independence, the maintenance of which requires the subordination of all domestic considerations.' This famous passage provided one of the first and most influential formulations of what

---

[3] Rochau, *Grundsätze*, p. 33.

came to be called the 'primacy of foreign policy'. By the late nineteenth century the primacy of foreign policy had become both a descriptive statement about historical reality and a normative statement about political priorities. Its advocates argued that, since the state's struggle for survival is the central fact of political life, foreign affairs ought to have precedence over domestic considerations. Against this position, a number of scholars have argued for a primacy of internal politics. To these people, most of whom have been influenced by some kind of Marxism, international relations are essentially the function of domestic struggles for power. Like its antithesis, this belief in the primacy of internal politics involves a political as well as a historiographical programme. Its advocates want to direct our attention to the real sources of foreign policy and to the need for domestic political change.[4]

In its most extreme form, neither of these positions is very satisfactory. In the world of international affairs, states do struggle to defend their interests, but how these interests are defined and how well they can be defended always depend on the alignment of political and social forces at home. At certain historical moments, either foreign or domestic politics may seem more important, but neither is 'primary' because they are never really separate. Both are part of the same process; each persistently helps to shape and is in turn shaped by the other.

It is ironic that in Germany, where the primacy of foreign policy was long in fashion, this interrelationship of foreign and domestic affairs seems especially intense. Indeed one of the most abiding features of the German question is the way in which it blurs the distinction between external and internal politics. This was true for the Holy Roman Empire, whose institutions made no clear distinction between what was foreign and what was domestic. In a different way it remained true for the German Confederation, which tried to regulate political relations within as well as among its member states. Throughout its existence, the Confederation's supporters viewed it as a source of both international and domestic stability, while its opponents wanted to replace it with a new instrument of national power and internal reform.

The revolution of 1848 had clarified but not resolved both the domestic and the international dimensions of the German question.

---

[4] Leopold von Ranke, *Die grossen Mächte. Politisches Gespräch. Mit einem Nachwort von Theodor Schieder* (Göttingen, 1955). On the concept, see Ernst-Otto Czempiel, 'Der Primat der auswärtigen Politik: Kritische Würdigung einer Staatsmaxime', *PV* 4/2 (1963), 266–87.

After two years of high hopes and missed opportunities, in 1850 the question of German identity seemed as open as it had been on the eve of the revolution. Neither parliamentary compromise nor Prussian diplomacy had been able to impose a union anchored in Berlin; Schwarzenberg's tentative efforts on behalf of a fusion of the German lands with the Habsburg monarchy had come to nothing. As we saw in Chapter 11, the weak federative bonds forged by Metternich in 1815 once again seemed to be the solution that divided Germans least. Thus it was that, in May 1851, the diet of a reconstituted German Confederation gathered at Frankfurt to provide a forum for national affairs.

As in 1815, the Confederation's success or failure depended on the ability of the two major German states to work together. Would Austria and Prussia be able to put behind them the bitter conflicts that had brought them to the brink of war? Would their common fear and hatred of upheaval be enough to cement a new conservative coalition? Or would Prussia's unfulfilled ambitions continue to challenge Austria's fragile primacy over German affairs? Count Prokesch, the Habsburgs' ambassador in Berlin, was not optimistic about the chances for harmony: 'One cannot hope for a reconciliation of the two powers' interests or for resolute co-operation against the revolution. From Frankfurt I expect nothing besides a continuation of the old game.' Of course to many conservatives the 'old game' was not the worst alternative—as long as it continued to be played according to the usual rules and for the customary limited stakes. Leopold von Ranke, for instance, assured Edwin von Manteuffel in 1852 that Austro-Prussian competition was 'a fundamental fact of German life and, properly understood, makes both states strong'.[5]

For most Austrians to 'understand properly' their competition with Prussia meant viewing it from a European perspective rather than within the narrower confines of the 'German question'. Few statesmen in Vienna wanted to struggle with Berlin for hegemony over the German lands, but they did want to ensure German support for the monarchy's various interests. This meant that, in Schwarzenberg's words, they had to 'win over the Prussians, draw them into our policies and keep them there'. The problem was that winning over the Prussians might require granting them greater authority over German affairs, which the Austrians were not prepared to do. From 1850 to 1866 policy-makers in Vienna floundered in the face of what Roy Austensen has called their

---

[5] Lutz, *Habsburg*, p. 393; Gerlach, *Revolution*, p. 61, n. 155.

central dilemma: 'devising policies consistent with the fact that Prussia was at the same time Austria's most dangerous rival and her most important ally'.[6]

In Berlin, opinion was divided over whether Austria was primarily a rival or an ally. Moderate liberals, both inside and outside the government, wanted to expand Prussia's power and influence over the other German lands. This could only be done at Austria's expense. Most conservatives, on the other hand, were inclined to see foreign policy as an instrument of counter-revolution. Stahl, for instance, called Austro-Prussian co-operation 'Germany's power and unity . . . a God-given bulwark against revolution that we should not recklessly abandon'.[7] For many Prussian conservatives, the ideal arrangement was some new version of the Holy Alliance through which the three great eastern monarchies could guarantee stability at home and abroad. The Olmütz agreement and the reconstitution of the Confederation seemed to signal the triumph of this viewpoint, whose advocates were greatly encouraged when it was announced that Otto von Bismarck had been appointed to lead the Prussian delegation at Frankfurt.

Bismarck was thirty-six years old when he went to Frankfurt to assume his post in the summer of 1851. That he was completely without diplomatic experience did not go unnoticed by his critics in Berlin: Prince William, the king's brother and heir apparent, expressed his dismay that 'this *Landwehrleutnant*' had been given such an important post; liberal newspapers predicted a sharp decline in Prussia's standing within the Confederation. But Bismarck had friends at court and he had shown himself to be a resolute defender of monarchical authority during the darkest days of the revolution. Moreover, his background, appearance, and personal style represented those social forces on which the Hohenzollern had so often depended. His mother's family, the Menckens, were successful civil servants with strong ties to the landed élite; the Bismarks were Junkers, held by ancient roots to Pomerania's sandy soil. After a brief and unsuccessful career as a subaltern bureaucrat, Bismarck had taken up the life of a country squire, occupied with running his estates but given to personal eccentricities and excess. 'And so I vegetate,' he wrote to a friend in his thirtieth year, 'without particular desires or anxieties, in a quite

---

[6] Lutz, *Habsburg*, p. 392; Austensen, 'Making', p. 861. The best source for Austrian policy in this period is Srbik (ed.), *Quellen*.
[7] Herre, *Nation*, p. 144.

harmonious but also quite boring condition.' Two years later three things changed his life: he underwent a religious conversion, got married, and was drawn into the crisis of Prussian politics that began with the calling of the United *Landtag* in 1847. As an outspoken opponent of reform in that body, he started on the political path that would lead him to his first major appointment four years later.[8]

A consistent critic of Radowitz, in December 1850 Bismarck had delivered an eloquent and widely publicized defence of the Olmütz agreements. But he was by no means an uncritical supporter of conservative diplomacy. While he may have deplored Radowitz's methods, he was no less dissatisfied with Prussia's subservient status in German affairs. Even before he arrived in Frankfurt, therefore, Bismarck had begun to express his concern that Austria's primacy in the Confederation would always put Prussia at a disadvantage. In June 1851 he wrote to Manteuffel that however useful the diet might be in dealing with 'general police and military matters', separate treaties on commercial, military, and legislative affairs would probably be more effective 'in satisfying our needs . . . within the territory given over to us by nature [des uns durch die Natur angewiesenen geographischen Gebiets]'.[9]

From the outset, the new Prussian representative proved to be a reluctant subordinate and difficult colleague. On petty matters of protocol (such as who had the right to smoke in the diet's chambers) and on major questions of policy, Bismarck did not pass up a chance to challenge Austrian pre-eminence. Throughout 1851 and 1852 he managed to turn the three main issues before the diet— the liquidation of the fleet acquired during 1848, the drafting of new laws governing the Press, and the possible extension of the *Zollverein* to include Austria—into a confrontation between the two great powers. In all three, the Prussian position prevailed.

As he made clear in a series of letters written to Leopold von Gerlach at the end of 1853, Bismarck had come to realize that the present arrangement of German affairs was untenable. This did not mean that he was prepared to speak the language of German patriotism: 'We must not let ourselves, either in our own and

---

[8] The literature on Bismarck is immense. Pflanze, *Bismarck*, has a clear, balanced treatment of his politics up to 1871. Gall, *Bismarck*, gives an elegantly written, up-to-date account of his entire career. Engelberg, *Bismarck*, is especially good on his family background and early life. The quotation is from Rothfels (ed.), *Bismarck*, p. 3, which contains a convenient selection of documents. The definitive edition of Bismarck's works is the so-called Friedrichsruhe Ausgabe (15 vols.; Berlin, 1923–33).

[9] Engelberg, *Bismarck*, p. 389.

through others' phrases, be entangled with "German politics".'
But, while he did not doubt the primacy of Prussian interests, he
also saw that 'our policy has no theatre of operations other than
Germany'. Since Austria refused to yield to Prussia's German
aspirations, some sort of a confrontation with Vienna was
inevitable: 'We each seek to breathe the same air, one of us must
weaken or be weakened, and until then we must be enemies, a fact
that cannot be ignored . . . no matter how unwelcome it might also
be.'[10] As an early expression of Bismarck's attitudes these letters are
significant, but they had no impact on Prussian policy. No one in
power in Berlin—least of all a conservative like Leopold von
Gerlach—was prepared to accept the apparent logic of Bismarck's
position. The first important impetus for a reordering of German
affairs came not from Frankfurt or Berlin, but rather from events
on the eastern flank of the Habsburg's realm.

For centuries the Habsburgs had been deeply involved with
developments along Europe's south-eastern rim, first as the self-
appointed guardians of Christendom against the Turks, then as
eager beneficiaries of the Ottoman Empire's long decline. At mid-
century there were new sources of tension in this perennially
troubled area. In 1849 Vienna threatened military action in order to
stop the Turks from harbouring Polish and Hungarian exiles; four
years later, Austrian troops blocked Turkish efforts to retaliate
against rebellious Montenegrins. In both these enterprises, Austria
had been supported by Russia. Understandably enough, in 1853 the
tsar expected Austrian help when Britain and France sought to
check Russian expansion into Ottoman territory. But Count Buol,
who had become Foreign Minister after Schwarzenberg's sudden
death in 1852, tried to avoid having to commit Austria to either the
Russians or the British and French by mediating between the two
groups. 'We are seeking to pacify on every side,' he declared in July
1853, 'and above all to avoid a European complication, which
would be particularly detrimental to us.'[11] No one was willing to
talk peace that summer. In September the British and French fleets
sailed into the Dardanelles; two weeks later, emboldened by this
support, the Turks declared war against Russia. In March 1854
Britain and France entered the war and began military action
against Russia in the Crimea. Throughout the winter of 1853–4 the
Russians had tried to enlist support or at least a declaration of
neutrality from Vienna. Buol, however, feared the destabilizing

[10] Rothfels (ed.), *Bismarck*, p. 170. See Engelberg, *Bismarck*, pp. 412–13.
[11] Rich, *War*, p. 67.

effects of Russian expansion into the Balkans and was also worried that alienating France might jeopardize Austria's position in Italy.

Buol knew that, if he were to take action to contain Russia, he would need the support of the German states, and especially of Prussia. Such support was not easy to get. The Prussian government, much like its Austrian counterpart, was divided between advocates and opponents of Russia. Frederick William IV was characteristically incapable of choosing between them. ('My dear brother-in-law goes to bed a Russian and wakes up an Englishman,' noted the tsar acerbically.)[12] Finally, in April 1854 Prussia agreed to a defensive alliance with Austria. Buol then proceeded to deliver an ultimatum demanding that Russia cease all military action south of the Danube and withdraw from the principalities of Moldavia and Wallachia, which Russian troops had occupied the year before. After the Russians complied with these demands, Buol's apparent willingness to go to war against them faded. Even though he entered into an alliance with Britain and France in December 1854, he was resolved to stay out of the conflict. Following the fall of the Russian fort of Sebastopol in September 1855, he delivered a new ultimatum with which he sought to force Russia to make peace. This time, his mediation efforts worked and the fighting came to an end.

It may be, as Buol's scholarly defenders have recently claimed, that the Austrian statesman played a bad hand as well as he could. Nevertheless, his policies were a disaster for Austria. Among the German states, Buol had outraged Russia's admirers and frightened those who did not want to be drawn into a European conflict from which they had nothing to gain. During the height of the crisis in 1854, some German statesmen, such as Count von der Pfordten from Bavaria and Beust from Saxony, had sought ways to protect the Confederation's neutrality. Much more important than its impact on German relations was the effects of Buol's policy on Austria's international position. His co-operation with Britain and France did not earn him trust or respect in London and Paris, but it did infuriate the Russians, who accused their former ally of perfidious ingratitude. In short, the final result of Buol's torturous diplomatic manœuvring had been to sacrifice an essential source of support without getting anything in return. It is difficult, therefore, not to agree with Norman Rich's judgement that 'Austria, not Russia, was eventually the greatest loser in the Crimean War.'[13]

[12] Gall, *Bismarck*, p. 161.
[13] Rich, *War*, p. 198. Historians have usually been harshly critical of Austrian

Austria's position after 1856 was especially dangerous because one result of the eastern crisis had been to narrow the boundaries of great power politics. In the late 1850s both Britain and Russia turned away from European affairs and devoted themselves to domestic problems. Consequently, Austria's choice of allies was limited to either its long-time rival, Prussia, or Bonapartist France. Without the active help of one of these powers, the Habsburgs would have little chance to defend their exposed flanks. By some unfriendly combination of the two, Austria would almost surely be defeated.

Throughout the eastern crisis, Bismarck had bombarded his superiors in Berlin with letters and memoranda urging them to exploit to the fullest Austria's indecision and embarrassment. Free from the responsibilities of power, Bismarck could suggest an array of alternatives that must have seemed outrageous to his cautious correspondents: an alliance with Russia or France, the creation of a bloc of armed neutrals, a political offensive against Austria in the Confederation. For most conservatives, an opening towards Paris was out of the question, since they saw Louis Napoleon as an illegitimate child of revolution and therefore an unworthy ally. Bismarck, however, had been recommending *rapprochement* with France for several years; as far as he was concerned, the legitimacy of Napoleon's regime was a question for the French to decide; other states had only their own interests to consider. In 1855, before the military situation in the Crimea had been resolved, Bismarck spent some time in Paris, where he met the emperor to lay the foundation for what would become an essential element in his diplomatic strategy against Austria.[14]

Bismarck was not the only observer to realize how the political climate had changed in 1854–5. Everywhere in central Europe, people began to acquire a new sense of political possibility. The eastern crisis, combined with the social, economic, and cultural developments that we examined in Chapters 12 and 13, gradually

policy during this period: see, for example, Friedjung, *Kampf*. Recently, however, Buol and his colleagues have found some eloquent defenders: Winfried Baumgart, *Der Friede von Paris, 1856: Studien zum Verhältnis von Kriegsführung, Politik und Friedensbewahrung* (Munich and Vienna, 1972); Paul Schroeder, *Austria, Great Britain, and the Crimean War: The Destruction of the European Concert* (Ithaca and London, 1972). For an analysis of these new views, see Ann Saab's long review article in *CEH* 8/1 (1975), 51–67, and the comments in Rich, *War*, pp. 122–3.

[14] There is a good summary of these developments in Pflanze, *Bismarck*, pp. 102 ff.

helped to dispel the apathy and depression that had followed the revolution's defeat.

One of the first and most acute attempts to understand the significance of the new situation was Johann Gustav Droysen's two-part essay, 'Zur Charakteristik der europäischen Krisis', published in *Minerva* during the fall of 1854. While Droysen's point of departure was the impact of the eastern crisis on the balance of forces established in 1815, he recognized that this conflict was connected to a deeper crisis that was transforming 'every assumption and condition of European life, every social and political force, every spiritual and material factor'. As a result of these transformations, 'everything old is exhausted, counterfeit, decayed, helpless. And the new is still formless, purposeless, chaotic, and merely destructive.' What would this mean for Germany? Droysen did not conceal his hopes that, from the confusion of the present, a resolute Prussia would emerge to establish its leadership over the other German states and thus fulfil its mission to bring Germans together into a unified, Protestant nation. If there was little to nourish such hopes in the present character of Prussian policy, Droysen could call upon the past, evoking at the end of his essay that mythic vision of the *Befreiungskrieg* which was so important to Prussia's admirers: 'After 1806 came 1813, after Ligny, Belle-Alliance. In truth, we only need the cry "Forward", and everything will be set in motion.'[15]

Prussia's admirers were greatly encouraged when, in October 1857, the government announced that Prince William would temporarily assume his royal brother's duties. Although rumours had been circulating about Frederick William IV's mental and physical disabilities for several years, the court, firmly backed by the Manteuffel ministry, had managed to prevent a permanent transfer of power. Even when a regency was finally established, it was limited to a series of three-month terms. By October 1858, however, Frederick William's condition was clearly irreversible and William formally became Prince Regent. A staunch conservative by nature and conviction, William was none the less prepared to rule constitutionally. On the first day of his reign, he summoned the *Landtag* to validate his regency and a few weeks later he himself swore an oath of loyalty to the constitution. Moreover, William hated the sanctimoniousness and obscurantism so pervasive in his brother's circle. Religion, William promised, would no longer be used as a 'cover' for political purposes; education would be left in

---

[15] Reprinted in Droysen, *Schriften*, pp. 307–42.

the hands of the teachers. Finally, the regent seemed to promise a new, more vigorous foreign policy when he declared that 'Prussia must make moral conquests in Germany by means of wise domestic legislation, the elevation of morality, and the use of unifying means such as the *Zollverein* . . .' On 5 November William appointed a cabinet of 'liberal conservatives' under Prince Hohenzollern Sigmaringen, which included Rudolf von Auerswald, who had served with Hansemann in the March Ministry of 1848, and Freiherr von Schleinitz, who had been an active supporter of Radowitz.[16]

Although William had declared there would be 'no break with the past', a new era seemed to have begun, for Prussia and for Germany. There were, to be sure, some sceptics. Karl Marx, for example, dismissed the events of 1858 as a shift from 'weak eccentricities' to 'sober mediocrity'—an unkind but not altogether inaccurate assessment of the two rulers' personalities. Many contemporaries, however, were convinced that a fundamental change had taken place. Ernst Ludwig von Gerlach, now excluded from his position of power and influence, lamented that 'the blossoms have all vanished, how many of them without fruit'. Among liberals, there was widespread jubilation. 'One has', the *Kölnische Zeitung* wrote on 4 November, 'a joyful feeling of deliverance.'[17]

As governmental repression eased, political activity increased. In many parts of the kingdom, veterans of 1848 reappeared on the scene, assumed leadership roles, and tried to form new alliances. The first results of their efforts were apparent in the elections held in mid-November 1858. Levels of participation rose dramatically from the doldrums of 1855: from 39.6 to 50.2 per cent in the First Class, 27.2 to 37.1 in the Second, and 12.7 to 18.5 in the Third. More important, a majority of these voters supported liberal candidates. In the new *Landtag*, the number of conservatives dropped from over 200 to less than 60, while the liberals went from 60 to about 210. 'With their vote', reported the *Kölnische Zeitung*, 'the overwhelming majority of electors from all social strata declared their opposition to feudal views and policies.'[18]

Even before the regent's authority was formally established,

<hr>

[16] Huber, iii. 269 ff.

[17] Marx and Engels, *Works*, xvii. 70; Hamerow, *Foundations*, (1969–72), ii. 9; Weinandy, 'Wahlen', fo. 149.

[18] Parisius, *Deutschlands*, p. 16; Hess, *Parlament*, p. 24; Weinandy, 'Wahlen', fo. 158.

Bismarck had sought to convert William to his view of the German question. In the most elaborate of these efforts—a ninety-two page memorandum of March 1858 which is conventionally called the 'booklet'—Bismarck argued that conflict with Austria was unavoidable. In this conflict, Prussia could not look to the other German governments for assistance: 'Prussia will never fulfil its German mission until it stops putting so much weight on the sympathy of the middle states.' This did not mean, however, that Prussia was alienated from the German lands: 'There is nothing more German than Prussia's special interests properly understood.' This phrase marked a significant advance from his views of 1853. Then he had recognized that Germany was the only field upon which Prussia could expand; now he had begun to see that such expansion would involve a qualified endorsement of the German national cause. The new government in Berlin, however, was no more receptive to its ambassador's enthusiastic suggestions than Frederick William's had been. Instead, Prince William turned towards better relations with Austria, which required a new representative at Frankfurt. In March 1859 Bismarck was sent east, to become Prussian ambassador in St Petersburg.[19]

By the time Bismarck had taken up residence in what he called 'cold storage on the Neva', a new crisis was under way—this time on the southern flank of the Habsburg lands. Count Cavour, the Prime Minister of Piedmont, had been among the first to recognize that Austria's estrangement from Russia left her vulnerable to anyone able to secure French support. In the summer of 1858 Cavour signed a secret alliance with Napoleon. The following April he managed to lure Austria into a declaration of war against Piedmont, thereby ensuring French assistance. In the first major use of rail lines for military purposes, French troops crossed the Alps in record time and prepared to help Cavour drive the Austrians from their Italian lands.

As he watched these events unfold, Bismarck had no doubt how Prussia should act, preferably by 'moving our entire army south, with boundary stakes in their packs, which can be planted on the Bodensee or wherever Protestantism stops'.[20] As usual, such advice found little support in Berlin, where Prince William was torn between a sense of obligation towards Austria and a desire to improve Prussia's position in the Confederation. When Vienna argued that Articles Forty-six and Forty-seven of the *Schlussakte*

[19] Rothfels (ed.), *Bismarck*, p. 171. See Pflanze, *Bismarck*, pp. 122 ff.
[20] Gall, *Bismarck*, pp. 136–7.

compelled the German states to come to the Habsburgs' assistance, the Berlin government played for time by insisting that, since Austria fought as a European rather than as a German power, it was not entitled to aid unless federal territory was threatened. Privately, however, Prussian diplomats suggested Prussia might be willing to fight if William was given command of the German forces. These negotiations were still limping along when, following the Austrian defeats at the battles of Magenta and Solferino, Napoleon and Francis Joseph signed a hastily drafted armistice on 11 July.

Now Bismarck could do no more than lament the loss of yet another opportunity to strike against the Habsburgs:

Clinging to the Slavic–Romanian half-breed state on the Danube, whoring with pope and emperor, is at least as treasonable against Prussia and Protestantism, indeed against Germany, as the most shameless Rhenish Confederation. To France we can, at worst, temporarily lose a province, but we can lose all of Prussia to Austria, now and forever.[21]

Once again, Bismarck's superiors ignored him. In Berlin, as in the other German capitals, statesmen did not see the situation so dramatically; most of them believed that the Italian war had shifted but not transformed the international system. After all, Napoleon and Cavour might have won militarily, but neither achieved their final goals. Francis Joseph lost an Italian province, but immediately set out to reform Austrian domestic institutions. William had managed to anger the Austrians, but he had not altered the balance of power within the Confederation.

The Italian question did mark a new stage in the evolution of public involvement in political affairs. In contrast to the opaque complexities of the eastern crisis, events in Italy provided a cause that touched many Germans' interests and values. To Austria's conservative supporters, the line was clearly drawn: on the one side, social order, political legitimacy, and religious faith, on the other, Bonapartism, nationalist passions, and secularization. These people urged federal support for the Habsburg cause, even if that meant war with France. They were prepared, in the slogan of the day, 'to defend the Po on the Rhine'. For Austria's enemies, however, the advocates of Italian unity seemed to be fighting a battle parallel to their own. They naturally identified with 'courageous, progressive' Piedmont, 'which seemed to want to establish a lasting basis for orderly freedom on Italian soil'. In Italy, as in Germany, the Habsburgs appeared to be the enemies of

---

[21] Ibid. 136.

progress and nationhood. Only when Austria had been expelled from Italy and the German Confederation, wrote Heinrich von Treitschke in June 1859, would it be possible to imagine that this 'unholy *Mischstaat* could find a purpose to exist through its cultural mission in the slavic east'. A month later, another *kleindeutsch* liberal expressed his conviction that 'Germany (and perhaps Europe) is dividing into two increasingly committed and self-conscious parties. At the head of one is, willingly or not, the state of the Hohenzollern. . . . The conflict is not only political, but embraces the realms of the spirit, religion, education, economy, and so on.'[22]

During the summer of 1859, while the Italian war and its aftermath were stirring German opinion, Prussia's advocates met in various cities to consider the future: on 17 July left-wing liberals under the leadership of Hermann von Schulze-Delitzsch gathered at Eisenach; two days later, a more moderate group from the northern states assembled in Hanover with Rudolf von Bennigsen as its spokesman. These two groups merged in September to establish the *Nationalverein*, a 'national party' committed to 'the unity and free development of the entire fatherland'. From its headquarters in Frankfurt, the *Nationalverein* pledged to use 'all available legal means, especially spiritual labour, to bring the ends and means of our widespread movement more and more to the forefront of national consciousness'. How exactly this would effect national unity under Prussian leadership was never stated. The assumption seemed to be that it would be enough, as Johannes Miquel put it, 'to make the fruit ripe . . . for the moment that must come'. Even in the post-revolutionary era, therefore, liberals retained their faith in the power of ideas and education to shape an irresistible force of public opinion. 'We are not diplomats or statesmen,' Miquel proudly insisted, 'we represent the views of the nation, and therefore it is enough if we speak the truth.'[23]

Despite some half-hearted efforts to organize the *Volk*, the *Nationalverein* remained in the hands of educated and propertied Protestant élites: officials (especially judges), professors and pastors, lawyers and notaries, journalists, industrialists, and merchants. As we shall see, the organization was frequently divided by

[22] On Germans and Italian unification, see Altgeld, *Italienbild*; Ernst Portner, *Die Einigung Italiens im Urteil liberaler deutscher Zeitgenossen* (Bonn, 1959). Quotes from Portner, p. 38; Engelberg, *Widerstreit*, pp. 127–8; Duncker, *Briefwechsel*, p. 162.

[23] Mommsen, *Miquel*, pp. 196–7, 201. Huber, *Dokumente*, ii. 90ff., has the most important sources. Hamerow, *Foundations*, i, provides a good account of the *Nationalverein* in its historical setting.

disagreements over goals and tactics, but it never abandoned the tone and procedures of an educational society whose distinctively *bürgerlich* sociability was captured so beautifully in Raabe's *Guttmanns Reise*, a novel set at the *Nationalverein* meeting of 1860.[24]

The opponents of a *Kleindeutschland* also responded to the crisis of 1859. In a pamphlet entitled *Deutschland und der Frieden von Villafranca*, Julius Fröbel argued that the Italian crisis underscored the need for federal reform. Unlike the founders of the Nationalverein, Fröbel assumed that any answer to the German question had to take into account what he called the 'three natural elements in the German state system: Austria, Prussia, and the totality of small and medium-sized states'. To Fröbel, as to generations of German federalists, the third Germany was an essential counterweight to the bureaucratic centralization represented by both Austria and Prussia. It was necessary, therefore, that the other German states form their own separate confederation, 'which could be organized as a third German power according to their own ideas and interests and as such participate equally with Austria and Prussia in a triadic rule'.[25]

Fröbel was the most articulate and effective spokesman for the democratic, federalist wing of the *grossdeutsch* movement. Others opposed Prussia and supported Austria for quite different reasons. There were Catholics like Julius Ficker, who feared Protestant hegemony, particularists like Minister von Varnbüler from Württemberg, who wanted to defend the integrity of their states, liberals like the publisher Johann Freiherr von Cotta, who opposed Prussian authoritarianism, and of course Austrian patriots like Counts Auersperg and Arneth. So divided were these people among themselves that it was not until 1862 that they could establish an organization to oppose the *Nationalverein*. Even then, the *Reformverein* reflected rather than resolved their differences. Some *grossdeutsch* leaders, such as the Württemberg democrat Moritz von Mohl, viewed it as a reactionary front, while others, such as the Hanoverian Catholic Ludwig Windthorst, gave it only their most qualified support. As Franz Herre put it, the composition of the *Reformverein* 'was like the multicoloured map of the Confederation that it wanted to transform'.[26]

The degree to which the German question had emerged as a central concern for the political public was manifest in the

---

[24] O'Boyle, 'Nationalverein'.

[25] Herre, *Nation*, pp. 150 ff.

[26] Ibid, 156. On the *Reformverein*; see Huber, *Dokumente*, ii. 95; Real, *Reformverein*; and Hope, *Alternative*.

celebrations held in November 1859 to mark the centenary of Schiller's birth. In Austria, Germans used this occasion to reaffirm their national identity: 'Politically divided, fragmented in parties, filled with the passions of the times . . . all Germans are united in Schiller's spirit.' His birthday had special meaning for the Habsburgs' German subjects because it gave them a chance to show 'that we feel ourselves to be German and see ourselves as an inseparable part of Germany'. Elsewhere, however, the Schillerfest took on very different meanings. To the defenders of *Kleindeutschland*, 'our Schiller' was Protestant and liberal, a forerunner of a Germany without Austria. This was the Schiller Wilhelm Raabe remembered in 1872, when he wrote that the toasts exchanged in 1859—'Seid einig, einig, einig!'—represented the true beginning of national unification under Prussian leadership.[27]

In organizations like the *Nationalverein*, celebrations like the Schillerfest, and hundreds of articles and pamphlets, Germans struggled to formulate and realize a new definition of their national existence. The pages of Schulthess's *Europäischer Geschichtskalender*—itself a product of political renewal—are filled with reports of meetings, petitions, and debates over political issues and national questions. Johann Caspar Bluntschli, speaking to a gathering of German jurists, compared these multifarious activities 'to brooks which flow towards a great river, brooks which continually grow bigger until the river embraces them and carries them away'. Eventually, Bluntschli believed, all Germans would be swept away in a national movement towards unification and constitutionalism.[28]

In most histories of the *Reichsgründung*, the story of these popular movements is told in tandem with the story of Prussia's diplomatic and military triumphs. That popular movement and state action worked together is central to the *kleindeutsch* position, which sees Prussia as instrument and ally of the national will. Given the weight of this historiographical tradition, it is worth emphasizing just how small and divided the national political public was in the 1850s and 1860s: the *Nationalverein*, for example, never had more than 25,000 members. No doubt public opinion did play a role in the calculations of statesmen. As Bismarck by 1858 had come to

[27] Lutz and Rumpler (eds.), *Österreich*, p. 207; Herre, *Nation*, p. 146. On the Schiller celebrations, see Hohendahl, *Kultur*, pp. 198 ff.
[28] Hamerow, *Foundations*, i. 339. On the pamphlet literature, see Hans Rosenberg's monumental bibliography, *Publizistik*. Fricke *et al.* (eds.), *Parteien*, has a great deal of useful information on a variety of organizations.

realize, national enthusiasms could be used to further state interests. Nevertheless, Bismarck knew—and we should not forget—that the German question remained essentially a question of power relationships within and among the various states.

ii. THE 'NEW ERA'

During the late 1850s, the political climate changed in almost every important German state. In Bavaria, for example, the Pfordten ministry, which had been under attack since 1856, was forced to resign after the opposition's stunning electoral victory in 1858. Rather than run the risk of a prolonged conflict with the liberal *Landtag*, King Maximilian entered into a limited but productive alliance with the progressive political forces in his state. Even more dramatic was the new course set by Grand Duke Frederick of Baden, who worked with a liberal *Landtag* majority on a series of political, social, and economic reforms. With the appointment of August Lamey as Minister of the Interior. Badenese liberalism became, in the words of its leading historian, 'a governing party'. Nowhere else were political shifts as obvious as they were in Munich and Karlsruhe, but most German governments moved away from their reactionary policies, eased restrictions on public life, and opened dialogues with opposition groups. As a result, electoral participation increased, organizations multiplied, and a new generation of political leaders began to emerge. In 1862, when he returned home after a dozen years of exile in the United states, Friedrich Kapp marvelled at 'people's greater independence, their participation in political affairs, economic expansion, and self-confidence'.[29]

In the Habsburg lands, the new era came in the wake of fiscal crisis and military defeat. To the poet Anastasius Grün (the pseudonym for Anton Count von Auersperg), the bad news from Italy brought hope for change within the monarchy itself:

> Denn nur aus Unglück kommt Dir Heil,
> So will's Dein alt Verhängnis,
> Dem Volk erblüht das Segensteil
> Aus seiner Herrn Bedrängnis.

The existing system, wrote a conservative commentator, 'is thoroughly rotten and must collapse'. But what would take its

[29] Kapp, *Frühsozialisten*, p. 77.

place? 'Just as in 1848, the word *constitution* is on everyone's lips.' Unnerved by the realities of war and badly shaken by the experience of defeat, Francis Joseph was ready to consider changes that he had found unthinkable just a few months earlier. In an extraordinary manifesto, issued to the nation from Laxenburg Castle on 15 July 1859, the emperor promised to seek 'Austria's domestic welfare and external power through the effective development of her rich spiritual and material resources, as well as through timely [*zeitgemässe*] improvements in legislation and administration . . . .'[30]

Even before the end of the Italian campaign, the emperor had begun to dismantle neo-absolutism. In May, Buol, one of the chief architects of defeat, was replaced by Count Rechberg, who became Minister President and Foreign Minister. Bach and Kempen, whose officials and policemen had personified Austrian government in the 1850s, were both forced to resign. On the other hand, Bruck, who represented the regime's progressive elements, continued to press for liberal reform from his post in the Finance Ministry. In April 1860, when Bruck took his own life in the midst of a financial scandal, the monarchy was deprived of one of its most devoted servants.

Throughout the first half of 1860, as the economic and political consequences of the Italian war became increasingly painful, the government moved towards reform. In March the emperor assembled an expanded *Reichsrat* to advise him on legislative and budgetary matters as well to prepare for constitutional reorganization. There were, to be sure, still those who insisted that no formal bonds should separate the people and the dynasty: Archduke Albrecht, for instance, believed that unless the Habsburgs were unencumbered by constitutional restraint they would 'collapse in the face of their various nationalities . . . and the democratic, levelling tendencies of the time'. But even many arch-conservatives agreed with the *Reichsrat*'s conclusion that 'the existing system of organization can neither ensure nor enhance the monarchy's future success'. There was, however, much less agreement on what should replace the neo-absolutist system. As at the beginning of German constitutional development, two models were available: a corporate system that would be built upon a set of relatively autonomous *Länder* or a representative system that would

---

[30] Bibl, *Zerfall*, p. 255; Herre, *Franz Joseph* (1978), p. 165; Huber, *Dokumente*, vol. 2, pp. 27–29.

exert centralizing pressures on the Habsburgs' scattered territories.[31]

In October the emperor decided for the first of these: after giving Count Goluchowski responsibility for domestic policies in a reorganized cabinet, Francis Joseph issued a decree that granted considerable legislative authority to the various *Landtage* and established an appointed *Reichsrat* to confirm laws affecting the monarchy as a whole. This solution, the so-called October Diploma, satisfied no one. Most national groups, including the Germans, Czechs, and Poles, believed that their interests were under-represented. Even the Hungarians, whose special status within the monarchy had been recognized, did not believe they had been given the power they deserved. Those in favour of greater centralization, on the other hand, decried the devolution of authority towards the *Länder*, while progressives feared a resurgence of aristocratic influence. Given the range and depth of these criticisms, it is unremarkable that the October Diploma did nothing to ease the monarchy's fiscal woes, which were—as always—an important source of constitutional experimentation. Government bonds continued to require record premiums while the interest rate on government loans rocketed. According to the Minister of Finance, Ignaz von Plener, the government's desperate need for funds was the 'decisive' reason that Francis Joseph so swiftly abandoned the October solution.[32]

The signal that the emperor had once again changed course came in mid-December, when Anton von Schmerling replaced Goluchowski as Interior Minister. Schmerling was from an old bureaucratic family that had been ennobled in the eighteenth century. His own career had followed the tangled course of Austrian constitutionalism—he was one of those liberal jurists who had pressed for reform during the opening stage of the revolution, a member of the delegation that had demanded Metternich's resignation, a leader of the *grossdeutsch* party at Frankfurt, and then Justice Minister in Vienna, a post he resigned in 1851 in protest against neo-absolutism. Schmerling was self-confident to the point of arrogance, but he was not doctrinaire. Like many others in the post-revolutionary era, he was sensitive to the limits of change and, as he wrote in his autobiography, aware that 'every constitution and all

[31] Herre, *Franz Joseph*, p. 178; Huber, iii. 378.
[32] Franz, *Liberalismus* (1955), p. 124. Franz provides on a good summary of Austrian liberal movements. See also Winter, *Revolution*. The best treatment of the monarchy's financial difficulties is Brandt, *Neoabsolutismus*.

constitutional rights are always questions of power'. His problem was to find a system that would be progressive enough to resolve the monarchy's chronic fiscal and political problems, but not so progressive that it would be unacceptable to the emperor and the still formidable conservative élites.[33]

The result of Schmerling's efforts was a series of decrees conventionally referred to as the February Patent of 1861. At the centre of these laws was a redefined *Reichsrat*, which now had the power to approve and even to initiate legislation. The *Reichsrat* was a bicameral body, with a Chamber of Deputies chosen by the members of the territorial *Landtage*, who were themselves elected by voters divided into curias (in most territories these consisted of large landowners, chambers of commerce and trade, and urban and rural communities). Although it purported to be merely an extension of the October Diploma, the Patent of 1861 redefined the basis for Austrian public life by shifting political power back towards the centre, further increasing the Hungarians' special status, and strengthening the political position of the German *Bürgertum*. Moreover, the new *Reichsrat* was, despite the carefully drawn restrictions on its authority, a genuine parliament in which elected delegates were free to deliberate on important national issues. The continued role of the territorial *Landtage*—and the new local government act [*Gemeindegesetz*] passed in 1862—was supposed to guarantee that the interests of the monarchy's heterogeneous parts would be represented and protected.[34]

In the spring of 1861, when the *Reichsrat* convened amid great ceremonial splendour, many Austrians must have hoped that they now had a chance to reconcile the conflicting forces of centralization and local autonomy, monarchical authority and representative government, political cohesion and national identities, rural conservatism and urban liberalism, rigid Catholicism and fervid anti-clericalism. Perhaps in more tranquil times, some sort of reconciliation might have been possible. But the 1860s were by no means tranquil; instead of marking the opening of a new era, the February Patent remained no more than an episode in a period beset by that combination of foreign and domestic crises to which the Habsburgs were so vulnerable.

From the start, constitutional experimentation in Austria was

[33] Somogyi, *Zentralismus*, p. 7.
[34] Franz, *Liberalismus*, pp. 169 ff. Kann, *Empire*, ii, app. 4, gives the composition of the various diets.

inseparable from the monarchy's struggle to sustain its international position, a struggle that inevitably involved Austria's
relationship to the Habsburgs' Hungarian and Italian lands as well
as to the members of the German confederation. Francis Joseph
believed that he had been betrayed by the German states during the
Italian war; in the Laxenburg Manifesto he spoke of the way in
which 'our oldest and most natural allies had refused to see the
significance of these great questions'. Nevertheless, with Russia
still hostile and Britain apathetic about Austria's fate, he had no
choice but to enlist German Europe against continued pressures
from the French.

The emperor's advisers disagreed about the ends and means of
the monarchy's German policy. Schmerling retained a *grossdeutsch*
vision. He hoped that the February Patent would help open the
way for federal reform that would improve Austria's position in
the Confederation at the same time as it consolidated German
power within Austria itself. To do this, he was prepared to
mobilize opinion in the monarchy and the rest of the German lands
against Prussia and a *kleindeutsch* solution. But he did not want to
unleash nationalist sentiments. As he put it, Austria should seek
'political primacy in the Confederation without [evoking] political
nationalism'.[35]

Rechberg, who remained Foreign Minister throughout the
cabinet reorganizations of the early 1860s had a different view of
German politics. Like so many of the Habsburgs' loyal servants,
the Rechbergs came from the west. The family was originally
Swabian; Johann Bernhard's father had been Bavarian Foreign
Minister before moving to Vienna in 1825. Father and son had close
ties to Metternich, whose view of the world they tended to share.
The Foreign Minister's ideal, therefore, was an alliance of
conservative powers in defence of the status quo at home and
abroad. Since it would take time to draw Russia into such an
alliance, Rechberg's first aim was closer ties to Prussia—which he
had to achieve without surrendering Austrian pre-eminence in the
Confederation. Rechberg regarded any appeal to national sentiments as an invitation to disaster.[36]

[35] Herre, *Nation*, p. 204. By setting the Hungarian situation to one side, my
account inevitably distorts the full picture of Habsburg politics. It is worth noting
once again, therefore, that Austria was always more than a German power. On the
Hungarian problem, Louis Eisenmann's *Le Compromis Austro-Hongrois de 1867*
(Paris, 1904) is still worth reading.

[36] Elrod, 'Rechberg'.

At least on the surface, relations between Austria and Prussia improved in 1860. Francis Joseph and Prince William were personally reconciled when they met at Teplitz in July. Three months later they both journeyed to Warsaw to see Tsar Alexander, thus raising hopes among conservatives that a new version of the Holy Alliance was at hand. As concern over Napoleon III's aggressive foreign policy increased, Berlin and Vienna set up a joint military commission to discuss strategic co-operation. Count Karolyi, the Austrian envoy in Berlin, tirelessly pressed for a formal political agreement.

But there was still no consensus in the Prussian government about relations with Austria. Bismarck continued to argue for a diplomatic offensive against the Habsburgs. While he was in Berlin for medical treatment during the summer and autumn of 1859, he had even met some leaders of the liberal movement, whose national goals he seemed prepared to sponsor. Baron von Schleinitz, the Foreign Minister, was not a man for such adventures. He distrusted popular forces, feared France more than Austria, and saw the advantages of a condominium with Vienna. As long as William remained loyal to his brother monarch and faithful to Prussia's duties in the Confederation, Schleinitz was able to restrain Bismarck and his supporters. Nevertheless, as Ambassador Karolyi realized, Austro-Prussian relations would remain unsettled until policy-makers in Berlin decided the essential question: 'Would Prussia recognize that if we stand together we can easily confront every danger . . . or does she see this as an opportune time to secure her position in Germany at Austria's expense?'[37]

While the two German superpowers were trying to construct a new basis for their relationship, other German states began to search for ways to reform the Confederation, whose weaknesses had been so painfully apparent during the eastern crisis and the Italian war. One of the most elaborate of these reform proposals was prepared in October 1861 by Count Beust, the Minister President of Saxony. Beust began from the assumption that Germany would have to remain a confederation of states rather than become a federal state—a *Staatenbund* rather than a *Bundesstaat*. But, he asked, how could a confederation satisfy 'the needs of the national sense of community and the development of national power'? This would require a careful reshaping of power relations that recognized Prussia's ambitions while guaranteeing Austria's integrity and admitted popular involvement while preventing

[37] Böhme (ed.), *Reichsgründung*, p. 111.

revolutionary upheavals. To accomplish these goals, Beust suggested a complex set of institutions, including a tripartite executive (composed of a Prussian, an Austrian, and a representative of the 'third Germany'), a renovated diet (which would meet twice a year, once under Prussian, once under Austrian direction), and a representative assembly (indirectly elected by the state parliaments).[38] Beust's plan, while perhaps a bit too complicated, was not unreasonable. But like every answer to the German question, its intrinsic merits mattered less than whether it could attract the power necessary to put it into effect. The small and middle-sized states were characteristically disunited and indecisive, while the Austrians, who were initially sympathetic, eventually backed away from Beust's position.

The most dramatic reply to Beust came from Berlin. In December 1861 Count Bernstorff, who had replaced Schleinitz as Foreign Minister two months before, sent the Saxon Minister President a formal counterproposal on federal reorganization. The Prussian plan included some features suggested by the Badenese statesman, Franz von Roggenbach, but it was essentially a restatement of Radowitz's plan of 1849: a *kleindeutsch* federal state, which would be joined to Austria in a *grossdeutsch* Confederation. Vienna had no choice but to respond. Using a simplified version of the Beust plan, prepared by Baron von Dalwigk, Minister President of Hesse-Darmstadt, Rechberg set about trying to rally the German states in defence of a reformed Confederation. In February 1862 Austria, supported by Bavaria, Württemberg, Saxony, Hanover, Hesse-Darmstadt, and Nassau, formally rejected Bernstorff's proposals. These states signed a secret agreement in which they pledged to resist a *kleindeutsch* solution, even if this meant a Confederation without Prussia. Austro-Prussian relations were further strained in July, when Berlin formally recognized the kingdom of Italy, thereby evoking a sharp protest from Vienna and applause from those German liberals for whom Italian unification was a model to be emulated. When the diet met in August to consider Austrian plans for federal reform, they were vigorously opposed by Count Usedom, the leader of the Prussian delegation.[39]

At the same time that animosity between the two German

---

[38] Ibid. 106 ff. For Beust's own account, see his *Erinnerungen*. Rumpler's *Politik* is a good introduction to Beust's background and career.

[39] In addition to the documents collected in Srbik, *Quellen*, see Enno E. Kraehe, 'Austria and the Problem of Reform in the German Confederation, 1851–63', *AHR* 56 (1950–1).

powers divided the Confederation, a new source of tension arose over commercial policy. Since its beginnings, the *Zollverein* had been regarded by Prussia's admirers as both instrument and example of the Hohenzollern monarchy's leadership role in German affairs. During the new era, as public debate over national issues intensified, *kleindeutsch* and *grossdeutsch* elements argued about Prussia's supposed economic hegemony over the other German states. Matters came to a head in August 1862 when Berlin signed a commercial treaty with France that substantially lowered trade barriers between the two states. Free traders—including many who had begun to oppose governmental policies on other matters—strongly supported the treaty, while protectionists denounced it. The Austrians recognized that because they could never embrace the provisions of the Franco-Prussian treaty, its acceptance by the other German states would effectively end Austria's chances of joining the *Zollverein*. Rechberg, therefore, began to encourage opposition to the treaty among the *Zollverein* states and also offered to lead the Habsburg monarchy into an enlarged customs union with the rest of Germany. This new source of conflict had just begun to emerge when, in September 1862, Otto von Bismarck was named Minister President of Prussia.[40]

In order to understand how Bismarck moved from the fringe to the centre of power, we must retrace our steps and follow the emergence of the constitutional crisis that threatened to paralyse the Prussian political system. As we have seen, Prince William's regency initially had evoked widespread enthusiasm among Prussian liberals and their supporters throughout the German states. Buoyed by their success in the elections of 1858, the Prussian opposition vowed to avoid the errors that had undone them a decade earlier. Left- and right-wing liberals emphasized their common goals, co-operated in local organizations, and sought to work with the government on a programme of moderate reform. Meanwhile, a similar coalition of forces in the *Nationalverein* set about rallying Prussia's admirers throughout *Kleindeutschland*. *Nur nicht drängen!* ('Just don't push!') was the order of the day.

From the start, the liberals' honeymoon with William was based on illusory hopes and false premisses. Although the regent had little sympathy for his brother's reactionary style, he was no less committed to preserving the authority of the crown. Indeed, he was surprised and dismayed that his vague overtures towards

---

[40] On the *Zollverein* controversy, see Böhme, *Deutschlands Weg*; Hamerow, *Foundations*, ii, ch. 3.

reform met such a positive response among people whom he regarded as dangerous radicals. The men with whom William felt at home were not liberal parliamentarians but conservative army officers like Edwin von Manteuffel and Albrecht von Roon, who shared his values, training, and unqualified commitment to the military foundations of the Hohenzollern state.

William was profoundly convinced that these foundations were in need of repair—after all, Prussia's armed forces retained the size and structure given them half a century earlier. Military reform, William and his advisers realized, was complicated by the fact that the Prussian army was an instrument of both foreign and domestic politics. To defend the state from its enemies abroad, the army had to be a mass force based on conscription, but to defend the social order from domestic unrest it had to remain a politically reliable servant of the king. Roon addressed this issue in a memorandum of July 1858 that called for a substantial increase in the number of line regiments, but also a three-year term of service in which recruits could learn the necessary military skills and political values. Furthermore, Roon advocated a significant curtailment of the militia, which had been established to supplement regular forces in time of war. Like many of his brother officers, Roon doubted the militia's effectiveness and questioned its loyalty. Poorly trained and led by non-professionals, it seemed to be an unwholesome intrusion of civilian society into the military sphere. In September 1859 William endorsed Roon's proposal and appointed him chairman of a Military Reform Commission; two months later, he became War Minister.[41]

Under the best of circumstances, military affairs were filled with the potential for conflict between the government and the political opposition. Liberals objected to the fact that, by claiming a lion's share of the budget, the army sopped up funds that might be used for roads or schools. Moreover, liberals resented the arrogance of the officer corps, whose members often made no effort to conceal their contempt for the rest of the nation, a contempt that had had harsh political consequences during the revolution of 1848. To these persistent strains, Roon added a new source of friction by attacking the militia, which played a part in the liberals' cherished myth of 'national liberation'. The conflict over the army reforms, therefore, was more than a conflict between the military and civilians or between throne and parliament, it was also a conflict between two visions of Prussia's identity.

[41] There is a good summary of the army issue in Craig, *Politics*, ch. 4.

When Roon presented his reforms to the *Landtag* early in 1860, liberal parliamentarians were appalled. But, because both sides still hoped to avoid a direct confrontation, the Chamber passed a provisional budget in May, based on the government's promise not to go further with army reorganization until a regular bill had been passed. In fact, William had no intention of waiting, but rather pressed ahead with the formation of new line regiments. Neither he nor his officers believed that the army was subject to parliamentary control; its organization and character were the monarch's sacred responsibility. Nor did William intend to compromise on the key issues of three-year service and the role of the militia. By the time he became king after his brother's death in January 1861, the optimism and good will of the new era had been replaced by anger and recrimination.[42]

As liberals' relationship with the government deteriorated, divisions within their own ranks began to appear. In January 1861 seventeen delegates separated themselves from the liberal faction led by Georg von Vincke, took up seats on the far left of the Chamber, and issued a statement demanding resolute opposition to the government. This group became the nucleus of the *Deutsche Fortschrittspartei* founded that June. Because it included both moderates and democrats from the old political opposition, the *Fortschrittspartei* could not take a firm stand on some key issues, such as suffrage reform and social policies. But its programmatic statements and organizational efforts did mark an important milestone in the evolution of German participatory politics. In the Chamber elected at the end of 1861, the party had over a hundred members and, together with the other oppositional groups, made up a clear majority. Despite some tentative efforts at organizational renewal, the conservatives, who had dominated the parliament just a few years earlier, were reduced to a pitiful minority of fifteen.[43]

The life of the new Chamber was brief; after a majority rejected the military budget, the king dissolved the parliament and named a new cabinet of hardliners under Prince Hohenlohe-Ingelfingen. But from the elections held in May 1862, the *Fortschrittspartei* once again emerged victorious, this time with 138 seats and roughly one third of the popular vote. Together, the various liberal factions

---

[42] The literature on the Prussian constitutional conflict is discussed in Sheehan, *Liberalism*, p. 320, n. 6.

[43] The relevant documents on the formation of the *Fortschrittspartei* can be found in *EGK* (1861), 41 ff., and Mommsen, *Parteiprogramme*, pp. 132–5. Eugene N. Anderson, *The Prussian Election Statistics 1862 and 1863* (Lincoln, Nebraska, 1954), has a complete set of electoral data, while Hess, *Parlament*, provides information on the *Landtag's* social and political composition.

could claim 235 of the 352 delegates. Faced with this strong and stubborn opposition, the king and his advisers were uncertain about how to proceed. Manteuffel urged defiance, perhaps because he hoped to provoke violence, which the government could counter with *coup d'état* against the constitution. Others, apparently including Roon, were willing to consider a compromise. William himself vacillated between obstinacy and despair. In September, with another parliamentary defeat virtually certain, the king seemed on the verge of abdicating in favour of his son, whose reputation as a liberal sympathizer suggested the possibilities of a new political direction. Instead, Roon persuaded William to make one final effort to save the military reforms and protect the authority of the crown by asking Bismarck to head a new cabinet. On 20 September Bismarck, who had been transferred from St Petersburg to Paris three months earlier, arrived in Berlin. Four days later he was named Minister President and Foreign Minister.

The day before Bismarck's appointment was announced, the Chamber refused the military appropriations in the budget, which was then voted down by the upper house. The political conflict over the army was thus turned into a constitutional conflict over the parliament's budgetary powers. It should be noted, however, that virtually no one in the liberal camp wanted to impose a parliamentary government on the monarch. When they spoke of 'ministerial responsibility', liberals had in mind a minister's legal responsibility rather than his subordination to a parliamentary majority. Their goal remained that fruitful co-operation with the crown they thought they had finally achieved in the happy days of the new era.[44] Yet they were not ready to purchase this co-operation at any price—as Bismark quickly discovered when he made some tentative offers of a compromise settlement to liberal leaders.

As soon as Bismarck's efforts at accommodation were rebuffed, he made clear his intention to govern without parliamentary approval. On 30 September he declared that the king could rule with 'emergency powers' (*Notrecht*) when a constitutional deadlock paralysed the normal machinery of government. From this came Bismarck's famous 'gap theory', which held that, if compromise is impossible, then 'conflicts become a question of power. Whoever holds the power then proceeds according to his own will, for the life of the state cannot remain still even for a second.'[45]

[44] For example, see Eduard Lasker's essays from 1862 and 1863, reprinted in *Zur Verfassungsgeschichte Preussens* (Leipzig, 1874).

[45] Pflanze, *Bismarck*, p. 194. On the legal dimensions of the 'gap theory', see Huber, iii. 305 ff.

Few observers believed that the Bismarck ministry would have sufficient power to survive. To the liberal majority he personified everything wrong with Prussia. As one writer for the *Preussische Jahrbücher* put it, 'The conflict is now revealed for what it basically is—the battle of the *Bürgertum* against the Junker allies of absolutism.'[46] Nor did he have many admirers on the right, who remembered his outrageous dispatches from Frankfurt and feared his lack of scruples and restraint. At court, the queen was known to detest him, while the crown prince and his English wife supposedly had ties to the liberal opposition. But against these manifest weaknesses, Bismarck could set one overwhelming source of strength: as long as he retained the confidence of the king, he could count upon the formidable power of the state. This, he hoped, would buy him enough time to find a way of defeating or converting his liberal opponents.

As we know, Bismarck had long been convinced that Prussia should move vigorously to assume leadership over the German states and that such a move might involve co-operation with the national movement. 'Prussia's frontiers', he told the *Landtag* Budget Committee, 'do not favour a healthy political existence.' But, he continued, this matter 'will not be decided by speeches and majority opinions—that was the mistake of 1848 and 1849—but by blood and iron . . .'. Part bluff, part challenge to the liberal opposition, these famous words should not be taken from their polemical context. Nevertheless, they do underscore the fact that Bismarck, unlike so many others who had addressed the German question, recognized that his answer might depend on the use of force. However vague his goals and however fluid his strategy, he never failed to see this essential connection between means and ends.[47]

During his first year in office, Bismarck's only successes on the international front were negative ones. He was able to mobilize enough support in the federal diet to defeat Austria's reform proposals, which lost by a vote of 9–7 in January 1863. That summer, he managed to block another Austrian move when he persuaded William not to attend a meeting of German princes called by Francis Joseph. Without Prussia's participation, the princes would give no more than qualified support to the emperor's call for a reconstructed Confederation. As usual, a majority of the smaller states preferred the status quo to a dangerous choice between the

---

[46] Heffter, *Selbstverwaltung*, p. 414.
[47] Böhme (ed.), *Reichsgründung*, p. 129.

superpowers. At a meeting of the *Zollverein* states held in Munich between April and July, Bismarck was able to resist Bavarian efforts to bring Austria into the customs union. The Minister President's more positive efforts, however, came to nothing. His attempt to draw Napoleon into an anti-Austrian alliance was unsuccessful, while his offer to assist Russia in repressing the Polish rebellion of 1863 aroused widespread distrust among the other great powers.

Bismarck's lacklustre record abroad did nothing to dampen liberal opposition to his policies at home. Nor did the Minister President's efforts to break the liberals' will with a restrictive Press law, reprisals against liberal civil servants, and electoral intimidation have any impact. In municipal governments and scholarly meetings, local clubs and economic associations, popular pamphlets and newspapers, people condemned the return to reaction. When the government again dissolved the *Landtag* and held new elections in October 1863, the *Fortschrittspartei* and its allies once again scored impressive victories; between them they now had more than a two-thirds majority of the Chamber.

The Prussian liberals' success at the polls was repeated in state and local elections all over German Europe. Most city councils, including those of the major capitals like Vienna and Berlin, were in liberal hands. From the start, German liberals dominated the Austrian *Reichsrat*—in large part because of favourable suffrage regulations. In 1862 liberals captured a majority in the Hessian parliament; the following year, they controlled fifty-four of the Badenese *Landtag's* sixty-three seats. Even in Bavaria and Saxony, where they could not overcome the resistance of anti-liberal forces, progressive elements represented a growing, vital political movement. In Württemberg, Hanover, and Saxony, they established *Fortschrittsparteien* as a mark of solidarity with their embattled Prussian colleagues. Every year, there was a parliamentarians' convention in Frankfurt, to which came liberal leaders from every major state. Like the *Nationalverein*, this gathering seemed to reflect a broad, national formation that liberals wanted to believe represented enlightened opinion everywhere. It did not seem to be merely electoral hyperbole, therefore, when the Prussian *Fortschrittspartei* declared that 'the absolutist–aristocratic party' found itself confronted by 'the great liberal majority of the nation'.[48]

Although liberals were better organized and more united than

[48] *EGK* (1861), 45. Sheehan, *Liberalism*, p. 95, surveys the various *Landtag* election returns.

they had been in the 1840s, the movement continued to be weakened by the fragmented character of German public life. Some sort of a new era opened almost everywhere, but the precise character of the relationship between the government and the opposition differed widely from state to state. In Baden, as we have seen, liberalism came close to being a governing party, while in Prussia it faced a constitutional impasse with the crown. Austrian liberals co-operated with the government on some issues, bitterly opposed it on others. In Württemberg, liberals' relations with the government were complicated by the presence of a strong democratic movement on their left. Elsewhere—in Hanover, for example—the opposition remained united against a reactionary regime. Political traditions and constitutional forms, the personalities of the monarch and of the liberal leadership, the level of social development and the structure of political alignments all gave politics in the various states a distinctive character and style. Men like Bennigsen from Hanover, Sybel and Hoverbeck from Prussia, Karl Brater from Bavaria, Julius Hölder from Württemberg, and Ludwig Häusser from Baden could agree on general principles when they met at some annual convention, but they could not help but interpret these principles in the light of very different practical experience.[49]

A more important source of liberals' weakness than the diversity of their political experience was the shallowness of their social base. Once again, we should not overlook the progress liberals had made since the 1830s and 1840s; in some areas, they had even managed to create a cohesive, well-organized popular movement. But in most places, the opposition continued to depend on the efforts of local notables, whose personal prestige and informal connections provided the foundation for electoral campaigns and political agitation. Liberal leaders in state parliaments and national associations were usually from the educated or propertied sectors of the Bürgertum, men with the educational background, leisure time, and social status that participatory politics seemed to require. As usual, many German liberals combined parliamentary opposition with a bureaucratic position: for example, among the liberal delegates

[49] In addition to Sheehan, Liberalism, see Eisfeld, Entstehung, and the following works on individual states: on Bavaria, Blessing, Staat, chs. 3, 4; on Württemberg, Langewiesche, Liberalismus and Brandt, Parlamentarismus; on Hesse, Adalbert Hess, Die Landtags- und Reichstagswahlen im Grossherzogtum Hessen, 1865–1871 (Oberursel, 1958); on Baden, Gall, Liberalismus.

elected to the Prussian *Landtag* in 1862 were fifteen local government officials, six pastors, ten teachers and professors, and seventy-seven judicial officials.[50]

Of course, liberal support had to extend well beyond the small social élites of *Bildung* and *Besitz*. On petitions supporting the opposition, in local organizations, and among liberal voters, we find tradesmen, artisans, and even a few wage labourers. Liberal candidates did equally well in all three classes of the Prussian suffrage system; the clearest difference between liberal and conservative voters in Prussia was not between rich and poor but rather between city and countryside. However, the Prussian statistics also point to another, equally important characteristic of public life in the 1860s: despite the intense political energies unleashed by the constitutional crisis, no more than a third of Prussia's eligible voters went to the polls. Here the difference among the three suffrage classes is quite dramatic: in 1862, 61 per cent of the First, 48 per cent of the Second, but only 30 per cent of the Third Class participated. We do not have comparable figures for the other states, but there is every reason to believe that the situation was similar in most places. At the height of their power, liberals may have been able to claim that they were supported by the majority of politically active Germans, but this remained a majority of a minority. [51]

Before 1866, popular apathy, poor communications, and restrictive suffrage systems left most of the population outside electoral politics, apparently untouched by the efforts of either liberals or their enemies to mobilize them. Nevertheless, we can catch a glimpse of the two mass movements that would eventually challenge liberals' claim to speak for the *Volk*: political Catholicism and Social Democracy. Although the origins of these movements surely belong to our story, it is important to remember that, before 1866, both of them were small and scattered; most of their future constituencies remained silent or unorganized.

As we have seen, the relationship between liberals and Catholics had always been problematic. Occasionally, the two groups acted together against state repression; in some areas, Catholic notables blended with the local élites and provided leadership for liberal

[50] Some examples: Langewiesche, *Liberalismus*, pp. 224–5; Hess, *Parlament*, pp. 65–72, Becker, *Staat*, p. 104.
[51] See Anderson's electoral data (cited above, n. 43) and the local election studies cited in Sheehan, *Liberalism*, pp. 317–18, n. 16.

politics. Overall, however, the tension between the church and the liberal movement was greater than the impulse to co-operate. Liberals were often ready to work with the state against the church, which they saw as a source of cultural backwardness and political reaction, while Catholics characteristically viewed liberal demands for religious freedom as unjust interference in their mission to save souls. After mid-century, divisions between liberalism and Catholicism increased. The apparent ascendancy of science and materialism inspired anti-clericals at the same time that it evoked a powerful response from the church, which intensified its resistance to 'modern' cultural trends. More immediate and dangerous than cultural secularization was the rise of liberal nationalism, which directly threatened the church's political position in Italy and, as both sides were quick to realize, could leave Catholics an embattled minority within a Prussocentric Germany.

Against this backdrop of cultural and political conflict, a series of confrontations between liberals and Catholics occurred in a number of German states. Austrian liberals, for example, struggled to alter the privileged position granted to the church by the Concordat of 1855. Church–state relations were also of paramount importance to liberals in Baden, where the new era brought a series of laws aimed at regulating the clergy and increasing the state's control over education. Baden's liberals, like their counterparts in Württemberg and Hesse, were able to force the government to retreat from its efforts to establish concordats with the papacy.[52] Against these liberal attacks, Catholics were surprisingly slow to organize. In Baden, for example, church leaders did not begin to mobilize mass support until 1864, whereas in Prussia's western provinces a profound religious revival did not have political implications until after national unification. Jonathan Sperber's conclusion that Rhenish Catholicism's 'mass political potential remained latent' holds true for most of the German lands before 1866.[53]

In contrast to political Catholicism, which would eventually be able to mobilize a pre-existing constituency, the labour movement's social basis remained ill-defined and inchoate throughout the century's middle decades. As we have seen, 'class consciousness' among German working people had just begun to emerge.

[52] Boyer, *Radicalism*, ch. 1; Becker, *Staat*.

[53] Sperber, *Catholicism*, p. 98; Sperber provides a brilliant account of popular religious life and its political potential. Lenger, *Kleinbürgertum*, p. 223, describes some early successes of Catholic agitation. For a stimulating attempt to describe the long range significance of religious antagonisms, see M. L. Anderson, 'The Kulturkampf and the Course of German History', *CEH* 19/1 (1986).

Workers were still divided into a variety of social groups and political organizations; some were aware of their distinctive social identity, while others remained committed to liberal values. Too often, historians of the labour movement, in their eagerness to establish a powerful pedigree for Social Democracy, have tended to obscure this variety and political malleability by predating what Gustav Mayer called 'the separation of *bürgerlich* and proletarian democracy'.[54]

Throughout the 1860s, the relationship between liberalism and labour remained fluid and complex. In some places, people committed to organizing working men against both liberals and reactionaries returned to public life as repressive measures began to ease. Elsewhere, however, workers joined educational societies formed under liberal auspices and voted for liberal candidates. Consider, for example, the case of August Bebel, who was born in 1840, the son of a non-commissioned army officer; as a woodworker's apprentice in Wetzlar, Bebel read enlightenment literature and absorbed *bürgerlich* values. Naturally enough, when he moved to Leipzig and became interested in politics, Bebel joined a liberal *Bildungsverein* because, like most of his contemporaries, he subscribed to the same political goals as his liberal patrons: 'freedom of enterprise, movement, and residence, freedom to travel, associate, and meet'.[55]

Some liberals recognized that their future depended on the ability to attract and maintain the allegiance of men such as Bebel. Hermann Schulze-Delitzsch, for example, devoted a great deal of time and energy to persuading his colleagues to take the 'worker question' seriously. A radical member of the Prussian parliament in

[54] Gustav Mayer, 'Die Trennung der proletarischen von der bürgerlichen Demokratie in Deutschland, 1863–1870'; first published in 1912, Mayer's classic essay is reprinted in *Radikalismus*. The literature on Social Democracy is immense, as can be seen from the titles in Dieter Dowe's *Bibliographie zur Geschichte der deutschen Arbeiterbewegung, sozialistischen und kommunistischen Bewegungen von den Anfängen bis 1863* (Bonn, 1976), and Klaus Tenfelde and G. A. Ritter (eds.), *Bibliographie zur Geschichte der deutschen Arbeiterschaft und Arbeiterbewegung, 1863–1914* (Bonn, 1981). A good place to start is with Shlomo Na'aman's collection of documents, *Die Konstituierung der deutschen Arbeiterbewegung, 1862–3* (Assen, 1975). Ulrich Engelhardt's *'Nur vereinigt sind wir stark!'* (Stuttgart, 1977) is an exhaustive account of the early union movement.

[55] Bebel, *Leben*, p. 73. For another, quite different example, see John Breuilly and Wieland Sachse, *Joachim Friedrich Martens (1806–1877) und die Deutsche Arbeiterbewegung* (Göttingen, 1984). Balser, *Sozial-Demokratie*; Birker, *Arbeiterbildungsvereine*; Na'aman, *Impulse*; Toni Offermann, *Arbeiterbewegung und liberales Bürgertum in Deutschland, 1850–1863* (Bonn, 1979) all contain analyses of the relations between liberals and workers.

1848, Schulze had been persecuted during the reactionary 1850s; he returned to politics in the new era and became one of the founders of the *Kongress deutscher Volkswirte*, the *Nationalverein*, and the Prussian *Fortschrittspartei*. The best solution to workers' problems, Schulze believed, was some form of co-operative, through which they could pool their talents and resources to save, purchase, or produce. While co-operatives promised workers a chance to better themselves and a stake in the established order, they did not challenge either the sanctity of private property or the laws of supply and demand. Moreover, co-operatives could appeal to both wage-earners and artisans, thus circumventing a potential split in the labour movement. Finally, co-operatives continued the educational thrust of liberal political action; in them people learned to work together, be frugal, and accept responsibility; at the same time they seemed to be practical and down to earth. No wonder that, despite its rather limited practical success, the idea of co-operation appealed to so many social reformers.[56]

In 1863 Schulze's efforts to maintain liberal influence over workers took on a new urgency when Ferdinand Lassalle suddenly burst on to the political scene. Lassalle was one of those historical figures whose lives resemble art—in his case, part melodrama, part tragedy, part farce. Born in 1825, the son of a Jewish merchant from Breslau, Lassalle belonged to that generation of young German intellectuals whose ambitions collided with the repressive restrictions of *Vormärz* society. Like Marx, with whom he had a long, tension-filled relationship, Heine, and many others, Lassalle was drawn to radical politics. Throughout most of his adult life he was in and out of trouble with the police, including a brief prison term for insurrection in 1849. But there was always an individualistic, quixotic strain in Lassalle: for example, even while he was engaged in struggling for a new political order, he devoted himself to an eight-year court battle to win a favourable divorce settlement for Countess Sophie Hatzfeldt.[57]

In 1862 Lassalle became convinced that the liberals' struggle with the Prussian government was bound to fail. Early the next year he began to urge workers to break their ties with the liberal

[56] Schulze-Delitzsch's *Schriften* are available in a five volume collection edited by Friedrich Thorwart. The most recent biography is Rita Aldenhoff, *Schulze-Delitzsch. Ein Beitrag zur Geschichte des Liberalismus zwischen Revolution und Reichsgründung* (Baden-Baden, 1984). See also Conze, *Möglichkeiten*.

[57] In Hermann Oncken's classic biography, *Lassalle* (3rd edn., Stuttgart, 1920), he appears as a nationalist foil to Marx. The definitive treatment of his life is now Shlomo Na'aman, *Lassalle* (Hanover, 1970).

movement, establish independent organizations, and press for full democratization of state and society. In May 1863 he founded the *Allgemeiner deutscher Arbeiterverein*, which soon attracted an impressive number of supporters in Hamburg, Frankfurt, and a few Rhenish cities. At the same time, Lassalle held a series of secret meetings with Bismarck, whom he hoped to draw into an anti-liberal alliance on behalf of the labour movement. These meetings meant little to the Minister President, but they were an important symptom of Lassalle's impatience. Flamboyant, eloquent, and charismatic, he could inspire political passions but had little interest in the details of organization or the formulation of strategy. When his efforts did not bring him immediate success and the government continued to press charges against him for sedition, his political enthusiasms gave way to despair. In the spring of 1864 he became increasingly absorbed by a hopeless love affair with Helene von Dönniges, the daughter of a Prussian historian and diplomat. That August, he was mortally wounded in a duel with Helene's fiancé.

Schulze-Delitzsch, who was a special target of Lassalle's anti-liberal attacks, responded to his campaign by redoubling his efforts to persuade workers that their future lay with liberalism. But to some of Schulze's liberal colleagues, the so-called 'worker question' was a 'swindle', perpetrated by radical revolutionaries or demagogic reactionaries. Others had little interest in social problems, which seemed far less important than constitutional and national issues. Some, however, were prepared to make tentative efforts on behalf of working people. In 1863 a group of liberals formed the *Verband deutscher Arbeitervereine*, which sought to co-ordinate the activities of various labour organizations throughout the German lands. In addition, a few liberals were ready to support trade unions, whose right to organize was supported by a majority of the Prussian *Fortschrittspartei* in 1865.[58]

Liberals had good reason to hope that German workers would not desert them. When Lassalle died in 1864, his organization had only about 4,600 members, substantially less than the array of co-operatives and educational associations affiliated with liberalism. In many areas, such as Berlin, Lassalle had met with little or no success. Nevertheless, in the flash of his brief career the potential divisions between liberals and labour were clearly revealed. First,

[58] Schulze-Delitzsch, *Schriften*, ii. 211 ff. In addition to the works cited above, n. 54, see John Breuilly, 'Liberalism or Social Democracy: A Comparison of British and German Labour Politics, *c*.1850–1875', *EHQ*, 15/1 (1985), 3–42.

there were the differences in economic interest between employers and employees, those with property and those without. Second, there were differences on political issues such as the suffrage, which divided workers from moderate and right-wing liberals, and on the national question, which divided particularist elements within the labor movement from the advocates of *Kleindeutschland*. Finally, there were matters of social values and style that made it difficult for working people to feel that they were full-fledged members of organizations supposedly designed for their benefit. Even Schulze, whose sincere concern for their welfare was unmistakable, could not avoid a condescending tone when he addressed gatherings of workers. In time, this combination of economic, political, and social strains would drive ambitious, talented young men like August Bebel to join movements they could regard as truly their own.

The emergence of an independent labour movement, like the first stirring of political Catholicism, intensified the uneasiness many liberals felt about the masses. Throughout the 1860s, we find liberal politicians pointing out the perils of uncontrolled democracy, the unreliability of the mob, and the destructive passions of the uneducated. These dangerous elements seemed to be lurking just behind the educated and propertied ranks of enlightened opinion, always ready to support revolution or dictatorship. 'In the essence of democracy', wrote Karl Beidermann in the third edition of the *Staatslexikon*, 'there is a certain drive to assert itself directly, without limits or mediation. This is something it has in common with despotism.' This persistent fear of the *Volk*, which was characteristic of liberalism everywhere in Europe, because especially debilitating when German liberals tried to establish their right to influence their nation's future.[59]

iii. NATIONAL CONFLICTS AND DOMESTIC REALIGNMENTS

There was something tentative and uncertain about Austrian attempts to assume the initiative in German affairs during 1863. Rechberg's efforts to lead the monarchy into the *Zollverein* were persistently challenged by domestic opponents who, like the Chamber of Commerce in Lower Austria, did not want to see their interests sacrificed 'for the sake of maintaining a political position in Germany with uncertain prospects'.[60] Francis Joseph's campaign to

[59] *StL* (3rd edn.), iv. 345.
[60] Katzenstein, *Partners*, p. 76. See also Elrod, 'Rechberg', p. 445.

mobilize the German princes was also half-hearted. When it became clear that Prussia would not participate, the emperor gave up trying to persuade or force the smaller states to rally to his plan for federal reform. Instead, at their meeting in Frankfurt that August, the princes did little more than consume a sumptuous banquet, applaud a splendid speech by Francis Joseph, and enjoy an elaborate fireworks display—in which, it was widely noted, only the illuminated figure of Germania failed to ignite. Francis Joseph was even more reluctant to link his German policy to the emerging force of *grossdeutsch* public opinion. Not only did this kind of popular agitation go against all of the emperor's instincts, it would also have threatened the delicate balance of conflicting nationalities within the monarchy.

These difficulties remind us once again that the Austrians' German policy was always inseparable from their other interests and obligations, in Europe and within the monarchy itself. Economically, diplomatically, and politically, Austrian Germans may have been too German to regard the rest of German Europe as foreign, but they were too Austrian to consider becoming part of a purely German nation-state. For them, some kind of federal solution was essential. This meant that Francis Joseph's government was forced to remain in a defensive, largely reactive stance. As German affairs approached a decisive historical moment, the initiative for change would come from Berlin, not Vienna.

By the end of 1863, when their various plans for reform had clearly lost their momentum, Rechberg and his sovereign returned to seeking the alternative they had always preferred, a bilateral agreement with Berlin. They counted on William's goodwill, dynastic loyalties, and personal affection to incline him towards his young colleague in the Hofburg. The Austrians recognized that to move William in their direction, they would have to neutralize Bismarck's formidable opposition or win him over to their side. In any event, they preferred Bismarck to a liberal ministry, whose ties to national opinion throughout the German lands could creative a revolutionary force beyond diplomatic control. This conviction that, however difficult Bismarck might seem, there was something worse waiting in the wings, gave the Prussian leader a useful card to play in the diplomatic game that unfolded over the next three years. Again and again, when presented with a proposal he did not like, the Minister President claimed that to accept it would mean his replacement by the liberal opposition. As a result, Bismarck was often able to effect compromises on his terms, drawing Austria into a maze of tactical errors and strategic illusions.

Bismarck's skills as a spinner of diplomatic webs began to emerge late in 1863, when the old problem of Schleswig-Holstein suddenly took on a new form. Schleswig-Holstein was, the reader will recall, a residue of ethnic diversity and legal ambiguity in a world increasingly dominated by nationalism and state sovereignty. Dynastically tied to Denmark, the duchies were legally inseparable, although Holstein, which had a German-speaking majority, was part of the Confederation. In 1851 and 1852, after the turmoil of the revolution had subsided, the great powers signed a series of treaties in which they promised to defend Danish sovereignty in return for Copenhagen's promise not to annex Schleswig or change the duchies' constitutional status without consulting their estates. International treaties, however, are notoriously ineffective against national antipathies and state ambitions. Throughout the late 1850s and early 1860s, threatening moves by the Danish government, together with agitation by both Danes and Germans in the duchies themselves, kept the situation unstable and potentially inflammable. Things came to a head in March 1863, when King Frederick VII aroused German national passions by seeking to impose a new constitutional order on Schleswig without the promised consultation with the estates.[61]

On 15 November 1863 Frederick died without a direct heir. Because they saw the possibility of a succession crisis, the signatories of the treaty of 1852 had acknowledged the claim of Prince Christian of Glucksburg, both to Denmark and the duchies. However, immediately after Frederick's death, Christian's right to the duchies was challenged by the German Prince Frederick of Augustenburg, who declared himself duke of Schleswig-Holstein. The Augustenburg claim was supported by most German liberals, as well as by progressive rulers like Duke Ernst of Koburg, who provided him with a base of operations in the heart of central Europe. When the diet, which had been discussing the Schleswig-Holstein issue throughout the year, met on 21 November to consider the new situation, a majority of the German states favoured Augustenburg. Faced with the apparent challenge of Danish aggression, a rare consensus seemed to have emerged between the German governments and a broad spectrum of national opinion.

Against this consensus stood Austria and Prussia, who declared their willingness to support Christian's claims to the duchies if he

---

[61] Steefel, *Question*, is still worth reading. Huber, iii. 449 ff. has a good account of the constitutional issues.

agreed to abide by the guarantees set out in the treaties of 1851 and 1852. Despite the appeals of various organizations, including both the *grossdeutsch Reformverein* and the *kleindeutsch Nationalverein*, and, despite their own strong inclinations in favour of Augustenburg, the members of the Confederation had to be content with voting sanctions against Denmark for violating its treaty obligations. When the Danes ignored this, federal troops moved into Holstein in December and, without resistance, occupied most of the territory south of the Eider River.

Austria and Prussia had a common policy towards the duchies, but their motives and goals were quite different. Rechberg saw the Schleswig-Holstein problem as the occasion for creating the constellation of forces that he had always wanted: a Confederation dominated by an Austro-Prussian condominium directed against liberal nationalism and in favour of the status quo. His interest in Schleswig-Holstein *per se* was minimal; his principal aim was to lay the basis for a broad and lasting set of agreements with Berlin. This was not Bismarck's intention. Although he did not reveal his goals to anyone for another year, he was attracted by the idea of annexing the duchies to Prussia. Moreover, his agreement to work with Vienna in support of the treaties of 1852 was purely tactical, a way to keep the game going while he waited to see what would develop. Years later, while reflecting on the events of 1864 and 1865, which he considered among his greatest achievements, Bismarck told his friend Lothar Bucher that the central problem had been a matter of timing: 'The individual actions were, in themselves, trifles; to see that they dovetailed was the difficulty.' To maintain maximum flexibility, he had to co-operate with Vienna, prevent the great powers—especially England—from interfering on Denmark's behalf, defeat the Danes quickly and decisively, and do all of this without committing himself on the question of the duchies' future. He moved, slowly and carefully, testing the ground at each step, always probing for weakness, but always ready to retreat.[62]

In January 1864, without regard either to their partners in the Confederation or to the outraged cries of public opinion, Austria and Prussia delivered their demands directly to Denmark. When the Danes, overestimating their own strategic advantage and the responsiveness of the European powers, refused to accept this ultimatum, the two states sent troops under General Wrangel

---

[62] Pflanze, *Bismarck*, p. 240; Pflanze gives a clear and balanced analysis of Bismarck's policy in ch. 11.

across the Eider into Schleswig. A conference hastily assembled in London that June did no more than demonstrate Britain's unwillingness to defend the treaties of 1852. As a result, the two German powers resumed hostilities, moved their troops from the mainland to seize the island of Alsen and thus threatened Denmark itself. On 1 August, the Danes had to sue for peace.[63]

Throughout this crowded period, in his dealings with his Austrian allies, with the other European powers, and with the German states, Bismarck kept the question of the duchies' future open. For a while he apparently based his policy on the treaties of 1851–52, but he steadfastly rejected Austrian efforts to guarantee Christian's sovereignty in Schleswig-Holstein. At the London conference he had offered a bewildering variety of alternatives, including even an Augustenburg regime. In the final peace treaty between Denmark and Austria and Prussia, he had compelled Christian to surrender his sovereignty over the duchies, but left their ultimate fate still in doubt—an ideal solution from Bismarck's perspective since it gave him time to prepare a new sequence of moves.

For their share of the victory over Denmark, the Austrians had got nothing. Rechberg had involved them in a war for territory in which they had no real interest, risked a confrontation with the European powers, and alienated Augustenburg's supporters in the Confederation. Instead of the specific agreements and guarantees for which Rechberg yearned, Bismarck had provided vague promises and empty rhetoric about the need for monarchical solidarity against revolution. 'A true German and conservative policy', he wrote to his envoy in Vienna on 6 August, 'is only possible when Austria and Prussia are united and take the lead. From this high standpoint an intimate alliance of the two powers has been our aim from the outset.' But when he and William met with Francis Joseph and Rechberg at Schönbrunn a few days later, what he would do to get such an 'intimate alliance' remained studiously imprecise. Rechberg's efforts to acknowledge Prussia's influence over the duchies in return for Prussian help in reconquering Austria's lost Italian territories met with no success. Bismarck was not about to pay for what he hoped to get for nothing.[64]

When the Schönbrunn conference failed to yield any tangible benefits, Rechberg's rivals in the Austrian government stepped up

[63] On the Danish war, see Craig, *Politics*, pp. 182 ff.
[64] Böhme (ed.), *Reichsgründung*, pp. 143 ff. The Schönbrunn Convention is reprinted in Huber, *Dokumente*, ii. 175.

their attacks on his policy of *rapprochement* with Berlin. Biegeleben, with Schmerling's support, continued to argue that an alliance with France was the only way to protect the monarchy from Prussian aggression. Rechberg tried to recoup his losses by taking up once again the question of Austria's participation in the *Zollverein*. But here too he met stubborn resistance from Berlin. After he was not even able to establish the basis for future consideration of the matter, he had no choice but to acknowledge defeat; in October 1864, he resigned. However, contrary to his rivals' hopes, Rechberg's departure did not bring a clear-cut victory for the anti-Prussian camp. As Rechberg's successor, Francis Joseph chose Count Mensdorff-Pouilly, a conservative, well-connected, and absolutely loyal army officer without diplomatic experience. On 31 October, in a long address to the ministry, the emperor outlined the principles of his foreign policy: peace, co-operation with Prussia, protection of the other German states, good relations but no alliance with France, and long-term efforts towards better ties with Britain and Russia—in short, an essentially defensive programme, based upon a desire to avoid painful choices and dangerous commitments by searching for support from every possible source.

Under some circumstances this might have been an admirable policy, but in 1864 its net effect was to surrender the initiative to Bismarck, who was free to choose the time and place to begin the next stage in his anti-Austrian offensive. Throughout 1865 the Prussian Minister President moved with characteristic caution, preparing the ground for future action while keeping every possible option open. By the spring he had managed to convince King William that Prussia should annex Schleswig-Holstein, even if it meant war with Austria. Indeed there was now the danger that William, with strong backing from the military, would push harder and faster than Bismarck wished. Before any final, unalterable confrontation with Vienna, he wanted to be sure that France, the other key power on the European scene, would remain neutral. To this end, he entered into complex negotiations with Napoleon, encouraging the emperor's appetite for territorial expansion on the Rhine without committing himself on how this appetite might be satisfied. To Austria, Bismarck offered a perplexing mixture of accommodation and defiance, especially with regard to Schleswig-Holstein. By mid-year, Vienna was ready to trade Prussian annexation of the duchies for appropriate compensation elsewhere in central Europe, but Bismarck chose to keep the game going, embroiling the Austrians more and more in an open-ended and uneven struggle. In August 1865 he convinced them to sign the so-called Gastein Convention, which left the future of the duchies open, but separated them administratively, with Prussia controlling Schleswig, and Austria Holstein. The Habsburgs' continued vulnerability to political, diplomatic, and military harassment was thereby ensured.[65]

In 1864 and 1865 Bismarck displayed for the first time his extraordinary skills as a diplomat: patience, flexibility, and the ability to exploit his opponent's hopes, fears, and illusions. But while we should not undervalue his abilities, we should also note that Bismarck was extremely fortunate in having the adversaries he did. Francis Joseph and Rechberg were surely less gifted than he. More important, the Austrians had to confront a more imposing array of enemies: in addition to the Prussian threat in the German lands and the new Italian state's unfulfilled aspirations, the monarchy was beset with internal conflicts that undermined and eventually destroyed the constitutional settlement of 1861.

Schmerling, as we have seen, had introduced the February Patent in order to consolidate German rule at home and prepare a *grossdeutsch* offensive abroad. He met powerful resistance on both fronts, from Rechberg and the others who wanted to pursue a special relationship with Berlin, and from nationalities inside the monarchy who resisted the creation of unified representative institutions. From the start, the Hungarians and Croats refused to send delegates to the *Reichsrat*. Only the dynasty, they maintained, provided a link between the Habsburgs' varied lands. In 1863, when martial law was declared in Galicia during the rebellion in Russian Poland, the Poles joined the boycott. In confronting this opposition, Schmerling had only qualified support from the *Reichsrat's* liberal majority, which was eager to press its own constitutional agenda, including limitations on the emperor's emergency powers, ministerial responsibility, and revocation of the Concordat of 1855. The *Reichsrat* also clashed with the government on the perennial problem of state finances, which, despite stringent cost-cutting measures, continued to be plagued by budget deficits and high borrowing costs. Finally, German liberals were impatient with what they took to be Schmerling's excessive tact in dealing with recalcitrant nationalities; most German-

---

[65] The record of Francis Joseph's presentation of 31 Oct. 1864 is printed in Srbik, *Quellen*, iii. 357–8; the Gastein agreement can be found in Huber, *Dokumente*, ii. 182.

speaking liberals wanted constitutional consolidation, with or without the co-operation of the Hungarians.[66]

Sometime towards the end of 1864 Francis Joseph decided to abandon the course set in 1861. He had never been personally close to Schmerling, had always been doubtful about his foreign policy, and heard with growing dismay the critical voices raised against his government in the *Reichsrat*. In 1865, without consulting his ministers, the emperor initiated negotiations with Deak and other Hungarian leaders. That June he made a brief, conciliatory visit to Budapest, suspended the emergency regulations introduced in 1861, and appointed a new chancellor for Hungarian affairs. Faced with this *de facto* disavowal of his policy, Schmerling resigned. He was replaced by Count Richard Belcredi, the Habsburgs' viceroy in Bohemia, whose appointment as Minister of State was limited to the western half of the monarchy. In September the constitution of 1861 was formally suspended and the search for a new basis of rule began again.

Although his government also faced a constitutional impasse in 1865, Bismarck's problems were altogether easier to manage than those of his Austrian rivals. Prussia had nothing comparable to the Austrian nationality problem—her largest ethnic minority, the Poles, were, for the moment at least, totally subjugated. Moreover, the Prussian economy was flourishing, revenues continued to pour in, and the apparatus of government worked smoothly. While the authorities in Vienna were recklessly cutting back on vital military expenditures, Roon and his colleagues were spending freely to improve the Prussian army's training, organization, and equipment. The first fruits of these improvements were harvested in 1864, when the Prussian army's successful assault on the Danish positions at Düppel in April evoked patriotic enthusiasm throughout the kingdom. Some liberals began to fear that economic prosperity, bureaucratic efficiency, and military power rendered the regime impervious to their opposition. As early as January 1864 Heinrich von Sybel wrote, 'Our government goes its own way—it is impossible to put pressure on it with nothing more than agitation and moral suasion.'[67]

The Danish war revealed some important fissures in the opposition. Initially, Prussian liberals had joined with their colleagues throughout the German lands to support Augustenburg's claim to the

[66] See Somogyi, *Zentralismus*; Redlich, *Staats-und Reichsproblem*.
[67] Heyderhoff and Wentzcke (eds.) *Liberalismus*, i. 211.

duchies and to condemn Austria's and Prussia's refusal to support the true 'German' cause. But following Denmark's defeat, some liberals in Berlin began to look more favourably on a policy of annexation, which continued to be rejected by most nationalist spokesmen. The impulse towards accommodation with the government created by military victory and patriotic fervour was increased by liberals' continued support for official economic policies, especially free trade. Nevertheless, the liberal opposition continued to reject the military budget, protest Bismarck's unconstitutional regime, and criticize his foreign policy. Only a minority was won over by the Minister President's limited accomplishments and elliptical promises.[68]

To Prussia's admirers in the other German states, the persistence of the constitutional conflict seemed to threaten the very foundations of the *kleindeutsch* programme. Franz von Roggenbach, for instance, had long argued that Prussia was Germany's natural leader. 'There is no Prussian policy', he wrote in 1859, 'that would not be German and national.' Even before he became Baden's Foreign Minister in 1861, Roggenbach had been influential in creating a strong cadre of *kleindeutsch* supporters within Badenese liberalism. With the end of the new era, however, liberals' trust in Prussia began to ebb. 'A government that does not pay attention to its own parliament', the *Karlsruher Zeitung* declared a month after Bismarck took office, 'cannot create a German parliament, and without the will of the German people national unification cannot occur.' Grand Duke Frederick, who had tried to convince William to adopt a more conciliatory posture, rightly feared that the kingdom's reactionary policies would prevent the moral conquest of Germany that the regent had promised in 1858.[69]

In 1864 Baden had its own crisis, caused by the eruption of a religious struggle between liberals and Catholics. The immediate issue was a new school law, but the conflict drew its distinctive intensity from a nest of animosities between *grossdeutsch* Catholics and *kleindeutsch* liberals, peasants and city-dwellers, craftsmen and entrepreneurs, Catholic populists and Protestant élites. When Catholic leaders began to mobilize popular opposition to the government, many liberals responded by demanding tighter restrictions on the political activity of the clergy, who, they

[68] Winkler, *Liberalismus*, ch. 2. There is a good sampling of liberal opinion in Heyderhoff and Wentzcke, (eds.); *Liberalismus*, i; see, for example, August Lammers's letter of May 1865, pp. 244–5.

[69] Hermann Oncken (ed.), *Grossherzog Friedrich I. von Baden und die deutsche Politik von 1854–1871* (Leipzig and Berlin, 1927), i. 24 and 46 ff.; Gall, *Liberalismus*, p. 224.

believed, were seducing the gullible masses. At the end of 1865 the Lamey government, itself deeply divided about how to meet the Catholics' counteroffensive, had to confront a restless parliament in which a minority of liberals had formed a new party committed to an uncompromising struggle against clericalism. In fact, the combination of their own domestic divisions and the emerging crisis over German affairs paralysed Baden's liberals, who now found themselves caught between what Lothar Gall called 'the Scylla of Bismarckian power politics and the Charybdis of an apparent ultramontane reaction led by Austria'.[70]

In Bavaria, King Maximilian's death in 1864 had brought that state's new era to an end. Maximilian was replaced by his nineteen-year old son, Ludwig II, who had heady notions about his artistic mission—we have already mentioned his relationship with Richard Wagner—but no political skills or experience. Indeed, his character already showed signs of the eccentricity that would eventually give way to madness. Much to the displeasure of the liberal *Landtag*, Ludwig recalled von der Pfordten as Foreign Minister and began a policy of reconciliation with the church; when the king refused to receive a liberal delegation from Nuremberg, he was accused of violating the foundations of constitutionalism. But the Bavarian *Fortschrittspartei* itself was riven by disagreements on domestic and national issues. In October, outraged by the Gastein Convention's rejection of Schleswig-Holstein's right to self-determination and disappointed by his own party's opposition to universal suffrage, Karl Cramer, the leader of the Bavarian left, resigned from the *Fortschrittspartei*. He was soon joined by democrats from Nuremberg, Fürth, and the Palatinate.[71]

The defection of Bavarian liberalism's left wing was part of a broader pattern of political realignment that took place throughout the south-west in 1864 and 1865. Much of the leadership and support for this realignment came from Württemberg, where the split within the opposition was first articulated. As in most of the German lands, the various elements of the Württemberg opposition had co-operated during the first stages of the new era: in 1859 Austria's military defeats, fear of French aggression, and the hopes aroused by the new political climate in Berlin encouraged both liberals and democrats towards a pro-Prussian position. Gradually, however, the two groups drifted apart. By 1863, when some

[70] Gall, *Liberalismus*, p. 348.
[71] Eisfeld, *Entstehung*, p. 129.

important left-wing leaders returned from exile, impatience with the slow pace of domestic reform and distrust of Prussia had created serious tensions in Württemberg's *Fortschrittspartei*. In 1864 the left seceded and formed the *Volkspartei*, which was committed to the democratization of public life throughout the German lands.[72]

Like the Prussian liberals who had formed the *Deutsche Fortschrittspartei*, the Württemberg democrats wanted to create a national movement. In September 1865 they met with representatives from other states to draft a programme for a German *Volkspartei*, which called for the democratization of every state's constitution and administration, 'federal organization of the states under a central government and parliament, with neither Prussian nor Austrian leadership, and a mutual recognition of the principles of nationality and self-determination'. The democrats believed that the behaviour of the great powers in the Schleswig-Holstein affair had stripped away the last illusions that a nation could be made with Vienna or Berlin. It was necessary, therefore, to redefine German public life, break away from the alternatives of *klein-* as opposed to *grossdeutsch*, and return to the democratic traditions of 1848. 'The German *Volspartei* bases itself on the *Volk*, not the cabinets.' Unfortunately, the resonance of these ideals was limited. An active *Volkspartei* emerged in Saxony and in a few scattered cities in the south-west; elsewhere it attracted only small groups around isolated individuals—Johann Jacoby from Prussia, Leopold Sonnemann from Frankfurt, and Georg Friedrich Kolb from the Palatinate.[73]

The same events that pushed the left wing of political opposition towards the *Volk* in 1864 and 1865 led others to reconsider their relationship with the states. Some liberals recognized that, despite five or six years of agitation, they still lacked the power to persuade or compel their governments: the constitutional conflict in Prussia dragged on, Prussian and Austrian statesmen ignored public opinion, the Confederation was paralysed. No wonder that a few liberals began to look for a great leader, what Karl Bollmann called 'an armed Redeemer who will lead us to the promised land of national unity and independence, even if we must go through the Red Sea of all-out war'. Franz Ziegler declared, 'One would like to

[72] The best accounts of these developments are Langewiesche, *Liberalismus*' and Brandt, *Parlamentarizmus*.
[73] The programme was reprinted in *EGK* (1865), 109–10. See Weber, *Demokraten*; Hope, *Alternative*.

go with a Caesar, if we had one.' 'Times are grave enough', Viktor Böhmert wrote in October 1865, 'that a choice between unity and freedom is required.' There was no question what he would choose: a year earlier he had told Bennigsen that 'German unity is dearer to me than a few paragraphs in the Prussian constitution, over which a German parliament will eventually decide anyway'. But such cries of despair represented a recalculation rather than a renunciation of liberal values; all these men remained convinced that, once national unity had been achieved—no matter how—then freedom must follow.[74]

The doubts and divisions within the opposition were especially painful to the leaders of the *Nationalverein*, which was, as we have seen, a product of the new era's hope-filled beginnings. By 1865 the compromises upon which the *Nationalverein* had been based— between liberals and democrats, governments and public opinion, Prussians and other Germans—had clearly begun to unravel. Overall, the organization's membership had declined, from 23,000 in 1865 to 17,000 a year later. Equally important, some of its most energetic spokesmen had resigned or lost interest. Do not be too critical of the Nationalverein, Gustav Freytag wrote to Treitschke in November 1865, 'It is a kindergarten for undisciplined demo- crats, who gradually must become accustomed to the Prussian idea and parliamentary restraint.'[75] Within a few months the German opposition would have an opportunity to learn a great deal more about both Prussian ideas and parliamentary restraint.

iv. THE GERMAN CIVIL WAR

After having dined with Francis Joseph in January 1866, the British ambassador in Vienna reported to London that 'His Imperial Majesty trusted that the year would pass over quietly and peacefully, and that Austria might be able to devote herself . . . entirely to her internal organization.' This was, the emperor himself must have known, more wish than expectation. There is a lull in politics, Mensdorff wrote on 20 January, 'but the atmosphere is heavy . . . plenty of inflammable stuff is lying about'. Within days an incendiary message arrived from Berlin: the occasion was a pro-Augustenburg demonstration authorized by the Austrian

[74] Sheehan, *Liberalism*, p. 117; Oncken, *Bennigsen*, i. 647, 676. See also Goll- witzer, 'Cäsarismus'.

[75] Engelberg, *Bismarck*, p. 145. See also *EGK* (1865), 131, and the documents reprinted in Oncken, *Bennigsen*, i; Heyderhoff and Wentzcke (eds.), *Liberalismus*, i.

administration in Holstein, which triggered a harsh and threatening note from Bismarck declaring that, if Vienna did not take action against the revolutionary agitation in the duchies, it would be necessary to reconsider 'our entire policy'. When Austria sent an equally sharp reply, Bismarck did not bother to answer. Instead, what the Austrian envoy in Berlin described as an 'ominous stillness' settled over the Prussian Foreign Ministry.[76]

In fact, Bismarck was busy laying the foundation for war. On 21 February he told the king that only three alternatives were now open to him: a liberal ministry, a *coup d'état* against the constitution, or war. A week later, at an extraordinary-council of the king's military and civilian advisers, the Minister President got the king's permission to begin negotiating an alliance with the Italians, whose participation in an impending conflict with Austria seemed essential. Although he still tried to keep his options open, Bismarck now believed that the time for a decisive struggle against the Habsburgs had arrived. Within Prussia's ruling circle, some expressed misgivings about war but only the crown prince seems to have spoken in favour of peace.[77]

In contrast to the élite, there was little public enthusiasm for war in Prussia or in the other German states. Conservatives continued to reject any recourse to nationalism, which Hermann Wagener called 'a lawless, illegal principle that sets out to dissolve the Christian community of nations'. Instead, the traditional right clung to the ideal of Austro-Prussian co-operation. Writing on 8 May, when the momentum towards war was virtually unstoppable, Ludwig von Gerlach called the dualism between Vienna and Berlin 'the vital foundation, the real basis for a German constitution'. There were, Gerlach admitted, deficiencies in the Confederation, 'but they would not lead me to devastate my family or my fatherland'.[78]

Liberals had their own reasons for fearing an impending conflict. During the first months of 1866 the Prussian constitutional crisis continued with increasing bitterness on both sides. The government, in blatant violation of the constitution's provision on parliamentary immunity, sought to prosecute leading members of the opposition for sedition. In major cities, policemen battled angry crowds; the authorities confiscated newspapers, disciplined disloyal civil servants, and refused to validate the elections of liberal

[76] Clark, *Franz Joseph*, p. 333; Pflanze, *Bismarck*, p. 261.
[77] Engelberg, *Bismarck*, p. 569.
[78] Schoeps, *Preussen*, p. 47; Gerlach, *Revolution*, i. 61.

candidates for local office. In this repressive atmosphere, members of the opposition naturally feared that, if war broke out, the government would step up its campaign against them. 'With the first clash between Prussian and Austrian troops'. Karl Brater believed, 'the Prussian *Fortschrittspartei* will be silenced.' Whoever wins an Austro-Prussian war, Theodor Mommsen wrote, 'it can only harm the German nation'.[79]

Most of the opposition was convinced that the Bismarckian regime could never lead Prussia to victory. For decades, liberals had argued that only domestic reform could bring foreign political success—this was, after all, the apparent lesson of the great era of reform upon which the liberals had established their own claim to represent the national interest. How could a government that ruled in defiance of the constitution and in conflict with the 'real' *Volk* hope to mobilize the spiritual and physical resources necessary for victory? Bennigsen, after surveying the forces arrayed against Bismarck, was convinced that the apparently aggressive turn in Prussian policy must be a bluff since the Minister President could not possibly be planning to fight a war with so many enemies at court, in the parliament, and throughout the country.[80]

Most military experts took an equally dim view of Prussia's situation.

Prussia has had no great war for fifty years [Friedrich Engels wrote in June], Her army is, on the whole, a peace army, with the pedantry and martinetism inherent in all peace armies. No doubt a great deal has been done latterly, especially since 1859, to get rid of this; but the habits of forty years are not so easily eradicated.

Foreign observers had also noted the confusion and uncertainty in the mobilization of 1856, which had prompted William to insist on the controversial reform programme as soon as he became regent. The Austrians, on the other hand, were widely regarded as having one of the world's great armies. This reputation had been tarnished but not destroyed by the defeats of 1859, when the army had fought bravely and effectively. In comparison to their Prussian allies, the Austrians had done extremely well against the Danes. With a courageous officer corps, troops recently tested by major combat, a splendid cavalry, and artillery battalions newly equipped with rifled cannon, the Habsburgs' army seemed formidable

---

[79] Oncken, *Bennigsen*, i. 691; Wickert, *Mommsen*, iv. 63. See also the material in *EGK* (1866), 157 ff.
[80] Oncken, *Bennigsen* i. 694.

indeed. According to Engels, it would be very surprising if 'the superior leadership, organization, tactics, and morale of the Austrians' did not prevail 'in the first great battle'.[81]

The Prussians were weak where the Austrians were strong. Their cavalry could not be compared to the well-mounted cuirassiers, hussars, dragoons, and uhlans, who had distinguished themselves in the Italian campaign. Deployed among regular infantry regiments, the Prussian cavalry had no clearly defined mission, either as a decisive offensive force or as an intelligence gathering agency. Similarly, the Prussian artillery was equipped with inferior weapons because, despite Krupp's salesmanship and the urging of some experts, the army had been slow to adopt cast steel guns with rifled bores. Most of their cannon in 1866 were less accurate and less reliable than the Austrians'.

These weaknesses were balanced by the overwhelming superiority of the Prussian infantry. Recruited from the kingdom as a whole, well trained and newly reorganized for swift mobilization, the infantry reflected the distinctive strengths of Prussian state and society. By 1866 all Prussian soldiers were armed with the so-called needlegun (named for the long, sharp pin on its hammer), a breechloading rifle of considerable reliability and accuracy. For two reasons, the breechloader had enormous tactical significance: first, it was capable of firing five rounds per minute, roughly three times faster than a muzzleloader; second, it could be fired and reloaded from a prone position. Together, these two features of the needlegun enabled troops to produce prolonged, murderously accurate fire without exposing themselves to the enemy. The Prussians adopted tactics appropriate for their new weapons: a flexible order of advance in company level units, with further dispersal of the forward units after contact with the enemy had been made. Such tactics required discipline and effective leadership at the lowest levels of organization; without such leadership, the results could be chaos, aimless fire, exhausted ammunition supplies, and almost certain defeat. Concern about these dangers as well as institutional inertia had prevented the Austrians from adopting breechloaders or revising their tactics. As a result, the Austrians' equipment and tactics played to the Prussians' strengths. They retained slow muzzleloaders, disciplined and fairly rigid firing lines, and an emphasis on the decisive superiority of the mass

---

[81] Engels's remarks quoted in Craig, *Königgrätz*, p. 16, and Rothenberg, *Army*, p. 66. Both these works provide valuable analyses of the two armies. See also Showalter, *Railroads*.

bayonet assault. Although the punishing casualties resulting from this *Stosstaktik* were clear to some observers in the Danish war, it remained the centrepiece of Austrian tactical doctrine.

As important as the tactical innovations produced by the breechloader was the strategic revolution created by the railroad, which fundamentally and irreversibly transformed the basic elements of war—time, space, and mass. Just as soldiers were slow to see the advantages of breechloaders, which had been used by hunters for decades, many of them had been reluctant to accept the railroad's military potential. In the first half of the nineteenth century, troops had been moved by train to counter civil disorders—in May 1848, for example, Prussian soldiers had been sent by rail to Dresden—but few believed that a railroad would be able to stand up to the size and complexity of a major campaign. When Prussia tried to use trains during her brief mobilization before Olmütz in 1850, for example, the results were most discouraging. Moreover, at mid-century there did not seem to be enough lines to provide the kind of flexibility that strategy required. In 1859, however, the military advantages of the railroad became apparent when the French took eleven days to move an army the distance that would previously have necessitated a forced march of two months.

Railroads changed the scale as well as the tempo of war. By making it possible to move troops without the enormous quantity of supplies required by slow marches, trains enabled commanders to bring together much larger formations than had traditionally been possible. The battle of Königgrätz would involve about 440,000 men—more than had ever before gathered on a single battlefield. Of course with this new scale came profound problems of command, communication, and control, which new techno-logical advances such as the telegraph were just beginning to address. As Martin van Creveld has written, 'Co-ordinating men, weapons and trains, as well as maximizing each railway line's capacity and preventing congestion, demanded a type of pains-taking staff work . . . raised to a new level of accuracy in both time and space.'[82]

Among the first officers in Europe to grasp the importance of these changes in warfare was Helmuth von Moltke, who had been involved in railway development, both as a military specialist and an investor, since the 1840s. Moltke was born in 1800, the son of a German officer serving in the Danish army. At the age of eleven he

---

[82] Van Creveld, *Command in War*, p. 106. See also Van Creveld, *Supplying War*.

entered a cadet school, whose harsh and cheerless confines were his home until he received his commission eight years later. At twenty-two he switched to the Prussian army, which recognized his intellectual gifts and promoted him first to the *Allgemeine Kriegsschule*, then the Topographical Office, and finally, in 1832, to the General Staff. The select officers of the General Staff were the army's intellectual élite, with responsibility for planning, strategy, and organization. However, when Moltke became its chief in 1857, the General Staff was not at the centre of the command structure; it had neither direct access to the king nor an established place in the highest councils of war. This began to change in 1864 when Moltke was sent north to straighten out the the Prussian forces' confused chain of command during the Danish campaign; his success earned him the king's admiration and a place among the decision makers in the period of increasing tension between Prussia and Austria.[83]

Like Clausewitz, Moltke knew that strategic planning was necessary despite—or perhaps precisely because of—the imponderables and uncertainties of war. 'It is only the layman', he wrote, 'who thinks that he sees in the course of a campaign the previously determined execution of a minutely detailed and scrupulously observed plan.'[84] A plan, therefore, had to be flexible enough to provide options but detailed enough to ensure that troops could be deployed swiftly and efficiently. In the memoranda on an Austrian war that Moltke prepared after 1860, he emphasized the need for speed as well as the enormous advantages offered by the increasingly effective Prussian rail system. Because he understood how railroads had changed the tempo and scale of war, he was willing to qualify the importance orthodox strategists gave to the concentration of forces and to the advantage of interior lines of communication. The new technology, he believed, made it possible to move troops separately, bringing them together at the last minute for a decisive engagement. By 1866 he had evolved a plan he was confident could compensate for the numerical superiority of Austria and its German allies.

Moltke's career and position underscores a further, perhaps decisive advantage of Prussia over Austria; the intellectual calibre of its officer corps. Austrian officers were brave and loyal—no one

---

[83] There is a good account of Moltke's achievements in Van Creveld, *Command in War*, ch. 4. The standard biography is Eberhard Kessel, *Moltke* (Stuttgart, 1957). A convenient collection of Moltke's own writings is available in *Strategy: Its Theory and Application. The Wars for German Unification. 1866–71* (Westport, Ct, 1971).

[84] Craig, *Königgrätz*, p. 27. On Molkte and Clausewitz, see Howard's essay in Clausewitz, *On War*, pp. 29 ff.

doubted that—but they were not encouraged to reflect upon their profession. 'Except for purely technical studies,' one influential general insisted, 'soldiers should not be allowed to publish; otherwise both discipline and *esprit de corps* will be endangered.' Benedek, who had played a heroic role in the defeat of 1859 and was given command of the northern armies in March 1866, once declared that, 'I conduct the business of war according to simple rules and I am not impressed by complicated calculations.' In the age of the railroad, however, complicated calculations were unavoidable.[85]

Military considerations became increasingly important in the spring of 1866 when Bismarck and Mensdorff confronted one another—in Otto Pflanze's words—'like two boxers . . . the one aggressive, the other defensive'. Bismarck wanted to provoke the Austrians into making the kind of move that would guarantee William's willingness to fight and facilitate his own efforts to keep the great powers neutral. Mensdorff, on the other hand, tried to use Bismarck's enemies at court—the crown prince and princess, the queen, and others—to dissuade William from attacking his brother monarch. At the same time, Mensdorff, like Bismarck, was busy seeking support from France. But Mensdorff's ability to man-œuvre was limited, not simply by Bismarck's skills as a diplomatic provocateur but also by the Austrian army's organizational inferiority. Because Austria would take two or three weeks longer than Prussia to field an effective fighting force, it was impossible for Mensdorff to wait for Berlin to take the first aggressive step. At some point, diplomatic advantage would have to be sacrificed to military necessity.[86]

In early April Bismarck quickened the pace in his march towards war. On 8 April his representative in Florence signed a secret alliance with the Italians. The agreement, which was limited to three months, committed the two states to assist each other in the event of war with Austria. The next day the Prussian delegate in Frankfurt formally presented to the diet a reform plan that Bismarck had been circulating among German governments for the past several weeks. This proposal called for the creation of a national parliament, to be elected by direct, universal, equal suffrage, that would work with the states towards the creation of a new order for Germany. Considering his relations with the Prussian *Landtag*, Bismarck's parliamentary sympathies aroused a

[85] Rothenberg, *Army*, pp. 60, 62.
[86] Pflanze, *Bismarck*, p. 285.

certain amount of scepticism among German liberals, who viewed his scheme as a snare. Nor did the Prussian plan meet much enthusiasm in the other German capitals. Most observers seem to have recognized that, as the French ambassador in Berlin reported, Bismarck's project 'is merely a tool to irritate Vienna and create confusion in Germany. . . . I told him so, and he did not deny it.'[87]

The diet was still considering Bismarck's proposal on 21 April, when the authorities in Vienna responded to news of troop movements in Italy by ordering a partial mobilization. The Italians countered with mobilization orders of their own. Although Austria and Prussia continued to exchange notes calling for a mutual reduction of military preparations, the movement towards war had become almost irreversible. On 1 May King William finally decided that Prussia would have to fight. The next day he gave Moltke virtual command over his armed forces; on the day after that, full-scale mobilization began.

Frightened by the superpowers' rush to arms, the other German states vainly tried to find a path towards peace. On 9 May the diet took Saxony's side in its dispute with Prussia over military mobilization. Ten days later, Bavaria, Württemberg, Baden, Hesse-Darmstadt, Saxony-Weimar, Saxony-Meiningen, Saxony-Coburg, and Nassau declared their support for a complete demobilization within the Confederation. At the same time, the governments of these states rejected the potent mix of promises and threats with which Bismarck tried to enlist their aid against the Habsburgs. Moltke was not far wrong when he declared on 20 May that Prussia had no friends among the German states. Three weeks later, when war was in sight, another Prussian official ruefully remarked, 'We have only two allies—the duke of Mecklenburg and Garibaldi.'[88]

Public opinion was also anti-Prussian. In April the *National-verein*, after a bitter and prolonged debate, had voted to oppose a German war; at the end of May the *Abgeordnetentag*, an annual convention of German parliamentary delegates, agreed to condemn what it viewed as 'a war of cabinets which will serve only dynastic purposes'. With few exceptions, the liberal-dominated city councils joined in this chorus of anti-war sentiment, while seventeen chambers of commerce from the western provinces solemnly informed the king that 'the entire country is opposed to the

---

[87] Herre, *Nation*, p. 256.

[88] Ibid. 258. There is a full account of the Confederation's deliberations in Huber, iii, chs. 9, 10.

fratricidal war in Germany which threatens us'. The Catholic population in these areas was vehemently pro-Austrian and seems to have remained so even after hostilities began.[89]

Although the essential decisions were made in Vienna and Berlin, the final act in the long drama of Austro-Prussian conflicts was played out in Frankfurt, where the two powers had so often pressed their claims to speak for Germany. On 1 June Baron Kübeck, now the Austrian representative to the diet, declared that his government's mobilization was a response to Prussia's threatening moves in Schleswig-Holstein. He asked that the diet seek to resolve this matter and thereby remove the principal source of friction between the two states. Prussia claimed that Kübeck's appeal to the diet violated the Gastein agreement and directly threatened its interests in the duchies. On 7 June Manteuffel, the commander of the Prussian forces in Schleswig, crossed the Eider River into Holstein, but did not engage the Austrians, who withdrew into Hanover. Kübeck protested against Prussia's aggression and on 11 June demanded that the Confederation mobilize its forces against Berlin. Three days later, when the diet voted nine to five to accept this resolution, the Prussian representative declared that his government considered the Confederation to be dissolved.

Because so much has been written about Prussia's growing power and influence—especially through its role in the *Zollverein*— it is worth noting that almost every important German state lined up on the Austrian side in 1866. The majority of Prussia's supporters were enclaves or small principalities which were sovereign in name only. With the exception of Baden, which abstained from the final vote, the German *Mittelstaaten*, including all four kingdoms, opposed Berlin. To these governments, the Confederation, despite its many deficiencies, remained more attractive than Prussian domination.

In a proclamation 'To the German People', issued on 16 June, King William blamed the Confederation for Germany's fragmentation and weakness and announced Prussia's 'decision to take up the struggle for the national unity of Germany hitherto thwarted by the self-interest of the individual states'. William's words remind us of similar proclamations issued in 1813, when another Hohenzollern tried to mobilize the *Volk* in the name of German nationalism—but in pursuit of Prussian interests. It is by no means clear that

---

[89] Hamerow, *Foundations*, ii. 264, 271. See also Sperber, *Catholicism*, pp. 156–7 and the letters in Heyderhoff and Wentzcke (eds.), *Liberalismus*, i.

William's proclamation of 16 June found substantially more
support among ordinary Germans than Frederick William III's had
half a century before. To be sure, many Prussians rallied to the flag
once they heard the first reports of victory; in the other states,
kleindeutsch elements celebrated Prussia's success. But the majority
of Germans were either hostile towards or apathetic about Berlin's
attempt to reorder German affairs by force. As Theodor von
Bernhardi told the crown prince, 'I certainly would not say that it's
not a fine thing . . . to have public opinion on our side—but
German unity is a question of power.' That question would have to
be resolved on the battlefield.[90]

Prussia's first task was to secure the northern sector by
establishing military control over Hanover, Electoral Hesse, and
Saxony. This was done quickly and easily; only the Hanoverians
offered serious resistance and had to be defeated in a hard-fought
engagement at Langensalza. The Prussians moved with comparable
success against Austria's allies in the south. But the decision,
everyone knew, would come in the east, where the Austrians had
moved their forces along the rails north of Vienna, gathering them
in the fortress towns of north-eastern Bohemia. Despite the
numerical superiority of Austria and its allies, Moltke's plan called
for a bold—some felt foolhardy—offensive move into Bohemia by
two separate armies, which would unite once the enemy had been
forced to commit to a full-scale battle. In a series of preliminary
encounters, the needlegun was devastating; even when they were
victorious, the Austrians suffered three times as many casualties as
their foes.

By the time Moltke, accompanied by the king, Bismarck, and a
large contingent of courtiers, joined the main Prussian force in
Bohemia on 30 June, there was considerable confusion about the
enemy's location and intention. Moreover, communication
between the two Prussian armies was highly imperfect; during the
preceding week they had had considerable difficulty understanding
and obeying their orders. On 3 July Prince Frederick Charles, the
commander of the First Army, acting without the knowledge of his
commander-in-chief, ordered a frontal attack on a large Austrian

[90] Engelberg, *Bismarck*, p. 593. We do not, of course, have any satisfactory way
of measuring public opinion—too often, historians have taken the most outspoken
members of society as somehow representative of the rest. We do know that, in the
elections of 1867, participation was low and particularist sentiment was strong: see
Otto Büsch, 'Der Beitrag der historischen Wahlforschung zur Geschichte der
deutschen und europäischen Wählerbewegung', in Otto Büsch (ed.), *Wählerbewegung in der Europäischen Geschichte* (Berlin, 1980), especially pp. 16–17.

force whose existence he had discovered the night before. Thus began a battle that raged for seventeen hours along a front between the town of Sadowa and the Elbe river fort of Königgrätz. While the First Army engaged the Austrians all morning, the Second Army, under the crown prince, moved to attack their flank; it arrived in time to stabilize the centre of the Prussian front and raise havoc on the Austrians' right. By late afternoon, Benedek, having suffered heavy casualties, was forced to withdraw.

Contrary to patriotic legend, Königgrätz was not a model of military planning and leadership. The battle did not occur when and where Moltke had expected it, nor was he fully aware of its character and significance until it was well under way. Had the Austrians been somewhat better armed, or better led, or better served by the fortunes of war, the outcome could easily have been different. But once such victories occur, they always seem inevitable; in retrospect, the winners have to win. Those who were there—at least until they themselves began to believe the legends—knew otherwise. Late in the afternoon of 3 July someone in the king's entourage told Bismarck, 'You are now a great man. But if the crown prince had arrived too late, you would be the greatest scoundrel in the world.'[91]

Is it a mistake to end this book with Bismarck and the Prussian victories of 1866? Many contemporaries would not have thought so; they were convinced that the events of 1866 marked a revolutionary change in the course of German affairs. Theodor Mommsen, for example, who had been deeply pessimistic about the future before the war, now rejoiced that he could be alive 'when world history turns a corner . . . Germany has a future and that future will be determined by Prussia.' Königgrätz had an even more direct and significant impact on Richard Wagner: at the end of June, when the Prussians defeated his patron's Bavarian forces, he had called Bismarck a 'thoroughly un-German creature', but after the final Prussian victory he advised a friend to 'follow Bismarck and Prussia. . . . I can see no alternative.' 'One can learn a great deal in such times', Nietzsche wrote on 5 July. 'The ground, which seemed so firm and unshakeable, shifts; masks fall. Self-seeking impulses reveal their ugly features. Above all, one notices

[91] Craig, *Königgrätz*, p. xii. Van Creveld, who admires Moltke's leadership, none the less writes: 'The battle was an unforeseen one, fought as a last minute improvisation against an enemy whose whereabouts had not previously been discovered for forty-eight hours even though he was only a few miles away': *Command in War*, p. 140.

how slight is the power of thought.' What Nietzsche saw so darkly, Johannes Miquel regarded as cause to celebrate: 'The time of ideals is over. German unity has come from the world of dreams into the everyday world of reality.'[92]

To Miquel, 'German unity' meant Prussian domination over non-Austrian Germany. This was, of course, the most significant effect of Königgrätz, which enabled Bismarck to gather twenty-three northern states into a new federal system created and led by Berlin. The settlement of 1815 was thus dissolved. Moreover, Bismarck annexed to Prussia Hanover, Hesse-Kassel, Nassau, and the city of Frankfurt, thereby violating the principles of sovereignty and the habits of restraint upon which the Metternichian order had been based. With Austria's allies south of the Main River he dealt more gently: Hesse-Darmstadt (which lost some territory), Baden, Württemberg, and Bavaria signed separate treaties, paid an indemnity, and formed alliances that brought them within Prussia's sphere of influence. Following the war with France in 1870 these states would become part of the German Reich.

Such changes on the national scene obviously affected domestic political life throughout the German lands. The Prussian liberals split, with a significant number joining *kleindeutsch* forces in the other states to form the National Liberal Party. Elsewhere, anti-Prussian forces were mobilized by Catholics, particularists, and political radicals. These groups, together with a newly formed labour party, found a fertile terrain for their agitation in the democratically elected north German *Reichstag*. In Austria, the impact of defeat was felt almost at once; the government, desperate for support and stability, accommodated itself to the advocates of both Hungarian autonomy and German liberalism. Thus, at the same time that Bismarck established a new constitutional order for the Prussian sphere, Francis Joseph accepted the *Ausgleich*, which guaranteed Hungarian hegemony over the eastern half of the empire.

While none of these things would have happened the way they did without the victory of 1866, most of them had deeper historical roots. Liberalism's internal divisions, the growing pressure for greater Hungarian autonomy within the Habsburg monarchy, and the political mobilization of Catholicism, particularism, and the

---

[92] A. Wucher, *Theodor Mommsen* (Göttingen, 1956), 151; Ronald Taylor, *Richard Wagner. His Life, Art and Thought* (London, 1979), p. 30; Nietzsche, *Briefwechsel*, pt. 1 vol. ii. 138; Mommsen, *Miquel*, p. 371. For additional examples, see Faber, 'Realpolitik'.

labour movement had all been apparent were the war. Despite its obvious significance, therefore, Königgrätz quickened rather than created the political forces that would shape German history during the years ahead.

Even in German affairs, the lines of continuity stretching across 1866 should not escape our attention. The problem of national identity, which had become so pressing for German intellectuals in the middle of the nineteenth century, did not go away—indeed for many Germans, especially those living outside the Bismarckian Reich, the problem became increasingly painful. 'You claim that you have founded a Reich,' Grillparzer wrote in 1866, 'but all you have done is to destroy a *Volk*.' In the realm of power politics, the relations between Vienna and Berlin remained fraught with tension and peril. As Paul Schroeder has written, Bismarck 'overturned central Europe' to sever Germany's connection to Austria, but in the process managed to create a situation in which 'Prussia–Germany would one day be more tightly chained to Austria and her non-German interests than had ever been the case under the old Confederation'. Seen through the lens of historical experience, Eduard Lasker's remark in 1870 that 'history no longer recognizes a German question' appears woefully, poignantly inaccurate. The German question, which was so long a part of central Europe's political, social, and cultural existence, did not go away merely because a battle had been won. It is, after all, still with us.[93]

[93] Lutz, *Habsburg*, p. 485; Paul Schroeder, 'Austro-German Relations: Divergent Views of the Disjoined Partnership', *CEH* 11/3 (Sept. 1978), 307; Klaus Erich Pollmann, *Parlamentarismus im Norddeutschen Bund, 1867–1870* (Düsseldorf, 1985), 505.

Conclusion

OUR account of German history from the end of the eighteenth century to 1866 has been dominated by three themes. First, we saw how the development of bureaucratic and participatory institutions changed the character and capacities of governments throughout German Europe. Second, we followed the economic expansion in which the productivity of both agriculture and manufacturing increased, commercial activity intensified, and urban growth was encouraged. Finally, we examined the rising culture of print, which sustained new developments in literature, philosophy, and scholarship and also helped transform the rules and procedures of everyday life. Of course these three themes were inseparable; each depended on and reinforced the other. Neither bureaucratization nor popular participation would have been possible without economic growth and increasing literacy, just as industrialization required new governmental forms and cultural foundations.

We have seen how these three developments led to an erosion of traditional values and institutions. Bureaucratic theory and practice penetrated and eventually absorbed the personal, customary, locally based patterns of authority that had prevailed within the realm of *Herrschaft*. Economic change shattered the material foundations and institutional restraints upon which the traditional social order had rested; guilds, autonomous urban units, unfree agricultural labour all proved incompatible with a dynamic, expansionary economy. The culture of print—of books and newspapers, written rules and compulsory schools, railroad schedules and training manuals—injected into people's lives new ways of thinking and talking about the world, new manners and fashions, new ambitions and sentiments. Although the impact of these developments was uneven and incomplete, by the 1860s their influence was felt throughout the German lands. Measured against the historical condition of the late eighteenth century, German politics, society, and culture had been transformed.

While it is clear that these political, economic, and cultural changes combined to destroy the old regime, it was not inevitable that they would produce a unified German nation. In some ways, they may even have made political unification more difficult. For example, the integrated sovereign states created from the wreckage of the old Reich were potentially harder to absorb into a nation state than the fragile little polities they had replaced. By encouraging regional specialization, economic growth intensified regional divisions, inequalities, and rivalries within central Europe. Even literary culture, which was so crucial to the formation of national consciousness, was not easily harnessed to a politically feasible solution to the German question. Because our three themes did not inevitably lead to unification, they cannot be subsumed within a national narrative whose foreordained destination is Bismarck's Reich.

The rise of new political, economic, and cultural institutions did, however, effect a redistribution of power within German Europe—from the south and east towards the north and west, from Catholics to Protestants, and from Austria to Prussia. In political terms, the last of these was essential. Because of its character, location, and traditions, Prussia was able to master bureaucratic institutions, benefit from economic innovations, and use new cultural forms for its own ends. These advantages became relevant to the German question when policy-makers in Berlin decided to use force to impose their own version of nationhood. Thus, while the developments that we have followed in this book did not make a Prussian answer to the German question 'natural' or 'inevitable', they do help to explain why, once the fighting began, Prussia emerged victorious.

Bismarck was right: the German question was resolved by 'blood and iron'. After all, bloodshed attends the birth of every nation; sometimes more is needed to keep the nation alive. But once the blood has been spilled and the iron's work is done, the time comes for 'speeches and majority opinions'. Oratory and ceremony, constitutions and legislative programmes, schoolbooks and scholarship all must contribute to the project of nation-building. Here history has a special role to play—in John Pocock's words—both as 'record' and 'instrument' of national identity. Historians must cherish the memories of nation-building's heroic course, just as they must forget, or at least downplay, what Ernest Renan called 'those deeds of violence which have marked the origins of all political formation'.[1] The result of this historical

---

[1] My thinking about national history owes a great deal to the work of John Pocock, especially 'British History: A Plea for a New Subject', *JMH* 47/4 (1975), and 'The Limits and Divisions of British History: In Search of the Unknown Subject', *AHR* 87/2 (1982). The Renan quote is from 'What is a Nation?', in A. Zimmern (ed.), *Modern Political Doctrines* (London, 1939), 190.

process of remembering and forgetting is a narrative of the national past whose victorious conclusion comes to be seen as natural, inevitable, and just. In this narrative, violence must appear to be the midwife rather than the mother of the nation. For the Germany created between 1866 and 1871, this historiographical mission was brilliantly fulfilled by the great historians of the *Reichsgründung*, who established a persisently influential model of national history.[2]

There is nothing uniquely German about such a construction of the national past. All history, as Lucien Febvre has written, 'is determined by the aid of the present. Obsessed by it, we reject a whole series of latent possibilities which might otherwise have been realized and which evolution in its course may one day offer again to man in the garb of necessities.'[3] Beginning, as we must, from our own present, our view of German history must be different from those historians who basked in the glow of Bismarck's victories and celebrated the reconciliation of *Volk* and *Staat*. We can understand their enthusiasms and admire their scholarship, but we must formulate our own assessment of German history's latent possibilities and apparent necessities.

[2] On this historiographical tradition, see Sheehan, 'Problem' and Wolfgang Hardtwig, 'Geschichtsinteresse, Geschichtsbilder, und politische Symbole in der Reichsgründungsära und im Kaiserreich', in E. Mai and S. Waetzoldt (eds.), *Kunstverwaltung*.

[3] Lucien Febvre and L. Bataillon, *A Geographical Introduction to History* (London and New York, 1925), 305.

RULERS OF MAJOR GERMAN STATES

THE HOLY ROMAN EMPIRE

1658–1705	Leopold I
1705–1711	Joseph I
1711–1740	Charles VI
1742–1745	Charles VII
1745–1765	Francis I
1765–1790	Joseph II
1790–1792	Leopold II
1792–1806	Francis II

BADEN

1771–1811	Karl Frederick (Margrave until 1803, then Elector; after 1806 Grand Duke)
1811–1818	Karl
1818–1830	Ludwig I
1830–1852	Leopold
1852–1856	Ludwig II
1856–1907	Frederick I (Regent after 1852)

BAVARIA

1777–1799	Karl Theodor
1799–1825	Max Joseph IV (after 1806 King Maximilian I)
1825–1848	Ludwig I
1848–1864	Maximilian II
1864–1886	Ludwig II

BRANDENBURG PRUSSIA

1640–1688	Frederick William (the Great Elector)
1688–1713	Frederick II (after 1701 King Frederick I)
1713–1740	Frederick William I

1740–1786	Frederick II (the Great)
1786–1797	Frederick William II
1797–1840	Frederick William III
1840–1861	Frederick William IV
1861–1888	William I

THE HABSBURG MONARCHY

1657–1705	Leopold I
1705–1711	Joseph I
1711–1740	Charles VI
1740–1780	Maria Theresa
1780–1790	Joseph II
1790–1792	Leopold II
1792–1835	Francis II (after 1804 Francis I)
1835–1848	Ferdinand I
1848–1916	Francis Joseph

HANOVER

1727–1760	George II
1760–1820	George III
1820–1830	George IV
1830–1837	William IV
1837–1851	Ernest Augustus
1851–1866	George V

HESSE-DARMSTADT

1738–1768	Ludwig VIII
1768–1790	Ludwig IX (after 1806 Grand Duke Ludwig I)
1790–1830	Ludwig X
1830–1848	Ludwig II
1848–1877	Ludwig III

(ELECTORAL HESSE) HESSE-KASSEL

1751–1760	William VIII
1760–1785	Frederick II

1785–1821	William IX (after 1803 Elector William I)
1821–1847	William II
1847–1866	Frederick William (co-regent after 1831)

SAXONY

1763–1827	Frederick Augustus III (after 1806 King Frederick Augustus I)
1827–1836	Anton
1836–1854	Frederick Augustus II regent after 1830)
1854–1873	Johann

WÜRTTEMBERG

1677–1733	Eberhard Ludwig
1733–1737	Karl Alexander
1737–1793	Karl Eugen
1793–1795	Ludwig Eugen
1795–1797	Frederick Eugen
1797–1816	Frederick II (after 1806 King Frederick I)
1816–1864	William
1864–1891	Karl

GUIDE TO FURTHER READING

THE footnotes contain historiographical references on specific topics, to which the index provides a guide. The works discussed here are general treatments of the period.

The best single-volume work in English is Agatha Ramm, *Germany, 1789–1919* (London, 1967), which gives a lucid, balanced account, especially of political developments. Eda Sagarra's *Social History of Germany, 1648–1914* (New York, 1977) is a well-informed and clearly presented introduction to the subject. The second and third volumes of Hajo Holborn, *A History of Modern Germany* (New York, 1959–69), are sometimes brilliant but often disappointing. Finally, there is an English translation of Heinrich von Treitschke, *History of Germany in the Nineteenth Century* (7 vols., London, 1915–19), a richly textured narrative that repays careful reading. Unfortunately, Treitschke did not live to complete his work, which ends on the eve of the revolution of 1848.

The other classic account of the period, Franz Schnabel's *Deutsche Geschichte im neunzehnten Jahrhundert* (4 vols.; 3rd edn., Freiburg, 1949–59), is also fragmentary and incomplete. Nevertheless, Schnabel's accounts of certain aspects of the period, particularly his discussions of science and technology in vol. 3 and of religion in vol. 4, remain unsurpassed. Overall, the best general history of the first two-thirds of the century is Thomas Nipperdey, *Deutsche Geschichte, 1800–1866: Bürgerwelt und starker Staat* (Munich, 1983). In addition to Nipperdey, several other syntheses have recently appeared: perhaps the most useful of these are the relevant volumes in the series *Deutsche Geschichte*, edited by Joachim Leuschner: Rudolf Vierhaus, *Deutschland im Zeitalter des Absolutismus, 1648–1763*, Karl Otmar Freiherr von Aretin, *Vom Duetschen Reich zum Deutschen Bund* (Göttingen, 1980), and Reinhard Rürup, *Deutschland im 19. Jahrhundert* (Göttingen, 1978–84). The first two volumes of Hans-Ulrich Wehler's moumental *Deutsche Gesellschaftsgeschichte* (Munich, 1987) cover the years from 1700 to 1849. Although Wehler's emphasis is on social and economic developments, his work has extraordinary range and depth. For a guide to historical documents and other source materials, see Klaus Müller (ed.), *Absolutismus und Zeitalter der französischen Revolution (1715–1815)* (Darmstadt, 1982), and Wolfram Siemann (ed.), *Restauration, Liberalismus und nationale Bewegung (1815–1870)* (Darmstadt, 1982).

BIBLIOGRAPHY

Abel, Wilhelm, *Massenarmut und Hungerkrisen im vorindustriellen Deutschland* (Göttingen, 1972).
—— *Geschichte der deutschen Landwirtschaft vom frühen Mittelalter bis zum 19. Jahrhundert* (3rd ed., Stuttgart, 1978).
—— *Agricultural Fluctuations in Europe. From the Thirteenth to the Twentieth Centuries* (New York, 1980).
Abraham, Karl, *Der Strukturwandel im Handwerk in der ersten Hälfte des 19. Jahrhunderts und seine Bedeutung für die Berufserziehung* (Cologne, 1955).
Abrams, M. H., *The Mirror and the Lamp: Romantic Theory and the Critical Traditional* (London and New York, 1953).
—— *Natural Supernaturalism: Tradition and Revolution in Romantic Literature* (New York, 1971).
Abrams, Philip, and Wrigley, E. A. (eds.), *Towns in Societies: Essays in Economic History and Historical Sociology* (New York, 1978).
Achilles, Walter, *Vermögensverhältnisse braunschweigischer Bauernhöfe im 17. und 18. Jahrhundert* (Stuttgart, 1965).
Ackerknecht, Erwin, *Rudolf Virchow. Doctor, Statesman, Anthropologist* (Madison, Wis., 1953).
Altgeld, Wolfgang, *Das politische Italienbild der Deutschen zwischen Aufklärung und europäischer Revolution von 1848* (Tübingen, 1984).
Anderson, Eugene N., *Nationalism and the Cultural Crisis in Prussia. 1806–1815* (New York, 1939).
Anderson, Margaret L. *Windthorst: A Political Biography* (Oxford, 1981).
Andrian-Werburg, Victor Freiherr von, *Österreich und dessen Zukunft* (2 vols., Hamburg, 1842–7).
Angel-Volkov, Shulamit, 'The "Decline of the German Handicrafts": Another Reappraisal,' *VSWG* 61/2 (1974), 165–84.
Angermann, Erich, *Robert von Mohl, 1799–1875: Leben und Werk eines altliberalen Staatsgelehrten* (Neuwied, 1962).
Arendt, Hannah, *Rahel Varnhagen: The Life of a Jewish Woman* (New York and London, 1974).
Aretin, Karl Otmar von, *Heiliges Römisches Reich 1776 bis 1806: Reichsverfassung und Staatssouveränität* (2 vol., Wiesbaden, 1967).
—— *Bayerns Weg zum souveränen Staat: Landstände und Konstitutionelle Monarchie, 1714–1818* (Munich, 1976).
—— *Vom Deutschen Reich zum Deutschen Bund* (Göttingen, 1980).
—— (ed.), *Der Aufgeklärte Absolutismus* (Cologne, 1974).
Aris, Reinhold, *History of Political Thought in Germany from 1789 to 1815* (London, 1936).
Arndt, Ernst Moritz, *Sämmtliche Werke* i. *Erinnerungen aus dem äusseren Leben*, (Leipzig, 1892).
Artelt, Walter, and Rüegg, W. (eds.), *Der Arzt und der Kranke in der Gesellschaft des 19. Jahrhunderts* (Stuttgart, 1967).

Ash, Mitchell, and Woodward, William (eds.), *The Problematic Science: Psychology in 19th Century Thought* (New York, 1982).

Aubert, Roger, *et al.* (eds.), *The Church Between Revolution and Restauration* (New York, 1982).

Austensen, Roy, 'Austria and the "Struggle of Supremacy in Germany", 1848–1864', *JMH* 52/2 (June 1980), 195–225.

—— 'The Making of Austria's Prussian Policy, 1848–1852', *HJ* 27/4 (1984), 861–76.

Avineri, Shlomo, *Hegel's Theory of the Modern State* (Cambridge, 1972).

· Ayçoberry, Pierre, *Cologne entre Napoléon et Bismarck: La croissance d'une ville rhénane* (Paris, 1981).

Bab, Julius, and Handl, Willi, *Wien und Berlin. Vergleichendes zur Kulturgeschichte der beiden Hauptstädte Mitteleuropas* (Berlin, 1918).

Bähr, Otto, *Eine deutsche Stadt vor sechzig Jahren* (2nd edn., Leipzig, 1886).

Balser, Frolinde, *Die Anfänge der Erwachsenenbildung in Deutschland in der ersten Hälfte des 19. Jahrhunderts* (Stuttgart, 1959).

—— *Sozial-Demokratie 1848/49–1963: Die Erste Deutsche Arbeiterorganisation* (2 vols.; Stuttgart, 1962).

Barnard, F. M., *J. G. Herder on Social and Political Culture* (Cambridge, 1969).

Bátori, Ingrid, *Die Reichsstadt Augsburg im 18. Jahrhundert. Verfassung, Finanzen und Reformversuche* (Göttingen, 1969).

Baumgart, Franzjörg, *Die verdrängte Revolution: Darstellung und Bewertung der Revolution von 1848 in der deutschen Geschichtsschreibung vor dem ersten Weltkrieg* (Düsseldorf, 1976).

Bazillion, Richard J., 'Urban Violence and the Modernization Process in Pre-March Saxony, 1830–1831 and 1845.' *Historical Reflections.* 12/2 (1985), 279–303.

Bebel, August, *Aus meinem Leben* (3rd edn., Berlin, 1961).

Beck, Lewis White, *Early German Philosophy: Kant and his Predecessors* (Cambridge, 1969).

Becker, Josef, *Liberaler Staat und Kirche in der Ära von Reichsgründung und Kulturkampf. Geschichte und Strukturen ihres Verhältnisses in Baden, 1860–1876* (Mainz, 1973).

Becker, Josef *et al.*, (eds.), *Badische Geschichte. Vom Grossherzogtum bis zur Gegenwart* (Stuttgart, 1979).

Beenken, Hermann, *Das 19. Jahrhundert in der deutschen Kunst* (Munich, 1944).

Behler, Ernst, 'The Origins of the Romantic Literary Theory.' *Colloquia Germanica*, I/1 (1968), 109–26.

Beidtel, Ignaz, *Geschichte der österreichischen Staatsverwaltung, 1740–1848* (2 vols., Innsbruck, 1896).

Ben-David, Joseph, *The Scientist's Role in Society: A Comparative Study* (Englewood Cliffs, New Jersey, 1971).

Bendix, Reinhard, 'Province and Metropolis: The Case of Eighteenth-Century Germany', in Joseph Ben-David and Terry Clark (eds.), *Culture and its Creators. Essays in Honor of Edward Shils* (Chicago and London, 1977), 119–49.

Benecke, G., 'Ennoblement and Privilege in Early Modern Germany', *History*, (Oct. 1971), 360–70.

—— *Society and Politics in Germany, 1500–1750* (London and Toronto, 1974).

Berdahl, Robert M., 'Prussian Aristocracy and Conservative Ideology: A Methodological Examination', *Social Science Information*, 15/415 (1976), 583–99.

Berding, Helmut, 'Leopold von Ranke', in Hans-Ulrich Wehler (ed.), *Deutsche Historiker* (8 vols,; Gottingen, 1971–82), i. 7–24.

—— *Napoleonische Herrschafts-und Gesellschaftspolitik im Königreich Westfalen, 1807–1813* (Göttingen, 1973).

—— and H. P. Ullmann (eds.), *Deutschland zwischen Revolution und Restauration* (Königstein und Düsseldorf, 1981).

—— 'Die Emanzipation der Juden im Königreich Westfalen (1808–1813)', *AfS* 23 (1983), 23–50.

—— *et al.* (eds.), *Vom Staat des Ancien Regime zum modernen Parteienstaat. Festschrift für Theodor Schieder* (Munich and Vienna, 1978).

Bergstrásser, Ludwig (ed.), *Das Frankfurter Parlament in Briefen und Tagebüchern: Ambrosch, Rümelin, Hallbauer, Blum* (Frankfurt, 1929).

Berkner, Lutz, 'The Stem Family and the Developmental Cycle of the Peasant Household: An Eighteenth-Century Austrian Example', *AHR* 77/2 (Apr. 1972), 398–418.

Berlin, Isaiah, *Against the Current: Essays in the History of Ideas* (New York, 1980).

Berman, Russell, *The Rise of the Modern German Novel* (Cambridge and London, 1986).

Berney, Arnold, 'Reichstradition und Nationalstaatsgedanke (1789– 1815)' *HZ* 140/1 (1929), 57–86.

Berthold, Rudolf, 'Die Veränderungen im Bodeneigentum und in der Zahl der Bauernstellen, der kleinstellen und der Rittergüter in den preussischen Provinzen Sachsen, Brandenburg und Pommern während der Durchführung der Agrarreformen des 19. Jahrhunderts', *JbW* Sonderband (1978), 9–116.

—— 'Bevölkerungsentwicklung und Sozialstruktur im Regierungsbezirk Magdeburg und in den vier Börde-Kreisen von 1816 bis 1910,' in H. J. Rach and B. Weissel (eds), *Landwirtschaft und Kapitalismus* (Berlin, 1979), 91–362.

Beust, Friedrich von, *Aus drei Vierteljahrhunderten: Erinnerungen und Aufzeichnungen* (2 vols.; Stuttgart, 1887).

Bibl, Viktor, *Der Zerfall Österreichs* (2 vols., Vienna, 1922–4).

Biedermann, Karl, *Mein Leben und ein Stück Zeitgeschichte* (2 vols., Breslau, 1886).

—— *Deutschland im 18. Jahrhundert* (2 vols. in 4; repr. Aalen, 1969).

Bigler, Robert, *The Politics of German Protestantism: The Rise of the Protestant Church Elite in Prussia, 1815–1848* (Berkeley, Los Angeles, and London, 1972).

Binkley, Robert, *Realism and Nationalism, 1852–1871* (New York, 1935).

Birker, Karl, *Die deutschen Arbeiterbildungsvereine, 1840–1870* (Berlin, 1973).

Bismarck, Otto von, *Die gesammelten Werke* (15 vols.; Berlin, 1923–33).

Blackall, Eric, *The Emergence of German as a Literary Language, 1700–1775* (Cambridge, 1959).

Blackbourn, David, 'The *Mittelstand* in German Society and Politics, 1871–1914', *SH* IV:3 (1977), 409–33.

—— and Eley, Geoff, *The Peculiarities of German History: Bourgeois Society and Politics in Nineteenth-Century Germany* (Oxford, 1984).

Blaich, Fritz (ed.), *Entwicklungsprobleme einer Region: Das Beispiel Rheinland und Westfalen im 19. Jahrhundert* (Berlin, 1981).

Blanning, T. C. W., *Reform and Revolution in Mainz, 1743–1803* (Cambridge, 1974).

—— *The French Revolution in Germany: Occupation and Resistance in the Rhineland, 1792–1802* (Oxford, 1983).

—— *The Origins of the French Revolution Wars* (London and New York, 1986).

Blaschke, Karlheinz, 'Zur Bevölkerungsgeschichte Sachsens vor der industriellen Revolution', *Beiträge zur deutschen Wirtschafts- und Sozialgeschichte im 18. und 19. Jahrhundert* (Berlin, 1962), 133–69.

Blasius, Dirk, *Bürgerliche Gesellschaft und Kriminalität: Zur Sozialgeschichte Preussens im Vormärz* (Göttingen, 1976).

—— 'Bürgerliches Recht und bürgerliche Identität: Zu einem Problemzusammenhang in der deutschen Geschichte des 19. Jahrhunderts', in Helmut Berding *et al.* (eds.), *Vom Staat des Ancien Regime zum modernen Parteienstaat: Festschrift für Theodor Schieder* (Munich and Vienna, 1978), 213–24.

—— *Kriminalität und Alltag: Zur Konfliktgeschichte im 19. Jahrhundert* (Göttingen, 1978).

—— 'Bürgerliche Gesellschaft und bürgerliche Angst: Der Irre in der Geschichte des 19. Jahrhunderts: Eine Skizze', *Sozialwissenschaftliche Informationen für Unterricht und Studium*, 8/2 (1979), 88–94.

Bleek, Wilhelm, *Von der Kameralausbildung zum Juristenprivileg: Studium, Prüfung und Ausbildung der höheren Beamten des allgemeinen Verwaltungsdienstes in Deutschland im 18. und 19. Jahrhundert* (Berlin, 1972).

Bleiber, Helmut, *Zwischen Reform und Revolution: Lage und Kämpfe der schlesischen Bauern und Landarbeiter im Vormärz, 1840–1847* (Berlin, 1966).

Blessing, Werner K., *Staat und Kirche in der Gesellschaft: Konstitutionelle Autorität und mentaler Wandel in Bayern während des 19. Jahrhunderts* (Göttingen, 1982).

Blum, Jerome, *The End of the Old Order in Rural Europe* (Princeton, 1978).

Boberach, Heinz, *Wahlrechtsfrage im Vormärz: Die Wahlrechtsanschauung im Rheinland 1815–1849 und die Entstehung des Dreiklassenwahlrechts* (Düsseldorf, 1959).

Bock, Helmut, *Die Illusion der Freiheit. Deutsche Klassenkämpfe zur Zeit der französischen Julirevolution, 1830 bis 1831* (Berlin, 1980).

Böckenförde, Ernst-Wolfgang, 'Die Einheit von nationaler und konstitutioneller politischer Bewegung im deutschen Frühliberalismus', in id. (ed.), *Moderne deutsche Verfassungsgeschichte (1815–1918)* (Cologne, 1972), 27–39.

—— (ed.), *Moderne deutsche Verfassungsgeschichte (1815–1918)* (Cologne, 1972).

Böckh, Richard, *Der Deutschen Volkszahl und Sprachgebiet in den europäischen Staaten: Eine statistische Untersuchung* (Berlin, 1869).

Boehn, Max von, *Biedermeier: Deutschland von 1815–1847* (Berlin, 1923).

Böhme, Helmut, *Deutschlands Weg zur Grossmacht: Studien zum Verhältnis von Wirtschaft und Staat während der Reichsgründungzeit, 1848–1881* (Cologne and Berlin, 1966).

—— (ed.), *Die Reichsgründung* (Munich, 1967).

Böhmer, Günter, *Die Welt des Biedermeier* (Munich, 1968).

Boldt, Werner, *Die Anfänge des deutschen Parteiwesens. Fraktionen, politische Vereine und Parteien in der Revolution vom 1848* (Paderborn, 1971).

—— 'Konstitutionelle Monarchie oder parlamentarische Demokratie: Die Auseinandersetzung um die deutsche Nationalversammlung in der Revolution von 1848', *HZ* 216/3 (June 1973), 553–622.

Bolognese-Leuchtenmüller, B., *Bevölkerungsentwicklung und Berufsstruktur* (Vienna, 1978).

Borchardt, Knut, 'The Industrial Revolution in Germany, 1700–1914', in Carlo Cipolla (ed.), *The Fontana Economic History of Europe*, iv. (Glasgow, 1972–6).

Born, Stephan, *Erinnerungen eines Achtundvierzigers* (Leipzig, 1898; repr. Berlin and Bonn, 1978).

Borscheid, Peter, und Teuteberg, H. (eds.), *Ehe. Liebe. Tod: Zum Wandel der Familie, der Geschlechts- und Generationsbeziehungen in der Neuzeit* (Münster, 1983).

Botzenhart, Manfred, *Deutscher Parlamentarismus in der Revolutionszeit, 1848–1850* (Düsseldorf, 1977).

Boyer, John W., *Political Radicalism in Late Imperial Vienna. Origins of the Christian Social Movement, 1848–1867* (Chicago and London, 1981).

Bramstedt, E. K., *Aristocracy and the Middle Classes in Germany: Social Types in German Literature, 1830–1900* (rev. edn.; Chicago and London, 1964).

Brandt, Harm Hinrich, *Der österreichische Neoabsolutismus: Staatsfinanzen und Politik, 1848–1860* (2 vols.; Göttingen, 1978).

Brandt, Hartwig, *Landständische Repräsentation im deutschen Vormärz: Politisches Denken im Einflussfeld des monarchischen Prinzips* (Neuwied, 1968).

—— 'Gesellschaft, Parlament, Regierung in Württemberg. 1830–1840,' in Gerhard A. Ritter, (ed.), *Gesellschaft, Parlament und Regierung: Zur Geschichte des Parlamentarismus in Deutschland* (Düsseldorf, 1974), 101–18.

—— *Parlamentarismus in Württemberg, 1819–1870: Anatomie eines deutschen Landtags* (Düsseldorf, 1987).

Braubach, Max, 'Die kirchliche Aufklärung im katholischen Deutschland im Spiegel des "Journal von und für Deutschland" (1784–1792)', *HJb* 54 (1934), 1–63, 178–220.

—— *Maria Theresias jüngster Sohn: Max Franz: Letzter Kurfürst von Köln und Fürstbischof von Münster* (Vienna and Munich, 1961).

Braudel, Fernand, *Capitalism and Material Life, 1400–1800* (New York, 1973).

Brazill, William J., *The Young Hegelians* (New Haven, Conn., 1970).
—— 'Georg Herwegh and the Aesthetics of German Unification', *CEH* 5/2 (June 1972), 99–126.
Brederlow, Jörn, *'Lichtfreunde' und 'Freie Gemeinde': Religiöser Protest und Freiheitsbewegung im Vormärz und in der Revolution von 1848/49* (Munich, 1978).
Brinkmann, Carl, *Wustrau: Wirtschafts-und Verfassungsgeschichte eines brandenburgischen Ritterguts* (Leipzig, 1911).
—— *Der Nationalismus und die deutschen Universitäten im Zeitalter der deutschen Erhebung* (Heidelberg, 1932).
Brinkmann, Richard (ed.), *Romantik in Deutschland* (Stuttgart, 1978).
Bruford, W. H., *Theatre, Drama, and Audience in Goethe's Germany* (London, 1950).
—— *Culture and Society in Classical Weimar, 1775–1806* (Cambridge, 1962).
—— *Germany in the Eighteenth Century: The Social Background of the Literary Revival* (Cambridge, 1965).
—— *The German Tradition of Self-Cultivation. 'Bildung' from Humboldt to Thomas Mann* (Cambridge, 1975).
Brunner, Otto, *Land und Herrschaft. Grundfragen der territorialen Verfassungsgeschichte Südostdeutschlands im Mittelalter* (3rd edn., Brünn, Munich, and Vienna, 1943).
—— *Adeliges Landleben und europäischer Geist* (Salzburg, 1949).
—— *Neue Wege der Verfassungs-und Sozialgeschichte* (2nd edn., Göttingen, 1968).
Brunschwig, Henri, *Enlightenment and Romanticism in Eighteenth-Century Prussia* (Chicago and London, 1974).
Bryce, James, *The Holy Roman Empire* (New York, 1904).
Bücher, Max, *et al.* (eds.), *Realismus und Gründerzeit: Manifeste und Dokumente zur deutschen Literatur, 1848–1880* (2 vols., Stuttgart, 1976).
Büchner, Georg, *Leonce and Lena. Lenz. Woyzeck*, trans. Michael Hamburger (Chicago and London, 1972).
Bullik, Manfred, *Staat und Gesellschaft im hessischen Vormärz: Wahlrecht, Wahlen und öffentliche Meinung in Kurhessen, 1830–1848* (Cologne and Vienna, 1972).
Burney, Charles, *An Eighteenth-Century Musical Tour in Central Europe and the Netherlands (1775)*, ed. P. A. Scholes (Oxford, 1959).
Butler, E. M., *The Saint Simonian Religion in Germany: A Study of the Young German Movement* (Cambridge, 1926).
—— *The Tyranny of Greece Over Germany: A Study of the Influence Exercised by Greek Art and Poetry over the Great German Writers of the Eighteenth, Nineteenth, and Twentieth Centuries* (Cambridge, 1935).
Butterfield, Herbert, *Man on his Past: The Study of the History of Historical Scholarship* (Cambridge, 1955).
Cambridge Economic History of Europe, v–vii (Cambridge, 1965–78).
Carsten, F. L., *The Origins of Prussia* (Oxford, 1954).
—— *Princes and Parliaments in Germany from the Fifteenth to the Eighteenth Century* (Oxford, 1959).
Casanova, Giacomo, *History of my Life* (New York, 1966–71).

Cassirer, Ernst, *The Philosophy of the Enlightenment* (Boston, 1951).

Chadwick, Owen, *The Secularization of the European Mind in the Nineteenth Century* (Cambridge, 1975).

—— *The Popes and European Revolution* (Oxford, 1981).

Chandler, David, *The Campaigns of Napoleon* (New York, 1966).

—— *Napoleon* (London, 1973).

Christ, Karl, 'Barthold Georg Niebuhr,' in Hans-Ulrich Wehler (ed.), *Deutsche Historiker*, 8 vols.; Göttingen, vi. 23–36.

Cipolla, Carlo (ed.), *The Fontana Economic History of Europe* (6 vols.; Glasgow, 1972–6).

Clagett, Marshall (ed.), *Critical Problems in the History of Science* (Madison, Wisconsin, 1969).

Clark, C. W., *Franz Joseph and Bismark: The Diplomacy of Austria before the War of 1866* (Cambridge, Mass., 1934).

Clark, Robert, *Herder: His Life and Thought* (Berkeley and Los Angeles, 1955).

Clausewitz, Carl von, *On War*, ed. and trans. Michael Howard and Peter Paret (Princeton, 1976).

Coleman, William, *Biology in the Nineteenth Century* (Cambridge, 1971).

Conze, Werner, 'Die Wirkungen der liberalen Agrarreformen auf die Volksordnung in Mitteleuropa im 19. Jahrhundert', *VSWG* 38/1 (1949), 2–43.

—— *Möglichkeiten und Grenzen der liberalen Arbeiterbewegung in Deutschland. Das Beispiel Schulze-Delitzschs* (Heidelberg, 1965).

—— 'Vom "Pöbel" zum "Proletariat." Sozialgeschichtliche Voraussetzungen für den Sozialismus in Deutschland', in Hans-Ulrich Wehler (ed.), *Moderne deutsche Sozialgeschichte* (Cologne and Berlin, 1966), 111–36.

—— (ed.)., *Staat und Gesellschaft im deutschen Vormärz. 1815–1848* (Stuttgart, 1962).

—— (ed.), *Sozialgeschichte der Familie in der Neuzeit Europas* (Stuttgart, 1976).

—— and Engelhardt, Ulrich (eds.), *Arbeiterexistenz im 19. Jahrhundert* (Stuttgart, 1981).

—— and Kocka, Jürgen (eds.), *Bildungsbürgertum im 19. Jahrhundert* (Stuttgart, 1985).

Copleston, Frederick, *A History of Philosophy*, vii. *Modern Philosophy. Part 1. Fichte to Hegel* (Garden City, New York, 1965).

Craig, Gordon A. *The Politics of the Prussian Army, 1640–1945* (New York and Oxford, 1956).

—— *The Battle of Königgrätz: Prussia's Victory over Austria, 1866* (Philadelphia and New York, 1964).

—— *Problems of Coalition Warfare: The Military Alliance Against Napoleon, 1813–1814* (The Harmon Lectures, no. 7; Colorado Springs, 1965).

—— 'Command and Staff Problems in the Austrian Army, 1740–1914', in Michael Howard (ed.), *The Theory and Practice of War* (New York, 1966), 43–68.

—— *The End of Prussia* (Madison, Wisconsin, 1984).

Crew, David, *Town in the Ruhr: A Social History of Bochum, 1860–1914* (New York, 1979).

Croon, Helmuth, 'Die Einwirkungen der Industrialisierung auf die gesellschaftliche Schichtung der Bevölkerung im rheinisch-westfälischen Industriegebiet', *RV* 20/3 (1955), 301–16.

Dahlmann, F. C., *Die Politik auf den Grund und das Mass der gegebenen Zustände zurückgeführt* (2nd edn., 1847; repr. Berlin, 1924).

—— *Kleine Schriften und Reden*, ed. C. Varrentrapp (Stuttgart, 1886).

Dann, Otto, 'Die Anfänge politischer Vereinsbildung in Deutschland', in Ulrich Engelhardt *et al.* (eds.), *Soziale Bewegung und politische Verfassung* (Stuttgart, 1976), 197–232.

—— 'Geheime Organisierung und politisches Engagement im deutschen Bürgertum des frühen 19. Jahrhunderts. Der Tugendbund-Streit in Preussen', in Peter Christian Ludz (ed.), *Geheime Gesellschaften*. (Heidelberg, 1979).

—— *Lesegesellschaften und bürgerliche Emanzipation* (Munich, 1981).

Deák, István, *The Lawful Revolution. Louis Kossuth and the Hungarians, 1848–1849* (New York, 1979).

Demeter, Karl, *Grossdeutsche Stimmen 1848/49: Briefe, Tagebuchblätter, Eingaben aus dem Volk* (Frankfurt am Main, 1939).

—— *The German Officer Corps in Society and State, 1650–1945* (New York, 1965).

DeVries, Jan, *The Economy of Europe in an Age of Crisis, 1600–1750* (Cambridge, 1976).

—— *European Urbanization, 1500–1800* (Cambridge, 1984).

Dickinson, Robert E., *Germany. A General and Regional Geography* (London and New York, 1961).

Dickson, Peter, *Finance and Government under Maria Theresa, 1740–1780* (2 vols., Oxford, 1987).

Dictionary of Scientific Biography, ed. Charles C. Gillispie (15 vols.; New York, 1970 ff.).

Diefendorf, Jeffrey, *Businessmen and Politics in the Rhineland, 1789–1834* (Princeton, 1980).

Dilthey, Wilhelm, *Gesammelte Schriften* (18 vols., Leipzig, 1914 ff.).

—— 'Das 18. Jahrhundert und die geschichtliche Welt', in *Gesammelte Schriften*, iii (Leipzig and Berlin, 1927), 210–75.

—— *Leben Schleiermachers*, *Gesammelte Schriften*, xiii (Göttingen, 1970).

Dotterweich, Volker, *Heinrich von Sybel; Geschichtswissenschaft in politischer Absicht (1817–1861)* (Göttingen, 1978).

Dreitzel, Horst, 'Ideen, Ideologien, Wissenschaften: Zum politischen Denken in Deutschland in der frühen Neuzeit'. *Neue politische Literatur*, 25/1 (1980), 1–25.

Dreyfus, François, *Sociétés et mentalités à Mayence dans la seconde moitié du XVIIIe siècle* (Paris, 1968).

Droysen, Johann Gustav, *Geschichte der preussischen Politik (1855–86)* (2nd edn., 5 vols., Leipzig, 1868–86).

—— *Vorlesungen über das Zeitalter der Freiheitskriege* (2nd edn., 2 vols., Gotha, 1886).

—— *Briefwechsel*, ed. R. Hübner (2 vols., Stuttgart, 1929).

—— *Politische Schriften*, ed. Felix Gilbert (Munich and Berlin, 1933).

—— *Historik: Historisch-kritische Ausgabe*, ed. Peter Leyk (Stuttgart-Bad Cannstatt, 1977).

Droz, Jacques, *Le Libéralisme Rhénan, 1815–1848. Contribution à l'histoire du Libéralisme allemand* (Paris, 1940).

—— *Le romantisme allemand et l'État. Résistance et collaboration dans l'Allemagne napoléonienne* (Paris, 1966).

Düding, Dieter, *Organisierter gesellschaftlicher Nationalismus in Deutschland (1806–1847): Bedeutung und Funktion der Turner- und Sängervereine für die deutsche Nationalbewegung* (Munich, 1984).

Duffy, Christopher, *The Army of Frederick the Great* (London, 1974).

—— *The Army of Maria Theresa* (New York, 1977).

Duncker, Max, *Politischer Briefwechsel aus seinem Nachlass* (Stuttgart and Berlin, 1923).

Earle, Edward Mead (ed.), *Makers of Modern Strategy. Military Thought from Machiavelli to Hitler* (New York, 1966).

Earle, Peter (ed.), *Essays in European Economic History* (Oxford, 1974).

Edler, Erich, *Eugène Süe und die deutsche Mysterienliteratur (Berlin, 1932)*.

—— *Die Anfänge des sozialen Romans und der sozialen Novelle in Deutschland* (Frankfurt, 1977).

Eisfeld, Gerhard, *Die Entstehung der liberalen Parteien in Deutschland, 1858–70* (Hanover, 1969).

Elias, Norbert, *The Civilizing Process* (2 vols., New York, 1978–82).

Eliot, George, *Essays* (London, 1963).

Elrod, Richard, 'Bernhard von Rechberg and the Metternichian Tradition: The Dilemma of Conservative Statecraft'. *JMH* 56/3 (Sept. 1984), 430–55.

Elster, Ludwig, *et al.* (eds.), *Handwörterbuch der Staatswissenschaften* (4th edn., Jena, 1924).

Engelberg, Ernst (ed.), *Im Widerstreit um die Reichsgründung: Eine Quellensammlung zur Klassenauseinandersetzung in der deutschen Geschichte von 1849 bis 1871* (Berlin, 1970).

—— *Bismarck: Urpreusse und Reichsgründer* (Berlin, 1985).

Engelhardt, Ulrich (ed.), *Handwerker in der Industrialisierung: Lage, Kultur, und Politik vom späten 18. bis ins frühe 20. Jahrhundert* (Stuttgart, 1984).

—— Sellin, Volker, and Stuke, Horst (eds.), *Soziale Bewegung und politische Verfassung* (Stuttgart, 1976).

Engel-Janosi, Friedrich, *et al.* (eds.), *Fürst, Bürger, Mensch: Untersuchungen zu politischen und soziokulturellen Wandlungsprozessen im vorrevolutionären Europa* (Munich, 1975).

Engeli, Christian und Haus, Wolfgang (eds.), *Quellen zum modernen Gemeindeverfassungsrecht in Deutschland* (Stuttgart, 1975).

Engelsing, Rolf, 'Das häusliche Personal in der Epoche der Industrialisierung', *Jahrbuch für Sozialwissenschaft*, 20 (1969), 84–121.

—— *Zur Sozialgeschichte deutscher Mittel- und Unterschichten* (Göttingen, 1973).

—— *Der Bürger als Leser: Lesergeschichte in Deutschland, 1500–1800* (Stuttgart, 1974).

Epstein, Klaus, *The Genesis of German Conservatism* (Princeton, 1966).

Erning, Günter, *Das Lesen und die Lesewut: Beiträge zu Fragen der Lesergeschichte* (Bad Heilbrunn, 1974).

Evans R. J. W., *The Making of the Habsburg Monarchy, 1550–1700* (New York, 1979).

Evans, Richard J., *Death in Hamburg: Society and Politics in the Cholera Years, 1830–1910* (Oxford, 1987).

—— and Lee, W. R. (eds.), *The German Family: Essays on the Social History of the Family in Nineteenth- and Twentieth-Century Germany* (London, 1981).

—— *The German Peasantry: Conflict and Community in Rural Society from the Eighteenth to the Twentieth Centuries* (London and Sydney, 1986).

Eyck, Frank, *The Frankfurt Parliament, 1848–1849* (London, 1968).

—— (ed.), *The Revolutions of 1848–49* (New York, 1972).

Faber, Karl Georg, 'Realpolitik als Ideologie: Die Bedeutung des Jahres 1866 für das politische Denken in Deutschland', *HZ* 203/1 (1966), 1–45.

Falkson, Ferdinand, *Die liberale Bewegung in Königsberg, 1840–1848* (Breslau, 1888).

Fauchier-Magnan, Adrien, *The Small German Courts in the Eighteenth Century* (London, 1958).

Fehrenbach, Elisabeth, *Traditionelle Gesellschaft und revolutionäres Recht: Die Einführung des Code Napoleon in den Rheinbundstaaten* (Göttingen, 1974).

—— 'Zur sozialen Problematik des rheinischen Rechts im Vormärz', in Helmut Berding *et al.* (eds.), *Vom Staat des Ancien Regime zum modernen Parteinstaat: Festschrift für Theodor Schieder* (Munich and Vienna, 1978),

—— 'Verfassungs- und sozialpolitische Reformen und Reformprojekte in Deutschland unter dem Einfluss des napoleonischen Frankreich', *HZ* 228/2 (1979), 288–316.

Feuerbach, Ludwig, *The Essence of Christianity*, trans. George Eliot (New York, 1957).

Fichte, Johann Gottlieb, *Addresses to the German Nation*, ed. G. A. Kelly (New York and Evanston, 1968).

Fischer, Fritz, 'Der deutsche Protestantismus und die Politik im 19. Jahrhundert', *HZ* 171/3 (May 1951), 473–518.

Fischer, Wolfram, *Handwerksrecht und Handwerkswirtschaft um 1800: Studien zur Sozial- und Wirtschaftsverfassung vor der industriellen Revolution* (Berlin, 1955).

—— 'Der Volkschullehrer: Zur Sozialgeschichte eines Berufsstandes', *Soziale Welt*, 12/1 (1961), 37–47.

—— and Bajor, G. *Die soziale Frage: Neuere Studien zur Lage der Fabrikarbeiter in den Frühphasen der Industrialisierung* (Stuttgart, 1967).

—— *et al.*, *Sozialgeschichtliches Arbeitsbuch. I. Materialien zur Statistik des Deutschen Bundes, 1815–1870* (Munich, 1982).

Flinn, Michael, *The European Demographic System, 1500–1820* (Baltimore, 1981).

Flohr, Bernd, *Arbeiter nach Mass: Die Disziplinierung der Fabrikarbeiterschaft während der Industrialisierung Deutschlands im Spiegel von Arbeitsordnungen* (Frankfurt, 1981).

Fontane, Theodor, *Von Zwanzig bis Dreissig Werke*, ix. (Munich, 1967).

Forster, Georg, *Ansichten vom Niederrhein (1791) Werke,* ix. (Berlin, 1958).

—— *Im Anblick des grossen Rades: Schriften zur Revolution,* ed. R. R. Wuthenow (Darmstadt, 1981).

François, Étienne, 'La Population de Coblence au xviiie siècle', *Annales de démographie historique* (1975), 291–341.

—— *Koblenz im 18. Jahrhundert: Zur Sozial- und Bevölkerungsstruktur einer deutschen Residenzstadt* (Göttingen, 1982).

Franz, Georg, *Liberalismus: Die deutschliberale Bewegung in der habsburgischen Monarchie* (Munich, n.d. [1955]).

Fremdling, Rainer, *Eisenbahnen und deutsches Wirtschaftswachstum, 1840–1879* (Dortmund, 1975).

Frevert, Ute, *Krankheit als politisches Problem, 1770–1880: Soziale Unterschichten in Preussen zwischen medizinischer Polizei und staatlicher Sozialversicherung* (Göttingen, 1984).

—— *Frauen-Geschichte zwischen bürgerlicher Verbesserung und neuer Weiblichkeit* (Frankfurt, 1986).

Freytag, Gustav, *Bilder aus der deutschen Vergangenheit, Gesammelte Werke,* xvii–xxi (Leipzig, 1897–8).

Fricke, Dieter, *et al.* (eds.), *Die bürgerlichen Parteien und andere bürgerliche Interessenorganisationen vom Vormärz bis zum Jahre 1945* (2 vols.; Berlin, 1970).

Friedenthal, Richard, *Goethe: Sein Leben und seine Zeit* (Munich, 1963).

Friedjung, Heinrich, *Der Kampf um die Vorherrschaft in Deutschland, 1859–1866* (9th edn., 2 vols., Stuttgart and Berlin, 1912).

Friedrichs, Christopher, *Urban Society in an Age of War: Nördlingen, 1580–1720* (Princeton, 1979).

Friedrichs-Friedlaender, Carola, *Architektur als Mittel politischer Selbstdarstellung im 19. Jahrhundert: Die Baupolitik der bayerischen Wittelsbacher* (Munich, 1980).

Fries, H., and Schwaiger, Georg (eds.), *Katholische Theologen Deutschlands im 19. Jahrhundert* (3 vols.; Munich, 1975).

Fuller, J. F. C., *The Decisive Battles of the Western World,* ii. *From the Defeat of the Spanish Armada to the Battle of Waterloo* (London, 1955).

Gagel, Walter, *Die Wahlrechtsfrage in der Geschichte der deutschen liberalen Parteien, 1848–1919* (Düsseldorf, 1958).

Gagern, Heinrich von, *Deutscher Liberalismus im Vormärz: Heinrich von Gagern: Briefe und Reden, 1815–1848* (Berlin, Frankfurt, and Göttingen, 1959).

Gagliardo, John, *From Pariah to Patriot: The Changing Image of the German Peasant, 1770–1840* (Lexington, 1969).

—— *Reich and Nation; The Holy Roman Empire as Idea and Reality, 1763–1806* (Bloomington, 1980).

Gailus, Manfred, 'Zur Politisierung der Landbevölkerung in der Märzbewegung von 1848', in Peter Steinbach (ed.), *Probleme politischer Partizipation im Modernisierungsprozess* (Stuttgart, 1982), 88–113.

Gall, Lothar, *Benjamin Constant: Seine politische Ideenwelt und der deutsche Vormärz* (Wiesbaden, 1963).

—— 'Das Problem der parlamentarischen Opposition im deutschen

Frühliberalismus', in Kluxen and Mommsen (eds.), *Ideologien*, 153–70.
—— *Der Liberalismus als regierende Partei. Das Grossherzogtum Baden zwischen Restauration und Reichsgründung* (Wiesbaden, 1968).
—— *Bismarck. Der weisse Revolutionär* (Berlin and Vienna, 1980).
Gause, Fritz, *Die Geschichte der Stadt Königsberg in Preussen* (2 vols., Cologne, 1965–8).
Gay, Peter, *The Enlightenment: An Interpretation* (2 vols., New York, 1966–9).
—— *The Bourgeois Experience* (2 vols., New York and Oxford, 1984–6).
Gebhardt, Hartwig, *Revolution und liberale Bewegung: Die nationale Organisation der Konstitutionellen Partei in Deutschland, 1840/49* (Bremen, 1974).
Geismeier, Willi, *Biedermeier: Das Bild vom Biedermeier: Zeit und Kultur des Biedermeier: Kunst und Kunstleben des Biedermeier* (Leipzig, 1979).
Gerhard, Dietrich (ed.), *Ständische Vertretungen in Europa im 17. und 18. Jahrhundert* (Göttingen, 1969).
Gerhard, Ute, *Verhältnisse und Verhinderungen. Frauenarbeit. Familie und Rechte der Frauen im 19. Jahrhundert* (Frankfurt, 1978).
Gerlach, Ernst Ludwig von, *Von der Revolution zum Norddeutschen Bund . . . Aus dem Nachlass*, ed. H. Diwald (2 vols., Göttingen, 1970—).
Gerlach, Leopold von, *Denkwürdigkeiten* (2 vols., Berlin, 1891–2).
Gerloff, Wilhelm, 'Der Staatshaushalt und das Finanzsystem Deutschlands, 1820–1927', in Gerloff (ed.), *Handbuch der Finanzwissenschaft* (Tübingen, 1929), 1–69.
Gerrish, B. A., *A Prince of the Church: Schleiermacher and the Beginnings of Modern Theology* (Philadelphia, 1984).
Gerteis, Klaus, 'Bildung und Revolution: Die deutschen Lesegesellschaften am Ende des 18. Jahrhunderts', *AfK* 53/1 (1971), 127–39.
Gerth, Hans, *Die sozialgeschichtliche Lage der bürgerlichen Intelligenz um die Wende des 18. Jahrhunderts: Ein Beitrag zur Soziologie des deutschen Frühliberalismus* (Frankfurt, 1935).
Gervinus, G. Gottfried, *Leben von ihm selbst (1860)* (Leipzig, 1893).
—— *Einleitung in die Geschichte des neunzehnten Jahrhunderts*, ed. W. Boehlich (Frankfurt, 1967).
Geschichtliche Grundbegriffe: Historisches Lexikon zur politisch- sozialen Sprache in Deutschland, ed. Otto Brunner *et al.* (Stuttgart, 1972 ff.).
Gilbert, Felix, *Johann Gustav Droysen und die preussisch-deutsche Frage* (Munich and Berlin, 1931).
Gillis, John R., *The Prussian Bureaucracy in Crisis, 1840–1860: Origins of an Administrative Ethos* (Stanford, 1971).
Glaser, Hermann, *The German Mind of the Nineteenth Century* (New York, 1981).
Glass, D. V., and Eversley, D. E. C. (eds.), *Population in History: Essays in Historical Demography* (London, 1965).
Glassbrenner, Adolf, *Unterrichtung der Nation: Ausgewählte Werke und Briefe in drei Bänden* (Cologne, 1981).
Goethe, Johann Wolfgang von, *The Sorrows of Young Werther*, trans. Catherine Hutter (New York, 1962).

—— *Autobiography* (2 vols., Chicago and London, 1974).

—— *Werke* (Hamburger Ausgabe) (10th edn., 14 vols., Munich, 1974).

—— and Schiller, Friedrich, *Briefwechsel*, (Frankfurt, 1961).

Gollwitzer, Heinz, 'Der Cäsarismus Napoleons III. im Widerhall der öffentlichen Meinung Deutschlands', *HZ* 173/1 (1952), 23–75.

—— *Die Standesherren: Die politische und gesellschaftliche Stellung der Mediatisierten, 1815–1918* (Stuttgart, 1957).

—— *Ludwig I. von Bayern: Königtum im Vormärz* (Munich, 1986).

Goltz, Theodor Freiherr von der, *Geschichte der deutschen Landwirtschaft* (2 vols.; Stuttgart and Berlin, 1902–03).

Gooch, G. P., *Germany and the French Revolution* (London, 1920).

—— *History and Historians in the Nineteenth Century* (Boston, 1959).

Good, David, *The Economic Rise of the Habsburg Empire, 1750–1914* (Berkeley, Los Angeles, and London, 1984).

Goody, Jack (ed.), *Family and Inheritance: Rural Society in Western Europe, 1200–1860* (Cambridge, 1976).

Graf, Friedrich Wilhelm, *Die Politisierung des religiösen Bewusstseins: Die bürgerlichen Religionsparteien im deutschen Vormärz: Das Beispiel des Deutschkatholizismus* (Stuttgart, 1978).

Gregory, Frederick, *Scientific Materialism in Nineteenth Century Germany* (Boston, 1977).

Grillparzer, Franz, *Sämtliche Werke* (4 vols., Munich, 1962–5).

Gross, Hanns, 'The Holy Roman Empire in Modern Times: Constitutional Reality and Legal Theory', in James A. Vann and Steven W. Rowan (eds.), *The Old Reich: Essays on German Political Institutions, 1495–1806* (Brussels, 1974), 1–29.

Grosser, Dieter, *Grundlagen und Struktur der Staatslehre Friedrich Julius Stahls* (Cologne and Opladen, 1963).

Gruner, Wolf D., 'Die deutschen Einzelstaaten und der Deutsche Bund', in A. Kraus (ed.), *Land und Reich/Stamm und Nation* (Munich, 1984), iii. 19–36.

—— *Die deutsche Frage: Ein Problem der europäischen Geschichte seit 1800* (Munich, 1985).

Grünthal, Günther, 'Konstitutionalismus und konservative Politik: Ein verfassungspolitischer Beitrag zur Ära Manteuffel', in Gerhard A. Ritter, ed., *Gesellschaft, Parlament und Regierung: Zur Geschichte des Parlamentarismus in Deutschland* (Düsseldorf, 1974), 145–64.

—— *Parlamentarismus in Preussen, 1848/49–1858. Preussischer Konstitutionalismus, Parlament und Regierung in der Reaktionsära* (Düsseldorf, 1982).

Guggisberg, Kurt, *Karl Ludwig von Haller* (Frauenfeld and Leipzig, 1938).

Gutzkow, Karl, *Wally the Skeptic: A Novel*, trans. Ruth-Ellen Boetcher-Joeres (Bern and Frankfurt, 1974).

Haass, Robert, *Die geistige Haltung der katholischen Universitäten Deutschlands im 18. Jahrhundert* (Freiburg, 1952).

Habermas, Jürgen, *Strukturwandel der Öffentlichkeit: Untersuchungen zu einer Kategorie der bürgerlichen Gesellschaft* (Neuwied, 1962).

Haferkorn, Hans J., 'Zur Entstehung der bürgerlich-literarischen Intelligenz und des Schriftstellers in Deutschland zwischen 1750 und

1800', in Ulrich Dzwonek *et al.* (eds.), *Deutsches Bürgertum und literarische Intelligenz, 1750–1800* (Stuttgart, 1974).

Hahn, Hans Werner, *Geschichte des deutschen Zollvereins* (Göttingen, 1984).

Haines, M., 'Agriculture and Development in Prussian Upper Silesia, 1846–1913', *JEH* 42 (1982), 355–84.

Hajnal, J., 'European Marriage Patterns in Perspective', in D. V. Glass and D. E. C. Eversley (eds.), *Population in History, Essays in Historical Demography* (London, 1965), 101–43.

Haltern, Utz, 'Politische Bildung und bürgerlicher Liberalismus; Zur Rolle des Konversationslexikons in Deutschland', *HZ* 223/1 (1976), 61–97.

Hamburger, Michael, *Reason and Energy. Studies in German Literature* (New York, 1957).

Hamerow, Theodore S., 'The Elections to the Frankfurt Parliament', *JMH* 33/1 (Mar.1961), 15–32.

—— *The Social Foundations of German Unification, 1858–1871* (2 vols., Princeton, 1969–1972).

Hammerstein, Notker, 'Das politische Denken Friedrich Carl von Mosers', *HZ* 221/2 (1971), 316–38.

—— *Aufklärung und katholisches Reich: Untersuchung zur Universitätsreform und Politik katholischer Territorien des Heiligen Römischen Reiches Deutscher Nation im 18. Jahrhundert* (Berlin, 1977).

Handbuch der deutschen Wirtschafts- und Sozialgeschichte, ed. Hermann Aubin and Wolfgang Zorn (3 vols., Stuttgart, 1971–76).

Hansen, Joseph, *Rheinische Briefe und Akten zur Geschichte der politischen Bewegung, 1830–1845* (1919; repr. Osnabrück, 1967).

Hantsch, Hugo, *Die Geschichte Österreichs* (2 vols., Graz and Vienna, 1951–3).

Hardtwig, Wolfgang, 'Von Preussens Aufgabe in Deutschland zu Deutschlands Aufgabe in der Welt: Liberalismus und borussianisches Geschichtsbild zwischen Revolution und Imperialismus', *HZ* 231/2 (1980), 265–324.

—— 'Studentische Mentalität—politische Jugendbewegung—Nationalismus: Die Anfänge der deutschen Burschenschaft', *HZ* 242/3 (1986), 581–628.

Harnisch, Hartmut, 'Vom Oktoberedikt des Jahres 1807 zur Deklaration von 1816: Problematik und Charakter der preussischen Agrarreformgesetzgebung zwischen 1807 und 1816', *JbW* Sonderband (1978), 231–93.

—— 'Bevölkerungsgeschichtliche Probleme der industriellen Revolution in Deutschland', in K. Larmer (ed.), *Studien zur Geschichte der Produktivkräfte: Deutschland zur Zeit der industriellen Revolution (Berlin, 1979)*.

Harris, H. S., *Hegel's Development: Toward the Sunlight (1770–1801)* (Oxford, 1972).

—— *Hegel's Development: Night Thoughts (Jena 1801–1806)* (Oxford and New York, 1983).

Hartmann, Nicolai, *Die Philosophie des deutschen Idealismus* (1923–9) (2nd edn., Berlin, 1960).

Hassinger, Herbert, 'Der Stand der Manufakturen in den deutschen Erbländern der Habsburgermonarchie am Ende des 18. Jahrhunderts', in Friedrich Lütge (ed.), *Die wirtschaftiche Situation in Deutschland und Österreich um die Wende vom 18. zum 19. Jahrhundert* (Stuttgart, 1914), 110–76.

Hausen, Karin, 'Familie als Gegenstand historischer Sozialwissenschaft: Bemerkungen zu einer Forschungsstrategie', *GuG* 1/2/3 (1975), 171–209.

Haushofer, Heinz, *Die deutsche Landwirtschaft im technischen Zeitalter* (Stuttgart, 1972).

Häusler, Wolfgang, *Von der Massenarmut zur Arbeiterbewegung: Demokratie und soziale Frage in der Wiener Revolution von 1848* (Vienna and Munich, 1979).

Häusser, L., *Deutsche Geschichte vom Tode Friedrich des Grossen bis zur Gründung des Deutschen Bundes* (4 vols., Berlin, 1855–7).

Haym, Rudolf, *Aus meinem Leben: Erinnerungen (Aus dem Nachlass)* (Berlin, 1902).

—— *Herder nach seinem Leben und seinen Werken* (2 vols., Berlin, 1958).

Heer, F., *Der Kampf um die österreichische Identität* (Vienna, 1981).

Heffter, Heinrich, *Die deutsche Selbstverwaltung im 19. Jahrhundert. Geschichte der Ideen und Institution* (Stuttgart, 1950).

Hegel, Georg Wilhelm Friedrich, *Philosophy of Right*, trans. T. M. Knox (London, Oxford, and New York, 1952).

—— *Werke* (20 vols., Frankfurt, 1971-).

—— *Phenomenology of Spirit*, trans. A. V. Miller (Oxford and New York, 1979).

Heine, Heinrich, *Werke*, ed. M. Greiner (2 vols., Berlin and Cologne, 1962.

—— *Sämtliche Schriften* (6 vols., Munich, 1968–76).

—— 'Zur Geschichte der Religion und Philosophie in Deutschland (1834)' in *Beiträge zur deutschen Ideologie* (Frankfurt, 1971), 1–110.

—— 'Die romantische Schule' (1836), in *Beiträge zur deutschen Ideologie* (Frankfurt, 1971), 111–236.

Helfferich, Karl, *Georg von Siemens: Ein Lebensbild aus Deutschlands grosser Zeit* (3 vols., Berlin, 1921–3).

Helling, Gertrud, 'Zur Entwicklung der Produktivität in der deutschen Landwirtschaft im 19. Jahrhundert', *JbW* 1 (1966), 129–91.

Helmholtz, Hermann von, 'On the Relation of Natural Science to Science in General' (1862), in *Popular Lectures on Scientific Subjects* (New York, 1897), 1–32.

—— 'Autobiographical Sketch' (1877), *Popular Lectures on Scientific Subjects* (2nd ser., New York, 1903), 266–91.

Henderson, W. O., *The Zollverein* (Cambridge, 1939).

Henning, Friedrich-Wilhelm, *Bauernwirtschaft und Bauerneinkommen in Ostpreussen im 18. Jahrhundert* (Würzburg, 1969).

—— 'Die Betriebsgrössenstruktur der mitteleuropäischen Landwirtschaft im 18. Jahrhundert und ihr Einfluss auf die ländlichen Einkommens-verhältnisse', *Zeitschrift für Agrargeschichte und Agrarsoziologie*, 17/2 (1969), 171–93.

—— *Dienste und Aufgaben der Bauern im 18. Jahrhundert* (Stuttgart, 1969).

—— *Bauernwirtschaft und Bauerneinkommen im Fürstentum Paderborn im 18. Jahrhundert* (Berlin, 1970).

Henning, Hansjoachim, *Das westdeutsche Bürgertum in der Epoche der Hochindustrialisierung 1860–1914: Soziales Verhalten und soziale Strukturen*, i. *Das Bildungsbürgertum in den preussischen Westprovinzen* (Wiesbaden, 1972).

—— 'Soziale Verflechtungen der Unternehmer in Westfalen, 1860–1914', *Zeitschrift für Unternehmersgeschichte*, 23/1 (1978), 1–30.

—— *Die deutsche Beamtenschaft im 19. Jahrhundert. Zwischen Stand und Beruf* (Wiesbaden, 1984).

Herder, Johann Gottfried, *Sämmtliche Werke*, ed. B. Suphan (33 vols., Berlin, 1877–1913).

Hermand, Jost, and Windfuhr, M. (eds.), *Zur Literatur der Restaurations-Epoche, 1815–1848* (Stuttgart, 1970).

Hermann, Georg, *Das Biedermeier im Spiegel seiner Zeit* (1913; repr. Oldenburg and Hamburg, 1965).

Herre, Franz, *Nation ohne Staat: Die Entstehung der deutschen Frage* (Cologne and Berlin, 1967).

—— *Kaiser Franz Joseph von Österreich* (Cologne, 1978).

Herrmann, Ulrich (ed.), *Die Bildung des Bürgers* (Weinheim, 1982).

Herrmann, Wolfgang, *Deutsche Baukunst des 19. und 20. Jahrhunderts* (1932; repr. Basel and Stuttgart, 1977).

Hess, Adalbert, *Das Parlament, das Bismarck widerstrebte: Zur Politik und sozialen Zusammensetzung des preussischen Abgeordnetenhauses der Konflikts-zeit (1862–1866)* (Cologne and Opladen, 1964).

Heyderhoff, Julius, and Wentzcke, Paul (eds.) *Deutscher Liberalismus im Zeitalter Bismarcks: Eine politische Briefsammlung* (2 vols., Bonn and Leipzig, 1925–6).

Hintze, Otto, *Die Hohenzollern und ihr Werk* (Berlin, 1916).

—— *Gesammelte Abhandlungen* (2nd edn., 3 vols., Göttingen, 1962–7).

—— *The Historical Essays*, ed. Felix Gilbert (New York, 1975).

Hippel, Wolfgang von, *Friedrich Landolin Karl von Blittersdorff, 1792–1861* (Stuttgart, 1967).

Hobsbawm, E. J., *The Age of Revolution, 1789–1848* (Cleveland and New York, 1962).

Hock, Wolfgang, *Liberales Denken im Zeitalter der Paulskirche. Droysen und die Frankfurter Mitte* (Münster, 1957).

Hodgskin, Thomas, *Travels in the North of Germany* (1820; repr. New York, 1969).

Hoffmann, Walther, 'The Take-Off in Germany', in W. W. Rostow (ed.), *The Economics of Take-Off into Sustained Growth* (New York, 1963), 95–118.

—— *Das Wachstum der deutschen Wirtschaft seit der Mitte des 19. Jahrhunderts* (Berlin, Heidelberg, and New York, 1965).

Hofmann, Hanns, *Adelige Herrschaft und souveräner Staat: Studien über Staat und Gesellschaft in Franken und Bayern im 18. und 19. Jahrhundert* (Munich, 1962).

—— (ed.), *Die Entstehung des modernen souveränen Staates* (Cologne and Berlin, 1967).

Hohenberg, Paul, and Lees, Lynn, *The Making of Urban Europe, 1000–1950* (Cambridge, 1985).

Hohendahl, Peter Uwe, *Literarische Kultur im Zeitalter des Liberalismus. 1830–1870* (Munich, 1985).

Hölderlin, Friedrich, *Poems and Fragments*, ed. and trans. Michael Hamburger (Cambridge, 1980).

Honour, Hugh, *Romanticism* (New York, 1979).

Hope, Nicholas, *The Alternative to German Unification: The Anti-Prussian Party: Frankfurt, Nassau, and the two Hessen, 1859–1867* (Wiesbaden, 1973).

Howard, Michael, *War in European History* (London, Oxford, and New York, 1976).

Hubatsch, Walter (ed.), *Grundriss zur deutschen Verwaltungsgeschichte, 1815–1945* (Marburg/Lahn, 1975).

Hubbard, William, *Familiengeschichte: Materialien zur deutschen Familie seit dem Ende des 18. Jahrhunderts* (Munich, 1983).

Huber, Ernst Rudolf, *Deutsche Verfassungsgeschichte* (4 vols., Stuttgart, 1957–69).

—— *Dokumente zur deutschen Verfassungsgeschichte* (3 vols., Stuttgart, 1957–6).

—— and Huber, Wolfgang (eds.), *Staat und Kirche im 19. und 20. Jahrhundert, ii. Vom Ausgang des alten Reichs bis zum Vorabend der bürgerlichen Revolution* (Berlin, 1973).

—— (eds.), *Staat und Kirche im 19. und 20. Jahrhundert, ii. Staat und Kirche im Zeitalter des Hochkonstitionalismus und des Kulturkampfes, 1848–1890* (Berlin, 1976).

Huck, Gerhard (ed.), *Sozialgeschichte der Freizeit* (Wuppertal, 1980).

Humboldt, Wilhelm von, *Werke*, ed. A. Flitner and K. Giel (5 vols., Stuttgart, 1960–4).

Husung, Hans-Gerhard, 'Kollektiver Gewaltprotest im norddeutschen Vormärz', in W. J. Mommsen and G. Hirschfeld (eds.), *Sozialprotest, Gewalt, Terror* (Stuttgart, 1982), 47–63.

Ibbeken, R., *Preussen, 1807–1813* (Cologne and Berlin, 1970).

Iggers, Georg G., *The German Conception of History: The National Tradition of Historical Thought from Herder to the Present* (Middletown, Conn., 1968).

Ilien, Albert, and Jeggle, Utz, *Leben auf dem Dorf* (Opladen, 1978).

Imhof, Arthur E., *Einführung in die Historische Demographie* (Munich, 1977).

—— *Die gewonnenen Jahre. Von der Zunahme unserer Lebensspanne seit dreihundert Jahren oder von der Notwendigkeit einer neuen Einstellung zu Leben und Sterben* (Munich, 1981).

—— (ed.), *Historische Demographie als Sozialgeschichte. Giessen und Umgebung vom 17. zum 19. Jahrhundert* (2 vols., Darmstadt and Marburg, 1975).

—— (ed.), *Mensch und Gesundheit in der Geschichte* (Husum, 1980).

Imhof, Ulrich, *Das gesellige Jahrhundert. Gesellschaft und Gesellschaften im Zeitalter der Aufklärung* (Munich, 1982).

Jacoby, Johann, *Vier Fragen beantwortet von einem Ostpreussen* (Mannheim, 1841).

Jäger, Helmut (ed.), *Probleme des Städtewesens im industriellen Zeitalter* (Vienna, 1978).

Jahnke, Hans and Otte, M. (eds.), *Epistemological and Social Problems of the Sciences in the Early Nineteenth Century* (Dordrecht, 1981).

Jantke, Carl, *Der vierte Stand: Die gestaltenden Kräfte der deutschen Arbeiterbewegung im XIX. Jahrhundert* (Freiburg, 1955).

—— and Dietrich Hilger (eds.), *Die Eigentumslosen; Armutsnot und Arbeiterschicksal in Deutschland in zeitgenössischen Schilderungen und kritischen Beobachtungen bis zum Ausgang der Emanzipationskrise des 19. Jahrhunderts* (Munich, 1965).

Jászi, Oscar, *The Dissolution of the Habsburg Monarchy* (Chicago, 1929).

Jeggle, Utz, *Kiebingen: Eine Heimatgeschichte: Zum Prozess der Zivilisation in einem schwäbischen Dorf* (Tübingen, 1977).

Jeismann, Karl-Ernst, *Das preussische Gymnasium in Staat und Gesellschaft: Die Entstehung des Gymnasiums als Schule des Staates und des Gebildeten, 1787–1817* (Stuttgart, 1974).

Jessen, Hans (ed.), *Die deutsche Revolution 1848/49 in Augenzeugenberichten* (Düsseldorf, 1968).

Joeres, Ruth Ellen, and Maynes, Mary Jo (eds.), *German Women in the Enlightenment and Nineteenth Centuries: A Social and Literary History* (Bloomington, Indiana, 1986).

Johnson, Hubert, *Frederick the Great and his Officials* (New Haven and London, 1975).

Jung-Stilling, Heinrich, *Lebensgeschichte* (Munich, 1968).

Kaehler, Siegfried A., *Wilhelm von Humboldt und der Staat* (2nd edn., Göttingen, 1963).

Kaelble, Hartmut, *Berliner Unternehmer während der frühen Industrialisierung: Herkunft, sozialer Status und politischer Einfluss* (Berlin, 1972).

—— 'Sozialer Aufstieg in Deutschland 1850–1914,' *VSWG* 90/1 (1973), 41–71.

—— *Historical Research on Social Mobility. Western Europe and the USA in the Nineteenth and Twentieth Centuries* (New York, 1981).

Kaiser, Gerhard, *Pietismus und Patriotismus im literarischen Deutschland. Ein Beitrag zum Problem der Säkularisation* (2nd ed., Frankfurt, 1973).

—— *Gottfried Keller* (Frankfurt, 1981).

Kann, Robert, *The Multinational Empire: Nationalism and National Reform in the Habsburg Monarchy, 1848–1918* (2 vols., New York, 1950).

Kant, Immanuel, *Briefwechsel*, ed. Otto Schöndörffer (Hamburg, 1972).

—— *Critique of Pure Reason*, trans. Norman Kemp Smith (New York, 1965).

—— *Philosophical Correspondence 1759–99*, ed. and trans. Arnulf Zweig (Chicago, 1967).

—— *Political Writings*, ed. Hans Reiss (Cambridge, 1970).

—— *Prolegomena to any Future Metaphysics that will be able to present itself as a Science* (Manchester, 1953).

—— *Religion within the Limits of Reason Alone* (New York, 1960).

Kapp, Friedrich, *Vom radikalen Frühsozialisten des Vormärz zum liberalen Parteipolitiker des Bismarckreichs: Briefe 1843–1884*, ed. H. U. Wehler (Frankfurt, 1969).

Kaschuba, Wolfgang, *Volkskultur zwischen feudaler und bürgerlicher Gesellschaft: Zur Geschichte eines Begriffs und seine gesellschaftlichen Wirklichkeit* (Frankfurt and New York, 1988).

—— and Lipp, Carola, *Dörfliches Überleben: Zur Geschichte materieller und sozialer Reproduktion ländlicher Gesellschaft im 19. und frühen 20. Jahrhundert* (Tübingen, 1982).

Katz, Jacob, *Out of the Ghetto: The Social Background of Jewish Emancipation, 1770–1870* (Cambridge, Mass., 1973).

Katzenstein, Peter J., *Disjoined Partners: Austria and Germany since 1815* (Berkeley, Los Angeles, and London, 1976).

Kaufhold, Karl Heinrich, 'Umfang und Gliederung des deutschen Handwerks um 1800', in W. Abel *et al.* (eds.), *Handwerksgeschichte in neuer Sicht* (Göttingen 1978), 26–64.

Kehr, Eckart, *Der Primat der Innenpolitik: Gesammelte Aufsätze zur preussisch-deutschen Sozialgeschichte*, ed. H. U. Wehler (Berlin, 1965).

Kellenbenz, Hermann, 'Germany', in Charles Wilson and Geoffrey Parker (eds.), *An Introduction to the Sources of European Economic History, 1500–1800* (Ithaca, 1977).

Keller, G., *Werke, iv. Die Leute von Seldwyla. Sieben Legenden* (Zürich, 1965).

Kelly, Alfred, *The Descent of Darwin: The Popularization of Darwinism in Germany, 1860–1914* (Chapel Hill, 1981).

Kemiläinen, Aira, *Auffassungen über die Sendung des deutschen Volkes um die Wende des 18. und 19. Jahrhunderts* (Helsinki, 1956).

Kiesel, Helmuth, and Münch, Paul, *Gesellschaft und Literatur im 18. Jahrhundert. Voraussetzungen und Entstehung des literarischen Markts in Deutschland* (Munich, 1977).

Kisch, Herbert, 'Growth Deterrents of a Medieval Heritage: The Aachen Area Woollen Trades before 1790', *JEH* 26 (Dec. 1964), 517–37.

—— *Prussian Mercantilism and the Rise of the Krefeld Silk Industry: Variations on an Eighteenth-Century Theme* (Philadelphia, 1968).

—— 'The Textile Industries in Silesia and the Rhineland: A Comparative Study in Industrialization', in Peter Kriedte *et al.* (eds.), *Industrialization before Industrialization* (Cambridge, 1981), 178–200.

Kiszling, Rudolf, *Fürst Felix zu Schwarzenberg. Der politische Lehrmeister Kaiser Franz Josephs* (Graz and Cologne, 1952).

Klein, Ernst, 'Johann Heinrich Gottlob Justi und die preussische Staatswirtschaft', *VSWG* 42/2 (1961), 145–202.

Kleist, Heinrich von, *An Abyss Deep Enough: Letters*, ed. P. B. Miller (New York, 1982).

Klessmann, Christoph, 'Zur Sozialgeschichte der Reichsverfassungskampagne von 1849', *HZ* 218/2 (Apr. 1974), 283–337.

Klessmann, Eckhart (ed.), *Napoleons Russlandfeldzug in Augenzeugenberichten* (Düsseldorf, 1964).

—— (ed.), *Die Befreiungskriege in Augenzeugenberichten* (Düsseldorf, 1966).

Klingenstein, Grete, *Staatsverwaltung und kirchliche Autorität im 18. Jahrhundert: Das Problem der Zensur in der theresianischen Reform* (Munich, 1970).

—— *Der Aufstieg des Hauses Kaunitz: Studien zur Herkunft und Bildung des Staatskanzlers Wenzel Anton* (Göttingen, 1975).

Klopp, Onno, *Der König Friedrich II. von Preussen und seine Politik* (1861; 2nd edn., Schaffhausen, 1867).

Kluckhohn, Paul, *Die Idee des Volkes in Schriften der deutschen Bewegung von Moser und Herder bis Grimm* (Berlin, 1934).

Kluxen, Kurt, and Mommsen, Wolfgang J. (eds.), *Politische Ideologien und nationalstaatliche Ordnung; Festschrift für Theodor Schieder* (Munich and Vienna, 1968).

Koch, Rainer, *Demokratie und Staat bei Julius Fröbel, 1805–1893: Liberales Denken zwischen Naturrecht und Sozialdarwinismus* (Wiesbaden, 1978).

—— 'Die Agrarrevolution in Deutschland 1848', in *Die deutsche Revolution von 1848/49* (Darmstadt, 1983), 262–94.

—— 'Staat oder Gemeinde? Zu einem politischen Zeitkonflikt in der bürgerlichen Bewegung des 19. Jahrhunderts', *HZ* 283/1 (1983), 73–96.

Kocka, Jürgen, *Unternehmungsverwaltung und Angestelltenschaft am Beispiel Siemens,1847–1914: Zum Verhältnis von Kapitalismus und Bürokratie in der deutschen Industrialisierung* (Stuttgart, 1969).

—— 'The Study of Social Mobility and the Formation of the Working Class in the 19th Century', *Mouvement Social*, iii (April–June 1980), 97–117.

—— 'The Entrepreneur, the Family and Capitalism: Some Examples from the Early Phase of Industrialization in Germany', *German Yearbook on Business History* (1981), 53–82.

—— *Lohnarbeit und Klassenbildung. Arbeiter und Arbeiterbewegung in Deutschland, 1800–1876* (Berlin, 1983).

—— (ed.), *Bürger und Bürgerlichkeit im 19. Jahrhundert* (Göttingen, 1987).

Koehler, Benedikt, *Ästhetik der Politik. Adam Müller und die politische Romantik* (Stuttgart, 1980).

Kohl, Thomas, *Familie und soziale Schichtung: Zur historischen Demographie Triers, 1730–1830* (Stuttgart, 1985).

Kolakowski, Leszek, *Main Currents of Marxism* (Oxford, 1978).

Köllmann, Wolfgang, *Sozialgeschichte der Stadt Barmen im 19. Jahrhundert* (Tübingen, 1960).

—— 'Bevölkerung und Arbeitskräftepotential in Deutschland, 1815–1865. Ein Beitrag zur Analyse der Problematik des Pauperismus', Landesamt für Forschung, Nordrhein-Westfalen, *Jahrbuch* (1968), 209–54.

—— (ed.), *Bevölkerung in der industriellen Revolution* (Göttingen, 1974).

—— and Kraus A. (eds.), *Quellen zur Bevölkerungs-, Sozial- und Wirtschaftsstatistik Deutschlands, 1815–1875*, i. *Quellen zur Bevölkerungsstatistik Deutschlands, 1815–1875* (Boppard, 1980).

Komlos, John, *The Habsburg Monarchy as a Customs Union* (Princeton, 1983).

Koopmann, Helmut, *Das Junge Deutschland. Analyse seines Selbstverständnisses* (Stuttgart, 1970).

Kopitzsch, Franklin, 'Hamburg zwischen Hauptrezess und Franzosenzeit', in Wilhelm Rausch (ed.), *Die Städte Mitteleuropas im 17. und 18. Jahrhundert* (Linz, 1981), 181–210.

Koselleck, Reinhart, *Preussen zwischen Reform und Revolution. Allgemeines Landrecht. Verwaltung und soziale Bewegung von 1791 bis 1848* (Stuttgart, 1967).

—— *Kritik und Krise: Ein Beitrag zur Pathogenese der bürgerlichen Welt* (Freiburg and Munich, 1973).

—— (ed.), *Studien zum Beginn der modernen Welt* (Stuttgart, 1977).

Koszyk, Kurt, *Geschichte der deutschen Presse. ii. Deutsche Presse im 19. Jahrhundert* (Berlin, 1966).

Kraehe, Enno E., *Metternich's German Policy* (2 vols., Princeton, 1963–84).

Kramer, Helmut, *Fraktionsbindungen in den deutschen Volksvertretungen, 1819–1849* (Berlin, 1968).

Kraul, Margret, *Gymnasium und Gesellschaft im Vormärz: Neuhumanistische Einheitsschule, städtische Gesellschaft und soziale Herkunft der Schüler* (Göttingen, 1980).

—— *Das deutsche Gymnasium, 1780–1980* (Frankfurt, 1984).

Kraus, Antje, ' "Antizipierter Ehesegen" im 19. Jahrhundert: Zur Beurteilung der Illegitimität unter sozialgeschichtlichen Aspekten', *VSWG* 46/2 (1979), 174–215.

Kriedte, Peter, Medick, Hans, and Schlumbohm, Jürgen, (eds.), *Industrialization before Industrialization* (Cambridge, 1981).

Krieger, Leonard, *An Essay on the Theory of Enlightened Despotism* (Chicago and London, 1975).

The German Idea of Freedom: History of a Political Tradition (Boston, 1957).

—— *Ranke: The Meaning of History* (Chicago and London, 1977).

—— and Stern Fritz, (eds.), *The Responsibility of Power: Historical Essays in Honor of Hajo Holborn* (New York, 1969).

Kroner, Richard, *Von Kant bis Hegel* (2nd edn., Tübingen, 1961).

Kübeck von Kübau, Carl Friedrich, *Tagebücher*, ed. Max von Kübeck (3 vols. in 4; Vienna, 1909–10).

Kudlich, Hans, *Rückblicke und Erinnerungen* (3 vols. Vienna, Pest, and Leipzig, 1873).

Kügelgen, Wilhelm von, *Lebenserinnerungen des alten Mannes* (Stuttgart, 1951).

Kussmaul, Adolf, *Jugenderinnerungen eines alten Arztes* (Stuttgart, 1919).

Lahnstein, Peter (ed.), *Report einer 'guten alten Zeit': Zeugnisse und Berichte, 1750–1805* (Stuttgart, 1970).

Laing, Samuel, *Notes of a Traveller . . .* (London, 1842).

Landes, David S., *The Unbound Prometheus: Technological Change and Industrial Development in Western Europe from 1750 to the Present* (Cambridge, 1969).

940

Lang, Karl Heinrich Ritter von, *Aus der bösen alten Zeit: Lebenserinnerungen*, ed. V. Petersen (2nd edn., 2 vols., Stuttgart, 1910–13).
—— *Memoiren* (1842; repr. Stuttgart, 1957).
Lange, Friedrich Albert, *The History of Materialism* (3 vols., London, 1879–81).
Langewiesche, Dieter, *Liberalismus und Demokratie in Württemberg zwischen Revolution und Reichsgründung* (Düsseldorf, 1974).
—— 'Die Anfänge der deutschen Parteien: Partei, Fraktion und Verein in der Revolution von 1848/49', *GuG* 4/3 (1978), 324–61.
—— (ed.), *Die deutsche Revolution von 1848/49* (Darmstadt, 1983).
Langsam, W. C., *Francis the Good. The Education of an Emperor, 1768–92* (New York, 1949).
LaVopa, Anthony, *Prussian Schoolteachers: Profession and Office, 1763–1848* (Chapel Hill, 1980).
Lee, J. J., 'Aspects of Urbanization and Economic Development in Germany, 1815–1914', *Towns in Societies: Essays in Economic History and Historical Sociology* (New York, 1978), 279–94.
Lee, Lloyd E., 'Liberal Constitutionalism as Administrative Reform: The Baden Constitution of 1818', *CEH* 8/2 (June 1975), 91–112.
—— *The Politics of Harmony: Civil Service, Liberalism, and Social Reform in Baden, 1800–1850* (Newark, 1980).
Lee, W. R. *Population Growth, Economic Development, and Social Change in Bavaria, 1750–1850* (New York, 1977).
—— 'Germany', in id. (ed.), *European Demography and Economic Growth* (New York, 1979), 144–95.
Lees, Andrew, *Revolution and Reflection: Intellectual Change in Germany during the 1850s* (The Hague, 1974).
—— *Cities Perceived: Urban Society in European and American Thought* (New York, 1985).
Lempp, Richard, *Die Frage der Trennung von Kirche und Staat im Frankfurter Parlament* (Tübingen, 1913).
Lenger, Friedrich, *Zwischen Kleinbürgertum und Proletariat. Studien zur Sozialgeschichte der Düsseldorfer Handwerker 1816–1878* (Göttingen, 1986).
Leppmann, Wolfgang, *The German Image of Goethe* (Oxford, 1961).
Lewald, Fanny, *Meine Lebensgeschichte (1861–62)*, ed. Gisela Brinker-Gabler (Frankfurt, 1980).
List, Friedrich, *Schriften, Reden, Briefe* (10 vols. in 12; Berlin, 1927–35).
—— *The Natural System of Political Economy*, ed. W. O. Henderson (London, 1983).
List, Günther, 'Historische Theorie und rationale Geschichte zwischen Frühliberalismus und Reichsgründung', in B. Faulenbach (ed.), *Geschichtswissenschaft in Deutschland* (Munich, 1974), 35–53.
Ludz, Peter Christian (ed.), *Geheime Gesellschaften* (Heidelberg, 1979).
Lütge, Friedrich, *Geschichte der deutschen Agrarverfassung vom frühen Mittelalter bis zum 19. Jahrhundert* (2nd ed., Stuttgart, 1967).
—— (ed.), *Die wirtschaftliche Situation in Deutschland und Österreich um die Wende vom 18. zum 19. Jahrhundert* (Stuttgart, 1964).

Lutz, Heinrich, *Zwischen Habsburg und Preussen: Deutschland, 1815–1866* (Berlin, 1985).

—— and Rumpler, Helmut (eds.), *Österreich und die deutsche Frage im 19. und 20. Jahrhundert* (Munich, 1982).

Lutz, Rolland Ray, 'The German Revolutionary Student Movement, 1819–1833', *CEH* 4/3 (Sept. 1971), 215–41.

Maass, Ferdinand, *Der Josephinismus. Quellen zu seiner Geschichte in Österreich, 1760–1790* (5 vols.; Vienna, 1951–61).

Macartney, C. A., *The Habsburg Empire, 1790–1918* (London, 1968).

—— (ed.), *The Habsburg and Hohenzollern Dynasties in the Seventeenth and Eighteenth Centuries* (New York, 1970).

Mai, Ekkehard, and Waetzoldt, Stephan (eds.), *Kunstverwaltung: Bau- und Denkmal-Politik im Kaiserreich* (Berlin, 1980).

Mannlich, Johann Christian von, *Rokoko und Revolution. Lebenserinnerungen* (Stuttgart, 1966).

Marquardt, Frederick, 'A Working Class in Berlin in the 1840s?', in Hans-Ulrich Wehler (ed.), *Sozialgeschichte Heute: Festschrift für Hans Rosenberg zum 70. Geburtstag* (Göttingen, 1974), 191–210.

—— 'Sozialer Aufstieg, sozialer Abstieg und die Entstehung der Berliner Arbeiterklasse, 1806–1848', *GuG* 1/1 (1975), 43–77.

Marschalck, Peter, *Deutsche Überseewanderung im 19. Jahrhundert: Ein Beitrag zur soziologischen Theorie der Bevölkerung* (Stuttgart, 1973).

—— *Bevölkerungsgeschichte Deutschlands im 19. und 20. Jahrhundert* (Frankfurt, 1984).

Martens, Wolfgang, *Die Botschaft der Tugend: Die Aufklärung im Spiegel der deutschen Moralischen Wochenschriften* (Stuttgart, 1968).

Martin, Alfred von, 'Weltanschauliche Motive im altkonservativen denken', in Paul Wentzcke (ed.), *Deutscher Staat und deutsche Parteien (Meinecke Festschrift)* (Berlin, 1922), 342–84.

Martini, Fritz, 'Von der Aufklärung zum Sturm und Drang', in H. O. Burger (ed.), *Annalen der deutschen Literatur* (Stuttgart, 1952), 405–64.

—— *Deutsche Literatur im bürgerlichen Realismus, 1848–1898* (Stuttgart, 1962).

Marx, Karl, *Early Writings* (New York, 1975).

—— and Engels, Frederick, *Collected Works* (London, 1975–).

Masur, Gerhard, *Friedrich Julius Stahl: Geschichte seines Lebens. Aufstieg und Entfaltung, 1802–1840* (Berlin, 1930).

Matis, Herbert, *Österreichs Wirtschaft, 1848–1913: Konjunkturelle Dynamik und gesellschaftlicher Wandel im Zeitalter Franz Joseph I.* (Berlin, 1972).

Matzerath, Horst, 'Von der Stadt zur Gemeinde: Zur Entwicklung des rechtlichen Stadtbegriffs im 19. und 20. Jahrhundert', *Archiv für Kommunalwissenschaften*, 13/1 (1974), 17–46.

Mauersberg, Hans, *Wirtschafts- und Sozialgeschichte zentraleuropäischer Städte in neuer Zeit* (Göttingen, 1960).

—— *Die Wirtschaft und Gesellschaft Fuldas in neuer Zeit. Eine städtegeschichtliche Studie* (Göttingen, 1969).

—— *Wirtschaft und Gesellschaft Fürths in neuerer und neuester Zeit* (Göttingen, 1974).

Mayer, Gustav, *Radikalismus, Sozialismus und bürgerliche Demokratie*, ed. H. U. Wehler (Frankfurt, 1969).

Mayhew, Alan, *Rural Settlement and Farming in Germany* (New York, 1973).

Maynes, Mary Jo, *Schooling for the People: Comparative Local Studies of Schooling History in France and Germany, 1750–1850* (New York and London, 1985).

McClelland, Charles, *The German Historians and England: A Study in Nineteenth-Century Views* (Cambridge, 1971).

—— *State, Society, and University in Germany, 1700–1914* (Cambridge, 1980).

McLellan, David, *Karl Marx: His Life and Thought* (New York, 1973).

McLeod, Hugh, *Religion and the People of Western Europe, 1789–1970* (Oxford, 1981).

Meinecke, Friedrich, *Das Leben des Generalfeldmarschalls Hermann von Boyen* (2 vols., Stuttgart, 1896–9).

—— *Radowitz und die deutsche Revolution* (Berlin, 1913).

—— *Cosmopolitanism and the National State* (Princeton, 1970).

—— *Historicism. The Rise of a New Historical Outlook* (London, 1972).

—— *The Age of German Liberation, 1789–1815* (Berkeley, Los Angeles, and London, 1977).

Mendels, Franklin, 'Proto-Industrialization: The First Phase of the Industrialization Process', *JEH* 32/1 (Mar. 1972), 241–61.

Mendelsohn, E., 'The Emergence of Science as a Profession in Nineteenth-Century Europe', in Karl Hill (ed.), *The Management of Scientists* (Boston, 1964), 3–48.

Menhennet, Alan, *Order and Freedom: Literature and Society in Germany from 1720 to 1805* (London, 1973).

Metternich, Clemens von, *Memoirs, 1773–1815* (2 vols. New York, 1980).

Metternich-Winneburg, Prince Richard (ed.), *Aus Metternichs nachgelassenen Papieren* (8 vols., Vienna, 1881).

Milstein, Barney, 'Eight Eighteenth Century Reading Societies: A Sociological Contribution to the History of German Literature', *German Studies in America*, 2 (Bern and Frankfurt, 1972).

Milward, Alan S., and Saul, S. B., *The Economic Development of Continental Europe, 1780–1870* (London, 1973).

Minder, Robert, *Kultur und Literatur in Deutschland und Frankreich* (Frankfurt, 1962).

Mitterauer, Michael, 'Familiengrösse–Familientypen—Familienzyklus: Probleme quantitativer Auswertung von österreichischen Quellenmaterial', *GuG* 1/2/3 (1975), 226–55.

—— *Sozialgeschichte der Jugend* (Frankfurt, 1986).

—— and Sieder, Reinhard, *Vom Patriarchat zur Partnerschaft* (Munich, 1977).

—— —— *The European Family: Patriarchy to Partnership from the Middle Ages to the Present* (Oxford, 1982).

Möckl, Karl, *Der moderne bayerische Staat: Eine Verfassungsgeschichte vom aufgeklärten Absolutismus bis zum Ende der Reformepoche* (Munich, 1979).
—— 'Die bayerische Konstitution von 1808', in Eberhard Weis (ed.), *Reformen im rheinbündischen Deutschland* (Munich, 1984), 51–67.
Moeller, Robert G. (ed.), *Peasants and Lords in Modern Germany: Recent Studies in Agricultural History* (Boston, 1985).
Mohrmann, Renate (ed.), *Frauenemanzipation im deutschen Vormärz: Texte und Dokumente* (Stuttgart, 1978).
Möller, Helmut, *Die kleinbürgerliche Familie im 18. Jahrhundert: Verhalten und Gruppenkultur* (Berlin, 1969).
Möller, Horst, *Aufklärung in Preussen: Der Verleger, Publizist, und Geschichtsschreiber Friedrich Nicolai* (Berlin, 1974).
Mommsen, Wilhelm, *Johannes Miquel, i. 1828–1866* (Berlin and Leipzig, 1928).
—— *Die politischen Anschauungen Goethes* (Stuttgart, 1948).
—— *Deutsche Parteiprogramme* (2nd edn., Munich, 1964).
Montagu, Lady Mary Wortley, *The Complete Letters* (2 vols.; Oxford, 1965–7).
Montgomery, William, 'Germany', in Thomas Glick (ed.), *The Comparative Reception of Darwinism* (Austin and London, 1974), 81–116.
Moritz, Karl Philipp, *Anton Reiser* (1785; Berlin and Weimar, 1973).
Morsey, Rudolf, 'Wirtschaftliche und soziale Auswirkungen der Säkularisation in Deutschland', in Rudolf Vierhaus and Manfred Botzenhart (eds.), *Dauer und Wandel der Geschichte* (Münster, 1966), 361–83.
Möser, Justus, *Sämtliche Werke,* xii–xiii. *Osnabrückische Geschichte,* (Hamburg, 1964–71).
—— *Sämliche Werke,* ix. *Patriotische Phantasien und Zugenhöriges* (Hamburg, 1958).
Mosse, Werner E. *et al.* (eds.), *Revolution and Evolution. 1848 in German-Jewish History* (Tübingen, 1981).
Mossner, Ernest Campbell, *The Life of David Hume* (Edinburgh, 1954).
Mueller, Hans Eberhard, *Bureaucracy, Education and Monopoly: Civil Service Reforms in Prussia and England* (Berkeley, 1984).
Müller, Adam von, *Die Elemente der Staatskunst,* ed. J. Baxa (4 vols., Vienna and Leipzig, 1922).
—— *Schriften zur Staatsphilosophie,* ed. R. Kohler (Munich, n.d.).
Müller, Detlef, *Sozialstruktur und Schulsystem: Aspekte zum Strukturwandel des Schulwesens im 19. Jahrhundert* (Göttingen, 1977).
Müller, Friedrich, *Korporation und Assoziation: Eine Problemgeschichte der Vereinigungsfreiheit im deutschen Vormärz* (Berlin, 1965).
Müth, Reinhard, *Studentische Emanzipation und staatliche Repression: Die politische Bewegung der Tübinger Studenten in Vormärz, inbesondere von 1825 bis 1837* (Tübingen, 1977).
Mutton, Alice, *Central Europe: A Regional and Human Geography* (2nd edn., London, 1968).
Na'aman, Shlomo, *Demokratische und soziale Impulse in der Frühgeschichte der deutschen Arbeiterbewegung der Jahre 1862/63* (Wiesbaden, 1969).
Nahrstedt, Wolfgang, *Die Entstehung der Freizeit* (Göttingen, 1972).

Nickel, Dietmar, *Die Revolution 1848/49 in Augsburg und Bayerisch-Schwaben* (Augsburg, 1965).

Nicolson, Harold, *The Congress of Vienna: A Study in Allied Unity, 1812–1822* (London, 1946).

Niethammer, Lutz (ed.), *Wohnen im Wandel: Beiträge zur Geschichte des Alltags in der bürgerlichen Gesellschaft* (Wuppertal, 1979).

Nietzsche, Friedrich, *Briefwechsel: Kritische Gesamtausgabe*, ed. G. Colli and M. Montinari (Berlin and New York, 1975).

Nipperdey, Thomas, 'Verein als soziale Struktur in Deutschland im späten 18. und frühen 19. Jahrhundert', in H. Boockmann *et al.* (eds.), *Geschichtswissenschaft und Vereinswesen im 19. Jahrhundert* (Göttingen, 1972), 1–44.

—— 'Nationalidee und Nationaldenkmal in Deutschland im 19. Jahrhundert', in *Gesellschaft, Kultur, Theorie: Gesammelte Aufsätze zur neueren Geschichte* (Göttingen, 1976), 133–74.

—— *Deutsche Geschichte, 1800–1866: Bürgerwelt und starker Staat* (Munich, 1983).

Novalis [Friedrich von Hardenberg], *Werke, Tagebücher und Briefe*, eds. H.-J. Mahl and Richard Samuel (2 vols., Munich and Vienna, 1978).

Noyes, P. H., *Organization and Revolution: Working Class Associations in the German Revolutions of 1848–49* (Princeton, 1966).

Obenaus, Herbert, 'Finanzkrise und Verfassungsgebung zu den sozialen Bedingungen des frühen deutschen Konstitutionalismus', in G. A. Ritter, *Gesellschaft, Parlament, und Regierung* (Düsseldorf, 1974), 57–76.

—— *Anfänge des Parlamentarismus in Preussen bis 1848* (Düsseldorf, 1984).

Obermann, Karl, *Die deutschen Arbeiter in der Revolution von 1848* (2nd edn., Berlin, 1953).

—— 'Die Volksbewegung in Deutschland von 1844 bis 1846', *ZfG* 5/3 (1957), 503–25.

—— 'Wirtschafts- und sozialpolitische Aspekte der Krise von 1845–1847 in Deutschland, insbesondere in Preussen', *JbG*, 8 (1972), 143–74.

O'Boyle, Lenore, 'The German Nationalverein', *JCEA*, 16/4 (1957), 333–53.

—— 'The Image of the Journalist in France, Germany and England, 1815–1848', *CSSH* 10/2 (1968), 290–315.

—— 'The Problem of an Excess of Educated Men in Western Europe, 1800–1850', *JMH* 42/4 (1970), 471–95.

—— 'Learning for its own Sake: The German University as Nineteenth-Century Model', *CSSH* 25/1 (1983), 3–25.

Oestreich, Gerhard, *Geist und Gestalt des frühmodernen Staates* (Berlin, 1969).

Olsen, Donald, *The City as a Work of Art: London, Paris, Vienna* (New Haven and London, 1986).

Oncken, Hermann, *Rudolf von Bennigsen: Ein deutscher liberaler Politiker* (2 vols.; Stuttgart and Leipzig, 1910).

Orr, William J., 'East Prussia and the Revolution of 1848', *CEH* 13/4 (1980), 303–31.

Owen, John, *Travels into Different Parts of Europe in the Years 1791 and 1792* (London, 1796).

Pagenstecher, C. H. Alexander, *Lebenserinnerungen* (3 vols. in 1; Leipzig, 1913).

Pankoke, Eckart, *'Sociale Bewegung'*, *'Sociale Frage'*, *'Sociale Politik': Grundfragen der deutschen 'Socialwissenschaft' im 19. Jahrhundert* (Stuttgart, 1970).

Paret, Peter, *Yorck and the Era of Prussian Reform, 1807–1815* (Princeton, 1966).

—— *Clausewitz and the State* (New York, London, and Toronto, 1976).

Parisius, Ludolf, *Deutschlands politische Parteien und das Ministerium Bismarck* (Berlin, 1878).

—— *Leopold Freiherr von Hoverbeck: Ein Beitrag zur vaterländischen Geschichte* (2 vols. in 3; Berlin, 1897–1900).

Parry, Geraint, 'Enlightened Government and its Critics in Eighteenth Century Germany', *HJ* 6/2 (1963), 178–92.

Pascal, Roy, *The German Novel. Studies* (Toronto, 1965).

Paschen, Joachim, *Demokratische Vereine und preussischer Staat. Entwicklung und Unterdrückung der demokratischen Bewegung während der Revolution von 1848–49* (Munich and Vienna, 1977).

Pedlow, Gregory, *The Survival of Hessian Nobility, 1770–1870* (Princeton, 1988).

Perkins, J. A., 'The Agricultural Revolution in Germany, 1850–1914', *Journal of European Economic History*, 10 (1981), 71–118.

Petersdorff, H. von, *Friedrich von Motz* (Berlin, 1913).

Pfeifer, Gottfried, 'The Quality of Peasant Living in Central Europe', in William L. Thomas (ed.), *Man's Role in Changing the Face of the Earth* (Chicago, 1956), 240–77.

Pfizer, Paul, 'Gedanken über das Ziel und die Aufgabe des Deutschen Liberalismus' (1832), in *Deutsche Literaturdenkmale*, 144 (Berlin, 1911).

Pflanze, Otto, *Bismarck and the Development of Germany: The Period of Unification, 1815–1871* (Princeton, 1963).

Phayer, Michael, *Religion und das gewöhnliche Volk in Bayern in der Zeit von 1750–1850* (Munich 1970).

Pinson, Koppel S., *Pietism as a Factor in the Rise of German Nationalism* (New York, 1934).

Plaul, Hainer, 'The Rural Proletariat: The Everyday Life of Rural Labourers in the Magdeburg Region, 1830–1880', in Richard J. Evans and W. R. Lee (eds.), *The German Peasantry: Conflict and Community in Rural Society from the Eighteenth to the Twentieth Centuries* (London and Sydney, 1986), 102–28.

Poliakov, Leon, *The Aryan Myth: A History of Racist and Nationalist Ideas in Europe* (New York, 1971).

Pollard, Sidney, *European Economic Integration, 1815–1870* (London, 1974).

—— *Peaceful Conquest: The Industrialization of Europe, 1760–1970* (Oxford, 1981).

—— and Holmes, C. (eds.), *Documents of European Economic History*, i. *The Process of Industrialization, 1750–1870* (London, 1968).

Post, John D., *The Last Great Subsistence Crisis in the Western World* (Baltimore, 1977).

Pottle, Frederick A. (ed.), *Boswell on the Grand Tour: Germany and Switzerland, 1764* (New York, 1953).

Pounds, N. J. G., *An Historical Geography of Europe, 1500–1840* (Cambridge, 1979).
—— *An Historical Geography of Europe, 1800–1914* (Cambridge, 1985).
Prawer, S. S., *German Lyric Poetry: A Critical Analysis of Selected Poems from Klopstock to Rilke* (London, 1952).
—— *Heine: The Tragic Satirist: A Study of the Later Poetry, 1827–1856* (Cambridge, 1961).
—— (ed.), *The Romantic Period in Germany* (London, 1970).
Press, Volker (ed.), *Städtewesen und Merkantilismus in Mitteleuropa* (Cologne, 1983).
Prignitz, Christoph, *Vaterlandsliebe und Freiheit. Deutscher Patriotismus von 1750–1850* (Wiesbaden, 1981).
Raabe, Wilhelm, *Sämtliche Werke*, vi. *Der Hungerpastor* (Freiburg and Braunschweig, 1953).
Radowitz, Josef von, *Nachgelassene Briefe und Aufzeichnungen zur Geschichte der Jahre 1848–1853*, ed. W. Moring (1922, repr. Osnabrück, 1967).
Ranke, Leopold von, 'Über die Trennung und die Einheit von Deutschland' (1832), *Sämmtliche Werke*, xlix–l (Leipzig, 1887), 134–72.
—— *The Theory and Practice of History*, ed. Georg Iggers and Konrad von Moltke (Indianapolis and New York, 1973).
Rath, R. John, *The Viennese Revolution of 1848* (Austin, 1957).
Rausch, Wilhelm (ed.), *Die Städte Mitteleuropas im 17. und 18. Jahrhundert* (Linz, 1981).
—— (ed.), *Die Städte Mitteleuropas im 19. Jahrhundert* (Linz, 1983).
Raynor, Henry, *A Social History of Music. From the Middle Ages to Beethoven* (London, 1972).
Real, Willy, *Der Deutsche Reformverein: Grossdeutsche Stimmen und Kräfte zwischen Villafranca und Königgrätz* (Lübeck and Hamburg, 1966).
Reardon, Bernard, *Religion in the Age of Romanticism: Studies in Early Nineteenth-Century Thought* (Cambridge, 1985).
Rebmann, Georg Friedrich, *Kosmopolitische Wanderungen durch einen Teil Deutschlands* (1793; repr. Frankfurt, 1968).
Redlich, Joseph, *Das österreichische Staats- und Reichsproblem: Geschichtliche Darstellung der inneren Politik der habsburgischen Monarchie von 1848 bis zum Untergang des Reiches* (2 vols. Leipzig, 1920–6).
—— *Emperor Francis Joseph of Austria* (London, 1929).
Reed, T. J., *The Classical Centre: Goethe and Weimar, 1775–1832* (New York and London, 1980).
Reeves, Nigel, 'Heine and the Young Marx', *Oxford German Studies*, 7 (1972–3), 44–97.
Reif, Heinz, *Westfälischer Adel 1770–1860: Vom Herrschaftsstand zur regionalen Elite* (Göttingen, 1979).
Reiss, H., *The Political Thought of the German Romantics, 1793–1815* (Oxford, 1955).
Renger, Reinhard, *Landesherr und Landstände im Hochstift Osnabrück in der Mitte des 18. Jahrhunderts* (Götingen, 1965)
Repgen, Konrad, *Märzbewegung und Maiwahlen der Revolutionsjahre 1848 im Rheinland* (Bonn, 1955).

Reulecke, Jürgen, *Geschichte der Urbanisierung in Deutschland* (Frankfurt, 1985).

—— (ed.), *Die deutsche Stadt im Industriezeitalter* (Wuppertal, 1978).

—— and Weber, Wolfgang (eds.), *Fabrik-Familie-Feierabend: Beiträge zur Sozialgeschichte des Alltags im Industriezeitalter* (Wuppertal, 1978).

Rich, Norman *Why the Crimean War? A Cautionary Tale* (Hanover and London, 1985).

Richarz, Monika (ed.), *Jüdisches Leben in Deutschland. Selbstzeugnisse zur Sozialgeschichte, 1780–1871* (New York, 1976).

Riedel, Manfred, 'Vom Biedermeier zum Maschinenzeitalter: Zur Kulturgeschichte der ersten Eisenbahnen in Deutschland', *AfK* 43/1 (1961), 100–23.

Riehl, Wilhelm Heinrich, *Kulturgeschichtliche Charakterköpfe: Aus der Erinnerung gezeichnet* (Stuttgart, 1892).

—— *Die bürgerliche Gesellschaft* (1851, 9th edn., Stuttgart, 1897).

—— *Kulturstudien aus drei Jahrhunderten* (6th edn., Stuttgart and Berlin, 1903).

—— *Die bürgerliche Gesellschaft*, ed. Peter Steinbach (Frankfurt, 1976).

Riesbeck, J. C., *Travels through Germany in a Series of Letters* (3 vols., London, 1787).

Riesser, Jacob, *The Great German Banks and their Concentration in Connection with the Economic Development of Germany* (Washington, 1911).

Ringer, Fritz, *Education and Society in Modern Europe* (Bloomington, 1979).

Ritter, Gerhard, *Stein: Eine politische Biographie* (3rd rev. edn., Stuttgart, 1958).

—— *Frederick the Great. A Historical Profile* (Berkeley and Los Angeles, 1968).

Ritter, Gerhard, A. (ed.), *Gesellschaft, Parlament und Regierung. Zur Geschichte des Parlamentarismus in Deutschland* (Düsseldorf, 1974).

Rohr, Donald, *The Origins of Social Liberalism in Germany* (Chicago and London, 1963).

Rorty, Richard, *Philosophy and the Mirror of Nature* (Princeton, 1980).

Rose, Carol M., 'The Issue of Parliamentary Suffrage at the Frankfurt National Assembly', *CEH* 5/2 (June 1972), 127–49.

Rosenbaum, Heidi, *Formen der Familie: Untersuchungen zum Zusammenhang von Familieverhältnissen, Sozialstruktur und sozialem Wandel in der deutschen Gesellschaft des 19. Jahrhunderts* (Stuttgart, 1982).

Rosenberg, Hans, *Die Weltwirtschaftskrise von 1857–1859* (Stuttgart, 1934).

—— *Die nationalpolitische Publizistik Deutschlands. Vom Eintritt der Neuen Ära in Preussen bis zum Ausbruch der deutschen Krieges. Eine kritische Bibliographie* (2 vols., Munich and Berlin, 1935).

—— *Bureaucracy, Aristocracy, and Autocracy. The Prussian Experience. 1660–1815* (Cambridge, Mass., 1958).

—— *Probleme der deutschen Sozialgeschichte* (Frankfurt, 1969).

—— *Politische Denkströmungen im deutschen Vormärz* (Göttingen, 1972).

Rosenzweig, Franz, *Hegel und der Staat* (2 vols., Munich and Berlin, 1920).

Rössler, Hellmuth, *Zwischen Revolution und Reaktion. Ein Lebensbild des Reichsfreiherrn Hans Christoph von Gagern 1766–1852* (Göttingen, 1958).

Rothacker, E., 'Savigny, Grimm, Ranke. Ein Beitrag zur Frage nach dem Zusammenhang der Historischen Schule', *HZ* 128 (1923), 413–45.

Rothenberg, Günther, *The Army of Francis Joseph* (West Lafayette, Indiana, 1976).

—— *Napoleon's Great Adversaries: The Archduke Charles and the Austrian Army, 1792–1814* (Bloomington, 1982).

Rothfels, Hans (ed.), *Bismarck und der Staat: Ausgewählte Dokumente* (2nd edn., Stuttgart, 1953).

Rotteck, Carl von, *Gesammelte und nachgelassene Schriften mit Biographie und Briefwechsel*, ed. Hermann von Rotteck (5 vols., Pforzheim, 1841–3).

Runge, Philipp Otto, *Hinterlassene Schriften* (2 vols., Hamburg, 1840–1).

Rumpler, Helmut, *Die deutsche Politik des Freiherrn von Beust 1848–1850: Zur Problematik mittelstaatlicher Reformpolitik im Zeitalter der Paulskirche* (Vienna, 1972).

Rupieper, Hermann-Josef, 'Die Sozialstruktur der Trägerschichten der Revolution von 1848/49 am Beispiel Sachsen', in Hartmut Kaelble *et al Probleme der Modernisierung in Deutschland* (Opladen, 1978), 80–109.

Rürup, Reinhard, 'Die Judenemanzipation in Baden', *ZGO* 114 (1966), 241–300.

—— 'Kontinuität und Diskontinuität der "Judenfrage" im 19. Jahrhundert: Zur Entstehung des modernen Antisemitismus', in Hans-Ulrich Wehler (ed.), *Sozialgeschichte Heute: Festschrift für Hans Rosenberg zum 70. Geburtstag* (Göttingen, 1974), 388–415.

—— *Emanzipation und Antisemitismus* (Göttingen, 1975).

—— *Deutschland im 19. Jahrhundert, 1815–1871* (Göttingen, 1984).

Russell, John, *A Tour in Germany and Some of the Southern Provinces of the Austrian Empire in 1820, 1821, and 1822* (2nd edn., Edinburgh, 1828).

Saalfeld, Diedrich, *Bauernwirtschaft und Gutsbetrieb in der vorindustriel.. Zeit* (Stuttgart, 1960).

Sagarra, Eda, *Tradition and Revolution. German Literature and Society. 1830–1890* (New York, 1971).

—— *A Social History of Germany, 1648–1914* (New York, 1977).

Sammons, Jeffrey, *Six Essays on the Young German Novel* (Chapel Hill, 1972).

—— *Heinrich Heine: A Modern Biography* (Princeton, 1979).

Sandgruber, Roman, *Österreichische Agrarstatistik 1750–1918* (Munich, 1978).

—— *Die Anfänge der Konsumgesellschaft: Konsumgüterverbrauch, Lebensstandard und Alltagskultur in Österreich im 18. und 19. Jahrhundert* (Munich, 1982).

Schenda, Rudolf, *Volk ohne Buch: Studien zur Sozialgeschichte der populären Lesestoffe, 1770–1910* (Frankfurt, 1970).

—— *Die Lesestoffe der Kleinen Leute. Studien zur populären Literatur im 19. und 20. Jahrhundert* (Munich, 1976).

Scherer, Peter, *Reichsstift und Gotteshaus Weingarten im 18. Jahrhundert: Ein Beitrag zur Wirtschaftsgeschichte der Südwestdeutschen Grundherrschaft* (Stuttgart, 1969).

Schib, Karl, *Die Staatsrechtlichen Grundlagen der Politik Karl von Rottecks. Ein Beitrag zur Geschichte des Liberalismus* (Mulhouse, 1927).

Schieder, Theodor, *Friedrich der Grosse* (Berlin, 1983).

Schieder, Wolfgang, *Anfänge der deutschen Arbeiterbewegung* (Stuttgart, 1963).

—— 'Der rheinpfälzische Liberalismus von 1832 als politische Protestbewegung', in Heldmut Berding *et al.* (eds.), *Von Staat des Ancien Regime zum modernen Parteienstaat: Festschrift für Theodor Schieder* (Munich and Vienna, 1978), 169–96.

—— (ed.), *Liberalismus in der Gesellschaft des deutschen Vormärz* (Göttingen, 1983).

Schilfert, Gerhard, *Sieg und Niederlage des demokratischen Wahlrechts in der deutschen Revolution 1848/49* (Berlin, 1952).

Schiller, Friedrich, 'Die Schaubühne als eine moralische Anstalt betrachtet' (1784), *Sämtliche Werke*, xi. *Philosophische Schriften* (Stuttgart and Berlin, n.d.).

—— *Werke* (Nationalausgabe), xx. *Philosophische Schriften* (Weimar, 1962).

Schissler, Hanna, *Preussische Agrargesellschaft im Wandel: Wirtschaftliche, gesellschaftliche und politische Transformationsprozesse von 1763 bis 1847* (Göttingen, 1978).

Schivelbusch, Wolfgang, *The Railway Journey: Theories and Travels in the 19th Century* (New York, 1979).

Schlegel, August Wilhelm, *Vorlesungen über dramatische Kunst und Literatur Kritische Schriften und Briefe*, ed. E. Lohner (Stuttgart, 1966).

Schlegel, Friedrich, *Kritische Ausgabe*, ed. Ernst Behler *et al.* (Paderborn, Darmstadt, and Zurich, 1958 ff).

—— *Schriften zur Literatur*, ed. W. Rasch (Munich, 1972).

Schleiermacher, Friedrich, *On Religion: Speeches to its Cultured Despisers* (New York, 1958).

Schlumbohm, Jürgen, *Freiheit: Die Anfänge der bürgerlichen Emanzipationsbewegung in Deutschland im Spiegel ihres Leitwortes* (Düsseldorf, 1975).

Schmidt, Siegfried, *Robert Blum: Vom Leipziger Liberalen zum Märtyrer der deutschen Demokratie* (Weimar, 1971).

Schmoller, Gustav, *Zur Geschichte des deutschen Kleingewerbes im 19. Jahrhundert* (Halle, 1870).

Schnabel, Franz, *Deutsche Geschichte im Neunzehnten Jahrhundert* (4 vols., 3rd edn., Freiburg, 1949–59).

Schnädelbach, Herbert, *Philosphy in Germany, 1831–1933* (Cambridge, 1984).

Schneider, Franz, *Pressefreiheit und politische Öffentlichkeit. Studien zur politischen Geschichte Deutschlands bis 1848* (Neuwied and Berlin, 1966).

Schober, Joyce, *Die deutsche Spätaufklärung, 1770–1790* (Frankfurt, 1975).

Schoeps, Hans-Joachim, *Das andere Preussen: Konservative Gestalten und Probleme im Zeitalter Friedrich Wilhelms IV.* (5th edn., Berlin, 1981).

Scholz, Otfried, *Arbeiterselbstbild und Arbeiterfremdbild zur Zeit der industriellen Revolution: Ein Beitrag zur Sozialgeschichte des Arbeiters in der deutschen Erzähl-und Memoirenliteratur um die Mitte des 19. Jahrhunderts* (Berlin, 1980).

Schorske, Carl E., *Fin-de-siècle Vienna: Politics and Culture* (New York, 1980).

Schraepler, Ernst, *Handwerkerbunde und Arbeitervereine, 1830– 1853: Die politische Tätigkeit deutscher Sozialisten von Wilhelm Weitling bis Karl Marx* (Berlin, 1972).

Schramm, Percy Ernst, *Hamburg, Deutschland und die Welt* (Munich, 1943).
—— *Neun Generationen: Dreihundert Jahre deutscher 'Kulturgeschicte' im Lichte der Schicksale einer Hamburger Bürgerfamilie* (2 vols., Göttingen, 1963–4).
Schulin, Ernst, *Traditionskritik und Rekonstruktionsversuch. Studien zur Entwicklung von Geschichtswissenschaft und historischem Denken* (Göttingen, 1979).
Schulte, Regina, *Sperrbezirke: Tugendhaftigkeit und Prostitution in der bürgerlichen Welt* (Frankfurt, 1979).
Schulze-Delitzsch, Hermann, *Schriften und Reden*, ed. F. Thorwart (5 vols., Berlin, 1909–13).
Schurz, Carl, *Lebenserinnerungen* (3 vols., Berlin and Leipzig, 1912–30).
Schütz, Rüdiger, *Preussen und die Rheinlande: Studien zur preussischen Integrationspolitik im Vormärz* (Wiesbaden, 1979).
Sengle, Friedrich, *Biedermeierzeit: Deutsche Literatur im Spannungsfeld zwischen Restauration und Revolution, 1815–1848* (3 vols. Stuttgart, 1971–80).
Sharlin, Allan, 'Social Structure and Politics: A Social History of Frankfurt am Main, 1815–1864', unpublished diss. (Wisconsin, 1976).
—— 'From the Study of Social Mobility to the Study of Society', *AJS* 85/2 (Sept. 1979), 338–60.
Sheehan, James J., 'Conflict and Cohesion among German Élites in the Nineteenth Century', in Robert Bezucha (ed.), *Modern European Social History* (Lexington, Mass., 1972), 3–27.
—— 'Liberalism and Society in Germany, 1815– 1848', *JMH* 45/4 (Dec. 1973), 583–604.
—— *German Liberalism in the Nineteenth Century* (Chicago, 1978).
—— 'What is German History? Reflections on the Role of *Nation* in German History and Historiography', *JMH* 53/1 (1981), 1–23.
—— 'Some Reflections on Liberalism in Comparative Perspective', in H. Köhler (ed.), *Deutschland und der Westen* (Berlin, 1984), 44–58.
—— 'The Problem of Nation in German History,' in Otto Büsch and James J. Sheehan (eds.), *Die Rolle der Nation in der deutschen Geschichte und Gegenwart* (Berlin, 1985), 3– 20.
Shorter, Edward, *The Making of the Modern Family* (New York, 1975).
Showalter, Dennis E., *Railroads and Rifles: Soldiers, Technology, and the Unification of Germany* (Shoestring, 1975).
Sieder, Reinhard, *Sozialgeschichte der Familie* (Frankfurt, 1987).
Siemann, Wolfram, *Die deutsche Revolution von 1848/49* (Frankfurt, 1985).
Silberner, Edmund, *Johann Jacoby. Politiker und Mensch* (Bonn-Bad Godesberg, 1976).
Simon, Walter M., *The Failure of the Prussian Reform Movement, 1807–1819* (Cornell, 1955).
Simson, Eduard von, *Erinnerungen aus seinem Leben* (Leipzig, 1900).
Sked, Alan, *The Survival of the Habsburg Empire: Radetzky, the Imperial Army, and the Class War, 1848* (London, 1979).
Slicher van Bath, B. H., *The Agrarian History of Western Europe. A.D. 500–1850* (London, 1963).
Small, Albion, *The Cameralists: The Pioneers of German Social Policy* (Chicago, 1909).

—— *Origins of Sociology* (Chicago, 1924).

Smart, Ninian *et al.* (eds.), *Nineteenth Century Religious Thought in the West* (3 vols., Cambridge, 1985).

Smith, C. U. M., *The Problem of Life: An Essay in the Origins of Biological Thought* (New York and Toronto, 1976).

Smith, Clifford T., *A Historical Geography of Western Europe Before 1800* (New York and Washington, 1967).

Snell, John L., *The Democratic Movement in Germany. 1789–1914*, ed. and completed by Hans Schmitt (Chapel Hill, 1976).

Soliday, Gerald, *A Community in Conflict. Frankfurt Society in the Seventeenth and Early Eighteenth Centuries* (Hanover, N. H., 1974).

Solta, Jan, *Die Bauern der Lausitz: Eine Untersuchung des Differenzierungs-prozesses der Bauernschaft im Kapitalismus* (Bautzen, 1986).

Sombart, Werner, *Die deutsche Volkswirtschaft im neunzehnten Jahrhundert* (2nd edn., Berlin, 1909).

Sommer, Louise, *Die österreichischen Kameralisten in dogmengeschichtlicher Darstellung* (2 vols., Vienna, 1920–5).

Somogyi, Eva, *Vom Zentralismus zum Dualismus: Der Weg der deutschöster-reichischen Liberalen zum Ausgleich von 1867* (Wiesbaden, 1983).

Sorkin, David, 'Wilhelm von Humboldt: The Theory and Practice of Self-Formation (Bildung) 1791–1810', *JHI* 44/1 (Jan. 1983), 55–73.

—— *The Transformation of German Jewry, 1780–1840* (New York, 1987).

Sperber, Jonathan, *Popular Catholicism in Nineteenth-Century Germany* (Princeton, 1984).

Spiel, Hilde (ed.), *Der Wiener Kongress in Augenzeugenberichten* (Düsseldorf, 1965).

Spindler, Max (ed.), *Handbuch der bayerischen Geschichte*, iv. *Das neue Bayern, 1800–1870* (in 2 parts, Munich, 1974–5).

Spree, Reinhard, *Soziale Ungleichheit vor Krankheit und Tod: Zur Sozial-geschichte des Gesundheitsbereichs im Deutschen Kaiserreich* (Göttingen, 1981).

Springer, Anton, *Geschichte Österreichs seit dem Wiener Frieden 1809* (2 vols., Leipzig, 1863–5).

Srbik, Heinrich Ritter von, *Metternich: Der Staatsmann und der Mensch* (3 vols., Munich, 1925–54).

—— *Quellen zur deutschen Politik Österreichs 1859–66* (5 vols., Berlin and Leipzig, 1934–8).

—— *Geist und Geschichte vom Deutschen Humanismus bis zur Gegenwart* (2 vols., Munich and Salzburg, 1950–1).

Staatslexikon, ed. Carl von Rotteck and Karl Theodor Welcher (1st edn., 15 vols., Altona, 1846–8; 2nd edn., 12 vols., Altona, 1845–8; 3rd edn., 14 vols., Leipzig, 1856–66).

Stadelmann, Rudolf, and Fischer W., *Die Bildungswelt des deutschen Handwerks um 1800* (Berlin, 1955).

Stahl, Friedrich Julius, *Das monarchische Princip* (Heidelberg, 1845).

Steefel, Lawrence, *The Schleswig Holstein Question* (Cambridge, 1932).

Steffens, Heinrich, *Was ich erlebte* (Munich, 1956).

Stegmann, Dirk, *et al.* (eds.), *Deutscher Konservatismus im 19. und 20.*

Jahrhundert (Bonn, 1983).

Stein, Hans, 'Pauperismus und Assoziation: Soziale Tatsachen und Ideen auf dem westeuropäischen Kontinent vom Ende des 18. bis zur Mitte des 19. Jahrhunderts, unter besonderer Berücksichtigung des Rheingebiets', *IRSH* 1/1 (1936), 1–20.

Steinbach, Peter (ed.), *Probleme politischer Partizipation im Modernisierungsprozess* (Stuttgart, 1982).

Steinhausen, Georg, *Geschichte des deutschen Briefs* (2 vols., Berlin, 1889–91).

Sterling, Eleonore, *Judenhass: Die Anfänge des politischen Antisemitismus in Deutschland, 1815–1850* (Frankfurt, 1969).

Stern, J. P., *Re-Interpretations: Seven Studies in Nineteenth-Century German Literature* (London, 1964).

—— *Idylls and Realities: Studies in Nineteenth-Century German Literature* (London and Southhampton, 1971).

Strakosch, Henry, *State Absolutism and the Rule of Law: The Struggle for the Codification of Civil Law in Austria, 1753– 1811* (Sydney, 1967).

Streisand, Joachim (ed.), *Studien über die deutsche Geschichtswissenschaft* (2 vols., Berlin, 1963–8).

Süss, Edgar, *Pfälzer im Schwarzen Buch: Ein personengeschichtlicher Beitrag zur Geschichte des Hambacher Festes, des frühen pfälzischen und deutschen Liberalismus* (Heidelberg, 1956).

Swales, Martin, *The German Bildungsroman from Wieland to Hesse* (Princeton, 1978).

Sweet, Paul, *Wilhelm von Humboldt* (2 vols.; Columbus, Ohio, 1978–80).

Sydow, Anna von (ed.), *Wilhelm und Caroline von Humboldt in ihren Briefen*, iv. *1812–1815* (Berlin, 1910).

Tapié, Victor L., *The Rise and Fall of the Habsburg Monarchy* (London, 1971).

Teuteberg, Hans-Jürgen, 'Der Einfluss der Agrarreformen auf die Betriebsorganisation und Produktion der bäuerlichen Wirtschaft Westfalens im 19. Jahrhundert', in Fritz Blaich (ed.) *Entwicklungsprobleme einer Region: Das Beispiel Rheinland und Westfalen in 19. Jahrhundert* (Berlin, 1980), 167–276.

—— and Bernhard, Annegret, 'Wandel der Kindernahrung in der Zeit der Industrialisierung', in J. Reulecke and W. Weber (eds.), *Fabrik-Familie-Feierabend* (Wuppertal, 1978), 177–214.

—— and Wiegelmann, G., *Der Wandel der Nahrungsgewohnheiten unter dem Einfluss der Industrialisierung* (Göttingen, 1972).

Thielen, Peter, *Karl August von Hardenberg, 1750–1822* (Cologne and Berlin, 1967).

Tilly, Charles (ed.), *The Formation of Nation States in Western Europe* (Princeton, 1975).

—— (ed.), *Historical Studies of Changing Fertility* (Princeton, 1978).

—— *et al.* (eds.), *The Rebellious Century, 1830–1930* (Cambridge, Mass., 1975).

Tilly, Richard, *Financial Institutions and Industrialization in the Rhineland, 1815–1870* (Madison, 1966).

—— 'Los von England': Probleme des Nationalismus in der deutschen Wirtschaftsgeschichte', *ZGS* 134/1 (1968), 179–96.

—— 'Popular Disorders in Nineteenth-Century Germany: A Preliminary Survey', *JSH* 4/1 (1970), 1–40.

—— *Kapital, Staat und sozialer Protest in der deutschen Industrialisierung: Gesammelte Aufsätze* (Göttingen, 1980).

Tipton, Frank, 'Farm Labour and Power Politics: Germany, 1850–1914', *JEH* 34 (1974), 951–79.

—— 'The National Consensus in German Economic History,' *CEH* 7/3 (Sept. 1974), 195–224.

—— *Regional Variations in the Economic Development of Germany during the Nineteenth Century* (Middletown, Conn., 1976).

Toews, John Edward, *Hegelianism: The Path toward Dialectical Humanism 1805–1841* (Cambridge, 1980).

Träger, Claus (ed.), *Die Französische Revolution im Spiegel der deutschen Literatur* (Frankfurt, 1975).

Treitschke, Heinrich von, *History of Germany in the Nineteenth Century* (7 vols., London, 1915–19).

—— 'Bundesstaat und Einheits-Staat' (1864), in *Aufsätze, Reden und Briefe*, ed. Karl Schiller (Meersburg, 1929), iii. 9–146.

Tribe, Keith, 'Cameralism and the Science of Government', *JMH* 56 (June 1984), 163–84.

Turner, R. Steven, 'The Growth of Professorial Research in Prussia, 1818–1848—Causes and Context', in R. McCormmack (ed.), *Historical Studies in the Physical Sciences* (Philadelphia, 1971), 137–82.

—— 'University Reformers and Professorial Research in Germany, 1760–1806', in L. Stone (ed.), *The University in Society* (Princeton, 1974), ii. 495–531.

—— 'Helmholtz, Sensory Physiology, and the Disciplinary Development of German Psychology', in Mitchell Ash and W. Woodward (eds.), *The Problematic Science: Psychology in 19th Century Thought* (New York, 1982), 147–66.

—— 'The Prussian Professoriate and the Research Imperative. 1790–1840', in Hans N. Jahnke and M. Otte (eds.), *Epistemological and Social Problems of the Sciences in the Early Nineteenth Century* (Dordrecht, 1981), 109–22.

Ulmann, H. (ed.), *Denkwürdigkeiten aus dem Dienstleben des hessen-darmstädtischen Staatsministers Freiherrn du Thil, 1803–1848* (Stuttgart, 1921).

Ullmann, Hans Peter, 'Die öffentlichen Schulden in Bayern und Baden. 1780–1820', *HZ* 242/1 (1986), 31–68.

Valentin, Veit, *Geschichte der deutschen Revolution, 1848–1849* (2 vols., Berlin, 1930–1).

—— *Das Hambacher Fest* (Berlin, 1932).

Valjavec, Fritz, *Die Entstehung der politischen Strömungen in Deutschland, 1770–1815* (Munich, 1951).

Van Creveld, Martin, *Supplying War: Logistics from Wallenstein to Patton* (Cambridge, 1977).

—— *Command in War* (Cambridge, 1985).

Vann, James Allen, *The Making of a State: Württemberg, 1593–1793* (Ithaca and London, 1984).

—— and Rowan, Stevens W. (eds.), *The Old Reich: Essays on German Political Institutions, 1495–1806* (Brussels, 1974).

Virchow, Rudolf, *Briefe an seine Eltern 1839 bis 1864*, ed. Marie Rahl [geb. Virchow] (2nd edn., Leipzig, 1907).

Vierhaus, Rudolf, *Ranke und die soziale Welt* (Münster, 1957).

—— 'Deutschland vor der französischen Revolution', unpublished Habilitationsschrift (Münster, 1961).

—— 'Politisches Bewusstsein in Deutschland vor 1789', *Der Staat*, 6/2 (1967), 175–96.

—— 'Eigentumsrecht und Mediatisierung: Der Kampf um die Rechte der Reichsritterschaft, 1803–1815', in R. Vierhaus, (ed.), *Eigentum und Verfassung: Zur Eigentumsdiskussion im ausgehenden 18. Jahrhundert* (Göttingen, 1972), 229–57.

—— 'Bildung,' *GGB*, (1972), i. 508–51.

—— 'Aufklärung und Freimauerei in Deutschland', in Rudolf von Thadden *et al.* (eds.), *Das Vergangene und die Geschichte: Festschrift für Reinhard Wittram* (Göttingen, 1973), 23–41.

—— 'Ranke und die Anfänge der deutschen Geschichtswissenschaft', in B. Faulenbach (ed.), *Geschichtswissenschaft in Deutschland* (Munich, 1974), 17–34.

—— *Deutschland im Zeitalter des Absolutismus, 1648–1763* (Göttingen, 1978).

—— (ed.), *Eigentum und Verfassung: Zur Eigentumsdiskussion im ausgehenden 18. Jahrhundert* (Göttingen, 1972).

Vleeschauwer, H. J. de, *The Development of Kantian Thought* (London, 1962).

Vogel, Barbara, 'Beamtenkonservatismus. Sozial-und Verfassungsges-chichtliche Voraussetzungen der Parteien in Preussen im frühen 19. Jahrhundert', in Dirk Stegmann *et al.* (eds.), *Konservatismus im 19. und 20. Jahrhundert* (Bonn, 1983), 1–32.

Von Laue, Theodore, *Leopold Ranke. The Formative Years* (Princeton, 1950).

Vopelius, M. E., *Die altliberalen Ökonomen und die Reformzeit* (Stuttgart, 1968).

Vorländer, Karl, *Immanuel Kant: Der Mann und das Werk* (2 vols., Leipzig, 1924).

Wagner, Richard, *Gesammelte Schriften*, ed. J. Kapp (14 vols., Leipzig, n.d. [1914]).

Walker, Mack, *Germany and the Emigration, 1816–1885* (Cambridge, Mass., 1964).

—— *German Home Towns: Community, State, General Estate, 1648–1871* (Ithaca, New York, 1971).

—— *Johann Jakob Moser and the Holy Roman Empire of the German Nation* (Chapel Hill, 1981).

Walter, F., *Die österreichische Zentralverwaltung (1740–1792)* (2 vols., Vienna, 1938 and 1950).

—— *Österreichische Verfassungs- und Verwaltungsgeschichte von 1500–1955* (Vienna and Graz, 1972).

Wandruszka, Adam, *The House of Habsburg: Six Hundred Years of a European Dynasty* (Garden City, New York, 1965).

—— and Urbanitsch, Peter (eds.), *Die Habsburgermonarchie, 1848–1918* (2 vols. Vienna, 1973–5).

Ward, Albert, *Book Production, Fiction, and the German Reading Public, 1740–1800* (Oxford, 1974).

Weber, Christoph, *Aufklärung und Orthodoxie am Mittelrhein, 1820–1850* (Paderborn, 1973).

Weber, Max, *Economy and Society. An Outline of Interpretive Sociology* (2 vols., Berkeley, Los Angeles, and London, 1978).

Weber, Rolf, *Kleinbürgerliche Demokraten in der deutschen Einheitsbewegung, 1863–1866* (Berlin, 1962).

—— *Die Revolution in Sachsen, 1848/49: Entwicklung und Analyse ihrer Triebkräfte* (Berlin, 1970).

Weber-Kellermann, Ingeborg, *Die deutsche Familie: Versuch einer Sozialgeschichte* (Frankfurt, 1974).

—— *Die Familie* (Frankfurt, 1977).

Wehler, Hans-Ulrich, *Deutsche Gesellschaftsgeschichte*, i and ii (Munich, 1987).

—— (ed.), *Deutsche Historiker* (8 vols., Göttingen, 1971–82).

—— (ed.), *Sozialgeschichte heute: Festschrift für Hans Rosenberg zum 70. Geburtstag* (Göttingen, 1974).

Weinacht, Paul-Ludwig, *Staat: Studien zur Bedeutungsgeschichte des Wortes von den Anfängen bis ins 19. Jahrhundert* (Berlin, 1968).

Weinandy, Klaus, 'Die politischen Wahlen in den rechtsrheinischen Kreisen Sieg, Mülheim, Wipperfürth, Gummersbach und Waldbröl des Regierungsbezirkes Köln in der Zeit von 1849 bis 1870,' unpublished diss. (Bonn, 1956).

Weis, Eberhard, 'Montgelas' innenpolitisches Reformprogramm: Das Ansbacher Mémoire für den Herzog vom 30. 9. 1796', *ZBL* 33/1 (1970), 219–56.

—— *Montgelas, 1759–1799: Zwischen Revolution und Reform* (Munich 1971).

—— (ed.), *Reformen im rheinbündischen Deutschland* (Munich, 1984).

Wellek, René, *A History of Modern Criticism, 1750–1950* (4 vols.; New Haven, 1955).

Wentzcke, Paul, *et al.*, (eds.), *Darstellung und Quellen zur Geschichte der deutschen Einheitsbewegung im neunzehnten und zwanzigsten Jahrhundert* (10 vols., Heidelberg, 1957–78).

Wickert, Lothar, *Theodor Mommsen: Eine Biographie* (4 vols.; Frankfurt, 1959–80).

Wieland, C. M., 'Über deutschen Patriotismus: Betrachtungen, Fragen und Zweifel', (May 1793), in *Werke*, ed. W. Kurrelmeyer, xv (Berlin, 1930), 586–95.

Wiese, Benno von, *Friedrich Schiller* (Stuttgart, 1963).

Wilhelm, Theodor, *Die Idee des Berufsbeamtentums. Ein Beitrag zur Staatslehre des deutschen Frühkonstitutionalismus* (Tübingen, 1933).

Winkler, Heinrich August, *Preussischer Liberalismus und deutscher National-staat* (Tübingen, 1964).

—— *Mittelstand, Demokratie und Nationalsozialismus: Die politische Entwick-lung von Handwerk und Kleinhandel in der Weimarer Republik* (Cologne, 1972).

Winter, Eduard, *Der Josephinismus: Die Geschichte des österreichischen Reformkatholizismus, 1740–1848* (rev. edn., Berlin, 1962).

—— *Frühliberalismus in der Donaumonarchie von 1790– 1868* (Berlin, 1968).

—— *Revolution, Neoabsolutismus und Liberalismus in der Donaumonarchie* (Vienna, 1970).

Wirtz, Rainer, '*Widersetzlichkeiten, Excesse, Crawalle, Thumulte und Skandale*'. *Soziale Bewegung und gewalthafter sozialer Protest in Baden, 1815–1848* (Frankfurt, 1981).

Wollstein, Günther, *Das 'Grossdeutschland' der Paulskirche: Nationale Ziele in der bürgerlichen Revolution, 1848/49* (Düsseldorf, 1977).

Wrigley, E. A., *Industrial Growth and Population Change: A Regional Study of the Coalfield Areas of North-West Europe in the Later Nineteenth Century* (London, 1961).

Wunder, Bernd, *Privilegierung und Disziplinierung: Die Entstehung des Berufsbeamtentums in Bayern und Württemberg (1780–1825)* (Munich, 1978).

—— *Geschichte der Bürokratie in Deutschland* (Frankfurt, 1986).

Wutzmer, Heinz, 'Die Herkunft der industriellen Bourgeoisie Preussens in den vierziger Jahren des 19. Jahrhunderts', in H. Mottek *et al.* (eds.), *Studien zur Geschichte der industriellen Revolution in Deutschland* (Berlin, 1975), 145–63.

Ziebura, Gilbert, 'Anfänge des deutschen Parlamentarismus. Geschäfts-verfahren und Entscheidungsprozess in der ersten deutschen National-versammlung, 1848/49', in G. A. Ritter and G. Ziebura (eds.), *Faktoren der politischen Entscheidung (Festgabe für Ernst Fraenkel)* (Berlin, 1963), 185–236.

Ziekursch, Johannes, *Hundert Jahre schlesischer Agrargeschichte* (Breslau, 1927).

Zorn, Wolfgang, 'Typen und Entwicklungskräfte deutschen Unter-nehmertums im 19. Jahrhundert', *VSWG* 44/1 (1957), 57–77.

—— 'Schwerpunkte der deutschen Ausfuhrindustrie im 18. Jahrhundert', *JbbNS* 173 (1961), 422–47.

—— 'Die wirtschaftliche Integration Kleindeutschlands in den 1860er Jahren und die Reichsgründung', *HZ* 216/2 (Apr. 1973), 304–34.

Zunkel, Friedrich, *Der rheinisch-westfälische Unternehmer, 1834–1879: Ein Beitrag zur Geschichte des deutschen Bürgertums im 19. Jahrhundert* (Cologne and Opladen, 1962).

Zwahr, Hartmut, *Zur Konstituierung des Proletariats als Klasse: Strukturunter-suchung über das Leipziger Proletariat während der industriellen Revolution* (Berlin, 1978).

—— 'Zur Klassenkonstituierung der deutschen Bourgeoisie', *JbG* 18 (1978), 21–83.

INDEX